The Faber Companion
to Foreign Films

The Faber Companion to Foreign Films

RONALD BERGAN
and
ROBYN KARNEY

Copyright © 199[?] by Ronald Bergan and Robyn Karney

faber and faber
BOSTON • LONDON

This paperback edition first published in the United States in 1992
by Faber and Faber, Inc., 50 Cross Street, Winchester, MA 01890.
First published in Great Britain in 1992 by
Bloomsbury Publishing Limited, 2 Soho Square, London W1V 5DE.

A copy of the CIP entry for this book is available from the Library of Congress

Published in arrangement with Bloomsbury Publishing Limited

Cover design by Susan Silton
Book design by Geoff Green
Printed in Great Britain

Introduction

As ever-increasing numbers of travellers love to visit the Taj Mahal, the Kremlin, the Eiffel Tower, the castles of the Rhine, Mount Fujiyama, the Sistine Chapel and the pyramids, so growing numbers of movie lovers have come to relish Indian, Russian, French, German, Japanese, Italian or Arabic films—not to mention the riches that are coming our way from China, Argentina, Spain, Brazil, Turkey, the Philippines, West Africa, and indeed, almost every country in the world. For, in an age of internationalism, the cinema has proved itself the most international of arts.

However, as there are some people who prefer never to venture out of their own country and feel, like the Nancy Mitford character, that 'abroad is unutterably bloody and foreigners are fiends,' so there are cinema-goers who seldom take a journey into the world of non-English language films. Still residing in the minds of many is the idea that foreign-language films are somehow elitist, representing the 'serious', the 'heavy' and the 'intellectual' branch of the cinema industry. There is an element of truth in this, but it is secondary to the fact that foreign film cannot be categorized.

We hope and believe that this book will prove a valuable reference for students, buffs and committed foreign-film enthusiasts in that it collates a wealth of factual information in one volume. However, our major purpose has been to open an Aladdin's cave for those movie-lovers who are still intimidated by the challenge of the foreign film. In browsing through our pages, in using the book as a guide and a reference, it should become clear that the vast range of films from over 50 countries is as multifarious as the cultures that produced them. Here, you will find the best (and occasionally, the worst) of gangster movies, horror pics, whodunnits, Westerns, melodramas, musicals, war epics, love stories, comedies and tragedies, and realize that entertainment and escapism are not the preserve of Hollywood. Where the foreign film *does* often differ is in transcending formula, using experiment and innovation to amuse, shock, or provoke us into a new awareness and understanding of issues.

Most of the greatest films ever made come from outside the English-speaking world. Many European, African and Asian governments are generous in subsidising their film industries, treating them as part of their country's essential culture and allowing directors and producers the freedom to work without the commercial constraints that bedevil their British and American counterparts. The films are not, on the whole, products of big studios where decisions, at every stage, are taken by the front office. As a result, they tend to be personal and individual in their artistic expression, thus enabling us to enter into an alien culture even more easily than travel might do, since they illuminate the character of the people and the psychology of a nation.

More and more countries are producing films that are entering the international bloodstream. African nations like Mali, Burkino Faso (formerly Upper Volta), Mauritania and Senegal have given birth to directors of unique imagination such as Ousmane Sembène, Souleymane Cissé and Med Hondo; China is sending films of spectacular visual quality, as well as absorbing content, to a Western world ever more eager to receive them; and Denmark, neglected as a film-making country since the days of Carl Dreyer, is experiencing a renaissance which won it a prestigious double in 1988 when *Babette's Feast* took the Best Foreign Film Oscar, and *Pelle The Conqueror* carried off the Palme D'Or at Cannes. Foreign films have become an integral part of our cultural landscape and the barriers between the worlds of English- speaking cinema and the rest are disappearing daily. Over the last few decades we have grown used to seeing 'our' stars—Burt Lancaster, Donald Sutherland, Robert de Niro, John Gielgud—acting for Luchino Visconti, Frederico Fellini, Bernardo Bertolucci and Andrzej Wajda; Nastassia Kinski, Christopher Lambert, Isabella Rossellini and Charlotte Rampling move with ease between English-speaking and foreign films; Louis Malle can make *Atlantic City* in the United States and return to his native France a few years later for *Au Revoir Les Enfants*.

Of course, this cultural cross-fertilization is not new. From its earliest days, Hollywood has benefited from the influx of gifted Europeans. From Sweden came Greta Gustafsson (Garbo) and Ingrid Bergman (mother of Isabella Rossellini), from Germany Maria Magdelena Dietrich Von Losch (Marlene Dietrich) and from Austria Hedy Kiesler (Hedy Lamarr). Italy gave America Sofia Sciccolone (Sophia Loren), Egypt supplied Michael Shalhoub (Omar Sharif), from France came Charles Boyer and Maurice Chevalier. All of these, and many more stars familiar to us, began their careers in their native lands, appearing in many of the films which are dealt with in the following pages. Also under scrutiny here is a generous selection of the pre-Hollywood work of directors such as Ernst Lubitsch, Fritz Lang, Douglas Sirk (Detlef Sierck), Robert Siodmak, Billy Wilder, Roman Polanski, Milos Forman and Andrei Konchalovsky.

Hollywood has drawn inspiration from the foreign cinema, as a glance at the long list of Hollywood remakes will confirm: Akira Kurosawa's *Seven Samurai* became *The Magnificent Seven*; Julie Andrews starred in the remake of Germany's 1933 *Victor Und Viktoria*, while the French *Three Men And A Cradle* took only two years to become *Three Men And A Baby*. René Clair's *À Nous La Liberté* furnished Chaplin with the basis for his *Modern Times* and, more recently, the bath scene in *Fatal Attraction* was clearly lifted from Clouzot's classic thriller, *Les Diaboliques*. Woody Allen, who idolizes Ingmar Bergman ('The greatest artist that ever pointed a camera at anything') and Fellini, has paid his own tribute to them with *Interiors*, *A Midsummer Night's Sex Comedy*, and *Stardust Memories*.

Although, in the 1920s, the general public in Britain and America flocked to see silent masterpieces such as Eisenstein's *Battleship Potemkin*, Clair's *The Italian Straw Hat*, and Abel Gance's *Napoleon*, a wider appreciation of foreign films began to spread after World War II, when Italian, Japanese, German and French motion pictures were once more available in the Allied countries. The increasing awareness of the quality of these films was aided by the recognition given each year by the Academy of Motion Pictures, Arts and Sciences. Vittorio de Sica's *Shoeshine* was the first to receive a special award from the Academy in 1947 and, since 1956, with Fellini's *La Strada* the first winner, the Academy has given an Oscar, in competition, to the Best Foreign-Language Film.

Nowadays, there are few regular movie-goers who are not familiar with the names of directors such as Buñuel, Bergman, Truffaut, Kurosawa, Fassbinder, Malle and Fellini; or unacquainted with performers such as Brigitte Bardot, Jean Gabin, Jean-Paul Belmondo, Catherine Deneuve, Alain Delon, Marcello Mastroianni, Stéphane Audran, Toshiro Mifune, Klaus Kinski, Gérard Depardieu, Monica Vitti, Max Von Sydow, Isabelle Adjani and Karl-Maria Brandauer. With the mushrooming of small cinemas that show foreign films, the plentiful showings on British and American television, the proliferation of, and growing interest in, festivals all over the world, including Sydney, Toronto and Johannesburg, we can look forward to larger audiences than ever for foreign film.

We feel, therefore, that it is now appropriate to offer movie-goers an accessible guide for quick—and, we hope, entertaining and illuminating—consultation on plot, critical opinion, general context and credits. we have not attempted to suppress our personal likes and dislikes, our prejudices and blind spots, or our enthusiasms, but we have tried to give the reader enough objective information to be able to assess the type, quality, content and style of each work under discussion.

Selection Of Titles

Our book contains over 2,000 entries. As tens of thousands of foreign films have been made since the dawn of the cinema, our list is necessarily selective, but we set out to be as wide-ranging and far-reaching as possible. We hope that not only do we have almost every significant film—classics which have stood the test of time or works that are integral to cinema history—but big box-office successes and movies which, irrespective of quality or current appeal, are representative of trends, fashions, styles and developments.

Although we have included some films that are difficult to see for various reasons, our choice has been dictated, to a large extent, by films that have been publicly released or shown on television in Britain and/or the United States; those included in retrospectives at the National Film Theatre and other repertory cinemas in Britain, or the Museum of Modern Art and similar establishments in the USA; films with a reputation; films that are significant in the understanding of a film-maker's work as a whole, or of a specific country's film history; a large number of winners from the three major festivals at Cannes, Venice and Berlin; experimental, *avant-garde* and underground films; the purely commercial, and a small selection of opera films (as opposed to filmed opera) and documentaries.

In the case of several directors of exceptional stature and reputation—among them Jean Renoir, Fellini, Eisenstein, Robert Bresson, Buñuel and Kurosawa—we have dealt with their complete, or almost complete *oeuvres*. In the case of directors such as Kenji Mizoguchi and Yasugiro Ozu, who were phenominally prolific, we have included most of their mature extant works, together with examples of their early works of quality.

On the whole, we have omitted movies that are virtually impossible to see in their original foreign language versions, many of which were specifically shot in English for release in Britain and the USA or are only ever screened with an execrably dubbed sound track. These include 'Spaghetti' Westerns, Italian muscle epics; films, such as *The Young Girls Of Rochefort* and *Daughters Of Darkness*, released exclusively in English, or Jean-Pierre Melville's *The Red Circle*, shown only in a dubbed and mutilated version. On the other hand, a film such as Visconti's *The Leopard*, made simultaneously in English, can be seen in Italian and is, in any case, a major example of its director's work and is therefore included. Eisenstein's unfinished *Que Viva Mexico* has been omitted because it exists in so many forms, all mutilated, and is generally shown as *Time In The Sun* with a specially written English commentary. Others with an English commentary, however, such as the Russian *Tchaikowsky* or the Dutch documentary, *The Voice Of The Water*, are included because, commentary or no, the dialogue within the films is in its original language.

Names and Accents

We have tried to be as accurate as possible in the spelling of names, standardizing where there are discrepancies in source material. These occur very often when actors change the way their names are spelled; where Italians in French films or vice versa are billed with a variation in spelling; or, most significantly, when names are transcribed from languages with a different alphabet. The difficulty can be summarized by the case of the Russian director, Josef Heifitz. In the course of our researches, we have come across Mr Heifitz billed in the following forms: Iosif and Yosif Heifitz (National Film Theatre programmes), Josif Heifits (*Oxford Companion To Film*), Josef and Joseph Heifits (Leslie Halliwell's *Film Guide*), Iosif Kheyfits (Scheuer's *TV Film Guide*), Jozef Heifitz (Katz's *International Film Ecyclopaedia*) and Josef Heifets (Richard Roud's *The Cinema: A Critical Dictionary*). None of these gentlemen is wrong, and the Heifitz saga has been the least of our problems!

Accents have presented a major difficulty. In deference to the cultures whose work we discuss and in the interests of reference, we elected to use accents. Having done so, however, it became clear why so many English-language publications now omit them. Source material is contradictory and incomplete and often without the accents, while even the screen credits themselves vary in usage, non-usage or conflicting usage. Consequently, we have had to do our incomplete best and beg indulgence—particularly from the Czechs, Poles, Hungarians, Yugoslavs, Bulgarians and Scandinavians—towards errors and omissions.

Explanatory Notes

TITLES: Films are filed alphabetically, ignoring the article. Thus *The Story Of A Cheat* will be found under S. We have used the English-language title as known in Britain, but, when the American title differs, we have listed this beneath, as well as any *aka* (also known as) titles. All US and aka titles are cross-referred. Thus, if you look up Louis Malle's *Murmur Of The Heart*, you will be instructed to see *Dearest Love* for the entry, since that is the British release title.

There are exceptions to the English-language rule where the title of a film has never been translated or the film is best known under its original foreign title eg *La Dolce Vita* (filed under D). The original foreign title is given beneath the English-language title or titles. This, too, is cross-referred as described above.

COUNTRY OF ORIGIN: This generally relates to the original language of the movie, regardless of how many countries were involved in the production process financially and/or creatively, or in terms of locations. That French money, for example, helped to finance films by Youssef Chahine doesn't alter the fact that these films are Egyptian. There are exceptions—Helma Sanders-Brahms' *The Future Of Emily*, for example. Here we have combined French and German money financing a German director, a French cinematographer, a combined French and German cast, and locations in both countries, to justify the shared credit for country of origin.

DATE: This refers, wherever possible, to the date of the film's first release, generally in the country of origin. Sometimes this coincides with the foreign release date, but there are often gaps of some years.

RUNNING TIME: This is always a contentious subject. Pictures are often cut after festival showings or initial release, or on reaching the USA or Britain, or for television. There are distributor's cuts and/or censor's cuts and, on occasion, replacement of cut material. Needless to say, this can cause a deal of confusion and we have opted, as far as possible to give the original running time. Silent films, shot at a different speed and with their running times originally given in metres, pose a different problem. All silent film times are, therefore, approximate.

COLOUR: The abbreviations bw and col are used to indicate black-and-white or colour.

PRODUCTION COMPANY: As we have indicated in our notes on country of origin, films are very often co-productions, largely for financial reasons. We have tried to indicate the involvement of different countries where relevant eg MK2 Productions(Paris)/Austra(Brazil).

TECHNICAL CREDITS: These are given in the following order: director (d), screenplay (sc), cinematographer (ph) and composer (m). The music credit generally refers to the soundtrack composer, although the use of classical music is identified and, on occasion, pop music is identified by its performers. Silent films are denoted as such under the music credit. Where there *is* no music credit, the film had no music or, more rarely, there is no credit listed anywhere. In no more than two or three instances, a photography or writing credit may be missing because it is totally unavailable.

CAST: All leading players are named, as well as significant supporting cast.

TEXT: Each piece opens with a plot summary. We have tried to keep the surprises—not give away the murderer and so forth. We have generally matched players to leading roles except where role attributions have proved contradictory or unavailable. Plot is followed by critical comment and any information of special interest.

AWARDS: We have confined awards, given at the bottom of an entry, to the Best Film, Best Director, Best Actor and Best Actress as given at Cannes, Venice and Berlin, and to the Oscar winners for Best Foreign Film. The date given is the date of the award presentation.

to the arduous research problems, helping in setting up our master list of titles and contributed much of practical value from his own knowledge. When circumstances forced Hillel to leave before completion of the book, Richard Chatten graciously stepped into his shoes, bringing *his* knowledge and remarkable energy to the final hurdles.

The documentation and resources of the British Film Institute were indispensable. To the staff at the BFI, whose patience was sorely tried, our sincere appreciation for their help and courtesy. To all these we owe a debt of gratitude.

Our heartfelt thanks also to Gilbert Adair, Brian Baxter, Helen Bourne, Catriona MacGregor and Deborah Sharp for their generous assistance; to our editor Linda Doeser for the expertise she applied to an exceptionally onerous task; and to Kathy Rooney at Bloomsbury and our agent, Tony Peake of London Management, for their encouragement and their understanding.

Ronald Bergan
Robyn Karney
London 1988

Authors' Acknowledgements

It only remains to thank those who helped to make this undertaking possible.

Clive Hirschhorn's assistance was of immeasurable value. Not only did he offer advice and encouragement but, with astounding generosity, gave us unlimited use of his remarkable collection of reference books.

Joel Finler was on hand throughout with advice, erudition, the loan of research material and an eagle eye on the manuscript. He also made specific specialist contributions: the synopsis of *Une Vie Sans Joie*, for example, almost always given incorrectly, is accurate here, thanks to Joel's supplying it from his reservoir of personal work on Renoir.

Musicologist and critic Max Loppert guided us in the selection of opera films and answered queries on musical detail, while Tony Coghan's knowledge solved a few thorny problems.

Hillel Tryster brought unswerving dedication, enthusiasm and long hours

Acknowledgements for Revised Edition

Updating this book proved positively pleasurable thanks to the generous and invaluable assistance of several people. Ed Lewis gave *carte blanche* to visit his superbly programmed (and comfortable) cinema at the Riverside Studios; Michelle Nickel of Metro Pictures went to inordinate lengths to make screenings and videos available; Elizabeth Draper and Emma Davie of Electric Pictures were similarly helpful. Grateful thanks also to Pam Engel and Iris Kehr of Artificial Eye, Susan Santini and her staff at the London Film Festival, Katie Sumner of Frontline, my researcher David Oppedisano, my long-suffering editor at Bloomsbury Tracey Smith, and Jo Berry of Empire Magazine.

Robyn Karney
London 1992

1st Edition
Editor Linda Doeser
Editorial Assistant Leone Edwards
Consultant and
  Historian Joel W. Finler
Research Hillel Tryster
  Richard Chatten

2nd Edition
Editor Tracey Smith
Copy Editor Trish Burgess
Research David Oppedisano

a

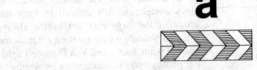

▶ **Aakaler Sandhane** see In Search Of Famine

Aan

▶ **aka Savage Princess**

India 1952 190 mins col
All India Film Corporation/Mehboob Productions

d **Mehboob**
sc **Chaudary, Ali Raza**
ph **Faredoon, A. Irani**
m **Naushad Dilip**
Dilip Kumar, Nimmi, Premnath, Nadira

Jai (Kumar), an heroic peasant, and his girl-friend, Mangala (Nimmi), help unseat a usurping prince and his savage sister, Aan (Nadira). The first Indian feature in Technic-olor, it was also one of the very few Indian films to reach the West before the advent of Satyajit Ray. Its exotic music, costumes, and spectacle, as much as the swashbuckling tale made it an immediate hit abroad where it was shown in a 130-minute version. Doubtless, the strong Western influence apparent in the film also added to its popular appeal.

▶ **Aanslag, De** see Assault, The

Abel

Netherlands 1986 105 mins col
De Cooperatieve Muziek Theater Vereniging Okkater UA

d **Alex Van Warmerdam**
sc **Alex Van Warmerdam**
ph **Marc Felperlaan**
m **Vincent Van Warmerdam**

Alex Van Warmerdam, Henri Garcin, Olga Zuiderhoek, Annet Malherbe, Loos Luca

Thirty-one-year-old Abel (Van Warmerdam) still lives with his mother (Zuiderhoek) and father (Garcin), and has not been outside the apartment for 10 years. Scared of facing life and isolated from other people – he views them only through a pair of binoculars – he is finally thrown out by his despairing father. Outside he meets and falls for a young woman (Malherbe), who happens to be having an affair with his father. This first feature by a former theatre director, who also plays the curious lead, is a quirky comedy that lampoons the absurdities of family life. The use of stage lighting and non-realist décor gives the film an extra satiric edge. Two hilarious set pieces are the arrival of a psychiatrist brought in to question an uncooperative Abel, and the disastrous visit of a girl invited over by the parents during which she is served herrings between a lagging conversation.

▶ **Abenteuer Des Prinzen Achmed, Die** see Adventures Of Prince Achmed, The

▶ **Abenteuer Des Werner Holt, Die** see Adventures of Werner Holt, The

▶ **Abhijan** see Expedition, The

▶ **Abismos De Pasión** see Wuthering Heights

▶ **À Bout De Souffle** see Breathless

▶ **Abschied** see Farewell

▶ **Abschied Von Gestern** see Yester-day Girl

▶ **Abus De Confiance** see Abuse Of Confidence

Abuse Of Confidence

▶ **Abus De Confiance**

France 1938 82 mins bw
Compagnie Commerciale Française
Cinématographique

d **Henri Decoin**
sc **Henri Decoin, Jean Boyer**
ph **L.H. Burel**
m **Georges Van Parys**
    Danielle Darrieux, Charles Vanel,
    Valentine Jessie, Pierre Mingand

A poor law student (Darrieux) gets a prominent historian (Vanel) to adopt her by pretending to be his long-lost daughter, and later has to defend a girl who committed a similar breach of confidence. One of a number of run-of-the-mill films that director Decoin made starring his wife Darrieux during their marriage from 1934 to 1940. The early scenes between her and Vanel, until the plot creaks to its court-room conclusion, are the best.

▶ **Abwärts** see Out Of Order

The Abyss

▶ **L'Oeuvre Au Noir**

Belgium 1988 110 mins col
La Sept/Films A2(Paris)/La Nouvelle
Imagerie(Brussels)

d **André Delvaux**
sc **André Delvaux**
ph **Charlie Van Damme**
m **Frédéric Devreese**
    Gian Maria Volonté, Jean Bouise,
    Philippe Léotard, Sami Frey, Anna
    Karina, Marie-Christine Barrault, Marie-
    France Pisier

Zenon (Volonté), a 16th-century Flanders physician and alchemist, spends some years wandering Europe to escape the Inquisition, which is after him for dissident writings, devilish medical practices (he actually cures the sick) and his bisexuality. He eventually returns, incognito, to his native Bruges, but is discovered and arrested. Delvaux's most expensive project (and his first in period) is a meticulous but somewhat stodgy adaptation of the last section of a 1976 novel by Marguerite Yourcenar, who died shortly before the film's completion. It's difficult to fault the acting of the large cast, led by the always splendid Volonté – here sporting a handsome head of white hair – and Van Damme's lighting photography is outstanding in helping to capture the brooding medieval atmosphere. However, for all its virtues, the work is episodic, lacks rigour, and remains uninvolving.

Accatone

Italy 1961 120 mins bw
Cino Del Duca/Arco

d **Pier Paolo Pasolini**
sc **Pier Paolo Pasolini**
ph **Tonino Delli Colli**
m **J.S. Bach**
    Franco Citti, Silvana Corsini, Franca
    Pasut, Roberto Scaringella, Adele
    Cambria

Accatone (Citti), a young pimp from the Roman slums, after trying to make an honest living, takes to thieving and is killed while escaping arrest. Pasolini, already a well-known novelist, poet, short-story writer and screenwriter, based his first feature on one of his novels. It drew on his intimate knowledge of sub-proletarian Rome and revealed his fatal attraction to the social outcast. It is brutal, realistic, unsentimental, and bustling with life, despite some rough edges. Particularly effective is the use of Bach on the soundtrack ironically counterpointing the world of pimps, prostitutes and street fighters. Citti, leading the cast of non-professionals, plays Accatone with a mixture of lethargy and vigour, seeking no sympathy. The director was to be murdered in 1975 by a young man from the same milieu.

Action Man

▶ **aka Leather And Nylon**
▶ **Le Soleil Des Voyous**

France 1966 95 mins col
Les Films Copernic-Fida

d   Jean Delannoy
sc Jean Delannoy, Alphonse Boudard
ph Walter Wottitz
m   Francis Lai
    Jean Gabin, Robert Stack, Margaret Lee,
    Suzanne Flon

A former crook (Gabin), now an aging, bored tycoon, links up with an American adventurer (Stack) to organize one last crime, the seizure of an army payroll. A run-of-the-mill gangster movie is almost saved by Gabin as his usual crusty, watchable self. In contrast, Stack, popular in Europe through TV's *The Untouchables*, is extremely wooden.

Act Of Aggression

▶ **L'Agression**

France   1975   102 mins   col
SNE Gaumont/Les Films Du Jeudi/Les Films De La Seine

d   Gérard Pirès
sc Gérard Pirès, Jean-Patrick Manchette
ph Silvano Ippoliti
m   Robert Charlebois
    Jean-Louis Trintignant, Catherine
    Deneuve, Claude Brasseur, Milena
    Vukotić

While driving off on holiday, a woman and her daughter are raped and murdered by a group of motorcyclists. So the husband and father decides to take the law into his own hands. Another French attempt to rival American crime thrillers of the 1970s, it contains unpleasant characters, a violent and sour screenplay, and is glibly directed. One remembers that the lovely blonde Deneuve, as the bitchy sister-in-law, used to make superior films.

▶ **Actors, The** see Players, The

An Actor's Revenge

▶ **Yukinojo Henge**

Japan   1963   113 mins   col
Daiei

d   Kon Ichikawa

sc Daisuke Ito, Teinosuke Kinugasa, Natto
    Wada
ph Setsuo Kobayashi
m   Yasushi Akutagawa
    Kazuo Hasegawa, Fujiko Yamamoto,
    Ayako Wakao, Ganjiro Nakamura

In the early 19th century, an *onnagata* (female impersonator) of the Kabuki theatre takes revenge on the three men who caused the death of his parents. The veteran screen actor, Hasegawa, not only gives an extraordinary performance as the hero/heroine, but also plays a daring bandit in the complex sub-plot. The Daieiscope screen is brilliantly used to create the impression of Japanese prints, the theatre stage and comic strips in this fascinating study of opposites – love/hate, illusion/reality, masculinity/femininity.

▶ **Adalen Riots, The** see Adalen 31

Adalen 31

▶ **aka The Adalen Riots**

Sweden   1969   115 mins   col
Svensk Filmindustri

d   Bo Widerberg
sc Bo Widerberg
ph Jörgen Persson
m   Duke Ellington and other composers
    Peter Schildt, Kerstin Tidelius, Roland
    Hedlund, Stefan Feierbach, Anita Björk

In 1931, a working-class family suffers during a lengthy strike at a paper mill in a small town in the north of Sweden, which ends with five workers being killed by soldiers. With its heart in the right place, the film is a colour-supplement socialist view of a tragic episode in modern Swedish history. The action takes place in sun-kissed, dappled surroundings, the camera even lingering on the beauty of blood on a white sheet covering a dead body.

Special Jury Prize Cannes 1969

Adam And Eve

▶ **Adam Y Eva**

Mexico   1956   78 mins   col
Costelaçion

d **Alberto Gout**
sc **Alberto Gout**
ph **Alex Phillips**
m **Gustave Cesar Carreon**
   Carlos Baena, Christiane Martel

In the Garden of Eden, Adam and Eve are happy until she is tempted to eat the forbidden fruit. Despite some good camerawork, this feeble and ludicrous version of Genesis created an exodus of audiences. Eve, played by Miss Universe 1953 with eye shadow and plucked eyebrows, had only a scream to utter.

▶ **Adam Y Eva** see Adam And Eve

L'Addition

▶ **aka The Patsy**

France 1983 87 mins col
Swanie/TF1/UGT-Top 1

d **Denis Amar**
sc **Denis Amar, Jean-Pierre Bastid, Jean Curtelin**
ph **Robert Fraisse**
m **Jean-Claude Petit**
   Richard Berry, Richard Bohringer, Victoria Abril, Farid Chopel

A young actor (Berry), after coming to the aid of a woman shoplifter, finds himself in prison where his sentence is increased following his supposed part in a break-out. A proficient and slick contemporary variation on the fatalistic pre-war French thrillers, but distinctly lacking their atmosphere and style.

▶ **Adeus Português, Um** see Portuguese Goodbye, A

Adieu Bonaparte

▶ **Al-Wedaa Ya Bonaparte**

Egypt 1984 120 mins col
Misr International/Lyric International/TF1 Films/Renn (Paris)

d **Youssef Chahine**
sc **Youssef Chahine**
ph **Mohsen Nasr**
m **Gabriel Yared**

Michel Piccoli, Mohsen Mohiedine, Mohsena Tewfik, Patrice Chereau

The experiences of an Egyptian family during the occupation of Alexandria by Napoleon and his army, and the uneasy friendship between a young Egyptian poet and one of Bonaparte's advisers. The exigencies of a big budget co-production might have accounted for a diminution in the great Chahine's poetry and power, but there are some spectacular scenes and excellent performances, notably from Chereau as a fanatical Bonaparte.

Adieu Léonard

France 1943 90 mins bw
Essor

d **Pierre Prévert**
sc **Pierre and Jacques Prévert**
ph **André Thomas**
m **Joseph Kosma (billed as Georges Mouqué)**
   Pierre Brasseur, Charles Trenet, Julien Carette, Jacqueline Bouvier

A crook (Carette) is blackmailed by a man (Brasseur) into murdering a wealthy imbecile (Trenet), but the would-be killer and victim escape together into the country. This whimsical farce, the second of the three features Pierre Prévert directed and co-scripted with his elder brother, was twice as long as the others and half as funny. Yet there is much to enjoy in the performances, though there was tension between Trenet and the director, because the latter had the popular singer imposed on him by the producer.

Adieu Les Beaux Jours

Germany 1933 95 mins bw
UFA

d **André Beaucler**
sc **Pierre France**
ph **Friedl Behn-Grund**
m **E.E. Buder, Raoul Ploquin**
   Brigitte Helm, Jean Gabin, Henri Bosc, Lucien Dayle, Henri Vilbert, Ginette Leclerc

A high class crook (Helm) steals a valuable necklace. While escaping to Spain, she gets involved with an innocent young advertising man (Gabin) who unwittingly helps her. Similar in plot to the later Dietrich-Gary Cooper film *Desire*, this German-made comedy-romance was a pleasant diversion, which gave audiences a chance to see the statuesque German star opposite the up-and-coming Gabin. Made in two languages, it was released in the USA and England in French versions for political as well as artistic reasons (most of the cast were French).

Adieu Philippine

France 1962 106 mins bw
Unitec/Alpha/Rome-Paris

d Jacques Rozier
sc Michèle O'Glor, Jacques Rozier
ph René Mathelin
m Jacques Denjean, Maxime Saury, Paul
   Mattei
   Jean-Claude Aimini, Yveline Céry,
   Stefania Sabatini, Vittorio Caprioli

In his last few months before military service, a young TV technician, on holiday, is torn between two girls. Rozier's first feature, using improvisation, amateur performers, hidden microphones and cameras in real locations, had a rough spontaneity very much in line with the aesthetics of the *nouvelle vague*. Disputes with the producer, delays in editing and its failure at the box office, prevented Rozier from making another film for 11 years.

The Adolescent

▶ aka An Adolescent Girl

▶ L'Adolescente

France 1978 90 mins col
Janus

d Jeanne Moreau
sc Jeanne Moreau, Henriette Jelinek
ph Pierre Gautard
m Philippe Sarde
   Simone Signoret, Laetitia Chauveau,
   Francis Huster, Hugues Quester

A 12-year-old Parisian girl (Chauveau), spending the summer of 1939 in the country with her grandmother (Signoret), falls for a young Jewish doctor (Huster), causing much

heartache. Moreau's second venture behind the camera (her debut film, *Lumière*, was made in 1975) is an old-fashioned and conventional tale of a sentimental education, overlaid with soppy lyricism. However, the playing of the innocent, confused girl and the wise old grandmother gives some dimension to the stock characters, and something of pre-war rural life is evoked.

▶ **Adolescente, L'** see Adolescent, The

▶ **Adolescent Girl, An** see Adolescent, The

▶ **Adolphe Or The Awkward Age** see Tender Age, The

▶ **Adolphe Ou L'Âge Tendre** see Tender Age, The

Adoption

▶ **Orökbefogadás**

Hungary 1975 89 mins bw
Hunnia

d Márta Mészáros
sc Márta Mészáros, Gyula Hernádi, Ferenc
   Grunwalsky
ph Lajos Koltai
m György Kovács
   Kati Berek, László Szabó, Gyon Gyver
   Vigh, Dr Arpad Perlaky, Péter Fried

When her married lover (Szabó) refuses to give her a child, a 42-year-old widowed factory worker (Berek) strikes up an intense friendship with an adolescent girl (Vigh). Well played as the leading character is, it is difficult to find her demands on others very sympathetic. Everyday sounds – factory noises, an alarm clock – add to the sense of alienation in this penetrating, intimist, uncomfortable film.

Best Film Berlin 1975

Adorable Creatures

▶ **Adorables Créatures**

France 1952 105 mins bw
Jacques Roitfeld/Sirius

d **Christian-Jaque**
sc **Charles Spaak, Jacques Companeez**
ph **Christian Matras**
m **Georges Van Parys**
   Daniel Gélin, Danielle Darrieux, Edwige Feuillère, Antonella Lualdi, Martine Carol

A Paris fashion executive (Gélin) remembers his past love affairs with four very lovely but very different women. This light-weight quartet of sex sketches, played with some class, provided the naughtiness lacking in English and American products at the time. Yet Gélin still ends up with a 'good' girl.

Adorable Julia

▶ **aka The Seduction Of Julia**

▶ **Julia, Du Bist Zauberhaft**

Austria 1962 97 mins bw
Wiener Mundus/Étoile(France)

d **Alfred Weidenmann**
sc **Johanna Sibelius, Eberhard Keindorff**
ph **Werner Krein**
m **Rolf A. Wilhelm**
   Lilli Palmer, Charles Boyer, Jean Sorel, Thomas Fritsch, Jeanne Valérie

Glamorous middle-aged Julia (Palmer), an actress on the London stage, embarks on one last fling with a younger man (Sorel), but finally realizes that her patient, adoring husband (Boyer) is the only man she really wants. Somerset Maugham's novel *Theatre* was the basis for this sugary, old-fashioned film, made with an eye on the international market. The charm of Palmer and Boyer can't disguise the faded air that hangs over the enterprise.

Adorable Liar

▶ **Adorable Menteuse**

France 1961 110 mins bw
Elefilm/Art Et Réalisation

d **Michel Deville**
sc **Michel Deville, Nina Companeez**
ph **Claude Lecompte**
m **Jean Dalve**
   Marina Vlady, Macha Meril, Michel Vitold, Jean-Marc Bory

A pretty 18-year-old girl is a compulsive liar, but when she genuinely falls for her 40-year-old neighbour (Vitold) her reputation makes him doubt her sincerity. A fairly breezy comedy which runs out of steam before the happy end, but Vlady makes a fetching fibber. The director, almost the same age as Godard and Chabrol, eschewed the *Nouvelle Vague* for commercial movies until the 1980s when he attempted to enter less conventional territory with films like *Death In A French Garden*.

▶ **Adorable Menteuse** see Adorable Liar

▶ **Adorables Créatures** see Adorable Creatures

▶ **À Double Tour** see Web Of Passion

Adrienne Lecouvreur

France 1938 110 mins bw
Georges Lampin/UFA

d **Marcel L'Herbier**
sc **Madame Simone**
ph **Fritz Arno Wagner**
m **Maurice Thiriet**
   Pierre Fresnay, Yvonne Printemps, Junie Astor, André Lefaur

Adrienne Lecouvreur, the famous 18th-century actress, loves Maurice De Saxe, son of the King of Poland, but when he goes off to war, she is poisoned by a rival for his love. The popular husband-and-wife team of Fresnay and Printemps tenderly acted out this tragic love story against a well-created background of theatre and aristocracy. The subject of four minor operas, it makes an attractive if minor film.

Adrift

▶ **Hrst Plna Vody**

Czechoslovakia 1969 108 mins col
Studio Barrandov-MPO

d **Jan Kadar**
sc **Jan Kadar, Elmar Klos, Imre Gyöngyössy**
ph **Vladimir Novotny**
m **Zdeněk Liška**

Rade Marković Milena Dravić, Paula Pritchett, Jožef Kroner

A happily married fisherman (Marković) becomes obsessed with a girl suffering from amnesia whom he rescued from the river but, after rejecting his love, she disappears again into the water. Freely adapted from Lajos Zilahy's best seller, *Something Is Adrift In The Water*, the film was being shot on the banks of the Danube in the summer of 1968 when it was interrupted by the arrival of Russian tanks. A year later, the cast and crew were reassembled to make this simple but intense tale, told in a rather complex manner, mixing past and present, real and imagined. It was helped considerably by the acting of Dravić as the wife and the striking looks of American fashion model Paula Pritchett as the river nymph.

▶ **Adua E Le Compagne** see Hungry For Love

▶ **Adulteress, The** see Thérèse Raquin

▶ **Adulterio All'Italiana** see Adultery Italian Style

Adultery Italian Style

▶ **Adulterio All'Italiana**

Italy   1966   93 mins   col
Fair Film

d   **Pasquale Festa Campanile**
sc   **Ottavio Alessi, Luigi Malerba, Pasquale Festa Campanile**
ph   **Roberto Gerardi**
m   **Armando Trovaioli**
     Catherine Spaak, Nino Manfredi, Maria Grazia Buccella, Vittorio Caprioli, Akim Tamiroff

When Marta (Spaak) learns that her husband Franco (Manfredi) has been dallying with her friend (Buccella), she decides to make him pay for it by inventing a fictitious lover. Franco falls for the ploy with unexpected, complicated and chaotic results. This is a wild farrago of largely coarse and repetitive farce in which credibility plays no part whatsoever. However, it is relieved by occasional scenes which, in degenerating into desperate parody, become extremely funny.

An Adventure Of Salvator Rosa

▶ **Un Avventura Di Salvator Rosa**

Italy   1939   97 mins   bw
Stella

d   **Alessandro Blasetti**
sc   **Ugo Scotti Berni**
ph   **Ugo Scotti Berni**
m   **Alessandro Cicognini**
     Gino Cervi, Luisa Ferida, Rina Morelli, Osvaldo Valenti

In the 17th century, a masked knight (Cervi) aids the peasants against the landed gentry, breaks up an unhappy marriage between a young duchess (Morelli) and a money-seeking count (Valenti), and woos a peasant beauty (Ferida). This is a typical spectacular costume drama from the leading director in Fascist Italy, who nevertheless managed some social insights. Although Blasetti made his name with this kind of escapist fare, his realist *Four Steps In The Clouds* (1942) was a great influence on post-war Italian cinema.

The Adventures Of Arsène Lupin

▶ **Les Aventures D'Arsène Lupin**

France   1956   103 mins   col
Chavane/SNE-Gaumont/Lambor-Costel Lazione

d   **Jacques Becker**
sc   **Jacques Becker, Albert Simonin**
ph   **Edmond Séchan**
m   **Jean-Jacques Grünewald**
     Robert Lamoureux, Liselotte Pulver, O.E. Hasse, Henri Rolland

Arsène Lupin (Lamoureux), man-about-town and gentleman thief in the Paris of 1912, is involved in several robberies, falls for a beautiful Baroness (Pulver) and is kidnapped by the Kaiser (Hasse). Lamoureux makes a stylish light-fingered job of Maurice Leblanc's famous character (the subject of a number of films), but it is the evocation of the last days of the *Belle Époque* that gives the film its appeal. Undemanding, commercial entertainment from a director capable of far better.

The Adventures Of Baron Münchhausen

▶ **Münchhausen**

    Germany 1943 134 mins col
    UFA

d   **Josef Von Baky**
sc **Berthold Bürger (pseudonym for Erich Kästner)**
ph **Werner Krien**
m   **Georg Haentzschel**
    Hans Albers, Wilhelm Bendow, Michael Bohnen, Marina Von Ditmar, Hans Brausewetter

At a costume ball in 1943, the Baron Münchhausen (Albers) recounts the story of his life to a young woman who thinks she's in love with him. He tells of his encounter with a magician in the 18th century who gave him the ability to make his wishes come true, one of them being never to age. The magic helps him get out of all kinds of scrapes, including one on the moon. The story of the extraordinary exploits of the mendacious Baron was ideally suited to the lavish production which matched anything from Hollywood at the time. The instigator of this extravagant German fantasy was Nazi propaganda minister Josef Goebbels (no mean liar himself) who wanted an international success to celebrate the 25th anniversary of UFA studios. Superbly photographed in Agfacolor, with breathtaking art direction by Emil Hasler and Otto Gulstorff, this enjoyable film took three years to make.

▶ **Adventures Of Don Quixote** see Don Quixote

The Adventures Of Goopy And Bagha

▶ **aka Goopy And Bagha**

▶ **Goopy Gyne Bagha Byne**

    India 1968 132 mins bw/col

    Purnima

d   **Satyajit Ray**
sc **Satyajit Ray**
ph **Soumendu Roy**
m   **Satyajit Ray**
    Tapan Chatterjee (Goopy), Robi Ghosh (Bagha), Santosh Dutta, Harindranath Chattopadhyay

Two wandering musicians encounter the King of Ghosts who offers them three wishes and a pair of magic slippers. Ray's first film to be made principally with children in mind, was adapted from a tale by his writer-artist grandfather. Its mixture of music, broad comedy, fantasy and romance, in the tradition of popular Indian cinema, made it Ray's biggest success in his own country. Westerners found the lengthy, whimsical picaresque tale less palatable, despite magic moments and an ending in bright colour in an otherwise black-and-white film.

The Adventures Of Prince Achmed

▶ **Die Abenteuer Des Prinzen Achmed**

    Germany 1926 65 mins bw
    (Restored print tinted)
    Comenius Film

d   **Lotte Reiniger**
sc **Lotte Reiniger**
ph **Animated film**
m   **Silent**

Prince Achmed rescues a princess from the clutches of assorted monsters and witches and is helped to a happy ending by Aladdin's lamp. The best-known work of animator Lotte Reiniger, who filmed it in the special silhouette technique which she invented herself, *Achmed* has the distinction of being the world's first feature-length animated film. Made over a three-year period in Potsdam, with the director's husband, Carl Koch, supervising the photography, it enjoyed world-wide success, although today's post-Disney audiences might find it a little limited. By 1954 only one print survived (held by the British Film Institute). From this, a new negative was made and, in the early 1970s, the original tinting instructions were found and applied under Reiniger's personal supervision. (She died in 1981, having settled in Britain).

The Adventures Of Rabbi Jacob

▶ **aka The Mad Adventures Of Rabbi Jacob**

▶ **Les Aventures De Rabbi Jacob**

France   1973   96 mins   col
Films Pomereu/Horse Films

d   **Gérard Oury**
sc **Gérard Oury, Danielle Thompson, Josy Eisenberg**
ph **Henri Decaë**
m   **Vladimir Cosma**
   Louis De Funès, Suzy Delair, Marcel Dalio, Claude Giraud

An anti-Semitic French businessman (De Funès), on his way to his daughter's wedding, unwittingly becomes involved with an Arab terrorist, disguises himself as a rabbi, and ends up at a barmitzvah. A broad comedy with a serious intent – an anti-Semite comes to like Jews – it has its amusing moments, although two men falling into a vat of chewing gum is not one of them. One of the few of the irascible De Funès' vehicles to make its appeal to a wider audience than his home fans.

The Adventures of Rémi

▶ **Sans Famille**

France   1958   100 mins   col
Societé De Productions Cinématographique/Européennes/ Francinex SA-Rizzoli

d   **André Michel**
sc **Pierre Véry**
ph **Robert Juillard**
m   **Paul Misraki**
   Pierre Brasseur, Gino Cervi, Bernard Blier, Joël Flateau

Rémi (Flateau), a little boy from a wealthy background, is sold to a wandering player (Cervi) by his foster parents, but is sought by an Englishman (Brasseur) acting for a wicked

uncle. This adaptation of Hector Malot's 19th-century children's classic, is colourful and incident-packed enough to appeal to sub-teenagers, but the many moments of excessive sentimentality might make hardier kids blow raspberries.

The Adventures Of Till Eulenspiegel

▶ **(US: The Bold Adventure)**

▶ **Les Aventures De Till L'Espiègle**

France   1956   90 mins   col
Les Films Ariane/Defa

d   **Gérard Philipe, Joris Ivens**
sc **Gérard Philipe, René Wheeler**
ph **Christian Matras**
m   **Georges Auric**
   Gérard Philipe, Jean Vilar, Nicole Berger, Fernand Ledoux

Till, a 16th-century Flemish folk-hero, organizes a liberation army and drives the occupying Spaniards from his country. Philipe enjoyed co-directing and starring in this lavish knockabout swashbuckler, but the genre was better served by Fairbanks in the 1920s, and by himself in *Fanfan The Tulip* (1951).

The Adventures of Werner Holt

▶ **Die Abenteuer Des Werner Holt**

E. Germany   1963   164 mins   bw
DEFA/VEB

d   **Joachim Kunert**
sc **Joachim Kunert, Claus Kuechenmeister**
ph **Rolf Sohre**
m   **Gerhard Wohlgemuth**
   Klause-Peter Thiele, Arno Wyzniewski, Manfred Karge, Gunter Junghans

Two young Nazi soldiers (Thiele and Wyzniewski) former schoolfriends, go different ways during the last days of the war, one questioning the cause, the other determined to defend Hitler to the end. Two years in the making, this anti-war, anti-Nazi epic impresses with its ambition and sincerity.

Rather cluttered with flashbacks and characters, it contains some spectacular battle sequences and the potent atmosphere of 1945.

Adventure Starts Here

▶ **Här Börjar Äventyret**

Sweden 1965 90 mins bw
Sandrew/Fennada

d   Jörn Donner
sc Jörn Donner
ph Jean Badal
m   Bo Nilsson
    Harriet Andersson, Matti Oravisto,
    Claude Titre, Göran Cederberg

A Swedish fashion-buyer (Andersson) on a trip to Berlin meets a Finnish architect (Oravisto) and her French ex-lover (Titre) but hesitates to fall in love again. Donner's third feature, and third film with his lover and future wife Harriet Andersson, is a personal tale consisting of a series of meetings, musings on language barriers, and fragmented memories with an indeterminate ending. Reviled at the time, this uneven film did show that there was a way to get out of the large shadow of Ingmar Bergman that hung over Swedish cinema.

The Adversary

▶ **aka Siddharta And The City**
▶ **Pratidwandi**

India 1970 100 mins bw
Priya

d   Satyajit Ray
sc Satyajit Ray
ph Soumendu Roy
m   Satyajit Ray
    Dhritiman Chatterjee, Jayashree Roy,
    Krishna Bose, Kalyan Chatterjee

A young man (Dhritiman Chatterjee), on the death of his father, is forced to give up his studies and look for a job in order to support his mother, sister and younger brother, but he is unable to compete in the rat race. Ray paints a perceptive portrait of a lethargic, rather insufferable, educated man trying to

cope with life in the vast and teeming city of Calcutta. The other characters are also beautifully observed in this funny, sad and bitter tale.

Aelita

USSR 1924 70 mins bw
Mezhrabpom

d   Yakov Protazanov
sc Fedor Ozep, Alexei Faiko
ph Yuri Zhelabuzhsky
m   Silent
    Julia Solntseva, Nikolai Batalov, Igor
    Ilinsky

Two Russian soldiers land on Mars and organize a revolution on the Soviet model against the autocratic ruler Queen Aelita (Solntseva). The Soviet cinema's first venture into science fiction is a delightful didactic comedy with futuristic set designs by Sergei Kozlovsky and interesting footage of 1920s Moscow. The screenplay (from a novel by Alexei Tolstoy) optimistically views the future from the standpoint of the USSR's New Economic Policy. Solntseva, making her screen debut, would soon become the wife of Dovzhenko and a remarkable director herself.

Aerograd

▶ **aka Frontier**
▶ **aka Air City**

USSR 1935 81 mins bw
Mosfilm-Ukrainfilm

d   Alexander Dovzhenko
sc Alexander Dovzhenko
ph Edouard Tissé, Mikhail Gindin
m   Dmitri Kabalevsky
    Semyon Shagaida, Stepan Shkurat, Sergei
    Stolyarov

A new city under construction in Siberia is almost destroyed by eight Japanese saboteurs smuggling dynamite across the border. Although rhetorical and overly patriotic, the rhythmic cutting and lyrical images make it one of the most unforgettable of Soviet films of the 1930s. Among the memorable scenes are a plane fight, a priest confronting a group of war widows, and the villain dying with the word 'Mama' on his lips.

L'Affaire Est Dans Le Sac

▶ **aka It's In The Bag**

> France 1932 47 mins bw
> Pathé/Nathan

d **Pierre Prévert**
sc **Jacques Prévert**
ph **Alphonse Gibory, Eli Lotar**
m **Maurice Jaubert**
> **Lora Hays, Julien Carette, Jacques Brunius, Etienne Decroux, Jacques Prévert, J.P. Dreyfus, Gildes**

A bored millionaire wishes his daughter only to marry a man who can amuse him. As his future son-in-law turns out to be a kidnapper, he gets more than he bargained for. The surreal humour of the first and best of the three features made by the Prévert brothers outraged the general public at the time. No-one could be shocked today by this delightful, irreverent, medium-length burlesque. It marked the first screen appearance of Carette, one of the French cinema's greatest comic character actors.

The Affair Lafont

▶ **Conflit**

> France 1939 85 mins bw
> Transatlantic

d **Leonid Moguy**
sc **Hans Wilhelm, Gina Kaus**
ph **Ted Pahle**
m **Wal-Berg**
> **Corinne Luchaire, Annie Ducaux, Raymond Rouleau, Armand Bernard**

A girl gives her illegitimate child to her barren married sister to bring up as her own, but tries to reclaim the child some years later. Similar to the superior Bette Davis weepie of the same year, *The Old Maid*, this reasonably diverting melodrama shifts the sympathy in favour of the sister fighting to keep the child she has nurtured, even to resorting to murder. This bias is further emphasized by the deeper

characterization from Ducaux as opposed to the mediocre Luchaire as the real mother.

▶ **Affair Of The Heart, An** see Switchboard Operator, The

The Affairs Of Dr Holl

▶ **aka Angelika**

▶ **Doktor Holl**

> W. Germany 1952 99 mins bw
> Friedrich Mainz-Sama

d **Rolf Hansen**
sc **Thea Von Harbou**
ph **Franz Weihmayr**
m **Mark Lothar**
> **Maria Schell, Dieter Borsche, Heidemarie Hatheyer**

The doctor (Borsche) who cures the invalid daughter of a wealthy industrialist marries her out of pity, believing she might not have long to live. Although Maria Schell as the suffering heroine smiles a lot through her tears, there is little for audiences to smile at in this cloying, clichéd concoction. The script was by Fritz Lang's former wife who had been an official screenwriter under the Nazis.

Afraid To Live

▶ **(US: The Confession Of Ina Kahr)**

▶ **Das Bekenntis Der Ina Kahr**

> W. Germany 1954 102 mins bw
> Omega

d **G.W. Pabst**
sc **Erna Fentsch**
ph **Günther Anders**
m **Erwin Haletz**
> **Curt Jurgens, Elisabeth Müller, Vera Molnar, Albert Lieven**

A much-betrayed wife (Müller) plans to poison both herself and her husband (Jurgens), and when he dies and she lives, she is accused of murder. A low point in Pabst's career, this routine battle-of-the-sexes melodrama has little substance or style. The wife gets off lightly, the film does not.

Africa Addio

Italy   1965   138 mins   col
Rizzoli

d   **Gualtiero Jacopetti, Franco Prosperi**
sc **Gualtiero Jacopetti, Franco Prosperi**
ph **Antonio Climati**
m   **Riz Ortolani**

With scenes, mainly of cruelty, perpetrated in different parts of Africa, this is another lurid, so-called documentary from Jacopetti, without even the humour that some might see in *Mondo Cane* to redeem it. It took over three years (according to the publicity) to photograph and collect these pictures of the bloody slaughter of wild life, the execution of people in the Congo, and barbaric tribal rituals. Under the guise of making anthropological points, the film obviously revelled in its material.

▶ **Africana, L'** see Woman From Africa, The

L'Âge D'Or

▶ **(US: The Golden Age)**

France   1930   60 mins   bw
Vicomte De Noailles

d   **Luis Buñuel**
sc **Luis Buñuel, Salvador Dali**
ph **Albert Dubergen**
m   **Wagner, Mendelssohn, Beethoven, Debussy**
    Gaston Modot, Lya Lys, Max Ernst, Pierre Prévert, Jacques Brunius, Luis Buñuel

Two lovers (Modot and Lys) constantly have their sexual desires thwarted by *bourgeois* society. With the logic of a dream, Buñuel's second film contains all the themes that would reappear in his future work. Owing much to Freud and to the Surrealist Manifesto, it set out to shock with anti-clerical images: a blind man being kicked, a cow on a bed and fellatio with the toe of a statue. As a result, it was banned for some years after the screen was splattered with ink by a Fascist group. What Henry Miller called 'a divine orgy' is still pretty potent today.

The Age Of Indiscretion

▶ **L'Eta Dell'Amore**

Italy   1953   85 mins   bw
I.C.S./Cormoran

d   **Lionello De Felice**
sc **Lionello De Felice, Franco Brusati, Vittorio Novarese**
ph **Mario Montuori**
m   **Mario Nascimbene**
    Marina Vlady, Pierre-Michel Beck, Aldo Fabrizi, Fernand Gravey

Two 15-year-olds, one the son of a well-to-do lawyer, the other the daughter of a widowed jailbird, fall in love, but suffer great pressure from the adults when the girl becomes pregnant. A well-meaning, uninspiring drama presenting all the adults as heavies. The young couple (Vlady and Beck) come off best in the acting department.

▶ **Age Of Infidelity** see Death Of A Cyclist

Age Of The Earth

▶ **Idade Da Terra**

Brazil   1980   158 mins   col
Glauber Rocha Prod. Artisticas

d   **Glauber Rocha**
sc **Glauber Rocha**
ph **Roberto Pires**
m   **Rogerio Duarte**
    Ana Maria Magalhaes, Mauricio Do Valle, Jece Valadão, Norma Benguel

A visionary argument between Marxism, Catholicism and African-derived beliefs, with scenes of folk rituals, the Mardi Gras, disputing political demogogues, and a historian in Brasilia. Rocha's first film shot in Brazil on his return from 10 years' exile and his last film before his death in 1981, aged 43, contains many of the elements of his past films: the ferment of juxtaposed images, the complex structure, the loud diatribes and repetitions.

However, the numbing effect of it all is to make *Cinema Novo*, which Rocha helped to found in the early 1960s – and of which this is an example – seem very old hat.

Agnus Dei

▶ **Égi Bárány**

Hungary   1970   90 mins   col
Mafilm Studio 1

d   **Miklós Jancsó**
sc **Miklós Jancsó, Gyula Hernádi**
ph **János Kende**
m   **National songs**
József Madaras, Márk Zala, Lajos Balázsovits, Daniel Olbrychski, Anna Széles, András Kozák

In a small religious peasant community in 1919, the Whites and Reds struggle for power, until an inspired Red leader emerges triumphant. A hymn of both despair and celebration in song, dance, and dialogue taken mainly from the Bible and Hungarian folk literature, orchestrated by the laterally-tracking camera and long takes that marked Jancsó's intensely personal style before it became self-parodic.

▶ **Agonia** see Agony

Agony

▶ **Agonia**

USSR   1975   148 mins   col
Mosfilm

d   **Elem Klimov**
sc **Semyon Lungin, Ilya Nusinov**
ph **Leonid Kalashnikov**
m   **Alfred Shnitke**
Alexei Petrenko, Anatoly Romashin, Velta Linei, Alisa Freindtlich

In the final days of the Romanov regime, the 'mad monk' Rasputin wields power at court. This forceful epic took nine years to make, then spent 10 more on the shelf, because the pre-*glasnost* Soviet authorities baulked at the orgies and at what they saw as a sympathetic portrayal of the doomed Tsar (Romashin). However, the latter is seen as a man completely out of touch with the people and political reality. To demonstrate this, the action is cleverly intercut with contemporary newsreels. Although the direction is sometimes a little feverish, it befits the character of Rasputin, a startling performance by Petrenko.

Agostino

Italy   1962   90 mins   bw
Baltea/Dino De Laurentiis

d   **Mauro Bolognini**
sc **Mauro Bolognini, Goffredo Parise**
ph **Aldo Tonti**
m   **Carlo Rustichelli**
Ingrid Thulin, John Saxon, Paolo Colombo

An attractive widow (Thulin) and her small son are enjoying their holiday at the Venice Lido, until a man (Saxon) begins to court the mother, alienating the child, who runs off and joins a street gang where he learns the brutal facts of life. One of Alberto Moravia's best stories, turned into a rather shallow film with an unnecessary narration to explain the boy's emotions. The Venetian locales, as usual, look good on the wide screen.

▶ **Agression, L'** see Act Of Aggression

▶ **Aguirre, Der Zorn Gottes** see Aguirre, Wrath Of God

Aguirre, Wrath Of God

▶ **Aguirre, Der Zorn Gottes**

W. Germany   1972   95 mins   col
Werner Herzog/Hessicher Rundfunk

d   **Werner Herzog**
sc **Werner Herzog**
ph **Thomas Mauch**
m   **Popol Vuh**
Klaus Kinski, Ruy Guerra, Helena Rojo, Cecilia Rivera

In the 16th century, a Spanish conquistador leads a hazardous expedition through the wilds of Peru in search of El Dorado. The fascination of this ponderous morality tale derives from the jungle atmosphere and pictorial flair, as well the intense performance of Kinski as Aguirre, the role that brought him international fame. Like his hero, the director had to overcome difficult conditions while filming in the Peruvian Andes. The final shot, an aerial view of the lone survivor on a raft, is masterful.

▶ **Ahdat Sanawouach El-Djamr** see Chronicle Of The Burning Years

▶ **Ah! Les Belles Bacchantes** see Femmes De Paris

Aida

Italy   1953   96 mins   col
Oscar Film

d   **Clemente Fracassi**
sc   **G. Castilli, A. Gobbi, V. Salvucci**
ph   **Piero Portalupi**
m   **Verdi**
     Sophia Loren (Aida, dubbed by Renata Tebaldi), Lois Maxwell (Amneris, dubbed by Ebe Stignani), Luciano Della Marra (Radames, dubbed by Giuseppe Campora), Afro Poli (Amonasro, dubbed by Gino Bechi)

Aida, an Ethiopian slave girl to Amneris, the King of Egypt's daughter, is torn between her love for Radames, an Egyptian army officer, and for her own defeated people. Without causing DeMille any loss of sleep, this colourful, faithful rendition of Verdi's grand opera was well served by the unseen singers and their embodiments. In the role turned down by Gina Lollobrigida, Sophia Loren, painted chocolate and striking in an Afro wig, came to the attention of the English-speaking world.

▶ **Aien Kyo** see Straits Of Love And Hate

▶ **Aigle À Deux Têtes, L'** see Eagle Has Two Heads, The

▶ **Ai No Borei** see Empire Of Passion

▶ **Ai No Corrida** see In The Realm Of The Senses

▶ **Ai No Kawaki** see Longing For Love

▶ **Air City** see Aerograd

▶ **Ajantrik** see Mechanical Man

A. K.

France   1985   75 mins   col
Greenwich Film Productions/Herald Ace

d   **Chris Marker**
sc   **Chris Marker**
ph   **Frans-Yves Marescot**
m   **Tohru Takemitsu**
     Akira Kurosawa and the cast and crew of *Ran*

A documentary on the location shooting of *Ran* in late 1984 on the slopes of Mount Fuji, including an interview with its 75-year-old director. This often too reverential impression of the Japanese master at work is nonetheless revealing about his methods and his relations with his crew. Marker also uses the subject for his own brand of poetic-philosophical celluloid essay on the Japanese and the filming of a film.

▶ **Akahige** see Red Beard

▶ **Akasen Chitai** see Street Of Shame

Åke And His World

▶ **Åke Och Hans Värld**

Sweden   1984   103 mins   col
Sandrew Film

d   **Allan Edwall**
sc   **Allan Edwall**
ph   **Jörgen Persson**
m   **Thomas Lindahl**
     Martin Lindström, Loa Falkman, Gunnel Fred, Katja Blomquist, Ulla Sjöblom, Suzanne Ernrup, Allan Edwall

Six-year-old Åke (Lindström), the son of a country doctor, commits a small misdemeanour and imagines that all sorts of punishments will befall him, from being struck down by the local pastor to being eaten by wolves. The film operates in the same delightful territory as *My Life As A Dog*, giving a child's eye view of quirky Swedish village life. It only falls short of the later film in that its scope is a little narrower. Åke, pronounced 'O-keh', is played by an exceptional nine-year-old, and the rest of the characters, seen through his eyes, ring true. Åke's world is beautifully captured by the photography of Persson (best known abroad for *Elvira Madigan*), and the director of this touching and funny film manages to avoid sentimentality.

▶ **Åke Och Hans Värld** see Åke And His World

▶ **Akibiyori** see Late Autumn

Akira

Japan 1988 124 mins col
Akira Committee

d **Katsuhiro Otomo**
sc **Katsuhiro Otomo, Izo Hashimoto**
ph **Katsuji Misawa**
m **Shoji Yamashiro**
   Animated cartoon figures

After World War III devastated the planet in 1988, Neo-Tokyo was built. Now, in the year 2019, the city is in crisis and chaos with unemployment rife, delinquent bikers on the rampage and warring factions everywhere. In a laboratory scientists control an experiment with Akira, an unseen creature believed by the authorities to spell destruction, and by the people to be a messiah of some kind. Tetsuo, a young biker injured in a fight, is hospitalized and taken over by Akira's power. 'Akira' is a massively popular Japanese comic strip and the film is no more nor less than an animated comic. Its pseudo-philosophical message is hopelessly confused, its science-fiction plot difficult to follow. Noisy and interminable, violent and unattractive, it is an amalgam of every violent American film one can think of. Definitely for specialist tastes only, its sole merit for others is the design and photography of some striking futuristic sets.

▶ **Al Asfour** see Sparrow, The

▶ **Albatros, L'** see Albatross, The

The Albatross

▶ **aka Love Hate**

▶ **L'Albatros**

France 1971 90 mins col
Balzac Films/Profilms/Bestar Productions

d **Jean-Pierre Mocky**
sc **Jean-Pierre Mocky, Claude Veillot, Raphael Delpard**
ph **Marcel Weiss**
m **Léo Ferré**
   Jean-Pierre Mocky, André Le Gall, Paul Muller, Marion Game

A criminal (Mocky), escaping from jail, forces a woman (Game) to drive him to the German border, but political intrigue enmeshes them and tragedy ensues. This sometimes powerful political thriller is undermined by implausible plotting, uncertain shifts from melodrama to satire, and an attempt to be all things to all parties.

▶ **Albero Degli Zoccoli** see Tree Of Wooden Clogs, The

▶ **Albert – Warum?** see Albert – Why?

Albert – Why?

▶ **Albert – Warum?**

W. Germany 1978 115 mins bw
HFF

d **Josef Rödl**
sc **Josef Rödl**
ph **Karlheinz Gschwind**
   Fritz Binner, Michael Eichenseer, George Schiessl, Elfriede Bleisteiner

Albert is a simple-minded gentle giant, considered an idiot by the Bavarian villagers because he stutters and has spent a while in a mental home. He loses control of the family farm to a cousin. Young director Rödl's graduation piece from the Munich Film School brings a small community brilliantly to life, while avoiding making judgements about ignorant attitudes. However, what makes the film memorable, is the remarkable performance of Fritz Binner, on whose own life Rödl based his screenplay.

Aleko

USSR   1953   60 mins   col
Lenfilm

d **Sidelov**
sc **A. Abramov, G. Roshal**
ph **A. Nazarov**
m **Rachmaninov**
   A. Ognivtsev, I. Zubkovskay, M. Reizen

A gypsy youth loves a married girl whose husband finally kills them both. The chance to see this rarely performed Rachmaninov opera, based on Pushkin's poem *The Gypsies*, is ruined by static direction, bad colour, and the lack of passion demanded by the sweeping music. However, this was a first attempt by the USSR to shoot an opera away from the confines of the stage against natural landscapes, foreshadowing more successful opera films.

▶ **Alerte En Méditerranée** see Hell's Cargo

Alexander Nevsky

USSR   1938   112 mins   bw
Mosfilm

d **Sergei Eisenstein**
sc **Sergei Eisenstein, Piotr Pavlenko**
ph **Edouard Tissé**
m **Prokofiev**
   Nikolai Cherkassov, Nikolai Okhlopov, Alexander Abrikosov, Dmitri Orlov

Prince Alexander Nevsky (Cherkassov) forms a people's army to drive brutal Teutonic invaders from the soil of Holy Russia in 1242. Although less experimental stylistically than Eisenstein's previous work (he had been charged with 'formalism' by the authorities), it has what the great Russian director called a 'symphonic structure' because of his close collaboration with Prokofiev. The result is an operatic, patriotic pageant offering stirring images and a dramatic use of music, particu-

larly in the brilliant Battle of the Ice sequence. Eisenstein's most enjoyable film was withdrawn at the time of the German-Soviet Pact in 1939, and only re-shown, appropriately, when the Nazis invaded the Soviet Union.

Alexander The Great

▶ **O Megalexandros**

Greece   1980   210 mins   col
RAI/ZDF/Angelopoulos Prod.

d **Theo Angelopoulos**
sc **Theo Angelopoulos**
ph **Ghiorgos Arvanitis**
m **Christodoulos Halaris**
   Omero Antonutti, Eva Kotamanidu, Grigoris Evangelatos, Michalis Yannatos

The bandit Alexander (Antonutti) takes a party of English aristocrats hostage, leading them to a mountain village where the peasants have overthrown the landowners and established a commune. Angelopoulos certainly takes his time in the telling of this allegory of Greek socialism, using slow pans, long takes and pauses, but it is superb to look at and often intriguing and mentally stimulating.

Alexandre

▶ **(US: Very Happy Alexandre)**
▶ **Alexandre Le Bienheureux**

France   1967   96 mins   col
Les Productions De la Guéville/
Madeleine Films/Les Films De la
Colombe

d **Yves Robert**
sc **Yves Robert, Pierre Levy Corti**
ph **René Mathelin**
m **Vladimir Cosma**
   Philippe Noiret, Françoise Brion, Marlène Jobert, Paul Le Person, Jean Carmet, Pierre Richard

After the death of his wife (Brion), Alexandre (Noiret) decides to lock himself up in his house with his dog and stay in bed all day, every day. After two months, he gets up and leads a holiday existence, until he is almost trapped into remarriage. As is the hero, so is the film – likeable, leisurely, unambitious.

Both Noiret and Kaly, the dog, are perfectly cast, the colour photography attractive, and the philosophy of sloth seductive. It's also rather misogynistic and forgettable.

▶ **Alexandre Le Bienheureux** see Alexandre

Alexandria – Why?

▶ **Iskindirya – Leh?**

Egypt 1978 125 mins col
Misr International Films (Cairo)/Oncic (Algeria)

d **Youssef Chahine**
sc **Youssef Chahine, Mohsen Zayed**
ph **Mohsen Nasr**
m **Fouad El Zaheri**
Mohsen Mohiedine, Naglaa Fathi, Farid Shawki, Ezzat El Alayli, Gerry Sundquist

In the Alexandria of 1942, while the Allied troops await Rommel, a film-mad schoolboy's hopes of becoming a star seem dashed when things go wrong at the end of a school play. The vitality and humour of the film is influenced by the Hollywood movies (particularly MGM musicals) into which the well-drawn characters escape from the wartime situation. This is the most immediately accessible of the great Egyptian director's works.

Best Director Berlin 1979

Alfredo Alfredo

Italy 1971 98 mins col
Rizzoli/Francoriz RPA

d **Pietro Germi**
sc **Leo Benvenuti, Tullio Pinelli, Piero De Bernardi**
ph **Aiace Parolin**
m **Carlo Rustichelli**
Dustin Hoffman, Stefania Sandrelli, Carla Gravina, Saro Urzi

A timid bank clerk (Hoffman) discovers after marriage that his wife (Sandrelli) is an oversexed bore, so he takes up with another girl (Gravina) only to find he can't get a divorce. Top Hollywood star Dustin Hoffman studiously learned his part in Italian before leaving for Rome, but Germi shot it in English and then dubbed it. Hoffman's talent was also wasted in this frenzied, intermittently funny, misogynistic satire on Italian customs and the divorce laws.

▶ **Al Grito De Este Pueblo** see Cry Of The People, The

▶ **Ali** see Fear Eats The Soul

Ali Baba And The Forty Thieves

▶ **Ali Baba Et Les Quarante Voleurs**

France 1954 90 mins col
Films Du Cyclope

d **Jacques Becker**
sc **Jacques Becker, Marc Maurette, Maurice Griffe, Jean Manse**
ph **Robert Le Fèbvre**
m **Paul Misraki**
Fernandel, Samia Gamal, Dieter Borsche, Henri Vilbert

Ali Baba (Fernandel), sent to buy a new wife for his brutal master, comes across a cave full of treasures and is discovered by the thieves. He returns to his village a changed man. Adapted from a Cesare Zavattini treatment of the Arabian Nights tale, this rather rambling, lacklustre vehicle for the popular horse-faced French comic, tries to bring in elements of social comment about the poor. Its main appeal lies in the handsome Moroccan locations shot in Eastman Colour.

▶ **Ali Baba Et Les Quarante Voleurs** see Ali Baba And The Forty Thieves

The Alibi

▶ **L'Alibi**

France 1937 82 mins bw
Tellus Films

d **Pierre Chenal**
sc **Marcel Achard**
ph **Ted Pahle, Jacques Mercanton**
m **Georges Auric, Jacques Dallin**

Erich Von Stroheim, Albert Préjean, Louis Jouvet, Jany Holt

A Parisian dance hostess (Holt), blackmailed into providing an alibi for a murderer (Stroheim), falls in love with a secret police agent (Préjean) sent to win her confidence. Other thrillers of the period were as sharply directed and written, but few had the inestimable advantage of the sparks set up between Stroheim's killer and Jouvet's police chief. The film was slightly spoiled by the dragged-in love interest and an insipid happy ending imposed by the producers.

▶ **Alibi, L'** see Alibi, The

Alice

▶ **Neco Z Alenky**

Czechoslovakia   1988   85 mins   col
Condor Features/Film Four International/Hessicher Rundfunk

d   **Jan Svankmajer**
sc   **Jan Svankmajer**
ph   **Svatopluk Maly**
m   **None credited**
   Kristina Kahoutova

Alice (Kahoutova, the only human among puppets), bored, sits in a room full of strange objects. When a stuffed white rabbit comes to life in his glass case, dresses up and leaves through an open table drawer, she follows him and falls down a deep tunnel to a cellar. She sets off in pursuit through a maze of subterranean vaults, meeting, among others, a hookah-smoking caterpillar, the Mad Hatter, the March Hare and the King and Queen of Hearts. 'My Alice is an interpretation of Carroll's, fermented by my own childhood with all its particular obsessions and anxieties,' explained the director of his first feature-length film. Svankmajer, well known for short, surreal and anarchic animation films, manages to remain faithful to the spirit of the children's classic while injecting it with his own black humour. There is certainly nothing cosy about this telling, which starts with, 'Now you will see a film...for children...perhaps,' and there are many innovations and variations along the way. When Alice lifts a spoon of jam to her lips, she

discovers the liquid turned into a drawing pin, and a bread roll suddenly spouts nails. Among the many vivid metamorphoses is the caterpillar forming itself out of a sock, two dolls' eyeballs and false teeth in a drawer. Brilliant as the conception is, the film at 85 minutes overstays its welcome in Wonderland and is continually disrupted by close-ups of Alice's lips telling the story, more disconcerting in the badly-dubbed English version.

▶ **Alice In Den Städten** see Alice In The Cities

Alice In The Cities

▶ **Alice In Den Städten**

W. Germany   1974   110 mins   bw
Filmverlag Der Autoren

d   **Wim Wenders**
sc   **Wim Wenders**
ph   **Robby Müller**
m   **Pop songs, Mahler**
   Rüdiger Vogler, Yella Rottländer, Liza Kreuzer

An almost wordless German photo-journalist (Vogler), numbed by recent assignments, travels down the east coast of America with a nine-year-old girl (Rottländer) in search of her grandmother. This gently amusing and melancholy road movie that foreshadows themes more deeply explored in *Paris Texas* (1984), was the first of four leisurely-paced, odd odysseys featuring Vogler. Wenders was much more comfortable with this low budget movie over which he had complete control, than on the international co-production of *The Scarlet Letter* from which he emerged as numbed as his photo-journalist character.

Alice Or The Last Escapade

▶ **Alice Ou La Dernière Fugue**

France   1977   93 mins   col
Filmel/PHPG

d   **Claude Chabrol**
ph   **Jean Rabier**
m   **Pierre Jansen**
   Sylvia Kristel, Charles Vanel, Jean

Carmet, André Dussollier, Thomas
Chabrol, Marcel Dalio

Alice Carrol (Kristel) suddenly gets into her
car and leaves her husband, but a huge storm
forces her to take refuge in a mysterious old
house where an old man (Vanel) and his valet
(Carmet) seem to expect her. A surprising
departure into fantasy for Chabrol which
doesn't really come off. In this half-hearted
homage to Lewis Carroll, there are psychological clues, an 'old dark house' movie pastiche and the beautiful Sylvia 'Emmanuelle'
Kristel looking as confused as her audience.

► **Alice Ou La Dernière Fugue** see
Alice Or The Last Escapade

The Alienist

► **O Alienista**

Brazil   1970   82 mins   col
Dos Santos/Barreto/Farias

d   **Nelson Pereira Dos Santos**
sc **Nelson Pereira Dos Santos**
ph **Dib Lutfi**
m   **Guilherme Maga'haes Vaz**
    Nildo Parente, Isabel Ribeiro, Arduino
    Colasanti, Irene Stafnaia

A new priest (Parente) comes to a small town
and builds an insane asylum for people who
do not agree with his ways and religion, but
the many homeless poor seek shelter within
its walls. Dos Santos, the doyen of the *Cinema
Nova* movement, used a famous 17th-century
tale to make a rather confused political parable on contemporary Brazil. However, there
is enough visual flair and caustic humour to
make it watchable.

► **Alienista, O** see Alienist, The

► **Ali: Fear Eats The Soul** see Fear
Eats The Soul

All About Loving

► **De L'Amour**

France   1964   90 mins   bw

Films De La Pleiade/Cocinor Marceau
(Paris)/Cinesocolo (Rome)

d   **Jean Aurel**
sc **Cecil Saint-Laurent, Jean Aurel**
ph **Edmond Richard**
m   **André Hodeir**
    Elsa Martinelli, Michel Piccoli, Martine
    Carol, Anna Karina, Joanna Shimkus,
    Philippe Avron, Jean Sorel, Bernard
    Garnier

Serge (Avron) pursues Hélène in a busy Paris
street and successfully seduces her; Werther
(Garnier) takes Sophie (Shimkus) to the dentist, Raoul (Piccoli), who seduces her; Sophie
deceives Raoul with her ex-husband (Sorel);
Raoul drops Sophie in favour of Mathilde
(Martinelli) to whom he shows films of his
conquests in which Sophie and Hélène –
remember Hélène? – appear. A sort of mini
La Ronde, 1960s style, which, aside from a
very tedious commentary read from the work
of Stendhal (which inspired the screenplay),
is not as crass as it sounds. Documentary
maker Aurel directs his first fiction film with
the lightest of touches, some inventive situations and an ironic edge, while the actors
are delightfully in command of themselves.
Footnote: Aurel was born aboard the Orient
Express as it passed through Romania one
day in 1925.

Allegro Non Troppo

Italy   1976   85 mins   col/bw
Bruno Bozzetto Film

d   **Bruno Bozzetto**
sc **Bruno Bozzetto, Guido Manuli, Maurizio**
    Nichetti
m   **Debussy, Dvořák, Ravel, Sibelius, Vivaldi,**
    Stravinsky
    Maurizio Nichetti, Nestor Garay,
    Maurizio Micheli, Maria Luisa
    Giovannini

Various animated sequences in colour set to
classical music are linked with live-action
scenes involving the producer, the conductor,
an orchestra of old ladies and a reluctant
animator (in monochrome). Not a patch on
Disney's *Fantasia*, the inspiration behind this
uneven pot-pourri, but there is some imaginative animation to be enjoyed between the
ponderously unfunny live-action sections.

Allez France

▶ **(US: The Counterfeit Constable)**

France   1964   86 mins   col
Le Film D'Art/Les Films Arthur Lesser/
Films Borderie

d   **Robert Dhéry**
sc **Robert Dhéry, Pierre Tchernia**
ph **Jean Tournier**
m   **Gérard Calvi**
    Robert Dhéry, Colette Brosset, Diana Dors, Jean Lefèbvre

A French rugby supporter crosses the Channel for the England-France match, gets lost, finds himself at a dentist's and in a policeman's uniform. Dhéry's comedy here is as subtle as a rugby scrum, and the joke of French-English misunderstandings wears pretty thin before the stock-shot finale of the match.

▶ **All Good Citizens** see All My Good Countrymen

All In Order

▶ **Ordnung**

W. Germany   1980   96 mins   bw
Marten Taege Film/ZDF

d   **Sohrab Shahid Saless**
sc **Sohrab Shahid Saless, Dieter Reifarth, Bert Schmidt**
ph **Ramin Molai**
m   **Rolf Bauer**
    Heinz Lieven, Dorothea Moritz, Ingrid Domann, Dagmar Hessenland

A prosperous Frankfurt engineer (Lieven), who suddenly decides to stop going to work, gets up early in the mornings, goes into the streets and shouts 'Wake up!'. He is eventually put into a mental clinic by his wife (Moritz) and friends. This powerful, low-budget, sociopolitical parable excellently directed by an Iranian exile in West Germany, effectively puts into question the notion of sanity and German values. The protagonist's provocative cry to Germans to wake up, becomes, in the end 'Auschwitz!' (a German play on words).

All My Good Countrymen

▶ **(US: All Good Citizens)**
▶ **Všichni Dobří Rodaci**

Czechoslovakia   1968   126 mins   col
Filmoře Studio Barrandov

d   **Vojtěch Jasný**
sc **Vojtěch Jasný**
ph **Jaroslav Kučera**
m   **Svatopluk Havelka**
    Radoslav Brozobohaty, Vlastimil Brodský, Vladimír Menšík, Drahoslava Hofman, Pavel Pavlovsky

The life in a small Moldavian village from the summer of 1945 to early 1968, punctuated by significant deaths. These the shooting of a postman (Pavlovsky), a young member of the local Communist Party, the death from blood poisoning of Joe the Lip (Menšík), a likeable thief, and that of František (Brozobohaty), a farmer who refuses to give up his land to the collective. Jasný, who first emerged as leader of the Czech 'New Wave' in 1957 with *September Nights*, a critique of Stalinist abuses in his country, won acclaim with this lyrical epic. But soon after its award at Cannes, the film was banned in Czechoslovakia, and Jasny left the country for Germany. Its brilliant blend of satire, drama and comedy, dream and reality, make it one of the finest features to emerge during the short 'Prague Spring'.

Best Director Cannes 1969

All Night Long

▶ **Toute Une Nuit**

Belgium   1982   89 mins   col
Avidia/Paradise/Gerick/Lyric/Partners/
Centre Bruxelles De L'Audiovisuel/Film
International/Cine 360

d   **Chantal Akerman**
sc **Chantal Akerman**
ph **Caroline Champetier**
m   **Mahler and a variety of songs**
    Angelo Abazoglou, Frank Aendenboom, Natalia Akerman, Véronique Alain, Paul Allio, Aurore Clément, Gabrielle Claes, Nicole Colchat

In Brussels on a hot summer's night, a number of couples meet, make love, part, dance, drink, eat, telephone each other and sleep. Although there is no plot and little dialogue, this series of amorous fragments, some sad, some happy, is a unique and strangely riveting experiment in narrative to which audiences must be prepared to bring their own imagination.

All Night Through

▶ **aka Restless Night**

▶ **Unruhige Nacht**

> W. Germany 1958 100 mins bw
> Realfilm
>
> d **Falk Harnack**
> sc **Hurst Bud Juhn**
> ph **Friedl/Behn-Grund**
> m **Hans-Martin Majewski**
>   **Bernhard Wicki, Ulla Jacobsson,**
>   **Hansjörg Felmy, Ann Savo**

A Protestant pastor (Wicki) called to administer the last rites to a German soldier (Felmy) about to be shot for desertion, discovers that the man deserted to help the Russian girl (Jacobsson) he loved. Based on the novel by Albrecht Goes, this dreary, badly shot 'good German' World War II drama, has only Wicki's pastor to give it some depth. It was in the same year that Wicki directed *The Bridge*, one of the best German films on World War II.

All Nudity Shall Be Punished

▶ **Toda Nudez Sera Castigada**

> Brazil 1973 102 mins col
> R.F. Faria
>
> d **Arnaldo Jabor**
> sc **Arnaldo Jabor**
> ph **Lauro Escorel**
> m **Paulo Santos**
>   **Darlene Glória, Paulo Porto, Paulo**
>   **Sacks, Paulo César Pereio**

When a widower (Porto) marries a prostitute, his teenage son (Sacks), supposedly ready to die defending the memory of his mother, is attracted to his new step-mother and a *ménage-à-trois* is set up. Banned in Brazil at the time, this baroque satire on middle-class hypocrisy is as unsubtle as its title. However, it is biting, exuberant and funny, with Darlene

Glória standing out amidst the overplaying as a variation on the tart with a heart of gold.

Allonsanfan

> Italy 1974 100 mins col
> Una Cooperativa Cinematografica
>
> d **Paolo and Vittorio Taviani**
> sc **Paolo and Vittorio Taviani**
> ph **Giuseppe Ruzzolini**
> m **Ennio Morricone**
>   **Marcello Mastroianni, Lea Massari,**
>   **Mimsy Farmer, Laura Betti**

A middle-aged Italian nobleman (Mastroianni) disillusioned by the 1816 Restoration in France, betrays the leader of a secret, revolutionary, Republican society to which he belongs. The Taviani brothers said that the film evoked 'the splendour of regression,' an equivocal statement on an equivocal film. It is never clear whose side the directors are on – the weak and regressive Mastroianni's or the bungling revolutionaries' – none of which is helped by some gimmicky camerawork and overemphatic direction. There is some splendour, however, in the more spectacular scenes.

All Screwed Up

▶ **aka Everything's Ready Nothing Works**

▶ **Tutto A Posto**

> Italy 1973 105 mins col
> Euro Intern Films
>
> d **Lina Wertmüller**
> sc **Lina Wertmüller**
> ph **Giuseppe Rotunno**
> m **Piero Piccioni**
>   **Luigi Diberti, Nino Bignamini, Lina**
>   **Polito, Sara Rapisarda**

A group of young people from the country come to Milan and form a commune to enable them to survive the economic evils of the big city. Any social or political points Wertmüller wants to make are blunted by her alienating self-indulgent style. Ham-fisted cutting and camerawork, and a deliberate attempt at bad taste – a ballet motif in an abattoir, for example – dull even the satire inherent in her subject. It was one of a series of her films that unaccountably gained a following in America during the 1970s.

All The Gold In The World

▶ **Tout L'Or Du Monde**

France   1961   100 mins   bw
Seca/Filmsonor/Cinériz/Royal Film

d   **René Clair**
sc   **René Clair**
ph   **Pierre Petit**
m   **Georges Van Parys**
     Bourvil, Philippe Noiret, Claude Rich, Colette Castel, Annie Fratellini, Francoise Dorléac

An obstinate peasant, his son and his cousin (all Bourvil) refuse to sell their land with its health-giving spring to property developers anxious to turn the place into a fashionable spa. Shot in natural locations (unusually for Clair) in rural France, this traditional, rather plodding bucolic comedy lacks the director's customary gentle touch. Some of the yokels vs city slickers satire – in which Clair ingeniously disclaimed taking any one side – and Bourvil in three roles provide some amusement.

▶ **All These Women** see Now About These Women

▶ **All The Youthful Days** see Boys From Fengkuei, The

Almost a Man

▶ **Un Uomo A Meta**

Italy   1966   100 mins   bw
Vittorio De Seta

d   Vittorio De Seta
sc   Vittorio De Seta, Vera Gherarducci, Fabio Carpi
ph Dario Di Palma
m   Ennio Morricone
     Jacques Perrin, Lea Padovani, Gianni Garko, Ilaria Occhini, Pier Paolo Capponi, Francesca De Seta

A young writer in the grip of a personal and artistic crisis, retreats further and further from

the real world, contemplates suicide, and is committed to a clinic for shock treatment. He escapes, returning to the home of his youth where he recollects the traumas of his past. A study of guilt and neurosis, told in a combination of flashback and flash forward, that is stronger on mood than on plot. An intelligent performance from Perrin helps to hold it together but Lea Padovani is wasted in a small part as his mother.

Best Actor (Jacques Perrin) Venice 1966

Aloïse

France   1975   120 mins   col
Unité Trois

d   **Liliane De Kermadec**
sc   **Liliane De Kermadec, André Téchiné**
ph **Jean Penzer**
     Isabelle Huppert, Delphine Seyrig, Marc Eyraud, Valérie Schoeller, François Chatelet

The life of Aloïse, the Swiss primitive painter whose work was accomplished during 40 years in a mental hospital to which she was committed after her emotional protests against World War I. A slow, detailed but absorbing look at an extraordinary woman and, in general, at the oppression of women in society. Both Huppert and Seyrig, who play Aloïse in youth and maturity respectively, give poignant performances.

Alone On The Pacific

▶ **Taiheiyo Hitoribochi**

Japan   1963   104 mins   col
Ishihara/Nikkatsu

d   **Kon Ichikawa**
sc   **Natto Wada**
ph **Yoshihiro Yamazaki**
m   **Yasushi Akatagawa, Tohru Takemitsu**
     Yujiro Ishihara, Masayuki Mori, Kinuyo Tanaka, Ruriko Asaoko

A young yachtsman takes three months to sail from Osaka to San Francisco on a 19-foot craft. Based on the 1962 true adventure of Kenichi Horie (Ishihara), it seemed an intractable filmic subject. But Ichikawa, using the wide screen to magnificent effect and integrating flashbacks to the sailor's life on shore, makes even the boring bits of the voyage interesting. The climactic scene, as the Golden Gate looms out of the mist, is genuinely moving.

Alphaville

▶ **Alphaville, Une Étrange Aventure De Lemmy Caution**

France 1965 98 mins bw
Chaumiane/Filmstudio

d   Jean-Luc Godard
sc Jean-Luc Godard
ph Raoul Coutard
m   Paul Misraki
    Eddie Constantine, Anna Karina, Akim Tamiroff, Howard Vernon, László Szabó

Private-eye Lemmy Caution (Constantine) is rocketed through space into a city run by dictator scientist Von Braun (Vernon), where individuality and love have been suppressed. Although actually filmed in contemporary Paris, an eerie futurist world has been superbly well created, and Godard's use of the trappings of American pulp fiction to make political statements is again telling. Constantine, the American in Paris, who made his name as Peter Cheyney's Caution in a number of cheap French thrillers, is perfect, as is Godard's then wife, the Danish-born Karina, as Von Braun's daughter.

Best Film Berlin 1965

▶ **Alphaville, Une Étrange Aventure De Lemmy Caution** see Alphaville

Alpine Fire

▶ **Höhenfeuer**

Switzerland 1985 117 mins col
Bernard Lang/SRG/WDR/Rex

d   Fredi Murer
sc Fredi Murer
ph Pio Corradi
m   Mario Beretta
    Thomas Nock, Johanna Lier, Dorothea Moritz, Rolf Illig

An adolescent girl has an incestuous relationship with her deaf-mute, younger brother on an isolated farm in the Alps, where the only other people they see are their strict parents and grandparents. Based on the director's own novel (originally set in Iceland), the film skilfully creates an atmosphere of Alpine mysticism, and never sensationalizes the subject. In what is virtually a four-hander, Thomas Nock, a moody boy tormented by his desires, and Johanna Lier, maternal and sexually provocative, are superb as the incestuous siblings.

Alraune

▶ **aka A Daughter Of Destiny**
▶ **aka Unholy Love**

Germany 1928 105 mins bw
Ama

d   Henrik Galeen
sc Henrik Galeen
ph Günther Krampf
m   Silent
    Brigitte Helm, Paul Wegener, John Loder, Ivan Petrovich

Alraune (Helm), born by artificial insemination from a hanged man and a prostitute, acquires a series of lovers, and takes revenge on the scientist (Wegener) who brought her up. Galeen, who contributed as screenwriter to the chilling *Nosferatu* and *Waxworks*, brought a similar menace to bear on this first screen version of H. Ewers' classic novel of 1900. As the perverse seductress, Brigitte Helm sometimes seems unsuitably to be repeating her role as the robotic woman in *Metropolis*, and there are some unintentional laughs. Yet the 'shocking' theme and the late Expressionist atmosphere make it superior to the 1930 sound remake (with Helm again), the 1952 version starring Hildegard Knef, and the rapidly vanished 1981 attempt featuring Nastassja Kinski.

Alsino And The Condor

▶ **Alsino Y El Cóndor**

Nicaragua 1982 89 mins col
Nicaraguan Film Institute/Cuban Film

Institute/Latin American Producers of Mexico/Costa Rican Film Cooperative

d   Miguel Littín
sc Miguel Littín, Isidora Aguirre, Tomás Turrent Pérez
ph Jorge Herrera, Pablo Martínez
m   Leo Brouwer
    Alan Esquivel, Dean Stockwell, Carmen Bunster, Alejandro Parodi

A 12-year-old peasant boy (Esquivel) from a jungle village in Nicaragua during the struggle against the Somoza dictatorship, dreams of flying like the helicopters he sees. Littín, a Chilean director, managed to combine 'magic realism' and a powerful depiction of war into a charming political allegory. This impressive first fiction film produced in Nicaragua after the Sandinista revolution, gained an Oscar nomination.

▶ **Alsino Y El Cóndor** see Alsino And The Condor

▶ **Älskande Pär** see Loving Couples

▶ **Älskar Innan** see Swedish Mistress, The

▶ **Alte Gesetz, Das** see Ancient Law, The

▶ **Al-Wedaa Ya Bonaparte** see Adieu Bonaparte

▶ **Amant De Cinq Jours, L'** see Infidelity

▶ **Amant De Poche, L'** see Lover Boy

▶ **Amants, Les** see Lovers, The

▶ **Amants De Teruel, Les** see Lovers Of Teruel, The

▶ **Amants De Vérone, Les** see Lovers Of Verona, The

▶ **Amants Du Tage, Les** see Lovers Of Lisbon, The

Amarcord

Italy   1973   123 mins   col
FC Produzione/PECF

d   Federico Fellini
sc Federico Fellini, Tonino Guerra
ph Giuseppe Rotunno
m   Nino Rota
    Puppela Maggio, Magali Noël, Armando Brancia, Ciccio Ingrassia

Memories of the seaside town of Rimini during the Fascist regime, particularly of one family with a sex-obsessed teenage son, an irascible anti-Fascist father, and an insane uncle. One of Fellini's most affectionate semi-autobiographical films, it is an often dream-like vision of the past (the title means 'I remember' in Roman dialect), as well as exaggerated, bawdy, funny and melancholy. Nino Rota's jaunty music and Danilo Donati's impressionistic art direction add to the special Fellini flavour, and the set-piece of the towns-people meeting a luxury liner is an inspired moment among many.

Best Foreign Film Oscar 1974

▶ **Amator** see Camera Buff

Amelia Or The Time For Love

▶ **aka A Time To Die**

▶ **Amélie Ou Le Temps D'Aimer**

France   1961   111 mins   bw
Port Royal Films/Indusfilms/Prima Film

d   Michel Drach
sc Michel Drach
ph Jean Tournier
m   Bach
    Jean Sorel, Marie-José Nat, Sophie Daumier, Clotilde Joano

An orphan girl (Nat) living on a small island off the Breton coast is in love with her cousin (Sorel), but he is more interested in the sea and a glamorous actress. Michel Drach's first major film is unashamedly romantic with a fine feel for the turn of the century. The dark-eyed Marie-José Nat, soon after to be the director's wife, made a heroine worth piping the eye for.

▶ **Amélie Ou Le Temps D'Aimer** see Amelia Or The Time For Love

▶ **Américain, L'** see American, The

The American

▶ **L'Américain**

France 1969 80 mins col
Films 13/Les Films Ariane

d Marcel Bozzuffi
sc Marcel Bozzuffi
ph Pierre Willemin
Jean-Louis Trintignant, Simone Signoret,
Marcel Bozzuffi, Bernard Fresson,
Françoise Fabian

A Frenchman (Trintignant), who has lived in America for 11 years, returns to his native town to settle down, but after meeting old friends and having a brief fling with an attractive middle-aged woman (Fabian), he leaves. The first film directed by Bozzuffi, the actor who was to gain international fame in *The French Connection* (1971), is a well-observed, bitter-sweet, small-scale, small-town drama with only a tenuous American connection. This minor stuff has a major cast, including Simone Signoret as a bar owner.

The American Friend

▶ **Der Amerikanische Freund**

W. Germany 1977 123 mins col
Road Movies/Wim Wenders-
Westdeutschen Rundfunk/Films Du
Losange

d Wim Wenders
sc Wim Wenders
ph Robby Müller
m Jürgen Knieper
Bruno Ganz, Dennis Hopper, Gérard
Blain, Liza Kreuzer, Nicholas Ray, Sam
Fuller, Daniel Schmid, Jean Eustache,
Lou Castel, Peter Lilienthal

A dying man (Ganz) unwillingly takes a job as a hit man in order to have money to leave to his widow. Wenders' first real success in the USA (the dialogue is partly in English) is an extremely loose adaptation from the Patricia Highsmith thriller *Ripley's Game*. But the flashy camerawork and too-conscious myth-making act against the story through which the director's real-life heroes Fuller, Ray and Hopper distractingly wend their way.

The American Soldier

▶ **Der Amerikanische Soldat**

W. Germany 1970 80 mins bw
Antiteater

d Rainer Werner Fassbinder
sc Rainer Werner Fassbinder
ph Dietrich Lohmann, Herbert Pajzold
m Peer Raben
Karl Scheydt, Elga Sorbas, Jan George,
Margarethe Von Trotta, Kurt Raab,
Rainer Werner Fassbinder

After serving in Vietnam, Ricky (Scheydt) returns from the USA to the Munich of his childhood, and carries out a series of murders for the police. Described by Fassbinder as 'what's left in the minds of the German people who see a lot of American gangster films,' this film is peopled by unsmiling, sadistic men in 1950s hats who make their women suffer. What matters is not so much the impenetrable plot or the self-conscious references, but the finely controlled visual style which expertly creates a desolate, absurdist world in the shadows.

▶ **Amerikanische Freund, Der** see American Friend, The

▶ **Amerikanische Soldat, Der** see American Soldier, The

▶ **Amiche, Le** see Girl Friends, The

▶ **Amici Per La Pelle** see Friends For Life

▶ **Ami De Mon Amie, L'** see My Girlfriend's Boyfriend

▶ **Amitiés Particulières, Les** see This Special Friendship

Un Ami Viendra Ce Soir

▶ **(US: A Friend Will Come Tonight)**

France 1946 120 mins bw
Francinex

d Raymond Bernard
sc Yvan Noë, Jacques Companeez
ph Robert Le Fèbvre

m Arthur Honegger
Michel Simon, Madeleine Solange, Louis
Salou, Saturnin Fabre, Marcel André,
Daniel Gélin

A group of French Resistance fighters pose
as inmates in a lunatic asylum in occupied
France in order to carry on sabotage unde-
tected. One of the first films about the Resistance to come out of liberated France, the
idea behind it was better than the execution.
The director, the son of playwright Tristan
Bernard, who had not shot a film for six
years, made the plot seem rather implausible
and paced it poorly. But there are some fine
character performances, especially by Simon,
top-billed in a smallish role.

▶ **Among People** see My Apprenticeship

▶ **Amor Brujo, El** see Love Bewitched,
A

L'Amore

▶ **(US: Woman**

▶ **aka Ways Of Love)**

Italy 1948 79 mins bw
Tevere Film

d   Roberto Rossellini
sc Roberto Rossellini, Tullio Pinelli,
Federico Fellini
ph Robert Juillard, Aldo Tonti
m   Renzo Rossellini
Anna Magnani, Federico Fellini

A film composed of two separate episodes: in
The Human Voice, a woman on the phone
tries to persuade her lover not to desert her;
and in *The Miracle*, a peasant woman is
seduced by a man she believes to be St Joseph
and thinks she will give birth to the New
Messiah. Rossellini's departure from Neo-
Realism was a homage to the awesome art of
actress Anna Magnani, first as a society
woman in an adaptation of Jean Cocteau's
monodrama, and then as a simple devout
peasant opposite Fellini who plays a man
who may or may not be St Joseph. The rather
theatrical and spurious film, only worth seeing
for Magnani, was banned in New York as
blasphemous.

▶ **Amore E Rabbia** see Love And Anger

▶ **Amore In Città** see Love In The City

▶ **Amor Es Una Mujer Gorda, El** see
Love Is A Fat Woman

Amorosa

Sweden 1986 113 mins col
Swedish Film Institute/Sandrew/Film
Sveriges TV-SVT 1

d   Mai Zetterling
sc Mai Zetterling
ph Rune Ericson
m   Roger Wallis
Stina Ekblad, Erland Josephson, Philip
Zanden, Catherine De Seynes, Olof
Thunberg

The story of Swedish novelist Agnes Von
Krusentjerna's strict upbringing, her controversial marriage, her scandalous writings, her
sexual fantasies and her mental breakdown.
Zetterling's first feature, *Loving Couples*
(1964), was based on a novel by the subject
of this one – her first Swedish film for 17
years. Ekblad has an intensity that makes her
series of tantrums and grotesque nightmares
(effectively rendered by the excellent camerawork) less monotonous than they might
have been. As these seem to take up most of
her time, it is difficult to know when she got
around to writing.

L'Amour À Mort

France 1984 93 mins col
Dussart/Les Films Ariane/Films A2

d   Alain Resnais
sc Jean Gruault
ph Sacha Vierny
m   Hans Werner Henze
Sabine Azéma, Pierre Arditi, Fanny
Ardant, André Dussollier, Jean Dasté

An archaeologist (Arditi) is pronounced dead
but recovers. The experience gives greater
intensity to his life and to his love for the
woman he lives with (Azéma). Resnais has
always ventured into areas where few film-
makers have dared go, this time depicting
resurrection as a fact. This leads to some

stylishly acted and filmed but rather stony-faced debates on the subject, frequently punctuated by shots of snowflakes (or feathers?) which are accompanied by Henze's haunting music.

▶ **Amour À Vingt Ans, L'** see Love At Twenty

▶ **Amour De Pluie, Un** see Loving In The Rain

▶ **Amour De Swann, Un** see Swann In Love

▶ **Amour En Fuite, L'** see Love On The Run

▶ **Amour En Question, L'** see Love In Question

L'Amour Fou

France 1968 256 mins bw
Marceau/Cocinor/Sogexport

d Jacques Rivette
sc Jacques Rivette, Marilu Tonilini
ph Alain Levent
m Jean-Claude Eloy
Jean-Pierre Kalfon, Bulle Ogier, André Labarthe, Denis Berry, Michele Moretti, Josée Destoop

A theatre group prepares to stage Racine's *Andromaque* while being filmed by a TV team. During the rehearsal, the director (Kalfon) replaces his wife (Ogier) in the lead with his former mistress (Destoop). The film, shot in both 35mm and 16mm, was developed from ideas of the cast and technicians, and improvised during filming. Its extreme length is integral to its meaning and texture, but the producers initially distributed it in a condensed two-hour version, disowned by Rivette. This led the director to follow up with *Out One* (1971) which originally ran 12 hours and 40 minutes, but was cut down to *Out One: Spectre* (1973) of four hours and 20 minutes. As they don't attempt to reach any conclusion, these intensely personal, cerebral and sensual films could have gone on for ever. For adventurous filmgoers with time on their hands.

▶ **Amour L'Après-Midi, L'** see Love In The Afternoon

▶ **Amour Par Terre, L'** see Love On The Ground

▶ **Amour Violé, L'** see Violated Love

Amphitryon

▶ **Aus Den Wolken Kommt Das Glück**

Germany 1935 93 mins bw
UFA/Alliance Cenenat

d Reinhold Schünzel
sc Reinhold Schünzel
ph Fritz Arno Wagner, Werner Böhne
m Franz Doelle
Willy Fritsch, Käthe Gold, Paul Kemp, Adele Sandrock, Aribert Wäscher

Jupiter (Fritsch) disguises himself as the mortal Amphitryon in order to make love to Alkmene (Gold), Amphitryon's faithful wife. The popular myth makes a charming and tuneful operetta with a minimum of spoken dialogue. Amusing anachronisms (Mercury on roller skates) and characterizations make one forget that musicals were an important part of Dr Goebbels' film programme.

Amsterdamned

Netherlands 1988 113 mins col
First Floor Features

d Dick Maas
sc Dick Maas
ph Marc Felperlaan
m Dick Maas
Huub Stapel, Monique Van de Ven, Serge-Henri Valcke, Hidde Maas, Lou Landré

A prostitute is murdered and suspended from a canal bridge in Amsterdam; two men collecting samples of water from a boat are slaughtered in the canal. And these are just for openers. Plainclothesman Eric Visser (Stapel) is assigned to the case and soon surmises that the killings are being carried out from within the depths of the city's waterways. In the course of his investigations he meets and falls in love with Laura (Van de Ven), whose ex-diver psychiatrist friend comes under suspicion... A movie much praised by English-speaking critics, it certainly offers an unusual premise and an ingenious use of its location – Amsterdam's complex canal routes – by having a psychotic killer on the loose under water. This allows for undue difficulty in tracking him down and an excellent boat chase substituting for the usual car chase. However, although a certain genuine tension is engendered, the movie is no more than a slightly sleazy, run-of-the-mill slasher tale in diving gear.

Ana And The Wolves

▶ **Ana Y Los Lobos**

Spain 1972 100 mins col
Elias Querejeta

d **Carlos Saura**
sc **Carlos Saura**
ph **Luis Cuadrado**
m **Luis De Pablo**
Geraldine Chaplin, Fernando Fernan-Gomez, José Maria Prada, José Vivó

Ana (Chaplin), an English governess, arrives at an old mansion in Spain where she becomes the object of the ravenous sexual desires of the three sons of a monstrous mother. One of Saura's least oblique attacks on the Franco regime, it is easy to read the three sons as representing aspects of Francoism. The film was passed by the censors only because they found it 'nonsense'. The mixture of farce, fantasy and melodrama may be a little disconcerting, but it is trenchant.

Anatomy Of A Marriage

▶ **La Vie Conjugale**

France 1963 193 mins bw
Films Borderie/Jolly Film/Terra Arco

d **André Cayatte**
sc **André Cayatte**
ph **Roger Fellous**
m **Louguy**
Marie-José Nat, Jacques Charrier, Georges Rivière, Macha Meril

The same events that lead to the breakdown

of the marriage of a young couple (Nat and Charrier) are seen from two opposite points of view. Originally two separate full-length features (later shown in one 112-minute version), under the titles *My Days With Jean Marc* and *My Nights With Françoise*, they contained the seed of a good idea which grew out of all proportion. Like many a marriage, it lasts too long, becoming flat and repetitive.

▶ **Ana Y Los Lobos** see Ana And The Wolves

The Ancient Law

▶ **aka Baruch**

▶ **Das Alte Gesetz**

Germany 1923 110 mins bw
UFA

d **E.A. Dupont**
sc **Paul Reno**
ph **Théodor Sparkühl**
m **Silent**
Ernst Deutsch, Henny Porten, Ruth Weyher, Hermann Vallentin

A Rabbi's son (Deutsch) goes against his father's wishes and becomes a famous actor, adored by the aristocracy. The first film by Dupont to gain international attention, it is psychologically perceptive and uses a more realist technique than earlier German expressionist works. The glimpses of contemporary German theatre in the mid-19th century (the film's period), though silent, are fascinating.

▶ **Andalusian Dog, An** see Chien Andalou, Un

And God Created Woman

▶ **aka And Woman Was Created**

▶ **Et Dieu Créa La Femme**

France 1956 92 mins col
Iena/UCIL/Cocinor

d **Roger Vadim**
sc **Roger Vadmi, Raoul Lévy**

ph **Armand Thirard**
m **Paul Misraki**
   Brigitte Bardot, Curt Jurgens, Jean-Louis Trintignant, Christian Marquand

An 18-year-old girl (Bardot), shortly after her marriage (to a wimpish Trintignant), finds she is attracted to other men, particularly her brother-in-law (Marquand). This was the film in which a new sex symbol reared her pretty, pouting, kittenish head, put St Tropez on the map, and brought French films out of the art house ghetto into mainstream cinema. (It earned $4 million in the USA alone.) Mostly shot on location, the rather silly, but certainly sensual, tale was a good excuse for Vadim (in his first feature) to display the amoral charms of his wife in various forms of dress (mainly jeans) and undress.

And Now My Love

▶ **Toute Une Vie**

   France 1974 150 mins col
   Les Films 13/Rizzoli

d **Claude Lelouch**
sc **Claude Lelouch, Pierre Uytterhoeven**
ph **Jean Collomb**
m **Gilbert Bécaud**
   Marthe Keller, André Dussollier, Charles Denner, Carla Gravina, Charles Gérard, Gilbert Bécaud

A wealthy Jewish girl (Keller), whose grandfather (Denner) was a cameraman in the early days of cinema, and whose father (also Denner) survived a concentration camp, falls in love with a petty thief (Dussollier). Three generations of a family treated in a glossy, superficial fashion, decked out with tearjerking 'philosophical' songs performed by Bécaud. La schmaltz!

And Quiet Flows The Don

▶ **Tikhi Don**

   USSR 1958 107 mins col
   Gorki Film Studio

d **Sergei Gerasimov**
sc **Sergei Gerasimov**
ph **Vladimir Rapoport**

m **Yuri Revitnin**
   Ellina Bystritskaya, Pyotr Glebov, Zinaida Kirienko, Danilo Ilchenko

The lives and events in and around a small village during and after World War I. This adaptation of Sholokov's lengthy novel (made in two parts, but reduced to one in Britain and the USA) flows slowly and quietly in a pleasing but academic manner, lacking the lyrical intensity of the great classics of the Soviet cinema in previous decades. There are some effective character vignettes and action scenes, such as the charge of the Cossacks, and good location shooting. In 1949, Gerasimov made a famous speech at the Cultural and Scientific Conference for World Peace in New York, in which he criticized the low moral standards of American films.

And Quiet Rolls The Dawn

▶ **Ek Din Prati Din**

   India 1979 94 mins col
   Mrinal Sen

d **Mrinal Sen**
sc **Mrinal Sen**
ph **K.K. Mahajan**
m **B.V. Karanth**
   Mamata Shankar, Gita Sen, Satya Banerjee, Sreela Majumdar

A night in the Calcutta tenement of a lower middle-class family, who are waiting anxiously for news of their daughter, also their breadwinner, who has failed to return home at the usual time. Sen's mordant, rigorous attack on social convention, shot in 21 days, is mainly confined to the house of the family who are trying to keep up appearances. 'I wanted to piss in the face of such decency,' commented the forthright director.

Andrei Rublev

   USSR 1966 185 mins bw
   Mosfilm

d **Andrei Tarkovsky**
sc **Andrei Tarkovsky, Andrei Mikhalkov-Konchalovsky**
ph **Vadim Yusov**

m   Vyacheslav Tcherniaiev
Anatoly Solonitsin, Ivan Lapikov, Nikolai
Grinko, Nikolai Sergeyev

Eight imaginary episodes in the life of the
great 15th-century icon painter Rubter
(Solonitsin) as he journeys through feudal
Russia, gradually abandoning speech, his art
and his faith, because of the cruelty he witnesses, but finally regains them. This slow,
powerful, impressive epic was shelved for
some years by the Soviet authorities, who felt
it was too 'dark' for the 50th anniversary of
the October Revolution, before being released
in a cut version (GB: 146 mins, US: 165
mins). This parable of the artist's position in
society ends with a sequence in which colour
and the CinemaScope screen do justice to the
paintings.

And So To Bed

▶ **Das Grosse Liebespiel**

Austria/W. Germany   1963   133
mins   bw
Team Film/Stadthallen Prod.

d   **Alfred Weidenmann**
sc **Herbert Reinecker**
ph **Georg Bruckbauer**
m   **Charly Niessen**
**Lilli Palmer, Hildegard Knef, Nadja
Tiller,
Daliah Lavi, Alexandra Stewart, Peter
Van Eyck, Thomas Fritsch, Martin Held**

A call girl teaches the ways of love to a
student who then seduces his teacher's wife,
whose husband has an erotic escapade with
his secretary who ... Another change rung on
the *La Ronde* theme, with a bed at the film's
centre, but a movie more likely to promote
thoughts of slumber than sex. Passing through
this monotonous, mechanical film, are a number of star performers who should have stayed
in their own beds.

And The Ship Sails On

▶ **E La Nave Va**

Italy   1983   132 mins   col
RAI/Vides/Gaumont

d   **Federico Fellini**

sc **Federico Fellini, Tonino Guerra**
ph **Giuseppe Rotunno**
m   **Gianfranco Plenizio, Giuseppe Verdi
Freddie Jones, Barbara Jefford, Victor
Poletti, Peter Cellier, Elisa Mainardi,
Norma West, Janet Suzman**

In 1914, a luxury liner, full of statesmen,
opera singers, aristocrats and a rhinoceros,
sails from Naples to an island where the ashes
of the world's greatest soprano (Suzman) are
to be scattered. Bordering on the precious at
times, it is a loving, critical, comic and moving
evocation of an era, coloured by the coming
war which is symbolized by Serbian refugees
boarding the ship. Fellini and art director
Dante Ferretti successfully celebrate artifice,
allied to Italian romantic opera and the crumbling pre-war society, with a dazzling ship, a
painted sky and a plastic sea in a Cinecitta
studio.

▶ **And The Wild Wild Women** see
Caged

▶ **And Woman Was Created** see And
God Created Woman

▶ **Angel** see Angelos

Angel Dust

▶ **Poussière D'Ange**

France   1987   94 mins   col
Président Films-U.G.C./Film De La
Saga/FR3 Films /La Sofica

d   **Edouard Niermans**
sc **Edouard Niermans, Jacques Audiard,
Alain Le Henry**
ph **Bernard Lutic**
m   **Leon Senza, Vincent-Marie Bouvot
Bernard Giraudeau, Fanny Bastien, Fanny
Cottençon, Jean-Pierre Sentier, Michel
Aumont, Gérard Blain**

Police inspector Simon Blount (Giraudeau) is
shattered when he discovers that his estranged
wife (Cottençon) is living with another man.
The man turns out to be a pimp implicated
in the murder of a prostitute who was the
mother of a bizarre girl (Bastien) whom
Blount has befriended. Although the film's
title might suggest something magical or

romantic, it is a cold, calculating, and contrived thriller very much modelled on American lines. Its strengths lie in Giraudeau's unshaven, dishevelled, baggy-eyed lush of a cop, and the sharp photography of night scenes and deserted locations.

Angèle

France 1934 162 mins bw
Films Marcel Pagnol

d **Marcel Pagnol**
sc **Marcel Pagnol**
ph **Willy**
m **Vincent Scotto**
 Orane Demazis, Henri Poupon, Annie Toinon, Fernandel, Jean Servais, Edouard Delmont

Seduced and abandoned, Angèle, (Demazis) a young, naive peasant girl, goes to Marseilles where she has a child and becomes a prostitute. The beautifully crafted script (from a Jean Giono short story) and the realistic Provençal background transcend the melodramatic plot of the fallen woman redeemed. By installing his troupe on a farm and using direct sound, Pagnol not only made the first important French talkie shot on location, but the first Neo-Realist film, as acknowledged by De Sica and Rossellini. In addition, Fernandel, as the simple-minded farm hand, emerged as a great tragicomic actor.

▶ **Angel Exterminador, El** see Exterminating Angel, The

▶ **Angelika** see Affairs Of Dr Holl, The

Angelina

▶ **L'Onorevole Angelina**

Italy 1947 90 mins bw
Lux/Ora

d **Luigi Zampa**
sc **Luigi Zampa, Suso Cecchi D'Amico, Piero Tellini, Anna Magnani**
ph **Mario Craveri**
m **Enzio Masetti**
 Anna Magnani, Nando Bruno, Ave Ninchi, Agnese Dubbini, Gianni Glori

Angelina (Magnani), a housewife, fights heroically to improve the living conditions of her neighbours in post-war Italy. Although made at the height of the Italian Neo-Realist movement by one of its minor members, this is really a star vehicle for the earthy, humorous and passionate Magnani, who appears in almost every scene.

Best Actress (Anna Magnani) Venice 1947

Angélique

▶ **Angélique, Marquise Des Anges**

France 1964 116 mins col
Francos/Films Borderie/Gloria/Fono

d **Bernard Borderie**
sc **Bernard Borderie, Claude Brûlé**
ph **Henri Pérsin**
m **Michel Magne**
 Michèle Mercier, Robert Hossein, Jean Rochefort, Giuliano Gemma

Angélique, the comely daughter of a penniless nobleman at the court of Louis XIV, is married off to a man who is later imprisoned for witchcraft. The first in a widely popular series of bodice-rippers, based on the books of Serge and Anne Golon which feature the adventures of a Forever Amber-like heroine, it is less fun than it should have been. The settings and costumes are colourful, and Mlle Mercier in the title role pouts prettily.

▶ **Angélique, Marquise Des Anges**
see Angélique

Angelos

▶ **aka Angel**

Greece 1982 126 mins col
Greek Film Centre

d **George Katakouzinos**
sc **George Katakouzinos**
ph **Tassos Alexakis**
m **Stamatis Spanoudakis**
 Michael Maniatis, Maria Alkeou, Dionyssis Xanthos, Katerina Helmi

A young homosexual (Maniatis) falls in love with a sailor (Xanthos) and leaves home to live with him. However, his lover soon persuades him into a life of degrading transvestite prostitution to earn them extra money. Not as melodramatic or sensationalist as it sounds, this debut film from a man who had worked as assistant on 60 previous films, is a sensitive and realistic portrait of a sub-culture. Based on a real-life case, it is a painful tale, containing some brutally explicit love scenes. Big box-office in Greece, it was also lauded at various festivals.

▶ **Angels Of The Streets** see Anges Du Péché, Les

▶ **Angemaeul** see Village In The Mist

Les Anges Du Péché

▶ **(US: Angels Of The Streets)**

France   1943   73 mins   bw
Synops
d   **Robert Bresson**
sc **Robert Bresson, Jean Giraudoux,
R. Bruckberger**
ph **Philippe Agostini**
m   **Jean-Jacques Grünewald
Jany Holt, Renée Fauré, Sylvie, Mila
Parély, Marie-Hélène Dasté**

A young novice (Fauré) devotes herself to the redemption of an ex-prisoner and murderer (Holt) even though it means sacrificing herself. Bresson's first feature, made when he was 36, has a religious intensity and rigour that overcomes some of its more melodramatic aspects. Although the film uses professional performers and was shot in a studio, the theme and images prefigure his later work.

Angi Vera

Hungary   1978   96 mins   col
Mafilm Studio/Hungarofilm
d   **Pál Gábor**
sc **Pál Gábor**
ph **Lajos Koltai**
m   **György Selmeczi
Veronika Papp, Erszi Pásztor, Éva
Szabó, Tamás Dunai, László Horváth**

When naive, 18-year-old Vera (Papp) criticizes management methods at the hospital where she works, she is sent for institutionalized training in the ways of the Party. Gradually corrupted by the system, she betrays a colleague and, in the process, her integrity. Her conversion to an honoured senior Party member is chilling in a sombre and gripping film that eloquently conveys the repressive climate of Stalinist Hungary in 1948. Coming from the Soviet bloc, the film's portrayal of the regime surprised and impressed critics in the West.

▶ **Angst** see Fear

▶ **Angst Des Tormanns Beim Elfmeter, Die** see Anxiety Of The Goalie At The Penalty, The

▶ **Angst Essen Seele Auf** see Fear Eats The Soul

Aniki-Bobo

Portugal   1942   70 mins   bw
Tobis
d   **Manoel De Oliveira**
sc **Manoel De Oliveira, Manuel Matos,
António Lopes Ribeiro, Nascimento
Fernandes**
ph **António Mendes**
m   **Jaime Silva
Nascimento Fernandes, Vital Dos Santos,
Antonio Palma, Armando Pedro**

The adventures of street urchins growing up in the slums of Oporto and on the banks of the river. This first feature by Portugal's only renowned director is, in style, much simpler than his later films, and gained some recognition abroad for its excellent location shooting and natural performances by the actual children of the area.

▶ **Ani Ohev Otach Rosa** see I Love You Rosa

▶ **Ani To Song Imoto** see Brother And His Younger Sister, A

▶ **Ankur** see Seedling, The

Anna

Italy 1951 95 mins bw
Dino De Laurentiis/Lux

d Alberto Lattuada
sc Giuseppe Berto, Dino Risi, Ivo Perilli,
Franco Brusati, Rodolfo Sonego
ph Otello Martelli
m Nino Rota
Silvana Mangano, Raf Vallone, Vittorio
Gassman, Gaby Morlay

Anna (Mangano), a nightclub singer, enters
a convent to avoid making a choice between
two men. The presence of three of Italy's
biggest stars of the 1950s, and the heady
mixture of the sacred and profane, ensured a
healthy box-office success at home and
abroad. However, the gaggle of screenwriters
and Lattuada's stolid direction only resulted
in a risible melodrama.

Anna

Finland 1970 83 mins col
Jörn Donner Productions

d Jörn Donner
sc Jörn Donner, Elija-Elina Bergholm
ph Heikki Katajisto
m Claes Af Geïjerstam
Harriet Andersson, Marjatta Packalen,
Tapio Rautavaara, Tapani Perttu

A 38-year-old woman becomes aware of the
passage of time during a holiday trip to the
Finnish archipelago, accompanied by her
young daughter and teenage maid. Andersson's expressive performance under her
husband's direction and some attractive
locations make this psychological mood piece
more watchable than it might have been.
However, the film is still rather enclosed and
self-consciously arty.

Anna Boleyn

▶ (US: Deception)

Germany 1920 100 mins bw
Messter/GMBH

d Ernst Lubitsch
sc Norbert Falk (billed as Fred Orbing)
ph Théodor Spärkuhl

m Silent
Emil Jannings, Henny Porten, Aud Egede
Nissen

Henry VIII (Jannings) is disappointed that
Anne (Porten) has not given him a son and
has her executed after he decides to marry
Jane Seymour (Nissen). Jannings, looking as
though he had stepped out of a Holbein
portrait, set the prototype for the lusty king
taken up by Charles Laughton in *The Private
Life Of Henry VIII* (1933), which displayed
a similar ironic approach to history. More
inventive and historically accurate than the
later film, this one had sets of Hampton Court
etc built at the UFA studios by architects
Kurt Richter and Poelzig.

▶ **Anna Di Brooklyn** see Anna Of
Brooklyn

Anna Karenina

USSR 1967 135 mins col
Mosfilm

d Alexander Zarkhi
sc Alexander Zarkhi, V. Katanian
ph Leonid Kalachnikov
m Rodion Chtchedrine
Tatiana Samoilova, Vassily Lanovoi,
Nikolai Gritzenko, Anastasia
Vertinskaya, Boris Goldaiev

Anna (Samoilova), married to an older man
(Gritzenko), falls in love with Vronsky (Lanovoi), a dashing officer, for whom she forsakes
her social position and even her beloved little
boy. Old-time director Zarkhi, using the
70mm screen effectively, comes closer to Tolstoy's romance than previous versions which
tended to ignore many of the important subsidiary characters and relationships. Samoilova, following such luminaries as Garbo and
Vivien Leigh, had her best role since *The
Cranes Are Flying* 10 years previously.

Anna Of Brooklyn

▶ (US: Fast And Sexy)
▶ Anna Di Brooklyn

Italy 1958 106 mins col

Circeo Cinematografica/France Cinema/ RKO

d **Reginald Denham, Carlo Lasticati**
sc **Ettore Margadonna, Luciana Corda, Joseph Stefano**
ph **Giuseppe Rotunno**
m **Alessandro Cicognini, Vittorio De Sica**
   Gina Lollobrigida, Dale Robertson, Vittorio De Sica, Peppino De Felippo, Amedeo Nazzari

A wealthy and attractive widow (Lollobrigida), returning from New York to her native Italian village in search of a husband, charms all the eligible bachelors except the handsome blacksmith (Robertson). This predictable, resistible romp at least had an eye-catching La Lollo and a witty performance by De Sica (who also 'supervised' the direction) as a gossiping priest.

Anne And Muriel

▶ **(US: Two English Girls)**

▶ **Les Deux Anglaises Et Le Continent**

France 1971 108 mins col
Films Du Carrosse/Cinétel/Simar

d **François Truffaut**
sc **François Truffaut, Jean Gruault**
ph **Nestor Almendros**
m **Georges Delerue**
   Jean-Pierre Léaud, Kika Markham, Stacey Tendeter, Sylvia Marriott, Philippe Léotard, Marie Mansart

At the turn of the century, an aspiring young French writer (Léaud) spends a holiday on the Welsh coast with two English sisters (Markham and Marriott) and falls in love with both of them. Truffaut's second adaptation of a novel by Henri- Pierre Roché is less successful than *Jules And Jim*, the first. This triangle, despite much delicacy and wit, is weighed down by the rather irritatingly over-sensitive characters. The desaturated colour was an attempt to recreate early two-tone Technicolor.

▶ **Année Dernière À Marienbad, L'**
see Last Year At Marienbad

Anne Trister

Canada 1986 115 mins col
Société Générale Du Cinéma Du Québec/Téléfilm Canada/ Société De Radio-Télévision Du Québec

d **Léa Pool**
sc **Marcel Beaulieu, Léa Pool**
ph **Pierre Mignot**
m **René Dupéré**
   Albane Guilhe, Louise Marleau, Lucie Laurier, Guy Thauvette, Hugues Quester, Nuvit Ozdogru

Anne Trister (Guilhe) is a 25-year-old Jewish painter living in Israel. The death of her father triggers an emotional crisis and, abandoning her lover (Quester), her mother and her studies, she goes to Canada to stay with her older female friend Alix (Marleau), a psychologist. Anne falls in love with Alix, plunging the latter's life into confusion, and their relationship is both enriched and further complicated by Alix's special bond with Sarah (Laurier), a rebellious, love-starved 10-year-old patient. An official entry at Berlin, this second feature by a maker of documentary and short films is an ambitious work that sets out to explore the voids created by bereavement, loss of self and change. Pool utilizes Anne's calling as an artist with originality, and treats the Lesbian theme intelligently, but the movie suffers from an overload of metaphor and unrelieved emotional intensity.

▶ **Anonimo Veneziano** see Anonymous Venetian, The

The Anonymous Venetian

▶ **Anonimo Veneziano**

Italy 1970 93 mins col
Ultra Film

d **Enrico Maria Salerno**
sc **Enrico Maria Salerno, Giuseppe Berto**
ph **Marcello Gatto**
m **Stelvio Cirpriani**
   Tony Musante, Florinda Bolkan, Toti Del Monte

An estranged couple spend a day together in

Venice remembering the high and low moments of their marriage, but the reconciliation is short-lived because the man is dying of an incurable disease. The debut film of Salerno, an established actor and theatre director, is a rather tedious tear-jerker with virtually only three protagonists – the constantly promenading couple and the wonderfully photogenic Venice. Naturally, the latter steals almost every scene.

▶ **À Nos Amours** see To Our Loves

Another Man, Another Chance

▶ **aka Another Man, Another Woman**

▶ **Un Autre Homme, Une Autre Chance**

> France   1977   128 mins   col
> Les Films Ariane/UA/Les Films 13

d   **Claude Lelouch**
sc   **Claude Lelouch**
ph   **Jacques Lefrançois**
m   **Francis Lai**
   Geneviève Bujold, James Caan, Jennifer Warren, Susan Tyrrell, Francis Huster

The French widow (Bujold) of a murdered photographer meets and falls in love with an American veterinary surgeon (Caan), whose wife was raped and slain in the Far West in the 1870s. A vain attempt by the ever-romantic Lelouch to remake his first success, *A Man And A Woman* (1966) into a Western. The muddled plot and unconvincing leads are not helped by the show-off style and pretentious use of the first bars of Beethoven's Fifth Symphony.

▶ **Another Man, Another Woman**
   see Another Man, Another Chance

Another Way

▶ **Egymásra Nézve**

> Hungary   1982   109 mins   col

Mafilm

d   **Károly Makk**
sc   **Károly Makk, Erzsébet Galgóczi**
ph   **Tamás Andor**
m   **László Dés**
   Jadwiga Jankowska-Cieslak, Grazyna Szapolowska, Jožef Kroner, Gábor Reviczky

The Lesbian love affair between two journalists in the period following the 1956 Hungarian uprising leads to the attempted murder of one by her husband and the death of the other. Hungary's senior director returned to his best form with this politically courageous, touching and intelligent plea for tolerance, based on the semi-autobiographical bestseller by his co-scriptwriter. The two Polish actresses as the doomed lovers, give remarkably perceptive performances.

Best Actress (Jadwiga Jankowska-Cieslak) Cannes 1982

À Nous La Liberté

▶ **(US: Freedom For Us)**

> France   1931   97 mins   bw
> Tobis

d   **René Clair**
sc   **René Clair**
ph   **Georges Périnal**
m   **Georges Auric**
   Raymond Cordy, Henri Marchand, Rolla France, Paul Olivier, Jacques Shelly, André Michaud

Two convicts, Louis (Cordy) and Emile (Marchand), escape from prison, but Emile is recaptured. Louis advances from gramophone salesman to owner of a huge, modern gramophone factory. Emile is released, finds work at the plant, rediscovers his old cellmate and, after things go wrong, they take to the road together as tramps. Making clever use of songs, sound effects, a horizontally panning camera, rhythmic dialogue and choreographed movements, Clair has created a sublime musical comedy satire on the work ethic and the dehumanizing effects of mass-production techniques. In a light-hearted manner, an analogy is made between prison and the factory, underlined by Lazare Meerson's striking Bauhaus sets dwarfing the workers. The film inspired Chaplin's *Modern Times*, in which there are similar sequences on the assembly line. Tobis, the production company, wanted to sue Chaplin, but Clair took it as the highest form of flattery, just as he, in his silent period, had doffed his beret to the great comic.

À Nous Les Petites Anglaises!

France 1976 112 mins col
Irene Silberman

d   Michel Lang
sc   Michel Lang
ph   Daniel Gaudry
m   Mort Shuman
     Rémy Laurent, Stéphane Hillel,
     Véronique Delbourg, Sophie Barjac,
     Brigitte Bellac

Because he has failed his English exam a middle-class, Parisian schoolboy (Laurent) is sent to England for his summer vacation instead of to St Tropez. What was intended as a punishment turns out to be the best time he has ever had. A certain freshness and authenticity among the youthful players, an air of improvisation, and holiday situations that many French and English teenagers could recognize, led to the success of this debut film from a young director. Not for anyone past the acne stage, though.

▶ **Ansikte Mot Ansikte** see Face To Face

▶ **Ansiktet** see Face, The

Answer To Violence

▶ **Zamach**

Poland 1958 83 mins bw
Illuzion Film Unit

d   Jerzy Passendorfer
sc   Jerzy Stefan Stawinski
ph   Jerzy Lipman
m   Adam Walacinski
     Bozena Kurowska, Grazyna Staniszewska,
     Zbigniew Cyncutis, Andrzej Kostenko,

Roman Klosowski, Tadeusz Lomnicki, Andrzej May, Jerzy Pichelski, Wojciech Siemion

In Warsaw during the winter of 1943-44, Polish hostages are executed by German firing squads. The Resistance decides to kill the man responsible, the General in command of the Warsaw SS, and the task is entrusted to a group of medical students. Few countries lost more lives in World War II than Poland, so it is perhaps not surprising that those years were still an obsession in 1958. A former member of the Cracow Resistance, Passendorfer has reconstructed a factual incident with an impressive concern for authenticity, ending up with a film with the flavour of a documentary. However, this approach works against the film because the action is far too slow and drawn out and characterization is almost non-existent. Worthy, and occasionally affecting, but a failure.

▶ **Antarjali Yatra** see Voyage Beyond

Anthracite

France 1980 90 mins col
Rush/Antenne 2

d   Edouard Niermans
sc   Edouard Niermans
ph   Bernard Lutic
m   Alain Jomy
     Jean-Pol Dubois, Jérôme Zucca, Bruno
     Cremer, Jean Bouise

At a Jesuit college for boys, one of the priest-teachers (Dubois), nicknamed 'Anthracite', is despised by colleagues and pupils alike for trying to teach by love rather than force. At the same time, Pierre (Zucca) suffers derision from his fellow pupils. The first feature by 37-year-old Jesuit-educated Niermans presents a bleak but realistic picture of the tensions and cruelty of school life, while avoiding many of the clichés of the genre. His second film, the very different *Angel Dust*, appeared seven years later.

Antigone

Greece 1960 93 mins bw
Norma Film Prod.

d George Tzavellas
sc George Tzavellas
ph Dinos Katsourdis
m Arghyris Kounadis
   Irene Papas, Manos Katrakis, Maro
   Kontou, Nikos Kazis

Antigone (Papas) is condemned to death for defying King Creon (Katrakis) by burying her two brothers killed in a quarrel over their succession to the throne of Thebes. Greek tragedy made filmic with no tricks so that Sophocles' poetic parable comes across with lucidity. Flashback and voice-over unobtrusively overcome the problem of long speeches by the chorus and messenger, thus giving more impact to the images, dominated by the excellent Irene Papas' dramatic beauty.

Antoine And Antoinette

▶ **Antoine Et Antoinette**

   France   1947   95 mins   bw
   SNEG

d Jacques Becker
sc Jacques Becker, Françoise Giroud,
   Maurice Griffe
ph Pierre Montazel
m Jean-Jacques Grünewald
   Roger Pigaut, Claire Maffei, Noël
   Roquevert

The everyday life of a young couple – he works for a printing firm, she is a shop assistant – is disrupted when they find they have won a lottery but lost the ticket. With a nod to René Clair's Le Million (1931), this beguiling romantic comedy, the first of Becker's Parisian 'loving couples' trilogy (including Rendez-Vous De Juillet, 1949 and Edward And Caroline, 1951), is interested less in plot than in the depiction of relationships and in affectionately filmed Paris locations.

▶ **Antoine Et Antoinette** see Antoine And Antoinette

Antonieta

   Mexico   1981   104 mins   col
   Gaumont/Conacine/Nuevo Cine

d Carlos Saura
sc Carlos Saura, Jean-Claude Carrière
ph Teo Escamilla
m José Antonio Zavala
   Isabelle Adjani, Hanna Schygulla, Ignacio
   Lopez Tarso, Carlos Bracho

A French author (Schygulla) goes to Mexico to research the life of Antonieta Rivas Mecadé (Adjani), Mexican patroness of the arts and liberal, who committed suicide in Notre Dame Cathedral in Paris in the 1920s. Denounced and hounded by the Spanish after Sweet Hours (1981), Saura fled to Central America where he made this big budget co-production, one of his least personal films. Although jumping back and forth between the present day and the past, it remains fairly static, with rather lifeless performances from the two female leads.

Antonio Das Mortes

▶ **Dragao Da Maldade Contra O Santo Guerreiro**

   Brazil   1969   95 mins   col
   Glauber Rocha/Mapa

d Glauber Rocha
ph Glauber Rocha
m Marlos Nobre, Walter Queiroz, Sergio
   Ricardo
   Mauricio Do Valle, Odete Lara, Othon
   Bastos, Hugo Carvana

A hired killer ends up siding with the peasants in their fight against the brutal landowners. Like Black God, White Devil (1962), this political allegory was set in the arid northeast of Brazil, and contains similar characters and characteristics: ritualized techniques drawing on the mystic cultural traditions of the country. Made under repressive conditions, it was Rocha's last radical cry from Brazil before almost 10 years' exile.

Best Director Cannes 1969

The Anxiety Of The Goalie At The Penalty

▶ **aka The Goalkeeper's Fear Of The Penalty Kick**

▶ **(US: The Goalie's Anxiety At The Penalty Kick)**

▶ **Die Angst Des Tormanns Beim Elfmeter**

W. Germany 1972 101 mins col
Filmverlag Der Autoren

d   Wim Wenders
sc Wim Wenders, Peter Handke
ph Robby Müller
m   Jürgen Knieper, Roy Orbison, and several
    pop groups
    Arthur Brauss, Kai Fischer, Maria
    Bardischewski, Erika Pluhar

A veteran goalkeeper (Brauss), who lets in a penalty without moving a muscle, meets up with a cinema cashier, goes to bed with her, and calmly strangles her in the morning. The film, based on Handke's first novel, uses the sporting metaphor to express the *angst* of modern life. Like the goalkeeper, the camera hardly moves. Each scene is separated by slow fades creating an atmosphere midway between the hypnotic and the soporific.

▶ **Any Number Can Win** see Big Snatch, The

Anyone Can Play

▶ **Le Dolci Signore**

Italy 1967 102 mins col
Documento Films

d   Luigi Zampa
sc Ruggero Maccari, Ettore Scola
ph Romano Dandi
m   Armando Trovaioli
    Ursula Andress, Virna Lisi, Marisa Mell,
    Claudine Auger, Jean-Pierre Cassel

Four contrasting married women each solve their sex problems by committing adultery. The 1960s saw an interminable string of Italian sex comedies that only slightly rib-tickled and titillated. This loosely scripted portmanteau picture was no exception.

▶ **Apa** see Father

Aparajito

▶ **aka The Unvanquished**

India 1956 127 mins bw
Epic Films

d   Satyajit Ray
sc Satyajit Ray
ph Subrata Mitra
m   Ravi Shankar
    Pinaki Sen Gupta, Karuna Bannerjee,
    Kanu Bannerjee, Sumiran Ghosjal

Apu (played by two boy actors, Gupta and Ghosjal) goes to Benares with his mother, then returns to his village where he begins his education. In the second part of Ray's great 'Apu trilogy' (the linking episode between the childhood in *Pather Panchali*, 1955 and the manhood in *The World of Apu*, 1959), we see Apu growing away from his mother (Karuna Bannerjee) and the village. The mother-son relationship is delicately observed, as are the contrasting scenes between the country and the city.

Best Film Venice 1957

▶ **... A Paty Jezdec Je Strach** see Fifth Horseman Is Fear, The

The Ape Woman

▶ **La Donna Scimmia**

Italy 1964 97 mins bw
Compagnia Cinematografica Champion/
Les Films Marceau/Cocinor

d   Marco Ferreri
sc Marco Ferreri, Rafael Azcona
ph Aldo Tonti
m   Teo Usuelli
    Annie Girardot, Ugo Tognazzi, Achille
    Majeroni, Filippo Pompa

A man (Tognazzi) discovers a monstrous woman (Girardot) covered with hair, marries her to exploit her at a funfair, falls in love with her and, after her death, travels with her embalmed body. No one could ever accuse Ferreri of good taste, but this cynical comedy has much vigour, and a hirsute Girardot brings some poignancy to the title role. Two endings were shot: a softened one terminating with the wife's death, and the other starker one. The latter, better, ending is more frequently shown.

► **A Porte Chiuse** see Behind Closed Doors

The Apple Game

► **Hra O Jablko**

Czechoslovakia 1976 101 mins col Krátky

d Véra Chytilová
sc Véra Chytilová, Kristina Vlachová
ph František Ulček
m Miroslav Kořinek
Jiří Menzel, Dagmar Bláhová, Evelyna Steimarová, Jiří Kodet, Nina Popeliková

A country girl (Bláhová), who works as a midwife at a maternity clinic, becomes pregnant by one of the doctors (Menzel). In her first film for 10 years in her native land, having been at odds with the Czech authorities, Chytilová continued in much the same anarchic vein. But the joky, jumpy, jazzy style had staled over the years, despite some funny moments and striking images (mostly of babies).

À Propos De Nice

France 1930 45 mins bw
Lozinski

d Jean Vigo
sc Jean Vigo
ph Boris Kaufman
m Silent

A satirical documentary on the famous Riviera resort. Under the influence of the experiments in montage of the Russian director Dziga Vertov, Vigo and Kaufman (Vertov's younger brother) brilliantly elaborated the simple contrast between the rich tourists and the poorer inhabitants of Nice. A woman suns herself until she becomes a skeleton, people walking along the promenade are compared with animals, a croupier rakes up passengers just arrived by train, and a girl at a café is stripped nude in a series of dissolves.

The latter scene was cut from the 35 mm version shown in Britain, but remained in the 16 mm print which was not subject to censorship.

► **Apu Sansar** see World Of Apu, The

The Arabian Nights

► **aka A Thousand And One Nights**
► **Il Fiore Delle Mille E Una Notte**

Italy 1974 155 mins col
PEA/Artistes Associés

d Pier Paolo Pasolini
sc Pier Paolo Pasolini
ph Giuseppe Ruzzolini
m Ennio Morricone
Ninetto Davoli, Franco Citti, Franco Merli, Ines Pellegrini

Ten interspliced tales of love and love-making, potions and betrayal, linked by the story of Mur-El-Din searching for his kidnapped slave girl. Pasolini took almost two years to complete this final and best segment of his trilogy of great story cycles, the others being *The Decameron* (1971) and *The Canterbury Tales* (1972). Filmed in Yemen, Eritrea, Iran and Nepal, it captures the beauties (landscape, buildings and people) of those countries, and the bawdy spirit of the original tales remains untramelled by Freudian or religious guilt.

► **Aranyer Din Ratri** see Days And Nights In The Forest

► **Archimède Le Clochard** see Archimède The Tramp

Archimède The Tramp

► **(US: The Magnificent Tramp)**
► **Archimède Le Clochard**

France 1958 91 mins bw
Filmsonor/Intermondia

d Gilles Grangier
sc Albert Valentin, Michel Audiard
ph Louis Page

m Jean Prodromidès
Jean Gabin, Darry Cowl, Bernard Blier,
Dora Doll, Julien Carette

Archimède (Gabin), a crusty old tramp, wrecks a bar in order to be able to spend the winter in jail, gets involved with a dog-stealing tramp and has various altercations with the rich. The script, based on an idea by Gabin, was a sketchy affair but it allowed the star at the end of his third decade in films, to display the full range of his mature mannerisms. He is as forceful as the film is feeble – it was the start of a decline in the material Gabin was to choose for the next two decades.

Best Actor (Jean Gabin) Berlin 1959

▶ **Ard, El** see Land, The

▶ **Ardh Satya** see Half-Truth

▶ **Ardiente Paciencia** see Burning Patience

Aren't We Wonderful?

▶ **Wir Wunderkinder**

W. Germany 1958 120 mins bw
Filmaufbau
d Kurt Hoffmann
sc Heinz Pauck, Günter Neumann
ph Richard Angst
m Franz Gröthe
Johanna Von Koczian, Hansjörg Felmy,
Wera Frydtberg, Robert Graf

An ex-Nazi, who has become a respected captain of industry in modern Germany, has his past exposed by a campaigning journalist, but is nonetheless honoured at his funeral. As the general level of West German films was lamentably low in the 1950s, this light satirical comedy came as a pleasant surprise. A pianist and a narrator in front of a small screen comment in a Brechtian manner on the rise and literal fall (down a lift shaft) of a Nazi, while at the same time finding room for a tender love story.

Are We All Murderers?

▶ **(US: We Are All Murderers)**

▶ **Nous Sommes Tous Des Assassins**

France 1952 95 mins bw
UGC
d André Cayatte
sc André Cayatte, Charles Spaak
ph Jean Bourgoin
m Raymond Legrand
Mouloudji, Raymond Pellegrin, Antoine
Balpêtre, Paul Frankeur, Georges
Poujouly

A former Resistance fighter (Mouloudji) is condemned to death for killing a policeman after the war, and awaits the guillotine with two other prisoners. Former lawyers Cayatte and Spaak followed up their previous success, *Justice Is Done* (1950) about mercy killing, with this heavy-handed and wordy, but nevertheless effective, condemnation of the death penalty. Audiences are left in ignorance as to whether the young killer is reprieved or not.

Special Jury Prize Cannes 1952

L'Argent

France 1928 195 mins bw
Cinémondial/Pathé
d Marcel L'Herbier
sc Marcel L'Herbier
ph Jules Kruger
m Silent
Pierre Alcover, Alfred Abel, Mary Glory,
Brigitte Helm, Raymond Rouleau,
Antonin Artaud

A tale of the constant rivalry between two business tycoons (Alcover and Abel), unscrupulously crushing anyone in their way, including friends and relations. The last and most ambitious of L'Herbier's great silent films was an expansive, updated adaptation of Zola's novel condemning big business. Unequivocally indicting the possession of vast wealth, the film had an enormous budget. A strong cast move through the huge, luminously photographed Art Deco sets. The mobility of the camera was another exciting element in a film that was known for many years only by reputation until it reappeared in the 1960s to general acclaim. Among the many bravura sequences is the camera skimming over the floor of the Stock Exchange, cross-cut with an aircraft taking off.

L'Argent

France　1983　84 mins　col
EOS/Marion's Films/FR3

d　**Robert Bresson**
sc　**Robert Bresson**
ph　**Emmanuel Machuel, Pasqualino De Santis**
m　**Bach**
　　Christian Patey, Sylvie Van Den Elsen, Michel Briguet, Caroline Lang

A young man passes a forged note in a photographer's shop, an action that leads him into theft and murder. Whatever one's views on Bresson's use of non-actors manipulated like expressionless puppets, his sparse editing, austere images, and severe Jansenist beliefs, the 76-year-old director remained true to his constant vision in this updating of a Tolstoy story. Non-Bressonians should abstain.

Best Director Cannes 1983

▶ **Argent De Poche, L'** see Small Change

▶ **Ariane** see Loves Of Ariane

Ariel

Finland　1988　74 mins　col
Villealfa Filmproductions

d　**Aki Kaurismäki**
sc　**Aki Kaurismäki**
ph　**Timo Salminen**
　　Turo Pajala, Susanna Häävisto, Matti Pellonpää, Eetu Hilkamo

Taisto (Pajala), a strong, silent loner, finds himself unemployed when the tin mine where he works in the snowy wastes of Lapland closes down. In an old convertible Cadillac, his only asset, he makes his way to the city, where he becomes involved with single-parent Irmeli (Häävisto) and her young son – a relationship which radically alters their lives. Part social comment, part thriller, Kaurismäki's film is a tightly constructed piece of gritty realism made with cool objectivity, a neat avoidance of clichés, and a certain wry humour to pierce its darker sides. The director and his brother, Mika, apparently form one third of Finland's small but significantly growing film industry which Aki started

bringing to acclaimed attention at festivals throughout Europe and the USA towards the end of the 1980s. Something of a maverick, his output is fairly prodigious and very varied – as well as variable. *Ariel* is the most conventional of his offerings and one of the most completely satisfactory. A thoroughly gripping piece, with Turo Pajala an attractive leading man.

Les Aristocrates

▶ **aka The Aristocrats**

France　1955　105 mins　bw
Gaumont

d　**Denys De La Patellière**
sc　**Roland Laudenbach, Denys De La Patellière**
ph　**Pierre Petit**
m　**René Cloërec**
　　Pierre Fresnay, Brigitte Auber, Jacques Dacqmine, François Guérin, Léo Joannon

An aging French aristocrat (Fresnay), locked into the style and habits of his past, comes into bitter conflict with his now grown-up children who try to push him into adapting to their modern way of life. This is the director's debut film and his inexperience shows in the lack of properly paced dramatic climaxes and a generally loose and choppy style. The acting, particularly from Fresnay, however, just about keeps the tale going. As the almost pathetically outmoded nobleman, living on dreams in his crumbling mansion which he refuses to modernize and clinging on to the last vestiges of dignity, he is a moving figure.

▶ **Aristocrats, The** see Aristocrates, Les

▶ **Armée Des Ombres, L'** see Army In The Shadows, The

Arms And The Man

▶ **Helden**

W. Germany　1958　96 mins　col
Casino Films

d Franz Peter Wirth
sc Johanna Sibelius, Eberhard Keindorff
ph Klaus Von Rautenfeld
m Franz Gröthe
   O.W. Fischer, Lilo Pulver, Ellen
   Schwiers, Ljuba Welitsch, Kurt Kasznar

Bluntschli (Fischer), a Swiss mercenary fleeing
the enemy, takes refuge in the bedroom of
Raina (Pulver), engaged to the Bulgarian
officer who put him to flight. Shaw's famous
anti-romantic comedy is given handsome settings and some good acting, but the film is
as talky as the play, which the stiff direction
does nothing to alleviate.

The Army In The Shadows

▶ **L'Armée Des Ombres**

   France   1969   143 mins   col
   Corona/Fono Roma

d Jean-Pierre Melville
sc Jean-Pierre Melville
ph Pierre Lhomme
m Eric De Marsan
   Lino Ventura, Simone Signoret, Jean-
   Pierre Cassel, Paul Meurisse, Claude
   Mann, Christian Barbier, Serge Reggiani,
   Alain Libolt, Paul Crauchet

Resistance fighter Philippe Gerbier (Ventura)
is arrested in Vichy France and sent to a
prison camp before being handed over to the
Gestapo. He is determined to track down the
informer who betrayed him and his group.
This is the main strand that weaves through
the bleakly atmospheric portrayal of the daring and complex workings of the French
Resistance in German-occupied Lyons during
World War II. Melville's third film on the
subject (he was himself in the *maquis*), based
on Joseph Kessel's novel, is a moving, truthful
and ultimately tragic view of the Resistance,
while not being afraid to glorify the heroism
of its members. These are given powerful
performances from a superb cast able to
express the moral ambiguities of the characters. Using the format of his gangster movies –
cool, classical images and a commanding use
of flashback – Melville turns the underworld
into the underground.

▶ **Arohan** see Ascending Scale

Arsenal

   USSR   1929   99 mins   bw
   VUFKU

d Alexander Dovzhenko
sc Alexander Dovzhenko
ph Danylo Demutsky
m Silent
   Semyon Svashenko, A. Buchma, Mikola
   Nademsky

The Bolsheviks' revolutionary struggles
against opposing forces and the problems of
collectivization in the Ukraine of 1918. The
Ukrainian Dovzhenko's highly symbolic and
lyrical account of his homeland's emergence
from feudalism expertly blends folklore, agit-
prop, drama, comedy and caricature. This
was the sort of plotless Soviet film (where a
tractor plays a leading role) that caused much
sniggering from some Western critics, but
nevertheless became a strong influence,
notably on documentary movements, in other
countries including Britain.

▶ **Artisten In Der Zirkuskuppel:
Ratlos, Die** see Artists At The Top Of
The Big Top: Disorientated

Artists At The Top Of The Big Top: Disorientated

▶ **Die Artisten In Der
Zirkuskuppel: Ratlos**

   W. Germany   1968   103 mins   col
   Kairos Film

d Alexander Kluge
sc Alexander Kluge
ph Günther Hörmann, Thomas Mauch
   Hannelore Hoger, Siegfried Graue, Alfred
   Edel, Bernd Höltz

A young circus director (Hoger), whose father
was killed in a trapeze accident, wants to
create the ideal circus, but gives it up and
goes into TV. Kluge's second and best-known
feature attempts to create an allegory of modern day Germany using four narrators,
including the director, newsreel footage, interviews, stills and acted scenes around the tired
old symbol of the circus as life. Influenced by

early Godard, much of it is wittily cerebral, but seemed fresher at the time when the new German cinema was emerging.

Best Film Venice 1968

▶ **Artists With The Ladies** see Coiffeur Pour Dames

Arturo's Island

▶ **L'Isola Di Arturo**

Italy 1962 102 mins bw
Champion Cinematografica/Titanus/
Metro

d **Damiano Damiani**
sc **Damiano Damiani, Ugo Liberatore, Enrico Ribulzi**
ph **Roberto Gerardi**
m **Carlo Rustichelli**
   Reginald Kernan, Key Meersman, Vanni De Maigret, Luigi Giuliani, Gabriella Giorcelli

Sixteen-year-old Arturo (De Maigret), whose mother is dead and whose strange and taciturn father, Wilhelm (Kernan), travels much of the time, lives a quiet life on an island in the Bay of Naples. One day Wilhelm returns, bringing a new young wife (Meersman) with him and, when he goes away again, Arturo falls hopelessly in love with his stepmother. Damiani has placed a story of adolescent turbulence in a beautiful and strongly atmospheric setting. However, in adapting a highly romantic novel (by Elsa Morante), character development has been neglected so that the protagonists drown in a sea of melodramatic plot. The casting, too, lets the piece down since the principals – with the exception of Key Meersman – don't have the expertise to overcome the weaknesses of the script.

Ascending Scale

▶ **Arohan**

India 1982 147 mins col
West Bengal Government

d **Shyam Benegal**
sc **Shama Zaidi**

ph **Govind Nihalani**
m **Purna Das Baul**
   Om Puri, Victor Banerjee, Noni Ganguly, Rajen Tarafdar, Gita Sen

A share-cropper, who is refused his rights, spends 10 years fighting for them in the courts. Benegal paints a horrifying picture of corruption and exploitation in modern India, based on an actual case history. Yet the film never sentimentalizes, but rather analyses the system that produces oppression of the individual.

▶ **Ascenseur Pour L'Échafaud** see Lift To The Scaffold

The Ascent

▶ **Voskhozhdenie**

USSR 1976 105 mins bw
Mosfilm

d **Larisa Shepitko**
sc **Larisa Shepitko, Juri Klepikov**
ph **V. Chuhnov**
m **Alfred Shnitke**
   Boris Plotkinov, Ludmila Poliakova, Vladimir Gostjuhin, Sergei Jakovlev, Anatoly Solonitsin

A small group of Soviet partisans during World War II escapes from the Germans across the snow and ice, but tragedy occurs when two of them leave the unit to forage for food. Far from the days of Socialist realism, the film depicts cowards and collaborators as well as heroes. Small figures in a brutal white landscape, suffering faces in close-up, and an incomparably powerful hanging scene, make a triumphant climax to Shepitko's four-feature film career. She was killed in a car crash in 1979 while preparing *Farewell*, later made by her widower, Elem Klimov.

Best Film Berlin 1976

▶ **Ascent to Heaven** see Mexican Bus Ride

▶ **Ashanti Sanket** see Distant Thunder

Ashes

▶ **aka The Lost Army**

▶ **Popioly**

Poland 1965 233 mins bw
Film Polski

d   **Andrzej Wajda**
sc **Aleksander Scibor-Rylski**
ph **Jerzy Lipman**
m   **Andrzej Markowski**
    Daniel Olbrychski, Pola Raksa, Boguslaw
    Kierc, Beata Tyszkiewicz, Piotr Wysocki

A Polish legion under General Dombrowski
fights on the side of Napoleon, hoping to free
their own country but, in reality, actually
helping to destroy the freedom of other
nations. Costing $3 million, a huge sum by
Polish standards, and running nearly four
hours (cut by 73 minutes in the USA), Wajda's
ambitious CinemaScope epic, based on the
classic neo-romantic novel by Stefan Zeromski, hoped for a wide international audience.
However, impressive as much of it is, particularly the battle scenes, it was too excessive
and meandering to realize its box-office
ambitions outside Poland.

Ashes And Diamonds

▶ **Popiol I Diament**

Poland 1958 104 mins bw
Film Polski

d   **Andrzej Wajda**
sc **Andrzej Wajda, Jerzy Andrzejewski**
ph **Jerzy Wojcik**
m   **Jan Krenz, Michal Kleotas Oginski**
    Zbigniew Cybulski, Ewa Krzyzanowska,
    Adam Pawlikowski, Bogumil Kobiela

On the last day of the war in 1945, Maciek
(Cybulski), the youngest member of a
Nationalist underground movement in a
provincial Polish town, is ordered to kill the
new Communist district secretary. As he waits
in a hotel during the night, he meets and falls
in love with a girl (Krzyzanowska) and learns
that there is something other to life than
killing. More mature and ironic than the two
preceding films in the trilogy (*A Generation*,
1954 and *Kanal*, 1957) about the resistance

in Warsaw as carried out by the young, this
is perhaps Wajda's finest work. The assassination scene, Maciek's death and the slow
motion polonaise climax are stunningly realized. The brilliant Cybulski embodied the
sceptical new generation in a complex characterization, and the film's enigmatic twilight
world communicated the 'Polish experience'
far beyond the country's frontiers.

Ashik Kerib

USSR 1988 78 mins col
Georgia Film Studio

d   **Sergo Paradjanov, Dodo Abashidze**
sc **Giya Badridze**
ph **Albert Yavuryan**
m   **Djavashir Kuliev**
    Yiur Mgoyan, Veronkia Metonidze,
    Levan Natroshvili, Sofiko Chiaureli, R.
    Chkhlkvadze, K. Stepanov

Ashik Kerib (Mgoyan), a young minstrel
rejected by a rich merchant as a suitor to his
daughter (Metonidze), leaves on a journey to
seek his fortune. On the way he plays at
weddings for the blind and the deaf-and-
dumb, is imprisoned by an evil sultan and
rides a flying horse back in time to win the
hand of the loved one. Although this Arabian
Nights tale, based on a story by Mikhail
Lermontov, is credited as co-directed with the
actor Abashidze, it is so richly adorned with
Paradjanov's exotic-erotic motifs that one not
only enters the world of the folk culture of
the Caucasus, but the great Georgian director's personal, idiosyncratic universe. What
comes across as strongly as ever is his love
of music, dance and gorgeous costumes, and
his identification with the misunderstood artist figure, although Paradjanov never uses his
own suffering at the hands of the Soviet
authorities in a self-pitying manner. Each
kaleidoscopic episode is as ravishing to look
at and as full of surprises as the next, up to
the happy ending when a white dove alights
on a black film camera, fluttering out of the
past into the present. The only disappoint-
ments are the flying horse, suggested merely
by helicopter shots, and the alienating use of
unsynchronized Azerbaijani dialogue with
Georgian voice-over. Paradjanov's last film,
it was dedicated to Andrei Tarkovsky, who

had recently died of cancer. When he made it, the director was aware that he, too, was dying of the same disease, to which he succumbed in July 1990.

As Long As You're Healthy

▶ **Tant Qu'on A La Santé**

France 1965 78 mins bw
Films De La Colombe

d **Pierre Étaix**
sc **Pierre Étaix, Jean-Claude Carrière**
ph **Jean Boffety**
m **Jean Paillaud**
   Pierre Étaix, Alain Janey, Denise Peronne

A little man (Étaix) is harassed wherever he goes – in the city crowds and traffic, at the doctor's surgery, on a camping site, and even on a desert island. The invention of Étaix, the dapper little French visual gagman, seems to be below his norm in his third feature. Chuckles there are, but he is best over a shorter distance. In fact, it was his 'shorts', including the Oscar-winning *Happy Anniversary* (1962), co-directed by Carrière, which made his reputation.

Aspern

France 1981 96 mins col
VO/Oxala

d **Eduardo De Gregorio**
sc **Michael Graham**
ph **Acácio De Almeida**
m **Mozart**
   Alida Valli, Jean Sorel, Bulle Ogier, Ana Marta

The biographer (Sorel) of the long-dead writer Jeffrey Aspern, visits the rambling villa in Lisbon where Aspern's aged mistress (Valli) and her niece (Ogier) live, in order to obtain some unpublished papers. De Gregorio, an Argentinian exile in Paris, relocated the well-known Henry James novella from 19th-century Venice to present-day Lisbon, mainly because the film was made with Portuguese money and was cheaper to shoot there. The updating and transplanting neither damaged

the tale significantly nor enhanced it much in this solid, atmospheric drama.

Asphalt

Germany 1929 114 mins bw
UFA

d **Joe May**
sc **Rolf Vanloo, Fred Majo, Hans Szekely**
ph **Günther Rittau**
m **Silent**
   Gustav Fröhlich, Betty Amann, Else Heller

A prostitute-thief (Amann) seduces a young policeman (Fröhlich) to avoid arrest and leads him accidentally to kill his rival for her love. This expressionistic drama holds a certain morbid fascination from the brilliant opening sequence of the lights in the big city to the inevitable tragic climax. The film came at the end of a series of what influential German critic Siegfried Kracauer termed 'Street Films', in which middle class characters, bored by their homes, are enticed by the forbidden attractions of the streets. One of the most famous examples is G.W. Pabst's *Joyless Street*.

The Assassin

▶ **(US: The Ladykiller Of Rome)**

▶ **L'Assassino**

Italy 1961 105 mins bw
Titanus/Vidas/SGC

d **Elio Petri**
sc **Elio Petri**
ph **Carlo Di Palma**
m **Piero Piccioni**
   Marcello Mastroianni, Salvo Randone, Micheline Presle, Andrea Checci

A day in the life of a prosperous antique dealer wrongly accused of murder, a situation which reveals and changes his personality. Told mostly in short, wry flashbacks, sometimes unrelated to each other or to the plot, the film relies heavily on Mastroianni who provides humour and pathos. Petri's debut feature was one of his more achieved Kafkaesque investigations into crime and a corrupt police force.

▶ **Assassin Habite Au 21, L'** see Murderer Lives At No. 21, The

▶ **Assassino, L'** see Assassin, The

▶ **Assassins Et Voleurs** see Lovers And Thieves

The Assault

▶ **De Aanslag**

Netherlands 1986 148 mins col
Cannon Netherlands

d   **Fons Rademakers**
sc **Gerard Soeteman**
ph **Theo Van Der Sande**
m   **Jurriaan Andriessen**
Derek De Lint, Mac Van Uchelen, Monique Van De Ven, Huub Van Der Lubbe, John Kraaykamp

Anton, who as a 12-year-old in Haarlem in January 1945, saw his whole family and 40 hostages killed by the Nazis, many years later encounters three people from that period who reopen his mental scars. The veteran Dutch director's fascinating examination of the changing political background of Europe works not only on the public and personal level, but as an exciting thriller. Its episodic structure, rather heavy symbolism, and many coincidences, do not hinder the illumination of moral questions or its ability to move.

Best Foreign Film Oscar 1986

Assault In Broad Daylight

▶ **(US: It Happened In Broad Daylight)**

▶ **Es Geschah Am Hellichten Tag**

Switzerland 1958 102 mins bw
Praesens Film

d   **Ladislao Vajda**
sc **Ladislao Vajda, Hans Jacoby, Friedrich Dürrenmatt**
ph **Heinrich Gaertner**
m   **Bruno Canfora**

Heinz Rühmann, Sigfrit Steiner, Siegfrier Löwitz, Michel Simon, Gert Fröbe

A police inspector gets on to the case of a child sex murder after an old pedlar has been forced into a false confession. What could have been a salacious melodrama is handled with intelligence and care, though it lacks pace. Rühmann as the cop and Simon, in the short part of the pedlar, both make an impact.

L'Astragale

France 1968 102 mins col
Films De La Pleiade/C.C.C. Filmkunst

d   **Guy Casaril**
sc **Guy Casaril**
ph **Edmond Richard**
m   **Joss Baselli**
Horst Buchholz, Marlène Jobert, Magali Noël, Claude Génia, Georges Géret

While escaping from prison to be with her Lesbian friend, a 19-year-old girl fractures her ankle bone (l'astragale) and is picked up by an ex-con (Buchholz) with whom she has a passionate affair and for whom she becomes a prostitute and thief. Albertine Sarrazin's best-selling autobiographical novel was given a shallow, showy treatment with plenty of nude love scenes. The freckled Marlène Jobert almost makes the heroine an object of contempt thanks to her self-indulgent performance coupled with the character's compliance in her own destiny.

Asya's Happiness

▶ **Istoriya Asi Klyachinoi, Kòtoraya Lyubila, Da Nie Vshla Zamuzh**

USSR 1967 98 mins bw
Mosfilm

d   **Andrei Mikhalkov-Konchalovsky**
sc **Yuri Klepikov**
ph **Georgy Rerberg**
Iya Savvina, Lyubov Sokolova, Alexander Surin, Gennady Yegorychev, Ivan Petrov

Asya (Savvina), a lame young woman who works as a cook in a small and remote Russian village, is pregnant by Stepan whom she loves but who turns his back on her.

Meanwhile, she meets tractor-driver Sasha during harvest time and they have a relationship. When Asya's baby is about to be born, Stepan changes his attitude, but she rejects him, happy to live alone with her son. The story of Asya herself is only an element in a film whose major achievement is to capture the essence of daily life in rural Russia – the landscape, the hardships, the character of the people. Using, aside from the superb Savvina, a largely non-professional cast, and turning an eloquent camera on authentic locations, Konchalovsky delivers a film rich in atmosphere and detail. However, Asya's independence, and the men's opinions on such issues as Vietnam and the Gulags (discussed while working the harvest), were sufficient to induce official nervousness and the film was promptly suppressed for 20 years. Since reaching Europe and the USA in the late 1980s, it has acted as a reminder of the quality of Konchalovsky's pre-Hollywood work, which places him in the forefront of Russian directors.

▶ **Asymvivastos** see Easy Road

L'Atalante

   France 1934 89 mins bw
   Nounez-Gaumont

d **Jean Vigo**
sc **Jean Vigo, Jean Guinée, Albert Riera**
ph **Boris Kaufman, Louis Berger**
m **Maurice Jaubert**
   Jean Dasté, Dita Parlo, Michel Simon, Gilles Margarites

A young barge captain (Dasté) takes his bride (Parlo) to live on his boat that plies the canals around Paris. Any telling of the simple story cannot do justice to the richness of Vigo's only full-length feature. The everyday life is filled with magical moments such as the mate (Simon) telling fantastic stories of his travels, a waltz on a phonograph, and Dasté searching for his sweetheart under water. Much of it was shot on location in severe weather conditions, contributing to Vigo's death of TB at the age of 29, just before completing the picture. Poorly received on first showing, it was badly cut and a popular song imposed upon it. Happily, it has since been restored to its original form.

▶ **Atame!** see Tie Me Up, Tie Me Down

At First Sight

▶ **(US: Entre Nous)**
▶ **Coup De Foudre**

   France 1983 110 mins col
   Partner's Productions/Alexandre Films/
   Hachette Première/Films A2/SFPC

d **Diane Kurys**
sc **Diane Kurys, Alain Le Henry**
ph **Bernard Lutic**
m **Luis Bacalov**
   Miou-Miou, Isabelle Huppert, Guy Marchand, Robin Renucci, Jean-Pierre Bacri, Patrick Bauchau

Two women's passionate friendship leads them to leave their husbands and set up a dress shop together. The true story of the director's mother and friend, most of it takes place in the Lyons of the 1950s, and is filled with the familiar nostalgic bric-à-brac of the period. The men are ineffectual creatures, and any suggestion of Lesbianism is dealt with somewhat coyly. But there is a throb of genuine feeling beneath the glossy surface, due largely to the performances of the four principals. The green-eyed Huppert and the dark-eyed Miou-Miou are elegantly framed on the CinemaScope screen.

▶ **Atithi** see Runaway, The

L'Atlantide

   France 1921 125 mins bw
   Thalman

d **Jacques Feyder**
sc **Jacques Feyder**
ph **Georges Specht, Victor Morin**
m **Silent**
   Stacia Napierkowska, Jean Angelo, Georges Melchior, Marie-Louise Iribe, Mohammed Ben Nuri

Two soldiers serving in North Africa rediscover the lost city of Atlantis where the queen has the power to make all men fall in love with her. Shot on location in the Algerian desert at a cost of two million francs, making it the most expensive French film to date, its exoticism and extravagance drew the crowds. In his first major film, Feyder's effective use of the spectacular sands could not overcome the miscasting of the plumpish Napierkowska as the supposedly seductive queen. This was the first of four versions of Pierre Benoît's novel.

L'Atlantide

▶ **aka Queen of Atlantis**

▶ **Die Herrin Von Atlantis**

Germany 1932 90 mins bw
Nero

d **G.W. Pabst**
sc **Ladislaus Vajda, Hermann Oberländer**
ph **Eugen Schüfftan, Ernst Koerner**
m **Wolfgang Zeller**
Brigitte Helm, Gustav Diessl, Tela Tschai, Heinz Klingenberg/(French version) Brigitte Helm, Jean Angelo, Pierre Blanchar, Florelle

Two soldiers, who have come across the lost city of Atlantis, fall under the hypnotic spell of its queen. Pabst's last film before the Nazis came to power, was made simultaneously in German, French and English (with the French cast), all three versions dominated by the statuesque presence of Brigitte Helm. Unlike Feyder's *L'Atlantide* (1921), with its genuine desert location, this campy, exotic fantasy takes place in a decor of dazzling white buildings studio sand, and artificial pools.

The Atonement Of Gösta Berling

▶ **(US: The Legend Of Gosta Berling)**

▶ **Gösta Berlings Saga**

Sweden 1924 190 mins bw
Svensk Filmindustri

d **Mauritz Stiller**
sc **Mauritz Stiller, Ragnar Hylten-Cavallius**
ph **J. Julius Jaenzon**
m **Silent**
Lars Hanson, Gerda Lundeqvist, Greta Garbo, Sixten Malmerfeldt

Gösta Berling (Hanson), a defrocked priest, becomes tutor to a well-off provincial family, and then returns to a dissipated life. This rambling family saga, almost a series of historical tableaux, is notable mainly for bringing Garbo to the world's attention. It was Stiller who discovered Greta Gustafson, renamed her, and got her to shed 10 kilos. The film lost about 45 minutes on foreign release, and much of its coherence. Garbo, however, stood out enough in the role of an Italian countess to catch the eye of Louis B. Mayer. The rest is history.

▶ **Att Älska** see To Love

▶ **Attentat, L'** see Plot

At The Meeting With Joyous Death

▶ **Au Rendez-vous De La Mort Joyeuse**

France 1972 82 mins col
Telecip/Artistes Associés

d **Juan Buñuel**
sc **Juan Buñuel, Pierre Maintigneux**
ph **Ghislain Cloquet**
m **Beethoven**
Françoise Fabian, Jean-Marc Bory, Yasmine Dahm, Jean-Pierre Darras, André Weber

After seeing her parents (Fabian and Bory) making love, an adolescent girl (Dahm) starts strange things happening in the Gothic house where she lives. These the shattering of windows and making the refrigerator and washing-machine move about wildly. The son of Luis Buñuel, making his first picture, seems to be a chip off the old block with his mischievous sense of the surreal. However, as social satire it lacks the bite of Buñuel Sr's work, although there is a feeling for suspense, and the mayhem unleashed at the end is well staged.

▶ **Auberge Rouge, L'** see Red Inn, The

▶ **Auch Zwerge Haben Klein Angefangen** see Even Dwarfs Started Small

▶ **Au-Delà Des Grilles** see Walls Of Malapaga, The

The Audience

▶ **L'Udienza**

Italy   1971   114 mins   col
Vides

d   Marco Ferreri
sc Marco Ferreri, Rafael Azcona
ph Mario Vulpiani
m   Teo Usuelli
    Enzo Jannacci, Ugo Tognazzi, Claudia
    Cardinale, Vittorio Gassman, Michel
    Piccoli, Alain Cuny

A young provincial (Jannacci) comes to Rome determined to communicate a personal message to the Pope but is constantly frustrated by Vatican officialdom. Ferreri's usual tendency to over-caricature and underline is held in check in this sardonic, Kafkaesque, anti-clerical tale, well acted by an experienced cast. Jannacci, a pop singer who had seldom acted, is excellent as the bewildered youth.

▶ **Aufstand, Der** see Uprising, The

▶ **Augen Der Mummie Ma, Die** see Eyes Of The Mummy, The

▶ **Au Hasard Balthazar** see Balthazar

▶ **Au Rendez-vous De La Mort Joyeuse** see At The Meeting With Joyous Death

Au Revoir Les Enfants

France   1987   104 mins   col
Nouvelles Éditions De Films/MK2
Productions/Stella Film (Munich)/NEF
(Munich)

d   Louis Malle
sc Louis Malle
ph Renato Berta
m   Schubert, Saint-Saëns
    Gaspard Manesse, Raphaël Fejtö,
    Francine Racette, François Negret,
    Philippe Morier-Genoud, Peter Fitz

January 1944. Jean Bonnet (Fejtö), an intelli-

gent and reserved boy, arrives at a Catholic boarding school in Fontainebleau, where he becomes friendly with Julien Quintin (Manesse), one of the brightest pupils at the school. Julien gradually discovers that Jean is one of three Jewish boys given refuge by Father Jean (Morier-Genoud), the head-master. But acting on an informer's tip, a Gestapo officer appears... Based by Malle on 'the most dramatic experience of my child-hood', the film is one of his very best, not only because he has managed to bring a fresh eye to bear on an oft-filmed period of sorrow and pity, but he has been able to move from broad comedy to pathos, from social comment to straight narrative with ease. Many emotions come into play in a key scene in which the boys watch Chaplin's *The Immigrant*, which offers them escape yet reminds them of people fleeing oppression in Europe. Another sequence which superbly lays bare the attitudes and atmosphere of the times takes place in an expensive restaurant, in which an elderly Jewish client is asked for his papers by the French police before some German officers come to the rescue. The film is a culmination of many of the director's preoccupations over the years – French collaboration during the Occupation, close mother-son relationships, and an unsentimental but affectionate view of children, as here in characterisations as natural as Vichy water.

Best Film Venice 1987

▶ **Aus Dem Leben Der Marionetten** see From The Life Of The Marionettes

▶ **Aus Den Wolken Kommt Das Glück** see Amphitryon

▶ **Aus Einem Deutschen Leben** see Death Is My Trade

▶ **Aussi Longue Absence, Une** see Long Absence, The

Austeria

Poland   1982   110 mins   col
Film Polski(Kadr Unit)

d   Jerzy Kawalerowicz

sc Tadeusz Konwicki, Jerzy Kawalerowicz,
    Julian Stryjkowski
ph Zygmunt Samosiuk
m   Leopold Kozlowski
    Franciszek Pieczka, Wojciech Pszoniak,
    Jan Szurmiej, Ewa Domanska

On the first day of World War I, a group of Jews flees from a Cossack army in Polish Galicia and finds itself trapped overnight in a border inn. Relationships develop, love affairs are snatched, the religious pray, hopes and fears are aired – both within the beleaguered band and between them and the innkeeper's family. Making his first film in five years, the distinguished director combines his gifts for intimate psychological drama with his penchant for history to re-create a vivid picture of a recently vanished world. Full of warmth and vitality, it captures the Jewish sense of humour which seems, uniquely, to draw inspiration from disaster.

Austerlitz

▶ **(US: The Battle Of Austerlitz)**

    France 1959 166 mins col
    CFPI/SCLF/Galatea/Michael Arthur/
    Dubrava

d   Abel Gance
sc Abel Gance, Roger Richebe
ph Henri Alekan, Robert Juillard
m   Jean Ledrut
    Pierre Mondy (Napoleon), Jean Mercure
    (Talleyrand), Martine Carol (Josephine),
    Jack Palance, Orson Welles, Michel
    Simon, Jean-Louis Trintignant, Leslie
    Caron, Claudia Cardinale, Rossano
    Brazzi, Jean Marais, Ettore Manni, Anna
    Moffo, Vittorio De Sica

Napoleon's strategy against, and subsequent defeat of, the Austro-Russian army at Austerlitz. Thirty years after making his silent masterpiece *Napoleon*, the 70-year-old director returned to his hero in a long, talky, academic and stilted pageant, made watchable by the familiar faces of the cast. It was cut by over an hour on release in the USA.

▶ **Austernprinzessin, Die** see Oyster
Princess, The

▶ **Autre Homme, Une Autre
Chance, Un** see Another Man, Another
Chance

An Autumn Afternoon

▶ **Samma No Aji**

    Japan 1962 115 mins col
    Shochiku/Ofuna

d   Yasujiro Ozu
sc Yasujiro Ozu, Kogo Noda
ph Yushun Atsuta
m   Kojun Saito
    Chishu Ryu, Shima Iwashita, Shinichiro
    Mikami, Keiji Sada

A widowed and aging company auditor (Ryu) arranges a marriage for his daughter (Iwashita), then finds himself alone except for his drinking cronies. During the shooting, Ozu's mother, with whom he had lived all his life, died. He was to follow her the next year. His valedictory film has a simplicity, mellowness and nostalgia that makes it a fitting finale to one of the most consistent and rewarding *oeuvres* in cinema.

Autumn Marathon

▶ **Osenny Marafon**

    USSR 1979 90 mins col
    Mosfilm

d   Georgy Danelia
sc Alexander Volodin
ph Sergei Vronski
m   Andrei Petrov
    Oleg Basilashvili, Natalia Gundareva,
    Marina Neyelova, Evgeni Leonov

A mild-mannered English-language teacher (Basilashvili) in Leningrad has a problem running between his wife (Gundareva) and mistress (Neyelova), as well as coping with his students, and prying neighbours. A wry comedy, from the Georgian satirist, Danelia, manages to combine humour with social comment on urban intellectual life in an adept manner. Its lack of bite is compensated for by the nicely observed gallery of obsessive characters, the droll playing and the Leningrad background.

Autumn Sonata

▶ **Hostsonaten**

Sweden 1978 97 mins col
Personafilm/ITC

d   **Ingmar Bergman**
sc **Ingmar Bergman**
ph **Sven Nykvist**
m   **Chopin, Bach, Handel**
    Ingrid Bergman, Liv Ullmann, Halvar
    Bjork, Erland Josephson, Gunnar
    Björnstrand

A world-renowned concert pianist (Bergman) returns to Sweden to visit the married daughter (Ullmann) she has not seen for many years, and has to face up to her feelings of guilt for having put her career above her family. As he did in *Persona*, Bergman places two women face to face with each other and their own inadequacies and, as in *Wild Strawberries*, there is the painful recognition that the past cannot be changed. With his masterly use of the close-up, and the flashback utilized as the subconscious, he creates a chamber work of almost Strindbergian intensity. This long night's journey into day, allows the director's namesake to give a remarkable performance, displaying every aspect of her screen personality over the years – naivety, sophistication, gaiety, and tragedy. It was Ingrid Bergman's first Swedish film for almost 40 years and, sadly, her last feature before her death.

▶ **Avenir D'Émilie, L'** see Future Of Emily, The

▶ **Aventures D'Arsène Lupin, Les** see Adventures Of Arsène Lupin, The

▶ **Aventures De Casanova** see Loves Of Casanova

▶ **Aventures De Rabbi Jacob, Les** see Adventures Of Rabbi Jacob, The

▶ **Aventures De Till L'Espiègle, Les** see Adventures Of Till Eulenspiegel, The

▶ **Aveu, L'** see Confession, The

The Aviator's Wife

▶ **La Femme De L'Aviateur**

France 1980 106 mins col
Les Films Du Losange

d   **Eric Rohmer**
sc **Eric Rohmer**
ph **Bernard Lutic**
m   **Jean-Louis Valero**
    Philippe Marlaud, Marie Rivière, Anne-
    Laure Meury, Matthieu Carrière

A post-office worker (Marlaud) meets a young girl (Meury) in a park and she agrees to help him spy on a pilot (Carrière), whom he suspects of seeing his older girlfriend (Rivière). The first of Rohmer's series called 'Comedies and Proverbs', is a delightful comedy of errors concerned with the illusions of love and the indiscretions of youth. In fact, the young dominate the sequence, in contrast to the more adult concerns of the previous 'Six Moral Tales'. It also introduces the figure of the exacting and spoiled young woman (here, as in *The Green Ray*, played by Rivière) who exasperates those around her, and some audiences too. Shot in Paris, using direct sound, the film provides a ravishing centrepiece in a verdant park.

▶ **Avrianos Polemistis** see Tomorrow's Warrior

L'Avventura

Italy 1960 145 mins bw
Cino Del Duca/PCE/Lyre

d   **Michelangelo Antonioni**
sc **Michelangelo Antonioni, Elio Bartolini,**
    Tonino Guerra
ph **Aldo Scavarda**
m   **Giovanni Fusco**
    Monica Vitti, Lea Massari, Gabriele
    Ferzetti, Dominique Blanchar

Anna (Massari) disappears when a group of wealthy people visit a Sicilian island by yacht, resulting in her architect fiancé (Ferzetti) and friend (Vitti) gradually coming together. This was the film in which, after five features in 10 years, Antonioni's style reached its maturity, redefining our views of time and space in the cinema. The long tracking shots, the limited dialogue and the strong relationship between the characters and their environment disconcerted some at the time, but average filmgoers should now take these in their stride. What matters in the plot is not the unsolved mystery story (as in *Blow Up* 1967, and *The Passenger* 1975), but the effect it has on the characters, especially the ravishing Vitti in her first role for the director whose lover she would become.

Special Jury Prize Cannes 1960

▶ **Avventura Di Salvator Rosa, Un**
see Adventure Of Salvator Rosa, An

Away From It All

▶ **Iz Zhizni Otdikhayushchikh**

USSR   1981   90 mins   col
Mosfilm

d   **Nikolai Gubenko**
sc   **Nikolai Gubenko**
ph   **Alexander Kniazhinski**
m   **Isaak Shvarts**
Zhanna Bolotova, Regimantas Adomaitis, Georgy Burkov, Rolan Bykov, Anatoly Solonitsin, Lydia Fedoseeva-Shukshina

An assorted group of late holiday-makers are thrown together at a Crimean seaside resort where they gossip, flirt, play cards, and eat. Here, also, a love affair blossoms between an educated woman and a taciturn man. The film is a beautifully observed, amiable, wry, Chekhovian satire on the Russians at play. A pinch of Tati and a soupçon of Fellini add to the pleasant dish which climaxes with a delightful farewell party. Only the rather too-leisurely central love story slows the film down.

Ay! Carmela

Spain   1990   95 mins   col
Iberoamericana Films/ELLEPI/TVE

d   **Carlos Saura**
sc   **Carlos Saura, Rafael Azcona**
ph   **José Luis Alcaine**
m   **Alejandro Masso**

Carmen Maura, Andres Pajares, Gabino Diego, Maurizio Di Razza

It is 1938 and the Spanish Civil War is raging. Republican supporters Carmela (Maura) and her husband Paulito (Pajares), a tacky but dedicated travelling cabaret act, entertain the soldiers, 'assisted' by Gustavete (Diego), a mute and helpless youngster whom they picked up in the devastation. After a gruelling stretch in the heart of battle-torn Aragon, Carmela persuades her husband to return to more peacable Valencia, but on the journey they encounter Franco's forces who take their truck and arrest them. When an Italian lieutenant who is keen on the theatre learns who they are, he commandeers their services to stage an entertainment for the troops and their prisoners. The show is a great success until Carmela, outraged at being a voice for Fascist propaganda, lets her feelings be known. Carlos Saura has not made a better film than this. His straightforward narrative, rooted in the horror and destruction of the Civil War, unfolds, for the most part, as a comedy, expertly controlled by the director and brilliantly executed by his stars and supporting cast. Saura creates an authentic atmosphere and makes strong political points. Although more realistic and uncompromising, the film puts one in mind of Lubitsch's immortal *To Be Or Not To Be* in its sharp, sly and funny dig at Fascism and military bureaucracy. Underlying the laughs, and the wonderful brio of the cabaret turns, is tenderness, poignancy and pain, and the movie audaciously ends on a tragic note. Pajares, one of Spain's best-known comedians, is superb as Paulito – weak, loving and instinctively understanding the game he must play for survival. And Carmen Maura, at the centre of the derring-do, is irresistibly extrovert, sexy, compassionate, funny and moving.

Best Actress (Carmen Maura) European Film Awards 1990

Aziza

Tunisia   1980   90 mins   col
SATPEC (Tunisia)/Radio Television Algeria/LATIF

d   **Abdel-Latif Ben Ammar**

sc **Abdel-Latif Ben Ammar, Toufik Jebali**
ph **Youssef Sharaqui**
m **Ahmed Malek**
　　Yasmine Khlat, Raouf Ben Amor, Dalila
　　Ramez, Mohammed Zinet

Aziza (Khlat), a young, obedient orphan girl,
moves with her old uncle and irresponsible
cousin (Amor) from the country to the big
city. When her uncle dies, she gets a job in a
textile factory and becomes, for the first time
in her life, economically independent. The
theme of the role of women in Arab society,
something that has concerned many of the
younger Arab directors, is here presented in
a direct, economical and affecting way in Ben
Ammar's third film. Its frankness on sensitive
issues and its compassionate portrayal of a
woman who finds her own worth (beautifully
played by the Lebanese Khlat) marked the
coming of age of Tunisian cinema.

▶ **Až Přijde Kocour** see When The Cat
Comes

Baara

Mali 1978 93 mins col
Souleymane Cissé Productions

d **Souleymane Cissé**
sc **Souleymane Cissé**
ph **Etienne Carton De Grammont**
m **Lamine Konté**
**Balla Moussa Keita, Baba Niaré,
Bubakar Keita, Oumou Diarra, Ismaïla
Sarr**

The investigations into the murder of a young
engineer (Balla Moussa Keita) who encouraged union activities at a local factory, opens
up a web of intrigue and corruption. Cissé
sets his superbly accomplished drama in
Bamako, the capital of Mali, thus moving
away from the folklore and tribal customs
central to many of his other films and to
black African films in general. It concentrates
on 'baara', translated as 'the world of work',
in a country just beginning to industrialize
and the problems that have derived from it.
The thriller storyline provides a base on which
Cissé builds a rich tapestry of African urban
life, pulsating with its particular rhythms and
colours.

▶ **Bab El Hadid** see Cairo Station

Babette Goes To War

▶ **Babette S'En Va-T'En Guerre**

France 1959 106 mins col
Iena

d **Christian-Jaque**
sc **Raoul Lévy, Gérard Oury**
ph **Armand Thirard**
m **Gilbert Bécaud**

**Brigitte Bardot, Jacques Charrier,
Hannes Messemer, Ronald Howard,
Francis Blanche**

In 1940, a French refugee girl is sent by
British intelligence from England to France
to use her feminine charms in a plot to kidnap
a Nazi general and delay the German invasion
of England. Bardot was at the height of her
fame when she embarked on this weary, witless war comedy, so it still made money.
During the shooting, she fell in love with her
handsome 22-year-old co-star Jacques Charrier, and they were married the same year, a
short-lived affair which was a kind of war in
itself.

▶ **Babette S'En Va-T'En Guerre** see
Babette Goes To War

Babette's Feast

▶ **Babettes Gaestebud**

Denmark 1987 105 mins col
Panorama Film International/Nordisk
Film/Danish Film Institute

d **Gabriel Axel**
sc **Gabriel Axel**
ph **Henning Kristiansen**
m **Per Norgaard**
**Stéphane Audran, Bodil Kjer, Brigitte
Federspiel, Jean-Philippe Lafont, Jarl
Kulle, Bibi Andersson**

On the bleak Jutland Peninsula in the 1870s
live two spinster sisters (Kjer and Federspiel),
daughters of the former pastor and founder
of an austere religious sect, who devote
themselves to keeping alive his memory and
his teachings in the tiny, remote community.
Subtle changes occur when Babette, a

Frenchwoman who has fled the war-torn Paris of 1871, turns up on their doorstep seeking refuge and becomes their cook-housekeeper. Fourteen years elapse before it is revealed that Babette is a *cordon bleu* cook – a fact which leads to a cathartic event for her, her employers and the community. This superb adaptation of the Karen Blixen (Isak Dinesen) novella remains true to its literary source with no loss to cinematic quality. Axel shifts from past to present and between voice-over narrative and dialogue with considerable skill, casting a spell over the spectator with an entrancingly bitter-sweet mix of comedy and deep poignancy. Audran, no stranger to meals in the films of her husband, Claude Chabrol, stands out among a large and flawless cast. A deserving winner in a particularly strong list of Foreign Oscar contenders.

Best Foreign Film Oscar 1987

▶ **Babettes Gaestebud** see Babette's Feast

Backstairs

▶ **Hintertreppe**

Germany 1921 60 mins bw
UFA

d **Leopold Jessner, Paul Leni**
sc **Carl Mayer**
ph **Karl Hasselmann, Willy Hameister**
m **Silent**
   Henny Porten, Wilhelm Dieterle, Fritz Kortner

Failing to hear from her distant lover (Dieterle), a servant girl (Porten) goes on a visit to the postman (Kortner). Unbeknown to her, the latter – handicapped mentally as well as physically – is morbidly infatuated with her and has been intercepting her lover's letters. This intimate piece, steeped in gloom and with a miscast leading lady, was not well-received by audiences of the day, but its Expressionistic style is interesting, as is writer Mayer's allegorical approach to character. Co-directed by Leni, who had a hand in the sets, it is mainly Jessner's work – a stage director known for his stylized use of staircases, the term *Jessnertreppe* was already part of the vocabulary of the German theatre before this film was made.

▶ **Bad Girls Don't Cry** see Night Heat

Bad Luck

▶ **Zezowate Szczescie**

Poland 1960 158 mins bw
WFF

d **Andrzej Munk**
sc **Jerzy Stefan Stawinski**
ph **Jerzy Lipman, Krzysztof Winiewicz**
m **Jan Krenz**
   Bogumil Kobiela, Maria Ciesielska, Barbara Kwiatkowska, Aleksander Dzwonkowski, Bronislaw Pawlik

Piszczyk (Kobiela), a middle-aged prisoner, relates the story of his unfortunate life to the warden: his failures as a boy scout, student, lover, soldier, prisoner-of-war, underground fighter and Stalinist bureaucrat. Munk's last completed work before his untimely death is a harsh satire on political and social conformity as represented by his pathetic hero. Naturally, the conformists in the Polish government at the time strongly criticized the film. Most movie critics, however, were more favourable and, despite its excessive length, the picaresque, poignant and humourous tale is a timely reflection of the painful history of Poland from the 1930s to the 1950s.

The Bad Sleep Well

▶ **Warui Yatsu Yoku Nemuru**

Japan 1960 151 mins bw
Tomoyuki Tanaka/Kurosawa

d **Akira Kurosawa**
sc **Akira Kurosawa, Hideo Oguni, Eijiro Kusaka, Ryuzo Kikushima, Shinobu Hashimoto**
ph **Yuzuru Aizawa**
m **Sasaru Sato**
   Toshiro Mifune, Masayuki Mori, Takashi Shimura, Chishu Ryu

The private secretary (Mifune) to a corrupt government official (Mori) marries his superior's daughter as part of a scheme to avenge his father's murder, for which he holds his father-in-law responsible. For his first independent production Kurosawa, leaning Westwards again, took an Ed McBain novel as the basis for this contemporary thriller. Although the Japanese style sits rather awkwardly on the American model, the use of the large 'Scope screen and the accomplished performances keep alive the interest in the rather complicated proceedings.

A Bad Son

▶ **Un Mauvais Fils**

France   1980   110 mins   col
Sara Films/Antenne 2/SFP

d   **Claude Sautet**
sc **Claude Sautet, Daniel Biasini, Jean-Paul Torok**
ph **Jean Boffety**
m   **Philippe Sarde**
    Patrick Dewaere, Yves Robert, Brigitte Fossey, Jacques Dufilho, Claire Maurier

Bruno (Dewaere), a young Frenchman, returns to Paris after serving five years in an American prison for drug trafficking. Readjustment proves difficult as he searches for work, faces his working-class father (Robert), who holds his past behaviour responsible for his mother's death, and has an affair with another ex-addict (Fossey), whose drug problems are not fully resolved. An excellent film from Sautet, who brings restraint to his usually glossy professionalism in this story of ordinary people in ordinary settings. It's a sympathetic, straightforward treatment, with Dewaere excellent, Fossey exhibiting the right degree of emotional fragility and actor-director Robert effective as the lonely and embittered father.

▶ **Baghe Sangui** see Garden Of Stones

▶ **Baie Des Anges, La** see Bay Of Angels

▶ **Baisers Volés** see Stolen Kisses

▶ **Báječni Muži S Klikou** see Those Wonderful Movie Cranks

▶ **Bakaruhaban** see Sunday Romance, A

Baker's Bread

▶ **Das Brot Des Bäckers**

W. Germany   1976   122 mins   col
Artus Film/ZDF

d   **Erwin Keusch**
sc **Erwin Keusch, Karl Saurer**
ph **Dietrich Lohmann**
m   **Condor**
    Günther Lamprecht, Bernd Tauber, Maria Lucca, Silvia Reize, Anita Lochner

Werner Wild (Tauber), apprentice to a small-town traditional baker Georg Baum (Lamprecht), moves to a bread factory in another town where his girlfriend (Lochnar) works. Georg's old-fashioned methods fail to meet the increased demand, until Werner returns to help him and he agrees to put his business on a co-operative basis. The first feature by Keusch, himself the son of a baker, is absorbing enough merely in the loving and detailed demonstration of the making of bread, rolls and cake. A lot more arises in this gentle, observant Brechtian tale (it is divided into captioned chapters) of the place of an 'artist' in a society where money is more important than dough.

The Baker's Wife

▶ **La Femme Du Boulanger**

France   1938   117 mins   bw
Marcel Pagnol Films

d   **Marcel Pagnol**
sc **Marcel Pagnol**
ph **G. Benoit, R. Lendruz, N. Daries**
m   **Vincent Scotto**
    Raimu, Ginette Leclerc, Charles Moulin, Charpin

A village baker (Raimu) refuses to bake bread when his attractive young wife (Leclerc) runs off with a handsome shepherd (Moulin), a situation which forces the breadless villagers to take action. Pagnol, combining the best of his humour with sympathetic characterizations of Provençal life, gives an individual drama of infidelity a collective dimension. The great Raimu is at his peak as the cuckold who welcomes back his errant wife warmly but reviles her cat for having been away – the kind of masterstroke seen throughout Pagnol's films.

▶ **Bakushu** see Early Summer

Le Bal

France 1984 112 mins col
S.A./A2/Massfil/Oncic

d **Ettore Scola**
sc **Ruggero Maccari**
ph **Ricardo Aronovich**
m **Vladimir Cosma**
   Jean-François Perrier, Marc Berman,
   Nani Noël, Danielle Rochard, Liliane
   Delval, Monica Scattini

Events in France from 1936 to the present day are reflected inside a ballroom by the changing music and the characters who have frequented the place over the years. A sort of 'La-Vie-En-Roseland' view of modern French history, drawing much of its imagery from movie mythology. But behind this and the caricature performances, one senses the pain of real events underlined with the potency of cheap music. Films speak in many ways. *Le Bal* manages to say a lot without a single line of dialogue.

Best Director Berlin 1984

La Balance

France 1981 102 mins col
Les Films Ariane/Films 42

d **Bob Swaim**
sc **Bob Swaim, M. Fabiani**
ph **Bernard Zitzermann**
m **Roland Bocquet**
   Nathalie Baye, Philippe Léotard, Richard
   Berry, Maurice Ronet

In order to nail a gang boss (Ronet), the Brigades Territoriales (élite French plainclothes police) coerce a petty crook (Léotard) into turning informer – 'la balance' in underworld parlance – using his relationship with a prostitute (Baye). Swaim is an American director resident in Paris, and this tough and exciting police thriller, set in the Casbah-like district of Belleville, was a huge commercial and critical success in France. But atmosphere and some brilliant set-pieces, such as a shoot-out in a traffic jam, don't quite compensate for the unsympathetic characters on both sides of the law.

Ballad

Sweden 1968 82 mins bw
Sandrew/Svenska Filminstitutet/Gösta Ågren

d **Gösta Ågren**
sc **Gösta Ågren**
ph **Per-Åke Dahlberg**
m **Bach and others**
   Vivian Gude, Stig Torstensson, Stefan
   Ekman, Jarl Lindblad, Lennart Snickars

An anti-Fascist journalist writing in Finland in the 1930s becomes aware that his neighbour and one-time friend, now recruited to the Fascist cause, is about to betray him. He goes into hiding, later joined by two friends, a man and a woman, and by using their logic they escape assassination. In spite of some plot points that are difficult to swallow, this is a stylish, serious-minded piece, with an underlying theme that examines the nature and possibilities of pacifism in the face of violence. It does so within a framework of a tense story, lyrically filmed against a summer landscape, and is an absorbing small film.

▶ **Ballada O Soldate** see Ballad Of A Soldier

Ballad Of A Soldier

▶ **Ballada O Soldate**

USSR 1959 89 mins bw
Mosfilm

d **Grigori Chukrai**
sc **Grigori Chukrai, Valentin Yoshov**
ph **Vladimir Nikolayev, Era Saveleya**
m **Mikhail Ziv**
   Vladimir Ivashev, Sharma Prokhorenko,
   Antonina Maximova, Nikolai Kryuchkov

A young soldier (Ivashev) on four days leave from the front travels by train, truck and on foot to visit his mother (Maximova). *En route* he meets various people affected by the war, and a girl (Prokhorenko) with whom he falls in love. This simple, sentimental and unrhetorical view of everyday life in wartime Russia continued the trickle of Soviet films welcomed in the West in the late 1950s. In fact, it was the first film from the USSR to enter an

American film festival – the San Francisco –
which it won.

Special Jury Prize Cannes 1960

Ballad Of Berlin

▶ **(US: The Berliner)**
▶ **Berliner Ballade**

W.Germany 1948 77 mins bw
Comedia Film

d **Robert Stemmle**
sc **Günter Neumann**
ph **Georg Krause**
m **Günter Neumann, Werner Eisbrenner**
   Gert Fröbe, Anton Zeithammer, Tatjana
   Sais, O.E. Hasse

The film starts 100 years in the future in a
peaceful, prosperous and rebuilt Germany.
Then, as though going back in time, it focuses
on the contemporary, immediate post-war
world. Otto Nobody (Fröbe), a reluctant soldier, returns from the front to a Berlin in ruins,
where he becomes prey to bureaucrats and
black marketeers. Like *Film Without A Title*,
this film with a title added a sense of irony
to the *Trümmerfilm* – works indulging in the
mood of resignation and self-pity experienced
by a defeated people. An awkward but interesting mixture of satire, songs, and sentiment,
it was one of the first post-war German
productions to be shown abroad. Gert Fröbe,
the future 'Goldfinger', made his screen debut
as the skinny hero.

The Ballad Of Narayama

▶ **Narayama-Bushi-Ko**

Japan 1958 98 mins col
Shochiku

d **Keisuke Kinoshita**
sc **Keisuke Kinoshita**
ph **Hiroyuki Kusuda**
m **Rokuzaemon Kineya, Matsunosuke**
   Nozawa
   Kinuyo Tanaka, Teiji Takahashi, Yuko
   Mochizuki, Eijiro Tono

The custom in a small, impoverished village
is for the elderly, on reaching the age of 70,
to be abandoned on a mountain top. Sixty-
nine-year-old Orin (Tanaka), living with her

son (Takahashi) and three grandchildren, prepares for her departure. When the day arrives,
the son carries his mother up the mountain
and tearfully leaves her. Less violent and
explicit than the later Imamura version of the
famous legend, it is also far more stylized,
echoing Kabuki theatre, and shot almost
entirely in studio settings. This makes the
barbaric customs more palatable, giving the
film an air of fantasy. Kinuyo Tanaka is as
wonderful as ever and the use of colour and
wide screen is superb.

The Ballad Of Narayama

▶ **Narayama-Bushi-Ko**

Japan 1983 130 mins col
Toei

d **Shohei Imamura**
sc **Shohei Imamura**
ph **Masao Tochizawa**
m **Shinichiro Ikebe**
   Ken Ogata, Sumiko Sakamoto, Tonpei
   Hidari, Takejo Aki

During the last century, an old woman prepares for death in a remote mountain village
in North Japan where the customs premature
burial for theft, and the abandonment of
anyone over 70 on the top of Mount Narayama. Imamura neither condemns nor con-
dones this imaginary primitive society,
derived from a novel by Shichiro Fukazawa
(also filmed by Keisuke Kinoshita in 1958),
but plainly seeks comparisons with the cruelty
of our own time. The point is rammed home
somewhat repetitiously, but the ritual sex and
violence, and the long final sequence when a
dutiful son carries his old mother up the
mountain slopes, cannot fail to impress and
shock.

Best Film Cannes 1983

▶ **Ballon Rouge, Le** see Red Balloon,
The

Balthazar

▶ **Au Hasard Balthazar**

France 1966 95 mins bw
Parc/Athos/Ardos/Svensk Industri

d   Robert Bresson
sc Robert Bresson
ph Ghislain Cloquet
m   Jean Wiener, Schubert
    Anne Wiazemsky, François Lafarge,
    Philippe Asselin, Nathalie Joyaut

The birth, life and death of a donkey which
passes from drawing a carriage to pulling a
plough, is ridden by children, becomes a
circus attraction, and turns a miller's grind-
stone before being shot by a customs officer
during a smuggling escapade. One of Bresson's more lyrical and accessible films, this
Christian parable sometimes edges into the
territory of children's animal movies. The
death of the donkey on the hillside surrounded by sheep, is a stunning sequence,
and it is not too frivolous to note that the
quadruped gives one of the best Bressonian
performances.

Special Jury Prize Venice 1966

Baltic Deputy

▶ **Deputat Baltiki**

USSR   1937   107 mins   bw
Lenfilm/Amkino

d   Alexander Zarkhi, Joseph Heifits
sc Alexander Zarkhi, Joseph Heifits, David
    Dell, Leonid Rakhmanov
ph Hoissaye Kaplan
m   Nikolai Tomofeev
    Nikolai Cherkassov, Marta Domasheva,
    Boris Livanov, Otto Zhakov

Incidents in the life of the distinguished Russian scientist and former Oxford professor
Klement Timiriazev (renamed in the film)
who, despite ostracism by colleagues, joined
the Bolsheviks in 1918 and became a hero of
the revolution. The 32-year-old Cherkassov
gives a remarkable portrayal, especially as a
70-year-old, in a film which ably balances
propaganda, action, humour and pathos.

▶ **Bambini Ci Guardano, I** see Children Are Watching Us, The

▶ **Bande À Part** see Outsiders, The

▶ **Bande Des Quatre, La** see Gang Of
Four, The

The Bandit

▶ **O Cangaceiro**

Brazil   1953   119 mins   bw
Vera Cruz

d   Lima Barreto
sc Lima Barreto, Rachel De Queiroz
ph Chick Fowle
m   Gabriel Migliori
    Alberto Ruschel, Marisa Prado, Milton
    Ribeiro, Vanja Orico

A rift develops between the leader (Ribeiro)
of a gang of *cangaceiros*, Brazilian bandits of
the Robin Hood type, and his young lieutenant (Ruschel), when the latter falls for a
schoolmistress captured by the group. The
first Brazilian film to become internationally
known is a poetic adventure played and
directed with gusto. Particularly striking
is the pulsating music, derived from folk
themes.

The Bandit

▶ **La Cucaracha**

Mexico   1959   90 mins   col
Ismael Rodriguez Productions

d   Ismael Rodriguez
sc José Balanos Prado, Ismael Rodriguez,
    José Luis Celis, Ricardo Garibay
ph Gabriel Figueroa
m   Raúl Lavista
    Emilio Fernández, Maria Felix, Dolores
    Del Rio, Pedro Armendáriz, Antonio
    Aguilar

A thoroughly battle-weary and demoralized
group of conscripts to Pancho Villa's cause
is given a new lease of life and courage by a
woman soldier, known as 'La Cucaracha'
(Felix), who falls in love with their leader,
Colonel Zeta (Fernández). He abandons her
for another woman (Del Rio) and is subsequently killed. Both women, La Cucaracha
now pregnant with his child, trek to the
mountains with the army. A brash, commercial exploitation of the Mexican Revolution,
exhibiting little flair or originality, but it's
highly entertaining to watch some of Hollywood's best-known native Mexicans going
through their paces, and Fernández, better-
known as a director, is superior to the overstated script and garish photography.

▶ **Banditi A Orgosolo** see Bandits At Orgosolo, The

The Bandits At Orgosolo

▶ **Banditi A Orgosolo**

Italy 1961 98 mins bw
Titanus

d **Vittorio De Seta**
sc **Vittorio De Seta, Vera Gherarducci**
ph **Vittorio De Seta**
m **Valentino Bucchi**
    **Michele Cossu, Peppeddu Cuccu,
    Vittorina Pisano**

A young Sardinian shepherd (Cossu), unjustly accused of a crime, flees with his flock, but becomes a bandit when his sheep die. This first feature by a documentary film-maker, played entirely by Sardinian peasants and made with minimum financial and technical facilities, impressed by its honesty and splendid photography. Its only compromise was the dubbing of the Sardinian argot into standard Italian.

▶ **Band of Outsiders** see Outsiders, The

▶ **Bangiku** see Late Chrysanthemums

▶ **Banshun** see Late Spring

▶ **Barefoot Savage** see Sensualità

▶ **Bariera** see Barrier

The Baritone

▶ **Baryton**

Poland 1984 95 mins col
'Zespoly Filmowe'/Perspektywa

d **Janusz Zaorski**
sc **Feliks Falk**
ph **Witold Adamek**
m **Jerzy Satanowski**
    **Zbigniew Zapasiewicz, Piotr Fronczewski,
    Malgorzata Pieczynska, Zofia Saretok,
    Aleksander Bardini**

In 1933, after 25 years abroad, the great singer 'Toni Taviatini' (Zapasiewicz) returns to his native town in Poland to give a performance marking his fiftieth birthday and to donate money towards the building of an opera house. Accompanied by an entourage that includes his faithless third wife (Pieczynska), who is carrying on with his scheming, ambitious male private secretary (Fronczewski), he checks in at a plush hotel where his life begins to fall apart. As most of the action takes place in the singer's hotel suite, and the screenplay by Falk, a director in his own right, is rather wordy, the film gives the impression – wrongly – that its source might have been a stage play. The quality of Zaorski's solid direction lies in the way the performers play against each other. Although a patina of irony lies over the fable, there is a sense of insidious fascism in the background, and the ending, in which the baritone has to mime to his own record, having lost his voice, gives the film deeper significance. Zapasiewicz in the title role cleverly combines cosmopolitan cynicism with encroaching insecurity.

Barocco

France 1976 102 mins col
Films La Boétie/Sara

d **André Téchiné**
sc **André Téchiné, Marilyn Goldin**
ph **Bruno Nuytten**
m **Philippe Sarde**
    **Isabelle Adjani, Marie-France Pisier,
    Gérard Depardieu, Jean-Claude Brialy**

A crook (Depardieu) kills his double, and takes his place and his girlfriend (Adjani). Together, the couple blackmail a politician and escape with the money to start a new life. The title gives some idea of what Téchiné was aiming for in this flamboyant parodic thriller. Unfortunately, the self-conscious and pretentious references to German Expressionism and *film noir* are inept, despite some atmospheric sets such as a red-light district where Pisier's seductive prostitute hangs out. Depardieu seems constrained and Adjani pouts.

Le Baron De L'Écluse

France 1959 94 mins bw

Filmsonor/Intermondia/Cinétel(Paris)/
Vides(Rome)

d   Jean Delannoy
sc Maurice Druon
ph Louis Page
m   Jean Prodromidès
    Jean Gabin, Micheline Presle, Blanchette
    Brunoy, Jacques Castelot, Jean Desailly

Baron Jérôme Napoléon Antoine (Gabin),
who lives on chance opportunities in Deauville, makes a killing at the casino and buys
a yacht he has been commissioned to sell. He
takes his former mistress Perle (Presle), an
adventuress, cruising on the canals, but is
stranded at a lock waiting for his commission
to arrive from the yacht's former owner. He
marries off the now petulant Perle to the local
wine millionaire, while he himself... This film
is a casually thrown together series of good-
natured episodes, elevated by Gabin's superb
performance as the monocled Baron who
retains his optimism despite the knowledge
that love has passed him by. The rest of the
acting is also at par, but it is the star's magic
presence which makes this a thoroughly pleasing and funny excursion.

▶ **Baron Fantôme, Le** see Phantom
Baron, The

Baron Munchausen

▶ **Baron Prásil**

    Czechoslovakia 1962 81 mins col
    Ceskoslovensky Film

d   Karel Zeman
sc Karel Zeman
ph Jiří Tarantik
m   Zdeněk Liška
    Miloš Kopecký, Hana Brejchová, Rudolf
    Jelinek, Jan Werich

On the moon, an astronaut meets the famous
liar Baron Munchausen (Kopecky) who
returns to earth with him to enact a number
of fantastic adventures. Using puppets, cartoons, special effects, and live-action against
painted backdrops, Czech animator Zeman
succeeded in creating a magical world, enticing to both children and adults. His inspiration sprang from the 1862 edition of G.A.

Burger's novel with drawings by Gustav
Doré, and the turn-of-the-century films of
conjurer and cinema pioneer, Georges Méliès.

▶ **Baron Prásil** see Baron Munchausen

Barren Lives

▶ **Vidãs Sêcas**

    Brazil 1963 135 mins bw
    Richers/Barreto/Trelles

d   Nelson Pereira Dos Santos
sc Nelson Pereira Dos Santos
ph Luiz Carlos Barreto, José Rosa
m   Leonardo Alencar
    Átila Iório, Maria Ribeiro, Orlando
    Macedo, Jofre Soãres, Gilvan and
    Genivaldo Lima

Around 1940, a poverty-stricken family – an
itinerant herdsman (Iório), his wife (Ribeiro)
and two young sons (Gilvan and Genivaldo
Lima) – are forced to wander the barren
sertao of Brazil, scratching out an existence.
A film of quiet dignity and compassion, it
recalls the best of the Italian Neo-Realists,
while the photography portrays the dry, harsh
Brazilian landscape exposed in a particular
light. By the use of subjective shots, Dos
Santos allows more identification with the
characters, but avoids self-pity. A landmark
in Latin-American cinema.

Barrier

▶ **Bariera**

    Poland 1966 83 mins bw
    Film Polski

d   Jerzy Skolimowski
sc Jerzy Skolimowski
ph Jan Laskowski
m   Krzysztof Komeda
    Jan Nowicki, Joanna Szczerbic, Tadeusz
    Lomnicki, Zygmunt Malonowicz

A disillusioned young medical student (Nowicki) travelling through modern Poland in
quest of the meaning of life, meets only
bureaucracy and materialism, but finally finds
satisfaction in a relationship with a young
woman tram driver (Szczerbic). Only in his

twenties at the time, Skolimowski became a mouthpiece for the cynical new Polish generation. This assured surreal satire presents a grim picture of his homeland, yet with an underlying quirky humour.

The Bartered Bride

▶ **Die Verkaufte Braut**

Germany 1932 80 mins bw
Reichaliga

d   Max Ophüls
sc Kurt Alexander, Jaroslav Kvapil, Max Ophüls
ph Reimar Kuntze, Franz Koch, Herbert Illing
m   Smetana
    Jarmila Novotná, Willy Domgraf-Fassbaender, Paul Kemp, Karl Valentin, Liesl Karlstad, Max Nadler

In a village in Bohemia in the mid-19th century, Mařenka (Novotná), the mayor's daughter, promised to a rich nitwit, tricks the marriage broker and her parents by marrying Jeník (Domgraf-Fassbaender). Not content merely to record a wonderfully sung performance of Smetana's delightful Czech opera (given here in German), Ophüls manages, by complex camera angles, to present his own comment on the filming of opera. Rarely seen, Ophüls' second feature-length film shows a master in the making.

▶ **Baruch** see Ancient Law, The

▶ **Barwy Ochronne** see Camouflage

▶ **Baryton** see Baritone, The

▶ **Bas-Fonds, Les-** see Lower Depths, The

▶ **Basilischi, I** see Lizards, The

▶ **Bas Ya Bahar** see Cruel Sea, The

▶ **Bataille Du Rail, La** see Battle Of The Rails

▶ **Batalla De Chile, La** see Battle Of Chile, The

▶ **Battaglia Di Algeri, La** see Battle Of Algiers, The

The Battle Of Algiers

▶ **La Battaglia Di Algeri**

Italy 1965 135 mins bw
Casbah/Igor

d   Gillo Pontecorvo
sc Franco Solinas
ph Marcello Gatti
m   Ennio Morricone, Gillo Pontecorvo
    Brahim Haggiag, Jean Martin, Yacef Saadi, Tommaso Neri

The guerrilla war for Algerian independence from the French in 1954 as seen through the eyes of some of the participants. Shot in the actual locations, mixing actors with those who fought in the battle and without recourse to any newsreel footage, the film probably comes closer to the truth and the complexities of the situation than any documentary could have. Although banned in France for some years, its main strength lies in its scrupulous attention to the views and problems on both sides.

Best Film Venice 1966

▶ **Battle Of Austerlitz, The** see Austerlitz

The Battle Of Chile

▶ **La Batalla De Chile**

Cuba/Chile 1977 287 mins bw
Equipe Tercer Ano Productions – in collaboration with Chris Marker

d   Patricio Guzman
sc Patricio Guzman
ph Jorge Mueller

A documentary on the 10 weeks in 1973 leading up to and including the overthrow of the Allende government by the CIA and the forces of General Pinochet. It is presented in three parts: 1) The Insurrection Of The Bourgeoisie 2) The Coup D'État 3) The Power Of The People. This remarkable record of a turbulent and tragic time in Chile was smuggled out of the country into Cuba where

Guzman, with a group of Cuban film-makers, took over four years to edit it. Stating its Marxist credentials, the film does not pretend to be objective, yet it is analytical and not uncritical of the Left. Apart from supporters of the former Chilean dictatorship, it would be hard for any spectator not to be moved and informed by the movie.

Battle Of The Rails

▶ **La Bataille Du Rail**

France 1946 87 mins bw
CGCF

d **René Clément**
sc **René Clément**
ph **Henri Alekan**
m **Yves Baudrier**
    Salina, Daurand, Lozach, Tony Laurent

A reconstruction of the resistance work, including sabotage of the railway link between the Occupied and Free Zones by French railwaymen during World War II. Clément brought the stark realism of his documentary shorts to bear on his first feature, a paean to the courage of the railway workers, with the men themselves re-enacting their actual exploits.

Best Film Cannes 1946
Best Director Cannes 1946

The Battleship Potemkin

▶ **(US: Potemkin)**
▶ **Bronenosets Potemkin**

USSR 1925 75 mins bw
Goskino

d **Sergei Eisenstein**
sc **Sergei Eisenstein**
ph **Edouard Tissé**
m **Silent**
    A. Antonov, Vladimir Barski, Grigori Alexandrov, M. Gomorov

An incident during the 1905 revolution when the crew of the battleship *Prince Potemkin* mutinied rather than eat rotting food, an action supported by some of the civilian population who were mown down by government troops. Made as part of the 20th anni-

versary of the Revolution, the film contains – in the massacre on the Odessa Steps (an invention of Eisenstein's) – one of the most memorable and exciting sequences in all cinema. Down a seemingly endless flight of steps march soldiers advancing on the fleeing citizens. A nurse is shot and the pram and baby bounce down the steps to destruction. The rapid montage, and the effects devised by using a trolley and a camera strapped to the waist of an acrobat, still take the breath away. The film that put Soviet cinema and Eisenstein on the international map.

▶ **Baule-Les Pins, La** see C'Est La Vie

▶ **Bayan Ko – Kapit Sa Patalim** see Bayan Ko: My Own Country

Bayan Ko: My Own Country

▶ **Bayan Ko – Kapit Sa Patalim**

Philippines 1984 108 mins col
Malaya Films (Manila)/Stephan Films (Paris)

d **Lino Brocka**
sc **José F. Lacaba**
ph **Conrado Baltazar**
m **Jess Santiago**
    Phillip Salvador, Gina Alajar, Claudia Zobel, Carmi Martin, Raoul Aragonn, Rez Cortez

Turing (Salvador), a worker at the Jefferson Printing Press, is given a loan by his boss on condition he doesn't join a trade union. During a strike, he becomes a scab but loses his job when he goes to the aid of pickets being attacked by hired thugs. Unable to pay his wife's hospital bill, he attempts to rob the plant, a decision which has tragic consequences. It is very much in line with those Hollywood films of doomed couples such as Fritz Lang's *You Only Live Once*, but given a political context. In fact, Lino Brocka is far more explicit in his condemnation of the system than he had been hitherto (the film got him charged with subversion by the Marcos regime), while still creating a hero who fails to embody any direct commitment to a cause. Despite some crudities of narrative, the film's force is undeniable.

Bay Of Angels

▶ **La Baie Des Anges**

> France   1962   90 mins   bw
> Sud-Pacifique

d   Jacques Demy
sc Jacques Demy
ph Jean Rabier
m   Michel Legrand
    Jeanne Moreau, Claude Mann, Paul
    Guers, Henri Nassiet

An ordinary bank clerk (Mann), who has had a streak of good luck at the Nice Casino, falls in love with a compulsive gambler (Moreau), who has left a husband and child to satisfy her craving. Shot very quickly on the French Riviera, this love story with a roulette wheel as the motif and the motive, is one of the most vivid evocations of gambling fever on film. The luminous photography and the hypnotic music add to the film's attraction.

The Beads Of One Rosary

▶ **Paciorki Jednego Rózańca**

> Poland   1979   111 mins   col
> PRF Zespoly Filmowe-Zespol Kadr

d   Kazimierz Kutz
sc Kazimierz Kutz
ph Wieslaw Zdort
m   Wojciech Kilar
    Marta Straszna, Augustyn Halotta, Jan
    Bógdol, Ewa Wiśniewska

In a provincial Polish town, a retired miner and his wife refuse to leave the small cottage the family has occupied for over 50 years when property developers want to destroy it in order to erect high-rise buildings on the site. The picture of individuals taking on large corporations always provides pleasure, and this likeable but soft-centred film is no exception. Non-professionals Straszna and Halotta as the elderly couple give the tale an authentic ring, but they are too often seen as eccentrics to be pitied rather than people fighting for their rights.

The Beast

▶ **La Bête**

> France   1975   102 mins   col
> Argos

d   Walerian Borowczyk
sc Walerian Borowczyk
ph Bernard Daillencourt, Marcel Grignon
m   Scarlatti
    Sirpa Lane, Pierre Benedetti, Guy
    Tréjean, Lisbeth Hummel, Elisabeth
    Kahson

An American heiress (Hummel), staying at the château of a marquis (Tréjean) whose son (Benedetti) she is about to marry, comes across the 18th-century diary of Romilda. She dreams of Romilda's sexual arousal by a mythological beast, half bear, half wolf. Another erotic fairy tale by Borowczyk became a *succès de scandale* because of the taboo subject of bestiality. But although it is never as shocking or as amusing as it sets out to be, the film provides a host of Freudian sexual symbols scattered throughout a story observed with the eye of a painter.

▶ **Beau Mariage, Le** see Good Marriage, A

▶ **Beau-Père** see Stepfather

Le Beau Serge

▶ **(US: Bitter Reunion)**

> France   1958   97 mins   bw
> AYJM

d   Claude Chabrol
sc Claude Chabrol
ph Henri Decaë
m   Emile Delpierre
    Gérard Blain, Jean-Claude Brialy,
    Bernadette Lafont, Michèle Meritz

A theology student (Brialy), suffering from TB, returns to his native village to discover his talented childhood friend, Serge (Blain), has become a hopeless drunk and is estranged from his pregnant wife. An inheritance from his first wife enabled the 28-year-old critic Chabrol to finance his debut feature, considered the first film of the *Nouvelle Vague*. This well-drawn view of a grey, unattractive small town – actually Sardent where the director spent the war years – is encased in a rather stiff Christian metaphor of salvation, ending with a death and a birth. Chabrol's personal style only emerged in his second film, *The Cousins* (1958) with the same two young male leads.

► **Beauté Du Diable, La** see Beauty And The Devil

► **Beauties Of The Night** see Night Beauties

The Beautiful Swindlers

► **Les Plus Belles Éscroqueries Du Monde**

France/Italy/Holland/Japan 1963 90 mins bw
Ulysse/Primex/Lux/Vides/Toho/Cesar

d 1) **Roman Polanski (Amsterdam)**
2) **Ugo Gregoretti (Naples)**
3) **Claude Chabrol (Paris)**
4) **Hiromichi Horikawa**
sc **Roman Polanski, Gérard Brach** 3) **Paul Gégauff**
ph 1) **Jerzy Lipman** 2) **Tonino Delli Colli** 3) **Jean Rabier** 4) **Asakazu Nakai**
m 1) **Krzysztof Komeda** 2) **Piero Umiliani** 3) **Pierre Jansen** 4) **Keitaro Miho**
1) **Nicole Karen, Jan Teulings** 2) **Gabriella Giorgelli, Guido Giuseppone** 3) **Jean-Pierre Cassel, Catherine Deneuve, Francis Blanche** 4) **Mie Hama, Ken Mitsuda**

1) A young French woman, a compulsive thief, cons a wealthy, middle-aged and married Dutchman into lending her his apartment, where she cons some jewellers out of a diamond necklace. 2) A pimp plans to marry off his girls to doddering old men. 3) A stupid German tourist buys the Eiffel Tower. 4) A bar girl goes home with a rich old musician who dies while eating noodles. A fifth episode, shot by Jean-Luc Godard with Jean Seberg, was dropped and released as a short. The biggest con of all was that perpetrated on the audience. Only Chabrol's contribution was mildly amusing in the whole tame enterprise.

Beauty And The Beast

► **La Belle Et La Bête**

France 1946 95 mins bw
André Paulve

d **Jean Cocteau**
sc **Jean Cocteau**
ph **Henri Alekan**
m **Georges Auric**
Jean Marais, Josette Day, Mila Parély, Michel Auclair, Marcel André, Nane Germon

Beauty (Day) goes to the Beast's castle to take the place of her father whom the Beast has threatened to kill, but he falls hopelessly in love with her, proposing to her nightly. Finally, when she reciprocates, the Beast turns into a handsome Prince. Cocteau stated that he discouraged his photographer, and the brilliant art director Christian Berard, from virtuosity in order to show unreality in realistic terms. But thankfully virtuosity is everywhere evident in the magical scenes in the Beast's castle. Jean Marais, behind extraordinary make-up, is touching, and Beauty is slightly disappointed when he turns into his romantic self. A fairy tale for children and intelligent adults.

The Beauty And The Beast

► **Skønheden Og Udyret**

Denmark 1983 90 mins col
Per Holst Filmproduktion/Danish Film Institute

d **Nils Malmros**
sc **Nils Malmros**
ph **Jan Weincke, Søren Berthelin**
m **Gunner Moller Pedersen, Purcell**
Line Arlien Søborg, Jesper Klein, Carsten Jørgensen, Eva Schjoldager, Brian Theibel

Sixteen-year-old Mette (Søborg) and her father (Klein) enjoy a close relationship built on love, mutual understanding and his pride in her. Left alone with her at Christmas while his wife is in hospital, he becomes aware that Mette has been concealing her romantic interest in Jonne (Jørgensen), a photographer, whom he considers a bad influence. Father feels that daughter has betrayed his trust, and his distress increases when Jonne becomes a constant visitor in his house. A stylish film in which the difficulties of a father-daughter relationship are well-delineated but, intrinsically, Malmros probes the individual psyches of his protagonists to reveal that the father is suffering from fear of losing his youth and needs to keep his daughter a little girl, while she is experiencing the growth of sexual awareness. Avoiding cliché, the director combines humour and pain, lending the story the weight of truth.

Beauty And The Devil

▶ **La Beauté Du Diable**

> France 1949 96 mins bw
> AYJM/Franco London

d René Clair
sc René Clair, Armand Salacrou
ph Michel Kelber
m Roman Vlad
   Michel Simon, Gérard Philipe, Simone Valère, Raymond Cordy, Nicole Besnard, Gaston Modot, Paolo Stoppa

Old Doctor Faust (Simon) is willing to sell his soul to Mephistopheles (Philipe), an agent of the Devil so that he can, in fact, look as young and handsome as the Prince of Darkness, and win the heart of the woman (Valère) he loves. Clair's clever conceit, therefore, is to allow Simon and Philipe to exchange roles midway. There is plenty of intelligence and wit in this ambitious version of the Faust legend, shot entirely among Léon Barsacq's splendid Baroque sets at Cinecittà in Rome, but it lacks delicacy and charm. However, the two great French actors are hard to resist.

Bébert And The Train

▶ **aka The Holy Terror**

▶ **Bébert Et L'Omnibus**

> France 1963 90 mins bw
> Les Productions De La Guéville

d Yves Robert
sc François Boyer
ph André Bac
m Philippe-Gérard
   Petit Gibus, Jacques Higelin, Jean Richard, Blanchette Brunoy, Michel Serrault, Pierre Mondy

Five-year-old Bébert (Gibus) gets lost on a train while travelling with his big brother (Higelin) and a frantic search ensues. Meanwhile, the brat causes a great deal of chaos. A pleasant, well-observed little film made by an actor who made his name as a director the year before with *War Of The Buttons*.

Unlike the previous film, with its hordes of kids, in this one Robert was able to concentrate on the delightful performance of Petit Gibus.

▶ **Bébert Et L'Omnibus** see Bébert And The Train

Bebo's Girl

▶ **La Ragazza Di Bube**

> Italy 1963 110 mins bw
> Lux/Ultra/Vides

d Luigi Comencini
sc Luigi Comencini, Marcello Fondato
ph Gianni Di Venanzo
m Carlo Rustichelli
   Claudia Cardinale, George Chakiris, Marc Michel, Dany Paris, Emilio Esposito

A country girl (Cardinale) falls in love with a man (Chakiris) she hardly knows. When he is imprisoned for 14 years for killing a Fascist policeman during the war, she prefers to wait for his release, despite an offer of marriage from a writer (Michel). Cardinale gives one of her best performances (opposite a wooden, unconvincing Chakiris) in a gentle film that excellently re-creates the 1940s atmosphere of an Italian village. Shot on location, it is a throwback to the Neo-Realist period, well understated until the mawkish ending.

Bed And Board

▶ **Domicile Conjugal**

> France 1970 97 mins col
> Films Du Carrosse/Valoria/Fida

d François Truffaut
sc François Truffaut, Claude De Givray, Bernard Revon
ph Nestor Almendros
m Antoine Duhamel
   Jean-Pierre Léaud, Claude Jade, Hiroko Berghauer, Daniel Ceccaldi, Barbara Laage

Antoine Doinel (Léaud) marries his sweetheart, does a variety of jobs, writes a novel, becomes a father, takes up with a Japanese girl, and returns to his wife, ready to face the responsibilities of adulthood. The fourth and penultimate film in the semi-autobiographical Doinel cycle has, like its hero, some difficulty in retaining its youth and innocence. Truffaut retreats into the past cinematic Paris of René Clair, Jacques Becker, and Jean Renoir – charming enough in itself.

Bed And Sofa

▶ **Tretia Mecht Chanskaya**

> USSR   1927   115 mins   bw
> Sovkino

d   **Abram Room**
sc **Victor Shklovsky**
ph **Gregori Giber**
m   **Silent**
    Nikolai Batalov, Ludmila Semenova, Vladimir Fogel

A married couple (Batalov and Semenova) have a small flat in Moscow. When an old friend (Fogel) of the husband's turns up in the city and is unable to find lodgings due to the housing shortage, he moves in with them. While the husband is away on business, sensual wife and attractive friend fall in love and have an affair but, after his initial outrage, the husband calms down and the three settle into a cosy, domesticated *ménage-à-trois* in which the wife virtually comes to assume the role of mother to her two boys... Rediscovered in the 1970s, Room's film has come to be regarded as a little masterpiece of the silent cinema. Aside from the extraordinary fluidity of his camera in a confined set and the splendidly natural performances of his cast, he deals with his subject in an almost casual, matter-of-fact way. Unusually frank for its period, it tells its tale with warmth, humour and absolute psychological truth, free of any trauma or sensationalism.

The Beekeeper

▶ **O Melissokomos**

> Greece   1986   112 mins   col
> Greek Film Centre/Marin Karmitz Productions/ERT 1/ Theo Angelopoulos

d   **Theo Angelopoulos**
sc **Theo Angelopoulos, Dimitris Nollas**
ph **Giorgos Arvanitis**
m   **Helen Karaindrou**

Marcello Mastroianni, Nadia Mourouzi, Serge Reggiani, Jenny Roussea, Dinos Iliopoulous

Spyros (Mastroianni), a morose retired schoolteacher, sets off on a trip around the beehive sites of Greece, taking his treasured beehives with him, and picks up an enigmatic young woman hitchhiker (Mourouzi) *en route*. 'A film on the silence of history, of love and of God,' is how the director describes his compelling metaphysical road movie. Set against the vividly caught landscape and small towns of Greece in winter, it sustains an atmosphere and even tempo throughout. Mastroianni's stoic performance proved that he had entered, in his sixties, the greatest period of acting in his career.

Before The Revolution

▶ **Prima Della Rivoluzione**

> Italy   1964   115 mins   bw
> Cineriz/Iride

d   **Bernardo Bertolucci**
sc **Bernardo Bertolucci**
ph **Aldo Scavarda**
m   **Gino Paoli, Ennio Morricone**
    Francesco Barilli, Adriana Asti, Alain Midgette, Morando Morandini

A middle-class youth (Barilli) in Parma is torn between radical politics and conformism, and between a passionate affair with his young aunt (Asti) and *bourgeois* marriage. He opts for respectability on both counts. Favourite themes such as father/son relationships and political/personal conflicts are already apparent in this richly textured and technically impressive second film by Bertolucci, still in his early twenties. But, like his hero, there is an element of the dilettante in the director's use of references to Marx, Freud and Stendhal, and the works of Verdi.

The Beggar Student

▶ **Der Bettelstudent**

> Germany   1936   75 mins   bw
> UFA

d   **Georg Jacoby**
sc **Walter Wasserman, H. Dilber**
ph **Ewald Daub**

m Carl Millöcker
   Marike Rökk, Carola Höhn, Ida Wüst,
   Johannes Heesters, Fritz Kampers

In German-occupied Cracow in 1704, as a practical joke, a revolutionary student (Heesters) is introduced as a duke to an aristocratic woman (Höhn), who falls in love with him. In the end, he turns out to be the nephew of the king. A typically light and lavish period operetta from UFA studios, by then under Nazi-government control. Full of pretty blondes, handsome soldiers, and plenty of anachronistic but pleasing melodies, the film appealed to audiences at home and abroad. It was remade in Germany in 1958 starring the Kessler twins.

The Beginning

▶ aka The Debut

▶ Nachalo

   USSR 1970 90 mins bw
   Lenfilm

d Gleb Panfilov
sc Yevgeni Gabrilovich, Gleb Panfilov
ph Dmitri Dolynin
m Vadim Bibergan
   Inna Churikova, Leonid Kuravlev,
   Valentina Telichkina, Yuri Klepikov,
   Mikhail Kononov

Pasha (Churikova), a lively working girl in a small town, is spotted performing in an amateur play and is offered the role of Joan of Arc in a forthcoming film. She goes to the city, leaving behind Arkady (Kuravlev), the married man she loves who has decided to go back to his wife. When the film is over, so is Pasha's new career, and she returns home to a welcome from her factory workmates, having gained a measure of maturity. Panfilov, making his second film, is adroit in inter-cutting his narrative with scenes from the film-within-a-film, even before Pasha is involved in the latter. *The Beginning* is a charming comedy, laced with pathos, made with exceptional lightness of touch, and offering an accomplished leading lady of extraordinary range.

▶ **Beguines, The** see Rempart Des Béguines, Le

Behind Closed Doors

▶ A Porte Chiuse

   Italy 1960 130 mins bw
   Fair Film/Rire Cinematografica/SGC

d Dino Risi
sc Marcello Coscia, Dino Di Palma, Sandro Continenza
ph Mario Montuori
m Piero Umiliani
   Anita Ekberg, Claudio Gora, Fred Clark,
   Ettore Manni, Gianni Bonagua

Olga Dubovich (Ekberg) is being tried for the murder of her wealthy lover from whose death she benefits. The evidence is so confusing that the prosecutor transfers the trial to the island where the crime took place and where Olga, back in familiar surroundings, is able to use her not inconsiderable charms as a trade-in for an acquittal – although that's not the end of the story. The plot belies the nature of Risi's film which is, in fact, a wild comic caper at the expense of Italian justice. It is very funny and Ekberg is a delight as the amoral enchantress, but the appeal is somewhat dissipated by the over-extended courtroom scenes in which the jokes wear a little thin.

Behold Thy Son

▶ Kiiroi Karasu

   Japan 1957 104 mins col
   Shochiku

d Heinosuke Gosho
sc Kennosuke Tateoka, Keije Hasebo
ph Yoshio Miyajima
m Yasushi Akutagawa
   Chikage Awashima, Yunosuke Ito, Koji
   Shitara, Kinuyo Tanaka, Masako
   Yasumura

When his father, whom he has never seen, returns home from an enforced 10-year sojourn in China, a young boy suffers intense feelings of resentment at the intrusion of a 'stranger', which increase when a baby sister is born. This is a moving and truthful exploration of a difficult father-son relationship, but it lets itself down in its latter stages with a melodramatic runaway sequence and a sentimental *rapprochement* between father and son.

▶ **Beiqing Chengshi** see City of Sadness, A

▶ **Bekenntis Der Ina Kahr, Das** see Afraid To Live

▶ **Beliye Nochi** see White Nights

▶ **Bell'Antonio, Il** see Handsome Antonio

Belle

Belgium 1973 93 mins col
Albina/La Nouvelle Imagerie

d **André Delvaux**
sc **André Delvaux**
ph **Ghislain Cloquet**
m **Frédéric Devreese**
    Jean Luc Bideau, Danièle Delorme,
    Adriana Bogdan, Roger Coggio

A middle-aged married professor (Bideau) who has an almost incestuous desire for his daughter, meets a mysterious woman (Delorme) in the woods and has an affair with her.The professor lectures on obscure writers, and director Delvaux is obscure in another sense. One is seldom sure what is dream and what is reality – is the woman in the woods real or imaginary? As the director himself stated, 'The imaginary can introduce things that haven't yet taken place but will happen in reality later on'. As always, his work is visually arresting, but tends to hover between the poetic and the arty.

La Belle Américaine

France 1961 101 mins bw/col
CCFC/Film D'Art/Panorama/Corflor

d **Robert Dhéry**
sc **Robert Dhéry, Pierre Tchernia, Alfred Adam**
ph **Ghislain Cloquet**
m **Gérard Calvi**
    Robert Dhéry, Louis De Funès, Colette Brosset, Alfred Adam, Bernard Lavalette, Annie Ducaux

When a Parisian factory worker (Dhéry) manages to buy a huge Cadillac (the 'beautiful American' of the title) at a bargain price, he gets into all kinds of trouble. Robert Dhéry became famous for his brilliant clowning in the London and Broadway hit review *La Plume De Ma Tante*. In his films, of which this was the most widely seen, he retains his zany comic skills, but only in short bursts. Unlike the supercar (seen in colour at the finale), Dhéry is not built for long distances.

Belle De Jour

France 1967 100 mins col
Paris Film/Five Film

d **Luis Buñuel**
sc **Luis Buñuel, Jean-Claude Carrière**
ph **Sacha Vierny**
    Catherine Deneuve, Jean Sorel, Michel Piccoli, Geneviève Page, Pierre Clémenti

The respectable wife of a doctor finds herself spending her afternoons working in a high-class brothel with kinky clients ... and enjoying it. This witty, erotic, elegant and subversive film, obviously encouraging sexual fantasies, began Buñuel's fertile last period of French works, pointedly aimed at *bourgeois* hypocrisy. 'My biggest commercial success ... I attribute more to the marvellous whores than to my direction,' said the 67-year-old Buñuel modestly. As chief whore, in an excellent cast, Deneuve grows more beautiful with each perversion, imagined or otherwise.

Best Film Venice 1967

La Belle Équipe

▶ **(US: They Were Five)**

France 1936 94 mins bw
Arys/Ciné Arts

d **Julien Duvivier**
sc **Julien Duvivier, Charles Spaak**
ph **Jules Kruger, Marc Fessard**
m **Maurice Yvain**
    Jean Gabin, Charles Vanel, Viviane Romance, Aimos, Raphael Medina

Five unemployed workers win a lottery and buy a country inn on the banks of the Marne, but their friendship is threatened by the vampish wife of one of them. A perfect example of French cinema of the Popular Front – believable working-class characters, their simple pleasures, lilting music, sunny open-air camerawork . . . and Gabin, the icon of the age. It loses its way a little when melodrama intervenes, but Duvivier shot alternative tragic and happy endings, the latter being more widely shown.

▶ **Belle Et La Bête, La** see Beauty And The Beast

▶ **Belle Fille Comme Moi, Une** see Gorgeous Bird Like Me, A

▶ **Belles De Nuit, Les** see Night Beauties

Bellissima

Italy   1951   113 mins   bw
Bellissima Films

d   **Luchino Visconti**
sc   **Luchino Visconti, Suso Cecchi D'Amico, Francesco Rosi**
ph   **Piero Portalupi, Paul Ronald**
m   **Franco Mannino**
Anna Magnani, Walter Chiari, Tina Apicella, Alessandro Blasetti

A woman from the slums determines to get her pretty seven-year-old daughter into films, but becomes disillusioned with Cinecitta, and refuses a screen test for her. Visconti's third feature already saw him moving into the realms of the 'woman's picture', and any attempt at Neo-Realism is blown away by Magnani's noisy larger-than-life performance. Alessandro Blasetti, an early Neo-Realist, is cast as a director, and there are some interesting glimpses of Cinecitta, one of Europe's biggest studios, contrasted with the steaming tenements of Rome.

Benjamin Or The Diary Of An Innocent Young Man

▶ **Benjamin Ou Les Mémoirs D'Un Puceau**

France   1966   104 mins   col
Parc/Marianne/Paramount

d   **Michel Deville**
sc   **Nina Companeez**
ph   **Ghislain Cloquet**
m   **Boccherini, Haydn, Mozart, Rameau**
Pierre Clémenti, Michèle Morgan, Catherine Deneuve, Michel Piccoli, Francine Bergé, Anna Gäel, Odile Versois

In the 18th century, a handsome 17-year-old orphan boy (Clémenti) is taken to live at the château of his wealthy aunt (Morgan) where he happily learns about sex from a variety of women of all ages and classes. The sort of film generally termed a 'romp', it has gorgeous costumes and settings, and a pleasant cast in becoming wigs that includes old hands Morgan and Piccoli, and Clémenti and Deneuve as attractive virgins. But its rococo ribaldry lacks sufficient charm and wit to sustain it. It was a huge success in France, presumably with those for whom Marivaux and Beaumarchais are closed books.

▶ **Benjamin Ou Les Mémoirs D'Un Puceau** see Benjamin Or The Diary Of An Innocent Young Man

Benvenuta

Belgium   1983   106 mins   col
La Nouvelle Imagerie (Brussels)/UGC/Europe 1/FR3 (Paris)/Opera-Film (Rome)

d   **André Delvaux**
sc   **André Delvaux**
ph   **Charlie Van Damme**
m   **Frédéric Devreese and extracts from, Mozart, Schumann, Brahms**
Fanny Ardant, Vittorio Gassman, Françoise Fabian, Matthieu Carrière, Claire Wauthion

François (Carrière), a writer from Alsace, has been commissioned to script a film from a novel which was something of a *cause célèbre* 20 years previously, and visits Jeanne (Fabian), the author, now living reclusively in Ghent, to discuss the material – how much is autobiographical, how much invention – and to plunder her memories of the story's several locales. True to his form, Delvaux plays an elaborate game with fantasy and reality, moving between the two, as between time and place, with consummate ease in a series of painterly images. François' vision of the story forms most of the action, with Benvenuta (Ardant, poker-faced) locked in an *amour fou* with Livio (Gassman, aging but attractive). But how much of it is Benvenuta's story, and how much is Jeanne's? For all its skill, this brew of eroticism, spiritual self-flagellation and quasi-poetic philosophizing, relentlessly ambiguous and indulgent, may strike some viewers as pretentious rather than intriguing.

▶ **Berg-Ejvind Och Hans Hustru** see Outlaw And His Wife, The

▶ **Berget Pa Manens Baksida** see Hill On The Dark Side Of The Moon, A

▶ **Bergkatze, Die** see Mountain Cat, The

Berlin-Alexanderplatz

Germany 1931 121 mins bw
Allianz Tonfilm/Capital

d **Phil Jutzi**
sc **Alfred Döblin, Hans Wilhelm**
ph **Erich Giese**
m **Allan Gray, Artur Guttman**
   Heinrich George, Bernhard Minetti,
   Margarete Schlegel, Albert Florath

Franz Biberkopf (George), a simple-minded ex-con, desperately tries to go straight, but his sexual obsession with Mieze (Schlegel) and his economic dependency on unsavoury characters lead to tragedy. Although Döblin himself collaborated on the screenplay of his great novel, which did for Berlin what Joyce's *Ulysses* did for Dublin (a direct influence), the structure and psychology of the tale were somewhat flattened out. It took Fassbinder, in his overwhelming 13-episode made-for-TV version (made in 1980 and running altogether 975 minutes), to do it full justice. But Jutzi gets strong performances from his cast, and the atmosphere of period Berlin is vividly captured.

▶ **Berlin: Die Sinfonie Einer Gross-stadt** see Berlin: Symphony Of A Great City

▶ **Berliner, The** see Ballad Of Berlin

▶ **Berliner Ballade** see Ballad Of Berlin

Berlin: Symphony Of A Great City

▶ **Berlin: Die Sinfonie Einer Gross-stadt**

Germany 1927 70 mins bw
Fox Europa

d **Walter Ruttmann**
sc **Karl Freund, Walter Ruttmann**
ph **Reimar Kuntze, Robert Baberske, Laszlo Shäffer**
m **Silent**

An impressionistic view of life in Berlin on a Spring day from dawn to midnight, the film took 18 months to make. Most of it was shot using cameras concealed in a removal van or in suitcases to catch people unawares. Edmund Meisel, who composed a jazzy score (since lost) for a 75-piece orchestra to accompany the film, worked with Ruttman on the editing to give it a rhythmic effect. Influenced by the montage developments of Eisenstein and Vertov, it led to further 'abstract' documentaries in the same style.

Bernadette

France 1988 118 mins col
Les Films De L'Étoile D'Or/Bernadette Association International S.A.

d **Jean Delannoy**
sc **Jean Delannoy, Robert Arnaut**
ph **Jean-Bernard Penzer**
m **Francis Lai**
   Sydney Penny, Jean-Marc Bory, Roland Lesaffre, Michèle Simonnet, Bernard Dhéran, Michel Duchaussoy, François Dalou, Arlette Didier

While collecting firewood in a grotto near Lourdes, Bernadette (Penny), the seriously asthmatic 15-year-old daughter of the near-destitute Soubirous family, has a spiritual vision of 'a beautiful lady in white'. Further visions follow, earning the girl the devotion of the poor, the derision of the *bourgeoisie* and the opprobrium of the State, the officers of which attempt to have her certified insane until the cynical Father Peyramale (Bory) comes to believe in her. The distinguished director, 79 when he made the film that he spent spent three years researching, brings unmistakable sincerity to the enterprise. Setting out to recount the facts – and Delannoy insists that not a single incident is his invention – of a very short and specific period in Bernadette's life, he does so with technical proficiency and a solid cast. The tone of the film is spiritual but not narrowly religious, and its stance neutral. The young American Sydney Penny, speaking excellent French and glowing with inappropriate health and beauty, convinces with the right quality of innocence, yet the film is simplistic, sometimes dull and suffers from an air of old-fashioned, clichéd unreality.

Bernadette Of Lourdes

► Il Suffit D'Aimer

France 1960 102 mins bw
EDIC-Films/S.E.N/Tamara(Paris)/Zebra Film/ Cineriz(Rome)

d Robert Darène
sc Gilbert Cesbron, Robert Darène
ph Marcel Weiss
m Maurice Thiriet
Danièle Ajoret, Madeleine Sologne, Bernard Lajarrige, Blanchette Brunoy, Lise Delamare, Henri Nassiet

Bernadette Soubirous (Ajoret), the sick daughter of a poverty-stricken family, sees a vision of the Virgin Mary. Her faith finally overcomes the disbelief and opposition of Church and State and, as thousands flock to the healing waters at Lourdes, she enters a convent where she dies, aged 35, from continued ill-health. It is interesting to compare this with Delannoy's large-scale colour movie almost 30 years later. Like its successor, this version is restrained, but covers Bernadette's entire life. The later scenes in the convent, contrasting the simple girl with the more educated nuns who continue to view her with a mixture of resentment, curiosity and awe, are the most interesting, and Ajoret, whose girlish qualities earlier on are a little synthetic, comes into her own. What emerges clearly from both films is that the undeniably absorbing subject seems to limit directorial imagination.

► Berührte, Die see No Mercy No Future

The Best Age

► Nejkrasnejsí Vek

Czechoslovakia 1968 80 mins bw
Barrandov Studio

d Jaroslav Papoušek
sc Jaroslav Papoušek
ph Josef Ort-Snep
m Karel Mares
Hana Brejchová, Věra Křesadlová, Jan Stöckl, Josef Sebánek, Jiří Sykora

An art school selects models for the sculpture class from a daily queue of hopefuls, who a group of pensioners. An elderly gentleman is chosen for his head but keeps dozing off; a young married woman with a baby agrees to pose in the nude whereupon her jealous husband smashes up the statues; a middle-aged coalman, recently injured, represents a wounded soldier . . . Papoušek's film is the work of a gentle miniaturist, wryly and affectionately recording day-to-day human absurdity. What he is really examining is the tendency to believe that one's best age is either past, or yet to come, as exemplified by the students' fascination with the old man's face, stamped with the marks of experience and impending death, while he envies them their youth. A charming piece, marred only by some moments of overstatement.

► Best Way, The see Best Way To Walk, The

The Best Way To Walk

► (US: The Best Way)
► La Meilleure Façon De Marcher

France 1976 90 mins col
Contrechamp/Speciality

d Claude Miller
sc Claude Miller, Luc Béraud
ph Bruno Nuytten
m Alain Jomy
Patrick Dewaere, Patrick Bouchitey, Christine Pascal, Claude Piéplu

When an instructor at a summer camp for boys accidentally discovers the son of the camp-owner in make-up and drag, he bullies him unmercifully, but it's the victim who gets the girl. The first film by the former assistant to Truffaut and Godard is a neatly made, sardonic but too pat tale of sexual identity. Dewaere as the bully, and Bouchitey as the camp camp counsellor, set up sexually ambiguous sparks leading to the rather embarrassing farewell party scene.

▶ **Bête, La** see Beast, The

▶ **Bête Humaine, La** see Human Beast, The

▶ **Betrayer, The** see Vanina Vanini

▶ **Bettelstudent, Der** see Beggar Student, The

Betty Blue

▶ **37°2 Le Matin**

France 1986 121 mins col
Claudie Ossard – Jean-Jacques Beineix

d   Jean-Jacques Beineix
sc Jean-Jacques Beineix
ph Jean-François Robin
m   Gabriel Yared
    Béatrice Dalle, Jean-Hugues Anglade,
    Consuela De Haviland, Gérard Darmon

Betty (Dalle), a young, disgruntled waitress, discovers a novel written by 35-year-old handyman, Zorg (Anglade), sets fire to his beach shack and takes off with him to Paris and then a provincial town where, disillusioned and on drugs, she goes mad. After the spectacular failure of *Moon In The Gutter*, Beineix recovered his reputation somewhat with this more realistic character study and narrative, but without sacrificing too much of his flamboyance. The torrid ephemeral affair of the central couple is depicted with frankness, and the playing, especially by new discovery Dalle, avoids the histrionics that the roles might have encouraged.

Between Time And Eternity

▶ **Zwischen Zeit Und Ewigkeit**

W. Germany 1956 97 mins col
Neue Terra

d   Arthur Maria Rabenalt

sc Robert Thoeren
ph Georg Bruckbauer
m   Bert Grund
    Lilli Palmer, Carlos Thompson, Willy
    Birgel, Ellen Schwiers

Nina (Palmer) is dying of a brain disease and, although her doctor husband has concealed the truth from her, she senses that she hasn't much time and goes off alone to a Mediterranean island where she falls in love with Manuel (Thompson), a handsome and carefree fisherman. There is absolutely nothing original or profound about this three-handkerchief weepie but, within its genre, it is entirely competent. The lovely Lilli Palmer (co-starring with her future husband after Rex Harrison) gives a sensitive and controlled performance, played out amid enticing Majorcan locations.

Between Two Wars

▶ **Zwischen Zwei Kriegen**

W. Germany 1977 83 mins bw
Harun Farocki

d   Harun Farocki
sc Harun Farocki
ph Axel Block, Melanie Walz, Ingo Kratisch
m   Mahler
    Jürgen Ebert, Michael Klier, Ingemo
    Engström, Hartmut Bitomsky

A series of six episodes and dialogues from 1917 to 1933 which set out a Marxist analysis of the causes of World War II and how it could have been avoided. Farocki took almost seven years to put together this film, which asks of the audience a certain political frame of reference and an ability to reflect on the arguments presented. With minimal means (it was made on a budget of less than $8,000), Farocki reconstructs the past by using visual synecdoche (the part for the whole) such as a bicycle toolbag and a shiny Horch automobile to stand for class differences. Although self-restrained and intellectual, there is a dramatic thread. The young hero (Ebert) hopes that 'science could blend with the dreams of the workers', joins the Communist party, sees the inevitability of the German industrial *bourgeoisie* supporting Hitler and commits suicide.

▶ **Between Two Worlds** see Destiny

Beware Of A Holy Whore

► **Warnung Vor Einer Heiligen Nutte**

W. Germany 1970 103 mins col
Antiteater-X Film/Nova International

d **Rainer Werner Fassbinder**
sc **Rainer Werner Fassbinder**
ph **Michael Ballhaus**
m **Peer Raben and extracts from Donizetti, Elvis Presley, Ray Charles, Leonard Cohen, Spooky Tooth**
   Lou Castel, Eddie Constantine, Hanna Schygulla, Marquard Böhm, Rainer Werner Fassbinder, Ulli Lommel, Margarethe Von Trotta, Kurt Raab, Ingrid Caven, Werner Schroeter

A German film crew sits around an old hotel at a Spanish seaside resort arguing, griping, drinking and making love, as they wait for the director (Castel), the star (Constantine) and money from Bonn. Fassbinder's bitter critique of himself and his own group of friends and hangers-on is also one of the most devastatingly honest views of film-makers and film-making ever put on screen. Apparently, much of the film reflected the actual shooting (in Sorrento, Italy) and the uglier side of the real people involved. Self-indulgent, self-righteous and self-pitying, it is also funny, provocative and well made. It ends with a quotation from Thomas Mann which was Fassbinder's own *cri de coeur* at the time: 'I tell you that I am often weary to death of portraying humanity without participating in what is human'.

Beyond Good And Evil

► **Oltre Il Bene E Il Male**

Italy 1977 127 mins col
Clesi Cinematografica/Lotar/Artemis/Artistes Associés

d **Liliana Cavani**
sc **Liliana Cavani, Franco Arcalli, Italo Moscati**
ph **Armando Nanuzzi**
m **Danièle Paris, Mahler, Schumann, Gounod, Schönberg**
   Dominique Sanda, Erland Josephson, Robert Powell, Virna Lisi, Philippe Leroy

In turn-of-the-century Rome, the German philosopher Nietzsche (Josephson) and his Jewish friend Paul Rée (Powell) meet a beautiful 20-year-old Russian girl, Lou Von Salomé (Sanda). They decide to set up an 'intellectual' *ménage-a-trois*. This is broken up through Nietzsche's jealousy and because anti-semitism causes Paul to try to poison himself. This fictionalized, febrile account of three people who defied convention is by a director with pretensions to do the same. To succeed it needed a little more intellect, less emotion, and a closer look at the truth. The performances range from the passive (Sanda) to the strident (Powell). There is even a lurid ballet depicting the struggle between Good and Evil, supposed to be Nietzsche's hallucination brought about by drugs. The result is neither Good nor Evil but Bad.

► **Beyond The Wall** see Destiny

Beyond The Walls

► **Me'Achorei Hasoragim**

Israel 1984 103 mins col
April Films

d **Uri Barbash**
sc **Benny Barbash, Eran Preis**
ph **Amnon Salomon**
m **Ilan Virtzberg**
   Arnon Zadok, Muhamad Bakri, Hilel Ne'eman, Assi Dayan, Boaz Sharaabi, Jacob Ayali, Iris Kanner, David Kedem

In an Israeli prison, Jewish criminals are housed with a number of Arabs being held on political charges. Their natural hostility is fuelled by the guards who pursue a divide and rule policy, and feelings are further inflamed by the arrival of an Israeli who sought contact with the PLO. Jewish Uri (Zadok) and Arab Issam (Bakri) find mutual respect when confined together away from the other prisoners, and unite to lead a prison strike. Barbash sets up an intelligent situation which he uses to examine the Arab-Israeli conflict but the metaphor of the title is not pursued. What we have is a prison drama, visually authentic and atmospheric, but peopled with every stereotype and offering the obligatory homosexual rape. It might just as well be the State Penitentiary, courtesy of Hollywood, but lacking the narrative tightness of the American genre.

▶ **Bez Konca** see No End

▶ **Bez Svidetelei** see Private Conversation, A

▶ **Bez Znieczulenia** see Rough Treatment

▶ **Bhumika** see Role, The

Les Biches

▶ **aka The Does**

France 1968 99 mins col
La Boetie/Alexandra

d Claude Chabrol
sc Claude Chabrol, Paul Gégauff
ph Jean Rabier
m Pierre Jansen
   Stéphane Audran, Jacqueline Sassard,
   Jean-Louis Trintignant

A rich and beautiful woman (Audran) picks up a student (Sassard) in Paris and takes her off to her villa in St Tropez, but the local architect (Trintignant) causes a rift in their Lesbian relationship. After seven years of rather paltry stuff, Chabrol re-established his reputation with this elegantly enacted, cool, callous and witty bisexual *ménàge-à-trois*. It was also the first film in which Audran (Mrs Chabrol since 1964) was given a role worthy of her subtle expressiveness. The character Sassard plays is called Why. You might well ask.

Best Actress (Stéphane Audran) Berlin 1968

▶ **Bicycle Thief, The** see Bicycle Thieves

Bicycle Thieves

▶ **(US: The Bicycle Thief)**

▶ **Ladri Di Biciclette**

Italy 1948 90 mins bw

PDS/ENIC
d Vittorio De Sica
sc Vittorio De Sica, Cesare Zavattini,
   Oreste Biancoli, Suso Cecchi D'Amico,
   Adolfo Franci
ph Carlo Montuori
m Alessandro Cicognini
   Lamberto Maggiorani, Lianella Carell,
   Enzo Staiola, Gino Saltamarenda

An unemployed man (Maggiorani) is offered a job as a bill-sticker provided he has a bicycle. He retrieves his own from the pawnbroker but it is stolen on his first day at work, and he spends a day with his small son (Staiola) desperately searching for it. After De Sica's success in the USA with *Shoeshine* (1946), David O. Selznick offered to produce his next film with a star like Cary Grant, but De Sica refused, raised the money himself, and continued his policy of working with non-actors in real locations. It paid off because it was this very un-Hollywood quality – the simplicity and underlying social criticism – that gave it wide appeal. At the time it seemed fragmentary and naturalistic, but it has a highly organized script, and is very moving.

Best Foreign Film Oscar 1949

▶ **Bidone, Il** see Swindlers, The

▶ **Bienvenido, Mr Marshall** see Welcome, Mr Marshall

The Big City

▶ **Mahanagar**

India 1963 131 mins bw
R.D. Bansal

d Satyajit Ray
sc Satyajit Ray
ph Subrata Mitra
m Satyajit Ray
   Anil Chatterjee, Madhabi Mukherjee,
   Vicky Redwood, Haren Chatterjee

The wife of an impoverished bank clerk takes a door-to-door job selling knitting machines to rich housewives in Calcutta, and thus becomes emancipated. Ray's warmth, humour, depth, and scrupulous attention to social detail – witness the scene in the home of an Anglo-Indian – are much in evidence in the first of his films to be given a contemporary urban setting. The convincing progress of the appealing Madhabi Mukherjee from timid housewife to sole breadwinner, is extremely satisfying, particularly in an Indian context.

Best Director Berlin 1964

▶ **Big Deal On Madonna Street** see Persons Unknown

A Big Family

▶ **Bolchaia Semia**

USSR   1955   105 mins   col
Lenfilm

d   **Josef Heifits**
sc **V. Kochetov, S.Kara**
ph **S. Ivanov**
m   **Venedikt Pushkov**
    Serge Lukyanov, Boris Andreyev, Vera Kuznetsova, Andrei Batalov, S. Kurilov, Vadim Medvedev, B. Bityukov, I. Arepina, Katya Luchko, Elena Savinova

Events in the lives of the Zhurbin family, all 10 of them, who make up three generations of dedicated shipyard workers, all living together under the eye of papa Zhurbin (Lukyanov). An old-fashioned, leisurely, heart-warming domestic portrait that Louis B. Mayer would have been pleased to call his own, were it not for the fact that Alexei's fiancée becomes pregnant by somebody else, and Viktor's wife leaves him rather than endure an unhappy marriage. Incidents such as these, emerging from 1950s Russia, caused the film to be rapturously received on release; if it's less impressive now, the reasons for the acting accolade remain apparent.

Best Acting Award (Complete Cast Ensemble) Cannes 1955

The Big Parade

▶ **Da Yuebing**

China   1986   103 mins   col
Guangxi Film Studio

d   **Chen Kaige**
sc **Gao Lili**

ph **Zhang Yimou**
m   **Qu Xiaosong**
    Wang Xueqi, Sun Chun, Lu Lei, Wu Ruofu, Guan Qiang, Kang Hua, Members of the Airborne Division of the People's Liberation Army

In China in 1984, 400 recruits, most of them in their teens and still raw, commence a year of gruellingly intensive training that will win some of them places in the National Day Parade in Peking's Tiananmen Square. Focusing on the hopes and fears of six central characters of contrasting ages and abilities, the film observes and records the relationship between the individual and the group, culminating in the immense parade itself. In the West, this movie has been received as a high-quality Chinese answer to the familiar American rookie-authority-patriotism genre. In China, however, the authorities regarded it as unacceptably critical of the People's Army and only allowed its release when Chen (*Yellow Earth*) Kaige made some adjustments, including, notably, the addition of the climactic Parade where he had intended only the empty square. To a Western viewer, it is a realistic drama with unmistakable elements of irony but no hint of subversion. A little dour, perhaps, and at times relentless in its portrayal of difficulties, but the compellingly naturalistic performances and strikingly sophisticated visual composition absorb and entertain.

The Big Snatch

▶ **(US: Any Number Can Win)**

▶ **Mélodie En Sous-Sol**

France   1963   112 mins   bw
Cipra-Cité Film/C.C.M.

d   **Henri Verneuil**
sc **Henri Verneuil, Albert Simonin, Michel Audiard**
ph **Louis Page**
m   **Michel Magne**
    Jean Gabin, Alain Delon, Viviane Romance, Dora Doll, José De Villalonga

An ex-con (Gabin) sets up one last job and enlists the help of a younger crook (Delon) to rob the casino at Cannes. Everything goes according to plan right up to the last minute until... The main interest in this competently-staged but conventional heist movie with a clever twist, is the coming together of the biggest star of the 1930s and the rising star of the 1960s. Also noteworthy is the appearance of Viviane Romance, who had played 'the vamp' opposite Gabin 27 years previously in *La Belle Equipe*.

▶ **Bijoutiers Du Claire De Lune, Les** see Heaven Fell That Night

▶ **Bilans Kwartalny** see Woman's Decision, A

The Birch Wood

▶ **Brzezina**

Poland   1970   99 mins   col
Tor/Zespoly Filmowe

d   **Andrzej Wajda**
sc   **Jaroslaw Iwaszkiewicz**
ph   **Zygmunt Samosiuk**
m   **Andrzej Korzyński**
    Olgierd Lukaszewicz, Daniel Olbrychski, Emilia Krakowska, Marek Perepeczko, Jan Domański

In the early 1930s, the tubercular Stanislaw (Lukaszewicz) returns from Switzerland to Poland to stay with his healthy, but bitter, forest warden brother (Olbrychski). He has a new lease of life and wins the love of the country girl (Krakowska) whom his brother secretly covets. Driven by 'censorship behind closed doors', Wajda turned to non-political literature for his material. Like the later *The Young Ladies Of Wilko*, this bitter-sweet drama was based on a book by Jaroslaw Iwaszkiewicz (who also wrote the screenplay). The general look of the film derives from Polish *art nouveau* paintings, and the direction is simple, slow, and understated. Like the contrasting brothers, the film moves between the pallid and the robust.

The Birds Come To Die In Peru

▶ **(US: Birds In Peru)**

▶ **Les Oiseaux Vont Mourir Au Pérou**

France   1968   98 mins   col
Universal France

d   **Romain Gary**
sc   **Romain Gary**
ph   **Christian Matras**
m   **Kenton Coe**
    Jean Seberg, Maurice Ronet, Danielle Darrieux, Pierre Brasseur, Jean-Pierre Kalfon

An insecure woman (Seberg), craving sex, leaves her husband (Brasseur) almost every night to search for it in a seaside brothel or on the beaches. One of the lowest points in Jean Seberg's sad life and career (she killed herself in 1979) was the first film directed by novelist-diplomat Romain Gary, her second husband. Like the birds of the title, this pretentious, salacious picture landed with a deadening thud.

▶ **Birds In Peru** see Birds Come To Die In Peru, The

▶ **Birds Of A Feather** see Cage Aux Folles, La

The Birds, The Bees And The Italians

▶ **Signore E Signori**

Italy   1965   115 mins   bw
Dear/RPA/Les Films Du Siècle

d   **Pietro Germi**
sc   **Pietro Germi, Luciano Vincenzoni, Age, Scarpelli**
ph   **Aiace Parolin**
m   **Carlo Rustichelli**
    Virna Lisi, Nora Ricci, Gastone Moschin, Alberto Lionello, Patrizia Valturri, Beba Loncar

Three separate short tales of sex in a small Italian town. 1) A man feigns impotence so that he can cuckold a husband without arousing suspicion 2) A henpecked husband leaves home and lives openly with a bar cashier 3) A young girl is seduced by most of the village men until her father reveals that she is underage. The Italian way with sex (at least in the movies) continued to provide endless amusement at home and abroad in the 1960s. This had more edge than most, and even managed to supply the occasional belly-laugh.

Best Film Cannes 1966

The Birth

► **Piravi**

India 1988 110 mins col
Film Folk/NFDCI

d Shaji
sc S. Jayachandran Nair
ph Sunny Joseph
m G. Aravindan, Mohan Sitara
Premji, S.V. Raman, Chandran Nair,
Mullaneyi, Kottara Gopalakrishnan

In an outlying rural village in southern India
an old man (Premji) is expecting his son home
from university to greet his sister's fiancé and
his family who are coming to visit. When the
young man fails to arrive, the old man journeys through the rain-sodden fields to the
ferry and thence to the bus station to wait
for his son. Day after day the boy fails to
appear, and day after day his father, confident
that he will come, makes the same journey.
Meanwhile, the daughter who tends the old
man discovers that her brother was arrested
and tortured and is probably dead. This directorial debut by a former award-winning
cameraman offers exquisite visuals, a con-
templative mood and a painful story. Unfortunately, its deliberate pace grows as
unbearable as the old man's poignant and
hopeless vigil, and the screenplay has missed
the opportunity for political comment, the
fate of the student seeming almost incidental
so exclusively does the film focus on the
father's plight.

► **Biruma No Tategoto** see Burmese
Harp, The

► **Bitteren Tränen Der Petra Von
Kant, Die** see Bitter Tears Of Petra Von
Kant, The

► **Bitter Reunion** see Beau Serge, Le

Bitter Rice

► **Riso Amaro**

Italy 1950 107 mins bw
Lux/De Laurentiis

d Giuseppe De Santis

sc Giuseppe De Santis, Carlo Lizzani,
Gianni Puccini
ph Otello Martelli
m Goffredo Petrassi
Silvana Mangano, Doris Dowling,
Vittorio Gassman, Raf Vallone

One of the many city women who come each
year to work in the rice fields of the Po valley,
falls for a petty crook who hopes to steal the
rice crop. To most of the public, *Bitter Rice*
means the voluptuous Mangano in thigh-
revealing shorts and torn nylons, her sizeable
breasts thrust forward, her seductive head held
high, standing in a rice paddy. The huge success of the steamy film and of the 19-year-old
actress, who married producer De Laurentiis
the same year, paved the way for other Italian
sexpots to join the international scene. Ostensibly a Neo-Realist exposé of the exploitation
of women workers, the film, in reality, exposes
only La Mangano and exploits the subject.

► **Bitter Spirit, The** see Eternal Love

The Bitter Tears Of Petra Von Kant

► **Die Bitteren Tränen Der Petra
Von Kant**

W. Germany 1972 124 mins col
Tango

d Rainer Werner Fassbinder
sc Rainer Werner Fassbinder
ph Michael Ballhaus
m Verdi, and a selection of pop records
Margit Carstensen, Hanna Schygulla, Irm
Hermann, Katrin Schaake, Eva Mattes

Petra Von Kant (Carstensen), a successful
fashion designer, conducts a sado-masochistic
relationship with her assistant Marlene (Hermann), until the arrival of Karin (Schygulla),
with whom Petra has a tempestuous love
affair. Fassbinder wrote the screenplay for
Carstensen, giving her plenty of scope to
emote and to change her wigs and gowns
frequently. This hermetic all-female chamber
piece, confined to the heroine's apartment
which is dominated by a brass bed, recalls an
old-fashioned melodrama of the 1920s despite
the Lesbianism – something the director might
have taken as a compliment.

▶ **Bizalom** see Confidence

Bizarre, Bizarre

▶ **Drôle De Drame**

France 1937 95 mins bw
Corniglion Molinier

d Marcel Carné
sc Jacques Prévert
ph Eugen Schüfftan
m Maurice Jaubert
   Françoise Rosay, Michel Simon, Louis
   Jouvet, Jean-Louis Barrault, Jean-Pierre
   Aumont

In Edwardian London, a bizarre chain of
events is set in motion when an English
mystery writer (Simon) has to pretend to a
visiting Bishop (Jouvet) that his wife (Rosay)
has been called away. A witty and anarchic
farce, played to perfection by the superb cast
and filmed in a cardboard London imagined
by art director Alexander Trauner. Among
the delights are Jouvet in a kilt and Barrault
as a vegetarian who murders butchers.

Black And White In Colour

▶ **La Victoire En Chantant**

France 1976 100 mins col
Reggance/SEP/Artco/Société Ivorienne
De Production

d Jean-Jacques Annaud
sc Jean-Jacques Annaud, Georges Conchon
ph Claude Agostini, Eduardo Serra,
   Nanamoudou Magassouda
m Pierre Bachelet, Mat Camison
   Jean Carmet, Jacques Dufilho, Catherine
   Rouvel, Jacques Spiesser, Dora Doll

When war is declared in Europe in 1914, a
group of self-satisfied French colonials at a
remote trading post in West Africa decide to
attack a nearby German fort and confusion
ensues. This first feature by a former TV-
commercial director, is a mildly amusing but
strained satire on colonialism. Nicely shot in
the Ivory Coast, and co-produced by the
former French colony, it was the Oscar-winner from a particularly poor bunch of nominations.

Best Foreign Film Oscar 1976

Black Brood

▶ **Camada Negra**

Spain 1977 85 mins col
El Iman

d Manuel Gutiérrez Aragón
sc José Luis Borau, Manuel Gutiérrez
   Aragón
ph Magi Torruella
m José Nieta
   José Luis Alonso, Maria Luisa Ponte,
   Angela Molina, Joaquín Hinojosa,
   Manuel Fadon, Emilio Fornet

Tatin (Alonso), aged 15 and too young to
join the Right wing terrorist group run by his
mother in memory of her late Falangist husband, privately vows to live by its three sacred
principles: revenge, secrecy and willingness to
sacrifice loved ones to the cause. The consequences of the decision are appalling, culminating in his brutal killing of his girlfriend
(Molina). Set in Madrid and directed and
acted with conviction, this obvious critique
of Franco's Spain makes connections between
gangsterism and political fanaticism, but constantly surprises with shifts of mood, sympathy and action. The title refers both to the
fanatical mother and her stepsons (one of
whom admits to being a former policeman)
and to a litter of black puppies that conceals
the hatch under which the gang's weapons
are hidden.

Best Director Berlin 1977

The Black Cannon Incident

▶ **Hei Pao Shi Jian**

China 1985 102 mins col
Xi'an Film Studio

d Huang Jianxin
sc Li Wei
ph Wang Xinsheng, Feng Wei
m Zhu Shirui
   Liu Zifeng, Gerhard Olschewski, Gao
   Ming, Wang Yi, Yang Yazhou, Ge Hui

A technical consultant-interpreter (Zifeng) on
a major Sino-German civil engineering project
is also a chess buff. One day, Party members
intercept a cryptic telegram he sent to a friend
about a lost chess piece (the black cannon).

Believing it to be a coded message, they relieve him of his post. His replacement, with little knowledge of German, makes a terrible mess of the project. Huang Jianxin, a young graduate of the Beijing Film Academy, made the wittiest and cheekiest satire on bureaucracy to have come out of China to date. It targets stupid and corrupt Party hacks, avaricious workers and noisy teenagers, and portrays a fine friendship between the hapless hero and a rather overbearing German engineer (Olschewski). The use of bold colours and clever camera effects adds to the pleasure.

Black God White Devil

▶ **Deus E O Diabo Na Terra Do Sol**

Brazil 1964 120 mins bw
Luiz Augusto Mendes/Copacabana

d **Glauber Rocha**
sc **Glauber Rocha**
ph **Waldemar Lima**
m **Bach, Villa-Lobos, folk songs**
   Yona Magalhaes, Geraldo Del Rey,
   Othon Bastos, Mauricio De Valle, Lidio
   Silva

When his boss tries to rob him, an impoverished cowman kills him, becomes an outlaw and a follower of a self-styled black saint who preaches bloodshed. The first of 25-year-old Rocha's essays on the *sertão*, the parched lands of north-east Brazil, is less fragmented and hysterical than his later work, and is an intoxicating synthesis of symbolism, realism and popular culture, often evoking directors as diverse as John Ford, Buñuel and Eisenstein.

Black On White

▶ **Mustaa Valkoisella**

Finland 1968 85 mins col
F. J. Filmi

d **Jörn Donner**
sc **Jörn Donner**
ph **Esko Nevalainen**
m **Georg Riedel**
   Jörn Donner, Liisamaija Laaksonen,
   Kristina Halkola, Lasse Martenson

A young businessman (Donner) leaves his wife (Halkola) and his perfect marriage to pursue an affair with a flighty secretary (Laaksonen) who wants no ties. Donner's first film in his homeland after making four features in Sweden is a gentle satire on the affluent society with a simple love triangle (and explicit sex scenes) at its centre. Without moralizing or melodrama, the director (himself excellent in the lead) calmly records the man's impossible quest for happiness. Despite the title, it is in eye-catching colour.

Black Orpheus

▶ **Orfeu Negro**

France 1958 106 mins col
Dispatfilm/Gemma/Tupan

d **Marcel Camus**
sc **Vinitius De Moraes, Jacques Viot**
ph **Jean Bourgoin**
m **Luis Bonfa, Antonio Carlos Jobim**
   Breno Mello, Marpessa Dawn, Ademar
   Da Silva, Lourdes De Oliviera

During carnival time in Rio, a philandering tram driver (Mello) accidentally kills his girlfriend (Dawn) and goes to seek her in the Underworld. The wide appeal of this crude transposition of the Orpheus myth to modern Rio lies in its exoticism, vigorous dancing, exciting music and the frenetic atmosphere of the Rio carnival, not in the veiled social comment or the naive acting. Marpessa Dawn, the lovely Eurydice, was the director's wife.

Best Foreign Film Oscar 1959
Best Film Cannes 1959

▶ **Black Peter** see Peter And Pavla

Black Rain

▶ **Kuroi Ame**

Japan 1988 123 mins bw
Imamura Productions/Hayashibara Group/Tohokushinsha Film Co.

d **Shohei Imamura**
sc **Shohei Imamura, Toshiro Ishido**
ph **Takashi Kawamata**

m   Toru Takemitsu
    Yoshiko Tanaka, Kazuo Kitamura, Etsuko
    Ichihara, Shoichi Ozawa, Norihei Miki,
    Keisuke Ishida

Yasuko (Tanaka) lives with her uncle (Kitamura) and aunt (Ichihara) in a small village near Hiroshima in 1950. The health of most of the villagers has been affected by the dropping of the A-bomb five years previously, and although Yasuko has been given a clean bill of health, no man will marry her for fear of contamination. Gradually, more and more people die of cancer until Yasuko herself is stricken on the eve of accepting the hand of Yuichi (Ishida), a nerve-racked young stonemason, who makes enigmatic carvings of malformed figures. As gloomy as its sounds – the nightmarish flashback scenes of the nuclear holocaust are devastating – the film, based on the 1966 novel by Masuji Ibuse, contains a balancing strain of black comedy and a meticulous examination of Japanese post-war rural society. The principal characters are all superbly well drawn and there is pleasure to be had from a number of subsidiary portrayals of the people who drift in and out of the narrative. Sometimes Imamura's tone hovers uncertainly between the ironic and the didactic, but his approach to the immensity of the human tragedy that underlies the story engenders disturbing emotions in the spectator.

Black Shack Alley

▶ **Rue Cases Nègres**

France 1983 106 mins col
Su Ma Fa Productions/Orca
Productions/NEF Diffusion

d   **Euzhan Palcy**
sc **Euzhan Palcy**
ph **Dominique Chapuis**
m   **Groupe Malavoi**
    **Garry Cadenat, Darling Legitimus, Douta
    Seck, Joby Bernabe, Francisco Charles,
    Marie-Jo Descas**

Young José (Cadenat), an orphan, lives with his grandmother (Legitimus) in Black Shack Alley, a collection of shacks attached to a cane plantation in Martinique. Grandma's ambition is to see the boy properly educated and thus able to escape the servitude of the plantation – an ambition which is finally real-

ized, but at the cost of her life through overwork. The first full-length feature from documentary-maker Palcy is an extremely moving evocation of poverty, dreams and black struggle during the 1930s, as well as a beguiling and funny tale of childhood and of loving relationships. The director draws outstanding performances from her cast, notably the full-blooded and entrancing Darling Legitimus, and her handling of the children on the plantation and in José's school is first class.

**Best Actress (Darling Legitimus) Venice
1983**

▶ **Black Thursday** see Gates Of The
Louvre, The

The Black Tulip

▶ **La Tulipe Noir**

France 1963 115 mins col
Mediterranée/Mizar/Agatha

d   **Christian-Jaque**
sc **Christian-Jaque, Henri Jeanson, Paul
    Andreota, Marcello Ciorciolini**
ph **Henri Decaë**
m   **Gerard Calvi**
    **Alain Delon, Virna Lisi, Akim Tamiroff,
    Dawn Addams, Francis Blanche, Adolfo
    Marsillach**

In 1789, Guillaume De Saint-Preux, seemingly cynical and corrupt, is in reality the legendary Black Tulip, masked scourge of the monarchy. When he receives a savage gash across his cheek – a mark which will identify him as a wanted outlaw – he sends for Julien, his idealistic twin brother to continue his exploits. Alain Delon, whose blank pretty-boy features had been used effectively by directors such as Clément, Visconti and Antonioni, here attempts to take on the mantle and buckle on the sword of Gérard Philipe. He looks rather than feels the twin parts in this overlong but reasonably diverting version of the Alexandre Dumas novel. Delon has the classic line in the dubbed version, 'The horse tossed me off!'.

▶ **Blade Of Satan's Bog** see Leaves
From Satan's Book

Blanche

France 1971 92 mins col
Telepresses/Abel Et Charton

d Walerian Borowczyk
sc Walerian Borowczyk
ph Guy Durban, André Dubreuil
m 13th-century music
   Ligia Branice, Michel Simon, Jacques
   Perrin, Georges Wilson, Lawrence
   Trimble

Blanche (Branice), beautiful, young and innocent, is married off to an aged nobleman
(Simon) who keeps her heavily guarded, but
her stepson (Trimble), a page (Perrin) and the
King (Wilson) manage to penetrate the castle.
The Paris-based Polish animator's second
live-action film began a series of erotic and
decorative period pieces, usually set in the
middle ages. Here, his pictorial sense – a two-
dimensional design that gives the film the
look of a tapestry or medieval painting –
overcomes much of the tiresome tushery.
Branice, the director's wife, compared to a
white dove throughout, flutters gently and
beautifully as the aptly named Blanche.

▶ **Blaue Engel, Der** see Blue Angel, The

▶ **Blaue Licht, Das** see Blue Light, The

▶ **Bláznova Kronika** see Jester's Tale,
A

▶ **Blechtrommel, Die** see Tin Drum,
The

Le Bled

France 1929 87 mins bw
Société Des Films Historiques

d Jean Renoir
sc Henri Dupuy-Mazuel, André Jaeger-
   Schmidt
ph Marcel Lucien, Morizet
m Silent
   Enrique Rivero, Jackie Monnier,
   Arquillière, Diana Hart, Manuel Raaby

Pierre (Rivero), a young Frenchman, sailing
to Algeria to join his prosperous farmer uncle,
meets a young woman on the boat (Monnier).

Once in his new country, he becomes romantically involved with her and, when she is
abducted, he manages to rescue her, paving
the way for 'happily-ever-after'. Made to celebrate the centenary of the first French colon-
ists who settled in Algeria in 1830, this
blatantly commercial film demonstrates that
Renoir, quite early in his career, had the gift
of breathing life into run-of-the-mill material.
There is a dramatically staged climactic chase
and the location photography is picturesque.
This film marked the end of the great director's silent output.

▶ **Blé En Herbe, Le** see Ripening Seed,
The

▶ **Bleierne Zeit, Die** see German Sisters, The

Blind Chance

▶ **Przypadek**

Poland 1981 122 mins col
Zespoly Filmowe

d Krzysztof Kieslowski
sc Krzysztof Kieslowski
ph Krzysztof Pakulski
m Wojciech Kilar
   Boguslaw Linda, Tadeusz Lomnicki,
   Zbigniew Zapa, Marzena Trybala, Jacek
   Borowski, Monika Godzdzik, Zygmunt
   Hubner

Witek (Linda), a promising young medical
student, lives three different variations on his
life, each of which begins with a rush to catch
a train. In the first case he gives up his studies
and, through a chance meeting on the train,
joins the Communist Party and takes a job
at a government drug addiction centre, but
falls in love with a girl who is a member of
the political underground. In the second tale
he misses the train, is arrested and ends up
working for the samizdat press. Lastly, he
again misses a train, meets an old girlfriend
at the station, marries her and becomes a
respectable doctor, but a cruel fate awaits
him. Made in 1981 but suppressed by the
authorities for five years, this film is complex
and original in structure, expertly executed
and very well acted. The director's ironic
humanism, now familiar from his 'short' films

about love and killing, is evident, as is his gift in capturing the atmosphere of a time and a place but, although undeniably absorbing, the aptly titled *Blind Chance* is ultimately confusing and unsatisfying. In treating notions of arbitrary fate Kieslowski involves us in an abstract game – who is Witek, did he exist, which was his story? The ending is a serious cop-out that leaves the viewer stranded even as it leaves the hero dead. (Note a reference to Woody Allen in the dialogue – a tribute from a European to an American master.)

A Blonde Dream

▶ **Ein Blonder Traum**

Germany 1932 87 mins bw
UFA

d Paul Martin
sc Walter Reisch, Billy Wilder
ph Günther Rittau, Otto Baecker
m Werner R. Heymann
Willy Fritsch, Lilian Harvey, Willi Forst, Paul Hörbiger

A young girl with film ambitions is cheated and robbed by a man pretending to be an American agent. Two window cleaners, both in love with her, come to her assistance. An effervescent comedy in which the doll-like Harvey sang and danced delightfully, and appeared in a mock-Expressionistic dream sequence of Hollywood. It was made at the same time in English in Germany with Jack Hulbert and Sonnie Hale replacing Fritsch and Forst, and retitled *Happy Ever After*.

A Blonde In Love

▶ **(US: Loves Of A Blonde)**

▶ **Lásky Jedné Plavovlásky**

Czechoslovakia 1965 82 mins bw
Barrandov Studios

d Miloš Forman
sc Miloš Forman, Jaroslav Papoušek, Ivan Passer
ph Miroslav Ondříček
m Evzen Illin
Hana Brejchová, Vladimir Pucholt, Joseph Sebánek, Milada Jezkova

A shy, romantic factory girl (Brejchová) in a small town depleted of men, falls in love with a visiting young pianist (Pucholt), but is made unwelcome by his parents when she pursues him to Prague. Following up the success of his first feature, *Peter And Pavla* (1963), Forman again used a simple plot to show young people in conflict with their elders in this Oscar-nominated movie. His gently mocking humour and keen eye for the minutiae of human behaviour is best demonstrated in the delightful sequence when a group of middle-aged army reservists cause a flutter among the sex-starved girls at a dance.

▶ **Blonder Traum, Ein** see Blonde Dream, A

Blood Of The Beasts

▶ **Le Sang Des Bêtes**

France 1949 20 mins bw
Forces Et Voix De La France

d Georges Franju
sc Georges Franju
ph Marcel Fradetal
m Joseph Kosma

The daily slaughter of animals in an abattoir is juxtaposed with images of everyday life in Paris not long after the carnage of World War II. Franju's first film since he co-directed a short with Henri Langlois in 1934, shows in cold and vivid detail, as never before or since, 'the bleeding flesh dripping down the screen,' as Godard described it. Those who have managed to keep their eyes on the screen find it a powerful and moving statement. Franju, a non-vegetarian himself, forces carnivores to face the reality in which they are participants.

Blood Of The Condor

▶ **Yawar Mallku**

Bolivia 1969 74 mins bw
Ukamau Limitada

d Jorge Sanjines
sc Jorge Sanjines, Oscar Soria
ph Antonio Eguino

m **Alberto Villalpando, Alfredo Dominguez, Gregorio Yana, Ignacio Quispe Marcelino Yanahuaya, Benedicta Mendoza Huanca, Vicente Salinas, and the people of the Kaata rural community**

Ignacio (Yanahuaya), head of a small community of Quechua Indians, and his wife Paulina (Huanca), having lost their children through illness, are anxious to have more, but Paulina seems unable to conceive. Hearing that others have the same problem, Ignacio visits the American Progress Corps clinic where, to his horror, he learns that the Americans are sterilizing Indian women to keep the population down. The villagers' reaction to this discovery leads to bloodshed. Not surprisingly, the Bolivian government banned this film, releasing it only when forced to do so by vociferous protest campaigns. Simple, honest and direct, this account of the gap between cultures, classes and ideologies both grips and appals. Everybody portrayed here is victim of a system, and Sanjines, in making the movie, both exposed political corruption and revealed the dawning of a wider political consciousness in his country.

The Blood Of The Poet

▶ **Le Sang D'Un Poète**

France   1930   58 mins   bw
Vicomte De Noailles

d **Jean Cocteau**
sc **Jean Cocteau**
ph **Georges Périnal**
m **Georges Auric**
   Lee Miller, Pauline Carton, Odette Talazac, Enrique Rivero, Jean Desbordes

A young poet passes through a mirror into a world where he sees a Mexican revolutionary executed and restored to life, opium smoking, a hermaphrodite, a boy killed in a snowball fight and living statues. Cocteau's first film, made when he was 41 and already famous, contains all the signs and symbols of his personal mythology evident in his poems, plays, novels and drawings. Thanks to the patronage of the Vicomte De Noailles, Cocteau was free to experiment with the new medium, exploring the creative process in arresting, dream-like images. Lacking the

mastery of his later films, it nevertheless had a great influence, particularly on the American *avant-garde*.

Blood On The Land

▶ **To Homa Vaftike Kokkino**

Greece   1965   120 mins   bw
Finos Films

d **Vassilis Georgiades**
sc **Nicos Foscolos**
ph **Nicos Dimopoulos**
m **Mimis Plessas**
   Nicos Courcoulos, Mary Chronopoulos, Yannis Voglis, Manos Katrakis

Peasants and landowners fight over land partition in the Greece of the early 1900s, and two enemy brothers fight over a woman. Despite some hair-tearing passions, and rather one-dimensional characterizations, this Oscar-nominated drama gets by on sincerity and some injection of genuine social consciousness. It was one of the last Greek films to be released before the military take-over in 1967 which led to a decline in creative film-making.

Blood Wedding

▶ **aka Red Wedding**

▶ **(US: Wedding In Blood)**

▶ **Les Noces Rouges**

France   1973   90 mins   col
La Boétie/Canaria

d **Claude Chabrol**
sc **Claude Chabrol**
ph **Jean Rabier**
m **Pierre Jansen**
   Stéphane Audran, Michel Piccoli, Claude Piéplu, Eliana De Santis, Clotilde Joano

The mayor (Piéplu) of a small town in the Loire valley discovers that his wife (Audran) is having an affair with his deputy (Piccoli), and decides to blackmail the latter into going along with a crooked property deal. Another variation on Chabrol's pet theme of infidelity leading to murder is as elegant, cool and blackly humorous as one expects from a director secure in his subject.

Blood Wedding

▶ **Bodas De Sangre**

> Spain 1981 72 mins col
> Emiliano Piedra

d   Carlos Saura
sc Carlos Saura, Antonio Gades
ph Teo Escamilla
m   Emillo De Diego
    Antonio Gades, Cristina Joyas, Juan
    Antonio Jiminez, Pilar Cardenas

Antonio Gades and his troupe rehearse and perform a flamenco ballet version of Lorca's tragedy in a empty dance studio. Forget the Lorca play, as Gades has done, and thrill to the Andalusian passion expressed in the eloquent movements of the heel-tapping dance and soulful song of the flamenco, seen through the eye of a rhythmic camera.

Blow-Out

▶ **La Grande Bouffe**

> France 1973 130 mins col
> Mara/Capitolina

d   Marco Ferreri
sc Marco Ferreri, Rafael Azcona
ph Mario Vulpiani
m   Philippe Sarde
    Marcello Mastroianni, Philippe Noiret,
    Ugo Tognazzi, Michel Piccoli, Andréa
    Ferréol

Four middle-aged men – a pilot (Mastroianni), a judge (Noiret), a master chef (Tognazzi) and a TV personality (Piccoli) – bored with life, meet at a secluded villa in order literally to eat themselves to death. Only Buñuel might have brought off this attempt to demonstrate that men (and women, here represented by the statuesque Andréa Ferréol) are victims of their appetites. Ferreri uses shock tactics and excremental schoolboy humour to make a wearisome, excessive movie about excess. It did no harm at the box-office though.

Blow To The Heart

▶ **Colpire Al Cuore**

> Italy 1982 105 mins col
> RAI/Antea Cinematografica

d   Gianni Amelio
sc Gianni Amelio, Vincenzo Cerami
ph Tonino Nardi
m   Franco Piersanti
    Jean-Louis Trintignant, Laura Morante,
    Fausto Rossi, Sonia Gessner, Vanni
    Corbellini, Laura Nucci

Camera-mad teenager Emilio (Rossi), son of Dario (Trintignant), meets two young acquaintances of his father's, Sandro (Corbellini) and unmarried mother Giulia (Morante). Having photographed the pair and formed an attachment to Giulia, Emilio sees Sandro dead in the street after a terrorist shooting, which leads to his keeping his father and Giulia under surveillance... Amelio's film, fluent and beautifully judged, has the issue of terrorism hovering over it like a miasma, but does not explore it. The director is essentially concerned with family relationships, examining the consequences on an only child of parents who keep themselves at a distance. (His mother, perfectly played by Morante, is forever typing while wearing earphones that effectively isolate her.) If certain questions are left unanswered, this is nevertheless a gripping and intelligent movie.

The Blue Angel

▶ **Der Blaue Engel**

> Germany 1930 98 mins bw
> UFA

d   Josef Von Sternberg
sc Robert Liebmann, Karl Zückmayer, Karl
    Vollmüller
ph Günther Rittau, Hans Schneeberger
m   Friedrich Holländer
    Emil Jannings, Marlene Dietrich, Kurt
    Gerron, Hans Albers

Professor Unrath (Jannings), an aging and puritanical schoolteacher, becomes infatuated by and marries Lola-Lola (Dietrich), a nightclub singer who deceives and humiliates him.

Commonly supposed to be Dietrich's first film, it was, in fact, the 28-year-old's seventeenth screen appearance. She had been a leading lady in B films and on stage when Sternberg, invited to Germany by Jannings to direct him in a screen version of Heinrich Mann's novel, saw potential sensuous, mysterious, glamorous star qualities in her. These qualities were fully exploited in the following six films he made with her in Hollywood. Her Lola-Lola, sitting on a chair huskily singing 'Falling In Love Again', in top hat, black stockings, bare thighs, clutching her knee, encapsulates an age and an impulse of German cinema. Beside her, Jannings, in his first talkie, seems out of date, though his crowing like a cock is a startling moment.

▶ **Bluebeard** see Landru

The Blue Light

▶ **Das Blaue Licht**

Germany 1932 77 mins bw
Sokal/Leni Riefestahl Film

d   **Leni Riefenstahl**
sc **Leni Riefenstahl, Béla Balázs**
ph **Hans Schneeberger**
m   **Giuseppe Becce**
    Leni Riefenstahl, Max Holzboer, Mathias Wieman, Beni Führer

A painter (Wieman) falls in love with a young girl (Riefenstahl) thought to be a witch because she alone in the Dolomite village can reach the top of a dangerous peak. When he discovers her secret route, she jumps to her death. Riefenstahl had appeared in four of Arnold Fanck's mountain films, and her first venture as a director was in a similar romantic vein, shot on location and emphasizing a Germanic mystical union with nature. It impressed Hitler so much that he asked her to make films for the Nazi party.

Blue Mountains

▶ **Golubye Gory Ely Nepravdopodobnaya Istoria**

USSR 1983 97 mins col

Gruziafilm Studios

d   **Eldar Shengalaya**
sc **Rezo Cheishvili**
ph **Levan Paatashvili**
m   **Giya Kancheli**
    R. Giorgobiani, V. Kakhniashvili, T. Chirgadze, D. Sumbatashvili, I. Sakvarelidze

Soso (Giorgobiani) arrives at a publishing company in a Georgian town to submit the manuscript of his new novel. It is autumn. Everybody appears interested, but their other concerns – will, for example, a picture fall off the wall on to an elderly editor's head? – prevent them from reading it. Winter comes, then Spring, then Summer. Still Soso haunts the offices, still nobody reads the book... The joke starts wearing thin around summer time and the ending is a little weak, but *Blue Mountains* is an anarchic and witty satire about the plight of the artist as victim. The decaying publishing house, which eventually crumbles away, is a splendid metaphor for bureaucracy, the movie is alive with dotty action, and the characterizations are splendidly detailed.

The Blue Veil

▶ **Le Voile Bleu**

France 1942 90 mins bw
CGC

d   **Jean Stelli**
sc **François Camaux**
ph **René Caveau**
m   **A. Theurer**
    Gaby Morlay, Elvire Popesco, Marcelle Géniat, Charpin, Larquey

A World War I widow (Morlay), whose child dies at birth, becomes a governess and devotes her life to the care of other people's children, even to the point of giving up a lover to be near her charges. Popular French star Gaby Morlay had them crying in the aisles with this unashamedly sentimental story. Although soppy, it does contain scenes of real pathos, and it is beautifully played. Hollywood didn't have to alter much in its 1951 remake starring Jane Wyman. The title refers to the headdress of the governess.

Blushing Charlie

▶ **Lyckliga Skitar**

Sweden   1970   96 mins   col
Sandrew

d   **Vilgot Sjöman**
sc **Vilgot Sjöman, Bernt Lundqvist, Solveig Ternström**
ph **Rune Ericson**
m   **Christer Boustedt, Lasse Werner, Gösta Wälivaara, Jan Carlsson**
    Bernt Lundqvist, Solveig Ternström, Lilian Johansson, Janet Petterson, Tomas Bolme

Charlie (Lundqvist), a confirmed bachelor, lives on a barge, drives a lorry for a living and, at weekends, drinks with jazz musician friends and chases after bunny girls. However, when pregnant Pia (Ternström) arrives to stay, Charlie, now involved in Left-wing politics, decides he'd like to marry her. Sjöman, following the recipe of his passingly notorious *I Am Curious-Yellow*, again makes a bid to combine frank sexual exploration and politics, resulting in a film which, although photographed with an excess of lyricism, is convincingly acted and directed until the hard-to-swallow dénouement.

The Boat

▶ **Das Boot**

W. Germany   1981   150 mins   col
Bavaria Atelier/Radiant Film

d   **Wolfgang Petersen**
sc **Wolfgang Petersen**
ph **Jöst Vacano**
m   **Klaus Doldinger**
    Jürgen Prochnow (The Captain), Herbert Grönemeyer, Klaus Wennemann, Hubertus Bengsch

In 1941, a German U-Boat goes on a dangerous mission from La Rochelle to Spain and back, hunted by Allied depth charges and air raids. At $12 million, the most expensive German film to date is a compendium of every submarine movie ever made, with all the expected claustrophobic horrors. Its main interest is not in the flat characterizations of the 'good' German crew – there is only one despised Nazi on board – but in the spectacular handheld camerawork, accurately depicting conditions under water. It was nominated for six Academy Awards.

The Boat Is Full

▶ **Das Boot Ist Voll**

Switzerland   1981   100 mins   col
Limbo Film/SRG/ZDF/ORF

d   **Markus Imhoof**
sc **Markus Imhoof**
ph **Hans Liechti**
    Tina Engel, Curt Bois, Hans Diehl, Martin Walz, Ilse Bahis, Gerd David

A group of Jewish refugees of all ages struggle to escape the Nazis across the Swiss border. They make it, only to be sent back to the waiting Germans by the Swiss in the village where they fetch up. Stylistically muted and unadorned, but with the camera picking up a complexity of small, telling detail, Imhoof's film is totally absorbing and quite chilling. What is different from other films of similar plot is that this is not so much an escape story or a memoir of victims of Nazi persecution, as an exposé of ordinary people's attitudes – bewilderment, suspicion, neutrality, hostility – to refugees whose plight they simply fail to comprehend. The acting is superb, notably from Tina Engel of Peter Stein's theatre company, and the 80-year-old veteran star, Curt Bois.

▶ **Bob Le Flambeur** see Bob The Gambler

Bob The Gambler

▶ **Bob Le Flambeur**

France   1955   100 mins   bw
Jenner/Cyme/Play Art/OGC

d   **Jean-Pierre Melville**
sc **Jean-Pierre Melville, Auguste Le Breton**
ph **Henri Decaë**
m   **Eddie Barclay, Jean Boyer**
    Roger Duchesne, Isabelle Corey, Daniel

Cauchy, Howard Vernon, Gérard Buhr, André Garret, Guy Decomble

Bob (Duchesne), a retired bank robber and inveterate gambler, has an unlucky streak, so he decides to mastermind a raid on the casino at Deauville. Melville's first original script and first entry into the world of *film noir* is an ironical variation on the plot of his favourite picture, John Huston's *The Asphalt Jungle* (1950). What is astonishing is how much its gritty, free-wheeling camera style and location shooting predates the French New Wave. Everything is already here, the jump cuts, the jazzy score, and the visual quotes. At the film's centre is Bob, the 'aging young man', played soulfully by Duchesne, masterfully expressing the man's moral code. Narrated by the director (billed merely as Melville), it reverberates with the atmosphere of the mean streets and brash nightclubs around Place Pigalle between dusk and dawn.

▶ **Boca Del Lobo, La** see Lion's Den, The

Boccaccio 70

Italy   1962   210 mins   col
CCC/Cineriz/Francinex/TCF

d   1) Federico Fellini 2) Luchino Visconti 3) Vittorio De Sica
sc 1)Federico Fellini, Tullio Pinelli, Ennio Flaiano 2) Luchino Visconti, Suso Cecchi D'Amico 3) Cesare Zavattini
ph 1) and 3) Otello Martelli 2) Giuseppe Rotunno
m   1) and 2) Nino Rota 3) Armando Trovaioli
    1) Anita Ekberg, Peppino De Filippo 2) Romy Schneider, Tomas Milian 3) Sophia Loren, Luigi Gillianni

1) A large, sexy model comes down from her billboard advertising milk to pursue a little puritan who campaigned against it. 2) A wife, on learning that her husband visits brothels, decides to charge him massive fees for her services. 3) A desirable woman offers herself as a prize in a raffle at a funfair, fixing the draw so a country bumpkin can win. Three of Italy's major directors (a fourth episode by Mario Monicelli was cut from most foreign

prints) provided three minor stories for a modern Decameron. They are respectively broad, dull and vulgar, but with Ekberg and Loren in the cast there are, to paraphrase Howard Hughes, four good reasons to see the picture.

▶ **Bodas De Sangre** see Blood Wedding

▶ **Boda Secreta** see Secret Wedding

La Bohème

France/Italy   1987   107 mins   col
Erato Films/La Sept/SFPC/Générale d'Images/Travelling Productions

d   **Luigi Comencini**
sc **Giuseppe Giacosa, Luigi Illica (libretto)**
ph **Armando Nannuzzi**
m   **Giacomo Puccini (conducted by James Conlon)**
    Barbara Hendricks (Mimi), Luca Canonici (Rodolfo – sung by José Carreras), Angela Maria Blasi (Musetta), Gino Quilico (Marcello), Richard Cowan (Schaunard), Ellero D'Artegna (Colline), Massimo Girotti (Old Suitor)

Penniless poet Rodolfo shares a Paris garret with Marcello, a painter, Schaunard, a musician, and Colline, a philosopher. One cold winter's evening, Mimi, a seamstress who lives in the same building, comes by to get a light for her lamp and she and Rodolfo fall in love. Things start to go badly after they have been living together for some months because of Rodolfo's jealousy and he drives her away. However, the real reason for his conduct is his concern for her health and his belief that she is too ill to continue to live in his damp and freezing atic. They are reconciled, but too late, and she dies in his arms. The best opera films manage to retain the spirit of the stage original while finding a way of translating the material into essentially cinematic terms. Comencini's approach is much more straightforward, using studio sets and seldom straining after filmic effects. However, it is never static. The use of close-ups of the singers is limited and discreet, but for one jarringly vulgar moment which shows Mimi, as seen in Roldolfo's mind, suddenly surrounded by fairy lights illuminating the attic. The second act at the Café Momus works best because film can encompass the bustling movement and various strands of the situation. The black American soprano Barbara Hendricks makes an exquisite and touching Mimi, and she is in splendid voice. Three days before shooting began the Spanish tenor José Carreras became seriously ill, but thankfully the soundtrack had already been recorded, so we hear his magnificent voice mouthed by the young Italian tenor Canonici. Unfortunately, Canonici's acting is an passionless as Carreras's singing is passionate. Only Mimi's hand was frozen, while his whole body seems so at times. But the uniformly good voices and the well-produced sound from the Orchestre National de France, should provide audiences with a fair share of goose-pimples. There is nothing in the film to really offend lovers of Puccini's most adored opera, and everything to please those new to it.

▶ **Bokhandlaren Som Slutade Bada** see Bookseller Who Gave Up Bathing, The

▶ **Bokser** see Boxer, The

▶ **Bolchaia Semia** see Big Family, A

▶ **Bold Adventure, The** see Adventures Of Till Eulenspiegel, The

Bombay Our City

▶ **Hamara Shaher**

India 1985 82 mins col
Anand Patwardhan

d Anand Patwardhan
ph Ranjan Palit, Anand Patwardhan
m Aavhan Natya Manch

Called by the *Times of India* 'quite clearly the best documentary ever made' in that country, Patwardhan's film allows the city and its people to speak for themselves in both words and pictures, without formal scripting or narration. The result is an intelligent and sympathetic examination of frailty, injustice, greed and complacency that has the unmistakable ring of truth. The camera catches several haunting images, such as that of people cooking their evening meal on the pavements against the glittering backdrop of the city at night, while a street voice sings of why 'we left our villages and came here'.

Bona

Philippines 1981 83 mins col
G.N.V. Productions

d Lino Brocka
sc Cenen Reamones
ph Conrado Baltazar
m Max Jocson
   Nora Aunor, Phillip Salvador, Rustica Carpio, Venchito Galvez, Nanding Josef

Eighteen-year-old Bona (Aunor) is infatuated with Gardo (Salvador), a bit player in movies, a womanizer and a violent lout. When she sees him set upon by some youths with a grudge, she goes home with him and stays overnight to tend his wounds. As a consequence her father beats her up, so she moves in with Gardo, caring for him with absolute devotion while his treatment of her becomes increasingly appalling. That the credibility of this film is not shaken when Bona, after an inordinately long time suddenly comes to grips with her self-imposed ordeal and shows a bit of mettle, is a tribute to the Philippines' foremost film-maker. Working from a tight script, Brocka makes the most of the highly dramatic moments and offers a vivid portrayal of community life in the poorer quarters of Manila. The film was financed by leading lady Aunor, the Philippines' most popular actress.

Le Bonheur

▶ **aka Happiness**

France 1965 79 mins col
Parc

d Agnès Varda
sc Agnès Varda
ph Jean Rabier, Claude Beausoleil
m Mozart
   Jean-Claude Drouot, Marie-France Boyer, Claire Drouot, Sandrine and Olivier Drouot

A young carpenter wants his wife to accept that he can be happily married and, at the same time, love his mistress. When his wife drowns herself, he lives happily ever after with his mistress and his two children. The idyllic colour landscapes, advertisement-style prettiness, and Mozart's music created an ambiguity and ironic reflection on the film's title, but also swamped its statement about an extended family. Its amorality provoked controversy, added to which the male lead's real-life family played his wife and children.

Special Jury Prize Berlin 1965

La Bonne Année

▶ **(US: Happy New Year)**

> France 1973 115 mins col
> Les Films 13(Paris)/Rizzoli Film(Rome)

d **Claude Lelouch**
sc **Claude Lelouch, Pierre Uytterhoeven**
ph **Claude Lelouch**
m **Francis Lai**
> **Lino Ventura, Françoise Fabian, Charles Gérard, Michou, André Falcon, Mireille Mathieu, Silvano Tranquilli**

Paroled from prison, jewel thief Simon (Ventura) who robbed the Cannes branch of Van Cleef and Arpels, arranges a reunion with his mistress, Françoise (Fabian). Meanwhile, he sets out to look for his accomplice, which leads him to recall the past events. Lelouch provides both a heist movie in which he nicely maintains the tension, and a love story about the attraction of opposites – Simon earthy, monogamous and uneducated, Françoise fashionable, liberated and intellectual. An entertaining movie, which begins with the convicts watching *A Man And A Woman*: partly the director's joke at his own expense, partly his comment on a changed social climate.

Les Bonnes Femmes

▶ **aka The Girls**

> France 1960 102 mins bw
> Paris/Panitalia/Hakim

d **Claude Chabrol**
sc **Paul Gégauff**
ph **Henri Decaë**
m **Paul Misraki, Pierre Jansen**
> **Bernadette Lafont, Stéphane Audran,**

Clothilde Joano, Lucile Saint-Simon, Claude Berri, Mario David

Four shop girls long to escape their monotonous existence: Ginette (Audran) sings at a tatty music hall, Jane (Lafont) simply wants a good time, Rita (Saint-Simon) drifts into a *bourgeois* marriage, and Jacqueline (Joano) yearns for romantic love, but is strangled by a sex murderer in the woods. Chabrol's early masterpiece offers a gallery of grotesques, macabre and farcical humour, but also poetry and tenderness. The mixture of compassion for the girls and contempt for their dreams created an ironic structure that disturbed the majority of critics when it first appeared, forcing Chabrol into making a series of potboilers.

La Bonne Soupe

▶ **(US: Careless Love)**

> France 1963 100 mins bw
> Belstar/Dear/Du Siècle

d **Robert Thomas**
sc **Robert Thomas**
ph **Roger Hubert**
m **Raymond Le Sénéchal**
> **Marie Bell, Annie Girardot, Claude Dauphin, Jean-Claude Brialy, Raymond Pellegrin, Franchot Tone, Christian Marquand, Bernard Blier, Daniel Gélin, Gérard Blain, Sacha Distel**

An aging woman tells the story of how she was seduced as a girl by a salesman, became a kept woman, married for money, made love to her son-in-law, and ended up a high-class prostitute. Felicien Marceau's hit boulevard comedy provided the source for this old-hat frolic, allowing a number of leading French actors (and Franchot Tone) to make passes at Marie Bell and Annie Girardot (as Bell's younger self). A sort of sexy version of *Un Carnet De Bal* in which Madame Bell had starred 26 years previously.

The Bookseller Who Gave Up Bathing

▶ **Bokhandlaren Som Slutade Bada**

> Sweden 1968 99 mins col
> Sandrew

d Jarl Kulle
sc Jarl Kulle
ph Rune Ericson
m Ulf Björlin
   Allan Edwall, Margaretha Krook, Jarl
   Kulle, Nils Eklund, Ingvar Kjellson

Middle-aged bachelor bookseller Jacob (Edwall) falls in love with sexy, sophisticated Amélie (Krook), a widow who has been living in France. They marry, Jacob gives up his Sunday afternoons at the river with his friends and the couple is blissfully happy until Amélie's brother reveals her past as a whore. Actor Jarl Kulle, well-known to followers of the Swedish cinema, made his directing debut with this bitter-sweet film in which tranquillity and nostalgia rub shoulders with sensual passion and farcical comedy. Jacob and his friend Krakow (Kulle), desperately trying to preserve life as a set of dreams and illusions, are poignantly realized in a beautifully controlled film, well acted and splendid to look at.

Boomerang

   Bulgaria 1979 90 mins col
   Bulgarofilm, Sofia

d Ivan Nichev
sc Svoboda Bucharova, Jenny Radeva
ph Victor Chichov
m Kiril Tsiboulka
   Lyuben Chatalov, Yavov Spassov, Nikolai
   Binev, Katya Paskaleva, Krassimira
   Damyanova

Mihail (Chatalov), recently graduated from Sofia University's journalism school, is determined to break into the highest professional and social echelons with a minimum of sacrifice, avoiding the usual period of probation in the provinces. How he cons his way into relationships that can advance him – notably with a clapped-out but influential novelist (Binev) – forms the substance of the plot. A sharp screenplay and perceptive direction give an inside view of the rat race in Bulgaria, surprisingly similar to our own, and probes the weaknesses of the political regime. Well-delineated characters are portrayed by an extremely accomplished cast, notably Chatalov as the handsome, arrogant Mihail, who becomes increasingly enmeshed in his own moral turpitude, causing his schemes to 'boomerang'.

▶ **Boot, Das** see Boat, The

▶ **Boot Ist Voll, Das** see Boat Is Full, The

Border Street

▶ **Ulica Graniczna**

   Poland 1948 110 mins bw
   Film Polski

d Alexsander Ford
sc Ludwik Starski, Alexsander Ford, Jan
   Fethke
ph Jaroslav Tuzar
m Roman Palester
   Maria Broniewska, Mieczyslawa
   Ćwiklińska, Jerzy Lesczyński, Wladyslaw
   Godik, Wladyslaw Walter

The lives of several families from different social classes in a neighbourhood of pre-war Warsaw are changed by the tragic events of the period. The respected doctor's family has to move into the Jewish ghetto, the father of an upper-class family joins the Resistance, and another family becomes pro-Nazi. The film climaxes with the Warsaw ghetto uprising. One of the first of a cluster of Polish films that emerged from the rubble of the war, it was made by an established pre-war director and a founder of Film Polski in 1945. In 1936, his *Street Of Youth*, which tried to reconcile Polish and Jewish youth, was banned. This one, returning to the theme with far more passion and anger, is marred by rather broad characterizations and rhetorical gestures, but the final sequences are well staged and the message got through to a wide audience in and outside Poland.

Borsalino

   France 1970 128 mins col
   Adel/Marianne/Mars

d Jacques Deray
sc Jacques Deray, Jean-Claude Carrière,
   Claude Sautet, Jean Cau
ph Jean-Jacques Tarbes
m Claude Bolling
   Jean-Paul Belmondo, Alain Delon, Michel
   Bouquet, Catherine Rouvel, Corinne
   Marchand

In the Marseilles of the 1930s, two petty

crooks join up and rise in the underworld until they control all meat supplies. The teaming of two of France's biggest box-office stars was a good commercial bet (Delon was the producer), and pre-dated buddy-buddy gangster movies like *The Sting* (1973). The two leads with tongues-in-cheek and borsalino hats on heads, the jazz score, and the period detail, passed most of the time agreeably enough. There was a less popular sequel, *Borsalino And Co* (1974).

▶ **Boucher, Le** see Butcher, The

▶ **Boudu Sauvé Des Eaux** see Boudu Saved From Drowning

Boudu Saved From Drowning

▶ **Boudu Sauvé Des Eaux**

France 1932 87 mins bw
Haik/CCF

d   Jean Renoir
sc Jean Renoir
ph Marcel Lucien
m   Raphael, Johann Strauss
    Michel Simon, Charles Grandval,
    Marcelle Hainia, Jean Dasté, Severine
    Lerczinska, Jacques Becker

A tramp, saved from drowning by a bookseller and taken into the latter's home, sets about seducing his rescuer's wife and mistress (the maid), before retreating thankfully to the banks of the Marne. The last and best of the four films that Renoir made with the extraordinary simian-faced Michel Simon, it is an exhilarating mixture of farce and drama through which runs the spirit of anarchy fighting *bourgeois* convention. The sense of Paris in the summer is heightened by the deep focus photography and direct sound.

Boule De Suif

▶ **Pyshka**

USSR 1934 65 mins bw
Mosfilm

d   Mikhail Romm
sc Mikhail Romm
ph Boris Volchok

m   Silent
    Galina Sergeyeva, Anatoli Goryunov, P.
    Repnin, Faina Ranevskaya, Andrei Fait

A Russian-made version of De Maupassant's famous short story attacking hypocrisy and selfishness, as demonstrated by the fate that befalls a brave and good-hearted prostitute known as Boule De Suif (Sergeyeva). During the Franco-Prussian War of 1870 she travels on a stagecoach with a group of aristocrats, merchants and their wives, and saves them from the threats of a Prussian officer by bestowing her favours on him. For this act, which the group was happy to encourage and accept, she is scorned and disdained. Sticking to the letter of the original, Romm also comes admirably close to capturing the French spirit in a compact, straightforward adaptation. Stylishly made and with a well-cast leading lady, it was the director's first film as well as the last of the Russian silents.

Boule De Suif

France 1945 105 mins bw
Artis Film

d   Christian-Jaque
sc Henri Jeanson
ph Lucienne Chevert
m   Maurice Paul Guillot
    Micheline Presle, Louis Salou, Alfred
    Adam, Suzet Mais, Roger Karl, Marcel
    Simon, Brochard

This is a workmanlike adaptation of De Maupassant's story of a prostitute in the Franco-Prussian war (see above), with a sympathetic and dignified Micheline Presle impressive in the title role. In this version, however, writer and director have cleverly combined plot elements from De Maupassant's other well-known work of the period, *Mademoiselle Fifi*, thus giving Boule De Suif an opportunity to take some audience-satisfying revenge on the Prussian officer to whom she is forced to give herself. The film had a strong impact at the time of its release because of its unmistakable resonances of World War II and the Nazi occupation of France.

The Boxer

▶ **Bokser**

Poland 1967 96 mins bw

Polski Film/Start

d   **Julian Dziedzina**
sc **Bohdan Tomaszewski**
ph **Mikolaj Sprudin**
    Daniel Olbrychski, Leszek Drogosz,
    Tadeusz Kalinowski, Malgorzata
    Wlodarska

A young blacksmith (Olbrychski), who has gained early recognition as an amateur boxer of outstanding talent, looks back over his tempestuous career as he waits in the dressing room for his Olympic final. Like his compatriot, Jerzy Skolimowski, who made *Walkover* two years previously, Dziedzina deals with the amateur side of the pet sport of the movies, showing it as far more skilful than brutal but no less exciting. The atmosphere of the arena at the Mexican Olympics is well caught, and 22-year-old Olbrychski (soon to become the favourite actor of Andrzej Wajda), using no stand-ins, is convincing as the boxer.

The Boxer

▶ **Boxer**

    Japan   1977   95 mins   col
    Toei

d   **Shuji Terayama**
sc **Shuji Terayama, Shiro Ishimori, Rio**
    Kishida
ph **Tatsuo Susuki**
m   **J.A. Seazer**
    Kentaro Shimizu, Bunta Sugawara

A retired boxer (Sugawara) leaves his wife and child in order to train a young featherweight (Shimizu) for the title. The experience Terayama gained as a sports writer before he became a theatre and film director came in useful for this drama of the ring, made to capitalize on the huge success of *Rocky* the year before. However, despite its surface resemblance to the Stallone hit – it also builds up to a big fight finale – the film has far more psychological insight, and there are also inserted tributes to great Japanese champions of the past. Pop singer Shimizu is dynamic in the lead, while most other roles are taken by members of Terayama's theatre group.

▶ **Boxer** see Boxer, The

Boy

▶ **Shonen**

    Japan   1969   97 mins   col
    Sozosha/ATG

d   **Nagisa Oshima**
sc **Tsutomu Tamura**
ph **Yasuhiro Yoshioka**
m   **Hikaru Hayashi**
    Tetsuo Abe, Fumio Watanabe, Akiko
    Koyama

A 10-year-old boy is trained by his parents to be knocked down by cars so that they can demand money from the frightened drivers before moving on to the next town. Structurally more conventional than Oshima's previous films, it is, nevertheless, an unusual story, taken from an actual case and told with remarkable social and psychological insight. The acting, the colour and the CinemaScope screen are all handled in a masterly manner.

Boy Meets Girl

    France   1984   100 mins   bw
    Abilene

d   **Leos Carax**
sc **Leos Carax**
ph **Jean-Yves Éscoffier**
m   **Jacques Pinault**
    Denis Lavant, Mireille Périer, Carroll
    Brooks, Elie Poicard, Anna Baldaccini

After breaking up with Florence (Baldaccini), the rootless Alex (Lavant), obsessed with a need for romantic fulfilment, falls in love with Mireille (Périer), but their attachment is doomed to fail. With his first feature, 22-year-old Carax joined Jean-Jacques Beineix, another precocious director, as one of France's brightest hopes. Shot in dazzling black and white in nocturnal Paris, and with the strange brooding personality of Denis Lavant (he plays the same role in Carax's second film *The Night Is Young*, 1986), the film, though hugely derivative – especially of early Godard – shows great promise. The appropriately simple title (the original given in English) reveals both the lack of plot and a nice sense of irony.

The Boys From Fengkuei

▶ **aka All The Youthful Days**

▶ **Feng-Kuei-Lai-Te jen**

Taiwan 1983 104 mins col
Evergreen Film Company

d **Hou Hsiao-hsien**
sc **Zhu Tianwen**
ph **Chen Kunhou**
m **Bach, Vivaldi**
   Niu Cheng-tse, Lin Xiuling, To Tsung-hua, Chang Shih

Three youths leave the small fishing village of Fengkuei, where they have grown up, to look for a more exciting life in the city of Kaohsiung. With no idea of what to expect and no sense of responsibility, they embrace all the experiences, both joyful and painful, that come their way, earning a living doing menial jobs in an export processing plant. This film, which would automatically be referred to as a rites-of-passage piece in the West, demonstrates a coming of age in the Taiwanese film industry. The exuberant and sincere central performances convince and involve, and the piece has an altogether more modern and universal approach than Taiwanese movies of a few years before. It is enjoyable, interesting and directed with sophistication by a director making his fourth feature.

▶ **Boys' School** see Disparus De St-Agil, Les

▶ **Božská Ema** see Divine Emma, The

The Branches Of The Tree

▶ **Shakha Proshakha**

India 1990 120 mins col
Erato Films/DD Productions/Soprofilms

d **Satyajit Ray**
sc **Satyajit Ray**
ph **Sandip Ray**
m **Satyajit Ray**
   Ajit Banerjee, Soumitra Chatterjee, Maradan Banerjee, Lily Charraborty, Deepankar De, Mamata Shankar, Ranjit Malik

Ananda Majunda (Ajit Banerjee), elderly widower and substantial public dignitary, is honoured on his seventieth birthday by the town which has been renamed after him. A man of the highest moral ethics and a belief in the essential necessity and dignity of work, he has four sons; three of them, all successful businessmen, live some distance away; the fourth, Proshanto (Chatterjee), once the most brilliantly gifted, sustained brain damage in an accident while studying in London and now, middle-aged, lives at home, depressive, mentally unstable and lost in his passion for classical music. When Ananda suffers a heart attack, the other sons, their wives and the one grandchild, arrive to stay in the house, which is also home to their senile grandfather. Confined, restless and thrown too close for comfort, the visitors reveal the cracks beneath the surface of their seemingly successful lives. Once again pursuing moral and intellectual themes, the veteran Ray makes perhaps his most challenging and complex film about human relationships, and about the creeping corruption endemic to late 20th-century society. The surface is simple, the contradictions simmering beneath it fraught with confusion, betrayal and human weakness. As in most of this director's work, there is a perceptive observation of human foibles, such control of the essential nuances and superb actors brilliantly cast. As a comment on the universal problems of life, particularly as they bear on the educated but materially ambitious middle classes, *Branches Of The Tree* is a salutary work. Ray both understands and chastises his characters, punctures their pomposity and identifies the imperfections in the father's well-intentioned moral rectitude. Most painful is the abyss that appears between ethics and compassion, forcefully demonstrated by the family's embarrassed disregard for the grandfather and their lack of effort to understand their damaged brother. This outstanding film was entirely financed by the French, Ray's greatest admirers, and co-produced by Gérard Depardieu.

▶ **Bratya Karamazovy** see Brothers Karamazov, The

▶ **Brave Soldat Schwejk, Der** see Good Soldier Schweik, The

Bread And Chocolate

▶ **Pane E Cioccolata**

Italy 1974 112 mins col
Verona Cinematografica

d Franco Brusati
sc Franco Brusati, Iaia Fiastri, Nino
Manfredi
ph Luciano Tovoli
m Daniele Patrucchi
Nino Manfredi, Anna Karina, Johnny
Dorelli, Paolo Turco

An uneducated working man (Manfredi) from
Naples gets a job as a waiter at a smart hotel
in Switzerland, but is arrested as an illegal
immigrant, and accused of indecent exposure
and murder. An amusing and touching illustration of a culture clash, and a graphic
depiction of a complacent and condescending
Switzerland, occasionally ruined by too much
sugar in the mixture.

Bread, Love, And Dreams

▶ **Pane, Amore, E Fantasia**

Italy 1953 90 mins bw
Titanus

d Luigi Comencini
sc Luigi Comencini
ph Arturo Gallea
m Alessandro Cicognini
Vittorio De Sica, Gina Lollobrigida,
Marisa Merlini, Roberto Risso

In a small rural village, the new sergeant of
police (De Sica), hoping to get married, chases
the midwife (Merlini) and the local spitfire
(Lollobrigida), who is in love with his deputy
(Risso). In the early 1950s this fast-moving
comedy seemed awfully saucy and elemental,
but now comes across as tame and artificial.
De Sica is amusing enough though, and the
film brought La Lollo to the world's attention. Being the top Italian money-maker up
to that time, it naturally engendered a sequel,
Bread, Love And Jealousy (1954), with the
same director and cast.

Bread, Love And Jealousy

▶ **Pane, Amore E Gelosia**

Italy 1954 98 mins bw

Titanus

d Luigi Comencini
sc Luigi Comencini, Vincenzo Talarico,
Ettore Margadonna
ph Carlo Montuori
m Alessandro Cicognini
Gina Lollobrigida, Vittorio De Sica,
Marisa Merlini, Roberto Risso

In a mountain village, the engagements of the
police sergeant (De Sica) to the midwife (Merlini), and that of the local beauty (Lollobrigida) to the sergeant's deputy (Risso) are
endangered by gossiping and suspicious neighbours. Partners are switched, an unknown
father turns up, and one of the women lands
in jail. A mildly amusing, likeable and well-
observed follow-up to *Bread, Love, And Dreams* has some lively playing by 'La Lollo' and
De Sica. More *Bread, Love...* films ensued, but
they got less and less nourishing.

▶ **Breakup, The** see Rupture, La

Breathless

▶ **À Bout De Souffle**

France 1960 90 mins bw
SNC

d Jean-Luc Godard
sc Jean-Luc Godard
ph Raoul Coutard
m Martial Solal
Jean-Paul Belmondo, Jean Seberg, Daniel
Boulanger, Jean-Pierre Melville

A young car thief kills a policeman and goes
on the run with his American girlfriend. Godard's first feature, from an idea by François
Truffaut and dedicated to Monogram Pictures
(Hollywood's all-B movie studio), attempted
to recapture the directness and economy of
the American gangster movie. This was
superbly achieved by the use of a handheld
camera, often with the cameraman in a
wheelchair, location shooting, and jump cuts
which eliminated the usual establishing shots
so that the film lives up to its title. This
greatly influential picture made the anarchic
Belmondo a star, revitalized Seberg's career,
and established Godard as a leading member
of the *Nouvelle Vague*.

Best Director Berlin 1960

▶ **Brennende Acker, Der** see Burning Earth, The

▶ **Breve Vacanza, Una** see Brief Vacation, A

The Bride Wore Black

▶ **La Mariée Était En Noir**

France 1967 107 mins col
Films Du Carrosse/Artistes Associés/De Laurentiis

d François Truffaut
sc François Truffaut, Jean-Louis Richard
ph Raoul Coutard
m Bernard Herrmann
   Jeanne Moreau, Jean-Claude Brialy, Michel Bouquet, Charles Denner, Claude Rich, Michel Lonsdale, Daniel Boulanger

After a bridegroom is shot on the steps of the church on his wedding day, his widow (Moreau) traces the group of men responsible and eliminates them one by one. Truffaut's most direct homage to Hitchcock was based, like *Rear Window*, on a novel by William Irish (Cornell Woolrich), and uses Hitch's frequent and distinctive composer, Bernard Herrmann. The result is slacker, more episodic and far more implausible than the Master would have allowed but still highly entertaining in itself. The glossy locales and splendid cameos from the victims give sturdy support to Moreau's intelligent performance as a meticulous avenging angel.

The Bridge

▶ **Die Brücke**

W. Germany 1959 106 mins bw
Fono/Jochen Severin

d Bernhard Wicki
sc Michael Mansfield, Karl-Wilhelm Vivier
ph Gerd Von Bönen
m Hans-Martin Majewski
   Volker Bohnet, Fritz Wepper, Franz Glaubrecht, Karl Michael Balzer, Günther Hoffman

In 1945, two days before the end of the war, seven schoolboys are drafted into the dregs of Hitler's army to defend an unimportant bridge against American tanks, which they do to the death. This powerful anti-war film, made in a semi-documentary style, was based on a true episode. One of the few good movies to come out of Germany in the 1950s, it was nominated for an Oscar.

▶ **Brief Encounters** see Short Encounters

A Brief Vacation

▶ **Una Breve Vacanza**

Italy 1973 106 mins col
Verona/Azor

d Vittorio De Sica
sc Cesare Zavattini
ph Giulio Battiferri
m Manuel De Sica
   Florinda Bolkan, Renato Salvatori, Daniel Quenaud, José Maria Prada, Teresa Gimpera

A Milanese factory worker (Bolkan), leading a squalid life with her macho husband (Salvatori) and children, contracts a lung disease and is sent to a sanatorium in the Alps. There she leads a happier life and discovers her true worth. Based on Apollinaire's epigram that 'sickness is the vacation of the poor,' De Sica's penultimate film reveals the deep humanist values which permeate most of his work. With Zavattini, his collaborator from way back, a gorgeous alpine setting and fine performances, especially from Bolkan, and allowing for some soap operatics, it is an appealing film with an effective feminist message.

Brightness

▶ **Yeelen**

Mali 1987 105 mins col
Les Films Cissé/Government of Mali

d Souleymane Cissé
sc Souleymane Cissé
ph Jean-Noël Ferragut, Jean-Michel Humeau
m Michel Portal, Salif Keita
   Issiaka Kané, Aova Sangere, Niamanto Sanogo, Soumba Traoré, Ismaíla Sarr, Balla Moussa Keïta

A young man (Kané), granted special magical powers, flees his jealous father (Sanogo) who plans to kill him. During the journey, the boy gains the wisdom with which to confront his father. A remarkably strange and beautiful film which draws us into the world of African ritual and legend. Some of the symbols might be obscure for those outside the culture, but there's no discounting their visual power. The performances, particularly that of the extremely handsome hero, are uniformly mesmeric.

▶ **Brink Of Life** see So Close To Life

▶ **Broken Commandment, The** see Sin, The

Broken Mirrors

▶ **Gebroken Spiegels**

Netherlands   1984   116 mins   col
Sigma Films

d   **Marleen Gorris**
sc **Marleen Gorris**
ph **Frans Bromet**
m   **Lodewijk De Boer, and an extract from Haydn's** *Stabat Mater*
      Lineke Rijxman, Henriette Tol, Edda Barends, Coby Stunnenberg, Anke Van't Hoff, Eddy Brugman

A sadistic killer kidnaps women and dumps their corpses on waste ground. In the Happy House brothel, presided over by a madame who keeps a gun, the women are united in their dislike of their work and their low opinion of men. This is, of necessity, a summary of the bare bones of a complex plot which focuses on certain relationships with absolute clarity, and whose parallel strands meet for the denouement. Using some of the same cast and the cameraman from *A Question Of Silence* made two years previously, writer-director Gorris here displays the same gifts of control and commitment, developed with intelligence and efficiency to create an absorbing and disturbing film. However, unlike its predecessor, this one is strident in its feminist message, transmitting violent and indiscriminate anti-male attitudes which, ultimately, undermine its own case and leave the viewer depressed rather than encouraged.

▶ **Bronenosets Potemkin** see Battleship Potemkin, The

The Brontë Sisters

▶ **Les Soeurs Brontë**

France   1979   115 mins   col
Gaumont

d   **André Téchiné**
sc **André Téchiné, Pascal Bonitzer, Jean Gruault**
ph **Bruno Nuytten**
m   **Philippe Sarde**
      Isabelle Adjani, Isabelle Huppert, Marie-France Pisier, Pascal Greggory, Patrick Magee

Emily (Adjani), Charlotte (Pisier) and Anne (Huppert) lead an isolated, claustrophobic life at the Haworth rectory in Yorkshire with their father (Magee) and brother Branwell (Greggory). Tragedy occurs when the latter, after a doomed affair with an older woman, turns to drink and drugs before dying at the age of 31. The decision to concentrate the plot around the sisters' relationship with their spoiled-genius brother would seem one way of avoiding the difficulties of presenting the tormented trio of writers on screen. Not so. The sluggish direction, and the almost caricature notion of what the Brontës were about – Emily spends her time stalking the moors in drag – cancel out the careful re-creation of period. The only interest comes from seeing three of France's most talented young actresses together. Lovers of kitsch are better advised to see the Hollywood version of 1946 called *Devotion*.

▶ **Brot Des Bäckers, Das** see Baker's Bread

A Brother And His Younger Sister

▶ **Ani To Song Imoto**

Japan   1939   100 mins   bw
Shochiku

d   **Yasujiro Shimazu**
sc **Yasujiro Shimazu**

ph **Toshio Ubukata**
m **Hikaru Saotome**
   **Shin Saburi, Michiko Kuwano, Kuniko
   Miyake, Ken Uehara**

The unmarried sister (Kuwano) of an office worker (Saburi) turns down a marriage proposal from the nephew (Uehara) of her brother's boss. She thinks that acceptance might damage her brother's prospects of promotion as the company is opposed to nepotism. Shimazu is considered the father of the 'home dramas' perfected by Ozu, Naruse and his pupil Gosho, and this typical drama of ordinary people is one of the best – and last – examples of his work in the genre. The rigidly conventional characters are not given much depth, but the small details of their domestic lives are carefully and lovingly drawn and the subtle shifts in mood give the narrative variety.

The Brothers Karamazov

▶ **aka The Murder Of Dmitri
   Karamazov**

▶ **Bratya Karamazovy**

   USSR   1968   220 mins   col
   Mosfilm

d **Ivan Pyriev**
sc **Ivan Pyriev**
ph **Sergei Vronsky**
m **Isaac Schwartz**
   **Mikhail Ulianov, Lionella Pyrieva, Kirill
   Lavrov, Andrei Myahkov, Marc Prudkin**

The effect of the murder of a dominating father on the lives of his three sons: the hedonistic Dmitri (Ulianov), the sceptical intellectual Ivan (Lavrov) and the devout Alyosha (Myahkov). Pyriev did not live to see the completion of his Dostoyevsky trilogy after *The Idiot* and *White Nights*, because he died during the making of this handsomely-mounted, extremely faithful (almost too much so) wide-screen adaptation of the great 19th-century novel, which had been filmed rather broadly 10 years before in Hollywood. It was completed by Ulianov and Lavrov, who both gave powerful performances. The film, released in the USA, was Oscar-nominated.

▶ **Brücke, Die** see Bridge, The

▶ **Bruno, L'Enfant Du Dimanche** see
Bruno – Sunday's Child

Bruno – Sunday's Child

▶ **Bruno, L'Enfant Du Dimanche**

   France   1968   90 mins   col
   Pro-Gé-Fi/Consortium Pathé/ Sirius
   (Paris)/Arthur Mathonet (Brussels)

d **Louis Grospierre**
sc **Alain Quercy, Louis Grospierre**
ph **Quinto Albicocco**
m **Jean-Pierre Bourtayre**
   **Christian Mesnier, Roger Hanin, Lena
   Skerla, Francine Bergé, Mary Marquet**

Thirteen-year-old Bruno (Mesnier), whose parents' divorce is about to come through, sees his father (Hanin), whom he adores, one Sunday in each month but, during the August holidays, they spend a long weekend together in Belgium. This is a very slight but touching film about a father-son relationship which sensitively delineates the problems each faces in their difficult situation. Careful direction avoids the pitfall of cloying sentiment, Hanin's performance is beautifully judged, and the Bruges locations are pleasing.

Brussels-Transit

▶ **Bruxelles-Transit**

   Belgium   1980   90 mins   bw
   Paradise Films

d **Samy Szlingerbaum**
sc **Samy Szlingerbaum**
ph **Michel Houssiau**
   **Hélène Lapiower, Boris Lehman, Jeremy
   and Micha Wald**

Malka Szlingerbaum (Lapiower), the director's mother, tells the story of her post-war journey from Poland to Belgium with her husband (Lehman) and of the struggles to make a new life for themselves. The first Yiddish feature since 1961 is also probably the first Yiddish experimental film. Samy Szlingerbaum commented that 'the film has two themes – on the one hand the way my mother remembers it, and on the other hand the way I remember my mother's stories'. Using voice-over narration, still photographs and long takes, set against a series of static compositions, this restrained and economical work manages to re-create the pain of displacement.

The Brute

▶ **El Bruto**

Mexico 1952 93 mins bw
Internacione Cinematografica

d **Luis Buñuel**
sc **Luis Buñuel, Luis Alcoriza**
ph **Agustín Jiménez**
m **Raúl Lavista**
Pedro Armendariz, Katy Jurado, Andrés Soler, Rosita Arenas

A simple-minded slaughterhouse worker (Armendáriz), employed by a decadent landowner (Soler) to scare his tenants, becomes the lover of his boss's wife (Jurado). Her jealousy is aroused when she finds out he has seduced the daughter (Arenas) of one of his victims. Shot in just 18 days, it 'could have been a good film..., but I was forced to change it completely'. Despite Buñuel's stricture, the film has a smouldering power and stifling atmosphere, and the theme of sexual passion balanced by gentle love breaks through the conventions of the plot.

▶ **Bruto, El** see Brute, The

▶ **Brutti, Sporchi E Cattivi** see Down And Dirty

▶ **Bruxelles-Transit** see Brussels-Transit

▶ **Brzezina** see Birch Wood, The

▶ **Büchse Der Pandora, Die** see Pandora's Box

▶ **Budapesti Měsěk** see Budapest Tales

Budapest Tales

▶ **Budapesti Měsěk**

Hungary 1976 91 mins col
Hunnia Studio

d **István Szabó**
sc **István Szabó**
ph **Sándor Sára**

m **Zdenkó Tamássy**
Maja Komorowska, Agi Mészáros, Ildiko Bánsági, András Bálint, Franciszek Piecza, Karoly Kováks

In the last days of World War II, a group of soldiers, civilians, and refugees take shelter in an abandoned streetcar by a riverbank. They decide to put it in working order and set off together to Budapest. Friendships, love affairs, and conflicts develop along the way. Szabó's fifth film in 12 years is plainly (but not so simply) an allegory of modern Hungarian history. The passengers on this streetcar named Hungary are representatives of a variety of opinions and obsessions, which they express in monologues to camera from time to time. Overloaded with symbols as the vehicle is while moving on its ponderous way, the film does raise some important questions and there are moments of genuine emotion and amusement.

Buffet Froid

▶ **(US: Cold Cuts)**

France 1979 93 mins col
Sara/Antenne 2

d **Bertrand Blier**
sc **Bertrand Blier**
ph **Jean Penzer**
m **Brahms**
Bernard Blier, Gérard Depardieu, Michel Serrault, Geneviève Page, Jean Carmet

A layabout (Depardieu) who lives in a deserted tower block is suspected by a crooked police inspector (Blier) of being the killer of an unknown man (Serrault) – only the first in a number of murder victims. Blier *fils* puts his father through his paces in this buffet of leftovers from better black comedies and droppings from Buñuel. None of the characters is convincing, even within the artificial conventions of the genre, and the director's notorious bad taste fails to shock this time.

▶ **Buraikan** see Scandalous Adventures Of Buraikan, The

Burglar

▶ **Vzlomshchik**

USSR 1987 89 mins col
Lenfilm

d   Valery Ogorodnikov
sc Valery Priyomykhov
ph Valery Mironov
m   Viktor Kisin
    Oleg Elykomov, Konstantin Kinchev, Yuri
    Tsapnik, Svetlana Gaitan, Polina
    Petrenko

Senka (Elykomov), who plays in a classical
boys' band, lives with his heavy-drinking
widowed father and his brother Kostya (Kin-
chev) who is a rock band singer. When Kostya
and his friends plan to steal a synthesizer
from the community centre where they perform, Senka warns the organizers of the place.
They take no notice, so he steals it himself,
but confesses when the police appear. This is
director Ogorodnikov's first feature, but it is
technically and visually sure of itself. The
focus on youth in the *glasnost* era adds to the
increasingly varied subject matter of Russian
films that are being shown in the West,
although this one doesn't seem too sure of its
themes which seem to muddle private and
public issues. Not great, but certainly interesting.

The Burmese Harp

▶ **(US: Harp Of Burma)**
▶ **Biruma No Tategoto**

    Japan 1956 116 mins bw
    Nikkatsu

d   Kon Ichikawa
sc Natto Wada
ph Minoru Yokoyama
m   Akira Ifukube
    Shoji Yasui, Rentaro Mikuni, Tatsuya
    Mihashi

A young soldier-musician (Yasui), in Burma
at the time of the Japanese capitulation, takes
on the role of a Buddhist priest and tries to
bury as many bodies as he can. Ichikawa's
first film to explore what he termed 'the pain
of the age', is a non-naturalistic odyssey in
visionary black and white images throbbing
with the anguish that war brings. Scripted by
the director's wife, it was one of the first of
a number of Japanese films concerned with
pacifist themes related to the defeat of Japan
in 1945.

Burning Angel

▶ **Palava Enkeli**

    Finland 1984 105 mins col
    Skandia Filmi

d   Lauri Törhönen
sc Claes Andersson, Hannele Törrönen,
    Lauri Törhönen
ph Esa Vuorinen
m   Hector
    Riita Viiperi, Tom Wentzel, Eeva
    Eloranta, Juuso Hirvikangas, Elina
    Hurme

Tuulikki (Viiperi), a newly graduated nurse,
takes up her first post which is in a mental
hospital. Inexperienced, and shocked at what
she sees, she is nonetheless assigned the special
care of a violent and pyromaniac patient
(Eloranta) to whom she dedicates herself. It
is a losing battle, fought while having to cope
with staff tensions and the sexual advances
of the doctors, with one of whom (Wentzel)
she has an unhappy affair. Apparently based
on the true case of a young Finnish psychiatric
nurse who cracked up, Törhönen's film is a
skilful and quite horrifying dissection of prevailing attitudes in Finnish mental asylums
which, alas, do not seem too different from
those elsewhere. Although depressing and
critical, the piece is leavened with humour,
thus managing to entertain, much as *One
Flew Over The Cuckoo's Nest* did. Viiperi,
making her debut, is impressive and, if the
film is a little over the top at times, it is
nevertheless compelling.

The Burning Earth

▶ **Der Brennende Acker**

    Germany 1922 80 mins bw
    Goron-Deulig Exklusiv Film

d   F.W. Murnau
sc Willy Haas, Thea Von Harbou, Arthur
    Rosen
ph Karl Freund, Fritz Arno Wagner
m   Silent
    Werner Krauss, Eugen Klöpfer, Wladimir
    Gaidarow, Eduard Von Winterstein, Stella
    Arbenina, Lya De Putti

An old peasant dies, leaving his farm to his
two sons. One of them, Johannes (Gaidarow),
determined to rise in the world, obtains a

post as secretary to a Count whose young wife, Helga (Arbenina), and daughter by a previous marriage (De Putti) both fall in love with him. When the Count dies Johannes, in order to get his hands on a piece of oil-rich land, marries Helga, thus setting in motion a train of misery, destruction and death. Murnau directs with a subtle and penetrating observation of human behaviour but it is, above all, for its visual quality that the film was acclaimed as a masterpiece by critics at the time: the brilliantly well-utilized deep-focus photography that captures the rustic harmony of the peasant farm interiors contrasted with the airy and elegant castle; the bleak snowbound winter landscape in opposition to the dramatic burning of the oil well. Alas and alack, much of the film is lost and the surviving reels have deteriorated in quality and are seldom shown. They are worth looking out for, however, since they belong to the *oeuvre* of a cinematic genius.

Burning Patience

▶ **Ardiente Paciencia**

Portugal 1983 79 mins col
Von Veitinghoff Filmproduktion/Prole Film/ZDF

d **Antonio Skarmeta**
sc **Antonio Skarmeta**
ph **João Abel Aboim**
m **Roberto Lecaros**
   Oscar Castro, Roberto Parada, Marcela Osorio, Naldy Hernandez

The great Chilean poet Pablo Neruda (Parada, a striking resemblance), living in Isla Negra, a seaside village, is the best customer of the young postman Mario (Castro) because the Nobel prize-winner gets mail from all over the world. Neruda helps and advises Mario in his courtship of Beatriz (Osorio), the local innkeeper's daughter, and the young man wins her hand by quoting from Neruda's love poems, passing them off as his own. This delightful poetic tale of an unlikely relationship, shot in Portugal by the Berlin-based director with a cast of other Chilean exiles, is warmly and humorously played, and directed with an undercurrent of the tragic circumstances to come. The wise and witty script subtly suggests the political events in the background and the film ends with the overthrow of Allende and the death of the poet soon after the coup in 1973. Unfortunately, at 79 minutes, the narrative is too compressed to allow the film to delve more expansively and deeply.

Bushido

▶ **Bushido Zankoku Monogatari**

Japan 1963 123 mins bw
Toei

d **Tadashi Imai**
sc **Naoyuki Suzuki**
ph **Makoto Tsuboi**
m **Toshiro Mayuzumi**
   Kinnosuke Nakamura, Masayuki Mori, Kyoko Kishida, Yoshiko Mita, Ineko Arima

An episodic tale, ranging over 300 years of history and demonstrating the consequences of 'bushido', the code of obedience to the feudal lord, as it affected one family. Imai's notion of exposing the brutal underbelly of honorable tradition is a fascinating departure for the Japanese cinema. Unfortunately, he fails to probe the history and moral conflicts of his subject, presenting instead an almost unrelieved excess of cruelty horrible to behold – beheadings, disembowellings, and the like. The film lacks narrative fluency and emotional drive, but is very well made and obviously seriously intentioned.

Best Film Berlin 1963

▶ **Bushido Zankoku Monogatari** see Bushido

Bus Number Three

▶ **Xiaozi Bei**

China 1980 90 mins col
Changchun Film Studio

d **Wang Jiayi, Luo Tai**
sc **Si Minsan, Zhou Yang, Wu Benwu, Sun Xionfei**
ph **Wu Guojiang**
m **Lei Zhengbang**
   Chen Yixin, Chi Zhiqiang, Wang Weiping, Yu Yangping

The events that take place on a city bus taken daily by workers, students, intellectuals, housewives and schoolchildren are depicted, and the lives of the two conductors, a hardworking young woman (Yixin) and an impatient and lazy man (Zhiqiang) are contrasted. The film's quirky humour, gentle romance and youthful vitality have plenty of appeal for the 'younger generation', the meaning of the Chinese title. This charming, episodic comedy, a departure for this country's film-makers in that it stresses individual achievement, gives a detailed picture of everyday life in modern China.

▶ **Buta To Gunkan** see Pigs And Battleships

The Butcher

▶ **Le Boucher**

France 1969 94 mins col
La Boetie/Euro International

d **Claude Chabrol**
sc **Claude Chabrol**
ph **Jean Rabier**
m **Pierre Jansen**
Stéphane Audran, Jean Yanne, Antonio Passalia, Mario Beccaria

Hélène (Audran), a schoolmistress in a small Périgord town, is courted by Popaul (Yanne), the shy local butcher who turns out to be a sex murderer. On the surface a thriller in the Hitchcock mode – the discovery of a mutilated body by a group of schoolchildren, and Hélène's awareness of Popaul's guilt while alone with him – the film is more of a subtle, compassionate psychological study of sexual frustration. The two leads are superb, supported by local people playing themselves.

Bwana Toshi

▶ **aka The Song of Bwana Toshi**

▶ **Bwana Toshi No Uta**

Japan 1965 115 mins col
Toho

d **Susumu Hani**
sc **Susumu Hani, Kunio Shimizu**
ph **Manji Kanau**
m **Tohru Takemitsu**

Kivoshi Atsumi, Hamisi Salehe, Tsutomu Shimomoto

A large firm sends one of its employees (Atsumi) to the wilds of Tanzania to prepare for the arrival of his company by getting houses built. At first wary and uncomprehending of each other, the Japanese and the Africans eventually come to understand each other's cultures and to learn from them. Hani, who made documentaries of African wildlife for Japanese TV, approaches the serio-comic tale without any condescension or sentimentality. The film is unusual, entertaining and doubly exotic (for Western audiences), while serving its humanistic message.

▶ **Bwana Toshi No Uta** see Bwana Toshi

Bye Bye Brazil

Brazil 1979 110 mins col
Carnaval Films/Aries Cinematografica/Gaumont (France)

d **Carlos Diegues**
sc **Carlos Diegues**
ph **Lauro Escorel Filho**
m **Chico Buarque, Roberto Menescal, Dominguinhos**
José Wilker, Betty Faria, Fabio Junior, Zaira Zambelli, Principe Nabor

The adventures of a tatty group of travelling players as they cross the vast North of Brazil. The troupe consists of a black strongman (Nabor), Salome (Faria) 'Queen of the Rhumba', and her lover Lord Cigano (Wilker), a magician. But wherever they go, even in the Amazon jungle, they find people prefer to watch TV rather than come to see them. Diegues, one of the leading lights in the *Cinema Novo* movement, uses the flamboyant performers and their garish show to comment, in a witty and equally flamboyant and garish manner, on what 'progress' has done to his country. The use of popular music from the States and an eye for the vulgar fetishes of the population – nightclubs, discos, portable radios and TV – give the film a satiric edge, as well as making a sad and pointed statement on the destruction of the culture of the Indians.

▶ **Byeleyet Parus Odinoky** see Lone White Sail

▶ **By Rocket To The Moon** see Woman In The Moon, The

By The Blood Of Others

▶ **Par Le Sang Des Autres**

France 1973 95 mins col
Kangourou Films/Les Films La
Boétie(Paris)/Merona
Produzione(Rome)/Cinévideo(Montreal)

d Marc Simenon
sc Jean Max
ph René Verzier
m Francis Lai
   Mariangela Melato, Yves Beneyton,
   Bernard Blier, Charles Vanel, Mylène
   Demongeot, Claude Piéplu

A young mental patient (Beneyton) in rural France brutally kidnaps a woman and her daughter and holds them hostage, demanding as his price for their release the company of the most beautiful girl in the nearby village. The local mayor, the prefect, the police chief, the doctor and the priest become involved in seeking a solution. Simenon, son of Maigret's creator Georges, delivers a proficient film dealing in a subject appropriate to the late 20th century. Sadly, however, neither the excellent cast (an incidental pleasure is a brief appearance by Demongeot, who co-produced the film) nor the basically interesting situation can triumph over a screenplay that quickly slides into predictability.

By The Bluest Of Seas

▶ **U Samovo Sinyevo Morya**

USSR 1936 1309 metres bw
Mezhrabpomfilm/Azerfilm

d Boris Barnet
sc K. Mints

ph M. Kirillov
m S. Pototski
   Elena Kouzmina, Lev Sverdline, Nikolai
   Krioutchkov, S. Svachenko, V. Sateieva

Two young Caspian fisherman (Sverdline and Krioutchkov) are shipwrecked on an island where they fall in love with the same bouncy girl (Kouzmina), who rejects them both. The blithest of Barnet comedies blissfully breaks the bonds of the studio by being filmed at a marine location. The players, particularly the delicious Kouzmina, and the director communicate the enjoyment they obviously had making it. Sadly, Barnet never again recaptured the spontaneity and joy of his pre-war films. He committed suicide in 1965.

By The Law

▶ **aka Dura Lex**

▶ **Po Zakonu**

USSR 1926 83 mins bw
Goskino

d Lev Kuleshov
sc Lev Kuleshov, Viktor Shklovsky
ph Konstantin Kuznetsov
m Silent
   Sergei Komarov, Alexandra Khokhlova,
   Vladimir Fogel, Pyotr Galadzhev, Porfiri
   Podobed

Five gold prospectors in the Yukon are isolated in a hut by storms and floods. One of them, an Irishman, goes berserk and kills two of the men. The remaining man is prevented by his wife from exacting instant retribution. 'It must be done by the law,' she says. They conduct a trial, find the Irishman guilty and hang him from a solitary tree. Based on Jack London's story The Unexpected, this strangely hypnotic work is divided into five 'acts', moving through a range of moods to the tense and bitter climax. At the centre is the riveting, stylized performance from Kuleshov's wife, Alexandra Khokhlova.

The Cabinet Of Dr Caligari

▶ **Das Kabinett Des Dr Caligari**

Germany 1919 73 mins bw
Decla-Bioskop

d **Robert Wiene**
sc **Carl Mayer, Hans Janowitz**
ph **Willy Hameister**
m **Silent**
Werner Krauss, Conrad Veidt, Friedrich Fehér, Lil Dagover, Hans Heinz Von Twardowski, Rudolf Lettinger

Caligari (Krauss), a fairground showman, hypnotizes his servant (Veidt) into committing murder at night and carrying off the girlfriend (Dagover) of the young hero (Fehér). The surprise ending enters the mind of a madman. Considered to be the first true example of Expressionism in the cinema, it was a great influence on German films for the next decade and on horror films in general. It has its risible moments today, but the weird and distorted sets (Walter Röhrig, Hermann Warm and Walter Reimann) and grotesquely angled photography still create a potent nightmarish atmosphere. In 1985, a print was shown that restored the colour tinting, original German intertitles and additional scenes.

Cabiria

Italy 1914 180 mins bw
Itala

d **Giovanni Pastrone**
sc **Giovanni Pastrone**
ph **Segundo De Chomon, Giovanni Tomatis, Augusto Batagliotti, Natale Chiusano**
m **Silent**
Italia Almirante Manzini, Lidia

Quaranta, Umberto Mozzato, Bartolomeo Pagano

The many adventures of the Sicilian slave girl Cabiria (Quaranta) with Maciste (Pagano), her strongman companion, and her love for Fulvio (Mozzato), a Roman, during the Second Punic War. The most expensive, the most spectacular and the longest film up to that date (even when generally shown less 32 mins), took over six months to shoot and contained technical innovations, such as dolly and crane shots and lighting from below. It was the first motion picture to merit a complete review in the Italian press, and its great success in America, where it opened the new Astor theatre, inspired D.W. Griffith to embark on his large-scale productions and influenced the Babylonian sequence in *Intolerance*. Yet Pastrone (working under the pseudonym of Piero Fosco) remained unknown for many years because the film publicized the name of Gabriele D'Annunzio, the most famous Italian writer of the day, who only wrote the intertitles.

▶ **Caccia Tragica** see Tragic Pursuit, The

▶ **Cadaveri Eccellenti** see Illustrious Corpses

▶ **Caduta Degli Dei, La** see Damned, The

La Cage Aux Folles

▶ **aka Birds Of A Feather**

France 1978 109 mins col
Les Productions Artistes Associés/DaMa Produzione

d   Edouard Molinaro
sc Marcello Danon, Edouard Molinaro,
    Francis Véber, Jean Poiret
ph Armando Nannuzzi
m   Ennio Morricone
    Ugo Tognazzi, Michel Serrault, Rémy
    Laurent, Claire Maurier, Benny Luke

Renato (Tognazzi) and Albin (Serrault) own
'La Cage Aux Folles', a nightclub where
Albin is the star drag queen. The two men,
lovers for 20 years, have brought up Renato's
son, the product of a fleeting heterosexual
liaison. The boy now wishes to marry, and
all hell breaks loose in the attempts to conceal
his background from his strait-laced future
in-laws. An old-fashioned bedroom farce with
a new angle, the movie is extremely funny,
and the relationship between Renato and
Albin is touching, thanks largely to the
accomplished acting of the two leads, particularly an outrageous Serrault. Originally a
long-running French play and, later, a successful Broadway musical, the film grossed a
fortune and gathered three Oscar nominations. However, the rush to cash in on its
success led to two progressively awful sequels,
La Cage Aux Folles II (1980) and *La Cage
Aux Folles III* (1985), with the same stars.

▶ **Cage Aux Rossignols, La** see Cage
Of Nightingales, A

Caged

▶ **(US: And The Wild Wild
Women)**

▶ **Nella Citta L'Inferno**

    Italy 1958 110 mins bw
    Riama Prod/Francinex

d   Renato Castellani
sc Renato Castellani
ph Leonida Barboni
m   Roman Vlad
    Anna Magnani, Giulietta Masina,
    Myriam Bru, Cristina Gajoni

The relationship in prison between an old
timer and a younger, inexperienced woman is
soon corrupted by their *milieu*. A film that
brings Magnani and Masina together in a
small space cannot be all bad, but this comes
close. They give good imitations of themselves

and then swop roles in this aimless and false
prison drama, punctuated by plenty of shouting and hysterics.

A Cage Of Nightingales

▶ **La Cage Aux Rossignols**

    France 1947 78 mins bw
    Gaumont

d   Jean Dréville
sc Noël-Noël, René Wheeler
ph Paul Cotteret
m   Paul Cloërec
    Noël-Noël, Micheline Francey, Georges
    Biscot, René Genin, Marguerite Ducouret

A drama with music in which an ex-reform
school boy (Noël-Noël) writes a novel based
on his experiences, and earns a living working
for a toy manufacturer while doing so. When
the novel is published, his girlfriend reads it
and, through her eyes, we see his story in
flashback. An unusual little film which offers
an adept mixture of past and present, together
with a realistic and sympathetic view of delinquent youth.

▶ **Caida, La** see Fall, The

▶ **Cairo: Central Station** see Cairo
Station

Cairo Station

▶ **aka Cairo: Central Station**

▶ **Bab El Hadid**

    Egypt 1958 95 mins bw
    Gabriel Talhamy

d   Youssef Chahine
sc Abdel Hay Adib, Mohamad Abou Youssef
ph Alvise
m   Fouad El Zahiry
    Farid Chawki, Hind Rostom, Youssef
    Chahine, El Baroudy, Sofia Sarwat,
    Naima Wasfy

Life in, on and around Cairo's teeming central
station, focusing on Quinawi, a poverty-
stricken, crippled newspaper vendor, obsessively and hopelessly in love with the prettiest
lemonade seller. His jealousies and fantasies

fuel his descent into madness and violence. This early film from Egypt's most distinguished director is bursting with ideas and themes – worker exploitation, the corrupting influence of the Coca-Cola culture, the dangers of sexual repression. And that's the trouble. A Neo-Realist approach encloses what is essentially a melodrama, leaving no room to explore these themes and presenting characters drawn in broad, simplistic brush strokes. However, Chahine himself is marvellous as the doomed Quinawi.

Calle Mayor

▶ aka Grande Rue

▶ (US: The Love Maker)

Spain 1956 95 mins bw
Play Art Iberia/Cesario Gonzales

d Juan Antonio Bardem
sc Juan Antonio Bardem
ph Michel Kelber
m Joseph Kosma
Betsy Blair, Yves Massard, René Blancard, Lila Kedrova, José Suarez

In a small Spanish town, a group of gamblers persuades a young stud (Suarez) from Madrid to make love and propose to a plain spinster (Blair) for a bet. But things aren't as simple as they seem. It was during the filming of this uncomfortable comedy-drama that Bardem was arrested and imprisoned on political grounds. He was released after two weeks as a result of an international outcry. The atmosphere of the stultifying town is well caught and so is the portrayal of *machismo*. The problem is the now rather dated view of an unmarried woman, not helped by Betsy Blair's repetition of her Oscar-nominated role in *Marty* the year before.

▶ Camada Negra see Black Brood

Camera Buff

▶ Amator

Poland 1979 112 mins col
Zespoly Filmowe-Film Polski

d Krzysztof Kieslowski
sc Krzysztof Kieslowski, Jerzy Stuhr
ph Jacek Petrycki

m Krzysztof Knittel
Jerzy Stuhr, Malgorzata Zajaczkowska, Ewa Pokas, Krzysztof Zanussi (as himself)

A factory worker (Stuhr) buys a home-movie camera to film his baby, but he becomes the official film-maker to his factory, wins a contest, and comes into conflict with his bosses. This wry satire explored the role and limits of the artist in Polish society, but was slightly blunted by the leading character's almost pathological obsession with his camera.

Camila

Argentina 1984 97 mins col
GEA Cinematografica(Buenos Aires)/Impala(Madrid)

d Maria Luisa Bemberg
sc Maria Luisa Bemberg, Beda Docampo Feijo, Juan Batista Stagnaro
ph Fernando Arribas
m Luis Maria Serra
Susu Pecoraro, Imanol Arias, Héctor Alterio, Elena Tasisto, Carlos Munoz

Camila (Pecoraro), an upper middle-class Catholic from a strict family, falls in love with Ladislao (Arias), a priest, who fights his feelings until he falls ill. The couple run away, outraging family, Church and state, and settle as husband and wife under assumed names in a distant village, but with a warrant out for their arrest. A bare outline fails to do justice to this powerful indictment of repression, set during the vicious dictatorship of De Rosas in 1847. Bemberg exposes the political complicity between Church and state – their cruel destruction of individual freedom – while making a strong feminist case: the ultimate tragedy occurs because Ladislao, not Camila, lacks the strength to defy the rules. Technically, the film is of a high order in all departments, and the director's incisive intelligence neatly avoids the conventions of period melodrama. Bemberg was denied permission to make the film (based on actual events) for several years because of its implied critique of contemporary regimes.

Camille Claudel

France 1988 174 mins col
Films Christian Fechner/Lilith Films/

Gaumont/A2 TV France/DD
Productions

d   **Bruno Nuytten**
sc **Bruno Nuytten, Marilyn Goldin**
ph **Pierre L'Homme**
m   **Gabriel Yared**
    Isabelle Adjani, Gérard Depardieu,
    Laurent Grevill, Alain Cuny, Philippe
    Clevenot, Madeleine Robinson, Katrine
    Boorman, Danielle Lebrun

The great French sculptor Auguste Rodin
(Depardieu) meets Camille Claudel (Adjani)
in Paris in 1883 when she approaches him
to give her lessons. She soon displays her
remarkable artistic talent and becomes his
chief assistant, eventually embarking on a
passionate affair with her master. However,
after Rodin refuses to abandon Rose (Leb-
run), his mistress for 20 years, Camille leaves
him to become her own woman. But the
prejudice of late 19th-century French bourgeois society and of her narrow-minded
mother (Robinson) and younger brother
Paul (Grevill), a Catholic poet and playwright, drives her to drink and madness.
Nearly three hours long, the first film by the
cinematographer of *Jean De Florette* and
Manon Des Sources is a soapy period melodrama set in the world of 'High Art' and
placed in the academic school of film-making. Yet there is much to recommend. The
period, which has been meticulously recreated, is given an added dimension by the
fact of its being a true story. Nuytten shows
the work that goes into sculpting, the artists'
passion for the materials, the way in which
the models have to be dehumanized in order
to humanize the statues, and the agony and
the ecstacy of creation. It is difficult not to
be moved and appalled by the plight of one
of the great 'invisible' female artists, driven
to despair by bourgeois society's double
standards. This resurrection could not have
taken place if the performance of Adjani
had been less riveting. She manages to
suggest the young girl's commitment to
sculpture, the sensuous lover, the indepen-
dently-minded woman, the alcoholic and
depressive. She is matched by Depardieu,
that Rodinesque actor of the French cinema,
less mannered and more restrained than
hitherto. Thanks mainly to this film, Camille
Claudel has finally entered the history of
art. For that alone it must be praised.

Best Actress (Isabelle Adjani) Berlin 1989

▶ **Camille Without Camellias** see
Lady Without Camellias, The

Camminacammina

▶ **aka Keep Walking**

▶ **aka Walking, Walking**

Italy   1983   165 mins   col
RAI

d   **Ermanno Olmi**
sc **Ermanno Olmi**
ph **Ermanno Olmi**
m   **Bruno Nicolai**
    Alberto Fumagalli, Antonio Cucciarre,
    Eligio Martel Lacci, Renzo Samminiatesi,
    Marco Bartolini

A vast caravan of pilgrims goes on a long
trek, following the light in the East in order
to welcome the birth of Christ. This humorous, moving, magical and irreverent re-enact-
ment of the Journey of The Magi is seen as
if through the eyes of children. In fact, it is
they who seem to have a stronger faith than
the querulous and squabbling adults (all
played by non-professionals). The caravan is
made up of ordinary Italian peasants with all
their strengths and weaknesses, giving the
event a believable reality. Olmi, who also
designed the costumes and sets, sees it almost
like a Western wagon train moving to the
promised land.

Camorra: The Naples Connection

▶ **Un Complicato Intrigo Di Donne, Vicoli e Delitti**

Italy   1985   106 mins   col
Cannon Productions/Italian
International

d   **Lina Wertmüller**
sc **Lina Wertmüller, Elvio Porta**
ph **Giuseppe Lanci**
m   **Tony Esposito**
    Angela Molina, Francisco Rabal, Harvey
    Keitel, Daniel Ezralow, Vittorio
    Squillante

A member of the notorious Rocco Family is
shot dead while assaulting Annunziata (Molina), an ex-whore turned Neapolitan hotelier.

The incident implicates Annunziata in a series of violent happenings involving sex, drugs, abduction and death. The film is a hodge-podge of crime and plot complication in the typically overheated style of this director, who offers much gratuitous sensationalism before finally revealing her moral focus – the fight of mothers against drug pushers who exploit and destroy their children. A long title for a long film with little depth.

Camouflage

▶ **Barwy Ochronne**

Poland   1977   100 mins   col
Tor Film Unit

d   **Krzysztof Zanussi**
sc **Tadeusz Wybult, Krzysztof Zanussi,**
ph **Edward Klosínski**
m   **Wojciech Kilar**
Zbigniew Zapasiewicz, Piotr Garlicki, Christine Paul, Marius Dmochowski, Magdalena Zawadska

At a summer seminar for linguistic students held at a country palace, a young, liberal-minded professor (Garlicki) finds himself at odds with an older, cynical colleague (Zapasiewicz) in particular and the whole university establishment in general. As in several previous Zanussi films, the plot unravels against an academic background, but it is really more about bureaucratic pettiness and the crushing of idealism. With his characteristic understatement and intelligence, Zanussi marks out his territory by showing the clash between two generations in a series of penetrating duologues. However, non-Polish speakers will miss certain important nuances.

▶ **Camp De Thiaroye** see Camp Thiaroye

Camp Thiaroye

▶ **Camp De Thiaroye**

Senegal   1988   152 mins   col
SNPC (Dakar)/ENAPROC (Algiers)/SATPEC (Tunis)

d   **Ousmane Sembène, Thierno Faty Sow**
sc **Ousmane Sembène, Thierno Faty Sow**
ph **Ismail Lakhdar Hamina**
m   **Ismaila Lo**
Ibrahima Sane, Sigiri Bakara, Hamed Camara, Ismaila Cissé, Ababacar Sy Cissé

November 1944. A force of black infantrymen from all over French West Africa disembark at Dakar in Senegal prior to repatriation to their countries of origin. They are marched to something little better than a POW camp with cramped living quarters and inedible food. A mutiny takes place, during which they take the French commanding officer hostage, but the camp is bombarded and most of the inmates slaughtered. This was Sembène's first film since *Ceddo* (1976) was banned in Senegal. The director, who fought for the Free French, centres his impressive film around the figure of Sergeant-Major Diatta (Sane), a Paris-educated intellectual with a French wife, who is contrasted with the French officers steeped in racism and bigotry. Despite its excessive length and several long-winded debates, the film vividly reveals a little-known aspect of the aftermath of World War II as seen through an African's eyes, and there are spectacular set pieces.

▶ **Cangaceiro, O** see Bandit, The

The Cannibals

▶ **Os Canibais**

Portugal   1988   98 mins   col
Folmargem (Portugal)/Gemini Films/La Sept (France)

d   **Manoel de Oliveira**
sc **Manoel de Oliveira**
ph **Mario Barroso**
m   **João Paes**
Leonor Silveira, Luis Miguel Cintra, Diogo Doria, Joel Costa, Pedro Da Silva, Rogerio Samora

On the wedding night of a viscount (Cintra) and his bride (Silveira), her secret lover (Doria) waits outside their bedroom. The Viscount then reveals that all his limbs are false as he removes then to consummate the marriage. Further bizarre events occur, culminating in a rash of cannibalism. This unconventional and macabre satire is fairly straightforward for a good half of the film, based as it is on the conventions of opera, decked out in gorgeous costumes and period décor. Gradually, however, anarchy begins to reign as the film becomes more and more grotesque, demanding an audience to throw off its preconceptions and go along with the humorous and poetic happenings. It ends with all the characters dancing together in a theatrical manner, followed by a duet between a fountain and an off-screen violin.

The Canterbury Tales

▶ **I Racconti Di Canterbury**

Italy 1971 109 mins col
UA/PEA/PAA

d Pier Paolo Pasolini
sc Pier Paolo Pasolini
ph Tonino Delli Colli
m Ennio Morricone
   Pier Paolo Pasolini, Hugh Griffith, Laura Betti, Tom Baker, Ninetto Davoli, Franco Citti, Josephine Chaplin, Jenny Runacre

Chaucer (Pasolini) is among the group of medieval pilgrims on their way to Canterbury who pass the time by telling each other stories. The presence of a number of English actors in the cast does not prevent the eight tales (including those of the Merchant, the Wife of Bath, and the Pardoner) from being filtered through Pasolini's Italian sensibility and, as the English classic was itself derived from *The Decameron* (the first in Pasolini's story-cycle trilogy), it hardly mattered. However, even non-purists might object to the coarsening of some of the episodes and the broad performances, while acknowledging the exuberance of the enterprise.

Best Film Berlin 1972

▶ **Caporal Épinglé, Le** see Vanishing Corporal, The

Capricious Summer

▶ **Rozmarné Léto**

Czechoslovakia 1968 75 mins col
Barrandov

d Jiří Menzel
sc Jiří Menzel, Vaclau Nyult
ph Jaromír Šofr
m Jiří Šust
   Rudolf Hrušínsky, Vlastimil Brodský, František Rehák, Jana Drchalová, Jiří Menzel, Mila Myslíková

The beautiful assistant (Drchalová) of an itinerant circus tightrope walker (Menzel) creates sexual tension among three middle-aged men (Hrusinsky, Brodsky and Rehák), who while away their time beside the lake of a sleepy provincial town. The film's gentle pace, seemingly uneventful plot and the soft colours reflect the season and the setting, but Menzel has packed it with a myriad of small comic incidents that add up to a more substantial whole. It is the sort of amusing, affectionate and observant bitter-sweet comedy that one expects from the minor master Menzel, who learnt to walk a tightrope for his own role in the film.

The Captain From Kopenick

▶ **Der Hauptmann Von Köpenick**

W. Germany 1956 93 mins col
Real Film

d Helmut Käutner
sc Karl Zuckmayer, Helmut Käutner
ph Albert Benitz
m Bernhard Eichhorn
   Heinz Rühmann, Hannelore Schroth, Martin Held, Erich Schellow

While in prison, Wilhelm Voigt (Rühmann) learns the regulations and procedures of the Prussian army from a handbook. On his release, unable to find work, he impersonates an army captain, commandeers soldiers on the streets of Berlin and takes over the city hall of the suburb of Köpenick in order to get himself a passport. This third screen version of Zuckmayer's 1931 play (filmed in the same year, and again in Hollywood in 1941, both by Richard Oswald) updated the action to that of the complacent Adenauer era, and shares some of the defects of the German cinema of the 1950s, namely a lack of style and teeth. The film, basically about the dangers of militarism, plays too much on the audience's sympathy for the imposter, and some clever satire and visual juxtapositions only make one wish it had taken more risks.

La Captive Du Désert

France   1990   100 mins   col
Titane/Double D/La Sept/Roger Diamantis/Films Saint-André Des Arts/ Jean Bernard Fetoux/SGGC/CNC/ Foundation Gan Pour Le Cinéma

d   Raymond Depardon
sc Raymond Depardon
ph Raymond Depardon
    Sandrine Bonnaire, with Dobi Kore, Dobe Wachinke, Atchi Wahi-Li, Fadi Taha, Badei Barka and the inhabitants of Chirfa, Orida and Djaba in Niger

A woman (Bonnaire) is held captive by a community of African rebel nomads in the desert. Isolated, lonely and worn out by the climate and living conditions, she unsuccessfully attempts to escape. Fifteen months later the nomads' reasons for their action are made known and she is released. Award-winning photo-journalist Depardon, making his first feature, based it on the true story of a Frenchwoman who was held by rebels in Chad in 1975. The result is a unique and truly remarkable film, almost devoid of dialogue, using only the natural sounds of the desert and capturing its monotonous beauty with a spare and truthful vision that is unforgettable. Bonnaire, stripped of glamour, is impressive; the small moments of respite, as when she teaches some of the tribeswomen a song, are quite wonderful. A most unusual experience, requiring patience and more than rewarding it.

Les Carabiniers

▶ aka The Soldiers
▶ (US: The Riflemen)

France   1963   80 mins   bw
Rome-Paris Films/Laetitia

d   Jean-Luc Godard
sc Jean-Luc Godard, Jean Gruault, Roberto Rossellini
ph Raoul Coutard

m   Philippe Arthuys
    Marino Masè, Albert Juross, Geneviève Galéa, Catherine Ribero

Two young peasants, lured by promises of booty, leave home to fight for King and Country only to be betrayed when a peace treaty is signed. The violent critical reaction in France to this seemingly dispassionate view of the horrors of war caused the film to be withdrawn after its initial release. But Godard's achievement was to create a powerful anti-war, anti-imperialist statement, using Brechtian distancing techniques, and literary devices, shooting in the grainy images of old newsreels in an unspecified time and place.

▶ Careless Love see Bonne Soupe, La

The Carmelites

▶ Le Dialogue Des Carmelites

France/Italy   1959   113 mins   bw
Champs-Elysées/Titanus

d   R. Bruckberger, Philippe Agostini
sc R. Bruckberger, Philippe Agostini
ph André Bac
m   Jean Françaix
    Jeanne Moreau, Alida Valli, Pascale Audret, Madeleine Renaud, Pierre Brasseur, Georges Wilson

Two young Carmelite novices take the veil almost on the eve of the French Revolution, and find themselves, their sister nuns and the convent itself caught up in the political events and violence that follow. This rather unwieldy film version of the Georges Bernanos novel is an interesting showcase for Moreau and Valli, but it fails to come to grips either with history or religion and is thus rather dull. The ending, when several nuns sacrifice themselves voluntarily to the guillotine, is moving and dramatic, but it's a long time to wait.

Carmen

Spain   1983   101 mins   col
Emiliano Piedra Productions

d   Carlos Saura

sc **Carlos Saura, Antonio Gades (inspired by Merimée & Bizet)**
ph **Teo Escamilla**
m **Paco De Lucia, Bizet**
    Antonio Gades, Laura Del Sol, Paco De Lucia, Cristina Hoyos, Juan Antonio Jimenez, Sebastian Moreno, José Yepes

Choreographer Antonio (Gades) casts an unknown girl (Del Sol) to dance the title role in his new ballet set to Bizet's *Carmen*. During the rehearsal period, he falls in love with her and they have an affair, although she has a husband, currently in jail on a drugs charge. She proves incapable of fidelity to either of them and, when he surprises her making love with a boy from the chorus in the dressing room, he stabs her in a fit of jealousy. Saura's film, using the well-tried but effective device of life mirroring art, tells the Carmen story twice – offstage and on. The edges tend, occasionally, to blur, but since the enterprise is really the foundation for a display of brilliant choreographic pyrotechnics, danced with breathtaking expertise and filmed with pulsating energy, no matter. A treat for lovers of the genre, with the added bonus of Bizet's music, some of it sung, using voices of the calibre of Regina Resnik and Mario Del Monaco.

Carmen

    France/Italy   1984   152 mins   col
    Gaumont/Production Marcel Dassault/
    Opera Film Produzione

d **Francesco Rosi**
sc **Francesco Rosi, Tonino Guerra (libretto by Meilhac & Halévy)**
ph **Pasqualino De Santis**
m **Georges Bizet (conducted by Lorin Maazel)**
    Julia Migenes-Johnson (Carmen), Placido Domingo (Don Jose), Ruggero Raimondi (Escamillo), Faith Esham (Micaela)

The narrative of Bizet's popular opera – a simple soldier's passion for a wayward and tempestuous gypsy leads to jealousy and murder – is followed exactly by Rosi's film, which uses the full *opéra comique* version (i.e. with spoken dialogue). The director opted for realism, filming on location in Andalucia,

which achieves authenticity on the one hand, but creates disruption on another: a vegetable cart, for example, rumbles into the midst of Jose and Micaela's duet to farcical effect, and too many big musical moments are diminished by long-shot cameras. The opening credit sequence, however, using slow-motion in the bullring, followed by a dramatic Corpus Christi procession, sets the tone for the events to come, rooting them firmly in the dark mystique of Spanish ritual. Julia Migenes-Johnson lights up the screen with a smoulderingly sexy Carmen, Domingo convinces as her victim, and Raimondi delivers a polished toreador. Purists will notice a musical excision in Act III, but this is a handsome, intelligent and entertaining opera film rather than a filmed opera.

Carmen Comes Home

▶ **Karumen Kokyo Ni Kaeru**

    Japan   1951   87 mins   col
    Shochiku

d **Keisuke Kinoshita**
sc **Keisuke Kinoshita**
ph **Hiroyuki Kusuda**
m **Chuji Kinoshita, Toshio Uzumi**
    Hideko Takamine, Toshiko Kobayashi, Takeshi Sakamoto, Shuji Sano, Chishu Ryu

A pretty Tokyo stripper (Takamine) pays a visit home to the little country village where she grew up and scandalizes the community, especially her father (Sakamoto), with her city ways. She learns the lesson that to return to one's past can be a dreadful mistake but, before she and her friend (Kobayashi) depart, they stage a strip show in an old barn and donate the proceeds to local charities. The first Japanese film to have been made and released in colour is a charming and light weight comedy on the surface, but it does have an underlying seriousness as we watch the tragicomic villagers falling victim to the worst aspects of the Coca-Cola culture. Takamine is effective as the flighty but likeable heroine. The following year saw a sequel, *Carmen's Pure Love*, also shot in colour, but the process was thought unsatisfacory and it was released in black and white.

Un Carnet De Bal

▶ aka Life Dances On

▶ aka The Dance Programme

France 1937 135 mins bw
Lévy Strauss/Sigma

d Julien Duvivier
sc Julien Duvivier, Jean Sarment, Pierre
Wolff, Bernard Zimmer, Henri Jeanson
ph Michel Kelber, Philippe Agostini
m Maurice Jaubert
Marie Bell, Françoise Rosay, Louis
Jouvet, Raimu, Harry Baur, Fernandel,
Pierre Blanchar, Pierre-Richard Willm

A rich, middle-aged widow (Bell) finds an old
dance card and decides to find out what
happened to the men whose names are on it.
She discovers an epileptic doctor (Blanchar),
a monk (Baur), a hairdresser (Fernandel), a
crooked nightclub owner (Jouvet), a skiing
instructor (Willm) and a small town mayor
(Raimu). A haunting waltz theme
accompanies this elegant but patchy sketch-
film which allows a galaxy of French stars
each to do a short turn. The film was so
successful that Duvivier was invited to Hollywood to make *The Great Waltz*. He repeated
the multi-story formula in four further films
with variable results.

Best Foreign Film Venice 1937

Carnival In Flanders

▶ La Kermesse Héroïque

France 1935 115 mins bw
Tobis/Regina

d Jacques Feyder
sc Jacques Feyder, Charles Spaak
ph Harry Stradling
m Louis Beydts
Françoise Rosay, Louis Jouvet, Jean
Murat, Alfred Adam, Bernard Lancret,
André Alerme

When Spanish troops enter a small town in
17th-century Flanders, the male inhabitants
disappear, leaving the women, including the
burgomaster's wife (Rosay), to enjoy the
attentions of their conquerors. Lazare Meerson's sets and costumes conjure up the period
with the eye of Jan Breughel (a character in
the film) and the witty script and performances have made this mock-heroic farce a
continual favourite. But it caused great
offence in Belgium for its presentation of the
Flemings in a less than heroic light, and was
liked by the Nazis for its sympathetic attitude
towards collaboration.

Best Director Venice 1936

Caroline Chérie

France 1951 135 mins bw
SNEG/Cinéphonie

d Richard Pottier
sc Jean Anouilh
ph Maurice Barry
m Georges Auric
Martine Carol, Jacques Dacqmine, Marie
Déa, Pierre Cressoy

Caroline and a young count (Dacqmine) are
in love, but the upheavals of the French
Revolution separate them. After a series of
affairs with others, they are reunited. Martine
Carol's appearance in the title role rocketed
her to stardom, the only fact of importance
to note about this slightly prurient, somewhat
tedious, run-of-the-mill costume drama, the
script of which does not do justice to its
writer's reputation.

Caroline Chérie

France 1967 105 mins col
Cineurop/Nordeutsche/Mancori

d Denys De La Patellière
sc Cecil Saint-Laurent
ph Sacha Vierny
m Georges Garvarentz
France Anglade, Jean-Claude Brialy,
Vittorio De Sica, Bernard Blier, Isa
Miranda

A beautifully photographed but otherwise
very poor colour remake of the French Revolution romance with Anglade in the role that
made Martine Carol famous. This version
offers a more *angst*-ridden and sexually
explicit account of Caroline's tribulations,

including rape and an enforced marriage
before she is finally reunited with her true
love (Brialy).

▶ **Caro Michele** see Dear Michael

▶ **Carrosse D'Or, Le** see Golden Coach, The

▶ **Carrozza D'Oro, La** see Golden Coach, The

Cartouche

▶ **aka Swords Of Blood**

France 1961 114 mins col
Les Films Ariane/Filmsonor/Vides

d   **Philippe De Broca**
sc **Philippe De Broca, Daniel Boulanger**
ph **Christian Matras**
m   **Georges Delerue**
    **Jean-Paul Belmondo, Claudia Cardinale,
    Odile Versois, Marcel Dalio, Philippe
    Lemaire, Jean Rochefort**

In the 18th century, Cartouche (Belmondo)
and Vénus (Cardinale) take over a Paris crime
syndicate in order to rob the rich and succeed
in antagonizing the foppish Chief of Police
(Lemaire).After his first four films, featuring
Jean-Pierre Cassel, De Broca switched to
Belmondo, an equally animated hero, for this
snappy, swashbuckling spoof. The film also
manages, with some expertise, to encompass
an element of drama and even tragedy.

▶ **Casa De Bernarda Alba, La** see
House Of Bernarda Alba, The

▶ **Casa Del Angel, La** see House Of
The Angel, The

Casanova

▶ **aka Fellini Casanova**

Italy 1976 163 mins col
PEA/TCF

d   **Federico Fellini**
sc **Federico Fellini, Bernadino Zapponi**
ph **Giuseppe Rotunno**
m   **Nino Rota**
    **Donald Sutherland, Tina Aumont, Cicely
    Browne, Carmen Scarpitta**

Episodes from the life of Giacomo Casanova
(Sutherland), the 18th-century Venetian
author, scientist and libertine who fornicates
mechanically with one girl after another until,
in this version, he has sex with an actual
automaton. After the warmth of Fellini's
three previous autobiographical films, this is
a cold, empty, repetitive study of a sexual
obsessive. There are, of course, a number of
eye-catching scenes, enhanced by Danilo
Donati's Oscar-winning costume design. Nino
Rota's music is as haunting as ever, and
Sutherland does his best behind extraordinary
make-up.

▶ **Cas Du Docteur Laurent, Le** see
Case Of Dr Laurent, The

The Case Of Dr Laurent

▶ **Le Cas Du Docteur Laurent**

France 1957 93 mins bw
Cocinor

d   **Jean-Paul Le Chanois**
sc **Jean-Paul Le Chanois, René Barjavel**
ph **Henri Alekan**
m   **Joseph Kosma**
    **Jean Gabin, Nicole Courcel, Sylvia
    Montfort, Arius Daxely**

A Paris doctor (Gabin) moves to the countryside to pioneer natural childbirth methods.
He meets with hostility from the locals and
opposition from the medical establishment
but, when an unwed mother gives birth without difficulty under his care, he wins over his
critics. An intelligent film, authenticated by
actual scenes of birth that are well-presented
and sensitively handled, and with an excellent
performance from Gabin.

▶ **Caso Mattei, Il** see Mattei Affair, The

▶ **Casque D'Or** see Golden Marie

▶ **Castle of The Spider's Web** see
Throne Of Blood

▶ **Castle Vogelöd** see Haunted Castle, The

▶ **Cat, The** see Chat, Le

Cat And Mouse

▶ **Le Chat Et La Souris**

France 1975 108 mins col
Les Films 13

d **Claude Lelouch**
sc **Claude Lelouch**
ph **Jean Collomb**
m **Francis Lai**
   **Michèle Morgan, Serge Reggiani, Jean-
   Pierre Aumont, Philippe Léotard, Valérie
   Lagrange**

The wife (Morgan) of a wealthy husband (Aumont), humiliated by his continual philandering, is tempted to push him off a skyscraper that he is in the process of having built, but does not. When he is later found shot, the detective investigating the case – named, in a delightfully improbable pun, Inspector Lechat (Reggiani) – suspects the widow of the crime. Lelouch has delivered a slick and glossy cop thriller, using flashbacks with skill, but it is all rather superficial and lacking in suspense or true drama. A disappointing vehicle for the lovely Michèle Morgan's return to films after an absence of eight years.

▶ **Catherine** see Vie Sans Joie, Une

▶ **Cathy Tippel** see Keetje Tippel

The Cat In The Bag

▶ **(US: The Cat In The Sack)**
▶ **Le Chat Dans Le Sac**

Canada 1964 74 mins bw
National Film Board Of Canada

d **Gilles Groulx**
sc **Gilles Groulx**
ph **Jean-Claude Labrecque**
m **John Coltrane, Couperin, Vivaldi
   Claude Godbout, Barbara Ulrich,**
   **Manon Blain, Véronique Vilbert, André
   Leblanc**

Barbara (Ulrich), an actress, and Claude (Godbout), a journalist, are a young couple living out 'the last days of their intimacy' during a winter in Montreal. Their estrangement personifies the dilemmas of a bilingual, bicultural country – she is Anglo-Canadian, and he québecois. The film that marked the beginning of Quebec cinema, and was the first feature of 33-year-old Groulx, a maker of short films, manages to be a personal history as well as an expression of the aspirations of French-speaking Canada. This is carried off by improvised techniques heavily influenced by Godard's early films, particularly *It's My Life*, with its monologues to camera, interviews, jump cuts and quotations, but it incorporates them into the freshly viewed Canadian experience.

▶ **Cat In The Sack, The** see Cat In The Bag, The

The Cat Shows Her Claws

▶ **La Chatte Sort Ses Griffes**

France 1959 102 mins bw
Paris-Elysée Films/Metzger & Woog/
Films Balar

d **Henri Decoin**
sc **Jacques Rémy**
ph **Pierre Montazel**
m **Joseph Kosma**
   **Françoise Arnoul, Horst Frank, Harold
   Kay, François Guérin, Bernard Lajarrige**

Cora (Arnoul) is a French Resistance worker known as The Cat. Suspecting, erroneously, that she has betrayed them, a group of her colleagues shoot her and leave her for dead, but she is rescued by the Germans. Major Von Hollwitz (Frank) makes her the subject of a brainwashing experiment and sends her back to the Resistance as a spy, but his plans come unstuck. Good locations, good photography and good acting, notably from Frank as the Nazi doctor who starts falling in love with his victim. Decoin directs with confident efficiency, but it is rather difficult to swallow the story, which has Arnoul performing some Pearl White-style heroics at the final fade.

Cats' Play

▶ **Macskajaték**

Hungary 1974 115 mins col
Hunnia Studio

d **Károly Makk**
sc **Károly Makk, János Tóth**
ph **János Tóth**
m **Péter Eötvös**
Margit Dayka, Elma Bulla, Margit Makay, Samu Balász

Mrs Orbán (Dayka), an elderly, widowed music teacher living in Budapest, focuses her life on her wealthy but paralyzed sister (Bulla) in Germany, with whom she communicates by letter and telephone, and on her old flame, Viktor (Balász), a retired opera singer who comes to dine every Thursday evening. When a friend from the past (Makay) appears and falls in love with Viktor, the balance and security of her existence are badly disturbed. As in his previous film, the award-winning *Love*, Károly Makk concentrates on the frailty, foibles and survival mechanisms of the old. The piece demands concentration, but is poignant, fragile and unsentimental, displaying fine judgement in direction and performance. Beautifully photographed, it effectively utilizes flashbacks to summon up the heroine's memories of youth.

▶ **Causa Kralik** see Payment In Kind

▶ **Cave Se Rebiffe, Le** see Counterfeiters, The

▶ **Caza, La** see Hunt, The

Ceddo

Senegal 1976 117 mins bw
Filmi Doomireev

d **Ousmane Sembène**
sc **Ousmane Sembène**
ph **Georges Caristan**
m **Manu Dibango**
Ismaila Diagne, Tabara N'Diaye, Moustapha Yade, Ousmane Camara, Mamadou Dioum

An Imam from the North tries forcibly to convert the population to Islam, using the king as his puppet. The king's daughter is kidnapped by a group that refuses conversion. Though their leader is slain and his followers defeated, his spirit lives on in the captive princess who returns to kill the Imam. As 70 per cent of the population of Senegal is Muslim, Black Africa's leading director again courted controversy in his own country, where the film was banned. It was his most daring and mature work in style and substance. Deeply rooted in African culture, it is a powerful allegory confounding European expectations of narrative.

Cela S'Appelle L'Aurore

France 1955 108 mins bw
Marceau/Laetitia

d **Luis Buñuel**
sc **Luis Buñuel, Jules Ferry**
ph **Robert Le Fèbvre**
m **Joseph Kosma**
Georges Marchal, Lucia Bosé, Gianni Esposito, Julien Bertheau, Henri Nassiet

In Corsica, a doctor (Marchal) falls in love with a widow (Bosé) when his wife is away on holiday, while his befriending of a peasant (Esposito) leads to murder. For his first film in Europe for 23 years, Buñuel chose to adapt an Emmanuel Roblès novel which he found to be 'a story so perfectly pure'. The film might have been perfectly pure melodrama, except for the director's spicing it with social consciousness. It was merely a sturdy stepping stone towards better works in his long career. Georges Marchal, the stony-faced male lead, unaccountably appeared in three further Buñuel films.

Céleste

W. Germany 1981 106 mins col
Pelemele/Bayerische Rundfunk

d **Percy Adlon**
sc **Percy Adlon**
ph **Jürgen Martin**
m **Franck**
Eva Mattes, Jürgen Arndt, Norbert Wartha, Wolf Euba, Joseph Manoth

The day-to-day existence of Céleste Albaret

(Mattes), a young, uneducated country girl, who came to work as housekeeper to the ailing author Marcel Proust (Arndt) in his Paris apartment in 1913 and stayed with him until his death nine years later. Though made in German, Adlon's adaptation is extremely faithful to Céleste's memoirs, and marvellously evokes the closed world in which Proust lived. Although offering no plot to speak of, the film is a subtle, humorous and touching study of the loyal relationship between a middle-aged homosexual intellectual and a simple, caring girl.

Celine And Julie Go Boating

▶ **Céline Et Julie Vont En Bateau**

France   1974   192 mins   col
Les Films Du Losange/Christian
Fletcher/Les Films 7/Rennes/Saga/Simar/
Vincent Malle

d   **Jacques Rivette**
sc   **Jacques Rivette, Eduardo Di Gregorio, Juliet Berto, Dominique Labourier**
ph   **Jacques Renard**
m   **Jean-Marie Senia**
      Dominique Labourier, Juliet Berto, Bulle Ogier, Marie-France Pisier, Barbet Schroeder, Nathalie Asnar, Philippe Clevenot

Celine (Berto), a magician in a cheap nightclub, meets librarian Julie (Labourier) in Montmartre and tells her how she sometimes works as governess to a little girl who lives in a strange suburban house with her widower father and two women. Celine and Julie enter the house and become involved in the repeated drama being played out within. Suggested by two Henry James stories, this brilliantly allusive comic meditation on the nature of fantasy manages to take in Lewis Carroll, Cocteau, Borges, Kafka, Proust, cartoons and Vincent Minnelli on the way. Although lengthy, it is the most approachable and accomplished of Rivette's films, and led critic David Thomson to call it 'the most important film made since Citizen Kane'.

▶ **Céline Et Julie Vont En Bateau**
see Celine And Julie Go Boating

▶ **Celui Qui Doit Mourir** see He Who Must Die

▶ **C'Era Una Volta** see Cinderella – Italian Style

▶ **C'Eravamo Tanto Amati** see We All Loved Each Other So Much

The Ceremony

▶ **Gishiki**

Japan   1971   123 mins   col
ATG/Argos

d   **Nagisa Oshima**
sc   **Tsutomu Tamura, Mamoru Sasaki, Nagisa Oshima**
ph   **Toichiro Narushima**
m   **Tohru Takemitsu**
      Kenzo Kawarazaki, Atsuko Kaku, Kei Sato, Nobuko Otowa, Maki Takayama

The history of Japan from the end of World War II to the present day is represented by the large and influential Sakurada family. Each stage is marked by a specific ceremony when the entire family gathers for an anniversary, a wedding or a funeral. 'Ceremonies are a time when the special characteristics of the Japanese spirit are revealed. It is this spirit that concerns and worries me,' commented Oshima on his most ambitious film to that date. It not only gave him the opportunity for some stunning stylistic devices and bizarre humour, but it also displayed a deeply ambivalent and revealing attitude to Japanese society.

▶ **Cerny Petr** see Peter And Pavla

▶ **Certo Giorno, Un** see One Fine Day

César

France   1936   117 mins   bw
Marcel Pagnol

d   **Marcel Pagnol**
sc   **Marcel Pagnol**
ph   **Willy**
m   **Vincent Scotto**
      Raimu, Orane Demazis, Pierre Fresnay, Charpin, André Fouché, Alida Rouffe

After his years in the merchant navy, Marius (Fresnay) runs a garage in Toulon. On the death of Panisse (Charpin), Fanny (Demazis) reveals to her adult son Césariot (Fouché) that he is really Marius's son. With much manoeuvring from grandfather César (Raimu), the lovers of 20 years before are reunited. The last part of Pagnol's trilogy (four years after the second, *Fanny*), was the only one he directed himself. Less fluent cinematically, the plot more predictable and the limited Demazis unable to suggest the passage of time, it still has Pagnol's delicious dialogue and Raimu's all-enveloping performance. Starting with *Marius*, the three films are fictionalized portraits of Marseilles life and characters described by a wonderful storyteller, a humorist who created pathos without sentimentality.

César And Rosalie

▶ **César Et Rosalie**

France 1972 105 mins col
Fildebroc/U.P.F./Mega Film

d   **Claude Sautet**
sc **Claude Sautet, Jean-Loup Dabadie**
ph **Jean Boffety**
m   **Philippe Sarde**
    Yves Montand, Romy Schneider, Sami Frey, Umberto Orsini

Rosalie (Schneider), the divorced mother of a little girl and mistress of César (Montand), runs off with an old flame (Frey). After various comings and goings, the two men become devoted friends and a *ménage-à-trois* is set up until Rosalie leaves. This see-sawing diversion, meandering along to a deliberately inconclusive ending, is a pleasant, amusing and polished – if somewhat rambling – offering, elevated by Montand's superb portrayal of a rough but kind self-made man.

▶ **César Et Rosalie** see César And Rosalie

C'Est La Vie

▶ **La Baule-Les Pins**

France 1990 100 mins col
Alexandre Films/S.G.G.C./Films A2/C.N.C.

d   **Diane Kurys**
sc **Diane Kurys, Alain Le Henry**

ph **Giuseppe Lanci**
m   **Philippe Sarde**
    Nathalie Baye, Richard Berry, Julie Bataille, Candice Lefranc, Alexis Derlon, Zabou, Jean-Pierre Bacri, Valeria Bruni-Tedeschi

Lyons, August 1958. Thirteen-year-old Frédérique (Bataille) and six-year-old Sophie (Lefranc), helped by their young nanny Odette (Bruni-Tedeschi) are excitedly packing for the annual holiday at the seaside. At the station their mother (Baye) announces she must go to Paris and will join them later. Arriving at La Baule, the children are reunited with their cousins and their jolly uncle (Bacri), torment the landlord and Odette, and eagerly await their mother's arrival and that of their father (Berry), who always joins them later. Gradually, the children become aware that all is not well between their parents, and learn that they are to live in Paris with their mother. Completing a trilogy based on her own memories that began with *Diabolo Menthe* (1977) and continued with the Oscar-nominated *Coup De Foudre* (1982), Diane Kurys has surpassed herself with this joyous, charming and painful evocation of childhood. The passage of holiday time is rich in small incidents, often funny, sometimes tender, and the director graphically reveals the gulf between childhood innocence and adult deceit as events unfold: the arrival of Baye's young lover, the violent quarrel between Baye and Berry, the spectre of divorce and change darkening the summer air. In a first-class cast all the children are superb and Kurys directs her subtle script with sensitivity but not sentimentality.

▶ **Cet Obscur Objet Du Désir** see That Obscure Object Of Desire

▶ **Chacal De Nahueltoro, El** see Jackal Of Nahueltoro, The

▶ **Chagrin Et La Pitié, Le** see Sorrow And The Pity, The

▶ **Chaika** see Seagull, The

▶ **Chained** see Mikaël

▶ **Chamade, La** see Heartbeat

▶ **Chambre Verte, La** see Green Room, The

The Champagne Murders

▶ **Le Scandale**

France   1967   110 mins   col
Universal (France)

d   **Claude Chabrol**
sc **Claude Brûlé, Derek Prouse, Paul Gégauff**
ph **Jean Rabier**
m   **Pierre Jansen**
    Anthony Perkins, Maurice Ronet, Stéphane Audran, Yvonne Furneaux, Suzanne Lloyd

The wealthy owner (Furneaux) of a champagne company, her former-gigolo husband (Perkins) and her secretary (Audran) plot to make an eccentric playboy (Ronet), who holds the key to a profitable takeover bid, believe himself to be a murderer. Chabrol flounders around in this grotesque and unpleasant thriller, using some clever contrivances and achieving a showy overhead final shot. Happily, he would soon return from the wilderness in which films like this had placed him.

Chapayev

USSR   1934   99 mins   bw
Lenfilm

d   **Sergei Vasiliev, Georgi Vasiliev**
sc **Sergei Vasiliev, Georgi Vasiliev**
ph **Alexander Sigayev**
m   **Gavril Popov**
    Boris Babochkin, B. Blinov, Leonid Kmit, Vavara Myasnikova

Red Army commander Chapayev (Babochkin), fighting against Czech and Kolchak forces during the Civil War of 1919, has to resist the attempts of a commissar to tame his impulsive and heroic nature. Shown to the public as the highlight of the fifteenth anniversary of Soviet cinema, the film was hailed at home and abroad as the first great Soviet success in the sound era. Although the directors (unrelated despite their shared surname) lacked the invention and genius of an Eisenstein or a Dovzhenko, the humanity of this modern folk tale makes it a good example of socialist realism.

▶ **Chapeau De Paille D'Italie, Un**
see Italian Straw Hat, The

Charles And Lucie

▶ **Charles Et Lucie**

France   1979   98 mins   col
Cythère Films/Les Films De La Chouette/Antenne 2

d   **Nelly Kaplan**
sc **Jean Chapot**
ph **Gilbert Sandoz**
m   **Pierre Perret**
    Daniel Ceccaldi, Ginette Garcin, Jean-Marie Proslier, Samson Fainsilber, Georges Claisse

Misfortune has reduced antique dealer Charles (Ceccaldi) to selling bric-à-brac, while former chanteuse Lucie (Garcin), her looks gone, is a charwoman. They fall victim to an elaborate con-trick which lands them in the South of France, penniless and pursued by gangsters and police alike, but it all ends happily. Firmly in the tradition of picaresque fantasy, Kaplan's film is charming, poignant, and sometimes witty, but remains little more than a light-weight divertissement.

Charles Dead Or Alive

▶ **Charles Mort Ou Vif**

Switzerland   1969   93 mins   col
Le Group 5

d   **Alain Tanner**
sc **Alain Tanner**
ph **Renato Berta**
    François Simon, Marcel Robert, Marie-Claire Dufour, André Schmidt

Charles, a middle-aged watchmaker (played by François, Michel Simon's son), opts out of the rat-race, abandoning business and family and moving in with an artist and his mistress. He retreats further and further from reality and ends as a willing accomplice to his son's decision to send him to an asylum. Switzerland's best-known and most accomplished director made an assured and intelligent debut with this film, suggesting the left-wing and sociological themes he would develop in later works.

▶ **Charles Et Lucie** see Charles And Lucie

▶ **Charles Mort Ou Vif** see Charles Dead Or Alive

▶ **Charme Discret De La Bourgeoisie, Le** see Discreet Charm Of The Bourgeoisie, The

Charulata

▶ **aka The Lonely Wife**

India   1964   124 mins   bw
R.D. Bansal

d **Satyajit Ray**
sc **Satyajit Ray**
ph **Subrata Mitra**
m **Satyajit Ray**
   Sailen Mukherjee, Madhabi Mukherjee, Soumitra Chatterjee, Shyamal Ghoshal, Geetali Roy

Towards the end of the 19th century, Charulata (Madhabi Mukherjee), the bored and neglected wife of a Calcutta intellectual (Sailen Mukherjee) deeply involved with his English-language political journal, falls in love with Amal (Chatterjee), a young poet and her husband's cousin. She sees in Amal a man who would appreciate her for herself and encourage her own writing, but it is an illusion. This subtle masterpiece of Ray's middle period, based on a story by his beloved Rabindranath Tagore, is a warm, wry and rounded picture of the breaking up of a middle-class marriage. The garden scene where the wife (a delicately beautiful performance) swings higher and higher as Amal sits writing, is equal to similar outdoor moments in the work of Renoir and suggest a sexuality that is unusual in the context of Indian cinema.

Best Director Berlin 1965

▶ **Chasers, The** see Young Have No Morals, The

▶ **Chastnaya Zhizn** see Private Life

Le Chat

▶ **aka The Cat**

France   1971   88 mins   col
Lira Films/Cinétel

d **Pierre Granier-Deferre**
sc **Pascal Jardin, Pierre Granier-Deferre**
ph **Walter Wottitz**
m **Philippe Sarde**
   Jean Gabin, Simone Signoret, Annie Cordy, Jacques Rispal

Julien and Clemence (Gabin and Signoret), an aging married couple, spend their days in their shabby house on the edge of Paris, locked in mutual hatred and contempt. They barely ever speak, are intent on causing each other misery and Julien has transferred the love he once had for his wife to his cat. Adapted from a novel by Georges Simenon, this is unlikely film material since the action is minimal, the environment hermetically sealed and the dialogue almost non-existent. However, by dint of inspired casting and a sensitivity in imparting meaning to objects and small gestures, Granier-Deferre almost manages to sustain our interest. It is a little drawn out and the flashbacks that remind us of the couple's youth are superfluous – particularly as we are left in the dark as to why their love turned to hate – but the leads' wholehearted double act is marvellous to watch.

Best Actor (Jean Gabin) Berlin 1971
Best Actress (Simone Signoret) Berlin 1971

▶ **Chat Dans Le Sac, Le** see Cat In The Bag, The

▶ **Chat Et La Souris, Le** see Cat And Mouse

▶ **Chatte Sort Ses Griffes, La** see Cat Shows Her Claws, The

▶ **Cheat, The** see Wanton, The

▶ **Cheated, The** see Duped, The

▶ **Cheats, The** see Youthful Sinners

▶ **Chelovek S Kinoapparatom** see Man With The Movie Camera, The

▶ **Chère Louise** see Louise

The Chess Player

▶ **Le Joueur D'Échecs**

France   1927   10,809 feet

Société Des Films Historiques

d **Raymond Bernard**
sc **Raymond Bernard, Jean-José Frappa**
ph **Joseph-Louis Mundviller, Marc Bujard, Willy Faktorivitch**
m **Silent (original score Henri Rabaud)**
    Pierre Blanchar, Charles Dullin, Édith Jehanne, Camille Bert, Pierre Batcheff, Marcelle Charles-Dullin, Jacky Monnier

In the year 1776 Poland is under Russian rule. A clandestine liberation movement is led by the young nobleman Boleslas Vorowski (Blanchar). Both Boleslas and the orphaned Sophie Novinska (Jehanne) have been raised by the enigmatic Baron Von Kempelin (Dullin), a maker of life-sized automata. Sophie is torn between her fraternal devotion to Boleslas and her love for Serge Oblomoff (Batcheff), a young Russian officer. After an insurrection, Boleslas, a price on his head, hides in a chess-playing automaton. The miraculous machine comes to the attention of Catherine II (Marcelle Charles-Dullin), who wishes to test her chess skills against it. Restored in 1990 by Kevin Brownlow and his team from an incomplete French negative confiscated by the Nazis early in the war and from different prints in Paris, Holland, Berlin and Luxembourg, *The Chess Player* emerged from its years of oblivion as a rediscovered masterpiece of the silent cinema. The big-budget production was shot in some 35 major sets at the Joinville studios outside Paris, as well as in the forest of Fontainebleau, San Moritz, and on the plains of Poland, using 1500 Polish cavalrymen. The tale, based on the novel by Henry Dupuy-Mazuel, is told with great sweep and passion, enhanced by the remarkable art direction of Jean Perrier and costumes by Eugène Lourié. But what is most extraordinary is the way Bernard focuses on the intimate feelings of the characters against the political background; his images are eloquent without resorting to the grandiloquence found in Abel Gance's *Napoleon* of the same year. In one scene in a garden the emotions of the four leading characters are explored through a series of close-ups, while fireworks explode in the background and a Polish patriot is executed. The climax involving the automata cut with the masked ball at the Winter Palace is one of the truly great sequences in cinema. The full impact of the film can only be felt when combined with the magnificent original score by Henri Rabaud, who worked closely with the director.

The Chess Players

▶ **Shatranj Ke Khilari**

India 1977 135 mins col
Devki Chitra

d **Satyajit Ray**
sc **Satyajit Ray**
ph **Soumendou Roy**
m **Satyajit Ray**
    Sanjeev Kumar, Saeed Jaffrey, Richard Attenborough, Amjad Khan

In Lucknow in 1856, two indolent chess-obsessed noblemen, neglecting their families, continue to play while the Maharajah, an effete poet-musician, is being dethroned by the British East India Company. Ray's first film in Hindi (and English delivered by Attenborough's Scots accent) is quietly humorous and sharply-observed, as well as being acute about Anglo-Indian relations in Victorian times. The attempt to link the chess playing to the wider political games is less successful.

▶ **Cheval D'Orgueil, Le** see Proud Ones, The

▶ **Chichi Ariki** see There Was A Father

▶ **Chieko-Sho** see Portrait Of Chieko

Un Chien Andalou

▶ **(US: An Andalusian Dog)**

France 1928 17 mins bw
Luis Buñuel-Salvador Dali

d **Luis Buñuel**
sc **Luis Buñuel, Salvador Dali**
ph **Albert Dubergen**
m **Silent**
    Simone Mareuil, Pierre Batcheff, Jaime Miravilles, Salvador Dali, Luis Buñuel

An open eye is slashed in half with a razor, ants emerge from the palm of a hand, breasts dissolve into buttocks, priests are pulled along the ground, dead donkeys lie on two pianos

... Made under the influence of André Breton's Surrealist Manifesto, this series of unconnected incidents designed to have the logic of a dream, was the cinematic equivalent of the surrealist's automatic writing. And so Buñuel's career as a director began with one of the most startling and most famous images in all cinema – the cutting of the eye. The film is still, as Jean Vigo stated in 1930, 'a work of major importance in every respect'. It was financed by Buñuel's mother, as well as the Vicomte de Noailles and 'money won by a friend on the lottery'. The music of Wagner, Beethoven, and a tango was added as a sound track in 1960.

La Chienne

France   1931   100 mins   bw
Braunberger-Richebé

d   Jean Renoir
sc Jean Renoir
ph Théodor Sparkühl, Roger Hubert
    Michel Simon, Janie Marèze, Georges
    Flament, Jean Gehret

An unhappily-married clerk (Simon) falls for a prostitute (Marèze), steals from his employer to satisfy her demands, and kills her out of jealousy of her pimp (Flament). Renoir demonstrates his ability to turn an amoral little melodrama into a work of unsentimental naturalism, creating characters rather than types. By filming in the noisy streets of Montmartre, without using any dubbed sound, a real, habitable world is created. But if the film imitated life, so life imitated the film. During the shooting, Simon became infatuated with Marèze who fell for Flament. The film completed, Flament drove along the Riviera with Marèze in his new American car and had an accident in which she was killed. *La Chienne* – an English translation of the title (The Bitch) was deemed unfit – was remade by Fritz Lang as *Scarlet Street* (1945).

▶ **Chiens, Les** see Dogs, The

▶ **Chikamatsu Monogatari** see Crucified Lovers, The

▶ **Chikuzan Hitori Tabi** see Life Of Chikuzan, The

▶ **Chikuzan Travels Alone** see Life Of Chikuzan, The

The Childhood Of Maxim Gorky

▶ **Detstvo Gorkovo**

USSR   1938   101 mins   bw
Soyezdetfilm

d   Mark Donskoi
sc Mark Donskoi, I. Grudzev
ph Pyotr Yermolov
m   Lev Schwartz
    Alexei Lyarsky (Maxim Gorky), Y.
    Valbert, M. Troyanovski, Valeria
    Massalitinova

Young Alexei Pyeshkov (later Maxim Gorky) arrives to live with his struggling grandparents in a small riverside town. With his eccentric bickering relations, the peasants and the workmen, the boy experiences early joys and sorrows, and learns to love the people and landscape of his country suffering under the Tsar. The first film in the Gorky trilogy, on which Donskoi's fame rests, is rich in humour, character and period detail, faithful to the vision of the great Marxist proletarian writer. Outstanding is Massilitinova's old grandmother.

The Children Are Watching Us

▶ **I Bambini Ci Guardano**

Italy   1943   85 mins   bw
Scalera/Invicta

d   Vittorio De Sica
sc Cesare Zavattini, Vittorio De Sica,
    Cesare Giulio Viola, Adolfo Franci,
    Margherita Maglione, Gherardo Gherardi
ph Giuseppe Caracciolo
m   Renzo Rossellini
    Isa Pola, Luciano De Ambrosis, Adriano
    Rimoldi, Giovanna Cigoli

A four-year-old boy (De Ambrosis) watches the break-up of the marriage of his middle-class parents, an unfaithful mother (Pola) and a suicidal father (Rimoldi). After directing and acting in four sentimental comedies, De

Sica suddenly made a breakthrough with a dramatic, humane and sharply realistic work. It was also his first important collaboration with the writer Cesare Zavattini, who was to contribute to virtually all his following films. Here, with the recently-orphaned De Ambrosis, De Sica showed himself a sensitive director of children as he was to prove still further in *Shoeshine* and *Bicycle Thieves*. One of the first Neo-Realist films, it was influential in changing the face of Italian cinema, although financially unsuccessful.

▶ **Children In Uniform** see Mädchen In Uniform

Children Of Hiroshima

▶ **Genbaku No Ko**

Japan 1952 97 mins bw
Kendai Eiga Kyokai/Gekidan Mingei

d **Kaneto Shindo**
sc **Kaneto Shindo**
ph **Takeo Itoh**
m **Akira Ifukube**
   Nobuko Otowa, Chikako Hoshawa, Niwa Saito

In 1952, seven years after the dropping of the first atomic bomb, a schoolteacher returns to Hiroshima to visit her parents' grave and to discover how her friends and ex-pupils have lived since that horrendous day. The brief but harrowing flashback reconstruction of the bombing clouds the rest of the humanist tale of the aftermath. The film is surprisingly free from bitterness, although it cannot disguise the revulsion most people feel about the event.

▶ **Children Of Paradise** see Enfants Du Paradis, Les

China Is Near

▶ **La Cina E Vicina**

Italy 1967 95 mins bw
Vides Cinematografica

d **Marco Bellocchio**
sc **Marco Bellocchio, Elda Tattoli**
ph **Tonino Delli Colli**

m **Ennio Morricone**
   Paulo Graziosi, Glauco Mauri, Elda Tattoli, Daniela Surina, Pierluigi Apra

When Vittorio (Mauri), the elder brother of a wealthy land-owning family, becomes a Socialist candidate, his younger brother (Apra), who has become a Maoist, does everything he can to disrupt his campaign. Their sister (Tattoli) is indifferent until she meets and falls in love with Vittorio's Party manager (Graziosi).Bellochio, who made an impressive debut with *Fists In The Pocket*, which dealt with family oppression, again uses the metaphor of the family to analyse the way revolutionary activity is absorbed into the *bourgeois* state. With a controlled camera style, the film is sharply ironic about Italian politics, casting its net of mockery far and wide. The performers successfully take on the tone of the picture.

Special Jury Prize Venice 1967

▶ **Chinese Girl, The** see Chinoise, La

Chinese Roulette

▶ **Chinesisches Roulette**

W. Germany 1976 86 mins col
Alatros/Films Du Losange

d **Rainer Werner Fassbinder**
sc **Rainer Werner Fassbinder**
ph **Michael Ballhaus**
m **Peer Raben**
   Margit Carstensen, Ulli Lommel, Anna Karina, Macha Meril, Brigitte Mira, Andrea Schober, Volker Spengler

A crippled girl (Schober) tricks her businessman father (Lommel) and her mother (Carstensen) into going to their country house with their lovers (Karina and Spengler) on the same weekend. There they play a series of games culminating in Chinese Roulette, a truth game that reveals more than they bargained for. It was during the shooting (at photographer Ballhaus's *schloss*) of this bizarre and bitter comedy of bad manners that Fassbinder started on the hard drugs that were to lead to his premature death only six years later. Yet, the roaming camera movements, the aesthetic framing and colour photography make it one of the most controlled and formalistic of his films. Some of the more melodramatic elements of the screenplay are acceptable due to the exemplary ensemble playing.

▶ **Chinesisches Roulette** see Chinese Roulette

La Chinoise

▶ **aka The Chinese Girl**

> France 1967 95 mins col
> Production De La Guéville/Parc/Simar/Anouchka/Athos

d **Jean-Luc Godard**
sc **Jean-Luc Godard**
ph **Raoul Coutard**
m **Stockhausen**
   Anne Wiazemsky, Francis Jeanson, Jean-Pierre Léaud, Juliet Berto

One summer vacation in Paris, a group of young people, including an actor, a painter, a student, an economist and a philosopher, set up a Maoist cell to try to put their theories into revolutionary practice. With this lively, polemical comedy thriller, Godard moved more directly towards the Maoist commitment, which only crystallized with the events of 1968, so prophetically set out here. Many of the debates about *bourgeois* ideology that would take place on the streets of Paris less than a year later are already being expounded by his characters. But it's certainly not only a film of words; there are actions and relationships revolving around Wiazemsky (Godard's new wife) as a student at Nanterre trying to balance her personal and political life. Appropriately, red is the dominant colour of the photography.

Special Jury Prize Venice 1967

▶ **Chips Are Down, The** see Jeux Sont Faits, Les

▶ **Chistoye Nebo** see Clear Sky

▶ **Chloë In The Afternoon** see Love In The Afternoon

Chocolat

> France 1988 105 mins col
> Cinémanuel/MK2 Productions/Cerito Films/SEPT/Caroline Productions/TFI Films

d **Claire Denis**
sc **Claire Denis, Jean-Pol Fargeau**
ph **Robert Alazraki**
m **Abdullah Ibrahim**
   Isaach De Bankolé, Giulia Boschi, François Cluzet, Kenneth Cranham, Mireille Perrier, Emmet Judson Williamson, Cécile Ducasse, Jean-Claude Adelin

France, whose childhood was spent in a far-flung corner of the Cameroons where her father was a French government administrator, pays a return visit to the now independent country. She hitches a lift with a black American now settled there and during the ride she conjures up memories of her childhood: her friendship with the black servant Protée (De Bankolé) to whom her mother was attracted, the comings and goings to their isolated home, which included the arrival of the motley crew and passengers from a crashed light aircraft and, most disturbingly, a young priest gone 'native' (Adelin) whose presence sows serious discord. Claire Denis's feature marks a debut of extraordinary accomplishment, wonderfully cast and acted, especially by De Bankolé, an actor of compelling presence, and by Cécile Ducasse as the child France. Beautiful to look at, the movie is a complex, many-faceted view of French colonialism. The black-white relationships are delineated with sensitivity, while the sense that ultimate harmony is doomed by misperception and 'progress' hovers sadly in the air. An intriguing, dignified film.

▶ **Choses De La Vie, Les** see Things Of Life, The

Christiane F.

▶ **Christiane F. Wir Kinder Vom Bahnhof Zoo**

> W. Germany 1981 131 mins col

Solaris Film/Maran Film/Popular Film/
CLV

d   Ulrich Edel
sc Herman Weigel
ph Justus Pankau, Jürgen Jürges
m   David Bowie, Jürgen Knieper
    Natja Brunckhorst, Thomas Haustein,
    Jens Kuphal, Rainer Wölk

Thirteen-year-old Christiane (Brunckhorst)
gets involved with the teenage drug scene in
Berlin, and has an affair with Detlef
(Haustein) who works as a male prostitute
in order to pay for the dope. Their cold-
turkey attempt goes for naught when they
visit friends at the Zoo station, main hangout
for addicts, pushers and hustlers. Edel, a TV
director making his first feature, based it on
a bestseller, itself written up from Christiane's confessions to two *Stern* reporters.
First-time actors and a semi-documentary
style contribute to a bleak and harrowing
film in which the director has eliminated
any suggestion of glamour by using bleached
out colour and close-ups to convey the full
physical horrors of heroin addiction. Salutary, and not a pleasant way to pass the
time.

► **Christiane F. Wir Kinder Vom
Bahnhof Zoo** see Christiane F.

Christ Stopped At Eboli

► **Cristo Si E Fermato A Eboli**

Italy   1979   155 mins   col
Vides/RAI/Action/Gaumont

d   Francesco Rosi
sc Francesco Rosi, Tonino Guerra, Raffaele
    La Capria
ph Pasqualino De Santis
m   Piero Piccioni
    Gian Maria Volonté, Alain Cuny, Paolo
    Bonacelli, Lea Massari, Irene Papas,
    François Simon

In 1935, doctor-painter-writer Carlo Levi
(Volonté) is exiled from Turin to a primitive
southern village because of his anti-Fascist
views. There he learns to understand the
national character which he finds amusing,
irritating and sympathetic. Like Levi's reactions in Volonté's brilliantly nuanced performance, one might react to Rosi's leisurely,

often too literary film in the same way. The
authentic mountain village background and
characters offer an interesting insight into the
place and period. A television version runs
240 minutes.

► **Chromata Tis Iridas, Ta** see Colours
Of Iris, The

Chronicle Of A Death Foretold

► **Cronaca Di Una Morte Annunciata**

Italy   1987   110 mins   col
Italmedia/Soprofilms/Les Films Ariane/
FR3 Films

d   Francesco Rosi
sc Francesco Rosi, Tonino Guerra
ph Pasqualino De Santis
m   Piero Piccioni
    Rupert Everett, Gian Maria Volonté,
    Ornella Muti, Anthony Delon, Irene
    Papas, Lucia Bosé

Twenty years after a handsome youth (Delon)
was murdered for supposedly deflowering a
beautiful virgin (Muti), leading to the ruin of
her glittering marriage to a wealthy man
(Everett) who abandons her, the community's
doctor (Volonté) returns to investigate the
circumstances of the death. Set in a small and
steamy Colombian town, Rosi's adaptation
of Gabriel Garcia Marquez' novel concentrates on the misplaced codes of honour,
machismo and revenge which led the girl's
twin brothers to commit the brutal crime, and
exposes the hypocritical conspiracy of silence
which made possible the killing of an almost
certainly innocent man. Told in flashback, the
film has epic sweep and visual power, but is
somewhat slow and static, and lacking in a
strong authorial voice.

Chronicle of A Love

► **(US: Story Of A Love Affair)**
► **Cronaca Di Un Amore**

Italy   1950   96 mins   bw
Villani Films

d   Michelangelo Antonioni

sc Michelangelo Antonioni, Danièle D'Anza,
    Silvio Giovaninetti, Francesco Maselli,
    Piero Tellini
ph Enzo Serafin
m   Giovanni Fusco
    Lucia Bosé, Massimo Girotti, Ferdinando
    Sarmi, Gino Rossi, Marika Rowsky

An adulterous wife (Bosé) and her impoverished lover (Girotti) consider the murder of
her rich husband, but he dies – by accident
or suicide – and they have to live with the
guilt of their intention. Antonioni was 38
years old before he found 'a man from Turin
who was willing to finance a film for me'.
Already his personal stamp is noticeable in
the cool, elegant style in contrast to the Neo-
Realist manner of many of his Italian contemporaries, and to his own documentaries. Foreshadowing his later work are the intricate
camera movements, the use of an urban landscape and an unsolved mystery. The plot was
in the tradition of American thrillers such as
The Postman Always Rings Twice which had
inspired Visconti's *Ossessione* (1942) also featuring Girotti.

The Chronicle Of Anna Magdalena Bach

▶ **Chronik Der Anna Magdalena Bach**

W. Germany 1967 93 mins bw
IDI/RAI/Franz Seitz/Kuatorium Junger
Deutscher Film/ Straub-Huillet/
Filmfonds/Tele Pool

d   Jean-Marie Straub
sc Jean-Marie Straub, Danièle Huillet
ph Ugo Piccone
m   Johann Sebastian Bach
    Gustav Leonhardt, Christiane Lang,
    Paolo Carlini, Katrin Leonhardt, Rainer
    Kirchner, Ernst Castelli

The daily life of Johann Sebastian Bach
(Leonhardt) – his conflicts with his patrons,
his work as a composer and musician, his
relationships with his family – as seen through
the eyes of his second wife (Lang). Straub's
second feature, which took 10 years to prepare, is totally convincing in its historical
accuracy and musical authenticity, with most
of the roles taken by professional musicians.
Thus Leonhardt, playing Bach, both the man
and the music, contributes to making this an
almost documentary account of instrumental-
ists at work during the 18th century. The
chronicle is interspersed with concerts and
landscape scenes, and the use of direct sound
and extremely long takes helps the frozen
images to supplement, rather than distract
from, the music.

Chronicle Of A Summer

▶ **Chronique D'Un Été**

France 1961 90 mins bw
Argos Films

d   Jean Rouch, Edgar Morin
sc Jean Rouch, Edgar Morin
ph Roger Morillers, Raoul Coutard, Jean-
    Jacques Tarbes, Michel Brault

One summer, a cross-section of Parisians are
asked by anthropologist film-maker Rouch
and sociologist Morin to respond to the question 'Are You Happy?'. Edited down from 25
hours of interviews, the film takes a fascinating ethnological approach to the French. The
development of light-weight sound and ciné
equipment helped create the style which was
called for the first time *cinéma-vérité* (a
translation of Dziga Vertov's *Kino Pravda*) to
publicize the film. The ambitious document
ends with the interviewees reacting to themselves on screen.

Chronicle Of The Burning Years

▶ **aka Chronicle Of The Years Of The Brazier**

▶ **aka Chronicle Of The Years Of Embers**

▶ **Ahdat Sanawouach El-Djamr**

▶ **aka Chronique Des Années De Braises**

Algeria 1975 175 mins col
ONCIC

d   Mohammed Lakhdar-Hamina
sc Mohammed Lakhdar-Hamina, Rachid
    Boujedra
ph Marcello Gatti
m   Philippe Arthuys
    Mohammed Lakhdar-Hamina, Jorge
    Voyagis, Leila Shenna, Cheik Nourredine

The history of Algeria from 1939 to 1954, the year of the beginning of the revolution, is reflected in the lives of the people in two impoverished villages who rise up against the French colonial presence. One of the most ambitious and expensive productions ever to come out of the Third World, it has the look of a Hollywood epic woven through with Arab culture. Spectacular though it is, Lakhdar-Hamina, one of the pioneers of Algerian cinema, and Boujedra, the great Algerian novelist, still succeed in presenting a personal view of events. Still, a smaller film might have created deeper characters.

Best Film Cannes 1975

▶ **Chronicle Of The Years Of Embers** see Chronicle Of The Burning Years

▶ **Chronicle Of The Years Of The Brazier** see Chronicle Of The Burning Years

The Chronicles Of The Grey House

▶ **Zur Chronik Von Grieshuus**

Germany 1925 172 mins bw
UFA

d   **Arthur Von Gerlach**
sc **Thea Von Harbou**
ph **Fritz Arno Wagner**
m   **Silent**
    Arthur Kraussneck, Paul Hartmann, Lil Dagover, Rudolf Forster, Gertrud Welcker

In the Middle Ages, Hinrich (Hartmann), heir to the Castle Grieshuus, marries Greta (Dagover), a commoner. Hinrich kills his brother (Forster) in a duel over his inheritance and Greta dies in childbirth. After eight years of wandering, Hinrich returns to be reunited with his son. A film (based on an 1884 novella by Theodor Storm) known more by reputation than by experience, it has been difficult to see at its original length, and a 42-minute condensed version is the only evidence most critics have of its quality. Influenced more by Swedish melodramas than the German *Caligari* tradition, it is striking for its location shooting – the castle overlooking a melanch-

oly moor is particularly effective – and its atmospheric lighting. Von Gerlach, a shadowy figure in the German cinema, died of apoplexy soon after completing this, his fourth film. Of the others only *Vanina* (1922) is extant.

▶ **Chronik Der Anna Magdalena Bach** see Chronicle Of Anna Magdalena Bach, The

▶ **Chronique Des Années De Braises** see Chronicle Of The Burning Years

▶ **Chronique D'Un Été** see Chronicle Of A Summer

Chuquiago

Bolivia 1977 87 mins col
Grupo Ukamau

d   **Antonio Eguino**
sc **Oscar Soria**
ph **Antonio Eguina, Julio Lencina, Juan Miranda**
m   **Alberto Villalpando**
    Nestor Yujra, Edmundo Villaroel, David Santalla, Tatiana Aponta, Alejandra Quispe

Four stories about four people from different social strata in La Paz, the capital of Bolivia: an Indian boy (Yujra) working for a drink vendor, a restless teenage son (Villaroel) of workers, a middle-aged lower middle-class functionary and playboy (Santalla) and a university student and spoiled daughter (Aponta) of the *haute bourgeoisie*. Antonio Eguino, the photographer on the once-banned *Blood Of The Condor*, reached a wider audience with this movie, the most expensive to be made in Bolivia by Bolivians, which became the country's biggest box-office success ever, at home and abroad. Made under the military regime, it naturally lacks a political dimension, yet audiences may come to their own conclusions on the lives so skilfully depicted.

The Churning

▶ **Manthan**

India 1976 133 mins col

Gujarat Co-operative Milk Marketing Federation

d   **Shyam Benegal**
sc **Vijay Tendulkar**
ph **Govind Nihalani**
m   **Vanraj Bhatia**
    Girish Karnad, Smita Patil, Naseeruddin Shah, Anant Nag, Amrish Puri

A government team, headed by veterinary surgeon Dr Rao (Karnad) and his assistant (Nag), arrive in the village of Gujarat to help set up a milk co-operative. They encounter many obstacles, not least from the local moneylender (Puri), who also owns the local dairy. Consolidating the reputation established earlier with his debut film, *The Seedling*, Benegal offers another and even more assured study of rural life. Ostensibly about the virtues of the co-operative movement, the film can be taken on many levels – as a tale of class intrigue and hostilities, a view of women's emancipation or as a series of humorous, sharply observed and, superbly photographed studies of village life. The only weakness comes in some of the romantic scenes. Benegal's films, which carry a powerful plea for equality and justice, usually manage to pay for themselves, and, being in Hindi, they reach a wider audience in India than many other fine films in regional languages.

► **Chûte De La Maison Usher, La** see Fall Of The House Of Usher, The

Le Ciel Est À Vous

► **(US: The Woman Who Dared)**

France   1944   105 mins   bw
Raoul Ploquin

d   **Jean Grémillon**
sc **Albert Valentin, Charles Spaak**
ph **Louis Page**
m   **Roland Manuel**
    Madeleine Renaud, Charles Vanel, Jean Debucourt, Anne Vandenne, Raymonde Vernay

Thérèse and Pierre Gauthier (Renaud and Vanel), a *bourgeois* couple with two children, suddenly develop a passion for flying. Thérèse becomes a pilot and, after many crises, breaks the women's non-stop, long distance flight record. A film about flying that has few aerial sequences, doesn't show the heroine at the controls of the plane or a pilot's subjective view, is quite an achievement. Although not overtly political, it was also a brave film to make in Vichy France which stressed that a woman's place is in the home. With his customary tenderness and restraint, Grémillon, a most under-rated director outside France, charts the movements of the marriage and the obsession, in one brilliant passage using a parallel between music and flying. Renaud's and Vanel's performances also take flight.

► **Cielo Sulla Palude** see Heaven Over The Marshes

Cigalon

France   1935   70 mins   bw
Les Films Marcel Pagnol

d   **Marcel Pagnol**
sc **Marcel Pagnol**
ph **A. Assouad**
m   **Vincent Scotto**
    Arnaudy, Henri Poupon, Madame Chabert, Alida Rouffe, Jean Castan, Léon Brouzet, Charles Blavette

Cigalon (Arnaudy), once a grand chef in the best hotels, runs the only restaurant in a village in Provence until Madame Toffi (Chabert), ex-laundress, opens a rival restaurant just opposite. War is declared, culminating in a battle over a 'rich' client, followed by a merger i.e. marriage. A comedy as delicious as the 200-franc meal served in the film, and played with the verve usual in Pagnol's *oeuvre*. However, as with *Merlusse*, he was dissatisfied with the first shooting and refilmed it a few weeks later. In the premier attempt, Poupon played the title role, but was more at ease here as The Client.

► **Cina E Vicina, La** see China Is Near

Cinderella – Italian Style

► **(US: More Than A Miracle)**
► **C'Era Una Volta**

Italy   1967   103 mins   col

Champion Films/Concordia

d   **Francesco Rosi**
sc **Tonino Guerra, Raffaele La Capria,
    Giuseppe Patroni Griffi, Francesco Rosi**
ph **Pasquale De Santis**
m   **Piero Piccione
    Sophia Loren, Omar Sharif, Dolores Del
    Rio, Georges Wilson, Leslie French,
    Carlo Pisacane**

A Spanish nobleman (Sharif), under family
pressure to marry which he does his best to
ignore, falls in love with a beautiful peasant
girl (Loren). Misunderstandings and the
deceits practised by others keep them apart
until the intervention of a priest, now become
an angel, helps them to a happy ending.
This curious confection from Rosi, concocted
from several Italian fairy tales, is photographed to recall the look of storybook
illustrations. Acted with a light touch, the
film is charming and sometimes funny, but
is hampered by being overlong for its
content.

Cinema Paradiso

▶ **Nuovo Cinema Paradiso**

Italy 1988 124 mins col
Les Films Ariane (Paris)/Cristaldifilm
(Rome)/TFI/RAI/TRE/Forum Pictures
(Spain)

d   **Giuseppe Tornatore**
sc **Giuseppe Tornatore**
ph **Blasco Giurato**
m   **Ennio Morricone
    Philippe Noiret, Jacques Perrin, Salvatore
    Cascio, Mario Leonardi, Agnese Nano,
    Antonella Attili, Pupella Maggio,
    Leopoldo Trieste**

Salvatore (Cascio), a little boy whose father
has been killed in World War II, lives with
his harassed mother in the grimness of a
small, war-torn Sicilian village where the local
priest rules with a rod of pious iron. He finds
refuge from the daily misery of life by sneak-
ing into the cinema where he becomes a thorn
in the side of Alfredo (Noiret), the projectionist. In time, Alfredo becomes his friend
and mentor, teaching the boy to take over
his job but ultimately encouraging him to
leave the stifling confines of the village. Years

later Salvatore (Perrin) is in Rome, a successful film-maker but a failed human being.
Tornatore's film travels a lengthy timespan in
a series of seamless and visually impressive
episodes, giving us three Salvatores (Leonardi
is the adolescent) for the price of one and a
marvellous collection of vintage movie clips
from the world's cinema. It was made in the
same year as Scola's *Splendor* (which it beat
in competition at Cannes) to which it has
been endlessly compared due to the similarity
of theme – the lure of film as seen through
the eyes of a child, culminating in the death
of the picture palace. Both movies achieve
wit and poignancy and are a must for true
lovers of the cinema. But, for all its expertise
and the accolades with which it has been
showered, *Cinema Paradiso* is finally the lesser
achievement, increasingly resorting to sugary
clichés, overlong and ultimately failing to
make its point with sufficient clarity.

Special Jury Prize Cannes 1989

Best Foreign Film Oscar 1989

▶ **Ciociara, La** see Two Women

Circle Of Deceit

▶ **Die Fälschung**

W. Germany 1981 109 mins col
Bioskop-Film/Artemis-Film (Munich)/
Argos Films (Paris)

d   **Volker Schlöndorff**
sc **Volker Schlöndorff, Jean-Claude Carrière,
    Margarethe Von Trotta, Kai Hermann**
ph **Igor Luther**
m   **Maurice Jarre
    Bruno Ganz, Hanna Schygulla, Jerzy
    Skolimowski, Gila Von Weitershausen,
    Jean Carmet**

A West German journalist (Ganz) in the
throes of marital conflict is sent to the Lebanon with his photographer (Skolimowski).
Once there, he gets caught up in events that
compromise his professional integrity, has an
affair with an old friend (Schygulla), now the
widow of an Arab, and stabs an Arab civilian
in panic, all the while undergoing a crisis of
conscience, until he finally returns home to
his wife. Schlöndorff's film is an uneasy mix

of personal and political concerns. Actually filmed in war-torn Lebanon, the scenes of civil strife and daily atrocities have a terrifying and dramatic immediacy, but the hero's indulgent preoccupation with self, his political confusion and his half-baked opportunism, as well as his clichéd domestic situation, amount to an irritating character who fails to serve any deeper political purpose the director might have had.

The Citadel

▶ **El Kalaa**

▶ **aka La Citadelle**

Algeria 1988 98 mins col
Le Centre Algérien De L'Art Et L'Industrie Cinématographique

d   **Mohamed Chouikh**
sc **Mohamed Chouikh**
ph **Allel Yahyaoui**
m   **Djawad Fasla**
    Khaled Barkat, Djillali Ain Tedelles,
    Fettouma Ousliha, Fatima Belhadj, Momo

In the little Algerian village of El Kalaa lives Sidi (Tedelles), a merchant who already has three wives but, to their distress, decides to acquire a fourth. Meanwhile, his son Kaddour (Barkat) is making overtures to Aissa (Momo), a married woman, and is deceived by a stranger and the local shaman into believing that he can make her his. Aissa's husband complains to Sidi that Kaddour attacked his wife, but unknown to all of them, Sidi and Aissa have become lovers. Nonetheless, Sidi plans a punishment for his son. The romantic comings and goings, and the curious lesson that the son is taught by his father are really of less substance or interest in this film than the careful unfolding of village life and the portrayal of women's lot in a claustrophobic, rigid and male-dominated society. Chouikh, formerly an actor with the Algerian National Theatre, brings a sharp and uncompromising eye to the proceedings, offering an authentic revelation of life as it is lived in a remote mountain village where Muslim law and ancient custom prevail.

▶ **Citadelle, La** see Citadel, The

The Citizen

▶ **Nagarik**

India 1952 120 mins bw
Film Guild

d   **Ritwik Ghatak**
sc **Ritwik Ghatak**
ph **Ramananda Sengupta**
m   **Hariprasanna Das**
    Satindra Bhattacharya, Prabha Devi,
    Shobha Sen, Ajit Banerjee, Ketaki Devi

In the teeming city of Calcutta, a young college graduate (Bhattacharya) is unable to get a job that would allow him to marry the girl (Ketaki Devi) he loves. When his father dies, things go from bad to worse and he, his mother (Prabha Devi) and unmarried sister (Sen) move from a middle-class neighbourhood into the working-class slums. Ghatak's first feature, made three years before Satyajit Ray's watershed *Pather Panchali*, was only released in 1977, two years after the director's death. The main strength of the film is its neo-realist depiction of the city which forms the background to a *petit-bourgeois* family with illusions of upward social mobility. The weaknesses come in some of the theatrical acting, some erratic editing and lighting (not surprising as it was made with little money under difficult circumstances) and a belief that the use of the 'Communist Internationale' on the sound track at the end is sufficient to make a Marxist point.

▶ **Città Delle Donne, La** see City Of Women

City Of Pirates

▶ **La Ville Des Pirates**

France 1983 121 mins col
Les Films Du Passage (Paris)/Metro Films (Lisbon)

d   **Râúl Ruiz**
sc **Râúl Ruiz**
ph **Acácio De Almeida**
m   **Jorge Arriagada**
    Hugues Quester, Anne Alvaro, Melvil
    Poupaud, André Engel, Duarte De
    Almeida

A surrealist fantasy involving a murderous child (Poupaud), a dreamy girl (Alvaro), who might be his mother, a schizophrenic pirate (Quester) who keeps her prisoner on a rocky island, incestuous relationships, a castration and a rape. It is impossible to give a synopsis of Ruiz's delirious baroque tale and even more difficult to compare it to anything else in contemporary cinema. Elusive and allusive as the film is, defying definitive interpretation, the surprising imagery and the bizarre humour hold the interest in this *reductio ad absurdum* of storytelling.

A City of Sadness

▶ Beiqing Chengshi

Taiwan 1989 160 mins col
3-H Films/Era International

d   **Hou Hsiao-hsien**
sc **Wu Nianzhen, Zhu Tianwen**
ph **Chen Huai'en**
m   **Tachikawa Naoki, Zhang Hongyi**
     Li Tianlu, Chen Songyong, Gao Jie, Tony Leung, Wu Yifang, Xin Shufen

The Lin family, headed by elderly widower Lin Ah-Lu (Tianlu), is one of many families who were forced to change their way of life when Taiwan reverted to Chinese sovereignty after Japanese colonial rule in 1945. Lin and his eldest son, Wen-Heung (Songyong), refurbish their Japanese-style nightclub and reopen it as the Little Shanghai. The second son is reported missing on forced service and the third son, Wen-Leung (Jie), who went to work as a translator for the Japanese in Shanghai, returns with a nervous breakdown and is hospitalized. The youngest son, Wen-Ching (Leung), deaf and mute since a childhood accident, gets drawn into the struggle for Taiwanese independence. Audiences with an understanding of the political and historical context in which this long and complex panorama of Taiwanese life is situated would certainly gain a great deal more from Hsiao-hsien's demanding film. Others with enough patience and intellectual curiosity will be rewarded by the meticulously recreated background and the human drama in the foreground. By concentrating on four contrasting sons, one of whom never appears, many of

the shadier aspects of that chaotic period of Taiwan's history are clarified, helped by the voice-over extracts from the diary of a nurse (Xin Shufen) who marries the youngest son. But the director's extensive use of medium and long shots distance the spectator and prevent too much involvement with the excellently portrayed characters.

Best Film Venice 1989

City Of Women

▶ La Città Delle Donne

Italy 1980 140 mins col
Opera Film/Gaumont(France)

d   **Federico Fellini**
sc **Federico Fellini, Bernardino Zapponi**
ph **Giuseppe Rotunno**
m   **Luis Bacalov**
     Marcello Mastroianni, Anna Prucnal, Bernice Stegers, Ettore Manni, Donatella Damiani

Snàporaz (Mastroianni), a middle-aged businessman, is enticed off a train and finds himself in a world completely dominated by women. As more and more bizarre adventures overtake him, it is clear that he is moving through his own fears and fantasies about women. This rather simple-minded and self-indulgent anti-feminist allegory has the advantage of Fellini's visual and emotional mastery and for much of its excessive length, there is a great deal to wonder at. But it lacks Nino Rota's essential musical collaboration, as well as any recognizable characters, although Mastroianni makes what he can of the pathetic and ridiculous hero.

▶ Ciulinii Baraganului see Thistles Of Baragan, The

Claire's Knee

▶ Le Genou De Claire

France 1970 106 mins col
Films Du Losange

d   **Eric Rohmer**
sc **Eric Rohmer**

ph **Nestor Almendros**
   Jean-Claude Brialy, Aurora Cornu,
   Laurence De Monaghan, Béatrice
   Romand, Gérard Falconetti

Prior to his marriage to a Swedish woman, a diplomat in his thirties (Brialy) takes a brief summer holiday at the lake resort of Annecy. Encouraged by his Romanian novelist friend (Cornu), he flirts with two sisters, but is only satisfied when he gets to fondle the knee of the elder one (De Monaghan), a sensuous beauty. Rohmer's lucid prose and witty observation delights as much as the shimmering background to his film. The actual moment when Brialy fulfils his desire is as erotic as any heavy-breathing bed play.

▶ **Clan Des Siciliens, Le** see Sicilian Clan, The

▶ **Classe Operaia Va In Paradiso, La** see Working Class Go To Heaven, The

Class Relations

▶ **Klassenverhältnisse**

W. Germany 1984 127 mins bw
Janus Film/Hessischer Rundfunk

d **Jean-Marie Straub, Danièle Huillet**
sc **Jean-Marie Straub, Danièle Huillet**
ph **William Lubtchansky**
   Christian Heinisch, Mario Adorf,
   Manfred Blank, Harun Farocki, Kathrin
   Bold, Libgart Schwarz, Laura Betti, Anne
   Bold, Alfred Edel, Andi Engel

Sixteen-year-old Karl Rossmann (Heinisch), sent from Prague to America, is unexpectedly welcomed by a rich uncle (Adorf). After failing in business, Karl sets out across country with two tramps, gets a job as an elevator-boy in a hotel and becomes a servant to an ex-opera singer (Betti). Wherever he goes, he feels he has been unjustly treated, but his goodness and integrity remain intact. Much of the original dialogue has been retained in Straub and Huillet's adaptation of Kafka's *Amerika*, as has the irony and moments of slapstick comedy; only the unfinished novel's final chapter in Oklahoma has

been omitted. The America that Kafka never saw was created by filming surroundings in Germany that could be anywhere. The directors' most approachable film, it demonstrates their characteristic 'minimalist' style of paring down each scene to its essentials (usually only one actor on screen at a time), restraining any expression and, as the title suggests, bringing out more social than psychological elements of the picaresque tale.

Clean Slate

▶ **Coup De Torchon**

France 1981 128 mins col
Les Films De La Tour/Les Films
A2/Little Bear

d **Bertrand Tavernier**
sc **Jean Aurenche, Bertrand Tavernier**
ph **Pierre William Glenn**
m **Philippe Sarde**
   Philippe Noiret, Isabelle Huppert, Jean-
   Pierre Marielle, Stéphane Audran, Guy
   Marchand

Lucien Cordier (Noiret), lackadaisical law officer and general laughing stock of a West African township in 1938, undergoes a complete transformation of character when, after shooting a pair of pimps, he sets out to get rid of everybody who is a thorn in his side, including his wife whose death he contrives, and his mistress whom he frames. Noiret is excellent in a film which offers some quirky humour and a good sense of atmosphere, and some entertainment is to be had from this portrait of a man seized by a form of mania, provided one doesn't look for any coherency of motivation. Tavernier has translated, adapted and distorted a novel by Jim Thompson set in the Deep South, and, in so doing, has muddied its motivations.

Clear Sky

▶ **Chistoye Nebo**

USSR 1961 109 mins col
Mosfilm

d **Grigori Chukrai**
sc **Daniel Khrabrovitsky**

ph **Sergei Poluyanov**
m **Mikhail Ziv**
   Nina Drobysheva, Yevgeny Urbansky, N.
   Kuzmina, Vitali Konyayev

A young woman (Drobysheva) meets and falls in love with a famous test pilot (Urbansky). She has his child and waits for him to come back from the war. When he returns, he is unjustly accused of treachery and stripped of his membership of the Party but, after Stalin's death, he is recognized as a 'Hero of the Soviet Union'. Watching this competently directed romantic drama, it is difficult to imagine its impact in the USSR at the time. When the ex-hero is told he cannot rejoin the Party, a huge effigy of Stalin looks down on him. The film ends with a symbolic shot of an iced-over river beginning to thaw. Aside from the historical interest of the piece, the acting of the leads is extremely good and many of the scenes have a ring of truth, despite the sprinkling of clichés throughout.

▶ **Cléo De 5 À 7** see Cleo From 5 To 7

Cleo From 5 To 7

▶ **Cléo De 5 À 7**

France   1961   90 mins   bw-col
Rome-Paris Films

d **Agnès Varda**
sc **Agnès Varda**
ph **Jean Rabier**
m **Michel Legrand**
   Corinne Marchand, Antoine Bourseiller,
   Dorothée Blanck, Michel Legrand, José-
   Luis Villalonga

Two hours in the life of a spoiled nightclub singer as she waits for the medical verdict on whether she is to live or die. Rabier's camera captures the sheen of Paris where every trivial incident takes on a new significance for the heroine. In fact, everything is seen in such *Nouvelle Vague* brilliance that the anxiety of the protagonist (the coolly beautiful ex-model Marchand) gets somewhat buried. The silent comedy Cleo watches shows Varda's colleagues Jean-Luc Godard, Anna Karina, Eddie Constantine and Jean-Claude Brialy enjoying themselves.

▶ **Cloak, The** see Overcoat, The

Clochemerle

▶ **aka The Scandals of Clochemerle**

France   1947   93 mins   bw
Cinéma Productions

d **Pierre Chenal**
sc **Gabriel Chevallier**
ph **Robert Le Fèbvre**
m **Henri Sauguet**
   Brochard, Maximilienne, Simone Michels,
   Jane Marken, Paul Demange, Félix
   Oudart, Saturnin Fabre

The progressive mayor (Brochard) of a small, conservative French village decides to build a public convenience in the town square, much to the horror of the inhabitants. As nobody in British or American films ever went to the lavatory or even possessed one until the 1960s, this mildly amusing comedy which revolved round a latrine, was a big hit abroad. But Chevallier seemed to have coarsened the satire in the adaptation from his own bestseller.

Closely Observed Trains

▶ **(US: Closely Watched Trains)**

▶ **Ostře Sledované Vlaky**

Czechoslovakia   1966   92 mins   col
Ceskoslovensky Film

d **Jiří Menzel**
sc **Jiří Menzel, Bohumil Hrabal**
ph **Jaromír Šofr**
m **Jiří Pavlik**
   Václav Neckár, Jitka Bendová, Libuše
   Havelková, Vladimir Valenta, Josef Somr,
   Jiří Menzel, Nadia Urbanková

During the German Occupation, a young trainee railway guard (Neckár) at a remote country station desperately tries to lose his virginity with, among others, the station master's wife (Havelková). He finally achieves his goal with a Partisan girl (Urbanková), who calls herself Victoria Freie (the underground password), before tragedy strikes. Menzel's first solo-directed film is closely observed, satiric, touching, anti-heroic and humorous, very much in the Czech new wave tradition of the 1960s. It is also perfectly balanced between comedy and tragedy. The director wanted a happy ending, but co-writer Hrabal, on whose novel the film was based, persuaded him to retain the tragic conclusion.

Best Foreign Film Oscar 1967

▶ **Closely Watched Trains** see Closely Observed Trains

Close To The Wind

▶ **Oss Emellan**

Sweden 1969 110 mins col
Omega Film/Filmmakarna/'Oss Emellan' Inc

d **Stellan Olsson**
sc **Stellan Olsson, Per Oscarsson**
ph **Jesper Höm, Lasse Dahlqvist**
m **Joe Hill, Tage Sivén**
   Per Oscarsson, Bärbel Oscarsson, Lina Oscarsson, Boman Oscarsson, Maria Oscarsson, Beppe Wolgers, Christina Johansson

Per (Oscarsson), an unsuccessful artist with three children, devotes his energies to attempting a life of individualistic non-conformism, while his wife Bärbel teaches at the local school to support them. Per's excesses of behaviour are infinite and the unveiling of pornographic designs to the board that has commissioned a mural. In his debut film, Olsson retains control of a tricky subject by recognizing the contradictions inherent in opposing a social system without having a coherent alternative to offer, and by creating an impressively naturalistic world for his protagonist. Per Oscarsson's close involvement in the project includes the casting of his wife and children, called by their own names in the film and thus helping to blur the lines between fiction and reality. The movie, which analyses the artist's role in society, does so in tones of parody and deploys some wonderfully contrary images: episodes of marital discord are set against lyrical backgrounds, while Per's idyllic outing on the beach with his mistress is accompanied by grey skies and blustery wind.

Clothes Make The Man

▶ **Kleider Machen Leute**

Germany 1940 102 mins bw
Terra-Filmkunst

d **Helmut Käutner**
sc **Helmut Käutner**
ph **Ewald Daub**
m **Bernhard Eichhorn**
   Heinz Rühmann, Hertha Feiler, Hilde Sessak, Hans Sternberg, Fritz Odemar, Rudolf Schündler, Erich Ponto

Wenzel (Rühmann), a daydreaming tailor's apprentice in a small Tyrolean town, gives in to fantasy and cuts the Mayor's new dress suit to fit himself. Sacked for this action, he leaves town with only the suit to his name and is everywhere mistaken for a nobleman. Encouraged by a puppet master (Ponto), he goes to Goldbach, pretending to be Stroganov (Odemar), a Russian Count who is expected there by Fräulein Von Serafin (Sessak), who falls in love with him. To complicate matters further, the real Stroganov turns up... Basing his third film on a novella by the 19th-century Swiss-German Romantic, Gottfried Keller, Käutner has made a thoroughly entertaining film from a well-constructed screenplay. Aside from its obvious merits of directorial quality, and a story in which romance and humour is the veneer applied to an ironic comment on the hypocritical surface of *bourgeois* values – all show and no substance – the film offers other pleasures. These spring from Käutner's exceptional eye for incidental but telling visual detail that contribute to his loving and critical evocation of period folksiness, from which the deceiver emerges as worthier than the deceived.

The Clowns

▶ **Il Clowns**

Italy 1970 92 mins col
RAI/Leone/O.R.T.F./Bavaria Film (Munich)

d   Federico Fellini
sc Federico Fellini, Bernardino Zapponi
ph Dario Di Palma
m   Nino Rota
    Riccardo Billi, Tino Scotti, Fanfulla,
    Carlo Rizzo, Freddo Pistoni (and other
    Italian and French clowns), Pierre Etaix,
    Annie Fratellini, Anita Ekberg, Victoria
    Chaplin, Maya Morin

Fellini and a comically clumsy film crew
investigate the art of the circus clown by
watching and talking to still active, as well
as former, exponents of the profession. He
also remembers the Rimini of his childhood
when the circus came to town. 'My films
owe an enormous amount to the circus. For
me the clowns were always a traumatic
visual experience, ambassadors of a vocation
of a showman,' Fellini has stated. Here the
great Italian ringmaster of the cinema affectionately returns to the root of his inspiration, absorbing it masterfully into his own
personal vision.

▶ **Clowns, II** see Clowns, The

Coach To Vienna

▶ **Kocár Do Vidne**

    Czechoslovakia   1966   80 mins   bw
    Ceskoslovensky Film, Barrandov
    Studio

d   Karel Kachyna
sc Jan Procházka, Karel Kachyna
ph Josef Illík
m   Jan Novák
    Iva Janzurová, Jaromír Hanzlík, Ludek
    Munzar

In 1944 in Czechoslovakia, young peasant
woman Christa (Janzurová) watches the Germans hang her husband for stealing two
bags of cement. She buries him and then her
farm wagon is commandeered by an Austrian soldier and his seriously wounded German colleague who order her to drive them
to the frontier. Appearing to comply, she
plans her revenge..... Centring on Janzurová's almost silent and compellingly
strong performance, this tightly constructed
film eloquently describes the brutalizing
effects of war and the tragic pointlessness of

revenge. It is unfortunate that a work of
grim horror, made with clear-sighted intelligence and irony, should have an English
title that so misleadingly evokes a period
romance.

Cobra Verde

    W. Germany   1988   111 mins   col
    Concorde Film. A Werner Herzog Film
    Production. In co-operation with ZDF &
    the Ghana Film Industry Corp.

d   Werner Herzog
sc Werner Herzog
ph Viktor Ruzicka
m   Popol Vuh
    Klaus Kinski, King Ampaw, José Lewgoy,
    Salvatore Basile, Peter Berling

Francisco Manoel Da Silva (Kinski), an
abused and exploited Brazilian peasant,
becomes the notorious bandit Cobra Verde.
He is sent off to revive the Brazilian slave
trade in West Africa, where he confronts the
mad King of Dahomey. Another manic trip
by Herzog and Kinski into the more untamed
territories of the world (this was made under
difficult conditions in Ghana) has plenty of
stunning photography of exotic locations. But
the narrative, based loosely on Bruce Chat-
win's novel *The Viceroy Of Ouidah*, is shapeless and halting, and the flaxen-haired Kinski
is a more ludicrous and unsympathetic figure
than any of his previous incarnations of
obsessive heroes have been. The putative
theme of slavery and colonialism is also dubi-
ously expounded.

▶ **Cobweb Castle** see Throne Of Blood

▶ **Cochecito, El** see Wheelchair, The

Cocktail Molotov

    France   1980   100 mins   col
    Alexandre Films/Antenne 2

d   Diane Kurys
sc Diane Kurys, Philippe Adrien, Alain Le
    Henry
ph Philippe Rousselot
m   Yves Simon

Élise Caron, Philippe Lebas, François Cluzet

After a quarrel with her parents, 18-year-old Anne (Caron) leaves home and decides to go and live on a kibbutz. Her boyfriend Frédéric (Lebas), also her first lover, and his friend Bruno (Cluzet), learning of her departure, go after her with the intention of bringing her home. In Venice their car and her possessions are stolen and the trio are forced to hitch-hike back to France. In her second feature (following *Peppermint Soda*) Diane Kurys again demonstrates her acute gifts for observing the behaviour and emotional nuances of young people, and her talent for drawing excellent performances from well-chosen young actors. The film is simple and has charm, but although set against a hovering backdrop of May 1968, seems only cursorily aware of these events. The road movie context of the film is at odds with its intimate concerns and the whole package adds up to no more than a pleasing, well-observed, but ultimately forgettable tale.

▶ **Coeurs Verts, Les** see Naked Hearts

Coiffeur Pour Dames

▶ **(US: Artists With The Ladies)**

France   1932   71 mins   bw
Joinville

d   **René Guissart**
sc **Paul Armont, Marcel Garbidon**
ph **Enzo Riccioni**
m   **Claude Pigault, Fernand Vimont**
    Fernand Gravey, Mona Goya, Irene Brilliant, Nina Miral

An ordinary barber (Gravey) from the country makes a great hit in Paris as a fashionable hairdresser and ends up with a string of beautiful women getting in his hair. Also busy with their scissors were the American censors who snipped about five 'lewd' minutes of the film. Nonetheless, much of Gravey's charm and the light comedy with songs survived. It was remade 20 years later with Fernandel.

▶ **Cold Cuts** see Buffet Froid

Cold Days

▶ **Hideg Napok**

Hungary   1966   101 mins   col
Mafilm Studio

d   **András Kovács**
sc **András Kovács**
ph **Ferenc Szécsényi**
    Zoltán Latinovits, Iván Darvas, Adám Szirtes, Tibor Szilágyi, Margit Bara, Eva Vas, Mari Szémes

In 1946, four ex-soldiers await trial in a Hungarian prison cell for their involvement in the army's massacre of over 3,000 people in the Yugoslav town of Novi Sad in 1942. Their conversation reveals the part each played in the event, their attitudes towards it, and the concerns which now preoccupy them. Kovács tells his tale in the form of a jigsaw puzzle, his visual approach linking the cold white cell walls with the snow that covered Novi Sad, and evoking the gruesome details of mass murder in swift, subtle images: a pile of discarded clothes, a distant huddle of figures, the echo of shots. A superb exercise in tension building and a penetrating, horrifying exposé of the processes which blunt man's humanity.

La Collectionneuse

France   1967   90 mins   col
Films Du Losange/Rome-Paris

d   **Eric Rohmer**
sc **Eric Rohmer**
ph **Nestor Almendros**
m   **Blossom Toes, Giorgio Gomelsky**
    Patrick Bachau, Daniel Pommereulle, Haydée Politoff, Alain Jouffroy

An artist (Bachau) and an antique dealer (Pommereulle) share a friend's villa in St Tropez with a bikini-clad nymphette (Politoff) who sleeps with a different boy each night. The two older men try to resist being added to her collection. The third of Rohmer's Six Moral Tales (and the first of feature length), made just before *My Night With Maud*, is, in the director's words, 'less concerned with what people do than with what is going on in their minds while they are doing it'. As in most of his films, the main action is in the witty analytical dialogue spoken among hedonistic settings, although it never becomes static, and Rohmer establishes the theme of resistance to sexual temptation, making sure that the lure is tantalizingly erotic.

Special Jury Prize Berlin 1967

Colonel Redl

▶ Redl Ezredes

Hungary/W. Germany/
Austria   1984   149 mins   col
Mafilm Studio Objectiv/Mokep/Film
Und Fersehen/ZDF/ORF

d   **István Szabó**
sc   **István Szabó, Peter Dobai**
ph   **Lajos Koltai**
m   **Extracts from Schumann, Chopin, Liszt
and others
Klaus Maria Brandauer, Hans-Christian
Blech, Armin Müller-Stahl, Gudrun
Landgrebe, Jan Niklas, László Mensáros,
Eva Szabó and 50 further featured players**

Alfred Redl (Brandauer), a humble railwayman's son, is fiercely patriotic and ambitious. He earns a place at the military academy and eventually becomes head of military intelligence to the Austro-Hungarian Empire in its dying days. He is both bisexual and Jewish and, in seeking to conceal these facts, he betrays his fellow officers, becomes a spy, and ends up shooting himself in one last act of honour. There are many complex and interweaving strands of plot and character examination present in this work which Szabó based on John Osborne's play, *A Patriot For Me*. The director has composed a very handsome film of epic sweep, but never loses sight of his central concern – the ambiguity of Redl's nature and the ease with which he tells the lies that destroy him. Brandauer, as in Szabó's *Mephisto*, is magnificent.

Special Jury Prize Cannes 1986

The Colour Of Pomegranates

▶ Tsvet Granata

▶ aka Sayat Nova

USSR   1969   73 mins   col

Armenfilm

d   **Sergo Paradjanov**
sc   **Sergo Paradjanov**
ph   **Suren and M. Shakhbazian**
m   **Tigran Mansurian
Sofico Chiaureli, M. Aleksanian, V.
Galstian, G. Gegechkori, O. Minassian**

Imagined and actual episodes from the life of the 18th-century Armenian poet Arutiun Sayadin, known as Sayat Nova, in which he rises from carpet weaver's apprentice to court minstrel and then to archbishop. Paradjanov was imprisoned for various 'crimes' in 1974 and released in 1977, the year a faded 16mm copy of this extraordinary film was smuggled into the West. Six years later, with the full cooperation of the Soviet authorities, it was shown widely and to acclaim in its original condition. A visual experience that defies description, its eloquent imagery and often obscure symbols are derived from Armenian paintings, poetry and history. As a friend of the director remarked, 'Paradjanov makes films not about how things are, but how they would have been had he been God'.

The Colours Of Iris

▶ Ta Chromata Tis Iridas

Greece   1974   100 mins   col
George Papalios

d   **Nikos Panayotopoulos**
sc   **Nikos Panayotopoulos**
ph   **Nikos Kavoukidis**
m   **Stamatis Spanoudakis
Nikitis Tsakiroglou, George Dialegmenos,
Vangelis Kazan, George Moschides**

During the shooting of a commercial on a beach, a portly middle-aged man, wearing a brown suit and carrying an umbrella, walks into the sea and is not seen again. Nico (Tsakiroglou), a composer, carries out his own investigation into the incident when the police drop the case. With the fall of the repressive regime of the Colonels, there was naturally a sudden burgeoning of liberated works of art, of which this striking, *avantgarde*, absurdist comedy is a good example. Homages are made to Godard, to French and American *policiers*, and to Greece's most distinguished director, Theo Angelopoulos. Political satire is also strongly present in the depiction of the police as both sinister and comic. Much of the film is rather too self-regarding and clever for its own good, but there is a lot to admire and to be surprised at.

▶ **Colpire Al Cuore** see Blow To The Heart

Come And See

▶ **Idi I Smotri**

USSR 1985 142 mins col/bw
Byelarusfilm/Mosfilm

d **Elem Klimov**
sc **Ales Adamovich, Elem Klimov**
ph **Alexei Rodionov**
m **Oleg Yanchenko, Mozart**
   Alexei Kravchenko, Olga Mironova,
   Liubomiras Laucevicius, Vladas Bagdonas

Teenaged Florya (Kravchenko) is taken off by a group of anti-German partisans, fighting in the woods of Byelorussia in 1943. They disappear and he is left to wander, gun in hand, until he rejoins them at the end as an active and hardened participant. Klimov's film is a product of mixed merits. Florya's ordeal, which turns his hair grey and wrinkles his young face, is undeniably moving, and there are some striking visual set-pieces. However, from the moment early on when the boy discovers his village is destroyed and his family dead, the viewer joins him in witnessing an unbroken series of Nazi atrocities, until the assault of deranged images on the senses leads to numbed detachment.

▶ **Comédie Du Bonheur, Le** see Comedy Of Happiness, The

The Comedy Of Happiness

▶ **Le Comédie Du Bonheur**

France 1940 108 mins bw
Paulvé/Scaleta

d **Marcel L'Herbier**
sc **Marcel L'Herbier**
ph **Massimo Terzano**
m **Jacques Ibert**
   Michel Simon, Ramon Novarro, Louis

Jourdan, Micheline Presle, Alermé, Doumel

A banker (Simon), whose altruistic tendencies have led his family to put him in a mental institution, escapes and ends up in a boarding house full of sad residents. He hires a troupe of carnival players to give them the illusion of happiness. Subtle, whimsical and witty (with additional dialogue by Jean Cocteau), this made-in-Rome picture was an excellent vehicle for the ebullient anarchic talents of Michel Simon. It also has an interestingly diverse cast, including former silent star Ramon 'Ben Hur' Novarro, and 21-year-old Louis Jourdan in one of his first films. L'Herbier's aesthetic sense is evident in the costumes and decoration of the carnival scenes.

Comic Strip Hero

▶ **(US: The Killing Game)**
▶ **Jeu De Massacre**

France 1967 95 mins col
Francinor/Coficitel/AJ Films/Films Modernes

d **Alain Jessua**
sc **Alain Jessua**
ph **Jacques Robin**
m **Jacques Loussier**
   Jean-Pierre Cassel, Claudine Auger,
   Michel Duchaussoy, Eléonore Hirt, Guy Saint-Jean

Pierre (Cassel) is a creator and writer of comic strips which his wife Jacqueline (Auger) illustrates. The couple's routine is disrupted by the visit of Bob (Duchaussoy), a young stranger who claims to live the experiences of Pierre's heroes and says that he is being pursued by a gang after his life. In dealing with the clashing and merging of imagination and reality, Jessua is traversing territory similar to that of his *Life Upside Down*, this time resolving his situation with inventiveness that is rooted nearer to sanity than madness. It's a good-natured film, full of incidents to hold the attention, well acted, cleverly designed and with the comic strips (drawn by Guy Peellaert) used to enhance the tale.

Coming Out

East Germany 1990 109 mins col

DEFA

d   **Heiner Carow**
sc   **Wolfram Witt**
ph   **Martin Schlesinger**
m   **Stefan Carow**
     **Mathias Freihof, Dagmar Manzel, Dirk
     Kummer, Michael Gwisdek, Walfriede
     Schmitt, Axel Wandtke**

Philipp (Freihof), an idealistic literature teacher in East Berlin, forms a relationship with Tanya (Manzel) and moves in with her. A chance meeting with an old schoolmate (Wandtke), with whom he was sexually involved, reawakens doubts as to his heterosexuality and he begins to investigate the underground gay life of the city with dramatic and often unhappy results for himself, Tanya and Mathias (Kummer), a young boy who falls in love with him. *Coming Out* (which has the same title in Germany), is a very frank and quite affecting account of the pitfalls of homosexuality, particularly under a repressive regime. As a piece of film-making, however, it is no more than adequate and suffers – perhaps understandably – from some heavy-handed didacticism and lingering melodramatic overstatement. Nonetheless, it has its moments, among them a lengthy spectacle in a bar where everybody appears to be in drag or some other form of fancy dress, and the sequence which shows the monumental difficulty of securing a ticket for the opera. Doubtless life is complicated in different ways since the wall came down.

▶ **Commare Secca, La** see Grim
Reaper, The

The Commissar

▶ **Komissar**

     USSR   1967   110 mins   bw
     Gorky Studios

d   **Aleksandr Askoldov**
sc   **Aleksandr Askoldov**
ph   **Valery Ginsberg**
m   **Alfred Schnittke**
     **Nonna Mordyukova, Rolan Bykov, Raisa
     Nedashkovskaya, Vasily Shukshin, Pavlik
     Levin, Ludmilla Volinskaya**

The Red Army takes over a town after its surrender and Commissar Clavdia Vavilova (Mordyukova) tells her commander she is pregnant. Instead of being court-martialled, she is billeted with a poor Jewish family consisting of a tinsmith (Bykov), his wife (Nedashkovskaya), his mother and six children. After the birth of her child, the Commissar makes the agonizing decision to leave the baby with the loving family and rejoin her regiment. Made in 1967, this powerful and vivid recreation of the life of a struggling Jewish family during the 1920 Civil War was released 20 years later after a screening at the Moscow Film Festival. One of the rare Soviet films to deal with Russian anti-Semitism, it caused controversy, particularly since Askoldov, whose debut film this was, refused to cut the flash-forward to the Jewish Holocaust, which the Commissar imagines. One of the most moving aspects of the film is the way in which a close relationship is built up between the initially arrogant Commissar and the wary family, symbolized by the mixing of a Russian lullaby and an old Hebrew song after the baby is born. The performances are all splendid, especially that of the huge, blonde leading lady learning to come to terms with the bitter Jewish humor of the tinsmith. The cramped quarters of the cottage are contrasted with the vast world outside by spectacular use of the large screen, as in the cross-cutting during the birth of the baby when the Commissar remembers how she and her comrades pushed a huge gun through the desert. There is also a creative manipulation of sound, especially in the horse stampede sequence. Altogether a remarkable film.

Best Film Berlin 1987

▶ **Communicants, The** see Winter
Light

▶ **Compagni, I** see Organizer, The

Company Limited

▶ **Seemabaddha**

     India   1971   112 mins   bw
     Barat Shumshere Rana

d   **Satyajit Ray**
sc   **Satyajit Ray**
ph   **Soumendu Roy**
m   **Satyajit Ray**
     Barun Chanda, Sharmila Tagore,

Parumita Chowdhary, Harindranath
Chattopadhyaya, Haradhan Banerjee

Shyamal Chatterjee (Chanda) has, via a university education, worked his way up in industry. He lives in privileged circumstances in
Calcutta, aping a middle-class English lifestyle, and is angling for a seat on the company
board. This he achieves by politically questionable contrivance. The social and moral
distance which Chatterjee has travelled from
his roots is subtly unveiled in the guided tour
of his haunts which he proudly gives his
visiting sister-in-law (Chowdhary). Completing the trilogy begun with *Days And Nights
In The Forest*, followed by *The Adversary*,
this film continues Ray's examination of
trends in urban Indian life, concentrating on
a young man caught between ambition and
his natural integrity. The work bears all the
hallmarks of Ray's style and concerns, and
displays his sense of irony at both its most
charming and its most pointed.

▶ **Compartiment Tueurs** see Sleeping
Car Murders, The

▶ **Complicato Intrigo Di Donne,
Vicoli e Delitti, Un** see Camorra: The
Naples Connection

▶ **Comrades Of 1918** see Westfront 1918

▶ **Condamné À Mort S'est Éch-
appé, Ou Le Vent Souffle Où Il
Vent, Un** see Man Escaped, Or The
Wind Bloweth Where It Listeth, A

▶ **Condé, Un** see Cop, The

The Conductor

▶ **Dyrygent**

Poland 1979 110 mins col
PRF/Film Polski – Group X

d **Andrzej Wajda**
sc **Andrzej Kijowski**
ph **Slawomir Idziak**
m **Beethoven**
**John Gielgud, Krystyna Janda, Andrzej
Seweryn, Jan Ciercierski, Tadeusz
Czechowski**

A famous Polish-born conductor (Gielgud)

returns to his birthplace after 50 years in the
USA. Although old and dying, he is able to
electrify the struggling provincial orchestra,
something their own conductor (Seweryn) has
never been able to do. The younger man's feeling of inadequacy puts a strain on his
marriage. One of John Gielgud's most distinguished and distinguishing features is his
mellifluous voice, but here we are deprived of
it by the Polish dubbing. Yet even with a borrowed voice and his obvious inexperience as a
conductor, he gives a fine performance of a
character that is not fully realized in the writing. The screenplay keeps hinting at deeper
meaning without actually revealing it, leaving
us with neither a significant parable nor a realistic look at the failures of provincial culture.

The Confession

▶ **L'Aveu**

France 1970 160 mins col
Corona/Pomereu/Selena

d **Costa-Gavras**
sc **Jorge Semprun**
ph **Raoul Coutard**
**Yves Montand, Simone Signoret, Gabriele
Ferzetti, Michel Vitold, Jean Bouise**

In 1951, Czech foreign minister Artur London
(Montand) was arrested, imprisoned and tortured during a political purge. After attacking
the far Right with enormous success in *Z*,
Costa-Gavras turned his attention to the Stalinist Left. Based on London's book about his
experiences, the screenplay's static and wordy
nature is not sufficiently tempered by the
direction or the playing. However, some of
the interrogation scenes which lead to the
false confession of the title cannot fail to have
an impact.

▶ **Confession Of Ina Kahr, The** see
Afraid To Live

The Confessions Of Winifred
Wagner

▶ **Winifred Wagner Und Die
Geschichte Des Hauses
Wahnfried 1914-1975**

W. Germany 1976 104 mins bw
Syberberg Film/ORF

d **Hans Jürgen Syberberg**
ph **Dietrich Lohmann**
m **Wagner**

An interview with the 78-year-old, English-born wife of Richard Wagner's son Siegfried in which she recounts her life at Wahnfried, the Wagners' house at Bayreuth, and talks about their family squabbles, her running of the Festival, her relationship with Hitler, and her views on the conductors and the artists she worked with. This fascinating interview with a formidable woman exists in a five-hour form, but is no less riveting in the released shorter version. Almost the entire film is made up of medium close-ups or head shots of Winifred, who addresses Syberberg and the camera unselfconsciously, hardly ever needing to be prompted. She stares out at us without a qualm and describes Hitler as 'a kindly uncle ... absolutely sweet with the children,' and 'if Hitler walked through the door today, I should be just as pleased and happy to see him as I ever was'.

Confidence

▶ **Bizalom**

Hungary 1979 117 mins col
Mafilm/Objectiv Studio

d **István Szabó**
sc **István Szabó**
ph **Lajos Koltai**
    Ildikó Bánsági, Peter Andorai, O.
    Gombick, Karoly Csaki

Two fugitives (Bánsági and Andorai), hiding from the Fascists in 1944, are thrown together and forced to pose as man and wife in a small room in the suburbs of Budapest. Although both are married, they find some sexual gratification with each other but lack mutual confidence. A chamber work in both senses, the film is as muted and as subtle as the colours used. It stands or falls on the performances of the two leads, as it is virtually a two-hander. They are as convincing as the often irritating and irrational roles allow them to be, and the threat from the world outside is made palpable.

▶ **Confidentially Yours** see Finally Sunday

Conflagration

▶ **aka The Flame Of Torment**
▶ **Enjo**

Japan 1958 96 mins bw
Daiei

d **Kon Ichikawa**
sc **Keiji Hasebe, Natto Wada**
ph **Kazuo Miyagawa**
m **Toshiro Mayazumi**
    Raizo Ichikawa, Ganjiro Nakamura,
    Tatsuya Nakadai

A young acolyte (Ichikawa) comes to study at the Golden Pavilion in Kyoto, where he sees tourists violating its beauty. Disillusioned by the post-war world, he despairingly sets fire to the holy temple in order to preserve it from contamination. As in all of Ichikawa's major films, this superb adaptation of Mishima's novel, *Temple Of The Golden Pavilion*, is a study of a man pushed to extremes. Beautifully photographed – witness the final shot of the burning temple as seen from the mountain – and deeply disturbing, it remains the director's own favourite.

▶ **Conflit** see Affair Lafont, The

The Conformist

▶ **Il Conformista**

Italy 1969 115 mins col
Mars/Marianne/Maran

d **Bernardo Bertolucci**
sc **Bernardo Bertolucci**
ph **Vittorio Storaro**
m **Georges Delerue**
    Jean-Louis Trintignant, Stefania
    Sandrelli, Dominique Sanda, Gastone
    Moschin, Pierre Clémenti, Enzo Taroscio

The childhood trauma of having shot a chauffeur who tried to seduce him, together with his own repressed homosexuality, is a strong factor in making Marcello (Trintignant) contract a *bourgeois* marriage and offer his services to the Fascist party for whom he is asked to assassinate his former professor. Bertolucci's most successful combining of his Freudian and political preoccupations is an ironic and stylish study of pre-war Italy, hauntingly evoked by Storaro's camera. Trintignant brings great conviction to the title role, and there are enticing performances from Sandrelli and Sanda who get to dance a tango together.

► **Conformista, II** see Conformist, The

The Confrontation

► **aka Sparkling Winds**

► **Fenyes Szelek**

Hungary 1969 85 mins col
Mafilm Studio

d **Miklós Jancsó**
sc **Gyula Hernádi**
ph **Tamás Somló**
m **Paul Arma**
   **Lajos Balázsovits, Andrea Drahota,
   András Bálint, Kati Kovács, András
   Kozák, Benedek Tóth**

In 1947, after the Communist Party has come to power in Hungary, a group of revolutionary students set out on a glorious summer's day to win over a nearby Catholic school to their cause, but they are manipulated by higher Party officials. Jancsó's first film in colour, of which he makes dazzling symbolic use, is conceived in choreographic and folk-opera terms. The film echoes the 1968 student movements in the West (the girls anachronistically wear mini-skirts) with an understanding of the Hungarian context of which Jancsó is such a singular and invigorating observer.

Congress Dances

► **Der Kongress Tanzt**

Germany 1931 92 mins bw
UFA

d **Erik Charrell**
sc **Norbert Falk, Robert Liebmann**
ph **Carl Hoffmann**
m **Werner Heymann**
   **Conrad Veidt, Willy Fritsch, Lilian
   Harvey, Lil Dagover, Gibb McLaughlin**

A shopgirl (Harvey) wins the affections of Tsar Alexander (Fritsch) during the 1814

Congress of Vienna. Complications occur, stirred up by a scheming Prince Metternich (Veidt) and a vampish countess (Dagover), when he returns to Russia leaving a double in his place. Made in Germany in three different language versions (Henri Garat replaced Fritsch in the French one), this frothy musical comedy was more concerned with romantic than political intrigues, and sets them in ornate drawing rooms, beer-gardens, and at grand balls. The feather-light script was directed with equivalent weight, and the film helped set a style for early screen musicals in Europe and Hollywood.

► **Conjugal Bed, The** see Queen Bee

The Consequence

► **Die Konsequenz**

W. Germany 1977 100 mins bw
Solaris Film/WDR

d **Wolfgang Petersen**
sc **Alexander Ziegler, Wolfgang Petersen**
ph **Jörg Michael Baldenius**
m **Nils Sustrate**
   **Jürgen Prochnow, Ernst Hannawald,
   Walo Lüond, Edith Volmann, Erwin
   Kohlund**

Martin (Prochnow), a homosexual actor imprisoned for a relationship with a minor, falls reciprocally in love with a warder's young son. When they try to make a life together, family pressures and interference lead them to tragedy. Petersen's film, shot in monochrome tones appropriate to the pall of oppression that hangs over it, is an excellent drama that is both a plea for tolerance and an indictment of the prejudice that leads to using prisons as instruments of persecution.

► **Constans** see Constant Factor, The

The Constant Factor

► **Constans**

Poland 1980 96 mins col
PRF-Zespol Filmowy

d **Krzysztof Zanussi**

sc **Krzysztof Zanussi**
ph **Slawomir Idziak**
m **Wojciech Kilar**
   Tadeusz Bradecki, Zofia Mrozowska,
   Malgorzata Zajaczkowska, Cezary
   Morawski

Witold (Bradecki) travels the world for his job in Polish international exhibitions, trapped by his complex nature which believes that life can be ordered by mathematical equations, and incapable of accommodating to petty corruption. His mother dies as a result of his inept handling of a bribe to a doctor, and he ends up as a window cleaner. Although cold and polemical, this outspoken tale is told with a good deal of visual flair, and the characters are analysed with precision.

▶ **Conte De Printemps** see Tale Of Springtime, A

Contempt

▶ **Le Mépris**

France   1963   103 mins   col
Rome-Paris Films

d   **Jean-Luc Godard**
sc **Jean-Luc Godard**
ph **Raoul Coutard**
m   **Georges Delerue**
    Brigitte Bardot, Michel Piccoli, Jack
    Palance, Fritz Lang, Giorgia Moll

A scriptwriter (Piccoli) is increasingly despised by his wife (Bardot) as he tries to set up a film in Rome of *The Odyssey* with an American producer (Palance), to be directed by Fritz Lang. Godard has slyly used Alberto Moravia's novel *Il Disprezzo* to make his own sharp comment on international film-making, using colour, wide screen and a multilingual cast. The first third of the movie, however, is concerned with the breakdown of a marriage in a remarkable flowing sequence set in the apartment of the couple (Bardot and Piccoli are superb). Palance ('When I hear the word culture I reach for my chequebook') brings an imposing presence to bear on the fascinating proceedings.

▶ **Contes Immoraux** see Immoral Tales

The Contract

▶ **Kontrakt**

Poland   1980   111 mins   col
PRF-Zespol Filmowy

d   **Krzysztof Zanussi**
sc **Krzysztof Zanussi**
ph **Slawomir Idziak**
m   **Wojciech Kilar, with extracts from**
    Schubert, Strauss, Debussy
    Maja Komorowska, Tadeusz Lomnicki,
    Magda Jaroszowna, Krzysztof Kolberger,
    Ignacy Machowski, Leslie Caron

A Warsaw physician arranges the civil marriage of his son, (Lomnicki), but the new young wife (Komorowska) refuses to go through with the subsequent church ceremony. Unperturbed, her father-in-law proceeds with the wedding party. It is a day of both wild carousal and unpleasant events, at the end of which the groom sets the house on fire. This is Zanussi at his least metaphorical, making an ironic, even comic, film that examines a sector of well-to-do Polish society which is, inevitably, on the brink of collapse. Interesting and entertaining, the film has an authentic cosmopolitan flavour, with dialogue moving easily between Polish, French, English and German.

Conversation Piece

▶ **Gruppo Di Famiglia In Un Interno**

Italy   1974   121 mins   col
Rusconi/Gaumont

d   **Luchino Visconti**
sc **Luchino Visconti, Suso Cecchi D'Amico,**
    Enrico Medioli
ph **Pasqualino De Santis**
m   **Franco Mannino**
    Burt Lancaster, Helmut Berger, Silvana
    Mangano, Claudia Cardinale, Claudia
    Marsani

A reclusive professor (Lancaster), living a well-ordered existence among his 18th-century art collection in his Rome apartment, has his tranquillity disturbed and his latent homosexuality aroused after reluctantly agreeing to let his top flat to a Countess (Mangano), her 'kept boy' (Berger) and her daughter (Marsani). Visconti's penultimate film was directed after a serious illness, which may account for some of its weaknesses. But the plot, although treated as drama, resembles a 1940s Hollywood screwball comedy in which an egghead learns to let his hair down, and is nothing short of ludicrous. Lancaster seems bemused throughout, and if one can believe Berger as a revolutionary student then one can believe anything. However, a tedious and repetitive sequel, *Le Cop II*, with the same team, followed in 1991.

Le Cop

▶ **Les Ripoux**

> France   1985   106 mins   col
> Film 7

d   **Claude Zidi**
sc   **Claude Zidi, Didier Kaminka**
ph   **Jean-Jacques Tarbes**
m   **Francis Lai**
      Philippe Noiret, Thierry Lhermitte, Régine, Grace De Capitani, Julien Guiomar

A veteran plain clothes policeman (Noiret), who happily turns a blind eye to all crime as long as he's paid off, has to educate his priggish new partner (Lhermitte) in his ways. The subject of police corruption and brutality could have been treated as a cynical satire, but it has been turned into an extremely amiable, often very funny, soft-hearted cop comedy. Noiret is such a lovable old rogue that one can't help being on his side.

The Cop

▶ **Un Condé**

> France   1970   98 mins   col
> Stephen Films(Paris)/Empire Films(Rome)

d   **Yves Boisset**
sc   **Claude Veillot, Yves Boisset**
ph   **Jean-Marc Ripert**
m   **Antoine Duhamel**
      Michel Bouquet, Françoise Fabian, Gianni Garko, Michel Constantin, Rufus, Bernard Fresson, Henri Garcin

A nightclub owner is murdered and his sister Hélène (Fabian) beaten up by members of a gang whose leader has police and political connections, Hélène's friend Dan (Garko) shoots the gang leader and unleashes a vendetta with the police, led by Inspector Favenin (Bouquet). Controversial in 1970, when its release was delayed because of ministerial objections to the portrayal of the police as corrupt thugs, this film now is no more than a violent crime thriller. It is directed and played (notably by Bouquet) with maximum efficiency, using techniques reminiscent of Jean-Pierre Melville's *policiers*, but the characters are largely two-dimensional and the excessive brutality becomes a bit much to take.

Cop Au Vin

▶ **Poulet Au Vinaigre**

> France   1984   109 mins   col
> MK2

d   **Claude Chabrol**
sc   **Claude Chabrol, Dominique Roulet**
ph   **Jean Rabier**
m   **Matthieu Chabrol**
      Jean Poiret, Stéphane Audran, Michel Bouquet, Lucas Belvaux, Jean Topart, Josephine Chaplin, Pauline Lafont

A crippled woman (Audran), living with her teenage postman son (Belvaux) in a small provincial town, is determined not to sell her house to a local cartel. When one of the members of the cartel is killed, Inspector Lavardin (Poiret) arrives to investigate. This mordant view of the nastiness of the provincial *bourgeoisie*, in Chabrol's commercial thriller mode, only really comes alive some way into the film with the arrival of the sardonic cop of the title. Basically sympathetic, in Poiret's clever performance, his 'lively methods' give the movie a moral ambiguity. The rest of the characters are one-dimensional, but it's done with style, and there are at least two Chabrolian meals to relish. Poiret and Chabrol recreated the cop character in *Inspector Lavardin* in 1986.

▶ **Coquille Et Le Clergyman, La** see Seashell And The Clergyman, The

▶ **Corbeau, Le** see Raven, The

▶ **Corde Raide, La** see Lovers On A Tightrope

▶ **Counterfeit Constable, The** see Allez France

The Counterfeiters

▶ **Le Cave Se Rebiffe**

France   1961   98 mins   bw
Cité Films/Compagnia Cinematografica Mondiale (Rome)

d   **Gilles Grangier**
sc **Albert Simonin, Gilles Grangier, Michel Audiard**
ph **Louis Page**
m   **Francis Lemarque, Michel Legrand**
    Jean Gabin, Martine Carol, Bernard Blier, Ginette Leclerc, Frank Villard, Maurice Biraud, Françoise Rosay

A small-time crook (Villard), together with a couple of friends, plans a forgery operation using the skills of Robert (Biraud), an engraver and the husband of his mistress (Carol). A professional mastermind (Gabin) is persuaded out of retirement to run the racket, and he and Robert double-cross the others and make off with the loot. A compact, small-scale comedy-thriller, marred by a somewhat limp and repetitive screenplay, but kept entertaining by crisp direction and its superior casting.

▶ **Coup De Foudre** see At First Sight

Coup De Grâce

▶ **Der Fangschuss**

W. Germany   1976   95 mins   bw
Bioskop Film/HR/Argos Films

d   **Volker Schlöndorff**
sc **Genevieve Dorman, Margarethe Von Trotta, Jutta Bruckner**
ph **Igor Luther**
m   **Stanley Myers**
    Margarethe Von Trotta, Matthias Habich, Rudiger Kirschstein, Matthieu Carrière, Valeska Gert

A German army unit, sent to keep Communism at bay in the Baltic during 1919–1920, is billeted on the now war-ravaged estate of a once wealthy family. Their commander, Erich (Habich), obsessed with all aspects of soldiering, attracts the unwelcome love of Sophie (Von Trotta), daughter of the mansion who, spurned by him, finally devotes herself to the Bolshevik cause. A complicated work, dealing in ideologies, the film nonetheless focuses largely on the nature and consequences of Sophia's hopeless passion. The bleak winter landscape is realistically evoked in the black and white photography but, while the film intrigues, it fails to come to grips with the dark undersides of human emotion at which it continually hints.

▶ **Coup De Torchon** see Clean Slate

▶ **Couple, Un** see Love Trap, The

▶ **Courage Fuyons** see Courage – Let's Run

Courage – Let's Run

▶ **Courage Fuyons**

France   1978   98 mins   col
Productions De La Guéville/Gaumont

d   **Yves Robert**
sc **Jean-Loup Dabadie, Yves Robert**
ph **Yves Lafaye**
m   **Vladimir Cosma**
    Jean Rochefort, Catherine Deneuve, Philippe Leroy-Beaulieu, Robert Webber, Dominique Lavanant

Middle-aged Martin (Rochefort), the insignificant proprietor of a small Paris chemist shop, gets involved in the 1968 riots and ends up in Amsterdam with glamorous singer Eva (Deneuve). Later reunited with his wife, he longs for Eva, and gets her after his wife leaves him for her lover. Robert's handsomely filmed comedy begins with Martin and Eva in Amsterdam and flashes back, via Martin's reflections, to the events that brought them there, then moves back into present time. This device, plus Rochefort essaying two other roles as members of his family, keeps things moving, but does little to elevate what is, in the end, a rather old-fashioned and silly story, jam-packed with ill-assorted characters and plot complications.

Cousin Angelica

▶ La Prima Angelica

Spain   1973   105 mins   col
Elias Querejeta

d   **Carlos Saura**
sc **Carlos Saura**
ph **Luis Cuadrado**
m   **Spanish popular melodies**
    José Luis López Vázques, Lina Canalejas,
    Maria Clara Fernández De Loayza,
    Fernando Delgado

A shy, balding, 45-year-old bachelor (Váz-quez) returns from Barcelona to his home town of Segovia after many years. There, he finds his cousin Angelica (Canalejas), whom he had loved as a child, now married to a Fascist (Delgado). He relives his childhood days at the time of the Civil War. What gives this plaintive 'remembrance of things past' drama a certain interest is that the middle-aged actor plays his nine-year-old self, rather in the manner of the old man's childhood memories in Bergman's *Wild Strawberries*. 'For years I have been studying how memory, imagination and close reality form a complex and fascinating whole,' Saura says. The film achieves its aims within its rather rigid structure.

Cousin Cousine

France   1975   95 mins   col
Les Films Pomereu

d   **Jean-Charles Tacchella**
sc **Jean-Charles Tacchella, with Danièle**
    Thompson
ph **Georges Lendi, Eric Faucherre, Michel**
    Thiriet
m   **Gérard Anfosso**
    Marie-Christine Barrault, Victor Lanoux,
    Marie-France Pisier, Guy Marchand,
    Ginette Garcin

Two married couples, who meet at a wedding which makes them in-laws, become entangled with each other's spouses. In the case of Marthe (Barrault) and Ludovic (Lanoux), they hold on to their virtue in the face of their partner's adultery until they decide they love each other and must go away together. A big hit in the US, this polished and some-times charming comedy, with elements of satire directed at the hypocrisy of the French *bourgeoisie*, is ultimately a little tedious in its superficiality – the ingredient which fre-quently appears as the limiting factor in Tac-chella's work.

The Cousins

▶ Les Cousins

France   1959   110 mins   bw
AJYM

d   **Claude Chabrol**
sc **Claude Chabrol**
ph **Henri Decaë**
m   **Paul Misraki**
    Jean-Claude Brialy, Gérard Blain,
    Juliette Mayniel, Claude Cerval

Simple, good-hearted country cousin Charles (Blain) comes to study at the Sorbonne in Paris where he stays at the luxury apartment of Paul (Brialy), his cynical town cousin. Charles works hard but fails his exams, Paul doesn't but passes and gets Charles's girl (Mayniel). Chabrol's second film is a riveting and perverse study of decadent Parisian stud-ent life, with a touch of Cocteau's *Les Enfants Terribles*. The City of Light is captured by Decaë's camera as if seen through the amazed eyes of Blain.

Best Film Berlin 1959

▶ **Cousins, Les** see Cousins, The

▶ **Čovek Nije Tica** see Man Is Not A Bird

The Cow

▶ Gav

Iran   1968   101 mins   bw
Caspain Studios

d   **Daryush Mehrjui**
sc **Daryush Mehrjui, Golam Hossein Suedi**
ph **Fereydun Ghovanlu**
m   **Hormoz Farhat**
    Ezat Entezami, Ali Nasirian, Jamshid
    Mashayekhi, Shojazedeh, Jafar Vali

Mashdi Hassan (Entezami) owns the only

cow in his little village and cherishes it to the point of mania. While he is absent on busness the cow dies and, to protect him, the villagers tell him it strayed. Paralyzed with both grief and disbelief, Hassan gradually assumes the cow's identity and slides into madness. Mehrjui's film is carefully structured to capture the detail and atmosphere of life and landscape in his chosen milieu, moving to a minutely observed study of the processes of madness. The images are well-judged and the editing is imaginative but, alas, once Hassan's madness is total and a resolution has to be found, the piece loses its focus and gives way to chaos and frenzy.

The Cow And I

▶ **La Vache Et Le Prisonnier**

France 1959 119 mins bw
Cyclope/Omnia

d **Henri Verneuil**
sc **Henri Verneuil, Henri Jeanson, Jean Manse**
ph **Roger Hubert**
m **Paul Durand**
Fernandel, René Havard, Albert Rémy, Bernard Musson

A French prisoner-of-war (Fernandel) escapes from a German labour farm, taking with him his favourite cow, Marguerite, to avoid suspicion. Among his various adventures on his way to the French border, he encounters other escapees disguised as Germans, has a skirmish with an amorous bull, and gets involved in military manoeuvres. A charming and quite touching comedy-drama in which the equine-faced French comic vies for the acting honours with his bovine co-star.

Crainquebille

France 1922 70 mins bw
Trarieux Films

d **Jacques Feyder**
sc **Jacques Feyder**
ph **L.H. Burel**
m **Silent**
Maurice De Féraudy, Françoise Rosay, Félix Oudart, Jean Forest

Crainquebille (De Féraudy), a poor but honest Parisian vegetable seller, is arrested and tried for telling a policeman to go to hell. Anatole France's story (the basis for two further film versions in 1933 and 1954) provided Feyder with one of his most experimental and brilliant works. It combines realistic location shooting with extraordinary dream sequences. Apart from the splendid De Féraudy in the title role, it gave Feyder's wife, Rosay, her first chance to shine on screen.

The Cranes Are Flying

▶ **Letyat Zhuravli**

USSR 1957 94 mins bw
Mosfilm

d **Mikhail Kalatozov**
sc **Victor Rosov**
ph **Sergei Urusevski**
m **M. Vainberg**
Tatiana Samoilova, Alexei Batalov, Vasili Merkuriev, Alexander Shvorin

When a young hospital worker (Samoilova) hears that her fiancé (Batalov) has been killed in the war, she refuses to believe it, yet she marries a man (Shvorin) she does not love. It has a happy ending. One of the first films after the 'thaw' which seemed to usher in a new liberty in Soviet cinema, is an unpretentious, lyrical love story that benefits from some sweeping camerawork and a touching performance from Samoilova (the great-niece of Stanislavsky). It was shown to acclaim in America in 1959 under a USA-USSR cultural exchange programme.

Best Film Cannes 1958 and Special Award to Samiolova

The Crazy Family

▶ **Gyakufunsha Kazoku**

Japan 1984 107 mins col
Art Theatre Guild/Directors Company/Kokusai Hoei

d **Sogo Ishii**
sc **Yoshinori Kobayashi, Fumio Konami, Sogo Ishii**
ph **Masaki Tamura**

m **1984**
   Katsuyo Kobayashi, Mitsuko Baisho,
   Yoshiki Arizono, Yuki Kudo, Hitoshi
   Ueki

The Kobayashi family moves into a spacious urban house. It is a dream come true – until grandfather's visit disturbs the balance of Kobayashi *père*'s mind. He becomes obsessed with digging a cellar for the old man to live in, his excavations become wilder and wilder, the family falls apart, the house is destroyed, and they all end up living happily in a space between two motorway flyovers! Played loud and fast, Ishii's third feature treats the theme – of crisis in a nuclear family with urban ambition – in a series of painful and ugly episodes presented in the style of a comic strip. Satire and slapstick rain blows on their targets in a film beautifully photographed by one of Japan's best cinematographers, and with a bizarre final sequence of special effects designed by *avant-garde* structuralist Takashi Ito.

Crazy Love

Belgium   1987   87 mins   col
Multimedia, in cooperation with the
Ministries of Culture of the Flemish and
French Communities

d   **Dominique Deruddere**
sc **Marc Didden, Dominique Deruddere**
ph **Willy Stassen**
m   **Raymond Van Het Groenewoud**
    Josse De Pauw, Geert Hunaerts, and
    Amid Chakir, An Van Essche, Florence
    Béliard

The life of Harry Voss told in three episodes. As a 12-year-old boy (Hunaerts) in 1955, he discovers romantic enchantment through a movie about a knight and a princess (Béliard), and is subsequently disillusioned by learning about sex too early and in bad circumstances. In 1962, during his last year at school, Harry (Du Pauw) has developed an extreme form of facial acne and is humiliated by a whorish girl who, upon seeing his boils, recoils from him. By 1976 the adult Harry lives in a nether world of drugs and alcohol. A chance meeting with an old schoolfriend (Chakir) just out of prison ends in their stealing a still warm

corpse. It turns out to be that of a beautiful girl, the dream princess of Harry's childhood... For a directorial debut of startling assurance, intelligence and sensitivity, Dominique Deruddere turned to the nightmare writings of America's Charles Bukowski for his subject. The result is a film which is at once, like its 'hero', nauseating and compelling. Famous for its scene where Harry, at the school dance, wraps his head in toilet paper to dance with the prettiest girl (Van Essche), the dark and bizarre story invites compassion and even elicits the odd smile while it shocks. Beautifully acted, photographed in often dream-like images and uncompromising in the treatment of its theme, *Crazy Love* requires a strong stomach, but the effort of endurance should prove worth it for most viewers.

▶ **Creeps** see Dreszcze

▶ **Cria!** see Raise Ravens

▶ **Cria Cuervos** see Raise Ravens

Cries And Whispers

▶ **Viskingar Och Rop**

Sweden   1972   95 mins   col
Svensk Filminstituten

d   **Ingmar Bergman**
sc **Ingmar Bergman**
ph **Sven Nykvist**
m   **Chopin, Bach**
    Harriet Andersson, Ingrid Thulin, Liv
    Ullmann, Kari Sylwan, Erland Josephson,
    George Arlin, Henning Moritzen

Agnes (Andersson), riddled with cancer, is dying in the family mansion, cared for by the faithful old retainer. Her two sisters (Thulin, frigid and suicidal and Ullmann, earthy and reckless) return home to give her comfort. Only the most extravagant superlatives could hope to convey the visual, aural and acting artistry of this film, the action of which occurs mostly in an agony of suffering silence, punctuated by the cries and whispers of the title. Unremittingly bleak and harrowing, it is a powerful document about dying, and reactions to dying, made by a master. Nykvist won the cinematography Oscar but, for all its beauty and emotionally charged use of blood colours, it needs a strong stomach to watch it.

Crime And Punishment

▶ **Crime Et Châtiment**

France   1935   110 mins   bw
CGPC

d   **Pierre Chenal**
sc **Marcel Aymé, Pierre Chenal, Christian Stengel, Wladimir Strijewski**
ph **Colas, Joseph-Louis Mundwiller**
m   **Arthur Honegger**
     Pierre Blanchar, Harry Baur, Marcelle Géniat, Madeleine Ozeray

Raskolnikov (Blanchar), a tormented student, kills a pawnbroker, and then plays mouse to the cat of Police Inspector Porfiry (Baur). Pierre Chenal, recently rediscovered in his eighties after years of neglect, had established his reputation as a leading French director of the 1930s with this taut, atmospheric adaptation of the Dostoevsky classic. Against the claustrophobic studio sets, Blanchar and Baur display their brilliant acting skills. The film looks even better when compared with Sternberg's stilted Hollywood version which appeared in the same year.

Best Actor (Pierre Blanchar) Venice 1935

Crime And Punishment

▶ **Crime Et Châtiment**

France   1956   110 mins   bw
Champs Elysée Productions

d   **Georges Lampin**
sc **Charles Spaak**
ph **Claude Renoir**
m   **Maurice Thiriet**
     Robert Hossein, Jean Gabin, Ulla Jacobsson, Bernard Blier, Marina Vlady, Gaby Morlay

René Brunel (Hossein), a Left Bank student, commits murder and robbery, to prevent his sister (Jacobsson) from having to marry a wealthy suitor (Blier), but is drawn to confess by the psychological wiles of a police inspector (Gabin). Dostoevsky's great complex novel has here been updated to modern Paris, and turned into just another *policier*. The idea of making Raskolnikov a young Parisian Existentialist in a duffle coat might have seemed a good one but, as morosely and flatly played by Hossein, it fails to generate any sense of the inner torment or tragedy of the character. Gabin and Blier keep the botched enterprise from sinking completely into the Seine.

Crime And Punishment

▶ **Prestupleniye I Nzaniye**

USSR   1970   200 mins   bw
Gorky Studio

d   **Lev Kulidzhanov**
sc **Lev Kulidzhanov, Nikolai Figurovsky**
ph **Vyacheslav Shumsky**
m   **Piotr Pakevich**
     Georgi Taratorkin, Viktoria Fyodorova, Irina Gosheva, Innokenti Smoktunovsky, Yevgeni Lebedev

Raskolnikov (Taratorkin), a former student living in poverty in St Petersburg, murders a pawnbroker and her daughter. Gradually, through his relationship with various characters, and his confrontation with Porfiry (Smoktunovsky), the prosecutor, Raskolnikov confesses to the murder. The ninth version of Dostoevsky's most-filmed novel follows the plot and sub-plot more closely than its predecessors. Yet the director has opted to stress the insane streak in Raskolinov at the expense of the intellectual, so that Taratorkin rolls his eyes and gesticulates for most of the film's rather tedious 200 minutes. The best scenes are those with Smoktunovsky, and the period atmosphere is well caught.

▶ **Crime De Monsieur Lange, Le**
see Crime Of Monsieur Lange, The

▶ **Crime Et Châtiment** see Crime And Punishment

▶ **Crimen De Cuenca, El** see Crime Of Cuenca, The

The Crime Of Cuenca

► **El Crimen De Cuenca**

Spain 1980 92 mins col
Incine/Jet Films

d **Pilar Miró**
sc **Pilar Miró, Salvador Maldonado**
ph **Hans Burmann**
m **Antón García Abril**
**José Manuel Cervino, Daniel Dicenta,
Amparo Soler Leal, Fernando Rey, José
Vivó, Héctor Alterio**

After a quarrel with two farmers, an illiterate shepherd disappears. His parents insist that the local police charge the two men (Cervino and Dicenta) with his murder. A priest (Vivó), a politician (Rey) and a magistrate (Alterio) collude, for their own purposes, to have the innocent men convicted...Miró, one of Spain's few female film directors, has also become one of the most controversial. Her first film *The Engagement Party* (1976) was banned for a time because of its explicit sex scenes, and this stark exposé of a legal conspiracy and of torture inflicted on prisoners, caused a storm of protest from the Civil Guard. Naturally, when it was released in Spain a year later, it packed in the public.

The Crime Of Monsieur Lange

► **Le Crime De Monsieur Lange**

France 1935 85 mins bw
Obéron

d **Jean Renoir**
sc **Jacques Prévert, Jean Renoir, Jean Castanier**
ph **Jean Bachelet**
m **Jean Wiener, Joseph Kosma**
Jules Berry, René Lefèvre, Florelle, Nadia Sibirskaïa, Sylvie Bataille, Henri Guisol

A group of exploited workers take over a publishing house when its crooked boss Batala (Berry) absconds, making them believe he is dead. After they have made a success of the co-operative, Batala returns to regain control, but Lange (Lefèvre), a writer of pulp Westerns, kills him. Shot in 25 days, this classic film of working-class solidarity, pre-

sented in the language of ironic black comedy, expressed the optimism of the Popular Front better than more didactic efforts. The two contrasting central actors – evil Berry and good Lefèvre – are superb, as is Renoir's use of the courtyard setting, and the famous 360-degree pan when Lange murders Batala is a *tour de force*.

The Criminal Life Of Archibaldo De La Cruz

► **aka Rehearsal For A Crime**
► **Ensayo De Un Crimen**

Mexico 1955 91 mins bw
Alianza Cinematografica

d **Luis Buñuel**
sc **Luis Buñuel, E. Ugarte**
ph **Augustín Jiménez**
m **Jorge Perez**
Ernesto Alonso, Ariadna Welter, Miroslava Stern, Rita Macedo

Because of a childhood experience of the death of a maid in erotic circumstances, Archibaldo (Alonso) grows up into a psychopathic woman-killer, although he is constantly thwarted in his efforts to carry out a murder. Still working within the budget and style limitations of Mexican cinema, Buñuel came up with one of his best black comedies of the period. It not only pokes wicked fun at the decadent *bourgeoisie* and at the Latin male, but at some of the director's own obsessions – foot fetishism, *l'amour fou*, and surrealism.

The Crimson Curtain

► **Le Rideau Cramoisi**

France 1952 43 mins bw
Argos

d **Alexandre Astruc**
sc **Alexandre Astruc**
ph **Eugen Schüfftan**
m **Jean-Jacques Grünewald**
Jean-Claude Pascal, Anouk Aimée, Madeleine Garcia, Jim Gérald

A young officer (Pascal), is billetted on a *bourgeois* couple (Gérald and Garcia) with a beautiful daughter (Aimée). To his astonishment, the girl makes advances to him and they embark on a silent nocturnal affair, carried out with some difficulty since her bedroom leads off that of her parents. The intrigue culminates in a surprise tragic ending. Astruc, novelist and film critic, who coined the phrase *camera-stylo*, wrote that cinema should be 'a means of writing as supple and as subtle as that of written language'. In this, his first film, the director practised what he preached, achieving a stylish, unusual and moving work in which narrative takes the place of dialogue and the camera and silent presences of the actors convey the drama. This little gem of a short feature, demonstrating the maxim that less is more, remains the best work of Astruc, whose later, longer films tend towards the turgid and lack clarity of purpose.

▶ **Cristo Proibito, II** see Forbidden Christ, The

▶ **Cristo Si E Fermato A Eboli** see Christ Stopped At Eboli

▶ **Cronaca Di Un Amore** see Chronicle of A Love

▶ **Cronaca Di Una Morte Annunciata** see Chronicle Of A Death Foretold

▶ **Cronaca Familiare** see Family Diary

▶ **Crook, The** see Simon The Swiss

The Crossing Of the Rhine

▶ **(US: Tomorrow Is My Turn)**

▶ **Le Passage Du Rhin**

  France   1960   125 mins   bw
  Franco-London/Gibe/Jonia/UFA

d   **André Cayatte**
sc **André Cayatte, Armand Jammot**
ph **Roger Fellous**
m   **Louiguy**
    Charles Aznavour, Nicole Courcel,
    Georges Rivière, Cordula Trantow

Two French POWs, a baker (Aznavour) and a journalist (Rivière), escape separately from the German farms where they have been forced to work, but meet up again in Paris after various advantures. This plodding, conventional, but well-intentioned escape story has the advantage of a sympathetic portrayal by Aznavour, and the disadvantage (for English-speaking audiences) of a moronic American commentary. Judges at Venice might have been swayed by its depiction of the Germans also suffering during the war.

Best Film Venice 1960

▶ **Crossroads** see Crossways

Crossways

▶ **aka Crossroads**

▶ **aka The Shadows Of The Yoshiwara**

▶ **Jujiro**

  Japan   1928   80 mins   bw
  Shochiku

d   **Teinosuke Kinugasa**
sc **Teinosuke Kinugasa**
ph **Kohei Sugiyama**
m   **Silent**
    J. Bandoha, A. Tschihaya, Yujiko
    Ogawa, I. Sohma

A young man, tormented by thinking he has killed a rival on an archery ground, takes refuge with his sister who has killed her seducer. This was one of the few Japanese silents to be distributed in the West and critics spoke of German Expressionist influence: fragmentary close-ups, a claustrophobic atmosphere of *angst* and dark impressionistic décor. However, it is said that Kinugasa had not seen any German films at that time. Even more like *Caligari* and the like, is his long-lost *A Page Of Madness* (1926), the major cinematic rediscovery of the early 1970s.

Crows And Sparrows

▶ **Wuya Yu Maque**

  China   1949   113 mins   bw
  Kunlun

d   **Zheng Junli**

sc Chen Baichen, Shen Fu, Wang Lingu, Xu
    Tao, Zheng Junli, Zhao Dan
ph Miao Zhenhua, Hu Zhenhua
m   Wang Yunjie
    Zhao Dan, Wu Yin, Wei Heling, Sun
    Daolin, Li Tianji, Ouyang Yunzhu

When the corrupt landlord (Tianji) of a
Shanghai boarding house decides to sell up
and move to Taiwan, the tenants must find
another home and therefore hardship. They
a teacher (Daolin) and his family, a pedlar
(Dan), a clerk (Heling), students and workers.
As the Red Army approaches, the tenants
gain their rights. One of the last fruits of a
fertile period in the cinema of pre-revolution-
ary China, it was also a landmark in its move
towards a style not far removed from Italian
Neo-Realism. Both the dialogue and the acting are vibrant and authentic, and the principal location (the boarding house) teems with
life. At first, Junli's first solo directorial effort
was subject to censorship from the Nationalist
Kuomintang government, but when the Communists came to power during post-pro-
duction, much of the cut dialogue was
restored and more anti-KMT slogans were
added with relish.

▶ **Crucible, The** see Witches of Salem,
The

The Crucified Lovers

▶ **Chikamatsu Monogatari**

    Japan 1954 110 mins bw
    Daiei

d   Kenji Mizoguchi
sc Yoshitaka Yoda
ph Kazuo Miyagawa
m   Fumio Hayasaka
    Kazuo Hasegawa, Kyoko Kagawa, Eitaro
    Shindo, Sakae Ozawa, Yoko Minamida

In late 17th-century Kyoto, a merchant's wife
(Kagawa) and a young clerk (Hasegawa) take
flight from the powerful influence of the Sho-
guns, and find themselves at the mercy of an
avaricious society. Although based on a play
by the 18th-century playwright Chikamatsu,
there is little in the fluid filmic narrative to
suggest its theatrical origins. Mizoguchi gives
us a vivid picture of a complex mercenary

system, as well as a love story which builds
in emotion. The gleaming photography of
Miyagawa – the camera keeping a discreet
distance where necessary – and the performances, contribute to the impact of one of the
best films of the director's great last phase.

The Cruel Sea

▶ **Bas Ya Bahar**

    Kuwait 1971 107 mins bw
    Falcon Productions

d   Khalid Siddik
sc Abdel-Rahman Saleh, Saad Faraj, Walaa'
    Salah El-Din, Khalid Siddik
ph Tewfik El-Amir
m   Bo Tarik
    Saad Faraj, Hayat El-Fahad, Mohammed
    Mansour, Amal Bakr

A young man (Mansour), whose father
(Faraj) was maimed by a shark in his days
as a pearl diver, is determined to make enough
money so that he can marry a rich merchant's
daughter (Bakr). But he also has to pay the
price for extracting pearls from the cruel sea.
The first feature to be made in the tiny Gulf
state of Kuwait is a pearl in itself. Not only
does Siddik's debut film authentically and
atmospherically recreate the harsh pre-oil
boom society, but it points an accusatory
finger at mercantile exploitation, the inferior
position of women and the *negative* effect of
religion.

The Cry

▶ **(US: The Outcry)**

▶ **Il Grido**

    Italy 1957 102 mins bw
    SPA/Robert Alexander

d   Michelangelo Antonioni
sc Michelangelo Antonioni, Elio Bartolini,
    Ennio De Concini
ph Gianni Di Venanzo
m   Giovanni Fusco
    Steve Cochran, Alida Valli, Dorian Gray,
    Betsy Blair, Lynn Shaw, Gabriella
    Pallotta

A worker (Cochran) in a sugar refinery in the
Po valley wanders with his little daughter

from place to place in search of love after the mother (Valli) of his child has deserted him for another man. The film directed just before *L'Avventura* made Antonioni an international name is morose and meandering with unconvincing performances from an international cast including Hollywood stalwart Cochran as an Italian worker. The desolate landscapes, rather obviously reflecting the hero's mental state, are well captured by Di Venanzo's camera.

The Cry

▶ **Krik**

Czechoslovakia 1963 80 mins bw
Ceskoslovensky Film, Barrandov Studio

d **Jaromil Jires**
sc **Ludvik Askenázy, Jaromil Jires**
ph **Jaroslav Kučera**
m **Jan Klusák**
   Eva Limánová, Josef Abrhám, Eva Kopecká, Dr J. Kvapil

When Ivana (Limánová) goes to hospital for the birth of her first baby, both she and her husband Slavek (Abrhám), a young TV repair man, reflect on their lives as a couple. Meanwhile, Slavek goes about his usual business and finds that his world and his daily encounters assume a new significance. This feature by a young and talented director overloads its message – a plea for a better world, put across by the unrealistic device of Slavek's encountering every kind of intolerance and threat in a single day – but it is choc-full of charm and youthful vitality, adding up to a well-wrapped package of small pleasures.

The Cry Of The People

▶ **Al Grito De Este Pueblo**

Argentina 1972 65 mins col/bw
Grupo Tercer Cine

d **Humberto Rios**
sc **Humberto Rios**
ph **Mario Diez**
m **Folk music**

A documentary on Bolivia from the disastrous Chaco war with Paraguay in 1932 to the present-day military dictatorship, using newsreels, commentary and interviews. Although angry at the appalling exploitation and conditions of the majority of the population, the film is rooted in hard facts and statistics that examine the reasons for the oppression and avoids being a mere salve to the liberal conscience. The images of mine workers, or of Indians trying to survive on the land, eloquently show suffering, while the commentary explains how the old tin barons have been replaced by even worse exploiters such as Standard Oil and Shell. The film stands with the short documentaries of the Cuban, Santiago Alvarez, and Fernando E Solanas's *The Hour Of The Furnaces*, which use the cinema as a powerful weapon for change.

▶ **Csend Es Kiáltás** see Silence And Cry

▶ **Csillagosok, Katonák** see Red And The White, The

Cuba Si!

France 1961 58 mins bw
Films de la Pléiade

d **Chris Marker**
sc **Chris Marker**
ph **Chris Marker**
m **E.G. Mantici, J. Calzada**

An account of the early days of the Cuban Revolution and the building of the new nation, including two interviews with Castro. It ends with the Bay of Pigs fiasco, which took place in April 1961 during the cutting of the film which had been shot a few months previously. Castro is the star of this personal, passionate and influential documentary which Marker made to celebrate the second anniversary of the Revolution. The anti-American tone of the ending caused the French government to ban the film until 1963, but Marker published the text and stills. However, these couldn't amply communicate his expert use of sound, image and text that makes his films so special.

▶ **Cucaracha, La** see Bandit, The

Current

▶ **Sodrásban**

Hungary 1963 86 mins bw
Hunnia Studio

d   István Gaál
sc István Gaál
ph Sándor Sára
m   András Szöllösy, Vivaldi, Frescobaldi
    Andrea Drahota, Marianne Moór, Sándor
    Csikós, János Harkányi, András Kozák

A group of teenage friends, between school
and college, hang around the streets of a
small town, play soccer, flirt, joke and go
swimming. When one of their number is
drowned, everything changes. After starting
off as a Hungarian 'teen movie about kids on
a summer vacation, the film's moral purpose
soon becomes clear. The death of the boy
makes the young people come to terms for
the first time with their own mortality, and
to realize how shallow and immature they
have been. Gaál, in his debut feature, copes
skilfully with the in mood, while fine visual
use is made of the setting, dominated by the
river. However, the theme is slighly over-
stressed and some of the acting is a little
rough edged.

▶ **Curse, The** see Xala

▶ **Curtain Rises, The** see Entrée Des
Artistes

▶ **Cybèle Ou Les Dimanches De
Ville-D'Avray** see Sundays And Cybèle

The Cycle

▶ **Dayereh Mina**

Iran 1974 102 mins col
Telfilm

d   Daryush Mehrjui
sc Daryush Mehrjui, Golam Hossein Saedi
ph Houshang Beharlou
    Esmail Mohammadi, Ezat Entezami,
    Frouzan, Said Kangarani, Ali Nasirian

A father (Mohammadi) and his son (Kangar-
ani) come to Teheran for the old man to be
treated for a persistent illness. The innocent
boy, in an effort to pay for his father's cure,
succumbs to the corruption around him,
becoming a shrewd and unscrupulous middle-
man in the city. 'I wanted to reveal this drama
in all its absurdity and painfulness, before
which I can express nothing but a feeling of
profound horror,' stated Mehrjui, who made
his name in 1968 with *The Cow*, which took
a less virulent view of society. Banned for
three years, this remarkable and dark look at
the Shah's Iran, manages to get many of its
points across with black and bitter humour,
and a striking visual quality. The central
theme of the trafficking in contaminated
blood is even more powerful today in a world
confronting AIDS.

Cyrano De Bergerac

France 1990 135 mins col
Hachette Première/Camera One/Films
A2/DD Productions/U.G.C.
Coproductions

d   Jean-Paul Rappeneau
sc Jean-Paul Rappeneau/Jean-Claude
    Carrière
ph Pierre Lhomme
m   Jean-Claude Petit
    Gérard Depardieu, Anne Brochet, Vincent
    Perez, Jacques Weber, Roland Bertin

Cyrano de Bergerac (Depardieu), Gascon
army officer, fearless swordsman and brilliant
poet, is afflicted with an abnormally long nose
which prevents him from declaring his love
for his beautiful cousin Roxane (Brochet).
When Roxane falls in love with Christian
(Perez), a handsome but inarticulate young
officer in Cyrano's regiment, the older man
pours out his soul in letters written on Christian's behalf. Many years afterwards, when it
is too late, Roxane discovers the truth. Staying close to the form and content of Edmond
Rostand's famous 19th-century romantic
play, Rappeneau and Carrière have constructed an epic and impressive film. Handsomely mounted and well acted, it captures
the 17th-century French atmosphere in a
series of rumbustious set pieces – particularly
effective in the opening sequence, set in a
theatre, which introduces the main characters.
Depardieu plays Cyrano with sincerity, vigour, and clarity, though he is perhaps slightly
too earthy and insufficiently graceful to be a

natural for the role. Nonetheless, the pain inherent in the character is ultimately very affecting. However, for all its high ambition and evident virtues, the director has allowed the more sombre aspects of the story to become overshadowed by a little too much sound and fury, and comic touches which topple into buffoonery. The English-language subtitling was written by Anthony Burgess.

Best Actor (Gérard Depardieu) Cannes 1990

Cyrano Et D'Artagnan

France 1963 145 mins col
Circe-Astarte Productions(Paris)/G.E.S.I.
Ciné/Agata Film(Rome)

d **Abel Gance**
sc **Abel Gance, Nelly Kaplan**
ph **Otello Martelli**
m **Michel Magne**
   José Ferrer, Jean-Pierre Cassel, Sylva

Koscina, Daliah Lavi, Michel Simon, Philippe Noiret

The musketeer D'Artagnan (Cassel) and the long-nosed poet Cyrano De Bergerac (Ferrer, reprising his Oscar-winning Hollywood role), join forces in trying to prevent revolution in Paris, and become involved in complicated *amours* with two attractive ladies of the court (Koscina and Lavi). This is an out-and-out swashbuckling romance, done with a modicum of dash, style and humour, much heroic swordplay and a handsome sense of period. However, the plot, drawn from both Edmond Rostand and Dumas *père*, is a somewhat rambling affair and the triviality of the exercise belies the then 75-year-old Gance's well-deserved reputation and achievements as a pioneer of the cinema.

▶ **Czlowiek Z Marmur** see Man Of Marble

▶ **Czlowiek Z Zelaza** see Man Of Iron

d

Daisies

▶ **Sedmikrásky**

Czechoslovakia 1966 76 mins col
Bohumil Smida-Ladislav Fikar

d **Věra Chytilová**
sc **Ester Krumbachová, Věra Chytilová**
ph **Jaroslav Kučera**
m **Jiří Šlitr, Jiří Šust**
　Jitka Cerhová, Ivana Karbonavá, Julius Albert

Brunette Marie I (Cerhová) and blonde Marie II (Karbonavá) are two bored girls who decide to respond to the consumer-orientated society by playing a number of outrageous pranks on those who belong to it, and by destroying material goods. Chytilová's first collaboration with leading Czech screenwriter Krumbachová (who also designed the film), and her second with her cameraman husband Kučera was the most adventurous and anarchic Czech movie of the 1960s. Its bold use of colour and range of visual effects perfectly underline the sardonic comedy, which ends in a slapstick orgy of destruction at a banquet. It shocked Czech government officials who withheld its release for a year. It was then welcomed enthusiastically at home and abroad.

▶ **Dama Do Cine Shanghai, A** see Lady From The Shanghai Cinema, The

▶ **Dama S Sobachkoi** see Lady With The Little Dog, The

▶ **Dame Aux Camélias, La** see Lady Of The Camellias, The

Les Dames Du Bois De Boulogne

▶ **(US: Ladies Of The Park)**

France 1946 90 mins bw
Films Raoul Ploquin

d **Robert Bresson**
sc **Jean Cocteau, Robert Bresson**
ph **Philippe Agostini**
m **Jean-Jacques Grünewald**
　Maria Casarès, Elina Labourdette, Lucienne Bogaërt, Paul Bernard

When Jean (Bernard) confesses to Hélène (Casarès) that he no longer loves her, she vows revenge. Hélène contrives a meeting between Jean and Agnès (Labourdette), a woman of 'easy virtue' whom he thinks to be devout and chaste. They fall in love and marry. After the wedding ceremony, Hélène reveals the truth. Bresson's second feature film was his last to use professional performers and to be shot in a studio. The transposition of an interpolated story in Diderot's *Jacques Le Fatalist* to a 20th-century *haute bourgeois* setting with few plot changes, plus the cold abstraction of the images might have been the cause of its commercial failure, but it brilliantly lays bare the ethical issues of the fable, and dramatic tension is created between the verbal flights of Cocteau and Bresson's natural austerity.

The Damned

▶ **Les Maudits**

France 1947 105 mins bw
Spéva Films

d **René Clément**
sc **René Clément, Jacques Rémy**

ph **Henri Alekan**
m **Yves Baudrier**
   Henri Vidal, Florence Marly, Kurt
   Kronefeld, Jo Dest, Anne Campion,
   Michel Auclair

A group of Nazi officials and assorted hangers-on, realizing their days are numbered as the end of the war approaches, take a U-boat from Oslo and head for South America. One of the women is seriously hurt in an attack by a destroyer, so they land on the French coast and kidnap a doctor (Vidal) who becomes the hero of the piece. Clément offers a thriller-style entertainment, topical when it was made, combined with some satisfying anti-Nazi propaganda. A strong cast convinces as the group of desperate nasties, and the director does well to keep things interesting within the claustrophobic confines of the submarine.

Best Film Cannes 1947

The Damned

▶ **aka Götterdämmerung**

▶ **La Caduta Degli Dei**

   Italy/W. Germany   1969   164
   mins   col
   Praesidens/Pegaso

d **Luchino Visconti**
sc **Nicola Badalucco, Enrico Medioli,**
   Luchino Visconti
ph **Armando Nannuzzi, Pasquale De Santis**
m **Maurice Jarre**
   Dirk Bogarde, Ingrid Thulin, Helmut
   Berger, Renaud Verley, Helmut Griem,
   René Kolldehoff, Umberto Orsini,
   Charlotte Rampling

The conflicts within the powerful Essenbeck family of munitions manufacturers, operating in Germany during the growth of Nazism. The first of Visconti's 'German decadence' trilogy (followed by *Death In Venice* and *Ludwig*) is a ludicrously baroque and garish caricature of the 20th century's most tragic era. It sets out to examine the ideological and economic link between the Nazis and the capitalist *bourgeoisie*, but gets hypnotized by the Nazi regalia. The jackboot- kissing Helmut Berger in Dietrich drag romps with the Boys in the Bund, while the rest of the British,

Swedish, French, Italian and German cast mouth banalities in whichever of the languages the film is shown in.

▶ **Dance Programme, The** see Carnet De Bal, Un

Dangerous Moves

▶ **La Diagonale Du Fou**

   Switzerland   1983   110 mins   col
   Arthur Cohn

d **Richard Dembo**
sc **Richard Dembo**
ph **Raoul Coutard**
m **Gabriel Yared (based on César Franck)**
   Michel Piccoli, Alexandre Arbatt, Leslie
   Caron, Liv Ullmann, Daniel Olbrychski,
   Michel Aumont

The World Chess Championship is played in Geneva between the Soviet Grand Master (Piccoli) – suffering a heart condition but supported by all the accoutrements of the blessing of the Kremlin – and the former world champion (Arbatt) who defected five years previously. This film, which can be read as a metaphor for the Cold War, offers a great deal for chess lovers, and first-time director Dembo builds up a certain amount of suspense in the moves and countermoves which are echoed by the offstage strategies of the opposing camps. However, there is little character development, the personalities are rather shallow and two-dimensional, and the Hollywood honour comes as something of a surprise.

Best Foreign Film Oscar 1984

Daniel Takes A Train

▶ **Szerencsés Daniel**

   Hungary   1983   92 mins   col
   Mafilm (Hunnia Studio)

d **Pál Sándor**
sc **Zsuzsa Tóth**
ph **Elemér Ragályi**
m **György Selmeczi**
   Péter Rudolf, Sándor Zsótér, Kati Szerb,
   Mari Törőcsik, Dezső Garás, Gyula
   Bodrogi

After the 1956 Hungarian uprising, Daniel (Rudolf) and his friend Gyuri (Zsótér) – a soldier on the run – travel to a small town on the Austrian border. Gyuri knows he must leave Hungary but Daniel, looking for his girlfriend, is trapped in conflict and uncertainty. As a political drama, the film hedges its bets by taking an even-handed look at the options on offer to the protagonists; as a piece of film-making, it is constantly absorbing. Sándor draws marvellous performances from his cast, the camera is inventive (notice the tracking shot at the railway station), and the storyline is full of surprises, both wry and tragic.

► **Dans La Ville Blanche** see In The White City

Danton

France 1982 136 mins col
Films Du Losange/Groupe X/Gaumont/
TF1/SFPC/TM

d **Andrzej Wajda**
sc **Jean-Claude Carrière**
ph **Igor Luther**
m **Jean Prodromidès**
  Gérard Depardieu, Wojciech Pszoniak, Anne Alvaro, Roland Blanche, Patrice Chéreau, Angela Winkler, Roger Planchon

The clash between the warmly idealistic Danton (Depardieu) and the coldly pragmatic Robespierre (Pszoniak) over the way the French Revolution should go, ends with Danton on the guillotine. At the time of its release, most critics made an analogy between the central ideological conflict and that of General Jaruzelski and Lech Waleska in contemporary Poland, although the film was based on a 1931 play by Stanislawa Przybyszewska. Perhaps their theories added interest to this long-winded, visually conventional film with a posturing central performance by Depardieu.

► **Daoma Zei** see Horse Thief

Dark Eyes

► **Oci Ciornie**

Italy 1987 117 mins col
Excelsior Film/RAI 1

d **Nikita Mikhalkov**
sc **Alexander Adabakhian, Nikita Mikhalkov (with the collaboration of Suso Cecchi D'Amico)**
ph **Franco Di Giacomo**
m **Francis Lai**
  Marcello Mastroianni, Silvana Mangano, Marthe Keller, Elena Sofonova, Vsevolod Larionov, Innokenti Smoktunovsky

On board ship, Romano (Mastroianni), an aging Italian *roué*, tells his story to an amiable Russian (Larionov). When a poverty-stricken student, Romano had married a beautiful heiress (Mangano) and had lived in indolent luxury, taking refuge in buffoonery, mistresses and lone visits to spas. At one such, he met and seduced the married Anna (Sofonova) who fell in love with him and fled, whereupon he pursued her to her home in the Russian provinces... Working from several short stories by Chekhov, of which the most evident is *The Lady With The Little Dog* (the 'lady' here is Anna, the 'dark eyes' of the title), Mikhalkov has made what the American critic Pauline Kael termed 'a massive hunk of Italo-Russian kitsch'. The material encompasses a range of mood from poignant to farcical, dominated by Mastroianni, every inch the star, moving back and forth between youth and age. Unfortunately, it's an uncomfortably exhibitionistic performance, and the film as a whole is crowded with overstated stereotypes and insistent close-ups. The women are fine, the clothes stunning and the sense of period convincing.

Best Actor (Marcello Mastroianni) Cannes 1987

Dark Habits

► **Entre Tinieblas**

Spain 1984 95 mins col
Tesauro

d **Pedro Almodóvar**
sc **Pedro Almodóvar**
ph **Angel L. Fernández**

m Cam España
   Cristina Pascual, Julieta Serrano, Marisa
   Paredes, Carmen Maura, Mari Carillo,
   Lina Canalejas, Manuel Zarzo, Chus
   Lampreave

Ensconced in a tumble-down convent in Madrid is a tiny band of nuns calling themelves the Humble Redeemers. The Mother Superior (Serrano) is a heroin-addicted Lesbian, while her faithful followers, Sisters Snake, Manure, Sin and Rat, are similarly afflicted with sacrilegious tendencies. Into their midst comes Yolanda (Pascual), a sultry nightclub singer and drug addict whose lover has killed himself and whose presence unleashes numerous intrigues and sets off several catastrophes. Almodóvar's third feature was released several years after it was made, cashing in on the international success of *Woman On The Verge Of A Nervous Breakdown* (1988). *Dark Habits* already exhibits the director's trademarks: an anarchic and original imagination, marvellous use of garish colour, offbeat humour and even Carmen Maura, albeit in a small role. However, the film itself is something of an undergraduate exercise, puerile, tasteless and tedious, in spite of the splendid performances.

Darkness

▶ **Tamas**

   India 1987 297 mins col
   Blaze Entertainment

d **Govind Nihalani**
sc **Govind Nihalani**
ph **V. Murthy, Govind Nihalani**
m **Singh Bandhu, Vanraj Bhatia**
   Om Puri, Deepa Sahi, Amrish Puri,
   Bhishram Sahni, Deena Pathak, Saeed
   Jaffrey

During the partitioning of India and Pakistan in 1947, various religious and political groups gather to put forward their own points of view, mostly through violent means. A simple Hindu untouchable (Om Puri) finds his position threatened in what has become Muslim Pakistan, and he and his wife (Sahi) try to find a safe home as they move through the turmoil around them. The film by Nihalani,

the distinguished Bombay film-maker, raised strong objections from conservative religious elements – so much so that the director had an armed guard at his house. Accused of reopening old wounds, he claimed that the film, based on a celebrated 1974 novel by Bhishram Sahni, is both a grim reminder and a warning that 'politicians, manipulating the religious for their own ends, can still cause untold misery and are doing so at this very moment'. Not really taking a political side, the film concentrates on the destruction brought about by bitter sectarian divisions. Nihalani's achievement is that the characters representing this divide are never ciphers but real human beings. (An exception occurs in the shaky accents and performances of a British colonial couple.) Indians had no trouble sitting through over four hours of it (it was released in a 150-minute version elsewhere), but it was also shown in six parts on Indian and British TV, easier to absorb than at one long sitting.

The Dark Side Of The Moon

▶ **aka The Man in the Moon**

▶ **Manden I Maanen**

   Denmark 1986 94 mins col
   Film-Cooperative Denmark

d **Erik Clausen**
sc **Erik Clausen**
ph **Morten Bruus, Jens Schlosser**
m **John Høybe**
   Peter Thiel, Catherine Poul Dupont,
   Christina Bergtsson, Kim Jansson,
   Tavuzer Cetinkaya

A prisoner (Thiel) is released 16 years after being jailed for killing his wife. Reticent and introspective, he adjusts slowly to society, steeling himself to approach his daughter (Bergtsson) who views him only as her mother's murderer. Dark it certainly is (there is not one daylight setting), and bleak, with Denmark presented as a loveless place, where people speak slowly and monosyllabically. But a ponderous and pretentious tendency is offset by the intense film debut of Peter Thiel who is strangely watchable, as unattractive as he is, and the almost expressionistic photography and lighting.

▶ **Dastforoush** see Pedlar, The

▶ **Daughter Of Destiny, A** see Alraune

Daughter Of The Nile

▶ **Nilouhe, Nuer**

Taiwan 1988 91 mins col
Fu Film Productions

d   **Hou Hsiao-hsien**
sc **Zhu Tianwen**
ph **Ch'en Huai-en**
m   **Ch'en Cihyuan, Chang Hung-yi**
    Yang Lin, Kao Jai, Yang Fan, Li Tien-lu

A schoolgirl (Lin), washing, cooking and
doing the housework for her father, grandfather, elder brother and younger sister, as
well as working at a Kentucky Fried Chicken
fast food joint after school, can only escape
by reading the comic strip *Daughter Of The
Nile*. Brisker, and more substantial than
Hsiao-hsien's first big international success *A
Summer At Grandpa's*, the film has as much
warmth and gentle observation as that picture. Yang Lin, a popular singer in Taiwan,
Kao Jai, an owner of fashion boutiques, and
Li Tien-lu are perfect as the drudge, her ne'er-
do-well brother and loving grandfather
respectively. Only some of the tenuous
allusions to the comic strip may escape the
Western spectator.

Daughters Of China

▶ **Zhonghua Nuer**

China 1949 92 mins bw
Northeast Film Studios

d   **Ling Zhifeng, Zhai Jiang**
sc **Yan Yiyan**
ph **Qian Jiang**
m   **Tung Yeng Orchestra**
    **Zhang Zheng, Yueh Shen, Bo Li, Tai Pu-
    hua, Chou-Su-Fei, Xie Yan**

During the Japanese invasion of North-east
China in 1936, a peasant woman (Zheng)
joins the resistance and finds herself in a
guerilla group with seven other women,
headed by Commissar Yun (Shen). After liberating an important town, they run into a
large Japanese force with tragic but heroic
consequences. The film, which can claim to
be the first production under the new government of the People's Republic of China, was
based on a real incident – the martyrdom of
eight women fighting the Japanese. It was a
perfect subject to inspire national unity and
point the way towards the New China style
of films. Although the women are pictured as
superheroines and symbols, much of the life
in the army, as well as the relationships among
the characters, is invested with an affecting
naturalism.

David

W. Germany 1979 125 mins col
Vietinghof Filmproduktion/Pro-ject Film
Produktion/ Filmverlag Der Autoren/
ZDF/Dedra Pictures

d   **Peter Lilienthal**
sc **Jurek Becker,Ulla Zieman, Peter
    Lilienthal**
ph **Al Ruban**
m   **Wojciech Kilar**
    **Mario Fische, Torsten Henties, Walter
    Taub, Irena Vrkljan, Eva Mattes**

When Rabbi Singer (Taub) has his synagogue
burnt down and his bald head scarred with a
swastika by the Nazi persecutors, his daughter
(Mattes) and teenage son David (Fische) go
into hiding. The girl is given refuge by a
shoemaker in return for money, but David
goes on the run alone, taking odd jobs, and
finally acquiring false papers to get to Israel.
A small tale about a major chapter in history,
the film is overlong and attempts no new
insights into or comments on the Holocaust.
However, although no more than competent
in all departments, it is nonetheless a moving,
and occasionally powerful, document.

Best Film Berlin 1979

▶ **Dawandeh** see Runner, The

Daybreak

▶ **Le Jour Se Lève**

France 1939 95 mins bw
Vog/Sigma

d   **Marcel Carné**
sc **Jacques Prévert, Jacques Viot**
ph **Curt Courant, Philippe Agostini**
m   **Maurice Jaubert**
     **Jean Gabin, Jules Berry, Arletty,
     Jacqueline Laurent, René Génin, Mady
     Berry, Bernard Blier**

A worker (Gabin) gets involved with the mistress (Arletty) of a shady showman (Berry) and kills him in a jealous confrontation over an innocent flower-seller (Laurent). He then barricades himself in his small room during the night as the police and crowds wait below. The most celebrated of the pessimistic poetic realist films of the Carné-Prévert partnership makes memorable atmospheric use of the dark tenement set (designed by Alexandre Trauner) and of Gabin's tragic stature almost, matched by the hypnotically suave villainy of Berry. Although most of the film is told in flashback as Gabin thinks back over the past, it is the image of the oppressively small room in which he is trapped, that lingers in the mind. When RKO bought the rights for an inferior 1947 remake called *The Long Night* with Henry Fonda, it shamelessly tried to destroy all prints. Happily it failed to do so.

▶ **Dayereh Mina** see Cycle, The

Day For Night

▶ **La Nuit Américaine**

France   1973   116 mins   col
Films du Carrosse/PECF/PIC

d   **François Truffaut**
sc **François Truffaut, Jean-Louis Richard,
     Suzanne Schiffman**
ph **Pierre-William Glenn**
m   **Georges Delerue**
     **Jacqueline Bisset, Valentina Cortese,
     Jean-Pierre Aumont, Jean-Pierre Léaud,
     Alexandra Stewart, François Truffaut,
     Dani, Jean Champion, David Markham**

During the filming of a melodrama called *Meet Pamela*, the juvenile lead (Léaud) falls hopelessly in love with the married international star (Bisset), an actress (Cortese) keeps forgetting her lines, the male lead (Aumont) is killed in a crash, time and money

begin to run out, and someone has a baby. 'Are films more important than life?' asks Léaud at one stage. Truffaut, himself playing the director, answers in the affirmative with this exuberant celebration of movie-making, even if the plainly lousy film being shot seems hardly worth the trouble. But the enthusiasm he feels comes across forcefully and so does the involved process of creating a film. Incidentally, novelist Graham Greene appears in an uncredited bit part.

Best Foreign Film Oscar 1973

A Day In The Country

▶ **Une Partie De Campagne**

France   1936   45 mins   bw
Panthéon/Films De La Pléiade/Pierre
Braunberger

d   **Jean Renoir**
sc **Jean Renoir**
ph **Claude Renoir, Jean Bourgoin**
m   **Joseph Kosma**
     **Sylvie Bataille, Georges Darnoux, Jane
     Marken, Paul Temps, Jacques Brunius,
     Gabriello, Gabrielle Fontan, Jean Renoir**

A tradesman, his wife, daughter and future son-in-law take a rare Sunday trip to the country where they picnic, go boating and fishing, and where the daughter falls in love with a young holiday-maker. The idyll ends on a regretful note. Originally Renoir only intended to make an hour-long film based on Guy De Maupassant's short story, shot on location in the countryside of the Île De France. However, the summer of 1936 was particularly rainy so the project was abandoned with only two sequences to shoot. In 1946, two intertitles were added to explain the missing passages, and it has been delighting audiences ever since. Renoir's glowing, witty, sensuous tribute to the countryside through which a river runs has seldom been surpassed.

Day Of Wrath

▶ **Vredens Dag**

Denmark   1943   105 mins   bw
Palladium

d   **Carl Dreyer**
sc **Carl Dreyer, Poul Knudsen, Mogens
    Skot-Hansen**
ph **Karl Andersson**
m   **Poul Schierbeck**
    **Thorkild Roose, Lisbeth Movin, Sigrid
    Neiiendam, Preben Lerdoff Rye, Anna
    Svierkier**

In 17th-century Denmark, a pastor (Roose) is cursed by a dying witch (Svierkier). His wife (Movin) then commits adultery with a younger man (Rye), the discovery of which kills the pastor, and she in turn is burned as a witch. Dreyer's 10 years of silence after *Vampyr* was broken with this rather ponderous, measured and academic study of people caught in a web of superstition. One cannot deny the splendid interior compositions or fail to recognize the glimmerings of Dreyer's austere genius. The film, one of his most famous, was taken as an allegory for occupied Denmark, so Dreyer took refuge in Sweden until after the war to avoid reprisals.

Days And Nights In The Forest

▶ **Aranyer Din Ratri**

India   1969   115 mins   bw
Priya

d   **Satyajit Ray**
sc **Satyajit Ray**
ph **Soumendu Roy**
m   **Satyajit Ray**
    **Soumitra Chatterjee, Sharmilia Tagore,
    Shubhendu Chatterjee, Samit Bhanja**

Four young men spend their country holiday in an unused bungalow where they come into contact with the villagers, meet a rich family, and develop relationships with women, before returning to their urban existence. Chekhov and Jean Renoir (with whom Ray worked) come to mind, especially in the magical picnic scene, but the subtle revelation of character through the purposefully slow tempo and the deceptively simple cinematic effects are all the master Indian director's own.

▶ **Days Of Hope** see Man's Hope

Days Of 36

▶ **Imeres Tou 36**

Greece   1972   120 mins   col
Finos Film

d   **Theo Angelopoulos**
sc **Theo Angelopoulos**
ph **Georges Arvanitis**
    **Georges Kiritsis, Thanos Grammenos,
    Yannis Kandilas, Christoforos Chimara,
    Takis Dukakos**

A man (Grammenos) is arrested for the assassination of a politician. He protests his innocence and holds a deputy (Kiritsis) hostage in his cell, threatening to kill the man and himself unless he is released. The first of Angelopoulos' triptych about recent Greek history (*The Travelling Players* and *The Huntsmen* followed), is based on actual events in 1936. Made during the reign of the Colonels, the film subtly undermines that regime in its portrayal of official incompetence. The prison governors and politicians are struck by a paralysis of indecision, finally breaking the deadlock by violent means in which justice has no place. The film is brilliantly photographed and, given its physical confines, its acreage of silence and the fact that the prisoner keeps himself out of sight for a good deal of the time, the high level of tension is a real achievement, especially considering the director's penchant for drawing things out.

▶ **Da Yuebing** see Big Parade, The

▶ **Deadlier Than The Male** see Murder À La Carte

▶ **Dear Detective** see Dear Inspector

Dearest Love

▶ **(US: Murmur Of The Heart)**

▶ **Le Souffle Au Coeur**

France   1971   118 mins   col
Nouvelles Éditions/Marianne/Vides
Cinematografica/Franz Seitz

d   **Louis Malle**
sc **Louis Malle**

ph **Ricardo Aronovich**
m **Charlie Parker, Sidney Bechet, Gaston Freche, Henri Renaud**
   Lea Massari, Benoît Ferreux, Daniel Gélin, Fabien Ferreux, Jacqueline Chauveau, Michel Lonsdale

Fifteen-year-old Laurent (Benoit Ferreux) is wrestling with the ache of adolescent sexual longings while his mother (Massari), though successfully married, has a lover with whom she is undergoing a crisis. After an illness leaves Laurent with a heart murmur, his mother takes him to a health spa where they each meet with sexual rejection, and their mutual sympathy and love culminates in bed. Malle treats incest with subtlety and sensitivity but the film is fundamentally about the pains and pleasures of adolescence and, as the mother makes clear, theirs is a one-off encounter, appropriate to that moment only. Played out in the context of 1950s middle-class family life, this truthful, funny, observant and affectionate work is served by first-class performances, notably from Massari who handles her task with exquisite finesse.

Dear Inspector

▶ **(US: Dear Detective)**

▶ **Tendre Poulet**

   France   1977   105 mins   col
   Les Films Ariane/Mondex Films

d   **Philippe De Broca**
sc **Michel Audiard, Philippe De Broca**
ph **Jean-Paul Schwartz**
m   **Georges Delerue**
    Annie Girardot, Philippe Noiret, Catherine Alric, Guy Marchand, Roger Dumas, Simone Renant

Lise (Girardot), divorcée and mother, is also a police inspector. While engaged on an important murder investigation, she romances with a professor of Greek (Noiret), an old acquaintance whom she met again through accidentally knocking him down in the street. The leads – Noiret confused, pompous and endearing, Girardot confused, madcap and endearing – shine in this charming comedy thriller, full of inventive gags, serious *policier* undertones and touching romance. Although De Broca's taste for the eccentric here degenerates on occasion into uncomfortable contrivance, there is much to enjoy in a light-hearted fashion.

Dear Irene

▶ **Kaere Irene**

   Denmark   1971   102 mins   bw
   Kollektiv Film

d   **Christian Braad Thomsen**
sc **Christian Braad Thomsen, Mette Knudsen**
ph **Dirk Brüel**
m   **Blue Sun**
    Mette Knudsen, Sten Kaalø, Ebbe Kløvedal, Agneta Ekmanner, Erik Nørgaard, Katrine Behrendt

Irene (Knudsen), who married Claus (Klovedal) some years ago because she could not get an abortion, is locked into an affair with Ebbe (Kaalø), who is very much in love with her. He leaves his journalist's job on a conventional newspaper in order to express his revolutionary views, while she, obsessed with asserting her independence, is cruelly unfaithful to him. The debut feature of the Marxist critic Thomsen is impressive. Shot in *cinéma vérité* style, it achieves a casual and convincing realism, while the events of the plot mask complex layers of social and political argument. A film about commitment and contradiction, about difficulties of choice, loneliness and isolation, and the political versus the personal, it grips on the surface level, too – especially as played by Knudsen, whose destructive and confused Irene is nonetheless sympathetic.

Dear John

▶ **Kare John**

   Sweden   1964   111 mins   bw
   Sandrew

d   **Lars Magnus Lindgren**
sc **Lars Magnus Lindgren**
ph **Rune Ericson**
m   **Bengt-Arne Wallin**
    Jarl Kulle, Christina Schollin, Helena Nilsson, Morgan Andersson, Synnove Liljeback

Anita (Schollin), an unmarried mother, works as a waitress in a small coastal town. John (Kulle) is a sailor whose barge anchors there for a weekend which they spend together. When he has to leave, she thinks she will never see him again. A skilfully constructed love story, tender but sensual, about two young people fearful of being hurt, but irresistibly drawn together. Lindgren uses flashback techniques with control, his stars act with sensitivity and conviction, and the photography makes palpable the clear light of a Swedish summer.

Dear Michael

► **Caro Michele**

Italy 1976 108 mins col
FLAG Production

d **Mario Monicelli**
sc **Suso Cecchi D'Amico, Tonino Guerra**
ph **Tonino Delli Colli**
m **Nino Rota**
   Mariangela Melato, Delphine Seyrig, Aurore Clément, Marcella Michelangeli, Lou Castel, Fabio Carpi

A middle-class Roman family finds its long-standing traditions and ideals challenged by the changing climate of the times, culminating in the free-thinking, free-living zany Mara (Melato) giving birth to the child of their rebellious son, Michael. When Michael, who is abroad fighting for some unspecified revolution, is killed, Mara, mother of the family's sole male heir, finds the problems of choice between individualism and conformity devolving on her. Working from a novel by the distinguished Russian, Natalia Ginzburg, Monicelli has made a literate and good-spirited film in which he strikes a convincing balance between sympathy for, and criticism of, his characters. Standing out in a first-rate cast is the accomplished and deliciously uninhibited Melato. Michael, to whom everyone writes letters and who serves to link the action, remains offscreen.

Best Director Berlin 1976

Death By Hanging

► **Koshikei**

Japan 1968 117 mins bw
Sozosha

d **Nagisa Oshima**

sc **Tsutomu Tamura**
ph **Yasuhiro Yoshioka**
m **Hikaru Hayashi**
   Yun-Do Yun, Kei Sato, Fumio Watanabe, Toshiro Ishido, Masao Adachi

An intelligent young Korean (Yun) is being hanged for the rape and murder of two Japanese girls, but his body refuses to die. The characters act out the man's story in seven chapters. Oshima's startling, angry and blackly humorous film begins like a documentary on the death penalty, becoming more and more unreal as the arguments are pursued. The main subject that emerges is the shameful treatment by the Japanese of the Korean minority, a fact of crucial importance to an understanding of the film.

Death In A French Garden

► **Péril En La Demeure**

France 1985 101 mins col
Gaumont/Elefilm/TFI Films

d **Michel Deville**
sc **Michel Deville, Rosalinde Damamme**
ph **Martial Thury**
m **Extracts from Brahms, Schubert, Enrique Granados**
   Michel Piccoli, Nicole Garcia, Anemone, Christophe Malavoy, Richard Bohringer, Anaïs Jeanneret

David (Malavoy) arrives to teach music to Viviane (Jeanneret), the young and sexually precocious daughter of a wealthy industrialist (Piccoli) and his wife, Julia (Garcia). Seduced by Julia, he finds himself entangled in a web of deception, voyeurism and murder, with a hired homosexual killer who is after his affections. Deville has delivered a stylish and accomplished film, beautiful to look at. However, its manipulative mix of thriller, sophisticated critique of *bourgeois* mores and suggested allegory, alternately dark and playful in tone, adds up to a superficial exercise which is sometimes tedious, sometimes engrossing.

Death In Venice

► **Morte A Venezia**

Italy 1971 128 mins col
Alfa Cinematografica

d **Luchino Visconti**
sc **Luchino Visconti, Nicola Badalucco**
ph **Pasquale De Santis**
m **Mahler**
   Dirk Bogarde, Bjorn Andresen, Silvano Mangano, Marisa Berenson, Mark Burns

Von Aschenbach, an aging and celebrated composer in poor health and suffering a crisis of his creative powers, visits Venice. There he becomes possessed by the beauty of a young Polish boy, Tadzio (Andresen), to whom he never speaks but who appears to embody his ideals of physical beauty and spiritual purity. He remains in Venice, in spite of a cholera epidemic, until ill health and his obsession combine to kill him. Visconti's transposition of Thomas Mann's novel is intelligent and sensitive, and evokes *fin-de-siècle* Venice to breathtaking perfection. The flashbacks examining Von Aschenbach's crisis are clumsy, and the intellectual heart of the novel is, perhaps, ultimately impossible to film. The transformation of Mann's writer into a composer is doubtless an attempt to overcome the difficulties and, although the device works well, the suggestion that Aschenbach – in the slightly too English, too young guise of Bogarde – composed the works of Gustav Mahler is a little unsettling. The Cannes Festival jury awarded its special twenty-fifth anniversary prize to Visconti for this film in particular, and his *oeuvre* in general.

Death Is My Trade

▶ **Aus Einem Deutschen Leben**

   W. Germany   1977   145 mins   col
   WDR (Cologne)/Iduna-Film (Munich)

d **Theodor Kotulla**
sc **Theodor Kotulla**
ph **Dieter Naujeck**
m **Eberhard Weber**
   Götz George, Elisabeth Schwarz, Kurt Hübner, Kai Taschner, Sigurd Fitzek, Peter Franke, Hans Korte, Walter Czaschke

The life, from 1922 until 1946, of Franz Lang (George), a German working-class patriot who joins the Nazi Party in 1924 and distinguishes himself by dedicated hard work and application. Himmler appoints him to an important post at Dachau and, seven years later, he is commandant at Auschwitz, respon-sible for carrying out the Final Solution. After the war, he writes his memoirs and dies without exhibiting a hint of remorse. Although given a fictitious name here, Lang is actually the notorious Rudolph Höss (not to be confused with Hess), portrayed here as a rather ordinary man, unquestioningly committed to his duty. If this is, in itself, a comment on the German high command's skill in securing faith in its ideology, Kotulla's film actually offers no comment and no apology. A detached, ordered account of events makes for a historical document, all the more chilling for its lack of emotion and the seeming normality of its protagonists.

Death Occurred Last Night

▶ **La Morte Risale A Ieri Sera**

   Italy   1970   98 mins   col
   Lombard Film/Filmes/C.C.C. (Berlin)

d **Duccio Tessari**
sc **Biagio Proietti, Duccio Tessari, Arthur Brauner**
ph **Lamberto Caimi**
m **Gianni Ferrio**
   Raf Vallone, Frank Wolff, Gabriele Tinti, Gillian Bray, Eva Renzi

When 25-year-old Donatella Berzhagi disappears, the police are offhand with her desperate father (Vallone), until he explains that she has a mental age of three and suffers from a tendency to nymphomania. To find her abductor, Inspector Lambert (Wolff) institutes a manhunt throughout a world inhabited by participants in every kind of call-girl racket. On the surface this is a slick thriller, trading in the currency of sleaze, but don't be fooled – Tessari has made an intelligent study of a milieu, using his plot to carry a series of observant character studies and pointing to a society composed of lonely and unhappy people, conveyed in some powerful and inventive images.

Death Of A Bureaucrat

▶ **La Muerte De Un Burocrata**

   Cuba   1966   84 mins   bw
   I.C.A.I.C.

d **Tomás Gutiérrez Alea**

sc **Alfredo Del Cueto, Ramón Suárez, Tomás Gutiérrez Alea**
ph **Ramón Suárez**
m **Leo Brouwer**
  Salvador Wood, Silvia Planas, Manuel Estanillo, Gaspar De Santelices, Carlos Ruiz De La Tejera, Omar Alfonso

After an exemplary worker is buried, clutching his union card, his widow (Planas) finds she needs it to claim her pension. The fruitless attempts of her nephew (Wood) to obtain an exhumation order lead to his visit to the cemetery at night and a series of further complications. This amusing satire not only takes a swipe at Red red-tape, but pays tribute to a whole range of other films on the way. Laurel and Hardy, Harold Lloyd, Buñuel and Bergman are all evoked, but it is to Alea's credit that they become integral to this inventive narrative.

Death Of A Cyclist

▶ **(US: Age Of Infidelity)**
▶ **Muerte De Un Ciclista**

  Spain 1955 85 mins bw
  Guion/Suevia/Trionfalcine

d **Juan Antonio Bardem**
sc **Juan Antonio Bardem**
ph **Alfredo Fraile**
m **Isrido Maiztegui**
  Lucia Bosé, Alberto Closas, Carlos Casaravilla, Otello Toso, Bruna Corra

A university professor (Closas), driving with his mistress (Bosé) who is married to an important man, knocks down a worker on a bicycle. Fearing their affair will be discovered, they leave the man to die in the road. Their subsequent guilt leads to a further tragedy. Bardem's most famous work was a decent attempt to make a socially critical film under Franco's regime. The milieu of the rich and the contrasting poor districts of Madrid are well caught in this bitter comment on contemporary Spain. Unfortunately, censorship forced Bardem to punish the adulterous woman in a melodramatic ending.

Death Of A Friend

▶ **Morte Di Un Amico**

  Italy 1959 87 mins bw

Universalcine

d **Franco Rossi**
sc **Giuseppe Berto, Oreste Biancoli, Pier Paolo Pasolini, Franco Riganti**
ph **Toni Secchi**
m **Mario Nascimbene**
  Gianni Garko, Spiros Focas, Didi Perego, Angela Luce, Anna Mazzucchelli, Fanfulla

Bruno (Focas), a delinquent layabout who lives with and is kept by a prostitute (Luce), succeeds in persuading quiet, respectable Aldo (Garko), his best friend since childhood, to join him in his own way of life. The ensuing catastrophes end in Aldo's tragic death. Rossi exercises commendable restraint and subtlety in dealing with a storyline and characters tailormade for overheated treatment. Focas and Garko convince and, although compassion tips over into sentimentality, this essentially small film is nonetheless affecting.

The Death Of Maria Malibran

▶ **Der Tod Der Maria Malibran**

  W. Germany 1971 104 mins col
  Werner Schroeter

d **Werner Schroeter**
sc **Werner Schroeter**
ph **Werner Schroeter**
m **Brahms, Beethoven, Thomas, Stravinsky, Mozart, Cherubini, Handel, Puccini, Rossini, and various popular standards**
  Magdalena Montezuma, Candy Darling, Annette Tirier, Christine Kaufmann, Ingrid Caven

A series of unrealistic tableaux enact the short life of Maria Malibran (Montezuma), the 19th-century Spanish prima donna, who died during a performance, at the age of 28 in 1836, from injuries received in a riding accident. High camp has to be the description of this perverse but curiously hypnotic and beautiful 'biopic', with no discernible plot, no direct dialogue (there are Shakespearian soliloquies etc), or direct singing (the voices are mostly disembodied) and a vast range of anachronistic melodies including 'St Louis Blues'. 'Mad genius' Schroeter was the only man Rainer Werner Fassbinder considered his artistic equal.

The Death Of Mario Ricci

▶ **La Mort De Mario Ricci**

Switzerland 1983 101 mins col
Pegase Fils/Television Suisse Romande/
Swanie Productions/FR3 (Paris)/Tele
München

d   **Claude Goretta**
sc **Claude Goretta, Georges Haldas**
ph **Hans Liechti**
m   **Arié Dzierlatka, Christian Bonneau, and
extracts from Vivaldi and Monteverdi
Gian Maria Volonté, Heinz Bennent,
Mimsy Farmer, Magali Noël, Jean-
Michel Dupuis**

Having been partly crippled in the course of
duty in South America, a Swiss TV journalist
(Volonté) returns home to interview a world-
famous expert on famine who lives in an
Alpine village. He discovers that the man is
on the verge of a nervous breakdown, and
learns that mystery surrounds the death of
Mario Ricci, an Italian worker killed in a
motorcycle smash. Compelling visual images
hint at the dark secrets harboured by a community, but the film lets itself down with too
many sub-plots, red herrings and existential
meanderings. A worthy, sometimes interesting, but finally unsatisfying piece, held
together by its technical expertise and excellent casting.

**Best Actor (Gian Maria Volonté) Cannes
1983**

The Death Ray

▶ **Luch Smerti**

USSR 1925 125 mins bw
Goskino

d   **Lev Kuleshov**
sc **Vsevolod Pudovkin**
ph **A. Levitski**
m   **Silent**
    **Porfiry Podobed, Sergei Komarov,
Vsevolod Pudovkin, Alexandra
Khokhlova, Vladimir Fogel, Lev Kuleshov**

A group of Fascist spies tries to steal the
Death Ray, an invention of a Soviet scientist
(Podobed), but they are eventually foiled by
a series of subterfuges. Mysterious masked
men, women brandishing guns and sinister
figures in black tights prowling across roof-
tops are all elements reminiscent of the Feuillade serials, but the film is original in its use
of mobile cameras, quick cutting and breathless pacing. (Pudovkin was nearly killed performing a stunt, when he fell from a three-
storey building.) All great fun, accidents
apart, but it failed to amuse Soviet officialdom
who thought it lacked 'meaningful' content
and stripped Kuleshov of much of his company's budget. What the po-faced commissars
did not see was its prediction of the growth
of Fascism.

▶ **Debut, The** see Beginning, The

The Decameron

▶ **Il Decamerone**

Italy 1971 111 mins col
PEA/Artemis/UA

d   **Pier Paolo Pasolini**
sc **Pier Paolo Pasolini**
ph **Tonino Delli Colli**
m   **Pier Paolo Pasolini, Ennio Morricone
Franco Citti, Ninetto Davoli, Angela
Luce, Patrizia Capparelli, Pier Paolo
Pasolini, Jovan Jovanovic, Gianni Rizzo**

Eight of Boccaccio's tales, set mostly around
14th-century Naples, including those of the
seducing nuns, the three jealous brothers who
murder their sister's lover, a false saint, a
deceiving husband, and the man who travels
to buy horses but finds himself caught up in
a series of disasters. The first in Pasolini's
lively and colourful trilogy based on famous
story cycles (*The Canterbury Tales* and *The
Arabian Nights* followed) included the director as Giotto working on a fresco as the pivot
around which Boccaccio's tales of sexual
deception revolved. Pasolini chose many ordinary Neapolitans to appear among the cast
of 54 to populate this re-creation of the
teeming Naples of the Middle Ages.

Special Jury Prize Berlin 1971

▶ **Decamerone, Il** see Decameron, The

▶ **Deception** see Anna Boleyn

▶ **De Cierta Manera** see One Way Or Another

▶ **Déclin De L'Empire Américain, Le** see Decline Of The American Empire, The

The Decline Of The American Empire

▶ **Le Déclin De L'Empire Américain**

Canada 1986 101 mins col
Corporation Image M&M/National Film Board Of Canada/Téléfilm Canada/ Sociéte Générale Du Cinéma Du Québec

d   **Denys Arcand**
sc **Denys Arcand**
ph **Guy Dufaux**
m   **F. Compierre**
    Dominique Michel, Dorothée Berryman, Louise Portal, Geneviève Rioux, Pierre Curzy, Rémy Girard, Yves Jacques, Daniel Brière

Four history professors discuss their contrasting sex lives while preparing a gourmet dinner in a country mansion. Meanwhile, their four female guests conduct a similar discussion in a sauna. Later, at the dinner, talk consists of fashionable and wide-ranging intellectual exchange until one of the women (Michel) announces that she has slept with two of her hosts, including the married Rémy (Girard) whose wife (Berryman) is present. Arcand's film is a cynical and observant conversation piece in which the protagonists' attitudes to sex serve to unmask their personalities, their deeper political concerns and their positions in the battle of the sexes. Dense, perhaps, but intelligent and interesting.

Dédée

▶ **Woman Of Antwerp**

▶ **Dédée D'Anvers**

France 1948 95 mins bw
Sacha Gordine/André Paulvé

d   **Yves Allégret**
sc **Yves Allégret, Jacques Sigurd**
ph **Jean Bourgoin**
m   **Jacques Besse**
    Simone Signoret, Marcel Pagliero, Bernard Blier, Marcel Dalio, Jane Marken

When Dédée (Signoret), a prostitute around the docks at Antwerp, falls for a sailor (Pagliero), her pimp (Blier) causes trouble that leads to tragedy. The first of three doom-laden melodramas that Allégret made with his then wife Signoret, was filmed in the kind of poetic realism which Marcel Carné made popular before the war. Without approaching the quality of such films as *Quai des Brumes* (1938), it depicts the dockside low life with conviction. Above all, there is 27-year-old Signoret, shining in her first important role.

▶ **Dédée D'Anvers** see Dédée

Le Défroqué

▶ **aka The Renegade Priest**

France 1953 111 mins bw
SFC/SNEG

d   **Léo Joannon**
sc **Léo Joannon, Denys De La Patellière**
ph **Nicolas Torporkoff**
m   **Jean-Jacques Grünewald**
    Pierre Fresnay, Pierre Trabaud, Nicole Stéphane, Marcelle Géniat, René Blancard

In a German prison camp, a defrocked priest (Fresnay) rails against the Church and religion, but his unselfish acts inspire a young fellow prisoner (Trabaud) to take up the priesthood after the war. In addition, it takes two deaths on his conscience to bring the heretic back to God. The Protestant Fresnay followed up his convincing portrayals of Catholic holy men in *Monsieur Vincent* and *Isle Of Sinners* with another brilliant performance in the devotional mode. While in no way competing with the two true religious artists of the cinema – Dreyer and Bresson – Joannon manages in a modest manner to make a telling drama with a highly emotional ending that only an actor of Fresnay's calibre could carry off.

Best Director Berlin 1954

A Degree Of Murder

▶ **Mord Und Totschlag**

W. Germany 1967 87 mins col
Rob Houwer Films

d Volker Schlöndorff
sc Gregor Von Rezzori, Niklas Franz, Arne
Boyer
ph Franz Rath
m Brian Jones
Anita Pallenberg, Hans P. Hallwachs,
Manfred Fischbeck, Werner Enke, Angela
Hillebrecht

A girl (Pallenberg) accidentally kills her boyfriend in a quarrel over a revolver. She persuades a stranger (Hallwachs), in exchange
for some money, to help her dispose of the
body which, via a sexual encounter with her,
he does. They place it in a hole in a construction site and, as the bulldozers are about to
dig it up, she is planning a trip to Greece
with another young man whom she has just
met. In his second film, Schlöndorff confirms
the competence he displayed in his first, *Young
Torless*. It is a naturalistic and convincing
piece, but so determinedly neutral in its examination of a bunch of drifters that the point
is not altogether clear. While it is happening,
though, this rather amoral but well-paced tale
is fairly absorbing. The acting is fine, but
Pallenberg's claim to fame would remain her
liaison with Keith Richard of The Rolling
Stones rather than her thespian abilities. Ex-
Stones guitarist Jones composed the music
shortly before his death.

▶ **Déjeuner Sur L'Herbe, Le** see
Lunch On The Grass

▶ **De L'Amour** see All About Loving

▶ **De Mayerling À Sarajevo** see
Sarajevo

▶ **Demise Of Father Mouret, The**
see Sin Of Father Mouret, The

Il Demonio

Italy 1963 100 mins bw

Titanus/Vox Film (Rome)/Cocinor/
Marceau (Paris)

d Brunello Rondi
sc Ugo Guerra, Brunello Rondi, Luciano
Martino
ph Carlo Bellero
m Piero Piccioni
Daliah Lavi, Frank Wolff, Giovanni
Cristofanelli, Luca Pascarella, Lea Eusso,
Giuseppe Macaluso

Purif (short for Purification), who lives in an
isolated mountain village with her family and
is passionately in love with Antonio (Wolff),
is plagued by voices and visions, and is
believed to be possessed by the devil.
Attempts to exorcise her fail, she is driven
out of the village, and meets Antonio, now
married to someone else, who succumbs to
his desire for her then kills her. An unexpectedly convincing performance from international Israeli glamour girl Dahlia Lavi lends
credence to this first feature from Rondi,
which he based on a documented anthropological study. He is clearly committed to the
material and handles the cast and atmosphere
well, but falls into the trap of concentrating
his narrative in episodes of abnormal behaviour, bypassing daily life rather than placing
Purif's story in opposition to it.

▶ **Demonios En El Jardin** see Demons
In The Garden

▶ **Demonio Y Carne** see Susana

Demons In The Garden

▶ **Demonios En El Jardin**

Spain 1982 105 mins col
Producciones Cinematograficas/Luis
Megino

d Manuel Gutiérrez Aragón
sc Manuel Gutiérrez Aragón, Luis Megino
ph José Luis Alcaine
m Javier Iturralde
Angela Molina, Ana Belen, Eusebio
Lazáro, Imanol Arias, Alvaro Sanchez-
Prieto

Two brothers, Oscar and Juan (Lazáro and
Arias), living in a provincial Spanish town in
1942, both love Ana (Belen). She marries

Oscar but loves Juan who has made her rival, Angela (Molina), pregnant. Juan abandons Angela, who gives birth to his illegitimate son. Ten years later the family, spearheaded by the grandmother, decide that 10-year-old Juanito (Sanchez-Prieto), whose nature combines the opposing temperaments of his father and uncle, must be raised in their midst. This complex study of sexual mores, political attitudes and family relationships, by one of Spain's most accomplished directors, unfolds against the background of Franco's regime. Aragón employs subtle symbolism and a poetical style, but sweetens the pill of weighty themes and fiery emotions with some well-judged irony and black humour.

▶ **Dentellière, La** see Lacemaker, The

Le Départ

Belgium 1966 91 mins bw
Elisabeth

d **Jerzy Skolimowski**
sc **Jerzy Skolimowski, Andrzej Kostenko**
ph **Willy Kurant**
m **Krzysztof Komeda**
Jean-Pierre Léaud, Catherine Duport, Jacqueline Bir, Paul Roland

A young ladies' hairdresser (Léaud), crazy about racing cars, dreams of driving his employer's Porsche in a rally, but all his machinations and dreams come to nothing. When the Polish authorities banned *Hands Up!* (1967), Skolimowski left the country to become, like his friend Roman Polanski, an international itinerant film-maker, carrying his vision and acid humour with him. The playful irony, the freewheeling, sharp photography, and the presence of Jean-Pierre Léaud (the darling of directors François Truffaut and Jean-Luc Godard), cloaked it in the French New Wave influence. But the fact that it was shot in Brussels, that surreal city of surrealists, gave it a different visual edge, and a more maniacal quality.

Deprisa, Deprisa

▶ **aka Fast, Fast**

Spain 1981 98 mins col

Elias Querejeta/Les Films Molieire/ Consortium Pathé

d **Carlos Saura**
sc **Carlos Saura**
ph **Teo Escamilla**
m **Spanish songs**
José Antonio Valdelomar, José Maria Hervas Roldan, Jesus Arias Aranzeque, Berta Socuellamos Zarco

Three young criminals are joined by Angela (Zarco), a waitress who can shoot with the best of them and who has an affair with one of the boys (Valdelomar). When a man is killed during a robbery, spiralling disaster follows, leaving Angela the sole survivor of the gang. Saura's film, sharp and – like its title – fast, takes a non-moralistic look at the punks from Madrid's urban waste land who spend their ill-gotten gains on drugs and fast cars. The director recruited his actors from the milieu he portrays and, ironically, Valdelomar was arrested for a bank robbery shortly before the film's Spanish première, while Aranzeque was caught making a getaway from a raid a few months later. Saura was apparently upset by these developments, as well as by the sensationalist press coverage given to them.

Best Film Berlin 1981

▶ **Deputat Baltiki** see Baltic Deputy

▶ **Derman** see Remedy

▶ **Dernier Combat, Le** see Last Battle, The

▶ **Dernière Femme, La** see Last Woman, The

Les Dernières Vacances

▶ **(US: The Last Vacation)**

France 1948 95 mins bw
Productions Cinématique/Les Films Constellation

d **Roger Leenhardt**
sc **Roger Breuil, Roger Leenhardt**
ph **Philippe Agostini**
m **Guy Bernard**
Roger Leenhardt, Michel François, Renée

Devillers, Pierre Dux, Odile Versois, Jean D'Yd

Jacques (François) and Juliette (Versois) are 16-year-old cousins who have spent many summer holidays together with their families at the ancestral estate in Southern France. But when the family, fallen on hard times, must sell the property, the children plot to drive potential buyers away. Made up mainly of two long flashbacks – the daydreams of Jacques while in the classroom – the film is bathed in an impressionistic glow that represents a memory of summer holidays. Yet, it avoids sentimentality and clichés of nostalgia, the tone being reminiscent of Renoir's *A Day In The Country*. Leenhardt, whose only other feature was *Le Rendez-vous De Minuit* (1962), though he made various shorts of interest, was much admired by the *Nouvelle Vague* directors for his independent qualities and intelligence. Godard and Truffaut gave him roles in *A Married Woman* and *The Man Who Loved Women*, respectively.

▶ **Dernier Métro, Le** see Last Metro, The

▶ **Dernier Milliardaire, Le** see Last Millionaire, The

▶ **Dernier Tournant, Le** see Last Bend, The

Derzu Uzala

USSR-Japan   1975   140 mins   col
Mosfilm/Toho

d   Akira Kurosawa
sc Akira Kurosawa, Yuri Nagibin
ph Asakazu Nakai, Yuri Gantman, Fyodor Dobronravov
m   Isaak Shvartz
    Maxim Munzuk, Yuri Solomin, M. Bichkov, V. Khrulev, V. Lastochin

A Russian scientist (Solomin) is sent with a party of soldiers to make a topographical survey of the wilds of Siberia at the turn of the century. He relies greatly on his hunter-guide Derzu Uzala (Munzuk), whose knowledge of nature saves his life more than once.

Based on the journals of Vladimir Arseniev, the film contains a splendid performance from Munzuk as a wily, noble savage. There is also one memorable set-piece of the building of a shelter during a storm, rendered magnificently on the 70mm screen with its six-track stereo sound, but most of the lengthy film is of the undemanding Disney real-life adventure sort.

Best Foreign Film Oscar 1975

The Deserter And The Nomads

▶ **Zbehovia A Poutníci**

Czechoslovakia   1968   102 mins   col
Koliba Film Studio (Bratislava)/Ultra Film (Rome)

d   Juro Jakubisko
sc Juro Jakubisko, Karol Sidon
ph Juro Jakubisko
m   Štepan Koníček
    Štefan Ladižinský, August Kubán, Gejza Ferenc, Jana Stehnová, Helena Grodová

Death (Kubán) is personified in three stories set in World Wars I, II and III. In the first, a gypsy soldier (Ferenc), deserting the battlefield, meets Death at a wedding in his own village. In the second, a Russian army captain (Ladižinský) orders an itinerant egg seller to be shot for spying for the Germans. In the future, after a nuclear holocaust, a young girl (Stehnová) and an old man try to find other survivors. This three-part fresco reveals an original but undisciplined talent in Jakubisko. The first episode, taking its imagery from peasant art, becomes excessive in its colour distortions and camera movements; the second is more restrained stylistically, but more familiar thematically; the third lacks the shock element necessary, while making a tenuous attempt to link it to the first episode. Yet much of it is involving and the film is an example of the last experimental gasp of film-makers just before the Prague Spring ended.

▶ **Deserto Rosso, Il** see Red Desert, The

Destiny

▶ **(US: Between Two Worlds)**

▶ **aka Beyond The Wall**

▶ **Der Müde Tod**

Germany 1921 79 mins bw
Decla-Bioscop

d   Fritz Lang
sc Fritz Lang, Thea Von Harbou
ph Erich Nietzschmann, Fritz Arno Wagner,
    Hermann Salfrank
m   Silent
    Lil Dagover, Walter Janssen, Bernhard
    Goetzke, Eduard Von Winterstein,
    Rudolph Klein-Rogge, Karl Huszar

A honeymoon is destroyed when the husband
(Janssen) disappears with a sinister stranger
(Goetzke), who turns out to be Death. The
wife (Dagover) pleads with him for her husband's life and he strikes a series of bargains
with her, which she ultimately loses, but which
project her into several different situations of
love and death in Arabia, Venice and China.
The plotting of this film is far too intricate
to recount here, but it's an intricacy which
applies equally to its themes, switches of style,
details of character and incident, and extravagant settings. A dark and mystical allegory,
Destiny was Lang's first notable critical success, and remains impressive for its range of
mood and the mastery of its visual composition.

Destiny Of A Man

▶ **aka Fate Of A Man**

▶ **Sudba Cheloveka**

USSR 1959 98 mins bw
Sovexportfilm/Mosfilm

d   Sergei Bondarchuk
sc Y. Lukin, F. Shakhmagonov
ph Vladimir Monakhov
m   V. Basnov
    Sergei Bondarchuk, Zinaida Kirienkova,
    Pavlik Boriskin, V. Markin, P. Volkov

During World War II, Andrei Sokolov (Bondarchuk) leaves his young wife (Kirienkova)
and children for the front. He is captured and

sent to a concentration camp from which he
escapes. On returning home, Andrei learns of
the death of his family. 'In the beginning I
led a very ordinary life...' is how the hero of
the film, based on the novel by Mikhail
Sholokhov, begins his story. The distinguished Soviet actor Bondarchuk, in his
first film as director, takes on the task of
interpreting this life of an 'ordinary' Russian
man, who has to dig deep into his resources
for physical and mental survival. As both
director and actor Bondarchuk succeeds to a
great extent, even if at times he treads rather
heavily. The realism of the fighting, of the
camps and of the bitter aftermath of war is
powerfully captured, and the optimistic ending, though predictable, is still moving. The
film won the best film award at the first
Moscow Film Festival.

Détective

France 1985 95 mins col
Sara Films/JLG Films

d   Jean-Luc Godard
sc Alain Sarde, Philippe Setbon
ph Bruno Nuytten
m   Schubert, Wagner, Chopin, Liszt,
    Honegger, Chabrier, Ornette Coleman,
    Jean Schwarz
    Nathalie Baye, Claude Brasseur, Johnny
    Hallyday, Laurent Terzieff, Jean-Pierre
    Léaud, Alain Cuny, Stéphane Ferrara

Various people investigate various suspects in
a murder that was committed in a Paris hotel
two years previously. Dedicated to John Cas-
savetes, Clint Eastwood and Poverty Row
director Edgar G. Ulmer, Godard's film is a
wordy, witty, banal and stimulating set of
variations on a B-movie theme. The joky
murder mystery plot goes out the window as
Godard's camera prowls around the hotel,
more interested in the antics of his
accomplished cast.

▶ **Detenuto In Attesa Di Giudizio**
see Why?

▶ **Detstvo Gorkovo** see Childhood Of
Maxim Gorky, The

▶ **Deuda Interna, La** see Veronico Cruz

▶ **Deus E O Diabo Na Terra Do Sol** see Black God White Devil

▶ **Deutschland, Bleiche Mutter** see Germany, Pale Mother

▶ **Deutschland Im Herbst** see Germany In Autumn

▶ **Deux Anglaises Et Le Continent, Les** see Anne And Muriel

▶ **Deuxième Souffle, Le** see Second Breath

▶ **Deux Lions Au Soleil** see Two Lions In The Sun

▶ **Deux Ou Trois Choses Que Je Sais D'Elle** see Two Or Three Things I Know About Her

Les Deux Timides

France   1928   66 mins   bw
Albatros/Sequana

d   **René Clair**
sc   **René Clair**
ph   **Robert Batton, Nicolas Roudakoff**
m   **Silent**
     Maurice De Féraudy, Pierre Batcheff,
     Vera Flory, Jim Gérald, Françoise Rosay

A mouse running across a courtroom causes a shy young lawyer (Batcheff) to lose a case and almost to lose his fiancée (Flory) to a rival suitor (Gérald). His prospective father-in-law (De Féraudy) is the other timid character of the title. Clair's last silent film was, like *The Italian Straw Hat* immediately preceding it, based on a wordy Labiche-Michel farce. It is funny and gentle, and seems to have no need for dialogue (the sign of a good silent film?) as the images speak volumes. The acting, particularly of De Féraudy and Rosay, the latter as a dragon aunt, helps it along.

▶ **Deveti Krug** see Ninth Circle, The

Devi

▶ **aka The Goddess**

India   1960   93 mins   bw
Satyajit Ray Productions

d   **Satyajit Ray**
sc   **Satyajit Ray**
ph   **Subrata Mitra**
m   **Ali Akbar Khan**
     Chabi Biswas, Sharmila Tagore, Soumitra Chatterjee, Karuna Bannerjee

A young woman (Tagore) is persuaded by her fanatical father-in-law (Biswas) that she is the reincarnation of the goddess Kali. She becomes an object of mystical reverence much to the despair of her educated husband (Chatterjee). Ray emerged from his great 'Apu Trilogy' to make a less expansive work, its theme even more strongly illustrative of the clash between ancient and modern beliefs. The well-organized plot has a less universal appeal, and the more dramatic style leans on occasion towards melodrama. However, the visual images are striking and there are intriguing glimpses into religious fervour on the sub-continent.

The Devil

▶ **(US: To Bed... Or Not To Bed)**
▶ **Il Diavolo**

Italy   1963   103 mins   bw
Dino De Laurentiis

d   **Gian Luigi Polidoro**
sc   **Rodolfo Sonego**
ph   **Aldo Tonti**
m   **Piero Piccioni**
     Alberto Sordi, Inge Sjorstrand, Ulf Palme, Ulla Smidje, Barbo Wastenson

When Amadeo Ferretti (Sordi), a small-town Italian, takes a trip to Sweden without his wife, his imagination takes flight with fantasies of possible romantic encounters. However, reality turns out quite differently. The girls he meets view him as no more than a kindly soul and a good friend, while he himself withdraws from the voracious demands of more mature women. The thick-set, lovable and comically gifted Sordi is very engaging in this efficiently made, funny film which, though clearly to the taste of the jury at Berlin, is no more than an engaging piece of fluff.

Best Film Berlin 1963

▶ **Devil And The Flesh, The** see Susana

The Devil And The Nun

▶ **aka Mother Joan Of The Angels**

▶ **Matka Joanna Od Aniolów**

Poland   1960   108 mins   bw
Film Polski

d   **Jerzy Kawalerowicz**
sc **Jerzy Kawalerowicz, Tadeusz Konwicki**
ph **Jerzy Wójcik**
m   **Adam Walacinski**
    Lucyna Winnicka, Mieczyslaw Voit, Anna Ciepielewska, Maria Chwalibóg

In a 17th-century Polish convent a priest (Voit), investigating demonic possession among the nuns, becomes the object of desire of the Mother Superior (Winnicka). Based on actual events at Loudun, also the subject of an Aldous Huxley novel, a John Whiting play, a Ken Russell film and a Krzysztof Penderecki opera, it was one of the first post-war Polish films not dealing with the theme of war to be seen in the West. The stylized narrative, design and performances make for a powerful allegory of Good vs Evil, Chastity vs Eroticism.

Special Jury Prize Cannes 1961

The Devil By The Tail

▶ **Le Diable Par La Queue**

France   1969   93 mins   col
Fildebroc/Les Productions Artistes Associés/Produzioni Europée Associate Films

d   **Philippe De Broca**
sc **Philippe De Broca, Daniel Boulanger**
ph **Jean Penzer**
m   **Georges Delerue**
    Yves Montand, Maria Schell, Jean Rochefort, Jean- Pierre Marielle, Madeleine Renaud, Marthe Keller, Xavier Gélin

In order to entice guests to her château, now turned into a hotel to make ends meet, the Marquise (Renaud) gets a young mechanic (Gélin) to sabotage the cars of motorists who stop at his garage and to convey them to the hotel while the 'repairs' are being carried out. One such guest turns out to be a bank robber (Montand) on the run. Much of De Broca's efforts to make a light, escapist, crazy comedy are helped by a pretty setting, Delerue's cod classical music and old hands, Montand, Rochefort and Renaud, who blissfully sail through it all. The balloon is weighed down occasionally by some unfunny slapstick and overdrawn caricatures.

Devil In The Flesh

▶ **Le Diable Au Corps**

France   1947   110 mins   bw
Transcontinental

d   **Claude Autant-Lara**
sc **Jean Aurenche, Pierre Bost**
ph **Michel Kelber**
m   **René Cloërec**
    Micheline Presle, Gérard Philipe, Jean Debucourt, Denise Grey, Jacques Tati

During the last months of World War I, a young married woman (Presle) has an affair with a 17-year-old schoolboy (Philipe) while her husband is at the front. The film of Raymond Radiguet's precocious semi-autobiographical novel caused outrage in some quarters for its non-condemnatory and sympathetic portrayal of lovers cuckolding a soldier away at war. The controversial aspect now diminished, the film can be seen as a sensuous and romantic love story, framing two touching performances, notably from 25-year-old Philipe (the same age as Presle), who shot to international stardom on the strength of it.

The Devil, Probably

▶ **Le Diable, Probablement**

France   1977   95 mins   col
Sunchold/GMF

d   **Robert Bresson**
sc **Robert Bresson**
ph **Pasqualino De Santis**

m **Philippe Sarde**
   Antoine Monnier, Tina Irissari, Henri De
   Maublanc

A young man (Monnier), horrified by the physical and spiritual pollution in the world, rejects politics, religion and psychoanalysis and pays a junkie friend to shoot him in Père Lachaise cemetery. Bresson's most didactic film, probably. Different groups offering a panacea for the world's ills are rather simply taken off, while smoke fills the sky and large trees are felled. It is all very earnest and schematic, but the uncluttered images and autumnal photography give it a touch of grace.

Special Jury Prize Berlin 1977

▶ **Devil's Envoys, The** see Visiteurs Du Soir, Les

The Devil's Eye

▶ **Djävulens Öga**

   Sweden 1960 90 mins bw
   Svensk Filmindustri

d **Ingmar Bergman**
sc **Ingmar Bergman**
ph **Gunnar Fischer**
m **Scarlatti**
   Jarl Kulle, Bibi Andersson, Nils Poppe,
   Stig Järrel, Gunnar Björnstrand

Because, as the proverb says, 'a woman's chastity is a sty in the devil's eye', the devil (Järrel) sends Don Juan (Kulle) to earth to deflower Virtue (Andersson), the daughter of a naive country parson (Poppe). Although demonstrating Bergman's metaphysical preoccupations, this rather heavy-handed comedy that shifts uneasily between an extremely theatrical Hell and the realism of the pastor's household, has been justifiably dismissed as a minor aberration by the great director. Perhaps he deserved a divertissement between the starkness of *The Virgin Spring* and *Through A Glass Darkly*.

The Devil's General

▶ **Des Teufel's General**

   W. Germany 1955 124 mins bw

Real Film

d **Helmut Käutner**
sc **Georg Hurdalek, Helmut Käutner**
ph **Albert Benitz**
m **Archive music**
   Curt Jurgens, Victor De Kowa, Karl
   John, Marianne Koch, Werner Fuetterer

Caught between patriotism and loyalty to his comrades on the one hand, and revulsion against the Nazi regime on the other, General Harras (Jurgens) of the Luftwaffe deliberately crashes his new bomber rather than be a party to the continuance of the war. Ironically, he is honoured as a martyred hero of the Reich. Käutner's film is based on a play by Carl Zuckmayer which is, in turn, loosely based on the life of Ernst Udets, the highest-ranking German air ace to have survived World War I, who committed suicide on the eve of World War II because of his horror of Hitler's regime. Jurgens is excellent, and the movie, although overlong, is well made and engrossing.

Best Actor (Curt Jurgens) Venice 1955

The Devil Strikes At Night

▶ **aka Nazi Terror At Night**

▶ **aka Nights When The Devil Came**

▶ **Nachts Wenn Der Teufel Kamm**

   W. Germany 1957 105 mins bw
   Divina

d **Robert Siodmak**
sc **Werner Jörg Lüddecke**
ph **George Krause**
m **Siegfried Franz**
   Claus Holm, Mario Adorf, Hannes
   Messemer, Anne Marie Düringer, Werner
   Peters

In 1944 the German authorities are baffled by the murders of 80 women, all strangled. An outside investigator finds the killer, a Gestapo member, but the Gestapo covers up and pins the crime on an innocent minor official. Siodmak's third film in Germany after his long and successful sojourn in Hollywood is a model of tasteful restraint, as well as a demonstration of the director's expertise in handling suspense. The screenplay was based on the true case, found documented in Gestapo files, of the mentally deranged Bruno Luedtke, who was secretly liquidated. The film gives a chilling glimpse into the ruthlessness, solidarity and complete moral rot which characterized the Nazi edifice.

The Devil's Wanton

▶ **Fängelse**

Sweden   1949   80 mins   bw
Terrafilm

d   **Ingmar Bergman**
sc **Ingmar Bergman**
ph **Göran Strindberg**
m   **Erland Von Koch**
     Doris Svedlund, Birger Malmsten, Eva Henning, Hasse Ekman, Stig Olin, Irma Christenson, Anders Henriksson

A director (Ekman) discusses an idea with an alcoholic writer friend (Malmsten) who suggests that they film the true story of a prostitute (Svedlund) he once knew who eventually killed herself. The appalling details of her wretched life then take over the action. Another of those early Bergman's only released abroad when his fame had travelled, this film points the way to the director's later explorations of unhappiness, but, while long on *angst*, it is short on conviction. It is more amusing to read some reviews of yesteryear which find one critic stating that the film 'finds Bergman in bleak mood'. Little did he guess what was yet to come!

▶ **Devuchka S Korobkoi** see Girl With The Hatbox

▶ **Devyat Dnei Odnogo Goda** see Nine Days Of One Year

▶ **Diable Au Corps, Le** see Devil In The Flesh

▶ **Diable Par La Queue, Le** see Devil By The Tail, The

▶ **Diable, Probablement, Le** see Devil, Probably, The

▶ **Diabolique** see Diaboliques, Les

Les Diaboliques

▶ **(US: Diabolique)**

▶ **aka The Fiends**

France   1954   114 mins   bw
Filmsonor/Vera Films

d   **Henri-Georges Clouzot**
sc **Henri-Georges Clouzot, Jérôme Géronimi, Frédéric Grendel, René Masson**
ph **Armand Thirard**
m   **Georges Van Parys**
     Simone Signoret, Vera Clouzot, Paul Meurisse, Charles Vanel

Nicole and Christina (Signoret, and the director's wife, Vera Clouzot) join forces to murder Christina's sadistic husband (Meurisse). They dump his corpse in the swimming pool of the seedy and unpleasant school where he is the headmaster but, by the next day, it has disappeared. He keeps turning up in the most unlikely places. Is he dead or alive? The answers are revealed only in the last terrifying moments of this masterpiece of suspense from the director of *The Wages of Fear*. Original, and very well made, this much-acclaimed film is a must for all fans of the genre.

▶ **Diabolo Menthe** see Peppermint Soda

▶ **Diagonale Du Fou, La** see Dangerous Moves

▶ **Dialogue Des Carmelites, Le** see Carmelites, The

Diary For My Children

▶ **Napló Gyermekeimnek**

Hungary   1982   107 mins   bw
Mafilm Studio/Hungarofilm

d   **Márta Mészáros**
sc **Márta Mészáros, Balázs Fakan, András Szeredás**
ph **Miklós Jancsó Jr**
m   **Zsolt Döme**
     Zsuzsa Czinkóczi, Anna Polony, Jan Nowicki, Tamás Tóth, Mari Szémes, Pál Zolnay

In 1947 orphaned Juli (Czinkóczi) returns

with her grandparents to Budapest from the USSR where members of the Hungarian underground had fled. The family find the country greatly changed, the old-style Communism replaced by a rigid bureaucratic regime in which Juli's aunt Magda (Polony), in whose luxury flat they stay, is a high flyer. Disliking both Magda and her politics, Juli begins her quest for freedom and independence. Mészáros brings her fine intelligence and a penetrating eye for detail to an analytical critique of recent Hungarian history. Utilizing the past – Juli's memories lyrically filmed – she brings her heroine to terms with the present in an engrossing story that embraces the individual, the family and the state, making the political personal and vice versa. The Hungarian authorities withheld this film from the West for two years after its completion.

Special Jury Prize Cannes 1984

Diary For My Loves

▶ **Napló Szerelmeimnet**

    Hungary   1987   130 mins   col/part bw
    Mafilm Budapest Studio for
    Hungarofilm

d   **Marta Mészáros**
sc **Marta Mészáros, Eva Pataki**
ph **Nyika Jancso**
m   **Zsolt Dome**
    Zsuzsa Czinkoczi, Anna Polony, Jan Nowicki, Irina Kouberskaya, Adel Kovats

It is 1951 and 18-year-old Juli (Czinkoczi) wants to become a film-maker. Unable to get a place at the Budapest film school, she is forced by her despised aunt-cum-foster mother, Magda (Polony), who is a colonel in the State Security Corps, to study economics in Moscow. Once there, she swaps places with a fellow student and attends the State Institute of Cinematography. Dividing her time between Budapest and Moscow, she also pursues her other burning goals: to trace her father who disappeared during Stalin's show trials and to keep contact with and work for the release of Janos, a former colleague of Magda's, now imprisoned on phoney charges. By 1956 Juli has met all her objectives with the help of new friends and teachers, but finds herself marooned in Moscow as a result of the Hungarian uprising. The second film in

Mészáros' trilogy, between *Diary For My Children* (1982) and *Diary For My Father And My Mother* (1990), continues Juli's story, using the same principal actors. The virtues of its predecessor – an uncompromising exposé of East European politics, a fine and intelligent eye for detail, and a sense of the power of images – informs its sequel, although this time around the director offers a more complex view of her protagonist's attitudes and fate. It is finally a bleak tale in which circumstances, albeit more hopeful for some, seem to prevail over the will of the individual more oppressively than in the previous 'Diary'. If some of Mészáros' references are elusive, this partly autobiographical portrait of a young woman fighting a world that defeats her is, nonetheless, absorbing.

Diary Of A Chambermaid

▶ **Journal D'Une Femme De Chambre**

    France   1964   98 mins   bw
    Speva/Ciné Alliance/Filmsonor/Dear

d   **Luis Buñuel**
sc **Luis Buñuel, Jean-Claude Carrière**
ph **Roger Fellous**
    Jeanne Moreau, Georges Géret, Michel Piccoli, Françoise Lugagne, Daniel Ivernel, Jean-Claude Carrière

Célestine (Moreau) takes up a post as chambermaid to a middle-class, provincial family, and becomes the catalyst that reveals their sexual, religious and social repressions. Both she and the sadistic valet Joseph (Géret) achieve their *petit bourgeois* ambitions. More acid and less lightweight than Renoir's 1945 Hollywood version of Mirbeau's novel, the film, foot fetishism and all, is pure Buñuel. By updating the story and making Joseph a member of the French Fascist party, Buñuel brings the social satire into sharper focus. Moreau – sexy, cruel and cool – is wonderful.

Diary Of A Country Priest

▶ **Journal D'Un Curé De Campagne**

    France   1950   120 mins   bw
    UGC

d   **Robert Bresson**

sc **Robert Bresson**
ph **L.H. Burel**
m   **Jean-Jacques Grünewald**
    Claude Laydu, Jean Riveyre, Armand
    Guibert, Nicole Ladmiral, Nicole Maurey

A young priest (Laydu) unable to resolve the problems of his small parish and assailed by self-doubt, dies alone of stomach cancer murmuring 'All is Grace'. The first truly Bressonian film in which he used non-actors, natural sound, pared down images and real locations to tell a spiritual tale. Bernanos' book published in 1936 seemed a most unlikely subject for the cinema, but Bresson managed to convey the solitude and inner anguish of the characters by their external behaviour and by shots of them in isolation while using the literary device of the first person narrative.

Diary Of A Lost Girl

► **Tagebuch Einer Verloren**

   Germany   1929   110 mins   bw
   G.W. Pabst

d   **G.W. Pabst**
sc **Rudolf Leonhardt**
ph **Sepp Allgeier**
m   **Silent**
    Louise Brooks, Fritz Rasp, Josef
    Rovensky, Edith Meinhard, Vera
    Pawlowa

A girl (Brooks) from a wealthy family is seduced by her pharmicist father's assistant (Rasp), becomes pregnant, is placed in a reform school, and ends up in a brothel. Adapted from a cheap contemporary novel, Pabst's film is a vivid exploration of a corrupt society in which sex and money dominate social relationships, despite the heavy cutting by the censors. (Apparently the film ends about half-way through the original script.) The eloquent faces in close-up have no need for dialogue, nor do sequences such as that when the headmistress of the reform school makes the girls march like puppets to the rhythm of her cane. However, what lingers in the mind is the exquisite bob-haired Louise Brooks exerting her *femme fatale* fascination, continuing the impact she made in Pabst's *Pandora's Box* of the same year.

► **Diary Of A Shinjuku Burglar** see
   Diary Of A Shinjuku Thief

Diary Of A Shinjuku Thief

► **(US: Diary Of A Shinjuku**
   Burglar)

► **Shinjuko Dorobo Nikki**

   Japan   1968   94 mins   col/bw
   Sozosha

d   **Nagisa Oshima**
sc **Nagisa Oshima, Tsutomu Tamura,**
    Mamoru Sasaki, Masao Adachi
ph **Yasuhiro Yoshioka, Seizo Sengen**
    Tadanori Yokoo, Rie Yokoyama, Moichi
    Tanabe, Tetsu Takahashi, Kei Sato

A young student (Yokoo) is caught shoplifting in a bookshop by a girl (Yokoyama), masquerading as an assistant, with whom he goes on to have a sexually unfulfilled affair. After seeking sexual advice, they finally find ecstasy while a street riot is breaking out. Using black and white with colour inserts and mixing realistic and theatrical acting, *cinéma vérité* techniques and Brechtian intertitles, Oshima has made an explosive agit-prop movie equating sexual liberation with revolution. Coming hot on the heels of the student riots of 1968, its impact has cooled only marginally.

► **Diavolo, Il** see Devil, The

► **Dieu A Besoin Des Hommes** see
   Isle Of Sinners

► **Diexue Shuang Xiong** see Killer,
   The

► **Dillinger E Morto** see Dillinger Is
   Dead

Dillinger Is Dead

► **Dillinger E Morto**

   Italy   1969   90 mins   col
   Pegaso Film

d   **Marco Ferreri**
sc **Marco Ferreri, Sergio Bazzini**
ph **Mario Vulpiani**
m   **Teo Usuelli**
    Michel Piccoli, Anita Pallenberg, Annie
    Girardot

While his wife (Pallenberg) is in bed with a headache, an industrial designer (Piccoli) spends an evening at home, making himself a meal, watching TV and seducing the maid (Girardot). He finds a package containing an old 45-calibre revolver and decides to kill his wife and go off to Tahiti. This bleak study of alienation allows a man's life to be laid bare in one evening and one setting, using a cast of only three. The objects in the protagonist's house take on a significance (he manufactures masks) by means of the careful camerawork, compositions and colour and the film reveals Ferreri at his most controlled.

► **Dimanche À La Campagne, Un** see Sunday In The Country

► **Dimanche De La Vie, Le** see Sunday Of Life, The

► **Dimenticare Venezia** see Forget Venice

Directed By Andrei Tarkovsky

► **Regi – Andrej Tarkovskij**

Sweden   1988   101 mins   col
Swedish Film Institute

d   **Michal Leszczlowski**
sc **Michal Leszczlowski**
ph **Arne Carlsson**
m   **None credited**
    Erland Josephson (narration), Larisa Tarkovsky

A documentary about the making of Andrei Tarkovsky's last film, *The Sacrifice* (1985), in Sweden, including footage of the director at work, excerpts from the finished film, interviews with the actors and members of the crew, and voice-over readings from the Russian director's book, *Sculpting In Time*. The enterprise derived from 50 hours of video tape shot on sets and locations by Carlsson, the assistant cameraman on *The Sacrifice*, and then cut into shape by Leszczlowski, the film's co-editor. Originally Tarkovsky had planned to collaborate on the project, but the illness that took his life in December 1986, at the age of 54, had already left him too weak to talk about his work, so the interviews with

him were those previously seen on television. The film as a whole takes its subject's 'genius' at face value, so audiences requiring a more objective critical study might be disappointed by the hagiographic tone, and those who are less than fans might remain unconvinced. But anyone interested in the process of film-making would find fascination in Tarkovsky's direction of the actors and his punctilious preparation of camera set-ups. Particularly interesting is the revelation that the shooting of the now famous 10-minute take of the burning house was first done with a jammed camera, and the house had to be reconstructed only to be destroyed again.

► **Dirty Hands** see Mains Sales, Les

Dirty Mary

► **(US: A Very Curious Girl)**
► **La Fiancée Du Pirate**

France   1969   106 mins   col
Cythère

d   **Nelly Kaplan**
sc **Nelly Kaplan, Claude Makovski**
ph **Jean Badal**
m   **Georges Moustaki**
    Bernadette Lafont, Georges Géret, Michel Constantin, Julien Guiomar, Jean Paredes, Claire Maurier

Marie (Lafont) lives with her mother in a small shack on the outskirts of a village. When her mother is killed in a hit-and-run accident and disputes arise over burial expenses, she decides to organize the funeral herself. She then takes revenge on the leading citizens of the village, who have treated her with scorn. Extrovert Lafont was perfect in this extrovert social satire, first as a sloppy despised servant girl, then as a seductive woman. Kaplan's film has verve, some good gags, and lively music, but it leans too far towards stereotypes, including that of a Lesbian.

Dirty Money

► **Un Flic**

France   1972   98 mins   col
Corona (Paris)/Oceania/Euro (Rome)

d   Jean-Pierre Melville
sc Jean-Pierre Melville
ph Walter Wottitz
m   Michel Colombier
    Alain Delon, Richard Crenna, Catherine
    Deneuve, Ricardo Cucciolla, André
    Pousse

An overworked Paris police commissioner,
intent on smashing a drug-smuggling operation, gets a fortuitous lead through a bank
robbery in a distant seaside town. He also
has an affair with a girl (Deneuve) who turns
out to be the gang leader's mistress. The last
feature from Melville, chief purveyor of the
gangster genre in France, is a study of disen-
chantment and betrayal, juxtaposing time and
locations in an almost experimental form to
create a disjunctive mood. The set-piece in
which a load of heroin is lifted off a moving
train by helicopter is terrific, and Delon's
embittered cop is effective.

The Discreet Charm Of The Bourgeoisie

▶ **Le Charme Discret De La Bourgeoisie**

France 1972 105 mins col
Greenwich

d   Luis Buñuel
sc Luis Buñuel, Jean-Claude Carrière
ph Edmond Richard
m   Galaxie Musique
    Fernando Rey, Delphine Seyrig, Stéphane
    Audran, Bulle Ogier, Jean-Pierre Cassel,
    Paul Frankeur, Michel Piccoli, Julien
    Bertheau

A small group of friends, members of the
wealthy middle class, gather at a house for
dinner only to find their host absent. Further
attempts to take a meal together are continually frustrated by a series of bizarre events,
mostly dreamed by the participants. This best
and most assured of the four anecdotal surrealist satires of Buñuel's final years is a
blistering but witty assault on the director's
constant targets – the church, the state and
the army. The masterful shifting of different
levels of consciousness, the depiction of collective phobias and the ensemble playing of
the impeccable cast are sophisticated joys.

Best Foreign Film Oscar 1972

Les Disparus De St-Agil

▶ **(US: Boys' School)**

France 1938 103 mins bw
Francinex/Vog
m   Christian-Jaque
sc J.H. Blanchon
ph Marcel Lucien
m   Henri Verdun
    Michel Simon, Erich Von Stroheim, Aimé
    Clariond, Armand Bernard, Mouloudji

At St Agil, a boys' boarding school, pupils
mysteriously disappear. A group of boys
decides to take action and discovers a forger
and murderer on the premises. Christian-
Jaque made his name with this atmospheric
and enjoyable black comedy. In the school
building, with its sliding doors and secret
underground rooms, lurk Simon as a drunken
art master and Stroheim as an eccentric language teacher, both having a fair old time.

Distant Thunder

▶ **Ashanti Sanket**

India 1973 101 mins col
Palaka Movies

d   Satyajit Ray
sc Satyajit Ray
ph Soumendu Roy
m   Satyajit Ray
    Soumitra Chatterjee, Babita, Sandhya Roy

In a small Bengali village in 1943, the school-
teacher-priest-doctor and his wife begin to see
the causes – and the horrifying effects – of
famine on their community. Often criticized
for ignoring the bitter realities of his country,
Ray here takes a more political line while
retaining his gentle wit and humanism. The
village movingly becomes a microcosm for
the wider sufferings of India, giving more
weight to the statistic (seen at the end) that
over five million people died at the time.

Best Film Berlin 1973

▶ **Dites-Lui Que Je L'Aime** see This
Sweet Sickness

Diva

France 1981 117 mins col

Les Films Galaxie/Greenwich Film Production

d   Jean-Jacques Beineix
sc Jean-Jacques Beineix, Jean Van Hamme
ph Philippe Rousselot
m   Vladimir Cosma, and arias by Catalani and Gounod
    Frédéric Andrei, Roland Bertin, Wilhelminia Wiggins Fernandez, Thuy An Luu, Dominique Piñon, Anny Romand, Richard Böhringer

A young postal messenger (Andrei) illicitly records a recital by his opera idol (Fernandez), but the possession of the cassette unwittingly leads him into a complicated quagmire of corruption and murder. Beineix's debut feature begins promisingly enough with an intriguing idea and some startlingly adventurous camerawork. Alas, it soon becomes an overlong confusion of both style and content, mixing fact and fantasy, violence and romance – with a nod to Feuillade in its hallucinatory quality – to degenerate into a flashy package of ultra-chic designer images and punk aesthetics of little meaning and less coherence. Nonetheless, there is evidence of a stylish talent looking for a home, and the movie is not without a modicum of entertainment value.

Divine

France   1935   80 mins   bw
Eden

d   Max Ophüls
sc Colette, Jean-Georges Auriol, Max Ophüls
ph Roger Hubert
m   Albert Wolff
    Simone Berriau, Georges Rigaud, Gina Manès, Philippe Heriat, Catherine Fonteney

A country girl (Berriau) goes to Paris where she becomes a chorus girl, gets involved with a dope-peddling snake charmer (Heriat) and his girlfriend (Manès), falls in love with a handsome milkman (Rigaud) and returns to the country with him. 'My biggest flop,' was Ophüls comment, and most critics, except François Truffaut who called it 'a little masterpiece', agree with him. Its weakness lies in the miscasting of the female lead

and the sentimental view of the superiority of the country over the wicked city. Actually, the director is defeated by his own expertise in re-creating the delightful and exciting atmosphere of the music-hall – including a 360-degree pan when 'Divine' first arrives at the theatre – so that the alternative espoused by the film can only seem dull.

The Divine Emma

▶ Božská Ema

Czechoslovakia   1979   111 mins   col
Filove Studiu Barrandov

d   Jiří Krejčík
sc Zdeněk Mahler, Jiří Krejčík
ph Miroslav Ondříček
m   Zdeněk Liška, Svatopluk Havelka, and operatic extracts from Bizet, Mozart, Verdi, Wagner, Puccini, Ponchielli, Richard Strauss, Dvořák, Smetana and Leoncavallo
    Božidara Turzonovová (singing dubbed by Gabriela Beňačková), Juraj Kukura, Miloš Kopecký, Jiří Adamíra, Cestmír Randa

The world-famous soprano Emma Destinn (well-played by Turzonovová) returns to her native Czechoslovakia when World War I breaks out. Suspected (correctly) of being a Czech sympathizer and (incorrectly) a spy, she is confined to her estate and forbidden to sing. The simple-minded mix of fact and fiction will be immediately recognizable to all followers of the Hollywood biopic, who will also relish the appearances of other 'real-life' characters such as Caruso and Toscanini. Opera-lovers will revel in the generous supply of arias, beautifully sung by the soprano generally regarded as the nearest thing to the great Diva herself, although Emma's propensity to burst into song on any and every occasion (Hollywood again) grows a little tiresome. Ondříček's camera does justice to the period settings.

Divorce Italian Style

▶ Divorzio All'Italiana

Italy   1961   108 mins   bw

Lux/Vides/Galatea

d   **Pietro Germi**
sc **Pietro Germi, Ennio De Concini, Alfredo
    Giannetti**
ph **Leonida Barboni**
m   **Carlo Rustichelli**
    **Marcello Mastroianni, Daniela Rocca,
    Stefania Sandrelli, Leopoldo Trieste**

An indolent Sicilian nobleman (Mastroianni)
can only marry his pretty cousin (Sandrelli)
by arranging for his stupid wife (Rocca) to
be seduced, so that he can kill her with
impunity as a jealous husband defending his
honour. The first, and best, of a number of
'Italian style' sex comedies of the 1960s
delightfully satirizes the Italian male and
the country's laws on divorce and *crime
passionnel* in its Oscar-winning script. Mastroianni, with sleeked-down hair and waxed
moustache, is just the right side of caricature,
and there are a number of hilarious visual
jokes.

▶ **Divorzio All'Italiana** see Divorce Italian Style

▶ **Djävulens Öga** see Devil's Eye, The

Docteur Petiot

France   1990   102 mins   col
MS Productions/Sara Films/Canal/Sofica

d   **Christian De Chalonge**
sc **Dominique Garnier, Christian De
    Chalonge**
ph **Patrick Blossier**
m   **Michel Portal**
    **Michel Serrault, Pierre Romans,
    Zbigniew Horoks, Berangère Bonvoisin**

During the Nazi occupation of Paris, Marcel
Petiot (Serrault), a somewhat eccentric and
volatile doctor and a brilliant diagnostician,
runs a busy medical practice, aided by his
devoted wife (Bonvoisin) – by day, that is.
By night he repairs to a second house he
owns to welcome Jews whose escape he has
arranged and who are carrying large sums of
money secreted according to his instructions.
Once there, they are murdered and incinerated
by the good doctor, until a fire a few years

later draws attention to his deeds. A master
of disguise, Petiot escapes – for a time. This
bizarre tale is an expressionistic retelling of
France's most notorious murderer and is fascinating. De Chalonge presents Paris in an
unfamiliar and threatening light, all looming
buildings and dank underground passages,
unfolding his tale with an eye for grotesque
detail. Finally unsatisfactory because there is
no character development and no background
given to Petiot, it nonetheless holds the interest, not least thanks to an extraordinary performance from the wonderful Michel Serrault,
who delivers a spellbinding *tour de force* of
manic complexity.

Doctor In The Village

▶ **Dorp Aan De Rivier**

Netherlands   1958   92 mins   bw
N.V. Nationale Filmproductie
Maatschappij

d   **Fons Rademakers**
sc **Hugo Claus**
ph **Eduard Van Der Enden**
m   **Jurriaan Andriessen**
    **Max Croiset, Mary Dresselhuys,
    Bernhard Droog, Jan Teulings, Hetty
    Beck, Fritz Butselaar**

The eccentric Doctor Van Taeke (Croiset)
settles in a little village on the banks of the
River Meuse early in the century. He dedicates himself to caring for the poor in the
community and to puncturing the pomposity
of the local authorities, of whom he eventually
falls foul, and has to leave. This was the
debut feature of Holland's best-known director, and one can only feel grateful that his
later films had more appeal. The doctor's
story is told in flashback as the reminiscences
of the local poacher, known as Deaf Cis
(Droog) – a device which, on this occasion,
deflates the narrative energy. Rademakers
appears to emulate Pagnol in his anecdotal
treatment of village life, but the characterization is superficial, sometimes to the point of
parody, and most of the major incidents are
either bizarre or cloying. The lead performance is the saving grace and the director,
who started his career in the theatre, does
exhibit a certain technical command of the
medium.

Doctor Mabuse, The Gambler

▶ **Doktor Mabuse, Der Spieler**

Germany   1922   265 mins (Part I 153
mins; Part II 112 mins)   bw
UFA

d   Fritz Lang
sc Fritz Lang, Thea Von Harbou
ph Carl Hoffman
m   Silent
    Rudolph Klein-Rogge, Alfred Abel,
    Gertrud Welcker, Lil Dagover, Paul
    Richter, Bernhard Goetzke

Master criminal Dr Mabuse (Klein-Rogge), a
man of many disguises, builds an underworld
empire with the intention of taking over the
world, but is finally foiled by the forces of
good. Made at a time of political turmoil in
Germany, Lang's early masterpiece is a
superb study of a decadent society, foreshadowing the coming of Hitler. Unfortunately, it is still mainly known in its pared
down 101-minute version, which lost its essential serial-type form. The evil genius Mabuse,
of course, did not die. Lang brough him back
in two sequels, *The Testament Of Dr Mabuse*
(1933), and *The Thousand Eyes Of Dr Mabuse*
(1961).

Dodes'kaden

Japan   1970   140 mins   col
Yonki No Kai/Toho

d   Akira Kurosawa
sc Akira Kurosawa, Hideo Oguni, Shinobu
    Hashimoto
ph Takao Saito
m   Tohru Takemitsu
    Yoshitaka Zushi, Kin Sugai, Junzaburo
    Ban, Kiyoko Tange, Michiko Hino

Life in a shanty town in which people live
with their fantasies – an old man and a boy
build an imaginary dream house, a silent man
is obsessed by the idea of his wife's infidelity
and a mentally retarded adolescent thinks he
is a tram, repeating the sound 'dodes'kaden,
dodes'kaden'. Kurosawa's first film in colour
is a sporadically interesting but uninvolving

and rather indigestible mixture of realism,
social comment, melodrama and fantasy. The
director himself painted the poster-style walls
which make an impression as oddball as the
characters.

▶ **Does, The** see Biches, Les

The Dogs

▶ **Les Chiens**

France   1978   99 mins   col
AJ Films/AMS Prod/Les Films De La
Drouette/Pacific Films

d   Alain Jessua
sc Alain Jessua, André Ruellan
ph Etienne Becker
m   René Koering
    Gérard Depardieu, Victor Lanoux, Nicole
    Calfan, Pierre Vernier, Gérard Sety

A young doctor (Lanoux) sets up practice in
a new city isolated by mountains. He learns
that the inhabitants defend themselves with
guard dogs, trained and sold by Morel
(Depardieu), in an attempt to maintain order
and peace. When the mayor is murdered it
becomes evident that there is complicity
between the townsfolk, so the doctor and his
girlfriend (Calfan) try to escape. Set in a
hideously impersonal new French town, the
film sets out to create a microcosm of an
extreme right-wing state where racism is rampant and civil rights negligible. But the whole
thing is played in such a heavily melodramatic
manner and directed with such ambiguity –
the tone shifts between irony, lyricism and
didacticism – that the film itself becomes as
unpleasant as the events it depicts.

▶ **Dog's Life, A** see Mondo Cane

▶ **Doktor Holl** see Affairs Of Dr Holl,
The

▶ **Doktor Mabuse, Der Spieler** see
Doctor Mabuse, The Gambler

▶ **Dolce Corpo Di Deborah, Il** see
Sweet Body Of Deborah, The

La Dolce Vita

▶ **aka The Sweet Life**

Italy   1960   174 mins   bw
Riama/Pathé

d   **Federico Fellini**
sc   **Federico Fellini, Ennio Flaiano, Tullio Pinelli, Brunello Rondi**
ph   **Otello Martelli**
m   **Nino Rota**
     Marcello Mastroianni, Anouk Aimée, Yvonne Furneaux, Magali Noël, Alain Cuny, Anita Ekberg, Nadia Gray, Valeria Ciangottini, Annibale Ninchi, Lex Barker

Gossip columnist and would-be serious writer Marcello (Mastroianni), is caught in the morass of decadent Roman society in which he rootlessly and amorally wanders in search of himself. Perhaps Fellini's most famous film, *La Dolce Vita* was given a re-release in a new print in 1987, thus allowing re-appraisal. Its notorious set-pieces (a vast statue of Christ is flown over Rome; Marcello and a bored heiress pick up a prostitute for a *ménage-à-trois*; Nadia Gray hosts an orgy at which she performs an immortal striptease) have lost their capacity to shock, but the imaginative brilliance and periodic wit of their construction is now clearly evident. The director places his study of crippling *ennui*, loss of self and the pursuit of false values in an artificially contrived world of shoddy pleasures. It is photographed with striking attention to heightened images and atmosphere on the large screen, which brings excitement and lends cohesion to the episodic nature of the work.

Best Film Cannes 1960

▶ **Dolci Signore, Le** see Anyone Can Play

The Doll

▶ **Lalka**

Poland   1968   159 mins   col
Kamera Film Unit

d   **Wojciech Has**
sc   **Wojciech Has, Kazimierz Brandys**

ph   **Stefan Matyaskiewicz**
m   **Wojciech Kilar**
     Beata Tyszkiewicz, Marius Dmochowski, Jan Kreczmar, Tadeusz Kondrat, Tadeusz Fijewski, Janina Romanówna

Stanislaw Wokulski (Dmochowski), a middle-aged man who failed to realize his youthful dreams of becoming an inventor, is now a wealthy merchant, a liberal and a philanthropist. He falls in love with Isabela (Tyszkiewicz), the remote and beautiful daughter of a Count, but is looked down upon because of his humble origins. She, however, marries him to save her father from financial ruin and brings him only pain. A film which combines a straightforward tale of unrequited love with a sharply satirical observation of Polish society during the turbulence of the mid-19th century, exposing snobbery and greed and charting all manner of frustrations. It is a visually rich evocation, but it wanders off into curious enigmatical distractions which remain puzzling, making it sometimes difficult to follow but worth the trouble.

The Doll With Millions

▶ **Kukla S Millionami**

USSR   1928   83 mins   bw
Mezhrabpom

d   **Sergei Komarov**
sc   **Fedor Ozep, Oleg Leonidov**
ph   **Konstantin Kuznetsov, Evgeni Alexeyev**
m   **Silent**
     Vladimir Fogel, Igor Ilinsky, G. Grauvhenko, A. Voytsik, Sergei Komarov

A rich widow dies leaving the key to her fortune hidden inside a doll. But which doll? Two of her greedy relatives, a penniless dandy (Fogel) and his maladroit brother (Ilinsky), both living in Paris, hurry back to Moscow in rival pursuit of the doll with millions. This chaotic comedy combines elements of the slapstick of Mack Sennett, the witty sophistication of Komarov's earlier *The Kiss Of Mary Pickford*, and an episodic narrative resembling the much-filmed Russian novel *The Twelve Chairs* by Il'f and Petrov. Most of the fun is derived from the brilliant comic playing of Fogel and Ilinsky.

▶ **Domani Accadra** see It's Happening Tomorrow

▶ **Domenica D'Agosto** see Sunday In August

▶ **Domicile Conjugal** see Bed And Board

▶ **Dom Na Trubnoi** see House On Trubnaya Square, The

▶ **Dom Za Vesanje** see Time Of The Gypsies

Dona Flor And Her Two Husbands

▶ **Dona Flor E Seus Dois Maridos**

Brazil   1976   110 mins   col
Carnaval Films

d   **Bruno Barreto**
sc   **Bruno Barreto**
ph   **Maurilo Salles**
m   **Chico Buarque De Holanda**
Sonia Braga (Dona Flor), Jose Wilker, Mauro Mendonca, Dinorah Brillanti, Nelson Xavier

Shortly after the profligate and sexually accomplished Vadinho drops dead at a carnival, his widow remarries a respectable but sexually dull man. On the anniversary of her first husband's death, he reappears to her in tangible form and shares her bed. This Brazilian cousin to Noel Coward's *Blithe Spirit* provides some fun, and Braga is both attractive and sexy. However, it's a one-joke movie which veers unmistakably in the direction of soft porn rather than romantic charm.

▶ **Dona Flor E Seus Dois Maridos** see Dona Flor And Her Two Husbands

Dona Herlinda And Her Son

▶ **Dona Herlinda Y Su Hijo**

Mexico   1986   90 mins   col

Clasa Films Mundiales

d   **Jaime Humberto Hermosillo**
sc   **Jaime Humberto Hermosillo**
ph   **Miguel Erhenberg**
m   **Popular Mexican songs**
Arturo Meza, Marco Antonio Trevino, Leticia Lupersio, Guadalupe Del Toro, Angelica Guerrero

A young music student (Meza) and a doctor (Trevino) have a homosexual relationship, but the latter's mother (Del Toro) wants him to marry. Everyone is satisfied when he marries and his mother, wife (Lupersio), child and boyfriend live together under one roof. Hermosillo, an openly gay Latin-American film-maker, has used his insider's knowledge to make a deliciously alert social comedy about a macho-dominated culture and sexual hypocrisy. The film's sustained joke is that everyone pretends not to know about the heroes' gayness. It was the first of the director's low-budget films to gain a wide and appreciative audience.

▶ **Dona Herlinda Y Su Hijo** see Dona Herlinda And Her Son

Donatella

Italy   1956   101 mins   col
Sudfilm

d   **Mario Monicelli**
sc   **Roberto Amoroso, Mario Monicelli, Piero Tellini, Sandro Continenza, Ruggero Maccari**
ph   **Tonino Delli Colli**
m   **Xavier Cugat**
Elsa Martinelli, Gabriele Ferzetti, Walter Chiari, Aldo Fabrizi, Xavier Cugat, Abbe Lane

Donatella (Martinelli), humble secretary to a wealthy household, is mistaken for the heiress to the family fortune by a visiting lawyer who, accordingly, pays court to her. Reminiscent of those Hollywood romantic comedies based on the mistaken identity idea that were popular a decade or two earlier, this is a disappointing flim-flam and its dated air and American flavour is emphasized by the appearance of Latin American music king Cugat, and his vocalist wife Lane. However, the luscious Martinelli, (discovered by Kirk Douglas), returning to Italy from Hollywood made an impression.

Best Actress (Elsa Martinelli) Berlin 1956

▶ **Dongdong De Jiaqui** see Summer At Grandpa's, A

Don Giovanni

France-Italy-Germany   1979
184 mins   col
Opera Film Produzione (Rome)/
Gaumont/Caméra One/Antenne-2
(Paris)/Janus Films (Frankfurt)

d   **Joseph Losey**
sc **Joseph Losey, Patricia Losey, Frantz
    Salieri (libretto by Lorenzo Da Ponte)**
ph **Gerry Fisher**
m   **Mozart (conducted by Lorin Maazel)
    Ruggero Raimondi (Giovanni), Kiri Te
    Kanawa (Elvira), Edda Moser (Anna),
    Jose Van Dam (Leporello), Kenneth
    Riegel (Ottavio), Teresa Berganza
    (Zerlina), John Macurdy (the
    Commendatore), Malcolm King (Masetto)**

Don Giovanni, the object of vengeance by Donna Anna whose father he killed, the object of the affection of Donna Elvira whom he has abandoned, and the seducer of peasant girl Zerlina on her wedding day, is finally dragged down to Hell. Although superbly sung by singers who, for the most part, look right in the roles, and shot in and around handsome Palladian villas in northern Italy, Losey's attempts to make the conventions of opera 'filmic' have an air of desperation about them. For example, the two static arias of Ottavio have him standing up in a boat being rowed along and walking over sleeping peasants. During the 'Catalogue' aria, a vulgar parade of nubile young women is displayed. Other perversions the introduction of a young man in black (Isabelle Adjani's brother), and the fact that Giovanni seems to fall into a glass-blower's vat rather than journey to the depths of Hell.

Don Juan 73 Or If Don Juan Were A Woman

▶ **Don Juan 73 Ou Si Don Juan
  Était Une Femme**

France   1973   94 mins   col
Filmsonor/Marceau/Paradox/
Filmes(Rome)

d   **Roger Vadim**
sc **Roger Vadim, Jean Cau, Jean Pierre
    Petrolacci**
ph **Henri Decaë, Andréas Winding**
m   **Michel Magne
    Brigitte Bardot, Jane Birkin, Maurice
    Ronet, Mathieu Carrière, Robert Hossein,
    Robert Walker Jr**

Jeanne (Bardot) confesses to her cousin, a young priest (Carrière), that she has committed a murder and tells him of the men she has driven to destruction. Eleven years after their last film together, B.B. and the director who made and married her (they were divorced amicably in 1957), concocted this modernized, distaff version of the Don Juan legend. It was as arty as it was salacious, and also proved that the 39-year-old former sex kitten no longer had the power to create a stir. The film caused her to decide to retire from the screen after 21 years. Vadim continued unabashed.

▶ **Don Juan 73 Ou Si Don Juan
  Était Une Femme** see Don Juan 73
  Or If Don Juan Were A Woman

▶ **Donkey Skin** see Magic Donkey, The

▶ **Donna Del Fiume, La** see Woman
  Of The River

▶ **Donna Scimmia, La** see Ape Woman,
  The

▶ **Don Quichotte** see Don Quixote

Don Quixote

▶ **aka Adventures Of Don Quixote**
▶ **Don Quichotte**

France   1933   82 mins   bw

Vandor/Nelson/Wester

d **G. W. Pabst**
sc **Paul Morand, Alexandre Arnoux**
ph **Nikolas Farkas**
m **Jacques Ibert**
   **Feodor Chaliapin, Dorville, Renée
   Valliers, Mady Berry, Mireille Balin,
   Vladimir Sokoloff**

Don Quixote (Chaliapin), whose mind is full
of tales of chivalry, fancies himself as a knight
errant, and sets out on many adventures with
his squire Sancho Panza (Dorville). Realizing
that it would be almost impossible to repro-
duce the vastness and depth of Cervantes'
novel, Pabst, in the first film of his five-year
sojourn in France, opted for episodes from the
tale punctuated by songs. As these were
rendered by the great Russian bass Chaliapin
(in one of the rare surviving film records of
him), there were few complaints. It was simultaneously shot in English, with George Robey
replacing Dorville. Eerily, considering the
contemporary rise of Nazism in Germany, the
film ends with a book-burning in which a copy
of *Don Quixote* seems to survive the flames.

Don't Let It Kill You

▶ **(US: No Good To Die For That)**

▶ **Il Ne Faut Pas Mourir Pour Ça**

Canada 1967 75 mins bw
Cinak

d **Jean Pierre Lefèbvre**
sc **Jean Pierre Lefèbvre, Marcel Sabourin**
ph **Jacques Leduc**
m **Andrée Paul**
   **Marcel Sabourin, Monique Champagne,
   Suzanne Grossman, Claudine Monfette**

Abel (Sabourin) is a bizarre, child-like young
man who collects insects and who keeps model
airplanes in cages and books in the fridge. His
life is divided into three by his relationships
with his dying mother (Champagne) and his
girlfriends, the blonde, English-speaking
Mary (Grossman) and the dark quebécoise
Madeleine (Monfette). Lefèbvre, the most
prolific and original of French Canadian film-
makers, made his name with this, his third
movie (and first in 35 mm) the title of which
comes from a Georges Brassens song that
states that 'no idea is worth dying for'. The

central character is alienated and detached
from society, something the film's minimalist
style conveys through a sparsity of close-ups
and cuts and by the use of selective sound
effects. Though without any strong narrative
line and teetering on the whimsical, it forces
one into a reappraisal of received ideas of
society and commitment.

Don't Look Now . . . We're Being Shot At!

▶ **La Grande Vadrouille**

France 1966 130 mins col
Les Films Corona

d **Gérard Oury**
sc **Gérard Oury, Georges and André Tabet**
ph **Claude Renoir**
m **Georges Auric**
   **Terry-Thomas, Bourvil, Louis De Funès,
   Claudio Brook, Marie Dubois, Benno
   Sterzenbach**

A British bomber crew, forced to bale out
over Paris, land in some odd places – the
conductor's dressing room at the Opera, for
example – and have to make their escape to
the Free Zone. How they do so, together with
a couple of Frenchmen and a nun, forms the
content of a wild, protracted and only
occasionally amusing farce. Some eye-catching locations and photography bring relief to
a film where Bourvil and De Funès (neither
at his best) speak fractured English on a
flimsy plot pretext.

▶ **Donzoko** see Lower Depths, The

▶ **Doomed** see Living

▶ **Doro No Kawa** see Muddy River

▶ **Dorp Aan De Rivier** see Doctor In
The Village

Dossier 51

France 1978 108 mins col
Elefilm/Société Française De Production/
Maran Film

d **Michel Deville**

sc **Michel Deville, Gilles Perrault**
ph **Claude Lecompte**
m **Jean Schwarz, Schubert**
**François Marthouret, Claude Marcault,
Jenny Clève, Roger Planchon, Françoise
Lugagne**

A rising French diplomat (Marthouret) is the
target of a secret agency that wishes to control
him. Using a variety of bugging and tracking
devices, they try to find out everything about
him and trap him into an indiscretion.
Deville's cold and complex thriller stands out
among spy stories by the way the spectator
becomes the eavesdropper and agent, watching the development of plot through video
screens and overhearing conversations on
tape. The hero, or target, is seen almost
exclusively in long shot, and the process rather
than the character becomes the focus of attention. It was said that the Soviet embassy in
Paris asked for a print of this expertly made
adaptation of Gilles Perrault's best seller.

Double Suicide

▶ **Shinjo Ten No Amijima**

Japan 1969 106 mins bw
Hyogensha/Nippon Art Theatre Guild

d **Masahiro Shinoda**
sc **Taeko Tomioka, Masahiro Shinoda**
ph **Toshiro Narushima**
m **Tohru Takemitsu**
**Shima Iwashita, Kichiemon Nakamura,
Hosei Komatsu, Yasuke Takita**

Social and moral restraints lead a married
newspaper seller (Nakamura) and the prostitute with whom he is having a passionate
affair to kill themselves in a love-in-death
pact. The formalized playing and the painted
backdrops betray the film's origin – a 1720
puppet play by Chikamatsu. However, within
the stylization, Shinoda has injected realistic
sex scenes and a bloody ending. An added
interest is that both the plain wife and the
beautiful prostitute are played by the splendid
Shima Iwashita.

Douce

▶ **(US: Love Story)**

France 1943 106 mins bw

Société Parisienne De L'Industrie
Cinématographique

d **Claude Autant-Lara**
sc **Jean Aurenche, Pierre Bost**
ph **Gaston Thonnart**
m **René Cloërec**
**Odette Joyeux, Jean Debucourt,
Marguerite Moreno, Roger Pigaut,
Madeleine Robinson**

There are tragic consequences when Douce
(Joyeux), the young daughter of an aristocratic family, falls for a manservant (Pigaud)
in their large Parisian house around
Christmas 1887. This is one of four light and
elegant films that Autant-Lara made during
the war from Aurenche-Bost scripts and starring the charming Joyeux. It makes for
slightly musty but civilized entertainment.

▶ **Doulos, Le** see Doulos – The Finger
Man

Doulos – The Finger Man

▶ **Le Doulos**

France 1962 108 mins bw
Rome-Paris Films/CCC

d **Jean-Pierre Melville**
sc **Jean-Pierre Melville**
ph **Nicolas Hayer**
m **Paul Misraki**
**Serge Reggiani, Jean-Paul Belmondo,
Monique Hennessy, Michel Piccoli, Jean
Desailly, Fabienne Dali**

Maurice(Reggiani), just out of jail, takes refuge with a girlfriend (Hennessy) and seeks
out Silien (Belmondo) to help him organize
a safe-cracking job. Silien obtains the tools
for Maurice then informs on him, sending
him back to jail, and has his girlfriend killed.
He then organizes Maurice's escape, but...
Cast and shot with all Melville's usual command, this is nonetheless a disappointment.
There is much violence and gun-play and
cops'n'robbers action, but the characterization lacks depth, and the particular loyalties
and treacheries of the underworld which so
fascinate this director and which would
coalesce so brilliantly in *Second Breath* are
here ambiguous and incoherent – in spite of

the 9-minute 38-second take of which Melville was especially proud. Belmondo portrays a brutal and unsympathetic meanie whose constant changes of heart and behaviour are hard to fathom.

▶ **Do Widzenia Do Jutra** see See You Tomorrow

Down And Dirty

▶ **aka Ugly, Dirty and Mean**

▶ **Brutti, Sporchi E Cattivi**

Italy 1976 115 mins col
Compagnia Cinematografica Champion

d **Ettore Scola**
sc **Ettore Scola, Ruggero Maccari**
ph **Dario Di Palma**
m **Armando Trovaioli**
   Nino Manfredi, Maria Luisa Santella,
   Francesco Anniballi, Maria Bosco,
   Giselda Castrini

A large family, headed by the aging, one-eyed Giacinto (Manfredi), lives in squalor in one rat-infested room in a shanty town on the outskirts of Rome. He lavishes his attention on an obese prostitute (Santella) who causes problems when she moves in with his abused wife, sons and daughters. Scola treats his poverty-stricken characters far less kindly than the directors of the Neo-Realist movement to whom he considers himself an heir, who saw the poor as innocent victims of a brutal system. No less critical of a system that breeds poverty, he does show its degrading effects in graphic, grotesque, scatological detail. Although much of the film is Ugly, Dirty and Mean, Scola establishes an ironic, often comic distance, and the cast – nonprofessionals apart from Manfredi – are as repulsively watchable as required.

Best Director Cannes 1976

Down The Ancient Stairs

▶ **Per Le Antiche Scale**

Italy 1975 102 mins col
Italian International Film/Les
Productions Fox Europa

d **Mauro Bolognini**
sc **Raffaele Andreassi, Mario Arosio, Tullio**
   Pinelli, Bernardino Zapponi, Sinko
   Solleville Marie
ph **Ennio Guarneri**
m **Ennio Morricone**
   Marcello Mastroianni, Françoise Fabian,
   Marthe Keller, Barbara Bouchet, Lucia
   Bosé

In an insane asylum in Tuscany in 1930, Dr Bonnacorsi (Mastroianni) pursues a chemical cure for schizophrenia while conducting affairs with the asylum director's wife, the wife of another doctor, and a nurse. He has not been outside the walls for eight years, but when his new assistant (Fabian) arrives, rebuffs his sexual advances, and discredits his research, he leaves. At the station he encounters a new form of madness – Fascism. Bolognini's attempt at a political allegory is strained, obtuse and unconvincing, while his glamorous leads contrast unpleasantly with scenes of risibly caricatured lunatics. The talents wasted included those of Pierre Blaise (*Lacombe Lucien*), who was killed in an accident shortly after this film.

Do You Remember Dolly Bell?

▶ **Sjecas Li Se Dolly Bell**

Yugoslavia 1981 90 mins col
Sutjeska Film/TV Sarajevo

d **Emir Kusturica**
sc **Abdulah Sidran**
ph **Vilko Filač**
m **Zoran Simjanović**
   Slavko Štimac, Ljiljana Blagojević,
   Slobodan Aligrudić, Borislav Stjepanović

Sixteen-year-old Dino (Štimac), son of a Muslim-Marxist father (Aligrudić) in Sarajevo in the early 1960s, loses his virginity to teenage prostitute 'Dolly Bell' (Blogojević) and acquires maturity. This is the first feature by 26-year-old Kusturica, who would win the Cannes Grand Prix with his second, *When Father Was Away On Business*, also written by the Muslim Sidran. As can be expected from someone who studied under Jiří Menzel in Prague, the film is a beautifully perceptive, bitter-sweet comedy full of delightful eccentric touches. The background details and the natural performances blow like a breath of fresh air through some of the more conventional 'rites of passage' moments.

▶ **Drachenfutter** see Spicy Rice

▶ **Dragao Da Maldade Contra O Santo Guerreiro** see Antonio Das Mortes

▶ **Drageurs, Les** see Young Have No Morals, The

▶ **Dragon's Food** see Spicy Rice

▶ **Drama Of Jealousy** see Jealousy, Italian Style

Drama Of The Rich

▶ **Fatti Di Gente Perbene**

Italy 1974 115 mins col
Filmarpa(Rome)/Lira Films(Paris)

d **Mauro Bolognini**
sc **Sergio Bazzini, Mauro Bolognini**
ph **Ennio Guarnieri**
m **Ennio Morricone**
   Giancarlo Giannini, Catherine Deneuve, Fernando Rey, Marcel Bozzuffi, Corrado Pani, Tina Aumont, Laura Betti, Ettore Manni, Paolo Bonacelli

Linda (Deneuve), daughter of the distinguished Professor Murri (Rey), confesses to her brother Tullio (Giannini) that her marriage to Count Bonmartini (Bonacelli) is unhappy and that she fears for her life. Tullio takes matters into his own hands and the family becomes enmeshed in scandal and murder. Bolognini has exhumed the records of the actual Murri case that shook Italy early in the century, but has long been forgotten. It is likely to remain so because the director has, alas, failed to bring it to life, merely glancing off the surface of the known facts without examining character or motive and failing to engender suspense. It looks splendid, but the almost operatic visual grandeur doesn't help. Acting honours go to Bozzuffi's relentless magistrate.

▶ **Drame De Shanghai, Le** see Shanghai Drama, The

▶ **Dramma Della Gelosia – Tutti** see Jealousy, Italian Style

Dream Flights

▶ **Polioty Vo Sne Naiavou**

USSR 1983 90 mins col
Aleksandr Dovzhenko Kiev Film Studios

d **Roman Balayan**
sc **Victor Merezhko**
ph **Vilen Kaliuta**
m **Vadim Khrapachev**
   Oleg Yankovsky, Ludmila Gurchenko, Oleg Tabakov, Ludmila Ivanova, Ludmila Zorina, Elena Kostina

About to turn 40, Sergei (Yankovsky) rebels against the responsibilities of work and family, only to find that his girlfriend (Kostina) has lost interest in him, while his wife (Zorina), unable to tolerate his infidelities, throws him out. Several adventures and disasters later, he ends up alone in a haystack after his birthday party. Light in tone and splendidly acted by Yankovsky as the male-menopausal philanderer, the film is somewhat ambiguous. On the one hand it deals in the attractive notion of individualism defying convention; on the other, it exposes its protagonist as an immature man who lets everybody down and deserves his rejection. Some efficient set-pieces and an in-joke or two – Sergei wanders into a film location where Mikhalkov is directing – make for a pleasing but forgettable film.

▶ **Dreams** see Journey Into Autumn

Dreams

Japan 1990 119 mins col
Akira Kurosawa USA/Warner Bros

d **Akira Kurosawa**
sc **Akira Kurosawa**
ph **Takao Saito, Masaharu Ueda**
m **Shinichiro Ikebe**
   Mitsuko Naisho, Toshihiko Nakano, Mitsunori Isaki, Mie Auzuki, Akira Terao, Mieko Harada, Masayuki Yui,

Shu Nakajima, Sakae Kimura, Yoshitaka Zushi, Martin Scorsese, Toshie Negishi, Hisashi Igawa, Chosuke Ikariye, Chishu Ryu

An anthology of eight episodic 'dreams', each with a protagonist elliptically identified as 'I': *Sunshine Through The Rain* recounts the tale of a young boy who spies upon the wedding procession of spirit foxes, only to find that they have left a dagger at his home with which he is to kill himself unless he asks their forgiveness. *The Peach Orchard* tells of peach-tree spirits in the form of traditional *hina* dolls, who express their anger at the destruction of an orchard. When a boy tells the spirits how he too misses the orchard, it briefly appears in all its former glory. *The Blizzard* follows a four-man team of mountain-climbers caught in a howling snowstorm. The fatigued team falls asleep and the leader finds himself wooed by a seductive female spirit to accept this snowy death... *The Tunnel* concerns an officer who, confronted by a platoon of dead soldiers marching through a long tunnel, accepts the responsibility for their deaths. In *Crows* a young man enters a Van Gogh painting and meets the artist himself (Martin Scorsese), who then hastily walks away through a cornfield full of crows. *Mount Fuji In Red* is a cautionary vision of the great mountain destroyed by exploding nuclear reactors. *The Weeping Demon* takes place in a world ravaged by nuclear war, where a human meets a one-horned mutant who takes him to a valley where two- and three-horned demons live out their remaining days in agony. *Village Of The Watermills* is set in an idyllic village where the inhabitants have achieved a balance with nature and an old man describes the natural way of life. The 80-year-old Kurosawa has always been master of the evocative image and *Dreams* is no exception. Each of the episodes which, together, represent the director's multi-faceted style, dazzles through colour and superbly wrought *mise-en-scène*, rather than dialogue or structure, but the anthology's overall message is disjointed. Outside of the obvious cautionary tales concerning environmental issues, Kurosawa hints at meaning rather than making it manifest in these stories of spirits, both ancient and modern. Although it issues from a director who, over the years, created sweeping, complex epics as no other, this American-financed film is no more than a series of postcards which, despite their superb beauty, ultimately convey nothing more than the most simplistic of moral messages.

▶ **Dreigroschenoper, Die** see Threepenny Opera, The

▶ **Drei Von Der Tankstelle, Die** see Three Men And Lilian

Dreszcze

▶ **aka Creeps (US: Shivers)**

Poland   1981   106 mins   col
Film Polski

d   **Wojciech Marczewski**
sc **Wojciech Marczewski**
ph **Jerzy Zielinski**
m   **Andrzej Trzaskowski**
    Teresa Sawicka, Wladyslaw Kowalski, Teresa Marczewska, Tomas Hudziec, Jerzy Binczycki, Marek Kindrat

In 1950s Poland, Stalinism takes over. Young Tomek (Hudziec) is sent to a youth indoctrination camp after his father (Kowalski) has been arrested, a neighbour has committed suicide and religion condemned. When father and son meet again, the boy is a changed being. A chilling account of one of Poland's many recent dark periods as it affected children. An autobiographical excursion for Marczewski, who uses some telling images to reflect his theme: a recurring shot of a leaking roof seems to echo the slow seep of poison into young minds. Made just after the Gdansk riots, the film played for a successful three weeks in Poland before being banned and withdrawn as the country's official Oscar entry.

Special Jury Prize Berlin 1982

▶ **Drevo Zhelanya** see Wishing Tree, The

▶ **Dritte Generation, Die** see Third Generation, The

▶ **Drôle De Drame** see Bizarre, Bizarre

▶ **Drôle D'Endroit Pour Une Rencontre** see Strange Place To Meet, A

▶ **Drôle De Paroissien, Un** see Heaven Sent

Drunken Angel

▶ **Yoidore Tenshi**

Japan 1948 102 mins bw
Toho

d   Akira Kurosawa
sc Akira Kurosawa, Keinosuke Vegusa
ph Takeo Ito
m   Fumio Hayasaka
    Takashi Shimura, Toshiro Mifune,
    Reisaburo Yamamoto, Chieko Nakakita,
    Michiyo Kogure, Norika Sengoku

When a young gangster (Mifune) comes to a doctor's surgery one night to have a bullet removed, the alcoholic doctor (Shimura) discovers his patient has tuberculosis, and finds himself involved in the man's world and destiny. Although Kurosawa's first important film has been compared with the Italian Neo-Realists for its evocation of post-war misery, it comes closer to a Warner Bros. gangster film of the 1930s, the James Cagney role being taken by Mifune. It made the latter a star, and it marked the first of his invaluable performances in all but one of Kurosawa's films until the mid-1960s.

▶ **Dry Summer** see Waterless Summer

▶ **Dubarry Von Heute, Eine** see Modern Dubarry, A

▶ **Du Bist Die Welt Für Mich** see You Are The World For Me

▶ **Due Soldi Di Speranza** see Two Pennyworth Of Hope

▶ **Dulces Horas** see Sweet Hours

The Duped

▶ **aka The Cheated**

▶ **aka The Dupes**

▶ **Al Makhdou-Oun**

Syria 1971 102 mins bw
The General Film Organization

d   Tewfik Saleh
sc Tewfik Saleh
ph Bahjat Hayder
m   Salhi El-Ouadi
    Mohamed Kheir-Halouani, Abderrahman,
    Al-Rachy, Bassam Lotfi, Abou-Ghazala

Three Palestinians, an old man, a young man and a teenage boy, living in poverty in Syria, try to find a means of crossing the desert into Kuwait to find work and freedom. A lorry driver agrees to smuggle them across the borders, hidden in the tank of an empty petrol van. Based on a novel, *Men Under The Sun*, by Palestinian writer Ghassan Kanafani, who was killed by a car bomb in Beirut in 1972, the film is a searing comment on the treatment of Palestinians by fellow Arabs, as well as being a gripping adventure of man against nature. The structure of the screenplay by the Egyptian director is initially confusing, shifting in time and space between the three leading characters, but once the relentless journey gets under way, it follows a strong, direct line. The fine photography creates a palpable impression of blistering heat under a cruel sun. In one scene the camera retreats until a man is a tiny dot in the desert. The climax is a potent symbol of a people dumped on the rubbish pile by history.

▶ **Dupes, The** see Duped, The

▶ **Dura Lex** see By The Law

▶ **Durante L'Estate** see During The Summer

▶ **Du Rififi Chez Les Hommes** see Rififi

During The Summer

▶ **Durante L'Estate**

Italy 1971 105 mins col
Palumbo Film/RAI

d   Ermanno Olmi
sc Fortunato Pasqualino, Ermanno Olmi
ph Ermanno Olmi
m   Bruno Lanzi
    Renato Parracchi, Rosanna Callegari, and
    a cast of unbilled non-professionals

A solitary, materially poor, and idealistic self-styled professor weaves a fantasy universe in

192   Duty Free Marriage

which his fellow creatures are ennobled by the realization of their potential and the discovery of their dignity. He gives substance to his vision by conferring honours on ordinary mortals of his choice. One summer, he meets and falls in love with a girl whom he sees as a sort of madonna princess, but he is arrested for fraudulently awarding titles. Although overlong and sometimes too leisurely, Olmi's film, originally made for Italian television, is full of imagination and sensitivity. The 'professor' is a Christ figure, whose positive qualities are a beacon of light in a world dark with cynicism, violence and destruction, and the absolute simplicity with which the piece is played and directed lends it conviction.

▶ **Du Sjak Aere Din Hstru** see Master Of The House

▶ **Dusman** see Enemy, The

Duty Free Marriage

▶ **Vámmentes Házasság (Finnish: Tullivapaa Avioliittor)**

Hungary/Finland 1980 101 mins col
Mafilm Hunnia Studio/Finnish Film Foundation

d János Zsombolyai
sc Ákos Kertész, Matti Ijäs, János Zsombolyai, Ildikó Kóródy, K.K. Suosalmi, Olli Soinio
ph Elemér Ragályi
m Omega Group
   Mari Kiss, Tom Wentzel, Cecilia Esztergályos, Ági Margittay, Juha Hyppönen, Päävo Piskonen

Mari (Kiss) is anxious to join her boyfriend who has defected to Finland, but is reluctant to lose her Hungarian passport. She persuades Pekka (Wentzel), a Finnish businessman, to agree to a marriage of convenience. Set partly in Budapest, partly in Helsinki, and enacted by an attractive cast, this movie successfully combines carefree comedy with a more serious consideration of moral dilemmas. There are some very funny sequences as Mari and her friends scheme to get out of Hungary; once gone, she and Pekka have to face the attraction that has grown between them and deal with the guilt of deceiving his family who

gives the couple a warm welcome and a large wedding – the dramatic high-point of an interesting and enjoyable film.

▶ **Duvar** see Wall, The

▶ **Dvadtsat Dnei Bez Voini** see Twenty Days Without War

▶ **Dvorianskoe Gnezdo** see Nest Of Gentlefolk, A

▶ **Dwadzat Schest Dnej Is Shisni Dostojewskogo** see Twenty Six Days In The Life Of Dostoevsky

The Dybbuk

▶ **Dybbuk**

Poland 1938 128 mins bw
Fencke Films

d Michael Wasynski
sc Al Kacyzna, Marek Arenstein
ph Albert Wywerka
m Henryk Kon
   Abraham Morevski, R. Samberg, Moishe Lipman, Lili Liliana, Leon Liebgold, Dina Halpern

In a Jewish *shtetl* in mid-19th century Poland, a young man (Liebgold), wishing to marry the daughter (Liliana) of his father's friend (Lipman), calls up the Devil to help him, and dies. The girl then becomes possessed by a *dybbuk*, the soul of a dead person that enters the body of a living one, until the rabbi (Morevski) exorcises it. One of the last, and most celebrated, examples of Yiddish films made in Europe before the war, it was adapted from a play by S. Anski, steeped in the folklore and traditions understood by Jewish audiences. Wasynski's well-crafted, technically proficient film expanded the plot, explaining certain aspects of the story to make it more widely appreciated.

▶ **Dybbuk** see Dybbuk, The

▶ **Dyrygent** see Conductor, The

▶ **Dzieje Grezechu** see Story Of Sin, The

e

The Eagle Has Two Heads

▶ **(US: Eagle With Two Heads)**

▶ **L'Aigle À Deux Têtes**

France 1948 93 mins bw
Les Films Ariane/Sirius

d **Jean Cocteau**
sc **Jean Cocteau**
ph **Christian Matras**
m **Georges Auric**
    **Edwige Feuillère, Jean Marais, Sylvia
Monfort, Edouard Dermithe, Yvonne De
Bray**

In a small mid-European kingdom in the 19th
century, a young anarchist (Marais), who
happens to be the double of the dead king,
breaks into the palace in order to kill the
queen (Feuillère), but falls in love with her.
The consequences are, nonetheless, tragic.
Cocteau's high-flown romantic melodrama,
an international stage success, was brought
to the screen by its author with the same two
leads as in the Paris production. Feuillère is
majestic, vulnerable and tragic, but 35-year-
old Marais in *lederhosen* is difficult to accept
as the fiery young revolutionary. Although
Cocteau's cinematic sense is too great to make
the film look stagey, the screenplay smacks
too much of the theatre. It is thus the most
minor of his own directed films.

▶ **Eagle With Two Heads** see Eagle
Has Two Heads, The

The Ear

▶ **Ucho**

Czechoslovakia 1969 93 mins bw

Svabik-Procházka Production Group,
Barrandov Studios

d **Karel Kachyna**
sc **Jan Procházka, Karel Kachyna**
ph **Joseph Illik**
m **Svatopluk Havelka**
    **Jirina Bohdalová, Radoslav Brzobohaty,
Gustav Opocensky, Miloslav Holub,
Lubor Tokos, Borijov Navrátil, Jiri Cisler**

Ludvik (Brzobohaty), a senior government
official, and his wife Anna (Bohdolová) attend
a reception for party functionaries at which
his senior and mentor is deposed. Other
officials are arrested and the couple return
home convinced that a similar fate awaits
Ludvik, particularly since there are security
police outside and every room in the house
would seem to be bugged. He spends the
night destroying possibly incriminating papers and preparing for the fateful knock on
the door while his wife rounds on him,
accusing him of cowardice and provoking a
bitter quarrel. Described by the critic Derek
Malcolm as 'a kind of amalgam of *Who's
Afraid of Virginia Woolf?* and political parable', *The Ear* was suppressed by the Soviet
authorities after the Prague invasion and
resurfaced only in 1989. In the event, if its
message no longer contains surprises, its
structure and domestic context do, being
unusual and imaginative. The acrimonious
domestic row and the political paranoia both
carry the sharp ring of unpalatable truth and
bring an occasional wry and unexpected smile.
Kachyna is a distinguished veteran of what
was once the Czech New Wave, and this
tightly controlled and excellent films shows
why.

▶ **Early Autumn** see End Of Summer,
The

Early Spring

▶ **Soshun**

Japan 1956 108 mins bw
Shochiku

d **Yasujiro Ozu**
sc **Yasujiro Ozu, Kogo Noda**
ph **Yushun Atsuta**
m **Takayori Saito**
   **Ryo Ikebe, Chikage Awashima, Keiko
   Kishi, Chishu Ryu**

A young clerk (Ikebe), bored with his office work and his wife (Awashima), has a brief affair with the firm's flirt (Kishi) during an office outing. When his wife hears about it, she leaves him. The characteristically slight plot, involving a modern Japanese couple, unravels slowly with great formal beauty, economy, lucidity and humour. The film opens with the start of a working day in Tokyo, thereafter limiting the outdoor scenes to brief glimpses or to pauses in the action.

Early Summer

▶ **Bakushu**

Japan 1951 135 mins bw
Shochiku

d **Yasujiro Ozu**
sc **Kogo Noda, Yasujiro Ozu**
ph **Yuharu Atsuta**
m **Senji Ito**
   **Setsuko Hara, Chishu Ryu, Kuniko
   Miyake, Chikage Awashima, Chiyeko
   Higashiyama, Ichiro Sugai**

Twenty-eight-year-old Noriko (Hara), who lives with her aged parents (Higashiyama and Sugai), her older brother (Ryu) and his wife (Miyake) and their two small sons, is under pressure to marry. But she rejects the suitors acceptable to the family and marries a man of her choice. The simple plot gives no indication of the meticulous observation, humour and pain, nor the delicacy of the playing of some 19 characters. Ozu's unique use of the spatial and the temporal is totally assured and those encountering his art for the first time should soon find themselves in tune with his rhythm and elliptical narrative technique.

▶ **Earrings Of Madame De ..., The**
see Madame De ...

Earth

▶ **Zemlya**

USSR 1930 90 mins bw
VUFKU

d **Alexander Dovzhenko**
sc **Alexander Dovzhenko**
ph **Danylo Demutsky**
m **Silent**
   **Semyon Svashenko, Stepan Shkurat,
   Mikola Nademsky, Yelena Maximova**

Collectivization in the Ukraine is implemented in the face of opposition from the Kulaks (landowners). After the leader of the village committee is shot by a resentful Kulak, the peasants become more united than ever. One of the supreme masterpieces of the Soviet cinema, it was not seen in its entirety until 1958. The authorities censored those scenes where the dead man's betrothed mourns him, naked and hysterical, and where the peasants urinate in the tractor's radiator. Even truncated, this political poem made an enormous impact in the West. Using choreographed images, counterpoints, juxtapositions and a final long elaborate parallel montage, Dovzhenko has created an indelible image of a rural paradise earned by the blood of the peasants.

▶ **Earth, The** see Land, The

▶ **Earth Entranced** see Land In Anguish

Eastern Wind

▶ **Hamsin**

Israel 1982 88 mins col
Nachsoh Films

d **Daniel Wachsman**
sc **Daniel Wachsman, Danny Verete, Jacob
   Lifshin**
ph **David Gurfinkel**
m **Raviv Gazit**
   **Shlomo Tarshish, Hemda Levy, Ruth
   Geler, Shawaf Yassin, Daou Selim, Zvika
   Cornfeld, Shmuel Shilo**

Gedalia Birmann (Tarshish) is a Jewish farmer in Galilee whose family has been closely connected with that of his chief Arab labourer Khaled (Yassin) for two generations. Further, Gedalia's sister (Levy) and Khaled are involved in an illicit love affair. Now the Israeli authorities are to appropriate the Arab land, thus destroying the established order with tragic results. Wachsman's film is well-made and very well acted, skilfully drawing together themes of class conflict, racial tension, and eroticism. A rare and uncompromising Israeli excursion into liberal argument, it is thought provoking and disturbing and caused much controversy at home.

Easy Road

▶ **Asymvivastos**

Greece   1979   110 mins   col
Greca Film

d   **Andreas Thomopoulos**
sc   **Andreas Thomopoulos**
ph   **Dimitris Vernikos**
m   **Mikis Theodorakis, George Theodorakis, Andreas Thomopoulos**
Paul Sideropoulos, Betty Levanon, Elen Manyiati, Vera Kruzka, Stavros Xenidis, Kostas Vrettas

Paul (Sideropoulos), a composer of ballads and a street troubador, is a former postgraduate medical student who dropped out in order to seek a new, freewheeling life and avoid commitment. Things change when he falls in love with a divorced mother of two children, assumes responsibility for the family and returns to his studies, only to be disillusioned by the corruption of the medical profession. This movie – it's title an echo of *Easy Rider* – is a commercially cunning little package, combining, as it does, a sharp look at the realities of modern day life, while offering something for the youth market in its hero's attitudes and its generous dose of music. These latter elements come off best, thanks largely to Sideropoulos' relaxed, attractive style of acting and singing.

▶ **Ebreo Errante, L'** see Wandering Jew, The

The Eclipse

▶ **L'Eclisse**

Italy   1962   125 mins   bw
Cineriz/Iteropa/Paris Film

d   **Michelangelo Antonioni**
sc   **Michelangelo Antonioni, Tonino Guerra, Elio Bartolini, Ottiero Ottieri**
ph   **Gianni De Venanzo**
m   **Giovanni Fusco**
Monica Vitti, Alain Delon, Francisco Rabal, Lilla Brignone, Louis Seigner

Vittoria (Vitti) leaves her lover (Rabal) of four years and begins an affair with Piero (Delon), a stockbroker, but finally opts for solitude rather than marriage or a failing relationship. *The Eclipse* – the title refers to the wiping out of emotions between men and women in modern industrial society – completes what is now seen as Antonioni's trilogy of alienation begun with *L'Avventura* and continuing with *La Notte* (both 1960). The film centres on the superb Vitti, through whose eyes we see the buildings and landscape echoing her emptiness. Perhaps the symbolic intentions are too plain, but nobody could deny the bravura of the stock exchange sequence or the haunting beauty of the final shots – 52 of them – of a city bereft of living creatures.

Special Jury Prize Cannes 1962

▶ **Eclisse, L'** see Eclipse, The

▶ **École Buissonnière, L'** see Passion For Life

▶ **Écoute Voir...** see See Here My Love

Ecstasy

▶ **Extase**

Czechoslovakia   1933   90 mins   bw
Elektra

d   **Gustav Machaty**
sc   **Gustav Machaty, Franz Horky, Vitezslav Nezval, Jacques A. Koerpel**
ph   **Jan Stallich, Hans Androschin**
m   **Giuseppe Becce**

Hedy Kiesler (later Lamarr), Aribert
Mog, Jaromír Rogoz, Leopold Kramer

A child bride whose husband is impotent, has
an affair with a roadway engineer and is
granted a divorce, but declines to go away
with her lover when her ex-husband commits
suicide. Because of the teenage Hedy's one or
two demure nude scenes in an idyllic pastoral
setting, the film caused a rumpus; Pope Pius
XII denounced it, Hitler banned it, and the
offending scenes were excised from most
European and American versions. The gorgeous star's husband, German munitions
magnate Fritz Mandl, spent millions trying
to buy up all the prints. It was much ado
about nothing on, but it helped win Hedy a
Hollywood contract. (Louis B. Mayer
changed her name to Lamarr because he
thought Kiesler sounded too much like a
slang word for buttocks.) The film itself, shot
partly on location, is full of lyrical beauty
and stylish eroticism, and Hedy's kiesler is
hardly seen.

▶ **Edipo Re** see Oedipus Rex

Edith And Marcel

▶ **Édith Et Marcel**

France 1983 162 mins col
Les Films 13/Parafrance

d   **Claude Lelouch**
sc **Claude Lelouch**
ph **Jean Boffety**
m   **Francis Lai**
    **Evelyne Bouix, Jacques Villeret, Francis
    Huster, Marcel Cerdan Jr, Jean-Claude
    Brialy, Jean Bouise, Charles Gérard,
    Charles Aznavour**

The love affair between singer Edith Piaf and
champion boxer Marcel Cerdan, idols of
France in the 1940s, ending with his death in
a plane crash, is parallelled with the romance
between an ordinary plump army private (Villeret) and a wealthy woman (Bouix) with
whom he corresponds. Lelouch, known for
seeing 'la vie en rose', made a superficial and
artificial entertainment out of a passionate
and exciting story, adding a completely pointless and dull sub-plot. Evelyne Bouix
struggled vainly to suggest 'the little sparrow',

with some of her songs actually sung by Piaf
and others by Mama Bea. When Patrick
Dewaere, originally chosen to play Cerdan,
committed suicide just before shooting, Cerdan's son switched from his role as technical
advisor to take that of portraying his father.

▶ **Édith Et Marcel** see Edith And Marcel

▶ **Édouard Et Caroline** see Edward
And Caroline

Edvard Munch

Norway 1974 210 mins col
Norsk Rikskringkasting/Sveriges Radio

d   **Peter Watkins**
sc **Peter Watkins**
ph **Odd Geir Saether**
    **Geir Westby (Munch), Gro Fraas, Eli
    Ryg, Knut Khristiansen, Nils-Eger
    Pettersen, Morten Eid**

A portrait of the great Norwegian Expressionist painter Edvard Munch (1863-1944) and
the hypocritical, puritanical society of Christi-
ana (later Oslo), where he lived his tormented
life. The English director Watkins concentrates mainly on the artist's early years
(derived mainly from Munch's memoirs), his
mother's and younger sister's deaths, his brother's suicide, his own ill-fated affair with a
married woman (Fraas) and his struggle to
maintain his sanity. This is done with a controlled intensity that reflects the visual world
of Munch, as well as getting to grips with the
artistic process itself. Although too long and
repetitive (even in the 167-minute version
released in the USA), it is one of the most
remarkable film biographies to date and the
antithesis of Ken Russell's vulgar efforts. The
non-professional cast, particularly Westby, is
wonderful.

Edward And Caroline

▶ **Édouard Et Caroline**

France 1951 99 mins bw
UGC/CICC

d   **Jacques Becker**
sc **Jacques Becker, Annette Wademant**

ph **Robert Lefèbvre**
m **Jean-Jacques Grünewald**
  Daniel Gélin, Anne Vernon, Jacques
  François, William Tubbs, Jean Galland

A struggling young pianist and his wife (Gelin and Vernon) quarrel on the evening he is to play at her rich uncle's fancy soirée to help launch his career. The best of Becker's comedies with a contemporary Paris setting, it is as light as a feather and twice as rib-tickling. Without much plot, the action, taking place in just a few hours, bubbles along towards the cheerful reconciliation of its appealing young couple.

▶ **Eeny Meeny Miny Moe** see Who Saw Him Die?

Effi Briest

▶ **Fontane Effi Briest**

  W. Germany 1974 140 mins bw
  Tango/Filmverlag Der Autoren

d   **Rainer Werner Fassbinder**
sc **Rainer Werner Fassbinder**
ph **Jürgen Jürges, Dietrich Lohmann**
m   **Saint-Saëns**
    Hanna Schygulla, Wolfgang Schenck, Ulli
    Lommel, Karl-Heinz Böhm, Ursula Stratz

Seventeen-year-old Effi (Schygulla), forced into marriage with an aristocrat (Schenck) twice her age, has a brief affair with a young officer (Lommel). Six years later, the husband discovers love letters and challenges the ex-lover to a duel. Fassbinder has been as faithful as possible to Theodor Fontane's famous 1895 novel on the restraints of a hidebound society, complete with narration and printed extracts, but this is no academic transposition. The elegant monochrome photography (bright fades punctuate the short scenes), the stylized framing (many a mirror image), and the finely shaded performances put it among the director's finest achievements. The radiant Schygulla, having appeared in almost all of Fassbinder's films since 1965, then went her own way for four years after a row about money.

▶ **Effrontée, L'** see Impudent Girl, An

▶ **Égi Bárány** see Agnus Dei

▶ **Egy Erkölcsös Éjsz** see Very Moral Night, A

▶ **Egymásra Nézve** see Another Way

An Egyptian Story

▶ **Hadduta Misriya**

  Egypt 1982 130 mins col
  Misr International

d   **Youssef Chahine**
sc **Youssef Chahine, Fakhry El-Leithy**
ph **Mohsen Nasr**
m   **Gamal Karraze**
    Mohiel Dine, Ussama Nadir, Magda-l-
    Khatib, Leila Hamada, Haman

An Egyptian film director (Dine) goes to London for open-heart surgery. While on the operating table, hovering between life and death, he reviews his life and the events in his country that affected it. Like Bob Fosse's *All That Jazz*, which this film coincidentally and superficially resembles in theme and structure, this is also a personal recollection of the director's own open-heart operation not long before. But unlike the show-bizzy American film's director, Chahine's hero is part of the political process. In this rich, energetic, rather meandering memoir, scenes from Chahine's own films are replayed against their autobiographical and historical context – the end of the war, the fall of Farouk and the Suez crisis.

▶ **Ehe Der Maria Braun, Die** see Marriage Of Maria Braun, The

▶ **Eien No Hito** see Eternal Love

$8\frac{1}{2}$

▶ **Otto E Mezzo**

  Italy 1963 188 mins bw
  Cineriz

d   **Federico Fellini**
sc **Federico Fellini, Ennio Flaiano, Tullio**
    Pinelli, Brunello Rondi
ph **Gianni De Venanzo**

m **Nino Rota**
   **Marcello Mastroianni, Claudia Cardinale,
Anouk Aimée, Sandra Milo, Rosella Falk,
Barbara Steele**

A famous movie director, unable to find the
inspiration to start his new film and harried
by people in the industry, his wife and his
mistress, retreats into personal recollections,
dreams and fantasies. Fellini's seventh solo
effort (plus three collaborations counting a
half each) is one of the most celebrated creations about the inability to create. The problem is that no matter how visually stunning,
exhilarating, and surprising the film was on
first viewing, it cannot avoid being self-indulgent, satirically shallow, and as spiritually
bankrupt as the director – played by Mastroianni as a calculated self-portrait of Fellini.
It remains, however, a compendium of every
Fellini theme and stylistic device, good and
bad.

Best Foreign Film Oscar 1963

1860

Italy 1934 75 mins bw
Cines

d **Alessandro Blasetti**
sc **Alessandro Blasetti, Gino Mazzucchi,
Emilio Cecchi**
ph **Anchise Brizzi, Giulio De Luca**
m **Nino Medin**
   **Giuseppe Gulino, Aida Bellia, Gianfranco
Giachetti, Mario Ferrari**

The events surrounding the battle of Calat-
afimi in May 1860 when the Sicilians rose up
and defeated the troops of the King of Naples.
Among the rebels is a young shepherd (Gulino) who carries a message to Garibaldi in
Genoa requesting support. The use of non-
professional actors, actual landscapes and
regional dialects makes Blasetti's intimate epic
a precursor of Neo-Realism, and a direct
influence on Visconti. The main difference is
that the film presents the peasants, whose
faces are seen being inspired by an unseen
Garibaldi, as part of the historical process
and not as individual victims. But rhetorical
postures are avoided and Blasetti succeeded
in creating a restrained, elegant and poetic
work in the midst of the many pretentiously

grandiose films being made in Fascist Italy at
the time.

▶ **Eijanaika** see Why Not?

▶ **Einmal Ku'damm Und Zurück** see
Girl In A Boot

▶ **Ek Din Prati Din** see And Quiet Rolls
The Dawn

▶ **Ekti Jiban** see Portrait Of A Life

El

▶ **(US: This Strange Passion)**

Mexico 1952 100 mins bw
Nacional Film/Tepeyac

d **Luis Buñuel**
sc **Luis Buñuel, Luis Alcoriza**
ph **Gabriel Figueroa**
m **Hernandez Breton**
   **Arturo De Cordova, Delia Garces, Luis
Beristain, Aurora Walker**

A 40-year-old male virgin (De Cordova) marries a beautiful young girl (Garces) and then
falls victim to paranoid jealousy which leads
him to attempted murder and a monastery.
One of Buñuel's finest black comedies from
his Mexican period continues the theme of
l'amour fou first dealt with in *L'Âge D'Or*
(1930). He transforms a basic Latin-American
melodrama into a biting anti-clerical satire,
full of bizarre touches such as having his
protagonist jab a knitting needle through a
keyhole when he thinks he is being spied
upon.

▶ **E La Nave Va** see And The Ship Sails
On

El Dorado

Spain 1988 151 mins col
Iberio-Americana TV/Chrysalide Films/
Canal Plus/FR 3

d **Carlos Saura**
sc **Carlos Saura**

ph **Teo Escamilla**
m **Alejandro Masso**
  Omero Antonutti, Lambert Wilson,
  Eusebio Poncela, Gabriela Roel, Inés
  Sastre, José Sancho, Féodor Atkine

In 1560, Pedro De Ursúa, accompanied by his mistress, 300 Spanish soldiers and 300 natives, set out from Peru to search for the legendary land of El Dorado. As the expedition travelled ever deeper into the jungle, it met with increasing disaster, and Ursúa's position was forcibly usurped by the conquistador Lope De Aguirre, who went mad and was killed by his few surviving soldiers. Excavating the same ground as Werner Herzog's *Aguirre, The Wrath Of God*, Carlos Saura has made a lavish and beautiful epic, reported to be the most expensive Spanish production to date ($8million). A faithful account of history, the film features some startling set-pieces (the graphic carving up of the horses for food, for example) but, alas, it simply fails to ignite. It drags its heavy load with insufficient action to hold the interest and does so for rather too long. Antonutti and Wilson, Aguirre and Ursúa respectively, are highly competent, but lack the necessary bite.

Electra

▶ **Elektra**

  Greece 1962 113 mins bw
  Finos

d **Michael Cacoyannis**
sc **Michael Cacoyannis**
ph **Walter Lassally**
m **Mikis Theodorakis**
  Irene Papas, Aleka Katselli, Yannis
  Fertis, Phoebus Rhazis

Electra (Papas) and Orestes (Fertis) plot the death of their mother Clytemnestra (Katselli), whom they believe to have been responsible for their father's murder. Because of political and financial pressures, Cacoyannis turned from modern to Ancient Greece with the first and best of his rather uninspiring Euripides trilogy, (*The Trojan Women*, 1971 and *Iphigenia*, 1976 followed), all featuring Irene Papas chewing the scenery – in this case the barren landscape around Mycenae. The old story

still grips despite unnecessary flashbacks and overpowering close-ups.

▶ **Electra, My Love** see Elektreia

▶ **Elektra** see Electra

Elektreia

▶ **aka Electra, My Love**
▶ **Szerelmem, Elektra**

  Hungary 1974 76 mins col
  Hunnia Film

d **Miklós Jancsó**
sc **Gyula Hernádi, L. Gyurkó**
ph **János Kende**
m **Popular Hungarian songs**
  Mari Töröcsik, György Cserhalmi, Jószef
  Madaras, Lajos Balázsovits

On the Hungarian plains, Elektra (Töröcsik) and her brother Orestes (Cserhalmi) fight against the tyranny of Egisto (Madaras). Through one of Jancsós most stylized and choreographed narratives can just be discerned the Electra myth. All the elements of the director's personal visual vocabulary are rather too densely packed in – the horsemen, the whips, the nudes, the dances, the folk songs, the extraordinary tracking shots and extremely long takes. But there are comical scenes, such as Egisto perched on a gigantic ball, and the surprising and optimistic ending when a red helicopter called *Revolution*, flying from East to West, comes down from the sky to rescue the hero and heroine. The message may be simple, but the symbols are strong.

Eléna Et Les Hommes

▶ **(US: Paris Does Strange Things)**

  France 1956 95 mins col
  Franco London/Les Films Gibé/Electra Compania Cinematographica

d **Jean Renoir**
sc **Jean Renoir**
ph **Claude Renoir**
m **Joseph Kosma**

Ingrid Bergman, Mel Ferrer, Jean Marais, Magali Noël, Juliette Greco, Jean Richard

An impoverished Polish princess (Bergman) sets out to find herself a rich husband among her many admirers in the Paris of the 1880s. She is finally faced with three choices – an elderly but wealthy boot magnate (Richard), a conquering soldier-hero (Marais) and an aristocratic dilettante (Ferrer). 'For a long time I had been dying to make a film with Ingrid Bergman. I wanted to see her laughing and smiling on the screen,' said Renoir, who rescued the Swedish star from the gloom of her four Rossellini films and restored her popularity. Bergman has seldom been more beguiling than in this, one of Renoir's most artificial films. Love is at the centre of a Paris of parades, ballad singers, salons and street carnivals, captured by Claude Renoir's camera as a series of popular prints. It sets out to prove, rather ingenuously, that 'Dictatorship has no chance in a country where affairs of the heart are so important'.

▶ **Éléphant Ça Trompe Énormément, Un** see Pardon Mon Affaire

The Elephant God

▶ **Joi Baba Felunath**

India   1978   112 mins   col
RDB

d   **Satyajit Ray**
sc   **Satyajit Ray**
ph   **Soumendu Roy**
m   **Satyajit Ray**
Soumitra Chatterjee, Siddartha Chatterjee, Santosh Dutta, Utpal Dutta

Private detective Feluda (Soumitra Chatterjee), on holiday in Benares with his teenage cousin (Siddartha Chatterjee), gets involved in the mysterious theft of a valuable gold statuette, the Elephant God. This follow-up to *The Golden Fortress* reintroduces the Indian Sherlock Holmes and his young Dr Watson in an enjoyable tale, told with all of Ray's affection and artistry. A range of picturesque characters, including a phoney holy man, and

a wonderful use of the Benares setting puts it in the Feuillade serial tradition.

▶ **Eles Nao Usam Black Tie** see They Don't Wear Black Tie

▶ **Elippathayam** see Rat-Trap

Elisa, My Life

▶ **aka Elisa, My Love**
▶ **Elisa, Vida Mía**

Spain   1977   125 mins   col
Elías Querejeta

d   **Carlos Saura**
sc   **Carlos Saura**
ph   **Teo Escamilla**
m   **Erik Satie**
Geraldine Chaplin, Fernando Rey, Norman Brisky, Isabel Mestres, Joaquín Hinojosa

Elisa (Chaplin), estranged from her husband (Brisky), visits her father (Rey), whom she has not seen for many years, at his cottage in the Segovian hills. He is writing a biography from her point of view and, gradually she begins to see things with his perspective. Saura's interest in memory, shifting chronology and different narrative devices is at its most complex in this drama of identity. 'The things that bother me are less clear than under Franco,' Saura said in 1976, and the film seems to express this opaque state. Yet the ambiguity – it seldom separates memory from imagination – and the subtle performances of Chaplin and Rey, pay some dividends.

Best Actor (Fernando Rey) Cannes 1977

▶ **Elisa, My Love** see Elisa, My Life
▶ **Elisa, Vida Mía** see Elisa, My Life

El Topo

▶ **aka The Mole**

Mexico   1971   124 mins   col
Producciones Panicas

d Alejandro Jodorowsky
sc Alejandro Jodorowsky
ph Raphael Corkidi
m Alejandro Jodorowsky
    Alejandro Jodorowsky, Mara Lorenzio,
    Brontis Jodorowsky, Paula Romo, Robert
    John, David Silva

Gunfighter El Topo (Alejandro Jodorowsky), accompanied by his seven-year-old son, sets out on an avenging journey, massacring a group of murderers and going on to defeat rival master gunfighters in the desert. All is achieved by means of deception, which leads him to seek redemption. Jodorowsky's epic is divided into four sections, subtitled Genesis, Prophets, Psalms and Apocalypse, and is top-heavy with allegory and symbolism, both Christian and Pagan. Crudely derivative – Fellini, Buñuel and Sergio Leone are the more obvious influences – it gathered a hysterically enthusiastic and youthful cult following its release in New York but, to more considered critics, it is a pretentious philosophical mess, liberally spattered with blood and violence. There are, however, one or two highly original sequences, and it is strikingly photographed against a dramatically beautiful landscape.

Elvira Madigan

Sweden 1967 95 mins col
Europa/Janco

d Bo Widerberg
sc Bo Widerberg
ph Jörgen Persson
m Mozart
    Pia Degermark, Thommy Berggren,
    Lennart Malmer

Elvira (Degermark), a tightrope artist, and Sixten (Berggren), a married army officer, fall in love, run away together, and enjoy an idyll in the countryside. Totally shunned by the 19th-century Swedish society whose moral code they have outraged, their passion ends in death. Widerberg's film version of a true story is lyrically photographed in soft focus and slow motion, and well acted – largely to the strains of Mozart's Piano Concerto No 21 (2nd movement). Some regard the film as an overblown and sentimental cigarette commercial; others find the lover's unrealistic and

tragic quest for happiness almost unbearably moving.

Best Actress (Pia Degermark) Cannes 1967

The Emigrants

▶ **Utvandrarna**

Sweden 1971 190 mins col
Svensk Filmindustri

d Jan Troell
sc Jan Troell, Bengt Forslund
ph Jan Troell
m Erik Nordgren
    Max Von Sydow, Liv Ullmann, Eddie
    Axberg, Svenolof Bern, Allan Edwall,
    Alina Alfredsson

A group of poor Swedish peasants, forced to emigrate to the USA because of hardship at home, survive a cramped voyage before optimistically settling down in Minnesota. Based on the novels of Vilhelm Moberg, this slushy, slow, solemn saga and its sequel The New Land (1973) did well in the New World but failed dismally in the Old. One almost forgets that Van Sydow and Ullmann, as the loving couple surviving disasters against beautiful landscapes, were the linchpins of many a Bergman film

Emil And The Detectives

▶ **Emil Und Die Detektive**

Germany 1931 73 mins bw
UFA

d Gerhard Lamprecht
sc Billy Wilder
ph Werner Brandes
m Schmidt-Boelke
    Rolf Wenkhaus, Fritz Rasp, Kaethe
    Haack, Olga Engl, Inge Landgut

Young Emil (Wenkhaus) becomes a hero when he tracks down a notorious thief with the help of the child population of Berlin. This first of five film versions of Erich Kastner's children's novel outstrips all the rest, including one from Walt Disney Studios in 1964. Lively and amusing, with good location photography, it never condescends to a youthful audience, allowing adults to enjoy it, too.

▶ **Emil Und Die Detektive** see Emil And The Detectives

Emitai

Senegal 1972 103 mins col
Films Domirev

d **Ousmane Sembène**
sc **Ousmane Sembène**
ph **Michel Remaudeau**
   Robert Fontaine, Michel Remaudeau,
   Pierre Blanchard, Ibou Camara, Ousmane
   Camara

The French arrive in a small West African village to recruit soldiers for their World War II armies, but meet with resistance. However, the colonized community's attempt to protect its traditional values and way of life has a tragic outcome. Leading Senegalese director Sembène's film, made on a tiny budget, is no less exemplary in its choices and judgement than a more expensive venture. The story, told from the point of view of the oppressed with a stoical regard for the truth that informs much as a documentary might, is poignant and salutary.

Emmanuelle

France 1974 94 mins col
Trinacra/Orphée

d **Just Jaeckin**
sc **Jean-Louis Richard**
ph **Richard Suzuki, Marie Saunier**
m **Pierre Bachelet**
   Sylvia Kristel, Marika Green, Daniel
   Sarky, Alain Cuny

The bored wife of a French embassy official in Bangkok, urged by her libertine husband to explore all the possibilities of sex, finds herself in bed with, among others, a Lesbian archaeologist and an elderly roué. This glossy soft porn package dressed up (or undressed) as art, with Kristel on display, was a huge international hit and spawned a mulitude of Emmanuelle sequels (and derivative copies) even worse than their begetter.

The Emperor Of California

▶ **Der Kaiser Von Kalifornien**

Germany 1936 100 mins bw
Luis Trenker Film

d **Luis Trenker**
sc **Luis Trenker**
ph **Albert Benitz, Heinz Von Jaworsky**
m **Giuseppe Becce**
   Luis Trenker, Viktoria Von Ballasko,
   Werner Kunig, Karl Zwingmann,
   Bernhard Minetti, Luis Gerold

In 1834, John Sutter (Trenker), a revolutionary, has to flee from Switzerland to America. In California, he becomes the leader of an immigrant community and later gains power as a Senator and a US Army General, until he is finally brought down. Blaise Cendrar's novel *L'Or* was originally to have been a Hollywood project for Sergei Eisenstein, but when that fell through Trenker applied to Universal to direct it. After they gave *Sutter's Gold* to James Cruze, Trenker made his own rival version in the same year. Some locations were filmed in America, but many others were shot in North Italy and Berlin. In fact, the film's splendid camerawork, clever montage and imaginative use of sets give it more of a feeling for the grandeur of the Old West than the second-rate Hollywood edition. Because Trenker made films under the Third Reich, the work was banned by both the Americans and Russians after the war.

Best Film Venice 1936

Empire Of Passion

▶ **(US: Phantom Love)**

▶ **Ai No Borei**

Japan 1978 105 mins col
Argos/Oshima

d **Nagisa Oshima**
sc **Nagisa Oshima**
ph **Yoshio Miyajima**
m **Tohru Takemitsu**
   Kazuko Yoshiyuki, Tatsuya Fuji,
   Takahiro Tamura, Takuzo Kawatani,
   Akiko Koyama

In a village in 1895, an old rickshaw man is murdered by his wife (Yoshiyuki) and her young lover (Fuji). Three years later, the old man's ghost appears, reawakening their guilt and leading to the exposure of their crime. This companion piece to *In The Realm Of The Senses* is less sexually explicit but equally steamy and cruel. Oshima's control of the medium is evident in this ghost story with an *amour fou* at its centre, but the social conviction and complexity of his earlier films seems to have evaporated. This has one keen eye on the audience's emotions and the other on the box-office.

Best Director Cannes 1978

The Empress Yang Kwei Fei

▶ **aka Princess Yang Kwei Fei**

▶ **Yokihi**

Japan 1955 125 mins col
Daiei-Shaw Brothers

d **Kenji Mizoguchi**
sc **Yoda Yoshikata**
ph **Kohei Sugiyama**
m **Hayasaka Fumio**
    Masayuki Mori, Machiko Kyo, So Yamamura, Sakae Ozawa

When the emperor of China marries a scullery maid on the death of his wife, the new empress is destroyed by jealousies and intrigue around her. Undeterred by the big budget spectacle requirements of the Shaw Brothers of Hong Kong, Mizoguchi triumphantly retains his reputation. The exquisite colour, costumes and decor are used almost as *leitmotifs* to counterpoint the emotions of the characters, especially the glowing Kyo in the title role. Sadly, the director would not live long enough (he died a year later) to experiment in colour on the wide screen.

The Empty Canvas

▶ **La Noia**

Italy 1964 118 mins bw
CC Champion/Concordia

d **Damiano Damiani**
sc **Damiano Damiani, Tonino Guerra, Ugo Liberatore**
ph **Roberto Gerardi**
m **Luis Bacalov**

Bette Davis, Horst Buchholz, Catherine Spaak, Isa Miranda, Lea Padovani, Georges Wilson

A young painter (Buchholz), obsessed by his deficiencies as an artist, falls in love with a model (Spaak) whom he brings home to the family estate to meet his mother (Davis). When she refuses to remain faithful to him, he becomes insanely jealous. The novels and stories of Alberto Moravia have seldom made good movies and this plodding, pompous film is no exception. Consolation comes (as always) from Bette Davis, amusing to watch as an Italian matriarch in her first foreign language film. But as for the rest...an empty screen might have been preferable.

The Empty Table

▶ **Shokutaku No Nai Ie**

Japan 1985 142 mins col
Marugen Building Group/Haiyu-za Film Production/ Herald Ace

d **Masaki Kobayashi**
sc **Masaki Kobayashi**
ph **Kozo Okazaki**
m **Tohru Takemitsu**
    Tatsuya Nakadai, Mayumi Ogawa, Kie Nakai, Kiichi Nakai, Takeyuki Takemoto, Shima Iwashita, Mikijiro Hira

Kidoji (Nakadai), a high-powered electronics academic is the head of a family which is disintegrating as a result of the arrest of his eldest son (Kiichi Nakai) for terrorist activities. Public disgrace walks hand-in-hand with private grief; he refuses to visit the boy in jail, and his wife loses her sanity. Kobayashi tells his story – primarily one of family relationships – in a series of shifting time blocks, and fills it with hints of political argument and examinations of moral responsibility. However, the dilemmas are presented rather than explored, and done so with a disciplined restraint that suggests something weightier than is actually present. It's a well-made, interesting film that never rises to the level of one's expectation.

▶ **En Cas De Malheur** see Love Is My Profession

The Enchanted Desna

▶ **Zacharovannaya Desna**

USSR 1964 81 mins col
Mosfilm

d   **Julia Solntseva**
sc **Alexander Dovzhenko**
ph **A. Temerine**
m   **Gavril Popov**
    Yevgeni Samoilov, Volodya Gontcharov,
    E. Bondarenko, Zinaida Kirienkova, V.
    Orlovsky

During World War II, a soldier (Samoilov)
on retreat finds strength in his memories, both
sad and happy, of the Ukraine of his youth
and in the beauty of his homeland. 'If Dovzhenko had lived, I would never have become
a director; all that I do I consider as propaganda, defence and illustration of Dovzhenko,' stated Solntseva on the filming of her
husband's three unrealized scenarios. The
third and best (after *Poem Of The Sea* and
The Flaming Years) astonishes with its eye-
boggling rhetorical images in 70mm and
stereophonic sound. Perhaps it lacks Dovzhenko's unique lyricism, but its amalgam of
illusion and reality, legend and Ukrainian
nationalism is very much in the tradition of
Zvenigora. For what it's worth, *The
Enchanted Desna* is one of Godard's favourite
films.

The Endless Land Of Alexis Droeven

▶ **Le Grand Paysage D'Alexis Droeven**

Belgium 1981 88 mins col
Les Films De La Drève(Brussels)/
RTBF(Liège)/Radio-Cinés SA(France)

d   **Jean-Jacques Andrien**
sc **Jean-Jacques Andrien, Franck Venaille**
ph **Georges Barsky**
m   **Monteverdi, Wagner**
    Jerzy Radziwilowicz, Nicole Garcia,
    Maurice Garrel, Jan Decleir, the
    inhabitants of the Aubel district

When dairy farmer Alexis Van Droeven (Garrel) dies, his son Jean-Pierre (Radziwilowicz)
returns to bury him. It is only from the
speeches at Alexis' graveside that the young
man learns of his father's struggles for political rights and, from his aunt (Garcia), that
Alexis wanted to save him from inheriting a
life of isolation and hardship. Jean-Pierre
must now decide whether to sell the farm or
carry it on. Andrien spent three years in the
Aubel district, living among the farming community of his ancestry to gather his material.
The result is a complex story of family
relationships and socio-political problems,
using flashback to portray key incidents in
the late Alexis' life. Spare and intelligent, the
film is outstandingly beautiful in its evocation
of landscape and won the best cinematography prize at Berlin.

The End Of A Day

▶ **La Fin Du Jour**

France 1939 108 mins bw
Regina/Filmsonor

d   **Julien Duvivier**
sc **Julien Duvivier, Charles Spaak**
ph **Christian Matras**
m   **Maurice Jaubert**
    Victor Francen, Louis Jouvet, Michel
    Simon, Madeleine Ozeray, Arthur Devere,
    Gabrielle Dorziat, Sylvie

The feuds, friendships, loves and hates of a
group of elderly actors and actresses in a
retirement home threatened with closure. The
film offers a feast of French ensemble acting
with Michel Simon standing out as a pathetic
prankster who hides the fact that he had only
ever been an understudy in his career. Duvivier ably balances comedy and sentiment in
virtually one setting.

▶ **End Of Innocence** see House Of The
Angel, The

The End Of St Petersburg

▶ **Konyets Sankt-Peterburga**

USSR 1927 122 mins bw
Mezhrabpom

d   **Vsevolod Pudovkin**

sc **Nathan Zarkhi**
ph **Anatoli Golovnya**
m **Silent**
   Ivan Chuvelov, Vera Baranovskaya, A.P.
   Khristiakov, V. Obolenski

In 1917, an uneducated peasant boy (Chuvelov) arrives in St Petersburg in time to witness the October Revolution, including the storming of the Winter Palace and the fall of Kerensky. Commissioned, like Eisenstein's *October,* as part of the tenth anniversary celebrations of the Revolution, and shot concurrently using the same sites and events, Pudovkin's was the more popular film with the public and officialdom – perhaps because it was made more human by having a central figure with whom audiences could identify, and was rather less stylized. Nevertheless, it also contained its share of marvellous montage sequences, such as the high-angle shot of the top hats of businessmen contrasted with the faces of dead soldiers in the trenches.

The End Of Summer

▶ **aka Early Autumn**

▶ **Kohayagawa-Ke No Aki**

   Japan   1961   103 mins   col
   Toho

d **Yasujiro Ozu**
sc **Yasujiro Ozu, Kogo Noda**
ph **Asakazu Nakai**
m **Toshiro Mayuzumi**
   Ganjiro Nakamura, Setsuko Hara, Yoko Tsukasa, Michiyo Aratama, Yumi Shirakawa

When an elderly man (Nakamura) decides to take up with his former mistress, his three daughters – one a widow about to remarry, another engaged and the third married – become extremely upset. The father dies of a heart attack. One of Ozu's bleakest films starts out in a light, anecdotal manner, gradually getting harsher, but all the time enriching our knowledge of family relationships. The film also contains one of Ozu's greatest characters in the wily old father.

▶ **Endstation Freiheit** see Slow Attack

The Enemy

▶ **Dusman**

   Turkey   1979   160 mins   col
   Guney Filmcilik

d **Zeki Ökten**
sc **Yilmaz Güney**
ph **Cetin Tunca**
m **Yavuz Top**
   Aytac Arman, Gungor Bayrak, Guven Sengil, Kamil Sonmez, Sevket Altug

A poor uneducated labourer, with a discontented wife, can find no work until he gets a job poisoning stray dogs. One of the four extraordinary films directed by proxy from a detailed script by Yilmaz Güney, serving a long prison sentence in Turkey, it is a powerful, passionate plea for social justice. What puts it beyond a tract is the gritty, sometimes quirky depiction of everyday life as lived by the disinherited.

▶ **Enemy Of The People, An** see Ganashatru

▶ **Enfance Nue, L'** see Naked Childhood

▶ **Enfant Sauvage, L'** see Wild Child, The

Les Enfants Du Paradis

▶ **(US: Children Of Paradise)**

   France   1945   195 mins   bw
   Pathé

d **Marcel Carné**
sc **Jacques Prévert**
ph **Roger Hubert**
m **Joseph Kosma, Maurice Thiriet**
   Arletty, Jean-Louis Barrault, Pierre Brasseur, Marcel Herrand, Maria Casarès, Louis Salou, Pierre Renoir, Gaston Modot, Jane Marken

In the 19th-century Paris of Louis Philippe, among the crowds that throng the boulevards, are the classical actor Frédéric Lemaître (Brasseur), the mime Debureau (Barrault), the criminal Lacenaire (Herrand), the aristocrat Comte Montray (Salou), the elusive courtesan Garance (Arletty), and the simple Nathalie (Casarès), all of whose fates are intertwined. This richly entertaining and intensely romantic evocation of an epoch, with vivid sets by Alexandre Trauner, came about because the Occupation forced Carné and Prévert to make 'escapist' films. The larger-than-life characters and performers, the ironic dialogue, the narrative skill and sweep of the whole production has placed this on many critics' lists as one of the greatest films ever made.

► **Enfants Gâtés, Des** see Spoiled Children

► **Enfants Terribles, Les** see Strange Ones, The

The Engagement

► **(US: The Fiancés)**

► **I Fidanzati**

Italy 1963 84 mins bw
Titanus Sicilia/Ventidue Dicembre/SEC

d **Ermanno Olmi**
sc **Ermanno Olmi**
ph **Lamberto Caimi**
m **Gianni Ferrio**
  Carlo Cabrini, Anna Canzi

A young man gladly accepts a welding job in Sicily which will take him away from his fiancée in Milan for 18 months, because he thinks the separation will be good for their relationship. However, loneliness and an unfamiliar environment make him long to see her again. Olmi's strength lies in the depiction of humble people (played here by a pair of non-professionals), whose problems he highlights without condescension or preaching. The film's use of natural sounds and actual locations creates an alienating environment in which there are pockets of warmth and humanity.

The Enigma Of Kaspar Hauser

► **(US: Every Man For Himself And God Against All)**

► **aka The Mystery of Kaspar Hauser**

► **Jeder Für Sich Und Gott Gegen Alle**

W. Germany 1974 110 mins col
ZDF

d **Werner Herzog**
sc **Werner Herzog**
ph **Jorge Schmidt-Reitwein**
m **Albinoni, Pachelbel, Di Lasso**
  Bruno S, Walter Ladengast, Brigitte Mira, Hans Musaus, Willy Semmelrogge

In the early 19th century, a strange young man, who seemed to have had no contact with human beings since his childhood, appeared in the town square at Nuremburg. He became an attraction in society until killed one day by an unknown assailant. Herzog's fascination with the outsider fixes itself on Kaspar Hauser, the ultimate misfit. The mysterious side of the true tale is, however, mainly ignored in favour of a stilted examination of the confrontation between innocence and corruption, and some obvious satire on social conventions. What makes the film riveting is the disturbing and remarkable presence of Bruno S, a man who spent 22 years in various institutions, including prison, before Herzog discovered him.

Special Jury Prize Berlin 1975

► **Enjo** see Conflagration

► **Ensayo De Un Crimen** see Criminal Life Of Archibaldo De La Cruz, The

Enthusiasm

► **aka Symphony Of The Don Basin**

► **Entuziazm**

USSR 1931 96 mins bw
Kiev Film Studio/ Ukrainfilm

d **Dziga Vertov**
sc **Dziga Vertov**
ph **Zeitlin**
m **N. Timofeyev**

A documentary on the industrial and agricultural workers in the Donets Coal Basin in the Eastern Ukraine, and their efforts to fulfil the Five Year Plan. No, it is not as boring as it sounds. In fact, this 'symphony of noise', this 'futuristic visual poem', much admired by Chaplin, not only celebrates workers in the building of the Soviet Union but the art of cinema. Enthusiasm for both his subject and his style permeates Vertov's first sound film, contrasting the old order and the new through didactic, dynamic montage. As in *The Man With The Movie Camera*, one's attention is drawn to the making of the film itself as a contribution to the modernization programme, epitomizing Lenin's statement, 'Of all the arts, for us cinema is the most important'.

► **Entotsu No Mieru Basho** see Where Chimneys Are Seen

Entr'acte

France 1924 22 mins bw
Ballets Suédois

d **René Clair**
sc **Francis Picabia**
ph **Jimmy Berliet**
m **Silent**
   Jean Borlin, Inge Fries, Francis Picabia, Man Ray, Georges Auric, Marcel Achard, Marcel Duchamp, Erik Satie, Georges Charensol, Rolf De Maré

A number of crazy characters rush around Paris where they end up at a funeral chasing a runaway hearse. This Dada joke was conceived by the painter and poet Picabia in order to be shown during the interval between the two acts of his ballet *Relâche* (music by Satie). Clair shot it in three weeks at various well-known locations in the city, intending it as a tribute to the pioneers of screen comedy, including Chaplin. An exercise in pure cinema – no plot, visual surrealism such as speeded-up motion and balletic slow motion – it is more interesting than funny, as it features many members of the French *avant-garde* of the day, and shows the emergence of a new genius of the cinema.

Entrée Des Artistes

► **(US: The Curtain Rises)**

France 1938 90 mins bw
Regina

d **Marc Allégret**
sc **Henri Jeanson, André Cayatte**
ph **Christian Matras**
m **Georges Auric**
   Louis Jouvet, Odette Joyeux, Claude Dauphin, Bernard Blier, Janine Darcey, Dalio, Carette, Sylvie

At the Paris Conservatory, two drama students (Joyeux and Darcey) fight over a fellow student (Dauphin), who is later accused of murdering one of them. Far more interesting than the melodramatic plot is the background of the cafés, the school and, particularly, the lessons with Jouvet – delightfully himself as a drama teacher. The film also proved to be a springboard for the careers of the young Joyeux, Dauphin and Blier.

► **Entre Nous** see At First Sight

► **Entre Tinieblas** see Dark Habits

► **Entuziazm** see Enthusiasm

Equinox Flower

► **Higan-Bana**

Japan 1958 118 mins col
Shochiku

d **Yasujiro Ozu**
sc **Kogo Noda, Yasujiro Ozu**
ph **Yuharu Atsuta**
m **Takanobu Saito**
   Shin Saburi, Fujiko Yamamoto, Kinuyo Tanaka, Ineko Arima, Keiji Sada

A young woman (Yamamoto) wishes to marry the man of her choice, but her obstinate father (Saburi) objects. although her mother (Tanaka) understands. Eventually he is won round. 'Colour is all right once in a while, but if you see it all the time, it's like eating *tendon* (seafood on rice). You get fed up with it,' said Ozu on the making of his first colour film. Actually, it was the producers who wanted it in colour to show off Yamamoto's beauty. Not only did it give the film a more modern look, but also showed the director becoming more interested in the younger generation, although he doesn't take sides. Here, the whole family is subjected to his gentle irony and loving detail. An example of Ozu's meticulous working methods on the film was recalled by Tanaka who, in a very short scene, had to say the line 'Yes, that's so' over 40 times before the director was satisfied.

▶ **Eredità Ferramonti, L'** see Inheritance, The

Erendira

Mexico 1982 105 mins col
Les Films Du Triangle/Films
A2/Ministère De La Culture(France)/
Cine Qua Non(Mexico)/Atlas Saskia
Film/Austra(W. Berlin)

d **Ruy Guerra**
sc **Gabriel García Márquez**
ph **Denys Clerval**
m **Maurice Lecoeur**
  **Irene Papas, Claudia Ohana, Michel
  Lonsdale, Oliver Wehe, Rufus, Blanca
  Guerra, Ernesto Gomez Cruz**

For accidentally burning down the mansion of her tyrannical grandmother (Papas), Erendira (Ohana) is forced to sell her virginity to the highest bidder. After seeking refuge in a convent and then escaping to marry Ulysses (Wehe), the son of the police chief, she and her lover plan to kill her grandmother. Márquez's screenplay (from two of his own stories) is a cruel fairytale of an ogrish woman, an innocent maiden and an ineffectual Prince Charming. The director goes in for the most bizarre images of Latin Grand Guignol, shot amid grotesque surreal settings. Eccentric, funny and often plain silly, the film has some memorable nightmarish sequences. The performances of the baddies are suitably over the top.

Ernesto

Italy 1979 98 mins col
Clesi Cinematografica/José Frade
Productions/ Albatros Produktion

d **Salvatore Samperi**
sc **Barbara Alberti, Amadeo Paganini,
  Salvatore Samperi**
ph **Camillo Bazzoni**
m **Carmelo Bernaola
  Martin Halm, Michele Placido, Virna
  Lisi, Turri Ferro, Lara Wendel**

Ernesto (Halm), a young Jewish boy in Trieste at the turn of the century, has his sexual initiation via a male worker at his uncle's factory whom he subjugates then discards. He visits a female prostitute successfully, then finds himself attracted to a twin brother and sister. He settles for heterosexuality with the girl. Samperi's promising debut with *Grazie Zia* (1968) rather fizzled out as his attempts at serious analysis of social and sexual problems became blurred by the dominance of his gift for soft porn. *Ernesto* exemplifies the problem, although it is a handsome film and not unenjoyable.

Eroica

▶ **aka Heroism**

Poland 1957 83 mins bw
Kadr/WFF/WFD

d **Andrzej Munk**
sc **Jerzy Stefan Stawinski**
ph **Jerzy Wojcik**
m **Jan Krenz
  Barbara Polomska, Leon Niemszyk,
  Edward Dziewonski, K. Rudzki, Roman
  Klosowski**

Subtitled *A Heroic Symphony In Two Movements*. 1) *Scherzo Alla Polacca* tells of a black marketeer during the Nazi occupation who accidentally becomes involved with the Polish underground movement. 2) *Ostinato Lugubre* explains how the morale of the inmates of a concentration camp was kept high by making them believe one of their number had escaped. Munk's second feature, an ironic and ambivalent study of heroism during the war, disconcerted audiences accustomed to the romantic and passionate treatment of the subject by his contemporaries.

Erotikon

Sweden 1920 85 mins bw
Svensk Filmindustri

d   **Mauritz Stiller**
sc **Rellits and Nedron (pseudonym for Stiller and Arthur Nordren)**
ph **Henrik Jaenzon**
m   **Silent**
    Lars Hanson, Karin Molander, Tora Teje, Anders De Wahl

An entomologist (De Wahl), who lectures on the sex life of beetles, is happy to give up his sophisticated wife (Teje) to his sculptor friend (Hanson) because he has fallen for a simple girl (Molander) who wins his affections with her delicious stuffed cabbage. The most celebrated of Stiller's comedies, but not the best, it was his last before moving on to more sombre works, and anticipates Bergman's *Smiles Of A Summer's Night* in its sexual manoeuvres and graceful wit. The highlight is the performance of Karin Molander, who starred in all the director's early comedies and was his most favoured incarnation of the 'modern' heroine. Renowned for his successful promotion of the liberated woman on screen, nonetheless, it is for discovering Garbo that Stiller will be best remembered.

Erotissimo

France   1968   100 mins   col
Les Films De La Pléiade/Les Films Des Deux-Mondes (Paris)/Kinesis (Rome)

d   **Gérard Pirès**
sc **Nicole De Buron, Gérard Pirès, Pierre Sisser**
ph **Jean-Marc Ripert**
m   **William Sheller**
    Annie Girardot, Jean Yanne, Francis Blanche, Dominique Maurin, Venantino Venantini

Philippe (Yanne) is preoccupied with a tax inspector's investigations into his business, leading his wife (Girardot) to believe he has lost interest in her. She embarks on a series of seductive ploys to reawaken his flagging desires, but to no avail, and her decision to take a lover collapses through lack of courage. All, however, ends happily, but not before this derivative and frenzied farce degenerates into tedium. Filmed in the style of an extended commercial, Pirès appears to be taking a sideswipe at consumerism and advertising (the

film's misleading title refers to a brand of cooking oil), but he has nothing new to say.

Escalier C

France   1985   101 mins   col
Films 7/FR3 Films

d   **Jean-Charles Tacchella**
sc **Jean-Charles Tacchella, Elvire Murail**
ph **Jacques Assuérus**
m   **Raymond Alessandrini**
    Robin Renucci, Jean-Pierre Bacri, Catherine Leprince, Jacques Bonaffé, Jacques Weber, Mony-Rey

Lafont (Renucci), a rarefied, egocentric, malicious art critic, and a ruthless womanizer, is jolted by a series of encounters and experiences into reconsidering his character. The film's title refers to the floor of the apartment block where Lafont lives and periodically crosses paths with his neighbours, who a gay artist whose affection he does nothing to discourage. What begins as an intriguing character study degenerates into a superficial and soft-centred film, largely populated by stereotypes, and of no particular distinguishing features.

▶ **Escape To Nowhere** see Silent One, The

▶ **Es Geschah Am Hellichten Tag** see Assault In Broad Daylight

▶ **Es Geschah Am 20 Juli** see Jackboot Mutiny

▶ **Espions, Les** see Spies, The

▶ **Espiritu De La Colmene, El** see Spirit Of The Beehive, The

▶ **Espoir** see Man's Hope

▶ **Eta Dell'Amore, L'** see Age Of Indiscretion, The

▶ **État De Siège** see State Of Siege

▶ **Et Dieu Créa La Femme** see And God Created Woman

▶ **Été Meurtrier, L'** see One Deadly
Summer

Eternal Love

▶ **aka The Bitter Spirit**

▶ **Eien No Hito**

Japan 1961 107 mins bw
Shochiku

d   Keisuke Kinoshita
sc Keisuke Kinoshita
ph Hiroshi Kusuda
m   Chuji Kinoshita
    Hideko Takamine, Yoshi Kato, Keiji
    Sada, Kiyoshi Nonmura, Tatsuya
    Nakadai, Yasushi Nagata, Nobuko Otowa

Sharecropper's daughter Sadako (Takamine)
awaits the return of her sweetheart, Takashi
(Sada) from the war. Meanwhile, Heibei
(Nakadai), son of the wealthy local landowner
is invalided out of the army and forces himself
on Sadako who is left with no choice but to
marry him. For almost three decades, until
the death of Takashi which releases Sadako
from her bitter memories and longings, the
couple live through a miserable marriage,
leavened only by occasional affection. With a
cast led by the accomplished Hideko Takamine, always a sympathetic heroine, Kinoshita
manages to stay just this side of melodrama
in his portrait of an ill-conceived marriage.
The film is compassionate as well as sentimental and lyrical, and its most notable and
imaginative feature is the music: a startlingly
un-Japanese score for Flamenco guitar, with
vocal interpolations used as a linking commentary. After the initial shock, it proves
surprisingly effective.

The Eternal Mask

▶ **Die Ewige Maske**

Austria/Switzerland 1935 88
mins bw
Progress Films

d   Werner Hochbaum
sc Leo Lapaire
ph Oscar Schnirch
m   Anton Profes
    Peter Petersen, Mathias Wieman, Olga
    Tschechowa, Tom Kraa, Thekla Ahrens

A young doctor (Wieman) suffers an acute
nervous breakdown following the death of a
patient he injected with a new serum contrary
to the orders of his superior (Petersen). The
only film for which Hochbaum is remembered
is a vivid and eerie depiction of a psychotic
state realized through Expressionistic devices
reminiscent of *The Cabinet Of Dr Caligari*
(1919).

▶ **Eternal Return, The** see Love Eternal

▶ **Éternel Retour, L'** see Love Eternal

▶ **Étoile Du Nord, L'** see Northern Star,
The

Europa 51

▶ **(US: The Greatest Love)**

Italy 1952 118 mins bw
Ponti/De Laurentiis/Lux

d   Roberto Rossellini
sc Roberto Rossellini, Sandro De Leo,
    Mario Pannunzio, Ivo Perilli, Brunello
    Rondi
ph Aldo Tonti
m   Renzo Rossellini
    Ingrid Bergman, Alexander Knox,
    Giulietta Masina, Ettore Giannini

A frivolous American society woman living
in Rome causes the death of her son. She
seeks redemption by giving her life up to
helping the underprivileged, but is certified
insane. The second collaboration between
Bergman and her director husband was an
improvement on the first, *Stromboli* (1950),
mainly because she was more at ease among
professional actors. Although equally as naive
and melodramatic as its predecessor, the film
carries through it a genuine feeling of spirituality, especially from the moment Bergman's
face in shadow comes into the light when she
sees the hope of salvation.

Even Dwarfs Started Small

▶ **Auch Zwerge Haben Klein
Angefangen**

W. Germany 1970 96 mins bw
Herzog

d   **Werner Herzog**
sc **Werner Herzog**
ph **Thomas Mauch**
m   **Florian Fricke, Spanish folk music**
    Helmut Döring, Gerd Gickel, Paul
    Glauer, Gisela Hertwig

A group of dwarfs living in a penal institution on a bleak island take advantage of the Prison Governor's absence to indulge in an escalating series of acts of rebellion and destruction. Already taking giant strides down the unbeaten track in his second feature, Herzog cast dwarfs in all the roles. Although it produced the desired bizarre and blackly comic effect, the film is too systematic and forced to provide a distorted mirror-image of society. At least it gave more roles to 'small people' than even *The Wizard Of Oz*, and was happily free from any pity or easy solutions.

Evening Bell

▶ **Wan Zhong**

China 1987 89 mins col
August First Film Studio/China Film

d   **Wu Ziniu**
sc **Wu Ziniu, Wang Yifei**
ph **Hou Yong**
m   **Ma Jianping**
    Tao Zeru, Liu Ruolei, Ge Yaming

A few months after World War II a small unit of Chinese soldiers attempts to persuade a larger unit of starving Japanese troops to surrender. However, the Japanese continue their wartime atrocities and resort to cannibalism. The gentle title of this film, held up for two years before being released, masks a stark and cruel saga. The director, one of the 'Fifth Generation' school, has created an impressive wide-screen epic in the manner of his earlier *The Last Day Of Winter* (1986). The painful tale is told in a taciturn, almost abstract, symmetrical style, never playing up the sensationalism of the subject nor underlining any message. The images themselves are eloquent testimony enough.

Evening Dress

▶ **(US: Menage)**
▶ **Tenue De Soirée**

France 1986 85 mins col

Hachette Première/DD Productions/Ciné Valse

d   **Bertrand Blier**
sc **Bertrand Blier**
ph **Jean Penzer**
m   **Serge Gainsbourg**
    Gérard Depardieu, Michel Blanc, Miou-Miou, Michel Creton, Mylène Demongeot

A macho homosexual criminal (Depardieu) accosts a couple in a bar one night and persuades them into burglary and a *ménage-à-trois*, but he turns out to have designs on the nondescript little husband rather than the gorgeous wife, with surprising consequences. Blier's predilection to shock is here let loose on an outrageous black comedy which upends conventional *bourgeois* notions of morality. Depardieu is superb, but it is Michel Blanc's conversion into a camp queen that is the highlight of the fun.

Best Actor (Michel Blanc) Cannes 1986

▶ **Every Man For Himself** see Slow Motion

▶ **Every Man For Himself And God Against All** see Enigma Of Kaspar Hauser, The

Everything For Sale

▶ **Wszystko Na Sprzedaz**

Poland 1968 105 mins bw
Film Polski

d   **Andrzej Wajda**
sc **Andrzej Wajda**
ph **Witold Sobociński**
m   **Andrzej Korzyński**
    Andrzej Lapícki, Beata Tyszkiewicz,
    Daniel Olbrychski, Elzbieta Czyżewska

During the making of a film the leading man, who leads a complicated personal and professional life, is killed while trying to jump on to a moving train. In 1967, aged 40, the short-sighted actor Zbigniew Cybulski, who starred several times for Wajda, died in the manner depicted in this ambiguous and earnest tribute, although his name is never mentioned here. The less charismatic Olbrychski plays the actor, and Lapicki is good as the Wajda surrogate.

▶ **Everything's Ready Nothing Works** see All Screwed Up

Eve Wants To Sleep

▶ **Ewa Chce Spac**

Poland   1957   98 mins   bw
Syrena Film Unit/Film Polski

d   **Tadeusz Chmielewski**
sc **Tadeusz Chmielewski, Andrzej Czekalski**
ph **Stefan Matyjaszkiewicz, Josef Stawiski**
m   **Henryk Czyz**
    Barbara Lass, Stanislaw Mikulski,
    Ludwik Benoit, Zygmunt Zintel

Sixteen-year-old Eve (Lass) arrives at technical school a day too soon and, in her attempts to find somewhere to sleep, encounters thieves and police helping each other plan a jewel robbery. A crazy comedy, in which even the film crew gets involved in the end, blew like a gust of fresh air from Poland in the late 1950s.

Evil Eden

▶ **La Mort en Ce Jardin**
▶ **aka La Muerte En Esta Jardin**

France/Mexico   1956   105 mins   col
Dismage Producciones Tepeyac

d   **Luis Buñuel**
sc **Luis Alcoriza, Luis Buñuel, Raymond Queneau, Gabriel Arout**
ph **Jorge Stahl Jr**
m   **Paul Misraki**
    Georges Marchal, Simone Signoret, Charles Vanel, Michel Piccoli, Michèle Girardon, Tito Junco

When anti-military rebellion erupts in a remote Central American tin-mining settlement, a group of French people led by Chark (Marchal), an escaped prisoner, make for Brazil via the river. The party consists of the town prostitute (Signoret), a compromised priest (Piccoli), an old innkeeper (Vanel) who goes mad, and the latter's deaf-mute daughter (Girardon). Forced to abandon their boat, the fugitives trek through the jungle, enduring all manner of hardship and deprivation. This is a straightforward adventure yarn, indeed, a potboiler, populated by a colourful mix of goodies and baddies, but Buñuel's familiar

targets – greed and hypocrisy – are still in evidence. The cast doesn't quite live up to its promise, but the film boasts richly textured photography and lighting which make the locations tangibly real.

▶ **Ewa Chce Spac** see Eve Wants To Sleep

▶ **Ewige Maske, Die** see Eternal Mask, The

The Executioner

▶ **(US: Not On Your Life)**
▶ **El Verdugo**

Spain   1963   110 mins   bw
Naga/Zebra

d   **Luis Berlanga**
sc **Luis Berlanga, Rafael Azcona, Ennio Flaiano**
ph **Tonino Delli Colli**
m   **Miguel Asins Arbó**
    Nino Manfredi, Emma Penella, José Isbert, José Luis Lopez Vázquez

An undertaker's assistant (Manfredi), who marries an executioner's daughter (Penella), agrees to take over his father-in-law's job but finds he can't go through with it. Despite cuts by Franco's censor, the film is not only a condemnation of capital punishment but contains social criticism spiked with gallows humour. Typical is the scene where the executioner is reluctantly dragged along to perform his macabre duty on a calm and dignified political prisoner.

The Expedition

▶ **Abhijan**

India   1962   150 mins   bw
Abhijatrik Calcutta

d   **Satyajit Ray**
sc **Satyajit Ray**
ph **Soumendu Roy**
m   **Satyajit Ray**
    Soumitra Chatterjee, Waheeda Rehman, Robi Ghosh, Ruma Guha Thakurta

A taxi driver (Chatterjee) gets involved with a variety of characters including drug smugglers, white-slavers, and a prostitute. The film is closer in style and in its picaresque plot to commercial Indian cinema (it even borrows Hindi star Waheeda Rehman) than to the best of Ray's work, but there is enough of the director's humanity and humour to make it more than run of the mill.

▶ **Experiment In Evil** see Testament Of Dr Cordelier, The

▶ **Extase** see Ecstasy

The Exterminating Angel

▶ **El Angel Exterminador**

Mexico 1962 95 mins bw
Ininci/Films 59

d **Luis Buñuel**
sc **Luis Buñuel, Luis Alcoriza**
ph **Gabriel Figueroa**
m **Alessandro Scarlatti, Paradisi, Gregorian Chants**
Silvia Pinal, Enrique Rambal, Jacqueline Andere, Claudio Brook, José Baviera, Rosa Elena Durgel

The guests at a high-society party find themselves unable to leave the room where they are gathered. As days pass without food, water or servants (who have all managed to leave), their social façade crumbles, revealing bestial qualities beneath. One of Buñuel's most effective parables is a savage attack on the *bourgeoisie*, launched in his mature blackly humorous and surreal manner. 'Basically I simply see a group of people who couldn't do what they want to . . . that kind of dilemma, the impossibility of satisfying a simple desire, often occurs in my movies.' Typical moments such as the introduction of a bear and a flock of sheep into the manor are reminders of *L'Âge D'Or*. After *Viridiana* the year before, the director himself proved he had entered his golden age.

The Extraordinary Adventures Of Mr West In The Land Of The Bolsheviks

▶ **Neobychainiye Priklucheniya Mistera Vesta V Stranya Bolshevikov**

USSR 1924 2600 m bw
Goskino

d **Lev Kuleshov**
sc **N. Asseiev**
ph **A. Levitski**
m **Silent**
Porfiry Podobed, Boris Barnet, Alexandra Khokhlova, Vsevolod Pudovkin

Accompanied by Jed (Barnet), his faithful cowboy aide, Mr J. West (Podobed), president of the YMCA, leaves the USA for a tour of the Soviet Union, his head full of images of leering evil Bolsheviks. When he gets to the USSR, a petty gang exploits his prejudices, but he soon gets to know the real Russian people. Kuleshov, who wrote the first theoretical studies of montage, put his researches at the service of this gag-filled satire. Using mobile cameras, quick cutting and sequences derived from American chase films, the film manages to deride the West's stereotyped view of 'mad, savage, Russians', while creating its own stereotyped Americans – the Harold Lloyd-type Mr West, clutching an American flag, and Jed firing six-guns and roping motorcyclists like steers from the top of a Moscow taxi.

The Eyes Of The Mummy

▶ **Die Augen Der Mummie Ma**

Germany 1918 55 mins bw
Projektions – AG

d **Ernst Lubitsch**
sc **Hans Kräly, Emil Rameau**
ph **Alfred Hansen**
m **Silent**
Pola Negri, Emil Jannings, Harry Liedtke, Max Laurence

A young English painter (Liedtke) rescues a girl (Negri) from an Egyptian tomb where she is being kept prisoner by a resurrected mummy (Jannings) who then pursues her to London. The first of six films that the alluring, dark-eyed, black-haired Negri made with Lubitsch in Germany, it was also the director's first important picture. Curiously, he received no credit on screen in the USA. Lubitsch used tracking shots to create horror, while Jannings was chilling in the leading role.

Eyes Without A Face

▶ **(US: The Horror Chamber Of Doctor Faustus)**

▶ **Les Yeux Sans Visage**

France 1959 90 mins bw
Champs Elysées/Lux

d **Georges Franju**
sc **Jean Redon**
ph **Eugen Schüfftan**
m **Maurice Jarre**
  Pierre Brasseur, Alida Valli, Edith Scob,

Juliette Mayniel

A plastic surgeon (Brasseur), responsible for the car crash in which his daughter (Scob) is hideously disfigured, gets his assistant (Valli) to kidnap and murder beautiful girls so that their facial tissue may be grafted on to his daughter's face. Unlike Hollywood's approach to this sort of material, Franju attempted to film this horror movie in a realistic and, above all, frightening manner, although it remains often poetic and haunting. However, it is too conscious of elevating the sordid tale and of its debts to Cocteau and early German cinema.

Fabian

W. Germany 1980 116 mins col
Regina Ziegler/UA

d **Wolf Gremm**
sc **Wolf Gremm, Hans Borgalt**
ph **Jürgen Wagner**
m **Charles Kalman**
   Hans P. Hallwach, Silvia Janisch,
   Brigitte Mira, Hermann Lause, Ivan
   Desny

Although Fabian (Hallwach), who works in an advertising agency in pre-war Berlin, sees the injustices around him, he spends his nights prowling the bars, brothels and nightclubs and enjoying the easy women. Eventually, reality intrudes when a friend (Lause) commits suicide, and he finds himself in love with a woman (Janisch) who becomes a film star. We're in the familiar *Cabaret* territory of decadent Berlin in the late 1920s, but Gremm brings some new insights to his serio-comic view of the era. He also manages to recapture the look of German movies of the time, but the sex scenes are more realistic.

The Face

▶ **(US: The Magician)**

▶ **Ansiktet**

Sweden 1958 103 mins bw
Svensk Filmindustri

d **Ingmar Bergman**
sc **Ingmar Bergman**
ph **Gunnar Fischer**
m **Erik Nordgren**
   Max Von Sydow, Ingrid Thulin, Gunnar
   Björnstrand, Naima Wifstrand, Åke
   Fridell, Bibi Andersson

Vogler (Von Sydow), a 19th-century mesmerist and magician, is stopped, with his troupe by officials at the gates of Stockholm and subjected to severe questioning in an attempt to reveal him as a fraud. A favourite Bergman theme, that of the duality of the artist, is forcefully expounded in this tragicomic Gothic study of a man, part charlatan part Messiah, which Von Sydow's mask/face expresses admirably. The character is, figuratively, a cousin to the wordless actress in *Persona* (1966), also called Vogler (Elizabeth).

Special Jury Prize Venice 1959

The Face Of Another

▶ **Tanin No Kao**

Japan 1966 121 mins bw
Hiroshi Teshigahara Productions

d **Hiroshi Teshigahara**
sc **Kobo Abe**
ph **Hiroshi Segawa**
m **Tohru Takemitsu**
   Tatsuya Nakadai, Machiko Kyo, Mikijiro
   Hira, Miki Irie

A scientist (Nakadai), whose face was disfigured in an industrial explosion, hides behind a handsome mask. In this disguise he seduces his wife (Kyo), and then accuses her of adultery. Like Teshigahara's most celebrated film, *Woman Of The Dunes*, this is an allegorical drama, also scripted by Kobo Abe from his own novel, but with a deeper interest in the psychology of the characters. Bizarre it certainly is, and a little distasteful, especially in the depiction of the parallel story of a beautiful woman (Irie, a half-Japanese model), with a hideously scarred left profile, in love with her brother. A lot of heavy significance is placed on questions of identity that remain unresolved, but it does work as a sombre study in alienation.

Face To Face

▶ **Ansikte Mot Ansikte**

Sweden   1975   136 mins   col
Dino De Laurentiis/Cinematograph

d   **Ingmar Bergman**
sc **Ingmar Bergman**
ph **Sven Nykvist**
m   **Mozart**
    Liv Ullmann, Erland Josephson, Gunnar Björnstrand, Aino Taube-Henrikson, Kari Sylwan

A psychiatrist has a nervous breakdown while staying with her grandparents when her husband and daughter are away. Originally made as a four-part series for Swedish TV, this painful, obsessive and airless psycho-drama has the doleful, expressive and lovely face of Liv Ullmann in close-up as the main field of vision. The audience often feels awkwardly excluded from the intimacy created between the Norwegian actress and the director with whom she had lived for five years.

▶ **Fadern** see Father, The

Falbalas

▶ **(US: Paris Frills)**

France   1945   112 mins   bw
Essor

d   **Jacques Becker**
sc **Jacques Becker,**
ph **Nicolas Hayer**
m   **Jean-Jacques Grünewald**
    Raymond Rouleau, Micheline Presle, Jean Chevrier, Gabrielle Dorziat

A top Parisian fashion designer (Rouleau), a successful seducer of women, falls in love with the fiancée (Presle) of a friend (Chevrier), a situation which leads to tragedy. Becker's dazzling but withering look at the world of *haute couture* shows him to be a master stylist in his own right. But the characters and situations don't have the freshness and appeal

typical of his next three Parisian romantic comedies, *Antoine And Antoinette*, *Edward And Caroline* and *Rendez-vous De Juillet*.

The Falcons

▶ **Magasiskola**

Hungary   1970   90 mins   col
Mafilm

d   **István Gaál**
sc **István Gaál**
ph **Elemér Ragályi**
m   **András Szöllösy**
    Ivan Andonov, György Bánffy, Judit Meszléri

A visitor (Andonov) to a falcon-training camp ruled by an iron disciplinarian (Bánffy) finally flees in horror. The film draws an impressive analogy between the taming of birds and a way of life which requires blind obedience. An atmosphere of menace is carefully built up, ending with the hero in a hostile landscape among vibrating telephone wires. A sensitive director of meagre output, Gaál gained international recognition with this picture.

The Fall

▶ **La Caida**

Argentina   1958   86 mins   bw
Argentine Sono

d   **Leopoldo Torre-Nilsson**
sc **Beatriz Guido, Leopoldo Torre-Nilsson**
ph **Alberto Etchebehere**
m   **Juan Carlos Paz**
    Elsa Daniel, Duilio Marzia, Lydia Lamaison, Carlos Lopez Monet

A strictly brought-up young girl (Daniel), on the verge of womanhood, lodges with an eccentric family. Her relations with the parents, their precocious children and a young lawyer, give her a new perspective on life. Torre-Nillsson and his wife Beatriz Guido consolidated the international success of *The House Of The Angel* with a further claustrophobic exploration into Argentinian family structures, seen through the eyes of a virginal girl, played perfectly in both cases by Elsa Daniel.

The Fall

▶ **A Queda**

Brazil 1978 120 mins col
Zoom Cinematográfica/Daga/Nelson
Xavier

d **Ruy Guerra, Nelson Xavier**
sc **Ruy Guerra, Nelson Xavier**
ph **Edgar Moura**
m **Milton Nascimento, Ruy Guerra**
Nelson Xavier, Lima Duarte, Isabel
Ribeiro, Maria Sílva, Hugo Carvana

When José (Carvana) is killed in an accident
on a building site where he worked, his friend
Mario (Xavier) attempts to gain compensation for his widow (Sílva). Although the
management refuses to accept responsibility,
Mario, at the cost of his marriage and his
job, fights on. A sequel to Guerra's acclaimed
The Guns from which sequences are quoted,
it follows the lives of three of the soldiers
from the earlier film. However, during the 15
years between the two films, *Cinema Novo*
had shifted its attention from the peasants to
the urban working class. Guerra directs his
powerful attack on Brazilian capitalism from
different stylistic angles – using still photos,
cinéma vérité techniques and genuine interviews with workers – all combining in a
complex and successful aesthetic whole.

Best Film Berlin 1978

▶ **Fall Jägerstätter, Der** see Refusal,
The

The Fall Of The House Of Usher

▶ **La Chûte De La Maison Usher**

France 1928 48 mins bw
Les Films Jean Epstein

d **Jean Epstein**
sc **Jean Epstein**
ph **Georges Lucas, J.A. Lucas**
m **Silent**
Marguerite Gance, Jean Debucourt,
Charles Lamy, Pierre Hot, Halma

Roderick Usher (Debucourt) buries his sister
(Gance) alive in the large family mansion, but
she returns after death to take her revenge.
Coming out of the French *avant-garde* movement, Epstein recreated the eerie lyricism of
the Edgar Allan Poe story by the device of
slow motion (one of the first times the technique was used in a fictional film) and surreal
sets. Despite a certain over-stylization, there
is much impressive imagery – long, windswept
corridors, the mist-shrouded trees, the burial
with four men carrying a white coffin – and
the macabre features of Marguerite Gance
(wife of Abel Gance) as the *revenant*. Luis
Buñuel was the assistant director.

▶ **Falsche Bewegung** see Wrong
Movement

▶ **Fälschung, Die** see Circle Of Deceit

▶ **Famiglia, La** see Family, The

The Family

▶ **La Famiglia**

Italy 1987 127 mins col Films
Ariane/Cinemax/Massfilm/Cinecitta

d **Ettore Scola**
sc **Ruggero Maccari, Furio Scarpelli, Ettore**
Scola
ph **Ricardo Aronovich**
m **Armando Trovajoli**
Vittorio Gassman, Fanny Ardant,
Stefania Sandrelli, Andrea Occhipinti, Jo
Champa

A saga spanning the period between the birth
of Carlo (Gassman) in 1906 to the day when
he celebrates his eightieth birthday in the
home where four generations of his Italian
upper middle-class family are gathered.
Carlo's main regret is his lost love (Ardent),
the older sister of the woman he married
(Sandrelli). As in *Le Bal* (1984), Scola has
limited himself to a single set – a large apartment where shots of the passage denote the
passage of time – to tell a tale that stretches
through the years. Unlike *Le Bal*, however,
the film only reflects obliquely on the historical and political events taking place outside,

while concentrating on a series of touching and comic vignettes, including a trio of constantly bickering maiden aunts. Photographed mostly in soft focus with a Nino Rota-style music score, it creates a real feeling of family, the damage that time has wreaked on its members and the healing qualities of nostalgia. Unfortunately, like its hero, the film begins to slow down, become confused and ramble a bit as the years go by. But Gassman (and his younger selves) hold the family portrait together, surrounded by a splendid array of other performers.

Family Diary

▶ **Cronaca Familiare**

Italy 1962 122 mins col
Titanus/Metro

d **Valerio Zurlini**
sc **Valerio Zurlini, Mario Missiroli**
ph **Giuseppe Rotunno**
m **Goffredo Petrassi**
   Marcello Mastroianni, Jacques Perrin, Salvo Randone, Sylvie, Valeria Ciangottini

When his younger brother Lorenzo (Perrin) dies from an untreatable disease, Enrico (Mastroianni) is grief-stricken. He leaves the newspaper office where he works to sit in his lodgings and reflect on Lorenzo's short and unhappy life, the circumstances which separated them in childhood, and those that later brought them together in a close and loving relationship in which he tried to act as protector. This leisurely, elegaic and intolerably sad film, played with sensitivity and absolute conviction, is directed with well-gauged fidelity to the semi-autobiographical novel by Vasco Pratolini on which it is based. Zurlini is a superb visual artist, and he evokes feelings, events and atmosphere by use of an Impressionist-painter style to moving and memorable effect, displaying a subtle eye for the significance of small moments.

Family Game

▶ **Kazoku Geemu**

Japan 1983 107 mins col
ATG/New Century Producers/Nikkatsu

d **Yoshimitsu Morita**
sc **Yoshimitsu Morita**
ph **Yonezo Maeda**
   Yusaku Matsuda, Ichirota Miyagawa, Junichi Tsujita, Juzo Itami, Saori Yuki

The Numatas are the perfect Japanese nuclear family: submissive wife, hardworking, self-important husband who drinks too much and limits his communication with his two boys to anxiety over their school marks. When yet another in a long line of tutors is hired to coach the bored and recalcitrant younger son, the outcome is surprising. This absurdist satire – a funny, intriguing, ambiguous critique of the aspirations and lifestyle of modern industrial society – is set largely inside the family's high rise apartment with its panoramic view of factories. Morita, a leading director of what is loosely termed the New Japanese cinema, owes a clear debt to the old: clean, crystalline images are framed with a formalism and breathtaking sense of composition somewhat reminiscent of Ozu, but his sense of the ridiculous is very much his own. Alas, the latter tends to the coarse-grained and lets him down in the undisciplined closing sequences of a beautifully played movie that is full of unexpected tenderness.

Family Life

▶ **Zycie Rodzinne**

Poland 1971 93 mins col
Tor Unit Film Polski

d **Krzysztof Zanussi**
sc **Krzysztof Zanussi**
ph **Witold Sobociński**
m **Wojciech Kilar**
   Daniel Olbrychski, Jan Nowicki, Jan Kreczmar, Maja Komorowska, Halina Mikolajska

After six years in Warsaw, a design engineer (Olbrychski) reluctantly returns to his family home, a dilapidated mansion in the country. There he has to come to terms with his alcoholic father and slightly deranged sister, as well as with his own life. Zanussi's second film is more traditional than his first, *The Structure Of Crystals*, although it has the same questioning intelligence. A controlled, melancholy mood piece, sustained by good acting and careful lighting, it is lacking in emotion.

The Fanatics

▶ **Les Fanatiques**

France 1957 92 mins bw
Cinégraph/Coopérative Générale Du
Cinéma/Les Films Régent

d **Alex Joffé**
sc **Alex Joffé, Jean Levitte**
ph **L.H. Burel**
m **Paul Misraki**
   **Pierre Fresnay, Michel Auclair, Grégoire
   Aslan, Françoise Fabian, Tilda Thamar**

A political hit-man (Fresnay) is detailed to blow up the private plane carrying a South American dictator (Aslan) home from France. When, at the eleventh hour, the General changes his flight to a regular airline carrying 50 other passengers, the hit-man's assistant (Auclair) balks at carrying out the assassination. This French approach to the kind of high-tension thriller popular in Hollywood was made with formula expertise and acted, notably by Fresnay, with cold, mechanical efficiency. Although offering some excitement, the film was already rather old hat by the time of its release abroad in 1960. Today, in the age of the hijack, it is more interesting, with its moral argument about the killing of innocent civilians no longer the preserve of commercial film-makers.

▶ **Fanatiques, Les** see Fanatics, The

▶ **Fanfan La Tulipe** see Fanfan The Tulip

Fanfan The Tulip

▶ **Fanfan La Tulipe**

France 1951 104 mins bw
Filmsonor/Les Films Ariane/Amato

d **Christian-Jaque**
sc **René Wheeler, Jean Fallet, Christian-
   Jaque**
ph **Christian Matras**
m **Georges Van Parys, Maurice Thiriet**
   Gérard Philipe, Gina Lollobrigida, Noël

Roquevert, Marcel Herrand, Geneviève
Page, Sylvia Pelayo

To escape a shotgun (or sword) wedding, the happy-go-lucky Fanfan (Philipe) is persuaded to join the army of Louis XV (Herrand) by the recruiting officer's daughter (Lollobrigida). She tells him that his destiny is to marry the king's daughter and, no sooner is he made a soldier than he rescues the princess (Pelayo) and Madame Pompadour (Page) from coach robbers. After almost single-handedly defeating the Austrian army, Fanfan realises all his dreams. This satire on Douglas Fairbanks-style movies and historical romance moves at a rapid pace without sacrificing splendid comic characterisations or witty lines. The last and best of three films made by the dashing Philipe for Christian-Jaque, it merrily swashbuckled its way into the international hit category.

Best Director Cannes 1952

▶ **Fängelse** see Devil's Wanton, The

▶ **Fangschuss, Der** see Coup De Grâce

Fanny

France 1932 128 mins bw
Marcel Pagnol/Braunberger-Richebe

d **Marc Allégret**
sc **Marcel Pagnol**
ph **Nicolas Toporkoff**
m **Vincent Scotto**
   **Raimu, Orane Demazis, Pierre Fresnay,
   Charpin, Alida Rouffe, Robert Vattier**

Fanny (Demazis), expecting the child of Marius (Fresnay) who left her to go to sea, marries Panisse (Charpin), an elderly widower. When Marius returns, his father César (Raimu) persuades him to renounce any claim on the child. The second and best-directed of the so-called *Pagnol Trilogy* picks up exactly where *Marius* ended, retaining the latter's vitality, warm humour and depth of character. The performances (excepting the pudding-faced Demazis, Pagnol's then wife) are a joy to behold – witness Raimu's feigned indifference at not hearing from his son – and Pagnol's dialogue displays supreme comic skill. The film's success enabled him to build his own studio near Marseilles.

Fanny And Alexander

▶ **Fanny Och Alexander**

Sweden 1982 188 mins col
AB Cinematograph/Svensk
Filminstituten/Swedish TV One/
Gaumont

d **Ingmar Bergman**
sc **Ingmar Bergman**
ph **Sven Nykvist**
m **Daniel Bell**
    Gunn Wallgren, Börje Ahlstedt, Christina Schollin, Bertil Guve, Pernilla Alwin, Gunnar Björnstrand, Jan Malmsjö, Ewa Froeling, Erland Josephson, Harriet Andersson

The well-to-do, loving and ebullient Ekdahl family gathers to celebrate Christmas. After the actor-father of 10-year-old Alexander (Guve) and eight-year-old Fanny (Alwin) dies, their mother marries a sadistic minister whose cruelty leads Grandmother Ekdahl's Jewish friend and lover to rescue them. Happiness and balance is restored as new babies are born and the family gathers once more to celebrate. Bergman's most optimistic film creates pure enchantment as comedy, tragedy, romance, realism and fantasy blend into a perfect evocation of childhood, place and period (turn-of-the-century Sweden), caught in glowing images by Sven Nykvist. Announced as Bergman's final film, it offers a superlative culmination of his 37 years as one of the cinema's greatest artists.

Best Foreign Film Oscar 1983

▶ **Fanny Och Alexander** see Fanny And Alexander

The Fantastic Night

▶ **La Nuit Fantastique**

France 1942 89 mins bw
U.T.C.

d **Marcel L'Herbier**
sc **Louis Chavance**

ph **Pierre Montazel**
m **Maurice Thiriet**
    Fernand Gravey, Micheline Presle, Saturnin Fabre, Charles Granval

A student (Gravey), who works as a night porter, continually dreams of a mysterious woman in white (Presle). When he meets her in reality, he finds she has a father (Fabre) and a fiancé (Granval), both of them unpleasant. He and the woman have a series of fantastic adventures, so that he is still not sure whether he's dreaming or not. The most widely-known of L'Herbier's sound films is a comedy-fantasy tinged with pessimism. Although restricted by certain conventions of commercial French cinema, the former *avant-garde* director created a palpable enough dream world for the audience to identify with the dreamer-hero.

Fantômas

France 1913 75 mins bw
Gaumont

d **Louis Feuillade**
sc **Louis Feuillade**
ph **Guérin**
m **Silent**
    René Navarre, Bréon, Georges Melchior, Renée Carl, Jane Faber

Fantômas (Navarre), arch-criminal and master of disguise, continues to defeat Inspector Juve (Bréon) and ace-reporter Fandor (Melchior). Feuillade's first great success was a serial in three episodes based on an extremely popular series of detective novels by Pierre Souvestre and Marcel Allain. While they are unread (and unreadable) today, the film, with its chases, robberies, and kidnappings, brilliantly mixing real locations with studio settings, can still be enjoyed. The director's genius for location is best seen in the shoot-out on the Quai De Bercy between Fantômas and Juve, using wine barrels as shields. Feuillade went on to make four further Fantômas serials, and the character has been revived in later films.

Fantômas

France 1964 105 mins col

P.A.C./S.N.E.G.(Paris)/P.C.M.(Rome)

d **André Hunebelle**
sc **Jean Halain, Pierre Foucaud**
ph **Marcel Grignon**
m **Michel Magne**
   **Jean Marais, Louis De Funès, Mylène
   Demongeot, Marie-Hélène Arnaud,
   Robert Dalban**

Fandor, a journalist, invents a sensational interview with the infamous criminal Fantômas and publishes it as the real thing. A displeased Fantômas kidnaps the newspaperman, demanding a follow-up article telling the truth but, on his release, Fandor is held for police questioning. His editor writes another hoax piece and Fandor is again seized by Fantômas. This ham-fisted dreary and feeble film is a travesty of Feuillade's famous silent serial. There are one or two striking set-pieces and the short-lived novelty of Jean Marais essaying a double role as journalist and villain, but De Funès' hammy performance as the police inspector is dreadful and, as the film is often released with excrutiating dubbing, it is best avoided.

▶ **Fantôme De La Liberté, Le** see
Phantom Of Liberty, The

▶ **Fantômes Du Chapelier, Les** see
Hatter's Ghosts, The

▶ **Faraon** see Pharaoh

▶ **Farceur, Le** see Joker, The

Farewell

▶ **Abschied**

Germany 1930 71 mins bw
UFA

d **Robert Siodmak**
sc **Emeric Pressburger, Irma Von Cube**
ph **Eugen Schüfftan**
m **Erwin Bootz**
   **Aribert Mog, Brigitte Horney, Vladimir
   Sokoloff, Emilia Unda, Konstantin Mic**

Life in a boarding house in West Berlin populated by a range of characters, including a ruined baron (Sokoloff), a skirt-chasing Russian emigré (Mic), a young salesman (Mog) and the girlfriend (Horney) he must leave. After his debut co-directing the silent *People On Sunday*, Siodmak made his first solo feature, a kind of anti-*Grand Hotel* comedy-drama. The film's imaginative manipulation of sound, the fluent use of the enclosed area of the *pension*, and the vivid character sketches, launched the director into his often neglected but excellent German period (necessarily brief, thanks to Hitler).

Farewell

▶ **Proshchanie**

USSR 1981 126 mins col
Mosfilm

d **Elem Klimov**
sc **Larisa Shepitko, Rudolf Tyurin, German
   Klimov**
ph **Alexei Rodionov, Yuri Skhirtladze, Sergei
   Taraskin**
m **V. Artyomov, A. Shnitke**
   **Stefaniya Stayuta, Lev Durov, Alexei
   Petrenko, Leonid Kryuk, Vadim
   Yakovenko**

An old village in Siberia is to be destroyed and its peasant community, locked into ancient ritual, resettled in a development of faceless apartment blocks. Darya (Stayuta) opposes the move, preferring to die rather than acquiesce, while her son works as foreman of the operation. The whole period, from the announcement of the scheme to its completion, is covered, presenting a conflict between the old order and the new, and a record of the price that has to be paid for progress. Klimov's film unfolds in a controlled, schematic style, focusing on the landscape as the centre of its debate. The result is a finely composed work which reflects a dilemma only too familiar in the West. Larisa Shepitko, Klimov's wife, was to direct *Farewell*, but was killed in a motor smash in 1980.

The Farewell

▶ **Jaahyvaiset**

Finland 1982 90 mins col

Oy Mainos TV Raklam/Swedish Film Institute/Sveriges TV2

d Tuija-Maija Niskanen
sc Eija-Elina Bergholm
ph Esa Vuorinen, Lasse Karlsson
Carl-Axel Heiknert, Sanna Hultman, Pirkko Nurmi, Kerstin Tidelius, Gunnar Björnstrand

A child grows to womanhood in an upper-class family at the time of World War II, and clashes with her stern father over many matters, including her right to live as a Lesbian. This first feature by one of Finland's few women directors, succeeds in creating a claustrophobic atmosphere by confining most of the action to the old family mansion. However, though the psychology of the heroine is well explored, the theme is familiar from many other films about oppressive Scandinavian families.

Far From the War

▶ **Yuanlizhanzhengde Niandai**

China 1988 88 mins col
August First Film Studio

d Hu Mei
sc Li Baolin
ph Zhang Li
m Zheng Qiufeng
Huang Zongluo, Wang Xueqi, Zhu Lin

A veteran soldier (Zongluo), now in retirement and left alone with no orders to follow, has to take individual decisions for the first time in many years. He has great difficulty in adjusting to civilian life and communicating with his military cadet son (Xueqi) and his young family. The second film by 32-year-old Hu Mei after *Army Nurse*, which was based on many of the director's own experiences in the military, concentrates on the psychology of an old soldier and questions the values of the society he fought for. But Hu Mei, like many of her contemporaries known as Fifth Generation directors, does not go for easy answers and looks with a humorous and perceptive eye at various sides of the situation through different members of one family. Although the characters could be taken to represent different aspects of Chinese opinion, she does not force the

wider perspective, but fits the ideas into a neat plot.

Far From Vietnam

▶ **Loin De Vietnam**

France 1967 115 mins bw/col
SLON

d Jacques Demy, Jean-Luc Godard, Claude Lelouch, Alain Resnais, Joris Ivens, Agnès Varda, Chris Marker, William Klein, Ruy Guerra
sc Over 38 writers,
ph photographers,
m musicians,
and performers in a co-operative effort

Thirteen reflections on the war in Vietnam, including newsreel shots of American bombing, demonstrations in the USA, a speech by Fidel Castro, a North Vietnamese travelling theatre, an anti-war song from folk-singer Tom Paxton, and Jean-Luc Godard behind a 35 mm camera explaining why he found it impossible to make a film on Vietnam. The question he asks is 'What possible help can a film-maker contribute to the Vietnamese struggle?' The rest of the film tries to answer it in various ways, some more satisfactorily than others. Alain Resnais and his writer Jacques Sternberg offer another interesting self-enquiry by showing an intellectual trying to justify his reluctance to take a moral stand on the war. On the whole, it was a timely propaganda piece, financed by Chris Marker's SLON independent company. It may still have lessons for us today.

▶ **Färö – Dokument 1979** see Färö 1979

Färö 1979

▶ **Färö – Dokument 1979**

Sweden 1979 103 mins col
Cinematograph

d Ingmar Bergman
sc Ingmar Bergman
ph Arne Carlsson
m Svante Pettersson, Sigvard Huldt, Dag

and Lena, Ingmar Nordströms, Strix Q,
Rock De Luxe, Ola And The Janglers
Richard Östman, Ulla Silvergren, Annelie
Nyström, Per Broman, Irene Broman

Ingmar Bergman (off-camera) conducts a
series of interviews with the inhabitants of
the small Baltic island of Farö where he lives
and where he has set a number of his films.
Ten years earlier, Bergman had made *The
Farö Document*, when he felt the central
government was killing the life and traditions
of the island. Many of the same people he
spoke to a decade earlier talk eloquently
about the place, and Bergman narrates and
watches them go about their work, which
includes the gruesome slaughter of a pig. It
makes for a fascinating, affectionate and
rather melancholy home movie by one of the
world's greatest directors.

Farrebique

France   1947   85 mins   bw
L'Écran Français/Les Films Etienne
Lallier

d   **Georges Rouquier**
sc **Georges Rouquier**
ph **André Dantan**
m   **Henri Sauguet**

The life of a peasant family in a remote area
of South-west France from December 1944
to November 1945, including the struggles in
work, the harvesting, an engagement, a death,
and baking of bread. Rouquier's first feature
was made in his native Massif Central, using
a family known to him. This personal involvement, the affectionate and detailed rendering
of the people's lives and the lyricism of the
cutting and camerawork make it one of the
finest of documentaries. The stunning time-
lapse photography on the coming of spring
was actually shot by Daniel Sarrade and
Maurice Delille in the Jardin Des Plantes in
Paris.

▶ **Fast And Sexy** see Anna Of Brooklyn

▶ **Fast, Fast** see Deprisa, Deprisa

▶ **Fate Of A Man** see Destiny Of A Man

Father

▶ **Apa**

Hungary   1966   95 mins   bw
Hungarofilm-Mafilm Studio 3

d   **István Szabó**
sc **István Szabó**
ph **Sándor Sára**
m   **János Gonda, Mahler**
    **András Bálint, Miklós Gábor, Kati
    Solyom, Klari Tolnay, Dani Erdélyi**

A growing boy (Bálint) attempts to come to
terms with truths about his dead father
(Gábor) whom he remembers only as a hero
who helped the Jews during the war. He has
a Jewish girlfriend, (Solyom) and, after the
1956 uprising, they both begin to question
their parents' generation. Szabó's second film,
told in a technically assured fragmentary
style, explores a subject that forms the basis
for most of his work – the relationship of
Hungary's post-war generation to the past.
Here it is symbolized by a sensitively and
humorously observed personal history, acted
with great conviction, especially by Bálint.

The Father

▶ **Fadern**

Sweden   1969   100 mins   col
Svenska Filminstitutet

d   **Alf Sjöberg**
sc **Alf Sjöberg**
ph **Lars Björne**
m   **Torbjörn Lundquist**
    **Georg Rydeberg, Gunnel Lindblom, Lena
    Nyman, Jan-Olaf Strandberg, Tord Stal**

A retired army captain (Rydeberg) and his
wife (Lindblom) continually fight over Berta
(Nyman), their beloved daughter. Because the
father plans for Berta to board out, and the
mother is determined to keep her at home,
the latter schemes to destroy her husband
mentally. 'The border between theatre and
film is as flexible as the people in Strindberg's
work – there is no set form saying how a film
should be made. *In absurdum* – everything in
film is really theatre.' So said Sjöberg about
the transposition of his acclaimed Royal Dramatic Theatre of Stockholm production to
the screen, using the same cast. It was man-

aged without much loss or any real gain. What we have been given is the chance to see some wonderful acting in Strindberg's powerful play, in its original language, directed by a specialist in his work. Sjöberg's most famous film remains the excellent *Miss Julie* (1950).

Father And Son

▶ **Fuzi Qing**

Hong Kong 1981 96 mins col
Feng Huang Motion Picture Company

d **Allen Fong (aka Fong Yuk-Ping)**
sc **Chan Chiu, Lee Bik-Wah, Cheung Kin-Ting**
ph **Patrick Wong**
m **Violet Lam**
   Shek Lui, Lee Yu-Tin, Cheng Yu-Or, Chan Sung, Yan Sin-Mei, Cheung Kwok-Ming, Kung Yee

After graduating with a degree in film in America, Law Ka-Hing (Yu-Or) returns to Hong Kong for his father's funeral. He reflects on his childhood and adolescence in a hillside shanty town, pursuing a fantasy world through comic books, magic lantern shows and attempts to make home movies – all of which causes conflict with his father and leads him into trouble at school. This first independent feature from a Hong Kong television director is clearly an autobiographical piece, reflecting the struggles of a would-be film-maker and confirmed fantasist to realize his ambitions in the face of his father's desire to push him into more traditional pursuits. Fong draws a vivid picture of the squalid environment and depicts the complex father-son relationship with truth. This is an entertaining film and refreshing in its departure from the all-pervasive martial arts genre from Hong Kong.

▶ **Father Master** see Padre Padrone

▶ **Fatti Di Gente Perbene** see Drama Of The Rich

Faust

Germany 1926 136 mins bw
UFA

d **F. W. Murnau**
sc **Hans Kyser**
ph **Carl Hoffmann**
m **Silent**
   Gösta Ekman, Emil Jannings, Camilla Horn, Wilhelm Dieterle, Yvette Guilbert

Faust (Ekman), an elderly professor, sells his soul to the devil in exchange for a return to his youth. Murnau's last film in Germany prior to going to Hollywood was a lavish studio production, with the masterly sets, constructed by the leading German designers Robert Herlth and Walter Röhrig, related to the camera set-ups to avoid any staginess. The chiaroscuro, the imagery derived from Romantic painters such as Caspar David Friedrich, and the magical photography, all cast a spell. There are imposing performances too from Ekman, Jannings (Mephistopholes), and Horn (Marguerite) in a part intended for Lillian Gish.

▶ **Faustrecht Der Freiheit** see Fox

▶ **Faute De L'Abbé Mouret, La** see Sin Of Father Mouret, The

▶ **Favoris De La Lune, Les** see Favourites Of The Moon

Favourites Of The Moon

▶ **Les Favoris De La Lune**

France 1984 101 mins col
Philippe Dussart Co/FR3/Ministère De La Culture/RAI TV

d **Otar Iosseliani**
sc **Otar Iosseliani, Gérard Brach**
ph **Philippe Theaudière**
m **Nicolas Zourabichvili**
   Katja Rupé, Jean-Pierre Beauviala, Christiane Bailly, Mathieu Amalric, Alix De Montaigu, Pascal Aubier

The separate paths of dozens of Parisian thieves constantly criss-cross as money, paintings and *objets d'art* are passed from one to another. For a good while the film seems to be a series of incoherent incidents concerning inexplicable characters. But Iosselliani, a Georgian in Paris, has a scheme which becomes clearer if not more involving. What the kaleidoscopic method reveals is the greed and emptiness of Western *bourgeois* society. The tiny details begin to add up, but the camera never lingers long enough for us to get to know any of the characters, mostly played by the director's friends. There are rewards, but they are few and far between.

Special Jury Prize Venice 1984

Fear

▶ **Angst**

▶ **aka La Paura**

W. Germany-Italy 1954 91 mins bw
Minerva/Ariston/Aniene

d **Roberto Rossellini**
sc **Roberto Rossellini, Sergio Amedei, Franz Graf Treuberg**
ph **Peter Heller**
m **Renzo Rossellini**
   Ingrid Bergman, Mathias Wieman, Kurt Kreugar, Elsie Aulinger

The wife of a German factory owner is black-mailed by the mistress of the man she had an affair with while her husband was in a POW camp. The final film Rossellini made with his then-wife Bergman was an unwieldy psychological thriller about a marriage in crisis, the theme of four of their six uneven collaborations. (The Rossellinis' own marriage was nearing its end.) Based on a story by Stefan Zweig, the picture displayed many of the faults and the virtues of that curious teaming of Hollywood Swede with Neo-Realist Italian.

Fear Eats The Soul

▶ **(US: Ali: Fear Eats The Soul**

▶ **aka Ali)**

▶ **Angst Essen Seele Auf**

W. Germany 1973 94 mins col
Tango Film

d **Rainer Werner Fassbinder**
sc **Rainer Werner Fassbinder**
ph **Jürgen Jürges**
m **Selections from archive material**
   Brigitte Mira, El Hedi Ben Salem,

Barbara Valentin, Irm Hermann, Peter Gauhe, Rainer Werner Fassbinder

Emmi (Mira), a lonely, widowed charlady, strikes up a friendship with Ali (Ben Salem), a Moroccan mechanic who is equally lonely and half her age. Their relationship meets with outraged disapproval and hostility, particularly when they marry. A serious and realistic articulation of its milieu, this film explores racism (and other pejudices), doing so through a fairly straightforward use of narrative, modelled on Hollywood melodramas of the 1950s, particularly Douglas Sirk's *All That Heaven Allows*.

▶ **Feine Gesellschaft Beschränkte Haftung** see High Society Limited

▶ **Fellini Casanova** see Casanova

Fellini Satyricon

▶ **aka Satyricon**

Italy 1969 129 mins col
PAA/UA/PEA

d **Federico Fellini**
sc **Federico Fellini, Bernadino Zapponi, Brunello Rondi**
ph **Giuseppe Rotunno**
m **Nino Rota, Ilhan Mimaroglu, Tod Dockstader, Andrew Rudin**
   Martin Potter, Hiram Keller, Max Börn, Capucine, Magali Noël, Alain Cuny, Salvo Randone, Lucia Bosé, Tanya Lopert

In Rome *circa* 500 AD, two students (Potter and Keller) go their different ways after fighting over a pretty boy (Börn). They have many adventures before meeting up again, some of which a drunken orgy, imprisonment on a galley ship and a duel with the Minotaur. This adaptation of Petronius' witty fragment is overblown and over-indulgent, but with one or two moments of the director at his grotesque best. It is really *La Dolce Vita* in Ancient Rome with Fellini looking ponderously and with assumed disapproval at the immoral goings-on of a pre-Christian society (and by implication today's), and the 'spiritual' episode is not far from Cecil B. DeMille territory.

Fellini's Roma

▶ **aka Roma**

Italy 1972 128 mins col
Ultra/UA

d   **Federico Fellini**
sc **Federico Fellini**
ph **Giuseppe Rotunno**
m   **Nino Rota**
    Peter Gonzales, Stefano Majore, Britta
    Barnes, Pia De Doses, Fiona Florence,
    Renato Giovannoli, Federico Fellini, Gore
    Vidal

Fellini, making a documentary on Rome, recalls his arrival in the city in his early twenties, the seedy pre-war music halls and the brothels. In present day Rome there is a gigantic traffic jam, the discovery of ancient Roman murals underground and an ecumenical fashion show. On the same lines as *The Clowns, Amarcord,* and *Intervista,* this blend of fantasy, autobiography and documentary is orchestrated by Fellini into a 'nostalgic carefree diary,' as the *maestro* called it. Some of the brew gives off a bad odour, but there are many delicious moments such as the young man's first night in Rome (a splendid bustling set), the very funny music hall scene, the traffic jam (mostly filmed at Cinecittá) and the last screen appearance of Anna Magnani, caught unawares late at night.

▶ **Female Prisoner, The** see Woman
In Chains

▶ **Femme D'À Côté, La** see Woman
Next Door, The

▶ **Femme De L'Aviateur, La** see Aviator's Wife, The

▶ **Femme De Mon Pote, La** see My
Best Friend's Girl

La Femme De Nulle Part

▶ **aka The Woman From Nowhere**

France 1922 70 mins bw
Cosmograph

d   **Louis Delluc**

sc **Louis Delluc**
ph **Alphonse Gibory, Georges Lucas**
m   **Silent**
    Eve Francis, Roger Karl, Michel Duran,
    Gine Avril, André Daven

A woman (Francis), who sacrificed everything for love, returns to the house from which she had fled with her lover years before. An air of disillusionment pervades the penultimate of Delluc's few films (he died of tuberculosis, aged 33, in 1924), a fantasy expertly intermingling memory and sensations. Eve Francis, the director's wife, gives a poignant portrayal in the title role. The Prix Louis Delluc (instigated in 1937) is awarded annually to the best French film of the year.

▶ **Femme Douce, Une** see Gentle Creature, A

▶ **Femme Du Boulanger, La** see Baker's Wife, The

▶ **Femme Est Une Femme, Une** see
Woman Is A Woman, A

La Femme Infidèle

▶ **aka The Unfaithful Wife**

France 1968 98 mins col
Films de la Boétie/Cinégai

d   **Claude Chabrol**
sc **Claude Chabrol**
ph **Jean Rabier**
m   **Pierre Jansen**
    Stéphane Audran, Michel Bouquet,
    Maurice Ronet, Stephen Di Napoli,
    Michel Duchaussoy

A respectable middle-class husband (Bouquet), complacently happy in his marriage, discovers that his wife (Audran) has been having an affair with another man (Ronet). He confronts the lover, suddenly strikes him dead and attempts to get rid of the body. The marriage is saved. Chabrol followed his return to form in *Les Biches* with the even more superior 'Hélène cycle' – films in which his wife Audran played Hélène in variations on the theme of marital infidelity leading to murder. Here, in the first and best, his sharp scalpel is applied brilliantly to the *bourgeois* marriage. He is particularly good in showing that, although passions seethe beneath the surface, the niceties of life (such as family meals) must continue. The three performers at each corner of the triangle match the director's skill and subtlety.

▶ **Femme Mariée, Une** see Married Woman, A

▶ **Femme Ou Deux, Une** see Woman Or Two, A

Femmes De Paris

▶ **(US: Peek-A-Boo)**

▶ **Ah! Les Belles Bacchantes**

France 1954 85 mins col
Optimax/Lux

d **Jean Loubignac**
sc **Robert Dhéry**
ph **René Colas**
m **Gérard Calvi**
Robert Dhéry, Colette Brosset, Louis De Funès, Raymond Bussières, Rosine Luguet, The Bluebell Girls

With the arrival of a variety show in his town, Inspector Leboeuf (De Funès) goes to the rehearsals to make sure it accords with standards of decency and ends up taking part in the show. This is a more or less straightforward record of Robert Dhéry's *Crazy Show*, a stage hit of its time, enveloped by a tenuous plot. Neither the revue – a series of comedy sketches, performed mostly by Dhéry and his wife Brosset and spiced with plenty of 'tasteful' nude scenes – nor the narrative have enough amusing moments to commend them.

▶ **Feng-Kuei-Lai-Te jen** see Boys From Fengkuei, The

▶ **Fenyes Szelek** see Confrontation, The

▶ **Ferestadeh** see Mission, The

▶ **Ferroviere, Il** see Railroad Man, The

▶ **Fête À Henriette, La** see Holiday For Henrietta

Les Fêtes Galantes

France 1965 90 mins col
S.N.E.G.(Paris)/Studio
Bucuresti(Bucharest)

d **René Clair**
sc **René Clair**
ph **Christian Matras**
m **Georges Van Parys**
Jean-Pierre Cassel, Geneviève Casile, Philippe Avron, Jean Richard, György Kovács, Alfred Adam

The army of the Prince De Beaulieu (Richard) lays siege to that of the Maréchal D'Allenberg. Inside the fortress, provisions dwindle while, without, Beaulieu and his lot pass the time in gourmandizing. Joli-Coeur (Cassel), a soldier on the losing end, is sent by the Princess (Casile) to fetch her lover, and has to survive several dangerous hurdles before the siege ends. So does the viewer. Set in the 18th century and pleasing to look at, Clair's film is a knockabout farce that cocks a snook at aristocratic leadership and sympathizes with peasant soldiery. Alas, the jokes are so repetitious and overworked, the characterization so thin and the entire enterprise so heavy-handed that there's little to enjoy in what was, sadly, Clair's last film.

▶ **Feu De Paille, Le** see Fire In The Straw

Le Feu Follet

▶ **aka Will O' The Wisp**

▶ **aka A Time To Live And A Time To Die**

▶ **(US: The Fire Within)**

France 1963 121 mins bw
Nouvelles Editions/Arco

d **Louis Malle**
sc **Louis Malle**
ph **Ghislain Cloquet**
m **Erik Satie**
Maurice Ronet, Lena Skerla, Yvonne Clech, Hubert Deschamps, Jeanne Moreau, Alexandra Stewart

An alcoholic writer (Ronet) leaves a clinic determined to kill himself, but decides to find out first if any of his friends can give him a reason to change his mind. They can't and he calmly shoots himself through the heart. Commenting on the commercial failure of the critically well-received film, Malle said, 'It is such a harsh subject and it's such a depressing movie'. But this poignant, unsentimental study of a spoiled and selfish man still deserving of pity, transcends the merely depressing because of the director's perception and authority, and Ronet's superb performance. Pierre Drieu La Rochelle, the author of the 1931 novel on which the film was based, killed himself in 1945 after having collaborated with the Nazis.

Special Jury Prize Venice 1963

▶ **Feu Mathias Pascal** see Late Mathias Pascal, The

Fever

▶ **Goracza**

Poland 1981 122 mins col
Film Polski, Warsaw Unit

d   **Agnieszka Holland**
sc **Krzysztof Teodor Toeplitz**
ph **Jacek Petrycki**
m   **Jan Kanty Pawluskiewicz**
    Olgierd Lukaszewicz, Barbara Grabowska, Adam Ferency, Tomasz Miedzik, Boguslaw Linda, Ryszard Sobolewski

In 1905, Poland is a troubled country, partitioned between Tsarist Russia, Germany and the Hapsburg Empire. The Russian sector suffers most from oppression, and it is there that a group of anarchists manufactures a bomb and plots to assassinate the Tsar's governor. This is Polish film-making at its best, with a strong and well-controlled narrative line, first-class photography and acting, and a sensitive, in-depth script that subtly reveals the motives and the temperaments of the individual anarchists as the bomb is passed from one to the other. Leon (Lukaszewicz), son of a rich industrialist, is the cold and objective leader; Kielza (Ferency), a simple peasant, is easily betrayed; Kama (Grabowska), the only woman, suffers

a breakdown after she fails to carry out the assassination and ends up insane. A salutary political drama, it engenders the tension of a gripping thriller.

Best Actress (Barbara Grabowska) Berlin 1981

A Few Days With Me

▶ **Quelques Jours Avec Moi**

France 1988 131 mins col
Sara Films/Cinéa Films/Films A2

d   **Claude Sautet**
sc **Claude Sautet, Jerome Tonnerre, Jacques Fleschi**
ph **Jean-François Robin**
m   **Philippe Sarde**
    Daniel Auteuil, Sandrine Bonnaire, Jean-Pierre Marielle, Dominique Lavanant, Danielle Darrieux

Martial (Auteuil), heir to a supermarket empire run by his mother (Darrieux), ends a stay in a psychiatric hospital where he has been attempting to come to terms with his chronic indifference to life. Sent away from Paris to check on some of the family businesses round the country, he stops in Limoges and dines with the greedy, *petit bourgeois* store manager (Marielle) and his objectionable wife (Lavanant). The next day he decides to stay in Limoges, rents an apartment and spirits away Marielle's maid (Bonnaire), with whom he proceeds to enjoy an idyllic love affair for a few days. If the plot, into which several complications infiltrate, takes a little swallowing, this is nonetheless Sautet at his delightful best. He has created a gallery of well-observed secondary characters who revolve round Auteuil, and a set of often funny situations which puncture middle-class pretension and hypocrisy. A well-made romantic comedy, very entertaining and visually pleasing, with the laid-back, sexy Bonnaire and the attractive and versatile Auteuil both perfectly cast.

▶ **Fiancée Du Pirate, La** see Dirty Mary

▶ **Fiancés, The** see Engagement, The

▶ **Fidanzati, I** see Engagement, The

▶ **Fiends, The** see Diaboliques, Les

▶ **Fièvre Monte À El Pao, La** see Republic Of Sin

Fifi La Plume

France   1964   80 mins   bw
Les Films Montsouris

d   **Albert Lamorisse**
sc **Albert Lamorisse**
ph **Pierre Petit, Maurice Fellous**
m   **Jean-Michel Defaye**
    Philippe Avron, Mireille Nègre, Henri Lambert, Raoul Delfosse, Michel De Ré

Fifi (Avron), a burglar specializing in the theft of clocks and watches, escapes from a raid into a circus arena. One thing leads to another, with Fifi becoming the circus birdman and discovering that he can actually fly. He does, across France, before settling down in Brittany with the pretty bareback rider (Nègre). Albert (*Red Balloon*) Lamorisse takes to the skies again with a piece of whimsy that offers some imaginative comic touches and a certain charm. However, the enterprise is too artificial, too sprawling and too unsure of its purpose to hold much appeal for adults.

The Fifth Horseman Is Fear

▶ **... A Paty Jezdec Je Strach**

Czechoslovakia   1965   100 mins   bw
Barrandov Film Studio

d   **Zbyněk Brynych**
sc **Zbyněk Brynych, Jan Kališ, Milan Nejedlý, Ester Krumbachová, Ota Koval**
ph **Jan Kališ**
m   **Jiří Sternwald**
    Miroslav Macháček, Olga Scheinpflugová, Ilja Prachař, Josef Vinklář

During the Nazi occupation of Czechoslovakia, the Jewish Dr Braun (Macháček) is asked to remove a bullet from a wounded Resistance fighter. After the operation, he begins a nightmarish search for morphine through the streets of Prague. Begun as a realistic portrait of the life of Czech Jews under the Nazis, the script was reconceived (by Krumbachová) as an expressionist Orwellian fable that transcended the specific (there are some shots of contemporary Prague). The ominous atmosphere is created by acute camera angles, shock editing and harsh lighting, in contrast to the understated nature of the performances. It is an impressive attempt to show, in the director's words, that 'Fascism is an international disease capable of emerging in many contexts'.

▶ **Fille Aux Yeux D'Or, La** see Girl With The Golden Eyes, The

▶ **Fille Du Puisatier, La** see Well-Digger's Daughter, The

▶ **Film D'Amore E D'Anarchia** see Love And Anarchy

▶ **Film Ohne Titel** see Film Without A Title

▶ **Film Without A Name** see Film Without A Title

Film Without A Title

▶ **(US: Film Without A Name)**

▶ **Film Ohne Titel**

W. Germany   1947   100 mins   bw
Camera Film

d   **Rudolf Jügert**
sc **Helmut Käutner, Ellen Fechner, Rudolf Jügert**
ph **Igor Oberberg**
m   **Bernard Eichhorn**
    Hans Söhnker, Hildegard Knef, Irene Von Meyendorff, Willy Fritsch, Fritz Odemar

A screenwriter (Odemar) and an actor (Fritsch) imagine a story of an employer (Söhnker) who falls in love with his maid (Knef), told from different points of view and with alternative endings. One of the very first post-war German film exports was an expertly witty piece, not only on human relationships but on the problems of making a comedy in that war-torn country. These problems were not solved in the German cinema for many years.

▶ **Fimpen** see Stubby

▶ **Final Accord** see Final Chord

Final Chord

▶ **(US: Final Accord)**

▶ **Schlussakkord**

Germany   1936   100 mins   bw
UFA

d   **Detlef Sierck**
sc **Kurt Heuser, Detlef Sierck**
ph **Robert Baberske**
m   **Kurt Schröder, excerpts from Beethoven,
    Handel, Tchaikovsky
    Willy Birgel, Lil Dagover, Maria Von
    Tasnady, Theodor Loos, Maria
    Koppenhöfer, Albert Lippert, Kurt Meisel**

When her husband, an embezzler who fled
to New York, commits suicide, Hanna (Von
Tasnady) returns to Germany to find her
small son. The boy is now in the care of an
orchestral conductor (Birgel) and his faithless
wife Charlotte (Dagover), who is locked into
an affair with a villainous clairvoyant (Lippert). Hanna takes a job as governess to her
son and, after many highly charged complications, a harmonious resolution is found.
Sierck (Douglas Sirk) claimed here to have
consciously attempted, for the first time, to
divest himself of theatrical and literary influences on his work. In fact, it is highly theatrical – literally so, with productions of Handel's
Judas Maccabaeus and a children's theatre
performance of *Snow White And The Seven
Dwarfs* featured, while Beethoven's *Ninth
Symphony* in concert lends both the 'chord'
and 'accord' implicit in the title. Though
highly schematic, this is, above all, an out-and-out melodrama, rich in visual and
emotional resonances which signal the style
for which the director became universally
regarded. Over the top, but absorbing.

Finally Sunday

▶ **(US: Confidentially Yours)**

▶ **Vivement Dimanche**

France   1983   117 mins   bw
Les Films Du Carrosse/A2/Soprofilms

d   **François Truffaut**
sc **François Truffaut, Suzanne Schiffman,
    Jean Aurel**
ph **Nestor Almendros**
m   **Georges Delerue
    Fanny Ardant, Jean-Louis Trintignant,
    Philippe Laudenbach, Caroline Sihol,
    Philippe Morier-Genoud**

A real-estate agent (Trintignant), accused of
the murder of his wife and her lover, goes
into hiding while his secretary (Ardant)
attempts to prove his innocence. As he had
done in several other films, and with far more
aplomb, Truffaut took an American pulp
novel (this time *The Long Saturday Night* by
Charles Williams) as the basis for a comedy
thriller. Shot in monochrome in a strained
effort to capture the style of 1940s Hollywood,
it is a self-regarding, hollow, mildly amusing
cinéphile's game. However, Fanny Ardant
proves to be the most attractive and versatile
of French actresses.

The Finances Of The Grand Duke

▶ **Die Finanzen Des Grossherzogs**

Germany   1923   80 mins   bw
Pagu

d   **F.W. Murnau**
sc **Thea Von Harbou**
ph **Karl Freund, Franz Planer**
m   **Silent
    Mady Christians, Harry Liedtke, Alfred
    Abel, Robert Scholz**

The Grand Duchess Olga (Christians), in love
with an insolvent Grand Duke (Liedtke),
decides to bail him out of his financial difficulties. She writes him an embarrassing letter
which is stolen, giving rise to mirth as it is
passed from hand to hand among several
people. The chief attraction of this film is
Mady Christians' delightful performance, its
chief interest the novelty of Murnau tackling
such frivolous fare. (It was based on an anti-Semitic novel but the racial slant was
removed.) Sadly, only incomplete prints of
this film survive, depriving modern audiences
of the beautiful landscape photography shot
in Yugoslavia.

► **Finanzen Des Grossherzogs, Die**
see Finances Of The Grand Duke, The

► **Fin Du Jour, La** see End Of A Day, The

Finis Terrae

France   1929   90 mins   bw
Société Générale Des Films

d   Jean Epstein
sc Jean Epstein
ph Joseph Barth, Joseph Kottula
m   Silent
    Fishermen of the islands of Ouessant and
    Bannec

The everyday lives of the fisherfolk on remote islands off the coast of Brittany. A precursor of Neo-Realism and very much in the tradition of the ecological documentaries of Robert Flaherty, the film was a strange departure for a director who had just astonished audiences with *The Fall Of The House Of Usher*. Although his aesthetic style kept the human dimension at a distance, the film showed Epstein's expert handling of non-professional actors.

► **Finyé** see Wind, The

► **Fiore Delle Mille E Una Notte, Il**
see Arabian Nights, The

Fire Festival

► **Himatsuri**

Japan   1985   120 mins   col
Gunro/Seibu Group/Ciné Saison

d   Mitsuo Yanagimachi
sc Kanji Nakagami
ph Masaki Tamura
m   Tohru Takemitsu
    Kinya Kitaoji, Kiwako Taichi, Ryota
    Nakamoto, Norihei Miki, Rikiya Yasuoka

In a coastal village in South-west Japan, a lumberjack in his forties (Kitaoji) has a mystical relationship with the goddess of the mountains. Seeing the fishing grounds polluted, speculators moving in and traditions being eroded, he turns a gun on his family and himself. Yanagimachi has used an actual event to create a mysterious parable of change – the young replacing the old, the modern encroaching upon the ancient. Some of the symbolism might confuse Western audiences, but the imagery of the sea and forest, the startling moments in the narrative and the visuals, and the pyrotechnics of the festival of the title make a deep impression.

Fire In The Straw

► **Le Feu De Paille**

France   1939   89 mins   bw
Véga

d   Jean-Benoît Levy
sc Jean-Benoît Levy, Henri Troyat
ph Marcel Lucien
m   Marcel Lattès
    Lucien Baroux, Orane Demazis, Jean
    Fuller, Jeanne Helbling, Aimos

A once-famous actor (Baroux) sees his son (Fuller) rise to fame in the movies while his own career fades. But the son's popularity does not last, and he discovers what his father has long known – acting is a precarious career. This well-characterized serio-comic story takes place against a somewhat unconvincing show business background and the leads, while competent, are hardly charismatic. The film was advertised in the US as the last picture to be exported from France before the Nazi occupation.

The Firemen's Ball

► **Hoří, Má Panenko**

Czechoslovakia   1967   73 mins   col
Barrandov/Carlo Ponti

d   Miloš Forman
sc Miloš Forman, Ivan Passer, Jaroslav
    Papoušek
ph Miroslav Ondříček
m   Karel Mares
    Vaclav Stockel, Josef Svet, Josef Kolb,
    Jan Vostřcil, František Debelka

During a small-town firemen's ball, a beauty contest fizzles out when the contestants refuse to leave the cloakrooms, the raffle prizes are stolen, someone has a heart attack, and a house burns down. After his more gently ironic previous films, Forman's rather gross satire on simple people with some sharp side swipes at petty bureaucracy caused 40,000 Czech firemen to resign in protest until it was explained that the picture was merely allegorical. Very popular in the West, the film was the last Forman made in his homeland before his self-imposed exile in America.

Fires On The Plain

▶ **Nobi**

Japan 1959 108 mins bw
Daiei

d **Kon Ichikawa**
sc **Natto Wada**
ph **Setsuo Kobayashi**
m **Yasushi Akutagawa**
   Eiji Funakoshi, Osamu Takizawa, Micky Curtis, Mantaro Ushio

On an island in the Philippines a soldier (Funakoshi), part of the retreating Japanese army, is forced to hide in the jungle where he encounters death, disease, starvation and cannibalism. This grim and gruesome, but dignified, film is a worthy companion piece to Ichikawa's other anti-war masterpiece, *The Burmese Harp* (1956). Its visual intensity is increased by keeping the dialogue to a minimum.

▶ **Fire Within, The** see Feu Follet, Le

First Name Carmen

▶ **Prénom Carmen**

France 1983 85 mins col
Sara/A2/Jean-Luc Godard Films

d **Jean-Luc Godard**
sc **Jean-Luc Godard, Anne-Marie Miéville**
ph **Raoul Coutard**
m **Beethoven, Tom Waits**
   Maruschka Detmers, Jacques Bonnaffé, Myriem Roussel, Christophe Odent, Jean-Luc Godard

Carmen (Detmers), a member of a gang of thieves and the lover of a security guard she met during a bank hold-up, uses the making of a film by her director uncle as a cover for a kidnapping. This is Godard at his most mischievous, playing wittily with Mérimée's *Carmen* (no Bizet, but a Beethoven string quartet rehearsed and played), a B-film plot – it ends wih the dedication 'In Memoriam Small Pictures' – and. notions of cinema. Above all, it offers Godard in a hilarious and mocking self-portrait.

Best Film Venice 1983

The First Teacher

▶ **Pervy Uchitel**

USSR 1965 98 mins bw
Kirghizfilm/Mosfilm

d **Andrei Mikhalkov-Konchalovsky**
sc **Chingiz Aytmatov, Boris Dobrodeyev**
ph **Georgy Rerberg**
m **Vyacheslav Ovchinnikov**
   Bolot Beishenaliev, Natalia Arinbasarova, Idris Nogaibayev, D. Kouioukova, M. Kychtobaiev

In 1923, an ex-Red Army Officer (Beishenaliev) opens a new school in a Kirghiz village, gradually winning over the hostile community, but when he falls in love with a beautiful 16-year-old girl (Arinbasarova) whom the local Kulak demands to marry, conflict and violence erupt. Set against an inhospitable landscape, Konchalovsky's first feature is partly a folk tale, replete with gnarled peasants and primitive customs, and partly a realistic account of genuine hurdles to progress. Technically, too, it combines cliché with some imaginative and persuasive images, and conveys a sense of menace that is controlled and convincing.

Best Actress (Natalia Arinbasarova) Venice 1966

▶ **Fist In His Pocket** see Fists In The Pocket

Fists In The Pocket

▶ **(US: Fist In His Pocket)**
▶ **I Pugni In Tasca**

Italy 1965 113 mins bw
Doria

d **Marco Bellocchio**
sc **Marco Bellocchio**
ph **Alberto Marrama**
m **Ennio Morricone**
    **Lou Castel, Paola Pitagora, Liliona
    Gerace, Marino Masè, Pier Luigi Troglio**

In a middle-class family consisting of a blind widow (Gerace) and her children – three brothers, two of whom are epileptics, and their half-crazed sister (Pitagora) – the eldest son (Masè), breadwinner and only normal member is prevented from marrying and living a full life. His younger brother (Castel) decides to free him by killing off the rest of the family. Twenty-five-year-old Bellocchio borrowed £28,000 from his family to make this searing critique of repressive Italian *bourgeois* family life, based on a script he wrote while following a film course at the Slade school in London under Thorold Dickinson. A remarkable first feature, it is notable for its intensity, claustrophobic atmosphere, and a powerful performance from Castel as the *deus ex machina*.

Fitzcarraldo

W. Germany 1982 158 mins col
Werner Herzog/Project Filmproduktion/
Zweite Deutsches Fernsehen/Wildlife
Films

d **Werner Herzog**
sc **Werner Herzog**
ph **Thomas Mauch**
m **Popol Vuh**
    **Klaus Kinski, Claudia Cardinale, José
    Lewgoy, Paul Hittscher, Miguel Angel
    Fuentes**

In an attempt to realize his dream of establishing an opera house in the Peruvian jungle at the turn of the century, an eccentric Irish rubber baron called Fitzgerald (Fitzcarraldo to the natives), has to have a massive steamship hauled over a mountain. 'If I should abandon this film I should be a man without dreams . . . I live my life or end my life with this project,' Herzog stated characteristically. Whether one thinks that this grandiose screwball epic might have been no worse with less effort, one can't help but admire the tenacity and daring of the director's determination to live his films. More interesting than this long

haul is *Burden Of Dreams*, Les Blank's documentary on the hazardous making of the film, which originally cast Jason Robards (who fell ill with jungle fever) in the role taken here by the grimacing Kinski.

Best Director Cannes 1982

Five Boys From Barska Street

▶ **Piatka Z Ulicy Barskiej**

Poland 1953 115 mins col
Film Polski

d **Alexsander Ford**
sc **Alexsander Ford, Kazimierz Kozniewski**
ph **Jaroslav Tuzar, Karel Chodura**
m **Kazimierz Serocki**
    **Tadeusz Janczar, Aleksandra Slaska,
    Andrzej Kozák, Mieczyslaw Stoor**

A gang of five boys are put on probation for robbery with violence in post-war Warsaw. Their kindly probation officer gets them jobs and helps them reject their old values and come to terms with society. Poland's leading director of the 1950s was entrusted with his country's first major production in colour. What emerged was a propagandist piece that parallels the rehabilitation of the delinquents with the reconstruction of Poland. In fact, it is not dissimilar to preachy American or British models of the genre. Ford was a sympathetic director of young people, as he had already proved in earlier 'street' films – *The Legion Of The Street* (1932) and *Border Street* (1948). The assistant on this film was Andrzej Wajda, whose first feature, *A Generation*, the following year was to give a very different view of Polish youth.

▶ **Five-Day Lover, The** see Infidelity

Five Evenings

▶ **Pyat' Vecherov**

USSR 1980 101 mins bw/col
Mosfilm

d **Nikita Mikhalkov**
sc **Aleksander Adabashyan, Nikita
    Mikhalkov**

ph **Pavel Lebeshev**
m **Yu. Mikhailov**
   Ludmila Gurchenko, Stanislav Liubshin,
   Valentina Telichkina, Larisa Kuznetsova,
   Igor Nefedov, Aleksander Adabashyan

Sasha (Liubshin), who claims to be the chief engineer of the Soviet Union's largest chemical plant, has arrived in Moscow on leave. A man of volatile temperament, he impulsively visits Tamara (Gurchenko) with whom he was romantically involved when the war broke out. She has never married and, over the course of five evenings characterized by revelations and vicissitudes, they resolve their relationship. This adaptation of a play by Alexander Volodin is only partially successful. It retains the running gags and act breaks that belong in the theatre, while an attempt to be cinematically adventurous in the closing sequences (black and white gives way to colour) is sentimental and contrived. However, as in his other films, Mikhalkov displays a pronounced gift for handling actors and it is the presence of his performers, notably the accomplished Gurchenko, that holds it together. The period, too, is interesting: 1957, when Khruschev was beginning to loosen the bonds of Stalinist austerity, conveyed in a series of images that signal the change.

Five Women Around Utamaro

▶ **(US: Utamaro And His Five Women)**
▶ **Utamaro O Meguru Gonin No Onna**

Japan 1946 94 mins bw
Shochiku

d **Kenji Mizoguchi**
sc **Yoshitaka Yoda**
ph **Shigeto Miki**
m **Hisato Osawa, Tamezo Mochizuki**
   Minosuke Bando, Kinuyo Tanaka, Kotaro
   Bando, Hiroko Kawasaki

Utamaro (Minosuke Bando), the legendary 18th-century Edo artist, gains his inspiration from the many courtesans who surround him. Jealousies and intrigues, however, are rife among the female entourage, as well as among

his other friends. Although scenarist Yoda stated that the film was, unconsciously, a portrait of the director, it is consciously about the problems of artists in general and Utamara in particular. It also suggests the link between erotic and creative impulses, and exquisitely evokes the period. One of Mizoguchi's most stylized works, *Utamaro* is also somewhat confusing in its treatment of complex relationships.

▶ **Flambierte Frau, Die** see Woman In Flames, A

A Flame In My Heart

▶ **Une Flamme Dans Mon Coeur**

France 1987 110 mins bw
Garance/La Sept(Paris)/
Filmograph(Geneva)

d **Alain Tanner**
sc **Myriam Mézières, Alain Tanner**
ph **Acácio De Almeida**
m **Bach**
   Myriam Mézières, Benoît Régent, Aziz
   Kabouche, André Marcon, Jean-Gabriel
   Nordman, Biana

Mercedes (Mézières), a Parisian actress, decides to break up with her uneducated Arab lover (Kabouche), which proves easier said than done due to his unbalanced persistence and their mutual sexual attraction. She finally escapes him by holing up in a hotel, then picks up Pierre (Régent), a journalist, on the Métro and goes to live with him. During his absence on an assignment, she disintegrates and, on his return, he takes her to Cairo although their relationship is by now very shaky. Although Tanner is still dealing with the alienation of the individual, familiar from his better films, he does so here with a mixture of pretentious attitudinizing and soft porn that manages to be at once tasteless and boring. The technique of the piece appears as a sort of retarded excursion into the New Wave, while the content, similarly, is a sketchy and incoherent nod to the 'permissive' past.

▶ **Flame Of My Love** see My Love Has Been Burning

▶ **Flame Of Torment, The** see Conflagration

Flame Top

▶ **Tulipää**

Finland 1980 135 mins col
P-Kino Oy/Finnish Film Foundation

d Pirjo Honkasalo, Pekka Lehto
sc Pirjo Honkasalo, Pekka Lehto
ph Kari Sohlberg, Pertti Mutanen, Raimo Paananen
m Heikki Valpola
   Åsko Sarkola, Rea Mauranen, Kari Franck, Esko Salminen, Åri Suonsuu

An account of the adult life of Maiju Lassila (Sarkola), the prolific Russian-Finnish writer who began as a successful businessman in Russia at the turn of the century, made a glittering marriage which soon collapsed, and became a Socialist revolutionary forced to flee to Finland. There, he led a mysterious existence and an unusual love-life, practising politics through his pen under several pseudonyms. The directors, concentrating largely on Lassila's affair with the failed actress, Olga (Maurinen), and his life during the German occupation of Finland have found a visionary, almost epic approach to an unpromising subject and have re-created a period of upheaval in a series of gripping images. The film, very controversial in Finland, took eight years to make.

The Flaming Years

▶ **aka History Of The Burning Years**

▶ **aka The Turbulent Years**

▶ **Povest' Plamennykh Let**

USSR 1961 105 mins col
Mosfilm

d Julia Sointseva
sc Alexander Dovzhenko
ph Fyodor Provorov, Alexei Temerine
m Gavril Popov
   Nikolai Vingranovsky, Boris Andreyev, Svetlana Zhgun, Zinaidi Kirienko, Sergei Loukianov, Vassili Merkouriev

Ivan Orlyuk (Vingranovsky), a soldier of infinite courage and patriotism, fights in World War II, overcoming continual wounding in battle, and survives to marry his brave school-teacher sweetheart (Zhgun). Continuing her homage to her late husband, the great Dovzhenko, Solntseva has achieved a memorable use of 70mm, creating a series of skilful, fluid, imaginative and affecting images. Alas, the content is rather less impressive, being an overt piece of flag waving to the indomitable spirit of Russia, symbolized by the ever-smiling Ivan. The simplistic story grows tedious and the director lacks her husband's conspicuous gifts that might have served to enliven his script. Nonetheless, it is a landmark in the use of the 70mm screen, its photography beautifully controlled by the experienced Provorov.

Best Director Cannes 1962

▶ **Flamme Dans Mon Coeur, Une**
see Flame In My Heart, A

The Flavour Of Green Tea Over Rice

▶ **Ochazuke No Aji**

Japan 1952 115 mins bw
Shochiku/Ofuna

d Yasujiro Ozu
sc Yasujiro Ozu, Kogo Noda
ph Yuharu Atsuta
m Ichiro Saito
   Shin Saburi, Michiyo Kogure, Koji Tsuruta, Keiko Tsushima, Kuniko Miyake

A middle-aged, middle-class couple find that their childless marriage has gone stale. The husband (Saburi) is a creature of habit with simple tastes, and the snobbish wife (Kogure) goes off on jaunts with other wives. They finally come together again in the kitchen when they share a bowl of *ochazuke* (green tea over rice). The delicate flavour of Ozu is seen in the subtle playing and camerawork. One of his brightest and funniest films, full of sly little surprises, it was considered by the director to be 'not very well made'.

Les Fleurs Sauvages

▶ **aka Wild Flowers**

Canada 1982 153 mins col/bw
Cinak

d   Jean Pierre Lefèbvre
sc Jean Pierre Lefèbvre
ph Guy Dufaux
m   Raoul Duguay
    Marthe Nadeau, Michèle Magny, Pierre
    Curzi, Claudia Aubin, Eric Beausejour

Seventy-year-old Simone (Nadeau) arrives for
her annual visit to her daughter's family in
rural Quebec. Michèle (Magny), her photographer husband (Curzi) and the two children are happy to see her. The week passes
in carefree summer pursuits in which Simone,
rooted in a more restrained and less loving
past, does her best to join with equanimity.
Originally shot on 16mm with the lowest of
budgets, Lefèbvre's film is technically
accomplished, sensitive and beautifully acted.
This is a perceptive and naturalistic tale of
family life, which initially reveals the barriers
and tensions beneath the surface of the
mother-daughter relationship when Michèle
presents her mother with a welcoming vase
of wild flowers – a gift that is subtly dispar-
aged. Michèle's quiet acknowledgement of a
gap in understanding between them remains
private, while Simone, too, keeps her criti-
cisms and resentments to herself. Unfortunately, the film is far too long and is disrupted
by the ill-judged use of voice-overs and black-
and-white sequences to express private
thoughts.

▶ **Flic, Un** see Dirty Money

▶ **Flickorna** see Girls, The

Floating Clouds

▶ **Ukigumo**

Japan 1955 123 mins bw
Toho

d   Mikio Naruse
sc Yoko Mizuki
ph Masao Tamai

m   Ichiro Saito
    Hideko Takamine, Masayuki Mori,
    Mariko Okada, Daisuke Kato

A solitary woman (Takamine), returning to
Japan after serving as a nurse at the front in
South-east Asia, seeks out a soldier (Mori)
she fell in love with there. But they have no
control over their destiny because he cannot
leave his invalid wife and she must suffer
degradation. One of the most popular of
Naruse's subtle, pessimistic melodramas flows
relentlessly towards the heartfelt conclusion.
Naruse has remarked of his characters that
'If they try to move forward even a little, they
quickly hit a wall'. But they struggle on
bravely, especially the women, played here
(as in 16 other Naruse films) by the remarkable Hideko Takamine.

Floating Weeds

▶ **Ukigusa**

Japan 1959 119 mins col
Daiei

d   Yasujiro Ozu
sc Yasujiro Ozu, Kogo Noda
ph Kazuo Miyagawa
m   Takanobu Saito
    Ganjiro Nakamura, Haruko Sugimura,
    Machiko Kyo, Ayako Wakao, Hiroshi
    Kawaguchi

A troupe of travelling players visits a remote
island town where lives the ex-mistress (Sugi-
mara) of the leading actor (Nakamura) with
whom she had had a son. Complications arise
when the actor's present lover (Kyo) becomes
jealous. This close remake of Ozu's silent
1934 film, A Story Of Floating Weeds, has a
mellowness lacking in the bitterer earlier film,
but retains much of the comedy of the theatre
scenes. It also has glowing colour photography by the great Miyagawa, who had worked
for Kurosawa (Rashomon) and Mizoguchi
(Ugetsu Monogatari), but only this once with
Ozu.

▶ **Fontane Effi Briest** see Effi Briest

▶ **För Att Inte Tala Om Alla Dessa
Kvinnor** see Now About These Women

The Forbidden Christ

▶ **Il Cristo Proibito**

Italy   1950   100 mins   bw
Excelsa

d   **Curzio Malaparte**
sc **Curzio Malaparte**
ph **Gabor Pogany**
m   **Curzio Malaparte**
**Raf Vallone, Elena Varzi, Gino Cervi,
Alain Cuny, Rina Morelli, Philippe
Lemaire, Anna Maria Ferrero**

Bruno (Vallone), a soldier, returns to Tuscany
after 10 years of war and captivity to learn
that his young Partisan brother was betrayed
to the Nazis. Bent on revenge, he receives no
help from the war-weary villagers; even his
family refuses to tell what it knows. Events
spiral and he is led into killing the wrong
man. The only film made by writer Malaparte
is an allegory on themes of guilt and expiation
which, while not always coherent and sometimes heavy-handed, is nonetheless powerful.
It is redolent with striking images of death
and encounters of telling irony, caught by an
adventurous camera and given stylized playing (very successful from Vallone, less so
elsewhere). Well-known for shifting his
allegiances between Communism and Fascism, Malaparte claimed to have renounced
politics with this gripping film, inspired by
accounts of an actual incident. It was a box-
office disaster, causing him to abandon future
film plans and return to journalism.

Forbidden Fruit

▶ **Le Fruit Défendu**

France   1952   103 mins   bw
Gray Films

d   **Henri Verneuil**
sc **Henri Verneuil, Jacques Companeez, Jean
Manse**
ph **Henri Alekan**
m   **Paul Durand**
**Fernandel, Françoise Arnoul, Claude
Nollier, Sylvie, Jacques Castelot**

A respectable doctor (Fernandel), a widower
living with his mother (Sylvie), takes a second

wife (Nollier), but gets involved with a young
prostitute (Arnoul). Georges Simenon's novel
Lettre À Mon Juge was the basis for this
absorbing little drama. The Belgian author's
favourite theme – the deep passions that lie
beneath the surface of stifling middle-class
respectability – is well articulated by the film,
which seemed terribly daring to English-
speaking audiences in the early 1950s (Arnoul
reveals a breast). Fernandel, not just a funny
face, gives one of his rare serious performances.

Forbidden Games

▶ **aka The Secret Game**
▶ **Jeux Interdits**

France   1952   102 mins   bw
Robert Dorfmann

d   **René Clément**
sc **Jean Aurenche, Pierre Bost**
ph **Robert Juillard**
m   **Narcisco Yepes**
**Brigitte Fossey, Georges Poujouly,
Amedée, Laurence Badie, Jacques Marin**

In 1940, as refugees flee the Germans, an
orphaned five-year-old girl and the young
son of a peasant family who takes her in,
build a cemetery for animals, stealing crosses
from the churchyard to do so. Clément's
direct and simple approach and the wonderfully natural performances he obtained from
the young Poujouly (discovered at a camp
for deprived children) and Fossey (who
returned to films as an adult) make for a
moving document on the effects of war on
children. It is topped and tailed by two
justly famous sequences – the column of
refugees being strafed by Nazi planes and
the final crane shot revealing the little girl in
a sea of displaced persons.

**Best Foreign Film Oscar 1952
Best Film Venice 1952**

Forbidden Relations

▶ **Visszaesök**

Hungary   1983   90 mins   col
Mafilm

d Zsolt Kézdi-Kovács
sc Zsolt Kézdi-Kovács
ph János Kende
   Lili Monori, Miklós B. Székely, Mari
   Töröcsik, József Horváth, József Tóth

In a remote farming community, a widow
(Monori) finds solace in the arms of a man
(Székely) whom she discovers to be her half-
brother. Despite social ostracism and a term
of imprisonment, they decide to live as a
married couple and have children. This tale
of brother-sister incest is directed in a measured, objective manner, eschewing melodramatics and presenting a love affair that
seems as natural as the beautifully caught
surroundings. (Although making them half-
siblings takes away half the shock.) The couple play with touching honesty and there is a
strong performance from Töröcsik as their
mother, literally trying to wash her feelings
of guilt away.

The Forest

▶ Kaadu

   India 1973 123 mins col
   LN Combines

d Girish Karnad
sc Girish Karnad
ph Govind Nihalani
m B.V. Karanth
   G.S. Nataraj, Amrish Puri, Nandini,
   Lokesh, Kalpana Sirur, Uma Shivakumar

Kitti (Nataraj), a 10-year-old boy,
accompanies his aunt (Nandini) on a nocturnal visit to the witchdoctor in the forest to
obtain a spell to stop his uncle (Puri) spending
his nights with a widow (Shivakumar). After
adventures in and around the same forest, he
watches helplessly as his aunt is raped on her
way to visit the witchdoctor for a second
time. The first film directed by the writer-
actor Karnad is, like Satyajit Ray's *Pather
Panchali*, a tale told through the eyes of a
child. But the haunting, lucid, and finally
tragic drama stands on its own considerable
merits. Karnad's story, based on an autobiographical novel, with its underlying violence,
superstition and rigid sexual codes, reveals a
darker side to Indian rural life than Ray's
film.

▶ **Forest of Hanged Men** see Lost
Forest, The

▶ **Forest Of The Hanged, The** see
Lost Forest, The

Forever My Love

▶ Sissi/Sissi-Die Junge Kaiserin/
  Sissi-Schicksalsjahre Einer
  Kaiserin

   Austria 1955/1956/1957 317 mins col
   Erma-Film

d Ernst Marischka
sc Ernst Marischka
ph Bruno Mondi
m Anton Profes
   Romy Schneider, Karl-Heinz Böhm,
   Gustav Knuth, Walther Reyer, Magda
   Schneider, Vilma Degischer

Young Franz Joseph, the Hapsburg Emperor
(Böhm), falls in love with Elizabeth (Sissi),
the sister of the Bavarian princess whom his
mother has arranged for him to marry. He
marries Sissi instead, much to his mother's
chagrin, but she brings a breath of fresh air
to the Court, wins the slavish devotion of the
formerly unhappy Hungarians, falls dangerously ill but recovers, and tours Austria's
Italian states with her husband, once again
captivating a hostile populace. Such is the
plot of this laboured marathon, comprising
three consecutive films, but generally shown
as one – substantially cut but still interminable. Part-operetta, part Hollywood-style
biopic, the tone is cloying, the technique
uneven, and the leading lady (Romy Schneider) too lightweight. Nonetheless, this film
proved massively successful, attracting large
lines at the box-office. An appeal, perhaps, to
a world hungry for nostalgia?

▶ **Forfolgelsen** see Witch Hunt

Forget Venice

▶ Dimenticare Venezia

   Italy 1979 107 mins col
   Rizzoli Film/Action Film

d Franco Brusati

sc **Franco Brusati, Jaj Fiastri**
ph **Romano Albani**
m **Benedetto Ghiglia, Saverio Mercadante, Gluck**
  Erland Josephson, Mariangela Melato, Eleonora Giorgi, David Pontremoli, Hella Petri, Fred Personne

Middle-aged Nicky (Josephson) and his male lover arrive to stay with Marta, Nicky's widowed and ailing sister, in her country house near Venice. Marta's adopted niece, Anna, lives with her, and the visit of the men sets in motion a series of childhood memories – played in flashback – for Nicky (happy recollections) and Anna (desperately miserable). Dealing, presumably, with the potency and the healing effects of memory, Brusati's film is stylish and elegant, but amounts to little more than a languid and superficial examination of his theme. Worse, his characters are rather boring. Forget it.

Fort Saganne

France 1984 190 mins col
Albina Productions/Films A2/SFPC

d **Alain Corneau**
sc **Henri De Turenne, Alain Corneau, Louis Gardel**
ph **Bruno Nuytten**
m **Philippe Sarde**
  Gérard Depardieu, Philippe Noiret, Catherine Deneuve, Sophie Marceau, Michel Duchaussoy, Salah Teskouk

Charles Saganne (Depardieu), a young man of simple peasant stock, joins the military and is posted to a garrison in the French Sahara. Overcoming initial setbacks, he develops into a heroic leader of men until his flame is extinguished by World War I. Along the way and among other things, he joins issue with the aggressive colonel (Noiret), enjoys a fling with a sophisticated Parisian journalist (Deneuve), marries the innocent daughter (Marceau) of a superior *bourgeois* family and performs an amputation on a tribal chieftain with the contents of a tool box. Adapted from a prizewinning novel by Louis Gardel, based on the real-life exploits of his grandfather, and filmed on location in France, Tunisia and Mauritania, this saga of Empire-building cost upwards of $6,000,000, making it one of

France's most expensive films ever. A starry cast, led by the virile Depardieu, go through their expert paces, enhanced by superb CinemaScope photography, and directed by Corneau with enough style and sense of period to overcome most of the clichés. This is the epic adventure movie revisited and it works.

Fortunella

Italy 1958 96 mins bw
Dino de Laurentiis/Les Films Marceau (Paris)

d **Eduardo De Filippo**
sc **Federico Fellini, Tullio Pinelli, Ennio Flaiano**
ph **Aldo Tonti**
m **Nino Rota**
  Giulietta Masina, Paul Douglas, Alberto Sordi, Franca Marzi

The homeless Fortunella (Masina) works for (and sleeps with) Peppino (Sordi), a weak-willed junk merchant, and is protected by a raffish professor (Douglas). But she imagines that she is the illegitimate daughter of a Prince who will someday claim her. Whimsical it sounds, and whimsical it is, with Masina repeating her repertoire of Chaplinesque mannerisms from *La Strada* and *Cabiria*, but without the controlling vision of her husband behind the camera. De Filippo had a good crack at making a Fellini film out of a Fellini script. Apart from the presence of Masina, and Nino Rota's music, there is the realistic setting on the banks of the Tiber intruded upon by the fantasy of wandering players, and a pleasing mixture of comedy and pathos.

The Forty First

▶ **Sorok Pervyi**

USSR 1927 80 mins bw
Mezhrabpom

d **Yakov Protazanov**
sc **Boris Lavryenov, Boris Leondinov**
ph **Pyotr Yermolov**
m **Silent**
  Ada Voitsik, Ivan Koval-Samborski, I. Strauch

During the civil war in Turkestan, a Red woman soldier takes prisoner a member of the retreating White army. They find themselves alone on an island where they fall in love, but she remembers her duty to the cause and kills him – her forty-first victim. Skilfully shot in desert locations in two months, the film's wide popularity was probably due more to the romantic than the political or visual aspects of the action tale, although the romance was the weakest element. It was remade in colour by Grigori Chukhrai in 1956.

Four Adventures Of Reinette And Mirabelle

▶ **Quatre Aventures De Reinette Et Mirabelle**

France 1986 95 mins col
CER/Les Films Du Losange

d **Eric Rohmer**
sc **Eric Rohmer**
ph **Sophie Maintigneux**
m **Ronan Girre, Jean-Louis Valero**
   Joëlle Miquel, Jessica Forde, Philippe Laudenbaum Yasmine Haury, Marie Rivière, Béatrice Romand, Fabrice Luchini

Four adventures lived by Mirabelle (Forde), a student of ethnology at the Sorbonne, and Reinette (Miquel), an art student. The first takes place in the country, where Reinette lives and they initially meet, later becoming flatmates in Paris. Here they find themselves having to cope with an obnoxious waiter, a kleptomaniac and an art dealer. Rohmer, with a small crew, very little money, a screenplay that was improvised as he went along and two unknown teenage actresses among a few of his regulars, has worked a tiny miracle. The performances of the two girls are beguilingly natural as Rohmer contrasts their attitudes – country girl Reinette with rigorous principles, the city girl more pragmatic. As a film of sketches, it cannot stand up to Rohmer's more ambitious work, but he shows in his 66th year that 'youth is not a question of age'.

▶ **Four Bags Full** see Pig Across Paris, A

▶ **Four Chimneys** see Where Chimneys Are Seen

The Four Days Of Naples

▶ **Le Quattro Giornate Di Napoli**

Italy 1962 119 mins bw
Titanus/MGM

d **Nanni Loy**
sc **Nanni Loy, Pasquale Festa Campanile, Massimo Franciosa, Carlo Bernardi**
ph **Marcello Gatti**
m **Carlo Rustichelli**
   Regina Bianchi, Aldo Giuffre, Lea Massari, Jean Sorel, Franco Sportelli, Charles Belmont, Gian Maria Volonté

In 1943, when the occupying Germans rounded up all males aged from five to 50 to send to Nazi camps, the people of Naples rose up and drove them out after an epic battle in the streets. This grim and powerful cinematic reconstruction of an heroic event was nominated for an Oscar in 1962, losing out to the inferior *Sundays And Cybèle*.

The Four Hundred Blows

▶ **Les Quatre Cents Coups**

France 1959 94 mins bw
Films Du Carrosse/SEDIF

d **François Truffaut**
sc **François Truffaut**
ph **Henri Decaë**
m **Jean Constantin**
   Jean-Pierre Léaud, Claire Maurier, Albert Rémy, Patrick Auffray, Robert Beauvais

A 12-year-old Parisian boy, Antoine Doinel (Léaud), neglected by his mother and stepfather, plays truant and takes to petty crime. He is placed in a reform school, but escapes to the coast. Truffaut, a harsh critic on the influential magazine *Cahiers du Cinéma*, was challenged by his movie producer father-in-law to make a film himself. His first feature, based on his own deprived childhood, was an immediate success which helped to launch the *Nouvelle Vague*, and started a series of films following Doinel through adolescence, marriage, fatherhood and divorce. From the start there was an extraordinary rapport between the director and his alter-ego, and much of the film's freewheeling quality is due to Léaud's spontaneous performance. The freeze of the child's face as he runs towards the sea, is one of cinema's most celebrated endings. Incidentally, both Truffaut and Jeanne Moreau can be glimpsed briefly.

Note: The title comes from a colloquial expression, *Faire les quatre cents coups*, meaning to get into a lot of trouble or to be a real troublemaker.

Best Director Cannes 1959

Four Nights Of A Dreamer

▶ **Quatre Nuits D'Un Rêveur**

France   1971   87 mins   col
Albina/Del Orso

d   **Robert Bresson**
sc **Robert Bresson**
ph **Pierre Lhomme**
m   **Brazilian folk songs**
    Isabelle Weingarten, Guillaume Des Forêts, Maurice Monnoyer, Jérôme Massart

One night a young artist (Des Forêts)) sees a girl (Weingarten) on the Pont Neuf trying to commit suicide. They talk, and meet on subsequent nights until her lover returns and she leaves the artist. Like his previous picture, *A Gentle Creature* (1969), Bresson's second colour film was based on Dostoevsky, this time the oft-lensed *White Nights*. The strength of the film lies in the enchanting nocturnal background of the bridges of Paris and the *bateaux mouches* gliding up the Seine, rather than in the blank and enigmatic young characters that drift around in the foreground unaware of the surrounding beauty. The intrusion of hippies into the Bressonian world seems curiously false.

Four Steps In The Clouds

▶ **Quattro Passi Fra Le Nuvole**

Italy   1942   90 mins   bw
Cines

d   **Alessandro Blasetti**

sc **Cesare Zavattini, Giuseppe Amato, Piero Tellini, Aldo De Benedetti**
ph **Vaclav Vich**
m   **Alessandro Cicognini**
    Gino Cervi, Adriana Benetti, Giuditta Rissone

A dull, unhappily married, travelling confectionery salesman (Cervi) meets a pregnant girl on a bus who begs him to pretend to be her husband for one night for the sake of her family. Anticipating the Neo-Realists by using humble characters and backgrounds, the film helped cheer up audiences in war-torn Italy. Since then non-Italians have been able to appreciate its genuine wit and charm. It was remade in France in 1957 as *The Virtuous Bigamist* starring Fernandel.

The Fourteenth of July

▶ **(US: July 14)**

▶ **Quatorze Juillet**

France   1932   98 mins   bw
Tobis

d   **René Clair**
sc **René Clair**
ph **Georges Périnal, Louis Page**
m   **Maurice Jaubert**
    Annabella, Georges Rigaud, Pola Illery, Paul Olivier, Raymond Cordy

On Bastille Day in Paris, a flower-girl (Annabella) and her taxi-driver boyfriend (Rigaud) meet various people. A child is born, a woman dies, there is a hold-up, and a drunkard (Olivier) is blissfully unaware of his surroundings. Clair's films have the same reputation for gaiety as Paris, the city he loved. This light, inconsequential comedy is quintessentially Clair, and the last of his pre-war 'Paris' pictures. Actually, the city is more the wittily artificial creation of Russian emigré set designer Lazare Meerson, who created the ideal space for Clair's choreographed characters.

The Fourth Man

▶ **Die Vierde Man**

Netherlands   1983   102 mins   col

De Verenigde Nederlandsche
Filmcompagnie

d **Paul Verhoeven**
sc **Gerard Soeteman**
ph **Jan De Bont**
m **Loek Dikker**
    **Jeroen Krabbé, Renée Soutendijk, Thom
    Hoffman, Dolf De Vries, Geert De Jong**

Amsterdam novelist Gerard (Krabbé) gives a
lecture in another town and sleeps with the
mysteriously thrice- widowed Christine (Soutendijk), treasurer of the literary society. He
discovers that she is engaged to Herman
(Hoffman), a young man he spied at the
station who has entered his quasi-religious
visions. Finally, Gerard has sex with Herman
and tries to warn him that Christine spells
destruction.... A novel by Gerard Reve – gay,
Catholic and a best-selling Dutch author –
has become a wonderfully overwrought film,
combining Christian guilt, homo-erotic imagery, black humour and high Gothic camp.
Verhoeven's direction is assured, his actors
expert.

▶ **Fourth Marriage Of Dame Margaret, The** see Parson's Widow, The

Fox

▶ **aka Fox And His Friends**
▶ **Faustrecht Der Freiheit**

W. Germany 1975 123 mins col
Tango

d **Rainer Werner Fassbinder**
sc **Rainer Werner Fassbinder, Christian
    Hohoff**
ph **Michael Ballhaus**
m **Peer Raben**
    **Rainer Werner Fassbinder, Peter Chatel,
    Harry Baer, Ulla Jacobsson, Adrian
    Hoven, Karl-Heinz Böhm**

A carnival barker (Fassbinder) who wins a
fortune in a lottery, is manipulated into
investing in his upper-class boyfriend's family
business with disastrous consequences.
Although an honest and lucid look at homosexual relationships, *Fox* is even more concerned with class exploitation, as conveyed in
Fassbinder's no-nonsense narrative. He himself makes a sympathetic but weak central

figure, especially in the cruellest scene when
the snobbish family humiliates him at the
dinner table.

▶ **Fox And His Friends** see Fox

Fragment Of An Empire

▶ **Oblomok Imperii**

USSR 1929 81 mins bw
Sovkino

d **Friedrich Ermler**
sc **Friedrich Ermler, Katerina Vinogradskaya**
ph **Yevgeni Schneider**
m **Silent**
    **Fyodor Nikitin, Yakov Gudkin, Ludmila
    Semyonova**

A young man (Nikitin), who lost his memory
in World War I and regained it ten years
later, takes a trip to Leningrad where he is
reunited with his lost wife (Semyonova) and
where he finds everything has changed under
the new Soviet order – customs, the landscape
and even the name of the city (from St
Petersburg). Ermler's most celebrated film
combines political parable with social satire
most effectively. Its humanity and the splendid location photography give the piece its
well-earned reputation.

The Fragrance Of Wild
Flowers

▶ **Miris Poljs Kog Sveca**

Yugoslavia 1977 93 mins col
Centar Film

d **Srdjan Karanović**
sc **Rajko Grlić, Srdjan Karanović**
ph **Živko Zalar**
m **Zoran Simjanović**
    **Ljuba Tadić, Sonja Divać, Nemanja Zivić,
    Rastislava Gacić, Olga Spiridonović**

Ivan Vasiljevic (Tadić), a famous actor, suddenly leaves a play rehearsal, walks out on
his career and his wife (Spiridonović), and
decides to sail down the Danube on an old
barge operated by his friend Stinky (Zivić).
But escape is not as simple as it seems. After
the Black Cinema (the sombre Yugoslavian
movement in the cinema of the 1960s), a new

wave of film-makers emerged, more concerned with individual than national identity. Kranović described his second feature as a 'kind of documentary fairy tale', by which he presumably meant that fantastic elements grow out of a realistic situation. It is at its best when it ironically and warmly observes the many characters (mostly played by non-professionals) that Tadić, himself a well-known stage and screen actor, meets on his journey.

▶ **Française Et L'Amour, La** see Love And The Frenchwoman

Francisca

Portugal 1981 166 mins col
V.O. Filme

d **Manoel De Oliveira**
sc **Manoel De Oliveira**
ph **Elso Roque**
m **João Paes**
    Teresa Meneses, Diogo Dória, Mário Barroso, Rui Mendes, Glória De Matos, Lia Gama

Camilo Castelo Branco (Barroso) and José Augusto (Dória) are both in love with the exquisite Fanny (Meneses), who finally marries José. Meanwhile, the two men are close friends and spend much time in philosophical conversation. De Oliveira, Portugal's most distinguished director, was already 73 when he made this film, based on a romantic novel by Agustina Bessa Luís. She, in turn, drew her material from the real-life triangular story, recorded in a novel by Camilo and the diaries of José and Fanny. It is a highly formal work, creating climaxes of unhappiness and self-destruction through slowly unfolding dialogue that reveals the pride, sadism, spite, vanity and despair of the characters, and building atmosphere through richly-detailed Velasquez-like compositions. An unusual, complex and rewarding piece.

Françoise Steps Out

▶ **Rue De L'Estrapade**

France 1953 95 mins bw
Cinéphonic/SGGC/Filmsonor

d **Jacques Becker**
sc **Annette Wademant**
ph **Marcel Grignon**
m **Georges Van Parys**
    Louis Jourdan, Anne Vernon, Daniel Gélin, Jean Servais, Micheline Dax

When Françoise (Vernon) discovers that her racing driver husband (Jourdan) has been unfaithful, she moves into a small flat in Paris, only to be pestered by a Left Bank crooner (Gélin). The last of Becker's enchanting modern Parisian comedies has all his characteristic warmth and observation. It summed up the director's credo: 'I believe in the possibility of entertaining friendship and in the difficulty of maintaining love...And I believe above all in Paris'. Vernon and Gélin are as charming a partnership here as they were in Becker's *Edward And Caroline*, and Louis Jourdan makes an effective return to a French film in between his less than inspired work in Hollywood movies.

▶ **Frantic** see Lift To The Scaffold

▶ **Frau Im Mond, Die** see Woman In The Moon, The

▶ **Frau, Nach Der Man Sich Sehnt, Die** see Woman That Men Yearn For, The

▶ **Freedom For Us** see À Nous La Liberté

Freedom Is Paradise

▶ **SER**

USSR 1989 75 mins col
Mosfilm

d **Sergei Bodrov**
sc **Sergei Bodrov**
ph **Yuri Skirtladze**
m **Alexander Raskatov**
    Volodya Kozyrev, Alexander Bureyev, Svetlana Gaitan, Vitautas Tomkus

Thirteen-year-old Sasha (Kozyrev) is an inmate of a residental school for problem children. His mother is dead and his father, whom he has never known, is in prison far across the country. The boy, who has FIP (Freedom in Paradise) tattooed on his wrist, is determined to escape and find him. He runs away frequently but, although wily and enterprising, is invariably caught and returned to the institution... This is a gentle and touching piece, whose underlying theme is more concerned with social deprivation than Communist oppression. Events unfold during a hot Russian summer and the people Sasha meets during his various journeys are largely kind folk; even the authority figures are refreshingly free of brutality. The freckled, defiant Kozyrev is a definite plus, the film itself likeable without being memorable.

French Cancan

▶ **(US: Only The French Can)**

France　1955　105 mins　col
Franco London/Jolly

d　**Jean Renoir**
sc　**André-Paul Antoine**
ph　**Michel Kelber**
m　**Georges Van Parys**
　　Jean Gabin, Françoise Arnoul, Maria Felix, Jean-Roger Caussimon, Gianni Esposito

The impresario (Gabin) who opened the Moulin Rouge in Montmartre in 1880, falls for a young laundress (Arnoul) whom he tries to make into a star – much to the annoyance of his fiery mistress (Felix). Renoir's return to film-making in France after 15 years' absence is an exuberant, colourful homage to the theatre of *La Belle Epoque*. (Edith Piaf and Patachou appear briefly as stars of the day.) The hackneyed story, based on the life of Ziegler, founder of the Moulin Rouge, is the stuff of many a Hollywood biopic, but expounded with delicate period taste and affection. It also gave Renoir the opportunity to work with Gabin again, having made three films with him in the 1930s.

Frenzy

▶ **(US: Torment)**

▶ **Hets**

Sweden　1944　101 mins　bw
Svensk Filmindustri

d　**Alf Sjöberg**
sc　**Ingmar Bergman**

ph　**Martin Bodin**
m　**Hilding Rosenberg**
　　Stig Järrel, Alf Kjellin, Mai Zetterling, Olof Winnerstrand, Märta Arbin, Gunnar Björnstrand

A sensitive schoolboy (Kjellin), victimized by a sadistic Latin teacher (Järrel) and misunderstood at home, turns for love to a young alcoholic prostitute (Zetterling). Twenty-six-year-old Ingmar Bergman's first screenplay, based on a recollection of one of his schoolmasters, prefigured some of the themes of his early films as director – young lovers at odds with society, the humiliation of the weak by the strong. Sjöberg's highly-charged Expressionist picture, rather too close to its title for comfort, not only launched Bergman, but the teenage Zetterling, and instigated the renaissance of Swedish cinema.

▶ **Freudlose Gasse, Die** see Joyless Street

Fric-Frac

France　1939　120 mins　bw
Maurice Lehmann

d　**Claude Autant-Lara, Maurice Lehmann**
sc　**Michel Duran**
ph　**Armand Thirard**
m　**Casimir Oberfeld**
　　Fernandel, Michel Simon, Arletty, Hélène Robert, Andrex

A gullible jeweller's assistant (Fernandel), through his infatuation with a jewel thief (Arletty), becomes unwittingly involved in a plan to rob his employer's shop. A film to defeat any sub-title writer since it was conceived almost entirely in (now dated) slang with the language an essential part of the humour. But the trio of top performers and the jolly plot are enough to keep non-French speakers content. Autant-Lara was virtually the sole director, but his producer boss claimed a co-credit.

Frida

▶ **Frida Naturaleza Viva**

Mexico　1984　108 mins　col
Cooperativa Buten

d **Paul Leduc**
sc **José Joaquín Blanco, Paul Leduc**
ph **Angel Goded**
m **Saint-Saëns, popular Spanish music**
   Ofelia Medina, Juan José Gurrola, Max
   Kerlow, Salvador Sánchez, Claudio
   Brook, Cecilia Toussaint

The gifted Mexican painter Frida Kahlo (Medina), wife of Diego Rivera (Gurrola), committed Communist and close friend of Leon Trotsky (Kerlow), is on her deathbed. She reflects on her life and art, and on her many physical afflictions that began with polio in childhood and culminated in the amputation of a leg. This is an impressionistic view of a remarkable woman that slowly comes together, like an emotional jigsaw puzzle, in a series of haunting images, some moving, some painful and ugly, others enchanting, but all dominated by the dramatically powerful presence of Medina. Every frame exhibits a depth and range of colour, light and texture appropriate to its subject and its setting, be it the watermelons of Diego, the surrealist portraits by Frida, Mexican Indians singing by firelight or the bullet-scarred pillars of an imposing public building. However, it must be acknowledged that, with its lack of narrative, its minimal dialogue and sequences of excruciating slowness, the film initially requires much patience and concentration.

▶ **Frida Naturaleza Viva** see Frida

Friends And Husbands

▶ **Heller Wahn**

   W. Germany 1982 106 mins col
   Bioskop-Film(Munich)/Les Films Du
   Losange(Paris)

d **Margarethe Von Trotta**
sc **Margarethe Von Trotta**
ph **Michael Ballhaus**
m **Nicolas Economou**
   Hanna Schygulla, Angela Winkler, Peter
   Striebeck, Christine Fersen, Franz
   Buchriese

Olga (Schygulla), strong, confident and an expert in Classical Romantic literature, is the emotional mainstay of her husband, her lover and her son. Ruth (Winkler), a gifted but unfulfilled and suicidally depressive artist, is married to Franz (Striebeck), a university

colleague of Olga's, on whom she is utterly dependent but who undermines her. The women meet and develop a close friendship which initially helps Ruth, but finally destroys both of them and Franz. Continuing her exploration of bonds between women begun with *Sisters, Or The Balance Of Happiness* and perfected in *The German Sisters*, Germany's most formidable woman director now takes it a step further in exposing the destructive potential of such relationships. Magnificently played by Schygulla and Winkler, and emotionally charged beneath its leisurely surface, this complex and intelligent film touches on many thorny issues and is distinctly devoid of comfort.

Friends For Life

▶ **Amici Per La Pelle**

   Italy 1955 100 mins bw
   Cines

d **Franco Rossi**
sc **Franco Rossi, Leo Benvenuti, Piero De**
   Bernardi, Ugo Guerra, Giandomenico
   Giagli
ph **Gabor Pogany**
   Geronimo Meynier, Andrea Scire, Luigi
   Tosi, Paolo Ferrari, Dina Perbellini

A motherless schoolboy goes to stay in the stable environment of his friend's family. However, when the two youngsters quarrel, the boy leaves for the Middle East with his businessman father, a decision which proves to be a painful wrench for both youngsters. This compassionate and sensitive study of the closed world of childhood, tinged with an adult's sentimentality, has two remarkable juvenile leads.

▶ **Friend Will Come Tonight, A** see
Ami Viendra Ce Soir, Un

▶ **Fröken Julie** see Miss Julie

From The Life Of The Marionettes

▶ **Aus Dem Leben Der**
   Marionetten

   W. Germany 1980 104 mins col/bw
   ITC

d   **Ingmar Bergman**
sc **Ingmar Bergman**
ph **Sven Nykvist**
m   **Rolf Wilhelm**
    Robert Atzorn, Christine Buchegger,
    Martin Benrath, Rita Russek, Lola
    Muethel, Walter Schmidinger

A rich, youngish businessman (Atzorn), going through a marriage crisis with his independent dress-designer wife (Buchegger), murders a prostitute in the back room of a nightclub. Bergman's second film made during his short tax exile in Germany is superior to the misconceived *The Serpent's Egg* (1977). Opening with a murder in a blood red room, most of the film is shot in stark monochrome with an intense whiteness in the dream sequences. Balanced between the distancing device of Brechtian titles and the use of large close-ups, Bergman has created a tightly controlled case history in the German idiom. Outstanding is a depressing monologue by an aging gay man (Schmidinger), one of the rare male homosexuals in Bergman's *oeuvre*.

▶ **Frontier** see Aerograd

▶ **Frühlingssinfonie**   see   Spring Symphony

▶ **Fruit Défendu, Le** see Forbidden Fruit

▶ **Fruits De La Passion, Les** see Fruits Of Passion, The

The Fruits Of Passion

▶ **Shina Ningyo**

▶ **aka Les Fruits De La Passion**

France/Japan 1981 83 mins col
Argos(Paris)/Terayama(Tokyo)

d   **Shuji Terayama**
sc **Shuji Terayama, Pauline Réage**
ph **Tatsuo Susuki**
m   **J.A. Seazer**
    Klaus Kinski, Isabelle Illiers, Arielle
    Dombasle, Peter, Kenichi Nakamura,
    Takeshi Wakamatsu

In the 1920s, English aristocrat Sir Stephen (Kinski) takes his willing slave 'O' (Illiers) to Hong Kong, where he installs her in a brothel while he takes his pleasure elsewhere. But Sir Stephen becomes jealous of one of her clients (Nakamura) and shoots him dead. The film was meant as a sado-masochistic follow-up to Oshima's *In The Realm Of The Senses* and *Empire Of Passion*, and French producer Anatole Dauman got Terayama to adapt the pseudonymous Pauline Réage's sequel to the erotic novel *The Story Of O*. In French, Japanese and some 'English', the film, when trying for some narrative coherence, is a badly acted, badly scripted disaster. When Terayama is left to explore his own fantasies, echoing earlier works, the picture has some morbid fascination. The brothel Madam is played effectively by the transvestite Peter, the Fool in Kurosawa's *Ran*.

▶ **Frustration** see Ship Bound For India, A

Full Moon In Paris

▶ **Les Nuits De La Pleine Lune**

France 1984 102 mins col
Les Films Du Losange/Les Films Ariane

d   **Eric Rohmer**
sc **Eric Rohmer**
ph **Renato Berta**
m   **Elli and Jacno**
    Pascale Ogier, Tcheky Karyo, Fabrice
    Luchini, Christian Vadim, Virginie
    Thevenet

A young trainee textile designer (Ogier), working in the centre of Paris but living with her boyfriend in the suburbs, gains some independence by finding a small apartment for herself in the capital. Rohmer, master of the minutiae of relationships, captures the way people, whatever their level of articulacy, talk things through. Here, however, he just manages to skate on the right side of the thin line that separates an interesting film from a trivial one about trivial young people. Pascale Ogier (daughter of Bulle Ogier), who also designed the sets, died prematurely in October 1984 aged 24.

Best Actress (Pascale Ogier) Venice 1984

The Funeral

▶ aka Funeral Rites

▶ Ososhiki

   Japan 1985 123 mins col
   Itami/N.C.P

d   Juzo Itami
sc Juzo Itami
ph Yonezo Maeda
m   Joji Yuasa
    Tsutomu Yamazaki, Nobuko Miyamoto,
    Kin Sugai, Shuji Otaki, Ichiro Zaitsu,
    Nekohachi Edoya, Chishu Ryu

When elderly Mr Amamiya dies suddenly, it
falls to Wabisuke (Yamazaki), the actor husband of the dead man's actress daughter
(Miyamoto, director Itami's wife), to assume
the role of chief mourner. The bereaved couple hurry off a film set to their country house
where the three-day wake is to be held, and
where Wabisuke swots up his duties from a
video called 'The ABC Of Funerals'. Such is
the tone of Itami's black comedy, peopled
with a gallery of richly drawn supporting
characters ranging from the pompous undertaker, through the Rolls Royce-owning,
money grubbing priest (Ryu), to 'the
deceased's fussy brother obsessed with the
comfort of the corpse. The director cruelly
satirizes the breach in the observance, but
rescues his irreverence from tastelessness with
the sincerity of the widow's address and the
solemnity of the cremation. Actor Itami's first
comedy as director is somewhat heavy-
handed (the more accomplished *Tampopo*
would follow), but it is inventive and amusing.

▶ Funeral Rites see Funeral, The

A Funny Dirty Little War

▶ No Habra Mas Penas Ni Olvido

   Argentina 1983 79 mins col
   Aries Cinematografica Argentina

d   Hector Olivera
sc Roberto Cossa, Hector Olivera
ph Leonardo Rodriguez Solis
m   Oscar Cardoza Ocampo
    Federico Luppi, Hector Bidonde, Victor

Laplace, Miguel Angel Sola, Graciela
Dufau, Angel Sola

In 1974, after Peron has returned to power
following 18 years in exile, a wave of violence
erupts as different factions, all professing loyalty to the president, fight among themselves.
In the sleepy town of Colonia Vela, administrator Fuentes (Luppi), together with a small
motley band, occupies the town hall in an act
of resistance against the army. Complications
proliferate, as does the cold-blooded murder
of defenceless civilians, for Olivera is much
concerned with the role of essentially innocent
folk rebelling against a messy regime. The
film is fast, furious and funny – a penetrating
political satire which hits its targets with a
mixture of broad comedy and brutal images.

Special Jury Prize Berlin 1984

Furia

   Italy 1946 90 mins bw
   Franchini/AGIC

d   Goffredo Alessandrini
sc Goffredo Alessandrini
ph Pierot Portalupy
    Isa Pola, Rossano Brazzi, Gino Cervi,
    Adriana Bennetti, Umberto Spadaro

Pola, bored with her marriage to wealthy
horse breeder Cervi, has a steamy affair with
stud keeper Brazzi who then marries Cervi's
daughter. But he and Pola still can't keep
their hands off each other, while stable-hand
Spardaro lusts after her with violent consequences. Neo-Realist Alessandrini tended to
utilize his style in the service of the box-office
and this uncompromising portrait of lust,
acted and directed with conviction, was no
exception. Don't search for meaning.

▶ Furong Zhen see Hibiscus Town

▶ Fussgänger, Der see Pedestrian, The

The Future Is Woman

▶ Il Futuro È Donna

   Italy 1984 100 mins col
   Faso Film(Rome)/UGC-Top No
   1(Paris)/Ascot Film(West Berlin)

d   Marco Ferreri
sc Marco Ferreri, Dacia Maraini, Piera
    Degli Esposito
ph Tonino Delli Colli
m   Carlo Savina, plus 12 Italian pop songs
    Ornella Muti, Hanna Schygulla, Niels
    Arestrup, Maurizio Donadoni, Michèle
    Bovenzi, Ute Cremer

Gordon (Arestrup) and his wife Anna (Schygulla) have decided against having children because of the nuclear threat. At a disco one evening, Anna rescues Malvina (Muti), a young woman who is being harassed by some youths. Learning that Malvina is pregnant and homeless, Anna takes her back with them, thus beginning a cycle of tensions, jealousies, reconciliations, leave-takings and returns. Although strongly cast (Schygulla and Muti are as sexy a pair as ever there was) and offering several dramatic and threatening images, Ferreri's film degenerates into an incoherent triangle that promises much but delivers little. As suggested by the title, there is a message about the expendability of men lurking somewhere in the script (Maraini and Esposito are well-known Feminists), together with the idea that parental instincts cannot be dictated by intellectual argument, but the themes are expressed with dreary pretension.

The Future Of Emily

▶ L'Avenir D'Émilie

France/W. Germany 1984 116
mins col
Les Films Du Losange(Paris)/Helma
Sanders Filmproduktion/Literarisches
Colloquium(Berlin)

d   Helma Sanders-Brahms
sc Helma Sanders-Brahms
ph Sacha Vierny
m   Jürgen Knieper
    Brigitte Fossey, Hildegarde Knef, Ivan
    Desny, Herman Treusch, Camille
    Raymond, and the voice of Mathieu
    Carrière

Movie star Isabelle (Fossey) completes a film in Berlin and leaves for Normandy to see her parents (Knef and Desny) and her young daughter Emily (Raymond) who lives with them during her frequent absences. Her arrival is complicated by a call from her leading man (Treusch) who is romantically pursuing her. Mother and daughter spend a long night exchanging their innermost thoughts, and Isabelle makes plans with Emily which both know will not materialize. With sensitivity, imagination, control and razor-sharp insight, Sanders-Brahms has delivered a multi-layered essay on life, art, parenthood and the patterns of generations. She is brilliantly well-served by her actresses, including young Camille Raymond, and the result is a powerful, if more loving, cousin to Bergman's *Autumn Sonata*, exploring similar territory about life versus art and mother-daughter relationships.

▶ Futuro È Donna, Il see Future Is Woman, The

▶ Fuzi Qing see Father And Son

g

Le Gai Savoir

▶ **aka The Joyful Wisdom**

France 1969 95 mins col
ORTF/Anouchka/Batavia Atelier

d Jean-Luc Godard
sc Jean-Luc Godard
ph Georges Leclerc
m Revolutionary Cuban hymn
  Jean-Pierre Léaud, Juliette Berto

Patricia Lumumba and Emile Rousseau sit in an empty TV studio and talk about the media, education and language, occasionally interrupted by street scenes. Godard was commissioned by French TV to make an adaptation of fellow Swiss Jean-Jacques Rousseau's classic *Emile*, but it became very much his own treatise on 'progressive' education. Cut during and after the events of May 1968, this stimulating two-character conversation piece was a key film in Godard's career. At one stage Léaud says, 'We must start again from zero,' and Godard's own return to zero resulted in a break from all commercial film-making until 1972. With Jean-Pierre Gorin, he shot a series of ciné-tracts in 16mm and later video. They *Pravda*, *Vent D'Est*, and *Vladimir And Rosa*.

Galia

▶ **aka I And My Lovers**

France 1965 105 mins bw
Speva/Ciné Alliance/Variety

d Georges Lautner
sc Georges Lautner, Vahe Katcha
ph Maurice Fellous
m Michel Magne, Bach (The Swingle Singers)

Mireille Darc, Venantino Venantini, Françoise Prévost, Jacques Riberolles

A badly-treated wife (Prévost) is rescued from a suicidal leap into the Seine by a passer-by (Darc). The latter visits the husband (Venantini), who believes his wife dead after seeing the suicide note and they carry on an affair. However, the wife decides to save her rescuer by killing her husband. The only reason for this absurd melodrama having had a fairly profitable release in Britain and the USA must have been the sexy disrobed presence of ex-model Darc. The film also had a veneer of chic and cheek.

The Gambler

▶ **Le Joueur**

France 1958 105 mins col
Franco-London

d Claude Autant-Lara
sc Jean Aurenche, Pierre Bost, François Boyer
ph Jacques Natteau
m René Cloërec
  Gérard Philipe, Liselotte Pulver, Nadine Alari, Bernard Blier, Jean Danet, Françoise Rosay, Carette

While waiting for his aunt to die and leave him her fortune, an aging general (Blier) lives and gambles in Baden-Baden at the expense of an adventurer who is the lover of his daughter (Pulver). Her tutor (Philipe), who is in love with her, arrives intending to rescue her from her sordid lot but is defeated by the consequences of the gambling fever that affects everybody. A somewhat overblown and melodramatic adaptation of the 1866 novella by Dostoevsky, the showy and garish colour and design actually suit the milieu.

The dashing hero of the French cinema, Philipe, is as beguiling as usual, while Pulver is touching as the tragic victim of her father's dissolute habits. Among the many screen versions of this subject was a 1949 Hollywood contribution, titled *The Great Sinner* and starring Gregory Peck.

▶ **Game Of Love, The** see Ripening Seed, The

▶ **Gamlet** see Hamlet

Ganashatru

▶ **aka An Enemy Of The People**

India 1988 100 mins col
National Film Development Corporation Of India

d **Satyajit Ray**
sc **Satyajit Ray**
ph **Barun Raha**
m **Satyajit Ray**
   Soumitra Chatterjee, Ruma Guhathakurta, Dhritiman Chatterjee, Dipanker Dey, Subhendu Chatterjee

Dr Ashok Gupta (Soumitra Chatterjee), chief medical officer in a small West Bengal town whose prosperity is dependent on visitors to the local temple, discovers that the temple's water supply is contaminated and causing an epidemic of disease. His demands for action threaten the vested interests of the authorities, among them the unscrupulous mayor (Dhritiman Chatterjee) who is Gupta's brother. The doctor continues his fight in growing isolation as the bureaucracy and the townspeople hound and discredit him... Ray's first film in four years after an enforced absence through illness is a skilful adaptation of Ibsen's *An Enemy Of The People*. Updating the Norwegian original to the present and brilliantly transposing its concerns to an Indian context whose themes the battle between superstition and science, Ray and his superb cast have created an acutely intelligent film. If much of the action is necessarily static, the dramatic effect is heightened when Ray does venture beyond the interiors. If *Ganashatru* fails to reveal the full scope of its maker's art, his delicate touch with domestic relationships, his simmering anger at ignorance and his precisely observant eye are intact.

Le Gang

France 1976 103 mins col
Adel Productions(Paris)/Mondial Ti-Fi(Rome)

d **Jacques Deray**
sc **Alphonse Boudard, Jean-Claude Carrière**
ph **Silvano Ippoliti**
m **Carlo Rusticelli**
   Alain Delon, Maurice Barrier, Roland Bertin, Laura Betti, Giampiero Albertini, Nicole Calfan

It is 1945 and the French police, busy weeding out Nazi collaborators from their ranks, are somewhat disorganized. Taking advantage of this, Robert (Delon) assembles a gang which embarks on a series of daring robberies, commencing with the interception of a bullion consignment. Finally cornered by the law, Robert escapes, only to meet his end in ironic circumstances. Deray's film, full of imaginative, almost quaint characters and situations, tells its tale in flashback from the point of view of Robert's mistress (Calfan) as his mournful gang gathers round his deathbed. However, although not evidently intended as a parody of the genre, it is so amiable and free from violence that it's good for little more than lazy family entertainment. Delon, sporting cheeriness, reckless bravado and a curly wig, sums up the tone.

The Gang Of Four

▶ **La Bande Des Quatre**

France 1988 160 mins col
Pierre Grise Productions (France)/Limbo Film (Switzerland)

d **Jacques Rivette**
sc **Jacques Rivette, Pascal Bonitzer, Christine Laurent**
ph **Caroline Champetier**
   Bulle Ogier, Benoit Regent, Laurence Cote, Fejria Deliba, Bernadette Giraud, Inês De Medeiros, Nathalie Richard

A celebrated drama teacher (Ogier) has chosen to work only with women in a Parisian studio theatre. The exclusive class, 'the gang of four' (Deliba, Giraud, Cote, Medeiros), live together in a small suburban house. While working on a version of Marivaux's *Double Inconstance*, their lives are disrupted by a mysterious man (Regent), the lover of a former student actress (Richard). Once again Rivette uses the theme of the interplay between theatre and life, and explores the way in which women relate to one another, enacted against a background of a strange city called Paris. (The director's obsessions date back to his first feature, *Paris Belongs To Us*, 1960.) It may be felt that over two-and-a-half hours is more than enough time to spend with these self-absorbed, loquacious characters, but Rivette's elegant technique is at its best when allowed a leisurely pace in which to develop the witty intricacies of his plots. In this case, the camera dwells lovingly on the faces of the contrasting women and there are many spellbinding moments, particularly the bravura opening sequence which follows a girl from a café, through the streets of Paris and into a room where she immediately begins a rehearsal.

▶ **Garde À Vue** see Inquisitor, The

Garden Of Stones

▶ **Baghe Sangui**

Iran 1976 84 mins col
N.I.R.T.

d **Parviz Kimiavi**
sc **Parviz Kimiavi**
ph **Freydoun Ghovaniou**
  Darvich Khan, his family, and villagers of Balvarad

An elderly shepherd (Khan), living in the semi-desert of the Iranian hinterland, has a mystic vision which leads him to construct an elaborate garden of stones attached to dry tree branches. The garden is dedicated to an unknown god and he worships there daily. The word spreads, however, and soon other villagers come to join him in his strange and private shrine, thus destroying the spell. Using

a non-professional cast who project simplicity and convinction, Kimiavi has constructed a spare and beguiling mixture of fable and reality. He manages a handful of gently ironic digs at established values, but dialogue is kept to a minimum, leaving the tale best told by its attractive and well-judged images.

Special Jury Prize Berlin 1976

The Garden Of The Finzi-Continis

▶ **Il Giardino Dei Finzi-Contini**

Italy 1970 95 mins col
Documento Film/CCC Filmkunst

d **Vittorio De Sica**
sc **Tullio Pinelli, Valerio Zurlini, Franco Brusati, Vittorio Bonicelli, Ugo Pirro, Alain Katz**
ph **Ennio Guarnieri**
m **Manuel De Sica**
  Dominique Sanda, Lino Capolicchio, Helmut Berger, Romolo Valli, Fabio Testi, Inna Alexeiff, Camillo Angelini-Rota

The opulent Ferrara mansion inhabited by the cultivated, Jewish Finzi-Contini family is already a ghetto created by their wealth, when the coming of Fascism forces them to retreat further behind its walls. The younger members, Micol and Alberto (Sanda and Capolicchio) open up the tennis courts when Jews are barred from the club, and spend the summer caught in ambiguous relationships complicated by the intrusion of politics and war, and the need to allegiances. The film, famously, ends with the Finzi-Contini dynasty assembled in the schoolroom awaiting deportation. This tragic testament to Italy's involvement in the Holocaust brought De Sica out of the directorial wilderness in which he had languished for some years. His august reputation was deservedly restored by this hauntingly beautiful, intelligent and tasteful film.

Best Foreign Film Oscar 1971
Best Film Berlin 1971

▶ **Garm Hava** see Hot Winds

Gate of Hell

► **Jigokumon**

> Japan   1953   90 mins   col
> Daiei

d **Teinosuke Kinugasa**
sc **Teinosuke Kinugasa**
ph **Kohei Sugiyama**
m **Yasushi Akutagawa**
> **Machiko Kyo, Kazuo Hasegawa, Isao Yamagata, Koreya Senda**

A 12th-century feudal warlord (Hasegawa) desires a married woman (Kyo), but she kills herself rather than submit to him. Filled with remorse, he becomes a monk. One of the few Kinugasa films known in the West, its director studied with Eisenstein and this was the first Japanese picture to use a western colour process (Eastmancolor). Although it makes a strong visual impact – it won the Oscar for costume design – and Kyo and Hasegawa are outstanding, the simple tale nonetheless conforms to the strict conventions of the *Jidai-Geki*, the popular Japanese period films.

> **Best Foreign Film Oscar 1954**
> **Best Film Cannes 1954**

► **Gate of Lilacs** see Gates Of Paris

Gates Of Paris

► **aka Gate of Lilacs**
► **Porte Des Lilas**

> France   1957   95 mins   bw
> Filmsonor/Rizzoli

d **René Clair**
sc **René Clair, Jean Aurel**
ph **Robert Le Fèbvre**
m **Georges Brassens**
> **Pierre Brasseur, Georges Brassens, Henri Vidal, Dany Carrel, Raymond Bussières, Amedée**

Juju (Brasseur), a drunken drifter, and his troubadour friend (Brassens) offer refuge to a gangster (Vidal), who repays them by making a play for Juju's girlfriend (Carrel). However, Juju accidentally kills the gangster. This is the sort of dark-toned film not usually associated with its director. Perhaps the critics who attacked the picture on first release, failed to see that, beneath the shadows of the underworld setting, it contains a modicum of wit, charm and poetry. However, the stylized sets and the somewhat stilted script surround it with an aura of faded artificiality that might have worked two decades previously in the hands of Marcel Carné and Jacques Prévert.

The Gates Of The Louvre

► **(US: Black Thursday)**
► **Les Guichets Du Louvre**

> France   1974   92 mins   col
> Les Films Du Parnasse/Saga/ORTF/Les Films Du Limon

d **Michel Mitrani**
sc **Michel Mitrani, Albert Cossery**
ph **Jean Tournier**
m **Mort Shuman**
> **Christine Pascal, Christian Rist, Judith Magre, Alice Sapritch, Michel Auclair, Michel Robin**

It is 'Black Thursday', a July day in 1942 when 13,000 Parisian Jews were rounded up and taken to a stadium before deportation and eventual extermination. Paul (Rist), a non-Jewish student, helps to rescue Jeanne (Pascal), a girl whose family has been arrested. They fall in love, but she decides to return to her people. With the breakthrough of Marcel Ophüls' *The Sorrow And The Pity*, after over 25 years of silence about the complicity of the French in the Final Solution, this shameful period began to be aired in fictional films. This notable example overcomes many of the pitfalls in the plot that could have become mawkish and moralistic – Jewish families being split, the love affair and the parting – because Mitrani handles them with taste and restraint. The characters, whether victims or oppressors, are never stereotyped, only the young lovers lack depth.

Gates Of The Night

► **Les Portes De La Nuit**

> France   1946   106 mins   bw
> Pathé

d **Marcel Carné**

sc Jacques Prévert
ph Philippe Agostini
m   Joseph Kosma
    Pierre Brasseur, Yves Montand, Nathalie
    Nattier, Serge Reggiani, Jean Vilar,
    Saturnin Fabre, Raymond Bussières,
    Julien Carette

Among various doomed lovers in a *quartier* in immediate post-war Paris are a Resistance hero (Montand) and a young woman (Nattier) whose husband was a black-marketeer and brother a collaborator. The film marked the end of the great Carné-Prévert partnership and the sombre poetic-realist tradition of which they formed such an important part. Since the film-makers failed to take account of the optimistic post-war mood in France, it was reviled on its release and failed miserably at the box-office. Today, the gloomy, rather pretentious fable is of interest for its heady 1940s atmosphere, the expensive studio sets by Alexander Trauner and the famous theme song, called 'Autumn Leaves' in English. Twenty-five-year-old Montand and the insipid Nattier replaced Jean Gabin and Marlene Dietrich, who both turned down the lead roles at the last moment.

▶ **Gattopardo, Il** see Leopard, The

▶ **Gav** see Cow, The

▶ **Gebroken Spiegels** see Broken Mirrors

▶ **Geheimnisse Einer Seele** see Secrets Of A Soul

▶ **Gehenu Lamai** see Girls, The

▶ **Geisha** see Gion Festival Music

▶ **Genbaku No Ko** see Children Of Hiroshima

General Della Rovere

▶ **Il Generale Della Rovere**

    Italy 1959 137 mins bw
    Zebra/Gaumont

d   Roberto Rossellini

sc Roberto Rossellini, Sergio Amedei, Diego
    Fabbri, Indro Montanelli
ph Carlo Carlini
m   Renzo Rossellini
    Vittorio De Sica, Hannes Messemer,
    Sandra Milo, Giovanna Ralli, Anne
    Vernon

A con man (De Sica), persuaded by the Nazis to pose as an Italian general and Resistance leader to discover who the partisans are, begins to identify with his role and dies a martyr. After some years in disfavour, Rossellini regained some of his prestige by returning to the subject of war and resistance with which he made his name in the 1940s. Rather stodgily directed, and with an unconvincing patriotic ending, it nevertheless has a fine performance from De Sica and poses some important questions.

Best Film Venice 1959

▶ **Generale Della Rovere, Il** see General Della Rovere

The General Line

▶ **aka Old And New**

▶ **Generalnaya Linya**

▶ **aka Staroye I Novoye**

    USSR 1929 90 mins bw
    Sovkino

d   Sergei Eisenstein
sc Sergei Eisenstein
ph Edouard Tissé
m   Silent
    Marfa Lapkina, Vasya Buzenkov, Kostya
    Vasiliev, Chukhamarev

A peasant woman (Lapkina) is converted to the socialist principles of agriculture and fights to maintain collective farming in her community. After *October* (1927) displeased the powers that were, Eisenstein tried to toe the Party line with his last silent film, but got into hot water again. Apparently the satirically humorous treatment of some of the peasants was not to its liking, and neither were the advanced editing techniques. However, the film, centred around identifiable human characters, works equally as art and propaganda. The 'tonal montage', as the director called it, is at its best in the demonstration of the cream separator and the courtship of a bull and cow.

▶ **Generalnaya Linya** see General Line, The

A Generation

▶ **Pokolenie**

Poland 1954 85 mins bw
Film Polski

d   Andrzej Wajda
sc Bohdan Czeszko
ph Jerzy Lipman
m   Andrzej Markowski
    Tadeusz Lomnicki, Urszula Modrzynska,
    Roman Polanski, Zbigniew Cybulski

A young man (Lomnicki) involved with the Resistance, who helps fighters from the Warsaw Ghetto uprising in 1942 to escape, and who falls in love with a girl (Modrzynska) who leads a youth group, grows in maturity and acquires qualities of leadership from his experiences. The title refers to Poland's 'lost generation', that of most of the people in their twenties whose first feature film this was – the director, the screenwriter, the photographer, the composer and many of the actors. It formed the realistic first part of an (unplanned) war trilogy that made Wajda's name and put Polish cinema firmly on the map. Compared with *Kanal* (1957) and *Ashes And Diamonds* (1958) it is over-simplistic, but the youthful fervour carries it off.

Genesis

India 1986 109 mins col
Scarabée Films (Paris)/Mrinal Sen
Productions (Calcutta)/Les Films De La
Drève (Brussels)/Cactus Film (Zurich)

d   Mrinal Sen
sc Mrinal Sen, with Mohit Chattopadhya
ph Carlo Varini
m   Ravi Shankar
    Shabana Azmi, Naseeruddin Shah, Om
    Puri, M.K. Raina

The Farmer and The Weaver eke out a bare existence in a ruined and deserted village. The Woman arrives, disturbing the balance between the two men who both desire her. She becomes pregnant and leaves, they fight, and the Trader's machines come to rebuild the village. Heavy with symbolism, the film's message is nonetheless explicitly simple: the poor will remain poor, being always at the mercy of the powerful and prosperous. Beautifully photographed – often in images that seem too contrived and manicured for the landscape they represent – *Genesis* is, for all its virtues of intelligence and social conscience, a somewhat alienating and passionless piece that keeps the viewer distanced from its nameless protagonists.

▶ **Genou De Claire, Le** see Claire's Knee

▶ **Genroku Chushingura** see Loyal 47 Ronin, The

Les Gens Du Voyage

▶ **aka The Wanderers**

France 1938 123 mins bw
Tobis

d   Jacques Feyder
sc Jacques Feyder, Jacques Viol
ph Franz Koch
m   Wolfgang Zilzer
    Françoise Rosay, André Brûlé, Fabien
    Loris, Mary Glory, Sylvie Bataille

A lady lion tamer (Rosay) gives refuge to her husband (Brûlé), a fugitive from justice, in the circus where she performs. Meanwhile their son (Loris) is having an affair with the bareback rider (Glory) and there are jealousies and intrigues among the circus folk. One of Feyder's last films, it isn't exactly the greatest show on earth, but it skillfully juggles the variegated elements of the plot. Rosay, of course, can make any cliché seem new-minted. The film was simultaneously made in a German version, entitled *Fahrendes Volk*, with Hans Albers in the role of the husband.

A Gentle Creature

▶ **Une Femme Douce**

France 1969 87 mins col
Parc/Marianne

d **Robert Bresson**
sc **Robert Bresson**
ph **Ghislain Cloquet**
m **Jean Wiener**
   Dominique Sanda, Guy Frangin, Jane
   Lobre

A young woman (Sanda) marries a pawn-broker (Frangin) but finds she cannot adapt her life to his. She toys with murdering him, but kills herself instead. Using colour for the first time, Bresson brought a more overt sensuality and 'modernity' to his work than hitherto. Visually composed almost entirely of blue and green tones, the plot (a Dostoevsky story transposed to contemporary Paris) and acting are mainly grey. By eschewing all psychology, the film never begins to explain the miserable girl's motives. It was the screen debut of 20-year-old fashion model Dominique Sanda, one of the rare Bresson discoveries who went on to make a career in acting.

Georgette Meunier

Switzerland/West Germany 1988 82 mins col
DFFB/Rey–Coquais-Stöcklin

d **Tania Stöcklin, Cyrille Rey–Coquais**
sc **Tania Stöcklin, Cyrille Rey–Coquais,**
   Felix Schnieder-Henninger
ph **Ciro Cappellari, Anka Schmid**
m **Nikolaus Utermohlen**
   Tiziana Jelmini, Thomas Schunke, Dina
   Leipzig, Detlev Knops

Georgette (Jelmini) and her brother Emile (Schunke) are locked in a passionately incestuous relationship until, in their late teens, their father packs Emile off to military service abroad and sends Georgette to a convent. Misery drives her to marry a dull pharmacist whom she accidentally kills, and she is imprisoned for manslaughter. When Georgette is released, her combined unhappy experiences cause her to embark on a vengeful killing spree in which she almost succeeds in wiping out the entire male population of the village where she lives and works. This joint debut feature by Stöcklin (Swiss) and Rey–Coquais (French) is a curiosity which has cult status written all over it. A pointless exercise in the macabre that is often repulsive, it nonetheless displays a measure of virtuosity in the creation of unexpected and often compelling images. Stylish, certainly, but whether, as its creators claim, the movie 'owes a debt to Fassbinder and feminism' or is just a load of drivel, is another matter.

▶ **Germania, Anno Zero** see Germany, Year Zero

The German Sisters

▶ **Die Bleierne Zeit**

W. Germany 1981 107 mins col
Bioskop

d **Margarethe Von Trotta**
sc **Margarethe Von Trotta**
ph **Franz Rath**
m **Nicolas Economou**
   Jutta Lampe, Barbara Sukowa, Rüdiger
   Vogler, Doris Schade, Verenice Rudolph

Two contrasting sisters – a feminist journalist (Lampe) and a Baader Meinhof activist (Sukowa) – are brought closer when the latter is imprisoned, goes on hunger strike and dies, although the official version of 'suicide' is refuted by the remaining sister. Inspired by real-life sisters Christiane and Gudrun Ensslin, the film never really answers the interesting questions it raises: how much does our upbringing affect our political beliefs and what is the best way to combat the injustices in Western society? However, it does have the force to unsettle, and is beautifully acted.

Best Film Venice 1959

Germany In Autumn

▶ **Deutschland Im Herbst**

W. Germany 1978 134 mins col
Autoren/Hallelujah/Kairos

d **Alf Brustellin, Alexander Kluge,**
   Maximiliane Mainka, Edgar Reitz, Katja
   Rupé, Hans Peter Cloos, Volker
   Schlöndorff, Rainer Werner Fassbinder,
   Bernhard Sinkel, Beate Mainka-
   Jellinghaus, Peter Schubert, Heinrich Böll
sc **Heinrich Böll, Peter Steinbach**
ph **Jürgen Jürges, Bodo Kessler, Dietrich**
   Lohmann, Michael Ballhaus, Colin
   Mounier, Jörg Schmidt-Reitwein

m Ennio Morricone, Tchaikowsky, Mozart
Hannelore Hoger, Katja Rupé, Hans
Peter Cloos, Angela Winkler, Franziska
Walser, Vadim Glowna, Helmut Griem,
Mario Adorf, Rainer Werner Fassbinder,
Armin Meier

A dozen West German film-makers contribute
their reportage, political statements and artistic comments on the political situation in their
country after the kidnap and murder of the
industrialist, Hans Martin Schleyer. Two episodes in particular stand out in this illuminating anatomy of West Germany seen
principally from the Left: Böll on the subject
of German TV's refusal to air Sophocles'
Antigone on the grounds of its being too
provocative; and Fassbinder's brave and painful piece of autobiographical film, in which
he is seen trying to drop his lover and talk
politics to his mother while on drink and
drugs.

Germany, Pale Mother

▶ **Deutschland, Bleiche Mutter**

W. Germany   1980   109 mins   col
Literarisches Colloquium/WDR

d   Helma Sanders-Brahms
sc Helma Sanders-Brahms
ph Jürgen Jürges
m   Jürgen Knieper
Eva Mattes, Ernst Jacobi, Elisabeth
Stepanek, Angelika Thomas

Just after her marriage, on the eve of the
German invasion of Poland, a young woman
(Mattes) sees her husband (Jacobi) go off to
join the German army. She and her daughter
(Stepanek) struggle for survival during the
long war years until the husband returns, an
embittered and brutal man. Sanders-Brahms
(born 1940) based her most celebrated film
on her own mother's experiences during and
after the war. It works as a harrowing personal document of a woman's courage, but
the director weighs the character down with
the symbolic burden suggested by the title
(taken from the first line of Brecht's 1933
poem 'Deutschland'). As such it becomes
spurious, melodramatic and over-extended.
The splendid Eva Mattes makes us suffer with
the mother in more ways than one.

Germany, Year Zero

▶ **Germania, Anno Zero**

Italy   1947   78 mins   bw
Tevere/Sadfilm

d   Roberto Rossellini
sc Roberto Rossellini, Carlo Lizzani, Max
Kolpet
ph Robert Juillard
m   Renzo Rossellini
Edmund Moeschka, Franz Kruger,
Barbara Hintz, Werner Pittschau, Erich
Gühne

In Occupied Berlin, a 12-year-old boy
(Moeschka), trying to feed his family, poisons
his sickly father to lessen the burden but,
unable to live with the deed, he throws himself
off a ruined building. For his last Neo-Realist
film, Rossellini took his cameras to a destitute
post-war Berlin, using only one professional
actor (Kruger), as the father. Despite the
weaknesses in exposition and execution, the
director's compassion shines through, and the
documentary material is fascinating. The final
section when the child, isolated from others
and society, finds a moment to play before
dying, is Rossellini at his poignant best.

Germinal

France   1963   110 mins   bw
Marceau-Cocinor/Metzger & Woog/
Laetitia

d   Yves Allégret
sc Charles Spaak
ph Jean Bourgoin
m   Michel Magne
Jean Sorel, Berthe Grandval, Claude
Brasseur, Bernard Blier, Lea Padovani,
Simon Valère

Etienne (Sorel) gets a job in a French coal-
mining town during the 1860s, and leads the
exploited miners in a strike for better conditions. Emile Zola's monumental novel
about social and economic conditions in 19th-
century industrial France has been robbed of
its power by a dull screenplay, a subdued
leading man, and direction that is generally
underpowered, apart from the excellent handling of the strike scenes. Although it was
filmed in Hungary, both place and period

convince, but the film emerges as little more than a period melodrama that fails to capitalize on the opportunities offered by Zola's rich tapestry.

Gertrud

Denmark   1964   116 mins   bw
Palladium

d   **Carl Dreyer**
sc **Carl Dreyer**
ph **Henning Bendtsen, Arne Abrahamsen**
m   **Jørgen Jersild**
    Nina Pens Røde, Bendt Rothe, Ebbe Rode, Baard Owe, Axel Strøbye

Gertrud (Pens Røde) leaves her husband for a young musician only to find he cannot give her his total love. Later she rejects the marriage proposals of three men in succession, finally accepting that her ideal will never be realized. Made after a 10-year gap, Dreyer's final film takes the form of a series of duologues photographed with an almost immobile camera and immensely long takes, and given stylized performances. It was critically ill-received on its release by those whose definition of action in the cinema is severely limited. The action here is in the dialogue and emotions which create a film of exceptional intensity and warmth and after the pain and torment of the protagonist (a mesmerising Pens Røde), a serenity achieved in the best of chamber music.

Gervaise

France   1956   116 mins   bw
Angnes Delahaye/Silver/CLCC

d   **René Clement**
sc **Jean Aurenche, Pierre Bost**
ph **Robert Juillard**
    Maria Schell, François Périer, Suzy Delair, Mathilde Casadeus, Armand Mestral

In the Montmartre of 1850, washerwoman Gervaise (Schell) is left with two children by her lover. She marries a roof repairer (Périer) and opens her own laundry, but difficult circumstances lead her and her husband to drink. The fifth screen adaptation of Zola's *L'Assommoir* was the most lavish and convincing portrait of the bustling place and harsh period. Despite the severe limitations of her superficial performance, Maria Schell impressed the Venice Film Festival jury.

Best Actress (Maria Schell) Venice 1956

Get Out Your Handkerchiefs

▶ **Préparez Vos Mouchoirs**

France   1978   108 mins   col
Les Films Ariane/CAPAC/Belga/SODEP

d   **Bertrand Blier**
sc **Bertrand Blier**
ph **Jean Penzer**
m   **Georges Delerue, Mozart, Schubert**
    Gérard Depardieu, Patrick Dewaere, Carole Laure, Riton, Michel Serrault

Raoul (Depardieu), finding his wife (Laure) sexually unresponsive, decides to present her with a lover (Dewaere) but he has no luck either. It takes a 13-year-old boy (Riton) to solve her problem and make her pregnant. Neither as ribald nor as funny as it sets out to be, the film has a great deal of old-fashioned charm. Depardieu and Dewaere, the leads in Blier's *Going Places* (1974), play with a lightness reminiscent of the New Wave days of Belmondo and Brialy.

Best Foreign Film Oscar 1978

▶ **Ghare-Baire** see Home And The World, The

▶ **Gharibeh-Va-Meh** see Stranger And The Fog, The

▶ **Giardino Dei Finzi-Contini, Il** see Garden Of The Finzi-Continis, The

▶ **Gift** see Poison

The Gift Of God

▶ **Wend Kuuni**

Upper Volta   1982   70 mins   col
National Cinema Centre

d   **Gaston J.M. Kaboré**
sc **Gaston J.M. Kaboré**
ph **Sekou Ouedraogo, Issaka Thiombiano**

m **René B. Guirma**
   Serge Yanago, Rosine Yanago, Joseph Nikiema, Colette Kaboré

In pre-colonial days, a small boy (Serge Yanago), found wandering lost in the bush and unable to speak, is adopted by a young couple (Nikiema and Kaboré). The boy spends his days silently tending their goats in the fields, sometimes with their young daughter (Rosine Yanago) who dreams that his speech will come back and he will be able to tell her what happened to him and where he comes from. Kaboré's concise first feature shows sensitivity and a simplicity of expression in a beautifully photographed story of an African childhood. The two children appear wonderfully natural under his careful direction.

Gigi

France 1948 109 mins bw
Codo-Cinéma

d **Jacqueline Audry**
sc **Pierre Laroche**
ph **Gérard Perrin**
m **Marcel Landowski**
   Danièle Delorme, Gaby Morlay, Yvonne De Bray, Frank Villard, Jean Tissier

In turn-of-the century Paris, Gigi (Delorme), a young girl trained to be a courtesan by her aunt (Morlay), opts for true love and marriage to a rake (Villard) whom she reforms. This charming, faithful adaptation of Colette's novel had the advantage of a close collaboration between the director, her screenwriter husband and the novelist herself. It was the first of a successful trilogy of films based on Colette stories, all directed by Audry and all starring the delicate Danièle Delorme, and, of course, was the subject of the award-winning Hollywood musical, starring Leslie Caron.

Ginger And Fred

▶ **Ginger E Fred**

Italy 1986 127 mins col
PEA(Rome)/Revcom Films/Les Films Ariane/FR3 Films (Paris)/Stella Films/Anthea(Munich)

d **Federico Fellini**
sc **Federico Fellini, Tonino Guerra, Tullio Pinelli**
ph **Tonino Delli Colli, Ennio Guarnieri**
m **Nicola Piovani**
   Giulietta Masina, Marcello Mastroianni, Franco Fabrizi, Frederick Von Ledebur, Augusto Poderosi, Martin Maria Blau, Toto Mignone

Before the war, dancers Amelia Bonetti (Masina) and Pippo Botticella (Mastroianni) performed a cabaret as Ginger and Fred in homage to the great Hollywood duo. Many years have passed since they went their separate ways; now they are reunited by an invitation to resurrect their act for a popular TV programme. A simple story in which Fellini simultaneously pays a nostalgic and affectionate tribute to old troupers and digs the knife into the crass commercialism of Italian television – at whose hands he has suffered with the indiscriminate mangling of his films. Masina, serene without being coy, and a flabby, balding Mastroianni are a delight as the couple, now past it but able to relive their former glory for a few magical moments. This is the director at his most warmly accessible.

▶ **Ginger E Fred** see Ginger And Fred

▶ **Gion Bayashi** see Gion Festival Music

Gion Festival Music

▶ **(US: Geisha)**

▶ **Gion Bayashi**

Japan 1953 100 mins bw
Daiei

d **Kenji Mizoguchi**
sc **Yoshikata Yoda**
ph **Kazuo Miyagawa**
m **Ichiro Saito**
   Michiyo Kogure, Ayako Wakao, Seizaburo Kawazy, Cheiko Naniwa, Eitaro Shindo

An elderly geisha (Kogure) trains a young girl (Wakao) in the ancient art, but the novice soon realizes that her romantic vision of her role is a far cry from the sordid reality. Almost a remake of Sisters Of The Gion (1936), it is one of Mizoguchi's finest chamber works, being a sensitive and thoughful study of two contrasting geishas (superbly played) and of the reduced status of their calling after World War II.

▶ **Gion No Shimai** see Sisters Of The Gion

▶ **Giornata Particolare, Una** see Special Day, A

▶ **Gioventù Perduta** see Lost Youth

▶ **Girasoli, I** see Sunflower

The Girl Friends

▶ **Le Amiche**

Italy 1955 90 mins bw
Trionfalcine

d   Michelangelo Antonioni
sc Suso Cecchi D'Amico, Alba De Cespedes, Michelangelo Antonioni
ph Gianni Di Venanzo
m   Giovanni Fusco
Eleanora Rossi Drago, Valentina Cortese, Yvonne Furneaux, Gabriele Ferzetti, Franco Fabrizi, Madeleine Fischer, Annamaria Pancani

Clelia (Drago), who has done well in Rome as a fashion designer, returns to her native Turin where she becomes involved in the affairs of four of her *haute bourgeois* girl friends. Adapted from a Cesare Pavese story, the film manages to hold 10 characters in balance, giving almost equal weight to their individuality and the shifting pattern of relationships. The elaborate social groupings and Antonioni's ability to set people meaningfully against landscapes is best illustrated by the extended sequence of an afternoon on the beach. The film, which won a prize at Venice, proves that Antonioni's greatness did not begin with *L'Avventura* (1960).

A Girl From Lorraine

▶ **La Provincial**

France 1980 112 mins col
Phoenix/Gaumont/FR3/SSR

d   Claude Goretta
sc Claude Goretta, Jacques Kirsner, Rosina Rochette
ph Philippe Rousselot
m   Arié Dzierlatka
Nathalie Baye, Bruno Ganz, Angela Winkler, Patrick Chesnais, Pierre Vernier

With great expectations, 30-year-old Christine (Baye) leaves her friends, local choir and dog in her small home town in Lorraine to find work in Paris. After having an affair with a married Swiss businessman (Ganz), struggling to make a living and avoiding temptation, she returns home disillusioned. Goretta followed *The Lacemaker* with another fable about a 'typical ordinary Frenchwoman', as Christine is described. To go by the film, this means priggish, humourless and rather dull. Like the life in Paris, the screenplay is too obviously loaded against her in order to prove the contentious point that existence in the provinces, no matter how hard, is morally superior to that in the big bad city.

The Girl From Stormycroft

▶ **(US: A Girl From The Marsh Croft)**

▶ **Tosen Fran Stormytorpet**

Sweden 1917 96 mins bw
Svenska Biografteatern

d   Victor Sjöström
sc Victor Sjöström, Esther Julin
ph Henrik Jaenzon
m   Silent
Greta Almroth, Lars Hanson, Karin Molander, Georg Blomstedt

Helga (Almroth) becomes a social outcast when she gives birth to an illegitimate baby, but eventually wins the respect of the remote rustic community by refusing to let the father (Hanson) court damnation by taking an oath on the Bible denying responsibility. She eventually wins the love of a young man (Blomstedt) who has also faced unjust opprobrium. With 32 films already behind him, Sjöström became an international figure with this, the first of several adaptations from novels by Selma Lagerlöf. The plot has its inconsistencies and crudities, but the superb underplaying and the director's ability to create a believable community make it one of his finest films. It was remade by Detlef Sierck (Douglas Sirk) in Germany in 1935.

▶ **Girl From The Marsh Croft, A** see
Girl From Stormycroft, The

Girl In A Boot

▶ **Einmal Ku'damm Und Zurück**

W. Germany 1983 96 mins col
Cinecom/Neue Filmproduktion/Sender
Freies

d **Herbert Ballmann**
sc **Jürgen Engert**
ph **Ingo Hamer**
m **Jürgen Knieper**
   **Ursela Monn, Christian Kohlund, Evelyn
   Meyka, Peter Schiff, Peter Seum**

East Berliner Ulla (Monn), whose father (Schiff) is a hard-line Party member, has a clandestine affair with Thomas (Kohlund), the cook at the Swiss Embassy. (Food is a nicely used recurring image.) Hiding Ulla in the boot of Thomas's car, the couple make a series of visits to the Western sector until a car accident in which Ulla is injured exposes them. Ballmann, who lived in East Berlin and made documentaries there, captures the details of daily life behind the wall, contrasting the struggles of the inhabitants with the cavalier consumerism of their privileged neighbours. The film is not, however, a didactic piece, being more concerned with Ulla who opts to sacrifice Thomas and stay at home, not for political reasons but because her roots are there.

The Girl In Black

▶ **To Koritsi Me Ta Mavra**

Greece 1955 93 mins bw
Hermes

d **Michael Cacoyannis**
sc **Michael Cacoyannis**
ph **Walter Lassally**
m **Argyris Kounadis, Manos Hadjidakis**
   **Ellie Lambetti, Georges Foundas, Dimitri
   Horne, Eleni Zafiriou, Stefanos Stratigos**

On the remote fishing island of Hydra, Marina (Lambetti) is persecuted by her neighbours for her widowed mother's indiscretions. A visiting Athenian writer (Foundas) tries to take her back to the mainland, but his attempts to save her end in near tragedy. Ellie Lambetti, the beautiful star of Cacoyannis' first film, the comedy *Windfall In Athens*, impressed even more as an actress of tragic stature in this controlled but passionate story. The German-born British Lassally gave it the keen-edged black and white photography it needed.

The Girl Rosemarie

▶ **(US: Rosemary)**

▶ **Das Mädchen Rosemarie**

W. Germany 1958 100 mins bw
Roxy

d **Rolf Thiele**
sc **Rolf Thiele, Erich Kuby, Jo Herbst, Rolf
   Ulrich**
ph **Klaus Von Rautenfeld**
m **Norbert Schultze**
   **Nadja Tiller, Peter Van Eyck, Carl
   Raddatz, Gert Fröbe, Mario Adorf, Horst
   Frank**

The diary of a murdered Frankfurt prostitute reveals that she was blackmailing her wealthy and powerful clients, some of them the investigators of the crime itself. This biting satire on Adenauer's Germany was based on a real case that opened up a cesspool of corruption within the Establishment. The slickly-made film had more impact in pre-Fassbinder days, but it's still a good exposé and Tiller, a former Miss Austria, is seductive in the title role.

▶ **Girls, The** see Bonnes Femmes, Les

The Girls

▶ **Flickorna**

Sweden 1968 100 mins bw
Sandrew

d **Mai Zetterling**
sc **Mai Zetterling, David Hughes**
ph **Rune Ericson**

m **Michael Hurd**
  Bibi Andersson, Harriet Andersson,
  Gunnel Lindblom, Gunnar Björnstrand,
  Erland Josephson, Frank Sundströom

Three actresses – Liz (Bibi Andersson), Marianne (Harriet Andersson), Gunilla (Lindblom) – are in a production of Aristophanes'
Lysistrata. Each has an unhappy personal
life, suffering boorish husbands, married lovers, and so forth, and the play begins to
influence them. Led by Liz, they begin to
stand up for their rights as women. Casting
some of the leading lights of Swedish film,
Mai Zetterling brings her not inconsiderable
experience to bear on a feminist plea, usefully
intercutting the action with the Aristophanes
classic. Unfortunately, she overstates her case,
making all the men either ineffectual or
unpleasant and the women visibly militant,
and so loses the argument.

The Girls

▶ **Gehenu Lamai**

  Sri Lanka 1977 110 mins bw
  Lester James Peries Productions

d **Sumitra Peries**
sc **Sumitra Peries**
ph **M.S. Anandan**
m **Nimal Mendis**
  Vasanthi Chaturani, Ajith Jinadasa,
  Jenita Samaraweera, Trilicia
  Gunawardana, Chitra Wakista

Kusum (Chaturani), daughter of a poor village family, wins a scholarship to boarding
school. On her visits home she looks after her
crippled father, acts as mentor to her younger
sister Soma (Samaraweera) and has a secret
love affair with her cousin (Jinadasa) to which
her aunt puts a stop. Soma wins a beauty contest and goes off to a movie career, but
becomes pregnant, and Kusum, unhappy, fails
her exams and must face a bleak future. This
first feature is the work of Sri Lanka's first
woman director – an achievement in itself. It's
a modest, straightforward film in both style
and content and, by Western standards, somewhat old-fashioned in its particular brand of
simplicity. As a glimpse of Sinhalese rural
values it's interesting and rather sad, but the
director has missed opportunities to develop
both her characters and her subject.

▶ **Girls In Uniform** see Mädchen In
Uniform

The Girl With A Suitcase

▶ **La Ragazza Con La Valigia**

  Italy 1960 135 mins bw
  Titanus (Rome)/S.G.C. (Paris)

d **Valerio Zurlini**
sc **Leo Benvenuti, Piero De Bernardi, Enrico**
  Medioli, Giuseppe Patroni Griffi, Valerio
  Zurlini
ph **Tito Santoni**
m **Mario Nascimbene**
  Claudio Cardinale, Jacques Perrin,
  Luciana Angelillo, Corrado Pani, Romolo
  Valli, Gian Maria Volonté

Aida (Cardinale), a nightclub singer, is
seduced by, and leaves her job for, Marcello
(Pani), a rich idler who then abandons her.
When she follows him to his family home in
Parma, he instructs his 16-year-old brother
Lorenzo (Perrin) to get rid of her, but the
couple fall in love before circumstances force
them to part. Zurlini, one of the most sensitive, economical and visually aware of Italian
directors of the period, has made a poignant
film of some depth, at the centre of which is
a lost soul ill-equipped to find redemption.
Cardinale and Perrin are excellent, but beware
of badly cut versions: the film's original British release lost 39 minutes, and was thus
severely distorted.

The Girl With The Golden Eyes

▶ **La Fille Aux Yeux D'Or**

  France 1961 105 mins bw
  Madeleine

d **Jean-Gabriel Albicocco**
sc **Jean-Gabriel Albicocco, Pierre Pelégri,**
  Philippe Dumarçay
ph **Quinto Albicocco**
m **Narciso Yepes, Arcangelo Corelli**
  Marie Laforêt, Paul Guers, Françoise
  Prévost, Jacques Verlier, Françoise
  Dorléac

A man (Guers) working in the world of *haute
couture* falls for a girl (Laforêt) of whom he

knows nothing. He soon discovers that she is the lover of a female colleague (Prévost), and becomes a threat to their relationship. It would be hard to guess that this chic, arty, stylized Lesbian tale, set in and around the Paris fashion houses of the 1960s, was based on a Balzac story. Albicocco in his first feature, strains too hard to be stylish and provocative, attributes which come naturally to his wife, Laforêt.

Girl With The Hatbox

▶ **(US: When Moscow Laughs)**

▶ **Devuchka S Korobkoi**

> USSR　1927　61 mins　bw
> Mezhrabpom

d　**Boris Barnet**
sc　**V. Tourkine, V. Cherchenievitch**
ph　**B. Frantzisson, B. Filshin**
m　**Silent**
　　Anna Sten, Vladimir Fogel, I. Koval-Samborski, V. Milhailov

While travelling on a train, Natasha (Sten), a Moscow milliner, meets a homeless student (Koval-Samborski) from the provinces. In order to get accomodation, he pretends to be married. After getting mixed up in a lottery squabble and stringing him along, she finally obliges him by marrying him. Barnet's first solo effort is a charming satirical comedy in the American style, that also owes much to Lev Kuleshov's experimental workshop. A model of cinematic storytelling, it includes some splendid location scenes in the wintry countryside and in Moscow's busy streets. Making her screen debut in the lead was the irresistible Anna Sten who, seven years later, was to have a disastrous Hollywood career.

The Girl With The Red Hair

▶ **Het Meisje Met Het Rode Haar**

> Netherlands　1981　114 mins　col
> Movies Filmproductions

d　**Ben Verbong**
sc　**Ben Verbong, Pieter De Vos**
ph　**Theo Van Der Sande**
m　**Nicola Piovani**
　　Renée Soutendijk, Peter Tuinman, Ada

Bouwman, Loes Luca, Robert Delhez, Lineke Rijxman

The wartime experiences of Hannie (Soutendijk), a Dutch Resistance worker who overcomes her reluctance to use a gun, has an affair with her colleague Hugo (Tuinman) and is caught and shot by the Germans when her distinctive red hair, dyed for protection, begins to grow out. The tale is told as a flashback recollection by An (Luca), the girl who trained Hannie, but is used as the basis for a feminist examination of Hannie's situation. This is an intriguing idea, but Verbong's message is a dreadful muddle, appearing to blame Hannie's tragedies on her impulsive temperament, 'typical' of redheads. Even the well-worn path of Resistance activities is retrod without imagination or sufficient tension.

▶ **Gishiki** see Ceremony, The

▶ **Giulietta Degli Spiriti** see Juliet Of The Spirits

▶ **Giuseppe Verdi** see Life And Music Of Giuseppe Verdi, The

The Given Word

▶ **O Pagador De Promessas**

> Brazil　1962　98 mins　bw
> Oswaldo Massaini

d　**Anselmo Duarte**
sc　**Anselmo Duarte**
ph　**Chick Fowle**
m　**Gabriel Migliori**
　　Leonardo Vilar, Dionizio Azevedo, Gloria Menezes, Geraldo Del Rey, Carlos Torres

A poor farmer (Vilar) drags a huge cross to the village church as an offering to Santa Barbara for saving his injured donkey. The priest (Azevedo) learns that he made his vow to do this at a voodoo ceremony, refuses him entry, and a battle of wills is fought, ending in the farmer's death. Adapted from a successful Brazilian play, Duarte's film retains its stage origins in confining the action largely to the steps of the church. A simple folk drama, brought to life with plenty of convincing atmosphere, but the central conflict becomes boring because the protagonists – both as written and played – are two-dimensional stereotypes.

Best Film Cannes 1962

▶ **Gläserne Himmel, Der** see Glass Heaven, The

The Glass Heaven

▶ **Der Gläserne Himmel**

W. Germany 1988 87 mins col
Avista Film/Voissfilm/Nina Grosse Film

d **Nina Grosse**
sc **Nina Grosse**
ph **Hans Bücking**
m **Flora St Loup**
   Helmut Berger, Silvie Orcier, Agnes Fink, Maria Harmann, Tobias Engel, Circe

Businessman Julien (Berger) lives an uneventful life with his wife (Harmann) and his bedridden mother (Fink) until he becomes haunted by a nightmare in which he sees a woman strangled in an aquarium. On his way to work one day, he sees the woman from his dreams and follows her into a bar. She disappears, but he recognizes a customer as the killer from his dream. and becomes involved with Bichette (Orcier), a prostitute who is friendly with the man... This is an exceptionally stylish debut film, boasting several imaginative ideas and unusual images. The resolution is a touch predictable but, until then, Grosse keeps up the momentum of her mysterious events, creating some nail-biting tension. She is helped by solid performances and excellent camerawork.

▶ **Goalie's Anxiety At The Penalty Kick, The** see Anxiety Of The Goalie At The Penalty, The

▶ **Goalkeeper's Fear Of The Penalty Kick, The** see Anxiety Of The Goalie At The Penalty, The

▶ **Gobbo, Il** see Hunchback Of Rome, The

▶ **Godard's Passion** see Passion

▶ **Goddess, The** see Devi

▶ **God Needs Men** see Isle Of Sinners

Gods Of The Plague

▶ **Götter Der Pest**

W. Germany 1970 91 mins bw
Antitheater-X Film

d **Rainer Werner Fassbinder**
sc **Rainer Werner Fassbinder**
ph **Dietrich Lohmann**
m **Peer Raben**
   Harry Baer, Hanna Schygulla, Margarethe Von Trotta, Günter Kaufmann, Ingrid Caven

Franz (Baer) comes out of jail and meets an old pal (Kaufmann) with whom he plans to rob a supermarket. The men are betrayed by two girls (Schygulla and Van Trotta) who both love Franz. Like Fassbinder's first feature, *Love Is Colder Than Death*, his third was influenced by Hollywood *film noir* as filtered through the French New Wave. Far too cool and self-conscious to work as a crime movie or even as pastiche, it does make an impact as a melancholy study of characters trapped in an unfriendly milieu, including the gloomy 'Lola Montes' nightclub. Except for a spectacular long-take helicopter shot, it is Fassbinder at his most austere. Günter Kaufmann, who dies beautifully at the end, was the illegitimate son of a black GI and a Bavarian woman. Fassbinder met him in 1969, fell in love and put him in his next few films.

Goha

France/Tunisia 1957 90 mins col
Films Franco Africains

d **Jacques Baratier**
sc **Georges Schéhadé**
ph **Jean Bourgoin**
m **Maurice Ohana**
   Omar Chérif (later Sharif), Zina Bouzaiane, Lauro Gazzolo, Gabriel Jabbour

A clever young man (Chérif), under the guise of stupidity, woos the bride of the town's wise man and helps a blind musician. Lovely colour, exotic locations and handsome 25-year-old Omar Sharif, still five years away from international stardom, make this Arab folk tale extremely pleasing. Baratier, in his debut feature, manages to switch from humour to drama with maturity.

▶ **Going Places** see Making It

Gold

Germany 1934 120 mins bw
UFA

d **Karl Hartl**
sc **Rolf Vanloo**
ph **Günther Rittau, Otto Baecker, Werner Böhne**
m **Hans-Otto Borgman**
Hans Albers, Brigitte Helm, Friedrich Kayssler, Lien Deyers, Michael Bohnen

A scientist (Albers) creates an atomic reactor able to change lead into gold, but destroys the machine rather than have it used for evil ends. It is now difficult to believe that after World War II the US government had this plodding but atmospheric science fiction drama screened for scientists to see whether it showed the Germans capable of producing nuclear power. It did not, but it was a tribute to the film's prescience. Hollywood re-used the underwater lab scenes for *The Magnetic Monster* (1953).

▶ **Golden Age, The** see Âge D'Or, L'

The Golden Coach

▶ **La Carrozza D'Oro**

▶ **aka Le Carrosse D'Or**

Italy 1952 100 mins col
Panaria/Hoche

d **Jean Renoir**
sc **Jean Renoir, Renzo Avanzo, Jack Kirkland, Giulio Macchi, Ginette Doynel**
ph **Claude Renoir**
m **Vivaldi**
Anna Magnani, Odoardo Spadaro,
Duncan Lamont, Nada Fiorelli, Ralph Truman, Ricardo Rioli, Paul Campbell

In 18th-century Peru, an actress (Magnani) with a touring Commedia Dell'Arte troupe is wooed by a bullfighter (Rioli), a soldier (Campbell) and the Viceroy (Lamont). When the latter presents her with a golden coach from Europe, she donates it to the church and opts for her first love – the theatre. Renoir conceived the *opera-buffa* type script while listening to Vivaldi, and the film contains much of the exuberance, and the dark undertones, of the Italian baroque composer. Based on a one-act play by Mérimée, it is a rich illustration of the theme of the tension between life and theatre. Only the casting of the somewhat coarse-grained Magnani as the centre of attraction seems a little perverse. It was a favourite film of Truffaut, who named his production company Les Films Du Carrosse after it.

Golden Eighties

France/Belgium 1986 96 mins col
La Cecilia (Paris)/Paradise Films (Brussels)/Limbo-Films (Zurich)

d **Chantal Akerman**
sc **Chantal Akerman, Leora Barish, Henry Bean, Pascal Bonitzer, Jean Gruault**
ph **Gilberto Azevedo, Luc Benhamou**
m **Marc Herouet**
Delphine Seyrig, Myriam Boyer, Fanny Cottençon, Lio, Charles Denner, Jean-François Balmer, John Berry, Nicolas Tronc

Jeanne Schwartz (Seyrig) and her husband own a clothes boutique in a shopping mall where their son Robert (Tronc) works. He, along with several other men, is infatuated with Lili (Cottençon), manageress of the hairdressing salon, whose assistant Mado (Lio) loves Robert. Everybody's lives are complicated by the arrival of Eli (Berry), Jeanne's pre-war lover, who tries to persuade her to go away with him. Akerman, feminist director of often minimalist and low-key films, has turned her hand to a musical in which the themes of love, sex and commerce are closely linked. If the undertones are bitter-sweet and sometimes cynical, the surface glints diamond-bright as the characters play out their destinies to the accompaniment of a lively score and witty, sometimes raunchy, lyrics, with a stylistic nod towards Jacques Demy (*The Umbrellas Of Cherbourg*). An original and intelligent film, with the graceful Seyrig glowing at its centre.

Golden Marie

▶ **Casque D'Or**

France 1952 96 mins bw
Speva/Paris

d **Jacques Becker**
sc **Jacques Becker, Jacques Companeez**
ph **Robert Le Fèbvre**
m **Georges Van Parys**
   Simone Signoret, Serge Reggiani, Claude Dauphin, Raymond Bussières, Gaston Modot

In turn-of-the-century Paris, an honest carpenter (Reggiani), drawn into a world of pimps, prostitutes and petty crooks because of his passion for gangster's moll Marie (Signoret), is driven to murder. Becker's lovingly recreated Paris of the past almost equals the radiance of Renoir *père et fils*. Despite the *crime passionnel* plot, the film throbs with the affirmation of love and friendship. The glowing sensuality of Signoret is reflected in the wonderful open air scenes and the warm morning sunshine as the lovers awake together.

Gold Of Naples

▶ **L'Oro Di Napoli**

Italy 1955 135 mins bw
Gala/Ponti-De Laurentiis

d **Vittorio De Sica**
sc **Vittorio De Sica, Cesare Zavattini, Giuseppe Marotta**
ph **Otello Martelli**
m **Alessandro Cicognini**
   Vittorio De Sica, Sophia Loren, Totò, Paolo Stoppa, Silvana Mangano, Pasquale Cennamo, Lianella Carrell, Giacomo Furia, Alberto Farnese, Erno Crisa

Four Neapolitan sketches. 'The Racketeer': a little man (Totò) outwits a bullying racketeer (Cennamo) who has imposed upon him and his wife (Carrell); 'Pizza On Credit': a wife (Loren) loses her wedding ring during a rendezvous with a lover (Farnese), arousing the suspicions of her husband (Furia); 'The Gambler': an inveterate gambler (De Sica) continues to believe himself lucky even after squandering his family's fortune; 'Theresa': a prostitute (Mangano) marries a mentally unbalanced young man (Crisa) and uses sexual therapy to help him. One of the better portmanteau films, with some good jokes and good performances from Mangano, Totò, 20-year-old Loren and De Sica, although the film could be seen as the beginning of De Sica's decline as a director. Perhaps it was just as well that only four of the original six sketches survived for import, because it might have overstayed its welcome.

Gold, Silver, Bad Luck

▶ **Oro, Plata, Mata**

Philippines 1982 194 mins col
Experimental Cinema of the Philippines

d **Peque Gallaga**
sc **José Javier Reyes**
ph **Rody Lacap**
m **José Gentica V**
   Manny Ojeda, Liza Lorena, Sandy Andolong, Cherie Gil, Fides Cuyugan Asensio

Two aristocratic families are gathered together to celebrate the birthday and coming-out of debutante Maggie (Andolong), but the gaiety is dispelled by the possibility of a Japanese invasion. The families, with their servants, flee to a primitive hunting lodge in the mountains where they live a precarious and fraught existence. One of the most ambitious and epic films to be made in the Philippines has a fine sweep and vigour, especially astonishing as it is former production designer Gallaga's solo directorial debut. Yet it is too diffuse, derivative (Visconti comes to mind), exceptionally bloody (tongues cut out, fingers chopped off, knives plunged into chests) and, despite some implied social criticism, rather suspect politically.

The Golem

▶ **Der Golem: Wie Er In Die Welt Kam**

France 1920   75 mins   bw
UFA

d   **Paul Wegener, Carl Boese**
sc **Paul Wegener, Henrik Galeen**
ph **Karl Freund, Guido Seeber**
m   **Silent**
    Paul Wegener, Albert Steinruck, Ernst Deutsch, Lyda Salmonova

In 16th-century Prague, a rabbi (Steinruck) creates a monster (Wegener) out of clay to help his people fight against the Emperor's expulsion of the Jews from the ghetto. The most eye-catching of the various versions of the ancient Jewish legend, mainly because of the Expressionistic sets by Hans Poelzig, and the use of chiaroscuro to create a Gothic effect. Wegener's lumbering gait was imitated by Boris Karloff in *Frankenstein* (1931).

The Golem

▶ **aka The Legend Of Prague**
▶ **Le Golem**

France 1936   95 mins   bw
AB

d   **Julien Duvivier**
sc **Julien Duvivier, André-Paul Antoine**
ph **Jan Stallich, Vaclav Vich**
m   **Joseph Kumok**
    Harry Baur, Roger Karl, Ferdinand Hart, Charles Dorat, Germaine Aussey

A rabbi (Dorat) brings the Golem (Hart) back to life in order to frighten the Emperor Rudolf II (Baur) into freeing the Jews from the slavery to which they have been reduced. The first sound version of the Jewish folk legend, almost a sequel to the 1920 remake, had the advantage of actually being shot in Prague. But despite good special effects and Baur's strong presence, it lacked the atmosphere and narrative drive of the earlier film.

▶ **Golem, Le** see Golem, The

▶ **Golem: Wie Er In Die Welt Kam, Der** see Golem, The

▶ **Golfos, Los** see Hooligans, The

Golgotha

France 1935   100 mins   bw
Ichtys Film

d   **Julien Duvivier**
sc **Joseph Reymond**
ph **Jules Kruger, René Ribault, Marie Fossard, Robert Juillard**
m   **Jacques Ibert**
    Harry Baur, Robert Le Vigan, Jean Gabin, Charles Grandval, André Bacque, Edwige Feuillère

The Passion and the Crucifixion of Christ. Duvivier's straightforward, well-crafted account of the life of Christ was the first sound film to be made on the subject tackled earlier in Cecil B. DeMille's superior *The King Of Kings* (1927). The cast was a curious one with Gabin as Pontius Pilate and Le Vigan as Christ. (Le Vigan, who became a Nazi collaborator, killed himself after the war.) Harry Baur made an imposing Herod.

▶ **Golubye Gory Ely Nepravdopo-dobnaya Istoria** see Blue Mountains

A Good Marriage

▶ **Le Beau Mariage**

France 1981   97 mins   col
Les Films Du Losange/Les Films Du Carrosse

d   **Eric Rohmer**
sc **Eric Rohmer**
ph **Bernard Lutic**
m   **Roman Girre, Simon Des Innocents**
    Béatrice Romand, André Dussollier, Feodor Atkine, Arielle Dombasle, Huguette Faget

A 25-year-old art student (Romand) breaks off an affair with a married man (Atkine) and determines to get a husband of her own. Unfortunately, she decides on a handsome, well-to-do lawyer (Dussollier) who has no intention of marrying. The title of Rohmer's elegant, witty and touching 'Comedy and Proverb' refers to an ideal rather than an actual event. The film is also a wry comment on the contradictions that exist in a liberated woman with some old-fashioned ideas. As usual the backgrounds are meticulously observed – this time Le Mans is the principal setting.

Best Actress (Béatrice Romand) Venice 1981

Good Morning

▶ **Ohayo**

Japan 1959 97 mins col
Shochiku

d **Yasujiro Ozu**
sc **Yasujiro Ozu, Kogo Noda**
ph **Yuharu Atsuta**
m **Toshiro Mayuzumi**
Chishu Ryu, Kuniko Miyake, Yoshiko Kuga, Keiji Sada, Masahiko Shimazu, Koji Shidara

Two young boys (Shimazu and Shidara), living with their parents (Ryu and Miyake) in suburban Tokyo, are refused a TV set. Told to shut up by their father, they take a vow of silence, refusing even to say 'good morning' to a neighbour. Returning to the theme of juvenile rebellion he had dealt with in *I Was Born But...* 28 years previously, Ozu here treats it with less depth but with the gentle, mocking affection and mastery of his late works. A sensitive use of colour and fine performances make the film an all-round pleasure.

The Good Soldier Schweik

▶ **Der Brave Soldat Schwejk**

W. Germany 1960 96 mins bw
CCC/Filmkunst-Weinfilm/Lionex

d **Axel Von Ambesser**
sc **Hans Jacoby**
ph **Richard Angst**
m **Bernhard Eichhorn**
Heinz Rühmann, Ernst Stankowski,

Ursula Borsodi, Senta Berger, Erika Von Thellmann

Schweik (Rühmann), a good-hearted, garrulous dog salesman, is reluctantly drafted into the Austrian army of 1914. Enmeshed in red tape and harassed by police, doctors, priests and officers, he makes his eventful way towards the moment when he is captured by his own troops. Jaroslav Hasek's classic novel brilliantly conveys both the obscenity of war and its absurdity through one of the greatest comic characters in all literature. Unfortunately, this pedestrian adaptation never begins to approach the glories of the novel, although there are glimmerings of what might have been in Rühmann's performance if only he had been surrounded by artists with more vision.

▶ **Goopy And Bagha** see Adventures Of Goopy And Bagha, The

▶ **Goopy Gyne Bagha Byne** see Adventures Of Goopy And Bagha, The

▶ **Goracza** see Fever

A Gorgeous Bird Like Me

▶ **(US: Such A Gorgeous Kid Like Me)**

▶ **Une Belle Fille Comme Moi**

France 1972 98 mins col
Films Du Carrosse/Columbia

d **François Truffaut**
sc **François Truffaut, Jean-Loup Dabadie**
ph **Pierre William Glenn**
m **Georges Delerue**
Bernadette Lafont, Claude Brasseur, Charles Denner, Guy Marchand, André Dussollier, Philippe Léotard

Camille Bliss (Lafont), a woman convicted of murder, tells a criminologist (Dussollier) the tale of her involvement with a singer (Marchand), a rat catcher (Denner) and a lawyer (Brasseur). An uncomfortable blend of French and American farce (it was based on an American novel by Henry Farrell), social document and black comedy, the film is not one of Truffaut's most accomplished works. The 'gorgeous' Lafont may wield immense power over the men in the film, but her strident performance might not seduce audiences quite so easily.

The Gospel According To Saint Matthew

▶ **Il Vangelo Secondo Matteo**

Italy   1964   142 mins   bw
Arco/Lux

d   **Pier Paolo Pasolini**
sc **Pier Paolo Pasolini**
ph **Tonino Delli Colli**
m   **Bach, Mozart, Prokofiev, Webern, Negro Spirituals**
Enrique Irazoqui (Christ), Susanna Pasolini (Mary), Mario Socrate (John the Baptist), Marcello Morante (Joseph)

The birth, life, teachings and death on the cross of Jesus Christ. Pasolini's second feature seemed a strange choice for a Marxist, but it is an attempt to take Christ out of the opulent church and present him as an outcast Italian peasant. Applying Neo-Realist methods, the director shot the film in Calabria, using the expressive faces of non-professionals including that of his mother as the Virgin Mary. Although considered by some critics as the greatest screen version of the 'greatest story ever told', it might have been more adventurous had not the Church helped to finance it.

Special Jury Prize Venice 1964

▶ **Gösta Berlings Saga** see Atonement Of Gösta Berling, The

Goto, Island Of Love

▶ **Goto, L'Ile D'Amour**

France   1968   93 mins   bw
Euro-Images/Les Productions René Thévenet

d   **Walerian Borowczyk**
sc **Walerian Borowczyk, Dominique Duvergé**
ph **Guy Durban, Paul Cotteret**
m   **Handel**
Pierre Brasseur, Ligia Branice, Ginette
Leclerc, René Dany, Jean-Pierre Andréani

Goto III (Brasseur) is a cruel dictator who rules over a small island, cut off from the world, where most of the population toil in the stone quarries. Goto's wife, Glossia (Branice), loves Gono (Andréani) with whom she hopes to flee. But things take a nasty turn. The Polish-born Borowczyck, in France since 1959, pursued the bitterly ironic surrealist vein of his animated films into his first live-action feature. Despite claims by the director that 'it is a realistic film', it creates an absurd and nightmarish world, full of nostalgic paraphenalia like music-boxes, phonographs and ancient instruments of torture. Given his truly surreal vision, it's not surprising that Borowczyk received the Max Ernst prize in 1967.

▶ **Goto, L'Ile D'Amour** see Goto, Island Of Love

▶ **Götterdämmerung** see Damned, The

▶ **Götter Der Pest** see Gods Of The Plague

Goupi-Mains-Rouges

▶ **(US: It Happened At The Inn)**

France   1943   95 mins   bw
Minerva

d   **Jacques Becker**
sc **Jacques Becker, Pierre Véry**
ph **Pierre Montazel, Jean Bourgoin**
m   **Jean Alfaro**
Fernand Ledoux, Georges Rollin, Blanchette Brunoy, Robert Le Vigan

When a member of the powerful but bickering Goupi family is killed and another suspected of the crime, the patriarch (Ledoux) decides to take the law into his own hands. Shot on location in the Charente, this outrageous black comedy with extravagant characters is nevertheless rooted in the reality of rural life. Owing much to Pagnol and Renoir, Becker's second feature (based on a novel by Pierre Véry) was a great success in Occupied France because of its affirmation of national identity.

▶ **Graal, Le** see Lancelot Of The Lake

▶ **Graduate First** see Passe Ton Bac D'Abord

▶ **Grail, The** see Lancelot Of The Lake

Le Grand Amour

France 1969 col 85 mins
CAPAC

d **Pierre Étaix**
sc **Pierre Étaix, Jean-Claude Carrière**
ph **Christian Guillouet**
m **Claude Stieremans**
Pierre Étaix, Annie Fratellini, Nicole Calfan, Ketty France, Louis Mais

Pierre (Étaix) and Florence (Fratellini, Étaix's real-life wife) are a reasonably happy married couple. One day, Pierre falls madly in love with his new young secretary (Calfan). While his wife is away on vacation, he tries to change his personality and woo her, but finds he is no Don Juan. There are many good visual gags running through this amiable comedy, and Étaix, working for the first time in colour, times most of them reasonably well. The problem lies in the fact that greater comedians, such as Max Linder and Buster Keaton, did the same sort of thing much better.

▶ **Grand Amour De Beethoven, Un**
see Life And Loves Of Beethoven, The

▶ **Grand Blond Avec Une Chaussure Noire, Le** see Tall Blond Man With One Black Shoe, The

Le Grand Chemin

France 1987 107 mins col

d **Jean-Loup Hubert**
sc **Jean-Loup Hubert**
ph **Claude Lecomte**
m **Georges Granier**
Anemone, Richard Bohringer, Antoine Hubert, Vanessa Guedj, Christine Pascal, Raoul Billerey, Pascale Roberts

In 1958 Louis (Hubert), a Parisian boy of nine, is taken and left by his pregnant mother to spend his summer vacation with her childhood friend Marcelle (Anemone) and her lover Pelo (Bohringer) in an isolated village in Brittany. There he makes friends with their 10-year-old neighbour, Martine (Guedj), a mischievous girl who shows him her hideouts and how to climb to the roof of the church. From his initial distrust of the couple he boards with, he learns about their secret distress and how to cope on his own. Most of the beauty and strength of this humorous and poignant film comes from the natural performances of Antoine Hubert, the director's son, reliving his father's childhood, and 11-year-old Vanessa Guedj, the latter giving one of the funniest and most anarchic portrayals by any actress of whatever age for many a day. In contrast to the childish couple is the childless one, to which Anemone and Richard Bohringer bring characterizations of increasing depth as the story evolves. However, the film is strongest in its city child's-eye view of rural life. In the beginning the country is seen as a sinister, bizarre and inhospitable place, but as the boy becomes seduced by the people and the environs, so do we. It is all done with such conviction that it overcomes the somewhat too neat and symmetrical plot – boy acting as catalyst in bringing the estranged couple together again, a symbolic nursery for a dead baby, a new child being born and a touch-and-go happy ending worthy of Hollywood.

▶ **Grande Bouffe, La** see Blow-Out

▶ **Grande Guerra, La** see Great War, The

La Grande Illusion

▶ **aka Grand Illusion**

France 1937 117 mins bw
Cinedis

d **Jean Renoir**
sc **Jean Renoir, Charles Spaak**
ph **Christian Matras, Claude Renoir**
m **Joseph Kosma**
Pierre Fresnay, Erich Von Stroheim, Jean Gabin, Marcel Dalio, Julien Carette, Gaston Modot, Dita Parlo, Jean Dasté

Three French soldiers, the working-class Maréchal (Gabin), the middle-class Rosenthal (Dalio) and the aristocrat Boïeldieu (Fresnay), are held prisoner in a fortress run by Commandant Von Rauffenstein (Von Stroheim). Boïeldieu dies so that his fellow POWs can escape. The script of Renoir's most popular film was touted around for three years before Gabin finally got it produced. Based on a true story of World War I told to the director by a friend, it is not only a moving anti-war statement but a rich exploration of class loyalties and transcending friendships. The fluid, deep-focus camerawork, the set pieces such as the singing of the 'Marseillaise' during theatricals, and the extraordinary performances make it one of the cinema's most enduring masterpieces, and it was awarded a prize at Venice for the best artistic ensemble.

▶ **Grande Rue,** see Calle Mayor

Les Grandes Familles

▶ **(US: The Possessors)**

France   1958   93 mins   bw
Filmsonor/Intermondia

d   **Denys De La Patellière**
sc   **Michel Audiard, Denys De La Patellière**
ph   **Louis Page**
m   **Maurice Thiriet**
     Jean Gabin, Jean Desailly, Bernard Blier, Pierre Brasseur, Jean Murat, Louis Seigner, Emmanuele Riva

The patriarch (Gabin) of a rich and powerful family with controlling interests in banking, the press and the arts, has doubts about the fitness of his weak son (Desailly) to succeed him, while trying to do down his rivals and keep the large family together. Gabin's imposing presence as an actor keeps the whole film together – an enjoyable, literate, old-fashioned entertainment. Based on the first third of Maurice Druon's 1948 three-part novel, the film's solid virtues and its veteran star made it popular at home and abroad.

▶ **Grandes Manoeuvres, Les** see Summer Manoeuvres

▶ **Grandeur Nature** see Life Size

▶ **Grande Vadrouille, La** see Don't Look Now . . . We're Being Shot At!

▶ **Grand Illusion,** see Grande Illusion, La

Le Grand Jeu

France   1934   115 mins   bw
Films De France

d   **Jacques Feyder**
sc   **Jacques Feyder, Charles Spaak**
ph   **Harry Stradling, Maurice Forster**
m   **Hanns Eisler**
     Pierre-Richard Willm, Marie Bell, Françoise Rosay, Charles Vanel

A Foreign Legionnaire (Willm) goes to Morocco to forget a coquettish Parisian society woman, only to find her double in the person of a cabaret singer. In order to create a strange ambiguity, Marie Bell, in a dual role, was dubbed by another actress for the Moroccan scenes. After a short sojourn in Hollywood where he directed Garbo in The Kiss (1929), Feyder returned to France and solidified his reputation with three successful films featuring his wife Françoise Rosay, beginning with this exotic, erotic romance.

▶ **Grand Manoeuver, The** see Summer Manoeuvres

▶ **Grand Meaulnes, Le** see Wanderer, The

▶ **Grand Paysage D'Alexis Droeven, Le** see Endless Land Of Alexis Droeven, The

▶ **Grands Chemins, Les** see Of Flesh And Blood

Grazie Zia

▶ **aka Thank You, Aunt**

Italy   1968   96 mins   bw
Doria Film

d   **Salvatore Samperi**
sc   **Sergio Bazzini, Salvatore Samperi, Pier Luigi Murgia**
ph   **Aldo Scavarda**
m   **Ennio Morricone**

Lou Castel, Lisa Gastoni, Gabriele
Ferzetti, Luisa De Santis, Massimo
Sarghielli

Alvise (Castel), seeking release from the world
that awaits him as heir to a wealthy industrialist, develops a psychosomatic paralysis that
confines him to a wheelchair. Placed in the
care of his brilliant, beautiful and liberated
doctor aunt (Gastoni), he draws her into a
series of elaborate and increasingly erotic
fantasies and games which lead to the loss of
her independence. Samperi, admitting to the
obvious influence of Bellocchio, Losey, Polanski and Buñuel, made this first feature at the
age of 24. He fails to explore the drives behind
Alvise's vicious behaviour, but succeeds in
creating a suffocatingly enclosed world,
evoked by accurate and intelligent images.
The leads are first-class and, if the piece is
derivative and lacking in cohesion, it is nonetheless undeniably talented.

The Great Adventure

▶ **Det Stora Aventyret**

Sweden 1953 80 mins bw
Sandrew/Bauman

d Arne Sucksdorff
sc Arne Sucksdorff
ph Arne Sucksdorff
m Lars Erik Larsson
   Anders Norberg, Kjell Sucksdorff, Arne
   Sucksdorff

Two young boys (Norberg and Kjell
Sucksdorff) in north Sweden attempt to tame
a wild otter but the animal longs to return to
the forests and lakes. What struck most adult
spectators was the brilliant photography of
wintry landscapes and wildlife, while children,
the main audience worldwide, identified with
the young heroes' adventures among the animals in this charming and beautiful little film.

The Great Consoler

▶ **Velikii Uteshitel**

USSR 1933 97 mins bw
Mosfilm

d Lev Kuleshov
sc Lev Kuleshov, Alexander Kurs
ph Konstantin Kuznetsov, G. Kabalov

m Zinovi Feldman
   Konstantin Khokhlov, I. Novoseltsev,
   Alexandra Khokhlova, Andrei Fayt

While serving a three-year prison sentence,
Bill Porter (Khokhlov), who wrote under the
name of O. Henry, sees the suffering of
safecracker Jimmy Valentine (Novoseltsev).
In a story, the writer transforms Jimmy into
a hero who rescues a girl trapped in a bank
vault. Reading it is Dulcy (Khokhlova), a
naive shop assistant, who has to wake up to
reality when she loses her job. Kuleshov, a
great admirer of American films and literature
(*By The Law* was based on a story by Jack
London), presents his 'interrogation' of O.
Henry's short story, *A Retrieved Reform*, in
three different narratives and styles – realistic,
burlesque and symbolic. This daring, novel,
but rather heartless film, which includes a
Western pastiche, was accused of 'intellectual-
ism' and American influences by officialdom,
and it was the last work of interest that
Kuleshov directed.

▶ **Greatest Love, The** see Europa 51

The Great War

▶ **La Grande Guerra**

Italy 1959 bw
DD/Gray

d Mario Monicelli
sc Mario Monicelli, Luciano Vincenzoni,
   Age, Furio Scarpelli
ph Giuseppe Rotunno, Roberto Gerardi
m Nino Rota
   Vittorio Gassman, Alberto Sordi, Silvana
   Mangano, Folco Lulli, Bernard Blier,
   Romolo Valli

Two shirking soldiers (Gassman and Sordi)
enjoy themselves with women in the town
while a World War I battle rages. Learning
that their company has been wiped out, they
gain a sense of duty and return to the front,
but are captured and shot for refusing to give
information. Like *What Price Glory?*, which
it resembles, this uneven film moves from low
comedy to high drama, though not with the
same ease. The two male leads, and Mangano
as a prostitute, give likeable but predictable
performances.

Best Film Venice 1959
Best Director Venice 1959

► **Green Mare, The** see Green Mare's Nest, The

The Green Mare's Nest

► **(US: The Green Mare)**

► **La Jument Verte**

France   1959   105 mins   col
Raimbourg/Star Presse/S.N.E.G./Sopac Films/Zebra Film

d   **Claude Autant-Lara**
sc **Jean Aurenche, Pierre Bost**
ph **Jacques Natteau**
m   **René Cloërec**
    Bourvil, Sandra Milo, Francis Blanche, Yves Robert, Valérie Lagrange, Julien Carette

When Honoré (Bourvil) inherits the estate of his father, a horse dealer who became wealthy after a green filly was born to one of his mares, a jealous neighbour (Robert) plots against him. Honoré later takes his revenge by cuckolding him. Even if the French naughtiness has diminished for today's audiences, it is still an enjoyable, admirably performed, slightly silly romp. It was the film in which Bourvil (born André Raimbourg) first became widely known outside France.

The Green Ray

► **(US: Summer)**

► **Le Rayon Vert**

France   1986   92 mins   col
Les Films Du Losange

d   **Eric Rohmer**
sc **Eric Rohmer, Marie Rivière**
ph **Sophie Maintigneux**
m   **Jean-Louis Valero**
    Marie Rivière, Lisa Heredia, Vincent Gautier, Eric Hamm, Marc Vivas, Béatrice Romand

A Parisian secretary (Rivière) is let down at the last minute by a friend with whom she was going on holiday. Not knowing what to do, she takes herself off to Cherbourg, then to the mountains and, lastly, Biarritz, but is bored and depressed everywhere, until she

meets the man of her dreams. Unlike Rohmer's previous films, the dialogue of this comedy of manners was entirely improvised, creating both the tedium and the fascination of real speech. How one reacts to the film may be greatly related to how one reacts to the overly fastidious girl. The title, taken from the Jules Verne novel, refers to the last ray of sunset, the green of which is supposed to make observers more aware of the feelings and perceptions of others. Rohmer's films have much the same effect.

Best Film Venice 1986

The Green Room

► **La Chambre Verte**

France   1978   94 mins   col
Les Films Du Carrosse/UA

d   **François Truffaut**
sc **François Truffaut, Jean Gruault**
ph **Nestor Almendros**
m   **Maurice Jaubert**
    François Truffaut, Nathalie Baye, Jean Dasté, Jean-Pierre Moulin, Antoine Vitez

An obituary writer (Truffaut), obsessed with death, makes a shrine of his dead wife's bedroom and fills an old chapel with memento mori. A girl he meets (Baye) concludes that the only way he could love her would be if she were dead. Perhaps Truffaut's darkest film, through which he himself walks in an expressionless and self-important manner, was an adaptation from two of Henry James's short stories, *Altar Of The Dead* with some ideas from *The Beast Of The Jungle*. It is to the director's credit that he created a morbid atmosphere without recourse to baroque or melodramatic methods.

The Green Wall

► **La Muralla Verde**

Peru   1969   110 mins   col
Amaru Producciones Cinematográficas Del Peru

d   **Armando Robles Godoy**
sc **Armando Robles Godoy**

ph **Mario Robles Godoy**
m **Enrique Pinilla**
   Julio Alemán, Sandra Riva, Raul Martin

An urban family – a father (Alemán), mother (Riva) and son (Martin) – try to make a home for themselves in the wilds, having to break down 'the green wall' of the jungle to do so. But a poisonous serpent invades their Garden of Eden. The first Peruvian film to gain attention in the USA interestingly demonstrates that pastoral bliss is threatened by civilization and nature itself. The Peruvian jungle makes a compelling background to the simple story which is rather spoiled by too much visual gimmickry.

Gribiche

France   1925   90 mins   bw
Albatros

d **Jacques Feyder**
sc **Jacques Feyder**
ph **Maurice Forster, Maurice Desfassiaux**
m **Silent**
   Jean Forest, Françoise Rosay, Rolla Norman, Cécile Guyon, Alice Tissot

When Gribiche (Forest), a young boy from a deprived background, returns a lost handbag to its wealthy owner (Rosay), she offers to adopt and educate him. Believing himself to be an obstacle to his widowed mother's remarriage, he accepts. An observant tale of social differences and human motivation – Gribiche's benefactress is more concerned with outward show than inner feelings, for example. Feyder has invested the story with an edge of satire that makes this film an ironic antidote to the Mary Pickford-style dramas about orphans saved by the kindly rich. As always, *grande dame* Rosay (Feyder's wife) is wonderful to watch, and Forest, who had played a not dissimilar role in the same director's *Visages D'Enfants* earlier that year, is excellent.

Gribouille

▶ **(US: Heart Of Paris)**

France   1937   85 mins   bw
André Davin

d **Marc Allégret**
sc **Marc Allégret, H.G. Lustig, Marcel Achard**
ph **G. Benoit, Armand Thirard, Michel Kelber**
m **Georges Auric**
   Raimu, Michèle Morgan, Jeanne Provost, Gilbert Gilles, Jean Worms, Carette, Jacques Gretillat

While serving on a jury, the owner of a sports shop (Raimu) takes pity on a penniless young woman (Morgan) on trial for manslaughter. Knowing his wife (Provost) would object to employing someone on probation, he gets her a job in his shop by asking a friend to recommend her. Matters are complicated when the wife suspects her husband of falling for the girl. Although the plot has a melodramatic base, the film keeps a comic tone throughout, only occasionally tipping over into pathos. Except for the extraordinarily hammy court case that begins it, this comedy of behaviour has witty dialogue and perfect playing, notably from the imposing Raimu as the big lummox or *gribouille* of the title. The lovely 17-year-old, almond-eyed Morgan made an immediate impression in her screen debut. It was also the first film appearance of a young but already portly Bernard Blier in a small role.

▶ **Grido, Il** see Cry, The

The Grim Reaper

▶ **La Commare Secca**

Italy   1962   100 mins   bw
Cinematografica Cervi

d **Bernardo Bertolucci**
sc **Bernardo Bertolucci, Sergio Citti**
ph **Gianni Narzisi**
m **Carlo Rustichelli, Piero Piccioni**
   Francesco Ruiu, Giancarlo De Rosa, Vincenzo Ciccora, Alvaro D'Ercole, Romano Labate

An investigation into the murder of a prostitute in Rome reveals different perspectives of different people on the events of her last day. Twenty-two-year-old Bertolucci's first film was based on a five-page outline by Pasolini, with whom the young man had worked as assistant on *Accatone*, and in whose style he attempted to make it. But Bertolucci was less engaged with the Roman proletariat that Pasolini loved, and the film became merely an interesting cinematic exercise. Each episode as told to the unseen investigator was filmed in a different style. It is, as the director admits, the film of 'someone who had never shot one foot of 35mm before but who had seen lots and lots of films'.

Grisbi

▶ **aka Honour Among Thieves**

▶ **Touchez Pas Au Grisbi**

France   1953   90 mins   bw
Del Duca/Antares

d   Jacques Becker
sc Jacques Becker, Maurice Griffe
ph Pierre Montazel
m   Jean Wiener
    Jean Gabin, Jeanne Moreau, Lino
    Ventura, Gaby Basset, Daniel Cauchy

After a bank robbery, the gangsters and their molls get involved in a fight to the death over the loot. What primarily interested Becker was not the cops and robbers plot based on a *série noire* novel by Albert Simonin, but the relationships of friendship and betrayal among the characters. It also gave the cast a chance to explore the depths of their roles, particularly Gabin in his poignant portrayal of a man afraid of growing old. Ventura, making his first screen appearance, was spotted in a wrestling ring by Becker.

Best Actor (Jean Gabin) Venice 1954

▶ **Grosse Liebespiel, Das** see And So To Bed

▶ **Gruppo Di Famiglia In Un Interno** see Conversation Piece

▶ **Guerre Des Boutons, La** see War Of The Buttons, The

▶ **Guerre D'Un Seul Homme, La** see One Man's War

▶ **Guerre Est Finie, La** see War Is Over, The

▶ **Guichets Du Louvre, Les** see Gates Of The Louvre, The

▶ **Güney's The Wall** see Wall, The

Gunnar Hede's Saga

▶ **aka The Judgement**

Sweden   1922   70 mins   bw
Svenska Bio

d   Mauritz Stiller
sc Mauritz Stiller
ph Julius Jaenzon
m   Silent
    Mary Johnson, Einar Hanson, Pauline
    Brunius, Stina Borg, Adolf Olchansky

Hede (Hanson), a dreamer with more interest in playing the violin than in his parents' plans for him to be a mining engineer, is eventually sent packing by his mother when he persists in his dalliance with Ingrid (Johnson), a gypsy girl. He becomes a strolling fiddler before following in his grandfather's footsteps by heading north after the reindeer herds. An accident leaves him in a dazed, hallucinating state and he is returned to the family estate where Ingrid nurses him back to health. The best of Stiller's three adaptations from the novels of Selma Lagerlöf, made between *Sir Arne's Treasure* (1919) and *Gosta Berling's Saga* (1924), it is a subtle realization of an artist's spiritual regeneration after the literal journey to the frozen North and a metaphoric one to the depths of despair. In images of luminous beauty, the film lingers lyrically and often surrealistically on the life of travelling entertainers and the different landscapes through which the hero moves, contrasted with the gloomy shadows of the ancestral house.

The Guns

▶ **Os Fuzis**

Brazil   1963   110 mins   bw
Copacabana Films/Embracine/Daga Films

d   Ruy Guerra
sc Ruy Guerra
ph Ricardo Aronovich
m   Moscir Santos

Átila Iório, Nelson Xavier, Maria Gladys, Leonides Bayer, Hugo Carvana, Mauricio Loyola

A Holy Man exhorts starving peasants in North East Brazil to follow a sacred ox which will bring rain. Meanwhile, soldiers occupy the nearby town to protect the Mayor's food supply, and senseless incidents of violence occur, culminating in an ex-soldier, infuriated by peasant apathy, firing on the troops. The peasants kill and devour the sacred ox. This is an early product from *Cinema Novo*, curiously static, yet quivering with the tension of underlying violence. A bleak and depressing illustration of a situation that requires revolution, the film offers no solutions as to how that might occur – except for the climactic killing of the ox which indicates the seeds of changed thinking as the peasants abandon the restrictive shibboleths of the church.

Special Jury Prize Berlin 1964

▶ **Gyakufunsha Kazoku** see Crazy Family, The

▶ **Gycklarnas Afton** see Sawdust And Tinsel

La Habañera

Germany 1937 95 mins bw
Bruno Duday/UFA

d   **Detlef Sierck**
sc **Gerhard Menzel**
ph **Franz Weihmayr**
m **Lothar Brühne**
    Zarah Leander, Karl Martell, Ferdinand Marian, Julia Serda, Boris Alekin

Swedish Astrée (Leander), on a visit to Puerto Rico, falls in love with the place and with a wealthy landowner (Marian) whom she marries. Ten years pass: the sultry island is in the grip of a fever epidemic and Astrée is desperately homesick. When her husband dies, she leaves for Sweden with her son and a Swedish scientist (Martell). An over-the-top melodrama, produced as a vehicle for Leander whom the Germans hoped would step into the departed Dietrich's shoes, the film has acquired added interest. Screenwriter Menzel went on to work for the Nazis and, even in this piece, insidiously favours Aryan notions of physical and mental health. The director, of course, is Douglas Sirk, who left Germany after this film which displays the characteristics his work would develop in Hollywood. Melodrama or no, Sirk views his subject with ironic detachment, and captures mood and atmosphere with skilfully deployed light play, mirror images, and a cleverly fluid camera which points to a vision at intelligent odds with the material.

▶ **Hadaka No Shima** see Island, The

▶ **Hadduta Misriya** see Egyptian Story, An

Hail Mary

▶ **Je Vous Salue, Marie**

France 1984 78 mins col
Pegase/JLG Films/Sara Films/TV Romande/Channel 4

d   **Jean-Luc Godard**
sc **Jean-Luc Godard**
ph **Jean-Bernard Menoud, Jacques Firmann**
m **Bach, Dvořák, John Coltrane**
    Myriem Roussel, Thierry Rode, Philippe Lacoste, Malachi Jara Kohan, Anne Gautier, Juliette Binoche

Marie (Roussel), the teenage daughter of a petrol station manager, dating Joseph (Rode), a cab driver, is told by her visiting Uncle Gabriel (Lacoste) that she is to have a child, although she's a virgin. Condemned by the Pope and some Church organizations, and acclaimed by some other Christians, Godard's updated reinterpretation of the Nativity is one of his most controversial films. The Virgin Birth is presented as a reality – the mystery for Godard is womanhood and birth in general. This he explores through stunning images of nature and the nude figure of his heroine, the latter photographed chastely without voyeurism or sexism. The ending has an irony and poetry that only Godard at the height of his powers could achieve. The film is generally shown with a short by Anne-Marie Miéville, Godard's long-time collaborator, called *The Book Of Mary*.

▶ **Hai Zi Wang** see King Of The Children

▶ **Hakai** see Sin, The

▶ **Hakayitz Shel Aviya** see Summer of Aviya, The

▶ **Hakuchi** see Idiot, The

▶ **Hal, El** see Transes

Half Of Heaven

▶ **La Mitad Del Cielo**

  Spain 1986 127 mins col
  Louis Megino

d **Manuel Gutiérrez Aragon**
sc **Manuel Gutiérrez Aragon, Luis Megino**
ph **José Luis Alcaine**
m **Milladoiro**
  **Angela Molina, Fernando Fernán Gomez,
  Margarita Lozano, Monica Molina,
  Nacho Martinez, Antonio Valero**

Widowed Rosa (Angela Molina) arrives in
Madrid from the country with her daughter
(Monica Molina), works as a nurse, runs a
small stand in a meat market and finally
becomes the owner of one of the capital's
finest restaurants, an important hang-out for
Franco's politicos. This view of Spain under
Franco in the 1960s as revealed through three
generations of women – Rosa (a spellbinding
performance from Angela Molina), her
daughter and her dead mother (Lozano, seen
as a ghost) – is sharply satirical and mildly
surreal. Although still overcluttering his
screenplay with symbols, Aragon, one of the
leading exponents of the New Spanish Comedy, shows a confidence in a more linear
narrative than hitherto in his work, and the
film gains from the use of his splendid repertory company of actors.

Half-Truth

▶ **Ardh Satya**

  India 1983 130 mins col
  Neo Films Associates

d **Govind Nihalani**
sc **Vijay Tendulkar**
ph **Govind Nihalani**
m **Ajit Verman**
  **Om Puri, Smita Patil, Amrish Puri,
  Naseeruddin Shah, Shafi Inamdar, Achyut
  Potdar, Sadashiv Amrapurkar**

Anant (Om Puri), a young policeman with
faith in law and justice, becomes depressed
when he sees the ease with which a known
criminal, whom he tries to apprehend, goes
free. His disillusion drives him to drink and
violence, causing pain to his girlfriend (Patil)
and bringing him into conflict with his father
(Amrish Puri). This is the second film (the
first was *Aakrosh*, 1981) directed by one of
India's finest colour cinematographers. *Half-
Truth* exposes the corruption in the police
force, but what distinguishes Nihilani's
approach is his belief that the police themselves are victims of a larger corruption that
rules the state. In Anant, he presents an
individual coming into crisis with a system
and having to make choices. How he makes
them is the stuff of the drama in a well-made
movie that startled and impressed the cinema-
going public in India, where confidence in the
police has been eroded and this kind of critique is rare. On the surface, the movie offers
the entertainment of a good crime actioner
more familiar in Hollywood.

▶ **Hamara Shaher** see Bombay Our City

▶ **Ha Megjön József** see When Joseph
  Returns...

Hamlet

▶ **Gamlet**

  USSR 1964 150 mins bw
  Lenfilm

d **Grigori Kozintsev**
sc **Grigori Kozintsev (based on Boris
  Pasternak's translation of Shakespeare)**
ph **Jonas Gritsyus**
m **Shostakovich**
  **Innokenti Smoktunovsky (Hamlet),
  Michail Nazvanov (Claudius), Elza
  Radzin-Szolkonis (Gertrude), Yuri
  Tolubeyev (Polonius), Anastasia
  Vertinskaya (Ophelia), S. Oleksenko
  (Laertes)**

The Russians filmed Shakespeare's most famous tragedy to commemorate the 400th anniversary of the playwright's birth. It is, of
course, impossible for an English audience to
judge the language, but Kozintsev's approach
to the plot is clear. Smoktunovsky's Prince
of Denmark is no vacillating dreamer but,
like everything else in the film, muscular and

volatile. The images, enriched by the dramatic Shostakovich music, are bold, sweeping and powerful with, for example, the Ghost a giant armour-clad figure who brings a palpable sense of terror with him. This *Hamlet* is a study in the sinister manipulations of medieval statecraft, played in an Elsinore that immures its inhabitants in a convincing fortress of stone and iron that requires large armies to penetrate it. Swift-moving, and with the text considerably cut, it is a memorable and exciting experience.

Hamlet Goes Business

▶ **Hamlet Liikemaailmassa**

Finland 1987 86 mins bw
Villealfa Filmproductions

d **Aki Kaurismaki**
sc **Aki Kaurismaki**
ph **Timo Salminen**
m **extracts from classical and popular music**
   Pirkka-Pekka Petelius, Kati Outinen,
   Elina Salo, Esko Saminen, Kari
   Väänänen, Turo Pajala

Hamlet's father is murdered by his uncle who then marries his mother. Now heir to his father's industrial empire, Hamlet sets out to take revenge, mistreating his girlfriend Ophelia who drowns herself in the bath. In the end, and many corpses later, the hapless 'hero' is himself destroyed by his only ally, the chauffeur. The undoubtedly gifted Kaurismaki has here concocted an undergraduate exercise in which the plot more or less follows Shakespeare's original, departing from it at the film-maker's whim, and including an occasional line of dialogue from the famous text to incongruous effect. This Hamlet (well played by Petelius) is fat, cunning and loathesome, Ophelia is a bore, Laertes – here called Lauri Polonius – a whimpering neurotic, Gertrude a passive, suburban housewife, and Rosencrantz and Guildenstern a pair of parody thugs. Only Claudius, renamed Klaus, carries any conviction as a character. There appears to be little purpose or meaning in this thoroughly unpleasant deconstruction of the world's most famous play and the enterprise is saved from complete disaster only by some superb *noir*-style photography and a compelling soundtrack which ranges

from rockabilly to Tchaikovsky. It must be said that in certain critical quarters around the world this film has been much liked.

▶ **Hamlet Liikemaailmassa** see Hamlet Goes Business

▶ **Hamnstad** see Port Of Call

▶ **Hamsin** see Eastern Wind

Handcuffs

▶ **Lisice**

Yugoslavia 1970 80 mins bw
Jadran Film

d **Krsto Papić**
sc **Mirko Kovač, Krsto Papić**
ph **Vjenceslav Orešković**
m **Miljenko Prohaska, Boško Petrović,**
   Silvije Glojnarić
   Fabijan Šovagović, Adem Čejvan, Jagodar
   Kaloper, Fahro Konjhodžić

During the celebrations at a Croatian village wedding in 1948, a decorated war hero (Čejvan) rapes the bride (Kaloper) and is then arrested for pro-Stalinist views. Despite the protestations of the groom (Šovagović), the drunken village men hunt down the deflowered bride. Set at the time of Stalin's attack on Yugoslavia for deviating from Soviet ideology, this powerful, blackly pessimistic tale reflects the uncertainties of the period. Innuendo and double meanings pervade the narrative in which cruelty and repression contrast starkly, and in an original manner, with the gaiety of folkloric singing and dancing.

The Hand In The Trap

▶ **La Mano En La Trampa**

Argentina 1961 90 mins bw
Angel(Buenos Aires)/UNINCI(Madrid)

d **Leopoldo Torre-Nilsson**
sc **Beatriz Guido, Leopoldo Torre-Nilsson,**
   Ricardo Muñoz Suay, Ricardo Luna
ph **Alberto Etchebehere, Juan Julio Baena**
m **Cristóbal Halffter, Atilio Stampone**
   Elsa Daniel, Francisco Rabal, Leonardo

Favio, Maria Rosa Gallo, Berta Ortegosa, Hilda Suarez

Laura (Daniel), a convent schoolgirl, comes to spend her summer holidays in her family's large old house, and discovers that her Aunt Inés (Gallo), whom she believed was dead, has been living on the top floor in solitary confinement since the rich and handsome Cristóbal (Rabal) broke off his engagement to her. Laura approaches Cristóbal and finds herself caught in an unforeseen relationship with him. Daniel again takes on the role of the unsmiling virgin in one of Torre-Nilsson's effective depictions of the narrowness of a crumbling Catholic *bourgeois* family, which lives by an empty code of 'honour'. At times too contrived, it does, nevertheless, tell the story vividly, and conveys, by fine camerawork, the mustiness of the house and the contrasting bright superficiality of the young people outside.

▶ **Händler Der Vier Jahreszeiten, Der** see Merchant Of Four Seasons, The

The Hands Of Orlac

▶ **Orlacs Hände**

Austria 1925 50 mins bw
Pan

d **Robert Wiene**
sc **Ludwig Nerz**
ph **Günther Krampf, Hans Andreschin**
m **Silent**
Conrad Veidt, Alexandra Sorina, Fritz Kortner

A pianist (Veidt) loses his hands in a railway accident and has new ones successfully grafted on. Because they are the hands of a convicted murderer, his character changes as he becomes afraid of succumbing to their evil influence. Wiene's *The Cabinet Of Dr Caligari* (1919) began the vogue for Expressionism in German cinema, of which this is a further example. All the elements are here: shadowy streets, dimly-lit rooms and characters on the verge of madness. The plot, based on Maurice Renard's novel, is melodramatic, and so is much of the acting. Better was the 1935 MGM version called *Mad Love* which introduced

Peter Lorre to Hollywood; worse was a 1960 Franco-British effort.

Handsome Antonio

▶ **Il Bell'Antonio**

Italy 1960 105 mins bw
Cina Del Duca/Arco/Lyre Cinematographique

d **Mauro Bolognini**
sc **Pier Paolo Pasolini, Gino Visentini**
ph **Armando Nannuzzi**
m **Piero Piccioni**
Marcello Mastroianni, Claudia Cardinale, Pierre Brasseur, Tomas Milian, Rina Morelli

Antonio (Mastroianni), a man with a reputation as a ladykiller, returns to his native Sicily to make an arranged marriage to a young woman (Cardinale). After he has proved impotent on his wedding night, the marriage is annulled and he is held up to public ridicule. The impotence of the Sicilian male in Vitaliano Brancati's novel was seen as a metaphor for Fascist Italy, a theme which is lost in this updating. Yet much of the satire on macho attitudes still holds true, despite Bolognini's tendency towards caricature. This is especially noticeable in Brasseur's performance as the father, but Mastroianni is perfect as the limp male.

▶ **Hands On The City** see Hands Over The City

Hands Over The City

▶ **aka Hands On The City**
▶ **Le Mani Sulla Citta**

Italy 1963 105 mins bw
Galatea

d **Francesco Rosi**
sc **Enzo Provenzale, Enzo Forcella, Raffaele La Capria, Francesco Rosi**
ph **Gianni De Venanzo**
m **Piero Piccioni**
Rod Steiger, Salvo Randone, Guido Alberti, Angelo D'Alessandro, Guglielmo Metafora

When deaths result from the collapse of a building in a poor district of Naples, the disaster becomes an important factor in the forthcoming municipal elections. Rosi's sombre, realistic, and angry drama is an early example of his favourite theme – political corruption. Rod Steiger lent his name and weight to the role of a political boss in a cast that consisted mainly of non-professionals.

Best Film Venice 1963

Hanussen

Hungary/West Germany 1988 117 mins col
Mafilm Objektiv Studio (Budapest)/CCC Filmkunst(West Berlin)

d **István Szabó**
sc **István Szabó, Péter Dobai**
ph **Lajos Koltai**
m **György Vukán**
Klaus Maria Brandauer, Erland Josephson, Ildikó Bánsági, Károly Eperjes, Adriana Biedrzynska, Grazyna Szapolowska

Klaus Schneider (Brandauer), an Austrian army corporal, is wounded in the head towards the end of World War I. Treated at a military hospital by the Jewish Dr Bettelheim (Erland Josephson), with whose nurse Betty (Bánsági) he enjoys an affair, Schneider begins having presentiments of the future, convincing Bettelheim that he is clairvoyant. After the war he finds himself in great demand among the business community until, with an old army friend (Eperjes) acting as his manager, he becomes a professional, changes his name to Erik-Jan Hanussen and stages public displays of his gifts. His arrest on a charge of charlatanism hints at his own future when the Nazi party, alarmed by his predictions, decides to intervene. *Hanussen* completes a trilogy that began with *Mephisto* in 1981 and continued with *Colonel Redl* in 1984. It has, as its connecting link, the magnetic and formidable Brandauer as the doomed character, at odds with the powers that be, at the centre of each. As with its predecessors, this film is directed, photographed and acted with an epic sweep surrounding an essentially personal tale. Szabó's ability to evoke period, atmosphere, and the

corruption that lurks beneath the surface of glamour is intact and the story, apparently based on a real-life character, is, like the other two films, a powerfully ironic comment on Man's blindness to the consequences of his actions.

Happiness

▶ **Schaste**

USSR 1934 90 mins bw
Moskino Kombinat

d **Alexander Medvedkin**
sc **Alexander Medvedkin**
ph **Gleb Troianski**
m **Mussorgsky (re-issued version)**
Piotr Zinoviev, Elena Egorova, L. Nenascheva, W. Uspenski, G. Mirgoryan

Khmyr (Zinoviev), a poor peasant, and his wife Anna (Egorova) are dispossessed of their small farm for failing to pay their heavy taxes. He is sent off to the wars and returns after the Revolution to a collective farm where the couple finally find happiness. Two years before making this amusing satire, Medvedkin was in charge of the Ciné-Train that travelled all over the Soviet Union making films on the spot and showing them to the local people. In 1971, Chris Marker made *The Train Rolls On* about it, which included an interview with the director, as a prelude to the revelatory showing of this feature unknown in the West. Using burlesque, music-hall jokes, surrealism, masked figures and folk-tale images, it succeeds in producing what the title promises. Although finally orthodox in its praise for collectivization, it recalls the radical Soviet cinema of a decade earlier – surprising during the period of strict Socialist Realism.

▶ **Happiness** see Bonheur, Le

Happy Day

Greece 1976 105 mins col
Greek Film Centre

d **Pantelis Voulgaris**
sc **Pantelis Voulgaris**
ph **George Panousopoulos**

m **Dionysis Savopoulos**
   A large, unidentified cast

During the Greek civil war, the Government establishes concentration camps for political prisoners on a number of islands. In one such camp, the prisoners go about their meaningless tasks, such as killing flies and storing them in jars. Punishments being bound to a pole in a tidal basin for days. At the climax, the prisoners put on a show for the visit of Queen Frederika. Voulgaris, who was incarcerated on an island during the junta of 1967-1974, adapted a book by a former inmate of the earlier repression, giving it the ironic English title, *Happy Day*. However, instead of filming a realistic portrayal of actual events, the director has opted for a symbolic, almost allegorical study of authority and resistance. But the daring decision not to characterize individuals – they are seen mostly in long shot – and to take a satiric rather than tragic tone is more often alienating than involving, even though the final vaudeville makes it point quite efficiently

Happy Gypsies

▶ **aka I Even Met Happy Gypsies**

▶ **Sreo Sam Cak I Srecne Cigane**

▶ **aka Skulpjaci Perja**

   Yugoslavia   1967   90 mins   col
   Avala

d **Aleksander Petrović**
sc **Aleksander Petrović**
ph **Tomislav Pinter**
m **Gypsy melodies**
   Bekim Fehmiu, Olivera Vučo, Bata
   Zivojinović, Gordana Jovanović, Mija
   Aleksić

Bora (Fehmiu), a gypsy dealer in goose-feathers travels a great deal away from his wife and children. On one trip he meets a girl (Jovanović) whose lecherous stepfather he kills. These gypsies are far from happy (so is the screenplay), but the music and colour and the rare and authentic depiction of their life on the vast Yugoslavian plains, holds the attention. Among some of Yugoslavia's leading actors was Gordana Jovanović, an illiterate 16-year-old gypsy girl virtually playing herself. The film was nominated for the Best

Foreign Film Oscar in 1967, as was Petrović's *Three* the previous year.

Special Jury Prize Cannes 1967

▶ **Happy New Year** see Bonne Année, La

Harakiri

▶ **Seppuku**

   Japan   1962   135 mins   bw
   Shochiku

d **Masaki Kobayashi**
sc **Shinobu Hashimoto**
ph **Yoshio Miyajima**
m **Tohru Takemitsu**
   Tatsuya Nakadai, Shima Iwashita, Akira
   Isahama, Rentaro Mikuni

The end of civil war in 1630 leaves many Samurai unemployed. One (Nakadai) visits a feudal lord and threatens harakiri in the hope that he be taken on. When denied, he insists on carrying out the ritual suicide. While remaining true to the traditions of the Japanese period film, Kobayashi manages to criticize the rigid codes of honour which are basic to their subject. The brutal tale, beautifully composed on the wide screen, is skilfully told in flashbacks.

Special Jury Prize Cannes 1963

▶ **Här Börjar Äventyret** see Adventure Starts Here

Hard Times

▶ **Tempos Difíceis, Este Tempo**

   Portugal   1988   96 mins   bw
   João Botelho/Artificial Eye (London)

d **João Botelho**
sc **João Botelho**
ph **Elso Roque**
m **António Pinho Vargas**
   Luis Estrela, Julia Britton, Isabel De
   Castro, Ruy Furtado, Inés Medeiros,
   Henrique Viana, Lia Gama, Joaquim
   Mendes, Pedro Cabrita Reis

World's End is a grimy industrial town where Tomaz Cremalheira/Gradgrind (Estrela), retired from business, devotes himself to providing a rational eduction for his children. Many years later he marries his daughter Luisa (Britton) off to his best friend, the factory owner José Grandela/Bounderby (Viana). But Grandela soon suspects his wife of having an affair with Julio/James Harthouse (Reis), accuses an innocent worker, Sebastião/Stephen Blackpool (Mendes) of robbery and is forced to acknowledge a poor old woman as his mother. These are the bare bones of the Dickens novel, although Botelho's adaptation sticks reasonably close to the original plot, while transferring it to present-day Portugal. However, the director utilizes the story principally for an exercise in style as an attempt to 'return to the dignity of the early days of cinema', in particular the work of D. W. Griffith. There are certainly echoes of silent cinema in many of the superb, lowering black and white images, but the minimalist acting and passionless approach is closer to the cinema of Jean-Marie Straub. Unfortunately, Dickens' rich characters and choice dialogue have lost so much vigour in the rigid approach that what remains is a beautiful but cold artefact.

▶ **Harp Of Burma** see Burmese Harp, The

Harry Munter

Sweden 1969 101 mins col
Sandrew

d   **Kjell Grede**
sc   **Kjell Grede**
ph   **Lars Björne**
m   **Dvořák, Johann Strauss, folk music**
     Jan Nielsen, Carl-Gustaf Lindstedt, Gun Jönsson, Georg Adelly, Elina Salo

Harry Munter (Nielsen), a precociously brilliant schoolboy, is responsible for an electronic invention which an American company wants to market, thus offering his struggling parents a new start in the US. However, Harry is more concerned with a group of variously unhappy people who depend on him (Munter means happiness), causing a clash between his idealism and the demands of the real world. In his second film (*Hugo And Josephine* was first), Grede employs the same lyrical camera, and once again looks at the world through youthful eyes, but this time in a setting of oppressive and repressive urban wasteland. He deals with shifting planes of reality in an almost Fellini-esque manner that is only partially successful and is uncertain of his tone in charting Harry's journey to maturity. Nonetheless, his young hero as played by Nielsen, is interesting in an often appealing film.

Harvest

▶ **Regain**

France 1937 122 mins bw
Marcel Pagnol

d   **Marcel Pagnol**
sc   **Marcel Pagnol**
ph   **Willy**
m   **Arthur Honegger**
     Gabriel Gabrio, Fernandel, Orane Demazis, Edouard Delmont, Marguerite Moreno, Robert Le Vigan

A poacher (Gabrio), wishing for fatherhood, coaxes an itinerant girl (Demazis) away from her simple knifegrinder companion (Fernandel) and sets up house with her in a deserted village which they bring back to life. Filmed in the sunlight and space of Provence, Pagnol does justice to the Jean Giono novel on which he based the film. Although the pantheism is a little overstrained – waving wheat and golden bread – it never detracts from the human comedy and the realism of the characters.

Harvest: 3000 Years

▶ **Mirt Sost Shi Amit**

Ethiopia 1975 138 mins bw
Haile Gerima

d   **Haile Gerima**
sc   **Haile Gerima**
ph   **Eliot Davis**
m   **Tesfaye Lema**
     Haregeweyn Tefferi, Melaku Mekonnen, Kasu Asfaw, Adane Melaku, Werke Abraha

A family of tenant farmers scratches a precarious living on the property of a ruthless landlord. The father (Mekonnen) dreams of a better life for his son (Melaku) and daughter (Abraha), but they are evicted from the land and the only hope is revolution. Gerima, an Ethiopian director trained at the University of California, has purposefully cast his characters as symbols of Third World exploitation. Nevertheless, although the particular situation is seen as a microcosm of Ethiopian peasant society, the people are still of flesh and blood. Music and song is used effectively to comment on the action, which gathers pace towards the optimistic conclusion.

▶ **Hasta Cierto Punto** see Up To A Point

▶ **Hatred** see Mollenard

▶ **Hatsukoi Jigoku-Hen** see Inferno Of First Love, The

The Hatter's Ghosts

▶ **Les Fantômes Du Chapelier**

France 1982 129 mins col
Horizon Productions/Films A2/SFPC

d   Claude Chabrol
sc   Claude Chabrol
ph   Jean Rabier
m   Matthieu Chabrol
    Michel Serrault, Charles Aznavour,
    Monique Chaumette, Aurore Clément,
    Christine Paolini

In a small provincial town, a hatter (Serrault) murders his bed-ridden wife and other local women while continuing his life as a respected citizen who meets his tradesmen cronies nightly at a café. Though sticking quite closely to the particulars of the Georges Simenon story, Chabrol, in fine wry form, has made a film right up his own dark, provincial alley. The portrayal of the rainy town has the perfect, enclosed, semi-artificial atmosphere in which the mad hatter does his bad deeds. Michel Serrault, investing him with a walk that recalls Jean-Louis Barrault's in Renoir's *The Testament Of Dr Cordelier*, gives one of his quirkiest and finest performances.

The Haunted Castle

▶ **aka Castle Vogelöd**
▶ **Schloss Vogelöd**

Germany 1921 75 mins bw
Decla Bioscop

d   F.W. Murnau
sc   Carl Mayer
ph   Fritz Arno Wagner, Laszlo Scheffer
m   Silent
    Arnold Korff, Lulu Keyser-Korff, Lothar
    Mehnert, Paul Bildt, Olga Tschechowa,
    Paul Hartmann

A group of people gathered for a hunting party at a mysterious castle are joined by a beautiful Baroness (Keyser-Korff) whose first husband died in suspicious circumstances. Certain strange goings-on eventually cause one of the guests to confess to the man's murder. Murnau's early, pre-*Nosferatu* chiller reveals some of the glories to come, especially in his handling of nightmares dreamt by the denizens of the castle and in the flashback scenes. However, the melodramatic story is rather complicated and is not much clarified by a surfeit of intertitles from a director who was to break new ground by using none in *The Last Laugh*, three years later.

▶ **Hauptmann Von Köpenick, Der**
see Captain From Kopenick, The

Havinck

Netherlands 1987 99 mins col
Riverside Pictures

d   Franz Weisz
sc   Ger Thijs
ph   Giuseppe Lanci
m   Egisto Macchi
    Willem Nijholt, Will Van Kralingen, Anne
    Martien Lousberg, Carolien Van Den
    Berg, Coen Flink

Robert Havinck (Nijholt), a partner in a successful law firm, is married to Lydia (Van Kralingen) and has a 15-year-old daughter, Eva (Lousberg). When Lydia kills herself in a car crash, he begins to investigate why she acted as she did. This is a rather Bergmanesque tale in theme and character –

a godless world in which a man cut off from his feelings destroys a woman in touch with hers. Flashbacks are skilfully used to bridge past and present, and the Italian camera crew has caught the Dutch light to perfection. However, it is difficult to identify with such a cold fish of a hero.

The Hawks And The Sparrows

▶ **Uccellacci E Uccellini**

Italy 1966 88 mins bw
Arco Film

d **Pier Paolo Pasolini**
sc **Pier Paolo Pasolini**
ph **Mario Bernardo, Tonino Delli Colli**
m **Ennio Morricone, Domenico Modugno**
   Totò, Ninetto Davoli, Rossana Di Rocco,
   Renato Capogna, Pietro Davoli

A father (Totò) and son (Ninetto Davoli) become vagabonds and, accompanied by an intellectual talking bird, set out on a picaresque journey to emulate St Francis of Assisi's mission to the birds. Following his *The Gospel According To St Matthew*, Pasolini presents a tragicomic fable which shows two delightful innocents caught, like many Italians, between the Church and Marxism. A running (or rather walking) debate takes place in which the bird recounts left-wing parables, there are newsreels of the 1964 funeral of Togliatti, the Italian Communist leader, and quotations from a range of thinkers. This fairy story does not end happily ever after, but on a note of qualified optimism. The duo of the wizened Totò and the curly-haired simpleton Davoli, reappeared in another magic fable in the Pasolini episode from *The Witches* in the same year.

▶ **Häxan** see Witchcraft Through The Ages

▶ **Heartbeat** see Schpountz, Le

Heartbeat

▶ **La Chamade**

France 1968 105 mins col
Les Films Ariane/Les Productions
Artistes Associés(Paris)/P.E.A.(Rome)

d **Alain Cavalier**
sc **Françoise Sagan, Alain Cavalier**
ph **Pierre Lhomme**
m **Maurice Leroux**
   Catherine Deneuve, Michel Piccoli, Roger
   Van Hool, Irène Tunc, Jacques Sereys

Lucile (Deneuve) lives luxuriously in the home of Charles (Piccoli), her middle-aged benefactor and occasional lover, moving in a dazzling social set until she meets Antoine (Van Hool), a comparatively penurious proof-reader. After much vacillation and a brief descent into the bottle, she enjoys an idyllic summer before recognizing her need for Charles. Working from her own book, Sagan and the director have come up with a slight romance that accurately catches the surface gloss of her once-fashionable work, but misses her novelist's nuances of character. A fragile entertainment that gets by on technical proficiency and accurate casting.

The Heartbreakers

▶ **Die Heartbreakers**

W. Germany 1983 113 mins col
Tura Film/Pro-Jekt Film Produktion im
Filmverlag Der Autoren/WDR

d **Peter F. Bringmann**
sc **Matthias Seelig**
ph **Helge Weindler**
m **Lothar Meid**
   Sascha Disselkamp, Mary Ketikidou, Uwe
   Enkelmann, Mark Eichenseher, Michael
   Klein

A group of teenage Rhine rockers set up a pop group in the mid-1960s to emulate British beat stars, but internal squabbles and inadequate talent lead to a disastrous first concert. An affectionate, often funny, nostalgic comedy, played by a likeable sextet of young actors, it is a refreshing change from the *angst* that dominates many of the films that come out of West Germany. However, the love interest between an aspiring German Mick Jagger (Disselkamp) and the female vocalist (Ketikidou) slows up the tempo and the running jokes are rather strained.

▶ **Heartbreakers, Die** see Heartbreakers, The

Heart Of A Mother

▶ **Serdtze Materi**

USSR 1966 100 mins bw
Gorky Studio

d **Mark Donskoi**
sc **Zoya Voskhresenskaya, Irina Donskaya**
ph **Mikhail Yakovitch**
m **R. Khozac**
  **Elena Fadeyeva, Danili Sagal, Rodion
  Nakhapetov, Nina Menichkova, Gennady
  Tchertov**

When the father of the Ulyanov family dies
suddenly, mother (Fadeyeva) is left with the
burden of caring for her six offspring. Subsequently, her eldest son and daughter are,
respectively, executed and exiled to Siberia
for their part in a plot to kill the Tsar, the
family is uprooted from its contented life in
a town on the Volga, and the second son,
Vladimir Ilyich (Nakhapetov), much affected
by events, commits himself to the Revolutionary cause, eventually taking the name Lenin.
Donskoi's film, the first in his studies of the
Russian leader's early life, is a work of
impressive visual beauty, capturing landscape
and period in sharp but lyrical images. If
mother herself is portrayed as somewhat
remote and enigmatic, the film as a whole
opts for a warmth which humanizes this
respectful and nostalgic journey into recent
history.

Heart Of Glass

▶ **Herz Aus Glas**

W. Germany 1976 94 mins col
Werner Herzog

d **Werner Herzog**
sc **Werner Herzog, Herbert Achternbusch**
ph **Jörg Schmidt-Reitwein**
m **Popul Vuh**
  **Josef Bierbichler, Stefan Guttler, Clemens
  Scheitz, Sepp Müller, Volker Prechtel**

In a 19th-century Bavarian village, a mystical
nomadic shepherd supplies a glass factory
owner with the lost secret formula for a very
precious glass and prophesies the coming of
the industrial era. 'The film is meant to convey
an atmosphere of hallucination, of prophecy,
of the visionary and of collective madness,'
quoth the director. Known for going to any

lengths to make a film (vide *Fitzcarraldo*),
Herzog had his actors perform under hypnosis to achieve the above effect. This impenetrable and hermetic film is pretty hypnotic
for some of the time and soporific at others,
but the landscapes are visually arresting.

▶ **Heart Of Paris** see Gribouille

The Heat Line

▶ **La Ligne De Chaleur**

Canada 1988 88 mins col
ACPAV

d **Hubert-Yves Rose**
sc **Micheline Lanctôt**
ph **Michel Caron**
m **Richard Grégoire**
  **Gabriel Arcand, Simon Gonzales, Gérard
  Parkes**

Robert (Arcand), recently divorced and
adjusting to life alone, takes his young son
(Gonzales) from Montreal to Florida, where
his father, whom he has not seen for years,
has died. They drive the father's car back to
Canada but very little goes smoothly on the
way home. Like many road movies, from
whatever country, this bleak, well-handled
French Canadian example of the genre is
about loneliness, alienation and loss, with the
road leading towards some kind of illumination. Hubert-Yves Rose, who dedicated the
picture to his own father, concentrates on the
father-son relationships – Robert's with his
dead father, and his own with his son. This
develops skillfully thanks to the fine central
performances and that of Parkes, who plays
a loquacious dying stranger they meet. The
climatic contrast between the cold of Canada
and the heat of Florida is used to good effect.

Heaven Fell That Night

▶ **(US: The Night Heaven Fell)**

▶ **Les Bijoutiers Du Claire De
Lune**

France 1957 91 mins col
Iena Productions/U.C.I.C.(Paris)/
C.E.I.A.P.(Rome)

d **Roger Vadim**

sc **Roger Vadim, Peter Viertel**
ph **Armand Thirard**
m **Georges Auric**
    **Brigitte Bardot, Stephen Boyd, Alida
    Valli, Pepé Nieto, José Marco Davo**

Ursula (Bardot), a convent girl holidaying in
Spain, runs off to the hills for an idyllic
interlude of love and sex with handsome
Lamberto (Boyd). The trouble is that Lamberto is a criminal layabout who previously
murdered Ursula's uncle and seduced her
aunt (Valli) and the police are hot on his
heels. A real piece of drivel and its only *raison
d'être* is to give audiences an eyeful (in CinemaScope) of Mrs Roger Vadim. Apparently,
the filming was dogged with difficulties –
unusually appalling weather for Spain, animosity between the leads – but one can't help
feeling that a smooth ride would have made
little difference.

Heaven Over The Marshes

▶ **Cielo Sulla Palude**

    Italy   1949   120 mins   bw
    Bassoli-Arx

d **Augusto Genina**
sc **Augusto Genina**
ph **G.R. Aldo**
m **Antonio Veretti**
    **Ines Orsini, Mauro Matteucci, Giovanni
    Martella, Assunta Radico, Francesco
    Tomalillo**

Maria Goretti (Orsini), a poor peasant girl,
resists a farmhand's repeated attempts to
seduce her and he finally kills her. This is a
true story of a religious girl who chose to be
murdered rather than to be dishonoured by
rape, became a folk heroine and was canonized 50 years later, soon after this film was
made in tribute to her. Veteran director Genina, working on location in the desolate,
malaria-infested Pontine marshes near Rome
where the incident took place, has made a
powerful and poignant film, drawing convincing performances from his cast of local farm
people, and helped by the finely judged camera of the brilliant G.R. Aldo. Originally
over-long, and at moments too slow, it is
generally shown less 20 minutes, which is to
its advantage. Genina, who entered films as
a scriptwriter in 1913 and died in 1957,

directed approximately 150 films during his
career, ranging from early melodramas to
Fascist propaganda.

Best Director Venice 1949

Heaven Sent

▶ **(US: Thank Heaven For Small
    Favors)**

▶ **Un Drôle De Paroissien**

    France   1963   83 mins   bw
    Film D'Art/A.T.I.L.A.

d **Jean-Pierre Mocky**
sc **Michel Servin, Alain Moury, Jean-Pierre
    Mocky**
ph **L.H. Burel**
m **Joseph Kosma**
    **Bourvil, Francis Blanche, Jean Poiret,
    Jean Yonnel, Jean Tissier, Jean Galland**

The Lachesnaye family, high-born aristocrats,
have fallen on hard times and must resort to
stripping off the doors and panelling of their
Paris apartment for use as firewood. They are
also threatened with eviction, but never waver
from their conviction that they were not born
to work. One of them, the ultra-religious
Georges (Bourvil), takes the sound of coins
dropping into the church offertory as a sign
from the Lord and embarks on a project for
removing money from poor-boxes to save his
family... A thoroughly light-weight but
delightfully irreverent comedy, which Mocky
directs at a terrific pace. It errs on the side
of predictability and superficiality, but the
splendid performances, notably from Bourvil,
Blanche and Galland, all in sparkling form,
make for satisfying entertainment.

He Died With His Eyes Open

▶ **On Ne Meurt Que 2 Fois**

    France   1985   106 mins   col
    Swaine Productions/TF1 Films

d **Jacques Deray**
sc **Jacques Deray, Michel Audiard**
ph **Jean Penzer**
m **Claude Bolling**
    Michel Serrault, Charlotte Rampling,

Elisabeth Depardieu, Xavier Deluc,
Gérard Darmon, Jean-Pierre Bacri

When the body of a brutally murdered man, his eyes open, is found on a piece of waste ground in Paris, Inspector Staniland (Serrault) is called in. His investigations lead him to the dead man's beautiful, mysterious and promiscuous mistress (Rampling) with whom he develops a bizarre and obsessive relationship. The major attraction of this film is Serrault's superb performance which lends authority and flesh and blood – characteristics conspicuously missing in everyone else – to his character. The ultra-chic sleaze of the film's milieu is well-captured, and there are a couple of intriguing ideas afloat in the screenplay, but it's all really rather silly and somewhat tasteless.

Heimat

▶ aka Homeland

W. Germany 1983 924 mins bw-col
Edgar Reitz/WDR/SFB

d Edgar Reitz
sc Edgar Reitz, Peter Steinbach
ph Gernot Roll
m Nicos Mamangakis
   Marita Breuer, Dieter Schaad, Kurt
   Wagner, Jörg Hube, Rüdiger Weigang,
   Karin Rasenack, Jörg Richter, Peter
   Harting

Life in a fictitious German village between 1919 and 1982, revolving around Maria (Breuer) and the Simon family into which she marries. An amusing, moving, absorbing and seldom boring high-class soap opera which mirrors modern German history through the eyes of ordinary people, and in which the characters age and develop convincingly. Particularly fascinating is the Nazi era as viewed from this standpoint. The film comes as close as any has to explaining how the evil of Hitler's ideology filtered down to taint otherwise decent citizens. The swastikas on buildings, frighteningly, lose their usual potency to become a natural feature of the decor; while the sudden shifting of former Party members to become American allies is dealt with satirically but subtly. The character of the composer who takes us through the modern era is Reitz's surrogate (he was himself a

musician). The 2,000-page screenplay took five years and four months to shoot and lasts 15½ hours. Although the director insists that it was made to be seen on the big screen, it is more practical and cheaper to see on TV with no great loss of impact. Only the constant change from monochrome to colour and back is often irritatingly arbitrary.

▶ Hei Pao Shi Jian see Black Cannon Incident, The

▶ Heir To Genghis Khan, The see Storm Over Asia

▶ Helden see Arms And The Man

▶ Heller Wahn see Friends And Husbands

Hell's Cargo

▶ (US: S.O.S. Mediterranean)

▶ Alerte En Méditerranée

France 1937 104 mins bw
Vega

d Léo Joannon
sc Léo Joannon
ph Marcel Lucien
m Michel Michelet
   Pierre Fresnay, Rolf Wanka, Kim
   Peacock, Nadine Vogel

Three naval officers, French, German and English, are at odds, but combine to help each other after a murder is committed during a sailors' brawl in Tangier, where they are on leave. What ensues is an action-packed (if sometimes rather far-fetched) adventure, involving the pursuit of a freighter carrying illicit cargo, and the saving of passengers aboard a French liner whose lives are imperilled by poisonous, gas-filled seas. The acting is initially a little stiff and the continuity somewhat jumpy, but the movie – clearly calculated to involve the emotions of all the nationlities it represents – provides an exciting climax in Mediterranean waters, as well as some uplift about abandoning national prejudices.

The Herd

▶ **Sürü**

Turkey 1978 118 mins col
Güney Film

d **Zeki Ökten**
sc **Yilmaz Güney**
ph **Izzet Akay**
m **Zülfü Livaneli**
   **Tarik Akan, Melike Demirag, Tuncel
   Kurtiz, Levent Inanir, Meral Niron**

A nomadic herdsman (Akan) who has married a woman (Demirag) from a tribe with which his family has an ancient feud, takes a flock of sheep to sell in Ankara. On the way, some sheep die and others are stolen and in the big city, the man is paid much less by a dealer than he was promised. Finally, his wife dies. Like *The Enemy* and *Yol*, this abrasive, violent and lyrical film was supervised by Güney from prison. Apparently it was scripted in a room shared by 80 other prisoners. Without preaching or sentimentality, the film exposes the hardships and injustices of the society. The one cinema that dared show it in Turkey was closed down after a bomb attack. Güney's films are themselves bombshells.

▶ **Herkulesfürdöi   Emlék**   see
Improperly Dressed

The Heroes Are Tired

▶ **(US: Heros And Sinners)**

▶ **Les Héros Sont Fatigués**

France 1955 105 mins bw
Terra Film

d **Yves Ciampi**
sc **J.L. Bost, Yves Ciampi**
ph **Henri Alekan**
m **Louiguy**
   **Yves Montand, Maria Felix, Jean
   Servais, Curt Jurgens, Elisabeth Manet,
   Gérard Oury, Gert Fröbe**

On the coast of the West African state of Liberia, a group of whites, mainly French, but including the odd German, play out a series of dramas that embrace diamond smuggling, marital discord, sensual affairs and strange political alliances. One can only assume that the title of this film is intended ironically, as the group are all on the verge of moral dereliction and do not appear to have any claim to heroism, past or present. Extravagantly overwritten and parading the art of coarse acting, the film offers every atmospheric cliché in the book to do with oppressive heat, insect-ridden interiors, rampant sexuality, booze-sodden verbosity, and 'the natives are restless tonight'. What a waste of the cast!

▶ **Heroism** see Eroica

▶ **Heros And Sinners** see Heroes Are Tired, The

▶ **Héros Sont Fatigués, Les** see Heroes Are Tired, The

▶ **Herr Arnes Pengar** see Sir Arne's Treasure

▶ **Herrin Von Atlantis, Die** see Atlantide, L'

Herr Puntila And His Servant Matti

▶ **Herr Puntila Und Sein Knecht Matti**

Austria 1955 95 mins col
Bauerfilm

d **Alberto Cavalcanti**
sc **Alberto Cavalcanti, Vladimir Pozner,
   Ruth Wieden**
ph **André Bac, Arthur Hämmerer**
m **Hanns Eisler**
   **Curt Bois, Hans Engelmann, Maria Emo,
   Edith Prager**

In Finland, Puntila (Bois), a well-to-do landowner, is generous, selfless and high-minded when under the influence of alcohol; sober, he is dictatorial, cruel, and exploitative. It is his chauffeur Matti (Engelmann) who has to bear the main brunt of his changing moods and who has to pacify the girls to whom Puntila proposes when he is drunk. Based on Bertolt Brecht's 1941 comedy of class, it is the only film adaptation of one of his plays that pleased him. In fact, Brecht gave Cavalcanti, that most cosmopolitan of directors, advice on the filming. The faithful screenplay and the performances are a delight, but considering that the original idea for the play came from a character in Chaplin's *City Lights*, it might have been more cinematically conceived.

▶ **Herr Puntila Und Sein Knecht Matti** see Herr Puntila And His Servant Matti

▶ **Herz Aus Glas** see Heart Of Glass

▶ **Hets** see Frenzy

He Who Must Die

▶ **Celui Qui Doit Mourir**

France   1957   126 mins   bw
Indusfilms

d   **Jules Dassin**
sc **Jules Dassin, Ben Barzman**
ph **Jacques Natteau**
m   **Georges Auric**
    Jean Servais, Carl Mohner, Pierre Vaneck, Melina Mercouri, Fernand Ledoux, Maurice Ronet, Gert Fröbe, Grégoire Aslan, Roger Hanin, Nicole Berger

In 1921, in a small Greek village under Turkish domination, the preparations for a Passion play are interrupted by the arrival of refugees from the mountains. Based on the Kazantzakis novel *Christ Recrucified*, Dassin's second film in France was one of his most ambitious. In spite of the obvious symbolism and some artiness, much of it succeeds because of the sincerity and passion of the direction and cast, including Melina Mercouri, Dassin's wife-to-be, in only her second film.

Hibiscus Town

▶ **Furong Zhen**

China   1986   135 mins   col

Shanghai Film Studio/China Film Corporation

d   **Xie Jin**
sc **Ah Cheng**
ph **Lu Junfu**
m   **Ge Yan**
    Liu Xiaoqing, Jiang Wen, Zheng Zaishi, Zhu Shibin, Xu Songzi, Zhang Guangbei, Xu Ning, Liu Linian

Hu Yuyin (Xiaoqing), owner of a popular beancurd stall in a small village in southern Hunan province, is accused by a hard-line government employee (Songzi) of enriching herself at the expense of the Party. During the Cultural Revolution, Hu becomes a street sweeper and the lover of fellow worker Qin (Wen), a discredited intellectual and composer who is imprisoned as an anti-revolutionary, leaving her pregnant. However, in 1979 Qin is released and Hu gets back her beancurd stall. Xie Jin, most famous in the West for *Two Stage Sisters* (1964) and one of the few Chinese directors to continue making films during and after the Cultural Revolution, answered the criticism that he was merely an opportunistic hack with a picture detailing some of the sins committed in the 1960s. Although this huge hit in China lost over 30 minutes in the export version, it remains a powerful and fascinating study of an era as seen through the eyes of a brave victim. The main strength of the film is its avoidance of rhetoric and stereotypes – even the local activist villains are shown to be all too human – and its ability to between political and social satire, comedy and realism within the framework of a sweeping melodrama.

The Hidden Fortress

▶ **Kakushi Toride No San-Akunin**

Japan   1958   123 mins   bw
Toho

d   **Akira Kurosawa**
sc **Akira Kurosawa, Ryuzo Kikushima, Hideo Oguni, Shinobu Hashimoto**
ph **Ichio Yamazaki**
m   **Masaru Sato**
    Toshiro Mifune, Misa Uehara, Minoru Chiaki

A Samurai leader (Mifune) offers his protection to the beautiful heiress (Uehara) of a feudal lord. She is fleeing with her treasure on a perilous journey to sanctuary during the civil wars in medieval Japan. Kurosawa embellishes a typical Japanese Western plot with a great deal of humour, excitement and magic. His use of the wide screen for the first time gives added visual sweep to the story.

Best Director Berlin 1959

▶ **Hideg Napok** see Cold Days

▶ **Higan-Bana** see Equinox Flower

High And Low

▶ **Tengoku To Jigoku**

Japan 1963 142 mins bw
Toho

d   **Akira Kurosawa**
sc **Hideo Oguni, Ryuzo Kikushima, Eijiro Hisaito, Akira Kurosawa**
ph **Asakazu Nakai, Takao Saito**
m   **Masaru Satu**
    Toshiro Mifune, Kyoko Kagawa, Tatsuya Nakadai, Tsutomu Yamakazi, Tatsuya Mihashi

Gondo (Mifune), a shoe manufacturer, faces a moral dilemma when the son of his chauffeur is mistaken for his own and kidnapped: if he pays the ransom, he will face financial ruin. The internationally-minded Kurosawa based this film on a detective novel by Ed McBain, but makes it very much his (and Japan's) own in tone and flavour. When Gondo decides to pay the ransom, the action moves into gripping high gear, wonderfully paced by the master director who invests his characters, notably the detectives, with a three-dimensional reality that lifts the piece above the Hollywood thriller formula which inspired it. The title refers to the social positions of the kidnapper, driven by envy, and his wealthy victim.

High Society Limited

▶ **Feine Gesellschaft Beschränkte Haftung**

W. Germany 1982 100 mins col
Ottokar-Runze-Filmproduktion

d   **Ottokar Runze**
sc **Uwe Dallmeier, Henning Gissel, Carlheinz Heitmann**
ph **Michael Epp**
m   **Hans-Martin Majewski**
    Lilli Palmer, Elisabeth Bergner, Hardy Kruger, Vadim Glowna, Gerhard Olschewski, Wolf Roth

Tenants of a building are evicted by developers. One of them, a poverty-stricken but saintly old lady (Bergner), unwittingly gets a ride with a couple of would-be bank robbers (Glowna and Olschewski) to a mansion on the banks of the Elbe. At that very moment, the mansion's owner, a glamorous multi-millionairess (Palmer), is being dispossessed of everything she owns by a bank consortium, thanks to the fraudulent actions of her manager. Old lady arrives with robbers, who hold everybody hostage, while we learn that the two women are sisters... A direr piece of drivel is difficult to imagine. The ludicrous plot and characters render this supposed comedy embarrassingly unfunny, while its vague attempts at substance – the poor will enter the kingdom of heaven, decent-minded citizens are driven to crime in order to pay the rent – are shapeless and clumsy. However, Lilli Palmer is exquisite even while being ridiculous, and it is interesting to see Bergner in the twilight of her years.

Hill of Death

▶ **Kozara**

Yugoslavia 1962 130 mins bw
Bosna Film

d   **Veljko Bulajić**
sc **Ratko Djurović, Stevan Bulajić**
ph **Aleksander Sekulović**
m   **Vladimir Kraus-Rajterić**
    Bert Sotlar, Milena Dravić, Olivera Marković, Mihajlo Kostić, Bata Zinojinović

In 1942 the mighty German army descends on the mountain village of Kozara, bombing indiscriminately and executing all suspected Partisans. A band of the latter, led by Vuksha (Sotlar), fights back courageously, losing most of its number in the process. This is a conventional and predictable war film about the local heroes of Yugoslavia, with little of interest to offer in its depiction of characters and relationships. However, the battle scenes are extremely well done, sparing no details but avoiding sensationalism, and the images of men and machines against the landscape are very striking.

A Hill On The Dark Side Of The Moon

▶ **Berget Pa Manens Baksida**

Sweden 1983 105 mins col
MovieMakers/Svenska Filminstitut/SVT 1/Sandrews

d **Lennart Hjulström**
sc **Agneta Pleijel**
ph **Sten Holmberg, Rolf Lindström**
m **Lars-Erik Brossner**
Gunilla Nyroos, Thommy Berggren, Lina Pleijel, Bibi Andersson, Ingvar Hirdwall, Iwar Wiklander

The last years in the life of Sonya Kovalevsky (Nyroos), the brilliant Russian mathematician, who died of pneumonia in 1891 aged 41, after becoming Sweden's first woman professor. Her loveless marriage having ended in her husband's suicide, the lonely, rootless and work-obsessed Sonya finds her world upended by a cataclysmic love affair with her namesake and compatriot, Professor Maxim Kovalevsky (Berggren), who preaches doctrines of sexual equality and individual freedom, but is cruelly contained in his emotions. A film of ambitious intentions which attempts to air political and feminist issues, but degenerates into an *angst*-ridden account of sexual passion and destructive jealousy, accompanied by inappropriate music, and failing to develop its characters who languish in picturesque seasonal landscapes. Nyroos gives a brave performance as the academic whose rationality deserts her in the face of her feelings, while Berggren does his best in support. For all its flaws, though, the film has its compelling moments – not least in the silent commentary provided by the presence of Sonya's adoring but unhappy young daughter (Pleijel).

▶ **Himatsuri** see Fire Festival

▶ **Himmel Über Berlin, Der** see Wings Of Desire

▶ **Hintertreppe** see Backstairs

Hiroshima Mon Amour

France 1959 91 mins bw
Argos/Comei/Pathé/Daiei

d **Alain Resnais**
sc **Marguerite Duras**
ph **Sacha Vierny, Takahashi Michio**
m **Giovanni Fusco, Georges Delerue**
Emmanuele Riva, Eiji Okada, Bernard Fresson, Stella Dassas, Pierre Barbaud

A French actress (Riva), filming in Hiroshima, has a brief affair with a Japanese architect (Okada). She tries to come to terms with the tragedy of his city while recalling her love for a German soldier in Nevers during the war. Resnais in his remarkable first feature, after 11 years of making short films, managed by a complex use of the flashback device to change the cinema's concept of subjective time. The past and present, personal and public anguish, Hiroshima and Nevers, intermingle in a masterly manner. It is also innovative in the use of sound (the past is silent), tracking shots and the literary but cinematic text by a leading modern novelist.

▶ **Histoire D'Adèle H, L'** see Story Of Adèle H, The

▶ **Histoires Extraordinaires** see Spirits Of The Dead

▶ **Histoire Simple, Un** see Simple Story, A

▶ **Historia Official, La** see Official Version, The

▶ **History Of The Burning Years** see Flaming Years, The

Hitler, A Film From Germany

▶ **Hitler, Ein Film Aus Deutschland**

W. Germany 1977 420 mins col
TMS/Solaris/Westdeutscher Rundfunk/ Ina/BBC

d **Hans Jürgen Syberberg**
sc **Hans Jürgen Syberberg**
ph **Dietrich Lohmann**
m **Wagner, Mozart, Beethoven**
   Harry Baer, Heinz Schubert, Peter Kern,
   Hellmut Lange, Rainer Von Artenfels,
   Martin Sperr, Johannes Buzalski

A phantasmagoric panorama of German history, culture and mythology, before, during and after Hitler, in four parts – 'The Grail', 'A German Dream', 'The End Of A Winter's Tale' and 'We Children Of Hell'. Following his stimulating investigations into the German psyche in *Ludwig – Requiem For A Virgin King, Ludwig's Cook, Karl May* and *Winifred Wagner*, Germany's most original and eclectic director opens his most copious Pandora's box of tricks to reveal 'the Hitler in us all'. An extensive use of puppets, back projection, visual quotes from *Caligari* and the German films of Fritz Lang, newsreels, interviews, narration, and burlesque, shows how Hitler was the great impresario/film director who mesmerized the masses. Syberberg's film does not seek to mesmerize, but to provoke audiences to thought and even anger.

▶ **Hitler, Ein Film Aus Deutschland**
see Hitler, A Film From Germany

Hoa-Binh

France 1970 90 mins col
Madeleine Films/Parc Film/Productions
De La Guéville/C.A.P.A.C.

d **Raoul Coutard**
sc **Raoul Coutard**
ph **Georges Liron**
m **Michel Portal**
   Phi San, Xvar Ha Moi, Le Qynh, Danièle
   Delorme, Huynh Cazenas, Xuan Ha

Tri (Qynh) goes to fight for the Vietcong, leaving behind his wife Thu (Ha Moi), 10-year-old son Hung (Phi San) and tiny daughter. Thu becomes ill, the village is razed by fire and the family takes refuge in the overcrowded and unwelcoming home of relatives. When Thu dies in hospital, Hung goes to Saigon with his baby sister, whom he eventually places in a nursery run by a sympathetic French nurse (Delorme) while he

scratches a living from odd jobs. Coutard, the distinguished New Wave and combat photographer, lived in Vietnam for many years and made his directorial debut with this vivid evocation of an almost permanently war-torn society, seen through the eyes of a child. The title means 'Peace', and is implicitly ironic, since the children don't even know what peace is. The director's stance is determinedly neutral and even-handed – some would say wishy-washy – with both sides voicing more or less the same sentiments as a background to Hung's movingly impassive acceptance of his fate.

▶ **Höhenfeuer** see Alpine Fire

The Hole

▶ **Le Trou**

France 1959 123 mins bw
Play-Art/Filmsonor/Titanus

d **Jacques Becker**
sc **Jacques Becker, José Giovanni, Jean**
   Aurel
ph **Ghislain Cloquet**
   Philippe Leroy, Marc Michel, Jean
   Keraudy, Michel Constantine, Raymond
   Meunier

Four long-term prisoners plan an escape which entails digging a tunnel through the prison vaults and into the Paris sewers. Doubts arise when a newcomer joins them in the cell. Becker, in his last film before his death in 1960 aged 54, seemed to be taking a new direction by using non-professional actors and a more austere camera style. With only natural noises on the sound track, he builds a meticulously detailed account of the characters' life in a small space and the preparations for escape.

▶ **Hole, The** see Onibaba

Holiday For Henrietta aka Henriette

▶ **La Fête À Henriette**

France 1952 113 mins bw

Regina/Filmsonor

d **Julien Duvivier**
sc **Julien Duvivier, Henri Jeanson**
ph **Roger Hubert**
m **Georges Auric**
Dany Robin, Michel Auclair, Hildegard Knef, Michel Roux, Saturnin Fabre, Julien Carette, Henri Crémieux, Louis Seigner

Two screenwriters (Crémieux and Seigner) keep changing the adventures of a young shopgirl (Robin) in Paris on Bastille Day. They are finally soft-hearted enough to give her day out a happy, romantic ending. The evocation of Paris is reminiscent of René Clair's *The Fourteenth of July* (1932), more in atmosphere than in lightness of touch. The central idea of writers influencing the course of the film is not fully explored, but the cast and plot make for pleasant entertainment. Its charm is more apparent when compared with the leaden Hollywood remake, *Paris When It Sizzles* (1963).

▶ **Hol Volt, Hol Nem Volt** see Hungarian Fairy Tale, A

The Holy Innocents

▶ **Los Santos Inocentes**

Spain   1984   105 mins   col
Ganesh Producciones Cinematograficas/ Televisí Española

d **Mario Camus**
sc **Antonio Larreta, Manuel Matji, Mario Camus**
ph **Hans Burmann**
m **Antón García Abril**
Alfredo Landa, Terele Pávez, Francisco Rabal, Augustín González, Juan Diego

Husband Paco (Landa), and wife, Régula (Pávez), exploited workers on the estate of a wealthy family in Franco's Spain in the 1960s, have to cope with a badly retarded child and Régula's mentally deficient and incontinent brother (Rabal). Their hopes rest in their son and elder daughter, but these are dashed by their feudal circumstance. It is difficult to be sure of Camus' intentions. His dark tale is lit with incidents of audacious black humour

and is ravishingly filmed in a magnificent landscape, the only compensation for those who, he seems to be saying, are born to suffer. The story is told in the form of recollections by the suffering peasant couple's son and is formally, but rather oddly, divided into episodes. Religious parable or political fable – who knows? But it has some sharply original moments and a performance of outstanding dimensions from Rabal as the madman, simultaneously pathetic and repulsive.

Best Actor (Alfredo Landa and Francisco Rabal) Cannes 1984

▶ **Holy Terror, The** see Bébert And The Train

The Home And The World

▶ **Ghare-Baire**

India   1984   140 mins   col
National Film Development Corporation Of India

d **Satyajit Ray**
sc **Satyajit Ray**
ph **Soumendou Roy**
m **Satyajit Ray**
Soumitra Chatterjee, Victor Banerjee, Swatilekha Chatterji, Gopa Aich, Jennifer Kapoor, Manoj Mitra

In 1907, Nikhil Choudhury (Banerjee), the wealthy and cultivated owner of a Bengali estate, decides that his wife (Chatterji) should leave the seclusion of the women's quarters. He introduces her to his friend Sandip (Chatterjee), a fiery and attractive leader of a nationalist movement. She falls in love with the man and and his cause, and he moves into the Choudhury home for a time, leaving political upheaval, personal betrayal and bloodshed in his wake. Ray adapted this dignified and poignant film from a novel by Tagore. At the centre of events is Nikhil, withdrawn from the world into the elegant refinements of his home, but eventually – and too late – deciding to act. This is the director in resigned mood, perhaps a little bitter in his sense of futility but, if it is not his most likeable or completely achieved work, it nonetheless holds the attention, and the three principals are superb.

▶ **Homeland** see Heimat

▶ **Homme De Cendres, L'** see Man Of Ashes

▶ **Homme De Nulle Part, L'** see Late Mathias Pascal, The

▶ **Homme De Rio, L'** see That Man From Rio

▶ **Homme Et Une Femme, Un** see Man And A Woman, A

▶ **Homme Et Une Femme: Vingt Ans Déjà, Un** see Man And A Woman: Twenty Years Later, A

▶ **Homme Qui Aimait Les Femmes, L'** see Man Who Loved Women, The

▶ **Homme Qui Me Plaît, Un** see Love Is A Funny Thing

▶ **Homme Sans Visage, L'** see Shadowman

▶ **Hon Dansade En Sommar** see One Summer Of Happiness

▶ **Hong Gaoliang** see Red Sorghum

▶ **Honour Among Thieves** see Grisbi

The Hooligans

▶ **Los Golfos**

Spain 1959 90 mins bw
Films 59

d   Carlos Saura
sc Mario Camus, Carlos Saura, Daniel Sueiro
ph Juan Julio Baena
m   Perico El Del Lunar
    Manuel Zarzo, Luis Marín, Oscar Cruz, Juanjo Losado, Ramón Rubio, Rafael Vargas, Maria Mayer

To finance their friend Juan (Cruz) in his ambition to become a bullfighter, a group of slum boys, living on the outskirts of Madrid, turn to crime and get one of their number killed. In spite of some uneven scripting and direction in the middle third of the film,

Carlos Saura, making his feature debut, displays several of the gifts which would distinguish his later, better work. He portrays his chosen milieu with authenticity, his characters with objective sympathy, and achieves some visually poetic moments. However, it is with the final scenes in the bullring that the then young director most impresses with his energy and his uncompromising exposé of brutality to both man and beast.

▶ **Hora Da Estrela, A** see Hour Of The Star

▶ **Hora De Los Hornos, La** see Hour Of The Furnaces, The

▶ **Hoří, Má Panenko** see Firemen's Ball, The

Horizon

▶ **Horizont**

Hungary 1971 87 mins bw
Mafilm Studio

d   Pál Gábor
sc Gyula Marosi, Pál Gábor
ph János Zsombolyai
m   János Gonda
    Péter Fried, Lujza Orosz, Szilvia Marossy, Zoltán Vadász, József Madaras

Karesz (Fried), 16 years old, rebellious but aimless, drops out of school and, to please his factory-worker mother (Orosz) whose dream is to see him better himself, works as an office messenger. He gets himself the sack and, resisting all help and persuasion, abandons his half-hearted attempts to resume his education. Gábor gives an absorbing picture of dispossessed youth, a familiar problem seen here from the perspective of the particular difficulties which bedevil the Eastern Bloc. Script and director make no attempt to compromise Karesz's unsympathetic personality – his cavalier disregard for the older generation, for example. An honest approach, but one that alienates audience sympathy in a film which, aside from some unnecessary symbolism, is exemplary.

▶ **Horizont** see Horizon

▶ **Horloger De St-Paul, L'** see Watchmaker Of St Paul, The

▶ **Horror Chamber Of Doctor Faustus, The** see Eyes Without A Face

Horse

▶ **Uma**

Japan 1941 129 mins bw
Toho

d **Kajiro Yamamoto**
sc **Kajiro Yamamoto**
ph **Akira Mimura (summer), Hiroshi Suzuki
(autumn), Hiromitsu Karasawa (spring),
Takeo Ito (winter)**
m **Shigeaki Kitamura
Hideko Takamine, Kahoru Futaba,
Kamatari Fujiwara, Chieko Takehisa**

The young daughter (Takamine) of a large, poor farming family lavishes her attention on her pet mare, much to her parents' disapproval. In spring, the horse gives birth to a colt, but debts force the heartbroken girl to sell it. The authenticity of this poignant, beautifully shot, bucolic tale of a girl and a horse was enhanced by the round-the-year shooting of the seasons and the documentation of horse-breeding in Japan. Akira Kurosawa, who was editor and assistant director, proposed marriage during the shooting to Takamine, the Japanese Shirley Temple, a veteran of 16 at the time. Her mother refused, as she did not feel he had much of a future. It was on the strength of Kurosawa's stunning second unit work that he was given his first film, *Judo Saga*, to direct.

Horse Thief

▶ **Daoma Zei**

China 1986 88 mins col
Xi'an Film Studio

d **Tian Zhuangzhuang**
sc **Zhang Rui**
ph **Hou Yong, Zhao Fei**
m **Qu Xiaosong
Tseshang Rigzin, Dan Jiji, Jayang
Jamco, Daika, Drashi**

In a remote and impoverished village in Tibet, Nordu (Rigzin), concerned for the welfare of his wife and son, takes to horse-stealing. After repenting in public at a religious ceremony, he kills a sacred ram, becomes a thief again, and ends up a doomed outcast. Zhuangzhuang is a member of an elite group of directors, known as the 'Fifth Generation', who spearheaded the Chinese cinema's renaissance and *Horse Thief*, filmed on location in Tibet and western China, has been called both minimalist and expressionist. Its rich concentration of extraordinary imagery, filled with showy effects – camera angles, dissolves, superimposition, montage, slow fades – and its depiction of (sometimes incomprehensible) ritual observances, renders it memorable chiefly for its visual qualities. Awesomely mysterious, full of religious overtones, and haunted by images of death, the film nevertheless lacks any clearly discernible ideology or theme, but is an expansive and rewarding piece of pure cinematic art.

▶ **Hostsonaten** see Autumn Sonata

L'Hôtel De La Plage

France 1977 111 mins col
Production 2000

d **Michel Lang**
sc **Michel Lang**
ph **Daniel Gaudry**
m **Mort Shuman
Daniel Ceccaldi, Myriam Boyer, Francis
Lemaire, Guy Marchand, Jean-Paul
Muel, Anne Parillaud, Michel Robin**

August, and the Hôtel De La Plage in Brittany is overflowing with holiday-makers. The guests families with small children, families with teenagers, a divorced philanderer with his equally inconstant mistress, a bachelor and his elderly mother... To phrase it kindly, Michel Lang is no Jacques Tati. His first film, *A Nous Les Petites Anglaises*, was about English holiday-makers in Ramsgate; his second attempts a jolly romp about the French *en vacances*, but home ground hasn't helped. It is a clumsy, episodic and simpering collection of clichés, in which a lot of dreary people of all ages are preoccupied with romance, actual or longed-for. Awful, but a popular hit in France on its initial release.

Hôtel Du Nord

France 1938 110 mins bw
Sedif/Imperial
d **Marcel Carné**
sc **Henri Jeanson, Jean Aurenche**
ph **Armand Thirard**
m **Maurice Jaubert**
**Annabella, Louis Jouvet, Jean-Pierre
Aumont, Arletty, Jane Marken, Bernard
Blier, François Périer**

Among the residents of a rundown hotel on
the Canal Saint-Martin in Paris, are a young
couple (Aumont and Annabella) who make
a suicide pact, and a bitter murderer on the
run (Jouvet) with his lively mistress (Arletty).
'Atmosphere! Atmosphere!' cries Arletty, and
we get plenty of it, mostly from Alexander
Trauner's set and the subtle lighting. Though
lacking the depth and irony of Jacques Prévert
(Carné's collaborator on six films), the writers
gave the director the opportunity to create a
poetic bitter-sweet drama and the splendid
cast a chance to shine.

Hôtel Du Paradis

France 1986 113 mins col
Umbrella-Portman Films (London)/
Pierson Production (Paris)/Film Four
International/London Trust Productions/
Atenne 2 (Paris)
d **Jana Bokóva**
sc **Jana Bokóva**
ph **Gérard De Battista**
m **Rodolfo Mederos**
**Fernando Rey, Marika Rivera, Carola
Regnier, Fabrice Luchini, Berangère
Bonvoisin, Hugues Quester**

A group of variously displaced persons con-
verge and cross paths at the Hotel Du Paradis,
a somewhat seedy but characterful and welcoming Parisian establishment run by the
exotic Marika (Rivera), who provides a home
from home for her guests. The latest arrivals
are Joseph Goldman (Rey), an aging actor
and former concentration camp inmate, with
his spinster sister (Regnier) who acts as his
devoted keeper. Joseph strikes up a friendship
with Frédérique (Bonvoisin), a beautiful but

rootless photographer, attempting to escape
her relationship with her live-in lover... The
distinguished Czech-born documentarist,
Jana Bokóva, resident in Britain (where,
unusually, she found the financing for her
film), is no stranger to exile and spent the
first years of her own in Paris. This, her debut
feature, displays her fine sense of atmosphere
and detail, reeks of authenticity and boasts a
uniformly excellent cast led by Rey at his
best. However, the piece is so meandering
and so lacking in any conventional narrative
line, that it finds itself stranded between documentary and feature conventions without
satisfying either. Although very well photographed, *Hotel Du Paradis* is a rare case of
a film which is more likely to please audiences
on TV than in the cinema and, indeed, it
counts Britain's Channel 4 among its backers.

Hotel Terminus: The Life
And Times Of Klaus Barbie

France 1988 267 mins col
Memory Pictures
d **Marcel Ophüls**
ph **Seven documentary cameramen**

Klaus Barbie, known as the 'Butcher of
Lyons', was extradited to France from Bolivia
where he had gone in 1951. He was tried in
1987 and given life imprisonment. Gestapo
chief and torturer extraordinary, Barbie was
responsible for the transportation and death
of most of Lyons' Jewish population, including the children. After the war, he proved of
use to Allied governments, notably that of
the United States and, with their connivance,
made his escape to a comfortable life in South
America. The entire Barbie saga is one of
moral ambiguity and corruption on an unim-
aginable scale: not only are the clear and
familiar atrocities of the Nazi regime
exhumed, but so is the hypocritical and self-
interested attitude of French citizenry, both
during the war and now, of American intelligence officers and of Barbie's South American
friends and business colleagues. It was one of
the latter who eventually betrayed him, merely
out of pique at being done down in a business
deal. Marcel Ophüls, whose *The Sorrow And
The Pity*, about the Nazi occupation of

France, was a landmark in documentary film-making, has here delivered a four-and-a-half hour film composed of interviews with myriad 'witnesses' – friends, enemies, victims, collaborators, lawyers and seemingly innocuous citizens of Lyons. Condemning themselves from their own mouths, the testimonies, brilliantly drawn from them by a relentless Ophüls, make for a film that is as compelling as it is horrifying. The cumulative effect is to expose human weakness at its most depressing, and the fact that no French funding could be found for the enterprise leaves one with the bleak impression that little has changed in Barbie's world of prejudice, blindness and self-interest.

Hot Winds

▶ **Garm Hava**

India   1973   136 mins   col
Unit 3 MM/Film Finance Corporation

d   **M.S. Sathyu**
sc **Kaifi Azmi, Shama Zaidi**
ph **Ishan Arya**
m   **Ustad Bahadur Khan, Aziz Ahmed, Khan Warsi**
    Balraj Sahni, Gita, Jamal Hashmi, Badar Begum, Dinanath Zutshi, A.K. Hangal, Rajendra Raghuvanshi

In 1947, after independence and partition, Halim Mirza (Zutshi) and his son Kazim (Hashmi) join the Muslim exodus to Pakistan. Halim's brother Salim (Sahni), a prosperous manufacturer whose daughter is betrothed to Kazim, opts to remain in India. Gradually, anti-Muslim prejudice catches up with him and each member of his family, causing severe and escalating domestic and business problems. When Kazim returns to fetch his fiancée and is arrested, the result is tragedy. In an ambitious debut film, Sathyu has succeeded in creating a rich mosaic of the problems that dominated his country in a period of upheaval rarely dealt with in the Indian cinema. His portraits of Salim and his family unveil the customs, textures and temperaments of the individuals, revealing their differing responses to bewildering change. The character of the grandmother (Begum), rooted in the past, is particularly poignant. This is an absorbing

human drama that culminates in the protagonists' growth to positive political involvement.

The Hour Of The Furnaces

▶ **La Hora De Los Hornos**

Argentina   1968   260 mins   col/bw
Grupo Cine Liberacion/Arger Film

d   **Fernando E Solanas**
sc **Fernando E Solanas**
ph **Octavio Getino, Fernando E Solanas**
m   **Various**

Part I: 'Neo-colonialism And Violence' deals with the history of Argentina. Part II: 'Act For Liberation' comprises notes and testimonies on the liberation struggles of the Argentinian people Part III: 'Violence And Liberation' considers the meaning and use of violence in the process of liberation. This masterpiece marks a way forward in didactic political documentaries. Solanas presents a dazzling array of newsreel material, extracts from films by Fernando Birri, Léon Hirszman, Joris Ivens and Humberto Rios, interviews, intertitles, songs, poems and new material with the camera zooming in on the faces of the people as evidence in his indictment and analysis of the effects of neo-colonialism on Argentina. This devastating film, made clandestinely, ends with a two minute close-up of the face of the dead Che Guevara, to whom the film is dedicated along with 'all who have died fighting to liberate Latin America'.

Hour Of The Star

▶ **A Hora Da Estrela**

Brazil   1985   96 mins   col
Raiz Produces Cinematograficas

d   **Suzana Amaral**
sc **Suzana Amaral, Alfredo Oroz**
ph **Edgar Moura**
m   **Marcus Vinicius**
    Marcelia Cartaxo, José Dumont, Tamara Taxman, Umberto Magnani, Denoy De Oliveira

Macabea (Cartaxo), a poor, naive, innocent

and plain peasant girl, comes to Rio and labours inadequately as a typist, while dreaming of romance and of becoming a movie star. A novella by the renowned Brazilian novelist, Clarice Lispector, was the basis for this compassionate portrait of a deprived person whose fate is preordained by society. Macabea can break her chains only in death, which comes in circumstances both tragic and ironic. A poignant, intelligent and much acclaimed first feature from a director who began her career in her late thirties, after raising nine children.

Best Actress (Marcelia Cartaxo) Berlin 1986

Hour Of The Wolf

▶ **Vargtimmen**

Sweden   1967   89 mins   bw
Svensk Filmindustri

d   **Ingmar Bergman**
sc   **Ingmar Bergman**
ph   **Sven Nykvist**
m   **Lars Johan Werle**
　　Liv Ullmann, Max Von Sydow, Erland Josephson, Gertrud Fridh, Gudrun Brost, Ingrid Thulin

An artist (Von Sydow), living with his wife (Ullmann) at their summer island home, is subject to terrible nightmares and hallucinations. Bergman used the eerie landscape of the island of Fårö (where he himself lived) to reflect the descent into madness of his hero at odds with society. The gloom of one of his most haunting and frightening films is relieved by an enchanting extract from a puppet performance of *The Magic Flute*.

House For Swap

▶ **Se Permuta**

Cuba   1984   103 mins   col
ICAIC

d   **Juan Carlos Tabio**
sc   **Juan Carlos Tabio, Raul Garcia**
ph   **Julio Valdes**
m   **Juan Marquez**
　　Rosita Fornes, Isabel Santos, Mario Falmaseda, Ramoncito Velos

Gloria Perdomo (Fornes), a middle-aged matron, spends her entire time manipulating others in her single-minded quest for better and better accommodation. Her daughter Yolanda (Santos) becomes engaged to a carefree graphic designer (Falmaseda) and Gloria makes elaborate plans to move in with the couple while convincing an elderly lady to move out of her 'mansion'. Meanwhile, Yolanda takes an interest in Pepe (Velos), a serious civil engineer, who is himself engaged and is thinking of moving. Based on a popular stage play, Tabio's lively first feature treats the problems of Cuba's housing shortages and the extreme lengths to which people will go to secure decent accommodation as a broad social comedy, punctuated with a multitude of visual and verbal gags. Though unpolitical and non-didactic on the surface, like the director's later satire *Plaff!* (1988), the film uses a number of humorous stylistic devices and picaresque anecdotes to make wry comments on the failure of the government to counter the desperate individual solutions to what should be a collective responsibility.

The House Of Bernarda Alba

▶ **La Casa De Bernarda Alba**

Spain   1981   104 mins   col
Paraiso Films

d   **Mario Camus**
sc   **Mario Camus, Antonio Larreta, Marisa Ibarra**
ph   **Fernando Arribas**
m   **Angel Alvarez**
　　Irene Gutierrez Caba, Ana Belén, Florinda Chico, Enriqueta Carballeira, Vicky Peña

Bernarda Alba, newly widowed, is the cruelly tyrannical ruler of a household of women: her insane mother, her servants and her five daughters ranging in age from 39 downwards. She imposes eight years of mourning on the family in conditions tantamount to a prison sentence, but when the eldest daughter's newly inherited wealth leads to her betrothal to a man 15 years her junior the lid comes off the boiling cauldron of repressed sexuality which haunts all five sisters in varying degrees. Federico Garcia Lorca's internationally renowed stage play – a powerful indictment of repressive Spanish custom – is tailormade for the visual and atmospheric accessories that the cinema can provide. Mario Camus, who specializes in literary adaptations, brings this hotbed of passions and dark tragedy to the screen with absolute fidelity to the original (but with too measured a pace), while at the same time skilfully opening it out from the confines of the one room in which it is generally played in the theatre. Alba herself (Caba), one of the great monsters of European drama, also serves as a political emblem, hinting at the ruthlessness of Fascism, the suffocating influence of the Church and the iniquities of the class system. Camus and his carefully chosen cast control the melodrama very well; he also has an eye for striking compositions and utilizes a superbly atmospheric soundtrack. A respectable film of undoubted quality that often absorbs and always interests but which, for all its virtues, never quite manages to achieve real emotional impact.

House Of Lovers

▶ **Pot-Bouille**

France 1957 118 mins bw
Paris/Panitalia

d Julien Duvivier
sc Henri Jeanson
ph Michel Kelber
m Jean Wiener
Gérard Philipe, Danielle Darrieux, Dany Carrel, Anouk Aimée, Jane Marken, Jacques Duby, Henri Vilbert, Claude Nollier

Penniless Octave Mouret (Philipe) arrives in Paris at the turn of the century to take up a job as assistant in a draper's shop run by Madame Hédouin (Darrieux). She takes a fancy to him, as do two girls (Carrel and Aimée) in the house where he lodges. A charming, often wickedly witty rendering of Zola's novel of snobbery and ambition among the *bourgeoisie*. An alert eye for the period, a stylish cast led by Philipe in his element, and a light erotic touch (the seduction scenes were considered quite naughty at the time) made it a return to form for Duvivier and his last film of merit.

▶ **House Of Pleasure** see Plaisir, Le

The House Of The Angel

▶ **(US: End Of Innocence)**

▶ **La Casa Del Angel**

Argentina 1957 73 mins bw
Argentina Sono Film

d Leopoldo Torre-Nilsson
sc Beatriz Guido, Leopoldo Torre-Nilsson, Martin Rodriguez Mentasti
ph Anibal Gonzalez Paz
Elsa Daniel, Lautaro Murua, Giullermo Battaglia, Jordana Fain, Berta Ortegosa

In the 1920s, a sheltered young girl (Daniel) growing up in the repressive Catholic morality of a *bourgeois* family is made to feel shame for the rest of her life over her first love affair which turned horribly wrong. Although Torre-Nilsson had previously directed seven films (co-directing two with his father Leopoldo Torres-Rios), it was this claustrophobic Gothic drama that put him – and Argentina – on the cinematic map. Like the successes that followed, it was based on a novel by his wife, Beatriz Guido, and broke away from the then staple Argentinian product of superficial comedies and melodramas.

The House On Trubnaya Square

▶ **Dom Na Trubnoi**

USSR 1928 64 mins bw
Mezhrabpom

d Boris Barnet
sc B. Zoritch, Anatoly Marienhov, V. Cherchenievitch, V. Chklovski, Nikolai Erdman
ph E. Alekseyev
m Silent
Vera Maretskaya, Vladimir Fogel, E. Tiapkina, S. Komarov, Boris Barnet, Anna Sten

A young country girl (Maretskaya) comes to Moscow and finds herself skivvying for a *petit-bourgeois* couple in a tenement on Trubnaya Square. But she is revitalized when she sees a play about Joan of Arc, and rebels when her employers refuse to let her go to a workers' co-operative stage show. At the very beginning the camera cranes down on the building of the title and we are introduced to the lovingly and sharply observed characters who inhabit it. A film jam-packed with delights includes an amusing scene of amateur theatricals, comically entangled relationships, a superb villain and some free-wheeling urban location shooting.

▶ **Hra O Jablko** see Apple Game, The

▶ **Hrst Plna Vody** see Adrift

▶ **Hsia Nu** see Touch Of Zen, A

▶ **Huang Tudi** see Yellow Earth

Hugo And Josephine

▶ **Hugo Och Josefin**

Sweden 1967 82 mins col
Sandrew

d   Kjell Grede
sc Maria Gripe, Kjell Grede
ph Lars Björne
m   Torbjörn Lundquist
    Maria Öhman, Fredrik Becklén, Beppe
    Wolgers, Inga Landgré, Helena Brodin

Lacking playmates, Josephine (Öhman) is lonely and unhappy until she meets Hugo (Becklén), whose conscientious-objector father is in prison, and who spends most of his time in the woods and fields. The children become close friends, sharing their thoughts and many adventures. Grede's debut feature enchants with its portrayal of the magic innocence of childhood, seen entirely from the children's point of view and conveyed quite unselfconsciously. The lyrical photography makes for overwhelming visual beauty and enhances a film that is free of sentimentality, a delight for children, and a poignant journey into the past for adults.

▶ **Hugo Och Josefin** see Hugo And Josephine

Hugs And Kisses

▶ **Puss Och Kram**

Sweden 1966 96 mins bw
Sandrews

d   Jonas Cornell
sc Jonas Cornell
ph Lars Swanberg
m   Bengt Ernryd
    Sven-Bertil Taube, Agneta Ekmanner,
    Häkan Serner, Lina Granhagen, Rolf
    Larsson

A down-at-heel bohemian writer (Serner) is taken into the home of a rich friend (Taube) whose wife becomes torn between her vain but steady husband and the unpredictable carefree guest. The quality of this witty, sophisticated comedy of sexual manners was obscured by the fuss over one scene when the elegant heroine (played by the director's wife) looks at herself naked in the mirror. The British censor showed the film to the press before deciding whether to excise it. The reaction of the scribes was favourable, as they vociferously claimed that pubic hair was not in itself obscene. It was shown uncut and hailed as one of the most promising debuts of many a year. Unfortunately, Cornell has not fulfilled the promise, but the film can be enjoyed today without the attendant hullabaloo.

▶ **Huis Clos** see No Exit

The Human Beast

▶ **La Bête Humaine**

France 1938 99 mins bw
Paris Films

d   Jean Renoir
sc Jean Renoir
ph Curt Courant
m   Joseph Cosma
    Jean Gabin, Simone Simon, Julien
    Carette, Fernand Ledoux, Jean Renoir

A train driver (Gabin) falls in love with the young wife (Simon) of a railwayman (Ledoux), whom the couple plan to kill. In this film, Renoir perhaps came closest to the dark mood of fatalistic 'poetic realism' that characterized the work of Marcel Carné and Julien Duvivier in the 1930s. The beautifully crafted screenplay, though updated, remained faithful to Zola's 1890 novel, and provided opportunities for the powerful brooding presence of Gabin, the enchanting pekinese profile of Simon, and at least two unforgettable sequences – the Paris-Le Havre run (actually filmed on a moving train) and the railwaymen's ball counterpointing a murder.

The Human Condition

▶ **Ningen No Joken**

> Japan   1958-1961   208 mins (No Greater Love), 181 mins (Road To Eternity), 190 mins (A Soldier's Prayer)   bw
> Shochiku

d   **Masaki Kobayashi**
sc   **Masaki Kobayashi, Zenzo Matsuyama**
ph   **Yoshio Miyajima**
m   **Chuji Kinoshita**
   Tatsuya Nakadai, Michiyo Aratama, So Yamamura, Eitaro Ozawa, Akira Ishihama, Shinji Nambara, Ineko Arima

In 1943, with Japan at war, Kaji (Nakadai), a young pacifist, accepts a job as a mine supervisor in Manchuria, where he finds the workers exploited and ill-treated. For rebelling against the bosses, he is arrested and tortured, then sent to the army. The second film deals with Kaji's life there. He finds similar brutality in the barracks. When Japan is defeated, he is interned in a labour camp. The last episode follows his escape in the snow and his efforts to get back to his wife (Aratama). This impressive and harrowing trilogy, based on Gomika's monumental novel, conveys its humanist message through an almost documentary-like visual treatment. Despite the handsome, courageous hero being too good to be true, the rest of humanity so consistently awful and the structure of the films similar, the whole experience is moving and memorable.

The Hunchback Of Rome

▶ **Il Gobbo**

> Italy   1960   103 mins   bw

Dino De Laurentiis Cinematografica/Orsay Films

d   **Carlo Lizzani**
sc   **Luciano Vincenzoni, Elio Petri, Tommaso Chiaretti**
ph   **Aldo Tonti, Leonida Barboni**
m   **Piero Piccioni**
   Gérard Blain, Anna Maria Ferrero, Ivo Garrani, Bernard Blier, Pier Paolo Pasolini, Teresa Pellati

In Rome in 1944, the Hunchback (Blain), a senior figure in the Italian Resistance famed for his ruthless courage, rapes Ninetta (Ferrero), the daughter of a collaborator, but subsequently falls in love with her. This does not prevent him from killing her father. After the liberation, she refuses his offers of help and turns to prostitution. He, only able to function by violence, leads a gang of criminals, but uses the profits to attempt the reclamation of whores... Lizzani's intriguing film is based on the life and death of a real-life hunchback, who flourished as a bandit during the Occupation. Dramatically well-photographed, this account of a man who hits back at a society prejudiced against his deformity is very absorbing until the director allows the Robin Hood element to romanticize and weaken the tale.

A Hungarian Fairy Tale

▶ **Hol Volt, Hol Nem Volt**

> Hungary   1986   98 mins   bw
> Mafilm-Objektiv Studio

d   **Gyula Gazdag**
sc   **Gyula Gazdag, Miklos Györffy**
ph   **Elemér Ragályi**
m   **Mozart arranged by István Mártha**
   Arpad Vermes, Mária Varga, František Hušák, Eszter Csákányi, Szilvia Tóth

During a performance of *The Magic Flute* at the Budapest opera house, Maria (Varga), a beautiful young woman, catches the eye of a handsome stranger. The couple, mutually enraptured, meet for the first and last time after the performance, a liaison that results in the birth of Maria's son, Andris (a wooden performance from young Arpad Vermes). When the boy is 10, his mother is killed in a freak accident and he escapes from the State custodians to seek the father whose details are on his birth certificate but who, unbeknown to him, is a fictitious person. Andris' odyssey lands him in a series of bizarre adventures at the same time as the official in charge of faking fathers grows disgusted with his job and runs amok. The premise of Gazdag's film, part surreal fairy tale, part anti-bureaucratic satire, derives from a Hungarian ploy to stamp out the stigma of illegitimacy by the simple expedient of according a fictitious father to children born out of wedlock. The idea is rich in possibilities but, from about the halfway mark, the focus disintegrates as Gazdag presents a rag-bag of ideas and styles, reality and fantasy, and a deal of tedious padding muddled together in what the director has declared 'a central European's version of Buñuelian cinema' in which 'Kafka meets Grimm'. This ambitious attempt to mix the vision of several other people is probably what sinks the enterprise, and its moments of charm and inventiveness are insufficient to rescue it. Nonetheless, the movie was well received at several European and Canadian festivals during 1987.

Hunger

▶ **Sult**

> Denmark 1966 110 mins bw
> Henning Carlsen (Copenhagen)/ABC Film (Oslo)/Sandrew/Svenska Filminstitutet (Stockholm)

d **Henning Carlsen**
sc **Henning Carlsen, Peter Seeberg**
ph **Henning Kristiansen**
m **Krzysztof Komeda**
> **Per Oscarsson, Gunnel Lindblom, Sigrid Horne-Rasmussen, Oswald Helmuth, Henki Kolstad**

Norway 1890. Pontus (Oscarsson), a penniless and starving writer, unable to keep down food even if he can get it, is thrown out of his lodgings and wanders the streets. Offered money for an article, he struggles to write it by the light of a street lamp and, thus engaged, encounters a beautiful woman (Lindblom) who invites him home. Her attempted seduction ends in humiliation for Pontus. In spite of a few misjudged moments – an unhappy use of distorted imagery, some

unnecessary characteristics invented for Pontus – Carlsen has made an excellent screen adaptation of Knut Hamsen's famous first novel. Boasting some wonderfully atmospheric locations and a strong evocation of the squalor of poverty, the film triumphs above all in Oscarsson's complex, truthful portrayal of a man, ravaged by hunger, whose mind is on the verge of disintegration.

Best Actor (Per Oscarsson) Cannes 1966

Hungry For Love

▶ **(US: Love À La Carte)**
▶ **Adua E Le Compagne**

> Italy 1960 150 mins bw
> Zebra

d **Antonio Pietrangeli**
sc **Ruggero Maccari, Ettore Scola, Antonio Pietrangeli, Tullio Pinelli**
ph **Armando Nannuzzi**
m **Piero Piccioni**
> **Simone Signoret, Marcello Mastroianni, Sandra Milo, Emmanuele Riva, Gina Rovere, Claudio Gora**

Following the official closing of brothels in Italy, four of the girls decide to pool their savings and open a restaurant. They make a go of it, until a wealthy former client causes problems. This is the sort of film that tries to give prostitutes a good name, but ends up giving Italian commercial cinema a bad one. Not that the acting of Signoret (as Adua) and company is anything but watchable, but the episodic plot is overstretched, clichés abound and it never gets to the heart, golden or otherwise, of the characters.

The Hunt

▶ **La Caza**

> Spain 1965 87 mins bw
> Elias Querejeta

d **Carlos Saura**
sc **Angelino Fons, Carlos Saura**
ph **Luis Cuadrado**
m **Luis De Pablo**
> **Ismael Merlo, Alfredo Mayo, José Maria**

Prada, Fernando Sanchez Polack, Emilio Guiterrez Caba, Violeta Garcia

Four men go on a day's rabbit-hunting outside Madrid. José and Luis (Merlo and Prada), middle-aged business partners, are failing to prosper and are each locked into an unhappy marriage. Paco (Mayo), who has not seen his former associates for several years, brings his young brother-in-law (Caba) with him. He has married well and exudes well-being and success. As the day passes, hostilities and resentments build up amid memories of the Civil War that lurk in the scarred and barren landscape, and the outing ends in bloodshed. Made in the repressive climate of Franco's Spain, Saura's third feature, which made his name, is a finely wrought metaphor for its times, presented as a taut, spare psychological thriller. The violent and shocking denouement grows naturally out of the inner crises of the characters, generated by boredom, frustration and anxiety in the languid heat. Powerful and unhappy stuff.

Best Director Berlin 1966

▶ **Hunters, The** see Huntsmen, The

Hunting Flies

▶ **Polowanie Na Muchy**

Poland 1969 108 mins col
Zeszpoly

d **Andrzej Wajda**
sc **Janusz Glowacki**
ph **Zygmunt Samosiuk**
m **Andrzej Korzyński**
   Malgorzata Braunek, Zygmunt Malanowicz, Ewa Skarzanta, Daniel Olbrychski, Joszef Pieracki

An ineffectual young translator (Malanowicz) is taken up by a glamorous, ambitious girl (Braunek) who tries to make him an artistic success by taking him away from his dull wife (Skarzanta) and introducing him to the right people. Wajda's first outright venture into comedy (few of his films find much to laugh at) is reminiscent of his compatriot Skolimowski's humour and milieu, but it is less focused and never exactly sure of its targets. For example, the film is plainly misogynistic

while being dedicated to women, an unconvincing irony. Nevertheless, there are some fiercely satirical jibes at certain sectors of Polish society.

The Huntsmen

▶ **(US: The Hunters)**

▶ **I Kynighi**

Greece 1977 165 mins col
Angelopoulos/INA Production

d **Theo Angelopoulos**
sc **Theo Angelopoulos, Stratis Karras**
ph **Ghiorgios Arvanitis**
m **Loukianos Kilaidonis**
   Vangelis Kazan, Georges Danis, Ilia Stamatiou, Stratos Pahis

A group of hunters in 1977, crossing a snowy mountainside in northern Greece, comes across the body of a Greek guerrilla fighter killed in 1949. At the subsequent inquest, each member of the hunting party, as well as various peasants and workers, speaks of his experiences during the civil war and the years that followed. Angelopoulos takes his time to unravel the various strands in this inquisition of the Right, using dream, memory and fantasy and the powerful symbol of the corpse as the silent accuser. The pastel shades, the languid pacing and the long takes are often justified in giving the spectator time to consider the issues or to think of something else.

▶ **Hurdes, Las** see Land Without Bread

▶ **Hustruer** see Wives

▶ **Hustruer Ti Ar Etter** see Wives (10 Years After)

▶ **Hypothèse Du Tableau Volé, L'** see Hypothesis Of The Stolen Painting, The

The Hypothesis Of The Stolen Painting

▶ **L'Hypothèse Du Tableau Volé**

France 1978 66 mins bw
L'Institut National De L'Audiovisuel

d   **Râùl Ruiz**
sc **Râùl Ruiz**
ph **Sacha Vierny**
m   **Jorge Arriagada**
    **Jean Rougeul, Gabriel Gascon, Chantal
    Paley, Jean Raynaud, Daniel Grimm**

An art collector (Rougeul) guides an unseen interviewer around six paintings by Frédéric Tonnerre, an academic painter of the Second Empire, in an attempt to solve the mystery of a missing seventh painting, which provoked a major scandal. Ruiz's intriguing and singular meditation on the possibilities and limitations of the pictorial in the cinema, is also a detective story with clues and a solution. Based on the novel *Baphomet* by Pierre Klossowski, brother of the painter Balthus and himself an artist, the film presents the six paintings as *tableaux vivants* in which the actors hold poses as they are minutely examined. It forces a reappraisal of one's approach to static paintings and to the narrative flow of films. Vierny's exquisite black and white photography helped bring the paintings to life. The film made the director, a Chilean exile in Paris, the darling of the *avant-garde*.

I Accuse

▶ **J'Accuse**

France 1919 150 mins bw
Pathé

d **Abel Gance**
sc **Abel Gance**
ph **L.H. Burel, Marc Bujart, Maurice Forster**
m **Silent**

Sévérin-Mars, Maryse Dauvray, Romuald Joubé, Maxime Des Jardine, Angèle Guys

The brutish François (Sévérin-Mars) seethes with jealousy because he knows his wife Edith (Dauvray) prefers his friend, the sensitive poet Jean (Joubé). But the war unites the men against a common enemy. Gance's biggest budget film to date, which he called 'a human cry against the bellicose din of armies,' begins with soldiers forming the letters of the title and ends with dead soldiers rising from their graves contrasted, in a split-screen sequence, with a victory parade to the Arc De Triomphe. This lengthy pacifist statement, depicting death, delusion and insanity in the trenches was actually shot during World War I with real soldiers under fire. However, much of its impact is weakened by the over-melodramatic triangular love story that takes up too much of the time. Gance remade this international success as a talkie in 1938, using many of the same techniques and sequences to less effect.

I Am Curious - Yellow

▶ **Jag Ar Nyfiken Gul**

Sweden 1967 121 mins bw
Sandrews

d **Vilgot Sjöman**
sc **Vilgot Sjöman**
ph **Peter Wester**
m **Bengt Ernryd**

Lena Nyman, Peter Lindgren, Börje Ahlstedt, Vilgot Sjöman, Magnus Nilsson

A sociologist (Nyman) conducts a series of interviews with workers, trade unionists, women and young people about the Swedish class structure and their roles in it. Meanwhile, she has a passionate affair with a visitor (Ahlstedt) to her father's apartment. They copulate in her bedroom, in front of the Royal Palace, in a tree, on the grass and in a pond. This is the film that broke a number of sexual taboos, and was released in the USA (where it was a huge box-office hit) only in New York and New Jersey after a court battle, and cut by 11 minutes in Great Britain. The film's loose narrative structure and the use of *cinéma vérité* interviews and newsreel material reflect part of the changing political and sexual climate in Europe in the late 1960s, but much of it is now more heavy going than heavy breathing. This *succès de scandale* was followed up by *I Am Curious - Blue* (1968) – yellow and blue being the two colours of the Swedish flag reflecting the director's comments on aspects of life in Sweden.

▶ **I And My Lovers** see Galia

The Ice Palace

▶ **Is-Slottet**

Norway 1987 78 mins col
Norsk Film

d **Per Blom**
sc **Per Blom**
ph **Halvor Naess**

Line Storesund, Hilde Nyeggen
Martinsen, Merete Moen, Sigrid Huun,
Vidar Sandem

Unn (Martinsen) and Siss (Storesund), two
11-year-old schoolgirls in a remote Norwegian village, develop a close friendship. One
afternoon they remove their clothes and
awaken mutual consciousness of their sexuality. The emotional shock of their feelings
disturbs both of them, particularly Unn.
Unable to face her friend the next day, she
wanders off to a huge frozen waterfall and
finds herself lost in the maze of a world made
of ice. Sensitivity to adolescence is demonstrated in Blom's film, as well as a compelling
feel for atmosphere and an eye for eerily
overwhelming beauty. The film sucks one into
a world of menace and isolation, the dark
tones of emotion powerfully counterpointed
by the dazzling white and green lights of the
ice palace. However, the Nordic *angst* and
lack of resolution finally exhausts and over-
whelms the viewer.

▶ **Ich Bin Ein Elefant, Madame** see
I'm An Elephant, Madame

▶ **Ich War 19** see I Was 19

▶ **Ich Will Doch Nur, Dass Ihr Mich
Liebt** see I Only Want You To Love Me

The Icicle Thief

▶ **Ladri Di Saponette**

Italy 1988 88 mins col/bw
Bambu'Srl/Reteitalia

d   **Maurizio Nichetti**
sc **Maurizio Nichetti, Mauro Monti**
ph **Mario Battistoni**
m   **Manuel De Sica**
    **Maurizio Nichetti, Caterina Sylos Labini,
    Federico Rizzo, Renato Scarpa, Heidi
    Komarek, Carlina Torta**

In an Italian TV studio a director (Nichetti)
is present while a critic introduces a screening
of his film, 'The Icicle Thief', a Neo-Realist
drama about a poverty-stricken family set in
the immediate post-war years. At home a
family is watching the programme, only
paying attention when the commercial breaks

occur and eventually being unable to distinguish between the movie and the breaks.
A power failure causes a scrambling of the
two and the desperate Nichetti, attempting
to intervene, finds himself in his own movie
and part of a total fusion and confusion of
illusion and reality. This is a bizarre confection made up of some clever ideas (not
unfamiliar from Woody Allen's *The Purple
Rose of Cairo*) and often very funny. The
film within the film is a superb pastiche of
Bicycle Thieves (1948), often poignant as
well as amusing, and the satire on the ruin
of film by television – an increasingly evident
concern of Italian film-makers – is pointed.
However, although there are many moments
to enjoy, not least Nichetti's impressive
double performance as himself and as the
put-upon father of his fictional family, the
exercise runs out of steam, degenerating into
tedious chaos and silliness.

Iconostasis

▶ **Ikonostasut**

Bulgaria 1969 94 mins bw
Sofia Film Studios

d   **Todor Dinov, Hristo Hristov**
sc **Todor Dinov, Hristo Hristov**
ph **Atanas Tassev**
m   **Milcho Leviev**
    **Dimiter Tashev, Emilia Radeva, Violetta
    Gindeva, Nikolai Ouzounov, Annie
    Spassova**

In a Bulgarian village, in the mid-19th century
during the final years of the Ottoman rule,
an itinerant master craftsman (Tashev) is
hired to design and carve the iconostasis (a
large screen set with icons) of a new church.
The heavy-drinking, slovenly artist gets a girl
(Gindeva) pregnant and is generally a disrup-
tive force among a peasant population beginning to rebel against their Turkish masters.
The complex historical background, the episodic structure and profusion of incident are
likely to confuse the average Western viewer,
but the different ways of life of the people
are vividly captured by Dinov, a leading
cartoon-maker, and Hristov, both making
their first feature.

▶ **Idade Da Terra** see Age Of The Earth

An Ideal Husband

▶ **Idealny Muzh**

USSR 1981 92 mins col
Mosfilm

d **Viktor Georgiyev**
sc **Viktor Georgiyev, from the play by Oscar Wilde**
ph **Fyodor Dobronravov**
m **E. Denisov**
   Yuri Yakovlev, Ludmila Gurchenko, Anna Tvelenyova, Eduard Martsevich, Pavel Kadochnikov

Mrs Cheveley (Gurchenko), an unprincipled upper-class schemer, attempts to blackmail Sir Robert Chiltern (Yakovlev) of the Foreign Office into protecting her business interests, and to bribe her former fiancé, Viscount Goring (Martsevich), into marrying her, but her chicanery backfires. Oscar Wilde's classic snipe at the morals of fashionable society works surprisingly well in the hands of a Russian director and cast, even though one is necessarily deprived of the pleasure of the Wildean language. There are one or two *faux-pas* – the view from a suite at Claridges, for example, discloses the Thames and the Houses of Parliament – but on the whole this is a creditable and pleasing entertainment from the USSR.

▶ **Idealny Muzh** see Ideal Husband, An

Identification Marks: None

▶ **Rysopis**

Poland 1964 76 mins bw
Panstwowa Wyzsza Szkola Filmowa w Lodzi

d **Jerzy Skolimowski**
sc **Jerzy Skolimowski**
ph **Witold Mickiewicz**
m **Krzysztof Sadowski**
   Jerzy Skolimowski, Elzbieta Czyżewska, Tadeusz Mins, Andrzej Zarnecki, Jacek Szczek

A young man is drafted into military service for two years. On the day of his departure, he visits his estranged wife and meets various other people, including an old school colleague turned playboy and a disabled war veteran, before just making it to the train on time. Twenty-five-year-old Skolimowski plays the hero and his wife, Czyzewska, portrays four different women in his first feature (for which he was also the art director), which already has his identification marks all over it: the lively, episodic structure full of telling incidents rather than a linear narrative, an off-centre humour, and non-conformism.

Identification Of A Woman

▶ **Identificazione Di Una Donna**

Italy 1982 131 mins col
Iter Film(Rome)/Gaumont(Paris)

d **Michelangelo Antonioni**
sc **Michelangelo Antonioni, Gérard Brach**
ph **Carlo Di Palma**
m **John Foxx**
   Tomas Milian, Daniela Silverio, Christine Boisson, Sandra Monteleoni, Giampaolo Saccarola

Niccolo (Milian), a 40-year-old divorced film director is searching for a particular female image for his next film. He and Mavi (Silverio), his aristocratic girlfriend, argue and he loses track of her. He then takes up with Ida (Boisson), a young actress, with whom he has an affair, but she also leaves him. After seven years of experimenting with video techniques, Antonioni, the former darling of the art circuit, returned to more familiar territory, but the film is a lugubrious exercise, like the thick fog that envelops Niccolo and Mavi on the road, and the hollow foundations of a villa referred to as 'the revenge of the void'. Every image, every aphorism is laden with a significance which the theme – the difficulty of loving someone fully in our times – cannot support. The picture has a plastic beauty, but it evoked the memory of Antonioni's past and the hope that, like the main character, he would find a more satisfying new project.

▶ **Identificazione Di Una Donna** see Identification Of A Woman

▶ **Idi I Smotri** see Come And See

The Idiot

▶ **L'Idiot**

France 1946 98 mins bw

Sacha Gordine/Lux

d **Georges Lampin**
sc **Charles Spaak**
ph **Christian Matras**
m **Maurice Thiriet**
   Gérard Philipe, Edwige Feuillère, Lucien Coëdel, Nathalie Nattier, Marguerite Moreno

The attempts of the saintly Prince Mishkin (Philipe) to bring tranquillity into the life of the tormented Nastasia Filipovna (Feuillère) are fraught with difficulties. Watching this competently directed and smoothly acted film, it is difficult to believe that it was adapted from one of the world's great novels. Nevertheless, though more modest than the Japanese and Soviet versions, it is more pleasurable in many ways, not least in the fine performances from Philipe and Feuillère. It was the first feature, and possibly the best, from Lampin, former assistant to René Clair and Abel Gance. He returned less successfully to Dostoevsky in 1956 with *Crime And Punishment* starring Jean Gabin.

▶ **Idiot, L'** see Idiot, The

The Idiot

▶ **Hakuchi**

Japan 1951 166 mins bw
Shochiku

d **Akira Kurosawa**
sc **Akira Kurosawa, Eijiro Hisaita**
ph **Toshio Ubukata**
m **Fumio Hayasaka**
   Masayuki Mori, Setsuko Hara, Toshiro Mifune, Takashi Shimura

Prince Kameda (Mori), saintly and unworldly, falls in love with Taeko (Hara), a kept woman, who is also loved by Kameda's wild-living friend Akama (Mifune). As can be seen from the above, Dostoevsky's novel has been transposed to Japan and the names of Prince Mishkin, Natasha and Rogozhin changed. It was also updated to the post-World War II era. Otherwise, Kurosawa's attempts to follow his favourite literary work slavishly were undermined by large cuts made by the producers. Furthermore, the film that

immediately followed on the heels of the international success of *Rashomon* suffered from some overacting, particularly from the miscast Hara. However, there are moments where the director manages to capture some of the original's greatness, filtered through his own sensibility.

The Idiot

▶ **Nastasia Filipovna**

USSR 1957 122 mins col
Mosfilm

d **Ivan Pyriev**
sc **Ivan Pyriev**
ph **Valentin Pavlov**
m **Nikolai Kryukov**
   Yuri Yakovlev, Julia Borisova, Nikita Podgorny, Leonid Parkhomenko, R. Maximova

Prince Mishkin (Yakovlev), a young and penniless nobleman, returns from Switzerland to St Petersburg and attempts to redeem Nastasia Filipovna (Borisova), a fallen woman. However, his Christ-like behaviour causes problems with her protector (Podgorny) and her passionate lover (Parkhomenko). Although much of the psychological and philosophical subtlety of the novel has been lost, a lot of its atmosphere and spirit have been retained. The first of Pyriev's lavish, rather academic Dostoevsky trilogy (*White Nights* and *The Brothers Karamazov* followed), it suffers from a somewhat operatic acting style.

▶ **Ieri, Oggi, Domani** see Yesterday, Today And Tomorrow

▶ **I Even Met Happy Gypsies** see Happy Gypsies

▶ **Így Jöttem** see My Way Home

▶ **I Had My Brother's Wife** see Waterless Summer

▶ **I Have A New Master** see Passion For Life

▶ **Ikimono No Kiroku** see I Live In Fear

▶ **Ikiru** see Living

▶ **Ikonostasut** see Iconostasis

I Live In Fear

▶ **aka Record Of A Living Being**

▶ **Ikimono No Kiroku**

Japan   1955   113 mins   bw
Toho

d   Akira Kurosawa
sc Shinobu Hashimoto, Akira Kurosawa,
    Hideo Oguni
ph Asakazu Nakai
m   Fumio Hayasaka
    Toshiro Mifune, Eiko Miyoshi, Takashi
    Shimura, Haruko Togo, Masao Shimizu,
    Yutaka Sada

A prosperous owner of a foundry (Mifune) decides to emigrate to Brazil with his large family because he believes that the effects of a nuclear war will be less there. The family, wishing to remain in Japan and not lose their share of his father's wealth, apply to the court to have him committed to an insane asylum. This is another of Kurosawa's films in which Mifune is the dynamo of the picture. Playing a much older man, bespectacled and stooped, he is a quirky figure difficult to identify with in the less successful, satirical first half, but becomes a tragic, Lear-like figure towards the end. Despite Mifune, and other good performances, this sombre contemporary tale seldom gets to grips with the complexities of its vast subject.

▶ **Illicit Interlude** see Summer Interlude

▶ **Ill Omen** see Sign Of Disaster

▶ **Illuminacja** see Illumination

Illumination

▶ **Illuminacja**

Poland   1973   91 mins   col
Tor

d   Krzysztof Zanussi
sc Krzysztof Zanussi

ph Edward Klosinski
m   Wojciech Kilar
    Stanislaw Latallo, Monika Denisiewicz-
    Olbrzychska, Malgorzata Pritulak,
    Edward Zebrowski

A young scientist (Latallo), who believes that everything in life can be handled through rational analysis, has this conviction shattered by his difficult affair with an older woman (Denisiewicz-Olbrzychska) and the death of a close friend in a climbing accident. Zanussi, who studied physics and philosophy at Warsaw University, claimed that 'The scientist is more interesting than anyone else as he is more responsible for the world than the usual people one finds in movies'. Although this statement might not convince everybody, the first major Polish film-maker in the generation after Wajda's certainly broke new ground in his cryptic, intelligent, ironic and ethical essays on the scientific mind. Non-scientists might be put off by the intercutting of documentary material, and non-Poles by the need to infer emotions hidden in the language.

Illustrious Corpses

▶ **Cadaveri Eccellenti**

Italy   1976   120 mins   col
PEA/UA

d   Francesco Rosi
sc Francesco Rosi, Tonino Guerra, Lino
    Jannuzzi
ph Pasqualino De Santis
m   Piero Piccioni
    Lino Ventura, Alain Cuny, Charles Vanel,
    Paolo Bonacelli, Marcel Bozzuffi, Max
    Von Sydow, Fernando Rey, Tina Aumont

A police inspector (Ventura), attempting to solve the murders of judges, prosecutors and leading politicians, but instructed to uphold the *status quo*, slowly reveals a Right-wing conspiracy to arouse public outrage against the Left. The original title is a pun on the name of a game where the head, torso and legs of a body are drawn in turn on a piece of paper, folded so that each player is unable to see the other's drawing. One of Rosi's most successful and acclaimed films resembles the game, as each new fact is revealed. Although the plot (in both senses) is unnerving, and the film is elegantly shot (except when Rosi can't resist strange camera angles and distortions), it is rather a cold exercise, never quite equal to its subject.

▶ **Il Ne Faut Pas Mourir Pour Ça**
see Don't Let It Kill You

I Love You Rosa

▶ **Ani Ohev Otach Rosa**

Israel   1971   91 mins   col
Noah Film

d   Moshe Mizrahi
sc Moshe Mizrahi
ph Adam Grinberg
m   Dov Seltzer
    Michal Bat-Adam, Gabi Otterman, Yossef Shiloah, Levana Finkelstein, Avner Hezkiahou, Moshe Tal

In 19th-century Jerusalem, Rosa (Bat-Adam), left widowed and childless at the age of 21, automatically belongs by Jewish law to the brother of her late husband. At the time, however, her brother-in-law, Nissim (Otterman), is only 11 years old, but his determination to do his duty does not waver, eventually maturing into love and desire... Rosa is clearly a name of resonances for Mizrahi whose *Madame Rosa* would win the Best Foreign Oscar six years later. This time he manages no more than a superficially charming exercise, generously laced with calculated doses of Jewish family comedy and sentimentality. The leads are controlled and appealing, but one is doubtful about the value of the flashback which has Rosa recounting her tale from the perspective of an ancient crone, now aged an amazing 107.

▶ **Il Suffit D'Aimer** see Bernadette Of Lourdes

▶ **Imagen Latente** see Latent Image

I'm An Elephant, Madame

▶ **Ich Bin Ein Elefant, Madame**

W. Germany   1968   100 mins   col
Iduna-Film

d   Peter Zadek
sc Robert Müller, Peter Zadek, Wolfgang Menge
ph Gerard Vandenberg
m   Andy Warhol and The Velvet Underground
    Wolfgang Schneider, Günther Lüders, Tankred Dorst, Heinz Baumann, Peter Palitzsch, Robert Dietl

In 1968, the climate of student protest filters into a West Bremen school, causing disruption and a widening gap between pupils and teachers, the latter divided between dogged conservatives and bemused liberals. At the centre of events is Rull (Schneider), an anarchic pupil who plays by his own rules, insulting protesters and reactionaries alike, but often as attractive as his behaviour is appalling. This is an original, provocative and energetic film, bursting with the youth icons of its period and offering the perceptive and often wittily presented observation that rebellion is frequently an expression of personal rather than political anarchy. Zadek, who lived in England for many years, displays an eclectic style, and takes no sides here.

▶ **Imeres Tou 36** see Days Of 36

I'm Jumping Over Puddles Again

▶ **Už Zase Skáču Přes Kaluže**

Czechoslovakia   1970   92 mins   col
Barrandov Film Studios

d   Karel Kachyna
sc Ota Hofman, Karel Kachyna
ph Josef Illík
m   Zdeněk Liška
    Vladimir Dlouhy, Karel Hlušička, Zdena Hadrbolcová, Vladimir Šmeral, Borivoj Navrátil, Božena Böhmová

Little Adam (Dlouhy), whose father trains and rides horses for the Imperial stables of the Austro-Hungarian Empire, dreams of the day when he will be old enough to participate, but contracts polio which paralyzes both his legs. Determined to ride, the boy fights his disability. Adapting and transposing an Australian autobiography by Allan Marshall to pre-World War I Moravia, Kachyna hymns a paean to courage, and to man's relationship with the noble horse, but the plot is thin and filled out with a deal of tediously repeated images, and some jarring tricks that disturb the beautiful photography. The film, largely seen through the eyes of the child, is best described as infuriatingly heart-warming.

▶ **Im Lauf Der Zeit** see Kings Of The Road

Immoral Tales

▶ **Contes Immoraux**

> France   1974   103 mins   col
> Argos

d   **Walerian Borowczyk**
sc   **Walerian Borowczyk**
ph   **Bernard Daillencourt, Guy Durban, Michel Zolat, Noël Véry**
m   **Maurice Le Roux, Guillaume De Machaut, traditional Spanish and Hungarian music**
Lise Danvers, Fabrice Luchini, Charlotte Alexandra, Paloma Picasso, Pascal Christophe, Florence Bellamy, Jacopo Berinizi

1) 'The Tide' – In 1974, a young man (Luchini) takes his virginal 16-year-old cousin (Danvers) to the beach to teach her the joys of sex; 2) 'Thérèse, The Philosopher' – In 1890, Thérèse (Alexandra), locked in a lumber-room by her aunt as a punishment, finds a book with erotic engravings that lead her to discover masturbation; 3) 'Erzsebet Báthory' – In 1620, the Countess Báthory (Picasso) rounds up the pretty maids of the village for nefarious purposes; 4) 'Lucrezia Borgia' – In 1498, Lucrezia (Bellamy) makes love to Pope Alexander VI (Berinizi). Borowczyk's fascination with the iconography of erotica and the emotions that lie beneath is more interesting than the monotonously bawdy storytelling in itself. The pictorial provocation was enough to make the film a commercial success.

L'Immortelle

> France   1962   100 mins   bw

Como/Tamara/Cocinor (Paris)/Dino De Laurentiis (Rome)/Hamle (Istanbul)

d   **Alain Robbe-Grillet**
sc   **Alain Robbe-Grillet**
ph   **Maurice Barry**
m   **Georges Delerue, Tashin Kavalcioglu**
Françoise Brion, Jacques Doniol-Valcroze, Guido Celano, Catherine Carayon, Sezer Sezin

In Istanbul, a French lecturer (Doniol-Valcroze) meets a mysterious woman (Brion), also a foreigner, who shows him around the city and then abruptly vanishes. His attempts to find her prove fruitless, until she reappears only to be lost to him again. Robbe-Grillet's screenplay for *Last Year In Marienbad* revealed a preoccupation with the image of the labyrinth. In his first film as director, a foreign city is a labyrinth in which the unnamed hero is lost linguistically, culturally, geographically and emotionally. The Turkish music, the threatening dogs, the incomprehensible language and the shrieking sirens emphasize his sense of alienation. 'The film is about a mythology which is that of the Orient, the Orient seen from Paris, a picture-postcard Orient,' Robbe-Grillet explained. This intriguing play on exotic and erotic stereotypes and the real and imaginary (the woman may only exist in the man's mind) is also a recognizable description of the nature of being uprooted.

Improperly Dressed

▶ **(US: Strange Masquerade)**
▶ **Herkulesfürdöi Emlék**

> Hungary   1977   89 mins   col
> Hunnia Studio/Hungarofilm

d   **Pál Sándor**
sc   **Zsuzsa Tóth**
ph   **Elemér Ragályi**
m   **Zdenkó Tamássy**
Endre Holman, Margit Dayka, Ildikó Pécsi, Sándor Szabó, Irma Patkós, Carla Romanelli, Dezsö Garás

After the collapse of the Communist Republic in the winter of 1919, János (Holman), wanted by the police for political offences, disguises himself as a woman and takes a job as an orderly at an isolated female sanatorium from where a contact is to help him escape across the border. Slow-paced, carefully directed and almost distractingly beautiful to look at, Sándor's film manages to use cross-dressing effectively for dramatic purposes, but, in avoiding the comic pitfalls, he loses the sexual ambiguity implicit in the situation – even though his protagonist comes to a new awareness of both feminine and masculine behaviour during his enforced transvestism. Overall, the film, like the microcosmic sanatorium, seems cut off from the political reality (despite the intrusion of White soldiers, one of whom is killed by János for making amorous advances), and from genuine passion (despite the Italian woman who discovers the young man's secret and makes love to him). The piece benefits immeasurably from Holman – wide-eyed, angularly handsome, beguilingly androgynous and conveying a mixture of grace and uneasiness in his female garb.

Special Jury Prize Berlin 1977

An Impudent Girl

▶ **L'Effrontée**

France   1985   97 mins   col
Oliane Films/Films A2/Telema/
Monthyon Films

d   **Claude Miller**
sc   **Claude Miller, Luc Beraud, Bernard Stora, Annie Miller**
ph   **Dominique Chapuis**
m   **Alain Jomy, and extracts from piano concertos by Beethoven, Mozart and Mendelssohn**
    Charlotte Gainsbourg, Bernadette Lafont, Jean-Claude Brialy, Raoul Billerey, Clothilde Baudon, Julie Glenn, Jean-Philippe Ecoffey

Thirteen-year-old Charlotte (Gainsbourg) lives with her widowed father and older brother. Shy, withdrawn, and feeling unloved because she is gawky, she relies on the housekeeper (Lafont) and a sickly younger child (Glenn) for company. When her idol Clara (Baudon), a famous piano prodigy her own age, comes to town to give a concert, Charlotte devotedly pursues her, with a series of unexpected consequences. Miller's proficient, sensitive and beautifully constructed work is,

in fact, a French extrapolation of Carson McCullers' *The Member Of The Wedding* although, curiously, the source is entirely uncredited. Brilliant as 27-year-old Julie Harris was in Fred Zinnemann's Hollywood version, this one has the advantage of a heroine who is the right age – and who gives a memorably delightful performance. Daughter of Jane Birkin and Serge Gainsbourg, the young star is admirably supported by a well-chosen cast. A charming, touching film.

In A Year With 13 Moons

▶ **In Einem Jahr Mit 13 Monden**

W. Germany   1978   129 mins   col
Tango Film/Pro-ject Film/Filmverlag Der Autoren

d   **Rainer Werner Fassbinder**
sc   **Rainer Werner Fassbinder**
ph   **Rainer Werner Fassbinder**
m   **Peer Raben**
    Volker Spengler, Ingrid Caven, Gottfried John, Elisabeth Trissenaar, Eva Mattes, Günther Kaufmann

Erwin (Spengler), driven by love for his business partner Anton (John), has undergone a sex-change operation and is now called Elvira. However, Anton has gone off to further his ambitions, leaving unhappy Elvira to a series of brutal and humiliating relationships with men. Finally, helped by Zora (Caven), a prostitute who later betrays her, and by his/her former wife, Elvira delves into the past in an effort to resolve the present. This tale is uncompromisingly pessimistic and told with the use of harsh colour, asymmetrical sets, shifting narrative techniques and a discordant sound-track to evoke the pain and ugliness of Erwin/Elvira's situation. In an introductory paragraph, the director explains that in a year of 13 moons – a planetary pattern which will have occurred six times in the 20th century – those vulnerable to depression often meet catastrophe. (The year here is 1978.) The film reflects Fassbinder's oft-expressed themes, but the images are elusive, contradictory, and quite unpleasant. Profound and disturbing, or flashy and pretentious? Make of it what you will.

▶ **Incompreso** see Misunderstood

▶ **Indagine Su Un Cittadino Al Di Sopra Di Ogni Sospetto** see Investigation Of A Citizen Above Suspicion

India Song

France   1975   120 mins   col
Sunchild Productions/Les Films
Armorial

d **Marguerite Duras**
sc **Marguerite Duras**
ph **Bruno Nuytten**
m **Carlos D'Alessio**
   Delphine Seyrig, Mathieu Carrière,
   Michel Lonsdale, Vernon Dobtcheff,
   Claude Mann

In Calcutta, Anne-Marie Stretter (Seyrig), a failed concert pianist and the pampered wife of the French vice-consul (Lonsdale) has numerous affairs to which her husband turns a blind eye. This evocation of heat and languor was filmed entirely in a house near Paris, the sounds as much as the camerawork giving the impression of India in the 1930s. The sound and images are often at variance, with a narrator commenting on a place and time other than that the camera is perceiving – generally in long, slow tracking shots. This 'Last Year In Calcutta' evolves like a repetitious and poetic dream, the characters going through a strange stylized ritual. Yet the physical distress of the beggar woman crying in the jungle and Anne-Marie's mental distress are palpable. The film was a follow-up to Duras' *Woman Of The Ganges* (1972), also set in a 'metaphorical India'.

▶ **Indische Grabmal, Das** see Tiger Of Eschnapur, The

▶ **In Einem Jahr Mit 13 Monden** see In A Year With 13 Moons

The Inferno Of First Love

▶ **Hatsukoi Jigoku-Hen**

Japan   1968   108 mins   bw

Hani Productions/Japan Art Theatre
Guild

d **Susumu Hani**
sc **Susumu Hani, Shuji Terayama**
ph **Yuji Okumura**
m **Akio Yashiro, Tohru Takemitsu**
   Akio Takahashi, Kuniko Ishii, Koji
   Mitsui, Kazuko Fukuda

Shun (Takahashi), a young metalworker, finds difficulty in making love to Nanami (Ishii), a nude model. He tells her of his unhappy childhood and of how he was sexually molested by his foster father (Mitsui). Gradually the couple becomes entangled in sordid events, resulting in a tragic ending. In condemning child abuse and the sexual exploitation of women by men, the film is often in danger of becoming the very thing it is criticizing. There are scenes of women posing in the nude, sado-masochistic games and a young boy and a girl being sexually molested, although the director is ostensibly making a moral point. The censors didn't see it this way and 20 minutes was cut from the film on its first US release. Be that as it may, sharp camerawork and telling flashbacks, realistic locations and the excellent non-professional actors reveal Hani as a forceful and talented director.

Infidelity

▶ **(US: The Five-Day Lover)**
▶ **L'Amant De Cinq Jours**

France   1961   95 mins   bw
Les Films Ariane/Filmsonor/Mondex
Films/Cineriz

d **Philippe De Broca**
sc **Daniel Boulanger, Philippe De Broca**
ph **Jean-Bernard Penzer**
m **Georges Delerue**
   Jean Seberg, Micheline Presle, Jean-
   Pierre Cassel, François Périer

Claire (Seberg), married to Georges (Périer), has an affair with bachelor Antoine (Cassel), who is being kept by her good friend Madeleine (Presle), a wealthy *couturière*. But the meetings at Antoine's apartment, five afternoons a week, come to a halt when their partners learn the truth. 'Love's a bubble. When it touches earth, it's over,' says Jean Seberg, and so is the film. De Broca's third film (Cassel also starred in *Playing At Love* and *The Joker*) is a classic sweet- and-sour *boudoir* comedy with a bored wife, staid husband, dashing young lover and the 'older' woman, done in a light and witty modern manner. It is well played by an excellent quartet, including the American Seberg, fresh from *Breathless*, as an English woman *(sic)* in Paris.

In For Treatment

► **Opname**

Netherlands 1979 92 mins col
Het Werkteater/VARA TV/Fugitive Cinema

d **Erik Van Zuylen, Marja Kok**
sc **Het Werkteater (from a scenario devised by the cast)**
ph **Robby Müller**
    Helmert Woudenberg, Frank Groothof, Hans Man In't Veld, Marja Kok, Daria Mohr, Herman Vinck

De Waal (Woudenberg), a middle-aged market gardener, is taken into hospital for extended exploratory treatment. The doctor tells his wife (Kok) that her husband has terminal cancer, but they conceal the information from him. Through his relationship with the young man (Groothof), himself a terminal patient, with whom he shares a room, De Waal realizes the truth and attempts to come to grips with it. In opening out its work for the screen, Het Werkteater retains the improvisational method of scripting that it uses for the stage, while employing the camera to create a convincing picture of hospital life. Restrained, accurate performances contribute to the veracity of the situation and the behaviour of the characters in a crisis of universal and ongoing interest. But the film loses its way towards the end, unsatisfactorily groping for philosophical expression instead of staying with the factual approach.

L'Ingénue Libertine

► **(US: Minne)**

France 1950 88 mins bw
Codo Cinéma

d **Jacqueline Audry**
sc **Pierre Laroche**
ph **Grignon**
m **Vincent Scotto**
    Danièle Delorme, Frank Villard, Jean Tissier, Claude Nicot

A romantic young woman (Delorme) is unable to make love to her possessive husband (Villard) who treats her like a child, until she gives into the advances of a philanderer (Nicot) and an old roué (Tissier). Following her successful adaptation of *Gigi*, starring Delorme, the year before, Audry tackled another Colette novel with the same sensitivity. Because of its hint of sexual misdemeanour, it was the first production released in Britain to gain the newly instigated 'X' certificate for films deemed suitable for adults only.

The Inheritance

► **L'Eredità Ferramonti**

Italy 1976 103 mins col
Flag Productions

d **Mauro Bolognini**
sc **Ugo Pirro, Sergio Bazzini**
ph **Ennio Guarnieri**
m **Ennio Morricone**
    Anthony Quinn, Fabio Testi, Dominique Sanda, Luigi Proietti, Adriana Asti, Paolo Bonacelli

Gregorio Ferramonti (Quinn) retires, having amassed a great fortune, and informs his family that they will inherit none of it. When his son Pippo (Proietti) marries Irene (Sanda), a local girl who works for him, she devotes herself to changing the *status quo*, eventually becoming Gregorio's mistress and his heir, while the rest of the family goes to pieces. Set in Rome in the 1880s, Bolognini's melodrama bears all the hallmarks of his painterly eye. It is a cornucopia of dazzlingly composed images and sumptuous period design which one should settle back and enjoy while its run-of-the-mill tale of greed, lust and the unworthiness of the rich plods along. The beautiful Sanda doesn't do much to justify her award.

Best Actress (Dominique Sanda) Cannes 1976

Innocence Unprotected

▶ **Nevinost Bez Zastite**

Yugoslavia 1968 78 mins bw/col
Avala

d   **Dušan Makavejev**
sc **Dušan Makavejev**
ph **Brank Perak, Stevan Miskovic**
m   **Vojislav Dostić**
    Dragolub Aleksić, Ana Milosavljević,
    Vera Jovanović, Bratoljub Gligorijević

Dragolub Aleksić, a circus strongman and
the writer-star-director of *Innocence Unprotected*, a Serbian film of 1942, reminisces
about the making of that picture and its
confiscation by the occupying Germans.
Other survivors of the original cast recall their
roles, and much of the film itself is shown, as
well as newreel footage. Although the extracts
from the film under discussion prove it to
have been a pretty awful melodrama, Makavejev is never snide about it. In fact, *his* title
refers not to the orphan heroine rescued by
the hero in the original film, but to the brave
and innocent people who made the film, to
whom he pays amusing and affectionate
homage.

Special Jury Prize Berlin 1968

The Innocent

▶ **aka The Intruder**

▶ **L'Innocente**

Italy 1976 125 mins col
Rizzoli

d   **Luchino Visconti**
sc **Suso Cecchi D'Amico, Luchino Visconti,**
    Enrico Medioli
ph **Pasqualino De Santis**
m   **Chopin, Liszt, Mozart, Gluck**
    Giancarlo Giannini, Laura Antonelli,
    Jennifer O'Neill, Didier Haudepin, Marc
    Porel

A wealthy Sicilian (Giannini) neglects his wife
(Antonelli) for his mistress (O'Neill). When
the wife tries to turn the tables on him by
taking a lover (Porel), events take a tragic
turn with the death of a child. Visconti's last
film, directed when he was very ill, was a
good example of Thomas Mann's expression,
'the voluptuousness of doom'. Adapted from
the book by Gabriele D'Annunzio, the poignant tale of sexual double standards is told
against sumptuous turn-of-the-century settings. Thankfully, there is little of the extravagant campness that mars much of Visconti's
late work. Elegant and restrained, it might
have been even better with a stronger cast.
With *The Leopard*, it is perhaps the best of
the 14 full-length films made by the Duke of
Modrone (Visconti), who died in the year of
its release.

▶ **Innocente, L'** see Innocent, The

Innocent Sorcerers

▶ **Niewinni Czarodzieje**

Poland 1960 91 mins bw
Film Polski

d   **Andrzej Wajda**
sc **Andrzej Wajda, Jerzy Skolimowski**
ph **Krzysztof Winiewicz**
m   **Krzysztof Komeda**
    Tadeusz Lomnicki, Zbigniew Cybulski,
    Roman Polanski, Jerzy Skolimowski,
    Krystyna Stypulkowska

A young bachelor doctor (Lomnicki), who
plays in a jazz band, finds difficulty in committing himself to his mannequin girlfriend (Styp-
ulkowska) and in coping with the problems
of his aimless friends. After his celebrated
war trilogy, Wajda took the West by surprise
with this ironic sex comedy which dealt
uncompromisingly with cynical modern Polish youth. Although it is now as dated as
many British and American films on the problems of young people in the newly-affluent
societies, it still has interest as one of the first
post-war Polish films to deal with contemporary issues, and as an influence on the films
directed a few years later by co-scenarist
Skolimowski and Roman Polanski, both
important members of the cast.

The Inquisitor

▶ **Garde À Vue**

France 1981 88 mins col

Les Films Ariane/T.F.1 Films

d **Claude Miller**
sc **Claude Miller, Jean Herman**
ph **Bruno Nuytten**
m **Georges Delerue**
   **Lino Ventura, Michel Serrault, Guy
   Marchand, Romy Schneider**

A wealthy lawyer becomes the prime suspect in a case of child rape and murder, and is detained for questioning on New Year's Eve. In this taut *policier*, confined almost entirely to the interrogation room, Miller cunningly plays with truth and lies so that the pendulum of guilt and innocence swings back and forth, while the inquisitor (Ventura) and the suspect (Serrault) engage in an extraordinary contest of cat and mouse. The parallel exposure of Serrault's appalling marriage (to Schneider in her last role before she committed suicide) is much less successful, although tantalizing. Ventura and Serrault are so mesmerizingly good that they render the holes in the plot almost invisible.

In Search Of Famine

▶ **Aakaler Sandhane**

India 1981 125 mins col
DK Films Enterprise

d **Mrinal Sen**
sc **Mrinal Sen**
ph **K.K. Mahajan**
m **Salil Chowdhury**
   **Dhritiman Chatterjee, Smita Patil, Sreela
   Majumdar, Gita Sen, Dipankar Dey,
   Rajen Tarafder**

When a film crew from Calcutta arrives in an isolated village to make a film about the disastrous famine of 1943, they encounter unexpected problems from the villagers who, caught in the grip of poverty and ignorance, are suspicious and hostile. Unable to bridge the terrible gap in understanding, the bewildered visitors return to the city without having achieved their object. One of the Indian cinema's most probing recorders of the country's social fabric, Sen has made a lively, truthful film, no less profound for perceiving the comedy in the situation of clashing worlds. An excellent piece, albeit somewhat too long and occasionally lacking clarity.

Special Jury Prize Berlin 1981

The Insect Woman

▶ **Nippon Konchuki**

Japan 1963 123 mins bw
Nikkatsu Corporation

d **Shohei Imamura**
sc **Keije Hasebe, Shohei Imamura**
ph **Masahisa Himeda**
m **Toshiro Mayuzumi**
   **Sachiko Hidari, Yitsuko Yoshimura,
   Hiroyuki Nagato, Seizaburo Kawazu,
   Sumie Sasaki**

An account of 45 years of the hard life of a woman (Hidari) who grafts with the industry of an ant to survive, be it as servant or whore. Her misfortunes begin when her foster father uses her as his mistress until, aged 20, she goes out into the world pregnant. Imamura's canvas is broad, crowded and extremely painful, reflecting the exploitation of women and the cruelty of human nature, as well as the problems brought to Japan by progress. Beautifully photographed, and with a superb performance from Hidari, aging from girlhood to late middle-age, it won 14 awards in its own country.

Best Actress (Sachiko Hidari) Berlin 1964

Insiang

The Philippines 1976 95 mins col
CineManila

d **Lino Brocka**
sc **Mario O'Hara, Lamberto E. Antonio**
ph **Conrado Baltazar**
m **Minda D. Azarcon**
   **Hilda Koronel, Mona Lisa, Ruel Vernel,
   Rez Cortéz**

Insiang (Koronel), an adolescent girl living with her fishmonger mother (Lisa) and other relatives in the notorious Tondo slums of Manila, is raped by her mother's young lover (Vernal) and abandoned by the man (Cortéz) she hoped to marry. She plans a revenge which destroys them all. Shown at Cannes in 1978, this was the first commercially produced Filipino film to appear at a major European Festival for 26 years and established Brocka's international reputation. With an economy of means – the camera quickly establishes character and situations – and sparse dialogue (in a Filipino dialect), Brocka does not rub our noses in the degradation but gives us a good whiff of it nevertheless. Although the rape happens off screen, there are some pretty nasty things that happen on it – understandably, given the sordid settings and the melodramatic plot. The film pivots on the central mother-daughter clash, exceptionally well-played by Koronel who appeared in over ten of Brocka's films, and the seldom-smiling Mona Lisa.

Inspecteur Lavardin

France   1986   103 mins   col
MK2/Antenne2/Suisse Romande TV

d   **Claude Chabrol**
sc **Claude Chabrol, Dominique Roulet**
ph **Jean Rabier**
m   **Matthieu Chabrol**
    Jean Poiret, Jean-Claude Brialy,
    Bernadette Lafont, Jacques Dacqmine,
    Hermine Claire, Jean-Luc Bideau

When a pillar of a French provincial community is found murdered, the renowned Inspecteur Lavardin arrives on the scene, only to find that the victim's widow (Lafont) is an old flame and that nothing in the case is what it appears to be. The redoubtable Lavardin (played with a nice dryness by Poiret) returns for a second neatly-scripted Chabrol detective tale after *Cop Au Vin*. It is full of surprises and an array of kinky characters, including a delightful Brialy (almost 30 years after appearing in Chabrol's first feature) as a gay uncle who paints glass eyes as a hobby. However, some may find the morality of the ending questionable.

▶ **Inspector Maigret** see Maigret Sets A Trap

Intermezzo

Sweden   1937   88 mins   bw
A.B. Svensk

d   **Gustaf Molander**
sc **Gustaf Molander, Gösta Stevens**
ph **Äke Dahlquist**
m   **Heinz Provost**
    Ingrid Bergman, Gösta Ekman, Inge
    Tidblad, Britt Hagman, Hans Ekman

Anna Hoffman (Bergman), a promising young pianist, is hired to give lessons to the little daughter of a famous concert violinist (Ekman). He and Anna fall in love and, forsaking his family, they go on an extended European concert tour with her as his accompanist until he realizes that their idyll is an interlude – an intermezzo – which cannot last. Directed by one of Sweden's most distinguished film-makers and played by the country's veteran leading man teamed with a young girl at the beginning of her career, this three-handkerchief weepie is restrained and irresistible. David O. Selznick saw it, imported Bergman to Hollywood two years later, remade the film in English co-starring her with Leslie Howard and thus launched her international career.

Interrogation

▶ **Przesluchanie**

Poland   1981 (released 1990)   117 mins   col
Zespoly Filmowa Unit X

d   **Ryszard Bugajski**
sc **Ryszard Bugajski with Janusz Dymek**
ph **Jacek Petrycky**
m   **Agnieszka Hundziak (consultant)**
    Krystyna Janda, Adam Ferency, Janusz
    Gajos, Agnieska Holland, Anna
    Romantowska, Bożena Dykiel

Tonia (Janda), a small-time entertainer, has a row with her husband one night, goes out and gets insensibly drunk with two 'admirers' and wakes up on the floor of an overcrowded prison. It transpires that the authorities, fabricating charges against one of her former lovers, wish her to give evidence on their behalf. She refuses, they persist and she is subjected to prolonged incarceration, interrogation and torture. Bugajski's graphically brutal protest against Stalinist repression is set in 1951, was made in 1981 and released in 1990 to some acclaim. It is an admirably uncompromising piece of work and should, perhaps, be compulsory viewing for those who doubt the depths to which the agents of oppressive regimes can sink. Basically, however, the film tells us nothing new and commits such unrelieved assault and battery on our sensibilities that it is difficult to recommend it. For connoisseurs of screen acting, however, Janda's astonishing performance lights up the rat-infested gloom of the enterprise.

Best Actress (Krystyna Janda) Cannes 1990

Interviews On Personal Problems

▶ **aka Several Interviews On Personal Matters**

▶ **Neskolko Intervyu Po Lichnyam Voprosam**

USSR 1979 94 mins col
Gruziafilm

d   **Lana Gogoberidze**
sc **Zaira Arsenishvili, Erlom Akhvlediani, Lana Gogoberidze**
ph **Nugzar Erkomaishvili**
m   **Gia Kancheli**
    Sofiko Chiaureli, Gia Badridze, Ketevan Orakhelashvili, Zhanri Lolashvili, Salome Kancheli

Sofiko (Chiaureli), a crusading journalist in her forties, travels extensively around the country interviewing women and getting involved in their problems. However, her career causes a conflict with her husband (Badridze), who would prefer her to pay more attention to her domestic duties. The theme of the dichotomy between a woman's career and her family obligations is a familiar one to Western audiences, but this first Georgian film to deal with feminist issues from a woman's perspective has an added interest. The interviews with various women – a librarian, a factory worker, a housewife etc – are ironically contrasted with the reality of their lives and that of the interviewee. This technically accomplished, emotionally involving film also touches on the Stalinist terror, during which the director herself lost both her parents.

Intervista

Italy 1987 105 mins col
Aljosha/RAI Uno/Cinecitta

d   **Federico Fellini**
sc **Federico Fellini, Gianfranco Angelucci**
ph **Tonino Delli Colli**

m   **Nino Rota**
    Federico Fellini, Marcello Mastroianni, Anita Ekberg, Sergio Rubini, Tonino Delli Colli, Maurizio Mein, Antonio Cantafora, Lara Vendel

While making his next film at Cinecitta, 'Maestro' Fellini, interviewed by a Japanese TV crew, reminisces about his first visit to the studio as a young reporter and takes the Japanese, and Marcello Mastroianni, on a nostalgic visit to Anita Ekberg's house in the country. Conceived as a tribute to Cinecitta's 50th anniversary, this affectionate divertissement, lightly balancing illusion and reality, is more of a self-homage from a director who has earned such a right. The centrepiece is a moving reunion between Marcello and a now mammothly proportioned Anita, who watch a scene from *La Dolce Vita* together. There is some dead wood and reprises from earlier films, but it's a trip Felliniphiles will enjoy.

In The Name Of The Father

▶ **Nel Nome Del Padre**

Italy 1971 107 mins col
Vides Cinematografica

d   **Marco Bellocchio**
sc **Marco Bellocchio**
ph **Franco Di Giacomo**
m   **Nicola Piovani**
    Yves Beneyton, Renato Scarpa, Lou Castel, Piero Vida, Laura Betti, Aldo Sassi

Angelo (Beneyton), an aloof non-conformist, disrupts a private Jesuit college where his fellow pupils are 'unteachables' from rich families. Angelo links up with a rebellious student (Sassi) to turn the school play into a weapon of subversion and ends up taking control of the college. Bellocchio remembers his own school experience as 'a kind of intellectual degradation in atmosphere', and the film is a vigorous portrayal of a reactionary and moribund institution. Surreal images abound as the empty rituals become increasingly exaggerated and meaningless. Not content, however, merely to depict such a place, Bellocchio attempts to broaden it into an allegory of Italian society, when the 'Fascist' hero takes over. Derivative (Vigo, Buñuel), overheated and somewhat cloudy, it is yet powerful enough to disturb.

In The Realm Of The Senses

▶ **Ai No Corrida**

Japan 1976 105 mins col
Argos/Oshima/Shibata

d **Nagisa Oshima**
sc **Nagisa Oshima**
ph **Hideo Ito**
m **Minoru Miki**
Tatsuya Fuji, Eiko Matsuda, Aoi Nakajima, Meika Seri

A married man (Fuji) and a geisha (Matsuda) retreat from the militarist Japan of 1936 into a world of their own where they obsessively act out their sexual fantasies. Finally, in a quest for the ultimate orgasm, she strangles and then castrates him. Oshima's first big commercial success was, for many, in the realm of pornography. For others, it was a serious treatment of the link between eroticism and death (a theme previously dealt with in *Last Tango In Paris*) and an artistic breakthrough in the representation of explicit sex on screen. No matter how powerful, passionate and stylish it is, the film takes some sitting through, unless watching more than an hour and a half of fornication appeals to you.

In The Town Of S

▶ **V Gorodye S**

USSR 1966 105 mins bw
Lenfilm

d **Josef Heifits**
sc **Josef Heifits**
ph **Ghenrih Marandzhan**
m **Nadejda Simonian**
Anatoly Papanov, Nonna Terentieva, Lidia Stykan, Igor Gorbachov, Andrei Popov, Alexei Batalov

Dr Ionych Startsev (Papanov) arrives to practise in a stiflingly *bourgeois* provincial town, where the only distraction is the cripplingly boring soirées given by the Turkin family with whose daughter (Terentieva) Startsev falls in love. She rejects him and, over the years, he degenerates into a friendless

money-grubber. The director of *The Lady With The Little Dog* (1960) has again turned to Chekhov for his material, using the playwright as a character to introduce the story. It is not as satisfying as the previous film, either in style or content, but the detailed evocation of the mood and period is superb and the few *longueurs* don't prevent enjoyment.

In The White City

▶ **Dans La Ville Blanche**

Portugal/Switzerland 1983 108 mins col
Metro Filme(Lisbon)/ Filmograph(Geneva)

d **Alain Tanner**
sc **Alain Tanner**
ph **Acácio De Almeida**
m **Jean-Luc Barbier**
Bruno Ganz, Teresa Madruga, Julia Vonderlinn, José Carvalho

Paul (Ganz), a ship's engineer, goes ashore at Lisbon and lodges in a little waterfront hotel where he falls in love with the maid (Madruga, excellent). He decides not to return to his ship, and wanders the city with a Super-8 camera, sending his wife the films as well as the news that he now loves two women. A compulsively watchable Bruno Ganz gives a marvellous portrayal of a man in crisis, alienated from his world and pursuing an elusive and ill-formulated freedom. Tanner reflects Paul's disjunction in his contrasting images of place – dazzling, sunbathed Lisbon on the sea, its evening backstreet shadows eerie and threatening; Switzerland where Paul's wife sits in ordered domesticity watching the films that reflect her husband's state of mind. Leisurely, complex, disturbing, the film is accompanied by a haunting saxophone score, while the pace and texture of the white city is tellingly caught by De Almeida's camera.

In The Wild Mountains

▶ **Ye Shan**

China 1986 99 mins col
Xi'an Film Studio

d Yan Xueshu
sc Yan Xueshu, Zhu Zi
ph Mi Jiaqing
m Xu Youfu
   Du Yuan, Yue Hong, Xin Ming, Xu
   Shouli, Tan Xihe

Two brothers and their wives farm in the mountains of Western China. One is lazy with a spirited, hard- working but infertile wife; the other, estranged from his wife and baby, lives with them and, encouraged by his admiring sister-in-law, is determined to make his fortune. Family differences escalate, causing break- up and scandal, until the women at last swap husbands. This is a leisurely, naturalistic and illuminating look at relationships and tradition in a simple Chinese community. Political statement is subtly implicit in gradual changes that we see taking place, but this is a human story, tender and funny, with just a hint of bitterness in its sweet resolution. The photography catches the countryside and the magnificent mountains in seductive, dewy textures and colours, the acting is first-class and the use of natural sound superb.

Intimate Lighting

▶ **Intimní Osvětleni**

   Czechoslovakia 1965 72 mins bw
   Ceskoslovenský Fzilm/Barrandov Studio

d Ivan Passer
sc Ivan Passer, Jaroslav Papoušek, Václav
   Šašek
ph Miroslav Ondříček, Jan Střecha
m Oldřich Korte
   Věra Křesadlová, Zdeněk Bezušek, Jan
   Vostřcil, Karel Blažek, Jaroslava Stědrá,
   Vlastimila Vlková

A professional 'cello player (Bezušek) comes to a provincial town with his fiancée (Křesdalová, Miloš Forman's second wife) to visit old friends. They eat, drink, play music and reminisce. Passer's second and last film in his native country is a tender, well-observed comedy about the everyday pleasures of life, the gentle humour concealing regret. The director had previously co-scripted Miloš Forman's first films, and left with him in 1969 for the USA.

▶ **Intimní   Osvětleni** see Intimate
Lighting

▶ **Intruder, The** see Innocent, The

Investigation Of A Citizen Above Suspicion

▶ **Indagine Su Un Cittadino Al Di Sopra Di Ogni Sospetto**

   Italy 1970 115 mins col
   Vera

d Elio Petri
sc Elio Petri, Ugo Pirro
ph Luigi Kuveiller
m Ennio Morricone
   Gian Maria Volonté, Florinda Bolkan,
   Salvo Randone, Gianni Santuccio

A top Rome police inspector (Volonté) slashes his girlfriend's throat and deliberately plants clues to see whether his own agents will be able to track him down. But he considers himself above suspicion. Flashy, rhetorical and emphatic when it needed more sobriety, subtlety and distance to score its political points, the film, nevertheless, created a furore in Italy on the Right (Petri is a Communist), and gained big box-office returns everywhere. Volonté is effective as the Fascist cop and the plot is gripping enough to overcome the stylistic weaknesses.

   Best Foreign Film Oscar 1970
   Special Jury Prize Cannes 1970

Invisible Adversaries

▶ **Unsichtbare Gegner**

   Austria 1978 109 mins col
   Valie Export

d Valie Export
sc Peter Weibel
ph Wolfgang Simon
   Susanne Widl, Peter Weibel, Dr Josef
   Plavee, Monika Helfer-Friedrich

Anna (Widl), a photographer and video artist, hears an announcement on the radio that invisible forces known as Hyksos are taking over the earth in the guise of human beings. During the day she makes love to her boyfriend (Weibel), develops erotic photographs, explores the streets of Vienna, interviews women on the topic of 'when is a human being a woman?' and visits her psychoanalyst.

A film as curious as the name of its debutante director, it caused controversy wherever it was shown and became a cult in Vienna. Frank in its sexuality, mixing dream and reality, it's a kind of feminist *Invasion Of The Body Snatchers*. Much of it is original, amusing (most of it intentionally) and complex. A film not only from the city of Freud, but from his mind.

The Invitation

▶ **L'Invitation**

> Switzerland 1973 100 mins col
> Citel Films/Group 5/Swiss TV(Geneva)/
> Planfilm(Paris)

d **Claude Goretta**
sc **Claude Goretta, Michel Viala**
ph **Jean Zeller**
m **Patrick Moraz**
> **Michel Robin, Jean-Luc Bideau, Jean Champion, Pierre Collet, Corinne Coderey, François Simon, Rosine Rochette**

When his mother dies Rémy (Robin), a mild-mannered, middle-aged bachelor, is given compassionate leave from his job. He buys a country house and gives his office colleagues a garden party where, as the afternoon wears on, social decorum wears off. This is a gentle session of eavesdropping on a group of recognizable types – loudmouthed joker, avuncular boss, giggly nymphet – who know each other well in one context, brought unfamiliarly together in another. Although Goretta has nothing new to say, the film is fluent and diverting and he and his excellent cast (notably Simon as the knowing and detached butler) offer some wry observations in attractive, well-photographed surroundings.

▶ **Invitation, L'** see Invitation, The

I Only Want You To Love Me

▶ **Ich Will Doch Nur, Dass Ihr Mich Liebt**

> W. Germany 1976 112 mins col
> Bavaria Atelier/Westdeutcher Rundfunk

d **Rainer Werner Fassbinder**
sc **Rainer Werner Fassbinder**

ph **Michael Ballhaus**
m **Peer Raben**
> **Vitus Zeplichal, Elke Aberle, Alexander Allerson, Ernie Mangold, Johanna Hofer**

Peter (Zeplichal), the only child of Bavarian innkeepers (Allerson and Mangold), tries in vain to please his parents. When he marries Erika (Aberle), he showers his wife with gifts he can ill afford. Rejection and hardship lead him to violence. Lack of parental love, a subject close to Fassbinder's own experience, is the theme of one of his most poignant and realist works, based on a true account from a book of interviews and originally made for television. The framing device of an interview (by real-life sociologist Erika Runge), with a number of flashbacks, gives us a deeper understanding of the protagonist than a straight narrative would have done.

Iphigenia

> Greece 1976 129 mins col
> Greek Film Centre

d **Michael Cacoyannis**
sc **Michael Cacoyannis**
ph **Ghiorgos Arvanitis**
m **Mikis Theodorakis**
> **Irene Papas (Clytemnestra), Costa Kazakos (Agamemnon), Costa Carras (Menelaus), Tatiana Papamosou (Iphigenia), Christos Tsangas (Odysseus), Dimitris Aronis (Calchas), Panos Michaopoulos (Achilles)**

After the abduction of Helen of Troy, her husband Menelaus, his brother King Agamemnon and the Greek fleet and armies are camped at Aulis. The high priest Calchas, conspiring with Odysseus King of Ithaca, persuades Agamemnon that the Greeks will only sail to victory if he makes a human sacrifice of his daughter, Iphigenia... Basing his screenplay on *Iphigenia In Aulis*, Cacoyannis completed his trilogy of Euripidean drama after *Electra* and *The Trojan Women* with what is undoubtedly the weakest of the three. The play itself has only survived in a chopped about form, but the director has compounded the difficulties by going all out for cinematic effects that are excessive and often superfluous and that weaken the heart of the drama by diffusing it. There *are* some striking images, such as the approach of Clytemnestra's retinue bringing Iphigenia to the island, and the performances are of a high order, but it is a muddle.

▶ **Iskindirya – Leh?** see Alexandria – Why?

The Island

▶ **Hadaka No Shima**

> Japan 1961 92 mins bw
> Kindai Eiga Kyokai

d **Kaneto Shindo**
sc **Kaneto Shindo**
ph **Kiyoshi Kuroda**
m **Hikaru Hayashi**
   Nobuko Otowa, Taiji Tonoyama, Shinji Tanaka, Masanori Horimoto

A man (Tonoyama) his wife (Otowa) and their two small sons are the only family on an island. Every day, year in and year out, the parents go to the mainland to fetch their only supply of water, and climb the hill to their home with the buckets on their backs. This human, moving, true and effective allegory unrolls beautifully on the wide screen, using no dialogue whatsoever. When the camera soars above the island in the end, we see it as the Earth on which humankind lives, works and dies. The performances, especially by Otowa, are stunning.

Isle Of Sinners

▶ **(US: God Needs Men)**
▶ **Dieu A Besoin Des Hommes**

> France 1950 100 mins bw
> Transcontinental

d **Jean Delannoy**
sc **Jean Aurenche, Pierre Bost**
ph **Robert Lefèbvre**
m **René Cloërec**
   Pierre Fresnay, Madeleine Robinson, Daniel Gélin, Andrée Clément, Jean Brochard, Sylvie

The island of Sein is a rugged and barren tract off the Britanny coast. Its inhabitants rely on pickings from shipwrecks to augment their meagre subsistence. When the priest decides that his flock is beyond redemption and leaves, the islanders persuade the simple verger (Fresnay) to execute some of the church rituals. Initially reluctant and confused, he comes to assume the full role of priesthood, even eschewing his fiancée in pursuit of his 'calling'. Adapted from a novel, based in turn on an obscure fragment of French history, this film attempts to explore definitions of sacrilege and divinity while, at the same time, portraying the Sein community as a primitive and feckless lot. The result is thematically confusing although the plot, played against a realistically stark and dramatic background, does capture the attention. Fresnay, an old hand at religious roles, is splendid and helps lend the piece some conviction.

▶ **Isola Di Arturo, L'** see Arturo's Island

Israel Why?

▶ **Pourquoi Israel?**

> France 1973 185 mins col
> Stephan Films/Parafrance/Compagnie D'Enterprise Et de Gestion

d **Claude Lanzmann**
sc **Claude Lanzmann**
ph **William Lubtchansky, Colin Mounier**

Three hours of travelogue and interviews with the citizens of Israel. They range from academics to lowly artisans, from the young to the old, and encompass native-born *sabras*, as well as long-time settled immigrants and tentative new arrivals of all nationalities. With the probing, incisive neutrality that would later inform his epic *Shoah*, Claude Lanzmann encourages his interviewees to reveal their hopes, fears, beliefs and, most tellingly, their differing viewpoints on vital and controversial issues. The film also reveals the challenge and beauty of the landscape and vividly captures incidents of daily life. With Israel becoming increasingly trapped in its political difficulties, this first-class piece of documentary film-making is of renewed interest.

▶ **Is-Slottet** see Ice Palace, The

▶ **Istoriya Asi Klyachinoi, Kòtoraya Lyubila, Da Nie Vshla Zamuzh** see Asya's Happiness

The Italian Straw Hat

▶ **Un Chapeau De Paille D'Italie**

France 1927 74 mins bw
Albatros

d **René Clair**
sc **René Clair**
ph **Maurice Desfassiaux, Nicolas Roudakoff**
m **Silent**
   Albert Préjean, Olga Tschechowa, Marise Maia, Alice Tissot, Yvonneck

Fadinard (Préjean), on the way to his wedding, finds his horse eating the straw hat of an errant wife who happens to be in a mildly compromising situation with a cavalry officer. He cannot get to the wedding until he has found an identical replacement for the *chapeau*. Clair made this version of the Labiche-Michel 19th-century farce into a classic silent film comedy, substituting many of the play's verbal jokes with visual ones, such as using an object to introduce each character in the chain of events. Made with clockwork precision, it ticks along at a fine pace, culminating in the hilarious wedding scene.

▶ **It Happened At The Inn** see Goupi-Mains-Rouges

▶ **It Happened In Broad Daylight** see Assault In Broad Daylight

▶ **It Happened In Europe** see Somewhere In Europe

It's Happening Tomorrow

▶ **Domani Accadra**

Italy 1988 90 mins col
Sacher Film/RAI

d **Daniele Luchetti**
sc **Daniele Luchetti, Franco Bernini, Angelo Pasquini**
ph **Franco Di Giacomo**
m **Nicola Piovani**
   Paolo Hendel, Giovanni Guidelli, Ciccio

Ingrassia, Angela Finocchiaro, Giacomo Piperno, Claudio Bigagli, Antonio Petrocelli

In 1848, in the disease-stricken swamplands of the Maremma area of Tuscany, a pair of *butteri* or cowboys (Hendel, Guidelli) must buy some medicine for a dying friend. Since they have no money, they turn to robbery, but their plan goes awry and they are hunted down by a trio of Austrian mercenaries and the robbery victim's son. For his first feature the 28-year-old director wanted to find an 'as yet unseen setting for an Italian film'. Certainly, there was no danger of familiarity breeding contempt for the well-photographed Tuscan location. The story itself is much more familiar, shifting equally between the dynamic and the leisurely. But the excellent, then unknown, leads bring an offbeat humour to this Italian, as distinct from 'spaghetti', Western, the style being more reminiscent of the Taviani brothers' social epics.

▶ **It's In The Bag** see Affaire Est Dans Le Sac, L'

It's My Life

▶ **(US: My Life To Live)**

▶ **Vivre Sa Vie**

France 1962 85 mins bw
Films De La Pléiade

d **Jean-Luc Godard**
sc **Jean-Luc Godard**
ph **Raoul Coutard**
m **Michel Legrand**
   Anna Karina, Sady Rebbot, André Labarthe, Brice Parain

When she can't pay her rent, Nana S. (Karina), a girl from the provinces, is gradually initiated into prostitution in Paris, finally becoming experienced. Using interview techniques, direct sound, long takes, texts, quotations and statistics, Godard gives this probing and dazzling examination of prostitution (in 12 chapters) a documentary tone. But, above all, it is a passionate celluloid love letter to Karina, the director's then wife. Close-ups of her are reminiscent of Louise Brooks, Lillian Gish and Falconetti, the latter tearfully watched by Karina in Dreyer's *The Passion Of Joan Of Arc*.

Special Jury Prize Venice 1962

Ivan

USSR   1932   85 mins   bw
Kiev Film Studio

d   **Alexander Dovzhenko**
sc **Alexander Dovzhenko**
ph **Danylo Demutsky, Yuri Yekelchik, Mikhail Glider**
m   **Igor Belza, Yuli Meitus, Boris Lyatoshinsky**
Pytor Masokha, Semyon Shagaida, D. Golubinsky, Stepan Shkurat

Three Ivans (a common Russian name) work on the construction of a hydro-electric dam on the Dnieper river in the Ukraine. Apart from the young peasant (Masokha) who is shaped into an ideal Soviet worker, the others are a worker killed in an accident and a youth who represents the future. Dovzhenko's first sound film opens with an explosion and continues with an array of aural experiments from the music to commentary via a loudspeaker. He brings the same lyricism to this industrial subject as he brought to the rural paradise of *Earth* two years previously. There are heroes and villains, slogans and speeches but, above all, there are powerful and poetic images that linger long after the noise has died away.

▶ **Ivan Groznyi** see Ivan The Terrible

▶ **Ivanovo Detstvo** see Ivan's Childhood

Ivan's Childhood

▶ **Ivanovo Detstvo**

USSR   1962   97 mins   bw
Mosfilm

d   **Andrei Tarkovsky**
sc **Vladimir Bogomolov, Mikhail Papava**
ph **Vadim Yusov**
m   **Vyacheslav Ovchinnikov**
Kolya Burlyaev, I. Tarkovskaya, Valentin Zubkov, E. Zharikov, Nikolai Grinko, V. Malyavina

When 12-year-old Ivan's family is wiped out by the Nazis, he is hell-bent on revenge and joins a detachment of Partisans who are able to use his size and agility for intelligence purposes. His superiors grow worried about him and send him to a safer area, but he rebels and is once again allowed dangerous assignments, with tragic results. Tarkovsky's film inevitably brings to mind Klimov's *Come And See* over two decades later but, where that film is determinedly grim and harrowing, its dazed protagonist wandering into the fight, this has a boy fully intent on his actions. Apart from a stark opening sequence where Ivan (Burlyaev) moves through swamp and forest near enemy lines, the director has opted for a plethora of cinematic effects, lyrically beautiful landscapes, and a treacly romantic sub-plot. This uncharacteristic softness from Tarkovsky is doubtless explained by the fact that this was his debut feature, and the first of several award-winning works.

Best Film Venice 1962

Ivan The Terrible

▶ **Ivan Groznyi**

USSR   1944 (Part I), 1946 (Part II)   99 mins (Part I) 88 mins (Part II)   bw (Part I), bw/col (Part II)
Mosfilm

d   **Sergei Eisenstein**
sc **Sergei Eisenstein**
ph **Edouard Tissé**
m   **Sergei Prokoviev**
Nikolai Cherkassov, Ludmila Tselikovskaya, Serafima Birman, Pavel Kadochnikov, Mikhail Nazvanov, Andrei Abrikosov, Vsevolod Pudovkin

The struggles of the 16th-century Tsar Ivan IV (Cherkassov) to establish himself, his love for the Tsarina Anastasia (Tselikovskaya), his political aims, and his conflict with the Boyars and the Church. Eisenstein began shooting his three-part epic (only two were completed) after more than two years of research, making sketches of every scene of the film. Stalin approved Part I, but as Ivan's character (in Cherkassov's powerful brooding central performance) became more complex he turned against it, and Part II (subtitled *The Boyars' Plot*) was not released until 1958. Taking its imagery from Grand Opera, the Japanese Kabuki Theatre and Russian icons, it is a slow-paced (the rapid montage of Eisenstein's early films has disappeared), opulent and absorbing work. It was the great director's final film. He died of a heart attack in 1948 aged 50.

I Was Born, But...

▶ **Umarete Wa Mita Keredo**

Japan 1932 100 mins bw
Shochiku/Kamata

d **Yasujiro Ozu**
sc **Akira Fushimi, Geibei Ibushiya**
ph **Hideo Shigehara**
m **Silent**
Tatsuo Saito, Hideo Sugahara, Tokkankozo, Mitsuko Yoshikawa, Takeshi Sakamoto

Two boys (Sugahara and Tokkankozo), aged 10 and eight, see their father (Saito), whom they love, kowtowing to his boss and playing the fool in order to ingratiate himself. Disgusted, they go on hunger strike until things become clearer to them. The first of Ozu's great films and a fine example of *shomin-geki*, or lower-middle-class domestic drama, of which he was to become a master. Although it reflects the melancholy theme of tainted innocence, the film is also wonderfully humorous, and the children a delight. Ozu was to use a similar plot in *Good Morning* in 1959.

I Was 19

▶ **Ich War 19**

E. Germany 1968 121 mins bw
Deutsche Film Artien Gesellschaft

d **Konrad Wolf**
sc **Konrad Wolf, Wolfgang Kohlhaase**
ph **Werner Bergmann**
m **Songs: Am Ro Jarama**
Jaecki Schwarz, Wassili Liwanow, Alexei Ejboshenko, Galina Polskich, Jenny Gröllmann

In the last days of World War II, Gregor Hecker (Schwarz), a young bilingual German, works as an officer with the Red Army's propaganda team in the suburbs of Berlin, attempting to get German soldiers to surrender and to win over the population. There are still pockets of resistance, like the fortress of Spandau held by SS men, but these are overcome. 'I am German; I was nineteen,' says Hecker's offscreen voice at the end of the film, which is really Konrad Wolf's story. Yet, though autobiographical, the film is not very personal. With the aid of newsreels, including some featuring the concentration camps, and dialogues with a vast range of Germans, Wolf meticulously and a bit drily reconstructs the epoch that saw the beginning of the German Democratic Republic.

▶ **Iz Zhizni Otdikhayushchikh** see
Away From It All

j

▶ **Jaahyvaiset** see Farewell, The

▶ **J'Accuse** see I Accuse

The Jackal Of Nahueltoro

▶ **El Chacal De Nahueltoro**

Chile 1969 95 mins bw
Cine Experimental De La Universidad
De Chile/Cinematográfica Tercer
Mundo

d **Miguel Littín**
sc **Miguel Littín**
ph **Héctor Ríos**
m **Sergio Ortega**
   Nelson Villagra, Shenda Román,
   Marcelo Romo, Héctor Noguera, Luis
   Alarcón

An illiterate peasant (Villagra), who killed a
widow and her five children, is hunted down
and captured. In prison, he is taught to read
and to understand social values. After being
rehabilitated, he is executed by a firing squad.
One of the best films to emerge from Chile
in the creative period just before and during
the presidency of Salvador Allende, it utilizes
a real case to denounce injustices in the
system. To create a raw and powerful authenticity, Littín shot in Nahueltoro and the prison where 'the jackal' was held and used
dialogue taken directly from interviews with
the prisoner himself. Most effective is the
bitter irony that pervades the narrative, in
which a man is taught to be literate in order
to read and sign his death warrant, and to
become a good Catholic in time to die within
the faith. The film became a centre of discussion all over the country and was shown
in prisons.

Jackboot Mutiny

▶ **Es Geschah Am 20 Juli**

W. Germany 1955 77 mins bw
Arca/Ariston

d **G.W. Pabst**
sc **W.P. Zibaso, Gustav Machaty**
ph **Kurt Hasse**
m **Johannes Weissenbach**
   Bernhard Wicki, Carl Ludwig Diehl, Carl
   Wery, Kurt Meisel, Erik Frey, Albert
   Hehn

A dramatic reconstruction of the 1944
attempt on Hitler's life by a group of army
officers. One of Pabst's last films, it was
neither more nor less distinguished than several other expiatory German films at the time.
Hitler is seen as an evil monster, surrounded
by weak and stupid sycophants, against whom
opposition might have been possible with a
few more Germans of the heroic character of
the army conspirators. Simple, preachy and
a little dull, it had much significance for
German audiences.

Jacob The Liar

▶ **Jakob Der Lügner**

E. Germany 1974 95 mins col
DEFA/East German TV

d **Frank Beyer**
sc **Gerd Gericke**
ph **Günther Marczinkowski**
m **Joachim Wetzlau**
   Vlastimil Brodsky, Erwin Geschonneck,
   Manuela Simon, Henry Hübchen, Blanche
   Kommerell, Armin Müller-Stahl

A Jewish ghetto in Poland in 1943. Jacob

Heym (Brodsky) is summoned to the Nazi guardhouse from which no one has ever been know to emerge, but he does, having overheard on the Gestapo radio that the Russians are advancing. He spreads the news but, frightened to say where he heard it, pretends that he has an illegal radio. He becomes a hero, pestered daily for news, and finds himself trapped in a cumulative series of lies which keep the hopes of his comrades alive. This is the nub of an extraordinary film which questions the value of truth in hopeless situations. Adapted from a novel by Jurek Becker, whose childhood was spent in a ghetto and a concentration camp, it's remarkable in wringing much full-blooded, absurdly funny comedy from a situation in which every resonance appals, and doing so without giving offence. There is poignancy, too (Jacob's relationship with a small girl, wonderfully played by Manuela Simon), and horror (the cold-blooded shooting of a ghetto resident), and the film's successful amalgam of ingredients rests in the truthful writing, brought to life by a superb cast in which Czech star Brodsky shines.

Best Actor (Vlastimil Brodsky) Berlin 1975

▶ **Jag Ar Nyfiken Gul** see I Am Curious - Yellow

▶ **Jakob Der Lügner** see Jacob The Liar

▶ **Jalsaghar** see Music Room, The

J.A. Martin Photographe

Canada   1976   101 mins   col
National Film Board of Canada

d   **Jean Baudin**
sc   **Jean Baudin, Marcel Sabourin**
ph   **Pierre Mignot**
m   **Maurice Blackburn**
Marcel Sabourin, Monique Mercure, Marthe Nadeau, Marthe Thierry, Jean Lapointe, Germaine Lemyre

At the turn of the century, in the backwoods of French Canada, photographer Joseph-Albert (Sabourin) lives with his wife Rose-Aimée (Mercure), his mother, and his five

children. Fifteen years of domestic drudgery for Rose-Aimée, and his having to grind out a living, has brought their marriage to an impasse of indifference which Rose-Aimée decides to cure by accompanying her husband on his annual cross-country business trip – a journey which proves to be packed with incident, both happy and sad. Baudin paints a portrait of a vanished era, nostalgic and affectionate, yet sympathetic to the difficulties of women. A little sentimental for some tastes, perhaps, but it's also a charming and sensitive love story, ravishing to look at, and making superb use of the period photographs 'taken' by its hero.

Best   Actress   (Monique   Mercure) Cannes 1977

▶ **Jana-Aranya** see Middle Man, The

▶ **Jänken** see Yankee, The

A Japanese Tragedy

▶ **Nihon No Higeki**

Japan   1953   116 mins   bw
Shochiku

d   **Keisuke Kinoshita**
sc   **Keisuke Kinoshita**
ph   **Hiroshi Kusuda**
m   **Chuji Kinoshita**
Yuko Mochizuki, Yoko Katsuragi, Masami Taura, Keiji Sata, Ken Uehara

A war widow (Mochizuki) makes every sacrifice to bring up her son (Taura) and daughter (Katsuragi), but they reject her when they grow up. The daughter has an affair with her married English teacher (Uehara) and the son is adopted by a wealthy man whose own child has died. This moving personal story, is a *haha-mono*, or 'mother picture', a popular genre in Japan. It is placed in its historical context by Kinoshita's use of newsreel footage. Use is also made of rapid cutting to the past in order to give the present more resonance. The tragic performance of Mochizuki adds more handkerchiefs to the audience's laundry bills.

Jazz Comedy

▶ **Vesyolye Rebyata**

USSR 1934 93 mins bw
Mosfilm

d **Grigori Alexandrov**
sc **Grigori Alexandrov, Nikolai Erdman, V. Mass**
ph **Vladimir Nilsen**
m **Isaac Dunayevsky**
   Lyubov Orlova, Leonid Utyosov, Maria Strelkova

A shepherd boy comes to the city and becomes a jazz band leader. After having been Eisenstein's assistant for almost eight years, Alexandrov began his career as director by introducing the Hollywood-style musical to the USSR. He made four pleasantly anarchic musicals, using a pre-recorded music track, of which this is the best known. So popular was it at the time, that there were 5,000 copies of the film in circulation. Orlova, the pretty blonde female lead and later the director's wife, became the first popular star of the Soviet cinema.

Jealousy, Italian Style

▶ **(US: Drama Of Jealousy**

▶ **aka The Pizza Triangle)**

▶ **Dramma Della Gelosia – Tutti I Particolare In Cronaca**

Italy 1970 106 mins col
Dean Film/Jupiter Generale
Cinematografica(Rome)/ Midega
Film(Madrid)

d **Ettore Scola**
sc **Age, Furio Scarpelli, Ettore Scola**
ph **Carlo Di Palma**
m **Armando Trovaioli**
   Marcello Mastroianni, Monica Vitti, Giancarlo Giannini, Manolo Zarzo, Marisa Merlini

Oreste (Mastroianni), a young Communist bricklayer, leaves his wife for gorgeous Adelaide (Vitti). All is bliss until she falls for his waiter friend Nello (Giannini). Plot complications increase, as does Adelaide's inability to choose. Finally she decides to marry Nello and disaster strikes. This contribution to that Italian genre which used dark, melodramatic plots to manufacture comedy, is moderately entertaining, with Scola managing – amid a characteristically Latin overdose of screaming and shouting – to achieve some delightful moments of political and social satire and a touch of pleasing parody (Fellini is one of his targets). The solid gold casting pays off.

Best Actor (Marcello Mastroianni) Cannes 1970

Jean De Florette

France 1986 122 mins col
Renn Productions/Films A2/RAI2/DD
Productions

d **Claude Berri**
sc **Claude Berri, Gerard Brach**
ph **Bruno Nuytten**
m **Jean-Claude Petit**
   Yves Montand, Gérard Depardieu, Daniel Auteuil, Elisabeth Depardieu, Ernestine Mazurowna, Marcel Champel

Jean (Depardieu), a hunchbacked tax collector from the city, with his wife (Elisabeth, Depardieu's real-life wife), and young daughter, Manon (Mazurowna), comes to farm some fertile land he has inherited. His neighbours, Ugolin (Auteuil) and his uncle César (Montand), covet the land so they plug up a half-buried spring with concrete to deprive Jean of water. The result is tragedy. In 1963, Marcel Pagnol turned the screenplay of his penultimate film, *Manon Des Sources* (1952) into a novel, adding a 'prequel' called *Jean De Florette*, which Berri turned into two highly successful separate movies. The director has been faithful to Pagnol's vision in the gorgeous sunbleached Provençal settings, the narrative thrust and towering performances of the three male leads – Auteil, comic, simple and touching; Montand earthy, charming and cunning; and Depardieu indomitable, loving and tragic in the title role. There were few people who did not want to see how the story developed in *Manon Des Sources* of the same year.

Jeanne Dielman

23, Quai Du Commerce 1080 Bruxelles

Belgium 1975 225 mins col

Paradise Films(Brussels)/Unité
Trois(Paris)

d **Chantal Akerman**
sc **Chantal Akerman**
ph **Babette Mangolte**
m **Beethoven (Bagatelle for Piano No 27)**
   Delphine Seyrig, Jan Decorte, Henri
   Storck, Jacques Doniol-Valcroze, Yves
   Bical

Forty-eight hours, from Tuesday to Thursday, in the life of discreet prostitute Jeanne Dielman, begin with her receiving a caller – daily occurrence, different callers – in between shopping, chores, neighbourly acts and caring for Sylvain (Decorte), her teenage son. After servicing Thursday's caller, Jeanne stabs him to death with a pair of scissors. The individual sequences selected by Akerman for her sober, minimalist work are filmed in real time, which both accounts for its immense length and draws the viewer into directly experiencing the preparation of a dish or the making of a bed. Opening with its title printed in the form of an address, the contents do resemble the small events which might make up a letter. The focus of the feminist argument is clouded by Akerman's failure to reveal the root cause of Jeanne's final action, but this still, bleak film remains original and intriguing for those with the patience to engage with it – and, of course, there is Delphine Seyrig shining at its centre.

Jeanne's House

▶ **La Maison De Jeanne**

France   1988   87 mins   col
MDG Productions/FR3

d **Magali Clément**
sc **Magali Clément**
ph **Pierre Novion**
m **Raymond Allessandrini**
   Christine Boisson, Benoît Régent, Marie
   Trintignant, Pascale Audret, Jean-Pierre
   Bisson, Michelle Goddet

Jeanne (Boisson) runs La Maison de Jeanne, a small hotel and restaurant in a country town, where she is surrounded by her sisters, their husbands and children. The place is full of laughter, music and love, with Jeanne taken completely for granted at its centre. However, the arrival of a pre-season hotel guest (Régent) begins slowly to change things and the family suddenly finds itself confronting the possibility of life without Jeanne. In her debut feature former actress Clément wished to 'fashion a sublime reality from everyday matters, since that is all there is' and almost wholly succeeds. An intelligent and deceptively simple film, it is perceptive about the interaction among members of a family, particularly the women. Its principal failing, however, is in being too cosily confident that audiences will find the characters as interesting and likeable as the screenplay seems to demand.

▶ **Jeder Für Sich Und Gott Gegen Alle** see Enigma Of Kaspar Hauser, The

Jenny

France   1936   105 mins   bw
Réalisations Artistiques
Cinématographique

d **Marcel Carné**
sc **Jacques Prévert, Jacques Constant**
ph **Roger Hubert**
m **Joseph Kosma, Lionel Cazeaux**
   Françoise Rosay, Albert Préjean, Charles
   Vanel, Jean-Louis Barrault, Roland
   Toutain, Lisette Lanvin

Jenny (Rosay), the manager of a nightclub of dubious reputation, gets involved with Lucien (Préjean), a member of a gang of criminals. Benoît (Vanel), the crooked owner of the club, employs his hunchback accomplice (Barrault) to help put an end to their affair. Meanwhile, Jenny's daughter (Lanvin) falls in love with Lucien and becomes her mother's rival. Carné, who had been assistant to Jacques Feyder on four films, was given a rather conventional melodramatic plot, concocted for Feyder's wife, Françoise Rosay, for his first directorial effort. Thanks to the superior dialogue co-written by the poet Prévert, with whom Carné was to make six further pictures, the excellent use of locations, an innate narrative sense and a terrific cast (including the composer Kosma), it gave a taste of the Carné-Prévert masterpieces to come.

▶ **Jenny Lamour** see Quai Des Orfèvres

A Jester's Tale

▶ **Bláznova Kronika**

Czechoslovakia 1964 80 mins bw
Gottwaldov

d   **Karel Zeman**
sc **Karel Zeman, Pavel Juráček**
ph **Václav Hunka**
m   **Jan Novák**
    **Petr Kostka, Miroslav Holub, Emilie
    Vašáryová, Valentina Thielová**

A young peasant (Kostka), forcibly con-
scripted during the Thirty Years War, is mistaken for a duke and accompanies a girl
(Holub) who is disguised as a jester on a
search for a country without war. As in his
Baron Munchhausen, Zeman wittily combines
romantic fantasy, pacifist allegory and historical reconstruction by mixing live action, animation, stylized sets and real locations. The
film won the Best Director's prize at the San
Francisco Festival.

▶ **Jésus De Montréal** see Jesus Of
Montreal

Jesus Of Montreal

▶ **Jésus De Montréal**

Canada 1989 119 mins col
Max Films (Montreal)/Gérard Mital
Productions (Paris)

d   **Denys Arcand**
sc **Denys Arcand**
ph **Guy Dufaux**
m   **Yves Laferrière, François Dompierre,
    Jean-Marie Benoît
    Lothaire Bluteau, Catherine Wilkening,
    Johanne-Marie Tremblay, Rémy Girard,
    Robert Lepage, Gilles Pelletier**

A small theatre group takes on the task of
mounting a Passion Play in Montreal. Daniel
Colombe (Bluteau), their lead actor-director,
with a cast that includes Constance (Trem-
blay), who works in a soup kitchen, Mireille
(Wilkening), a model, and Martin (Girard),
who does voice-overs, transforms the stuffy
original into a modern telling of the Passion.
A hit with critics and the public, it fails to
amuse the Church. Taken to hospital with

concussion during a struggle with police sent
in to close the show, Daniel believes himself
to be Jesus. After the relatively wide showing
of *The Decline Of The American Empire*
(1986), the 48-year-old French-Canadian
Arcand (who plays the Judge) drew his largest
audience ever with this acerbic allegory which
covers, among other things, according to the
publicity, 'the Brothers Karamazov, the dubbing of pornographic movies, the Big Bang,
the formula for Coca-Cola Classic, Hamlet's
soliloquy...organ transplants and Paul Newman's salad dressing'. It is both the film's
weakness and its charm that it attempts to
cram in too many targets and ideas, sometimes blurring the strong central theme of the
thin line that exists between fiction and reality.
It also leads to an unintentionally risible
climax. It is at its best when observing the
contrasting lives of the actors, and in the
performances, particularly from the remarkable Lothaire Bluteau.

Je T'Aime, Je T'Aime

France 1968 94 mins col
Parc/Les Productions Fox Europa

d   **Alain Resnais**
sc **Jacques Sternberg**
ph **Jean Boffety**
m   **Krzysztof Penderecki
    Claude Rich, Olga Georges-Picot, Anouk
    Ferjac, Van Doude, Annie Fargue,
    Georges Jamin**

A young man (Rich), saved from suicide, is
invited by scientists to participate in an experiment that sends him back in time for short
periods. Things go wrong and incidents from
his past occur in disordered fragments. The
main theme in Resnais' films is best expressed
by the opening lines of T.S. Eliot's *Burnt
Norton*: 'Time present and time past are both
perhaps present in time future, and time
future contained in time past'. This was brilliantly articulated in the director's first three
features, in which correlatives of time were
integral to the characters and structures of
the films. Here, by using a time-exploring
machine, it is rather like revealing the bare
mechanics behind a magician's act. But there
is not much in the hat. The man's past that
we see in non-chronological segments, often
dazzlingly conjured up, is not interesting

enough to encourage us to make the effort to piece it together, and the leads lack presence.

▶ **Jeu De Massacre** see Comic Strip Hero

▶ **Jeunes Loups, Les** see Young Wolves, The

▶ **Jeux De L'Amour, Les** see Playing At Love

▶ **Jeux Interdits** see Forbidden Games

Les Jeux Sont Faits

▶ **(US: The Chips Are Down)**

France   1947   91 mins   bw
Les Films Gibe

d   **Jean Delannoy**
sc **Jean-Paul Sartre**
ph **Christian Matras**
m   **Georges Auric**
    **Micheline Presle, Michel Pagliero,
    Fernand Fabre, Colette Ripert**

A Communist (Pagliero) who was killed in an uprising, and a woman (Presle) poisoned by her Fascist official husband meet in the afterlife and fall in love. They are sent back to earth with permission to remain there, provided they consummate their affair within 24 hours. They don't because they get caught up in political discussion and quarrels. The first of Sartre's attempts at an original screenplay is both an intellectually intriguing exercise, and a grim and depressing fable.

Je Vous Aime

France   1981   105 mins   col
Renn Productions

d   **Claude Berri**
sc **Claude Berri, Michel Grisolia**
ph **Etienne Becker**
m   **Serge Gainsbourg**
    **Catherine Deneuve, Jean-Louis
    Trintignant, Serge Gainsbourg, Gérard
    Depardieu, Alain Souchon**

Alice (Deneuve), mother of two children, each by a different father, neither of whom she

married, is living with Julien (Trintignant). It is Christmas and she has invited her former lovers Simon (Gainsbourg) and Patric (Depardieu), the father of her small daughter, to spend Christmas at her beautiful country house. During the festivities, she tells Julien that she has fallen in love with someone else and their four years together are over. He leaves and her liaison with Claude (Souchon), newly widowed and the father of a small son, flourishes – for a time... Claude Berri's account of a woman who, by her own admission, does not believe in the possibility of lasting relationships and who can materially afford the luxury of remaining single, is potentially interesting and he has constructed it as an exercise in time, utilizing a series of seamless flashbacks triggered off by Alice's memories. However, the film fails to fulfil its promise. Alice's character is underdeveloped and somewhat alienating, and there are some strange holes and confusions in the plotting – the son's father, for example, appears once for a few seconds, giving the lie to the impression we have formed that he belongs to Simon. In the end it is an inconsequential and disappointing diversion.

▶ **Je Vous Salue, Marie** see Hail Mary

Jew Süss

▶ **Jud Süss**

Germany   1940   85 mins   bw
Terra

d   **Veit Harlan**
sc **Veit Harlan, Ludwig Metzger, Eberhard
    Wolfgang Möller**
ph **Bruno Mundi**
m   **Wolfgang Zeller**
    **Ferdinand Marian, Werner Krauss,
    Heinrich George, Kristina Söderbaum**

Süss Oppenheimer (Marian), financial advisor and collector of taxes for the Duke of Württemburg, uses evil methods to gain power for himself and his people. Made with the personal encouragement of Josef Goebbels, this is one of the most notorious of the anti-Semitic films produced by the Nazis during the war. The script is a travesty of Lion Feuchtwanger's famous pro-Jewish novel of

1925, filmed previously in Britain in 1934. Harlan, the leading director of propagandist fiction films for the Third Reich, was charged with war crimes by the Allies. The case was dropped due to lack of evidence, and he returned to making films in Germany until 1962, two years before his death.

▶ **Jigokumon** see Gate of Hell

▶ **Jinruigaku Nyumon** see Pornographer, The

The Job

▶ **(US: The Sound Of Trumpets)**

▶ **Il Posto**

Italy　1961　90 mins　bw
24 Hores/Titanus

d　**Ermanno Olmi**
sc　**Ermanno Olmi**
ph　**Lamberto Caimi**
　　Sandro Panzeri, Loredana Detto, Tullio Kezich

A shy young man (Panzeri) from a poor family gets his first job in a large office in Milan, progressing from office boy to clerk. The entire non-professional cast was made up of the employees at the Edison building in Milan, with the exceptions of Panzeri, who later got a job in an office, and Olmi's wife, Loredana Detto, as the girl who befriends him. The director's second feature film is a humorous, sad and astute study of white-collar workers, contrasting the dehumanization of the work with their humanity. A film of an uneventful life, rich in brilliantly observed incidents. It is not for nothing that the sad-faced boy wears a hat like Buster Keaton's at the office party.

▶ **Jób Lázadása** see Revolt Of Job, The

Jofroi

France　1934　55 mins　bw
Les Auteurs Associés

d　**Marcel Pagnol**
sc　**Marcel Pagnol**
ph　**Willy**
m　**Vincent Scotto**
　　Vincent Scotto, Henri Poupon, André Robert, Annie Toinon, Charles Blavette

Jofroi (Scotto), an old peasant, sells some land to a neighbour (Poupon) and then objects to the new owner cutting down the trees. His protestations come in the form of various attempts at suicide. Pagnol's second film as sole director, and the first of the four works by Provençal writer Jean Giono to be made Pagnolian, came as a real breath of fresh air. The natural sound and settings gave this comic, ecological 'morality' tale an essential reality, though the performances, enjoyable as they are, are as broad as an oak.

▶ **Joi Baba Felunath** see Elephant God, The

▶ **Joi-Uchi** see Rebellion

The Joker

▶ **Le Farceur**

France　1960　90 mins　bw
A.J.Y.M.

d　**Philippe De Broca**
sc　**Daniel Boulanger, Philippe De Broca**
ph　**Jean Penzer**
m　**Georges Delerue**
　　Jean-Pierre Cassel, Anouk Aimée, Geneviève Cluny, Palau, Georges Wilson, Anne Tonietti, François Maistre

Dedicated philanderer Edouard (Cassel) searches for the perfect woman and thinks he's found her when he meets Hélène (Aimée), the bored and beautiful wife of a rich businessman. His rose-coloured spectacles, however, shatter when they go away together. De Broca's second film retains much of the charm and energy of his first, *Playing At Love*, as well as its eccentricity. (Edouard lives in a strange ménage that includes his illegitimate children, his elder brother who supports the family, a quaint old uncle – a gem from Palau – and several dogs.) Though there's much to enjoy, the joke is too thin to sustain, resulting in an overdose of frenzied vivacity from star and director in their efforts to keep up the momentum.

Le Joli Mai

France 1963 190 mins bw
Sofracima

d **Chris Marker**
sc **Chris Marker, Catherine Varlin**
ph **Pierre Lhomme**
m **Michel Legrand**

Interviews with ordinary people in the streets of Paris in May 1962 on the subjects of the day, including the Salan trial, the anti-OAS riots and current strikes. There is a linking commentary spoken by Yves Montand and sequences showing events and aspects of modern Paris. Compiled from 55 hours of interviews, this amusing, revealing and complex exercise in *cinéma vérité* has been boiled down to two-and-a-half hours (it lost 30 minutes in the English version narrated by Simone Signoret). Marker, whose three previous documentaries had been *Letter From Siberia*, *Description Of A Struggle (Israel)*, and *Cuba Si!*, brought the same foreigner's-eye view to bear on his own city.

Jom

▶ **Jom: Ou, L'Histoire D'Un Peuple**

Senegal 1982 80 mins col
Baobab Films/Zweites Deutschen
Fernsehen

d **Ababacar Samb Makharam**
sc **Ababacar Samb Makharam, Babacar Sine**
ph **Peter Chappell, Orlando Lopez**
m **Lamine Konté**
   Oumar Gueye, Amadou Lamine Camara, Zator Sarr, Ibou Camara, Oumar Seck, Oumi Sene

When the workers of a factory go on strike, the local sage (Gueye) encourages them with two stories that illustrate *jom* (the Wolof word for self-respect and integrity). One tells of a prince (Seck) who resisted the French colonizers, and the other relates how a dancer (Sene) defied her employers. This absorbing and brilliantly controlled mixture of socio-politics and African folk narrative is especially effective in its clever transitions from the past to the present. With the films of Ousmane Sem-

bène and Makharam, the Senegalese film industry has plenty of *jom*.

▶ **Jom: Ou, L'Histoire D'Un Peuple**
see Jom

Jonah Who Will Be 25 In The Year 2000

▶ **Jonas Qui Aura 25 Ans En L'An 2000**

Switzerland 1975 110 mins col
Citel/SSR/Action/SFP

d **Alain Tanner**
sc **Alain Tanner, John Berger**
ph **Renato Berta**
m **Jean-Marie Senia**
   Jean-Luc Bideau, Myriam Boyer, Jacques Denis, Roger Jendly, Dominique Labourier, Myriam Mezière, Miou-Miou, Rufus

In Geneva, a copy editor, a secretary, a rural worker and his factory-worker wife, a farmer and his wife, a teacher and a supermarket cashier are all trying, in different ways, to maintain the ideals of May 1968 in Paris and find alternatives to capitalism. Tanner and the English Marxist writer John Berger have created that rare species – a polemical comedy whose eight protagonists are warmly and vividly portrayed. The sub-Brechtian interpolations in black and white are superfluous though.

▶ **Jonas Qui Aura 25 Ans En L'An 2000** see Jonah Who Will Be 25 In The Year 2000

Joseph Kilián

▶ **Postava K Podpírání**

Czechoslovakia 1963 40 mins bw
Ceskoslovensky Film

d **Pavel Juráček, Jan Schmidt**
sc **Pavel Juráček, Jan Schmidt**
ph **Jan Curík**
m **Wiliam Bukovy**
   Karel Vasícek, Consuela Morávková, Pavel Bártl, Zbynek Jirmar

Herold (Vasícek), searching old Prague for a vague acquaintance named Joseph Kilián, wanders into a jazz concert taking place inside an imposing building. Nobody there can help him but, on impulse, he hires a cat for the day from a neighbouring cat-lending office. When he tries to return the animal, the office has disappeared and he finds himself trapped in a web of bureaucratic stonewalling. With his cat, he continues looking for Kilián... Deliberately Kafkaesque in story, tone and style, this short but intriguing allegory criticizes the 'personality cult' – a huge portrait of Stalin dominates the political posters in the music room – and paints a vivid picture of isolation, confusion and bureaucratic pettiness in a totalitarian regime. It is well made and funny, as well as disturbing and elusive.

▶ **Joueur, Le** see Gambler, The

▶ **Joueur D'Échecs, Le** see Chess Player, The

Jour De Fête

France 1947 87 mins bw
Francinex

d **Jacques Tati**
sc **Jacques Tati, Henri Marquet**
ph **Jacques Mercanton**
m **Jean Yatove**
   Jacques Tati, Guy Decomble, Paul Frankeur, Santa Relli, Maine Vallee, Roger Rafal, Beauvais

François (Tati), the postman in a small French village, decides to emulate the high-speed delivery of mail in the USA, something he witnessed in a documentary film shown at a travelling fair. It was as the vigorously cycling postman that Tati rode to everlasting comic fame in his first feature as director. Here we have the true descendant of the silent movie comedians, relying as he does on sight gags. What also emerges is his brilliant use of space – the tiny incident at the corner of the screen – an ability to create characters in a few revealing shots, and his slightly sentimental view of the old French values. *Jour De Fête* is an expanded version of Tati's short film *L'École Des Facteurs*, the success of which was responsible for the later feature. It was

shot in an unsatisfactory new colour process, but was released in black and white. However, since the 1970s, a partly hand-coloured print has been shown successfully.

▶ **Journal D'Un Curé De Campagne** see Diary Of A Country Priest

▶ **Journal D'Une Femme De Chambre** see Diary Of A Chambermaid

▶ **Journal D'Une Femme En Blanc, Le** see Woman In White

Journey Into Autumn

▶ **aka Dreams**

▶ **Kvinnodröm**

Sweden 1954 86 mins bw
Sandrew

d **Ingmar Bergman**
sc **Ingmar Bergman**
ph **Hilding Bladh**
   Eva Dahlbeck, Harriet Andersson, Gunnar Björnstrand, Ulf Palme, Inga Landgré, Naima Wifstrand

Susanne (Dahlbeck), a fashion photographer, and Doris (Andersson), a model, go to Gothenburg where Susanne seeks to revive an affair with a married man (Palme), and Doris flirts with a wealthy, retired diplomat (Björnstrand). The gap between illusion and reality is pointedly demonstrated in 'Women's Dreams', the title's literal translation, and beautifully embodied by sophisticated Dahlbeck and pert Andersson. By turns sunny and dark, the film shows Bergman moving from his spring into his summer.

Journey Of Hope

▶ **Reise Der Hoffnung**

▶ **aka Voyage Vers L'Espoir**

Switzerland 1990 110 mins col
Condor Pictures/Catpics

d **Xavier Koller**
sc **Xavier Koller, Feride Ciçekoglu**
ph **Elemér Ragályi**

m Jan Gabarek, Terje Rypdal, Arild
   Andersen
   Necmettin Çobanoglu, Nur Sürer, Emin
   Sivas, Mathias Gnädinger

Haydar (Çobanoglu) ekes out a bare living
farming a few sheep in a small mountain
village in South-East Turkey. Encouraged by
an optimistic postcard from his cousin who
has emigrated to Switzerland, he decides to
seek a new life there. Selling everything they
possess to pay for the journey and the papers,
and leaving their other six children behind,
Haydar, his wife Meryem (Sürer), and seven-
year-old Mehmet Ali (Sivas), set out on the
arduous trip via Istanbul and Italy to the
country they regard as Paradise. Nothing,
however, turns out as they expected and hope
becomes despair. Shot entirely on location in
Turkey, Italy and Switzerland, this film is
based on an amalgam of actual events that
befell poor Turks. It is a tale that is at once
inspiring in its portrait of the will to survive
and to seek a better life, appalling in its
picture of man's inhumanity and greed as the
smugglers of illegal immigrants ruthlessly
cause suffering, and heartbreaking as the
dreams of a simple family end in tragedy.
This film, acted, photographed and edited
with impeccable restraint, is haunting and
dignified, and gripping to watch.

Best Foreign Film Oscar 1990

Journey To Italy

▶ **aka The Lonely Woman**

▶ **(US: Strangers)**

▶ **Viaggio In Italia**

   Italy 1953 79 mins bw
   Italiafilm/Junior Film/Sveva Film

d **Roberto Rossellini**
sc **Roberto Rossellini, Vitaliano Brancati**
ph **Enzo Serafin**
m **Renzo Rossellini**
   **Ingrid Bergman, George Sanders, Natalia
   Ray, Leslie Daniels, Marie Mauban**

An English couple (Bergman and Sanders)
are travelling by car to Naples where they
intend to sell a villa left to them by an uncle.
Their marriage is going through a crisis, but
certain significant events reunite them. This
is an example of how a film can be buffeted
around on the waves of fashion and critical
opinion. With the appearance of this third
Rossellini-Bergman picture, after both *Stromboli* and *Europa '51* had flopped, the repu-
tations of the Italian director and his Swedish
actress wife reached their lowest ebb. The film
was attacked for being a clumsily made (the
shadow of a camera crane is seen at the end),
badly acted (Sanders and Bergman disliked
making it), sentimental woman's picture.
However, in the late 1950s, the directors of
the *Nouvelle Vague* and young critics claimed
it a masterpiece of narrative simplicity, a
penetrating semi-documentary on a marriage,
a camera's voyage into the Self. It happens
to be all these things, good and bad.

▶ **Jour Se Lève, Le** see Daybreak

▶ **Joyful Wisdom, The** see Gai Savoir,
   Le

Joyless Street

▶ **(US: The Street Of Sorrow aka
   Streets Of Sorrow)**

▶ **Die Freudlose Gasse**

   Germany 1925 139 mins bw
   Sofar Film

d **G.W. Pabst**
sc **Willi Haas**
ph **Guido Seeber, Kurt Oertel, Walter Robert
   Lach**
m **Silent**
   **Asta Nielsen, Werner Krauss, Greta
   Garbo, Valeska Gert, Agnes Esterhazy**

In Vienna following World War I, the
daughter (Garbo) of a middle-class father
ruined by inflation, is faced with entering a
brothel. In the course of her travails, she
encounters a kept woman (Nielsen), a butcher
(Krauss) and the brothel's Madame (Gert).
Although obviously filmed on a studio set,
the seedy view of post-war Vienna with its
profiteers and poverty seemed to bring a
change from Expressionism to Realism in the
German cinema. The melodramatic tale is of
little importance beside the performances of
the lovely but plump 20-year-old Garbo (in
her third and last film in Europe), contrasted

with the 42-year-old Nielsen at the height of her fame and popular cabaret artist Gert. Note for buffs: Marlene Dietrich is to be spied in a small part.

▶ **Joyu Sumako No Koi** see Love Of Sumako The Actress, The

Judex

France 1916 270 mins bw
Gaumont

d **Louis Feuillade**
sc **Louis Feuillade, Arthur Bernède**
ph **Klausse, A. Glattli**
m **Silent**
    René Cresté, Musidora, Bout De Zan, Edouard Mathé, Gaston Michel, Yvonne Dario

Judex (Cresté), a mysterious cloaked crusader, battles against evil forces in order to destroy the empire of an arch criminal. After the Minister of Interior had criticized Feuillade's greatest serial, *Les Vampires*, for its immoral heroes, the director created the adventures of a handsome righter of wrongs in 12 episodes, and achieved his biggest success. More carefully structured, more sanctimonious and less frightening than its predecessors, it was still vastly entertaining and thrilling. It prompted an inferior sequel serial *La Nouvelle Mission De Judex*, and two features, one directed by Feuillade's son-in-law Maurice Champreux in 1933, and another by Georges Franju in 1963.

Judex

France 1963 95 mins bw
Comptoir Français Du Film

d **Georges Franju**
sc **Jacques Champreux, Francis Lacassin**
ph **Marcel Fradetal**
m **Maurice Jarre**
    Channing Pollock, Francine Bergé, Edith Scob, Michel Vitold, Jacques Jouanneau, Sylva Koscina

Favraux (Vitold), a wicked banker, warned by Judex (Pollock), the righter of wrongs, that unless he reforms he will be punished, is apparently struck dead during a masked ball. Actually, he is held prisoner by Judex in his secret lair in order to trap Diana Monti (Bergé), a mistress of disguise, and prevent her from getting the inheritance of the banker's daughter (Scob). Louis Feuillade had been an influence on Franju's first films, now he was paid a direct homage in this remake of his 1916 serial. The casting of a real magician in the title role was an inspired idea, but the true magic came from Fradetal's re-creation of the starkly contrasting blacks and whites of Feuillade's surreal world. With Bergé in a cat suit and Pollock as the mysterious masked avenger bringing a dead dove back to life, Franju conjured up a lost era.

The Judge And The Assassin

▶ **Le Juge Et L'Assassin**

France 1976 125 mins col
Lira Films

d **Bertrand Tavernier**
sc **Jean Aurenche, Pierre Bost, Bertrand Tavernier**
ph **Pierre William Glenn**
m **Philippe Sarde**
    Philippe Noiret, Michel Galabru, Isabelle Huppert, Jean-Claude Brialy, Yves Robert, Renée Fauré

Judge Rousseau (Noiret) must decide whether an ex-army sergeant (Galabru), apprehended for a series of child murders, should be executed or whether he is insane. He develops a relationship with the man, a self-appointed holy avenger, and learns of the background that shaped his disturbed personality. For his third feature, Tavernier chose a complex subject, set in the 19th century against a background of political and economic unrest. The judge, well-played by Noiret, pursues the case with an energy that is part duty, part professional excitement and certainly part of a desire to achieve recognition and glory. An interesting and complex political parable that ultimately fails due to lack of clarity.

▶ **Judgement, The** see Gunnar Hede's Saga

Ju Dou

China   1990   94 mins   col
China Films Coproduction Corp/
Tukumashoten Pablo/Tokuma
Communications/China Film Import and
Export Group

d   **Zhang Yimou, Yeng Feng-Liang**
sc **Lui Heng**
ph **Gu Chang-Wei, Yang Lun**
m   **Zhao Ji-Pin**
    **Gong Li, Li Bao-Tian, Li Wei, Zheng
    Jian, Zhang Yi**

Jin-Shan (Li Wei), the elderly owner of a dye factory, brings his young third wife, Ju Dou (Gong Li), back to his home in a small village in China in 1920. He mistreats her badly, and Tian-Qing (Bao-Tian), his 40-year-old bachelor nephew, who works for his martinet uncle, overhears Ju Dou's cries of pain at night. The wife and the nephew soon establish a relationship, and when the uncle goes away they make love. She becomes pregnant and has a son which her husband believes is his own. The child grows up with hatred in his heart. The plot of this passionate melodrama resembles that of a Hollywood *film noir* of the 40s. But instead of the chiaroscuro of those films, this tale takes place against the rich colours of a dye factory, the red dye oozing like blood at certain appropriate moments, with yellow as the dominant colour. Although co-directed, it contains many of the striking large-screen pictorial qualities that ex-cameraman Yimou brought to his debut film *Red Sorghum* (1987), which also featured the sensuous Gong Li. Here, in a superbly-used small space, the directors manipulate their interlocking characters – all brilliantly played, especially the sinister child (Jian and Yi at different ages).

Judo Saga

▶ **aka Sanshiro Sugata**

▶ **Sugata Sanshiro**

Japan   1943   80 mins   bw
Toho

d   **Akira Kurosawa**
sc **Akira Kurosawa**
ph **Akira Mimura**

m   **Seichi Suzuki**
    **Susumu Fujita, Denjiro Okochi, Takashi
    Shimura, Yukiko Todoroki**

In the late 19th century, Sugata (Fujita) becomes a master of the new fighting style of Judo, gradually proving its superiority over the more established martial art of Ju-jitsu, and learns to gain spiritual peace at the same time. Thirty-three-year-old Kurosawa's first film immediately established him as a director to be reckoned with. Made at the height of World War II, it managed to avoid the patriotic and propagandistic aspects found in many Japanese films of the day, but told an exciting story of a young man's growth in a stylish manner. Xenophobia intrudes into the sequel, *Judo Saga, Part II (Zoku Sugata Sanshiro,* 1945), although it retains the pictorial and narrative strengths of the first.

▶ **Jud Süss** see Jew Süss

▶ **Juexiang** see Swan Song

▶ **Juge Et L'Assassin, Le** see Judge And The Assassin, The

▶ **Jujiro** see Crossways

Jules And Jim

▶ **Jules Et Jim**

France   1961   105 mins   bw
Films Du Carrosse/SEDIF

d   **François Truffaut**
sc **François Truffaut, Jean Gruault**
ph **Raoul Coutard**
m   **Georges Delerue**
    **Jeanne Moreau, Oskar Werner, Henri
    Serre, Marie Dubois, Vanna Urbino,
    Boris Bassiak, Sabine Haudepin**

Close friends, the German Jules (Werner) and the Frenchman Jim (Serre) are both in love with Catherine (Moreau). However, Jules marries her and takes her back to Germany. World War I separates the two friends and when they meet again afterwards, Catherine changes partners. Although Truffaut's invigorating tale of friendship and love is full of cinematic allusions (one to Chaplin's *The Kid*), and is a homage to Jean Renoir, it is a unique piece of film-making. The director, while remaining true to Henri-Pierre Roché's first novel (another was used for the less successful *Anne And Muriel*), employs a wide range of cinematic devices to express the shifting moods of the characters and plot, including stills and newsreels. The three leads are a delight, and 'Le Tourbillon', the song sung so charmingly by Moreau, became a hit as did the film.

▶ **Jules Et Jim** see Jules And Jim

▶ **Julia, Du Bist Zauberhaft** see Adorable Julia

Juliet Of The Spirits

▶ **Giulietta Degli Spiriti**

Italy 1965 145 mins col
Federiz/Francoriz

d **Federico Fellini**
sc **Federico Fellini, Tullio Pinnelli, Brunello Rondi, Ennio Flaiano**
ph **Gianni Di Venanzo**
m **Nino Rota**
   Giulietta Masina, Mario Pisu, Sandra Milo, Valentina Cortese, Sylva Koscina, Caterina Boratto, Valeska Gert

While her husband (Pisu) philanders, a bored middle-aged, middle-class Roman housewife (Masina) consults clairvoyants and mediums, and escapes into a world of the imagination drawn from the 'spirits' of her past, present and future. Following the male fantasies of $8\frac{1}{2}$, Fellini put his wife Masina under scrutiny in his first full-length colour feature. The brilliant photography by Venanzo and the opulent designs by Piero Gheradi can't alleviate the basic silliness of the character of the wife and her Vogueish dreams.

Juliette Or The Key Of Dreams

▶ **Juliette Ou La Clé Des Songes**

France 1951 90 mins bw
Sacha Gordine

d **Marcel Carné**

sc **Marcel Carné, Jacques Viot**
ph **Henri Alekan**
m **Joseph Kosma**
   Gérard Philipe, Suzanne Cloutier, Yves Robert, Jean Caussimon, Delmont

A young man (Philipe), sleeping in a prison cell, meets Juliette (Cloutier) in his dreams. He follows her far and wide, from a white village where the inhabitants have lost their memories to a mysterious Bluebeard's castle. Carné's attempt to return to the world of 1940s fantasy succeeds despite the whimsical and rather purposefully dated nature of the exercise. Weighing in its favour are the gentle performance of Philipe as the wide-eyed dreamer, the magical camera of Alekan and the sets by master designer Alexandre Trauner, who had worked with Carné over half a dozen times before. Against it was the playing of French-Canadian Cloutier (soon to become Mrs Peter Ustinov) and the imposed happy ending, neither of which did justice to the conception of Georges Neveux's play.

▶ **Juliette Ou La Clé Des Songes** see Juliette Or The Key Of Dreams

▶ **July 14** see Fourteenth of July, The

▶ **Jument Verte, La** see Green Mare's Nest, The

▶ **Junge Törless, Der** see Young Törless

▶ **Jungfrukällan** see Virgin Spring, The

Junoon

India 1978 141 mins col
Film-Valas

d **Shyam Benegal**
sc **Shyam Benegal**
ph **Govind Nihalani**
m **Vanraj Bhatia**
   Shashi Kapoor, Jennifer Kendal, Nafisa Ali, Shabana Azmi, Naseeruddin Shah, Shushma Seth

During the Indian Mutiny, the congregation of a British church is attacked. Anglo-Indian Charles Labadoor is killed, leaving his wife, Mariam (Kendal), and daughter, Ruth (Ali), to fend for themselves. Jhavad Khan (Kapoor), a Pathan nobleman who desires Ruth, abducts the family to his palace where, to the jealous horror of his wife, he intends, as is his Muslim right, to marry her. Thus begins the conflict between Christian and Muslim and, for Jhavad, terrible confusion as his code of honour prevents him taking Ruth by force, and his passion keeps him from his duty as a fighting man. Shyam Benegal is one of a handful of directors who demonstrate that, if Ray set the precedent and remains the master in India, he is not without honorable competitors. *Junoon* is a complex and intricate work (adapted from a short story based on diaries of true events) drawing together the threads of love and war, and giving, to a Westerner, a new perspective on the Mutiny. Intelligent and moving, it's exquisite to look at and offers several memorable images and sequences.

▶ **Jury Of One** see Verdict

Just Before Nightfall

▶ **Juste Avant La Nuit**

France 1971 107 mins col
Films de la Boétie/Columbia(Paris)/
Cinégai(Rome)

d **Claude Chabrol**
sc **Claude Chabrol**
ph **Jean Rabier**
m **Pierre Jansen**
   **Stéphane Audran, Michel Bouquet,
   François Périer, Anna Douking, Marina
   Ninchi**

Charles (Bouquet) murders his mistress, then confesses to his wife Hélène (Audran) and the victim's husband (Périer), neither of whom condemns him. In the final scene, Bouquet uses the word 'juste' 17 times in different ways, and Chabrol the moralist recognizes that justice has more than one interpretation. This classically photographed and structured picture is a reversal of *La Femme Infidèle*, being 'Le Mari Infidèle', but in both cases it is Bouquet married to Audran and living in Versailles, who does the killing and the con-

fessing. The main ironic point is that murder must not be permitted to disturb the surface of the *bourgeois* marriage. Chabrol takes wicked delight in presenting his own wife as the adulterous or betrayed wives in his films, and their work together makes for one of the most captivating husband-wife teams in cinema.

▶ **Juste Avant La Nuit** see Just Before Nightfall

Justice Est Faite

▶ **aka Let Justice Be Done**
▶ **(US: Justice Is Done)**

France 1950 105 mins bw
Silver Films

d **André Cayatte**
sc **André Cayatte, Charles Spaak**
ph **Jean Bourgoin**
m **Raymond Legrand**
   **Claude Nollier, Michel Auclair, Valentine
   Tessier, Jean Debucourt, Balpêtre,
   Raymond Bussières**

Elsa Lundenstein (Nollier) is brought to trial in the assize court at Versailles for the mercy killing of her lover. The proceedings are conducted with punctilious regard for the letter of the law by the court president (Balpêtre, intriguing and authoritative) before a jury of seven whose private lives and concerns are revealed to the movie audience. This is one of the most successful of ex-lawyer Cayatte's ironic examinations of French justice. Here, it is really the jury system itself that is on trial in a well-written (Spaak, too, was formerly a lawyer), tightly directed and beautifully acted film that could well have been titled, '*Has Justice Been Done?*'

Best Film Venice 1950

Best film Berlin 1951

▶ **Justice Is Done** see Justice Est Faite

▶ **Jutro** see Morning

k

▶ **Kaadu** see Forest, The

▶ **Kabinett Des Dr Caligari, Das** see Cabinet Of Dr Caligari, The

▶ **Kaere Irene** see Dear Irene

Kagemusha

Japan 1980 181 mins col
Toho/Kurosawa

d Akira Kurosawa
sc Akira Kurosawa, Masato Ide
ph Kazuo Miyagawa, Asaichi Nakai, Takao Sato, Masaharu Ueda
m Shinichiro Ikebe
    Tatsuya Nakadai, Tsutomu Yamazaki, Kenichi Hagiwara, Kota Yui, Hideji Otaki, Hideo Murata

In 16th-century Japan, a thief (Nakadai) is employed as the double, or *kagemusha*, of a clan leader, who later dies, in order to confuse the enemy. When the deception is uncovered, he is thrown out and wanders the countryside like a pariah. Kurosawa's first film for five years was the most expensive Japanese movie ever made (with the assistance of executive producers Francis Coppola and George Lucas, and a Twentieth Century-Fox distribution deal). The screen is well used to frame the epic grandeur of the subject with red sunsets, vivid rainbows, the multi-coloured flags of soldiers, and the dream-like battle scenes with horses and men dying in slow motion. Yet there is something lifeless about the pictorial composition, the cutting and the camera angles, and the story never fulfils its Shakespearean promise. The export version lost 22 minutes.

Best Film Cannes 1980

▶ **Kagi** see Odd Obsession

▶ **Kaiser Von Kalifornien, Der** see Emperor Of California, The

▶ **Kak Molody My Byli** see When We Were Young

▶ **Kakushi Toride No San-Akunin** see Hidden Fortress, The

▶ **Kalaa, El** see Citadel, The

Kameradschaft

▶ **aka La Tragédie De La Mine**

Germany 1931 92 mins bw
Nerofilm

d G.W. Pabst
sc Laszlo Wajda, Karl Otten, Peter Martin Lampel
ph Fritz Arno Wagner, Robert Baberske
    Ernst Busch, Alexander Granach, Fritz Kampers, Gustav Puttjer, Daniel Mendaille, Elizabeth Wenst

French miners are trapped below ground near the Franco-German border, and the Germans burrow through the underground frontier to rescue their comrades. Pabst used a screenplay based on a real mining disaster to illustrate his plea for the international solidarity of workers. Although there was some outdoor location shooting, the mine galleries were built entirely in the studio, cleverly creating the utmost realism while allowing for effective lighting. The film's bilingualism was part of its didactic purpose, and like its pacifist companion piece, *Westfront 1918*, its commendable message is to be applauded, even though it seems naively optimistic from our cynical post-World War II standpoint.

Kamikaze

France   1986   89 mins   col
Les Films Du Loup/ARP/Gaumont

d   **Didier Grousset**
sc **Didier Grousset, Luc Besson**
ph **Jean-François Robin**
m   **Eric Serra**
    Richard Bohringer, Michel Galabru,
    Dominique Lavanant, Riton Leibman,
    Kim Massee, Harry Cleven, Romane
    Bohringer

Fired from his job, electronics wizard Albert (Galabru) spends all his time at home watching TV. He finds the announcers nauseating and constructs an electronic gun to kill them during a live broadcast. Romain (Richard Bohringer), the detective assigned to the 'TV murders' case, follows a bizarre hunch and assembles a group of internationally acclaimed scientists to outwit the killer. Originally a Luc Besson project, it was handed over to his former assistant Grousset when Besson became involved with *The Big Blue*. The idea behind the screenplay is the highly pleasurable wish-fulfilment of many a TV viewer to be able to influence the affairs on the screen and eliminate those presenters he finds objectionable. In spite of some telling moments leading to a tense climax, the film, unfortunately, never quite lives up to its initial promise: the narrative loses its way by moving into flashy *policier* territory and the characters are barely credible.

Kamikaze 1989

W. Germany   1982   106 mins   col
Regina Ziegler Filmproduktion/Trio Film/Oase Filmproduktion

d   **Wolf Gremm**
sc **Wolf Gremm, Robert Katz**
ph **Xaver Schwarzenberger**
m   **Tangerine Dream**
    Rainer Werner Fassbinder, Günter
    Kaufmann, Boy Gobert, Arnold Marquis,
    Nicole Heesters, Brigitte Mira, Franco
    Nero

Inspector Jansen (Fassbinder) is sent to find out who sent a bomb threat to the president of a huge pop-media conglomerate known as The Combine. He tracks down suspects through slums, drug dens, mansions and the corrupt organization itself run by 'Blue Panther' (Gobert). The only excuse for seeing this bizarre version of the futuristic crime novel, *Murder On The Thirty-first Floor* by the Swedish writer Per Wahlöö, is the performance of the overweight Fassbinder, permitted to do as he pleased and enjoying himself in a phoney leopard-skin suit. (He kept the suit and wore it during the last year of his life.) Unfortunately, Gremm seems more dazzled by the brilliance of his vision of a society ruled by the most tawdry pop culture than critical of the values it represents. (Mind you, it looks good for a low-budget film shot in 25 days.)

Kanal

Poland   1957   97 mins   bw
Film Polski

d   **Andrzej Wajda**
sc **Jerzy Stefan Stawinski**
ph **Jerzy Lipman**
m   **Jan Krenz**
    Teresa Izewska, Tadeusz Janczar, Emil
    Kariewicz, Wienczylaw Glinski,
    Wladyslaw (later Vladek) Sheybal

During the 1944 Warsaw uprising, Polish partisans are pursued and trapped in the sewers by Nazi soldiers. The central film in Wajda's Resistance trilogy (between *A Generation* and *Ashes And Diamonds*) starkly recreates the claustrophobic nightmare of an actual wartime incident. There are weaknesses in the characterization and in some of the dialogue (heavy-handed symbolic references to Dante's *Inferno*), but its powerful theme and imagery helped awaken the world to the new Polish cinema.

Special Jury Prize Cannes 1957

Kangchenjunga

India   1962   102 mins   col

d   **Satyajit Ray**
sc **Satyajit Ray**
ph **Subrata Mitra**
m   **Satyajit Ray**
    Chabi Biswas, Karuna Bannerji, Anil
    Chatterjee, Anubhe Gupta, Subrata Sen,

Indrani Singh, Nilima Roy Chowdbury, Alakananda Roy, Arun Mukerjee

Indranath Choudhuri (Biswas), a wealthy and forceful man, takes his family to Darjeeling on holiday. There they get involved with a group of other holiday-makers who talk and drink tea among the Himalayan foothills as they wait for the mists to clear from the peak of Kangchenjunga. Among the people Indranath meets is a young, unemployed man (Mukherjee) who asks to marry his younger daughter (Chowdbury) and makes him see his acquisitiveness in a different light, while his older daughter (Chatterjee) tries to resolve the problems of her unhappy marriage. Shot in 26 days, Ray's first colour film and the first he scripted himself, explores one of his constant themes – the conflict between old and new. The entire action takes place during one afternoon and was filmed mostly on the winding roads above the valley against spectacular scenery, photographed in pastel shades. The director called it the most musical of his films, mainly because of the rhythm of the constant cross-cutting between the characters, all superbly cast, and the variations on a central theme. It is also a telling satire on the Indian *bourgeoisie* on holiday with their tendency to imitate English habits, while still making arranged marriages. Above all, one remembers the magic mountain in the background.

▶ **Kanojo To Kare** see She And He

Kaos

Italy 1984 188 mins col
RAI/Filmtre

d   **Paolo and Vittorio Taviani**
sc **Paolo and Vittorio Taviani**
ph **Giuseppe Lanci**
m   **Nicola Piovani**
    Margarita Lozano, Claudio Bigagli, Enrica Maria Modugno, Ciccio Ingrassia, Franco Franchi, Biagio Barone, Omero Antonutti

A group of four stories by Luigi Pirandello about peasant life in turn-of-the-century Sicily, concluding with an epilogue in which Pirandello (Antonutti) himself returns to his birthplace (Kaos). The ochre Sicilian landscape, stunningly photographed, is the main link between the peasant folk tales written and filmed without sentimentality or condescension by middle-class intellectuals. The film fully covers the gamut from tragedy to comedy, although the more serious narratives are more successful. As these – 'The Other Son' and 'Moon Sickness' – are placed before the semi-humorous 'The Jar' and 'Requiem', there are slightly diminishing returns. But the frank performances and flamboyant imagery make this one of the Taviani brothers' best efforts.

Kapo

Italy/France 1960 115 mins bw
Vides/Zebra(Rome)/Francinex(Paris)

d   **Gillo Pontecorvo**
sc **Franco Solinas, Gillo Pontecorvo**
ph **Goffredo Bellisario, Aleksandar Sekulović**
m   **Carlo Rustichelli**
    Susan Strasberg, Laurent Terzieff, Emmanuele Riva, Didi Perego, Gianni Garko

In a Nazi concentration camp, a doctor saves 14-year-old Parisian Jewess Edith (Strasberg) from extermination by giving her the identity of a non-Jewish political prisoner who has died. Sent to another camp, she becomes a Kapo, or prisoner-guard, a role which takes her over and corrupts her into brutality, until she comes to her senses and sacrifices her life. What does one say about this effort? Pontecorvo has jam-packed his film with every kind of tear-jerking cliché on offer and entrusted the debasement and regeneration of his heroine to a sadly inept actress. The result is an overheated melodrama which does a grave disservice to the enormity of its subject, although the horrors of the camps are realistically portrayed.

▶ **Käpy Selän Alla** see Skin Skin

▶ **Kare John** see Dear John

Karin, Daughter Of Ingmar

▶ **Karin Ingmarsdotter**

Sweden 1919 110 mins bw
Svenska Biographeatern

d   **Victor Sjöström**
sc **Victor Sjöström, Esther Julin**
ph **Henrik Jaenzon, Gustav Boge**
m   **Silent**
    Victor Sjöström, Tora Teje, Bertil
    Malmstedt, Tor Weijden, Nils Lundell

Old Ingmar (Sjöström) thwarts the proposed marriage of his daughter Karin (Teje) to Halvor (Weijden), because he fears the young man may become an alcoholic like his father. Karin marries the sober and industrious Eljas (Lundell), who takes to drink. Karin and Halvor eventually make their future together. Sjöström followed up his two-part *The Ingmarssons*, taken from Selma Lagerlöf's epic novel *Jeruselum In Dalecarlia*, with a section that takes place several years later. Although the temperance tale is a plodding and puritanical one, made even longer by copious intertitles, the film is full of marvellous exterior and interior images, with the great pioneer director showing himself a master of framing people in their environment.

▶ **Karin Ingmarsdotter** see Karin, Daughter Of Ingmar

▶ **Kärlek 65** see Love 65

▶ **Kärlek Och Journalistik** see Love And Journalism

▶ **Karumen Kokyo Ni Kaeru** see Carmen Comes Home

▶ **Katerina Ismailova** see Lady Macbeth Of Mtsensk

Katinka

▶ **Ved Vejen**

Denmark/Sweden 1988 96 mins col
Nordisk Film/The Danish Film Institute

d   **Max Von Sydow**
sc **Klaus Rifbjerg**
ph **Sven Nykvist**
m   **Georg Riedel**
    Tammi Ost, Ole Ernst, Kurt Ravn, Ghita
    Norby, Birthe Backhausen, Vibeke
    Hastrup, Bodil Lassen

Katinka (Ost), the wife of the station-master (Ernst) in a small Danish village at the turn of the century, daydreams about love and life, feelings she cannot express to her doltish husband. Her longed-for passion finally seems possible when the handsome new manager (Ravn) of the neighbouring estate falls in love with her, but because of social codes their love remains unconsummated. 'It's been a love story between me and the book for 25 years,' said the distinguished Swedish actor Max Von Sydow of the Herman Bang novel which formed the basis for his first film as director. As would be expected from someone who has performed in so many Ingmar Bergman films, and with Sven Nykvist, Bergman's constant photographer in tow, Von Sydow shows the influence of his master. However, despite the melancholy story framed by funeral scenes, the film is altogether sunnier, less complex and less *angst*-ridden than is usual with Bergman. Von Sydow reveals considerable control over his material, managing to breathe life generously into the simple triangle story. The acting is superb throughout and the beautiful images are tinged with sadness at a romance doomed never to flower.

Katzelmacher

W. Germany 1969 88 mins bw
Antieater-X

d   **Rainer Werner Fassbinder**
sc **Rainer Werner Fassbinder**
ph **Dietrich Lohmann**
m   **Peer Raben**
    Hanna Schygulla, Lilith Ungerer, Elga
    Sorbas, Doris Mattes, Rainer Werner
    Fassbinder, Harry Baer

In a bleak suburb of a big city, the lives of the bored young people are disturbed by the arrival of a Greek 'guest worker' (Fassbinder). The girls, especially Maria (Schygulla), take a fancy to him, and the boys beat him up. Fassbinder's second film, influenced by Godard, was based on the play he had written and staged successfully the year before. Using direct sound, limited dialogue and camera movements, he penetrates to the heart of xenophobia, an exploration developed later in films such as *Fear Eats The Soul*. Fassbinder himself plays the *Katzelmacher* (pejorative Bavarian slang for a foreigner) in a rare sympathetic role, while the rest of the cast effectively personifies ignorance.

▶ **Kazoku Geemu** see Family Game

▶ **Kdo Hledá Zlaté Dno** see Who Looks For Gold

Keep An Eye On Amelia

▶ **(US: Oh, Amelia!)**

▶ **Occupe-Toi D'Amélie**

France 1949 98 mins bw
Lux Film

d   Claude Autant-Lara
sc   Jean Aurenche, Pierre Bost
ph   André Bac
m   René Cloërec
     Danielle Darrieux, André Bervil, Grégoire
     Aslan, Jean Desailly

Amelia (Darrieux), a Parisian cocotte, is dividing her favours between a Balkan prince (Aslan) and a slightly dim-witted officer (Bervil) who is her self-appointed protector. Away on army manouevres, the latter leaves her to the care of his best friend (Desailly) who persuades her into a mock marriage to ensure his inheritance. An extremely lively, sparkling and skilful adaptation of a Feydeau farce, imaginatively directed by Autant-Lara who retains the theatrical proscenium, but moves out into the audience, the streets, and back again, to maximum effect. On release, the movie incurred some local bans in Britain and enraged American critics who, in the moralistic climate of the times, considered it lewd and immoral.

The Keepers

▶ **La Tête Contre Les Murs**

France 1958 98 mins bw
Atica/Sirius/Elpenor

d   Georges Franju
sc   Jean-Pierre Mocky
ph   Eugen Schüfftan
m   Maurice Jarre
     Jean-Pierre Mocky, Pierre Brasseur, Paul
     Meurisse, Anouk Aimée, Charles
     Aznavour, Edith Scob

A rebellious and wealthy young man (Mocky) is committed by his father to a mental home, escapes to Paris, and is returned before he

can prove his sanity. Much of Franju's first feature was shot in an actual asylum, the frightening reality of which sits uncomfortably with the fictional story (adapted from a 1949 Hervé Bazin novel about conditions in mental hospitals in the 1930s). Although there is some disturbing and poetic imagery, Franju's sense of a world hovering between sanity and madness, reality and fantasy is better developed in his next film, *Eyes Without A Face*.

▶ **Keep Walking** see Camminacammina

Keetje Tippel

▶ **(US: Cathy Tippel)**

Netherlands 1975 101 mins col
Rob Houwer Film

d   Paul Verhoeven
sc   Gerard Soeteman
ph   Jan De Bont
m   Rogier Van Otterloo
     Monique Van De Ven, Rutger Hauer,
     Eddie Brugman, Hannah De Leeuwe,
     Andrea Domburg

In 1881, the adolescent Keetje (Van De Ven) leaves Friesland for Amsterdam with her impoverished family, who hope to improve their lot. They barely manage to earn a living and Keetje and her elder sister (De Leeuwe) are forced into prostitution. Keetje, however, manages to work her way out of it, becomes a socialist and marries a wealthy man (Brugman). The box-office success of films such as *Turkish Delight*, which also starred Van De Ven and Hauer (here as a snobbish clerk), enabled Verhoeven to make bigger budget commercial productions, a rarity in Dutch cinema. This attempt to paint a realistic picture of the harsh working class life in the 19th century (based on autobiographical stories by Neel Doff) is far too glossy and superficial to convince, but the performance of Van De Ven as a spirited girl shines through and there is a certain amount of wit.

▶ **Kermesse Héroïque, La** see Carnival In Flanders

▶ **Key, The** see Odd Obsession

▶ **Kiiroi Karasu** see Behold Thy Son

▶ **Kilenc Hónap** see Nine Months

Killer!

▶ **(US: This Man Must Die)**
▶ **Que La Bête Meure**

France 1969 110 mins col
Les Films La Boétie(Paris)/Rizzoli
Films(Rome)

d **Claude Chabrol**
sc **Paul Gégauff**
ph **Jean Rabier**
m **Pierre Jansen, Brahms**
    Michel Duchaussoy, Caroline Cellier,
    Jean Yanne, Anouk Ferjac, Marc Di
    Napoli, Maurice Pialat

The young and only son of Charles Thénier
(Duchaussoy), a widower, is killed by a hit-
and-run driver whom the police are unable
to trace. Resolving to find and kill the killer,
Charles becomes involved – at first cold-
bloodedly, later genuinely – with Hélène (Cellier) whose brother-in-law, Paul (Yanne), he
has reason to believe is the object of his
pursuit. Complications multiply when the
boorish Paul's adolescent son (Di Napoli),
who detests his father, attaches himself to
Charles. The plot is based on a thriller by
Nicholas Blake (alias poet C. Day Lewis).
Chabrol has constructed a remarkably complex film, finely shaded to diagnose the subtle
shifts and contradictions in the balance of
human motives and behaviour. Extremely
well acted, notably by Yanne, it is further
illuminated by Rabier's expressive camera and
the effective use of a Brahms song. This is
Chabrol at his gripping best.

The Killer

▶ **Diexue Shuang Xiong**

Hong Kong 1989 111 mins col
Film Workshop

d **John Woo (Wu Yusen)**
sc **John Woo (Wu Yusen)**
ph **Yuen Chun-Wah, Lee Wai-Tak**
m **Lowell Lowe (Lu Guanting), James Wong**
    (Huang Zhan), Tang Shusen

Chow Yun-Fat (Zhou Runfa), Danny Lee
(Li Xiuxan), Sally Yeh (Ye Qianwen),
Chu Kong (Zhu Jiang), Shing Fui-On
(Cheng Kui'an), Ye Rongzu

Jeff (Yun-Fat), a hired hit-man, carries out a
killing in a nightclub during which he inadvertently injures the singer, Jennie (Yeh), who
needs a cornea graft as a result. Keeping his
identity hidden, Jeff befriends the girl and
accepts a final assignment to earn the money
to pay for her operation. The victim is a well-
known financier being guarded by two police
officers. They give chase but fail to catch the
killer, and a watch is put on him amidst
proliferating complications and escalating
violence. Meanwhile, a love affair blossoms
between Jeff and Jennie. John Woo is one of
Hong Kong's most experienced and prolific
directors, and has worked with a variety of
genres. Here, he is paying homage to both
American and French *film noir* and it has
become a favourite critics' game to trace
elements of Jean-Pierre Melville and Martin
Scorsese (as Woo himself originally intended),
not to mention Sergio Leone, Sam Peckinpath
et al. However, there are also clearly influences from the Chinese *wuxia pan*, or 'martial
chivalry' films of the 1960s, which lend the
work a distinctive nostalgic grace. All this
matters little from the point of view of an
ordinary moviegoer. *The Killer* is a hard-
edged, convincing, tightly constructed thriller
in its own right, filmed with immense style
and control and thoroughly entertaining for
fans of the genre.

▶ **Killing Game, The** see Comic Strip
Hero

King Lear

▶ **Korol Lir**

USSR 1970 139 mins bw
Lenfilm

d **Grigori Kozintsev**
sc **Grigori Kozintsev (from Boris Pasternak's**
    translation of the play by William
    Shakespeare)
ph **Jonas Gritsius**
m **Dmitri Shostakovich**
    Yuri Yarvet (Lear), Elsa Radzinya

(Goneril), Galina Volchek (Regan),
Valentina Shendrikova (Cordelia), Karl
Sebris(Gloucester), Oleg Dal (Fool)

Shakespeare's monumental late play about
the King who, having misjudged his daughters
and cast the youngest one out, is consigned
to madness and grief in the wilderness, is here
brought to the screen with a memorable mag-
nificence of visual imagery. Unfortunately,
however, the sureness of interpretation that
marked the director's *Hamlet*, is missing here.
This *Lear* (the king played as a merely irascible and neurotic old man, lacking the grandeur of kingship), is seen as an account of
the collapse of a badly governed society. As
such – and necessarily deprived of the original
language – it fails to satisfy many English-
speaking viewers.

King Of The Children

► **Hai Zi Wang**

China 1988 107 mins col
Xi'an Film Studio

d **Chen Kaige**
sc **Chen Kaige, Wan Zhi**
ph **Gu Changwei**
m **Qu Xiaosong**
   **Xie Yuan, Yang Xuewen, Chen Shaohua,
   Zhang Caimei, Xu Guoqing**

In a remote mountain district during the last
stages of the Cultural Revolution, a labourer
(Yuan), sent from the city to cultivate the
fields alongside peasants, is suddenly asked
to become a teacher although he is totally
unqualified. He refuses to follow the official
pedagogic line, and teaches his pupils not
only the three 'R's', but also how to understand the world around them. He is eventually
found out and incurs the wrath of the authorities. Dubbed affectionately as 'Goodbye
Mr Chopsticks', the third film from the 30-
year-old Kaige, visiting scholar at New York
University in 1988, has a great deal of intelligence, freshness and charm, with attractively
conceived locations. However, many of the
elements of the education it attacks, such as
the diligent copying of every character in a
dictionary, may be lost on Occidental audiences; certain situations seem synthetic and
the pace is rather slack at times.

Kings Of The Road

► **Im Lauf Der Zeit**

W. Germany 1976 176 mins bw
Wim Wenders Produktion

d **Wim Wenders**
sc **Wim Wenders**
ph **Robby Müller, Martin Shäfer**
m **Improved Sound Ltd/Axel Linstädt**
   **Rüdiger Vogler, Hanns Zischler, Liza
   Kreuzer, Rudolf Schündler, Marquard
   Böhm**

Robert (Zischler), fleeing his family, crashes
his Volkswagen into the river where Bruno
(Vogler), an itinerant film projector mechanic,
has parked his pantechnicon. Bruno offers
Robert a ride and they travel along the border
between East and West Germany for over a
week on the repair circuit. 'The Yanks have
colonized our subconscious,' says one of the
German friends in this leisurely (the original
title translates as 'in the course of time'),
complex, subtly comic, buddy-buddy road
movie. American rock music dominates their
listening and the image of the empty landscape as seen from the van recalls the wide
open spaces of the USA. Taking a gloomy
view of the present state of German cinema,
the film makes direct references to the silent
films of Fritz Lang and his exile in America.
Exile and borders are used both literally and
metaphorically throughout, effectively encap-
sulated by the use of the wide screen and the
black and white images. But the two leads
remain an enigma, because of the detached
view the director takes of them.

The Kiss Of Mary Pickford

► **Potselui Meri Pikford**

USSR 1927 70 mins bw
Mezhrabpom-RUS/Sovkino

d **Sergei Komarov**
sc **Sergei Komarov, V. Shershenevich**
ph **E. Alekseyev**
m **Silent**
   **Igor Ilinsky, Anna Sudakevich, E.
   Rozenstein, N. Sizova, Ya. Lents**

Dusya (Sudakevich), who works in a film

studio, is loved by Hoha Palkin (Ilinsky), but only has eyes for the stars she idolizes. When Palkin receives a kiss from the visiting Mary Pickford, he becomes an object of worship. The movie, though no more than an extended sketch and light as air, is funny and charming, and boasts an outstanding comedy performance from Ilinsky. It is also of interest that Komarov was a disciple of Kuleshov, whose theories of montage are put into practice here in the use of newsreel footage. Contrary to popular belief, this footage was not culled from archives, but was specially shot by the makers of the film during the 1926 visit to Moscow of Mary and her husband Douglas Fairbanks Sr.

► **Klassenverhältnisse**   see   Class Relations

► **Kleider Machen Leute** see Clothes Make The Man

The Knife

► **Het Mes**

Netherlands 1960 90 mins bw
Nederlandse Filmproductie
Maatschappij(Rotterdam)

d   **Fons Rademakers**
sc **Hugo Claus**
ph **Eduard J.R. Van Der Enden**
m   **Pim Jacobs**
    Reitze Van Der Linden, Ellen Vogel, Paul Cammermans, Marie-Louise Videc, Mia Goossen

During a school vacation, Thomas (Van Der Linden), 13 and fatherless, steals an oriental knife from an exhibition. His tutor, Oscar (Cammermans), confiscates it but Thomas steals it back, thus precipitating a series of emotional crises, particularly in his relationship with his mother (Vogel), whom he discovers to be locked into a degrading sexual relationship with Oscar. One of Rademakers' earliest films tells its story as a flashback recollection from Thomas, and entirely from his point of view. However, in spite of a convincing picture of Dutch small-town life, an interesting idea, and a startlingly mature

and uncompromising central performance from the boy, the resulting film is somewhat plodding and pedestrian, and the director's attempts at the occasional Bergmanesque sequence tend to come unstuck.

Knife In The Head

► **Messer Im Kopf**

W. Germany 1978 113 mins col
Bioskop-Film/Hallelujah-Film/WDR

d   **Reinhard Hauff**
sc **Peter Schneider**
ph **Frank Brühne**
m   **Irmin Schmidt**
    Bruno Ganz, Angela Winkler, Hans Hönig, Hans Brenner, Udo Samel, Carla Egerer

Biogeneticist Berthold Hoffman (Ganz) is calling for his estranged wife (Winkler) at a Left-wing youth centre when a police raid occurs and he is shot in the head. Waking in hospital, he has lost all memory and physical co-ordination. Against the odds, Hoffman determines to piece himself and his past together, but now has to battle against trumped-up charges of political subversion and murder. Hauff combines the elements of political thriller and psychodrama to explore the nature of human will and to warn against the dangers of a police state in West Germany. Ganz convinces, holding together a piece which, though intriguing, lacks depth and stylistic consistency, and leaves us to guess at the solution to its central mystery.

Knife In The Water

► **Noz W Wodzie**

Poland 1962 94 mins bw
ZRF Kamera

d   **Roman Polanski**
sc **Jerzy Skolimowski, Roman Polanski, Jajub Goldberg**
ph **Jerzy Lipman**
m   **Krzysztof Komeda-Trzcinski**
    Leon Niemczyk, Jolanta Umecka, Zygmunt Malanowicz

A married couple (Niemczyk and Umecka),

on their way to their boat, pick up a handsome freewheeling young man (Malanowicz) and invite him to join them on a sailing trip. The man and the boy struggle for ascendency, competing for the attention of the woman. Polanski, in his only Polish feature, using a spare and subtle style, turns a simple tale of three people on a boat into an absurdist drama of sexual rivalry and the generation gap. The acting of the threesome (Polanski dubbed his own voice for the unprofessional Malanowicz) is excellent, and the film gained an Oscar nomination and the director immediate fame.

Knights Of The Teutonic Order

▶ **Krzyzacy**

Poland   1960   180 mins   col
Studio Unit

d   **Alexsander Ford**
sc **Alexsander Ford, Jerzy Stefan Stawinski**
ph **Mieczyslaw Jahoda**
m   **Kazimierz Serocki**
     Urszula Modrzynska, Grazyna Staniszewska, Andrzej Szalawski

In the middle ages, Poland is invaded by Teutonic knights wishing to convert the people to Christianity, but their cruelty causes the population to take up arms against them. In order to commemorate the 550th anniversary of the Battle of Grunwald, Ford, the distinguished Polish director, was given a large budget to make this epic, wide-screen, colour version of Henryk Sienkiewicz's classic novel. One of the very first Polish period films of the post-war years, it provided a stark contrast to the many intense examinations of the country's contemporary history. This no doubt contributed to its enormous success at home and abroad, apart from its obvious spectacular pictorial qualities.

▶ **Kocár Do Vidne** see Coach To Vienna

▶ **Kohayagawa-Ke No Aki** see End Of Summer, The

▶ **Koks I Kulissen** see Ladies On The Rocks

▶ **Komissar** see Commissar, The

▶ **Komödianten** see Players, The

▶ **Kongbufenzi** see Terrorizer, The

▶ **Kongress Tanzt, Der** see Congress Dances

▶ **Konsequenz, Die** see Consequence, The

▶ **Kontrakt** see Contract, The

▶ **Konyets Sankt-Peterburga** see End Of St Petersburg, The

Korczak

Poland   1990   118 mins   bw
Filmstudio 'Perspektywa'/Regina Ziegler
Filmproduktion (Berlin/ZDF (Mainz)/
Erato Films (Paris)/BBC Films
(London)/Telmar Film International

d   **Andrzej Wajda**
sc **Agnieszka Holland**
ph **Robby Müller**
m   **Wojciech Kilar**
     Wojtek Pszoniak, Ewa Dalkowska, Piotr Kozlowski, Marzena Trybala, Wojciech Klata, Adam Siemion

After the Nazis invade Poland in 1939, Dr Janusz Korczak (Pszoniak), director of a Jewish orphanage, and his assistant Stephania (Dalkowska), are forced to transfer the home to the Warsaw ghetto. When deportation begins to seem inevitable, Korczak, who is outspoken in his criticism of the Nazis, refuses to flee the country or go into hiding. Instead, on 6 August 1942, the doctor and Stephania go with the children on the train to Treblinka. It is fitting that Wajda, himself a Resistance fighter and who made his reputation with his war trilogy, should return to his country's darkest days for what he claimed would be his final film. In a way, however, it seems as though the 64-year-old ailing director and senator of the new Polish People's Republic could not really face up to the tragic consequences of this true story. 'It has been difficult to come to terms with this reality,' says an end title after Wajda has pulled short of showing the children going to the gas chambers by imagining their souls released from the train and able to romp freely in the countryside. He also seems genuinely afraid to get too involved in the subject, and much of the screenplay is left trailing. Nevertheless, the appalling situation comes through with all its attendant heartbreak and Pszoniak makes of the film's hero a sardonic, melancholy and dignified figure. The monochrome photography of Robby Müller perfectly recaptures the time, as remembered through newsreels, as if there were no colour in Europe under the Nazi regime.

▶ **Koritsi Me Ta Mavra, To** see Girl In Black, The

▶ **Körkalen** see Phantom Carriage, The

▶ **Korol Lir** see King Lear

▶ **Korotkie Vstrechi** see Short Encounters

▶ **Korpinpolska** see Raven's Dance

▶ **Koshikei** see Death By Hanging

▶ **Koto** see Twin Sisters Of Kyoto

▶ **Ko To Tamo Peva** see Who's That Singing Over There?

▶ **Kozara** see Hill of Death

▶ **Kradezat Na Praskovi** see Peach Thief, The

▶ **Krajobraz Po Bitwie** see Landscape After Battle

▶ **Kreitzerova Sonata** see Kreutzer Sonata, The

▶ **Krestyaniye** see Peasants

The Kreutzer Sonata

▶ **Kreitzerova Sonata**

USSR 1987 135 mins col
Mosfilm Studio

d Mikhail Schweitzer, Sofia Milkina
sc Mikhail Schweitzer (based on the novel by Leo Tolstoy)
ph Mikhail Agranovitch
m Sofia Gubaidulina
Oleg Yankovsky, Irinia Seleznyova, Alexander Trofimov, Alia Demidova, Alexander Kalyagin, Dmitri Pokrovsky

On a long-distance train Pozdnyshev (Yankovsky) tells a travelling companion (Trofimov) the story of how he came to kill his wife, Lisa (Seleznyova). He charts his rocky marriage – his possessiveness, her boredom and their quarrels. Things come to a head when he suspects the piano-player Lisa of having an affair with a violinist (Pokrovsky) with whom she plays sonatas at soirées. Wanting to be as faithful to Tolstoy as possible, the directors have allowed Oleg Yankovsky, as the wandering man, to tell his sorry tale directly to the camera for much of the time, rather than using a voice-off narration, so that the cutting from the past back to the present dislocates the drama as soon as it gets going. Despite the actor's skill, the technique soon begins to pall (even though the first 25 minutes was cut for British distribution). Some of the stylistic problems of the film might be put down to its having been co-directed, as there seems to be a distinct change in approach about halfway through. The flashbacks in the first half are photographed in sensuous soft-focus lighting to create an art nouveau atmosphere with rather agitated camera movements. The second half is more controlled, realistic and penetrating, although the two protagonists (well played as they are) remain hollow, and the other characters hardly exist, notwithstanding all the Tolstoyan talk.

▶ **Krik** see Cry, The

▶ **Krótki Film O Miłości** see Short Film About Love, A

▶ **Krótki Film O Zabijaniu** see Short Film About Killing, A

▶ **Krzyzacy** see Knights Of The Teutonic Order

Kühle Wampe

▶ **aka Whither Germany?**

Germany 1932 90 mins bw
Praesens-Film

d **Slatan Dudow**
sc **Bertolt Brecht, Ernst Ottwald**
ph **Günther Krampf**
m **Hanns Eisler**
Hertha Thiele, Ernst Busch, Adolf
Fischer, Martin Wolter

During a time of depression and unemployment, the Bönike family is dispossessed of its home and moves to Kühle Wampe, a tent-city outside Berlin. The son commits suicide and the daughter marries a chauffeur who becomes a political activist. The only film that Brecht was involved in that did not distort his intentions was a co-operative venture using actors drawn from the theatre in the principal roles, supported by real workers. A passionate propaganda piece that included ballads in the manner of Brecht's plays, it pulled no punches. Thus the film fell foul of the censors who felt it 'endangered the safety of the state,' not realizing that the true danger was coming in the form of the Nazi party. Eventually, after a court case, it was passed for showing in a cut version. A year later, Brecht and Dudow, both Communists, were in exile. The latter was killed in a car accident in East Germany in 1963 leaving an unfinished film.

▶ **Kukla S Millionami** see Doll With Millions, The

▶ **Kumonosu-Jo** see Throne Of Blood

▶ **Kuroi Ame** see Black Rain

▶ **Kurutta Ippeiji** see Page Of Madness, A

▶ **Kvarteret Korpen** see Raven's End

▶ **Kvinnas Ansikte, En** see Woman's Face, A

▶ **Kvinnodröm** see Journey Into Autumn

▶ **Kvinnorna På Taket** see Women On The Roof, The

▶ **Kvinnors Väntan** see Waiting Women

Kwaidan

Japan 1964 164 mins col
Ninjin Club/Bungei

d **Masaki Kobayashi**
sc **Yoko Mizuki**
ph **Yoshio Miyajima**
m **Tohru Takemitsu**
Rentaro Mikuni, Ganjiro Nakamura,
Katsuo Nakamura, Michiyo Aratama,
Misako Watanabe, Keiko Kishi

Four ghost stories – 'The Black Hair', 'The Woman Of The Snow' (omitted in export prints on first release), 'Hoichi The Fearless' and 'In A Cup Of Tea' – based on tales by Lafcadio Hearn. Although taken from a Western writer, the tales ('kwaidan' means ghost story), peopled with samurais, Buddhist monks and lute players, are told in the haunting imagery derived from Japanese art. Eerie, beautifully composed using the wide screen shape, and somewhat overlong, the Oscar-nominated film took five years to prepare and one to shoot. It was the most expensive Japanese picture to date.

Special Jury Prize Cannes 1965

▶ **Kynighi, I** see Huntsmen, The

▶ **Kyritiko Xyprima** see Windfall In Athens

Lac Aux Dames

France   1934   90 mins   bw
SOPRA

d **Marc Allégret**
sc **Colette**
ph **Jules Kruger**
m **Georges Auric**
   Jean-Pierre Aumont, Simone Simon,
   Michel Simon, Illa Meery, Odette
   Joyeux, Rosine Déréan

An unemployed young engineer (Aumont)
takes a job as a lifesaver and swimming
instructor at a mountain lake resort. There
he gets involved with a rich woman (Déréan),
a mysterious child of nature called Puck
(Simone Simon), and a former girlfriend
(Meery) now turned crook. A Vicki Baum
novel was the basis for this slight but
satisfying romance set among attractive
Tyrolean scenery. It displays Allégret's delicacy of touch and sense of fantasy, and it
made stars of handsome Aumont and the
kittenish Simone Simon, both in their early
twenties.

The Lacemaker

▶ **La Dentellière**

France   1977   107 mins   col
Action/FR3/Citel/Janus

d **Claude Goretta**
sc **Claude Goretta, Pascal Lainé**
ph **Jean Boffety**
m **Pierre Jansen**
   Isabelle Huppert, Yves Beneyton, Florence
   Giorgetti, Anne Marie Düringer

A reticent, young Parisian hairdresser (Huppert) is nicknamed 'Pomme' because she likes
apples. While she is on holiday in Normandy,
with an outgoing friend (Giorgetti), she has
an affair with a university student (Beneyton).
However, back in Paris the gap in class and
education causes a rift and Pomme's breakdown. This discreet, observant study of an
incompatible couple is, like their relationship,
better in Normandy than in Paris, where the
situations, though recognizable, become contrived. Huppert does well to retain our sympathy, despite the obvious loading of the film
in her favour and the irritating passivity of
the role.

Lacombe Lucien

France   1974   137 mins   col
NEF/UPF/Vides/Hallelujah Films

d **Louis Malle**
sc **Louis Malle, Patrick Modiani**
ph **Tonino Delli Colli**
m **Performed by Django Reinhardt, André**
   Claveau, Irène De Trebert
   Pierre Blaise, Aurore Clément, Holger
   Löwenadler, Gilberte Rivet, Jacques
   Rispal, Thérèse Giehse

Lucien (Blaise), a 17-year-old peasant of mean
intelligence and dispossessed of family life,
falls in with the Gestapo, and moves in on
the Horns, a Jewish family in hiding. He
becomes entangled with the daughter, provokes the father's death, saves the girl and
her grandmother from execution and, after
the liberation, is shot. Louis Malle's film was
virtually the first French feature to air the
thorny issue of collaboration without
compromise and, while hailed as a masterpiece in certain circles, gave much offence in
others. The director treats Lucien with cool

objectivity, revealing the banality of his repellent actions. The wartime atmosphere of an occupied provincial town is authentic, and the terrifying dilemma of the Horns, at the mercy of their young captor, is expressed with the subtlety of understanding that distinguishes all Malle's best work. The acting is brilliant, notably from Holger Löwenadler as the once wealthy and fashionable Jewish Parisian tailor whose self-disgust drives him to give himself up to the Nazis.

▶ **Ladies Of The Park** see Dames Du Bois De Boulogne, Les

Ladies On The Rocks

▶ **Koks I Kulissen**

Denmark   1983   110 mins   col
Kommune Film

d   **Christian Braad Thomsen**
sc **Christian Braad Thomsen, Helle Ryslinge, Annemarie Helger**
ph **Dirk Brüel**
m   **Helle Ryslinge**
    Helle Ryslinge, Annemarie Helger, Flemming Quist Møller, Hans Henrik Clemmensen, Gyda Hansen, Aksel Erhardsen

Misse (Ryslinge), single and prone to falling for men who treat her like dirt, and Laura (Helger), married with two children, write and perform a provocative, self-mocking and somewhat risqué cabaret act. One winter, they find a certain personal liberation as they tour the show through Denmark, playing in small venues to bemused and occasionally outraged locals. A sometimes bleak, sometimes funny, and often charming film which clearly beats the feminist drum while accepting its heroines' emotional dependency on men. The claustrophobia of the tacky life on the road is well caught, and the women's act is both good and bad enough to be believable.

▶ **Ladri Di Biciclette** see Bicycle Thieves

▶ **Ladri Di Saponette** see Icicle Thief, The

The Lady From Constantinople

▶ **Sziget A Szárazföldön**

Hungary   1968   76 mins   bw
Mafilm Studio

d   **Judit Elek**
sc **Iván Mándy**
ph **Elemér Ragályi**
    Manyi Kiss (No further cast credits given)

An old lady, living on memories among the cluttered objects from her past, decides to exchange her apartment for a smaller one. She is thus temporarily brought into contact with other people until, resettled, she once again retreats into isolation. In this gem of a film Judit Elek, making her feature debut, builds up a character study and a picture of life in Budapest by the simplest of means: observation of small details. Unlike most Hungarian films seen abroad, it is not a political piece but a study of loneliness and human foibles, given truthful and unsentimental life by one of Hungary's leading stage actresses.

The Lady From The Shanghai Cinema

▶ **A Dama Do Cine Shanghai**

Brazil   1987   115 mins   col
Star/Raiz

d   **Guilherme De Almeida Prado**
sc **Guilherme De Almeida Prado**
ph **José Roberto Eliezer**
m   **Hermelino Nader**
    Antonio Fagundes, Maitê Proença, Paulo Villaça, José Lewgoy

Lucas (Fagundes), an estate agent, wanders into a cinema during a heatwave and picks up a mysterious married woman (Proença). Her even more mysterious husband subsequently buys a white-elephant apartment which Lucas has been trying to sell, and he moves into a hotel across the street where he can keep an eye on her. Lucas and the woman have an affair and their association leads him into a web of corruption and violence. Prado's latterday *film noir*, although not without atmosphere and the occasional intriguing idea, is a complicated pastiche on the Chandleresque school of plotting. Unfortunately, the film simply isn't clever enough to get away with it. The protagonists, particularly Lucas who becomes the Philip Marlowe figure in order to clear himself of murder, are boring and unattractive, the story is muddled to the point where it becomes crude parody rather than clever pastiche, and the film is unable to hold one's interest other than sporadically.

▶ **Ladykiller Of Rome, The** see Assassin, The

Lady Macbeth Of Mtsensk

▶ **Katerina Ismailova**

USSR 1966 116 mins col
Lenfilm

d **Mikhail Shapiro**
sc **Mikhail Shapiro (libretto: Dimitri Shostakovich, A. Preis)**
ph **Rostislav Davydov, V. Ponamarev**
m **Dimitri Shostakovich (conducted by Konstantin Simeonov) Galina Vishnevskaya (Katerina Ismailova), Artem Inozemtsev (Sergei, sung by V. Trepyak), Alexandrovich Sokolov (Boris, sung by A. Verdernikov), Nikolai Boyarksi (Zinovi, sung by V. Radziyevski), T. Gavirolova (Sonyetka, sung by V. Reka)**

Katerina, a peasant who has married into the *petit bourgeoisie*, is bored by her dull husband, oppressed by the codes to which she must subscribe and ill-treated by her father-in-law, Boris, whose bullying conceals his lust for her. She takes Sergei, a workman, as her lover, but Boris discovers the affair and has him flogged almost to death. Katerina poisons the old man, the first of a series of violent deaths that culminates in her own. Shostakovich's powerful opera, blending passion and social critique (Wajda used the same story for his *Siberian Lady Macbeth*), is given a gripping and naturalistic screen treatment by Shapiro, who capitalizes on its episodic structure to dramatic effect and utilizes outdoor locations that vividly capture the atmosphere. Vishnevskaya sings and acts superbly and the rest of the cast is well chosen and given

appropriate vocal doubles. Only a periodic discrepancy in synchronization mars an otherwise excellent contribution to opera as film.

The Lady Of The Camellias

▶ **La Dame Aux Camélias**

France 1981 121 mins col
Gaumont/Les Films Du Losange/FR-3/Opera Films

d **Mauro Bolognini**
sc **Jean Aurenche, Vladimir Pozner**
ph **Ennio Guarnieri**
m **Ennio Morricone Isabelle Huppert, Gian Maria Volonté, Bruno Ganz, Fabrizio Bentivoglio, Fernando Rey, Yann Babilée**

The rise and fall of Parisian courtesan Alphonsine Duplessis. This version (reputedly the 22nd), using flashback as Dumas *fils* rehearses his play, tells the story, not of tragic, romantic Marguerite Gauthier *à la* Garbo, but of the real-life woman on whom she was modelled. This Lady of The Camellias is conceived, and played by Huppert, as tough, ambitious and grasping. She comes complete with a drug-addicted father (Volonté) and a husband (Ganz), as well as a protector (Rey). The magnificent art direction and costumes recreate the lavishness of the Second Empire in all its decadent glory, and Bolognini directs with fluency and commendable lack of sentimentality.

The Lady Without Camellias

▶ **(US: Camille Without Camellias)**
▶ **La Signora Senza Camelie**

Italy 1953 105 mins bw
ENIC

d **Michelangelo Antonioni**
sc **Michelangelo Antonioni, Suso Cecchi D'Amico, Francesco Maselli, P.M. Pasinetti**
ph **Enzo Serafin**
m **Giovanni Fusco Lucia Bosé, Andrea Cecchi, Gino Cervi, Ivan Desny, Alain Cuny**

A shopgirl (Bosé) becomes a starlet at Cinecittà, and marries her producer (Cecchi), who pushes her beyond her talent in the role of Joan of Arc. Her failure as a star reduces her again to playing ingénues in tatty films. Antonioni's third feature accurately evokes the less glamorous side of the Italian film industry. As in his following picture, *The Girl Friends*, he is concerned with the position of and pressures on women in society. The beautiful Lucia Bosé shows great sensitivity in a role originally intended for Gina Lollobrigida.

► **Lady With The Dog, The** see Lady With The Little Dog, The

The Lady With The Little Dog

► **(US: The Lady With The Dog)**

► **Dama S Sobachkoi**

USSR   1959   90 mins   bw
Lenfilm

d   **Josef Heifits**
sc   **Josef Heifits**
ph   **Andrei Moskvin, D. Meschiev**
m   **Jiří Sternwald**
     Iya Savvina, Alexei Batalov, Ala Chostakova, N. Alisova

In the seaside resort of Yalta at the turn of the century, a married Moscow banker (Batalov) meets and falls in love with a beautiful woman (Savvina in an impressive debut), the unhappily married wife of a local petty official. She is on holiday alone, except for the company of her little dog. They continue their affair secretly in Moscow. The sensitive low-key direction subtly evokes the prose of Chekhov's short love story, and the contrast between Yalta in summer (brass bands, windy promenade *et al*), and Moscow in winter is vividly conveyed, reflecting the illicit lovers' psychology. This remains one of the most admired adaptations of Chekhov, although Heifits directed two others almost as good, *In The Town Of S* and *Duel*.

Special Jury Prize Cannes 1960

► **Lalka** see Doll, The

► **Lancelot Du Lac** see Lancelot Of The Lake

Lancelot Of The Lake

► **aka The Grail**

► **Lancelot Du Lac**

► **aka Le Graal**

France   1974   85 mins   col
Mara-Films/Laser Production/RTF

d   **Robert Bresson**
sc   **Robert Bresson**
ph   **Pasquale De Santis**
m   **Philippe Sarde**
     Luc Simon, Laura Duke Condominas, Humbert Balsan, Vladimir Antolek-Oresek, Patrick Bernard

The Knights of the Round Table, their numbers heavily depleted by death, return to King Arthur's court (Antolek-Oresek) after a long, bloody and fruitless quest for the Holy Grail. Their rituals become debased as they are riven by jealousies and rivalries, with Lancelot (Simon) and his relationship with Guinevere (Condominas) at the centre of their strife. The film's rich and burnished colours often stand in for language to powerful effect, and there is little romance about these knights, who are viewed through Bresson's characteristically austere eye. The actors play with a flat detachment that is curiously compelling. This is a uniquely original and hypnotic study of the loss of spirituality, caught in distinctive images that are at once stark and sensuous, with arrestingly realistic sounds, such as the clanking of armour, to accompany them.

The Land

► **aka The Earth**

► **El Ard**

Egypt   1968   130 mins   col
O.G.E.C.

d   **Youssef Chahine**
sc   **Hassan Fouad**
ph   **Abdel Halim Nasr**
m   **Ali Ismaïl**
     Nagwa Ibrahim, Mahmoud El Meligui,

Ezzat El Alaili, Yehia Chahine, Hamid Ahmed

A young peasant fights against rapacious property owners who are attempting to force him into the sale of his land. At first glance this would seem to be an old-fashioned tale of simple rural life, touching on the lure of urban attraction that threatens the peasants and featuring a pretty young girl who is much in demand. However, this impression is soon superseded by Chahine's mature and penetrating analysis of exploitation and social divisiveness, interpreted through powerful images and incidents that break the traditional view of the peasant as the 'eternal damned of the earth'. *The Land* subtly sows the seeds of a political thesis about the necessity for solidarity which Chahine would expand and develop in a trilogy composed of this film, *The Choice* (1970), and, most notably, *The Sparrow* (1973).

Land And Sons

▶ **Land Og Synir**

    Iceland 1980 94 mins col
    Isfilm

d **Ágúst Gudmundsson**
sc **Ágúst Gudmundsson**
ph **Sigurdur Sverrir Pálsson**
m **Gunnar Reynir Sveinsson**
    Sigurdur Sigurjónsson, Jón
    Sigurbjórnsson, Gudny Ragnarsdóttir,
    Jónas Tryggvason

In 1937, in a remote valley in northern Iceland, the rural landscape is glorious, but life is hard and lonely and the young are starting to drift south to Reykjavik. This leads to bitter conflict between a father and son, even though the latter (sensitively played by Sigurdur Sigurbjórnsson) is forcing himself to leave his beloved land and animals in the quest for future prospects. This is a rare opportunity to see a film from Iceland, a tiny country overshadowed by its better-known Scandinavian neighbours. Made for only £70,000, it was a tremendous success at home and recouped its costs in under two months – deservedly so, for it is refreshingly unsentimental, truthful and moving in its presentation of a real and painful problem and in its evocation of man's relationship with nature.

Land In Anguish

▶ **aka Earth Entranced**
▶ **Terra Em Transe**

    Brazil 1967 115 mins bw
    Mapa

d **Glauber Rocha**
sc **Glauber Rocha**
ph **Luiz Carlos Barreto**
m **Sergio Ricardo, Verdi, Carlos Gomes,**
    Villa Lobos
    Jardel Filho, José Lewgoy, Glauce Rocha,
    Paulo Autran, Paulo Gracindo, Danuza
    Leão

A journalist and poet (Filho) is killed by the police as he and his mistress (Rocha) drive from the headquarters of Vieira (Lewgoy), the governor of a province of El Dorado. As he dies, he recalls his shifting political involvement from support of Diaz (Autran), a mystic and reactionary politician, to Vieira's popular cause. Rocha, the leading member of the Brazilian *Cinema Novo* movement, launched into a vigorous attack on the 'permanent state of madness' that his country seemed to be living in since the military *coup d'état* of 1964. In his denunciation, he calls on every cinematic weapon at his disposal – shock montage, jump cuts, an ironic use of the samba and other Brazilian rhythms and a film-within-a-film technique. Some of the cultural and political references may be obscure to non-Latin Americans, but there is no mistaking the power with which they are delivered. Not surprisingly, the film was condemned in Brazil and banned outright for a period.

▶ **Land Of Desire, The** see Ship Bound For India, A

Land Of Promise

▶ **Ziemia Obiecana**

    Poland 1974 178 mins col
    Film Polski

d **Andrzej Wajda**
sc **Andrzej Wajda**
ph **Witold Sobociński, Waclaw Dybowski,**
    Edward Klosínski
m **Wojciech Kilar**

Daniel Olbrychski, Wojciech Pszoniak,
Anna Nehrebecka, Andrzej Seweryn

Three industrialists representing different eth-
nic groups in Poland – a Pole (Olbrychski),
a German (Seweryn) and a Jew (Pszoniak) –
build a textile factory in Lodz at the turn of
the century, but they encounter problems with
the overworked, underpaid workers. Over-
directed and under-characterized, this saga,
based on a novel by Nobel Prize-winner Wla-
dyslav Reymont, nevertheless vividly depicts
a society on the edge of change. The portrayal
of a ruthless Jew caused some Jewish groups
in the USA mistakenly to accuse the film of
anti-Semitism.

▶ Land Og Synir see Land And Sons

Landru

▶ aka Bluebeard

France   1962   115 mins   col
CC Champion/Rome-Paris Films

d   Claude Chabrol
sc Claude Chabrol, Françoise Sagan
ph Jean Rabier
m   Pierre Jansen
    Charles Denner, Michèle Morgan,
    Danielle Darrieux, Hildegard Knef,
    Juliette Mayniel, Stéphane Audran,
    Catherine Rouvel

The true story of the notorious Landru, who
charmed a number of unsuspecting women,
and then murdered them. After four flops in
a row, Chabrol hoped that this period piece
in colour, with a starry female cast, would be
a commercial hit, but it failed to deliver the
goods. No wonder! Although this stylized
treatment of the same subject as Chaplin's
Monsieur Verdoux (1947) had much of Chabrol's characteristic acid wit, Landru (Denner
with bald dome, bushy eyebrows and black
beard) was a cartoon figure, and the women
were treated with neither sympathy nor depth.

Landscape After Battle

▶ Krajobraz Po Bitwie

Poland   1970   11 mins   col
Film Polski

d   Andrzej Wajda
sc Andrzej Wajda, Andrzej Brzozowski
ph Zygmunt Samosluk
m   Zygmunt Konieczny
    Daniel Olbrychski, Stanislawa Celínska,
    Tadeusz Janczar

A group of concentration camp survivors
await repatriation in a disused barracks in
Germany in 1945. Two members of the group
have a love affair until the Jewish girl is
accidentally killed by an American guard.
The first of Wajda's series of works based on
Polish literary classics was taken from the
stories of Tadeusz Borowski, an Auschwitz
survivor who committed suicide in 1959 aged
29. The film, made in a non-realist, lyrical
style using subdued colour, not only portrays
a tender, fateful love story, but raises a polemical voice on the ambiguity of Polish
behaviour during the war.

Landscape In The Mist

▶ Topio Stin Omichli

Greece   1988   125 mins   col
Greek Film Centre/Greek Television/
Paradis Film (France)/RAI (Italy)

d   Theo Angelopoulos
sc Theo Angelopoulos, Tonino Guerra,
    Thanassis Valtinos
ph Giorgos Arvanitis
m   Eleni Karaindrou
    Michalis Zeke, Tania Palaiologou,
    Stratos Tzortzoglou, Eva Kotamanidou,
    Alika Georgouli

Two illegitimate children, Voula (Palaiolo-
gou) and her young brother Alexandros
(Zeke), having been told the lie that their
father lives in Germany, leave their mother
and board an express train to find him. Having no tickets, they are put off at an empty
station and the police are informed, but they
run away and are befriended by Orestes
(Tzortzoglou), a young man who works with
his grandfather's troupe of travelling players.
En route again, the pair are picked up by a
truck driver who rapes Voula before they
finally reach the German border. The Greece
of Angelopoulos is a cold and bleak place in
which unfulfilled people search for some
meaning to their existence. Although as solemn, elliptical, symbolic and snail-paced as

usual, this voyage has more poignancy and is more approachable than, say, *The Beekeeper*, the director's previous film, because of having children at its centre. As a result, the moments of happiness are more precious and the cruelty towards them more painful than if they had been adult protagonists. But, although beautifully photographed and played, especially by the pubescent girl, the film often seems perversely to exclude any brightness that might interfere with its stark vision.

Land Without Bread

▶ **Las Hurdes**

▶ **aka Terre Sans Pain**

Spain 1932 27 mins bw
Ramon Acin

d **Luis Buñuel**
sc **Luis Buñuel**
ph **Eli Lotar**
m **Brahms**

The 8,000 inhabitants of Las Hurdes, a remote and poverty-stricken area of Spain, try to survive on the barren land. After his two surrealist masterpieces, *Un Chien Andalou* and *L'Âge D'Or*, Buñuel turned towards social realism with this stark documentary on the poverty of the peasants. The searing and sombre commentary and photography, eschewing any rhetoric, were so effective in revealing this festering social evil, that the film was banned in Spain. Buñuel did not make another in his native land until *Viridiana* 29 years later.

▶ **Lao Jing** see Old Well, The

▶ **Lásky Jedné Plavovlásky** see Blonde In Love, A

The Last Battle

▶ **Le Dernier Combat**

France 1983 92 mins bw
Les Films Du Loup

d **Luc Besson**
sc **Luc Besson, Pierre Jolivet**
ph **Carlo Varini**

m **Eric Serra**
Pierre Jolivet, Jean Bouise, Fritz Wepper, Jean Reno

After a nuclear war, a man surviving on the top of a tower block buried by sand, makes contact with an aging doctor and a girl, and is set upon by a homicidal swordsman. Twenty-three-year-old Besson's impressive first feature is a fable of survival, played out against stark and striking black-and-white CinemaScope images of a wasteland of abandoned buildings and vehicles. However, it runs on lines familiar to apocalyptic films, and the decision to dispense with dialogue doesn't appear sufficiently justified.

The Last Bend

▶ **Le Dernier Tournant**

France 1939 90 mins bw
Gladiator Films

d **Pierre Chenal**
sc **Charles Spaak, Henri Torres**
ph **Claude Renoir, Christian Matras**
m **Jean Wiener**
Michel Simon, Fernand Gravey, Corinne Luchaire, Florence Marly, Robert Le Vigan

A young woman (Luchaire), living an isolated existence in the French Alps, falls for a handsome stranger (Gravey) with whom she plots to kill her elderly husband (Simon). The first film adaptation of James M. Cain's novel *The Postman Always Rings Twice* is remarkably faithful to the original though transposed to France. Chenal directs with vigour, and there is excellent character work from Simon and from Le Vigan as the nasty blackmailer. Only the lovers lack the eroticism one finds in the other three versions (two from Hollywood, and Italy's *Ossessione*).

The Last Bridge

▶ **Die Letzte Brücke**

Austria 1954 104 mins bw
Cosmopol Film

d **Helmut Käutner**
sc **Helmut Käutner, Norbert Kunze**
ph **Fred Kollhanek**

m   Carl De Groof
    Maria Schell, Bernhard Wicki, Barbara
    Rutting, Carl Mohner, Horst Haechler

Maria Schell portrays a German doctor who
is captured by Yugoslav Partisans (led by
Wicki) during World War II and forced to
tend their wounded. Her initial resistance to
co-operating is gradually overcome with her
growing realization that a suffering Yugoslav
is no different from a suffering German. A
very simple plot, beautifully paced and carefully controlled, reveals a strong anti-war
theme in this moving and intelligent, if slightly
sanitized movie. Interestingly, in view of Yug-
oslav-German animosity, it was filmed on
location in Yugoslavia with the co-operation
of that country's film trades union.

    Special Jury Prize Cannes 1954
    Best Actress (Maria Schell) Cannes 1954

The Last Day Of Winter

▶ **Zuihou Yige Dongri**

    China   1986   92 mins   col
    Xiaoxiang Film Studio

d   Wu Ziniu
sc Qiao Xuezhu
ph Yang Weidong
m   Wang Xilin
    Li Ling, Tao Zhergu, Hong Yuzhou,
    Zhang Xiaomin, Wu Meng

Three travellers arrive at a bleak prison camp
in central China to visit their relatives, incarcerated there for various crimes which are
depicted in flashback. Naturally, the meetings
and separations are charged with emotion.
The director, a contemporary of Chen (*Yellow
Earth*) Kaige and Tian (*Horse Thief*) Zhuangzhuang at the Peking Film Institute in
1978, managed to make this film despite having had his previous work, *Dove Tree*, about
an affair between a Chinese soldier and a
Vietnamese nurse, permanently banned. Like
the work of his former classmates, the film
breaks new ground in its subject matter – the
first to deal with a Chinese gulag – and its
epic use of the wide screen. Some of the
stylized flashbacks are more compelling than
others and the music is rather too insistent,
but the images of shaven-headed prisoners
jogging through the snow and details such as
a woman inmate being excessively grateful

for a gift of sanitary towels from her brother,
add up to a memorable experience.

Last Images Of The Shipwreck

▶ **Ultimas Imagenes Del Naufragio**

    Argentina   1989   129 mins   col
    Cinequanon/TVE Television Española

d   Eliseo Subielo
sc Eliseo Subielo
ph Alberto Basail
m   Extracts from Bach, Verdi, José G. and
    O. Cátulo Castillo
    Lorenzo Quinteros, Noemi Frenkel, Hugo
    Soto, Pablo Brichta, Sara Benitez, Andres
    Tiengo, Alicia Aller, Alfredo Stuart

Roberto (Quinteros), a married insurance
salesman and frustrated novelist, stops a
woman from throwing herself under a train.
He later discovers that the woman, Estela
(Frenkel) is a prostitute, and he offers to pay
her in return for details about her life to use
in his novel. After meeting her three socially
outcast brothers (Soto, Brichta, Tiengo),
Roberto is drawn deeper and deeper into the
life of the underworld and becomes increasingly attracted to Estela. The subject of artists' control over their material has always
been a tricky one for film-makers, but even
the best results, such as Fellini's *8½* (1963),
have a tendency to topple into pretentious-
ness. Played against the tragic background of
Argentinian history ('the apocalypse brigade'), Subielo's Pirandellian exploration into
the creative impulse manages, on the whole,
to retain its balance. It is most successful
when exploring the prostitute's family with
all its pathologies ('We're a family that's
always been in movement...but backwards.'),
and quirkily viewing the low life of Buenos
Aires. Less rewarding are the overloaded
dream images of plastic-shrouded subway
passengers and Christ descending from the
cross to eat some salami, as well as a misbelief
that slowness of pace equals profundity.

The Last Laugh

▶ **Der Letzte Mann**

    Germany   1924   73 mins   bw
    UFA

d **F.W. Murnau**
sc **Carl Mayer**
ph **Karl Freund**
m **Silent**
    Emil Jannings, Max Hiller, Maly
    Delschaft, Hans Unterkirchen

An old doorman at a luxury hotel, proud of his work and uniform, is reduced to being a lavatory attendant. The film that made Murnau's international reputation is mainly remarkable for being told without any intertitles. The camera tracking through hotel corridors, the distortions, the subjective shots, the drunken dream sequence, and Jannings' expressive performance made words superfluous. The unconvincing happy ending was tacked on at the insistence of producer Eric Pommer to make the piece more commercial.

The Last Metro

▶ **Le Dernier Métro**

France 1980 131 mins col
Les Films Du Carrosse/Andrea/SEDIF/
TF1/SFP

d **François Truffaut**
sc **François Truffaut, Suzanne Schiffman,**
    Jean-Claude Grumberg
ph **Nestor Almendros**
m **Georges Delerue**
    Catherine Deneuve, Gérard Depardieu,
    Jean Poiret, Heinz Bennent, Andréa
    Ferréol

In occupied Paris in 1942, a Jewish manager (Bennent) of a Montmartre theatre goes into hiding in the cellar of the building, while his wife (Deneuve) runs the company. This includes a member of the Resistance (Depardieu) and a homosexual director (Poiret), who are also in danger of being arrested by the Nazis. Truffaut stated that the film fulfilled three of his ambitions: to re-create on film the climate of the Occupation, to show the backstage life of the theatre, and to provide Deneuve with the role of a responsible woman. The film achieves all three, adeptly capturing the mood of the period and life in the theatre, although it could have delved deeper into the psychology of the characters, including that of the wife. There have certainly been better films about the time, but

few more entertaining and exciting or with such a top-notch cast.

The Last Millionaire

▶ **Le Dernier Milliardaire**

France 1934 90 mins bw
Pathé Natan

d **René Clair**
sc **René Clair**
ph **Rudolph Maté**
m **Maurice Jaubert**
    Max Dearly, Renée Saint-Cyr, Marthe
    Mellot, Raymond Cordy

A small European kingdom is saved from bankruptcy by the return of Banco (Dearly), a native-born millionaire who gets engaged to Princess Isabelle (Saint-Cyr) and runs the country, even though a knock on the head makes him temporarily insane. The last of Clair's features in France for 13 years was howled down by French Fascists at its first showing, presumably because they knew that the film had failed to get German financial backing. Although the comedy is a trifle strained and the decor rather airless, it is still an enjoyable Ruritanian fantasy, hardly more political than the Marx Brothers' *Duck Soup* the previous year.

The Last Stage

▶ **Ostatni Etap**

Poland 1948 120 mins bw
Film Polski

d **Wanda Jakubowska**
sc **Wanda Jakubowska, Gerda Schneider**
ph **Borys Monastryrski**
m **Roman Palester**
    Wanda Bartóvna, Huguette Faget,
    Barbara Drapinska, Stanislaw Zaczyk,
    Tatjana Gorecka

In the 'hospital' in the women's section of Auschwitz, Marta (Drapinska), a prisoner who acts as interpreter, sees others in the 'last stage', the final journey to the gas chambers and crematoria. As both Jakubowska and Schneider were former inmates of the notorious concentration camp, this searing, uncompromising testament has an immediacy and personal involvement missing from many later films on the subject. The documentary-like reconstruction of the day to day 'life' is even more affecting for being presented in a calm, almost matter-of-fact manner, rather than wallowing in degradation. The startling opening shots of the thinly-clad, shaven-haired barefoot women, the birth of a baby, sickness and death, and the prison orchestra playing Richard Strauss and Franz Lehar as the victims march to their fate, made an even greater impact when the film appeared in 1948. It also drew attention to a re-awakening Polish film industry.

The Last Supper

▶ **La Ultima Cena**

Cuba   1976   110 mins   col
Cuban Film Institute

d   **Tomás Gutiérrez Alea**
sc **Tomás Gutiérrez Alea, Tomás Gonzalez, Maria Eugenia Haya**
ph **Mario Garcia Joya**
m   **Leo Brouwer**
    Nelson Villagra, Silvano Rey, Luis Alberto García, José Antonio Rodriguez

A plantation owner casts 12 of his slaves to play the apostles in a re-creation of The Last Supper during Holy Week, urging them momentarily to forget their shackles, but when they revolt all but one are beheaded. This 'allegory of Christian liberalism', as the director describes it, has much in common with Buñuel's *Viridiana* (1961) in its content and caustic wit. Filmed in muted colours with a powerful black cast, the picture belabours its message in the final sequence, a symbol of the coming Socialist Cuba.

The Last Ten Days

▶ **aka The Last Ten Days of Adolf Hitler**

▶ **Der Letzte Akt**

Austria   1955   109 mins   bw
Cosmopol

d   **G.W. Pabst**
sc **Fritz Harbeck**
ph **Günther Anders, Hannes Staudinger**
m   **Erwin Haletz**

Oskar Werner, Albin Skoda, Lotte Tobisch, Willy Krause, Helga Kennedy-Dohrn

In the bunker, Hitler (Skoda) and his staff await the end. As part of his atonement for having made three historical films under the Nazis, Pabst brought his jaundiced eye to bear on Erich Maria Remarque's account of Hitler's final hours. Much of it is as heavy as a jackboot, but there are glimmerings of the pre-war Expressionist master at work, particularly in the mad-dance orgy near the end.

▶ **Last Ten Days of Adolf Hitler, The** see Last Ten Days, The

▶ **Last Vacation, The** see Dernières Vacances, Les

The Last Waltz

▶ **Der Letzte Walzer**

Germany   1934   94 mins   bw
Panorama

d   **Georg Jacoby**
sc **Dr Max Wallner, Georg F. Weber**
ph **Carl Drews**
m   **Oscar Straus**
    Camilla Horn, Ivan Petrovitch, Ernst Dumcke, Adele Sandrock, Max Guelsdorf, Hans Junkermann

A young couple in 19th-century St Petersburg overcome the wicked machinations of a Grand Duke and find happiness together. Based on Oscar Straus's stage operetta, this Ruritanian-style romance, one of a plethora of German screen musicals of the 1930s, was notable for its rich portrayal of the lifestyle of the Russian nobility. Glamorous leads (Horn and Petrovitch) and well-paced direction resulted in entertaining escapist fare.

▶ **Last Will Of Dr Mabuse, The** see Testament Of Dr Mabuse, The

The Last Woman

▶ **L'Ultima Donna**

▶ **aka La Dernière Femme**

Italy/France   1976   112 mins   col

Jacques Roitfeld/Flaminia

d **Marco Ferreri**
sc **Marco Ferreri, Rafael Azcona**
ph **Luciano Tovoli**
m **Philippe Sarde**
   **Gérard Depardieu, Ornella Muti, Michel
   Piccoli, Renato Salvatori, Zouzou,
   Nathalie Baye, Carole Lepers**

When the wife (Zouzou) of a young French
engineer (Depardieu) walks out on him and
their baby to join her friend (Lepers) in the
feminist movement, he takes up with an unlib-
erated woman (Muti), but feels threatened
when she and the wife plot to take his son
from him. For some of the time there is
amusement to be had from the role reversal
satire, and from Depardieu as the bemused
phallocrat unable to deal with women
asserting themselves. What, alas, is less pleasantly remembered, is the crude symbolism of
the ending when the hero castrates himself
with an electric carving knife.

Last Year At Marienbad

▶ **L'Année Dernière À Marienbad**

   France 1961 94 mins bw
   Terra/Tamara/Cormoran/Precitel/Como
   /Argos/Cinetel/Silver/Cineriz

d **Alain Resnais**
sc **Alain Robbe-Grillet**
ph **Sacha Vierny**
m **Francis Seyrig**
   **Delphine Seyrig, Giorgio Albertazzi,
   Sacha Pitöeff, Françoise Bertin**

In a vast baroque mansion with geometrically
designed gardens, a man (Albertazzi) tries to
convince a woman guest (Seyrig) that they
had had an affair the year before, and that
she should leave the man (Pitöeff) she is with.
Rejecting a chronological structure, this min-
gling of memory and imagination, past and
present, desire and fulfilment, can now be
seen as one of the cinema's most haunting
and erotic poems. The cryptic screenplay, the
stylized playing, the organ music, the tracking
shots down endless corridors, the dazzling
decor by Jacques Saulnier, and the mysteriously beautiful Seyrig (in her first feature) in
extravagant gowns and feathers, are all unforgettable.

Best Film Venice 1961

Late Autumn

▶ **Akibiyori**

   Japan 1960 125 mins col
   Shochiku

d **Yasujiro Ozu**
sc **Yasujiro Ozu, Kogo Noda**
ph **Yushun Atsuta**
m **Kojun Saito**
   **Setsuko Hara, Yoko Tsukasa, Chishu
   Ryu, Mariko Okada**

A widowed mother (Hara) attempts to find a
husband for her daughter (Tsukasa), but the
daughter mistakenly believes that her mother
wishes to remarry. 'I wanted to show life,
which seems complex, reveal itself as simple,'
Ozu stated about his third film on the theme
of arranged marriages. As always, Ozu has
made a film of great formal beauty, rich in
humour and emotion.

Late Chrysanthemums

▶ **Bangiku**

   Japan 1954 117 mins bw
   Toho

d **Mikio Naruse**
sc **Sumie Tanaka, Toshiro Ide**
ph **Masao Tamai**
m **Ichiro Saito**
   **Haruko Sugimura, Yuko Mochizuki,
   Chikako Hosokawa, Ken Uehara, Sadako
   Sawamura**

Four retired geishas contemplate their past
lives and their continuing unequal relationships with men. One attempts suicide, and
old lovers turn up. A subtle and detailed
tragicomic character study adapted from
three Fumiko Hayashi stories, the film gets
its effects by using an unfussy camera style
but with many set-ups per sequence. As in
most of Naruse's films, the women (superbly
played) suffer a kind of defeat but nevertheless
continue to fight on.

The Late Mathias Pascal

▶ **(US: The Living Dead Man)**
▶ **Feu Mathias Pascal**

   France 1924 169 mins bw

Albatros

d **Marcel L'Herbier**
sc **Marcel L'Herbier**
ph **René Guichard, Bourgassof, Jean Letort**
m **Silent**
   Ivan Mosjoukine (Ivan Mozhukhin),
   Michel Simon, Marcelle Pradot, Pierre
   Batcheff, Douvan, Lois Moran

Reading about his own death in the newspaper, Mathias Pascal (Mosjoukine) decides to take advantage of the situation and leave his family to start a new life. When he tires of the deception, he returns to face his past. The great Russian emigré actor Mosjoukine (as he was known in France), gained his international reputation as the cynical observer of life at the centre of L'Herbier's lively, witty, expressionistic version of Pirandello's ironic story. It was the last major work as art director by Cavalcanti. Assisted by Lazare Meerson, he devised sets and lighting that were influenced by German films of the time. Michel Simon, in one of his very earliest films, puts in an amusing appearance.

The Late Mathias Pascal

▶ **L'Homme De Nulle Part**

France 1937 98 mins bw
General Productions/Ala-Colosseum

d **Pierre Chenal**
sc **Roger Vitrac, Armand Salacrou, Pierre Chenal, Christian Stengel**
ph **Joseph-Louis Mundwiller, André Bac**
m **Jacques Ibert**
   Pierre Blanchar, Isa Miranda, Ginette Leclerc, Robert Le Vigan, Palau

When a henpecked Italian provincial (Blanchar) is mistakenly believed to be dead, he moves to Rome, assumes a new identity and falls in love with his landlord's daughter (Miranda). Unlike Marcel L'Herbier's stylized, silent, studio-shot 1924 version of the Pirandello story, Chenal's was filmed on location in Italy. It turned out to be a delightful, ironic comedy with an excellent script (some of it reflecting the influence of surrealist writer Vitrac) and fine performances, especially from Blanchar, very different from his Raskolnikov in Chenal's *Crime And Punishment* two years previously.

Latent Image

▶ **Imagen Latente**

Chile 1987 92 mins col
Chilenos-Ictus Prod.

d **Pablo Perelman**
sc **Pablo Perelman**
ph **Beltran Garcia**
m **Jaime De Aguirre**
   Bastian Bodenhofer, Maria Isquerdo, Gonzalo Robles, Gloria Munchmeyer, Elena Muñoz

In Santiago in 1983 an advertising photographer (Bodenhofer) begins a belated search for his younger brother who 'disappeared' in 1975, two years after the military coup. Unlike his brother, he has never been involved in politics, but he is prodded by the scorn of his politically active wife (Isquerdo) into reopening his brother's case. His actions bring him into greater contact with the political underground and he begins to fear that he may suffer the same fate as his brother. Like the central character, the spectator of this film (banned in Chile) is drawn from a comfortable position into a world where people live in constant fear of the barbaric government's cruelty. Most of the brutality is suggested by imaginings, memories and photographs, making it even more palpable than a direct depiction of torture might be. With the rather passive protagonist's voice-over and the way in which characters are seen through windows, screens and mirrors, the director creates a certain distance from the events, allowing the cool contemplation of the personal sufferings from political oppression. Thus a certain obliqueness creeps in, a latent image, but the film is no less powerful a film for that.

Late Spring

▶ **Banshun**

Japan 1949 108 mins bw
Ofuna

d **Yasujiro Ozu**
sc **Yasujiro Ozu, Kogo Noda**
ph **Yuharu Atsuta**
m **Senji Ito**
   Setsuko Hara, Chisu Ryu, Haruko Sugimura, Jun Usami

A widowed father (Ryu) lives happily with his daughter (Hara), who is somewhat past the usual marrying age. Feeling he is keeping her from matrimony, he leads her to believe that he is to remarry in order to free her. This was one of Ozu's own favourites, and he would return to the theme again and again over the next decade. (He never married and lived with his mother all his life.) It also marked the return of his screenwriter Noda after 14 years, and the beginning of the director's mature style: a simplicity of story, structure and tempo, with short incisive exteriors punctuating the domestic scenes. There is a notable Noh theatre sequence that lasts about three minutes.

Lazarillo

▶ **El Lazarillo De Tormes**

Spain 1959 109 mins bw
Hesperia Films

d **Cesar Ardavin**
sc **Cesar Ardavin**
ph **Manuel Berenguer**
m **Ruiz De Luna**
   Marco Paoletti, Juan José Menendez, Carlos Casaravilla, Margarita Lozano

A fatherless boy (Paoletti), abandoned by his mother, finds a living with a series of employers who a blind beggar, a miserly sacristan, a fake nobleman and a troupe of travelling players. He encounters vanity, cupidity and deception, and learns the skills of cunning and connivance in order to survive. A mildly satirical but otherwise stolid morality tale, enlivened by the young Italian actor's performance and an impeccable re-creation of 17th-century Castille.

Best Film Berlin 1960

▶ **Lazarillo De Tormes, El** see Lazarillo

Leap Into The Void

▶ **Salto Nel Vuoto**

Italy/France 1980 120 mins col
Clesi Cinematografica/M.K.2 Productions(Paris)

d **Marco Bellocchio**
sc **Marco Bellocchio, Piero Natoli, Vincenzo Cerami**
ph **Beppe Lanci**
m **Nicola Piovani**
   Michel Piccoli, Anouk Aimée, Michele Placido, Gisella Burinato

Mauro (Piccoli), a middle-aged bachelor judge, and Marta (Aimée), his spinster sister, live together in the family house of their childhood. Marta's confined existence, cooking, washing and ironing for her brother with only a housemaid for company, has disturbed her mental balance until Mauro attempts to have her disposed of with unexpected results. Two decades on from *Fists In The Pocket* Bellocchio's vibrant, explosive anger has mellowed into moody introspection. Issues of family, dependency and feminism are here (incest is side-stepped but the hint hovers). It's played with the expertise one would expect, and the art direction and photography are broodingly atmospheric. However, like the lighting, the film's themes are shadowy and confused, making heavy weather of two hours.

Best Actor (Michel Piccoli) Cannes 1980

Best Actress (Anouk Aimée) Cannes 1980

▶ **Leather And Nylon** see Action Man

Leaves From Satan's Book

▶ **Blade Of Satans Bog**

Denmark 1919 133 mins bw
Nordisk

d **Carl Dreyer**
sc **Edgar Høyer, Carl Dreyer**
ph **George Schneevoigt**
m **Silent**
   Helge Nissen, Halvard Hoff, Jacob Texiere, Hallander Hellemann, Ebon Strandin

Four episodes showing the activities of Satan (Nissen) through the ages: as a Pharisee at the time of Christ, as a Spanish Grand Inquisitor, as a police officer at work during the French Revolution and as a revolutionary monk in the Russo-Finnish war of 1918. Dreyer's second film was modelled on D. W.

Griffith's *Intolerance* (1916), although he doesn't intercut the four stories. Pompous, preachy and patchy, it nevertheless displays the beginnings of Dreyer's thematic preoccupations and pictorial sense, as well as an accomplished style of montage.

► **Lebende Leichnam, Der** see Living Corpse, The

► **Lebenszeichen** see Signs Of Life

► **Leçon Particulière, La** see Private Lesson, The

La Lectrice

France 1988 98 mins col
Eléfilm/AAA Productions/TSF
Productions/Ciné-5/Sofimage

d **Michel Deville**
sc **Rosalinde Deville, Michel Deville**
ph **Dominique Le Rigoleur**
m **Extracts from works of Beethoven arranged by Quentin Damamme**
   Miou-Miou, Régis Royer, Christian Ruché, Marianne Denicourt, Charlotte Farran, Patrick Chesnais, Brigitte Catillon, Maria Casarès

Constance (Miou-Miou) reads aloud to her lover a novel called *La Lectrice*. It is about Marie who, like Constance, loves books and decides to take up reading aloud to people as an occupation. The answers to her advertisement take Marie, variously, to read to teenage Eric (Royer), paralysed after an accident, an eccentric old woman (Casarés), the widow of a general, who celebrates Lenin's birthday, a child whose mother is too busy to attend to her, a company director (Chesnais) who is too stressed to read himself, and an elderly judge. In each case, Marie's expectations and determined professionalism are confounded by unexpected responses: all her clients want something other than her... Never a narrator of clarity, Deville here offers a massive conceit, photographed among the beauties of Arles in winter and highly stylized, which ultimately adds up to nothing. The first trick is to have Constance and Marie as the same person, so that the divide between truth and fiction is immediately blurred and very unsatisfactory (the device merely allows the beauti-

ful and accomplished Miou-Miou to hog every frame of the film). Interesting ideas are hinted at but remain unexplored, and although the film has imagination, a measure of comedy and eroticism and the occasional moment of genuine pain, it ultimately disappoints.

► **Leda** see Web Of Passion

The Left-handed Woman

► **Die Linkshändige Frau**

W. Germany 1977 119 mins col
Roadmovies

d **Peter Handke**
sc **Peter Handke**
ph **Robby Müller**
m **Bach**
   Edith Clever, Marcus Muehleisen, Bruno Ganz, Michel Lonsdale, Gerard Départieu, Bernhard Wicki

A woman (Clever), living in the Paris suburbs, no longer loves her husband (Ganz) and does not relate to her young son, her father, or her friends. Novelist-playwright-screenwriter Peter Handke's directorial debut (produced by Wim Wenders) is a study of a suburban woman's boredom, apathy and non-communication. But as the film follows the almost wordless creature while she wanders aimlessly about her house, it not only presents *ennui* on screen but creates it in the audience.

► **Legenda Del Santo Bevitore, La** see Legend Of The Holy Drinker, The

► **Legenda Suramskoi Kreposti** see Legend Of The Suram Fortress, The

► **Legend Of Gosta Berling, The** see Atonement Of Gösta Berling, The

► **Legend Of Prague, The** see Golem, The

The Legend Of The Holy Drinker

► **La Legenda Del Santo Bevitore**

Italy/France 1988 125 mins col

Cecchi Gora Group/Tiger
Cinematografica

d **Ermanno Olmi**
sc **Ermanno Olmi, Tullio Kezich**
ph **Dante Spinotti**
m **Stravinsky**
   **Rutger Hauer, Anthony Quayle, Sandrine
   Dumas, Dominique Pinon, Jean Maurice
   Chanet, Sophie Segalen**

Andreas (Hauer), an involuntary exile in
Paris, alcohol-dependent and destitute, lives
rough under the bridges of the Seine. One day
he is waylaid by a mysterious stranger
(Quayle) who insists on giving him some
money. Andreas accepts on condition that he
be allowed to repay it, whereupon, describing
himself as 'living a miracle, the miracle of conversion', the gentleman instructs him to return
the money to the statue of Saint Theresa of
Liseux at the church of Ste Marie de Batig-
nolles. The remainder of this rather overlong
film concerns itself with Andreas' efforts to
make good the bargain. Adapted from a novel
by Joseph Roth, an East European *émigré*
who died of drink in Paris in 1938, Olmi's
screenplay details the pain of exile and the tyranny of poverty in fine, painterly style. International star Rutger Hauer, his brilliant blue
eyes, angelic smile and saintly dignity transcending his filthy clothes, blackened teeth and
unavoidable humiliations, dominates every
frame of this richly atmospheric work which,
though often beguiling, is sometimes confusing (particularly in its flashbacks) and veers
uneasily between allegory, parable and whimsical fairy tale in between episodes of seeming
realism. Note that it was filmed and released in
various language versions, including English.

Best Film Venice 1988

The Legend Of The Suram Fortress

▶ **Legenda Suramskoi Kreposti**

USSR 1985 87 mins col
Georgianfilm Studio

d **Sergo Paradjanov, Dodo Abashidze**
sc **Vazha Gigashvili**
ph **Sergo Sixarulidze**
m **Dzhansugh K'Axidze**
   **Levan Uchaneishvili, Zurab Kipshidze,
   Dodo Abashidze, Veriko Andzhaparidze**

A mysterious force causes a medieval fortress
to crumble and collapse as soon as it is built.
In an attempt to solve the problem, the local
soothsayer demands that the son of the lover
who jilted her must brick himself up alive
inside the wall of the fortress for it to remain
standing and invincible. Based on a Georgian
legend, the film is dedicated to 'Georgian
warriors of all times who gave up their lives
for the Motherland'. Yet this is no conventional patriotic pageant, but a poetic, pic-
torially breathtaking, personal celebration of
the republic's history and folklore. Like Paradjanov's previous film, *The Colour Of Pomegranates*, the narrative is divided into
chapters, each embodying a specific religious
concept depicted in striking *tableaux vivants*,
emblematic gestures or formalized movement.
Specific meaning may be difficult to grasp,
but the overall experience is a unique and
sensuous one.

▶ **Lektion I Kärlek, En** see Lesson In
Love

Leningrad Cowboys Go America

Finland 1989 79 mins col
Villealfa Filmproductions/Swedish Film
Institute

d **Aki Kaurismäki**
sc **Aki Kaurismäki**
ph **Timo Salminen**
m **Mauri Sumén**
   **Matti Pellonpää, Kari Väänänen, Nicky
   Tesco and The Leningrad Cowboys**

In some remote spot in the tundra region the
inept rock musicians known as The Leningrad
Cowboys (an actual group) audition unsuccessfully for a Soviet official. He suggests they
make for the USA where 'they listen to any
old shit' and gives them the address of a
cousin (Tesco) in New York. With their autocratic manager, Vladimir (Pellonpää), and the
village idiot (Väänänen) who has followed
them, the boys arrive in America where they
buy a second-hand Cadillac and head across
the country via a succession of disastrous gigs
and assorted adventures to Mexico. Filmed
on location with his (and Salminen's) characteristic feel for landscape, and using a jumble
of Finnish and English dialogue, Kauris-

mäki's rock 'n' road movie is a fantastical comedy rich in his own brand of deadpan humour. There's a suggestion of homage to Jim Jarmusch in certain scenes and, indeed, the American director who is greatly admired by the Finn, plays the car salesman. A completely daffy movie with a lot of verve and charm, but not to all tastes.

Lenin In 1918

▶ **Lenin V 1918**

USSR   1939   133 mins   bw
Mosfilm

d   Mikhail Romm
sc Alexei Kapler, Tatiana Zlatogorova
ph Boris Volchok
m   Nikolai Kryukov
    Boris Shchukin (Lenin), Nikolai
    Okhlopkov, Vasily Vanin, Nikolai
    Cherkassov, Mikhail Gelovani

1918 sees Lenin as head of the new Soviet state, struggling ceaselessly to bring order out of the chaos of war, revolution and famine. Aiding him in his task is the writer Maxim Gorky (Cherkassov) and Stalin (Gelovani). The tremendous success of *Lenin In October* led to the making of this sequel with virtually the same team. Given the deficiencies of hagiography and the obvious attempt to show Stalin as Lenin's heir, there is a good deal of warmth and depth in Shchukin's portrayal (he was to have starred in a third Lenin film, but it was cancelled because of his death) and, minor inaccuracies apart, it is a good reconstruction of the period.

Lenin In October

▶ **Lenin V Oktiabrye**

USSR   1937   111 mins   bw
Mosfilm

d   Mikhail Romm
sc Alexei Kapler
ph Boris Volchok
m   Anatoli Alexandrov
    Boris Shchukin (Lenin), I. Golshtab
    (Stalin), Vasily Vanin, Nikolai Okhlopkov

Lenin's early political life, his exile and return to Russia to lead the October Revolution in 1917. Asked to make a film to celebrate the 25th anniversary of the October Revolution, Romm delivered, in a matter of months, this lively, human 'hagiopic', starring Lenin look-a-like Shchukin. The latter watched newsreels and studied Lenin's speech patterns in preparation for the role, which he played again in the sequel, *Lenin In 1918* (1939), and many more times.

▶ **Lenin V 1918** see Lenin In 1918

▶ **Lenin V Oktiabrye** see Lenin In October

▶ **Leone Have Sept Cabecas, Der** see Lion Has Seven Heads, The

▶ **Léon Morin, Prêtre** see Léon Morin, Priest

Léon Morin, Priest

▶ **Léon Morin, Prêtre**

France   1961   117 mins   bw
Rome-Paris Films

d   Jean-Pierre Melville
sc Jean-Pierre Melville
ph Henri Decaë
m   Martial Solal, Albert Raisner
    Jean-Paul Belmondo, Emmanuele Riva,
    Irène Tunc, Marielle Gozzi

In rural France during the German Occupation, a young atheist widow falls in love with the priest who converts her to religion. Not as pious as it sounds, Melville's quietly polemical film explores the psychology and humanity of the priest (a restrained Belmondo) and the woman (Riva) through a series of discussions, set against the finely detailed background of the period.

The Leopard

▶ **Il Gattopardo**

Italy   1963   205 mins   col
GTCF/Titanus/SNPC/GPC

d   Luchino Visconti
sc Luchino Visconti
ph Giuseppe Rotunno
m   Nino Rota
    Burt Lancaster, Claudia Cardinale, Alain

Delon, Paolo Stoppa, Serge Reggiani,
Leslie French

When his penniless nephew (Delon) marries
Angelica (Cardinale), the daughter of a merchant (Stoppa), the Prince of Salina (Lancaster) reflects sadly on the death of the
aristocratic world and the rise of the crass
bourgeoisie during the Risorgimento. This
gorgeous evocation of an era, faithfully
adapted from Giuseppe De Lampedusa's
novel, is full of superb set-pieces, particularly
the final ball which takes up 40 minutes of
screen time. In order to get the American
Lancaster to play the dying 19th-century Sicilian prince, Visconti agreed to allow 20th
Century-Fox to release the film internationally. Although it was overlong and
somewhat lethargic, it didn't justify Fox's
cutting (by about 44 minutes), dubbing, and
reprocessing of it in CinemaScope and Deluxe
Color. Visconti disowned this version, but
Lancaster's mellow performance still shines
through in both the maimed and original
versions.

Best Film Cannes 1963

Lesson In Love

▶ **En Lektion I Kärlek**

Sweden 1954 95 mins bw
Svensk Filmindustri

d Ingmar Bergman
sc Ingmar Bergman
ph Martin Bodin, Bengt Nordwal
m Dag Wirén
   Gunnar Björnstrand, Eva Dahlbeck,
   Harriet Andersson, Yvonne Lombard

A gynaecologist (Björnstrand) meets his
estranged wife (Dahlbeck) on a train to
Copenhagen where they relive their bumpy
past. One of Bergman's few comedies is an
entertaining if minor contribution to his
despatches from the battle of the sexes. The
lovely blonde Dahlbeck proved herself adept
at sophisticated comedy, a talent even better
used in the following year's *Smiles Of A
Summer Night*.

Let Joy Reign Supreme

▶ **Que La Fête Commence**

France 1975 120 mins col

Fildebroc

d Bertrand Tavernier
sc Bertrand Tavernier, Jean Aurenche
ph Pierre William Glenn
m Philippe D'Orléans
   Philippe Noiret, Jean Rochefort, Marina
   Vlady, Jean-Pierre Marielle

The intellectual and atheistic Philippe D'Orléans (Noiret), aided by a power-hungry priest
(Marielle), holds the reins of state for an
under-age Louis XV, and keeps the populace
in check, while his own life at court revolves
around his mistresses. A rather glib and traditional look at the rottenness of the Baroque
court and the horrors of life outside it, with
the usual orgies and rompings in masks. Tavernier's favourite actor, Noiret, seems to relish
the costumes, and the authentic music is by
the character he plays.

▶ **Let Justice Be Done** see Justice Est
Faite

Let's Hope It's A Girl

▶ **Speriamo Che Sia Femmina**

Italy 1985 119 mins col
Clemi Cinematografica/Producteurs
Associés/ Soprofilms/Films A2(Paris)

d Mario Monicelli
sc Leo Benvenuti, Piero De Bernardi, Suso
   Cecchi D'Amico, Tullio Pinelli, Mario
   Monicelli
ph Camillo Bazzoni
m Nicola Piovani
   Liv Ullmann, Catherine Deneuve, Philippe
   Noiret, Bernard Blier, Giuliana De Sio,
   Stefania Sandrelli, Athina Cenci

Elena (Ullmann), separated from her husband
Leonardo (Noiret), an impoverished count,
struggles to keep the family's crumbling
country property and rules over its inhabitants who, but for daft old Uncle Gugo
(Blier), are composed entirely of women. The
spirits and resolve of the family are resurrected when Elena's daughter Franca (De Sio)
becomes pregnant with the first (illegitimate)
grandchild. After making comedies for 50
years, it is not surprising that Monicelli
delivers a piece that is highly efficient, albeit
one that suffers from an excess of plot and
length. The tone is uncertain at times and the

film tends to sprawl like the old family mansion in it, but the Tuscan settings are ravishing and there is a gentle and unexpected suggestion of pro-feminist bias. The expert Franco-Italian cast, led by Sweden's Ullmann, contribute to an appealing if light-weight movie.

Letter From Siberia

▶ **Lettre De Sibérie**

> France   1958   60 mins   col
> Argos Films

d   **Chris Marker**
sc   **Chris Marker**
ph   **Sacha Vierny**
m   **Pierre Barbaud**

A personal documentary, filmed in Siberia, on various aspects of life there and attitudes towards it. 'I write to you from a far off country,' begins Marker's first full-length filmic letter, using texts, cartoons and a sequence repeated three times with a different commentary which brilliantly questions objectivity in non-fiction films. The humorous and poetic style tells us more about Marker than Siberia, but it beats all those boring travelogues.

Letter From The Wife

▶ **Stir Patra**

> India   1974   98 mins   bw
> Dhrupadi

d   **Purnendu Pattrea**
sc   **Purnendu Pattrea**
ph   **Shakti Banerjee**
m   **Ramkumar Chatterjee**
    Madhabi Mukherjee, Ashim Chakrabarti, Smita Sinha, Nimu Bhowmick

Mrinal (Mukherjee) has married into a prosperous family that expects her to accept the traditional role of the Indian wife. However, by writing poetry secretly she gains a measure of personal freedom. When one of her husband's relatives is forced into marriage with a half-wit, she rejects all that his family represents. Because this is an adaptation of a story by Rabindranath Tagore and it stars the superb Madhabi Mukherjee of *The Big City* and *Charulata*, comparisons with the

work of Satyajit Ray are inevitable. But Pattrea shows an individual visual talent and political sense and, although narrative and character are a little less assured than Ray's, it's a worthy addition to Tagore interpretations on screen.

Letters From A Dead Man

▶ **Pisma Myortvovo Chelovyeka**

> USSR   1986   87 mins   col
> Lenfilm

d   **Konstantin Lopushansky**
sc   **Konstantin Lopushansky, Vyacheslav Ribakov**
ph   **Nikolai Pokoptsev**
m   **Fauré, Giulio Gaccini**
    Rolan Bykov, I. Riklin, V. Mikhailov, V. Sabinin, N. Gryakalova

A Soviet city is devastated by a nuclear holocaust that happened by mistake. A Nobel Prize-winning scientist (Bykov) tries to make sense of events in a series of imaginary letters to his missing son while his wife is dying of radiation sickness and, elsewhere, the young and healthy shelter in an overcrowded bunker to which a group of orphaned children are denied entry. Shot in a murky, tinted monochrome to capture the haunting rubble-strewn landscape of nuclear disaster, Lopushansky's film is a depressing document of the horror that awaits us if the button is pressed with, surprisingly, some underlying wry humour.

Letters From My Windmill

▶ **Lettres De Mon Moulin**

> France   1954   120 mins   bw
> Cie Mediterranéene De Films – Eminente

d   **Marcel Pagnol**
sc   **Marcel Pagnol**
ph   **Willy**
m   **Henri Tomasi**
    Roger Crouzet, Henri Crémieux, Edouard Delmont, Henri Vilbert, Fernand Sardou

The author Alphonse Daudet (Crouzet) returns to Provence where he hears three tales – about monks who manufacture a new liqueur, how the Devil tricked a gourmand priest, and how a miller pretends his mill has been working for 18 years for a non-existent client. Originally three hours long, Pagnol's final film had a long prologue and epilogue cut on release. The loss was not severe, as this talkative and old-fashioned film could have done with even more pruning. But Daudet's tales, Pagnol's rich dialogue and the warm southern characters provide good rustic entertainment.

▶ **Lettre De Sibérie** see Letter From Siberia

▶ **Lettres De Mon Moulin** see Letters From My Windmill

▶ **Letyat Zhuravli** see Cranes Are Flying, The

▶ **Letzte Akt, Der** see Last Ten Days, The

▶ **Letzte Brücke, Die** see Last Bridge, The

▶ **Letzte Mann, Der** see Last Laugh, The

▶ **Letzte Walzer, Der** see Last Waltz, The

Les Liaisons Dangereuses 1960

France   1959   106 mins   bw
Films Marceau

d   **Roger Vadim**
sc   **Roger Vadim, Roger Vailland, Claude Brûlé**
ph   **Marcel Grignon**
m   **Jack Murray, Thelonius Monk**
     Gérard Philipe, Jeanne Moreau, Annette Vadim, Jeanne Valérie, Jean-Louis Trintignant

Valmont (Philipe) and his wife Juliette (Moreau) encourage each other's sexual conquests, until the wages of sin catch up with them. Good performances from Moreau and the dying Philipe, the display of Vadim's wife's body, and the cool ironic tone make this slickly directed updating of Laclos' 1782

epistolary novel one of the director's better efforts. The false denouement, with shooting, madness and fire, demonstrated that promiscuity doesn't pay – just in case audiences thought so from the tempting goings-on that preceded it.

▶ **Liebe Der Jeanne Ney, Die** see Love Of Jeanne Ney, The

▶ **Liebe In Deutschland, Eine** see Love In Germany, A

▶ **Liebe Ist Liebe** see Love Is Love

Liebelei

Austria   1932   85 mins   bw
Fred Lissa

d   **Max Ophüls**
sc   **Hans Wilhelm, Kurt Alexander**
ph   **Franz Planer**
m   **Theo Mackeben**
     Magda Schneider, Wolfgang Liebeneiner, Luise Ullrich, Willy Eichberger

A young officer (Liebeneiner) and the daughter of a violinist (Schneider) have a brief love affair, until he is killed in a duel over a married woman, and she jumps to her death. Far less ironic and more romantic than Arthur Schnitzler's play – witness the invigorating sleigh ride – the film's emphasis is on music, sound and camera movement rather than dialogue. It was Max Ophüls' first big success and the most memorable performance from Magda Schneider, mother of Romy.

The Life And Loves Of Beethoven

▶ **Un Grand Amour De Beethoven**

France   1937   135 mins   bw
Générales

d   **Abel Gance**
sc   **Abel Gance**
ph   **Robert Lefèbvre, Marc Fossard**
m   **Beethoven**
     Harry Baur, Annie Ducaux, Jany Holt, Jean-Louis Barrault

The great composer (Baur) has trouble with his hearing and with a girl who ignores him and prefers to marry a count, but another wins his heart. Gance was not at his best with dialogue as this rather leaden biopic demonstrates, but it does have the expected visual flourishes. The sequence when the hero loses his hearing, revealed by the silent shots of violins, bells and birds singing, is poignant and paradoxical. The loss of sound for Beethoven and the coming of sound for Gance were almost equally agonizing. Note that in the foreign release version Barrault, as the composer's nephew, has completely disappeared.

The Life And Music Of Giuseppe Verdi

▶ **Giuseppe Verdi**

> Italy 1938 123 mins bw
> Grandi Film Storici

d **Carmine Gallone**
sc **Carmine Gallone, Lucio D'Ambra**
ph **Massimo Terzano**
m **Giuseppe Verdi**
> **Fosco Giachetti, Germana Paolieri, Gaby Morlay, Maria Cebotari, Beniamino Gigli, Pierre Brasseur**

Verdi (Gachetti) comes to Milan, is rejected by the conservatory of music and marries. His young wife dies, his early operas flop and he falls in love with a singer (Paolieri).He later remarries, becomes a success and is then inspired to compose *Aida* by another young singer (Morlay). Apart from the chance to hear a liberal sprinkling of arias from the likes of Cebotari and Gigli, this biopic is really old opera hat. After 25 years in the business, veteran director Gallone made a second career out of workmanlike opera-related films such as *Manon Lescaut* (1939), *Rigoletto* (1947), *Il Trovatore* (1949), *Puccini* (1952), *Madame Butterfly* (1955) and *Tosca* (1956).

Life And Nothing But

▶ **Le Vie Et Rien D'Autre**

> France 1989 134 mins col

Hachette Première/AB Films/Little Bear/ Films A2/Sofinergie/CNC

d **Bertrand Tavernier**
sc **Jean Cosmos, Bertrand Tavernier**
ph **Bruno De Keyzer**
m **Oswald D'Andrea**
> **Philippe Noiret, Sabine Azema, Pascale Vignal, Maurice Barrier, François Perrot, Michel Duchaussoy**

Two years after the end of World War I the French are still dealing with the devastation of the countryside, the final body count and the problem of amnesiac survivors. Major Dellaplane (Noiret) is in charge of accounting for the latter; the beautiful Irène (Azema) is searching for her missing husband; country schoolteacher Alice (Vignal) seeks her fiancé. The paths of these three intertwine with unforeseen consequences. Tavernier's acclaimed film is effectively photographed in muted tones – even the clothes in low-key blues, greys and blacks complement and reflect the landscape – and offers a pungent evocation of the gruesome farce that was the war. The context is sombre, the atmosphere powerful, but the film is overlong and underpaced, and its plot resolution not entirely convincing. The by-now veteran Noiret, slightly too old for his role but exuding the required gravitas, together with a sense of irony that hovers over the film, heads an excellent cast. Flawed but intriguing.

▶ **Life Dances On** see Carnet De Bal, Un

Life Is A Bed Of Roses

▶ **La Vie Est Un Roman**

> France 1983 111 mins col
> Soprofilms/Films A2/Fideline/Les Films Ariane/Filmedis

d **Alain Resnais**
sc **Jean Gruault**
ph **Bruno Nuytten**
m **M. Philippe-Gérard**
> **Vittorio Gassman, Ruggero Raimondi, Geraldine Chaplin, Fanny Ardant, Pierre Arditti, Sabine Azéma, Robert Manuel**

In the early 1920s, at Count Forbek's château

dedicated to happiness, his guests take a special drug to become 'reborn' and forget their pasts. In 1982, the building has been turned into a progressive school. During the summer vacation, a teachers' conference is held there, while the few remaining children imagine a world of knights and dragons. Despite its ostensibly complex structure – shifting seamlessly between the past, the present and the imagined – it is one of Resnais' lightest and most approachable films. It is a Feuillade-like drama, a satiric-comedy on intellectuals, a musical, and a children's fantasy all rolled into one, linked by the theme that happiness and imagination cannot be forced upon one, and that only children have the secret. Taken separately, the first episode is visually appealing, the second is rather unfunny, the music is slight, and the comic-book stuff (seen only in long shot) is fey. But, as a whole, the film is entertaining.

Life Is A Long Quiet River

▶ **La Vie Est Une Longue Fleuve Tranquille**

France 1988 90 mins col
Telema/MK2/FR3 Films/Sofica/CNC

d   Etienne Chatiliez
sc Etienne Chatiliez, Florence Quentin
ph Pascal Lebegue
m   Gerard Kawczynski
Benoit Magimel, Hélène Vincent, André Wilms, Daniel Gelin, Catherine Hiegel, Christine Pignet, Patrick Bouchitey

In a fit of pique at her lover and employer, Dr Mavial (Gelin), nurse Josette (Hiegel) switches two babies at birth. Years later when Mavial's wife dies and he still doesn't marry her, she reveals the swap. The Le Quesnoys, middle class, wealthy and ultra-respectable, 'buy' back their rightful son, Momo, from the unemployed, illiterate and semi-criminal Groseilles, unleashing chaos and confusion in their own well-ordered household. Chatiliez, a highly successful director of quirky French commercials, made his debut with this wild comedy which cocks an energetic and hilarious snook at class differences. It collected several Césars and broke box-office records in France, even though it disappointingly peters out towards the end. Hélène Vincent's

uptight Mme Le Quesnoy is a gem of fine observation and young Magimel captivates as the amoral Momo.

Life, Love, Death

▶ **La Vie, L'Amour, La Mort**

France 1969 115 mins col/bw
Les Films 13/Les Films Ariane/Les Productions Artistes Associés (Paris)/ P.E.A. (Rome)

d   Claude Lelouch
sc Claude Lelouch
ph Jean Collomb
m   Francis Lai
Amidou, Janine Magnan, Marcel Bozzufi, Caroline Cellier

A factory worker (Amidou) at Simca, with a wife (Magnan) and mistress (Cellier), is condemned to death for the murder of nine prostitutes. Lelouch, the incurable romantic, turned uneasily to the subject of sex crime and capital punishment, but managed to control some of his usual excesses with the camera. Based on a number of case histories, the film conveys the hapless man's last days in serious black and white, while the flashbacks are in colour. Amidou's touching performance helps to counteract the director's manipulation.

The Life Of Chikuzan

▶ **aka Chikuzan Travels Alone**

▶ **Chikuzan Hitori Tabi**

Japan 1977 122 mins col
Kindai Eiga Kyokai/Jean-Jean Productions

d   Kaneto Shindo
sc Kaneto Shindo
ph Kiyomi Kuroda
m   Hikaru Hayashi
Chikuzan Takahashi, Ryuzo Hayashi, Nobuko Otowa, Dai Kanai, Mitsuko Baisho

Chikuzan Takahashi, the blind singer and player of the Shamisen, a Japanese stringed instrument, has led the life of a vagabond for 50 years since he was apprenticed to a blind beggar as a child. Shindo discovered the virtuoso player and singing chronicler in a neglected corner of Tokyo where students flocked to hear his music, and re-created his life in a visually and aurally sublime semi-documentary. Actors play him as a child and young man, while Chikuzan appears as himself, an old man, with no hint of self-pity.

The Life Of O-Haru

▶ **Saikaku Ichidai Onna**

Japan   1952   133 mins   bw
Shin Toho

d   **Kenji Mizoguchi**
sc **Yoshitaka Yoda**
ph **Yoshimi Kono**
m   **Ichiro Saito**
    Kinuyo Tanaka, Toshiro Mifune, Ichiro Sugai, Toshiko Yanane, Ataro Shindo

O-Haru (Tanaka), the daughter of a samurai, falls in love with a man (Mifune) from a lower class. After he is beheaded, she is forced to become the mistress of the head of a great clan in order to bear him an heir. Her duty done, she is dismissed from the palace and descends from marriage to a poor merchant, who is later killed, to becoming a prostitute and beggar. Meanwhile, her son has become a lord. Against a meticulously realized background of 17th-century Japan (mostly filmed in a bombed out park), Mizoguchi, without sentimentality or moralizing, delineates the sufferings of a woman (Tanaka giving one of the greatest of screen performances). Like most of the women of the period, his camera watches the moments of crisis and violence from a discreet distance, deepening our sympathy for the characters. The 52-year-old director, a number of whose previous films had been flops, risked everything to make this adaptation from Saikaku's classic picaresque novel. Happily, it marked his recognition in the West and led to further masterpieces in the last four years of his life.

Life Size

▶ **aka Love Doll**

▶ **Grandeur Nature**

Spain/France   1973   100 mins   col
Jet Film(Barcelona)/Uranus Productions/ Fox Europa-Films 66 (Paris)/ Verona(Rome)

d   **Luis Garcia Berlanga**
sc **Rafael Azcona, Luis Garcia Berlanga**
ph **Alain Derobe**
m   **Maurice Jarre, Johann Strauss**
    Michel Piccoli, Valentine Tessier, Rada Rassimov, Amparo Soler Leal, Manolo Alexandre

When Michel (Piccoli), a successful Parisian dentist, acquires a life-sized doll, he begins to treat it as human. He abandons his practice and his wife (Rassimov) to devote himself exclusively to life with the doll, whom he dresses and undresses, films in various positions and takes with him everywhere. His happy fantasy turns to horror when first the janitor, then his Spanish neighbours, make use of his precious possession... A bizarre portrait of fetishism which will shock some and amuse others. Piccoli carries off his role with aplomb and Berlanga, offering no explanations and delivering no judgement, directs with stylish expertise, rooting Michel's increasingly extreme behaviour in contexts of normalcy. He provides several well-observed supporting characters whose ability to accept and relate to the doll is free of perversion. However, its quality notwithstanding, the movie begins to pall by virtue of its simplicity.

Life Upside Down

▶ **La Vie À L'Envers**

France   1964   92 mins   bw
A.J. Films

d   **Alain Jessua**
sc **Alain Jessua**
ph **Jacques Robin**
m   **Jacques Loussier**
    Charles Denner, Anna Gaylor, Guy Saint-Jean, Nicole Gueden, Jean Yanne

An ordinary young Paris office worker (Denner), suddenly decides to retreat into his own inner world, giving up his loquacious new wife (Gaylor), his friends, work and possessions. He ends contentedly staring at a blank wall in the bare room of a mental clinic. The theme of alienation, a prevalent one in the 1960s, has seldom been explored with such wry wit and sensitivity, although the film's attitude to its hero remains ambiguous.

Audiences will have to make up their own minds whether he is to be admired, emulated, pitied or scorned. What is clear, however, is the subtle way in which the images in the film itself become more and more denuded, moving towards a blank screen. Inexplicably, the director never fulfilled the vast promise of this feature, which won the Best First Film award at Venice.

Lift To The Scaffold

▶ **(US: Frantic)**

▶ **Ascenseur Pour L'Échafaud**

France   1957   89 mins   bw
Nouvelles Editions De Films

d   Louis Malle
sc Louis Malle, Roger Nimier
ph Henri Decaë
m   Miles Davis
    Maurice Ronet, Jeanne Moreau, Georges
    Poujoly, Lino Ventura, Yori Bertin

A young man (Ronet) murders his boss with the complicity of the victim's wife (Moreau), but is nearly punished for another crime he did not commit. Twenty-five-year-old Malle's first solo feature overlaid a conventional, complicated and somewhat implausible plot with a dark atmosphere and psychological depth. Tension is also well built up, especially in the crucial scene in the lift of the title in which the hero is stuck. Decaë's vivid photography of the Paris locations would soon make him a favourite with the *Nouvelle Vague*, and the film launched Moreau into stardom after 10 years in pictures. The effective jazz score was improvised by Miles Davis and a group of European musicians while watching a screening of the film.

The Light Across The Street

▶ **La Lumière D'En Face**

France   1955   99 mins   bw
EGC/Fernand Rivers

d   Georges Lacombe
sc Louis Chavance, René Masson, René
    Lefèvre
ph Louis Page
m   Norbert Glanzberg

Brigitte Bardot, Raymond Pellegrin,
Roger Pigaut, Claude Romain

When the sexy wife (Bardot) of a jealous truck driver (Pellegrin), who spends most of his time trying to make money, falls for a garage mechanic (Pigaut), the result is murder. There is not much light in this murky low-life melodrama, but Bardot's wanton gamine appeal manages to shine through for the first time. A year later, Roger Vadim, her husband since 1952, used it to notorious effect in *And God Created Woman*, thus creating the legendary sex kitten known as BB.

Lights Of Variety

▶ **(US: Variety Lights)**

▶ **Luci Del Varieta'**

Italy   1950   94 mins   bw
Film Capitolium

d   Alberto Lattuada, Federico Fellini
sc Federico Fellini
ph Otello Martelli
m   Felice Lattuada
    Peppino De Filippo, Carla Del Poggio,
    Giulietta Masina, John Kitzmiller

A stage-struck young girl (Del Poggio) joins a third-rate vaudeville troupe and casts her spell on the manager and principal comic (De Filippo), until she leaves for better things. Fellini, who wrote songs and sketches for the music hall in his youth, wonderfully re-creates the world of a tatty troupe of performers, while seeing the humanity behind their stage make-up. Already, in his first film as director (he handled the actors, Lattuada the camera and action), Fellini established his Chaplinesque style.

▶ **Ligne De Chaleur, La** see Heat Line,
  The

La Ligne De Démarcation

France   1966   120 mins   bw
Rome-Paris Films/SNC

d   Claude Chabrol
sc Claude Chabrol, Colonel Rémy
ph Jean Rabier
m   Pierre Jansen

Jean Seberg, Maurice Ronet, Daniel Gélin, Stéphane Audran, Jacques Perrin, Jean Yanne, Noël Roquevert

In a small provincial town in Occupied France, a group of inhabitants attempts to smuggle two spies and a pair of fugitive Allied airmen across the border into Vichy territory. This film holds few surprises, portraying the usual struggles of Resistance fighters and the treachery of collaborators and informers common to the genre. This is an unexpected piece from Chabrol, but displaying his usual intelligence and craftsmanship, together with his slightly ironic sense of detachment in looking at the individuals – heroes and traitors alike – of a troubled period.

Lika, Chekhov's Love

▶ **aka Subject For A Short Story**

▶ **Siuzhet Dlya Nebloshova Rasskaza**

▶ **aka Lika, Lyubov Chekhova**

USSR   1968   90 mins   col
Mosfilm/Telsia(France)

d   Sergei Yutkevitch
sc   Leonid Malyugin
ph   Naum Ardashnikov
m   Rodion Schedrin
Nikolai Grinko, Marina Vlady, Iya Savvina, Yuri Yakovlev

Lika (Vlady), a beautiful singing teacher who was loved by Chekhov (Grinko), returns from Paris to St Petersburg in 1896 for the opening night of *The Seagull*, which turns out to be a scandalous flop. This sensitive, elegant and stylized episode from Chekhov's life could only have been made by a Russian director. Yutkevich and his performers, including French actress Marina Vlady (née Marina De Poliakoff-Baidaroff), capture the nuances of language and tone necessary for the portrayal of real events and people. But this is really the material for a short story and should perhaps have been the subject for a shorter film.

▶ **Lika, Lyubov Chekhova** see Lika, Chekhov's Love

Like Father, Like Son

▶ **(US: The Tailor's Maid)**

▶ **Padri E Figli**

Italy   1957   104 mins   col
Royal Film/Filmel-Lyrica

d   Mario Monicelli
sc   Age, Furio Scarpelli, Mario Monicelli, Leo Benvenuti, Luigi Emmanuele
ph   Leonida Barboni
m   Alessandro Cicognini
Vittorio De Sica, Marcello Mastroianni, Antonella Lualdi, Marisa Merlini, Franco Interlenghi, Franco Di Trocchio

A tale of five families, all connected to each other by love and/or marriage, focuses particularly on the pregnant nurse with four children, her childless sister and brother-in-law to whom she gives her youngest boy, and on the tailor's amorous daughter who falls for the doctor's son. This typically Italianate romp of the sort at which Monicelli excels is somewhat overcrowded with characters, but extrovert, charming, and funny. The acting honours go to De Sica as the weak, rascally and lovable tailor, and Mastroianni as Cesare the mechanic, who shares some of the best scenes with the little nephew (Di Trocchio) whom he and his wife adopt.

Best Director Berlin 1957

Lili Marleen

W. Germany   1980   120 mins   col
Roxy/CIP/Rialto/Bayerische Rundfunk

d   Rainer Werner Fassbinder
sc   Rainer Werner Fassbinder, Manfred Purzer, Joshua Sinclair
ph   Xaver Schwarzenberger
m   Peer Raben
Hanna Schygulla, Giancarlo Giannini, Mel Ferrer, Christine Kaufmann, Rainer Werner Fassbinder

A German singer (Schygulla) and a Swiss-Jewish composer (Giannini), in love with one another, are separated by World War II, but her song 'Lili Marleen', popular on both fronts, unites them forever. Fassbinder's attempt to ape a romantic Hollywood biopic, despite ironic touches, turns out even sillier than his model. The scene where the Gestapo tortures the hero with endless playings of a cracked record of the title song is pure Monty Python. Garish colour and campy back projection add to the artificiality.

Liliom

> France   1934   120 mins   bw
> Erich Pommer/Fox Europa

d   Fritz Lang
sc Fritz Lang (uncredited), Robert Liebman
ph Rudolph Maté, Louis Née
m   Jean Lenoir, Franz Waxman
    Charles Boyer, Madeleine Ozeray,
    Florelle, Pierre Alcover, Roland Toutain

A raffish carnival barker (Boyer) is killed in a knife fight, but is given one day to return to earth to see how his wife (Ozeray) and daughter are managing. Lang's adaptation of the Ferenc Molnar play, his only film made in France where he had fled the Nazis *en route* to the USA, was less sentimental and more amusing than the 1930 Hollywood version or the stage and screen musical *Carousel*. Particularly good were Boyer and the fantasy scenes in heaven.

Lina Braake

> W. Germany   1975   85 mins   col
> Sinkel/WDF

d   Bernhard Sinkel
sc Bernhard Sinkel
ph Alf Brustellin
m   Joe Haider
    Lina Carstens, Fritz Rasp, Herbert
    Botticher, Erica Schramm, Benno
    Hoffmann

Lina Braake (Carstens), a spry, 82-year-old woman has lost her house through the machinations of a bank. She meets a retired bankrupt gentleman (Rasp) in an old people's home and together they plot to defraud the bank of a large sum of money. Actually shot in an old people's home, with the inhabitants as extras, the film reveals a part of society rarely visited by film-makers. Thirty-five-year-old Sinkel's first feature shows a sensitivity towards its subject while managing to avoid sentimentality, before it moves unsteadily

from reality into fairytale. Its principal attraction is the co-starring of two veterans of German cinema, Carstens and Rasp, the latter having appeared in *Metropolis* almost 50 years earlier.

▶ **Linea Del Cielo, La** see Skyline

▶ **Linkshändige Frau, Die** see Left-handed Woman, The

The Lion Has Seven Heads

▶ **Der Leone Have Sept Cabecas**

> Congo   1970   103 mins   col
> Claude Antoine/Polifilm

d   Glauber Rocha
sc Glauber Rocha, Gianni Amico
ph Guido Cosulich
m   Congolese folk music
    Jean-Pierre Léaud, Rada Rassimov,
    Giulio Brogli, Gabriele Tinti

A CIA man, a Portuguese mercenary, a missionary priest, an ex-Nazi, puppet rulers, revolutionaries, and a blonde woman later crucified, act out Africa's colonial past and present. Rocha's first film abroad after his exile from Brazil is a highly symbolic, rhetorical, non-narrative cry for international revolution represented by the five languages that make up the original title – German, Italian, English, French and Portuguese. But this patchwork of protest theatre, carnival, caricature and political texts, moves in the direction of anarchy, madness and sado-masochism, only adding to the burdens of the Third World.

The Lion's Den

▶ **La Boca Del Lobo**

> Peru   1988   116 mins   col
> Producciones Inca Films/Tornasol Films/
> Televisión Española

d   Francisco J. Lombardi
sc Augusto Cabada, Giovanna Pollarolo,
    Gerardo Herrero
ph Teodoro Delgado
m   Bernardo Bonezzi
    Gustavo Bueno, Tona Vega, José Tejada,

Gilberto Torres, Bertha Pagaza, Antero Sanchez, Aristoteles Picho

In 1983 a platoon of government soldiers is dispatched to a remote Peruvian mountain village to seek out and put down the Communist guerrillas. When an Indian woman is raped by one of the soldiers, her tribe protests and the tough lieutenant Roca (Bueno) beats a man to death. He then orders all the villagers who witnessed his crime to be executed. Only the young private, Luna (Vega), refuses to fire. Seen through the eyes of the young, idealistic soldier who narrates, this uncompromising tale of oppression is not only a powerful political drama but an attack on the macho ethos of soldiery. The disturbed lieutenant, chillingly played by Bueno, believes only in proving 'he has balls' and that only the weak play by the rules. Although the psychological analysis of the lieutenant is a little too pat, the characterizations of the soldiers too familiar and the Russian roulette scene owes too much to *The Deer Hunter*, the images of a suffering people have the ring of painful reality. (The story is based on an actual event.) The scene where the Indians are made to sing the Peruvian national anthem shows in one stroke their alienation from their masters, and the climactic massacre is graphically bold.

The Lipstick

▶ **Il Rossetto**

Italy 1960 100 mins bw
Europa Cinematografica/Explorer/
CFPC-Medallion

d **Damiano Damiani**
sc **Damiano Damiani, Cesare Zavattini**
ph **Pier Ludovico Pavoni**
m **Giovanni Fusco**
 Laura Vivaldi, Pierre Brice, Giorgia Moll, Bella Darvi, Pietro Germi

A 13-year-old schoolgirl (Vivaldi) is infatuated with her handsome next door neighbour (Brice), leading to her involvement with a murder case in which he is heavily implicated. A competent and compact crime thriller in which suspense is well maintained, and to which added interest is given by the age of the heroine from whose point of view

the action is observed. An excellent feature debut for former documentary-maker Damiani.

▶ **Lisice** see Handcuffs

▶ **Liten Ida** see Little Ida

Little Ida

▶ **Liten Ida**

Norway 1981 79 mins col
Norsk Film A.S. Svensk Filminstituten

d **Laila Mikkelsen**
sc **Marit Paulsen, Laila Mikkelsen**
ph **Hans Welin, Kjell Vassdal**
m **Eyvind Solaas**
 Sunniva Lindeklejv, Lise Fjeldstad, Howard Halvorsen, Arne Lindtner Ness, Ellen Westerfjell

During the Nazi occupation of Norway in 1944, seven-year-old Ida (Lindeklejv) has to endure an incomprehensible agony of loneliness and malicious abuse because her mother takes up with a German soldier. Based on writer Paulsen's own memoirs, this grim tale of survival is filmed in authentically chilly landscapes, and offers an astonishing performance from Lindeklejv. Director Mikkelsen, telling her dreadful tale with absolute fidelity to truth, avoids the pitfalls of maudlin sentimentality to achieve a moving document of childhood and of an aspect of World War II.

The Little Matchgirl

▶ **La Petite Marchande D'Allumettes**

France 1928 29 mins bw
Jean Renoir & Jean Tedesco

d **Jean Renoir**
sc **Jean Renoir**
ph **Jean Bachelet**
m **Silent**
 Catherine Hessling, Jean Storm, Manuel Raaby, Amy Wells

Unable to sell her matches, the destitute girl

(Hessling) is reduced to striking them in a futile effort to keep warm, and comforts herself with dreams of a fantasy world. In the morning her tiny, frozen body is found dead in the snow. This poignant film was the last, and best, of the four silents Renoir made with his actress wife, noticeably drawing on her talent for mime. With the close collaboration of friends – Tedesco, Bachelet and Danish designer Eric Aës – the director devised an appropriate cinematic language for translating the world of Hans Christian Andersen to the screen, placing his actors in stylized sets, making use of double exposure and other tricks, and expanding the story to themes from other Andersen stories such as *The Tinder Box*, and *The Steadfast Tin Soldier* in which toys come to life.

The Little Nuns

► **Le Monachine**

> Italy 1963 100 mins bw
> Ferruccio Brusarosco

> d   **Luciano Salce**
> sc **Franco Castellano, Giuseppe Moccia**
> ph **Erico Menczer**
> m   **Ennio Morricone**
> **Didi Perugo, Catherine Spaak, Sylva Koscina, Amadeo Nazzari, Umberto Orsini**

The sound waves of commercial jets flying overhead are destroying the treasured fresco of a humble convent. The Mother Superior (Perugo) and a naive young nun (Spaak) journey to Rome to plead with the airline's executive. Mission accomplished, they also save the executive's job and find him a wife. An easily digested comedy, liberally seasoned with charm and enhanced by convincing performances.

The Little Soldier

► **Le Petit Soldat**

> France 1960 88 mins bw
> Georges De Beauregard/Société Nouvelle De Cinéma

> d   **Jean-Luc Godard**
> sc **Jean-Luc Godard**
> ph **Raoul Coutard**
> m   **Maurice Leroux**
> **Michel Subor, Anna Karina, Henri-Jacques Huet, Laszló Szábó, Paul Beauvais**

In Geneva, at the time of the Algerian War, a French secret agent (Subor), on a mission to kill a top man in the FLN, finds himself used as a pawn by both sides. Godard's second feature was banned by the French Ministry of Information (it was released with minor cuts in 1963) because of its ambivalent attitude to the Algerian War, and its reflection of brutality on both sides which affronted both Left and Right opinion. Other reasons might have been its matter-of-fact filming of torture, and the treatment of the political crisis as a confusing gangster movie. This powerful reflection of the period saw the debut of Anna Karina, whom Godard married in 1961. They separated five years and eight films later.

The Little Theatre Of Jean Renoir

► **Le Petit Théâtre De Jean Renoir**

> France 1969 100 mins col
> ORTF

> d   **Jean Renoir**
> sc **Jean Renoir**
> ph **Georges Leclerc**
> m   **Jean Wiener, Joseph Kosma, Octave Cremieux**
> **Jeanne Moreau, Fernand Sardou, Françoise Arnoul, Jean Carmet**

A film in four parts: 1) two old tramps find freedom in dreams; 2) a housewife is obsessed with an electric floor polisher; 3) Jeanne Moreau, in Belle Époque costume, sings 'Quand L'Amour Meurt'; 4) a husband whose wife has betrayed him with his best friend, accepts the situation rather than be parted from either. Renoir's adieu to the cinema 'after seven years of unwilling inactivity', actually made for TV and released in 1971, is an uneven divertissement, looking back on some aspects of his art. There is the studio artifice of his silents in the whimsical first tale, the second is an unfunny sung satire, Moreau's song is charming, and the last episode reminds us of Renoir's great humanity.

Little Vera

▶ **Malenkaya Vera**

USSR 1988 134 mins col
Gorky Studios

d **Vasili Pichul**
sc **Mariya Khmelik**
ph **Yefim Reznikov**
m **Vladmimir Matetski**
  Natalya Negoda, Andrei Sokolov,
  Liudmila Zaitseva, Yuri Nazarov,
  Alexander Alexeyev-Negreba, Andrei
  Fomin, Alexandra Tabakova

Vera (Negoda), her drunken, lorry-driver father (Nazarov, superb) and long-suffering, meal-obsessed mother (Zaitseva) live in a small apartment in a grey industrial town. Waiting for her higher education to commence, the girl, clearly suffering from terminal boredom and resentment of her parents, hangs about in coffee bars and dance-halls. Spurning Andrei (Fomin), who is in love with her, she picks up and sleeps with the attractive Sergei (Sokolov) and, announcing their intention to marry, moves him into the family home with catastrophic consequences for all of them. Widely acclaimed as an outspoken picture of Russian life that could not have been made pre-*glasnost*, Pichul's excursion into kitchen-sink realism holds no surprises for Western audiences other than the realization that the life of no-hopers is the same everywhere. The movie, well made and offering some fine nuances of observation, can be summed up in one word: bleak. This, in spite of evident attempts at anarchic humour. The characters (uniformly well played) are almost unrelievedly unsympathetic, their lives distasteful, and the film itself seems permeated with a similar disgust to that it awakens in the viewer. Additionally, the first half moves at a snail's pace, which, if it were a Hollywood saga set in the outskirts of Detroit, would have prompted us to leave before it got more interesting – which, to be fair, it does.

Little Wars

▶ **Petites Guerres**

Lebanon 1982 108 mins col
Maroun Baghdadi Film Production

d **Maroun Baghdadi**
sc **Maroun Baghdadi, Kamal Karin Kassar**
ph **Edward Lachman, Heinz Hollcher**
m **Gabriel Yared**
  Saroya Khoury, Nabil Ismael, Roger
  Hawa, Reda Khoury, Youssef Hosni,
  Rifaat Tarabay

Soraya (Khoury) is a student in love with Talal (Hawa), whose father, a wealthy feudal bey, has been kidnapped. Talal is forced by his domineering mother (Reda Khoury) to find his father's kidnappers and, if necessary, avenge his blood. At the same time, Soraya becomes friendly with Nabil (Ismael), a photographer and small-time conman involved in the Beirut Mafia. The title of this fast-moving political thriller, filmed entirely in Beirut and environs, refers to all the small rivalries that exist between gangs and clans, reflecting the larger civil war in the background and thus revealing the absurdity of the whole tragic situation. Baghdadi, whose debut feature this is, and who worked at Zoëtrope in Hollywood with Francis Coppola, directs crisply, conjuring up the atmosphere of a beautiful country devastated by war. The film comes closer to what 'ordinary' life is like in that benighted land than Volker Schlöndorff's comparable *Circle Of Deceit* (1981). There is an ironic approach to the way the Western media view the troubles, giving licence for any kind of wild behaviour among the young, such as the shooting down of the letters on a neon sign. All the while, however, as the characters play at civil war, the real one intrudes fatally.

The Little World Of Don Camillo

▶ **Il Piccolo Mondo Di Don Camillo**

Italy 1952 106 mins bw
Rizzoli/Amato/Francinex

d **Julien Duvivier**
sc **Julien Duvivier, René Barjavel**
ph **Nicolas Hayer**

m **Alessandro Cicognini**
   Fernandel, Gino Cervi, Sylvie, Franco
   Interlenghi, Vera Talqui

The parish priest (Fernandel) and the Communist mayor (Cervi) of an Italian village, usually at odds with each other, combine forces to help a modern Romeo and Juliet (Interlenghi and Talqui). Fernandel's portrayal of the scheming Camillo, who holds conversations with God, was so successful that it prompted several lesser sequels also based on the novels of Giovanni Guareschi. There are plenty of amusing situations, despite the unreality and overcuteness.

Live For Life

▶ **Vivre Pour Vivre**

   France 1967 130 mins col
   UA/Ariane/Vides

d **Claude Lelouch**
sc **Claude Lelouch, Pierre Uytterhoeven**
ph **Patrick Pouget**
m **Francis Lai**
   Yves Montand, Candice Bergen, Annie
   Girardot, Irène Tunc

A globe-trotting TV news reporter (Montand) leaves his wife (Girardot) after their holiday in Amsterdam, has an affair with an American fashion model (Bergen) in Kenya, the Congo, and Paris, is taken prisoner in Vietnam, and is reconciled with his wife in the French Alps. For this follow-up to his vastly successful *A Man And A Woman* (1966), Lelouch was given the money to run around the world, but made specious use of the Vietnam War and other troublespots as backgrounds to Montand's marital problems. Put together with the expert eye of a smooth huckster, it was nominated for an Oscar.

Living

▶ **aka Doomed**

▶ **(US: To Live)**

▶ **Ikiru**

   Japan 1952 143 mins bw
   Toho

d **Akira Kurosawa**

sc **Akira Kurosawa, Shinobu Hashimoto,**
   Hideo Oguni
ph **Asaichi Nakai**
m **Fumio Hayasaka**
   Takashi Shimura, Nabuo Kaneko, Kyoko
   Seki, Miki Odagiri

Discovering he is in the terminal stages of cancer, an elderly civil servant (Shimura) spends his last months initially in self-absorption, but then devotes himself to forcing through the building of a children's playground in the slums. One of Kurosawa's rare looks at modern Japanese society is a bleak one. The low key photography and the regretful flashbacks build a picture of a sterile society, counteracted by the touching central character of a man who dies happily.

The Living Corpse

▶ **Der Lebende Leichnam**

▶ **aka Zhivoi Trup**

   Germany/USSR 1928 108 mins bw
   Prometheus/Mezhrabpomfilm

d **Fedor Ozep**
sc **B. Gusman, Anatoly Marienhof**
ph **Anatoli Golovnya**
m **Silent**
   Vsevolod Pudovkin Maria Jacobini, V.
   Garden, Gustav Diessl

A husband (Pudovkin), whose wife (Jacobini) is unfaithful to him and who is unable to get a divorce, decides to kill himself. The fine acting of the great Russian director Pudovkin and the splendid camerawork add considerably to the quality of this version of Leo Tolstoy's play, made in two languages in Germany. Much admired at the time, the content, but not the style, has lost much of its impact over the years.

▶ **Living Dead Man, The** see Late Mathias Pascal, The

The Lizards

▶ **I Basilischi**

   Italy 1963 85 mins bw
   Galatea

d **Lina Wertmüller**
sc **Lina Wertmüller**
ph **Gianni Di Venanzo**
m **Ennio Morricone**
   Toni Petruzzi, Stefano Sattaflores, Sergio Ferrannino, Luigi Barbieri

In a sleepy southern Italian town a group of young men spend their time ogling the girls and vegetating in the sun. Not much happens in the film, nor to the aimless characters, but Wertmüller in her first feature displayed a sharp eye and a keen sense of humour, absent from most of her subsequent films.

▶ **Ljubavni Slucaj** see Switchboard Operator, The

▶ **Loin De Vietnam** see Far From Vietnam

Lola

France   1960   91 mins   bw
Rome-Paris/Euro-International

d **Jacques Demy**
sc **Jacques Demy**
ph **Raoul Coutard**
m **Michel Legrand**
   Anouk Aimée, Marc Michel, Jacques Harden, Elina Labourdette

Lola (Aimée), a cabaret singer and dancer in Nantes, tries to choose between three men, two of them sailors. Dedicated to Max Ophüls, Demy's first feature has the circular construction, long tracking shots and frothiness to remind one of the dedicatee, but it owes as much to *On The Town* (MGM, 1949) with its sailors on leave, chance encounters and fleeting love affairs. This modern fairytale brought Demy and the tall, brown-eyed enigmatic beauty, Anouk Aimée, international fame.

Lola

W. Germany   1981   114 mins   col
Rialto Film/Trio Film

d **Rainer Werner Fassbinder**

sc **Rainer Werner Fassbinder, Peter Märthesheimer, Pea Fröhlich**
ph **Xaver Schwarzenberger**
m **Peer Raben**
   Barbara Sukowa, Armin Müller-Stahl, Mario Adorf, Matthias Fuchs, Ivan Desny

A respectable middle-aged building commissioner (Müller-Stahl) falls helplessly in love with Lola (Sukowa), the star of a nightclub-cum-bordello and mistress of the owner, a sleazy building profiteer (Adorf). The flavour is of *The Blue Angel* updated (filled with 1950s kitsch) and revamped into a Douglas Sirkian melodrama, with Fassbinder's usual indictment of a corrupt, avaricious Germany. The garish pink and blue colours and non-naturalistic lighting helps create a heady atmosphere and consciously harks back to De Luxe Color of the late 1950s.

Lola Montès

France   1955   140 mins   col
Gamma/Florida/Oska

d **Max Ophüls**
sc **Max Ophüls, Annette Wademant, Franz Geiger**
ph **Christian Matras**
m **Georges Auric**
   Martine Carol, Anton Walbrook, Peter Ustinov, Oskar Werner, Will Quadflieg

The story of the famous courtesan Lola Montès (Carol), now become a circus attraction, including her love affairs with King Ludwig I (Walbrook), Liszt (Quadflieg) and a student (Werner), told by the ring master (Ustinov). Ophüls' final film, his only work in colour, treats the space of the CinemaScope screen (using masking and other devices) in an unprecedented and breathtaking manner. The crane shots and camera movements, plus a 360-degree revolve, have the virtuosity of a Liszt sonata. All this makes up for the discursive narrative and the deficiencies of the leading lady. The film, which lost a great deal of money and was shown in a heavily cut version for many years, should only be seen on the wide screen.

▶ **Lonely Wife, The** see Charulata

▶ **Lonely Woman, The** see Journey To Italy

Lone White Sail

▶ **Byeleyet Parus Odinoky**

USSR 1937 92 mins bw
Soyuzdetfilm

d **Vladimir Legoshin**
sc **Valentin Katayev**
ph **Bentsion Monastirsky, G. Garibian**
m **M. Rauchberger**
Igor But, Boris Runge, A. Melnikov, Ivan Peltser, A. Chekayevsky

Two young boys (But and Runge) hide a mutinous sailor (Melnikov) from the battleship *Potemkin* and help him to make contact with fellow revolutionaries in Odessa in 1905. A children's tale, in the best tradition of *Kidnapped*, it is told by Legoshin (a pupil of Eisenstein's) in an exciting, humorous and highly attractive manner. No matter that the adults are stereotyped, the children are delightful, fully-rounded, splendidly played creations. This immensely enjoyable film was popular at home and abroad with audiences of all ages.

The Long Absence

▶ **Une Aussi Longue Absence**

France 1961 96 mins bw
Procinex/Lyre/Galatea

d **Henri Colpi**
sc **Marguerite Duras, Gerald Jarlot**
ph **Marcel Weiss**
m **Georges Delerue**
Alida Valli, Georges Wilson, Jacques Harden

A widow (Valli), who owns a café in a Paris suburb, meets a tramp (Wilson) who may or may not be her husband who disappeared 15 years before in a prison camp. Colpi, who worked as editor on Alain Resnais' first features, made his directorial debut with this poetic, poignant, beautifully underplayed and simple story. A quiet revolution in the cinema.

Best Film Cannes 1961

Longing For Love

▶ **aka The Thirst For Love**

▶ **Ai No Kawaki**

Japan 1967 105 mins bw
Nikkatsu

d **Koreyoshi Kurahara**
sc **Shigeo Fujita, Koreyoshi Kurahara**
ph **Yoshio Mamiya**
m **Toshiro Mayuzumi**
Ruriko Asaoko, Tetsuo Ishidate, Nobuo Nakamura, Chitose Kurenai, Akira Yamanouchi

A young widow (Asaoko), living with her husband's family and enduring the unwelcome attentions of her father-in-law (Nakamura), finds herself infatuated with the family's young gardener (Ishidate). Her growing obsession, although secret, gradually becomes obvious to everybody except the boy himself. When she learns that one of the servant girls (Kurenai) is pregnant by the gardener, she is precipitated into an emotional crisis that leads to violence. This extraordinarily disturbing film about loneliness and sexual frustration combines irony, absurdity and, ultimately, tragedy in a finely balanced mix. An intimate work that probes the depths of its central character, it is acted with uncompromising truth by Asaoko, and directed with subtlety, skill and an effective touch of black humour.

Long Live The Lady!

▶ **Lunga Vita Alla Signora!**

Italy 1987 115 mins col
Raiuno/Cinemaundici

d **Ermanno Olmi**
sc **Ermanno Olmi**
ph **Maurizio Zaccaro**
m **Georg Philipp Telemann**
Marco Esposito, Simona Brandalise, Stefania Busarello, Simone Dalla Rosa, Lorenzo Paolini, Tarcisio Tosi, Marisa Abbate

Six boys and girls, top graduates of a catering school, are engaged to wait at table at a grand banquet of exotic foods being given in a medieval castle by 'La Signorina' (Abbate), a mysterious old lady. The multi-national guests are rich and titled shareholders of a giant conglomerate, gathered to approve the annual report and accounts. During the feast the veneer of sophistication breaks down. Libenzio (Esposito), one of the students, who has fallen for an 'angelic' guest, flees the castle when summoned to the lecherous old lady's room. This satire on the *haute bourgeoisie*, as seen through the eyes of a bespectacled, pimpled youth, is as Buñuelian as the gentle Olmi can become. Like the boy, the director, whose first film this was for five years, minutely observes, by turns fascinated and repulsed, the rituals of a strictly hierarchical, decaying society whose dominant symbol is the huge, ugly, deep-sea fish which the guests consume with relish, not put off by its resemblance to their ancient hostess. By the use of gestures, faces and looks more eloquent than dialogue, Olmi creates witty and sharp caricatures, as well as characters of flesh and blood. There is a marvellously flowing sequence, underscored by the music of Telemann, during the preparation for the banquet. After *Babette's Feast* and *Tampopo*, it was the third film released within a year in which food was used as a metaphor. But although it is more schematic and abstract than the other two pictures, the virtually wordless and plotless film, like the early *Il Posto* (1961), is rather more concerned with the foibles of the people than the allegory which they inhabit.

▶ **Lost Army, The** see Ashes

The Lost Forest

▶ **aka The Forest Of The Hanged**

▶ **aka Forest of Hanged Men**

▶ **Padurea Spinzuratilor**

Romania 1965 157 mins bw
Bucuresti Studios

d **Liviu Ciulei**
sc **Titus Popovici**
ph **Ovidiu Gologan**
m **Theodor Grigoriu**
  Victor Rebengiuc, Liviu Ciulei, Anna Széles, György Kovács

During World War I, when Romanians, Czechs, and Serbians are forced by the Austro-Hungarian Empire to fight against their fellow countrymen, a Romanian lieutenant (Rebengiuc) suffers from divided loyalties. He finally makes a decision that leads to his execution. Romanian films were sparse until Ciulei made an international breakthrough with this rigorous, carefully composed, anti-war drama shot in 'Scope. The acting and writing have an understated quality, unlike the Romanian propaganda epics that preceded it.

Best Director Cannes 1965

The Lost Honour Of Katharina Blum

▶ **Die Verlorene Ehre Der Katharina Blum**

W. Germany 1975 106 mins col
Paramount-Orion/WDR/Bioskop-Film(Munich)

d **Volker Schlöndorff, Margarethe Von Trotta**
sc **Volker Schlöndorff, Margarethe Von Trotta**
ph **Jöst Vacano, Peter Arnold**
m **Hans Werner Henze**
  Angela Winkler, Mario Adorf, Dieter Laser, Jürgen Prochnow, Heinz Bennent, Hannelore Hoger, Karl Heinz Vosgerau

Katharina Blum (Winkler) spends the night with Ludwig Goetten (Prochnow), a new acquaintance who is, unknown to her, under police surveillance. The encounter has serious repercussions: taken in for questioning, she is released to find herself mercilessly hounded by the press who turn her into an object of public opprobrium. In adapting a novel by Heinrich Böll, Schlöndorff and his wife have shifted some of the emphases of the original to make a statement on modern terrorism and police methods in Germany. However, Böll's attack on the yellow press remains powerfully intact in this well-paced if over-literal film.

The Lost One

▶ **Der Verlorene**

W. Germany 1951 90 mins bw
Arnold Pressburger

d **Peter Lorre**

sc **Peter Lorre, Benno Vigny, Axel Eggebrecht**
ph **Vaclav Vich**
m   **Willi Schmidt-Gentner**
    Peter Lorre, Karl John, Helmut Rudolph, Johanna Hofer, Richard Münch

A Nazi scientist (Lorre), who has murdered his fiancée and a woman who reminded him of her, changes his name and becomes a doctor in a refugee camp after the war. Nearly two decades after leaving Germany, Peter Lorre returned to direct his only film rather in the expressionistic manner of those that were being made there when he left. Although no Fritz Lang, Lorre does create a tangible atmosphere of evil which he manages to embody with his own hypnotic presence.

The Lost Son

▶ **Der Verlorene Sohn**

Germany 1934 102 mins bw
Deutsche Universal Film

d   **Luis Trenker**
sc **Luis Trenker, Reinhardt Steinbicker, Arnold Ulitz**
ph **Albert Benitz, Reimar Kuntze**
m   **Giuseppe Becce**
    Luis Trenker, Maria Andergast, Marian Marsh, Paul Henckels, Jimmie Fox

A mountain guide (Trenker) falls in love with an American girl (Marsh) he has rescued from death in the Alps. He then travels to the USA to find her, but only suffers in the Depression. They finally meet again by chance, but he returns to his girlfriend (Andergast) back home. With *The Emperor From California*, this film forms Trenker's American dyad, and gives a vivid and unforgettable picture of New York in the early 1930s, shot on location. The American section comes between some breathtaking mountain material (Trenker was an expert skier and alpinist), in the tradition of the popular *Bergfilm*, with their rather sentimental attitudes and idyllic images.

Lost Youth

▶ **Gioventù Perduta**

Italy 1948 84 mins bw

Carlo Ponti/Lux Film

d   **Pietro Germi**
sc **Pietro Germi, Mario Monicelli, Bruno Valeri, Leopoldo Trieste**
ph **Carlo Montuori**
m   **Carlo Rustichelli**
    Jacques Sernas, Massimo Girotti, Carla Del Poggio, Nando Bruno

A middle-class university student (Sernas) from a loving home stops at nothing, from big-time theft to the murder of his sweetheart when she stumbles on evidence against him. Directed with intelligent restraint by later comedy specialist Germi, the film – technically excellent in all departments – is a convincing character study of post-war delinquency. It was initially withheld by the Italian censors because of its suspected Left-wing bias, but the resultant publicity forced a release.

Lotna

Poland 1964 89 mins col
Film Polski

d   **Andrzej Wajda**
sc **Andrzej Wajda, Wojciech Zukrowski**
ph **Jerzy Lipman**
m   **Tadeusz Baird**
    Božena Kurowska, Jerzy Pichelski, Jerzy Moes, Adam Pawlikowski

The history of the Polish cavalry in its fight against the Germans in World War II as symbolized by an off-white horse that passes to various people in the military until it breaks its leg and is shot. Wajda, son of a cavalry officer who was killed in the war, made his first colour film as a visually arresting and sweeping tribute to the heroic horsemen who faced German tanks. But the episodic screenplay leans too heavily on the *Black Beauty* formula.

Louise

▶ **Chère Louise**

France 1972 105 mins col
Les Films Ariane/P.E.C.F.(Paris)/ C.C.C.(Rome)

d   **Philippe De Broca**
sc **Jean-Loup Dabadie**

ph **Ricardo Aronovitch**
m **Georges Delerue**
   **Jeanne Moreau, Julian Negulesco, Didi
   Perego, Yves Robert, Pippo Starnazza**

After the death of her mother, divorcée Louise, grown somewhat spinsterish, starts a new life as a teacher in Annecy. There, she befriends Luigi (Negulesco), a destitute Italian many years her junior, who becomes her live-in lover. A tried and trusted formula is given new life by Louise's attitude to her affair and her attempts both to keep and to free Luigi, lent conviction by Moreau's beautifully balanced performance. However,in an obvious decision to avoid sugary sentiment, De Broca also succeeds in robbing his film of real depth.

Loulou

France   1980   105 mins   col
Gaumont/Action Films

d **Maurice Pialat**
sc **Arlette Langmann**
ph **Pierre-William Glenn, Jacques Loiseleux**
m **Philippe Sarde**
   **Isabelle Huppert, Gérard Depardieu, Guy
   Marchand, Humbert Balsan**

A *bourgeois* businesswoman (Huppert) leaves her respectable lover (Marchand) to set up home with a working-class yobbo (Depardieu) who is solely preoccupied with booze and bed. Working within the naturalistic tradition, Pialat, with an unobtrusive camera, depicts a Zola-esque story about an incongruous couple drawn to each other by sex alone. One's attitude to the film might depend a great deal on one's reaction to the earthy Depardieu as Loulou – the name being a diminutive of Louis or, colloquially, meaning darling or lout.

Love

▶ **Szerelem**

Hungary   1971   92 mins   bw
Mafilm Studio/Ajay

d **Károly Makk**
sc **Tibor Déry**
ph **János Tóth**
m **András Mihály**
   **Lili Darvas, Mari Töröcsik, Iván Darvas,
   Erszi Orsolya**

With her husband János in jail on a trumped up political charge, Luca (Töröcsik) is left to take care of her old and dying mother-in-law (Darvas). She writes letters purporting to come from János in America, telling of his glittering success as a Hollywood film director, and reads them to the old lady. Luca becomes ostracized for her political connections and loses her job. Makk has made an exquisitely wrought film about love, falsehood (political and personal) and illusion. Whether the old lady believes in the letters is left deliberately ambiguous, as is the truth of her extravagant memories of a Viennese girlhood. Ferenc Molnar's widow, Darvas made this – her second and last film – just before her death and gave a memorable performance, almost matched by that of Töröcsik.

▶ **Love Affair: Or The Case of The Missing Switchboard Operator** see Switchboard Operator, The

▶ **Love À La Carte** see Hungry For Love

Love And Anarchy

▶ **Film D'Amore E D'Anarchia**

Italy   1973   108 Mins   col
Euro International Films

d **Lina Wertmüller**
sc **Lina Wertmüller**
ph **Giuseppe Rotunno**
m **Nino Rota**
   **Giancarlo Giannini, Mariangela Melato,
   Lina Polito, Eros Pagni, Pina Cei**

Tunin (Giannini), a simple farmer, commits himself to an anti-Fascist group that despatches him to assassinate Mussolini. He lodges in a whorehouse, the madame of which (Melato) became a political idealist when her lover was killed by the Fascists. Tunin falls in love with one of the prostitutes (Polito) and this, together with his oversensitive nature, impedes his mission and leads him to his own violent destruction. As is usual in her work, Wertmüller indulges in excess but, on this occasion, it comes into its own in creating a palpable sense of the period, with the Lautrec-like brothel and its anarchic inhabitants serving as a subtle metaphor for freedom.The film's thesis – romanticism is not a realistic basis for political activism – is a telling one, and director, cast and designers achieve an authentic evocation of the disturbed atmosphere and the look and feel of 1930s Italy while providing strong entertainment.

Best Actor (Giancarlo Giannini) Cannes 1973

Love And Anger

▶ **Amore E Rabbia**

Italy 1969 102 mins col
Castoro Film (Rome)/Anouchka Film (Paris)

d 1) **Carlo Lizzani 2) Bernardo Bertolucci 3) Pier Paolo Pasolini 4) Jean-Luc Godard**
sc 1) **Carlo Lizzani 2) Bernardo Bertolucci 3) Pier Paolo Pasolini 4) Jean-Luc Godard**
ph 1) **Sandro Mancori 2) Ugo Piccone 3) Giuseppe Ruzzolini 4) Alain Levent** m **Giovanni Fusco**
1) **Tom Baker 2) Julien Beck 3) Ninetto Davoli 4) Christine Guého, Nino Castelnuovo, Catherine Jourdan, Paolo Pozzesi**

1) *Indifference*: In a high-rise New York housing estate nobody takes any notice of a murder, a car crash or a police chase.
2) *Agony*: A dying man sees visions in his final agony. 3) *The Sequence Of The Paper Flower*: God speaks to an innocent young man walking down a street in Rome, and then strikes him dead. 4) *Love*: One couple observes another couple in a garden. Of these modern interpretations of New Testament parables, only Pasolini's 12-minute gem can be considered a success, while Godard's is intellectually teasing, and Bertolucci's gives an indulgent and dated glimpse of the Living Theatre at work. A fifth episode by Marco Bellocchio about student militants was cut from the US and UK versions.

Love And Journalism

▶ **Kärlek Och Journalistik**

Sweden 1916 60 mins bw
Svenska Bio

d **Mauritz Stiller**
sc **Harriet Bloch**
ph **Gustaf Boge**
m **Silent**
Richard Lund, Karin Molander, Jenny Tschernichin-Larsson, Stina Berg, Göran Cederborg

In search of a news story, young journalist Hertha (Molander) secures the post of maid in the household of Erik Bloome (Lund), a leading Antarctic explorer. She is unmasked and dismissed, but Bloome realizes he has fallen in love and sets out to find her... The picture is effectively stolen by the delightful Molander as the prototype of the intelligent, resourceful and emancipated 'modern' heroine of the day. This entertaining comedy was the first of many which Stiller directed in the late 'teens, and which clearly anticipate the work of Lubitsch in the 1920s. To those who identify the Swedish cinema (particularly Stiller's work) with more serious dramatic efforts, they come as a breath of fresh air.

Love And The Frenchwoman

▶ **La Française Et L'Amour**

France 1960 135 mins bw
Metzger & Woog/Paris Elysée Film

d 1) **Henri Decoin 2) Jean Delannoy 3) Michel Boisrond 4) René Clair 5) Henri Verneuil 6) Christian-Jaque 7) Jean-Paul Le Chanois**
sc 1) **Felicien Marceau 2) Louise De Vilmorin, Jacques Robert 3) Annette Wademant 4) René Clair 5) France Roche, Michel Audiard 6) Charles Spaak 7) Jean-Paul Le Chanois**
ph **Robert Lefèbvre**
m 1) **Joseph Kosma 2) Paul Misraki 3) Jean Constantin 4) Jacques Metehen 5) Norbert Glanzberg 6) Henri Crolla 7) Georges Delerue**
1) **Martine Lambert, Pierre-Jean Vaillard, Jacqueline Porel 2) Annie Sinigalia, Roger Pierre, Sophie Desmarets, Pierre Mondy 3) Valérie Lagrange, Pierre Michael, Paul Bonifas, Nicole Chollet 4) Marie-José Nat, Claude Rich, Yves Robert 5) Dany Robin, Paul Meurisse, Jean-Paul Belmondo 6) Annie Girardot, François Périer, Jean Poiret, Michel Serrault 7) Robert Lamoureux, Martine Carol, Sylvia Montfort, Simone Renant**

An anthology, taking a supposedly representative view of French women in relation to love at various stages of life, under the headings: 'Childhood', 'Adolescence', 'Virginity', 'Marriage', 'Adultery', 'Divorce', and 'A Woman Alone'. Inevitably light-weight, given the brevity of each episode, but the little stories are well written, directed and acted and the film has a lot of charm. Clair's episode, about a couple who are jolted by their first arguments *en route* to their honeymoon destination, is the most completely accomplished, but some might prefer the now engagingly old-fashioned 'Virginity' in which a young couple, forced to postpone their wedding, grapple with the problem of celibacy.

Love At Twenty

▶ **L'Amour À Vingt Ans**

France/Italy/Japan/W. Germany/
Poland 1962 123 mins bw
Ulysse-Unitec (Paris)/Cinesecolo
(Rome)/Toho-Towa (Tokyo)/Beta Film
(Munich)/Zespol Kamera (Warsaw)

d 1) **François Truffaut** 2) **Renzo Rossellini**
   3) **Shintaro Ishihara** 4) **Marcel Ophüls**
   5) **Andrzej Wajda**
sc 1) **François Truffaut** 2) **Renzo Rossellini**
   3) **Shintaro Ishihara** 4) **Marcel Ophüls**
   5) **Jerzy Stefan Stawinski**
ph 1) **Raoul Coutard** 2) **Mario Montuori**
   3) **Shigeo Hayashida** 4) **Wolfgang Wirth**
   5) **Jerzy Lipman**
m **Georges Delerue, Tohru Takemitsu, Jerzy**
   Matuszkiewicz
   1) **Jean-Pierre Léaud, Marie-France**
   Pisier
   2) **Eleanora Rossi Drago, Cristina Gajoni,**
   Geronimo Meynier 3) **Koji Furuhata,**
   Nami Tamura 4) **Christian Doermer,**
   Barbara Frey
   5) **Barbara Lass, Zbigniew Cybulski,**
   Wladyslaw Kowalski

1) Antoine Doinel falls for a music student, but spends an evening with her parents while she's out on a date. 2) The mistress of a young man warns off the innocent girl he thinks he loves. 3) A young factory worker murders a beautiful student. 4) A photographer falls in love with a woman after she has had his child. 5) Young people taunt a worker

who lived through World War II. Three successes out of five is not bad for a sketch film – Truffaut's delightful vignette, Ishihara's perverted but powerful tale and Wajda's painful episode – all linked by Cartier-Bresson photographs.

A Love Bewitched

▶ **aka Love The Magician**
▶ **El Amor Brujo**

Spain 1985 98 mins col
Emiliano Piedra Prod.

d **Carlos Saura**
sc **Carlos Saura, Antonio Gades**
ph **Teo Escamilla**
m **Manuel De Falla**
   Antonio Gades, Cristina Hoyos, Laura
   Del Sol, Juan Antonio Jimenez, Emma
   Penella

Two gipsy children, pledged in marriage by their fathers, grow up to fall in love elsewhere with tragic consequences. The culmination of the Saura-Gades Spanish dance trilogy (the others were *Blood Wedding*, 1981 and *Carmen*, 1983) is set in the splendidly stylized decor (by Gerardo Vera) of a studio with props representing a shanty town. Although the dancing is as passionate as ever, only enthusiasts of the genre will find it other than monotonous.

▶ **Love Doll** see Life Size

Love Eternal

▶ **(US: The Eternal Return)**
▶ **L'Éternel Retour**

France 1943 111 mins bw
André Paulvé

d **Jean Delannoy**
sc **Jean Cocteau**
ph **Roger Hubert**
m **Georges Auric**
   Jean Marais, Madeleine Sologne, Jean
   Murat, Yvonne De Bray, Piéral, Roland
   Toutain

Patrice (Marais) brings Nathalie (Sologne) to

the château of his recently widowed friend Mark (Murat) in the hope they will marry. However, Patrice and Nathalie fall hopelessly in love as a result of a love potion issued to them by Achille (Piéral), a vicious dwarf. They eventually find their apotheosis in death. Cocteau's updating of the Tristan and Iseult legend works on many levels and fails on others. Certainly, the presence of Cocteau, who was in constant attendance during the filming, is strongly felt in the dialogue and in the playing of the members of his stock company. But there is something a trifle ludicrous about the *liebestod* in the context of 'modern youth' in ski jerseys, apparel which became fashionable because of the film's huge success in France. Made during the Occupation, its Aryan lovers (Marais and Sologne lacking sexiness) were extremely pleasing to the Occupiers.

▶ **Love Game, The** see Playing At Love

▶ **Love Hate** see Albatross, The

A Love In Germany

▶ **Eine Liebe In Deutschland**

W. Germany 1983 132 mins col
CCC/Filmkunst/Gaumont/TF1/Stand'art

d Andrzej Wajda
sc Andrzej Wajda, Boleslaw Michalek, Agnieszka Holland
ph Igor Luther
m Michel Legrand
Hanna Schygulla, Marie-Christine Barrault, Armin Müller-Stahl, Piotr Lysak, Daniel Olbrychski

In a small German town during World War II, a married woman shopkeeper (Schygulla) breaks Nazi law by having an affair with a young Polish POW (Lysak). She is sent to a work camp and he is executed. Wajda's second film outside Poland, like *Danton* of the same year, uses the past to make a forced comparison with his homeland today. Here, the shifts from past to present only detract and distance us from the interesting drama based on a true incident as documented in Rolf Hochhuth's bestseller.

Love In Question

▶ **L'Amour En Question**

France 1978 100 mins col
Paris-Cannes-Alpes Cinema

d André Cayatte
sc André Cayatte, Jean Laborde
ph Jean Badal
m Olivier Dassault
Annie Girardot, Bibi Andersson, Michel Galabru, Michel Auclair

The Swedish wife (Andersson) of an elderly French architect is accused of plotting his murder with the aid of her English lover. Another of Cayatte's flat, didactic films dealing with aspects of the law, it throws up a few interesting sidelights on the contrast between the French and British legal systems. The casebook characters lack depth, though Annie Girardot does her best as an investigating judge.

Love In The Afternoon

▶ **(US: Chloë In The Afternoon)**
▶ **L'Amour L'Après-Midi**

France 1972 97 mins col
Films Du Losange

d Eric Rohmer
sc Eric Rohmer
ph Nestor Almendros
m Arié Dzierlatka
Bernard Verley, Zouzou, Françoise Verley, Daniel Ceccaldi, Malvina Penne, Babette Ferrier

Frédéric (Bernard Verley), a fairly young business executive, happily married to Hélène (Françoise Verley), meets up with Chloë (Zouzou), a friend from the past. They begin to see each other during his afternoon lunch breaks, but when Chloë offers herself to him, he returns to his wife. The last of Rohmer's Six Moral Tales is the first to present a married man with the choice between love and sex. The trouble is that, whereas the preceding films dealt with articulate, attractive, and interesting people, Frédéric is dull and unadmirable, representing rather unappealing *bourgeois* values which the director seems to uphold. (It was after seeing the

Verleys' wedding photographs that Rohmer decided they should play a married couple in the film.)

Love In The City

▶ **Amore In Città**

Italy 1953 110 mins bw
Faro

d **Dino Risi, Michelangelo Antonioni, Federico Fellini, Francesco Maselli, Cesare Zavattini, Alberto Lattuada, Carlo Lizzani**
sc **Aldo Buzzi, Luigi Malerba, Luigi Chiarini, Tullio Pinelli, Vittorio Vettroni**
ph **Gianni Di Venanzo**
m **Mario Nascimbene**
Antonio Cifariello, Livia Venturini, and non-professionals from the Centro Sperimentale Di Cinematografia, Rome

Six true episodes taken from newspaper reports were filmed in the locales where the events took place with the people involved in them. Screenwriter Zavattini, one of the major forces in the Neo-Realist movement, here as producer, tried to make an omnibus film that fulfilled his notions of objective reportage. It ends up being neither fish nor fowl. The only meat comes from Fellini, who subverted the whole venture by making an obviously fictional episode about a reporter at a matrimonial agency claiming to be a doctor representing a werewolf who thinks that marriage might cure him. Antonioni contributes a series of bleak interviews with young girls who survived suicide attempts, Zavattini and Maselli concentrate on a Sicilian girl seduced and abandoned in Rome, while Risi and Lattuada's subjects strain to be amusing. The Lizzani piece was cut from the print shown outside Italy because the authorities objected to its portrayal of prostitution.

Love Is A Fat Woman

▶ **El Amor Es Una Mujer Gorda**

Argentina 1987 80 mins bw
Movimiento Falso/Allart's Enterprises B.V.

d **Alejandro Agresti**

sc **Alejandro Agresti**
ph **Nestor Sanz**
m **Paul Michael Van Brugge**
Elio Marchi, Sergio Povés Campos, Carlos Roffe, Mario Luciani, Stella Fabrizzi, Enrique Morales

José (Marchi), a writer and journalist, rails against what he considers the exploitation of poverty by a visiting American film company and loses his job. Penniless and thrown out of his lodgings, he wanders the streets, sleeping where he can and encountering old acquaintances. José is obsessed with a quest for his 'disappeared' girlfriend with whom he lived during the years of the military regime and prefers to believe that she left him rather than face the truth that she was killed by the authorities. This elliptical work attacks complacency, examines hypocrisy and reveals the ugly legacy of political repression. The series of fragmented incidents that serve as narrative is too oblique to be entirely successful and the angry, embittered and self-deluding protagonist something of an enigma. However, the film, made on the thinnest of shoestrings, is constantly absorbing and powerfully atmospheric. It deals in characters who live on the margins of Buenos Aires society and its low-key, imaginatively angled black-and-white photography is reminiscent of the work of Orson Welles. Made partly with Dutch money, and processed in Holland where Agresti went after offending the Argentinian authorities, it is only his second feature, made when he was 26. He says of himself, 'The street is my real inspiration. I was raised on the streets, everything I put in my films is based on my experience of life on the streets.' And, indeed, it is the half-deserted city and its wandering, lost souls that continue to haunt the memory.

Love Is A Funny Thing

▶ **Un Homme Qui Me Plaît**

France 1969 95 mins col
Films Ariane/Films 13/UA

d **Claude Lelouch**
sc **Claude Lelouch, Pierre Uytterhoeven**
ph **Claude Lelouch**
m **Francis Lai**
Annie Girardot, Jean Paul Belmondo,

Maria Pia Conte, Marcel Bozzuffi, Farrah Fawcett, Peter Bergman

While working on a film in Hollywood, two married French people, an actress (Girardot) and a musician (Belmondo), have a brief affair. After travelling around to Las Vegas, Monument Valley and New Orleans, they agree to meet again one day in Nice. He turns up. She doesn't. At one stage of this picture Belmondo says to the movie director (Bergman) that there are too many films about aimless, wealthy people who think their affairs are important. Lelouch, ignoring the irony of the remark, blithely proceeds to make such a film, another superficial variation on his first hit, *A Man And A Woman* (1966). Nor does he bring a fresh French eye to the sightseeing scenes, pleasant as they are to look at, and the couple's rompings, in bed and elsewhere, are repetitive. The director would return to the USA with *Another Man, Another Chance* in 1977 with slightly better results.

Love Is Love

▶ **Liebe Ist Liebe**

Germany 1932 88 mins bw
UFA

d **Paul Martin**
sc **Robert Gilbert, Robert Liebmann, Max Kolpe**
ph **Günther Rittau, Otto Baecker**
m **Werner R. Heymann**
    Kaethe Von Nagy, Julius Falkenstein, Hans Albers, Frieda Richard, Hans Brausewetter

A young man quits his job after a big win on the horses, proceeds to lose both the money and his girl, and gets both back after a series of misunderstandings. A light-weight romantic comedy with the thinnest of plots, but boasting interesting Berlin locations, a charming and pretty leading lady in Von Nagy, and a dose of suitably pleasing waltz music.

Love Is My Profession

▶ **En Cas De Malheur**

France 1958 120 mins bw

Iéna/UCIL/Incom

d **Claude Autant-Lara**
sc **Jean Aurenche, Pierre Bost**
ph **Jacques Natteau**
m **René Cloërec**
    Jean Gabin, Edwige Feuillère, Brigitte Bardot, Franco Interlenghi, Nicole Berger

A wealthy middle-aged lawyer (Gabin) is smitten with a young client (Bardot) whom he is defending on a charge of theft. She steals him away from his long-suffering wife (Feuillère). The racy English title disguises a competent, well-acted melodrama, based on a Georges Simenon novel. It is fun to see the veteran Gabin being vamped by sex kitten BB. Although she has an obligatory nude scene, the film also gives her a chance to show some acting ability.

▶ **Love Maker, The** see Calle Mayor

The Love Makers

▶ **La Viaccia**

Italy 1961 106 mins bw
Titanus/Galatea/Arco(Rome)/
S.G.C(Paris)

d **Mauro Bolognini**
sc **Vasco Pratolini, Pasquale Festa Campanile, Massimo Franciosa**
ph **Leonida Barboni**
m **Piero Piccioni, Debussy**
    Jean-Paul Belmondo, Claudia Cardinale, Pietro Germi, Romolo Valli, Gabriella Pallotta, Paul Frankeur

When Ferdinando (Frankeur) takes control of the family farm, 'La Viaccia', he offers his nephew Amerigo (Belmondo) a job in his wine business. The young man takes up his position, but falls passionately in love with the première whore (Cardinale) in a Florentine brothel, thus ruining his prospects and his life. There are several intricacies to the plot, of course, but none of them matters over much. What impresses is the background against which this semi-dynastic melodrama is played – Florence in the 1880s filmed by Bolognini, one of the masters of visual beauty, atmosphere and period detail, all of which he evokes without any recourse to obvious glamour. Belmondo and Cardinale are good, but only as far as a slightly undernourished script allows.

▶ **Love Match** see Partie De Plaisir, Une

The Love Of Jeanne Ney

▶ **aka Lusts Of The Flesh**

▶ **Die Liebe Der Jeanne Ney**

Germany 1927 120 mins bw
UFA

d G.W. Pabst
sc Ladislas Vajda, Rudolf Leonhardt, Ilya Ehrenberg
ph Fritz Arno Wagner, Walter Robert Lach
m Silent
    Edith Jehanne, Uno Henning, Fritz Rasp, Brigitte Helm

Jeanne Ney (Jehanne) falls in love with the man (Henning) who killed her father in the Crimea during the Russian Revolution. The couple move to Paris, but are pursued by a sadistic political opportunist (Rasp) who schemes against them. Intended by UFA as a Hollywood-type romance set in rapidly changing locales, it was lighter and more naturalistically conceived than Pabst's other films of the period. Although the plot (from Ehrenberg's novel) is rather complicated, it is full of inventive sequences such as the officers' orgy reflected in a high mirror, and the shot of a bride weeping alone after a wedding, espied by lovers from a hotel bedroom.

The Love Of Sumako The Actress

▶ **Joyu Sumako No Koi**

Japan 1947 96 mins bw
Shochiku

d Kenji Mizoguchi
sc Hideo Nagata
ph Shigeto Miki
m Hisato Osawa
    Kinuyo Tanaka, So Yamamura, Eijiro Tono, Kikue Mori, Chiyeko Higashiyama

The noted stage director Hogetsu Shimamura (Yamamura) puts on the first Japanese production of Ibsen's *A Doll's House* with

Sumako (Tanaka), a new young actress, with whom he falls in love. He leaves his wife and daughter to tour with her, but both are determined to dedicate their lives to their art. This true and fascinating account of the rise of Western theatre in Japan and of one of the country's first actresses, is also a rich melodrama with a mirror image of life and the stage. It was the third of 10 films the tender tragedienne Tanaka made for Mizoguchi.

Love On The Ground

▶ **L'Amour Par Terre**

France 1984 125 mins col
La Cecilia

d Jacques Rivette
sc Jacques Rivette, Pascal Bonitzer, Marilu Parolini, Suzanne Schiffman
ph William Lubtchansky
    Jane Birkin, Geraldine Chaplin, Jean-Pierre Kalfon, László Szabó, André Dussollier, Facundo Bo

Two foreign actresses (Chaplin and Birkin) in Paris are requested by a rich and enigmatic playwright (Kalfon) to appear in a special play he has written for a single performance at his château. When a director tries to return after a decade to the territory of his most popular film, watch out! This time, instead of *Céline And Julie Go Boating*, Rivette provides Charlotte And Emily (the Brontë names are typical of the archness of the exercise) Go Boring. Yet there is some intellectual pleasure to be had from the game-playing, the decor and performances. Though most critics found it soporific, there were a few who thought it superior to the earlier film.

Love On The Run

▶ **L'Amour En Fuite**

France 1979 95 mins col
Les Films Du Carrosse

d François Truffaut
sc François Truffaut, Marie-France Pisier, Jean Aurel, Suzanne Schiffman
ph Nestor Almendros
m Georges Delerue
    Jean-Pierre Léaud, Claude Jade, Marie-France Pisier, Rosy Varte, Dorothée

Antoine Doinel (Léaud), separated from his wife (Jade) and young son, is involved with Sabine (Dorothée), until he meets Colette (Pisier, who also played Colette in *Love At Twenty*), a childhood sweetheart now a lawyer. Encouraged by her, he decides to write a novel. This is the last of the five Truffaut films following the adventures of his alter-ego Antoine Doinel, alias Léaud begun with *The Four Hundred Blows*, almost 20 years previously. Although as lightweight as the others, it cannot hide the pain at the loss of youthful spontaneity and the difficulties of obtaining durable love. The film is really a look back in affection at the previous episodes, with some footage from them. When Truffaut died, Léaud suffered a breakdown and was never the same again.

Lover Boy

▶ **L'Amant De Poche**

France 1977 94 mins col
Progefi/S.F.P./Gaumont

d **Bernard Queysanne**
sc **Bernard Queysanne, Pierre Pelégri**
ph **Alain Levent**
m **Laurent Petitgirard**
   Mimsy Farmer, Pascal Sellier, Stéphane Jobert, Bernard Fresson, Andréa Ferréol

Sixteen-year-old Julien (Sellier) is seduced by an American woman (Farmer) who buys him evening clothes and takes him to Tunisia for a weekend. After a last night together, she sends a message – via his father – that she loves him, and disappears. She is, in fact, a high-class whore, which leads to several plot complications. A light-hearted romp, verging on sexploitation, from the director of the much superior *Un Homme Qui Dort*.

The Lovers

▶ **Les Amants**

France 1958 88 mins bw
Nouvelle Editions

d **Louis Malle**
sc **Louis Malle, Louise De Vilmorin**
ph **Henri Decaë**
m **Brahms**
   Jeanne Moreau, Jean-Marc Bory, Alain Cuny, Judith Magre

A sensuous but bored provincial wife (Moreau), finds sexual gratification, a deeper love and a more meaningful life in an adulterous relationship with a young man (Bory), a house guest of her husband (Cuny). This chic, lyrical, erotic satire, which Truffaut called 'the first night of love in the cinema,' presumably because of its semi-nude love scenes to Brahms, caused a scandal in its day, made an international star of Moreau, and much money for the producers.

Special Jury Prize (Louis Malle) Venice 1958

Lovers And Thieves

▶ **Assassins Et Voleurs**

France 1956 85 mins bw
CLM/SNEG

d **Sacha Guitry**
sc **Sacha Guitry**
ph **Paul Cotteret**
m **Jean Françaix**
   Jean Poiret, Michel Serrault, Magali Noël, Clément Duhour

A middle-aged man about to commit suicide tells a burglar of how he shot the husband of his mistress and slipped the gun into the pocket of the very same burglar. Guitry, aged 72 and approaching death (he died a year later), had clearly run out of steam in this rather static, cynical boulevard comedy, but there were still some piquant lines and situations, and Poiret and Serrault always make an amusing team.

▶ **Lovers Like Us** see Savage, The

▶ **Lovers' Net** see Lovers Of Lisbon, The

The Lovers Of Lisbon

▶ **(US: Lovers' Net**

▶ **aka Port Of Shame)**

▶ **Les Amants Du Tage**

France 1954 123 mins bw
Enterprise Générale/Hoch/Fides

d **Henri Verneuil**
sc **Marcel Rivet, Jacques Companeez**

ph Roger Hubert
m Lucien Legrand
   Daniel Gélin, Françoise Arnoul, Marcel
   Dalio, Trevor Howard, Amalia Rodrigues

Pierre (Gélin) kills his wife for infidelity.
Acquitted, but distrustful of women, he settles
in Lisbon and falls in love with Kathleen
(Arnoul), the wealthy widow of an Englishman whose death she caused and which is
under investigation by an English policeman
(Howard). Romance is hardly a happy business in this lengthy film, which is a mixed
bag of realism and pretension in which the
actors don't seem entirely at ease.

▶ **Lovers Of Montparnasse, The** see
Montparnasse 19

The Lovers Of Teruel

▶ **Les Amants De Teruel**

   France   1962   90 mins   col
   Monarch/CD

d Raymond Rouleau
sc Raymond Rouleau, René-Louis Laforgue
ph Claude Renoir
m Mikis Theodorakis, Henri Sauguet
   Ludmilla Tcherina, Milko Sparemblek,
   Milenko Banovitch, Antoine Marin

A gypsy dancer (Tcherina) stars in a ballet
about a woman whose lover goes away for
three years to prove his worth. When he fails
to return she reluctantly marries, whereupon
her lover reappears and kills himself. She
follows suit. What lends the story interest is
that the tragic heroine's life begins to mirror
the Spanish legend she interprets. An attractive film, enhanced by the beauty and balletic
gifts of Tcherina.

The Lovers Of Verona

▶ **Les Amants De Vérone**

   France   1948   110 mins   bw
   CICC

d André Cayatte
sc André Cayatte, Jacques Prévert
ph Henri Alekan
m Joseph Kosma

   Pierre Brasseur, Serge Reggiani, Anouk
   Aimée, Marcel Dalio, Martine Carol

Two young people (Reggiani and Aimée)
understudying the roles of Romeo and Juliet
in a film being shot in Italy, find their love,
like that of the 'star-crossed lovers', blighted
by their families. Although this romance of
post-war gloom really needed Marcel Carné
to bring all the nuances of Prévert's script to
life, Cayatte, on the eve of his more didactic
period, does a creditable job. It was Prévert
who had the idea of writing the part of the
modern-day Juliet for 16-year-old Anouk
Aimée. Her glowing beauty and tender performance ensured that her first starring role
was not her last.

Lovers On A Tightrope

▶ **La Corde Raide**

   France   1960   90 mins   bw
   Panda Film

d Jean-Charles Dudrumet
sc Jean-Charles Dudrumet, Roland
   Laudenbach
ph Pierre Gueguen
m Maurice Jarre
   François Périer, Annie Girardot, Gérard
   Buhr

The bored wife (Girardot) of a wealthy
businessman (Périer) has an affair with a
motor mechanic who is after her money. He
attempts to dispose of her husband by tam-
pering with the latter's car, but the husband's
brother is mistakenly killed instead. Dudrumet's first film is a humdrum effort, lacking
both tension and credibility, despite good lead
casting.

A Lover's Return

▶ **Un Revenant**

   France   1946   90 mins   bw
   C.F.C.C.

d Christian-Jaque
sc Henri Jeanson, Louis Chavance,
   Christian-Jaque
ph Louis Page
m Arthur Honegger
   Louis Jouvet, Gaby Morlay, François

Périer, Ludmilla Tcherina, Marguerite Moreno

A successful ballet impresario (Jouvet), returns to the provinces to exhume a love affair that went wrong. A basically static and rambling exercise in nostalgia offers some wry Gallic reflection on the nature of love, a characteristically polished performance from the leading man, and some lively – albeit brief – distraction provided by the lovely ballet dancer, Tcherina.

Love's Crucible

▶ **Vem Dömer?**

Sweden 1921 88 mins bw
Svensk Filmindustri

d   Victor Sjöström
sc   Hjalmar Bergman, Victor Sjöström
ph   J. Julius Jaenzon
m   Silent
     Jenny Hasselqvist, Ivan Hedkvist, Tore Svennberg, Gösta Ekman, Knut Lindroth

In Renaissance Florence, Ursula (Hasselqvist) is in love with Bertram (Ekman), but is married against her will to the elderly sculptor Anton (Hedkvist). When her husband dies, Ursula is accused of murder from which only an ordeal by fire can exonerate her. This large production, aiming for an international market with a subject away from a Scandinavian setting and themes, was a commercial flop. Now it can be seen as one of Sjöström's neglected masterpieces, full of bravura sequences and images derived from the great Italian painters of the period. Most famous is the final scene using superimpositions, rhythmic disolves and a tracking shot dramatically to represent Ursula at the stake.

Love 65

▶ **Kärlek 65**

Sweden 1965 95 mins bw
Europa Film

d   Bo Widerberg
sc   Bo Widerberg
ph   Jan Lindeström
m   Bill Evans, Vivaldi
     Keve Hjelm, Anne-Marie Gyllenspetz,

Evabritt Strandberg, Ben Carruthers, Thommy Berggren

Keve (Hjelm), an established film director, is going through a difficult time in his marriage to Ann-Mari (Gyllenspetz), and is having problems with his leading man Thommy Berggren (playing himself). He takes up with Evabritt (Strandberg), the wife of a former student, but he can only find peace in flying kites. The reaction of most critics to this bleak, self-indulgent autobiography was to tell the director to 'go fly a kite'. Fragmented and fumbling, it has a morose, unsympathetic figure (a self-portrait?) at its centre. Some splendidly romantic images, and an interesting glimpse into the director's fantasies (a variation on Fellini's $8\frac{1}{2}$) are among the few things going for it.

▶ **Loves Of A Blonde** see Blonde In Love, A

Loves Of Ariane

▶ **Ariane**

Germany 1931 78 mins bw
Nero

d   Paul Czinner
sc   Paul Czinner, Carl Mayer
ph   Adolf Schlasy, Adolf Jansen
m   Mozart, Richard Strauss
     Elisabeth Bergner, Rudolf Forster, Annemarie Steinsieck, Hertha Guthmar

When Ariane (Bergner), an innocent Russian girl studying in Berlin, falls for a man-of-the-world (Forster), she pretends to be a coquette because she dislikes inexperienced women. Billy Wilder remade this charming little sophisticated comedy as *Love In The Afternoon* with Audrey Hepburn and Gary Cooper in 1957, not one of his best. On the other hand, Czinner's film is above his own average, with his future wife, Bergner, in her first talkie, this time only adding half a spoon of sugar to her performance.

Loves Of Casanova

▶ **Aventures De Casanova**

France 1947 101 mins bw
Sirius

d   **Jean Boyer**
sc **Marc G. Sauvajon**
ph **Charles Suin**
m   **René Sylvester**
    Georges Guetary, Hélène Dassonville,
    Noelle Norman, Jacqueline Gauthier,
    Claudette Falco

Casanova (Guetary) journeys from Venice to Paris to seek his fortune. *En route*, and after his arrival, he engages in a succession of romantic affairs with various attractive women. Yet another replay of the Casanova legend, this time in the form of a musical. The boyish, engaging cabaret star essaying the great lover is too wholesome for the role by far and, aside from some picturesque duelling and horse-riding and frequent bursts of song, the movie is innocuous, insipid and forgettable.

▶ **Loves Of Pharaoh, The** see Wife Of Pharaoh, The

▶ **Love Story** see Douce

▶ **Love The Magician** see Love Bewitched, A

The Love Trap

▶ **Un Couple**

    France   1960   84 mins   bw
    Balzac Films/La Société Discifilm

d   **Jean-Pierre Mocky**
sc **Raymond Queneau, Jean-Pierre Mocky**
ph **Eugen Schüfftan**
m   **Alain Romans**
    Juliet Mayniel, Jean Kosta, Francis
    Blanche, Véronique Nordey, Christian
    Duvaleix

Pierre and Anne (Kosta and Mayniel) have been happily married for three years when they decide that their relationship has palled and they must part. Pierre, in any event attracted to his fellow employee Véronique (Nordey), spends the night at a hotel, but the next day he and Anne meet at a party. A reconciliation takes place but doesn't last, as each is overcome by fresh doubts. In his

second film as director, actor Mocky deals frankly, sympathetically and sincerely with a realistic problem. Unfortunately, in spite of these promising ingredients and convincing performances from the leads, the director loses his grip and allows the piece to get out of hand. The supporting characters are unattractive stereotypes, and the external apparatus of his situations – the bizarre toy factory where Pierre works, for example – is crude and unhelpful. This lack of discipline would come to characterize Mocky's subsequent work.

Loving Couples

▶ **Älskande Pär**

    Sweden   1964   118 mins   bw
    Sandrew

d   **Mai Zetterling**
sc **Mai Zetterling, David Hughes**
ph **Sven Nykvist**
m   **Roger Wallis**
    Harriet Andersson, Gunnel Lindblom,
    Anita Björk, Gunnar Björnstrand, Eva
    Dahlbeck, Gio Petre

In the early 1900s, three contrasting expectant mothers (Andersson, Lindblom, Petre) think over their past relationships with men and how they came to be pregnant. Mai Zetterling suddenly emerged from being an ingenue in a number of insipid British films of the 1950s into a far from insipid director with this ironically titled social comedy-drama, hugely influenced by Ingmar Bergman. In fact, the film's main strength is in the excellent acting and camerawork from members of the Bergman stable. Co-adapted with her then husband, a British novelist, from the *roman fleuve* by Agnes Von Krusentjerna, the film suffers somewhat from over-elaboration and a self-conscious desire to shock.

Loving In The Rain

▶ **Un Amour De Pluie**

    France   1974   90 mins   col
    Lira Films/Claudia Cinematografica/
    Terra Film

d   Jean-Claude Brialy
sc Jean-Claude Brialy, Jean-Claude Carrière
ph Andreas Winding
m   Francis Lai
    Romy Schneider, Nino Castelnuovo,
    Bénédicte Boucher, Suzanne Flon, Alain
    David

A still young and glamorous woman (Schneider) takes a holiday with her 15-year-old daughter. Two romantic episodes ensue as mother has an affair with a mysterious Italian (Castelnuovo), and daughter her first adolescent flirtation with a youth, before they return home to their mundane existences. Competent, but superficial and forgettable, with Brialy – although himself a polished and experienced actor – missing the opportunity to draw real feeling from his protagonists.

The Lower Depths

▶ **Les Bas-Fonds**

    France   1936   92 mins   bw
    Albatros
d   Jean Renoir
sc Jean Renoir, Charles Spaak
ph Jean Bachelet
m   Jean Wiener
    Jean Gabin, Louis Jouvet, Vladimir
    Sokoloff, Jany Holt, Robert Le Vigan,
    Suzy Prim

A ruined Baron (Jouvet) befriends a thief (Gabin) and goes to live with him and other assorted losers in a doss house. 'I was not trying to make a Russian film. I wanted to make a human drama based on the play by Gorky,' stated Renoir about his very French, very free adaptation of a classic play. In fact, it differed so much from the original that the director sought and gained Gorky's approval before embarking on it. Less profound in tone, it still has two splendid performances from Gabin and Jouvet, the latter telling a tale while a snail climbs up his finger.

The Lower Depths

▶ **Donzoko**

    Japan   1957   124 mins   bw

    Toho
d   Akira Kurosawa
sc Akira Kurosawa, Hideo Oguni
ph Kazuo Yamasaki
m   Masaru Sato
    Toshiro Mifune, Isuzu Yamada, Kyoko
    Kagawa, Bokuzen Hidari

A pedlar (Mifune) wanted by the police goes to live in a hovel filled with human derelicts. Among these is an aging woman who loves a thief who loves a young girl. Kurosawa's version of Gorky's play is as Japanese as Renoir's was French, demonstrating the universality of the Russian original. Although most of the action takes place in one large room – effectively filmed with multiple cameras (witness the 180 degree camera reversals) – the visual fluidity and the extraordinary characterizations keep the picture alive.

Lowland

▶ **Tiefland**

    W. Germany   1954   98 mins   bw
    Leni Riefenstahl
d   Leni Riefenstahl
sc Leni Riefenstahl
ph Albert Benitz
m   Eugen D'Albert, Herbert Windt
    Leni Riefenstahl, Franz Eichberger,
    Bernhard Minetti, Aribert Wäscher,
    Maria Kappenhöfer

Don Sebastian (Minetti), an impoverished Spanish nobleman, marries the wealthy mayor's daughter (Kappenhöfer), but will not give up his mistress Marta (Riefenstahl), a flamenco dancer. She marries Pedro (Eichberger), a shepherd, but when Sebastian tries to take her back, Pedro kills him. Riefenstahl started filming this melodrama, based on D'Albert's *verismo* opera, in 1935, but was constantly interrupted during the war. The French confiscated the unfinished film after the war, but Riefenstahl regained, completed, edited and released it in 1954. Despite the picture's chequered history, it makes (except for the ending) an aesthetic whole. The pictorial beauty (1930s black-and-white textures) and spectacular mountain set pieces, compensate for some of the deficiencies of plot and performance. Rumours still abound that gypsies from the concentration camps were used as extras, a charge of which the director was cleared in 1949.

The Loyal 47 Ronin

▶ **Genroku Chushingura**

> Japan 1941-1942 222 mins bw
> Koa (Part I), Shochiku (Part II)

d **Kenji Mizoguchi**
sc **Kenichiro Hara, Yoshitaka Yoda**
ph **Kohei Sugiyama**
m **Shiro Fukai**
   Chojuro Kawarazaki, Yoshizaburo Arashi, Mantoyo Mimasu, Kenemon Nakamura

Following the forced harikari of Lord Asano, 47 of his ronin (disbanded samurai) avenge his death by trapping the court ruler who caused it. They are then condemned to death, but allowed the honour of taking their own lives. One of the most famous incidents in early 18th-century Japanese history became a success of the Kabuki theatre and the basis for some 20 screen adaptations, notably Inagaki's wide-screen and colour version of 1962, and Mizoguchi's, both in two parts. It started off being made under a new independent company, but Mizoguchi overshot the budget and Shochiku took over. One does not usually turn to Mizoguchi for such epic tales, but he avoids the excesses of the genre and creates a noble ritualistic tragedy.

▶ **Luch Smerti** see Death Ray, The

Lucia

> Cuba 1969 155 mins bw
> Cuban Institute of Art and Cinema

d **Humberto Solas**
sc **Humberto Solas, Julio Garcia Espinosa, Nelson Rodriguez**
ph **Jorge Herrera**
m **Leo Brouwer**
   Raquel Revuelta, Eslinda Nuñez, Adela Legra, Adolfo Liaurado, Ramon Brito

Three episodes about three women called Lucia: 1) in 1895, the aristocratic Lucia (Revuelta) kills the married man who aban-

doned her; 2) in 1932, the middle-class divorced mother Lucia (Nuñez) takes up with a young revolutionary; 3) in 1969, the agricultural worker Lucia (Legra) meets a teacher who will make her literate, but her truck-driver husband objects. One of Cuba's most ambitious films since the Revolution, it manages admirably to tell three stories in different styles while making sharp points about women's changing role in a 'macho' society.

▶ **Luci Del Varieta'** see Lights Of Variety

Ludwig

> Italy/France/W. Germany 1972 186 mins col
> Mega/Cinetel/Dieter Gessler/Divina

d **Luchino Visconti**
sc **Luchino Visconti, Enrico Medioli**
ph **Armando Nannuzzi**
m **Richard Wagner**
   Helmut Berger, Romy Schneider, Trevor Howard, Silvana Mangano, Helmut Griem, Gert Fröbe

The young Ludwig (Berger) ascends the throne of Bavaria, is forced to marry, becomes obsessed with the music of Wagner (Howard), indulges in homosexual orgies, goes mad, and is drowned. The poorest of Visconti's love-hate epics about a decaying European society is an extremely slow, long, rambling, academic and superficial soap opera. But the usually ham Berger is good and looks the part, and the Bavarian locations, castles, costumes and manners are depicted in loving detail.

Ludwig: Requiem For A Virgin King

▶ **Ludwig II: Requiem Für Einen Jungfräulichen König**

> W. Germany 1972 139 mins col
> TMS Film

d **Hans Jürgen Syberberg**
sc **Hans Jürgen Syberberg**
ph **Dietrich Lohmann**
m **Richard Wagner, Franz Lehar, Kurt Weill**

Harry Baer, Balthasar Thomas, Peter
Kern, Peter Moland, Günter Kaufmann

The inner and outer life, real and imagined,
of the mad castle-building King of Bavaria
(Baer), told in 28 chapters, or *tableaux-viv-
ants*. Cheaply made, and using a blend of
theatrical techniques such as backdrops and
back projections, this collage of German history, culture and psychology – at different
moments puerile, fatuous, stimulating, amusing and over-extended – says far more about
Ludwig than Visconti's plodding film on the
same subject. Among the *dramatis personae*
are a dwarf Wagner, Hitler dancing a tango
with Röhm, and Bismarck on a bicycle.

▶ **Ludwig II: Requiem Für Einen
Jungfräulichen König** see Ludwig:
Requiem For A Virgin King

▶ **Lulu** see Pandora's Box

▶ **Lulu The Tool** see Working Class Go
To Heaven, The

▶ **Lumière D'En Face, La** see Light
Across The Street, The

Lumière D'Été

▶ **(US: Summer Light)**

France   1943   112 mins   bw
Discina

d   Jean Grémillon
sc   Jacques Prévert, Pierre Laroche
ph   Louis Page
m   Roland Manuel
    Madeleine Renaud, Pierre Brasseur,
    Madeleine Robinson, Paul Bernard, Jane
    Marken, Georges Marchal

An ex-dancer (Renaud) runs an isolated
mountain hotel where the guests a number of
people with problems. This melancholy allegory about characters living on the edge of a
figurative and literal abyss, was made under
the restrictions of Vichy France. Nevertheless,
Grémillon managed a personal statement and
the script and performances are first rate.
Madeleine Renaud is outstanding, making the
third of four wartime films in a row for the
director.

La Luna

Italy   1979   142 mins   col
TCF/Fiction Cinematografica

d   Bernardo Bertolucci
sc   Bernardo Bertolucci, Giuseppe Bertolucci,
    Clare Peploe
ph   Vittorio Storaro
m   Verdi
    Jill Clayburgh, Matthew Barry, Laura
    Betti, Renato Salvatori, Alida Valli

An internationally renowned opera singer
(Clayburgh) has an almost incestuous
relationship with her spoiled teenage son
(Barry), who is searching for his (a) father.
The film, paying homage to Verdi, threads
together a series of splendid scenes (or arias
and duets) on the string of an opaque, operatic and Oedipal plot which doesn't really
hang together. The virtuosity, however, is
undeniable.

Lunch On The Grass

▶ **(US: Picnic On The Grass)**

▶ **Le Déjeuner Sur L'Herbe**

France   1959   91 mins   col
Compagnie Jean Renoir

d   Jean Renoir
sc   Jean Renoir
ph   Georges Leclerc
m   Joseph Kosma
    Paul Meurisse, Catherine Rouvel, Fernand
    Sardou, Ingrid Nordine

A pompous Parisian professor (Meurisse),
concerned with artificial insemination, finds
himself seduced by the mysteries of the
countryside and the farmer's daughter (Rouvel, her debut). At 65, Jean Renoir wished to
pay his most direct homage to his painter
father in this hymn to nature. Shot almost
entirely at Les Collettes, the Renoir family
home near Cannes, its sensuous colours and
sunlit images derive from the Impressionists.
But the satire is sour, the plot ponderous and
the characters mere cardboard.

▶ **Lune Dans Le Caniveau, La** see
Moon In The Gutter, The

▶ **Lunga Vita Alla Signora!** see Long Live The Lady!

▶ **Lupa, La** see She-Wolf, The

▶ **Lusts Of The Flesh** see Love Of Jeanne Ney, The

▶ **Lyckliga Skitar** see Blushing Charlie

M

Germany 1931 118 mins bw
Nero Film

d Fritz Lang
sc Thea Von Harbou, Paul Falkenberg,
Adolf Jansen, Karl Vash
ph Fritz Arno Wagner
m Karl Vollbrecht, Emil Hasler
Peter Lorre, Otto Wernicke, Gustav
Gründgens, Theodore Loos, Ellen
Widmann, George John

A psychopathic child murderer on the loose
in Berlin creates panic among mothers, and
in the underworld whose members are
hounded by the police in their search for the
killer. Fritz Lang's first sound film is a masterpiece of low-keyed expressionism, in which
fear permeates every brick of the dark alleys
and crumbling buildings which form its background. If Lang's choice of images and his
uncompromising examination of his subject
were both penetrating and progressive, he
had, in Peter Lorre, the ideal actor. His
bulbous eyes reflecting terror and self-loath-
ing in equal measure, Lorre made of *M* an
unforgettable figure which brought him international fame, but doomed him to playing a
succession of criminals in Hollywood.

Macho Dancer

Philippines 1988 125 mins col
Special People Productions

d Lino Brocka
sc Ricardo Lee
ph Joe Tutanes
Allan Paole, William Lorenzo, Daniel
Fernando, Jaclyn Jose, Princess
Punzaian, Bobby Samo

A young man (Paole), after being abandoned
by his manipulative soldier lover, comes from
the provinces to Manila where he becomes a
'macho dancer' (a striptease artist) in a gay
nightclub after befriending a streetwise fellow
dancer (Fernando) and a female prostitute
(Jose). During a search for a friend's sister
sold into prostitution, they encounter brutal
pimps and corrupt cops. Many of Brocka's
themes are again evident in a film that gained
the censure of the Aquino government – an
innocent being exploited in a wicked city, the
difference between love and sex, male and
female prostitution, police brutality –
wrapped up in a melodramatic plot set in the
seamy areas of Manila. Brocka's own tastes
incline him towards a more sympathetic treatment of the homosexual underworld than of
the heterosexual brothels, and a great deal of
footage is taken up by the nude acts in gay
clubs, including a number in which the hero
and his mate soap each other down. Despite
its attempt to be a lively exposé of a decadent
society, laced with rather simplistic ethical
notions, the film is lubricious and soapy (in
both senses) and Aids is conspicuous by its
absence.

▶ **Macht Der Männer Ist Die Geduld Der Frauen, Die** see Power Of
Men Is The Patience Of Women, The

▶ **Macskajáték** see Cats' Play

▶ **Mad Adventures Of Rabbi Jacob,
The** see Adventures Of Rabbi Jacob, The

Madame Bovary

France 1934 117 mins bw
Nouvelle Société De Film

d   Jean Renoir
sc Jean Renoir
ph Jean Bachelet
m   Darius Milhaud, Donizetti
    Valentine Tessier, Pierre Renoir, Fernand
    Fabre, Daniel Lecourtois

A romantic young woman (Tessier), soon bored with marriage to a dull country doctor, has affairs with other men, gets deeply into debt, and finally poisons herself. Renoir originally made a three-hour film of Flaubert's great 19th-century novel, but was forced to release it in a much shorter version. A further hour would have given the picture more breadth and, perhaps, depth, but the fatal miscasting of the title role would still have remained. Tessier, a close friend of the director, was too much the 'grande dame' in the part, too emotional, and not young enough. Neither the fine use of Normandy landscapes nor Pierre Renoir's well-judged performance as Dr Bovary compensate.

Madame Bovary

Germany 1937 94 mins bw
Terra Film

d   Gerhard Lamprecht
sc Hans Neumann, Erich Ebermayer
ph Karl Hasselmann
m   Giuseppe Becce
    Pola Negri, Aribert Wäscher, Ferdinand
    Marian, Werner Scharf

Emma Bovary (Negri), young and beautiful, marries a dull, middle-aged doctor in a French provincial town during the 19th century. Growing bored and restless, and the victim of an over-romantic nature, she runs up debts and has a couple of affairs, most cataclysmically with Léon (Scharf), a handsome friend of her husband with whom she falls in love. Gustave Flaubert's classic novel has fallen prey to three screen versions – Renoir's in French (1934), this one, and Hollywood (1949). Curiously, the last, directed by Vincente Minnelli with Jennifer Jones, is the most successful. Lamprecht's effort is competent, although the look and flavour retain a distinctly German air, but the film is mainly interesting as an opportunity to see the legendary and flamboyant Pola Negri, abandoned by Hollywood when the talkies came

and here attempting (with Hitler's approval) to remake her career in Germany. As Emma, she's okay – no more, no less.

Madame Butterfly

Italy/Japan 1955 114 mins col
Rizzoli/Toho

d   Carmine Gallone
sc Illica & Giacosa (libretto)
ph Claude Renoir
m   Giacomo Puccini (conducted by Oliviere
    De Fabritiis)
    Karuo Yachigusa (Cio-Cio-San, sung by
    Orietta Moscucci), Nicola Filacuridi
    (Pinkerton, sung by Giuseppe Campora),
    Michiko Tanaka (Suzuki, sung by Anna
    Maria Canali), Ferdinando Lidonni
    (Sharpless), Satoshi Nakamura
    (Yamadori, sung by Adelio Zagonara)

Made before the fashion for opera *as* film, this is very much opera *on* film, and thus somewhat stagy and static. However, it was notable as the first attempt to bring one of the most popular, famous and accessible works of the romantic repertoire to the screen, and the Japanese-Italian collaboration is a happy one. With Japanese-designed sets (ravishingly photographed by Renoir) and Japanese actors, the film offers a sense of authenticity while, musically, it is served by an excellent cast of Italian voices under a fine conductor.

Madame De ...

▶ (US: The Earrings Of Madame
De ...)

France 1953 102 mins bw
Franco London/Indus/Rizzoli

d   Max Ophüls
sc Max Ophüls, Marcel Achard, Annette
    Wademant
ph Christian Matras
m   Oscar Straus, Georges Van Parys
    Charles Boyer, Danielle Darrieux,
    Vittorio De Sica, Jean Debucourt, Lea Di
    Lea

A fickle society woman (Darrieux) sells her diamond earrings. They are acquired by her husband (Boyer) who gives them to his mistress (Di Lea) who loses them gambling. They are then bought by an Italian diplomat (De Sica) who gives them to *his* mistress – the society woman. Ophüls' penultimate film was another of his witty merry-go-round confections, where both the camera and the plot make giddy circles. Based on the novel by Louise De Vilmorin it has, like Viennese coffee, much whipped cream above the bitterness. The surface covering to the theme of the transitory nature of love consists of the elaborate period designs by Jean D'Eaubonne.

Madame Dubarry

▶ **(US: Passion)**

Germany 1919 85 mins bw
Union/UFA

d **Ernst Lubitsch**
sc **Fred Orbing (pseudonym of Norbert Falk), Hans Kräly**
ph **Théodor Sparkühl**
m **Silent**
    Pola Negri, Emil Jannings, Harry Liedtke, Reinhold Schünzel, Edouard Von Winterstein

The rise and fall of Jeanne (Negri), a woman of the people, who became the Countess Dubarry and mistress to King Louis XV (Jannings). The first of Lubitsch's ironical historical romances really established his own reputation and that of the German film industry abroad. The director's intentions were 'to humanize my historical characters. I treated the intimate nuances just as importantly as the mass movements and tried to blend them both together.' In this he succeeded, and with Negri and Jannings, and the lavish costumes and designs, the film was welcomed by British and American audiences as the height of European sophistication – an essence Lubitsch bottled and brought to Hollywood in 1923.

Madame Rosa

▶ **La Vie Devant Soi**

France 1977 105 mins col
Lira Films

d **Moshe Mizrahi**
sc **Moshe Mizrahi**
ph **Nestor Almendros**
m **Philippe Sarde**
    Simone Signoret, Claude Dauphin, Samy Ben Youb, Michal Bat Adam, Costa-Gavras

Rosa, a survivor of Auschwitz and an ex-prostitute, has run an unofficial nursery for the children of her colleagues. Now aging, ill, and tormented by failing memory, she is cared for by her sole remaining ward, Mohammed. When a doctor friend comes to persuade her that she must be moved, Mohammed carries out his promise to hide her, and she dies. Signoret, fat and herself aging, is charismatic as a big-hearted woman haunted by the ghosts of the Holocaust, and Ben Youb is enchanting as the young Arab orphan. However, Mizrahi's film, while unavoidably moving, is a heavily sentimentalized version of the racy and much tougher prize-winning novel by Emil Ajar (a pseudonym for Romain Gary) from which it was adapted, and which gave a more vibrant and truthful account of life in the Arab-Jewish *quartier* of Paris than the somewhat deodorized view here.

Best Foreign Film Oscar 1977

Mädchen In Uniform

▶ **aka Girls In Uniform**

Germany 1931 110 mins bw
Deutsche Film-Gemeinschaft

d **Leontine Sagan**
sc **Christa Winsloe (based on her novel), F.D. Andam**
ph **Reimar Kuntze**
m **Hansen Milde-Meissner**
    Dorothea Wieck, Hertha Thiele, Emilia Unda, Hedwig Schlichter

Manuela (Thiele), sent to boarding school, is away from home for the first time. A highly strung girl, she reacts badly to the school's aggressively authoritarian atmosphere, and finds solace only in the company of a sympathetic teacher (Wieck). The consequences of the relationship lead to the girl's attempted suicide. An all-female enterprise, this is a powerful film the Lesbian undertones of which lend it a strange, subtle eroticism. This, however, is secondary to the warning against the rigidity of austere and oppressive regimes. The very uniforms worn by the girls, and the methods by which the headmistress imposes her disciplines, prefigure the already looming Third Reich. An interesting political, as well as emotional, document.

Mädchen In Uniform

► **aka Children In Uniform**

W. Germany 1958 91 mins col
Les Films Modernes/S.N.C./CCC/
Filmkunst

d **Géza Radványi**
sc **Franz Hollering, F.D. Andam**
ph **Werner Krien**
m **Peter Sandloff**
   Lilli Palmer, Romy Schneider, Thérèse Giehse, Christine Kaufmann

A remake of Leontine Sagan's 1931 classic, with Lilli Palmer as the teacher and Romy Schneider as the tormented student who falls in love with her. This version is lacking in the weapons with which to hurt politically, and the Lesbian aspect is more explicit. With its two Technicolored international beauties in the lead, it is an artfully manicured copy of its predecessor, but retains the power to move.

► **Mädchen Rosemarie, Das** see Girl Rosemarie, The

Made In Italy

Italy 1965 102 mins col
Documento Film

d **Nanni Loy**
sc **Ettore Scola, Ruggero Maccari, Nanni Loy**
ph **Ennio Guarnieri**
m **Carlo Rustichelli**
   Anna Magnani, Sylva Koscina, Jean Sorel, Virna Lisi, Alberto Sordi, Catherine Spaak, Nino Manfredi, Lea Massari, Walter Chiari, Giulio Bosetti, Rosella Falk

A group of boisterous Italian workmen is

travelling to Stockholm on a plane which, *en route*, touches down at destinations throughout the length of Italy, including Rome, Naples, Sicily, Amalfi, Venice, Florence and Turin. The format is an excuse, and a good one at that, for a series of vignettes about Italian life. Employing a large star cast, together with an army of uncredited players, Loy presents a wry, sympathetic and loving look at his land and his compatriots which embodies social criticism, particularly of the Church, and is, by turns, funny and sad. Though the film crams in too much and is sometimes off-course, it is enjoyable, with Guarnieri's contrasting urban and rural photography not the least of its pleasures.

Made In Sweden

Sweden 1969 86 mins col
AB Svensk Filmindustri

d **John Bergenstrahle**
sc **Sven Fagenberg, John Bergenstrahle**
ph **Gunnar Fischer**
m **Bengt Ernryd**
   Lina Granhagen, Per Myrberg, Karl-Birger Blomdahl, Börje Ahlstedt, Ingvar Kjellson, Max Von Sydow

A committed journalist (Myrberg) who refuses to conform to the dictates of officialdom, follows up a rumour that a major Swedish financial organization is involved in gun-running on the Vietnam border. He secures the evidence to support the accusation. A promising debut by the director, who uses the relationship between his hero and girlfriend (Granhagen) to air intellectual issues, juxtaposes horrific documentary footage with telling irony, and defines the chasm between rich and poor, as well as commenting on war and corruption. Fresh insights, and good acting – the ubiquitous Von Sydow scores in a cameo as the industrialist villain – contribute to an intelligent and interesting socio-political film.

Special Jury Award Berlin 1969

Made In USA

France 1966 85 col
Rome-Paris Films/Anouchka Films/Sepic

d   Jean-Luc Godard
sc Jean-Luc Godard
ph Raoul Coutard
m   Schumann, Beethoven
    Anna Karina, Jean-Pierre Léaud, László
    Szabó, Yves Alfonso, Ernest Menzer

A young woman (Karina), in trying to discover the identity of her lover's killer, comes across agents of corruption and intrigue. Any attempt by the spectator to understand the plot in a conventional sense will be frustrated by Godard's elliptical style in which he continually breaks the narrative up with quotes, slogans, a song by a Japanese girl, a sound track that is often purposefully distorted and an attempt to make the audible visual with a long take of a tape-recorder. The film also makes references to the Ben Barka and Kennedy assassinations. This is Godard, in brilliant colours, continually redefining image in a spontaneous, topical, pop art manner.

▶ **Maestro e Margarita** see Master And Margarita, The

▶ **Magasiskola** see Falcons, The

The Magic Donkey

▶ **(US: Donkey Skin)**

▶ **Peau D'Âne**

    France 1970 90 mins col
    Mag Bodard/Marianne

d   Jacques Demy
sc Jacques Demy
ph Ghislain Cloquet
m   Michel Legrand
    Catherine Deneuve, Jacques Perrin,
    Delphine Seyrig, Jean Marais, Micheline
    Presle

In a fairytale kingdom, the King (Marais) swore to his wife on her death bed that he would not remarry unless his new wife was as beautiful as she. There seems to be only one person who fits this description – his daughter (Deneuve). However, with the magic aid of her fairy godmother (Seyrig), the Princess finally marries the handsome prince (Perrin) of a neighbouring kingdom and they all

live happily ever after. Demy's tribute to Walt Disney's *Snow White* (there is some animation), and Jean Cocteau's *Beauty And The Beast* (more than just the presence of Marais) has much charm and pleasant songs. However, its airy-fairy storytelling makes only tolerable enough kiddie fare, despite the Freudian side to Perrault's tale. Adults might enjoy Seyrig's witty Lilac Fairy most.

The Magic Flute

▶ **Trollflöjten**

    Sweden 1975 135 mins col
    TV2

d   Ingmar Bergman
sc Ingmar Bergman, (libretto by Emanuel Schikeneder)
ph Sven Nykvist
m   Mozart (conducted by Erik Ericson)
    Josef Köstlinger (Tamino), Irma Urrila (Pamina), Håkan Hagegård (Papageno), Ulrik Cold (Sarastro), Birgit Nordin (Queen of the Night)

Tamino and his bird-catcher friend Papageno are sent to rescue Pamina, the Queen of the Night's daughter from the clutches of Sarastro. But Sarastro is a wise priest who unites the lovers, Tamino and Pamina, after various ordeals. The darkness and gloom of Bergman's films suddenly gave way to the light and joy of Mozart's last operatic masterpiece. Shot in a studio reconstruction of the interior of the exquisite 18th-century Drottningholm Theatre, Bergman's production (sung in Swedish) is a paradigm of opera films, respecting the theatrical conventions yet making the experience cinematic. He also demystifies the enterprise by showing the singers backstage at the interval, playing chess, reading a comic and smoking. Pity, therefore, that the overture is used like a Coca-Cola commercial (faces in the audience of all ages and races), and that there are some perverse liberties taken with the text.

▶ **Magician, The** see Face, The

▶ **Magnificent Tramp, The** see Archimède The Tramp

▶ **Mahanagar** see Big City, The

Maigret Sets A Trap

▶ **(US: Inspector Maigret)**

▶ **Maigret Tend Un Piège**

> France   1957   120 mins   bw
> Intermondia/J.P. Guibert/Jolly Film

d   Jean Delannoy
sc Michel Audiard
ph Louis Page
m   Paul Misraki
    Jean Gabin, Annie Girardot, Jean
    Desailly, Olivier Hussenot, Lino Ventura

Inspector Maigret (Gabin) tries to trap a
killer, and discovers why a happily married,
wealthy, talented man should want to bump
off women at night. Gabin is perfect as
Georges Simenon's secure and steady sleuth,
and old-hand Delannoy expertly keeps up the
pace and suspense. Although a trifle extended
and not exactly living up to its opening
sequence of the killer choosing his weapon
from a butcher's shop, it is an enjoyable
whodunnit.

▶ **Maigret Tend Un Piège** see Maigret
Sets A Trap

Les Mains Sales

▶ **aka Dirty Hands**

> France   1951   103 mins   bw
> Fernand Rivers/Eden Production

d   Fernand Rivers
sc Jacques Bost, Fernand Rivers, Jean-Paul
    Sartre
ph Jean Bachelet
m   Paul Misraki
    Pierre Brasseur, Daniel Gélin, Claude
    Nollier, Monique Artur, Marcel André,
    Jacques Castelot

A young Communist (Gélin), fighting the
Nazis in a nameless country, is despatched
by his fellows to kill the boss of their faction,
who is considering selling out the cause by
compromise. Taking his wife (Artur) with
him, he finds himself unable to do the deed,
engaging, instead, in philosophical discussion,
until he finds his wife in the man's arms. This
is a screen adaptation of a successful and
controversial play by Sartre, which originally
starred Charles Boyer. Unfortunately, as a
film, it is very static and too wordy by half,
betraying its honorable origins while failing
to hold one's interest in spite of competent
actors who do their best.

▶ **Maison De Jeanne, La** see Jeanne's
House

▶ **Maître De Musique, Le** see Music
Teacher, The

▶ **Makhdou-Oun, Al** see Duped, The

Making It

▶ **(US: Going Places)**

▶ **Les Valseuses**

> France   1974   118 mins   col
> CAPAC/UPF/SN

d   Bertrand Blier
sc Bertrand Blier, Philippe Dumarçay
ph Bruno Nuytten
m   Stéphane Grappelli
    Gérard Depardieu, Miou-Miou, Patrick
    Dewaere, Jeanne Moreau, Jacques
    Chailleux, Brigitte Fossey, Isabelle
    Huppert, Jacques Rispal

Jean-Claude (Depardieu) and Pierrot (Dewaere) steal cars and break into houses, but
largely as a prelude to abducting, seducing
and otherwise exploiting women. No moral,
no judgement and no retribution interferes
with the unfolding of events in Blier's film,
adapted from his own novel, the original title
of which is French slang for 'testicles'. The
purpose of this slick caper, the high point of
which is the boys' encounter with Jeanne
Moreau as a just-released jailbird, is not
evident. By turns revolting, funny, and tedious, it cleverly utilizes Grappelli's score to
counterpoint the action but, when all is said
and done, it's a nasty shocker in chic dress.

Malabrigo

> Peru   1986   95 mins   col

Perfor Studio S.A./Channel 4/ZDF/
ICAIC

d **Alberto Durant**
sc **Alberto Durant, Jorge Guerra**
ph **Mario Garcia Joyo**
   **Charo Verastegui, Luis Alvarez, Luis
   Peirano, José M. Salcedo, Ricardo Blume**

Sonia (Verastegui) arrives at a Peruvian fishing village in search of her accountant husband, who has disappeared following an
explosion at the factory where he worked. At
the same time an insurance adjuster (Alvarez)
arrives at the village and together they
uncover dark dealings. The second feature by
the 34-year-old director is laden with atmosphere and a sense of mystery as it explores
the corruption of Peruvian society. It also has
a certain visual flair that is reminiscent of
Costa-Gavras's political thrillers. Unfortunately, the characters never advance much
beyond stereotypes and all suspense is dissipated at the climax by a protracted discussion
between a factory owner and the insurance
adjuster.

▶ **Malenkaya Vera** see Little Vera

Malevil

France 1981 119 mins col
NEF Diffusion/Stella Film(Munich)/
Antenne 2/Les Films Gibe/Télécip

d **Christian De Chalonge**
sc **Christian De Chalonge, Pierre Dumayet**
ph **Jean Penzer**
m **Gabriel Lared**
   **Michel Serrault, Jacques Dutronc, Robert
   Dhéry, Jean-Louis Trintignant, Jacques
   Villeret**

Malevil is a country château, in the wine
cellars of which the owner (Serrault) and a
small group of companions take refuge during
a nuclear attack on the village. In due course,
they emerge and begin to reclaim and cultivate
some land, encountering another band of
survivors, led by a rabid Fascist (Trintignant).
A timely and disturbing subject, in which the
burnt-out devastation of a futuristic holocaust
is brilliantly photographed in telling contrast
to the rustic idyll that precedes it. Unfortunately, when the two groups of survivors

meet, action, dialogue and plot topple over
into some obvious melodramatics that reduce
the the overall impact and quality of the film.

Malou

W. Germany 1980 93 mins col
Regina Ziegler

d **Jeanine Meerapfel**
sc **Jeanine Meerapfel**
ph **Michael Ballhaus**
m **Peer Raben**
   **Ingrid Caven, Grischa Huber, Helmut
   Griem, Ivan Desny, Marie Colbin, Peter
   Chatel**

A young German schoolteacher (Huber), in
the midst of spiritual crisis, attempts to come
to terms with the memory of her dead mother,
Malou (Caven), by travelling to Argentina
where Malou had lived a tragic existence.
This autobiographical journey of self-discovery has many interesting aspects, particularly the way in which the two women of
different generations take different roads to
reach a feminist awareness through suffering.
But the director often sacrifices our sympathy
by ponderously stating the obvious and striv-
ing to make the women representative rather
than individual. The presence of the splendid
Caven and other Fassbinder regulars in this
worthy movie makes unfavourable comparison with the latter's work inevitable.

▶ **Malu Tianshi** see Street Angel

Malva

USSR 1957 85 mins col
Kiev Film Studio

d **Vladimir Braun**
sc **Nikolai Kovarski**
ph **Vladimir Voitenko**
m **Igor Sciamo**
   **Zidra Ritenberg, Pavel Usovicenko,
   Anatoli Ignatiev, A. Tolbuzin, G. Yukhtin**

Malva (Ritenberg), a lusty girl who lives in a
small fishing village, doesn't wish to tie herself
down to one man and, consequently, finds
herself involved with four of them. Braun's

film (he died shortly after completing it) is adapted from a story by Maxim Gorki and emerges as an extremely static conversation piece, although it takes place largely outdoors on beaches and similar locations. Thus, in spite of excellent performances, notably from the strapping and lively leading lady, and exquisite colour photography in attractive settings, it's rather dreary.

Best Actress (Zidra Ritenberg) Venice 1957

▶ **Maman Et La Putain, La** see Mother And The Whore, The

Mamma Roma

Italy   1962   110 mins   bw
Arco/Cineriz

d   **Pier Paolo Pasolini**
sc **Pier Paolo Pasolini**
ph **Tonino Delli Colli**
m   **Vivaldi**
    Anna Magnani, Franco Citti, Ettore Garofolo, Silvana Corsini, Luisa Loiano

A woman, trying to escape her past as a prostitute, harbours middle-class ambitions for her teenage son. However, her former pimp threatens to tell the boy of his mother's profession unless she goes back 'on the game'. Pasolini's second film, like *Accatone* (1961), is a study of the sub-proletariat of Rome but, though it has a certain rude vigour derived from the volcanic Magnani and the location shooting, it lacks the debut picture's freshness and vitality.

▶ **Man About Town** see Silence Est D'Or, Le

A Man And A Woman

▶ **Un Homme Et Une Femme**

France   1966   102 mins   col
Les Films 13

d   **Claude Lelouch**
sc **Claude Lelouch, Pierre Uytterhoeven**
ph **Claude Lelouch**
m   **Francis Lai**
    Jean-Louis Trintignant, Anouk Aimée,

Pierre Barouh, Valérie Lagrange, Simone Paris

A racing driver widower (Trintignant) and a script-girl widow (Aimée) fall in love while visiting their children at the seaside resort of Deauville. Should they, shouldn't they, do they, don't they make it together? An ultra-chic love story told in glossy advertising images, with a certain freewheeling charm and attractive performers, is backed by the popular 'daba-daba-da' musical theme. The 'artistic' device of using colour and sepia came about because the director ran out of funds and couldn't afford any more colour stock. The film's huge success made Lelouch's international reputation and enough money for him never to run out of film again.

Best Film Cannes 1966,

Best Foreign Film Oscar 1966

A Man And A Woman: Twenty Years Later

▶ **Un Homme Et Une Femme: Vingt Ans Déjà**

France   1986   120 mins   col
Les Films 13/Sofica Cinergie/Sofimage

d   **Claude Lelouch**
sc **Claude Lelouch, Pierre Uytterhoeven, Monique Lange, Jérôme Tonnerre**
ph **Jean-Yves Le Mener**
m   **Francis Lai**
    Anouk Aimée, Jean-Louis Trintignant, Richard Berry, Evelyne Bouix, Marie-Sophie Pochat

When a former script-girl-turned-producer (Aimée) and a now middle-aged racing driver (Trintignant) decide to make a film about their affair of 20 years ago, they fall in love all over again. When Lelouch made *A Man And A Woman* on a shoestring budget in the 1960s and found himself with an unexpected mega-hit on his hands, he remarked that, all things being equal, the team would make a sequel in 20 years' time. And they did – complete with Francis Lai's music, the formula as before, and its two stars as attractive as ever.

▶ **Mandabi** see Money Order, The

► **Mandat, Le** see Money Order, The

► **Manden I Maanen** see Dark Side Of The Moon, The

► **Man Die Zijn Haar Kort Liet Knippen, De** see Man Who Had His Hair Cut Short, The

► **Mandragola, La** see Mandrake, The

The Mandrake

► **La Mandragola**

Italy 1965 99 mins bw
Arco Film (Rome)/Lux (Paris)

d Alberto Lattuada
sc Alberto Lattuada, Luigi Magni, Stefano Strucchi
ph Tonino Delli Colli
m Gino Marinuzzi Jr
Rosanna Schiaffino, Philippe Leroy, Totò, Jean-Claude Brialy, Romolo Valli, Nilla Pizzi

Callimaco (Leroy), a rich Florentine, determines to possess Lucrezia (Schiaffino), the strikingly beautiful wife of the notary, Nicia (Valli), who is desperately seeking a cure for her barrenness. Callimaco poses as a doctor and, by a series of cunning ploys, gets himself successfully into Lucrezia's bed. With style, wit and attention to detail, Lattuada has made an entertaining filmed version of the play by Machiavelli which, while still very much of a stage work, strikes just the right note of bawdiness and cynicism.

► **Manèges** see Wanton, The

A Man Escaped, Or The Wind Bloweth Where It Listeth

► **Un Condamné À Mort S'est Échappé, Ou Le Vent Souffle Où Il Vent**

France 1956 102 mins bw
GAU/SNE

d Robert Bresson

sc Robert Bresson
ph L.H. Burel
m Mozart
François Leterrier, Charles Le Clainche, Roland Monot, Maurice Beerblock, Jacques Ertand

Fontaine (Leterrier) of the French Resistance, imprisoned by the Nazis, plans his escape. When condemned to death, he puts the plan into action, accompanied by a newly acquired teenage cell-mate. André Devigny, on whose account of his own experiences the story was based, acted as technical adviser, and the film reconstructed his actual cell at Montluc, the fortress which would house Klaus Barbie in the 1980s. Bresson's camera stripped the action of all but the bare essentials, allowing the viewer to become totally involved with Fontaine's painstaking and ingenious preparations. A testament to courage and faith, all the more authentic for its use of non-professional actors and the director's spare, matter-of-fact style.

Best Director Cannes 1957

The Man From Majorca

► **Mannen Fran Mallorca**

Sweden 1984 105 mins col
Drakfilm/Svensk Filmindustri/Svenska Filminstitutet/SV2/Filmhuset KB/Crone Film Sales

d Bo Widerberg
sc Bo Widerberg
ph Thomas Wahlberg, Gunnar Nilsson, Hans Welin
m Björn Jason Lindh
Sven Wollter, Tomas Von Brömssen, Häkan Serner, Ernst Gunther, Margreth Weivers, Nina Gunke

While two plainclothes policemen keep watch on a call-girl's flat, a lone masked gunman robs a neighbouring post office. The detectives give chase, thus becoming involved in a case which grows in complexity and drags the special squad and the Minister of Justice into the web of suspicion. Widerberg, in tune with his liberal voice, points a finger at police methods and political corruption in a well-acted, well-scripted film. However, the director over-indulges in too many supposedly significant close-ups in a piece which, for all its professional excellence, is little more than a conventional *policier*.

Manila: In The Claws Of Neon

▶ **Maynila Sa Mga Kuko Ng Liwanag**

The Philippines   1975   125 mins   col
Cinema Artists

d   **Lino Brocka**
sc **Clodualdo Del Mundo Jr**
ph **Miguel Del Leon**
m   **Max Jocson**
    Rafael Roco Jr, Hilda Koronel, Tommy Abuel, Lou Salvador Jr, Jojo Abella, Joonee Gamboa

Julio (Roco Jr), a provincial fisherman, comes to Manila to look for his childhood sweetheart Ligaya (Koronel) who has disappeared. Before coming across Ligaya in sordid circumstances, Julio works under gruelling conditions on a building site and becomes an unwilling and ineffective male prostitute. Lino Brocka's film stood out among the 200 or so trashy pictures the Filipino cinema produced every year, mainly soap operas and kung fu-type adventures. While using elements of these popular films – sex, sentiment and violence – Brocka has tried to inject some social consciousness under its thick melodramatic surface. The director wanted 'to put a mirror before the audience'. Most effective are the depictions of the urban squalour of Chinatown and the waterside slums, but they are without any political context, not surprising as it was made some years into the martial law imposed by Marcos.

▶ **Man in the Moon, The** see Dark Side Of The Moon, The

Man Is Not A Bird

▶ **Čovek Nije Tica**

Yugoslavia   1965   80 mins   bw
Avala Film

d   **Dušan Makavejev**

sc **Dušan Makavejev**
ph **Aleksandar Petković**
m   **Petar Bergamo**
    Milena Dravić, Janez Vrhoveć, Eva Ras, Stojan Arandelović, Boris Dvornik, Roko

In a bleak industrial town in Slovenia, a visiting engineer (Vrhoveć) has an affair with a young and carefree hairdresser (Dravić), which does not prevent her making love to a truckdriver (Dvornik) she had known previously. With its guiltless eroticism, vertiginous images from hand-held cameras, and satiric attitude to authority, Makavejev's first feature came as a revelation from Eastern Europe. Its light side is balanced by its portrayal of the noisy, dirty, dehumanizing work done by industrial workers. The provocative ending cross-cuts between a performance of Beethoven's Ninth Symphony as a special event for local dignitaries at a factory, and the lovemaking of the heroine, finding her own 'Ode To Joy'.

▶ **Mani Sulla Citta, Le** see Hands Over The City

▶ **Manji** see Passion

A Man Like Eva

▶ **Ein Mann Wie Eva**

W. Germany   1983   89 mins   col
Schier-Straub/Trio/Impuls/Maran

d   **Radu Gabrea**
sc **Radu Gabrea, Laurens Straub**
ph **Horst Schier**
m   **Verdi (*La Traviata* with Maria Callas)**
    Eva Mattes, Liza Kreuzer, Werner Stocker, Charles Regnier, Carola Regnier, Charly Muhamed Huber

The relationships of the film director Eva (Mattes) with various people during the shooting of his version of The Lady Of The Camellias in a large mansion. He repulses his ex-lover Ali (Huber), marries the leading lady (Kreuzer) and seduces the leading man (Stocker). Although Rainer Werner Fassbinder (1946-1982) is not mentioned by name, this bizarre and dubious enterprise is an apochryphal portrait of him, played in a beard by his erstwhile star Eva Mattes. Gabrea directs in Fassbinder's own most Sirkian manner, but without his control of excess. Many of the bare facts of the director's life are here telescoped, trivialized and turned into melodrama. As Fassbinder did the same with his life, fans might not object.

▶ **Mannen Fran Mallorca** see Man From Majorca, The

▶ **Mannen På Taket** see Man On The Roof, The

▶ **Männer** see Men

▶ **Mann Wie Eva, Ein** see Man Like Eva, A

▶ **Mano En La Trampa, La** see Hand In The Trap, The

Man Of Ashes

▶ **Rih Essed**
▶ **aka L'Homme De Cendres**

Tunisia 1986 109 mins col
SATPEK/Ciné-Télé Films

d **Nouri Bouzid**
sc **Nouri Bouzid**
ph **Youssef Ben-Youssef**
m **Salah Mahdi**
   Imed Malaal, Khaled Ksouri, Habib Belhadi, Mohamed Dhrif, Mouna Noureddine, Mahmoud Bel-Hassen

Hachemi (Malaal), a young furniture maker in the Tunisian town of Sfax and about to be married, is haunted by childhood memories of being sodomized. Unlike his friend Farfat (Ksouri), who had the same experience and is publicly known (and ridiculed) as homosexual, Hachemi suffers privately, giving in to destructive introspection until a sympathetic prostitute initiates him into heterosexual sex. Bouzid's controversial first film is not so much about the pros and cons of homosexuality as about the power of masculinity in Tunisian society which is judged in relation to women. Efficiently filmed to give the flavour of a community where Muslim, Christian and Jew co-exist peacably, it's also an immature work, focusing on the surface hysteria rather than

the inner character of its protagonists. Consequently, what should provoke and move merely irritates – rather in the manner of an over-intense and tedious first novel.

▶ **Man Of Iron** see Railroad Man, The

Man Of Iron

▶ **Czlowiek Z Zelaza**

Poland 1981 152 mins col/bw
PRF/Filmowy

d **Andrzej Wajda**
sc **Aleksander Scibor-Rylski**
ph **Edward Klosínski**
m **Andrzej Korzyński**
   Jerzy Radziwilowicz, Krystyna Janda, Marian Opania

A radio reporter (Opania), expected to cover the 1980 shipyard strike at Gdansk from the official point of view, meets the son of 1950s worker hero Birkut (*Man Of Marble*) now married to a dissident film-maker (Janda). Wajda's sequel to *Man Of Marble* (1972), filmed under enormous pressure during the actual events, leaped off the screen like the day's headlines. The personal story is linked with the wider struggle for the recognition of Solidarity, thus making the film dependent to a large extent on its political topicality. As Wajda uses an unfussy narrative technique, it might soon seem as dated as yesterday's headlines.

Best Film Cannes 1981

Man Of Marble

▶ **Czlowiek Z Marmur**

Poland 1972 165 mins col
PRF/Zespol

d **Andrzej Wajda**
sc **Aleksander Scibor-Rylski**
ph **Edward Klosínski**
m **Andrzej Korzyński**
   Jerzy Radziwilowicz, Krystyna Janda, Michael Tarkowski, Tadeusz Lomnicki

As a basis for her graduation film project, a student (Janda) investigating the life of a bricklayer hero of the 1950s who has since been discredited, finds obstacles in getting at the truth. This bold, no-frills, no-holds-barred political tale is Wajda's reflection on Poland's immediate past, whereas the sequel, *Man Of Iron* (1981), looked at the present. Most effective are the black and white reconstructions of the newsreels of the time, and Radziwilow-icz's convincing performance as Birkut, the worker who stepped out of line. Wajda, too, was thought to have gone over the official limits, and the film's release was held up for four years. Although good polemical cinema, the nervous chain-smoking portrayal by Janda acts as an irritant.

Man Of Straw

▶ **L'Uomo Di Paglia**

> Italy   1958   95 mins   bw
> Vides/Lux Film

d   **Pietro Germi**
sc **Alfredo Giannetti, Leo Benvenuti, Piero De Bernardi, Pietro Germi**
ph **Leonida Barboni**
m   **Carlo Rustichelli**
    Pietro Germi, Luisa Della Noce, Franca Bettoja, Edoardo Nevola, Saro Urzi

A married man (Germi), father to a little son, falls in love with a young girl (Bettoja) and neglects his family in pursuit of the affair. Both he and the girl are painfully aware that their relationship cannot last but, when the parting comes, the effect on her is unexpected and tragic. Using many of the team, both in front of and behind the camera, from his previous film, *The Railroad Man*, Germi, working from an excellent screenplay, has delivered an honest, downbeat and perceptive tale of adultery, subtly conveying how life can never again be the same for the protagonist after this poignant interlude. The rest of the cast also give confident performances.

Manon

> France   1949   100 mins   bw
> Alcina

d   **Henri-Georges Clouzot**
sc **Henri-Georges Clouzot, Jean Ferry**
ph **Armand Thirard**

m   **Paul Misraki**
    Cecile Aubrey, Michel Auclair, Serge Reggiani, Gabrielle Dorziat

After the liberation, a former Resistance fighter (Auclair) rescues Manon (Aubrey), a collaborator, from the avenging villagers. They flee to Paris where Manon drives her lover to jealous rage by her involvement with profiteering and prostitution but, when he commits a murder, she leaves France with him, and ends up dying in the desert. A curious reworking of the Abbé Prévost's 18th-century novel, *Manon Lescaut*, the film fails to convince, due to sketchy characterization and underpowered casting. Not one of Clouzot's better efforts, his style is nonetheless evident in capturing the atmosphere of post-war, low-life Paris – sufficiently so to have made an impression on the Festival jury at Venice.

Best Film Venice 1949

Manon Des Sources

> France   1952   190 mins   bw
> Films Marcel Pagnol

d   **Marcel Pagnol**
sc **Marcel Pagnol**
sc **Willy**
m   **Raymond Legrand**
    Jacqueline Pagnol, Raymond Pellegrin, Henri Vibert, Rellys, Henri Poupon

Manon (Pagnol), a wild girl who lives in the hills, takes her revenge on the villagers, particularly Ugolin (Rellys) and his uncle Papet (Poupon), who indirectly caused her father's death. 'If water plays an important role in my work, it's because it is a major problem in Provence which is so often deprived of it,' Pagnol commented. The theme of water flows like a stream through his penultimate film, which originally ran almost five hours (when it was released commercially it lost two hours). Despite the pastoral beauty, the narrative suffered cruelly, and it flopped. Jacqueline Pagnol (formerly Bouvier), the director's wife, was unconvincing in the title role, and some of the other performances were too caricatured. An exception is Rellys, whose desperate declaration of love for Manon is one of the highlights. Claude Berri's 1986 remake (plus the 'prequel *Jean De Florette*) kept most of the wonderful dialogue, but rectified many of the acting and structural weaknesses.

Manon Des Sources

France 1986 114 mins col
Renn/A2/RAI 2/DD

d   Claude Berri
sc Claude Berri, Gérard Brach
ph Bruno Nuytten
m   Jean-Claude Petit
    Yves Montand, Daniel Auteuil,
    Emmanuelle Béart, Hippolyte Girardot,
    Elisabeth Depardieu

Ten years after watching her father die as a result of the plugging up of the spring on his land by two malicious neighbours, Manon (Béart) wreaks revenge on the whole community by depriving them of water. Of the two films, this continuation of *Jean De Florette* is the more pantheistic and, as the title suggests, more operatic. In fact, the film should not be approached as naturalistic drama: the Marcel Pagnol story (filmed by him in 1952) was conceived as an updated Greek tragedy transposed to Provence. Against the sensuous settings are rich portrayals from a mellow Montand and the unforgettable tragicomic Auteuil.

The Man On The Roof

▶ **Mannen På Taket**

Sweden 1976 109 mins col
Svensk Filmindustri

d   Bo Widerberg
sc Bo Widerberg
ph Odd Geir Saether, Per Källberg and
    others
m   Björn Jason Lindh
    Carl-Gustaf Lindstedt, Gunnel Wadner,
    Håkan Serner, Sven Wollter

When a tough policeman is killed by a sniper in Stockholm, a vast manhunt is put into operation. Based on a popular crime novel by Maj Sjöwall and Per Wahlöö, Widerberg's stylish and suspenseful thriller is divided into two distinct sections – detection and chase.

Both parts are familiar from Hollywood and TV cop dramas, but unfamiliar in settings and attitudes. A little less significance-searching might have made it even better entertainment.

Man's Hope

▶ **aka Days Of Hope**

▶ **Espoir**

▶ **aka Sierra De Teruel**

France-Spain 1939 73 mins bw
Corniglion/Molinier

d   André Malraux
sc André Malraux
ph Louis Page
m   Darius Milhaud
    Mejuto, Nicolas Rodriguez, José Lado

A small group of ill-equipped Republican fighters in the Spanish Civil War attempts to blow up a bridge to prevent arms and supplies reaching Franco's troops. The only feature directed by the esteemed French writer Malraux, based on his novel *L'Espoir*, was begun in 1938, but shooting was interrupted when General Franco took Barcelona. It was completed in Paris, but not shown until after World War II with altered editing and a prologue by Government minister Maurice Schumann. The film is remarkable for the feeling it gives of the actual war, although most of it was shot in a studio. The climax of the villagers carrying their dead down a mountainside is truly memorable.

▶ **Manthan** see Churning, The

▶ **Ma Nuit Chez Maud** see My Night With Maud

The Man Who Had His Hair Cut Short

▶ **De Man Die Zijn Haar Kort Liet Knippen**

Belgium 1966 95 mins bw
Belgium Ministry of Culture/Belgian TV

d André Delvaux
sc André Delvaux, Anna De Pagter
ph Ghislain Cloquet
m Frédéric Devreese
   Senne Rouffaer, Beata Tyszkiewicz,
   Hector Camerlynck

A married middle-aged lawyer (Rouffaer) falls idealistically in love with a pupil (Tyszkiewicz) at a girls' school where he teaches. When he meets her again years later, she has become a famous actress while he gradually loses his sanity. Delvaux's first feature already reveals a firm grip on grim material that veers between beauty and ugliness, illusion and reality, with a self-conscious reference to Flemish old masters. The title refers to the hero's compulsive visits to the barber which vividly symbolize his encroaching madness.

The Man Who Loved Women

► **L'Homme Qui Aimait Les Femmes**

   France 1977 119 mins col
   Les Films Du Carrosse/Les Productions
   Artistes Associés

d François Truffaut
sc François Truffaut, Michel Fermaud,
   Suzanne Schiffman
ph Nestor Almendros
m Maurice Jaubert
   Charles Denner, Brigitte Fossey, Leslie
   Caron, Nelly Borgeaud, Geneviève
   Fontanel, Nathalie Baye

Bertrand (Denner) dedicates his life to the indefatigable pursuit of women, for whom he has a limitless passion, until his obsession involves him in an accident and leads to his death. Truffaut attempts to examine what drives his protagonist by using the device of flashback as Bertrand writes his memoirs, but his tone is that of romantic comedy, the structure lacks shape, and the film obstinately refuses to cast light on its characters, making it no more than a superficial and sporadically entertaining exercise.

► **Man Without A Face, The** see
   Shadowman

The Man With The Movie Camera

► **Chelovek S Kinoapparatom**

   USSR 1928 90 mins bw
   VUFKU

d Dziga Vertov
sc Dziga Vertov
ph Mikhail Kaufman
m Silent

A montage of Moscow life showing the inhabitants – workers, shoppers, holiday-makers – and the machines that keep the city moving. The first full length film by Vertov (real name Denis Kaufman, whose brother was the photographer) is a joyous and spec-tacular constructivist celluloid poem dis-playing all the techniques of cinema at his disposal: split screen, dissolves, slow motion, and freeze frames. Yet the pyrotechnics are mostly entertaining and seldom abstract. Documentary and experimental film-makers still acknowledge its influence and Jean-Luc Godard formed the Group Dziga Vertov to produce his movies between 1968 and 1972.

Marcelino

► **Marcelino Pan Y Vino**

   Spain 1955 90 mins bw
   Charmartin Production

d Ladislao Vajda
sc José Maria Sanchez-Silva, Ladislao Vajda
ph Enrique Guerner
m Pablo Sarosabal
   Pablito Calvo, Rafael Rivelles, Juan
   Calvo, Antonio Vico, Isabel De Pomes,
   Fernando Rey

Abandoned at birth on the steps of a humble monastery, Marcelino (Pablito Calvo) is brought up by the gentle monks who impart a purity and compassion of spirit to the boy without curbing his high spirits. Finding a life-sized crucifix in the attic where he has been forbidden to go, he thinks the Christ figure is real and brings it food. Christ reaches out for it and thanks the boy... Made when audiences were less jaded and cynical, this Spanish fantasy is a gem and a delight.

Although undeniably sentimental even in its day, it has been directed, photographed and acted with great finesse and charm and Calvo, no more than six or seven, is irresistible.

▶ **Marcelino Pan Y Vino** see Marcelino

Il Mare

▶ **aka The Sea**

> Italy   1962   110 mins   bw
> Gianni Buffardi

d   **Giuseppe Patroni Griffi**
sc **Giuseppe Patroni Griffi, Alfio Valdarini**
ph **Ennio Guarnieri**
m   **Giovanni Fusco**
    Umberto Orsini, Françoise Prévost, Dino Mele

An actor (Orsini), visiting Capri in winter, meets a moody boy (Mele) who drinks heavily. In due course, they befriend a woman (Prévost) who has come to sell her house, and whose presence causes complications. Patroni Griffi's film is a beautifully constructed study of lonely and insecure people seeking, and failing to find, reassurance and comfort in one another. The director tells us little about his protagonists (they don't even have names), but doesn't need to because it is their particular circumstance – that of finding themselves in a cold, deserted place where unseasonal deadness triggers off their needs and emotions – with which the film is concerned. Beautifully photographed and acted with finesse, it is laced with ironic humour that keeps it from becoming either maudlin or overweighted with *angst*.

Marguerite De La Nuit

> France   1955   126 mins   col
> SNEG/Gaumont Actualités/Cino Del Duca

d   **Claude Autant-Lara**
sc **Ghislaine Autant-Lara, Gabriel Arout**
ph **Jacques Natteau**
m   **René Cloërec**
    Michèle Morgan, Yves Montand, Jean-

François Calvé, Massimo Girotti, Fernand Sardou, Palau

Old Dr Faust (Palau) signs away his soul to Mephistopheles (Montand), disguised as the drug-trafficking owner of a Pigalle night-club, in return for his lost youth. He wakes next morning as a handsome young man (Calvé) with whom Marguerite (Morgan) falls in love. Autant-Lara's rather limp updating of the Faust legend suffers from miscasting, garish lighting and mechanical tricks. It's only *raison d'être* seems to be the *art déco* settings by Max Douy (the action takes place in the 1920s), and some flashes of humour.

Maria Candelaria

> Mexico   1943   102 mins   bw
> Films Mundiales

d   **Emilio Fernández**
sc **Emilio Fernández, Mauricio Magdaleno**
ph **Gabriel Figueroa**
m   **Francisco Dominguez**
    Dolores Del Rio, Pedro Armendáriz, Alberto Galan, Margarita Cortes, Manuel Inclan

Maria (Del Rio), an Indian peasant girl, lives in a primitive community whose members stoned her mother to death after she had posed nude for an artist (Galan). Maria and her fiancé (Armendariz) are poverty-stricken, and he is jailed for stealing quinine for her malaria. To obtain funds, she poses for Galan, head only, but the locals make assumptions and history repeats itself. The exquisite Dolores Del Rio, showing few signs of age (at 38, she had been a star of the Hollywood silents), is excellent, and Figueroa's photography of the Mexican landscape is impressive. Although verbose and sometimes lacking in action, the film has surprising flashes of humour embedded in its sad and simple tale.

Best Film Cannes 1946

Maria Chapdelaine

▶ **aka The Naked Heart**

> France   1934   120 mins   bw
> Société Nouvelle De Cinématographie

d   Julien Duvivier
sc Julien Duvivier, Gabrielle Boissy
ph Jules Kruger, Georges Périnal
m   Jean Wiener
    Madeleine Renaud, Suzanne Despres,
    Jean Gabin, Jean-Pierre Aumont, André
    Bac, Alexandre Rignault

The Chapdelaines are a French Canadian family battling with the hardships of pioneer life in the icy wilderness, but determined to preserve their French custom and heritage. Both Maria's mother and her adored fiancé (Gabin), a fur trapper, die during a cruel winter, but she resists the temptation to escape to the city with a new suitor. Duvivier brought the full mastery of his poetic realism to bear on this sensitive adaptation of Louis Hemon's best-seller. Impeccably acted by all the cast, particularly Renaud in the title role, the film also benefits from some spectacular location photography, shot amid the Canadian snowscapes.

▶ **María De Mi Corazón** see Mary My Dearest

Marie – A Hungarian Legend

▶ **(US: Spring Shower)**

▶ **Tavaszi Zapor**

Hungary 1932 66 mins bw
Adolphe Osso

d   Pál Fejós
sc Ilona Fülöp, Pál Fejós
ph István Eiban, Pawerel Marley
m   László Angyal, Vincent Scotto
    Annabella, István Gyergyai, Karola Zala,
    Ilona Dajbukát, Erzsi Bársony

Maria Szabó (Annabella), a maid working for a rich family, is seduced by the fiancé (Gyergyai) of the daughter (Bársony) of the house. Turned out by the family, she gets a job as a waitress in an unsavoury tavern. When her baby is born, a group of local women take the child away from her, she becomes a drunk and dies. Fejós' first film in his native Hungary for nine years (after his sojourn in Hollywood and a couple of pictures in France) could reasonably be considered the best Hungarian film of the 1930s. Paradoxically, its strength is also its weakness. The trite melodramatic tale of woe, with a climax of gooey religiosity, is filmed in such a glowing way as to be reminiscent of the magical silent pictures of Sjöström and Murnau, and the ravishing Annabella puts one in mind of Gish and Pickford. The influence of Hollywood is seen in the amusing coda when Annabella, installed in 'Heaven's kitchen', saves her daughter from a fate similar to her own.

La Marie Du Port

France 1949 100 mins bw
Films Corona/Sacha Gordine

d   Marcel Carné
sc Marcel Carné, Louis Chavance
ph Henri Alekan
m   Joseph Kosma
    Jean Gabin, Nicole Courcel, Blanchette
    Brunoy, Carette, Claude Romain

Chatelard (Gabin), a world-weary restaurant owner from Cherbourg, escorts his mistress to the funeral of her father, a poor fisherman, in a little Breton port town. Once there, he becomes involved with her younger sister (Courcel). Director and cameraman capture the life and atmosphere of the port with realistic exactitude, while Gabin and Courcel convince as the couple – he sophisticated and cynical, she a willing novice in the game of love. Shades of irony lend an intriguing ambiguity to the romance but it is Carné (working from a novel by Georges Simenon) past his best.

▶ **Mariée Était En Noir, La** see Bride Wore Black, The

Marie Octobre

France 1958 102 mins bw
Orex/SF/Abbey/Doxa

d   Julien Duvivier
sc Julien Duvivier, Jacques Robert
ph Robert Le Fèbvre
m   Jean Yatove
    Danielle Darrieux, Serge Reggiani,
    Bernard Blier, Paul Meurisse, Noël
    Roquevert, Lino Ventura, Paul Guers,
    Paul Frankeur

A group of ex-Resistance fighters meets some years after the war for a reunion dinner. During the course of the evening one of their number is exposed as a traitor, and the obligatory consequence follows. An experiment on the lines of Hitchcock's *Rope*, the action takes place in one set, the director using long takes. Although verbose and rather stifling, the dramatic possibilities are fully exploited by the excellent cast.

▶ **Mariés De L'An Deux, Les** see Scoundrel, The

Marius

France   1931   125 mins   bw
Marcel Pagnol/Paramount

d   **Alexander Korda**
sc   **Marcel Pagnol**
ph   **Ted Pahle**
m   **Francis Grammon**
   Raimu, Pierre Fresnay, Orane Demazis, Charpin, Alida Rouffe, Robert Vathier

Marius (Fresnay), who works in his father's dockside café in Marseilles, is set to marry Fanny (Demazis) his childhood sweetheart, but the call of the sea is too strong for him, and he joins the merchant navy, unaware that Fanny is pregnant. Pagnol's entry into cinema was as producer, adviser, and screenwriter on the film of his successful play of the same name with almost the same cast. The warm atmosphere of the trilogy (*Fanny* and *César* followed) was immediately established, although it is the least cinematic of the three and rather crude when trying to expand the location, which is largely confined to César's café. No matter. The interest lies in character, the wisdom of the writing and the wonderful performances, especially from the great Raimu as the crabby but lovable César.

Marlene

W. Germany   1983   94 mins   col
OKO-Filmproduktion/Karel Dirka

d   **Maximilian Schell**
sc   **Meir Dohnal, Maximilian Schell**
ph   **Ivan Slapeta, Pavel Hispler, Henry Hauck**
m   **Nicholas Economou**
   Annie Albers, Bernard Hall, Marta Rakosnik, Patricia Schell, Ivana Spinell, William Von Stranz, Maximilian Schell, and the voice of Marlene Dietrich

A still from *Marlene* in the British Film Institute's monthly bulletin is captioned 'interview with an absent subject', which would seem to sum up Maximilian Schell's documentary. Having agreed to be interviewed for a film, the legendary German star then refused point blank to appear before the camera. Undaunted, Schell pressed on, giving us the star's (mostly ill-tempered) views on her art and those who helped to elevate her in it. What we look at is a detailed reconstruction of her Paris apartment, with the director's crew and producer trying to make the best of a bad job, a handful of interviews and a good selection of clips from her best-known movies. The high point is a disagreement between star and director where he walks out and provokes her wrath. Overall, in spite of some understandably chaotic fill-in material – editing machines and the like – this is a fascinating documentary, part homage, part critique from which, frankly, the great Dietrich emerges as an unpleasantly perverse and difficult woman, but with an appealing forthrightness that cuts through the cult of idolatry. By her absence, her presence is the stronger.

The Marquise Of O

▶ **Die Marquise Von O**

W. Germany   1976   107 mins   col
Janus/Films Du Losange

d   **Eric Rohmer**
sc   **Eric Rohmer**
ph   **Nestor Almendros**
m   **Roger Delmotte**
   Edith Clever, Volker Frächtel, Bruno Ganz, Peter Lühr, Edda Seippel, Eric Rohmer

A highly moral Marquise (Clever), a widow with two children, is drugged and then raped by Count F (Ganz), a lieutenant-colonel in the invading Russian army of Lombardy in the early 18th century. When she finds herself pregnant, the Marquise gets the Count to marry her, and they separate immediately after the ceremony. Shooting in Germany, in

German and with a German cast, the typically French Rohmer conjured up a restrained, ironic and touching version of Heinrich Von Kleist's classic novella. It is also intentionally funny in some of the more melodramatic moments. The film's pictorial beauty was inspired by painters such as Caspar David Friedrich.

Special Jury Prize Cannes 1976

▶ **Marquise Von O, Die** see Marquise Of O, The

Marriage Italian Style

▶ **Matrimonio All'Italiana**

Italy 1964 102 mins col
C.C. Champion (Rome)/Films Concordia (Paris)

d **Vittorio De Sica**
sc **Eduardo De Filippo, Renato Castellani, Tonino Guerra, Leo Benvenuto, Piero De Bernardi**
ph **Roberto Gerardi**
m **Armando Trovaioli**
   Sophia Loren, Marcello Mastroianni, Aldo Puglisi, Giovanni Ridolfi, Vito Moriconi, Generoso Cortini

Filomena (Loren) who met Domenico (Mastroianni) in a brothel, has been his mistress for 20 years but he now intends to marry a young girl. However, on hearing she is mortally ill, he rushes to her bedside and marries her as a last gesture, whereupon she 'miraculously' recovers, and reveals three grown-up sons. . . . The plot of this comedy, based on De Filippo's play *Filomena*, contains elements of both the erotically vulgar and the ludicrously silly, but is always extremely funny. Loren – sexy, uninhibited and cunning – is a delight and Mastroianni – vain, egotistical and bemused – is marvellous, while De Sica directs with inventiveness and the lightest of touches.

The Marriage Of Maria Braun

▶ **Die Ehe Der Maria Braun**

W. Germany 1978 119 mins col
Albatros/Trio/WDR/FDA

d **Rainer Werner Fassbinder**
sc **Peter Märthesheimer, Pea Fröhlich**
ph **Michael Ballhaus**
m **Peer Raben**
   Hanna Schygulla, Klaus Löwitsch, Ivan Desny, Gottfried John, George Byrd

Maria Braun (Schygulla) survives in Berlin through the war years while her husband (Löwitsch) is at the Russian front. On his return, he is imprisoned for killing a black GI who befriended her. She takes up with an industrialist (Desny) and rises to wealth and power. Fassbinder's biggest international box-office success is a dramatic and subtle picture of an indomitable woman and his most effective metaphorical onslaught on Germany's 'Economic Miracle' of the 1950s. Framed between photographs of Hitler and Helmut Schmidt, the story is filled with superbly conceived comic and soap opera incidents, giving Schygulla one of her best roles. The producers had wanted Romy Schneider for the part, but a meeting between the director and star ended up with him calling her a 'dumb cow', and she declaring she would never work with such a 'beast'.

Best Actress (Hanna Schygulla) Berlin 1979

A Married Woman

▶ **(US: The Married Woman)**

▶ **Une Femme Mariée**

France 1964 98 mins bw
Anouchka/Orsay

d **Jean-Luc Godard**
sc **Jean-Luc Godard**
ph **Raoul Coutard**
m **Beethoven, Claude Nougaro**
   Macha Méril, Philippe Leroy, Bernard Noël, Roger Leenhardt, Rita Maiden

A young Parisian wife (Méril) who moves between her airline pilot husband (Leroy) and her lover (Noël), is overly influenced by advertising and women's magazines. General De Gaulle objected greatly to this humorously erotic portrayal of French womanhood, no doubt thus contributing to its considerable box-office takings. Godard's depiction of the sex act by showing patterned portions of the anatomy has been much imitated and so has his feminist theme. But his use of sexuality for polemical purposes was far more effective in his films of the 1980s.

▶ **Married Woman, The** see Married Woman, A

Marry Me! Marry Me!

▶ **Mazel Tov Ou Le Mariage**

France   1968   90 mins   col
Renn Productions/Parafrance Films/
Madeleine Films

d   **Claude Berri**
sc **Claude Berri**
ph **Ghislain Cloquet**
m   **Emile Stern**
     Claude Berri, Elizabeth Wiener, Grégoire Aslan, Luisa Colpeyn, Prudence Harrington

When Isabelle (Wiener), daughter of a rich Antwerp diamond merchant, becomes pregnant by her lover Claude (Berri), he decides to marry her. Meanwhile, however, he becomes infatuated with his English teacher Helen (Harrington), rushes back to Paris from Belgium, and breaks off his engagement. Soon disillusioned with Helen, he is reunited with Isabelle and her family. Berri, playing the lead as well as writing and directing, has drawn on his own background to create a detailed portrait of Jewish family life, climaxing with the colourful wedding. It is an endearing film, presenting very real characters and a deal of wry light comedy, free of sugary sentiment or Jewish clichés.

The Marseillaise

▶ **La Marseillaise**

France   1938   135 mins   bw
CGT

d   **Jean Renoir**
sc **Jean Renoir**
ph **Jean Bourgoin**
m   **Joseph Kosma, Lalande Rameau, Mozart, Bach, Rouget L'Isle, Sauveplane**
     Pierre Renoir, Lise Delamare, Louis Jouvet, Julien Carette, Gaston Modot, Léon Larive

A group of volunteers march from Marseilles to Paris to take part in the downfall of the French monarchy in 1789. One of Renoir's favourite movies was also one of his least successful. His affection for it might have attached more to the comradely manner in which it was made rather than to its actual consummation. The collective production, financed by the French trades unions, was 'the film of the union of the French nation against a minority of exploiters, the film of the rights of man and of the citizen'. These were great claims for an episodic picture which lacked a grand design. Although there are some stirring moments with the people it is, ironically, the aristos – led by a touching Pierre Renoir as Louis XVI – who come off best.

▶ **Marseillaise, La** see Marseillaise, The

Martha

W. Germany   1974   95 mins   col
WDR

d   **Rainer Werner Fassbinder**
sc **Rainer Werner Fassbinder**
ph **Michael Ballhaus**
m   **Archive music**
     Margit Carstensen, Karl-Heinz Böhm, Gisela Fackeldey, Barbara Valentin, Adrian Hoven

Martha (Carstensen), a wealthy and selfish woman, marries a stranger (Böhm) whom she gradually discovers is a sadist. He tries to subdue her, but it is not until she is paralyzed in an accident that he becomes the dominant partner. If Fassbinder's previous film, *Fear Eats The Soul*, was his tribute to the Douglas Sirk of *All That Heaven Allows*, then this baroque extravagance is a homage to Sirk's *Written On The Wind*. Over the top it may be, and full of cinematic and private allusions, but there is no discounting the virtuosity of the direction, the bold use of colour, lighting and decor – and all shot on 16mm at a cost of the coffee break at Universal Studios.

Martin Roumagnac

▶ **(US: The Room Upstairs)**

France   1946   115 mins   bw
Alcina

d **Georges Lacombe**
sc **Pierre Véry**
ph **Roger Hubert**
m **Marcel Mirouze**
    Jean Gabin, Marlene Dietrich, Margo Lion, Daniel Gélin, Marcel André

Martin (Gabin), a builder in a dusty French provincial town, is hired to construct a house for Blanche (Dietrich), a sophisticated, cosmopolitan newcomer to the district. They have a passionate affair until he discovers that she is a high-class whore, whereupon he kills her and is tried for murder. Played as flashback from the courtroom, the film lost 16 minutes on release in Britain and 27 in the US where the Catholic Legion of Decency raised moral objections. In the event, the promise of so electric and starry a pairing as Gabin and Dietrich resulted in no more than a disappointingly old-fashioned, superficial and mediocre drama.

▶ **Marusa No Onna** see Taxing Woman, A

▶ **Marusa No Onna 2** see Taxing Woman's Return, A

Mary My Dearest

▶ **María De Mi Corazón**

Mexico 1983 100 mins col
Azteca Films/Universidad Veracruzana

d **Jaime Humberto Hermosillo**
sc **Gabriel García Márquez, Jaime Humberto Hermosillo**
ph **Angel Goded**
m **Joaquin Gutiérrez Heras**
    Héctor Bonilla, María Rojo, Ana Ofelia Murguia, Blanca Torres, Salvador Sánchez

Héctor (Bonilla), a small-time crook, is reunited with his former girlfriend María (Rojo) who persuades him to give up crime and join her in a touring magic show. One day, the van in which she is travelling breaks down and, in her frantic search for a telephone, she finds herself in a sanatorium for the mentally ill from which she cannot escape. One of Mexico's best-known directors, Hermosillo gathered together a dedicated group of actors, technicians, intellectuals and artists and engineered this independent production on a miniscule budget, free from the traditional constraints of the industry, thus starting a new trend. The film combines a naturalistic view of everyday *bourgeois* life with the fantastical and bizarre and does it well, building up inexorably to a horrifying conclusion. But the mixture of styles often undercuts the clarity of the piece and minimizes one's involvement with the characters.

Masculine-Feminine

▶ **Masculin-Féminin**

France 1966 104 mins bw
Anouchka/Argos/Svensk Filmindustri/Sandrews

d **Jean-Luc Godard**
sc **Jean-Luc Godard**
ph **Willy Kurant**
m **Francis Lai**
    Jean-Pierre Léaud, Chantal Goya, Michel Debord, Marlène Jobert, Catherine-Isabelle Duport

Paul (Léaud), fresh from military service, meets Madeleine (Goya), who gets him a job on the magazine where she works. But he is more interested in spending his time in Left-wing political activity and his relationship with the two girls (Duport and Jobert) with whom he shares an apartment. Godard's view of the generation of 'the children of Marx and Coca Cola' is represented by Léaud at the start of his six-film collaboration with the director in the late 1960s. (In fact, Léaud has made as many films with Godard as he did with his mentor, Truffaut.) Less engaging here than as Truffaut's Antoine Doinel, Léaud was able to create the right anarchic, questioning image of French youth typical of the attitude that led to the 'events' of May 1968 in Paris. The fragmented techniques and seemingly improvised style reflect the character, but disguise a firm structure. Brigitte Bardot can be glimpsed briefly on the Métro.

Best Actor (Jean-Pierre Léaud) Berlin 1966

▶ **Masculin-Féminin** see Masculine-Feminine

Maskerade

▶ **(US: Masquerade In Vienna)**

Austria 1934 101 mins bw
Tobis/Sascha

d **Willi Forst**
sc **Willi Forst, Walter Reisch**
ph **Franz Planer**
m **Willi Schmidt-Gentner**
   **Anton Walbrook, Paula Wessely, Olga
   Tschechowa, Peter Petersen, Walter
   Janssen, Hilde Von Stolz**

A ladies' man and celebrated artist (Walbrook) is the love object of an unsophisticated
young woman (Wessely), whom his friends
suspect of being the model in his painting of
a female nude in a ball-mask. A delightful
bitter-sweet comedy set in the favourite era
of pre-war romantic escapism – Vienna at the
turn of the century. The adult script, the
waltzing camera, and two fine leads in the
vulnerable Wessely and the suave Walbrook,
made it justifiably actor-singer Willi Forst's
most famous film as a director, and presented
an image of the Austria that most people had
before the *Anschlüss*.

▶ **Masquerade In Vienna** see Mas-
kerade

Masques

France 1987 100 mins col
MK2 Productions/Films A2

d **Claude Chabrol**
sc **Odile Barski, Claude Chabrol**
ph **Jean Rabier**
m **Matthieu Chabrol**
   **Philippe Noiret, Robin Renucci,
   Bernadette Lafont, Anne Brochet,
   Monique Chaumette, Pierre-François
   Duméniaud**

Writer Roland Woolf (Renucci) arrives to
stay at the country house of Christian Legagneur (Noiret), a famous TV game-show host
whom he is to interview. Woolf, in fact, is
really there to seek clues to the disappearance
of his sister, and soon discovers that his host's
niece-cum-ward (Brochet), is confined to bed
in the grip of a mysterious malady, and that
the affable Legagneur is, to put it mildly, not

what he seems. Directing with his customary
flair and efficiency – and with a couple of
obvious nods towards Hitchcock – Chabrol
unfolds a tale of murderous duplicity, with
Noiret immensely entertaining as the ambiguous centre of the action, but the enterprise is
pretty thin under its thick coating of style.

The Master And Margarita

▶ **Maestro e Margarita**

Yugoslavia/Italy 1972 101 mins col
Dunav Film (Belgrade)/Euro
International Film (Rome)/Tzigane Film
Productions

d **Aleksander Petrović**
sc **Aleksander Petrović, Barbara Alberti,
    Amedeo Pagani**
ph **Roberto Gerardi**
m **Ennio Morricone**
   **Ugo Tognazzi, Mimsy Farmer, Alain
   Cuny, Tasko Nacić, Danilo Stojković,
   Zlatko Madunić**

The brilliant playwright Nikolai Maksudov
(Tognazzi), known as The Master, attends the
dress rehearsal of his new play, 'Pontius Pilate', at a Moscow theatre during the 1920s.
The theatre manager and others object to the
play on ideological grounds but The Master,
supported by his girlfriend Margarita
(Farmer) and a mysterious Professor Woland
(Cuny), refuses to withdraw the piece. The
Master then discovers that the professor is
the Devil but, when he tries to alert people,
he is committed to a madhouse. Petrović
based his film on 'ideas' from Bulgakov's
novel, and has presented it as an explicit plea
on behalf of so-called 'dissident' artists, whose
plight he exposes in a mixture of formal
restraint, special effects and animation. It is
all expertly achieved, but an ambiguous ending which implies that the action has been a
hallucination suffered by the mad Nikolai,
dilutes the central theme and begs its
questions.

Master Of The House

▶ **aka Thou Shalt Honour Thy
   Wife**

▶ **Du Sjak Aere Din Hstru**

Denmark 1925 95 mins bw

Palladium

d   **Carl Theodor Dreyer**
sc **Carl Theodor Dreyer, Svend Rindom**
ph **George Schneevoigt**
m   **Silent**
    Johannes Meyer, Astrid Hölm, Mathilde
    Nielson, Clara Schönfeld

Since the collapse of his business, Victor (Meyer) has grown increasingly morose, ill-tempered, selfish and demanding. Unaware of his wife's (Hölm) struggle to feed and clothe him and their three children on limited means, he treats her with bullying and tyrannical disregard until her health cracks under the strain. When her mother sends her away to recuperate, his old nanny (Nielson) moves in and, treating him like a recalcitrant child, teaches him to mend his ways. Told with the utmost simplicity, its cramped studio-built apartment beautifully lit and capturing the bleak cold of a Danish winter, Dreyer's silent film is a minor masterpiece. The self-sacrifice of the wife is unbearably painful and the hard journey to self-recognition for the husband unexpectedly affecting. The nanny is a wonderful creation, almost but not quite sinister, and bringing the odd faint touch of humour to the proceedings. Fundamentally a tale of love and devotion, given emotional intensity by the camera's close concentration on faces and gestures, viewed today the movie is actually a feminist work of some depth and offers strong contemporary resonances.

▶ **Mat** see Mother

Matador

Spain   1986   115 mins   col
Andres Vicente Gomez Prod.

d   **Pedro Almodóvar**
sc **Pedro Almodóvar, Jesus Ferrero**
ph **Angel Luis Fernandez**
m   **Bernardo Bonezzi**
    Assumpta Serna, Nacho Martinez, Eva
    Cobo, Antonio Banderas, Bibi Andersson

Angel (Banderas), a 21-year-old from a very strict Catholic upbringing, is training to become a matador at the bullfighting school run by Diego (Martinez). After unsuccessfully attempting to rape his instructor's fashion model girlfriend (Cobo), he gives himself up to the police. There he confesses to two murders, but it becomes evident, partly due to his feminist lawyer (Serna), that others are responsible. Typically surreal, iconoclastic and kinky, the film continues Almodóvar's exploration into the link between violence and eroticism – a woman kills the men she brings to orgasm – couched in the camp language of 1950s screen melodrama, *Matador* can only alienate reactionaries and/or those who believe that less excess produces more success. As self-regarding and often juvenile as it is, the film has enough black humour and brashly colourful sequences to shock and charm at the same time.

Mata-Hari, Agent H.21

France   1964   99 mins   bw
Filmel/Les Films Du Carrosse/
Simar(Paris)/Fida
Cinematografica(Rome)

d   **Jean-Louis Richard**
sc **Jean-Louis Richard, François Truffaut**
ph **Michel Kelber**
m   **Georges Delerue**
    Jeanne Moreau, Jean-Louis Trintignant,
    Claude Rich, Frank Villard, Albert Rémy,
    Henri Garcin

Spying for the Germans in Paris during World War I, Mata-Hari (Moreau) is ordered to seduce a young captain (Trintignant) in order to keep him occupied while certain documents are stolen. Everything goes according to plan except that spy and soldier fall in love, thus sealing their doom. This account of the Mata-Hari legend offers a superbly sophisticated and versatile performance from Moreau, as well as some amusement early on while she masquerades as a Javanese nightclub dancer. However, the love affair is clichéd and the film lacks credibility, succeeding neither as espionage thriller nor as melodrama. An improvement, though, on the ghastly Garbo version.

The Match Factory Girl

Finland   1989   70 mins   col
Villealfa Filmproductions

d **Aki Kaurismäki**
sc **Aki Kaurismäki**
ph **Timo Salminen**
   Kati Outinen, Elina Salo, Esko Nikkari,
   Vesa Vierikko, Silu Seppala

Plain, shy, uneducated and poor, Iris (Outinen) works at a soul-destroying job on the assembly line of a match factory, supporting her mother and stepfather on her meagre earnings. At night she returns to their bleak, cramped and squalid apartment to cook for the ungrateful pair. Her only pleasure is in sentimental pop music, and she visits dancehalls in futile search of romance. Finally, sporting a garish and pathetic new dress, she is picked up by a wealthy businessman (Vierikko) in a disco. He cruelly abandons her and she later discovers she is pregnant. Thrown out by her parents, she resolves to extract a harsh revenge on those who have mistreated her. The prolific Kaurismäki's seventh feature is a tightly constructed, tightly edited, minimalist and pitiless study of poverty, loneliness and despair. Sketched with the matter-of-fact brush strokes of a Grimm fairy tale, the film, in spite of lacking credibility in one or two details, is thoroughly absorbing, from the visually striking opening sequence among the machines of the factory, to its denouement in which Iris' dignity is ironically restored. It might be best to ignore Kaurismäki's somewhat flamboyant claim that he 'decided to make a film that will make Robert Bresson seem like a director of epic action pictures', and appreciate the fine observation of this third work in his so-called 'working-class' trilogy. (The little-seen *Shadows In Paradise* (1986) was the first, *Ariel* (1988) the second.)

La Maternelle

France 1932 89 mins bw
Photosonor

d **Jean Benoît-Lévy, Marie Epstein**
sc **Jean Benoît-Lévy**
ph **Georges Asselin**
m **Edouard Flament**
   Madeleine Renaud, Paulette Elambert,
   Alice Tissot, Mady Berry, Henri Debain

Rose (Renaud), a teacher at a *maternelle* (nursery school) is devoted to the children, particularly a little girl abandoned by her prostitute mother. However, the child becomes distraught when Rose considers marrying. Benoît-Lévy and Marie Epstein (the sister of the distinguished director Jean Epstein) made a number of features in the 1920s and early 1930s about the plight of children, of which this is the most famous and widely seen. Deeply felt and wonderfully acted, it is still worth seeing, despite the inherent sentimentality and well-meant ending.

▶ **Matka Joanna Od Aniolów** see Devil And The Nun, The

▶ **Matrimonio All'Italiana** see Marriage Italian Style

The Mattei Affair

▶ **Il Caso Mattei**

Italy 1972 118 mins col
Vides Verona

d **Francesco Rosi, Tonino Guerra**
sc **Francesco Rosi**
ph **Pasqualino De Santis**
m **Piero Piccioni**
   Gian Maria Volonté, Luigi Squarzina,
   Peter Baldwin, Renato Romano, Franco
   Graziosi

The life and death in a mysterious plane crash in 1962 of Enrico Mattei (Volonté), the socialist oil magnate, the 'most powerful Italian since Augustus Caesar', is examined in flashback. Using a bold, semi-documentary cinematic style, Rosi in another of his incisive studies of corrupt post-war Italian power games, leaves the audience to choose from the hypotheses offered as to the cause of Mattei's death. Volonté has enough charisma to carry off the role of the man whose public behaviour interests Rosi far more than his private life.

Best Film Cannes 1972

A Matter of Dignity

▶ **To Telefteo Psemma**

Greece 1957 104 mins bw
Finos

d **Michael Cacoyannis**
sc **Michael Cacoyannis**
ph **Walter Lassally**
m **Manos Hadjidakis**
  Ellie Lambetti, Athena Michaelidou, Georges Pappas, Eleni Zafiriou, Minas Christides, Michel Nikolinakas

Chloe (Lambetti), daughter of a once-wealthy family on the brink of ruin, tries to save their situation by agreeing to marry a millionaire whose dullness she can barely tolerate. Photographed with graphic clarity and acted with expertise, this is one of the director's best melodramas, focusing with powerful truth and accuracy on its issues. The hollow values of the idle rich are ruthlessly exposed in the character of Chloe's mother (Michaelidou), obsessed with keeping up appearances even to the point of sacrificing her daughter; the gulf between rich and poor is made manifest in the tragic plight of the family servant. Chloe's painful journey to self-discovery carries moving conviction, thanks particularly to the beautiful Lambetti's striking mobility of expression.

▶ **Maudits, Les** see Damned, The

Mauvaise Graine

France   1933   80 mins   bw
Compagnie Nouvelle Cinématographique

d **Alexander Esway, Billy Wilder**
sc **Alexander Esway, H.G. Lustig, Billy Wilder**
ph **Paul Cotteret, Maurice Delattre**
m **Walter Gray, Franz Waxman**
  Danielle Darrieux, Pierre Mingand, Raymond Galle, Jean Wall, Michel Duran, Paul Escoffier

Henri Pasquier (Mingand), charming but idle, has his smart car removed and sold by his stern doctor father (Escoffier). The loss lands him in an awkward situation which he takes care of by impulsively stealing another vehicle, but is seen doing so by members of a professional gang who give chase. One thing leads to another and Henri becomes a member of the gang, falling in love with Jeanette (Darrieux), their attractive decoy. Filmed on location in Paris and Marseilles, this slight but appealing comedy-drama marks the first film Billy Wilder made outside Germany, prior to his great Hollywood career. Although it's a collaborative effort, the Wilder touch can be discerned in moments of imaginatively wry humour and the moral ambiguities of the characters and situation. The movie was a superb showcase for the beautiful and talented 17-year-old Danielle Darrieux.

▶ **Mauvais Fils, Un** see Bad Son, A

▶ **Mauvais Sang** see Night Is Young, The

▶ **Max** see Max Et Les Ferrailleurs

Max Et Les Ferrailleurs

▶ **aka Max**

France   1971   110 mins   col
Lira Films/Sonocam

d **Claude Sautet**
sc **Claude Neron, Claude Sautet**
ph **René Mathelin**
m **Philippe Sarde**
  Michel Piccoli, Romy Schneider, Bernard Fresson, François Périer, Georges Wilson

Max (Piccoli), a former magistrate-turned-police inspector, is obsessed by the fact that known gangsters go free for lack of evidence. Determined to redress the balance, he invests his time, skill and private income in schemes to push small-time crooks into big-time activities in order to nail them. His bizarre plans come unstuck when he falls in love with a prostitute (Schneider) who is the companion of Max's latest target, a petty junk thief. Sautet has come up with a nice idea for an unusual cop-and-gangster film, to which he brings the right wry tone. However, it falls apart because Max's behaviour loses credibility, there is insufficient action and Romy Schneider is uncomfortably miscast.

Max Havelaar

Netherlands   1976   170 mins   col
Fons Rademakers Productie/PT Mondial Motion Pictures

d **Fons Rademakers**
sc **Gerard Soeteman**
ph **Jan De Bont**
   Peter Faber, Sacha Bulthuis, Lerry
   Iantho, Elang Mohamad, Adenan
   Soesilaningrat

Civil servant Max Havelaar (Faber) is sent to Dutch colonial Java to try to reform a corrupt local system, but he is thwarted in his efforts by his own government and by mercantile interests. Rademakers' eighth film, his most expensive and expansive, was adapted from an 1859 novel by 'Multatuli' (Edouard Douwes Dekker), which attacked the colonial rule in the Dutch East Indies (now Indonesia). The film takes a less astringent approach than the book, and the portrayal of the idealistic Havelaar lacks nuance. However, the contrast between the scenes in Amsterdam and Java is effective and the recreation of the era is compelling. The best performances come from the Indonesian actors in a film which switches between Dutch and a Malay dialect.

▶ **Max, Mon Amour** see Max, My Love

Max, My Love

▶ **Max, Mon Amour**

   France 1986 94 mins col
   Greenwich Film Production/Films A2

d **Nagisa Oshima**
sc **Nagisa Oshima, Jean-Claude Carrière**
ph **Raoul Coutard**
m **Michel Portal**
   Charlotte Rampling, Anthony Higgins,
   Christopher Hovik, Victoria Abril, Anne-
   Marie Besse, Pierre Étaix

When a British diplomat (Higgins) in Paris discovers that his bored wife (Rampling) has rented an apartment where she can visit her lover Max, a chimpanzee (!), he invites the ape to come and live with them. The shade of Buñuel hovers over this witty, black comedy of manners that judiciously avoids the vulgarity inherent in the subject. In fact, this *ménagérie à trois* is often tender and sensitive, thanks mainly to the enigmatic and sensuous performance by Rampling, and is often hilarious, such as during the dinner party scene.

The only problem is that Max's character is not sufficiently developed.

Mayerling

   France 1935 96 mins bw
   Concordia Cinématographique/Nero

d **Anatole Litvak**
sc **Joseph Kessel, Irmgard Von Cube**
ph **Armand Thirard**
m **Arthur Honegger**
   Charles Boyer, Danielle Darrieux, Suzy
   Prim, Jean Debucourt, Vladimir Sokoloff

Crown Prince Rudolph (Boyer), heir to the Austro-Hungarian Empire, is forced into a loveless marriage, but subsequently falls passionately for 17-year-old Marie Vetsera (Darrieux), a girl of good family. When the Pope refuses Rudolph's request to annul his marriage, the lovers flee to Mayerling, the prince's hunting lodge, where they spend an idyllic 24 hours before he shoots her, and then himself, in a death pact. One of the most famous and poignant of romantic tragedies in history, *Mayerling* was impeccably cast and directed with taste and discretion. It made Boyer an idol of women the world over and led to a Hollywood contract for Litvak. Another French version (Max Ophüls' *Mayerling To Sarajevo*) was made in the 1940s, and Terence Young directed it with Omar Sharif and Catherine Deneuve in 1968, but this remains the definitive version. Sad footnote: A few days after the death of his beloved wife in 1978, Boyer committed suicide, thus echoing the fate of Rudolph.

▶ **Mayerling To Sarajevo** see Sarajevo

▶ **May Fools** see Milou In May

▶ **Maynila Sa Mga Kuko Ng Liwanag** see Manila: In The Claws Of Neon

▶ **Mazel Tov Ou Le Mariage** see Marry Me! Marry Me!

▶ **Me** see Naked Childhood

▶ **Me'Achorei Hasoragim** see Beyond The Walls

The Meadow

▶ **Il Prato**

Italy 1979 120 mins col
Filmtre/RAI

d   **Paolo and Vittorio Taviani**
sc **Paolo and Vittorio Taviani**
ph **Franco Di Giacomo**
m   **Ennio Morricone**
    **Isabella Rossellini, Michele Placido,
    Saverio Marconi, Giulio Brogi, Ermanno
    Taviani, Angela Goodwin**

Anthropology graduate Eugenia (Rossellini) earns a dull living in a Florence tax office; her long-standing lover Enzo (Placido) is an agronomist who dreams of reclaiming idle land; Giovanni(Marconi), a young Milanese magistrate, longs to be a film-maker. In Tuscany on business, Giovanni meets Eugenia, falls in love with her and they have an affair, but she has no intention of leaving Enzo. The Taviani brothers' portrait of three young professional people searching for fulfilment and wrestling with notions of happiness is a disappointment. Overlong and containing a gaudy Pied Piper story sequence that could happily be excised, the film is a blend of dreams and reality, of the over-intellectual and the over-emotional, in which the protagonists' behaviour grows increasingly irrational. The redeeming features are the exquisitely photographed Tuscan landscape, the excellent performances and the beautiful presence of Ingrid Bergman's and Roberto Rossellini's daughter.

Mechanical Man

▶ **aka Pathetic Fallacy**

▶ **Ajantrik**

India 1958 102 mins bw
West Bengal Government

d   **Ritwik Ghatak**
sc **Ritwik Ghatak**
ph **Dinen Gupta**
m   **Ali Akbar Khan**
    **Kali Bandyopadhyay, Gyanesh
    Mukhopadhyay, Satindra Bhattacharya,
    Gangapada Basu**

The greatest friend of Bimal (Bandy-opadhyay) is his ancient, broken-down taxi, the object of ridicule to the people of the small country town where he scrapes a living. This is a satirical comment on the attitude to machinery in a traditional society, as well as being an entertaining episodic tale, expertly told with humour and pathos. Ghatak, who died an alcoholic aged 49 in 1975, made only eight feature films, few of them known outside India until after his death. He has since been recognized as a key figure in the development of modern Indian cinema.

Medea

Italy 1969 118 mins col
San Marco/Number One/Janus

d   **Pier Paolo Pasolini**
sc **Pier Paolo Pasolini**
ph **Ennio Guarnieri**
m   **Pier Paolo Pasolini, Che Ringrazia, Elsa
    Morante
    Maria Callas, Giuseppe Gentile, Laurent
    Terzieff, Massimo Girotti, Margareth
    Clementi**

Jason (Gentile) arrives back in Corinth with Medea (Callas), the daughter of the King of Colchis and a high priestess with magical powers. After some years living with their two children, Jason tires of his 'barbarian' princess, but she wreaks a terrible revenge. It might have seemed a good idea to cast the fieriest of actresses from the operatic stage in the 'straight' part of Euripides' Medea, but the result was a damp squib. Much of the blame for the diva's disappointing (dubbed) performance must be laid at the door of Pasolini's wayward direction. At least this turgid mythological mish-mash contained some scenic splendour.

▶ **Meetings Of Anna, The** see Rendez-Vous D'Anna, Les

▶ **Megalexandros, O** see Alexander The Great

▶ **Megáll Az Idó** see Time Stands Still

▶ **Még Kér A Nép** see Red Psalm

▶ **Meilleure Façon De Marcher, La**
see Best Way To Walk, The

▶ **Meisje Met Het Rode Haar, Het**
see Girl With The Red Hair, The

▶ **Melissokomos, O** see Beekeeper, The

Melo

▶ **Der Träumende Mund**

France/Germany 1932 95 mins bw
Pathé/Nathan/Matador

d **Paul Czinner**
sc **Paul Czinner, Carl Mayer**
ph **Jules Kruger, René Ribault**
m **Beethoven, Wagner**
   Elisabeth Bergner, Anton Edthofor,
   Rudolf Forster, Margarete Hruby

The wife (Bergner) of an orchestra musician
falls in love with her husband's best friend, a
concert violinist. All three are tormented by
the situation, which she finally resolves by killing herself. Adapted from a mediocre play by
Henri Bernstein, it is a sad and romantic, if
rather tedious piece, of interest chiefly because
it introduced the famous German star to
American audiences and critics, who gave due
adulation to her transcendental qualities. This
version was simultaneously shot in French,
starring Gaby Morlay; then, in 1937, Czinner
remade it in English in Britain, again starring
his wife Miss Bergner, and calling it *Dreaming
Lips*. The German director Josef Von Baky
had another go at the story in the 1950s, eliminating the suicide, among other changes, and
casting Maria Schell as the wife, and it resurfaced yet again in a much better light in 1987
in Alain Resnais' version.

Mélo

France 1986 112 mins col
MK2/Films A2/CNC

d **Alain Resnais**
sc **Alain Resnais**
ph **Charlie Van Damme**
m **Philippe-Gérard**
   Sabine Azéma, Fanny Ardant, Pierre
   Arditi, André Dussollier, Jacques
   Dacqmine, Hubert Gignoux

Marcel (Dussollier), a celebrated violinist,
falls in love with Romaine (Azéma), the wife
of Pierre (Arditi), an old friend. But Marcel's
loyalty to Pierre is stronger than his love for
Romaine, and she commits suicide. Henri
Bernstein's boulevard drama of the 1920s had
already served as vehicles for the fragile talents of Elisabeth Bergner (1932, 1937) and
for Maria Schell (1953) before Resnais used
it as a consciously theatrical ensemble piece.
Yet, despite its being set behind a proscenium
arch, the brilliant camerawork and editing
make it a curiously satisfying cinematic
experience. Every nuance is caught in the
expert performances by the same four leads
as in his previous film, *L'Amour À Mort*,
giving the old-fashioned plot (it is set in the
1940s) a depth and resonance it lacked previously.

▶ **Mélodie En Sous-Sol** see Big Snatch,
The

▶ **Melody Haunts My Memory, The**
see You Only Love Once

▶ **Memorias Del Subdesarrollo** see
Memories Of Underdevelopment

▶ **Memórias Do Cárcere** see Memories Of Prison

Memories Of Prison

▶ **Memórias Do Cárcere**

Brazil 1984 187 mins col
Produçoes L. C. Barreto

d **Nelson Pereira Dos Santos**
sc **Nelson Pereira Dos Santos**
ph **José Medeiros**
m **Giya Kancheli**
   Carlos Vereza, Glória Pires, Jofre
   Soares, José Dumont, Wilson Grey

In 1936, the Brazilian author Graciliano
Ramos became a political prisoner, first in a
prison in Rio and then in a penal colony
together with 900 other convicts. He managed
to write down his experiences and published
his *Memoirs Of Prison* when he was finally
released. The extraordinary book was the
inspiration behind an almost equally extraordinary film. Set in the 1930s, it can also be

taken as a metaphor for Brazilian society in the 1980s and, although most of the cast are men, lead by Vereza as Ramos, it also shows his wife (Pires) gaining her independence. This is the second film by Pereira Dos Santos to be based on a work by Ramos, the first being the acclaimed *Barren Lives*.

Memories Of Underdevelopment

▶ **Memorias Del Subdesarrollo**

Cuba   1968   104 mins   bw
ICAIC

d   Tomás Gutiérrez Alea
sc Tomás Gutiérrez Alea, Edmundo Desnoes
ph Ramón Suárez
m   Leo Bower
    Sergio Corrieri, Daisy Granádos, Eslinda Nuñez, Beatriz Ponchora

A wealthy *bourgeois* intellectual (Corrieri) whose family flees to Miami when Castro comes to power, elects to stay and come to terms with the revolution. This most subtle and ironical investigation into the role of the intellectual in the new Cuba, proved – if proof were needed – that Third World cinema could hold its own in sophistication with that of European films. Edmundo Desnoes, on whose book it was based, appears as himself in a scene at a writers' conference.

Men

▶ **Männer**

W. Germany   1985   99 mins   col
Olga Film/ZDF

d   Doris Dörrie
sc Doris Dörrie
ph Helge Weindler
m   Claus Bantzer
    Heiner Lauterbach, Uwe Ochsenknecht, Ulrike Kriener, Janna Marangosoff, Dietmar Bär

When Julius (Lauterbach), a successful, happily married advertising executive, discovers that his wife (Kriener) is having an affair with Stefan (Ochsenknecht), a hippy artist, he rents a room in Stefan's apartment in order to spy on the unsuspecting couple, meanwhile developing a friendship with his rival. Doris Dörrie may have little new to say about the childish insecurities, double standards and reactionary prejudices of men, but she presents her material as a well-written, well-constructed comedy, bringing a fresh, detached, razor-sharp eye and a touch of surreal fantasy to bear on a thoroughly entertaining and intelligent film.

▶ **Menage** see Evening Dress

Ménilmontant

France   1924   50 mins   bw
Dimitri Kirsanov

d   Dimitri Kirsanov
sc Dimitri Kirsanov
ph Léonce Crovan
m   Silent
    Nadia Sibirskaïa, Yolande Beaulieu, Guy Belmont, Jean Pasquier

Two sisters, left alone and poor after their father has savagely murdered their mother, quarrel and part. They meet some years later, by which time one (Sibirskaïa) has become a prostitute and the other (Beaulieu) has had a child by a lover killed in a street fight. One of the most famous experimental films of the 1920s, it is a ciné poem which combines several styles – ultra-rapid montage, static compositions, hand-held camera movements, flashbacks and superimpositions. Yet its series of visual impressions makes narrative sense and has an emotional impact, and Sibirskaïa, a Russian emigré like the director, is remarkable.

▶ **Menschen Am Sonntag** see People On Sunday

Mephisto

Hungary   1981   144 mins   col
Mafilm (Studio Objectiv)/Manfred Durniok Productions

d   István Szabó
sc Peter Dobai, István Szabó
ph Lajos Koltai
m   Karl Millöcker, Mendelssohn, Reinitz,

Liszt, Johann Strauss, Franz Meissner,
Aldar Pege
Klaus Maria Brandauer, Ildikó Bánsági,
Krystyna Janda, Rolf Hoppe, György
Cserhalmi, Peter Andorai, Karin Boyd

Högen, an acclaimed actor in pre-war
Germany, famous for his interpretation of
Mephistopheles, is a man of Left-wing lean-
ings, hoping to establish a workers' theatre.
When, however, the Nazis take power, his
hunger for fame supersedes his principles and
silences his conscience and he sells out to the
oppressors, betraying his colleagues and his
family. Szabó's chilling study of compromise,
expertly directed and edited, was based on
the novel by Klaus Mann (son of Thomas),
itself drawing on the life of his uncle, actor
Gustav Grundgens. A gripping story of over-
weening ambition, steeped in creeping political corruption, the film is beautifully cast, but
it is Brandauer's monumental performance –
explosively committed and energetic – that
makes the film unforgettable.

Best Foreign Film Oscar 1982

▶ **Mépris, Le** see Contempt

The Merchant Of Four Seasons

▶ **Der Händler Der Vier
Jahreszeiten**

W. Germany   1971   89 mins   col
Tango Film

d   **Rainer Werner Fassbinder**
sc **Rainer Werner Fassbinder**
ph **Dietrich Lohmann**
m   **Rocco Granata plus archive material**
**Hans Hirschmüller, Irm Hermann, Hanna
Schygulla, Andrea Schober, Klaus
Löwitsch, Karl Scheydt**

Hans Epp (Hirschmüller), unable to achieve
any of his ambitions, which included joining
the Foreign Legion, embarks on a loveless
marriage and becomes a trader in fruit and
vegetables. He drinks heavily, beats his wife
and, finally, drinks himself deliberately to
death. The first of Fassbinder's works to
demonstrate the development of a schematic
and unambiguous style, it was also the first

to gain general praise and recognition in
Germany. Hans is the product of stifling *petit
bourgeois* values, and his disillusionment and
disintegration constitute the director's
pointed attack on those values. Well-acted,
and encompassing a measure of black humour, the film is both bleak in its vision and
enthralling in its presentation, and retains
sympathy for its hopeless chief protagonist.

Merlusse

France   1935   75 mins   bw
Les Films Marcel Pagnol

d   **Marcel Pagnol**
sc **Marcel Pagnol**
ph **A. Assouad**
m   **Vincent Scotto**
**Henri Poupon, André Pollack,
Thommeray, André Robert, Rellys**

Merlusse (Poupon), a schoolteacher hated by
his pupils, reveals an unsuspected warmth to
the boys left behind in the boarding school
during the Christmas holidays. It transpires
that the teacher frightened the boys because
he was afraid of them. Pagnol filmed this
sensitive story in the lycée in Marseilles where
he had been both pupil and teacher. Any
sentimentality is avoided by the disarming
playing and the ironic edge to the dialogue.
Unhappy with the technical aspects of the
first filming, Pagnol had the whole film reshot.

▶ **Mes, Het** see Knife, The

▶ **Meshi** see Repast

▶ **Messer Im Kopf** see Knife In The
Head

Messidor

Switzerland   1977   120 mins   col
Action/Gaumont/Citel

d   **Alain Tanner**
sc **Alain Tanner**
ph **Renato Berta**
m   **Arié Dzierlatka**
**Clémentine Amouroux, Catherine Rétoré,
Franziskus Abgottspon, Gérald Battiaz,
Hansjorg Bedschard**

Jeanne (Amouroux), a university student, and Marie (Rétoré), a shop assistant, meet at the roadside while hitch-hiking. Both are bored with their lives and decide to escape. When they run out of money they begin to hold up stores and become wanted criminals. Tanner observes his repellent, amoral heroines (convincingly played by two young newcomers) with a cold but fascinated eye as they travel across Switzerland – not the country of the tourist brochures, but one of crowded motorways, and roadside cafés. He may have given the lie to those who say the Swiss only produce cuckoo-clocks and chocolate, but chocolate is easier to digest than this controversial film.

Metello

Italy   1970   112 mins   col
Documento Film

d   **Mauro Bolognini**
sc **Luigi Bazzoni, Ugo Pirro, Suso Cecchi D'Amico, Mauro Bolognini**
ph **Ennio Guarnieri**
m   **Ennio Morricone**
    Massimo Ranieri, Lucia Bosé, Ottavia Piccolo, Tina Aumont, Frank Wolff

Metello (Ranieri), a young workman, becomes involved with the rise of the Italian labour movement towards the end of the 19th century. Over the years, he has affairs, marries, enjoys political triumph as a successful strike leader, and is twice imprisoned. In this film Bolognini combined his bent for 19th-century subjects with a later sense of political commitment. The result is a story that is somewhat well-worn, and overcrowded with scenes of riot and anarchy, but is nonetheless authentic in flavour, very well cast and exceedingly handsome to look at.

Best Actress (Ottavia Piccolo) Cannes 1970

Metropolis

Germany   1926   153 mins   bw
UFA

d   **Fritz Lang**
sc **Thea Von Harbou**
ph **Karl Freund, Günther Rittau**
m   **Silent**

Brigitte Helm, Alfred Abel, Gustav Frölich, Rudolf Klein-Rogge, Fritz Rasp

The down-trodden factory workers in a futuristic city are confused by a malign robot made in the image of the saintly girl (Helm) who tried to lead them towards justice. Lang was given an unprecedented budget to create the still impressive huge sets inspired by the New York skyline, such as flying machines moving between skyscrapers, and Eugen Schüfftan introduced a new special effects process combining life-size action with models. Despite its ridiculously naive ending – Capital and Labour reconciled by love – and a soppy romantic hero (Fröhlich), the film is a potent allegory of totalitarianism. In 1984, Giorgio Moroder added a rock music score, tinted sequences, and edited it down to 83 minutes with less disastrous results than anticipated.

Mexican Bus Ride

▶ **aka Ascent to Heaven**

▶ **Subida Al Cielo**

Mexico   1951   85 mins   bw
Producciones Isla

d   **Luis Buñuel**
sc **Juan De La Cabada, Manuel Altolaguirre, Luis Buñuel**
ph **Alex Phillips**
m   **Gustavo Pittaluga**
    Lilia Prado, Carmelita González, Esteban Márquez, Manuel Dondé, Roberto Cobo

A young man (Márquez) is hauled away on his wedding night by his grasping elder brothers, anxious to get him to the next town to ratify their dying mother's will. On the hazardous bus journey over the mountains, the bus gets stuck in a flooded river, a woman has a premature delivery, the young man is pursued by the local tart and there is an unscheduled banquet. Buñuel was particularly fond of this sardonic, quickly-made comedy, based on a real-life trip made by the director's friend, the poet Altolaguirre. It is one of his lightest films, while retaining the deeper themes of birth, copulation and death, and a delightful self-parodic dream sequence.

Michael Kohlhaas

West Germany   1979   95 mins   col

Horst Film GmbH and Co

d **Wolf Vollmar**
sc **Wolf Vollmar**
ph **Wolfgang Hannemann**
m **Peter Sandloff**
   Rolf Boysen, Alfred Schieske, Wilhelm Borchert, Wolfgang Buettner, Irene Marhold

Michael Kohlhaas (Boysen), a 16th-century horse trader, is forced to pay to go through a nobleman's land and has to leave two horses there while he obtains a licence. When he returns, he finds his horses dying and his assistant beaten. After a year of legal quibbling over compensation, in which the land-owner is backed by a corrupt court, Kohlhaas becomes an outlaw to fight for justice. Heinrich Von Kleist's 1810 story, based on an historical incident of a German Robin Hood, had been filmed less successfully in English by Volker Schlöndorff in 1968. This later version, originally made as a TV series but never transmitted, has a certain sweep, a cast of splendid German stage actors and lovely locations, but it obviously lost some depth by being reduced to feature-film length. Despite being an enjoyable enough romantic adventure, it might leave those audiences unacquainted with the Kleist work wondering why it is considered a classic of German literature.

The Middle Man

▶ **Jana-Aranya**

India 1975 131 mins bw
Indus

d **Satyajit Ray**
sc **Satyajit Ray**
ph **Soumendou Roy**
m **Satyajit Ray**
   Pradip Mukherjee, Satya Banerjee, Dipankar Dey, Lily Chakravarty, Aparna Sen

A young university graduate (Mukherjee) cannot find work in Calcutta after eight months of trying. In desperation, he takes a job as a middle man in a corrupt business that traffics in goods and prostitutes. One of Ray's most astringent comments on contemporary Indian society cleverly pinpoints the dilemma of choice between ethics and survival. His principal characters are viewed with less warmth than usual and the ending is rather contrived, but the depiction of the 'order-supply' business is enthralling.

The Middle Of The World

▶ **Le Milieu Du Monde**

Switzerland 1974 115 mins col
Action/Citel

d **Alain Tanner**
sc **John Berger, Alain Tanner**
ph **Renato Berta**
m **Patrick Moraz**
   Olympia Carlisi, Philippe Léotard, Juliet Berto, Jacques Denis

Adriana (Carlisi) comes from Italy to a small Swiss town to work as a waitress at a railway café. There she has an affair with Paul (Léotard), a married engineer. He tries to make her enter his *bourgeois* world, but she finally rejects it and him. Although a simple love story on the surface, it has a parable of the conflict between rich and poor, male and female and North and South embedded in it. Tanner spoke of its structure as 'a hundred little short films, each done in one take'. The title refers to a posh restaurant and also to Switzerland. The film, too, whatever its Left-wing objectives, comes out as neutral, because the characters are not well enough defined and the message is too elusive.

▶ **Mignon È Partita** see Mignon Has Left

Mignon Has Left

▶ **Mignon È Partita**

Italy 1988 90 mins col
Ellepi Film (Rome)/Chrysalide Film (Paris)/with R.A.I. and RAITRE

d **Francesca Archibugi**
sc **Francesca Archibugi, Gloria Malatesta, Claudia Sbarigia**
ph **Luigi Verga**
m **Roberto Gatto, Battista Lena**
   Stefania Sandrelli, Jean-Pierre Duriez, Leonardo Ruta, Céline Beauvallet,

Lorenzo De Pasqua, Daniele Zaccaria, Francesca Antonelli

Teenage Mignon Forbicioni (Beauvallet), owing to a family crisis of whose nature she is ignorant, is sent away from her well-heeled Parisian home to stay with the somewhat shabbier Italian branch of the family in Rome. Turning up her nose at their crowded conditions (five children including the baby) and oozing superiority from every pore, she antagonizes all her cousins, except the gentle, bookish and bespectacled Giorgio (Ruta), who breaks through her reserves and falls secretly and painfully in love with her. This debut film from an Italian woman director won a multitude of awards in its home country, but for all its evident virtues it adds up to little more than a bitter-sweet domestic comedy-drama, dispensed with a good measure of charm and some occasional poignancy. The most interesting (and best-played) character is the mother (Sandrelli) of the unruly Forbicionis, coping with her family, a husband who has a mistress, and her own longings. A pleasing film, generous in incident, it is the Italian equivalent of what Diane Kurys might have made in France, but lacking the French director's refinement.

Mikaël

▶ **(US: Chained)**

Germany　1924　74 mins　bw
Decla Bioskop

d　**Carl Dreyer**
sc　**Carl Dreyer, Thea Von Harbou**
ph　**Karl Freund, Rudolph Maté**
m　**Silent**
　　Benjamin Christensen, Walter Slezak, Nora Gregor, Robert Garrison

Zoret (Danish director Christensen), a renowned and elderly artist, is driven to despair when Mikaël (Slezak), his model and pupil whom he loves more than a son, is taken from him by Princess Zamikoff (Gregor). Dreyer's study of passion and loneliness could be considered the first film of his mature period. The *fin de siècle* sets, the expressionistic lighting and the 'decadent' subject of latent homosexuality show the work's German provenance, but Dreyer

keeps a steady hand on the helm, quietly penetrating into the deeper recesses of the artist's psychology. (Sigmund Freud himself makes an appearance.) Gregor became more widely known for her role in Renoir's *The Rules Of The Game*, and the handsome, 22-year-old Slezak would gain weight, lose his looks and become a favourite Hollywood villain.

▶ **Mikres Aphrodites** see Young Aphrodites

▶ **Milieu Du Monde, Le** see Middle Of The World, The

The Milky Way

▶ **La Voie Lactée**

France　1968　102 mins　col
Greenwich/Medusa

d　**Luis Buñuel**
sc　**Luis Buñuel, Jean-Claude Carrière**
ph　**Christian Matras**
m　**Luis Buñuel**
　　Laurent Terzieff, Paul Frankeur, Delphine Seyrig, Bernard Verley, Pierre Clémenti, Georges Marchal, Edith Scob, Michel Piccoli, Alain Cuny

Two tramps (Terzieff and Frankeur) set off from Paris to make a pilgrimage to the Spanish shrine of Santiago De Compostella. *En route* they meet various characters who expound in different ways on the six central 'mysteries' of Catholic dogma: the nature of God, Christ, the Virgin Mary, the Eucharist, divine grace, and evil. The first of Buñuel's four anecdotal French films of his last years (*The Discreet Charm Of The Bourgeoise, The Phantom Of Liberty,* and *That Obscure Object Of Desire* followed) is the fervent atheist director's most direct treatment of Catholicism. Many of the arguments may seem somewhat obscure to non-Catholic audiences, but it is as wryly amusing and mischievously anti-clerical and anti-Establishment as the other films, although Buñuel stated that it 'is neither for nor against anything at all'. Only Christian fundamentalists might take offence at some of the episodes, including the depiction of Christ (Verley) being dissuaded by the

Virgin Mary (Scob) from shaving off his beard.

Le Million

France   1931   89 mins   bw
Tobis

d   René Clair
sc René Clair
ph Georges Perinal
m   Georges Van Parys
Annabella, René Lefèvre, Paul Olivier, Louis Allibert, Vanda Gréville, Raymond Cordy

A young painter (Lefèvre) wins a large lottery prize but loses the ticket. His search for it takes him across Paris, where he ends up on the stage of the opera house. In his second sound film, with dialogue, music and sound effects recorded on a single track while it was being shot, Clair retained the ease of movement of his best silent work, with the added joy of integrated musical numbers. In fact, this funny, charming cinematic operetta had a great influence on the film musical.

The Mill On The Po

▶ Il Mulino Del Po

Italy   1949   105 mins   bw
Lux Film

d   Alberto Lattuada
sc Federico Fellini, Tullio Pinelli
ph Aldo Tonti
m   Ildebrando Pizzetti
Jacques Sernas, Carla Del Poggio, Giacomo Giuradei, Isabella Riva, Mario Besesti

A young farmer (Sernas) and the daughter (Del Poggio) of a small mill owner wish to marry, but public events overtake private concerns when the farmers' demands for agrarian reform lead to social unrest and revolt in which the young man is a leading participant. The film was adapted from Ricardo Bachelli's epic novel about the events in 1876 depicted here, and Lattuada has delivered an account that is both graphic and epic, if a little too episodic and crowded with incident.

The panoramas of the Po valley are authentic and effective, and the performances – particularly from real-life farmer and first-time actor Giuradei – excellent.

▶ **Milou En Mai** see Milou In May

Milou In May

▶ **(US: May Fools)**
▶ **Milou En Mai**

France   1989   108 mins   col
Nouvelle Editions De Films/TF1 Films/ Ellipi Film (Rome)

d   Louis Malle
sc Louis Malle, Jean-Claude Carrière
ph Renato Berta
m   Stéphane Grapelli
Michel Piccoli, Miou-Miou, Michel Duchaussoy, Dominique Blanc, Harriet Walter, Bruno Carette, François Berléand, Martine Gautier, Paulette Dubost

When Madame Vieuzac (Dubost) dies on a country estate in southwest France, Milou (Piccoli), her 60-year-old son, summons the family to the funeral. However, the events of May 1968 in Paris have spread to the provinces – the undertakers are on strike and Madame Vieuzac cannot be buried. The family whiles away the time by dividing up the matriarch's belongings, disputing the will and playing sexual games but, fearing that the revolution is at their gates, they take to the woods until they hear that order has been restored. Just as Louis Malle was one of the first directors to tackle the Nazi occupation, he leads the way again by approaching, however obliquely, that famous month in 1968 when all France was in turmoil. He seems less comfortable, though, with the political background than with making an enjoyable and amusing, old-fashioned, black comedy. (It resembles the films that Claude Atant-Lara used to make in the 1950s with Bourvil.) Milou, finely played by Piccoli, is the upholder of the best of traditional country values; he is unambitious, unacquisitive and loves nature. While he is the repository of all the director's sympathies, his *bourgeois* family are treated in a satiric manner, although Malle does not spare the young revolutionaries either. However, his soft-heartedness prevents the film from having the bitterness of a Buñuel or the acerbity of a Chabrol, both of whom would have handled the subject with more rigour, and the film is especially wayward when it moves into allegorical territory near the end. It also falls for the conventional wisdom that lesbians are only waiting for a good man to rescue them. Nevertheless, there is splendid ensemble playing, some excellent jokes and Stéphane Grappelli's lively jazz on the soundtrack.

▶ **Mimì Metallurgico Ferito Nel-l'Onore** see Seduction Of Mimì, The

▶ **Minne** see Ingénue Libertine, L'

Miquette

▶ **Miquette Et Sa Mère**

France   1950   95 mins   bw
Alcina

d   **Henri-Georges Clouzot**
sc **Henri-Georges Clouzot, Jules Ferry**
ph **Louis Née**
m   **Albert Lasry**
    Louis Jouvet, Danièle Delorme, Bourvil, Saturnin Fabre, Pauline Carton

Miquette (Delorme), confined to a strict girls' school, is courted by a naive and maladroit young man (Bourvil). The lovers are separated by her mother (Carton) and his uncle (Fabre), who sends him off to work in a travelling theatre run by a ham actor (Jouvet). But love finds a way. A surprisingly bright entry into the gloom of Clouzot's *oeuvre*, this version of an old boulevard comedy is treated with a delightfully light touch. In his cinematic use of the theatre, Clouzot puts one in mind of Renoir. However, the main joy comes from the choice cast and the hilariously disastrous climactic theatrical performance.

▶ **Miquette Et Sa Mère** see Miquette

▶ **Miracle Des Loups, Le** see Miracle Of The Wolves, The

Miracle In Milan

▶ **Miracolo A Milano**

Italy   1950   101 mins   bw
ENIC

d   **Vittorio De Sica**
sc **Cesare Zavattini, Vittorio De Sica**
ph **G.R. Aldo**
m   **Alessandro Cicognini**
    Francesco Golisano, Brunella Bovo, Emmo Gramatica, Paolo Stoppa

Toto (Golisano), a foundling rescued from a cabbage patch, grows into an optimist who loves his fellow men, thanks to the old lady who adopted him. Through force of circumstance, he becomes the youthful leader of a colony of homeless poor in Milan, and fights injustice with the help of a magic dove given to him by the ghost of his long-dead guardian. Following De Sica's starkly realistic *Bicycle Thieves*, this one is best described as a Neo-Realist fairytale. The plot is allegorical, the characters a mix of real and caricature, the exposition pure fable, and the background harsh. It is an imaginative film, very well received in its day, but nearly 40 years on it is a sentimental, whimsical and sometimes tedious hotchpotch, more suited to children than adults.

Best Film Cannes 1951

The Miracle Of Malachias

▶ **Das Wunder Des Malachias**

W. Germany   1961   122 mins   bw
Bernhard Wicki

d   **Bernhard Wicki**
sc **Heinz Pauck, Bernhard Wicki**
ph **Klaus Von Rautenfeld, Gerd Von Bonin**
m   **Hans-Martin Majewski**
    Horst Bollmann, Richard Munch, Christiane Nielsen, Günter Pfitzmann, Karin Moorbach, Kurt Ehrhardt

When a huge gambling casino opens near his monastery, attracting bad elements, Father Malachias prays for its destruction. God obliges with a miracle, but the cure becomes worse than the disease when the press, advertising agencies, big business and the Church begin to profit from the event. A serious, funny and very sharp satire on Germany's post-war 'economic miracle'. (Notice the banker who resembles Adenauer). What makes it more effective is that Wicki, whose *The Bridge* was one of the best German films in the 1950s on World War II, shoots this allegory in a realistic manner. Only its frightening ending, hinting at a nuclear holocaust, unbalances the tale somewhat. The gentle monk, through whose large eyes we see the corruption, is beautifully played by Bollmann.

Best Director Berlin 1961

The Miracle Of The Wolves

▶ **Le Miracle Des Loups**

France   1924   100 mins   bw
La Societé Des Romans Historiques
Filmés

d   **Raymond Bernard**
sc **Henry Dupuy-Mazuel, Jean-José Frappa**
ph **Marc Bujard, Maurice Forster**
m   **Silent (original score Henry Rabaud)**
    **Charles Dullin, Romuald Joube, Vanni-
    Marcoux, Yvonne Sergyl, Gaston Modot,
    Philippe Hériat, Armand Bernard**

Robert Cottereau (Joube), standard bearer to the Duke of Bourgogne (Vanni-Marcoux), is in love with Jeanne Fouquet (Sergyl), goddaughter of King Louis XI (Dullin). During a ball given by Bourgogne for the King, the Duke's favourite, Lord Châteauneuf (Modot), tries to rape Jeanne. It causes a rupture between the King and Bourgogne, and Robert and Jeanne are separated. Châteauneuf tries to undo any attempts at reconciliation between the two parties. When Jeanne, carrying a secret letter from the King to Bourgogne, is pursued by Châteauneuf's men, she is protected by a pack of wolves. At a cost of eight million francs, and shot with 15 cameras simultaneously, this sweeping chronicle was the most expensive French production to date and the first to be shown at the Paris Opéra, with a specially composed score by Henri Rabaud. Yet Bernard proved that finesse and intelligence were not incompatible with pageantry and vast panoramas. As a result of the film's critical and commercial success, the director was hailed 'the French D.W.Griffith'. Based on a novel by Dupuy-Mazuel, also the source for *The Chess*

Player (1927), it is full of rich pictorial invention and outstanding performances, especially from stage luminary Charles Dullin. There was a considerably inferior colour remake in 1961, directed by André Hunebelle.

▶ **Miracolo A Milano** see Miracle In Milan

▶ **Mirch Marsala** see Spices

▶ **Miris Poljs Kog Sveca** see Fragrance Of Wild Flowers, The

▶ **Miroir À Deux Faces, Le** see Mirror Has Two Faces, The

Mirror

▶ **aka A White White Boy . . .**

▶ **Zerkalo**

USSR   1974   106 mins   col/bw
Mosfilm Unit 4

d   **Andrei Tarkovsky**
sc **Andrei Tarkovsky, Aleksandr Misharin**
ph **Georgy Rerberg**
m   **Eduard Artemyev, Pergolesi, Bach,
    Purcell**
    **Margarita Terekhova, L. Tarkovskaya,
    Philip Yankovsky, Ignat Danilisev, Oleg
    Yankovsky, Innokenti Smoktunovsky
    (narrator)**

An artist (heard but not seen) reflects on three generations of his family, and his relationships – as both child and adult – with his mother and father, and those with his wife and small son. This intensely personal and somewhat impenetrable multi-layered film is best approached without searching too hard for specific meaning. It is full of haunting dream-like images, evoking memories and fantasies of Tarkovsky's private and public life in the form of a visual poem. The poems in the film were written and read by his own father, and his mother (Tarkovskaya) plays the old mother on screen. The mother as a young woman and the wife are played by the same actress (Terekhova), with her hair pinned up and let down.

The Mirror Has Two Faces

▶ **Le Miroir À Deux Faces**

France 1958 98 mins bw
Paris/Union

d **André Cayatte**
sc **André Cayatte, Gérard Oury**
ph **Christian Matras**
m **Louiguy**
  **Michèle Morgan, Bourvil, Ivan Desny,
  Elisabeth Manet, Gérard Oury, Sandra
  Milo, Sylvie, Jane Marken**

A sober, unambitious schoolmaster (Bourvil),
living with his mother (Sylvie), marries a very
plain woman (Morgan). After six dreary years
of marriage, the wife is transformed into a
beauty by plastic surgery and her husband's
indifference to her is transformed into jealousy. Credit must be given to make-up man
Charles Parker for doing the opposite of what
the plastic surgeon (Oury) does in the film,
by transforming Michèle Morgan into an ugly
duckling. Unsurprisingly, however, there is
no suspense while her 'new face' is being
revealed. As usual, Cayatte raises some interesting issues, but the script and direction are
only skin deep.

▶ **Mirt Sost Shi Amit** see Harvest: 3000
Years

Les Misérables

France 1934 305 mins bw
Pathé Natan

d **Raymond Bernard**
sc **Raymond Bernard, André Lang**
ph **Jules Kruger**
m **Arthur Honegger**
  **Harry Baur, Charles Vanel, Henry
  Krauss, Charles Dullin, Odette Florel,
  Jean Servais, Josseline Gaël, Orane
  Demazis**

Jean Valjean (Baur), sentenced to 10 years
hard labour for stealing a loaf of bread,
escapes from jail an embittered man. Helped
by a bishop, he regains his sense of compassion and forgiveness, adopting an
orphaned child as his own daughter. Changing his identity, he rises in the world but is
haunted by his Nemesis, Inspector Javert,
who is determined to recapture him. This
version of Victor Hugo's classic benefits from
the best of Valjeans (Fredric March is a close
contender) and an unrivalled Javert (Vanel),
and is probably the most detailed and faithful
adaptation of the original. If Bernard's
respectful direction is a little short of energy,
the film is nevertheless a must for lovers of
the material. It is generally shown in two
parts, titled *Jean Valjean* and *Cosette*, and is
the best of the six French versions of the film;
the most recent one, made in 1982, stars Lino
Ventura.

The Mission

▶ **Ferestadeh**

USA/W. Germany 1983 108
mins col
The New Film Group(Michigan)/Aria
Film Produktion(Munich)

d **Parviz Sayyad**
sc **Parviz Sayyad**
ph **Reza Aria**
  **Houshang Touzie, Parviz Sayyad,
  Mohammed B. Gaffari, Mary Apick,
  Hedyeh Anvar, Hatam Anvar, Kamran
  Nozad**

Douad (Touzie), a religious young Iranian,
arrives in New York on a mission to assassinate an opponent of Ayatollah Khomeini, only
to learn that the man has already been murdered. He is given another target, a former
colonel in the Shah's army, but a series of
accidental happenings push him into a personal relationship with the man and his family, and unmask the corruption of His
Eminence, a Muslim clergyman from whom
Douad is taking his orders. Parviz Sayyad's
previous film was the last made in Iran before
the Revolution and the director, one of his
country's finest, and his New Film Group
were forced into exile in the US, in spite of
having always courted trouble with the Shah's
authorities. *The Mission* is a marvellous piece
of work, well made and beautifully acted,
notably by Sayyad himself as the reluctant
assassin's ebullient quarry. Tense, ironic
and moving, the film understands and exposes the contradictions on both sides of the
conflict.

The Mississippi Mermaid

▶ **La Sirène Du Mississippi**

France 1969 123 mins col
Les Films Du Carrosse

d **François Truffaut**
sc **François Truffaut**
ph **Denys Clerval**
m **Antoine Duhamel**
   **Jean-Paul Belmondo, Catherine Deneuve,
   Michel Bouquet, Nelly Borgeaud, Marcel
   Berbert**

The mail-order bride (Deneuve) of a tobacco
planter (Belmondo) on the island of Réunion
turns out to be a dangerous imposter and a
thief. Taking his plot from a William Irish
mystery novel, Truffaut, while exploring the
possibilities of the thriller genre, has also tried
to make a love story. Unfortunately, though
it looks good on the wide screen, it is far too
allusive and knowing to be either exciting or
moving. There are homages to *Johnny Guitar,
Vertigo,* and the work of Renoir and Cocteau,
while the private eye featured in the plot is
named after the editor of *Cahiers Du Cinéma*
for which Truffaut was once a critic.
Belmondo and Deneuve, both at the height
of their popularity, play the game rather than
their roles.

Miss Julie

▶ **Fröken Julie**

Sweden 1951 87 mins bw
Sandrew

d **Alf Sjöberg**
sc **Alf Sjöberg**
ph **Göran Strindberg**
m **Dag Wirén**
   **Anita Björk, Ulf Palme, Max Von
   Sydow, Märta Dorff, Anders Henrikson**

Miss Julie (Björk), the daughter in a wealthy
19th-century household, chooses the highly
charged atmosphere of the Midsummer Night
revels to humiliate the valet, Jean (Palme),
and to attempt to will him to seduce her.
Although August Strindberg's famous play
about repression, both sexual and class, loses
some of its claustrophobia in this adaptation –
the action has moved from one room to take
in other areas of the mansion and the estate –

it gains by the complex flashback and flash
forward technique in which characters from
the past appear in scenes with those of the
present. Björk gives a remarkable performance as the neurotically defiant Julie.

Best Film Cannes 1951

Miss Oyu

▶ **Oyusama**

Japan 1951 96 mins bw
Daiei

d **Kenji Mizoguchi**
sc **Yoshitaka Yoda**
ph **Kazuo Miyagawa**
m **Fumio Hayasaka**
   **Kinuyo Tanaka, Nobuko Otowa, Yuji
   Hori, Kiyoko Hirai, Reiko Kongo**

In the Meiji period (1867-1912), a wealthy
bachelor (Hori) falls in love with Oyu
(Tanaka), a widow whose young son will lose
his inheritance if she remarries. Oyu's younger
sister (Otowa) agrees to marry him in name
only in order to form a bridge between the
two lovers. But the triangular arrangement
leads to jealousy and tragedy. *Miss Oyu* is
another fine vehicle for Tanaka, made and
played with great delicacy, style and emotion.
The long takes give the characters and
relationships time to breathe and deepen the
audience's experience.

▶ **Mistero Di Oberwald, Il** see Oberwald Mystery, The

▶ **Mistress, The** see Swedish Mistress,
   The

Misunderstood

▶ **Incompreso**

Italy 1966 105 mins col
Rizzoli Film Productions

d **Luigi Comencini**
sc **Leo Benvenuti, Piero Di Bernardi**
ph **Armando Nannuzzi**
   Anthony Quayle, Stefano Colegrande,

Simone Giannozzi, John Sharp, Adriana Facchetti

When the wife of an English consul in Rome dies suddenly, her husband (Quayle) begins to lavish affection on their younger son (Giannozzi), believing the older boy (Colegrande) to be unmoved by his mother's death. His desperate efforts to win his father's love end in tragedy. Based on Florence Montgomery's turn-of-the-century novel, this is a real tearjerker. Comencini, who made his name with a prize-winning short, *Bambini In Citta* (1946), about children in post-war Milan, has often shown his talent for working with youngsters. Here the two boys are extremely well handled, not only in the sentimental scenes but in the early ones, such as their battle with a formidable governess. The adults, including a dubbed Anthony Quayle, are less convincing. The ending, during which all stops are pulled out, works effectively for those willing to forgive its manipulative playing on the emotions.

► **Mitad Del Cielo, La** see Half Of Heaven

► **Mit Liv Som Hund** see My Life As A Dog

Mitsou

France   1957   95 mins   col
Ardennes Films

d   **Jacqueline Audry**
sc   **Pierre Laroche**
ph   **Marcel Grignon**
m   **Georges Van Parys**
     Danièle Delorme, Fernand Gravey, François Guérin, Claude Rich, Odette Laure, Gaby Morlay

In Paris during World War I, Mitsou (Delorme), a chorus girl, is in love with a handsome young lieutenant (Guérin) who throws her over because she lacks refined taste, social finesse and a knowledge of food and wine. Mitsou confesses all to her sugardaddy (a suave and sophisticated Gravey) who generously gives her a crash course in becoming a lady. With its suggestion of *Gigi*, it's easy to tell that the plot came from Colette, but the emaciated screenplay is

devoid of the novelist's piquancy. What we get is a feeble romance that, in spite of some frank moments, remains bland and lifeless. On the credit side, Delorme looks gorgeous, as do the sets and clothes, photographed in pleasing pastels.

► **Mitten Ins Herz** see Straight Through The Heart

► **Mitt Hem Är Copacabana** see My Home Is Copacabana

► **Miyamoto Musashi** see Samurai

Moderato Cantabile

France   1960   95 mins   bw
Raoul J. Levy/Iena Production(Paris)/
Documento Films(Rome)

d   **Peter Brook**
sc   **Marguerite Duras, Gérard Jariot, Peter Brook**
ph   **Armand Thirard**
m   **Antonio Diabelli**
     Jeanne Moreau, Jean-Paul Belmondo, Didier Haudepin, Valerie Dobuzinsky, Pascale De Boysson

The desperately bored and frustrated wife (Moreau) of a wealthy industrialist in the Gironde, who accompanies her son (Haudepin) to his piano lessons, one day hears a woman's scream from a nearby café, then sees her dead body. Obsessed with the murder, she frequents the café, becoming acquainted with a man (Belmondo) who purports to give her the information for which she hungers and to whom she grows increasingly attracted. Adapted from a novella by Duras and directed by international theatre guru Peter Brook with a spare, bleak style, this is very much a mood piece where words are used in place of action. A study of boredom and emotional sterility, in which Moreau expressively captures the despair of the woman and Belmondo the ambiguity of the man. Unfortunately, although the atmosphere and performances cast a certain spell, this is a rather airless and arty film.

Best Actress (Jeanne Moreau) Cannes 1960

A Modern Dubarry

▶ **Eine Dubarry Von Heute**

Germany 1927 110 mins bw
Felsom/UFA

d **Alexander Korda**
sc **Lajos Biro**
ph **Fritz Arno Wagner**
m **Silent**
   Maria Corda, Hans Albers, Alfred Abel,
   Jean Bradin, Julia Serda, Alfred Gerasch,
   Friedrich Kayssler

Toinette (Corda), a young Parisian coquette, is helped by one of her male friends to become a fashion model. She meets and falls in love with a man (Bradin) who, unbeknown to her, is the King of Astoria. Circumstance separates them and she continues to work her way up the ladder of success via a series of influential lovers until she and her king are reunited. A combination of frothy Gallic 'society' picture and Ruritanian romance – it comes complete with a revolution – this is an uneven piece in which the action grows over-complicated and then flags. The director's wife is well-showcased – part of the film's aim and object, as the Kordas were leaving to take up a contract with First National in Hollywood, prior to the producer-director becoming a key figure in the growth of the British film industry. Look out for Marlene Dietrich, passing through as a coquette.

▶ **Modigliani Of Montparnesse** see Montparnasse 19

▶ **Moglie Del Prete, La** see Priest's Wife, The

▶ **Moi Drug Ivan Lapshin** see My Friend Ivan Lapshin

▶ **Moi Universiteti** see My Universities

▶ **Mole, The** see El Topo

Molière

France 1978 188 mins col
Les Films Du Soleil Et De La Nuit/Les Films 13/Antenne 2/RAI

d **Ariane Mnouchkine**
sc **Ariane Mnouchkine**
ph **Bernard Zitzermann**
m **René Clemencic**
   Philippe Caubère, Joséphine Derenne,
   Brigitte Catillon, Claude Merlin, Roger
   Planchon

The life story of the great 17th-century French playwright Molière (Caubère), born Jean-Baptiste Poquelin, from his childhood and schooling, through his years with a troupe of travelling players until he gains the patronage of King Louis XIV, up to his death while playing the title role in *Le Malade Imaginaire*. Mnouchkine, founder-director of the Théâtre Du Soleil, has reconceived her epic stage production for the cinema, framing much of it in the manner of the master painters of the epoch. Some of the exciting theatrical quality of the original is dissipated, but the evocation of the theatre of the day and the unequal society – the contrast between the extreme poverty of the people and the opulence of the court – comes through strongly in this sprawling pageant. However, some of the sequences outstay their welcome, a mistake Molière, played with splendid conviction by Caubère, would not have made. It was initially made as $4\frac{1}{4}$ hours of television, to be shown in episodes, and was later cut for the cinema.

Mollenard

▶ **(US: Hatred)**

France 1937 89 mins bw
Corniglion/Molinier

d **Robert Siodmak**
sc **Charles Spaak**
ph **Eugen Schüfftan**
m **Darius Milhaud**
   Harry Baur, Gabrielle Dorziat, Albert
   Préjean, Dalio, Pierre Renoir, Jacques
   Baumer, Walter Rilla

Dunkirk-based Captain Mollenard (Baur), whose arms-trafficking activities cause the disruption of his ship and family, and earn him the enmity of his cold and spiteful wife (Dorziat), finds his happiness in the brothels of Shanghai. This curious but intriguing drama mixes realistic Dunkirk locations with Alexander Trauner's artificial atmospheric sets of murky ports. The two contrasting halves of the story are dominated by the wonderful Baur, given splendid support from an array of the most talented performers around.

▶ **Moment D'Égarement, Un** see Summer Affair, A

▶ **Momento Della Verità, Il** see Moment Of Truth, The

The Moment Of Truth

▶ **Il Momento Della Verità**

Italy/Spain 1964 110 mins col
Federiz/AS Films (Madrid)

d Francesco Rosi
sc Francesco Rosi
ph Gianni Di Venanzo, Aiace Parolin,
    Pasquale De Santis
m Piero Piccioni
    Miguel Mateo Miguelin, José Gomez
    Sevillano, Linda Christian, Pedro Basauri

A peasant boy (Miguelin) comes from Andalucia to Barcelona to seek his fortune in the bullring. Considered by many to be the greatest of all bullfighting movies, it stars one of Spain's most famous matadors. By the use of a telephoto lens, Rosi was able to show in close-up the unremitting slaughter of the bulls in a sacrificial ceremony to appease a savage god. Between the killings of the bulls, there is a story of sorts in which the young hero falls for Linda Christian playing herself.

▶ **Monachine, Le** see Little Nuns, The

▶ **Monde Du Silence, Le** see Silent World, The

▶ **Monde Sans Pitié, Un** see World Without Pity

Mondo Cane

▶ **aka A Dog's Life**

Italy 1961 105 mins col
Cineriz

d Gualtiero Jacopetti
sc Gualtiero Jacopetti (commentary)

ph Antonio Climati, Benito Frattari
m Nino Oliviero, Riz Ortolani

A documentary made up of approximately 30 episodes in the life of man and beast, filmed all over the world – New Guinea, Germany, Singapore, Portugal, Australia, America, and beyond. Admittedly it is well made, but the sole motive behind it seems to be to show us to ourselves in the worst possible light. Apart from a couple of sequences in which humans are made to look merely ridiculous, most of the material is concerned with cruelty, debasement and revolting carnage. One dignifies it with inclusion here because it was unique at the time (unhappily spawning some successors) and, terrifyingly, a massive box-office hit worldwide. Even the theme music became popular. Called by one critic, 'a hymn to death and mutilation embellished with a shrug and a giggle,' it is not for the sensitive.

The Money Order

▶ **Le Mandat**
▶ **aka Mandabi**

Senegal 1968 90 mins col
Films Domirêve (Dakar)/Comptoir
Français Du Film (Paris)

d Ousmane Sembène
sc Ousmane Sembène
ph Paul Soulignac
m Ousmane Sembène and traditional music
    Makourédia Gueye, Younousse N'diaye,
    Issa Niang, Moustapha Touré, Farba
    Sarr, Serigne Sow

Ibrahima (Gueye), an unemployed man living with his two wives and seven children in a poor suburb of Dakar, receives a letter from his nephew in Paris containing a money order for 250 francs. The news spreads through the neighbourhood and Ibrahima's troubles begin. Although France gave three million francs towards the production, this superb Senegalese satire was the first feature ever made by an all-African crew in a native African language, in this case, Wolof. Already in his second film (after the medium-length *Black Girl* of 1966, set in France), Sembène reveals his favourite theme – the hangover his country is suffering after nearly 400 years of colonial rule – through wry humour and pathos. It works not only as political allegory but as a social comedy, rooted in the African experience.

▶ **Monika** see Summer With Monika

▶ **Mon Oncle** see My Uncle

▶ **Mon Oncle Antoine** see My Uncle Antoine

▶ **Mon Oncle D'Amérique** see My American Uncle

Monsieur Hawarden

Belgium   1968   106 mins   bw
Sofidoc(Brussels)/Parkfilm(Amsterdam)

d   **Harry Kümel**
sc   **Jan Blokker, Harry Kümel**
ph   **Eduard J.R. Van Der Enden**
m   **Pierre Bartholomée**
     Ellen Vogel, Hilde Uitterlinden, Johan Remmelts, Dora Van Der Groen, Xander Fisher

Monsieur Hawarden, accompanied by his beautiful maid Victorine (Uitterlinden), arrives to stay at a remote farmhouse in the Ardennes. The household retainers gossip about the newcomers and develop rivalries over Victorine which end in her death. Hawarden leaves for Spa and resumes 'his' true identity, that of Meriora Gillibrand, daughter of Viennese aristocrats, has a brief affair with an officer, and returns – as Hawarden again – to the French farm... Filmed with a cool, stylish elegance and an eye for period detail, this deliberately slow-paced film unfolds in the manner of a mystery story. Based on a Flemish novel which took its inspiration from a true case, it made an impressive debut for Kümel, who only occasionally lapses into self-conscious or melodramatic effects. Vogel is powerfully convincing in the tragic title role.

Monsieur Hire

France   1989   80 mins   col
Cinéa/Hachette Première Et Cie/FR3 Films/CNC/SNCF

d   **Patrice Leconte**
sc   **Patrice Leconte**
ph   **Denis Lenoir**
m   **Michael Nyman**
     Michel Blanc, Sandrine Bonnaire, Luc Thuillier, André Wilms

Fastidious and reclusive, Monsieur Hire (Blanc) is a tailor by day and a *voyeur* by night. A loner, he is disliked and ridiculed by his neighbours, and when a local girl is found murdered, suspicion is pointed at him and he is hounded by the policeman (Wilms) in charge of the case. Meanwhile, Hire spends his evenings spying on the activities of Alice (Bonnaire), the beautiful girl in the apartment opposite. How he and the girl meet, and what develops as a result, it would be unfair to reveal. Working from a novel by Georges Simenon (previously filmed as *Panique* by Julien Duvivier in 1946), Leconte has manufactured a *policier*-cum-psychological thriller of impressive stylishness. Off-beat choices made in camerawork and editing help to create an atmosphere at once threatening and intriguing, while both the plot and screenplay structure play cat and mouse with the audience's emotions. The splendid Michel Blanc is superbly cast and the beautiful Bonnaire is a perfect foil. Tension, uncertainty and a measure of bizarre eroticism further grip one's attention, but in spite of these plaudits, the film does not withstand too close an examination of its supposed depths and insights.

Monsieur Hulot's Holiday

▶ **Les Vacances De Monsieur Hulot**

France   1953   91 mins   bw
Cady/Discina

d   **Jacques Tati**
sc   **Jacques Tati, Henri Marquet**
ph   **Jacques Mercanton, Jean Mouselle**
m   **Alain Romans**
     Jacques Tati, Nathalie Pascaud, Michèle Rolla, Valentine Camax

Monsieur Hulot (Tati), an amiable bachelor, spends his summer holidays at a small Breton seaside resort where he inadvertently triggers off a series of mishaps. Inspired by a sergeant he had known in the army and a clumsy architect called Hulot, Tati introduced his endearing, maladroit character in the first of four comic gems. Hulot, invariably wearing a hat, overcoat and rather too short trousers, smoking a pipe and walking as if against a strong wind, is not only an instigator of incidents but an observer of the idiosyncracies of the French middle class at the seaside. There is very little dialogue, the gentle humour residing in the body language and the eloquently organized sound track.

Monsieur Vincent

France   1947   113 mins   bw
EDIC/UGC

d   **Maurice Cloche**
sc **Jean Anouilh, Jean-Bernard Luc**
ph **Claude Renoir**
m   **Jean-Jacques Grünewald**
    Pierre Fresnay, Aimé Clairiond, Jean
    Dubucourt, Lise Delamare, Gabrielle
    Dorziat, Michel Bouquet

The life and work of the 17th-century Saint Vincent De Paul (Fresnay), who was in conflict with the rich and powerful because of his pioneer work among the poor. Although the film had some financial backing from the Catholic Church, this inspiring depiction of saintliness contains only a modicum of sermonizing. The beauty of the photography does not exclude the starkness of the poverty or the brutality of the age. Fresnay, growing from a young man to old age, carries even atheists along with him.

Best Foreign Film Oscar 1948
Best Actor (Pierre Fresnay) Venice 1947

Montparnasse 19

▶ **aka The Lovers Of Montparnasse**

▶ **(US: Modigliani Of Montparnesse)**

France   1958   110 mins   bw
Franco London Films/Astra

d   **Jacques Becker**
sc **Jacques Becker, Max Ophüls, Henri Jeanson**
ph **Christian Matras**
m   **Georges Van Parys, Paul Misraki, Bach**

Gérard Philipe, Lilli Palmer, Anouk Aimée, Gérard Séty, Lino Ventura, Lila Kedrova, Lea Padovani

The tubercular and alcoholic painter Modigliani (Philipe) leads a wild and dissolute life in Paris with his mistress (Palmer). He falls in love with Jeanne (Aimée), who follows him to the South of France. She becomes his mistress and his model and commits suicide before his untimely death. The twelfth of Becker's 13 films provides a vivid glimpse of the milieu and period of Modigliani's life but does not rank with the director's best work. The performance of his stellar lead was lacklustre, but the women were excellent and the action reasonably convincing. It was a troubled project: Ophüls, who was meant to direct the film, died, Becker quarrelled with co-writer Jeanson, and the artist's daughter was on the set to add to Becker's problems. Nonetheless, it is quite entertaining and occasionally moving.

The Moon In The Gutter

▶ **La Lune Dans Le Caniveau**

France   1983   130 mins   col
Gaumont/TF1 Productions/SFPC (Paris)/Opera Film Produzione (Rome)

d   **Jean-Jacques Beineix**
sc **Jean-Jacques Beineix**
ph **Philippe Rousselot**
m   **Gabriel Yared**
    Gérard Depardieu, Nastassja Kinski, Victoria Abril, Bertice Reading, Vittorio Mezzogiorno, Dominique Piñon

In his search for the rapist of his sister, who has since killed herself in despair, a stevedore (Depardieu) becomes involved with a wealthy girl (Kinski) whose alcoholic brother (Mezzogiorno) he suspects of the crime. Depardieu himself suggested Jean-Jacques (*Diva*) Beineix's second feature be called 'Film In The Gutter'. Based on a 1953 American crime novel by David Goodis, it was shot at Cinecitta among elaborate sets which give it an airless, stagey atmosphere steeped in the aesthetics of pop record sleeves. The film works as neither fantasy nor reality, and was rightly rounded on by the critics. However, it is the sort of bad arty movie that could easily become a cult in a few years.

▶ **Mörder Sind Unter Uns, Die** see
Murderers Are Among Us, The

▶ **Mord Und Totschlag** see Degree Of
Murder, A

▶ **More Than A Miracle** see Cinderella – Italian Style

Morning

▶ **Jutro**

Yugoslavia 1967 104 mins bw
Dunav Film

d **Purisa Djordjević**
sc **Purisa Djordjević**
ph **Mika Popović**
m **Miodrag Ilić-Beli**
  **Milena Dravić, Ljubisa Samardzić, Mija
  Aleksić, Neda Arnerić, Ljuba Tadić, Olga
  Jancevecka**

Events in the Serbian town of Cacak during
the last day of war and the first of peace,
involving the reactions of a diverse collection
of characters including victorious Partisans,
captured Germans, a Red Army officer, collaborators and, of course, the townspeople.
Djordjević, who himself left school at 17 to
join the Partisans, claims that there was both
more brutality and more tenderness during
1945 than he has succeeded in showing. Nonetheless, it is an affecting piece, the third and
most acclaimed of a quartet of films the
director has made on the war years and their
aftermath in Yugoslavia.

**Best Actress (Ljubisa Samardzić) Venice
1967**

▶ **Mort De Mario Ricci, La** see Death
Of Mario Ricci, The

▶ **Morte A Venezia** see Death In Venice

▶ **Morte Di Un Amico** see Death Of A
Friend

▶ **Mort en Ce Jardin, La** see Evil Eden

▶ **Morte Risale A Ieri Sera, La** see
Death Occurred Last Night

▶ **Morte-Saison Des Amours, La** see
Season For Love, The

Moscow Distrusts Tears

▶ **(US: Moscow Does Not Believe
In Tears)**

▶ **Moskava Slezam Ne Verit**

USSR 1979 148 mins col
Mosfilm

d **Vladimir Menshov**
sc **Valentin Chernykh**
ph **Igor Slabnevich**
m **Sergei Nikitin**
  **Vera Alentova, Alexei Batalov, Irina
  Muraveva, Alexander Fatiushin, Raisa
  Ryazanova, Boris Smorchkov**

Three young Russian girls share a room in a
Moscow workers' dormitory during 1958,
pursuing their careers and their love affairs.
Tonya (Ryazanova) achieves a happy and
settled marriage, Ludmila (Muraveva) an
unhappy marriage, and Katerina (Alentova),
the central protagonist, is abandoned with an
illegitimate child. Twenty years later –
denoted on screen by the ticking of a clock –
we meet them again. This is a competent,
well-acted diversion of a kind that would be
termed 'a woman's picture' in the West. The
film is chiefly interesting for being a good old
Hollywood romantic comedy-drama, with all
its familiar clichés and conventions transported to an unfamiliar – and unexpected –
setting.

Best Foreign Film Oscar 1980

▶ **Moscow Does Not Believe In
Tears** see Moscow Distrusts Tears

Moses And Aaron

▶ **Moses Und Aron**

Austria 1975 col
Janus Films/Austrian TV/ARD

d **Jean-Marie Straub**
sc **Jean-Marie Straub, Danièle Huillet (Text
  Arnold Schönberg)**
ph **Ugo Piccone**

m **Arnold Schönberg (Conductor Michael Gielen)**
   Guenther Reich, Louis Devos, Eva Csapo, Roger Lucas, Richard Salter, Werner Mann

Moses (Reich), through his brother Aaron (Devos), tries to communicate God's message to his people. In the wilderness, while waiting for Moses to return from Sinai, the people make a Golden Calf. Moses returns and smashes the tablets bearing the Command-ments. By shooting the opera in a Roman amphitheatre (in Italy) and using direct sound, Straub avoided the awkward tech-nique of dubbing. The singers could hear the orchestra through earphones, conveniently hidden under their head-dresses, and see the conductor on closed circuit TV screens. The result is a remarkably faithful and musically exciting rendering of Schönberg's religious and philosophical opera. He allows the work to unravel and flow, with few cuts per sequence, keeping the camera either fixed or continuouslyrevolving. Only the Act II orgy is unconvincing, represented as it is by one nude couple. The spoken Act III, for which Schönberg never got to write music, is staged in one long take.

▶ **Moses Und Aron** see Moses And Aaron

▶ **Moskava Slezam Ne Verit** see Mos-cow Distrusts Tears

Mother

▶ **Mat**

USSR 1926 90 mins bw
Mezhrabpom-Russ

d **Vsevolod Pudovkin**
sc **Nathan Zarkhi, Vsevolod Pudovkin**
ph **Anatoli Golovnya**
m **Silent**
   Vera Baranovskaya, A.P. Khristiakov, Nikolai Batalov, Ivan Koval-Samborski, Anna Zemtsova, Vsevolod Pudovkin

At the time of the abortive revolution of 1905, Pavel (Batalov), the son of a drunken father (Khristiakov) and an overworked mother (Baranovskaya), leads an illegal strike. The mother inadvertently gives her son away to the police, but gradually turns to Communism through her experience of injustice and suffer-ing. Pudovkin's first feature turns Maxim Gorky's rambling novel into a tightly con-structed narrative. The film's emotional and visual impact has not diminished with time, nor has Baranovskaya's performance. The remarkable montage – water is a constant visual metaphor, as in the scene of blocks of ice flowing rapidly in the river as the May Day demonstrators run through the streets – is never allowed to usurp the human factor. Mark Donskoi remade it in 1956, and Brecht's version for the Berliner Ensemble was filmed two years later.

The Mother And The Whore

▶ **La Maman Et La Putain**

France 1973 215 mins bw
Films Du Losange/Elites Films/Ciné Qua Non/Simar/V.M.

d **Jean Eustache**
sc **Jean Eustache**
ph **Pierre Lhomme, Jacques Renard, Michel Cenet**
m **Mozart, Offenbach**
   Jean-Pierre Léaud, Bernadette Lafont, Françoise Lebrun, Isabelle Weingarten, Jacques Renard

Alexandre (Léaud), who lives with the slightly older Marie (Lafont), picks up Veronika (Leb-run), a sexually liberated nurse. They set up a *ménage-a-trois*, until tensions within it force them to discuss options. Funny, irritating, obsessive, verbose, witty, provocative and erotic, this long film consists mainly of con-versations, stories, confessions and mono-logues delivered by the three brilliant players. It is the summation of the French New Wave. Eustache shot the film economically in his own apartment and in local bistros. The film's success led on to his last film, the bigger budgeted *Mes Petites Amoureuses*. He com-mitted suicide in 1981 aged 43.

Special Jury Prize Cannes 1973

▶ **Mother Joan Of The Angels** see Devil And The Nun, The

Mother Kuster Goes To Heaven

▶ **Mutter Küsters Fahrt Zum Himmel**

W. Germany 1975 120 mins col
Tango Film

d **Rainer Werner Fassbinder**
sc **Rainer Werner Fassbinder**
ph **Michael Ballhaus**
m **Peer Raben**
   Brigitte Mira, Margit Carstensen, Karl-Heinz Böhm, Ingrid Caven, Armin Meier

When Frau Kuster (Mira) learns that her husband has killed one of his bosses and committed suicide in protest against dismissals at his factory, she becomes politicized, and finally joins a Left-wing urban guerrilla movement. Like *Fear Eats The Soul*, also starring the remarkable Brigitte Mira, this bitterly ironic film (the woman is exploited by Left and Right) depicts a lonely, aging woman liberating herself. One of Fassbinder's most cohesive narratives, it continues and improves upon the theme of the pressures of industrial society on the individual as expounded in *Why Does Herr R Run Amok?*. Originally the film, made in 20 days, ended with Mother Kuster's being killed, but the director re-shot it so that she survives.

Mouchette

France 1967 90 mins bw
Parc/Argos

d **Robert Bresson**
sc **Robert Bresson**
ph **Ghislain Cloquet**
m **Monteverdi, Jean Wiener**
   Nadine Nortier, Jean-Claude Guilbert, Marie Cardinal, Paul Hébert, Jean Vimenet

Mouchette (Nortier), a 14-year-old village schoolgirl, the loveless, abused and humiliated daughter of an alcoholic father and a dying mother, drowns herself. Bresson returned to the work of Georges Bernanos, the author of *Diary Of A Country Priest* (1951). He changed the locale from the north to Provence for the sake of better weather for shooting, but there is little warmth in the film itself – a relentlessly oppressive detailing of a wasted young life. There is something almost sadistic in the way the girl is used, in the same manner as the donkey in his previous film *Balthazar*. Monteverdi's *Magnificat* adds the layer of spirituality that is supposed to be inherent in Bresson's economic method.

▶ **Moul Le Ya, Moul Le Ya** see Wheel, The

The Mountain Cat

▶ **(US: The Wildcat)**
▶ **Die Bergkatze**

Germany 1921 80 mins bw
Union/UFA

d **Ernst Lubitsch**
sc **Hans Kräly, Ernst Lubitsch**
ph **Théodor Sparkühl**
m **Silent**
   Pola Negri, Viktor Janson, Paul Heidemann, Wilhelm Diegelmann, Hermann Thimig

Rischka (Negri), the strong-willed and outspoken daughter of the chief of a comical band of mountain brigands, is attracted to Lieutenant Alexis (Heidemann) and demonstrates her affection by stealing his clothes and pelting him with snowballs. Rischka's father, however, wants her to marry a member of his gang... In this delightfully stylized and offbeat comedy, Lubitsch succeeded in satirizing the military while creating a bizarre imaginary world for which he drew on surrealism, expressionism and everything in between. The extraordinary sets are by stage designer Ernst Stern, but it is Negri, the cat of the title, who steals the show, giving one of her liveliest comedy performances in the days before she became a big star of costume pictures, none of which could hold a candle to this little gem.

▶ **Mourir À Madrid** see To Die In Madrid

▶ **Mourir À Tue-Tête** see Primal Fear

▶ **Mouton À Cinq Pattes, Le** see Sheep Has Five Legs, The

▶ **Mrigaya** see Royal Hunt, The

Mr Klein

France   1976   123 mins   col
Lira Films/Adel Productions/Nova Films (Paris)/Mondial Te-Fi (Rome)

d   **Joseph Losey**
sc   **Franco Solinas**
ph   **Gerry Fisher**
m   **Egisto Macchi, Pierre Porte**
     Alain Delon, Jeanne Moreau, Suzanne Flon, Michel Lonsdale, Juliet Berto, Louis Seigner, Francine Racette, Massimo Girotti

In 1942, Robert Klein, a womanizing antique dealer, remains untouched by the German occupation of Paris and indifferent to the fate of Jews under Nazi rule – until he is confused with another Robert Klein, a wanted man and a Jew. As he gets caught ever more tightly in the web of mistaken identity, Klein grows obsessed with finding his *doppelgänger*, and eventually assumes his identity. Co-produced by Alain Delon, excellent in the title role, this film is a blend of Kafkaesque nightmare and glossy thriller. Made with Losey's customary detachment, expertise and feel for atmosphere, it is a complex and absorbing examination of identity crisis, moral ambivalence, and the implications of French reaction to Hitler's invasion.

Muddy River

▶ **Doro No Kawa**

Japan   1981   105 mins   bw
Kimura Productions

d   **Kohei Oguri**
sc   **Takako Shigemori**
ph   **Shohei Ando**
m   **Kurato Mori**
     Nobutaka Asahara, Takahiro Tamura, Yumiko Fujita, Minoru Sakurai, Mariko Kaga, Makiko Shibata

Nine-year-old Nobuo (Asahara) makes friends with Kiichi (Sakurai), a boy of his own age who lives on a barge with his sister (Shibata) and their widowed mother (Kaga).

When Nobuo's parents (Tamura and Fujita) learn that the widow is a prostitute, they warn him not to visit the barge at night. The theme of friendship between children has been extensively covered in the Japanese cinema over the years, including works by Ozu and Shimizu, so this extremely promising first feature suffered somewhat from comparisons. The main flaws occur in the latter sequences, when Nobuo witnesses the sexual activities of his friend's mother. Nevertheless, most of the film minutely builds up a loving picture of children and their relationship with adults (all excellently played) against a well-observed background of riverside life in Osaka in 1956. The film received an Oscar nomination.

▶ **Müde Tod, Der** see Destiny

▶ **Muerte De Un Burocrata, La** see Death Of A Bureaucrat

▶ **Muerte De Un Ciclista** see Death Of A Cyclist

▶ **Muerte En Esta Jardin, La** see Evil Eden

▶ **Mujeres Al Borde De Un Ataque De Nervios** see Women On The Verge Of A Nervous Breakdown

▶ **Mulino Del Po, Il** see Mill On The Po, The

▶ **Mumia, El** see Night Of Counting The Years, The

▶ **Münchhausen** see Adventures Of Baron Münchhausen, The

▶ **Mur, Le** see Wall, The

▶ **Mura Di Malapaga, Le** see Walls Of Malapaga, The

▶ **Muralla Verde, La** see Green Wall, The

Murder À La Carte

▶ **(US: Deadlier Than The Male)**

▶ **Voici Les Temps Des Assassins**

France   1955   113 mins   bw

C.I.C.C./Agiman

d Julien Duvivier
sc Julien Duvivier, Maurice Bessy, Charles Dorat
ph Armand Thirard
m Jean Wiener
   Jean Gabin, Danièle Delorme, Gérard Blain, Germaine Kerjean, Lucienne Bogaërt, Robert Manuel, Gabrielle Fontan

Chatelin (Gabin),a good-hearted and elderly Paris restaurateur, is visited by a girl (Delorme) who claims to be the daughter of his ex-wife (Bogaërt). She tells him that her mother has died, leaving her alone and helpless, and he takes her in, in spite of the misgivings of his possessive mother (Kerjean). As time goes by, it turns out that her mother is alive, albeit half-crazed by drugs, and that she herself is a ruthless gold-digger. This film firmly belongs to the period of Duvivier's decline. The whole farrago is implausible and rather squalid, but nonetheless fairly compulsive thanks to the uninhibited and skilful performances of the women who surround an uncharacteristically docile Gabin – a quartet of vipers, completed by Chatelin's vindictive housekeeper (Fontan).

Murder Czech Style

► Vrazda Po Cesky

   Czechoslovakia 1966 87 mins bw (part col)
   Ceskoslovensky Film

d Jiří Weiss
sc Jan Otcenašek, Jiří Weiss
ph Jan Nemeček
m Zdeněk Liška
   Rudolf Hrušínsky, Kveta Fialová, Vaclav Voska, Vladimír Menšík, Vera Uzelacova, Libuse Svormová

František (Hrušínsky), a dull, overweight, middle-aged clerk in a provincial city, leads a boring and loveless existence until he meets Alice (Fialová), a beautiful colleague from Prague and, surprisingly, marries her. At her behest, the marriage is not consummated for some time and he discovers that she has a married lover in Prague. František plans several increasingly unlikely methods of revenge... Jiří Weiss's last Czech-made film before he moved to the West is an awful disappointment, particularly as it begins so promisingly. Hrušínsky's nondescript inadequate is beautifully played, and the details of his daily life are expertly observed by director and cameraman. However, halfway through, the story degenerates into a silly and pointless fantasy.

The Murderer Lives At No. 21

► L'Assassin Habite Au 21

   France 1942 90 mins bw
   Continental

d Henri-Georges Clouzot
sc Henri-Georges Clouzot
ph Armand Thirard
m Maurice Yvain
   Pierre Fresnay, Suzy Delair, Noël Roquevert, Pierre Larquey, Jean Tissier

A murder takes place in a boarding house full of eccentrics, each one a likely suspect. Clouzot, whose films are generally dark in character, made his feature debut with this delightful comedy-thriller of the *Thin Man* type. Fresnay is witty as the detective, but Delair as his bubble-headed assistant is irritating enough to drive anyone to murder.

► Murderers Among Us see Murderers Are Among Us, The

The Murderers Are Among Us

► (US: Murderers Among Us)
► Die Mörder Sind Unter Uns

   W. Germany 1946 87 mins bw
   Defa

d Wolfgang Staudte
sc Wolfgang Staudte
ph Friedl Behn-Grund, Eugen Klagemann
m Ernst Roters
   Hildegard Knef, Ernst Borchert, Arno Paulsen, Erna Sellmer, Robert Forsch

In the ruins of immediate post-war Germany,

a doctor (Borchert) who has witnessed the atrocities in a death camp is tormented by guilt. His former captain (Paulsen), by contrast, lives a contented family life, untroubled by the mass executions he carried out. Encouraged by his girlfriend (Knef), the doctor denounces the captain to the war crime investigators. Although a heavy-handed, plodding piece of bleak introspection, this film raises questions that compel attention, and is also interesting as one of the first productions to come out of Germany itself which faced the question of responsibility for the crimes of the Nazi era.

► **Murder Of Dmitri Karamazov, The** see Brothers Karamazov, The

Muriel

► **Muriel, Ou Le Temps D'Un Retour**

France 1963 116 mins col
Argos/Alpha/Eclair/Les Films De La Pléiade/Dear Films

d **Alain Resnais**
sc **Jean Cayrol**
ph **Sacha Vierny**
m **Hans Werner Henze**
   Delphine Seyrig, Jean-Pierre Kérien, Nita Klein, Jean-Baptiste Thierrée, Laurence Badie, Martine Vatel

A middle-aged woman (Seyrig) invites her lover (Kérien) of 20 years earlier and his niece (Klein) to stay with her and her stepson (Thierrée) in Boulogne. The latter, just returned from military service in Algeria, is haunted by the memory of a girl called Muriel, just as the ex-lovers are haunted by their past. Seemingly more realistic on the surface than Renais' previous film, *Last Year At Marienbad*, it is almost as stylized and metaphysical. The rhythmic dialogue and overlapping sounds, the ethereal Henze music, Boulogne shot in visionary colour, and the fragmented narrative technique give a resonance to the actions of a group of characters placed in mundane situations and surroundings but tortured by their memories. Arguably

Resnais' last great film until *Providence* 14 years later.

Best Actress (Delphine Seyrig) Venice 1963

► **Muriel, Ou Le Temps D'Un Retour** see Muriel

► **Murmur Of The Heart** see Dearest Love

► **Music In The Dark** see Night Is My Future

The Music Room

► **Jalsaghar**

India 1958 100 mins bw
Satyajit Ray

d **Satyajit Ray**
sc **Satyajit Ray**
ph **Subrata Mitra**
m **Satyajit Ray**
   Chabi Biswas, Padma Devi, Tulsi Lahin, Pinaki Sen Gupta, Kali Sarkar

An aristocratic provincial landowner (Biswas), forced to sell his crumbling mansion because of his extravagances, decides to spend the remains of his dwindling fortune on a last concert of classical Indian music. As a composer himself, music has always played an important role in Ray's films but never more so than in this exquisite early chamber work. The performance of Biswas as the declining reclining nobleman is as formalized as the elegiac concert finale, interrupted by a sudden storm.

The Music Teacher

► **Le Maître De Musique**

Belgium 1988 100 mins col
RTBF/K2 One

d **Gérard Corbiau**
sc **Gérard Corbiau, Andrée Corbiau, Patrick Iratni, Jacqueline Pierreux, Christian Watton**

ph **Walther Vanden Ende**
m **Mahler, Verdi, Bellini, Mozart,
Offenbach, Puccini, Schubert, Schumann
José Van Dam, Anne Roussel, Philippe
Volter, Sylvie Fennec, Patrick Bauchau,
Johan Leysen, Max Schreiber**

In the early years of the century operatic
baritone Joachim Dallayrac (Van Dam)
retires to his country home, accepting two
pupils, Sophie (Roussel), a beautiful and
admiring 18-year-old, and Jean (Volter), a
young singing pickpocket, for intensive training. Sophie and Jean fall in love and both
enter a singing contest run by the bisexual
Prince Scotti (Bauchau), who is attracted by
the young couple. Jean and Arcas (Schreiber),
Scotti's protégé, compete against each other
as Dallayrac lies dying. Kitsch and camp as
they come, this faintly ridiculous enterprise is
aimed at those whose taste in opera comes in
small tasty morsels and who believe that the
glamour behind the footlights extends far
beyond the opera house. However, even for
serious music-lovers, except those without a
sweet tooth, there are enough rich orchestral
sounds (from Le Nouvel Orchestre Sym-
phonique de la RTBF) and fine (dubbed)
voices (Dinah Bryant, Jérôme Pruett) singing
marvellous songs and arias (including a rarity
from Bellini's *Bianca And Fernando*), and the
forceful voice and presence of renowned
Belgian baritone José Van Dam. There is also
plenty for the eye, as the camera dwells on
lovely landscapes and exquisite décor, even if
much of it is reminiscent of chocolate commercials.

▶ **Musik I Mörker** see Night Is My
Future

▶ **Mustaa Valkoisella** see Black On
White

▶ **Mutter Küsters Fahrt Zum Himmel** see Mother Kuster Goes To Heaven

My American Uncle

▶ **Mon Oncle D'Amérique**

France 1980 126 mins col
Andrea Films/TF1

d **Alain Resnais**
sc **Jean Gruault**
ph **Sacha Vierny**
m **Arié Dzierlatka
Gérard Depardieu, Nicole Garcia, Roger
Pierre, Henri Laborit**

The lives of the manager of a small manufac-
turing plant (Depardieu), a committed actress
(Garcia), and a TV executive (Pierre) are
analysed in terms of the animal behaviourist
theories of Dr Henri Laborit. From the peak
of *Providence*, Resnais plunged into the
numbing banality of this semi-satire on modern French life which comes to the hardly
original conclusion that we are only what
society makes us. This is reached through the
stories of three unappealing characters compared mostly with laboratory rats by what
seems a parody professor who happens to be
playing himself. It is all put together with
Resnais' usual brilliant cutting technique.

Special Jury Prize Cannes 1980

My Apprenticeship

▶ **aka Out In The World**
▶ **(US: Among People)**
▶ **Vlyudyakh**

USSR 1939 98 mins bw
Soyezdetfilm

d **Mark Donskoi**
sc **Mark Donskoi, Ilya Grouzdez**
ph **Piotr Ermolov**
m **Lev Schwartz
Alexei Lyarsky, Varvara Massalitinova,
Mikhail Troianovski, V. Novikov**

The teenage Maxim Gorky (Lyarsky) gets
work on a ferry on the river Volga, becomes
a servant in a large household and an apprentice to ikon painters. He also begins to read
of and to observe the hardships of the society
around him. As in the first of Donskoi's
trilogy, *The Childhood Of Maxim Gorky*, there
is a rich gallery of characters, particularly
Massalitinova's wonderful old grandmother,
and a vivid depiction of the bustling riverside
life. It culminates with the heart-rending and
uplifting scene when the young man leaves
his grandparents for the first time. His adven-

tures are followed in *My Universities*, the following year.

My Best Friend's Girl

▶ **La Femme De Mon Pote**

France 1983 100 mins col
Renn Productions/Sara Films

d **Bertrand Blier**
sc **Bertrand Blier, Gérard Brach**
ph **Jean Penzer**
m **J. J. Cale, Mozart Serenade No 5, and 11 pop songs**
   Coluche, Isabelle Huppert, Thierry Lhermitte, Farid Chopel, François Perrot

While on holiday in the ski resort of Courchevel, Pascal (Lhermitte) acquires a new flame, Viviane (Huppert), whom he leaves in the care of his best friend Micky (Coluche). When Viviane throws herself at Micky, who can't resist her, the friendship of the boys is threatened. Blier's film is expertly played, naturistically directed, has much charm and attractive locations. However, the director seems unsure whether he is making a boulevard comedy or taking a profound look at the motivations and morality of his characters. The result is a superficial entertainment, larded with vague pretensions to something more. Interesting footnote: Popular comedian Coluche stood for the French presidency, and was killed in an accident.

My Friend Ivan Lapshin

▶ **Moi Drug Ivan Lapshin**

USSR 1986 99 mins bw (part col)
Lenfilm

d **Alexei Gherman**
sc **Eduard Volodarsky**
ph **Valery Fedosov**
m **Arkady Gagulashvili**
   Andrei Boltnev, Nina Ruslanova, Andrei Mironov, Alexei Zharkov, Yu. Kuznetsov

Ivan Lapshin (Boltnev), a police chief in a provincial Russian town, shares an apartment with his self-important immediate subordinate (Zharkov), and with a man who has a nine-year-old son. Lapshin's main activity in the cold winter of 1935 is to track down a notorious gang of criminals, but he finds time to make a clumsy attempt at romance with an actress (Ruslanova) and to take care of his best friend (Mironov) whose wife has died. The film opens in the present (in colour) and reverts to the past (black and white) via an unseen narrator who, it would seem, was the little boy living with Lapshin. Gherman based his third feature on stories written by his father Yuri, a well-known literary figure. It is a densely packed and richly detailed tapestry of life and conditions in the period just prior to the Stalin purges, made with perception and a naturalistic style, and offering performances as good as one could wish for.

My Girlfriend's Boyfriend

▶ **L'Ami De Mon Amie**

France 1987 102 mins col
Les Films Du Losange

d **Eric Rohmer**
sc **Eric Rohmer**
ph **Bernard Lutic**
m **Jean-Louis Valero**
   Emmanuelle Chaulet, Sophie Renoir, Eric Viellard, François-Eric Gendron, Anne-Laure Meury

In a new town outside Paris, Blanche (Chaulet) becomes friends with Lea (Renoir). They meet Alexandre (Gendron), an engineer, to whom Blanche is attracted. While Lea is on holiday, Blanche gets to know Lea's boyfriend Fabien (Viellard). Lea and Alexandre get together, and Blanche and Fabien... Like the preceding five of Rohmer's 'Comedies and Proverbs', the film involves rather trivial, egoistic young people, concerned only with their love lives. But Rohmer has proved (perhaps a little too often) that it is possible to make an interesting film about uninteresting people. His model for his pastel comedies of manners is the 18th-century playwright Marivaux. The main pleasure comes from watching modern youth indulging in the amorous games people have always played. Rohmer, as hedonistic as ever, provides his characters with good food, wine and sunshine, the camera lapping up the artificial lake, the woods and the futuristic buildings of Cergy-Pointoise.

My Home Is Copacabana

▶ **Mitt Hem Är Copacabana**

Sweden 1965 88 mins bw
Svensk Filmindustri

d **Arne Sucksdorff**
sc **Arne Sucksdorff, Flavio Migliaccio, Joâo Bethecourt**
ph **Arne Sucksdorff**
m **Radamés Gnatalli, Luciano Perrone, Luis Antonio
Leila Santos De Sousa, Cosme Dos Santos, Antonio Carlos De Lima, Josafa Da Silva Santos**

Four child outcasts from the underbelly of Rio make a home for themselves in a clifftop shelter and eke out an existence by begging, pilfering and executing a number of ingenious con-tricks. Documentary-maker Sucksdorff is a superior visual artist with a gift for judging the effect of a moment. However, in this feature he has constructed a semi-fictionalized tale in which the young protagonists are all angelic to look at and both calm and worldly-wise in accepting their lot. This is salutary, but somewhat hard to swallow. In short, the film is a half revealing, half romanticized view of grinding poverty and underprivilege, which raises questions, stretches credibility and is yet affecting.

My Life As A Dog

▶ **Mit Liv Som Hund**

Sweden 1985 100 mins col
AB Filmteknik/Svensk Filmindustri

d **Lasse Hallström**
sc **Lasse Hallström, Reidar Jönsson, Brasse Brännstrom, Pelle Berglund**
ph **Jörgen Persson, Rolf Lindström**
m **Björn Isfält
Anton Glanzelius, Manfred Serner, Anki Liden, Tomas Von Brömssen, Melinda Kinnamen**

Twelve-year-old Ingemar lives with his dog, elder brother and sick mother until he is sent away to stay with relatives in a small country village where he leads an eventful life. The depiction of a village that seems populated entirely by eccentrics, a boy's love for his dog from whom he is parted, and the death of his beloved mother may signal cuteness and senti-mentality, but Hallström's enchanting film of childhood, set in the 1950s, nimbly avoids such traps. That it is so amusing and moving can be put down to the unaffected playing of Glanzelius as the young hero, and to the magical camerawork.

▶ **My Life To Live** see It's My Life

My Love Has Been Burning

▶ **(US: Flame Of My Love)**

▶ **Waga Koi Wa Moenu**

Japan 1949 84 mins bw
Shochiku

d **Kenji Mizoguchi**
sc **Yoshitaka Yoda, Kaneto Shindo**
ph **Kohei Sugiyama**
m **Senji Ito
Kinuyo Tanaka, Mitsuko Mito, Kuniko Miyabe, Ichiro Sugai, Koreya Senda**

Eiko (Tanaka), a feminist in a Japanese province in 1884, has her school closed because of her politics and is distraught when Chiyo (Mito), a servant girl, is sold into slavery. She goes to Tokyo, where she becomes a Liberal Party activist and is imprisoned. On her release, heavily disillusioned by her experiences, she decides to go home and open another school, this time for the purpose of educating women to understand their role in society. Released in the West some three decades after it was made, this film reflects Mizoguchi's ongoing concern with the nature and position of women, and points to the flowering of his best work in the 1950s. Made quickly and cheaply, it is highly critical of society and politics in Japan, and sometimes brutal in its imagery. It was ill-received in his own country, where one critic accused it of being made 'by a wild animal' but, apart from tending to treat the characters as mouthpieces for ideas rather than as flesh and blood beings, it is an absorbing piece.

▶ **My Night At Maud's** see My Night With Maud

My Night With Maud

▶ **(US: My Night At Maud's)**

▶ **Ma Nuit Chez Maud**

France   1968   110 mins   bw
Films Du Losange/Films Du Carrosse/
Les Films De La Pléiade

d   **Eric Rohmer**
sc **Eric Rohmer**
ph **Nestor Almendros, Emmanuel Machuel**
m   **Classical selections**
    François Fabian, Jean-Louis Trintignant,
    Marie-Christine Barrault, Antoine Vitez

An engineer and devout Catholic (Trintignant), determined to marry the blonde girl
(Barrault) he has noticed in church, spends a
chaste night with the beautiful, dark, free-
thinking Maud (Fabian), although they are
mutually attracted. The film that made
Rohmer's international name, set in a snowy
Clermont Ferrand, proved that long intellectual discussions could be as cinematic as more
obviously visual material. As Rohmer has
stated, 'The people in my films are not
expressing abstract ideas . . . but revealing
what they think about relationships between
men and women, about friendship, love,
desire . . .'. Witty, erotic, profound and
deliciously performed, this fourth released of
his Six Moral Tales, was Oscar-nominated.

My Sister, My Love

▶ **Syskonbädd 1782**

Sweden   1966   96 mins   bw
Sandrew

d   **Vilgot Sjöman**
sc **Vilgot Sjöman**
ph **Lars Björne**
    Bibi Andersson, Per Oscarsson, Jarl
    Kulle, Gunnar Björnstrand, Tina
    Hedstrom, Berta Hall

When Jacob (Oscarsson) returns home after
several years' absence to learn that his sister
Charlotte (Andersson) is about to marry, he
is beset by jealousy. Brother and sister realize
they are in love and, by the time of her
wedding night – which he spends in a brothel –
she is carrying his child. The story climaxes
in both violence and regeneration. Although

played with dignity and restraint by the two
leads, and filmed with a Bergmanesque eye
for bleak and dramatic landscape, Sjöman's
study of incest suffers from a lack of cohesive
style or structure, is heavy-handed, and overloaded with neurotic incident. Like all of this
director's work, it fails to live up to its
aspirations, in spite of having drawn its inspiration from John Ford's Jacobean classic,
'Tis Pity She's A Whore.

▶ **Mystère Alexina** see Mystery Of
Alexina, The

▶ **Mystère De La Chambre Jaune,**
Le see Mystery Of The Yellow Room,
The

▶ **Mystère Picasso, Le** see Picasso
Mystery, The

The Mystery Of Alexina

▶ **Mystère Alexina**

France   1985   90 mins   col
Les Cinéastes Associés/T.F.1 Films

d   **René Ferét**
sc **Jean Gruault, René Ferét**
ph **Bernard Zitzermann**
m   **Anne-Marie Deschamps**
    Vuillemin, Valérie Stroh, Véronique
    Silver, Bernard Freyd, Pierre Vial

In the year 1858 Alexina (Vuillemin), fresh
from a convent, goes to teach in a small
boarding school where the owner's daughter,
Sara (Stroh), becomes her friend. Sexual
desire grows between them, whereupon they
discover that Alexina is really a young man.
Unperturbed, Sara rechristens him Camille
and he determines to marry her. René Ferét
based his film on the diary, edited by Michel
Foucault, of Herculine Barbin, a real-life
19th-century hermaphrodite, but the film
doesn't quite do justice to its poignant,
intriguing and ultimately tragic subject matter. The love affair is over-romanticized, and
insufficient attention is paid to psychological
and emotional processes, but Ferét tries hard
and, despite its shortcomings, the piece is
affecting.

▶ **Mystery of Kaspar Hauser, The**
see Enigma Of Kaspar Hauser, The

▶ **Mystery Of Picasso, The** see Picasso
Mystery, The

The Mystery Of The Yellow Room

▶ **Le Mystère De La Chambre Jaune**

France   1930   108 mins   bw
Film Osso

d   Marcel L'Herbier
sc   Marcel L'Herbier
ph   L.H. Burel
m   Edouard Flament
     Huguette Duflos, Kissa Kouprine, Roland
     Toutain, Belières

A journalist (Toutain), investigating a series of attacks on a professor's daughter (Duflos) by an unknown assailant, finds himself in some curious situations, not least in an 'old dark house'. One of the most effective of L'Herbier's sound films (second only to its sequel *The Perfume Of The Woman In Black*), this pacy, semi-serious yarn is based on the famous detective thriller by Gaston Leroux. Bringing with him some of his marvellous technical tricks from the silent days, the director adds the dimension of chilling sound effects and overlapping dialogue, while Burel's camerawork creates a sinister shadowy world.

My Sweet Little Village

▶ **Vesničkó Má Středisková**

Czechoslovakia   1985   100 mins   col
Barrandon Film Studio

d   Jiří Menzel
sc   Zdenek Sverak
ph   Jaromír Šofr
m   Jiří Šust
     János Bán, Marian Labuda, Rudolf
     Hrušínsky, Milena Dvorska, Ladislav
     Zupanic, Petr Cepek

The everyday events in a rural village, among them an adulterous affair, a teenager's crush on a schoolmistress, an accident-prone doctor's unorthodox methods, and the uneasy partnership between a small, fat truck driver and his tall, thin mentally-retarded workmate. Menzel, who made an international reputation in the 1960s with such films as the Oscar-winning *Closely Observed Trains* (1966) returned to favour with this sweet little Oscar-nominated movie. Edging on cuteness and without much bite, it is full of gentle comic touches and a real feel for a living community. Ban and Labuda make a wonderful Laurel and Hardy pairing.

My Uncle

▶ **Mon Oncle**

France   1958   116 mins   col
Spectra/Gray/Alterdel/Centaure

d   Jacques Tati
sc   Jacques Tati, Jacques Lagrange
ph   Jean Bourgoin
m   Alain Romans, Franck Borcellini
     Jacques Tati, Jean-Pierre Zola, Adrienne
     Servatie, Alain Becourt

Monsieur Hulot (Tati) cannot come to terms with the job he has at his brother-in-law's factory, nor with the ultra-modern gadget-filled home where his small nephew lives unhappily, so different from the shabby old boarding house where he himself resides. Despite the simplistic, sentimental nostalgia for the picturesque old Paris of the corner bistro and accordian music, Tati depicts a mechanized house in which the *bourgeois* inhabitants have become dehumanized in a series of brilliant and original sight and sound gags. Monsieur Hulot's second screen appearance was enough to put him among the immortals.

Best Foreign Film Oscar 1958
Special Jury Prize Cannes 1958

My Uncle Antoine

▶ **Mon Oncle Antoine**

Canada   1971   110 mins   col
National Film Board Of Canada

d   Claude Jutra
sc   Clément Perron
ph   Michel Brault
m   Jean Cousineau

Jean Duceppe, Jacques Gagnon, Lyne
Champagne, Olivette Thibault, Claude
Jutra, Hélène Loiselle

Fourteen-year-old orphan Benoit (Gagnon)
lives with his Uncle Antoine (Duceppe) and
family in a small provincial mining town
where Antoine keeps the local store, as well
as being the town's undertaker. One
Christmas Eve, during the 1940s, Uncle Antoine is called away from the festivities to fetch
a body, and takes Benoit with him. Antoine
gets drunk and, on their return home, Benoit
observes many incidents, including his aunt
in the embrace of the store clerk. This is a
rites-of-passage essay, both tender and funny
and, aside from some over-indulgence with a
zoom lens which disturbs the balance of
mood, it is a finely observed portrait of family
life in Quebec, made with a feeling for the
contrast between intimate interiors and open
winter landscape.

My Universities

▶ **Moi Universiteti**

USSR   1940   104 mins   bw
Soyezdetfilm

d   **Mark Donskoi**
sc **Mark Donskoi**
ph **Piotr Ermolov**
m   **Lev Schwartz**
    **Nilolai Valbert, Stepan Kaioukov, Nicolas
    Dorokhine, Plotnikov**

Having left home, Maxim Gorky (Valbert)
goes from job to job witnessing the exploitation of the workers, which makes him more
and more politically aware. There is a slight
falling off in the third part of Donskoi's
Gorky trilogy as it becomes more episodic
and didactic, but it is still packed with memor-

able sequences. One of them takes place in a
bakery where the wily boss talks all through
the night. The film ends symbolically with the
great Russian writer-to-be seeing the coming
of a better future. The three films, *The Childhood Of Maxim Gorky*, *My Apprenticeship*
and this one, based on Gorky's autobiography, are shot through with the author's observation, humanism and patriotism, adding up
to one of the masterpieces of Socialist Realism
in the cinema.

My Way Home

▶ **Így Jöttem**

Hungary   1964   109 mins   bw
Studio IV, Mafilm

d   **Miklós Jancsó**
sc **Gyula Hernádi**
ph **Tamás Somló**
m   **Zoltán Jenei**
    András Kozák, Sergei Nikonenko

Joská (Kozák), a Hungarian youth making
his way home across Russian-occupied
countryside near the end of World War II, is
arrested, interned, released, arrested again,
and sent to tend a herd of cows together with
Kolya (Nikonenko), a young Russian soldier.
The two transcend barriers of language as
well as nationality, to become close friends,
but Kolya becomes ill and dies while Joská
is fetching help. This stark and moving film,
eloquently conveying the dislocation of an
occupied country, was Jancsó's third solo
feature. It affirms his uniquely individual
style – choreographed camera work, interplay
of figures and landscape – as well as treating
the themes that would mark all his best work:
man alienated from himself and others by the
cruelty of war, the harshness of nature and
the unreliability of allegiances.

n

► **Nachalo** see Beginning, The

► **Nachts Wenn Der Teufel Kamm** see Devil Strikes At Night, The

► **Nackt Unter Wölfen** see Naked Among Wolves

Nada

France 1974 134 mins col
Films La Boétie(Paris)/Verona
Film(Rome)

d **Claude Chabrol**
sc **Jean-Patrick Manchette**
ph **Jean Rabier**
m **Pierre Jansen**
   **Fabio Testi, Michel Duchaussoy, Maurice
   Garrel, Michel Aumont, Lou Castel,
   Viviane Romance, Mariangela Melato,
   Katia Romanoff**

Nada (the Spanish for 'nothing') is the name
of a small and disparate group of terrorists
who decide to kidnap the American ambassador in Paris during his regular weekly visit to
a brothel. The plan unleashes conflicts within
the group and within the police, with the
former coming into uncompromisingly
bloody contact with the latter. In this articulation of the view that the destroyers of the
state and its protectors are two sides of the
same coin, Chabrol, while eliciting occasional
sympathy for the courage of his anarchists,
offers no comfort to the viewer. Very violent,
but punctuated with black humour and subtle
observation, this superlatively cynical exercise
is realized with expertise in all departments.

► **Nagarik** see Citizen, The

Naked Among Wolves

► **Nackt Unter Wölfen**

E. Germany 1963 125 mins bw
DEFA

d **Frank Beyer**
sc **Bruno Apitz**
ph **Günther Marczinowski**
   **Erwin Geschonneck, Gerry Wolff, Fred
   Delmare, Armin Müller-Stahl, Boleslaw
   Plotnicki, Krystyn Wójcik**

As the Americans draw near to the notorious
Buchenwald concentration camp in 1945, the
prison resistance group decides to revolt
rather than face elimination by the Nazi
guards. An unexpected and dangerous problem confronts them when a new prisoner
arrives, bringing a small boy hidden in a
suitcase... The negative qualities of the film
two-dimensional characters and the suggestion that all good men and true in the camps
were Communists. However, the subject is
compelling and, if the direction is a little flat,
it is nonetheless dignified and there is much
authentic detail – partly, no doubt, because
writer Apitz was himself an inmate.

Naked Childhood

► **(US: Me)**

► **L'Enfance Nue**

France 1968 80 mins col
Parc Film/Stephan Films/Renn
Productions/Les Films Du Carrosse

d **Maurice Pialat**
sc **Maurice Pialat, Arlette Langman**
ph **Claude Beausoleil**
   Michel Terrazon, Marie-Louise Thierry,

René Thierry, Marie Marc, Henri Puff,
Pierrette Deplanque

Ten-year-old François (Terrazon), abandoned
by his mother, is sent to a working-class foster
family where his behaviour is disturbed. After
several incidents, including his throwing a cat
down a stairwell to prove it can land on its
feet, he is removed. The second family, where
the parents (Marie-Louise and René Thierry)
are elderly, the grandmother (Marc) ancient
and a foster brother (Puff) awkward and shy,
proves a success, although François' tendency
to uncontrollable behaviour leads to a crisis.
Making his first full-length feature, Pialat
exhibits superb control of his subject, an
examination of childhood, which is never
allowed to become sentimental. The film tells
a simple and touching story with warmth and
directness, offering some splendid performances, notably from Marie Marc as the grandmother with whom François forms a deep
bond. As a distant cousin to both *The Four
Hundred Blows* and *The Two Of Us*, it is no
surprise to notice that François Truffaut and
Claude Berri were two of the producers.

▶ **Naked Heart, The** see Maria Chap-
delaine

Naked Hearts

▶ **Les Coeurs Verts**

France 1966 105 mins bw
Films Raoul Ploquin/Sodor Films

d **Edouard Luntz**
sc **Edouard Luntz**
ph **Jean Badal**
m **Serge Gainsbourg, Henri Renaud**
   **Gérard Zimmerman. Erick Penet, Marise
   Mair, Françoise Bonneau, Arlette Thomas**

Two juvenile offenders, Zim (Zimmerman)
and Jean-Pierre (Penet), meet in prison and
are released on the same day. Zim decides to
go straight and becomes a labourer, but Jean-
Pierre's efforts to do likewise peter out. Set
in the conurbations of outer Paris, Luntz's
first full-length feature is a triumph of *cinéma
vérité*, with non-professional actors communicating an authentic sense of truth. A detached
study of aimless youth in incoherent revolt,
revealing their haunts, lifestyles and insecurit-

ies without comment, the film has the authority of a documentary with the added impact
of Luntz's gift for the unexpected situation
and Badal's for the imaginative image.

▶ **Naked Night, The** see Sawdust And
Tinsel

Nana

France 1926 98 mins bw
Jean Renoir

d **Jean Renoir**
sc **Pierre Lestringuez**
ph **Jean Bachelet, Edmund Corwin**
m **Silent**
   **Catherine Hessling, Werner Krauss, Jean
   Angelo, Raymond Guerin-Catelain, Pierre
   Champagne, Valeska Gert, Pierre
   Philippe**

Nana has a fleeting triumph as a third-rate
actress, and briefly enjoys the life of an
admired courtesan before dying a horrible
death. Zola's celebrated novel provided
Renoir with the greatest challenge of his early
career. The film offers a hint of pleasures to
come, touching on the director's love of artifice and theatrical spectacle, his fascination
with class relations, the exploration of character within a wide social setting, the mixing of
comedy with tragedy. Hessling's Nana is light-
weight and doll-like, but Renoir subtly undercuts her performance by his sympathetic treatment of the male characters. The relatively
lavish production (it flopped at the box-office)
was designed by future director Claude Autant-Lara.

Nana

France 1955 100 mins col
Cigno Films

d **Christian-Jaque**
sc **Henri Jeanson, Jean Ferry, Albert
   Valentin**
ph **Christian Matras**
m **Georges Van Parys**
   **Martine Carol, Charles Boyer, Jacques
   Castelot, Elisa Cegani, Noël Roquevert,
   Jean Debucourt**

Nana (Carol), a luxury-loving girl from the slums, becomes a small-time actress-cum-courtesan at the height of the Second Empire. Involved with a man of substance (Boyer), she decides to run away with his rival, thus provoking fatal consequences. Emile Zola, on the whole, doesn't fare too well with film-makers. The best attempt at *Nana* was prob-ably Renoir's silent version in 1926, while Hollywood made a watchable but cleaned-up version with Anna Sten in 1934, and the Swedes took the liberty of turning it into a sexploitation film in 1971. Here, Christian-Jaque concentrates on spotlighting his beauti-ful wife (a mediocre performance) in authentic period settings of sumptuous opulence, into which Debucourt wanders as Napoleon III. The ugly underbelly and political implications of Zola's novel have, however, been ignored.

▶ **Naniwa Hika** see Osaka Elegy

▶ **Napló Gyermekeimnek** see Diary For My Children

▶ **Napló Szerelmeimnet** see Diary For My Loves

Napoléon

France   1927   270 mins   bw
WESTI/Société Générale De Films

d   **Abel Gance**
sc **Abel Gance**
ph **Jules Kruger**
m   **Silent**
    Albert Dieudonné, Wladimir Roudenko, Gina Manès, Nicolas Koline, Annabella, Antonin Artaud, Van Daële, Koubitsky, Abel Gance, Pierre Batcheff

The life of Napoleon: his childhood, military schooling, and rise to power. Abel Gance's unhistorical but historic film was first shown at the Paris Opera in a five-hour version. After its poor reception, it was released in various truncated forms until filmologist (*sic*) Kevin Brownlow's reconstruction, as close to the original as possible, was shown in 1980 complete with the triptychs – a triple screen process that anticipated Cinerama by 30 years. The film is a pyrotechnical display of almost every device of the silent screen and beyond, using hand-held cameras and one strapped to a horse's back, wide-angle lenses, superimposition and rapid cutting. The most famous set-piece is the symbolic sequence in which Napoleon (Dieudonné) sails back from Corsica in a storm, as the storm in the Con-vention rages. But Gance's view of Napoleon as a Nietzschean superman and the rhetorical devices with which he expresses it, makes the film, notwithstanding its greatness, as dema-gogic as its hero.

Napoléon

France   1955   190 mins   col
Filmsonor/CLM/Francinex

d   **Sacha Guitry**
sc **Sacha Guitry**
ph **Pierre Montazel**
m   **Jean Françaix**
    Daniel Gélin, Raymond Pellegrin, Sacha Guitry, Michèle Morgan, Danielle Darrieux, Orson Welles, Jean Marais, Yves Montand, Maria Schell, Jean Gabin, Erich Von Stroheim, Gianna-Maria Canale

Talleyrand (Guitry) recounts a series of anec-dotes about the life and loves of Napoleon which develop into dramatized illustration of the tales, with the little Corsican rebel who became Emperor of France played first by Gélin, then by Pellegrin. The film is a series of vignettes which act as the excuse for one of Guitry's witty all-star extravaganzas (only about half the mouth-watering cast is listed above!). The lovely Michèle Morgan is Jose-phine, and Von Stroheim's cameo has him impersonating Ludwig Van Beethoven. Expensively made – it was reputed to have cost a record $1.8 million – it looks good, and is three hours of light entertainment that casts no serious light on its huge subject.

▶ **Nara Livet** see So Close To Life

▶ **Narayama-Bushi-Ko** see Ballad Of Narayama, The

▶ **Narayama-Bushi-Ko** see Ballad Of Narayama, The

▶ **Nastasia Filipovna** see Idiot, The

The Nasty Girl

▶ **Das Schreckliche Mädchen**

West Germany 1989 92 mins col
Sentana Film

d Michael Verhoeven
sc Michael Verhoeven
ph Axel Del Roche
m Mike Herting, Elmar Schloter
   Lena Stoltze, Monika Baumgautner,
   Michael Gahr, Fred Stillkrauth, Elisabeth
   Bertram, Robert Giggenbach, Hans-
   Richard Müller

Sonja (Stoltze) is a much admired schoolgirl
in the small German town of Pfilzing, having
won an essay competition on the subject of
'Freedom In Europe'. But when she enters
for another competition in which the subject
is 'My Home Town During The Third Reich',
she finds the inhabitants unwilling to help
her. After her marriage to a schoolmaster
(Giggenbach), she doggedly continues in her
determination to uncover the truth, despite
personal danger to herself and her family.
Based on the true story of Anja Rosmus, the
film takes an extremely novel attitude to the
theme of German fascism, not only in the
past but in its worrying present-day form. By
using a format which allows characters,
especially Sonja (an exceptionally engaging
performance from 34-year-old Stoltze, both
as a teenager and married woman), to address
the audience directly, and many back projections in the manner of Hans Jürgen Syberberg, it takes on the style of a witty, satiric
fable. The only problem with this approach
is that there is sometimes too abrupt a shift
from the surreal to the real, and much of the
latter part loses some tension and dramatic
impact. But the 52-year-old Verhoeven's film
has a youthful vigour and freshness, and even
a certain attractive indiscipline in structure.

   Best Director Berlin 1990

▶ **Nattlek** see Night Games

▶ **Nattvardsgasterna** see Winter Light

Nazarín

Mexico 1958 94 mins bw
Manuel Barbachano Ponce

d Luis Buñuel
sc Luis Buñuel, Julio Alejandro
ph Gabriel Figueroa
   Francisco Rabal, Marga López, Rita
   Macedo, Jesús Fernández, Noe
   Murayama

Nazarín (Rabal), a humble and unworldly
priest, attempts to live by the precepts of
Christianity but is despised for his pains,
finding compassion only in a prostitute. One
of Buñuel's most astringent and forceful
attacks on formal religion, told in the manner
of a Christian parable, the film was ambiguous enough for it to win the International
Catholic Cinema Office award – a supreme
irony for the cinema's most famous anti-
Catholic atheist. The theme of the impossibility of leading a pure Christian life was
further explored in *Viridiana*, which didn't
win any awards from the Church.

▶ **Nazi Terror At Night** see Devil Strikes
At Night, The

▶ **Neco Z Alenky** see Alice

▶ **Nejkrasnejsí Vek** see Best Age, The

▶ **Nella Citta L'Inferno** see Caged

▶ **Nel Nome Del Padre** see In The
Name Of The Father

▶ **Neobychainiye Priklucheniya
Mistera Vesta V Stranya Bolsh-
evikov** see Extraordinary Adventures Of
Mr West In The Land Of The Bolsheviks,
The

▶ **Neokonchennaya Pyesa Dlya
Mekhanicheskogo Pianin** see
Unfinished Piece For Mechanical Piano

▶ **Neskolko Dnei Iz Zhizni I. I. Oblomov** see Oblomov

▶ **Neskolko Intervyu Po Lichnyam
Voprosam** see Interviews On Personal
Problems

The Nest

▶ **El Nido**

Spain 1980 97 mins col

A-Punto ELSA

d Jaime De Armiñán
sc Jaime De Armiñán
ph Teo Escamilla
m Joseph Haydn, anon 17th century
  Héctor Alterio, Ana Torrent, Luis Politti,
  Agustín González, Patricia Adriani

A wealthy old widower (Alterio) becomes enthralled by a 13-year-old girl. His priest, his maid, the girl's teacher, her father and a police sergeant all try to dissuade them both from the liaison which ends in death. This is a gentle, intriguing film on a taboo subject that manages to avoid prurience. Beautifully acted by Alterio and Torrent (the marvellous little girl in *The Spirit Of The Beehive* seven years before) and luminously photographed, it might have been even better had it been less literary and explored the subject with more irony.

A Nest Of Gentlefolk

▶ Dvorianskoe Gnezdo

USSR 1969 106 mins col
Mosfilm

d Andrei Mikhalkov-Konchalovsky
sc Valentin Yezhov, Andrei Mikhalkov-
  Konchalovsy
ph Georgy Rerberg
m Vyacheslav Ovchinnikov
  Leonid Kulagin, Irina Kupchenko, Beata
  Tyszkiewicz, A. Kostomolotsky, V.
  Sergachov, Nikita Mikhalkov

Disenchanted with the superficial glitter of Parisian society and with his frivolous wife (Tyszkiewicz), Fyodor Lavretsky (Kulagin) returns to his long-neglected estate in Russia, reflects on his past while sorting through the cobweb-covered *objets* of a lifetime, and falls unrequitedly in love with his neighbour's young daughter (Kupchenko). In adapting a work by Turgenev, Konchalovsky has focused on his central character, narrowing the novelist's range of observation, and creating a mood piece. He does so with superb visual sensitivity, evoking the atmosphere of lethargy and decay that has come to signify the texture of Russian *bourgeois* life just before the Revolution. Occasionally bordering on the monotonous, the film is nonetheless full of good things, not least the performance of Kupchenko.

Never On Sunday

▶ Pote Tin Kyriaki

Greece 1959 97 mins bw
Lopert/Melinafilm

d Jules Dassin
sc Jules Dassin
ph Jacques Natteau
m Manos Hadjidakis
  Melina Mercouri, Jules Dassin, Georges
  Foundas, Tito Vandis, Despo Diamantidou

An exuberant and contented waterfront prostitute (Mercouri) meets an earnest American (Dassin) who falls for her and, in Professor Higgins fashion, attempts to educate her to literature and a higher strain of music than *bouzouki*. A low-budget movie, that manages some wonderful views of Piraeus and a lot of Greek atmosphere, offers a mediocre performance from Dassin and a high-octane one from Mercouri which brought her international fame. A thoroughly good-natured romp which, in its day, seemed invitingly shocking and became a world-wide hit, as did the catchy but rather repetitive Oscar-winning title song.

Best Actress (Melina Mercouri) Cannes 1960

Never Strike A Woman – Even With A Flower

▶ Zénu Ani Květinou Neuhodis

Czechoslovakia 1966 100 mins bw
Barrandov Film Studio

d Zdeněk Podskalsky
sc Jaroslav Dietl, Zdeněk Podskalsky
ph František Valert
m Evzen Illín
  Vlastimil Brodsky, Hana Brejchová,
  Slávka Budínová, Jirina Bohdalová, Kveta
  Fialová

Ludvík (Brodsky), a middle-aged and married musician, is diffident and obliging, especially to women, wherein lies the secret of his charm. His several attempts at affairs all go awry, belying his reputation as an enviable philanderer, but result in his wife throwing him out, whereupon he has a surprise love affair with an innocent girl (Brejchová). Popular in his own country since 1958, Podskalsky's work has been virtually unknown in the West. This example is a comedy, filled with the kind of charmingly ridiculous situations which point to the silent cinema or the films of Lubitsch and Billy Wilder. If the story itself is unoriginal, the treatment is fresh and Brodsky's performance as the bewildered hero is a delight.

▶ **Nevinost Bez Zastite** see Innocence Unprotected

The New Angels

▶ **I Nuovi Angeli**

> Italy   1961   105 mins   bw
> Titanus/Galatea/Arco

d **Ugo Gregoretti**
sc **Mino Guerrini, Ugo Gregoretti**
ph **Tonino Delli Colli, Mario Bernardi**
m **Piero Umiliani**
   Non-professionals from Chianti, Milan, Naples, Agrigento, Riccione and Rome

In a series of eight episodes occurring across the length and breadth of the country, the attitudes and behaviour of contemporary Italian youth are demonstrated. The tales feature young people of differing classes and backgrounds, revealing their contrasting attitudes to progress, ambition, social mores and sexual ethics. Gregoretti's first film adopts a documentary style and approach and comes across as factual and informative, although the stories themselves are fictional. Utilizing some gentle irony and black humour, the director points up the contradictions that co-exist in the society of his time – the cowherd, for example, who would rather have his wife and baby starve than suffer the 'disgrace' of her taking a job as a waitress – in a pleasing if ephemeral exercise.

The New Babylon

▶ **Novyi Vavilon**

> USSR   1929   80 mins   bw
> Sovkino

d **Grigori Kozintsev, Leonid Trauberg**
sc **Grigori Kozintsev, Leonid Trauberg**
ph **Andrei Moskvin**
m **Silent**

Elena Kuzmina, Pyotr Sobelevsky, Sophie Magarill, D. Gutman, Vsevolod Pudovkin, Sergei Gerasimov

Louise (Kuzmina), a shop assistant in a luxury store (The New Babylon), sees the effects of the German advance on Paris on the cowardly *bourgeoisie* and the patriotic working class, and the collapse of the Commune of 1871. Kozintsev's and Trauberg's great silent period culminated with this dazzlingly inventive satire. Despite the symbolic intentions and episodic structure, there is a warmth in the performances of the proletarian characters and a realism in some of the sequences. But it is in the montage and the lighting used to contrast the rich and the poor that the film is at its best.

The Newcomer

▶ **Le Nouveau Venu**

> Benin   1979   87 mins   col
> Iris Films/International Tropic Films

d **Richard De Meideros**
sc **Richard De Meideros, René Ewagnion, Bouraima Lawani**
ph **Maxime Lefevre, Bouraima Lawani**
   Michel Djondo, Sikirou Ogoujobi, Ages Capo-Cichi, Sebastien De Souza

A young administrator of the new order is appointed to run a government office. His determination to increase output and efficiency brings him into conflict with the old-fashioned workers' leader who resents the challenge to his status and methods. The latter even resorts to putting an ancient spell on the new boss but undergoes a change of heart and mind. Yet another expression of the conflict between independence and the hangover of colonialism which characterizes many of the films from the Third World (Benin was formerly the French colony of Dahomey), this particular film is somewhat naive and simplistic, with a pat and unconvincing resolution. Nonetheless, it offers a slant on African custom and the problems of progress, doing so at an acceptable level of efficiency and with some warmth and humour.

▶ **New Gentlemen, The** see Nouveaux Messieurs, Les

The New Gulliver

▶ **Novyi Gulliver**

USSR 1935 85 mins bw
Mosfilm

d Alexander Ptoushko
sc Alexander Ptoushko, B. Roshal
ph N. Renkov
m Lev Schwartz

A reading of Swift's *Gulliver's Travels* to a group of Young Pioneers at a camp gives them dreams in which they see updated episodes from the book. Among the imaginings are a newsreel cameraman filming Gulliver being hauled into the Lilliputian capital, modern engineering techniques used to feed the 'giant' and the hero helping the oppressed in a class war. The world's first feature-length puppet film took Ptoushko three exhausting years to make; he had already shot a number of short puppet films and been responsible for the special effects for Dovzhenko's *Aerograd*. The manipulation of the wax dolls as caricature humans worked wonderfully as satire not far removed from Swift's own, and the Lilliput chapter lends itself easily to the Soviet ideology of the time.

The New Land

▶ **Nybyggarna**

Sweden 1972 205 mins col
Svensk Filmindustri

d Jan Troell
sc Jan Troell, Bengt Forslund
ph Jan Troell
m Bengt Ernryd, George Oddner
   Max Von Sydow, Liv Ullmann, Eddie Axberg, Monica Zetterlund, Pierre Lindstedt

Karl Oskar Nillson (Von Sydow) and his wife Kristina (Ullmann), Swedish immigrants to Minnesota in the 19th century, struggle to build a home, to farm their land and bring up a family, against all odds. Although the ending of this sequel to *The Emigrants*, even longer than the previous film, shows a third generation of Nillsons happy and assimilated in America, it does reveal a darker side to the saga. The hardships caused by nature are more brutally depicted, from a blizzard to a scorching desert, yet Troell still visualizes things from an idealized perspective. There are moving moments, but historical events such as the Civil War and the Indian wars are dragged in unconvincingly. The dyptich was the most expensive Swedish cinematic project to date.

New Tales Of The Taira Clan

▶ **Shin Heike Monogatari**

Japan 1955 113 mins col
Daiei

d Kenji Mizoguchi
sc Yoshitaka Yoda, Masashige Narusawa, Hisakazu Tsuji
ph Kazuo Miyagawa
m Fumio Hayasaka, Masaru Sato
   Raizo Ichikawa, Yoshiko Kuga, Narutoshi Hayashi, Michiyo Kogure, Ichijiro Oya, Eitaro Shindo, Ichiro Sugai

In 12th-century Japan, the soldier monks of the rich and powerful monasteries clash with the families of the samurai. When the young samurai Kiyomori Taira hears of a plot to assassinate Tadamori, the head of the Taira clan, he comes to the clan's rescue. After Tadamori's death, he assumes leadership, facing the monks and destroying their idols. One of Mizoguchi's last films shows a remarkable use of colour, ranging from pastel blues to deep red. Working closely with Miyagawa, the great cinematographer, the director decided on the colours which were to predominate in each scene. He also manages to keep the main characters in the complex plot in focus with a never-slacking narrative. The film is marginally less successful than his other late films, because it moved away from his 'woman' pictures into the more familiar and predictable samurai territory of Japanese cinema.

The Nibelungen

▶ **Die Nibelungen**

Germany 1924 118 mins (Part I – Siegfried); 131 mins (Part II - Kriemhild's Revenge) bw
Decla Bioskop/UFA

d Fritz Lang
sc Fritz Lang, Thea Von Harbou

ph Carl Hoffman, Günther Rittau, Walter
   Ruttmann
m Silent
   Paul Richter, Margarete Schon, Hanna
   Ralph, Bernhard Goetzke, Theodore Loos,
   Hans Adalbert Von Schlettow, Rudolf
   Klein-Rogge

Siegfried (Richter), married to Kriemhild
(Schon), journeys from Iceland to Burgundy
with Brunhild (Ralph) as a bride for his
brother-in-law Gunther (Loos). After many
adventures, magical and otherwise, Brunhild
has Siegfried killed by Hagen (Von Schlettow). Kriemhild gets her revenge on the Bur-
gundians. Lang's adaptation of the 13th-
century German saga is a superb example of
the craftsmanship at the UFA studios. The
stylized set designs by Otto Hunte, Erich
Kettelhut and Karl Vollbrecht create a mysterious beauty, especially the misty forest
(constructed in a Zeppelin hangar) and the
romantic castles. There is also a wonderful
dragon that the hero slays early in Part I and
a massively staged battle to end Part II. The
characters are deliberately one-dimensional as
befits the epic mode.

▶ **Nibelungen, Die** see Nibelungen, The

▶ **Nibelungen, Die** see Whom The Gods
   Wish To Destroy

▶ **Nicht Versöhnt, Oder Es Hilft Nur**
   see Not Reconciled, Or Only Violence

▶ **Nido, El** see Nest, The

▶ **Niewinni Czarodzieje** see Innocent
   Sorcerers

▶ **Night, The** see Notte, La

Night And Fog

▶ **Nuit Et Brouillard**

   France   1955   31 mins   bw/col
   Argos/Como/Cocinor

d Alain Resnais
sc Jean Cayrol
ph Ghislain Cloquet, Sacha Vierny
m Hanns Eisler

This is a tour of the ruins of Auschwitz in
the mid-1950s, filmed in colour but intercut
with black-and-white archive material of the
horrors that took place there not too many
years before. The peak of Resnais' eight short
films prior to his feature debut *Hiroshima,
Mon Amour* (1959), was reached with this
moving and thought-provoking documentary.
The carefully controlled commentary, narrated by Michel Bouquet and written by ex-
deportee Cayrol (later the screenwriter of
Muriel), as well as the gentle music, contrast
starkly with the newsreels of the concentration camp victims – the past intrudes upon
the present, memory precludes forgetting. The
theme and the long exploratory tracking shots
were to become characteristics of Resnais'
feature films.

Night Beauties

▶ **(US: Beauties Of The Night)**
▶ **Les Belles De Nuit**

   France   1952   89 mins   bw
   Franco-London/Film Rizzoli

d René Clair
sc René Clair
ph Armand Thirard
m Georges Van Parys
   Gérard Philipe, Gina Lollobrigida,
   Martine Carol, Magali Vendeuil, Paolo
   Stoppa, Raymond Bussières, Raymond
   Cordy

A shy young music teacher (Philipe) escapes
from his drab life into dreams of romantic
adventures in different epochs and places
where he encounters beautiful women derived
from acquaintances he meets in his waking
hours. Most of Clair's films have a dreamlike
atmosphere, so he was naturally at home
when creating dreams more overtly. The film
is not only an entertaining fantasy, but makes
an ironic comment on the interaction between
fact and fiction.

Night Games

▶ **Nattlek**

   Sweden   1966   105 mins   bw
   Sandrews

d **Mai Zetterling**
sc **Mai Zetterling**
ph **Rune Ericson**
m **Jan Johansson, George Riedel**
  Ingrid Thulin, Keve Hjelm, Lena Brundin,
  Naima Wifstrand, Jörgen Lindström

A sexually inhibited and disturbed man
(Hjelm), unable to come to terms with adult
life, recalls his mother-dominated childhood.
Mai Zetterling's second feature, adapted from
her own novel, caused a furore among moral-
ists who objected to its frank treatment of
sex. It is, in fact, a wickedly sensuous Strindbergian drama, handled with maturity and a
sharp eye for decadent details. However, the
theme, together with the presence of Thulin,
caused critics to compare the director
unfavourably with Bergman.

Night Heat

▶ **(US: On Any Street**
▶ **aka Bad Girls Don't Cry)**
▶ **La Notte Brava**

  Italy 1959 93 mins bw
  AJACE/Franco-London

d **Mauro Bolognini**
sc **Pier Paolo Pasolini**
ph **Armando Nannuzzi**
m **Piero Piccioni**
  Laurent Terzieff, Jean-Claude Brialy,
  Franco Interlenghi, Rosanna Schiaffino,
  Mylène Demongeot, Elsa Martinelli,
  Antonella Lualdi, Tomas Milian

Twenty-four hours in the life of three young
working-class Romans, on the make for
money and girls. Their activities selling stolen
firearms, trafficking with prostitutes and petty
theft. The day ends with a fight between them.
Bella-Bella (Interlenghi) is left unconscious,
Scintillone (Brialy) is arrested for causing a
fracas in a nightclub and Ruggeretto (Terzieff), after a night of carousal with a girl, ends
up forlorn and penniless. Pasolini's screenplay, albeit a little repetitive, is a cynical and
sharply observant dissection of the amorality
to which the hopelessly underprivileged Italian poor are driven in their desire for a better
life. Things have changed somewhat since the
film was made, of course, but it is still reasonably interesting and entertaining, if a little

slow at times. It is a pity that Bolognini
undercuts the impact of the piece by glam-
ourizing the fundamentally sleazy lives and
locales that are presented.

▶ **Night Heaven Fell, The** see Heaven
Fell That Night

Night Is My Future

▶ **aka Music In The Dark**
▶ **Musik I Mörker**

  Sweden 1948 87 mins bw
  Terra Film

d **Ingmar Bergman**
sc **Dagmar Edqvist**
ph **Göran Strindberg**
m **Erland Von Koch**
  Birger Malmsten, Mai Zetterling, Bengt
  Eklund, Naima Wifstrand, Gunnar
  Björnstrand

A young man (Malmsten) who has been
blinded determines to adjust to his affliction
and to live and work as an equal of the
sighted. He takes up the piano, and hires
a housekeeper-companion (Zetterling) to
whom he acts as a sort of Professor Higgins.
After several set-backs in the outside world,
the couple find love and fulfilment together.
Bergman's fourth film, only released outside
Sweden many years after he had found his
form and his fame, is mainly interesting in
demonstrating how far he progressed. There
are clear hints of the powerful imagery to
come, and a pointed picture of provincial
life but, overall, it is an over-earnest, sentimental and clichéd romantic melodrama –
although one would hesitate to join the
New York Times in calling it 'cinematic
juvenilia'.

The Night Is Young

▶ **Mauvais Sang**

  France 1986 119 mins col
  Les Films Plain Chant/Soprofilms/FR3
  Films

d **Leos Carax**
sc **Leos Carax**

ph **Jean-Yves Escoffier**

m **Prokofiev, Britten, Charlie Chaplin, David Bowie, Charles Aznavour, Serge Reggiani Denis Lavant, Juliette Binoche, Michel Piccoli, Hans Meyer, Carroll Brooks, Julie Delphy**

Alex (Lavant), a petty thief, joins two crooks (Piccoli and Meyer) in a plan to rob a laboratory of the drug to stop the spread of STBO (a disease which attacks only insincere lovers), but he is more interested in Anna (Binoche), the girlfriend of one of the crooks. Carax's second feature is almost a sequel to his debut film, *Boy Meets Girl*, in sharing a central character called Alex played by the glowering, antipathetic Lavant. They also share a soulful, passive, short-haired heroine and a visual flair. But, unlike the previous picture which had some resemblance to real life, this is filtered through other movies and pulp literature. Godard did it with more style and conviction in the 1960s.

The Night Of Counting The Years

▶ **El Mumia**

Egypt 1969 102 mins col
Egyptian Cinema General Organisation

d **Shadi Abdelsalam**

sc **Shadi Abdelsalam**

ph **Abdel Aziz Fahmy**

m **Mario Nascimbene**
Ahmed Marei, Zouzou El Hakim, Ahmad Hegazi, Nadia Loutfy, Gaby Karraz

In Thebes in 1881, Wanniss (Marei), the younger son of the chief of the Horrabat tribe, shocked to learn that the tribe has been robbing the mummies' tombs and selling the trophies to mercenary dealers, reveals the whereabouts of the tombs to a team of archeologists trying to discover the source of the valuable objects. Towering like a pyramid over the commercial dross of the Egyptian film industry, this first feature from former art director Abdelsalam is notable for its startling visual beauty. The brooding story evolves slowly against the glories of Ancient Egypt, captured in deep-focus photography and vividly contrasting colours.

The Night Of San Lorenzo

▶ **(US: Night Of The Shooting Stars)**

▶ **La Notte Di San Lorenzo**

Italy 1981 107 mins col
RAI/Ager Cinematografica

d **Paolo and Vittorio Taviani**

sc **Paolo and Vittorio Taviani, Giuliani De Negri**

ph **Franco Di Giacomo**

m **Nicola Piovani**
Omero Antonutti, Margarita Lozano, Claudio Bigagli, Massimo Bonetti, Norma Martelli, Enrica Maria Modugno

The Tuscan town of San Martino is threatened with destruction by the Nazis as the Americans advance in August 1944. Many flee and join up with a resistance group. A bloody battle between them and the Fascists takes place on the eve of Liberation. The Taviani brothers have used all the rhetorical devices at their disposal to illustrate an important moment in modern Italian history and in their own lives – the Tuscan-born directors were 13 and 15 respectively at the time. Many of the events in the film are seen through the eyes of a six-year-old girl. There are enough bravura and inspiring sequences in the rambling structure and among the simplistic gestures to make it worthwhile.

Special Jury Prize Cannes 1982

▶ **Night Of The Shooting Stars** see Night Of San Lorenzo, The

The Night Of Varennes

▶ **La Nuit De Varennes**

France 1982 155 mins col
Gaumont/Opéra Film/FR3

d **Ettore Scola**

sc **Sergio Amedei, Ettore Scola**

ph **Armando Nannuzzi**

m **Armando Trovaioli**
Marcello Mastroianni, Jean-Louis Barrault, Hanna Schygulla, Daniel Gélin, Harvey Keitel, Jean-Claude Brialy, Laura Betti, Andréa Ferréol, Michel Vitold

During 1791, the French King and Queen flee across their country in a coach that is finally captured by the people of Varennes. Following and observing them is a collection of people who the writer Restif De Bretonne (Barrault), Casanova (Mastroianni), well past his prime, and American revolutionary Tom Paine (Keitel). They have been joined by a countess (Schygulla) travelling with her hairdresser (Brialy), an Italian opera singer (Betti), a rich widow, an industrialist and a magistrate. The group spends the journey engaged in philosophical discussion and commentary on life, love, politics and history – which is about to sweep several of them away in the Revolution. On the credit side, it is a handsome film, glitteringly cast, mounted in the style of an ambitious pageant and directed with evident finesse. However, it becomes an overlong and rather tedious exercise. The characters fail to come to life and the screenplay sheds little light on the period. One very nice touch is that all that is seen of the ill-fated Louis and Marie Antoinette are their lower legs and feet.

Night Paths

▶ **(US: Ways In The Night)**

▶ **Wege In Der Nacht**

> W. Germany 1979 98 mins col
> Westdeutscher Rundfunk

d   **Krzysztof Zanussi**
sc **Krzysztof Zanussi**
ph **Witold Sobociński**
m   **Wojciech Kilar**
    Mathieu Carrière, Maja Komorowska,
    Horst Frank, Zbigniew Zapasiewicz,
    Irmgard Forst

A cultivated German officer (Carrière), billeted in a small Polish town in 1943, is bewitched by an older Polish baroness (Komorowska). She uses their relationship in order to obtain information and give it to the local partisans. The director, too, uses this romance for his own ends in order to analyse, in a series of dialogues, the nature of aesthetics, the difficulties of remaining civilized while in the uniform of a 'barbarian' and to cast doubt on whether people with similar backgrounds can transcend the historical circumstances that divide them. Dry and

dispassionate as much of it is, the use of small but significant events, such as the stripping of a Jew to 'determine' his race, effectively brings the greater horror into focus.

Nights Of Cabiria

▶ **Le Notti Di Cabiria**

> Italy 1956 110 mins bw
> Dino De Laurentiis/Les Films Marceau

d   **Federico Fellini**
sc **Federico Fellini, Ennio Flaiano, Tullio**
    Pinelli, Pier Paolo Pasolini
ph **Otello Martelli**
m   **Nino Rota**
    Giulietta Masina, Amadeo Nazzari,
    François Périer, Franca Marzi, Mario
    Passante, Dorian Gray

Cabiria (Masina) is a prostitute living on the outskirts of Rome. Life is hard, but she never loses her sunny smile or her faith in human nature, even when she is cruelly dumped by a glamorous film star (Nazzari) and – worse – the respectable man (Périer) who is going to marry her disappears with her life savings. The perennially attractive idea of the whore with the heart of gold is given the full Fellini treatment in its wonderful observation of detail, and the narrative is veined with humour as well as sadness. However, it's difficult to escape memories of *La Strada* with funny, Chaplinesque Masina on display, fighting unkind fate but hardly anyone's idea of a woman of the streets. It was made into the hit American musical *Sweet Charity* directed by Bob Fosse, with Gwen Verdon on Broadway and Shirley MacLaine on film.

Best Foreign Film Oscar 1957

▶ **Nights When The Devil Came** see Devil Strikes At Night, The

Night Train

▶ **Pociag**

> Poland 1959 100 mins bw
> Kadr Unit, Film Polski

d   **Jerzy Kawalerowicz**
sc **Jerzy Lutowski, Jerzy Kawalerowicz**

ph **Jan Laskowski**
m **Andrzej Trzaskowski**
   **Lucyna Winnicka, Leon Niemczyk,
   Zbigniew Cybulski, Teresa Szmigielowna,
   Roland Glowacki**

Suffering an inner crisis, Marthe (Winnicka) buys a ticket from a stranger for a crowded holiday train, and finds herself in a 'Men Only' sleeper with an unhappy doctor (Niemczyk). The police board the train in search of a killer... Some interesting and compassionate images are insufficient to hold this film together. Kawalerowicz seems uncertain as to whether he's making a psychological study of loneliness or a thriller and doesn't really succeed in either direction.

Night Zoo

▶ **Un Zoo De La Nuit**

Canada   1987   115 mins   col
Les Productions Oz/L'Office National
Du Film Du Canada

d **Jean-Claude Lauzon**
sc **Jean-Claude Lauzon**
ph **Guy Dufaux**
m **Jean Corriveau**
   **Gilles Maheu, Roger Le Bel, Lynne
   Adams, Lorne Brass, Germain Houde,
   Corrado Mastropasqua, Jerry Snell**

Marcel (Maheu), a drug dealer, is freed after two years in prison. Returning to his bare, chic apartment and a world of hi-fi, modern paintings and Harley Davidsons, he discovers that his former pusher, Charlie (Houde), the latter's new, psychopathically violent partner and a couple of corrupt cops are after him for the drugs and a substantial sum of money which he hid before being jailed. Marcel's girlfriend (Adams) has become a prostitute and wants nothing of their former relationship, and he is having a difficult time with his father (Le Bel), his parents having separated while he was locked up. It is quite astonishing to learn that Lauzon's painfully slow, somewhat incoherent and rather tacky piece won nine major Genie awards (the Canadian Oscar). Its maker attempts to run two parallel stories – that of Marcel's underworld plight, and his relationship with his father which, famously, culminates in them shooting an elephant at the zoo in lieu of a moose-hunting

trip which the old man is too ill to take. Liberally sprinkled with some sensationalist come-ons (Marcel is graphically raped by a man in prison in the first scene), and attempting to echo the high-tech thriller-style of Jean-Jacques Beineix with singular lack of success, *Night Zoo* is one to avoid.

▶ **Nihon No Higeki** see Japanese Tragedy, A

Nikita

▶ **aka La Femme Nikita**

France   1990   117 mins   col
Gaumont Production (Paris)/Cecchi Gori
Group/Tiger Cinematografica (Rome)

d **Luc Besson**
sc **Luc Besson**
ph **Thierry Arbogast**
m **Eric Serra**
   **Anne Parillaud, Jean-Hugues Anglade,
   Tcheky Karyo, Jeanne Moreau, Roland
   Blanche, Marc Duret**

After a raid on a pharmacy by Nikita (Parillaud) and her gang of punk henchmen ends in destruction and carnage, the uncontrollably violent and drug-addicted 19-year-old girl is sentenced to life imprisonment. Believing her to have potential as a state secret service assassin, agent Bob (Karyo) puts her into a training establishment where it takes four years to curb her rebellion and turn her into a beautiful woman and an accomplished weapon of destruction. Out in the world again, with a cover story, Nikita falls in love with Marco (Anglade), but has a problem reconciling the two sides of her life. Besson's throbbing thriller is an awesomely audacious affair insofar as its plot is almost insultingly ludicrous and incredible, there is little characterization and no attempt is made to comment on the social or political conditions which fuel its violence and its threat. However, the director is a master of the fashionably glossy and moody camera, skilful editing and use of a compelling soundtrack. The lissom, uninhibited and very beautiful Parillaud holds the questionable ingredients together – the scenes with veteran Moreau, hired to teach her how to be 'first a human being' and then a woman, are gems – and for all its fundamental worthlessness, the movie is thoroughly entertaining from start to finish, although the latter could profitably have come a little sooner.

▶ **Nilouhe, Nuer** see Daughter Of The Nile

Nine Days Of One Year

▶ **Devyat Dnei Odnogo Goda**

USSR 1961 110 mins bw
Mosfilm

d **Mikhail Romm**
sc **Mikhail Romm, Daniel Khrabrovitsky**
ph **German Lavrov**
m **D. Ter-Tatevosyan**
   Alexei Batalov, Innokenti Smoktunovsky, Tamara Lavrova, Nikolai Plotnikov

Nine separate days of a year in the life of a young scientist (Batalov), whose work has exposed him to radiation. Neither his neglected wife (Lavrova) nor his colleague (Smoktunovsky) can persuade him to give up his dangerous experiments. The years of Stalinism began to hang heavily on the films of Romm, but after the 'thaw' he emerged from mediocrity with this revealing and realistic glimpse into the world of Soviet science. It was not only the subject matter that was unusual, but the placing of discussion rather than action at its dramatic centre. The plot, which sometimes approaches Hollywood's idealistic view of the man of science, is elevated by the fine performances from the three leads and the craftsmanship of the direction.

Nine Months

▶ **Kilenc Hónap**

Hungary 1976 93 mins col
Hunnia Filmstudió

d **Márta Mészáros**
sc **Gyula Hernádi, Ildikó Kóródy, Márta Mészáros**
ph **János Kende**
m **György Kovács**
   Lili Monori, Jan Nowicki, Djoko Rodič

Juli (Monori), a worker in an iron foundry, has a passionate affair with János (Polish actor Nowicki), the foreman. When he dis-

covers that she has had a child by a married professor (Rodič), he becomes insanely jealous. But Juli retains her independence, despite having János's baby. As in most of the lowkey films of Mészáros, the central figure is a woman who, without being a rebel, refuses to bow to convention and who values her freedom. The fact that the heroine is squat and plain is relevant only because it is rare in films where women are more likely to be attractive. Most of the plot is taken up by the slow and largely uneventful relationship between Juli and János, against a nicely observed background of a small industrial town. Monori, who was pregnant at the start of shooting, allowed herself to be photographed in childbirth for the film's conclusion.

Nineteen Hundred

▶ **Novecento**

Italy 1976 175 mins (Part I); 165 mins (Part II) col
PEA/Artistes Associés/Artemis

d **Bernardo Bertolucci**
sc **Bernardo Bertolucci, Franco Arcalli, Giuseppe Bertolucci**
ph **Vittorio Storaro**
m **Ennio Morricone**
   Burt Lancaster, Robert De Niro, Gérard Depardieu, Dominique Sanda, Donald Sutherland, Sterling Hayden, Alida Valli, Laura Betti, Stefania Sandrelli

Italian history as seen through the lives of Olmo (Depardieu) and Alfredo (De Niro) born on January 27, 1901 (novecento means the 20th century), until Liberation Day on April 25, 1945. Olmo, the son of a peasant woman, and Alfredo, the son of the lord of the manor (Lancaster) grow up together as friends until differences in class and politics separate them. Bertolucci, turning away from the introspection of his previous films, tried to make a popular movie of the class struggle using the style of both American epics and the lyrical Soviet cinema of the 1930s. It is operatic (it opens with a clown announcing the death of Verdi), didactic, bombastic, mean, moody and magnificent to look at. The second part gets rather over-Baroque and violent (a cat and a boy's head being smashed against a wall is not for the squeamish), and

Sutherland and Betti are ludicrously caricatured Fascists. But, with the last 30 minutes –
symbolic of revolution and post-revolution –
it enters greatness.

▶ **1999-Nen No Natsu Yasumi** see
Summer Vacation 1999

▶ **Ningen No Joken** see Human Condition, The

The Ninth Circle

▶ **Deveti Krug**

Yugoslavia 1960 108 mins bw
Jadran Film

d   **France Štiglic**
sc **Zora Dirnbach**
ph **Ivan Marinček**
m   **Branimir Sakač**
    **Dušica Žegarac, Boris Dvornik, Desanka
    Lončar, Branko Tatić**

In Croatia in the early 1940s, Ruth (Žegarac),
the young, upper middle-class daughter of a
Jewish family, marries a Catholic boy (Dvornik) to avoid being sent to a concentration
camp like her father. The pretence is maintained with difficulty, until Ruth can no longer
bear to hide her true identity. The first Yugoslavian film to deal with the concentration
camp and the atrocities committed by the
Uštaše, the Croatian Nationalists who collaborated with the Nazis, opened up the way for
other films in the 1960s to deal with the
Occupation. Štiglic, in a taut and classical
style, avoids melodrama while boldly and
movingly shifting from the lighter first part
about the lives of the young people and the
marriage of convenience towards the inferno
of the camps.

▶ **Nippon Konchuki** see Insect Woman,
The

▶ **Nobi** see Fires On The Plain

Nobody's Wife

▶ **Señora De Nadie**

Argentina 1982 90 mins col

GEA Cinematográfica

d   **Maria Luisa Bemberg**
sc **Maria Luisa Bemberg**
ph **Miguel Rodriguez**
m   **Luis Maria Serra**
    **Luisina Brando, Julio Chavez, Rodolfo
    Ranni, China Zorrilla, Gabriela Acher,
    Susu Pecoraro**

After discovering her husband's extra-marital
affair, a wife (Brando) leaves him (Ranni)
and her two children to establish a new life
on her own. She makes friends with an
unhappy, young homosexual (Chavez), whom
she meets at a therapy group, placing his
friendship above her hypocritical marriage.
She also shares an apartment with a happily
promiscuous girl (Acher) and finds work with
an estate agent. Bemberg fought for four
years to have her script passed by the censor,
who considered it damaging to family life.
What it does, in a trenchant but non-strident
manner, is attack the type of stultifying upper-
middle-class Argentine marriage from which
the heroine liberates herself. When she leaves
her husband she says, 'I was Mrs Somebody,
now I'm Mrs Nobody.' Actually, she becomes
somebody from nobody, a change which Luis-
ina Brando admirably illustrates, and learns
to laugh at herself. Buenos Aires is well used
as a solid background to a convincing drama
of self-discovery.

▶ **Noces Rouges, Les** see Blood
Wedding

No End

▶ **Bez Konca**

Poland 1984 108 mins col
Zespoly Filmowe

d   **Krzysztof Kieslowski**
sc **Krzysztof Kieslowski, Krzysztof
    Piesiewicz**
ph **Jacek Petrycki**
m   **Zbigniew Preisner**
    **Grazyna Szapolowska, Maria Pakulnis,
    Aleksander Bardini, Jerzy Radziwilowicz,
    Artur Barcis, Michal Bajor**

The ghost of a dead lawyer (Radziwilowicz)
watches his wife (Szapolowska) and young

son (Bajor) as they struggle to survive without him. He also sees the way the case of a young worker, charged with organizing a strike, is handled by another lawyer (Bardini) with a different approach. Set during Poland's martial law in 1982, Kieslowski's film was not shown outside Poland until 1986. While plainly deeply felt, it is far too schematic, studied, slow and solemn to create the desired effect. Intensely acted by the two female leads – Pakulnis plays the wife of the accused worker – the film, like the solid ghost that wanders through it, resides in a kind of creative limbo.

No Exit

▶ **Huis Clos**

France 1955 99 mins bw
Les Films Marceau

d   **Jacqueline Audry**
sc **Pierre Laroche**
ph **Robert Juillard**
m   **Joseph Kosma**
    Arletty, Frank Villard, Gaby Sylvia, Nicole Courcel, Yves Deniaud, Danièle Delorme

A weak man (Villard), a sexy woman (Sylvia) and an embittered Lesbian (Arletty), strangers to one another and each with a dark past, find themselves walled up together in a hotel room where, since they are all actually dead, they are condemned to a vile eternity of dislike, wrangling and rivalry. Jean-Paul Sartre's famous play, the theme of which is 'hell is other people', travels badly to the screen. Wordy and static, it is neither particularly well photographed nor well acted, although Arletty remains an attraction. Audry attempts to buck things up by introducing cinema screens on which the characters can visualize incidents in their lives, and there are some new characters, but none of it really helps. The film initially ran into some censorship problems – uncharacteristically for France.

▶ **No Good To Die For That** see Don't Let It Kill You

▶ **No Habra Mas Penas Ni Olvido** see Funny Dirty Little War, A

▶ **Noia, La** see Empty Canvas, The

Noir Et Blanc

France 1986 80 mins bw
Les Films Du Volcan

d   **Claire Devers**
sc **Claire Devers**
ph **Daniel Desbois**
m   **Sung by Chorale Rhapsodes**
    Francis Frappat, Jacques Martial, Josephine Fresson, Marc Berman, Claire Rigollier

Antoine (Frappat), a shy, conventional, young accountant, takes a job at a health club and is persuaded to avail himself of the facilities. Gradually, a strange sado-masochistic relationship develops between him and his black masseur, Jacques (Martial), as each explores the attraction of pain in their increasingly violent massage sessions which lead to an inevitably horrifying conclusion. Winner of the 1986 *Camera D'Or* prize for a first film at Cannes, Devers' astonishingly accomplished debut movie (suggested by a Tennessee Williams story) is, in turn, enigmatic, droll, sickening and illuminating. Dispassionately observing the development of the relationship, the director eschews the actual depiction of violence, but succeeds in conveying it. Kinky, certainly, but skilful and imaginative.

▶ **Noi Vivi** see We The Living

No Mercy No Future

▶ **Die Berührte**

W. Germany 1981 108 mins col
Helma Sanders-Brahms Filmproduktion

d   **Helma Sanders-Brahms**
sc **Helma Sanders-Brahms, Rita G.**
ph **Thomas Mauch**
m   **Manfred Opitz, Harald Grosskopf**
    Elisabeth Stepanek, Hubertus Von Weyrauch, Irmgard Mellinger, Nguyen Chi Danh, Jorge Reis, Erich Koitzsch-Koltzack

The daughter of wealthy middle-class parents, Veronika Christoph (Stepanek), between bouts of enforced hospitalization and repeated attempts to kill herself, wanders Berlin searching for a Christ figure and giving herself to men on the fringes of society. She sleeps with a Ghanaian (Reis) and believes she has found her Christ. Back in hospital she has visions of her father burning on the Cross. Sanders-Brahms, one of Germany's most radical and adventurous directors, based this film on a letter she received from her co-credited screenwriter, Rita G., about the latter's life as a schizophrenic. Directed and acted with passionate commitment and conviction, this study of modern madness caused an outrage at Cannes and split critical opinion. Is it merely a farrago of sexual and hallucinatory sensationalism, conveyed in shocking images of great skill, or is it a work of multi-layered complexity, crowded with religious emblems, politico-historical allegory, scathing social attack and compassion?

▶ **Non Uccidere** see Thou Shalt Not Kill

▶ **Nora Inu** see Stray Dog

The Northern Star

▶ **L'Étoile Du Nord**

France   1982   124 mins   col
Sara Films/Antenne 2

d   **Pierre Granier-Deferre**
sc **Jean Aurenche, Michel Grisolia, Pierre Granier-Deferre**
ph **Pierre-William Glenn**
m   **Philippe Sarde**
    Simone Signoret, Philippe Noiret, Fanny Cottençon, Julie Jezequel, Jean Rougerie

In a Belgian boarding house in the 1930s, world-weary Edouard (Noiret) fascinates the landlady (Signoret) with his tales of Egypt, but he has blanked out the memory of his murder of an Egyptian millionaire aboard L'Étoile du Nord, the Paris to Amsterdam express. Despite some bizarre alterations to Georges Simenon's novel *Le Locataire*, previously filmed in 1939 (destroyed) and 1947, this is good old-fashioned story-telling, assured by the contribution of veteran screenwriter Aurenche. But most of the pleasure is

provided by the Signoret-Noiret duet and the careful period detail.

Nosferatu

▶ **Nosferatu, Eine Symphonie Des Grauens**

Germany   1921   72 mins   bw
Prana

d   **F.W. Murnau**
sc **Henrik Galeen**
ph **Fritz Arno Wagner**
m   **Silent**
    Max Schreck, Gustav Von Wangenheim, Greta Schroeder-Matray, Alexander Granach, Georg H. Schnell, Ruth Landshoff

Hutter (Wangenheim), a newly married clerk, travels to Transylvania to complete some business with Count Orlock alias Nosferatu, a vampire (Schreck). When the Count's secret is discovered, he is forced to leave his castle. He travels to Bremen (via a ship stricken by the 'plague') in order to take up residence there because he desires Ellen (Schroeder), Hutter's young wife whose picture he had seen. But the sacrifice of Ellen finally vanquishes the vampire. This film marked the first appearance on screen of Bram Stoker's Dracula. In fact, it was pirated from the 1897 novel and the characters' names were changed. (Recent prints restored Stoker's original names.) But the author's widow brought a successful action for breach of copyright and official prints of the film were destroyed, leaving only a few of poor quality. Later, longer and better prints were discovered. It remains arguably the eeriest and most magical of all the multitude of film versions of the famous supernatural tale. The use of real locations to create atmosphere instead of the usual stylized studio sets, the special effects – negative film and speeded-up motion to suggest a ghostly ride – and the spectral gaunt figure of Schreck's Dracula make the first work of Murnau's maturity also one of his best.

▶ **Nosferatu, Eine Symphonie Des Grauens** see Nosferatu

▶ **Nosferatu: Phantom Der Nacht**
see Nosferatu The Vampire

Nosferatu The Vampire

▶ **Nosferatu: Phantom Der Nacht**

W. Germany   1979   107 mins   col
Werner Herzog Filmproduktion/
Gaumont(Paris)

d   **Werner Herzog**
sc **Werner Herzog**
ph **Jörg Schmidt-Reitwein**
m   **Popul Vuh, Florian Fricke, Wagner,
    Gounod
    Klaus Kinski, Isabelle Adjani, Bruno
    Ganz, Walter Ladengast, Roland Topor,
    Dan Van Husen**

Jonathan Harker (Ganz) is sent from Wismar
to Transylvania to complete a property deal
with Count Dracula (Kinski). Dracula, who
has shown an interest in Harker's wife, Lucy
(Adjani), comes to Wismar, coffins and all.
Lucy gives herself up to him, hoping that the
vampire will linger beyond cock-crow and
thus be destroyed. Herzog's attraction to
bizarre characters (*Aguirre, Kaspar Hauser,
Stroszek*) led him naturally into the horror
genre. Although the director claimed that he
went back to the Bram Stoker novel for
inspiration, many of the sequences – as well
as Kinski's make-up – indicate a somewhat
slavish attempt to remake Murnau's 1922
classic version of the Dracula tale. In truth,
colour and sound have subtracted from,
rather than added to, the quality of this rather
irrelevant exercise. The film was released in
the USA with an English soundtrack, but
audiences found it so risible that the original
German was reinstated. There still remains
much to laugh (and shiver) at in the camp
Gothic proceedings and in Kinski's kinky
performance.

▶ **Nostalghia** see Nostalgia

Nostalgia

▶ **Nostalghia**

Italy   1983   126 mins   col/bw

Opera Film/Sovin Film/RAI

d   **Andrei Tarkovsky**
sc **Andrei Tarkovsky, Tonino Guerra**
ph **Giuseppe Lanci**
m   **Verdi, Beethoven, Russian folk music
    Oleg Jankovsky, Erland Josephson,
    Domiziana Giordano, Patrizia Terreno,
    Delia Boccardo**

At a spa in the Tuscan hills, a Russian poet
and musicologist (Jankovsky), researching the
life of an 18th-century composer, meets a
mysterious man (Josephson) who is convinced
that the end of the world is nigh. The Russian
is asked to cross an ancient sulphur pool from
side to side carrying a lighted candle as an
act of faith. Tarkovsky's first film outside the
USSR expresses, through his hero *in extremis*,
great homesickness. This enclosed, melancholy and poetic film is full of personal and
Christian symbols, such as birds bursting
forth from the breast of a statue of the
Madonna. Monochrome is used for the past
in Russia and desaturated colour for the
present. The extremely long takes, the camera
moving almost imperceptibly at times, create
an intense concentration on the many extraordinary images. But there are scenes of an
almost perverse obscurity and the final
sequence is tedious beyond belief.

No Tomorrow

▶ **Sans Lendemain**

France   1939   82 mins   bw
Gray Film/Ciné Alliance

d   **Max Ophüls**
sc **Hans Wilhelm (billed as Jean Villeme),
    Jacot**
ph **Eugen Schüfftan**
m   **Allan Gray
    Edwige Feuillère, Georges Rigaud, Daniel
    Lecourtois, Paul Azais, Gabriello,
    Georges Lannes**

A stripper (Feuillère) in a Montmartre nightclub meets her ex-lover (Rigaud) whom she
hasn't seen for ten years. She wishes him to
bring up her son, but in trying to keep the
truth of her profession from him and in
pretending she is wealthy, she gets involved
with a racketeer (Lannes). As usual Ophüls,

by an elegant sleight of hand, has transformed a novelettish story into a tragic romance. Edwige Feuillère suffers beautifully as the misused mother who becomes a *poule de luxe* in spite of herself, while the men are rather unsympathetic – whether by design or by accident one cannot be sure.

▶ **Not On Your Life** see Executioner, The

Not Reconciled, Or Only Violence Helps Where Violence Rules

▶ **Nicht Versöhnt, Oder Es Hilft Nur Gerwalt,Wo Gewalt Herrscht**

W. Germany   1965   53 mins   bw
Straub-Huillet

d   **Jean-Marie Straub**
sc   **Jean-Marie Straub, Danièle Huillet**
ph   **Wendelin Sachtler, Gerhard Ries, Christian Schwarzwald (Christian Blackwood), Jean-Marie Straub**
m   **Bartok, Bach**
    Heinrich Hargesheimer, Carlheinz Hargesheimer, Martha Ständer, Danièle Straub (Danièle Huillet), Henning Harmssen, Ulrich Hopmann

A half-century (1910-1960) in the lives of the middle-class Fähmel family, headed by the architect Heinrich (Heinrich Hargesheimer at 80, Carlheinz Hargesheimer at 35), and his wife Joanna (Ständer at 70, Straub as a young woman). In less than an hour, Straub deconstructs Heinrich Böll's *Billiards At Half-Past Nine*, a long novel about three generations, by, as he says, 'eliminating as much as possible any historical aura in both costumes and sets, thus giving the images a kind of atonal character'. The film also leaps backwards and forwards in time, giving the impression of the co-existence of past and present, thus making the point that Nazism didn't begin in 1933 or end in 1945. It may not convince those not reconciled to experimental cinema, but to others this first feature will astonish.

▶ **Notre Histoire** see Our Story

La Notte

▶ **aka The Night**

Italy   1961   121 mins   bw
Nepi Film/Silva Film (Rome)/Sofitepid (Paris)

d   **Michelangelo Antonioni**
sc   **Michelangelo Antonioni, Ennio Flaiano, Tonino Guerra**
ph   **Gianni Di Venanzo**
m   **Giorgio Gaslini**
    Marcello Mastroianni, Jeanne Moreau, Monica Vitti, Bernhard Wicki, Rosy Mazzacurati

Twenty four hours in the life of a Milanese novelist (Mastroianni) and his wife (Moreau), during which they visit a dying friend (Wicki) in hospital, go to a nightclub, meet a rich industrialist's daughter (Vitti) at a party, and face the emptiness of their lives and marriage. Following *L'Avventura*, Antonioni further explored an alienated couple placed in an unresponsive environment. Here, the background is the cold beauty of Milan's modern architecture, and the streets through which Moreau (in a role she detested) wanders in the longest and most impressive sequence.

Best Film Berlin 1961

▶ **Notte Brava, La** see Night Heat

▶ **Notte Di San Lorenzo, La** see Night Of San Lorenzo, The

▶ **Notti Bianche, Le** see White Nights

▶ **Notti Di Cabiria, Le** see Nights Of Cabiria

▶ **Nous Étions Un Seul Homme** see We Were One Man

▶ **Nous Ne Vieillerons Pas Ensemble** see We Will Not Grow Old Together

▶ **Nous Sommes Tous Des Assassins** see Are We All Murderers?

▶ **Nouveau Venu, Le** see Newcomer, The

Les Nouveaux Messieurs

▶ **(US: The New Gentlemen)**

France 1928 135 mins bw
Albatros/Séquence

d   **Jacques Feyder**
sc **Charles Spaak, Jacques Feyder,**
ph **Georges Périnal**
m   **Silent**
    Albert Préjean, Gaby Morlay, Henri
    Roussel

An electrician (Préjean) at the Paris Opera is
enamoured of a ballerina (Morlay) who has
an elderly and wealthy protector whom she
decides to leave. The electrician, who is a
politically ambitious trade unionist, decides
to become a deputé. It was following a French
ban on this lively satirical comedy that Feyder
accepted MGM's invitation to direct Garbo
in *The Kiss* in Hollywood. The film, which
pokes fun at rival politicians, was officially
felt to undermine 'the dignity of Parliament
and its ministers', a decision more farcical
than anything the screenplay dreamed up.
The contributions of Préjean, Périnal, and the
designer Lazare Meerson, are a reminder that
it doesn't quite have the *joie de vivre* of Rene
Clair's comedies of the period.

Nouvelle Vague

France 1990 90 mins col
Sara Films/Periphera/Canal Plus/Vega
Film

d   **Jean-Luc Godard**
sc **Jean-Luc Godard**
ph **William Lubtchansky, Christopher**
    Pollock, Frank Messmer
m   **Hindemith**
    Alain Delon, Domiziana Giordano,
    Roland Amstutz, Laurence Cote

A man (Delon) wandering the highways is
knocked down by a fast, smart car driven by
an attractive, rich, young Italian businesswoman (Giordano). She takes him to her
lakeside mansion where he slowly recovers
and enters into a love affair with her. Later,
she seemingly allows him to drown. Enter his
brother (Delon), as confident and domineering as his twin was hesitant and submissive.
Roles become reversed. Filmed in and around

Godard's grandparent's château on Lake
Geneva, where the director spent an idyllic
childhood, it is one of his most ravishing films
for some time, the camera sweeping over the
lakeside landscape and breathtakingly up to
the tops of the trees. There is also a sequence
of lateral camera movements worthy of Max
Ophüls. In addition to the feast of images, is
a feast of sound – musical and verbal. Shaped
like a melancholy oratorio (there are musical
chapters and Latin intertitles) for a spiritually
and ethically dead society, the screenplay
consists almost entirely of quotations, sometimes overlapping (causing severe problems
for the subtitles), from literary, philosophical
and film sources so that a falsely modest
Godard could claim to have been 'only the
conscious organizer of the film'. At the centre
is the fading handsomeness of Delon, bags
under his questing eyes, attempting to break
through the wall of words towards love.

▶ **Novecento** see Nineteen Hundred

▶ **Novembermond** see Novembermoon

Novembermoon

▶ **Novembermond**

W. Germany 1984 107 mins col
Ottokar Runze Filmproduktion(West
Berlin)/ Sun 7 Productions(Paris)

d   **Alexandra Von Grote**
sc **Alexandra Von Grote**
ph **Bernard Zitzermann**
m   **Egisto Macchi**
    Gabriele Osburg, Christiane Millet,
    Danièle Delorme, Stéphane Garcin, Bruno
    Pradal

In 1939, a Jewish girl by the somewhat
unlikely name of November (Osburg), leaves
Hitler's Germany for Paris. Courted by Laurent (Garcin), she falls in love with his sister
Férial (Millet) and they enjoy an idyllic affair
until the Nazi invasion. November ends up
in hiding with Férial and her mother (the
veteran Delorme) in Paris. Férial, to avoid
suspicion, takes a job with a pro-Nazi sympathizer and, at the liberation, is shot for her
pains. Von Grote joins the formidable list of
Berlin's female *auteurs* and made this film
under the auspices of Basis Film, the indepen-

dent company which has encouraged the work of Helke Sander, Helma Sanders-Brahms, Jutta Bruckner, and several others. All the more disappointing, therefore, that *Novembermoon* has so little insight to offer. In taking her story to France, the director fashions clichés of character and situation, and the only real interest of her heroine lies in the casting of Osburg who is sympathetically gauche.

▶ **Novyi Gulliver** see New Gulliver, The

▶ **Novyi Vavilon** see New Babylon, The

Now About These Women

▶ **(US: All These Women)**

▶ **För Att Inte Tala Om Alla Dessa Kvinnor**

Sweden 1964 80 mins col
Svensk Filmindustri

d Ingmar Bergman
sc Ingmar Bergman, Erland Josephson
ph Sven Nykvist
m Eric Nordgren
   Jarl Kulle, Georg Funkquist, Eva Dahlbeck, Karen Kavli, Harriet Andersson, Bibi Andersson, Gertrud Fridh

A pompous music critic (Kulle), attempting a biography of a famous cellist, is hampered in his efforts by a flock of the maestro's female companions. Bergman responded to the mixed critical reaction to his recent 'morbid' films by making a farce that pokes fun at critics. Also, to get away from any accusations of darkness, he decided to use colour for the first time to bring out the prettiness of the ornate sets and flamboyant 1920s costumes. Unfortunately, though well-played, it is a strained, airless and unfunny film. The critics were unamused, and Bergman returned to drama.

▶ **Noz W Wodzie** see Knife In The Water

▶ **Nuit Américaine, La** see Day For Night

La Nuit De Carrefour

France 1932 80 mins bw
Europa Films

d Jean Renoir
sc Jean Renoir
ph Marcel Lucien, Asselin
   Pierre Renoir, Winna Winfried, Georges Koudria, Georges Térof, Dignimont, G.A. Martin, Jean Mitry

When the body of an Amsterdam diamond dealer is found in mysterious circumstances in a small town north of Paris, Inspector Maigret (Renoir) is sent to investigate. Holding each member of the small community suspect in turn, he discovers a link with the Parisian underworld before finally solving the case. The first Simenon thriller to be adapted to the screen, this is a sadly neglected masterpiece of the early sound cinema, largely filmed on location and using direct sound. It effectively captures the atmosphere of the crossroads community with its dank fields, speeding cars, and mysterious inhabitants: the slightly sleazy garage owner, the sinister Dane with a black monocle, the latter's young sister (or wife?) who is attracted to Maigret – a remarkable erotic performance from Winna Winfried. In his first major film role, the director's elder brother gives a totally convincing portrayal of the famous detective.

▶ **Nuit De Varennes, La** see Night Of Varennes, The

▶ **Nuit Et Brouillard** see Night And Fog

▶ **Nuit Fantastique, La** see Fantastic Night, The

▶ **Nuits De La Pleine Lune, Les** see Full Moon In Paris

▶ **Nuits Rouges** see Shadowman

Numéro Deux

France 1975 90 mins col
Sonimage/Bela/SNC

d Jean-Luc Godard
sc Jean-Luc Godard, Anne-Marie Miéville
ph William Lubtchansky

m **Léo Ferré**
   Sandrine Battistella, Pierre Oudry,
   Alexandre Rignault, Rachel Stefanopol

The daily lives of a young couple (Battistella and Oudry), their two children and two grandparents (Rignault and Stefanopol). The wife feels imprisoned in the home, the husband is exhausted at work; she has chronic constipation, he cannot achieve an erection. Godard's 'home movie of family life' is an astonishing experiment in the use of video on to film. For nine-tenths of the duration, only part of the screen is used – two rectangles placed top-left and bottom-right – where different images are seen simultaneously. As always, Godard's manipulation of the medium cannot be separated from the message it contains. Here the relationship between the social, political and sexual is also tied up with how they are portrayed on the part-screen. It does take rather an effort to adjust to the method and it is even more frustrating on TV where the two images are reduced in size. Only at the end is there the relief of a full-screen image, like an orgasm or the end to constipation (number two/numéro deux?).

► **Nunta De Pietra** see Stone Wedding

► **Nun, The** see Religieuse, La

► **Nuovi Angeli, I** see New Angels, The

► **Nuovo Cinema Paradiso** see Cinema Paradiso

► **Nybyggarna** see New Land, The

▶ **Obchod Od Na Korze** see Shop On The High Street, The

The Oberwald Mystery

▶ **Il Mistero Di Oberwald**

Italy   1980   129 mins   col
RAI

d   Michelangelo Antonioni
sc   Michelangelo Antonioni, Tonino Guerra
ph   Luciano Tovoli
m   Richard Strauss, Schoenberg, Brahms
     Monica Vitti, Franco Branciaroli, Luigi
     Diberti, Elisabetta Pozzi, Paolo Bonacelli

The Queen (Vitti) of a middle European country at the turn of the century, in hiding for ten years after the assasination of the King, gives refuge to a fleeing anarchist poet (Branciaroli) who resembles her dead husband and who becomes her 'angel of death' lover. Returning to Italy after some years, and to Monica Vitti with whom he had last worked in 1964 on *The Red Desert*, Antonioni made the flawed but interesting experiment of shooting a film with a video camera, then transferring it on to 35mm. Some of the colours evoke the early two-tone colour processes, and others are decidedly muddy. But the most evident problem lies in the fact that the restrained, ascetic Antonioni is temperamentally at the opposite pole to the flamboyant, aesthetic Cocteau, upon whose *The Eagle Has Two Heads* the film is based. This fustian melodrama seems no less silly when played in such a muted manner by the splendid looking leads, than it did in the hammier method the piece requires (see Cocteau's own screen version).

▶ **Oblomok Imperii** see Fragment Of An Empire

Oblomov

▶ **Neskolko Dnei Iz Zhizni I. I. Oblomov**

USSR   1979   140 mins   col
Mosfilm

d   Nikita Mikhalkov
sc   Nikita Mikhalkov, Aleksander
     Adabashyan
ph   Pavel Lebechev
m   Eduard Artemyev
     Oleg Tabakov, Elena Solovei, Andrei
     Popov, Yuri Bogatyrev

Oblomov (Tabakov), a civil servant in his thirties, decides to take to his bed for the foreseeable future. There he stays, looked after by his servant Zakhar (Popov), until Andrei (Bogatyrev) gets him up and introduces him to the lovely Olga (Solovei), whom the slothful Oblomov marries. As Goncharov's great 1859 satire on the Russian aristocracy is as static as its indolent and infuriating hero, Mikhalkov has tricked out the narrative with copious flashbacks and dreams. Adapted from only a section of the novel, it has some scenes that do justice to the original. Overall, however, it lacks bite and, as played by Tabakov, Oblomov is not a harmful parasite, but an enviable charmer. At over two hours, it might produce an Oblomovist effect on the spectator.

The Occupation In 26 Pictures

▶ **Okupacija U 26 Slika**

Yugoslavia   1978   116 mins   col
Jadran Film/Croatia Film

d   Lordan Zafranovic

sc **Mirko Kovač, Lordan Zafranovic**
ph **Karpo Godina**
m **Alfi Kabiljo**
**Frano Lasic, Milan Strljic, Ivan Klemenc,
Boris Kralj**

Twenty-six events that take place in the first days of the Italian occupation of the coastal town of Dubrovnik during World War II and their effect on three friends from different backgrounds. Brilliantly contrasting the beauties of the medieval town with the nastiness of the Occupation, Zafranovic also reveals how much of the war is fought in the salons of powerful civilians. Some of these pictures are far from pretty, one in particular is as gruesome as any to be found in a modern horror film, but their purpose was part of a serious and uncompromising attempt to understand the reality of the events.

► **Occupe-Toi D'Amélie** see Keep An Eye On Amelia

► **Ochazuke No Aji** see Flavour Of Green Tea Over Rice, The

► **Oci Ciornie** see Dark Eyes

October

► **aka Ten Days That Shook The World**

► **Oktyabr**

USSR 1928 164 mins bw
Sovkino

d **Sergei Eisenstein**
sc **Sergei Eisenstein, Grigori Alexandrov**
ph **Edouard Tissé**
m **Silent**
Nikandrov, Vladimir Popov, Boris Livanov, soldiers of the Red Army, sailors of the Red Navy, and citizens of Leningrad

The 10 days in October 1917 when the Bolsheviks brought down the Kerensky government, showing the dismantling of the statue of Alexander III and the storming of the Winter Palace. The best of a number of films commissioned by the Soviet government to celebrate the tenth anniversary of the Revolution, it was also the most unpopular. Firstly, the official rejection of Trotsky, who had figured prominently in the film, necessitated his being expunged from it. Audiences were disorientated by its dynamic montage, the constantly contrasting images, its visual metaphors (Kerensky is seen as a mechanical peacock) and ambiguous attitude to religious relics – everything that makes the film such a rich experience today. A new print was released in 1967 with music by Shostakovitch on the sound track.

Odd Obsession

► **aka The Key**

► **Kagi**

Japan 1959 107 mins col
Daiei

d **Kon Ichikawa**
sc **Natto Wada, Keiji Hasebe, Kon Ichikawa**
ph **Kazuo Miyagawa**
m **Yasushi Akutagawa**
Ganjiro Nakamura, Machiko Kyo, Tatsuya Nakadai, Junko Kano, Tanie Kitabayashi, Ichiro Sugai, Jun Hamamura

Elderly Mr Kenmochi (Nakamura), obsessed and frightened by his growing impotence, encourages his daughter's fiancé (Nakadai) to show interest in his beautiful young wife in the hope that jealousy will restore his virility. His machinations lead to increasingly bizarre sexual situations, ending in the death of all concerned. Stylishly shot in appropriately muted colours and essentially exposing the unrewarding nature of lust and perversion, Ichikawa's film is an amalgam of morbidity and black farce. The denouement is frankly silly, but executed with the confident sense of tension and perverse air of normalcy which prevails throughout. An undeniably skilful and absorbing excursion into degeneracy, beautifully acted by Nakamura and Kyo, but a bleak and ugly tale which might offend the sensitive.

Special Jury Prize Cannes 1960

Oedipus Rex

► **Edipo Re**

Italy 1967 110 mins col
Arco

d **Pier Paolo Pasolini**
sc **Pier Paolo Pasolini**
ph **Giuseppe Ruzzolini**
m **Pasolini, Mozart, popular Roman songs, ancient Japanese music**
   Franco Citti, Silvana Mangano, Carmelo Bene, Julian Beck, Pier Paolo Pasolini, Alida Valli

Despite the warnings of the blind soothsayer Tiresias (Beck), Oedipus (Citti) unknowingly kills his father and marries his mother Jocasta (Mangano). When the truth is revealed, she kills herself and he puts out his eyes. Pasolini's splendid version of the great Greek tragedy was ravishingly filmed in Morocco, using the desert landscapes and Moorish architecture as backgrounds. Although faithful to Sophocles, it has a surprising prologue and epilogue set in modern times. This Oedipus ends up on the arm of his daughter Antigone, a common blind beggar walking through the streets of 1960s Rome. Perhaps this is an unessary straining after a universality the work already has, but it is cinematically effective. The interesting cast includes *avant-garde* film and theatre director Carmelo Bene as Creon, Julian Beck from New York's Living Theater, and Pasolini himself (typecast?) as the High Priest.

▶ **Oeil Du Malin, L'** see Third Lover, The

▶ **Oeuvre Au Noir, L'** see Abyss, The

Of A Thousand Delights

▶ **(US: Sandra)**

▶ **Vaghe Stelle Dell'Orsa**

Italy 1965 100 mins bw
Vides/Royal

d **Luchino Visconti**
sc **Luchino Visconti, Suso Cecchi D'Amico**
ph **Armando Nannuzzi**
m **César Franck**
   Claudia Cardinale, Jean Sorel, Michael Craig, Marie Bell, Renzo Ricci

Sandra (Cardinale), returning to Italy from America with her husband (Craig) to attend a memorial ceremony for her Jewish scientist father killed by the Nazis, has to face her mother (Bell), whom she believes responsible for his death, and her brother (Sorel) who has incestuous longings for her. Vivid black and white images and strong performances from the women are the main qualities of this operatic tale of guilt, betrayal and incest derived from the Electra myth. But the men are anaemic and the melodramatics override any characterization. The literal translation of the title is 'misty stars of the great bear', the opening line of a poem by Leopardi.

Best Film Venice 1965

▶ **Ofelas** see Pathfinder

▶ **Official Story, The** see Official Version, The

The Official Version

▶ **(US: The Official Story)**

▶ **La Historia Official**

Argentina 1985 115 mins col
Historias Cinematograficas/Progress Communications

d **Luis Puenzo**
sc **Aida Bortnik, Luis Puenzo**
ph **Felix Monti**
m **Atilio Stampone**
   Héctor Alterio, Norma Aleandro, Chela Ruiz, Chunchuna Villafane, Hugo Arana

Roberto (Alterio), a businessman, and his wife Alicia (Aleandro), a history teacher, live comfortably in a suburb of Buenos Aires with their adopted little daughter. Alicia, decent but complacent and intellectually moribund, is gradually made aware of the facts about children removed from detained and tortured parents and then given away. She comes to suspect that her own child might be one of them. Puenzo's film, both unbearably moving (a towering performance from Aleandro) and highly intelligent, weaves several interlocking themes into the centre of what he calls an 'intimate' film. The main focus is Alicia's gradual politicization and recognition of her own unwitting complicity. Her journey of self-discovery, however, exposes the horrors and the imminent collapse of the corrupt military regime under Galtieri.

Best Foreign Film Oscar 1985
Best Actress (Norma Aleandro) Cannes 1985

Of Flesh And Blood

▶ **Les Grands Chemins**

France   1963   95 mins   col
Films Du Saphrène/Films Copernic(Paris)/ Dear Film(Rome)

d   **Christian Marquand**
sc   **Christian Marquand, Paul Gégauff, Pierre La Salle**
ph **Andreas Winding**
m   **Michel Magne**
Robert Hossein, Renato Salvatori, Anouk Aimée, André Bervil, Jean Lefèvre, Andrée Turcy

En route to deliver a jeep in Grenoble, Francis (Salvatori) gives a ride to Samuel (Hossein), a conman and card-sharp, and Anna (Aimée), a young widow. The jeep breaks down near to a hotel owned by Anna and repairs take a week, during which time Francis works on a farm and has an affair with Anna. Samuel, however, cons the locals, who retaliate by crushing his hands in a barn door, thus triggering off a series of bizarre events that end in terrible bloodshed. For his directorial debut, actor Marquand turned to a novel by Jean Giono. The film is strong on mood and beautifully photographed in attractive colour, and there is an attempt to penetrate the depths of Giono's abstract themes about strange loyalties. However, the movie fails to get to the heart of the matter, partly because the casting is not ideal, while new characters – notably Anna – are introduced, along with extraneous sex and violence. (Could it be the hand of Roger Vadim, who 'supervised'?) Marquand's second career foundered forever on one more film, the notoriously awful *Candy* (1968).

▶ **Offret** see Sacrifice, The

▶ **Oh, Amelia!** see Keep An Eye On Amelia

▶ **Ohayo** see Good Morning

Ohm Krüger

Germany   1941   135 mins   bw
Tobis

d   **Hans Steinhoff**
sc   **Harold Bratt, Kurt Heuser**
ph **Fritz Arno Wagner**
m   **Theo Mackeben**
Emil Jannings, Franz Schafheitlin, Ferdinand Marian, Gustav Gründgens, Hedwig Wangel

Heroic Boers led by Paul Kruger (Jannings) fight against the brutal British in South Africa. British missionaries incite the natives to attack the Boers, many of whom are put into concentration camps. But there are victories and Kruger goes to London to negotiate with a whisky-swigging Queen Victoria (Wangel). One of the Nazi regime's biggest propaganda hits was made on a lavish scale with fine photography. Some of the crudities of the message in the long-winded screenplay were somewhat ameliorated by the impressive avuncular performance of Jannings (who also directed a few sequences) as the first president of South Africa. The film would probably be welcomed by the present South African regime. Steinhoff, Goebbels pet propagandist, died in a plane crash in 1945.

▶ **Oh, Sun** see Soleil Ô

▶ **Oiseaux Vont Mourir Au Pérou, Les** see Birds Come To Die In Peru, The

▶ **Oka Oorie Katha** see Outsiders, The

▶ **Oktyabr** see October

▶ **Okupacija U 26 Slika** see Occupation In 26 Pictures, The

▶ **Old And New** see General Line, The

▶ **Old Capital, The** see Twin Sisters Of Kyoto

The Old Country Where Rimbaud Died

▶ **Le Vieux Pays Où Rimbaud Est Mort**

Canada/France   1977   113 mins   col

Cinak/Filmoblic/Institut National De
L'Audiovisuel

d   **Jean Pierre Lefèbvre**
sc **Mireille Amiel, Jean Pierre Lefèbvre**
ph **Guy Dufaux**
m   **Claude Fonfrède**
    **Marcel Sabourin, Anouk Ferjac, Myriam
    Boyer, Mark Lesser, Germaine Delbat**

Québecois Abel (Sabourin) records his
impressions of visiting France, 'the Old
Country'. He stays in Paris, then goes to
Charleville, the home town of the woman
(Boyer) with whom he is having an affair,
and then on to the Côte D'Azur where he
meets a probation officer (Ferjac) who gains
his affection. Abel then decides to return to
Canada. This episodic exploration of the
relationship between France and French Canada takes the form of a letter home by the
film's taciturn hero, who observes and listens
'to see if there were still Frenchmen in
France – to see if they resembled me'. Much
of what he (and Lefèbvre, the most renowned
of Québecois directors) observes is amusing,
touching and surprising, despite the often self-
conscious use of long takes, a static camera
and quotes from Rimbaud on the sound
track.

The Oldest Profession

▶ **Le Plus Vieux Métier Du Monde**

France/Italy/W. Germany 1967 115
mins col
Gibé/Francoriz/Rialto/Rizzoli

d   **Franco Indovini, Mauro Bolognini,
    Philippe De Broca, Michel Pfleghar,
    Claude Autant-Lara, Jean-Luc Godard**
sc **Ennio Flaiano, Daniel Boulanger, Georges
    and André Tabet, Jean Aurenche, Jean-
    Luc Godard**
ph **Pierre Lhomme**
m   **Michel Legrand**
    **Michèle Mercier, Elsa Martinelli,
    Gastone Moschin, Jean-Claude Brialy,
    Jeanne Moreau, Raquel Welch, Martin
    Held, France Anglade, Jacques Charrier,
    Anna Karina, Jean-Pierre Léaud**

Five episodes illustrate prostitution through
the ages – prehistoric times, Ancient Rome,
the French Revolution, *La Belle Époque*, and

Paris in the year 2,000. Movie directors, one
of the newest professions, pay tribute to the
oldest profession, no doubt recognizing certain similarities – certainly in this commercial
venture. One has to sit through four sketches
ranging from the mildly amusing to the completely unfunny before coming to the Godard
chapter, the only one with artistic merit. Until
1968, prostitution was a major theme in his
films, and here he elaborates on it through
the eyes of a visitor from outer space.

▶ **Old Maid, The** see Vieille Fille, La

The Old Well

▶ **Lao Jing**

China 1987 130 mins col
Xi'an Film Studio

d   **Wu Tianming**
sc **Zheng Yi**
ph **Chen Wancai, Zhang Yimou**
m   **Xu Youfu**
    **Zhang Yimou, Liang Yujin, Lu Liping,
    Wu Tianming, Xie Yin**

In a dusty, barren village in the remote Tiah-
ang mountain region of China the inhabitants
have been digging for water for years at great
cost in resources and lives. The village's first
college graduate (Yimou) returns as a hydro-
geologist and organizes the villagers to dig
for another well. The undertaking ends in
disaster, killing his brother, while he himself
is trapped underground with the girl he loves
(Yujin). They are rescued but the struggle to
bring water to the village continues. An
intensely absorbing portrait of a backward
community resisting a move into the modern
world, as represented by the young graduate,
memorably played by the cinematographer of
Yellow Earth (1984) and *The Big Parade*
(1986) in his first appearance on the screen.
The 48-year-old director, head of the Xi'an
Film Studio since 1983, after having given
younger directors their first breaks, reveals an
ability to make a potent political statement
with flesh-and-blood characters in real situations.

▶ **Ole Dole Doff** see Who Saw Him Die?

Olivia

France 1950 96 mins bw
Memnon Films

d **Jacqueline Audry**
sc **Colette Audry, Pierre Laroche**
ph **Christian Matras**
m **Pierre Sancan**
  **Edwige Feuillère, Simone Simon, Claire
  Olivia, Yvonne De Bray, Suzanne
  Dehelly, Lesly Meynard, Rita Roanda**

In the 1880s Olivia (Olivia), an English girl,
attends a French boarding school run by two
sisters, Mademoiselle Julie (Feuillère) and
Mademoiselle Cara (Simon). She is enchanted
by the frivolous atmosphere, but it transpires
that staff and pupils are split into two factions,
and Olivia's gravitation towards Julie precipi-
tates a severe crisis. This film is based on the
autobiographical novel by Lytton Strachey's
sister, Dorothy Bussy. A colourful character,
she too subscribed to *Olivia's* epigraph – 'Love
has always been the chief business of my life'.
Like *Mädchen In Uniform*, this story of hothouse emotions with Lesbian undercurrents is
richly dramatic, but also contains humour and
presents the teachers as willing participants in
the relationships. Audry has brought this
material to the screen with tremendous style
and period authenticity and with a superbly
well-chosen cast, but it slightly disappoints in
lacking the required depths of passion.

▶ **Oltre Il Bene E Il Male** see Beyond
Good And Evil

▶ **Olvidados, Los** see Young And The
Damned, The

▶ **Olympia** see Olympiad

Olympiad

▶ **(US: Olympia)**
▶ **Olympische Spiele 1936**

Germany 1938 118 mins (Part I –
Festival Of The Nations) – 107 mins
(Part II – Festival Of Beauty) bw
Tobis

d **Leni Riefenstahl**

sc **Leni Riefenstahl**
ph **Hans Ertl and others**
m **Herbert Windt**

A documentary on the 1936 Berlin Olympics
attended by Hitler. A prologue links the ideals
of beauty in Greek antiquity with those of the
Third Reich. Part I concentrates on the track
events inside the stadium; Part II takes in
events around the stadium and in the Olympic
village. Riefenstahl was commissioned to film
the Games 'as a song of praise to the ideals of
National Socialism'. As there could be no
retakes of the great moments, the film was
organized with Nazi efficiency. The director
had over 30 cameramen as well as planes and
airships at her disposal, and spent two years
in the cutting room. Slow and reverse motion
make the diving sequence a *tour de force*, the
Marathon becomes an 'epic hymn to endurance'; the yacht racing under a darkened sky,
and the screen filling with thousands of girls
swinging clubs are some of the other remarkable sequences. But it is easy to be seduced by
the exceptional beauty of many of the images
into ignoring the sinister significance of the
swastikas, and to forget the persecution of the
Jews that was taking place outside the walls of
the stadium.

▶ **Olympische   Spiele   1936** see
Olympiad

▶ **On Any Street** see Night Heat

One Deadly Summer

▶ **L'Été Meurtrier**

France 1983 133 mins col
SNC/CAPAC/T.F.1 Films

d **Jean Becker**
sc **Sébastien Japrisot**
ph **Etienne Becker**
m **Georges Delerue**
  **Isabelle Adjani, Alain Souchon, Jenny
  Clève, Suzanne Flon, François Cluzet,
  Manuel Gélin, Maria Machado**

Elle (Adjani) comes to live in a small Provençal village with her crippled father and German mother. Nineteen, beautiful, sexually
provocative and extraordinarily moody, she
captivates Pin Pon (Souchon), moves in with

his family, and traps him into marrying her as part of a plan to avenge her mother's rape (which led to her birth). Japrisot, adapting his own novel, has constructed an intricate psychosexual mystery, using voice-over narrative which shifts from Pin Pon to Elle and, in so doing, subtly and shockingly reveals Elle's obsessions. Dialogue, action, and Adjani's mercurial performance gradually unfold a tale of mental derangement, the roots of which are explained in well-judged flashbacks. If the film is a mite too long and occasionally inclined to melodrama, it is nonetheless directed with care and conviction, its village life beautifully caught, and it provides an extra pleasure in the veteran Suzanne Flon's portrayal of a stone deaf but perceptive family aunt.

One Fine Day

▶ **Un Certo Giorno**

Italy 1969 105 mins col
Cinema s.p.a./Italnoleggio/Istituto Luce

d   **Ermanno Olmi**
sc **Ermanno Olmi**
ph **Lamberto Caimi**
m   **Gino Negri**
    Brunetto Del Vita, Maria Crosignani, Vitaliano Damioli, Lidia Fuortes, Raffaele Modugno

A middle-aged philandering advertising executive (Del Vita) runs down a workman on the day he is offered the managing directorship of his company. On trial for dangerous driving, he reassesses his job and marriage. The first of Olmi's films to deal with the middle classes is less moving and original than his studies of the lower echelons of society, although he applies the same perception and brings the same humanity to bear on his characters, avoiding easy satire on the advertising industry. This is achieved by his continuing use of non-professionals. The dialogue and events were based on conversations Olmi had with Del Vita, an advertising executive in real life.

One Life

▶ **Une Vie**

France 1958 88 mins col

Agnès Delahaie Production/Nepi Film

d   **Alexandre Astruc**
sc **Roland Laudenbach, Alexandre Astruc**
ph **Claude Renoir**
m   **Roman Vlad**
    Maria Schell, Christian Marquand, Ivan Desny, Antonella Lualdi, Pascale Petit, Marie-Hélène Dasté

Young, innocent and aristocratic Jeanne (Schell) marries Julien (Marquand), unaware that her handsome husband is a womanizer, but gradually comes to realize that he has no desire to be with her. Julien's affair with a friend's wife (Lualdi) leads to his death, leaving Jeanne and her son to face life alone. Astruc's refined treatment of De Maupassant's story catches the sexual tensions of the original, but otherwise misses its depths. Schell's cloying sweetness is no help, but Marquand, Lualdi and Petit are excellent, and the 19th-century country milieu is beautifully caught by Renoir's richly textured, almost impressionistic camerawork.

One Man's War

▶ **La Guerre D'Un Seul Homme**

France 1981 106 mins bw
Marion's Films/INA/ZDF(W. Germany)

d   **Edgardo Cozarinsky**
sc **Edgardo Cozarinsky with text by Ernst Junger**
ph **Newsreel cameramen**
m   **Hans Pfitzner, Richard Strauss, Schönberg, Franz Schreker**

French newsreels during the German occupation of 1940-1944 show the life in Paris: the theatre, fashions and sport, as well as propaganda on the progress of the war and the benevolence of the Third Reich. Counterpointing these bland commentaries of half-truths is a linking narration from the Paris diaries of Ernst Junger, a German officer critical of Nazism, and a superb use of music. Cozarinsky, a Jewish Argentinian exile living in Paris, uses a method that goes beyond the mere documentary into the realms of a meditation on history, disinformation, and the inability of people to see their own times with any clarity.

1 + 1 = 3

W. Germany 1979 85 mins col
Peter Genée & Von Fürstenberg
Produktion/Heidi Genée Filmproduktion

d Heidi Genée
sc Heidi Genée
ph Gernot Roll
m Andreas Köbner
   **Adelheid Arndt, Dominik Graf, Christoph
   Quest, Helga Storck, Dietrich Leiding**

Katarina (Arndt), an unmarried actress in
Munich becomes pregnant. Initially shocked
at the news, her boyfriend Bernhard (Graf)
later offers a proposal, and money for an
abortion. Both are refused, since Katarina is
determined to have her child while avoiding
the pitfalls of marriage as exemplified by her
sister's unhappy situation. Katarina takes a
holiday, meets divorced Jürgen (Quest) and
ends up living with him. It becomes clear that
his major enthusiasm is for the forthcoming
baby to whom Bernhard also continues to lay
claim... This committedly feminist film is, in
fact, played with much gentle comedy and
offers a heroine who is warm, wry and attractive, as well as steadfastly independent.
Involved in the chaos of her sister's life,
Katarina is constantly surrounded by children, and Genée sketches in the domestic
detail of life with an eye both caring and
sharp, while her male characters are bemused
inadequates rather than reactionary heavies.
The pacy narrative reveals a world that, even
when turbulent, is charmingly familiar.

One Sings, The Other Doesn't

▶ **L'Une Chante, L'Autre Pas**

France 1976 120 mins col
Ciné Tamaris/Société Française De
Production/Institut National De
L'Audiovisuel/Contrechamp(Paris)/
Paradise Films(Brussels)/Population
Films(Curaçao)

d Agnès Varda
sc Agnès Varda
ph Charlie Van Damme
m François Wertheimer
   **Valérie Mairesse, Thérèse Liotard, Robert
   Dadiès, Gisèle Halimi, Ali Raffi, Jean-
   Pierre Pellegrin, Rosalie Varda, Mathieu
   Demy**

Pauline (Mairesse), aged 17, helps her friend
Suzanne (Liotard), 22 and the unmarried
mother of two children, to procure an abortion. Pauline becomes a singer, travels the
world, and has children by her Iranian lover;
Suzanne returns to her parents' farm, educates
herself, and runs a family planning clinic.
They meet 10 years later at an anti-abortion
demonstration, and again 12 years after that,
this time having kept in touch. After a nine-
year absence from features, Varda made a
triumphant return with this irrefutably feminist film, which is somewhat marred by the
softness of its glossy, romantic approach.
Taking Simone De Beauvoir's maxim that
'Women are made, not born,' as her theme,
the director presents two friends of different
temperaments and backgrounds who both
face adversity but achieve independence and
fulfilment. Mairesse and Liotard are stunning.

One Summer Of Happiness

▶ **Hon Dansade En Sommar**

Sweden 1952 103 mins bw
Nordisk Tonefilm/Lennart Landheim

d Arne Mattsson
sc W. Semitjov
ph Göran Strindberg
m Sven Skjöld
   **Folke Sundqvist, Ulla Jacobsson, Edvin
   Adolphson, John Elfstrom, Irma
   Christensson**

Göran (Sundqvist), having recently finished
his studies, spends a summer in the country
with his uncle (Adolphson). He meets Kerstin
(Jacobsson), the innocent daughter of the
neighbouring farmer, and they fall in love.
The puritanical atmosphere and the opposition of the rigid pastor (Elfstrom) impose
constraints, but they manage to find some
happiness until their affair is destroyed by
tragedy. With the help of an excellent cast,
Mattsson gives a fresh and moving account
of young love, strengthened by the lyrical
photography of nature and landscape. This
is contrasted with the stark, low-angle shooting of the sequences with the pastor designed
to project the harsh religion which he rep-

resents. But the director's moral point remains unclear due to an unsatisfactory ending. The film's shimmering nude bathing/love scene caused much controversy at the time.

One Way Or Another

▶ **De Cierta Manera**

Cuba   1974   79 mins   bw
Instituto Cubano Del Arte E Industria Cinematográficos

d   **Sara Gómez**
sc **Sara Gómez, Tomás González Pérez**
ph **Luis García**
m   **Sergio Vitier**
    Mario Balmaseda, Yolanda Cuéllar, Mario Limonta, Guillermo Díaz

Two young lovers, a mulatto worker (Balmaseda) in a bus assembly factory and a middle-class schoolteacher (Cuéllar), learn about each other's backgrounds and the class prejudices they grew up with before embracing the revolution. Sara Gómez, who made a number of impressive short documentaries before her only feature, died from an asthma attack while it was being completed. The first Cuban film to be directed by a woman confronts the problems of being both black and female in the Third World. This is brilliantly done by Gómez (also known as Sara Gómez Yera), subverting a conventional love story by interjecting documentary footage, interviews and voice over and with the characters occasionally speaking directly to the camera.

▶ **One Wild Moment** see Summer Affair, A

Onibaba

▶ **aka The Hole**

Japan   1964   104 mins   bw
Kindai Eiga Kyokai/Tokyo Eiga

d   **Kaneto Shindo**
sc **Kaneto Shindo**
ph **Kiyomi Juroda**
m   **Hikaru Hayashi**
    Nobuko Otowa, Yitsuko Yoshimura, Kei Sato

In medieval times, on a remote plain, a widow (Yoshimura) and her mother-in-law (Otowa) kill wandering Samurai, put their bodies in a hole in the ground and sell their armour and valuables, until the daughter-in-law falls in love with one of them. This strange and violent folk-tale is marred by a penchant for sensationalism and sentimentality. But the strong performances, notably from Otowa, Shindo's regular star, and the eerie atmosphere, were partly responsible for its popularity in the West.

▶ **Only The French Can** see French Cancan

▶ **Onna No Rekishi** see Woman's Life, A

▶ **On Ne Meurt Que 2 Fois** see He Died With His Eyes Open

▶ **Onorevole Angelina, L'** see Angelina

On Purge Bébé

France   1931   62 mins   bw
Braunberger-Richebé

d   **Jean Renoir**
sc **Jean Renoir**
ph **Théodor Sparkühl, Roger Hubert**
    Michel Simon, Louvigny, Marguerite Pierry, Olga Valéry, Fernandel

Monsieur Follavoine (Louvigny), a porcelain manufacturer, attempts to clinch a deal with Monsieur Chouilloux (Simon) to supply the French army with 200,000 unbreakable chamber pots. Meanwhile, Follavoine's wife, obsessed with their baby's constipation, inflicts the purge on the hapless Chouilloux. Renoir's first sound picture, adapted from a Feydeau farce, is little more than a piece of filmed theatre. Shot quickly and cheaply, and using long takes on an artificial-looking set, with most of the action staged in front of a stationary camera, it nonetheless swiftly earned a substantial profit, thus enabling Renoir to make the Michel Simon picture he really wanted – *La Chienne*.

▶ **Open City** see Rome, Open City

Open Doors

▶ **Porte Aperte**

    Italy 1990 108 mins col
    Erre Prods/Urania Film

d **Gianni Amelio**
sc **Gianni Amelio, Vincenzo Cerami**
ph **Tonino Nardi**
m **Franco Piersanti**
    Gian Maria Volonté, Ennio Fantastichini, Renato Carpentieri, Renzo Giovampietro, Tuccio Musumeci, Silverio Blasi, Vitalba Andrea, Lydia Alfonsi

One morning in Palermo in 1937, Tommaso Scalia (Fantastichini) commits three murders. At the trial, one of the judges, Vito Di Francesco (Volonté), tries to protect the assassin from the death penalty, even though the accused himself shows little interest in being saved. The judge investigates, probes and questions, much to the disgust of the presiding judge (Giovampietro). But one of the jurors, a farmer (Carpentieri), is on his side. Although there are three brutal murders and a rape in the first few minutes, they are filmed in long shot or discreetly cut away, a technique that typifies the director's restrained approach to the whole of this true case history. But just as Amelio's earlier film *Blow To The Heart* (1982) was not specifically about terrorism, *Open Doors* has no interest in tackling the big themes of Fascism and the death penalty head on. Instead, it subtly concentrates on the character of the tolerant judge – Volonté oozing the milk of human kindness. The film fails to reveal enough about the man on trial and too many strands are left dangling. What, for example, happens to the young son of the murderer? He is not only neglected *in* the film, but also, unforgivably, *by* the film. For all its honesty, its excellent performances, smoothly prowling camera, brooding images, and the drama of the court case, this work finally lacks the edge that Franco Rosi might have brought to it. In addition, the portrayal of the liberal Dostoevsky-reading farmer living in a rural idyll, is an unconvincing Utopian image that softens the impact even further.

Opera Do Malandro

    Brazil 1986 108 mins col
    MK2 Productions (Paris)/Austra (Brazil)/T.F.1. Films

d **Ruy Guerra**
sc **Chico Buarque, Orlando Senna, Ruy Guerra**
ph **Antonio Luis Mendes**
m **Chico Buarque**
    Edson Celulari, Claudia Ohana, Elba Ramalho, Ney Latorraca, Fabio Sabag

Max (Celulari) is a pimp and profiteer, but passionately anti-Nazi and pro-American. During the period between Pearl Harbor and Brazil's declaration of war on Germany, his complicated activities involve him heavily with two women – his regular girlfriend who is a whore, and the criminally minded daughter of a wealthy German club owner – as well as with his friend, the corrupt police chief. Guerra's musical film is an eclectic, indeed, somewhat chaotic affair, being a loose attempt at a Brazilian version of *The Threepenny Opera*, combined with images and assumptions drawn from the Hollywood musical. Its political and social messages are somewhat hazy, but there is enjoyment to be had from some imaginative dance sequences and from the sheer ebullience of the piece.

Ophelia

    France 1962 105 mins bw
    Boreal

d **Claude Chabrol**
sc **Claude Chabrol, Martial Matthieu**
ph **Jean Rabier**
m **Pierre Jansen**
    André Jocelyn, Alida Valli, Claude Cerval, Juliette Mayniel, Robert Burnier

Yvan Lesurf (Jocelyn), son of a wealthy industrialist, is grief-stricken at his father's death and disturbed by the swift remarriage of his mother (Valli) to his uncle (Cerval). He behaves badly towards them and, on seeing Olivier's film of *Hamlet*, draws parallels with Gertrude and Claudius, and plots revenge. Chabrol plays an inventive, if not altogether successful, game in this film, delighting in the bizarre notions of his eccentric hero and upending the Shakespearian details to suit himself. Set in a gloomy mansion and its appropriate surroundings, the film is photographed with flair and cool detachment, well played, and enhanced by acid wit as well as some brilliant set-pieces.

▶ **Opname** see In For Treatment

Orage

> France 1938 85 mins bw
> André Daven

d **Marc Allégret**
sc **Marcel Achard, H.G. Lustig**
ph **Armand Thirard**
m **Georges Auric**
> **Charles Boyer, Michèle Morgan, Lisette Lanvin, Robert Manuel, Jean-Louis Barrault**

André Pascaud (Boyer) is indifferent to the wife (Lanvin) who adores him, while his brother-in-law Gilbert (Manuel) loves Françoise (Morgan) who doesn't reciprocate his feelings. At Gilbert's behest, André looks up Françoise in Paris and they fall passionately for one another, enjoying a brief idyll before his wife reclaims him and tragedy ensues. Adapted from a play by the popular Henri Bernstein, this triangular tale starts out well but ends up drowning in its own repetitive intensity. In one of her first major roles, Morgan's personality and looks make an impact, though her acting abilities were to improve substantially with experience. Boyer is as smooth, attractive and skilful as always, and Barrault lends the colour of his unique personality to a small role. A competently directed but disappointing romance.

Orchestra Rehearsal

▶ **Prova D'Orchestra**

> Italy 1978 72 mins col
> Daimo Cinematografica(Rome)/Albatros Produktion(Munich)

d **Federico Fellini**
sc **Federico Fellini, Brunello Rondi**
ph **Giuseppe Rotunno**
m **Nino Rota**
> **Balduin Baas, Clara Colosimo, Elisabeth Labi, Ronaldo Bonacchi, Ferdinando Villella, Giovanni Javarone, David Mauhsell, Francesco Aluigi, Andy Miller, Sibyl Mostert, Franco Mazzieri, Daniele Pagani, Filippo Trincia, Claudio Ciocca, Cesare Martignoni**

Orchestral musicians argue the merits of their respective instruments while waiting for a rehearsal that is to be filmed as a television documentary. When the German conductor (Baas) arrives, the ancient building is shaken by rumblings, the electricity fails and a demolition crew gets to work. Meanwhile, the musicians stage a revolt against the conductor's authoritarianism. However, by employing increasingly Hitlerian techniques and tone, he finally persuades them that to play together is their only salvation. This is clearly intended as an allegory about totalitarianism, but that's about all that *is* clear in this lumbering, banal and simplistic exercise. The music doesn't pass muster as a symphony, but is nonetheless beguiling and, sadly, Nino Rota's last score before his death.

Ordet

▶ **aka The Word**

> Denmark 1955 125 mins bw
> Palladium

d **Carl Dreyer**
sc **Carl Dreyer**
ph **Henning Bendtsen**
m **Poul Schierbeck**
> **Henrik Malberg, Emil Hass Christensen, Preben Lerdorff Rye, Caj Kristiansen, Birgitte Federspiel, Ejner Federspiel**

In a remote, West Jutland farming community, a severe father (Malberg) of three sons refuses to let one of them, Anders (Kristiansen), marry the daughter of a man with whom he has religious differences. When Inge (Birgitte Federspiel), his daughter-in-law, married to Mikkel (Christensen), dies in childbirth, Johannes (Rye), the visionary son, prays for her resurrection. Dreyer's penultimate work, based on a famous play by Kai Munk (already filmed by Gustaf Molander in 1943), is an extraordinary expression of spiritual optimism. Dreyer achieves the powerful effects by deceptively simple means. A tale of a miraculous resurrection brought about by human love could have been pious, sentimental and even risible – Dreyer makes it (using only 114 shots) into an enriching experience.

Best Film Venice 1955

▶ **Ordnung** see All In Order

▶ **Orfeu Negro** see Black Orpheus

The Organizer

▶ **I Compagni**

Italy 1963 130 mins bw
Lux/Vides/Mediteranée/Cinema/Avala

d Mario Monicelli
sc Age, Scarpelli, Mario Monicelli
ph Giuseppe Rotunno
m Carlo Rustichelli
Marcello Mastroianni, Renato Salvatori, Annie Girardot, Gabriella Giorgelli, Bernard Blier, François Périer, Folco Lulli

In turn-of-the-century Turin, the factory workers are on strike for better pay and conditions. They are helped to form a union by an impoverished aristocratic professor (Mastroianni). Monicelli, renowned for comedies tinged with a social purpose, successfully handles this poignant social drama tinged with humour. Although its relevance to present-day labour conditions is lessened by the rather picturesque and detailed period setting (often in the style of daguerrotypes), the film still packs a reasonable punch. The cast give well-rounded characterizations, particularly a myopic Mastroianni as the organizer, although the Italian title, 'Comrades', is closer to the plot's communal nature.

▶ **Orgueilleux, Les** see Proud Ones, The

Orion's Belt

▶ **Orions Belte**

Norway 1985 105 mins col
Filmeffekt

d Ola Solum

sc Richard Harris
ph Harald Paalgard
m Geir Bøhren, Bent Åserud
Helge Jordal, Sverre Anker Ousdal, Hans Ola Sørlie, Kjersti Holmen, Vidar Sandem, Jon Eikemo

Three sailors earn a living running tours in the North Sea and simultaneously practising minor thefts and fiddles on the side, until their old freighter puts ashore at the site of a Soviet spy installation and they become fatally involved in international politics and violence. A notably big-budget production by Norwegian standards, the film is strikingly located in the isolated Arctic reaches of Spitzbergen, but its content veers unevenly between serious ideology and over-the-top spy thriller. Efficiently made, it is often enjoyably gripping, but has ponderous stretches during which only the atmosphere and visual detail hold the attention.

▶ **Orions Belte** see Orion's Belt

▶ **Orlacs Hände** see Hands Of Orlac, The

▶ **Oro Di Napoli, L'** see Gold Of Naples

▶ **Orökbefogadás** see Adoption

▶ **Oro, Plata, Mata** see Gold, Silver, Bad Luck

▶ **Orphée** see Orpheus

Orpheus

▶ **Orphée**

France 1950 112 mins bw
André Paulvé/Films Du Palais Royal

d Jean Cocteau
sc Jean Cocteau
ph Nicolas Hayer
m Georges Auric
Jean Marais, François Périer, Maria Casarès, Marie Déa, Edouard Dermithe, Juliette Greco

The poet Orpheus (Marais) falls in love with the Princess of Death (Casarès), while her chauffeur, the angel Heurtebise (Périer), falls for the poet's wife Eurydice (Déa). When Heurtebise takes Eurydice to the Underworld through the looking-glass, Orpheus follows to get her back. Probably Cocteau's finest film, this is a perfect marriage between Greek legend and his own mythology. Although he uses reverse slow-motion and negative images to suggest the Underworld, the modern-day domestic life of Mr and Mrs Orpheus is filmed 'realistically', effectively elaborating the theme of the poet caught between the worlds of the real and the imaginary. This witty and haunting film can be considered the centrepiece of Cocteau's entire *oeuvre*, and of his Orphic trilogy (it comes between *The Blood Of The Poet* and *The Testament Of Orpheus*), in particular.

Osaka Elegy

▶ **Naniwa Hika**

Japan   1936   66 mins   bw
Daiichi

d   **Kenji Mizoguchi**
sc **Yoshitaka Yoda**
ph **Minoru Miki**
m   **Koichi Takagi**
    Isuzu Yamada, Seiichi Takegawa, Chiyoko Okura, Shinpachiro Asaka, Benkei Shiganoya

A young telephonist (Yamada) in a pharmaceutical company allows herself to be set up as the mistress of her married boss (Shiganoya) in order to resolve the debts of her drunken father (Takegawa) and put her brother (Okura) through school. When turned out by the boss, she resorts to prostitution. The title explains the tone, an elegy for the heroine and others like her. Yamada, the great actress who starred 20 years later in Kurosawa's *Throne Of Blood* and Ozu's *Tokyo Twilight*, is wonderful at the centre of the film, finally looking accusingly at the camera and, by implication, the audience. The film, with its twin masterpiece, *Sisters Of The Gion*, of the same year, brought fame to Mizoguchi and began his creative partnership with the unknown writer Yoshitaka Yoda, which lasted through more than 20 pictures.

▶ **Os Canibais** see Cannibals, The

▶ **Osenny Marafon** see Autumn Marathon

▶ **Os Fuzis** see Guns, The

▶ **Ososhiki** see Funeral, The

▶ **Oss Emellan** see Close To The Wind

Ossessione

Italy   1942   135 mins   bw
Industria Cinematografica Italiana

d   **Luchino Visconti**
sc **Antonio Pietrangeli, Mario Alicata, Gianni Puccini, Giuseppe De Santis, Luchino Visconti**
ph **Aldo Tonti, Domenico Scala**
m   **Giuseppe Rosati**
    Massimo Girotti, Clara Calamai, Juan De Landa, Elia Marcuzzo, Dhia Christiani

Gino (Girotti), a handsome drifter, and Giovanna (Calamai), the beautiful and desperately unhappy wife of Bragana (De Landa), an elderly and boorish innkeeper, have an affair which leads them to kill Bragana, whereupon their relationship drifts to inevitable tragedy. Significant both as the first film to be labelled Neo-Realist (by writer Pietrangeli) and the first to be directed by Visconti, *Ossessione* displays control, assurance, and the director's eye for detail. However, James M. Cain's study of fatal lust in rural America, *The Postman Always Rings Twice*, did not travel well to provincial Italy. Realistic it certainly is, but the reworking of the story's context, the addition of new characters, and Visconti's coolly distanced vision resulted, in spite of a couple of inspired moments, in a film that is curiously devoid of passion. The French had already attempted it as *Le Dernier Tournant* in 1939, but Hollywood would do it best in 1945 and 1981 under its original title.

▶ **Ostatni Etap** see Last Stage, The

▶ **Ostře Sledované Vlaky** see Closely Observed Trains

▶ **Otac Na Službenom Putu** see When Father Was Away On Business

Otello

Italy 1986 123 mins col
Cannon Productions (Rome)/Italian
International Film

d **Franco Zeffirelli**
sc **Franco Zeffirelli (libretto by Arrigo
Boito)**
ph **Ennio Guarnieri**
m **Giuseppe Verdi (conducted by Lorin
Maazel)**
**Placido Domingo (Otello), Katia
Ricciarelli (Desdemona), Justino Diaz
(Iago), Petra Malakova (Emilia), Urbano
Barberini (Cassio)**

Otello the Moor, military governor of Cyprus,
is deceived by Iago into believing that his
wife, Desdemona, is unfaithful, and murders
her. Verdi's late, great Shakespearean tragedy
is given the full panoply of cinematic embellishment: wonderful Greek locations, magnificent colour alternately vivid, burnished
and white, a superb re-creation of a Renaissance world after the manner of its paintings.
The principals, too, are cast from the best
available, and there are thus moments to
admire and enjoy. However, in an effort to
popularize the work and highlight its most
overtly passionate elements, Zeffirelli has
over-reached himself in an enterprise that is,
alas, hindered by a series of technical imperfections. Worse, the director has tampered
with Verdi's (and Shakespeare's) nuances, the
score has suffered unacceptable excisions, notably that of Desdemona's famous 'Willow
Song', and the camera has run riot with close-
ups and histrionic flourishes that serve finally,
to obscure the painful impact of both Shakespeare *and* Verdi.

Othello

USSR 1955 109 mins col
Mosfilm

d **Sergei Yutkevitch**
sc **Sergei Yutkevitch**
ph **Yevgeny Andrikanis**
m **Aram Khachaturian**
**Sergei Bondarchuk, Irina Skobotseva,
Andrei Popov, A. Maximova, Vladimir
Soshalsky, Evgeny Vesnik**

Othello (Bondarchuk) is led by his ensign
Iago (Popov) to believe that his wife Desdemona (Skobtseva) has been unfaithful to him

with his lieutenant Cassio (Soshalsky). Bondarchuk, following in the footsteps of Emil
Jannings and Orson Welles in the role of the
Moor on celluloid, gives an admirable but
rather passionless performance, concentrating
more on the character's nobility and baffle-
ment than on his rage and power. Skobotseva
(subsequently Bondarchuk's wife) is touching
as the doomed Desdemona. The faithful,
often academic adaptation (ironically marred
by the initial release in the UK and USA in
a dubbed English version with the songs
remaining in Russian), is filmed in striking
colours (except for an unfortunate moment
when Othello's face literally turns into a
green-eyed monster), with splendid costumes,
and has some inventive sequences, such as
the swearing of vengeance on the sea shore
amid the swirling waves.

Best Director Cannes 1956.

▶ **Otto E Mezzo** see 8½

Our Short Life

▶ **Unser Kurzes Leben**

East Germany 1981 110 mins col
DEFA

d **Lothar Warneke**
sc **Regine Kühn**
ph **Claus Neumann**
m **Gerhard Rosenfeld**
**Simone Frost, Gottfried Richter,
Hermann Beyer, Christian Steyer,
Dietrich Koerner**

Franziska (Frost), a young architect apprenticed to a famous professor who designs prestige projects such as theatres, has a great
future but a bad marriage. When the latter
collapses she decides to take a year away in
another town and experience life. She gets a
soulless job working for the planning department that builds high-rise flats, lives in a
hostel where she meets underprivileged citizens, has an unhappy affair and attempts to
rally the authorities to allow her to replan
the town. Franziska's hunger for life, her high
ambitions and enthusiasms and often damaging impulsiveness are universal and well conveyed by the lead actress, but there are no
amazing insights into life and politics in East
Germany, except for an authentic sense of

the sterility and inertia which is the by-product of bureaucratically controlled mass social programmes. Although the film has a few appealing moments, it is altogether less than memorable and the changes in Germany have rendered it somewhat outdated.

Our Story

▶ **Notre Histoire**

> France 1984 111 mins col
> Adel Productions/Sara Films/A2

d **Bertrand Blier**
sc **Bertrand Blier**
ph **Jean Penzer**
m **Martinu, Beethoven, Schubert, Laurent Rossi**
   Alain Delon, Nathalie Baye, Michel Galabru, Geneviève Fontanel, Gérard Darmon, Sabine Haudepin

Robert (Delon), befuddled with beer and feeling morose, encounters Donatienne (Baye) on a train. She tells him a 'story' about a girl who picks up a man on a train for a quick, never-to-be-repeated sexual encounter. Her story becomes a real incident between them, but Robert, believing he has found the love of his life, follows her...Blier, adopting methods clearly – and no doubt deliberately – culled from Buñuel, has delivered a mystifying muddle which veers back and forth between the surreal and the farcical, until the ending reveals the mystery. Ludicrous, irritating and seemingly interminable, it offers gold in the dross in the shape of the two leads, and some very inventive and funny sequences, but nothing keeps the tedium at bay(e)!

▶ **Outcast, The** see Sin, The

▶ **Outcry, The** see Cry, The

▶ **Out In The World** see My Apprenticeship

The Outlaw And His Wife

▶ **Berg-Ejvind Och Hans Hustru**

> Sweden 1917 136 mins bw
> Svenska Biografteatern

d **Victor Sjöström**
sc **Victor Sjöström, Sam Ask**
ph **J. Julius Jaenzon**
m **Silent**
   Victor Sjöström, Edith Erastoff, John Ekman, Nils Aréhn

Berg-Ejvind (Sjöström), wanted for stealing sheep to feed his starving family, falls in love with a rich land-owning widow (Erastoff, Sjöström's third wife) in mid-18th century Iceland. She abandons her estate and they flee to the mountains. After an idyllic summer together, winter brings tragedy. Although filmed in northern Sweden, Sjöström has suggested the grandeur of the Icelandic mountain landscape, the primitive setting for this tempestuous, passionately performed melodrama. Here can be seen the beginnings of the fatalism and animism that run through Swedish films to the present day, and the equating of summer with hope and winter with despair.

Out Of Order

▶ **Abwärts**

> W. Germany 1984 88 mins col
> Laura Film/Mutoskop Film/Maran Film/Dieter Geissler Film-production

d **Carl Schenkel**
sc **Carl Schenkel**
m **Jacques Zwart**
   Götz George, Renée Soutendijk, Wolfgang Kieling, Hannes Jaenicke, Klaus Wennemann

The lift of an office block jams between two floors. Trapped within are an executive (George) and his seductive former mistress (Soutendijk), a punk youth (Jaenicke), and a nondescript accountant (Kieling) clutching a briefcase filled with cash that he has embezzled. The predictable inter-relationships, as tempers fray in tandem with the lift cables, cannot avoid engendering a certain tension, particularly as Schenkel uses all the effective, if clichéd, devices of cut-aways and close-ups with maximum efficiency, but it is essentially a re-tread of a well-worn formula.

The Outsiders

▶ **aka Band of Outsiders**

▶ **Bande À Part**

France   1964   95 mins   bw
Anouchka/Orsay

d   Jean-Luc Godard
sc   Jean-Luc Godard
ph   Raoul Coutard
m   Michel Legrand
     Anna Karina, Sami Frey, Calaude
     Brasseur, Luisa Colpeyn

Two young men (Brasseur and Frey) and a
woman (Karina) plan to steal a great deal
of money hidden in the house where the
latter works, but things go awry and murder
is the result. Godard transposes a Hollywood
thriller format to a grey suburb of Paris
where his three protagonists act out their
fantasies. Needless to say, the director's
concerns are less with the plot than with the
isolation of the characters as seen lounging
in cafés, for example, or on the Métro. It
makes for a touching, refreshing and illuminating film.

The Outsiders

▶ **Oka Oorie Katha**

India   1977   114 mins   col
Chandrodaya Art Films

d   Mrinal Sen
sc   Mrinal Sen, Mohit Chattopadhyaya
ph   K.K. Mahajan
m   Vijay Raghava Rao
     Vasudeva Rao, Narayana Rao, Mamata
     Shankar, A.R. Krishna, Pradeep Kumar

Venkaiah (Vasudeva Rao), an anarchic old
man opposed to work, lives with his son
Kistaiah (Narayana Rao) on the outskirts
of a village in conditions of grinding poverty.
Kistaiah marries Nilamma (Shankar), who
brings some order to the house and encourages a more ambitious attitude in her husband, infuriating the old man who later
denies her a midwife on the grounds of
expense, thus causing her death. Set in a
virtually feudal context where the only power
resides with the landlords, Sen's film, devoid
of the analysis and irony which informs
much of his work, does no more than
present, without embellishment, a picture of
the consequences of poverty. It is unrelievedly and appallingly bleak and depress-

ing, with a compelling central performance
from Vasudeva Rao.

The Overcoat

▶ **aka The Cloak**

▶ **Shinel**

USSR   1959   78 mins   bw
Lenfilm

d   Aleksei Batalov
sc   L. Solovyov
ph   Ghenrih Marandzhan
m   N. Sidelnikov
     Rolan Bykov, Yuri Tolubeyev, A.
     Yezhkina, Y. Ponsova, T. Teykh

An insignificant and ill-paid clerk (Bykov)
spends his Christmas bonus on a necessary –
and tailormade – overcoat which becomes his
pride and joy. One night he is set upon in the
snow and robbed of the garment. Receiving
no help from the police, he tramps out into
the cold, catches a chill and dies. There's
more to it than that, but why spoil the tale?
Adapted from the story by Gogol, this poignant little parable is very watchable. It had
been made as a Russian silent in 1926, even
shorter at 65 minutes, and less persuasive, but
visually superb where this is perfectly
adequate.

▶ **Overgreppet** see Question Of Rape, A

The Oyster Princess

▶ **Die Austernprinzessin**

Germany   1919   70 mins   bw
Union Film/UFA

d   Ernst Lubitsch
sc   Hans Kräly, Ernst Lubitsch
ph   Théodor Sparkühl
m   Silent
     Ossi Oswalda, Harry Liedtke, Viktor
     Janson, Curt Bois, Julius Falkenstein

A 'dollar princess' (Oswalda), daughter of Mr
Quaker (Janson) the American 'oyster king',
hopes to gain a real title by marrying an
impoverished prince (Falkenstein) from an
old aristocratic Prussian family. Lubitsch's
first major satirical comedy (a genre in which

he would become a master) successfully opened UFA's first large theatre. In just over an hour, the 27-year-old director delivers plenty of juicy jibes at the parvenu Yankees and the decadent blue-bloods. Lubitsch discovery Oswalda, one of Germany's most popular stars of the 1920s, gives a delightful Mary Pickford-like performance.

▶ **Oyusama** see Miss Oyu

▶ **Paciorki Jednego Rózańca** see Beads Of One Rosary, The

Padre Padrone

▶ **aka Father Master**

Italy 1977 113 mins col
RAI

d   Paolo and Vittorio Taviani
sc Paolo and Vittorio Taviani
ph Mario Masini
m   Egisto Macchi
    Fabrizio Forte, Omero Antonutti, Saverio
    Marconi, Marcella Michelangeli, Gavino
    Ledda

In Sardinia, a father sends his small peasant son (Forte) to the mountains to look after the sheep all by himself. He is deprived of company and language throughout his teens, until education during military service enables him (now played by Marconi) to break away from his domineering father. This potentially fascinating story was based on the autobiography of Gavino Ledda, who appears at the beginning and end of the film. If the Taviani brothers had approached it in a more sober and detached manner, instead of overstating their case and allowing music to supply much of the emotion, the story might have been a moving one as well. However, there are interesting sidelights into primitive patriarchal Sardinian life.

Best Film Cannes 1977

▶ **Padri E Figli** see Like Father, Like Son

▶ **Padurea Spinzuratilor** see Lost Forest, The

▶ **Pagador De Promessas, O** see Given Word, The

A Page Of Madness

▶ **Kurutta Ippeiji**

Japan 1926 60 mins bw
Shin Kankaku-ha Eiga Renmei

d   Teinosuke Kinugasa
sc Yasunari Kawabata
ph Kohei Sugiyama
m   Minoru Muraoka, Toru Kurashima
    Masao Inoue, Yoshie Nakagawa, Ayako
    Iijima, Hiroshi Nemoto, Misao Seki, Eiko
    Minami

An elderly man (Inoue) works voluntarily at odd jobs in the lunatic asylum where his wife (Nakagawa) is confined (having attempted to drown her baby son in a fit of madness many years earlier), and hopes to set her free. Kinugasa rediscovered this film in his storeroom during the early 1970s, and made it available for release with a musical soundtrack added. It is a remarkable work of concentrated emotional power, seeking to understand the nature of insanity while offering a straight narrative (the wife's story) in flashback. Relying on its images, the film uses no inter-titles, displaying breathtaking technical virtuosity: the director employs every available camera device, in the style of German Expressionism which was unknown to him at the time. A masterpiece of imagination and control, it has not dated in 60-odd years.

▶ **Pai Mao Nu** see White-Haired Girl, The

Paisa

▶ **(US: Paisan)**

Italy   1946   115 mins   bw
OFI/Foreign Film Productions/Capitani

d   **Roberto Rossellini**
sc **Roberto Rossellini, Federico Fellini,
     Sergio Amedei**
ph **Otello Martelli**
m   **Renzo Rossellini**
     **William Tubbs, Gar Moore, Maria Michi,
     Carmelo Sazio, Robert Van Loon, Dots
     Johnson, Dale Edmonds**

Six episodes which take place from the first
Allied landings in Sicily to the day of victory,
concentrating on the encounters between the
Italian people and their liberators. They the
meeting of a black American soldier and an
urchin boy who steals his boots, a soldier
who tries to communicate with a Sardinian
peasant girl, a nurse who risks her life to join
her partisan-leader lover and the rounding up
and execution of partisans. The second of
Rossellini's post-war films, following *Rome,
Open City*, uses mainly non-professional
actors in often deliberately undramatic anec-
dotes. There are some weaknesses in the playing and partly improvised dialogue, but the
film has a passion and immediacy that is
difficult to deny and is a document of historical importance.

▶ **Paisan** see Paisa

▶ **Palava Enkeli** see Burning Angel

▶ **Palermo   Oder   Wolfsburg** see
Palermo Or Wolfsburg

Palermo Or Wolfsburg

▶ **Palermo Oder Wolfsburg**

W. Germany   1980   175 mins   col
Thomas Mauch Film Produktion/Eric
Franck

d   **Werner Schroeter**
sc **Werner Schroeter, Giuseppe Fava**
ph **Thomas Mauch**
m   **Alban Berg, folk music**
     Nicola Zarbo, Calogero Arancio, Padre

Face, Cavaliere Comparato, Magdalena
Montezuma

A naive young Sicilian (Zarbo), who leaves
his poverty-stricken family in Palermo to take
a job at the Volkswagen factory at Wolfsburg
in Germany, is tried for manslaughter after
he has stabbed two Germans for impugning
his honour. The low-key beginning is an
unexpected one from such a flamboyant director, but as the film moves along its three
hours (it was edited down from eight hours),
it becomes more and more extravagant and
operatic, which in some way diminishes its
plea for the oppressed. There are some sharply
observed episodes and the non-professional
Zarbo lends conviction to the central role.

Best Film Berlin 1980

Paltoquet

France   1986   92 mins   col
Elefilm/Erato Films

d   **Michel Deville**
sc **Michel Deville**
ph **André Diot**
m   **Dvořák, Janáček**
     **Fanny Ardant, Daniel Auteuil, Richard
     Bohringer, Philippe Léotard, Jeanne
     Moreau, Michel Piccoli, Claude Piéplu,
     Jean Yanne**

Five card players and a prostitute (Ardant)
gather each night in a bar run by The Bar
Owner (Moreau) assisted by a barman (Piccoli) who is a paltoquet or simpleton. A man
is murdered in a nearby hotel, and The Detective (Yanne) investigates. Shot virtually in one
set – what looks like a disused warehouse
pretends to be a sleazy bar – the film has the
air of a dated *avant-garde* drama of the 1930s.
Actually, the six client suspects are six characters in search of an *auteur* – waiting for
Godard. The cast is good enough to convince
that they believed in this pointless exercise in
deconstructing the cheap crime thriller genre.

Pandemonium

▶ **Shura**

Japan   1970   134 mins   bw

Matsumoto Productions/Art Theatre
Guild

d **Toshio Matsumoto**
sc **Shuji Ishizawa, Toshio Matsumoto**
ph **Tatsuo Suzuki**
m **Nishimatsu Fumikazu**
   **Katsuo Nakamura, Yasuko Sanjo, Juro
   Kira, Masao Imafuku, Tamotsu Tamura**

Gengobe (Nakamura), a samurai in love with
a geisha (Sanjo), finds out she has been promised to a rival samurai and he must buy her
if he wishes to keep her. But when Gengobe
discovers that he has been tricked and that
she is already married with a child, he carries
out a bloody vendetta. Matsumoto, in his
second film, has been entirely faithful to the
gruesome spirit of the original 18th century
Kabuki play upon which the screenplay is
based. Apart from the opening shot of the
setting sun in colour, the rest of the film is
shot in stark black-and-white as the characters move through the nocturnal plot and
counterplot, reminiscent of English Jacobean
tragedy. The static compositions, interrupted
by some surreal sequences, give the film a
formal beauty, while tension is maintained by
a tightly constructed script.

Pandora's Box

▶ **aka Lulu**
▶ **Die Büchse Der Pandora**

   Germany 1929 97 mins bw
   Nero Film

d **G.W. Pabst**
sc **G.W. Pabst, Laszlo Wajda**
ph **Günther Krampf**
m **Silent**
   **Louise Brooks, Fritz Kortner, Franz
   Lederer, Gustav Diessl, Alice Roberts,
   Carl Goetz**

Lulu (Brooks), a *femme fatale*, wreaks
emotional and physical havoc on Dr Schön
(Kortner), his son Alva (Lederer) and the
Lesbian Countess Geschwitz (Roberts) before
meeting her death at the hands of Jack the
Ripper (Diess). It was after seeing Louise
Brooks in Howard Hawks' *A Girl In Every
Port*, that Pabst asked her to play Lulu in his
adaptation of two of Frank Wedekind's plays.
The black, bobbed hair framing a pale kitten-

ish face, the intense eroticism of each
expression and gesture, has made Brooks one
of the icons of the cinema and inspired Pabst
to his greatest film. But it was many years
before the performance and the picture were
appreciated. The Germans objected to an
American in the lead, and the film was heavily
cut around the world. One print omitted Jack
the Ripper and showed Lulu joining the Salvation Army.

▶ **Pane, Amore, E Fantasia** see
Bread, Love, And Dreams

▶ **Pane, Amore E Gelosia** see Bread,
Love And Jealousy

▶ **Pane E Cioccolata** see Bread And
Chocolate

Panic

▶ **Panique**

   France 1946 98 mins bw
   Filmsonor

d **Julien Duvivier**
sc **Charles Spaak, Julien Duvivier**
ph **Nicolas Hayer**
m **Jacques Ibert**
   **Michel Simon, Viviane Romance, Paul
   Bernard, Charles Dorat, Max Dalban**

The blame for a woman's murder is shifted
on to a respectable man (Simon) by the real
culprit (Bernard) and his girlfriend
(Romance). Duvivier marked his return to his
homeland after his wartime sojourn in Hollywood with a taut thriller based on a Georges
Simenon novel. Freed from the sex-code
restrictions imposed on him in the USA, he
managed to get some 'oomph' into the love
scenes. It was also a reminder of what a
master of atmosphere Duvivier had been in
films like *Pépé Le Moko* (1937).

▶ **Panique** see Panic

▶ **Panny Z Wilka** see Young Ladies Of
Wilko, The

Paper Bird

▶ **Papirfüglen**

Norway 1984 95 mins col
Norsk Films A/S

d   **Anja Breien**
sc **Anja Breien, Knut Faldbakken**
ph **Erling Thurmann-Andersen**
m   **Jan Garbarek**
    **Elisabeth Mortensen, Björn Floberg, Per
    Sunderland, Bente Borsun, Svein Sturla
    Hungnes, Anne K. Krigsvoll**

Helen Stousland (Mortensen), lawyer and div-
orcee, comes across a crowd gathered in the
street around a dead man who fell from the
balcony of his apartment. On discovering that
it is her father (Sunderland), Helen begins a
quest to solve the mystery of his death. Was
it suicide, or was he murdered? She uncovers
horrifying facts about her father, as well as
discovering disturbing aspects about her own
relationship with him. At the same time she
develops an ambiguous romantic attachment
to a police detective (Floberg). Breien uses an
ostensibly conventional thriller plot to explore
the psychology of her heroine (played with a
sensuous yet intellectual intensity by Mortensen). What emerges is a study of stunted
emotions which only drugs, drink and sex
help to satisfy. But as tautly directed as it is –
flashbacks punctuate the narrative perfectly –
the screenplay is overloaded with revelations
leading to a rather far-fetched conclusion.

▶ **Papirfüglen** see Paper Bird

Paracelsus

Germany 1943 104 mins bw
Bavaria-Filmkunst

d   **G. W. Pabst**
sc **Kurt Heuser, G. W. Pabst**
ph **Bruno Stephan**
m   **Herbert Windt**
    **Werner Krauss, Mathias Wieman, Harald
    Kreutzberg, Martin Urtel, Harry
    Langewisch**

Paracelsus (Krauss), appointed town physician of medieval Basle, fights traditional
medicine, reactionary academics and greedy
merchants in an attempt to keep plague from
the city. The second of the three films directed
by Pabst for the Third Reich was shot at the
Barrandov studios outside occupied Prague
with a German crew. The script has all the
elements which appealed to his Nazi masters –
a rebel hero cleansing Germany of ancient
practices, anti-intellectualism ('Resolute
imagination can accomplish all things,' states
Paracelsus) and the replacement of Latin
(foreign influences) with the German language. Most of it is a stagey, plodding costume drama, with one or two scenes involving
the dancer Harald Kreutzberg to wake one
up.

Parade

France/Sweden 1974 85 mins col
Gray Film/Sveriges Radio

d   **Jacques Tati**
sc **Jacques Tati**
ph **Jean Badal, Gunnar Fischer**
m   **Charles Dumont**
    **Jacques Tati, Karl Kossmayer, Pia
    Colombo, Les 'Williams', Les 'Veterans',
    Les 'Sipolo', Bertilo**

Jacques Tati does a number of his famous
music-hall mimes of sportsmen, in between
various circus acts – a magician, acrobats,
clowns – in a circus tent in front of an
audience in Sweden. In every way it was sad
that this co-production was Tati's last film.
He used video techniques to record a series
of dismal and repetitive provincial circus acts,
occasionally enlivened by his own presence.
He also attempted to demonstrate his whimsical philosophy that everyone is a natural
clown by showing some comical members of
the audience and, rather in the manner of
Bergman's *The Magic Flute*, cutting to the
reactions of two children, with whom the film
finishes as they play endlessly with props in
an empty circus tent.

Parade Of The Planets

▶ **Parad Planyet**

USSR 1984 96 mins col

Mosfilm

d **Vadim Abdrashitov**
sc **Alexander Mindadze**
ph **Vladimir Shevtsik**
m **Vyacheslav Ganin, and extracts from Beethoven and Shostakovich**
    Oleg Borisov, Sergei Nikonenko, Sergei Shakurov, Alexei Zharkov, Pyotr Zaichenko, Aleksander Pashutin

Five territorial army comrades, called up on an exercise discover they are now considered too old to be useful, so mark their last meeting by journeying to the village where they would have been detailed to go, and experience a series of strange encounters. Abdrashitov's study of human beings who no longer fit into a world of masculine-orientated values – and those, such as women, who never did – is not without some interest, but it is an unyieldingly cryptic piece of which the dreamlike atmosphere and shadowy images serve only to obscure the director's intentions even further.

▶ **Paradise Place** see Summer Paradise

▶ **Paradistorg** see Summer Paradise

▶ **Parad Planyet** see Parade Of The Planets

Paraguelia

Greece 1980 95 mins col
Greca Film

d **Pavlos Tassios**
sc **Pavlos Tassios**
ph **Sakis Maniatis**
m **Kyriakos Sfetsas**
    Antonis Antoniou, Katerina Gogou, Sophia Roubou, Nikitis Tsakiroglou, Antonis Kafetzopoulos

Two brothers and their girlfriends are spending an evening at a *bouzouki* house. One of the boys pays the musicians for a 'paraguelia' – a session of music to which the customer dances solo and during which it is taboo for anyone else to take the floor. When somebody from another party insists on joining in, a fight breaks out, a man is killed and the elder brother (Antoniou) is tried for murder. Tas-

sios, one of the most popular and successful of the current crop of Greek directors, has delivered a drama redolent with passion and violence and enough *bouzouki* to enthral fans and discourage anyone who can't bear it. Characterization is pretty sketchy and there is some ill-judged voice-over poetry used as a narrative link, but it's crisply directed, efficiently acted and the fight scene is terrific.

▶ **Parapluies De Cherbourg, Les** see Umbrellas Of Cherbourg, The

Pardon Mon Affaire

▶ **Un Éléphant Ça Trompe Énormément**

France 1976 108 mins col
Les Films De La Guéville/Gaumont International

d **Yves Robert**
sc **Jean-Loup Dabadie, Yves Robert**
ph **René Mathelin**
m **Vladimir Cosma**
    Jean Rochefort, Claude Brasseur, Guy Bedos, Victor Lanoux, Danièle Delorme, Annie Duperey, Martine Sarcey

Middle-aged Etienne (Rochefort), although happily married to Marthe (Delorme), decides to pursue Charlotte (Duperey), the girl on an advertising poster. Numerous mix-ups later, he spends a night with her which ends in a farcical public exposure of his dalliance. Evidently drawing on *The Seven Year Itch* for some much-needed inspiration – Duperey's skirt being blown over her head by a hot-air grille is the most obvious pointer – Robert has come up with a rather meandering and unsubtle farce, full of sub-plots involving Etienne's three friends (Brasseur, Bedos and Lanoux). However, the mediocre enterprise is rescued by some superlative comedy performances, notably from Brasseur, who carries off some outrageous set-pieces with expertise, and Rochefort, whose versatile range of facial expressions is a delight. A sequel the following year, *Pardon Mon Affaire, Too*, was in some respects even more witless, but with the same cast again proving effective and Delorme's Marthe pivotal to the action. The original was remade by Gene Wilder in 1984 as *The Woman In Red*.

Les Parents Terribles

► **(US: The Storm Within)**

France 1948 98 mins bw
Sirius

d   **Jean Cocteau**
sc **Jean Cocteau**
ph **Michel Kelber**
m   **Georges Auric**
    Jean Marais, Yvonne De Bray, Gabrielle Dorziat, Marcel André, Josette Day

When the son (Marais) of a middle-class Parisian family announces his love for a young woman (Day), neither he nor his domineering mother (De Bray), who cannot accept his adulthood, knows that the girl is the mistress of his father (André). Making few cuts in his play of the same name, using only two settings, and keeping camera movement to a minimum, Cocteau retained the theatricality of his over-ripe melodrama. But the use of close-ups – witness the mouth of Marais and the eyes of De Bray as he tells her of his love – enabled the director 'to catch my wild beasts unawares with my tele-lens'. Although it enables us to appreciate the superb performances, excepting the 35-year-old Marais as the *maman*'s boy, it would have been happier kept behind a proscenium arch.

► **Parfum De La Dame En Noir, Le** see Perfume Of The Lady In Black, The

► **Paris Au Mois D'Août** see Paris In August

Paris Belongs To Us

► **Paris Nous Appartient**

France 1960 140 mins bw
AJYM/Films Du Carrosse

d   **Jacques Rivette**
sc **Jacques Rivette, Jean Gruault**
ph **Charles Bitsch**
m   **Philippe Arthuys**
    Betty Schneider, Gianni Esposito,

Françoise Prévost, Daniel Crohem, François Maistre, Jean-Claude Brialy

A group of young amateurs come together in the deserted Paris of summer to stage a performance of Shakespeare's *Pericles*, but there are sexual and political tensions; their composer dies and the producer kills himself. Because of lack of funds, Rivette's first feature was made over a period of two years, and strangely reflects its subject in the struggles of creation against all odds. Despite some of its aural and visual inadequacy and slackness, its austere style builds up an atmosphere of doom against a vividly realized Paris. Fellow *nouvelle vague* directors Chabrol, Demy and Godard make appearances.

► **Paris Does Strange Things** see Eléna Et Les Hommes

► **Paris Frills** see Falbalas

La Parisienne

► **Une Parisienne**

France 1957 90 mins col
Ariane/Cinetel/Filmsonor/Rizzoli/UA

d   **Michel Boisrond**
sc **Annette Wademant, Jean Aurel, Jacques Emmanual, Michel Boisrond**
ph **Marcel Grignon**
m   **Hubert Rostaing**
    Brigitte Bardot, Henri Vidal, André Luguet, Charles Boyer, Nadia Gray, Madeleine Lebeau, Noël Roquevert

The innocent yet enticing daughter (Bardot) of the President of the French Council (Luguet), marries her father's private secretary (Vidal). But when her husband takes to a rakish lifestyle, she decides to fight back by making eyes at an aging Prince (Boyer), flying with him to a Riviera resort. However, the romance is ruined when the two of them catch colds and the newly-weds are reunited. Frothy and saucy are the usual adjectives to describe this sort of light comedy, which would have been flat and insipid if not for the charms of the half-clad sex kitten. Actually, the film, directed by Boisrond (whose first feature in 1956 was the similar *Mam'zelle Pigalle*, also with B.B.) resembles nothing more than

American fluff of the period, with the addition of some Gallic spice. Boyer goes through the suave routine that made him a Hollywood dreamboat in the 1930s and 1940s.

▶ **Parisienne, Une** see Parisienne, La

Paris In August

▶ **Paris Au Mois D'Août**

France   1965   98 mins   bw
Sirius

d   Pierre Granier-Deferre
sc   R.M. Arlaud, Pierre Granier-Deferre
ph   Claude Renoir
m   Georges Garvarentz, Charles Aznavour
    Charles Aznavour, Susan Hampshire,
    Daniel Ivernel, Michel De Ré, Alan Scott,
    Jacques Marin

Department store salesman Henri (Aznavour), alone in Paris while his wife and children are away, meets an English girl (Hampshire) and shows her Paris. He pretends to be an artist, she a famous model, and they enjoy an idyllic affair. Granier-Deferre uses this run-of-the-mill romance as an excuse to explore Paris, so beguilingly photographed by Renoir that it transcends the selection of myths and clichés on offer. The combination of tiny Gallic Aznavour and English rose Hampshire (who married the director) is unusual, but whether it appeals is a matter of taste. A sweet, inconsequential outing.

▶ **Paris Nous Appartient** see Paris Belongs To Us

▶ **Paris Vu Par...** see Six In Paris

▶ **Par Le Sang Des Autres** see By The Blood Of Others

Parsifal

W. Germany   1982   255 mins   col
TMS Film(Munich)/Gaumont(Paris)

d   Hans Jürgen Syberberg
sc   Hans Jürgen Syberberg (after Wagner's text)
ph   Igor Luther
m   Richard Wagner (Conductor: Armin Jordan)
    Michael Kutter and Karin Krick (Parsifal I and II, sung by Rainer Goldberg), Edith Clever (Kundry, sung by Yvonne Minton), Armin Jordan (Amfortas, sung by Wolfgang Schöne), Robert Lloyd (Gurnemanz), Aage Haugland (Klingsor)

The tale of the redemption of the wounded Amfortas, Leader of the Knights of the Grail, by Parsifal, 'the innocent fool enlightened by pity'. It was inevitable that Syberberg, that chronicler of the German soul, should tackle Wagner's last opera, the synthesis of the composer's own religious and mystic beliefs. Syberberg's film, while demystifying the work, also presents it as an unassailable masterpiece. The action takes place on and around a gigantic death mask of Wagner and embraces a wide range of startling images, associations and film techniques – long takes, back projections, puppets, and *tableaux vivants*. The most daring device has Parsifal played both by a boy, who represents the 'fool', and a girl as the asexual symbol of purity he becomes after Kundry's kiss. This splendidly sung and acted kitsch celebration, is the most personal and imaginative of opera films.

The Parson's Widow

▶ **aka The Witch Woman**
▶ **aka The Fourth Marriage Of Dame Margaret**
▶ **Prästänkan**

Sweden   1920   4907 feet   bw
Svensk Filmindustri

d   Carl Dreyer
sc   Carl Dreyer
ph   George Schneevoigt
m   Silent
    Hildur Carlberg, Einar Rod, Greta Almroth, Olav Aukrust, Kurt Welin

Söfren (Rod), a young parson, who wins his first living in a country village, discovers to his dismay that, according to local custom, he has also inherited the previous incumbent's widow, Dame Margaret (Carlberg), an aged harridan who has already buried three parson husbands. Trapped because he can't marry his pretty fiancée (Almroth), he has his sweetheart masquerade as his sister and introduces her to the parsonage as a maid. Frustrated by the constant vigilance of the old hag, the young lovers set about doing away with her in a plan which goes sadly awry. Shot in a museum village in Norway, Dreyer's third film is a great improvement on his first two efforts and is an important step in his development. This delightfully funny, tender and ribald tale also reveals the director's continual fascination with psychology and with women in dominant roles. Though still under the lyrical influence of Sjöström and Stiller, Dreyer moved the acting further along the line towards naturalism. One of the most extraordinary performances comes from 77-year-old Carlberg, who reveals a humanity and warmth beneath her emaciated and forbidding exterior.

▶ **Partie De Campagne, Une** see Day In The Country, A

Une Partie De Plaisir

▶ **aka Love Match**

▶ **(US: Pleasure Party)**

France   1975   100 mins   col
La Boétie/Sunchild/Gerico

d   **Claude Chabrol**
sc **Paul Gégauff**
ph **Jean Rabier**
m   **Beethoven, Brahms, Schubert**
    Paul Gégauff, Danielle Gégauff, Clémence Gégauff, Paula Moore, Michel Valette, Pierre Santini

The anatomy of the breakdown of the marriage between an unfaithful husband and a wife he has subjected to his will. When she follows his suggestion that she take a lover, he is furious. Paul Gégauff, screenwriter on over a dozen of Chabrol's films, plays the monstrous husband opposite his real ex-wife and daughter. The director is obviously fascinated and disgusted by his friend's behaviour – Gégauff slaps his wife and forces her to kiss his foot – and the audience might feel the same. Finally, the loathesomeness of the man and the exhibitionism of the whole enterprise outweigh the interest. Gégauff, in

fact, was stabbed to death in 1983 by his second wife.

Partner

Italy   1968   105 mins   col
Red Film

d   **Bernardo Bertolucci**
sc **Bernardo Bertolucci, Gianni Amico**
ph **Ugo Piccone**
m   **Ennio Morricone**
    Pierre Clémenti, Stefania Sandrelli, Tina Aumont, Sergio Tofano, Giulio Cesare Castello

Jacob (Clémenti), a confused and shy young man, is ejected from the birthday party given for Clara (Sandrelli), whom he loves. He therefore creates Jacob II, his more confident double. Based loosely on Dostoevsky's short novel, *The Double*, it was updated to the Rome of 1968, with the central character played by Clémenti speaking French while all the rest speak Italian. The young man, divided into two, seems to represent Respectability/Rebellion – Bertolucci/Godard. It is, in fact, incoherent, undigested Godard, interesting as a typical product of 1968, that year of student revolt.

The Party And The Guests

▶ **(US: A Report On The Party And The Guests)**

▶ **O Slavnosti A Hostech**

Czechoslovakia   1966   71 mins   bw
Ceskoslovensky/Barrandov

d   **Jan Němec**
sc **Jan Němec, Ester Krumbachová**
ph **Jaromír Šofr**
m   **Karel Mares**
    Ivan Vyskocil, Jan Klusák, Jiří Němec, Zdenka Skvorecká, Helena Pejsková, Karel Mares, Jana Pracharová

Everybody at a large *al fresco* party seems to be enjoying themselves and they constantly reassure each other that they are. Only one man refuses to be happy and, when he leaves, he is pursued by the other guests with tracker dogs. This bitter political allegory, made by a group of friends, was denounced in the

National Assembly and had to wait for the Prague Spring before it could be released. Although many of the references are obscure to non-Czechs, the script (co-written by Němec's then wife, Krumbachová) and the visual conception carry a clear enough message.

▶ **Pasażerka** see Passenger

▶ **Pasqualino Settebellezze** see Seven Beauties

▶ **Passage Du Rhin, Le** see Crossing Of the Rhine, The

Les Passagers

▶ **aka Shattered**

France   1976   103 mins   col
Viaduc Productions/Trianon Productions(Paris)/ PIC(Rome)

d   **Serge Leroy**
sc **Christopher Frank, Serge Leroy**
ph **Walter Wottitz, Jacques Assuérus, Patrick Morin**
m   **Claude Bolling**
    Jean-Louis Trintignant, Mireille Darc, Bernard Fresson, Richard Constantini, Adolfo Celi

While air stewardess Nicole (Darc) sorts out their new Paris apartment, her husband Alex (Trintignant) goes to fetch his 11-year-old stepson Marc (Constantini) from school in Rome. Soon after their journey commences, Marc disconcerts a sceptical Alex by insisting that they are being followed by a van. And, indeed, they are. The driver, Fabio (Fresson), is a disbarred airline pilot and a former lover of Nicole's, now grown seriously disturbed and violent. This is an extremely well-crafted film which, on the surface, is a first cousin to Spielberg's *Duel*, with its overtones of elusive menace on the highway. However, the thriller elements are neatly interwoven into the central 'father-son' relationship and, with the aid of a skilfully used tracking camera, Leroy contrives constantly shifting balances of atmosphere, locale and emotion that hold one's interest right through to the brutal and gripping climax. Trintignant and Constantini make an excellent and appealing pair.

Passenger

▶ **Pasażerka**

Poland   1963   63 mins   bw
WFF Lódź/Kadr

d   **Andrzej Munk**
sc **Andrzej Munk, Zofia Posmysz-Piasecka**
ph **Krzysztof Winiewicz**
m   **Tadeusz Baird**
    Aleksandra Slaska, Anna Ciepielewska, Marek Walczewski, Jan Kreczmer, Irena Malkiewicz

In the 1960s, a coincidental meeting on board a liner between a former female guard (Slaska) at Auschwitz and one of the prisoners (Ciepielewska), who had been in her charge, triggers off a series of bitter memories. Munk, one of Poland's most promising directors, was killed in a car crash, at the age of 40, during the shooting. Three of the completed episodes were put together, plus a montage of stills with music and commentary. The powerful and haunting sequences in Auschwitz, and the play of past and present, guilt and expiation, shows every sign that it would have been his best film.

Passe Ton Bac D'Abord

▶ **aka Graduate First**
▶ **aka Pass Your Exam First**

France   1978   90 mins   col
Livardois Films/Renn Productions/ FR3/I.N.A.

d   **Maurice Pialat**
sc **Maurice Pialat**
ph **Pierre William Glenn**
m   **Patrick Juvet**
    Sabine Haudepin, Philippe Marland, Valérie Chassigneux, Annick Alane, Michel Caron

In a provincial city in the mining region of Northern France, a group of disillusioned students with no prospects other than dead-end jobs or unemployment, see little point in doing any work for their *baccalauréat*. Ignoring the futile dissertations of their teachers, they drift aimlessly round the local bistro or down to the coast; some engage in hollow sexual encounters; others go to Paris. Pialat's minutely detailed observation of dispossessed youth is made with an admirable combination of objectivity and compassion. The director's youthful cast is remarkable for a naturalness so complete as to become almost tedious, but which gives this rather dispiriting film the ring of truth. Shooting was interrupted and later resumed with a different crew and this, no doubt, accounts for certain technical discrepancies.

▶ **Pas Si Méchant Que Ça** see This Wonderful Crook

▶ **Passion** see Madame Dubarry

Passion

▶ **Manji**

Japan 1964 90 mins col
Daiei

d **Yasuzo Masumura**
sc **Kaneto Shindo**
ph **Setsuo Kobayashi**
m **Tadashi Yamauchi**
   Ayako Wakao, Kyoko Kishida, Yusuke Kawazu, Eiji Funakoshi

Sonoko (Kishida) falls in love with Mitsuko (Wakao), and the two girls have an affair. Sonoko's husband (Funakoshi) is tolerant of the situation, but she is herself thrown by the discovery that Mitsuko has a male lover. From then on, complications proliferate among the foursome, ending in a bizarre and ambiguous death pact. A film that often borders on the ludicrous and sometimes hints at sexploitation, it is also redolent of absurdist black comedy and never boring. Difficult as it is to be sure of the director's intentions, his control over the curious goings-on is undeniably skilled.

Passion

▶ **aka Godard's Passion**

France 1982 88 mins col
Sara Films/Sonimage/Films A2/Film et Video Productions/SSR

d **Jean-Luc Godard**
sc **Jean-Luc Godard**
ph **Raoul Coutard**

m **Mozart, Dvořák, Beethoven, Fauré**
  Jerzy Radziwilowicz, Hanna Schygulla, Michel Piccoli, Isabelle Huppert, László Szabó

A Polish film director (Radziwilowicz), trying to make a movie called *Passion*, has an affair with the owner (Schygulla) of the French motel where he and the crew are staying. Her husband (Piccoli) has to cope with a labour dispute at his factory led by a woman worker (Huppert). Meanwhile, money for the film is beginning to run out. The first and best of a number of films in the 1980s in which Godard directly confronted the nature of his own art – *First Name Carmen*, the made-for-TV *Rise And Fall Of A Little Film Company* (1986), and *King Lear* (1987) are principally about the making of a film. But the passion of the title does not apply only to film-making, it also has a sexual and religious (or blasphemous) sense. Through *tableaux vivants* based on the Old Masters, great music contrasted with traffic noise, and verbal dialectic, Godard continues to astonish, and annoy, those who want films to tell a story.

A Passion

▶ **(US: The Passion Of Anna)**

▶ **En Passion**

Sweden 1969 100 mins col
Svensk Filmindustri

d **Ingmar Bergman**
sc **Ingmar Bergman**
ph **Sven Nykvist**
m **Allan Gray, Bach**
  Max Von Sydow, Liv Ullmann, Erland Josephson, Bibi Andersson, Erik Hell, Hjördis Petterson

A man with a past (Von Sydow) has found peace living in remote seclusion, but is disturbed one day by a crippled woman (Ullmann) asking to use the telephone. In due course this chance encounter results in his becoming embroiled with the woman and her friends, a married couple (Josephson and Andersson) with problems. A homicidal maniac is at large, exacerbating the tensions of the foursome. Bergman's second excursion into colour, filmed on the bleak island of Fårö, is widely considered one of his best works. It is a penetrating examination of personal pain, bearing all the hallmarks of the director's unique style of expression – and those of his cast and cameraman – and is never less than interesting.

▶ **Passion De Jeanne D'Arc, La** see Passion Of Joan Of Arc, The

Passione D'Amore

Italy 1981 119 mins col
Massfilm(Rome)/Marceau Cocinor(Paris)

d **Ettore Scola**
sc **Ruggero Maccari, Ettore Scola**
ph **Claudio Ragona**
m **Armando Trovaioli**
   Bernard Giraudeau, Valeria D'Obici,
   Laura Antonelli, Jean-Louis Trintignant,
   Massimo Girotti, Bernard Blier

Army captain Giorgio (Giraudeau) is parted from his mistress Clara (Antonelli) when he is transferred to a frontier post. There, he is intrigued by the empty place set at dinner each evening for the indisposed Fosca (D'Obici), ward and cousin to the Colonel (Girotti). When Fosca does appear, Giorgio is shocked by her appalling ugliness, apparently aggravated by a neurotic illness. To Giorgio's horror, Fosca conceives a hopeless passion for him and, when he takes leave to visit Clara, she falls dangerously ill, thus drawing him into a fatal web of pity and obligation... Set in 1862 and making a reasonable attempt at period opulence à la Visconti, Scola's simplistic study in contrasts fails to make full use of the rich possibilities of the story. Thus, with its lack of characterization and a plethora of high emotional dramatics, it comes across as no more than a mildly entertaining and minor psycho-sexual excursion into *Grand Guignol*.

▶ **Passion, En** see Passion, A

Passion For Life

▶ **aka I Have A New Master**
▶ **L'École Buissonnière**

France 1949 94 mins bw
Cooperative Générale Du
Cinématographie Français

d **Jean-Paul Le Chanois**
sc **Elise Freinet, Jean-Paul Le Chanois**
ph **André Dumaître, Marc Fossard, Maurice Pecqueux**
m **Joseph Kosma**
   Bernard Blier, Juliette Faber, Edouard Delmont, Pierre Coste, Jean-Louis Allibert, Danny Caron

Pascal Laurent (Blier) is a dedicated schoolteacher of rare enthusiasm who brings new ideas and a modern approach into the classroom. His methods meet with opposition from the parents as well as from the old-guard staff, but the pupils are responsive. One of the great stalwarts of the French cinema, Bernard Blier can usually be relied upon to raise the level of a film. Not that there's much to raise here. It's a simple, old-fashioned and slightly sentimental story, competently executed and sometimes touching.

▶ **Passion Of Anna, The** see Passion, A

The Passion Of Joan Of Arc

▶ **La Passion De Jeanne D'Arc**

France 1928 114 min bw
Société Générale Des Films

d **Carl Dreyer**
sc **Carl Dreyer, Joseph Delteil**
ph **Rudolph Maté**
m **Silent**
   Renée Falconetti, Eugène Silvain, Maurice Schutz, Michel Simon, Antonin Artaud

The 29 examinations of Joan of Arc (Falconetti) on her last day before she was burned at the stake. Based on transcripts of the 18-month long trial, the screenplay telescopes the events into one day, thus providing the film with more formal intensity. Dreyer's constant and unforgettable use of long-held close-ups has led some critics to describe it as a film consisting entirely of close-ups. The faces of Joan's judges, wearing no make-up, are cruelly exposed to Maté's camera, but it is the agonized face of Falconetti, in her only film, that burns itself on the mind. It was said that Dreyer bullied her unmercifully to draw out the suffering he required. Since the nature of the material is intrinsically verbal, the images are frequently interrupted by long titles. Dreyer was given a free hand by his

French producers. He took 18 months – as long as Joan's 15th-century trial – to shoot in costly sets. Like most of the director's work, his first masterpiece was a critical but not a commercial success.

▶ **Pass Your Exam First** see Passe Ton Bac D'Abord

Pather Panchali

India   1955   122 mins   bw
Government of West Bengal

d **Satyajit Ray**
sc **Satyajit Ray**
ph **Subrata Mitra**
m **Ravi Shankar**
   Subir Bannerjee, Kanu Bannerjee, Karuna Bannerjee, Uma Das Gupta, Chunibala

Apu (Subir Bannerjee), a young boy lives in a small Bengal village with his parents, his sister and aged aunt (Chunibala) on the borderline of poverty. Out of an industry almost entirely dominated by formula, escapist musical films in Hindi, Ray suddenly appeared on the international scene with this masterpiece about Apu's childhood in the minority language of Bengali, and entirely altered notions of Indian cinema. He had great difficulty in raising funds for his debut film, the first of a trilogy based on a popular book by Bhibuti Bashan Bannerjee. He was about to abandon shooting after 18 months when he was rescued by the West Bengal government. The title means 'little song of the road', and the motif throughout is one of travel, of something beyond the confines of the tiny rural community. There are the travelling players viewed with wonder and delight by the child, and the lyrical sequence when Apu and his sister run through the long grass towards the railway line to see a train taking people to the big cities. The boy was to take this journey himself in the following film, *Aparajito*.

▶ **Pathetic Fallacy** see Mechanical Man

Pathfinder

▶ **Veiviseren** (Norwegian)/**Ofelas** (Lapp)

Norway   1987   86 mins   col

Filmkameratene/The Norway Film Development Co/Norsk Film

d **Nils Gaup**
sc **Nils Gaup**
ph **Erling Thurmann-Andersen**
m **Nils Aslak Valkeapää**
   Mikkel Gaup, Ingvald Guttorm, Ellen Anne Buljo, Inger Utsi, Svein Scharffenberg, Sara Marit Gaup, Helgi Skulasin, Knut Walle, Nils Utsi

On the frozen plains of Lapland many centuries ago, Aigin (Gaup), a teenage boy, returns from a hunting expedition to discover that his parents and younger sister have been butchered by a marauding band of Tchude warriors. He escapes to a nearby Lapp encampment, but the inhabitants, fearing the boy may have led the Tchudes to them, head for a larger settlement along the coast. Aigin remains behind and receives a visit from a holy man, Raste (Nils Utsi), who is tortured by the Tchudes to be their pathfinder. Aigin offers to lead them to the Lapps, but has a plan to deceive them. The first feature to be made in the Lapp language is a wonderfully exciting wide-screen adventure, with splendid Dolby sound magnifying every significant footstep in the snow. Underneath the 'boy's own' tale runs the spirit of the original Lapp legend *The Pathfinder And The Torch*, told around camp fires and passed from generation to generation, finishing up on the cinema screens of the world. The director's son, Mikkel Gaup, makes the perfect handsome hero and heads a convincing cast.

The Patriot

▶ **Die Patriotin**

W. Germany   1979   120 mins   bw/col
Kairos Film

d **Alexander Kluge**
sc **Alexander Kluge**
ph **Thomas Mauch, Jörg Schmidt-Reitwein, Werner Lüring, Günther Hörmann**
m **Beethoven, Mahler, Haydn, Sibelius and others**
   Hannelore Hoger, Dieter Mainka, Alfred Edel, Alexander Von Eschwege, Beate Holle

Gabi Teichert (Hoger), a history teacher in Frankfurt, investigates new ways of presenting Germany's past to a new generation. The teacher's investigation into the historical process becomes part of Kluge's own dialectical method of film-making. The film is a kaleidoscopic commentary on Germany's relationship to its past, starting with the statement that it is wrong to assume 'the dead are somehow dead'. In the process, use is made of newsreel material, interviews, speeded up takes of life in Frankfurt, fairy tales illustrated by magic lantern scenes and inserts real events such as the SPD party conference. Kluge's own voice is heard on the soundtrack in the role of a knee *(sic)* that belonged to a corporal killed at Stalingrad. Much of it is as illuminating as it is puzzling, enriching as it is irritating.

▶ **Patriotin, Die** see Patriot, The

▶ **Patsy, The** see Addition, L'

▶ **Pauline À La Plage** see Pauline At The Beach

Pauline At The Beach

▶ **Pauline À La Plage**

France   1983   95 mins   col
Les Films Du Losange/Les Films Ariane

d   **Eric Rohmer**
sc   **Eric Rohmer**
ph   **Nestor Almendros**
m   **Jean-Louis Valero**
   **Arielle Dombasle, Amanda Langlet,
   Pascal Greggory, Féodor Atkine, Simon
   De La Brosse, Rosette**

Pauline (Langlet) and her older, recently divorced cousin Marion (Dombasle) arrive to spend two weeks at the family's holiday cottage on the Normandy coast. Both of them get entangled with Pierre (Greggory), Marion's former lover, Henri (Atkine), a divorced anthropologist, and Sylvain (De La Brosse), a teenage boy. In the third of his 'Comedies and Proverbs', Rohmer shows his unique and witty way of placing an 18th-century plot of mistaken identity, sentimental subterfuge and an interplay of couples in a modern setting. As Rohmer is a summer director (few of his films take place in another season), he uses the beach setting and the warm evenings sensuously, and continues his

obsession with *'les jeunes filles en fleur'*. He also manages to laugh with and at his rather empty and vain characters, all impeccably and realistically played.

Best Director Berlin 1983

▶ **Paura, La** see Fear

▶ **Paura E Amore** see Three Sisters

Payment In Kind

▶ **aka The Rabbit Case**

▶ **Causa Kralik**

Czechoslovakia   1980   85 mins   col
Ustredni Pujdovna Filmu Praha

d   **Jaromil Jíres**
sc   **Jaroslav Dietl**
ph   **Jaromír Sofr**
m   **Vadim Petrov**
   **Milos Kopecky, Irena Hahnova, Jaroslav
   Satoransky, Karel Augusta, Alena
   Vranova**

An aging and ailing lawyer (Kopecky) comes out of retirement to help the inhabitants of the small country community where he lives. Prominent among his cases is that of an old peasant lady (Hahnova) who accuses her ne'er-do-well nephew (Satoransky) of spending her life savings. He says the money was a present, she claims it was a loan. The English titles of this gentle and amiable film refer to the fact that the old lady can only pay the lawyer with rabbits. But well-acted and well-observed as it is, all the characters seem just too nice and there is a vein of sentimentality running through the film, underlined by the music. One has the feeling that Jires, one of Czechoslovakia's talents in the 60s and early 70s, renowned especially for *Valerie And Her Week Of Wonders* (1970) and other fantasies marked by surrealism, had, like many of his contemporaries, crept into more cosy corners of film-making.

The Peach Thief

▶ **Kradezat Na Praskovi**

Bulgaria   1964   84 mins   bw
Bulgaria State Films

d   **Vulo Radev**
sc **Vulo Radev**
ph **Todor Stoyanov**
m   **Simeon Pironkov**
    Nevena Kokanova, Rade Markovich,
    Mikhail Mikhailov, Vassil Vachev

Towards the end of World War I in Turnovo, the medieval capital of Bulgaria, attractive Lisa (Kokanova) spends lonely days in her garden with its beautiful peach orchard while her husband, the colonel, supervises the local garrisons and POW camp. Lisa's life changes when Ivo (Markovich), a Serbian officer prisoner, breaks into her garden to steal peaches, an incident that leads to the couple's falling in love. A sensitively realized love story and beguilingly atmospheric, but the later stages of the film lose focus when the action overbalances into a *mélange* of political and military incident that weakens the impact of the ending. Acting and photography achieve a level of respectable competence, while the period reconstruction is notably fine.

The Pearls Of The Crown

▶ **Les Perles De La Couronne**

France   1937   120 mins   bw
Tobis

d   **Sacha Guitry, Christian-Jaque**
sc **Sacha Guitry**
ph **Jules Kruger, Marc Fossard**
m   **Jean Françaix**
    Sacha Guitry, Renée Saint-Cyr, Lyn
    Harding, Percy Marmont, Arletty,
    Raimu, Claude Dauphin, Jean-Louis
    Barrault, Jacqueline Delubac, Marguerite
    Moreno

The history of seven pearls given to a range of famous personages over the ages, and a number of contemporary people of different nationalities in search of them. Guitry's trilingual movie – French, English and Italian – was meant as a celebration of the coronation of Edward VIII. It happens to be more of a celebration of Guitry's style and wit. (He plays four parts, including François I and Napoleon III.) There is also an enjoyable string of cameos, among them Barrault as Bonaparte, Harding as Henry VIII and Guitry's wife, Delubac, as Mary, Queen of Scots and the Empress Josephine. However, most of the pearls are to be found in the dialogue rather than in the plot.

Peasants

▶ **Krestyaniye**

USSR   1935   120 mins   bw
Lenfilm

d   **Friedrich Ermler**
sc **Friedrich Ermler, Mikhail Bolshintsov, V.**
    Portnov
ph **Alexander Gintzburg**
m   **Venedikt Pushkov**
    A. Petrov, Ekaterina Korchagina-
    Alexandrovskaya, Nikolai Bogolyubov,
    Yelena Yunger

A dispossessed kulak (Petrov) tries to sabotage a collective by sowing suspicion among the peasants. After beating his pregnant wife (Yunger) to death when she declares she will dedicate her future child to the Revolution, his schemes are finally revealed. A fine, and neglected, example of the Soviet cinema of the mid-1930s, full of earthy humour and passion in its realistic depiction of peasant life. Memorable sequences are an eating contest and the murder scene. The narrative drive and human touches transcend its simple propagandist ending.

▶ **Peau D'Âne** see Magic Donkey, The

▶ **Peau Douce, La** see Silken Skin

The Pedestrian

▶ **Der Fussgänger**

W. Germany   1974   97 mins   col
ALFA/MFG

d   **Maximilian Schell**
sc **Maximilian Schell**
ph **Wolfgang Treu, Klaus König**
m   **Manos Hadjidakis**
    Gustav Rudolf Sellner, Ruth Hausmeister,
    Maximilian Schell, Alexander May,
    Manuel Sellner, Gila Von Weitershausen

The past begins to catch up with a wealthy and respectable West German industrialist (Gustav Rudolf Sellner), when a newspaper editor (May) reveals that, as a Nazi officer, he participated in the burning of an occupied building in Greece in 1943. The issues are explored in a TV debate in which the industrialist and what he represents are condemned. One of the many guilt-ridden German films over the last few decades says very little new, but says it reasonably well. An effective use is made of flashbacks to link the horror of the past with the present – references are made to Vietnam – and the Weimar Republic with the Germany of today. More predictable than pedestrian, it does have a surprising sequence of a tea party at which Peggy Ashcroft, Lil Dagover, Elisabeth Bergner and Françoise Rosay make cameo appearances.

The Pedlar

▶ **Dastforoush**

Iran 1987 95 mins col
Arts Bureau Of The Organization For The Propagation of Islamic Thought

d **Mohsen Makhmalbaf**
sc **Mohsen Makhmalbaf**
ph **Homayun Payvar, Mehrdad Fakhimi, Ali R. Zarindast**
m **Madjid Entezami**
  Zohreh Saramadi, Esmail Saramadian, Morteza Zarrabi, Behzad Behzadpoor

Three accounts of urban deprivation in contemporary Iran. The first (based on a story by Alberto Moravia) tells of a couple whose grinding poverty leads them to try and find someone to adopt their newborn daughter. The second concerns an unstable man who is laughed at by his neighbours and has only his aged mother for company. The last is about a youth, the pedlar of the title, who is suspected of betraying his fellow traffickers. The three stories chart a fascinating journey through the lower reaches of Iranian society, each one vividly portraying different aspects of it. Although there are glimmerings of hope throughout, what comes across is the unvarnished truth, often moving and sometimes humorous. Despite the name of the production company, non-Muslim audiences would have no feeling of being preached at. The only thing missing is a political context, hardly surprising considering the regime under which the film was made.

▶ **Peek-A-Boo** see Femmes De Paris

▶ **Pelle Erobreren** see Pelle The Conqueror

Pelle The Conqueror

▶ **Pelle Erobreren**

Denmark 1987 160 mins col
Per Holst Filmproduktion Aps/Danish Film Institute/Svensk Filmindustri

d **Bille August**
sc **Bille August**
ph **Jörgen Persson**
m **Stefan Nilsson**
  Max Von Sydow, Pelle Hvenegaard, Erik Paaske, Björn Granath, Axel Strøbye, Astrid Villaume

At the turn-of-the century, Lasse (Max Von Sydow), a widowed farmer, and his nine-year-old son Pelle (Hvenegaard), leave poverty-stricken Sweden for what they hope will be a better life on the Danish Baltic Island of Bornholm. But the father finds himself little more than a slave as a cowherd, while his son suffers at the rural school. Pelle decides to leave and conquer the world. Director August, refusing American money and the offer to make the film in English, settled for making only the first part (in Danish) of Nobel-Prizewinner Martin Andersen Nexoe's best-selling four-volume novel. The result is a stylistically old-fashioned, beautiful-to-look-at, unsentimental but moving epic of exploitation, with a cast of characters that includes the staples of period soap – the farm owner's alcoholic wife, a cruel foreman and a seduced and abandoned servant girl. The performances from Von Sydow and Hvenegaard are outstanding.

Best Film Cannes 1988
Best Foreign Film Oscar 1988

Pension Mimosas

France 1935 110 mins bw
Tobis

d **Jacques Feyder**
sc **Charles Spaak, Jacques Feyder**
ph **Roger Hubert**
m **Louis Beydts**

Françoise Rosay, Paul Bernard, Alermé, Lise Delamare

Louise (Rosay), the proprietor of the Pension Mimosas on the French Riviera, which caters for *habitués* of the Nice casinos, carries out a desperate ploy to save her shiftless godson (Bernard) from gambling and women. Like *Le Grand Jeu*, the year before, which concentrated on the inhabitants of a café, this comedy-drama centres on a small community, the hotel of the title. In the midst of the flow of well-defined characters stands Rosay's rich portrait of a woman whose passion for her 'son' is more than maternal. Lazare Meerson's vivid sets add to Feyder's splendid sense of place.

▶ **People Of France, The** see Vie Est À Nous, La

People On Sunday

▶ **Menschen Am Sonntag**

> Germany 1929 72 mins bw
> Studiofilm

d   Robert Siodmak, Edgar Ulmer
sc Billy Wilder, Curt Siodmak
ph Eugen Schüfftan
m   Silent
    Brigitte Borchert, Christl Ehlers, Annie Schreyer, Wolfgang Von Waltershausen, Erwin Splettstösser

Twenty-four hours in the lives of a group of Berliners on a day's outing, including a taxi driver, a salesman, a shopgirl and a model. This fresh, humorous and romantic semi-documentary (the people involved re-enact their real-life roles), shot in a freewheeling style on location, launched the careers of a number of film-makers who would all make it big in Hollywood. These are the first credits for the Siodmak brothers, Ulmer and Wilder. In addition, Schüfftan's photographic assistant was Fred Zinnemann.

Pépé Le Moko

> France 1936 90 mins bw
> Paris Film

d   Julien Duvivier

sc Henri Jeanson, Roger D'Ashelbe, Julien Duvivier
ph Jules Kruger
m   Vincent Scotto
    Jean Gabin, Mireille Balin, Gabriel Gabrio, Lucas Gridoux, Line Noro, Gilbert-Gil, Saturnin Fabre

Pépé Le Moko, high-powered jewel thief and bank robber forced to flee from his beloved Paris, lives in the Algerian Casbah as his only means of avoiding arrest. When he falls in love with a beautiful visiting Parisienne he leaves the Casbah to seek her, and is caught. The quintessential loner at his most attractively roguish, Gabin created one of the cinema's best loved anti-heroes in a film teeming with life, romance, suspense and humour. Under Duvivier's direction, the film is immaculately acted, and beautifully lit and photographed. It remains a classic of the genre, which Hollywood was swift to plunder, giving us *Algiers* with Charles Boyer and Hedy Lamarr in 1938 (rather good), and a semi-musical, *Casbah*, in 1948 with Tony Martin and Yvonne De Carlo (rather poor).

Peppermint Frappé

> Spain 1968 94 mins col
> Elias Querejeta Productions

d   Carlos Saura
sc Carlos Saura, Angelino Fons, Rafael Azcona
ph Luis Cuadrado
m   Luis De Pablo
    José Luis Lopez Vasquez, Geraldine Chaplin, Alfredo Mayo

Julian (Lopez Vasquez), a doctor, becomes obsessively infatuated with his brother's lively and attractive wife, Elena. Since she is unattainable, he sets out to transform Ana, his shy, plain nurse, into a replica of Elena, and seduces her with tragic consequences. The director dedicates his film to Buñuel, whose influence is evident in this treatment of a disturbed mind as Julian falls prey to illusions, dreams and memories, focused on his repressed religious upbringing. Geraldine Chaplin impresses in the dual roles of Elena and Ana in this controlled suspense story, illuminated by Saura's insight and imagination.

Peppermint Freedom

▶ **Peppermint Frieden**

W. Germany 1982 112 mins bw/part col
Nourfilm Produktion

d **Marianne S.W. Rosenbaum**
sc **Marianne S.W. Rosenbaum**
ph **Alfred Tichawsky**
m **Konstantin Wecker**
    Peter Fonda, Saskia Tyroller, Gesine Strempel, Hans Peter Korff, Cleo Kretschmer

After the war Marianne (Tyroller) and her family go to live in a small village in Germany's American zone. There, the little girl and her friends try to make sense of the war and of the peace through imaginary games and the hero-worship of an American soldier (Fonda) whom they call 'Mr Freedom'. (The 'Frieden' of the title actually means 'peace'). In her play-acting, and in a series of vivid dreams, Marianne tries to understand the contradictions, concealments and repressive teachings of the adult world. Working from a pacifist and feminist perspective, and drawing inspiration from her own childhood memories, the director defines her imaginative anti-war film as being about 'the birth of guilt'. A serious piece that is dense in content and surreal in style, it also encompasses a measure of humour.

▶ **Peppermint Frieden** see Peppermint Freedom

Peppermint Soda

▶ **Diabolo Menthe**

France 1977 101 mins col
Les Films De L'Alma/Alexandre Films

d **Diane Kurys**
sc **Diane Kurys**
ph **Philippe Rousselot**
m **Yves Simon**
    Eléonore Klarwein, Odile Michel, Anouk Ferjac, Michel Puterflam, Yves Renier

Thirteen-year-old Anne (Klarwein), withdrawn and a non-achiever, and her sister Frédérique (Michel), extrovert and into her first adolescent love affairs, are the daughters of a divorced Jewish couple. They live with their mother, attend a joyless and authoritarian school, and spend holiday time with their father with whom they are ill at ease. Kurys' debut feature is a gentle, observant and nostalgic piece, drawn from experiences of her own adolescence, and with the action occupying a year from the time of Kennedy's assassination. If the director betrays inexperience in her somewhat clumsy handling of the social and political climate of the times, she has an admirable command of her excellent cast – notably Klarwein – and is sensitive to the school milieu.

Perceval

▶ **Perceval Le Gallois**

France 1978 140 mins col
Les Films Du Losange/FR3/A.R.D./Gaumont/RAI (Italy)

d **Eric Rohmer**
sc **Eric Rohmer**
ph **Nestor Almendros**
m **Guy Robert**
    Fabrice Luchini, André Dussollier, Arielle Dombasle, Marc Eyraud, Marie-Christine Barrault

The young Welsh knight Perceval (Luchini) comes in his wanderings to a mysterious castle in which he sees the Holy Grail. In the morning, the castle is deserted and he rides away, only realizing too late what he had seen. He cannot find the place again and continues his quest for the Grail. Following his other excursion into the past in The Marquise Of O, Rohmer went even further back, almost to the beginning of French literature, for the inspiration of what is also a decidedly moral tale. Based on the unfinished 12th-century poem by Chrétien De Troyes, the film retains the verse form in a translation of the original Old French. Shot entirely on stylized painted sets, it gives the impression of being an animated medieval miniature. However, despite many incidental aural and visual pleasures, it takes a bit of sitting through at over two hours.

▶ **Perceval Le Gallois** see Perceval

The Perfume Of The Lady In Black

▶ **Le Parfum De La Dame En Noir**

France 1931 109 mins bw
Film Osso

d Marcel L'Herbier
sc Marcel L'Herbier
ph Georges Périnal
    Huguette Duflos, Roland Toutain, Kissa
    Kouprine, Belières

After solving *The Mystery Of The Yellow Room* for the professor's daughter (Duflos), the intrepid journalist (Toutain) comes once more to her rescue when she is haunted by the presence of her first husband whom she believes is dead. Even better than the previous film based on Gaston Leroux's novel, this sequel shows L'Herbier at his delirious best, revealing a marvellous mosaic of film techniques to serve the purposes of this labyrinthine thriller – mirror images, *trompe l'oeil* sets, fragmented cutting and inventive sound. Sadly, L'Herbier never reached this height again and was forced to 'accept forms of cinema which were the very ones I'd always avoided'.

▶ **Péril En La Demeure** see Death In A French Garden

▶ **Per Le Antiche Scale** see Down The Ancient Stairs

▶ **Perles De La Couronne, Les** see Pearls Of The Crown, The

Persona

Sweden 1966 81 mins bw
Svensk Filmindustri

d Ingmar Bergman
sc Ingmar Bergman
ph Sven Nykvist
m Lars Johan Werle
    Liv Ullmann, Bibi Andersson, Gunnar
    Björnstrand, Margaretha Krook, Jörgen
    Lindström

Elisabeth Vogler (Ullmann), a famous actress, is stricken with psychosomatic loss of speech and is placed in the care of Nurse Alma (Andersson) at a remote seaside cottage. The woman who has renounced language and the other, who talks incessantly, begin to understand one another and exchange identities. With *Persona*, the female face in close-up became Bergman's main field of vision. In this virtual two-hander, everything is written on the features of the superb female leads, including the spiritual anguish from which most Bergman characters suffer. The poetic and tragic face-to-face encounter is only cluttered by an extraneous prologue of brutal images, a strange young boy, and an ending of film burning in a projector.

▶ **Personal Column** see Snares

Persons Unknown

▶ **(US: Big Deal On Madonna Street)**

▶ **aka The Usual Unidentified Thieves**

▶ **I Soliti Ignoti**

Italy 1958 105 mins bw
Lux/Vides/Cinecitta

d Mario Monicelli
sc Age, Scarpelli, Suso Cecchi D'Amico,
    Mario Monicelli
ph Gianni Di Venanzo
m Piero Umiliani
    Vittorio Gassman, Renato Salvatori,
    Marcello Mastroianni, Totò, Memmo
    Carotenuto, Claudia Cardinale, Rosanna
    Rory

A group of incompetent amateur crooks plan an elaborate robbery of a pawn shop through an empty apartment next door, but end up merely stealing pasta and peas. This delightful comedy of errors, spoofing *Rififi*, is no less funny for being firmly rooted in social conditions of deprivation. The impeccable cast, the comic silent-film intertitles and the jaunty jazz score added to its popularity. It was remade by Louis Malle as *Crackers* in 1984 and given a San Francisco setting.

▶ **Pervy Uchitel** see First Teacher, The

Pestonjee

India 1988 114 mins col
National Film Development Corporation

d Vijaya Mehta
sc Vijaya Mehta, B.K. Karanjia
ph Rajan Kothari
m Vanraj Bhatia
    Naseeruddin Shah, Shabana Azmi,
    Anupam Kher, Veera Sorabjee, Chandu
    Parhi, Farrokh Mehta

Among the Parsee *bourgeoisie* of the late
1950s, Piroisha (Shah), the self-appointed
conscience of everyone around him and
especially of his closest friend Pestonjee
(Kher), loves Jeroo (Azmi) but hesitates to
propose to her. When she marries his best
friend he continues to love them both over
the years and prays for their health, happiness
and the blessing of children. But while Piroisha remains the same, the couple, so important in his life, change towards each other and
him. The third feature of Mehta, well known
as an actress in India, is a moving, tender
and witty Chekhovian tale of small but significant events in the lives of three people.
Meticulously recreating its time, place and
society, the film subtly delineates the changing
relationships over the years, similar in substance but not style to Truffaut's *Jules And
Jim* (1961).

Peter And Pavla

▶ **(US: Black Peter)**

▶ **Cerny Petr**

Czechoslovakia 1964 85 mins bw
Czechoslovak State

d Milôs Forman
sc Milôs Forman, Ivan Passer, Jaroslav
    Papoušek
ph Miroslav Ondříček
m Jiří Šlitr
    Ladislav Jakim, Pavla Martínková, Jan
    Ostrčil, Božena Matušková, Vladimír
    Pucholt

Teenage Peter (Jakim), finds his first job as a
trainee store detective not to his liking, has
problems of communication with his conservative father (Ostrčil) and makes little
headway with carefree Pavla (Martínková)

whom he takes dancing. After two shorts in
which he gave documentary material fictional
form – they were about talent and brass band
contests – Forman, in his first feature, gave
his fictional material documentary form.
Using non-professional actors, improvised
dialogue and shooting in the streets, the film
brought a new vitality into the Czech cinema.
This sharply observed, satiric, affectionate
and humorous movie, with a smattering of a
plot, was the launch of a career that led
Forman to bigger things and Hollywood.

▶ **Petite Marchande D'Allumettes,
    La** see Little Matchgirl, The

▶ **Petites Guerres** see Little Wars

La Petite Voleuse

France 1988 109 mins col
Orly Films/Renn Productions/Ciné Cinq/
Les Films du Carosse/Sedif

d Claude Miller
sc François Truffaut, Claude Givray;
    adaptation and dialogue Claude Miller,
    Luc Béraud, Annie Miller
ph Dominique Chapuis
m Alain Jomy
    Charlotte Gainsbourg, Didier Bezace,
    Simon De La Brosse, Raoul Billerey,
    Chantal Banlier

It is 1950. Sixteen-year-old Janine
(Gainsbourg), abandoned by her mother but
hopeful of her return, lives with her aunt and
uncle (Banlier, Billerey) in a small town.
Longing to be grown-up, the girl steals
clothes, make-up and, finally, money from
church funds, narrowly escaping prosecution.
She takes a job as a maid, loses her virginity
to a married man (Bezace), takes up with a
young thief (De La Brosse), becomes pregnant, is institutionalized, escapes and returns
home to a cold welcome... François Truffaut
had long intended to film this subject, Janine
a sort of female counterpart to Antoine
Doinel, but his premature death prevented it.
Working from the basis of a synopsis he left
behind, his former assistant, Claude Miller,
has given it life. In the event, one wonders
why he bothered. Set in post-war France, the
movie is jam-packed with incident and offers

many small details of mood and characterization which are admirable and even enjoyable. Fundamentally, however, although it is difficult to fault Gainsbourg's portrayal of a half-knowing, half-innocent and feisty delinquent, Janine is so uncompromisingly irritating and her story finally so uninteresting that the film becomes almost unendurably tedious. Comparisons have been drawn with Emily Lloyd and *Wish You Were Here*, but *Voleuse* has none of the charm of David Leland's film and little comparable period interest.

▶ **Petit Soldat, Le** see Little Soldier, The

▶ **Petit Théâtre De Jean Renoir, Le** see Little Theatre Of Jean Renoir, The

▶ **Petomane, Il** see Windbreaker, The

The Phantom Baron

▶ **Le Baron Fantôme**

France   1943   100 mins   bw
Consortium De Productions De Films

d   **Serge De Poligny**
sc **Serge De Poligny**
ph **Roger Hubert**
m   **Louis Beydts**
    Jany Holt, Odette Joyeux, Alain Cuny, Gabrielle Dorziat, Claude Sainval, André Lefauer, Jean Cocteau

In 1826 a Countess (Dorziat), her daughter, Elfy (Joyeux), and the latter's friend (Holt) arrive at the castle of the Countess's uncle, the Baron Carol (Cocteau), to learn that, during one of his sleepwalking fits, he has spirited himself and his possessions away. The trio moves into the manor next door where the girls pass their childhood. Ten years later, romantic love and its attendant problems enter their lives and the discovery of the crumbling Baron in a crypt brings revelations. On the face of it, this is an escapist period romance with an immensely complicated plot, tailor-made for wartime audiences. However, the hand of Cocteau, who wrote the effervescent dialogue, is everywhere evident in the fairytale elements that abound. A magical flavour, prefiguring *Beauty And The Beast*,

clings to much of it, but credit must go, too, to Poligny and Hubert for the atmosphere and striking visuals, by turns bleak, mysterious, frightening, pretty and poetic. The fantasy is realistically acted by a highly professional cast.

The Phantom Carriage

▶ **aka Thy Soul Shall Bear Witness**

▶ **aka The Stroke of Midnight**

▶ **Körkalen**

Sweden   1921   70 mins   bw
Svenska Bio

d   **Victor Sjöström**
sc **Victor Sjöström**
ph **J. Julius Jaenzon**
m   **Silent**
    Victor Sjöström, Hilda Borgström, Tore Svennberg Astrid Holm

The drunkard David Holm (Sjöström) has an accident on New Year's Eve, and relives the upright life he led before drink ruined him. He is finally reformed after seeing the carriage of death. Sjöström tells this simple moralistic folk tale with a brilliant array of flashbacks and eerie special effects. Shot mainly outdoors, with a fine lead performance by the director himself, it is widely considered to be his greatest Swedish film. It was mainly due to its success (and the decline of the Swedish cinema industry) that he found himself working in Hollywood as Victor Seastrom a few years later. The film was remade in France in 1939 and in Sweden in 1958.

▶ **Phantom Love** see Empire Of Passion

The Phantom Of Liberty

▶ **Le Fantôme De La Liberté**

France   1974   104 mins   col
Greenwich/20th Century-Fox

d   **Luis Buñuel**
sc **Luis Buñuel, Jean-Claude Carrière**
ph **Edmond Richard**
    Monica Vitti, Michel Piccoli, Jean-

Claude Brialy, Jean Rochefort, Adolfo Celi, Bernard Verley

A series of casually linked episodes moving from Toledo in 1808 and Goya's painting of *The Executions Of 3 May* to contemporary Paris, where various people try to grasp or shun, in Karl Marx's phrase, 'the phantom of liberty'. Buñuel's penultimate film is as mordantly comic, fluent and subversive as one would expect, but the loose, episodic structure and some easy jokes and targets betray a certain laziness. The best remembered sequence has elegant guests seated on individual lavatories around a table from which they excuse themselves to go and have a meal in a little room behind a locked door. The film ends with a close-up of the eye of an ostrich, the most unlikely bird to represent Buñuel's unflinching view of the world.

Pharaoh

▶ **Faraon**

Poland 1965 183 mins col
Film Polski, Kadr Unit

d   Jerzy Kawalerowicz
sc Tadeusz Konwicki, Jerzy Kawalerowicz
ph Jerzy Wójcik
m   Adam Walacinski
    George Zelnik, Barbara Bryl, Krystyna Mikolajewska, Piotr Pawlowski, Andrzej Girtler, Leszek Herdegen

Young Prince Rameses (Zelnik) incurs the disfavour of the powerful high priest Herihor (Pawlowski) when he takes a Jewish girl (Mikolajewska) as his mistress. Further conflict with the hierarchy results from his liberal and aggressive efforts to solve Egypt's severe economic and military problems. When his father the Pharaoh dies, he succeeds him and, as Rameses III, his battle with Herihor escalates, leading to duplicity and violence. An historical epic, complete with battle scenes, but more restrained and realistic than, say, its Hollywood counterparts, this visually striking film, marked by a fine sense of historical veracity, is also a fascinating dissection of the nature of power. Regrettably, it is sometimes shown in a severely cut version which distorts the scale and leaves gaps in the narra-

tive. In any version, Zelnik is not up to his task.

▶ **Philosoph, Der** see Three Women In Love

▶ **Piaf** see Sparrow Of Pigalle, The

▶ **Piatka Z Ulicy Barskiej** see Five Boys From Barska Street

The Picasso Mystery

▶ **aka The Mystery Of Picasso**
▶ **Le Mystère Picasso**

France 1956 78 mins col
Filmsonor

d   Henri-Georges Clouzot
sc Henri-Georges Clouzot, Pablo Picasso
ph Claude Renoir
m   Georges Auric
    Henri-Georges Clouzot, Pablo Picasso

Pablo Picasso, the 75-year-old modern master, talks to the film director Clouzot about his work and inspiration and creates paintings in front of the camera. An intriguing documentary and a valuable record of arguably the greatest artist of the 20th century at work, brilliantly captured by Claude Renoir, the grandson of August Renoir. Special transparent 'canvases' were prepared so that Renoir could film the paintings from behind. It is also an odd meeting between the passionate Spaniard, executing his paintings with furious rapidity, and the cool, punctilious French film-maker.

▶ **Piccolo Mondo Di Don Camillo, Il** see Little World Of Don Camillo, The

Pickpocket

France 1959 80 mins bw
Lux Films

d   Robert Bresson
sc Robert Bresson
ph L.H. Burel
m   Lully

Martin La Salle, Marika Green, Kassagi, Pierre Leymarie, Jean Pelegri, Pierre Étaix, Dolly Scal

A lonely young man (La Salle) embarks on a career as a pickpocket. Arrested, he reflects on the morality of a life of crime but, although temporarily deterred, returns to it, taking lessons from a master (Kassagi). 'With theft I entered by the back door into the kingdom of morality,' stated Bresson on this Jansenist tale (inspired by *Crime And Punishment*) of a sinner who finds redemption through the love of a woman (Green). The protagonist is deliberately kept blank and representational as he moves through the dark, untextured photography which concentrates on his hands, the tools of his trade. The first person narrative technique is used, as in *Diary Of A Country Priest* and *A Man Escaped*, and the visual economy is matched by the spare dialogue. A typical Bressonian exercise, it may be too stoical for those who prefer something less thin-blooded, but its final sequence was copied by Paul Schrader, an admirer of Bresson, in his own *American Gigolo*.

▶ **Picnic On The Grass** see Lunch On The Grass

▶ **Piège Pour Cendrillon** see Trap For Cinderella, A

▶ **Pièges** see Snares

Pierrot-Le-Fou

France 1965 110 mins col
Rome-Paris Films/Dino De Laurentiis/
Georges De Beauregard

d   Jean-Luc Godard
sc Jean-Luc Godard
ph Raoul Coutard
m   Antoine Duhamel
    Anna Karina, Jean-Pierre Belmondo,
    Dirk Sanders, Raymond Devos, Graziella
    Galvani, Sam Fuller

Ferdinand (Belmondo), dissatisfied with his Parisian life and his wife, sets off on a picaresque journey across France to the South with Marianne (Karina), getting involved

with her criminal activities along the way. Godard's stunning study of personal and global violence (there are references to Angola, Vietnam etc) uses colour in a dramatic and symbolic manner. Asked why there was so much blood in the film, Godard replied, 'It is not blood but red'. But most of all it is a tragedy about the transience of love. It is not difficult to see the Belmondo-Karina love-hate relationship as a reflection of the Godard-Karina marriage, then reaching its end. As American director Sam Fuller reflects in the picture, 'Film is like a battleground, love, hate, action, violence, death...in one word, Emotion'.

A Pig Across Paris

▶ **(US: Four Bags Full)**
▶ **La Traversée De Paris**

France 1956 90 mins bw
Franco London/Continentale

d   Claude Autant-Lara
sc Jean Aurenche, Pierre Bost
ph Jacques Natteau
m   René Cloërec
    Jean Gabin, Bourvil, Jeanette Batti,
    Louis De Funès, Georgette Anys

A wealthy artist (Gabin) and a simple cab driver (Bourvil) join up to transport four suitcases of blackmarket pork across Paris during the Occupation, avoiding German roadblocks, hungry dogs and collaborators. Although one of the first Occupation therapy French films to recognize that there was cowardice, stupidity, apathy and hypocrisy among the populace during the period, the movie is principally a competent comedy-thriller with two rattlingly good performances from the well-contrasted male leads.

Best Actor (Bourvil) Venice 1956

Pigs And Battleships

▶ **Buta To Gunkan**

Japan 1961 108 mins bw
Nikkatsu

d   Shohei Imamura

sc **Hisashi Yamanouchi**
ph **Shinsaku Himeda**
m   **Toshiro Mayuzumi**
    Hiroyuki Nagato, Yitsuko Yoshimura,
    Tetsuro Tamba, Sanae Nakahara

When a brothel, which services American sailors from a naval base at Yokosuka, is forced to close down, the owner (Nakahara) sets up a pig farm and places a former pimp (Nagato) in charge. A gang tries to steal the pigs, and chaos and death ensue. This is a splendid mix of melodrama, satire and black comedy, even though it somewhat labours the metaphor of prostitution in US-Japanese relationships. However, the American connection is triumphantly used in the climactic pig stampede, plainly a reference to the Western. At the film's centre is a quintessential Imamura heroine, played by Yoshimura, who retains her decency in the midst of corruption.

Pigsty

▶ **Il Porcile**

Italy 1969 90 mins col
Film Dell'Orso/Idi Cinematografica/
INDIEF/CAPAC(Paris)

d   **Pier Paolo Pasolini**
sc **Pier Paolo Pasolini**
ph **Tonino Delli Colli**
m   **C.A.M. Ghiglia**
    Pierre Clementi, Franco Citti, Jean-Pierre Léaud, Anne Wiazemsky, Ugo Tognazzi, Alberto Lionello

The story of a soldier cannibal (Clementi) in a medieval wasteland is interwoven with that of the son (Léaud) of an ex-Nazi industrialist (Tognazzi) in modern-day Germany. The young German, who is more attracted to pigs than to his fiancée (Wiazemsky), and the cannibal become sacrificial victims of their different societies. This strange, grotesque and rather silly parable is filmed with such calm beauty and underlying disgust that it seems to gain significance. *Theorem* and *Pigsty* were the only films in which Pasolini dealt directly with the hated middle classes; thereafter he was to leave the 20th century behind until his final film, *Salo*.

Pillars Of Society

▶ **Stützen Der Gesellschaft**

Germany 1935 82 mins bw
Krüger-Ulrich/UFA

d   **Detlef Sierck**
sc **Dr Georg C. Klaren, Peter Gillmann**
ph **Carl Drews**
m   **Franz R. Friedl**
    Heinrich George, Maria Krahn, Horst Teetzmann, Albrecht Schönhals, Suse Graf

Johann Tönnessen (Schönhals), having left Norway 20 years previously, is a successful rancher in America. Homesickness prompts him to accompany his circus-owner friend on a tour to his native land where he has a reunion with his ex-business associate Bernick (George), now his brother-in-law. Johann's presence reopens old wounds and triggers off new tensions, particularly as he attracts the hero-worship of Bernick's son (Teetzmann) and falls in love with his ward (Graf) who, it transpires, is actually his illegitimate daughter... This screen version of Ibsen's play is only partially successful. It comes across as standard melodrama, a genre on which Sierck (Douglas Sirk) would, of course, capitalize, and benefits from images which demonstrate the director's imaginative visual skills. However, apart from those sequences where he has opened the material out (the horses in the prologue and, again, at the circus and the climactic storm that spells destruction to Bernick), the piece remains obstinately and detrimentally rooted in its stage origins.

The Pink Telephone

▶ **Le Téléphone Rose**

France 1975 93 mins col
Gaumont

d   **Edouard Molinaro**
sc **Francis Véber**
ph **Gérard Hameline**
m   **Vladimir Cosma**
    Mireille Darc, Pierre Mondy, Michel Lonsdale, Daniel Ceccaldi, Françoise Prévost, Gérard Hérold

Naive, middle-aged provincial industrialist

Mondy is harassed by threatened strikes at his factory, as well as tax difficulties, leading him to consider a takeover by an American company. The latter instals him in the luxury of the Hôtel Georges V in Paris, and introduces him to Darc with whom he falls in love, only to discover that she is a high-class call-girl. He nevertheless abandons his wife (Prévost) to pursue a future with her. This film offers some impeccable acting, Mlle Darc's fair looks, and the suggestion of insight into ruthless business methods. Unfortunately, neither writer nor director seems certain whether this is a comedy, and Molinaro's crude direction only helps to wreck the enterprise.

▶ **Piravi** see Birth, The

Pirosmani

USSR   1971   84 mins   col
Gruziafilm

d   **Georgy Shengelaya**
sc   **Georgy Shengelaya, Erlom Akhvlediani**
ph   **Konstantin Apryatin**
m   **V. Kukhianidze**
    Avtandil Varazi, David Abashidze, Zurab Kapianidze, Teimuraz Beridze, Boris Tsipuria

The Georgian artist Niko Pirosmani (born 1863) roams the taverns of his native land, paying for his keep with his paintings, and finding solace in alcohol. Shengelaya, the son of pioneer Georgian film-maker Nikolai Shengelaya, has vividly captured the qualities of Pirosmani's art – the soft and subtle colours, the primitive forms, the wide-ranging subjects from animals and birds to ordinary people and historical figures. As not much is known about Pirosmani, who is played by the film's art director (Varazi), his life is recounted in a fragmented but naturalistic manner. An original and imaginative work.

▶ **Pisma Myortvovo Chelovyeka** see Letters From A Dead Man

Pixote

Brazil   1981   125 mins   col

Embrafilme/Hector Babenco

d   **Hector Babenco**
sc   **Hector Babenco, Jorge Duran**
ph   **Rodolfo Sanches**
m   **John Neschling**
    Marilia Pera, Fernando Ramos De Silva, Jorge Juliao, Gilberto Moura, Jose Nilson Dos Santos

During a routine police sweep of the squalid streets of São Paulo, Pixote (De Silva), an abandoned 10-year-old boy, the effeminate 17-year-old Lilica (Juliao) and another youth (Dos Santos) are taken to a detention centre. The three boys escape, aided by Lilica's lover (Moura) and get involved with a homosexual drug dealer and an aging alcoholic prostitute (Pera)... The plight of the three million homeless children in Brazil needs to be exposed and Babenco, who introduces the film, plainly has his heart in the right place. However, any political or social purpose the movie might have had gets lost in sensationalism. Unlike Güney's The Wall or Buñuel's The Young And The Damned, it creates disgust rather than outrage. The performances by actual street kids are horrifyingly natural; in fact, the child in the title role returned to his life of crime after making the film and was shot and killed by the police in 1987.

▶ **Pizza Triangle, The** see Jealousy, Italian Style

▶ **Plaf! – Demasiado Miedo A La Vida** see Plaff! – Too Afraid Of Life

Plaff! – Too Afraid Of Life

▶ **Plaf! – Demasiado Miedo A La Vida**

Cuba   1988   110 mins   col
Production Company ICAIC

d   **Juan Carlos Tabio**
sc   **Juan Carlos Tabio, Daniel Chavarria Reynoso**
ph   **Julio Valdès**
m   **None**
    Daisy Granados, Thais Valdès, Luis Alberto Garcia, Raúl Pomares, Alicia Bustamante, Jorge Cão

A jealous mother-in-law (Granados) tries to

undermine the marriage of her son (Garcia) to a modern girl (Valdès) by the use of Santeria, Cuba's unofficial African-based religion, but is constantly dodging the assaults of a mysterious egg-thrower. A quirky, funny film that is packed with surprises, it is also a pointed satire on many of the sacred cows of Cuban society – religious cults, soap opera and government control – while spoofing the film-making process itself. Tabio's 'alienating' effect of pretending the film is being made incompetently by including fluffs, bad editing and continuity, visible camera booms and the entire crew glimpsed in a mirror, reflects the prevailing attitude to Third World cinema and the inefficiencies of the country's bureaucracy. Typical is the filing cabinet in an office which blocks a door. In order to have it removed, a vast correspondence has to take place, resulting in a pile of letters obstructing the door. It is vigorously played by a cast led by the magnificent Granados, and if some of the jokes go 'plaff', many of them are bang on target.

Le Plaisir

▶ **(US: House Of Pleasure)**

France 1952 97 mins bw
Stera/CCFC

d **Max Ophüls**
sc **Jacques Natanson, Max Ophüls**
ph **Christian Matras, Philippe Agostini**
m **Joe Hajos (adapted from Offenbach)**
Claude Dauphin, Gaby Morlay, Madeleine Renaud, Danielle Darrieux, Ginette Leclerc, Jean Gabin, Pierre Brasseur, Simone Simon, Daniel Gélin, Jean Servais, Jean Galland

Three tales based on stories by Guy de Maupassant. 1) 'Le Masque' – an old man (Galland) finds his youth again by wearing a magic mask. 2) 'La Maison Tellier' – a group of prostitutes pays an annual holiday visit to the country. 3) 'La Modèle' – an artist (Gélin) in the habit of making mistresses of his models has to marry one (Simone) out of sympathy when she cripples herself during a suicide attempt. Each of the three complementary stories has memorable sequences which ensure that the film lives up to its title: the exhilarated camera moving with the masked dancer as he

whirls and whirls until he falls, the contrast between the brothel and the country, between shadow and light in the second story, and the trapped painter wheeling his wife along the beach in the last. Pleasure comes too from performances such as Renaud's Madame and Gabin as her lecherous peasant brother.

The Players

▶ **aka The Actors**
▶ **Komödianten**

Germany 1941 110 mins bw
Bavaria Filmkunst

d **G. W. Pabst**
sc **Axel Eggebrecht, Walter Von Hollander, G. W. Pabst**
ph **Bruno Stephan**
m **Lothar Brühne**
Käthe Dorsch, Hilde Krahl, Henny Porten, Gustav Diessl, Richard Häussler

In mid-18th century Germany, Philine Schröder (Krahl) runs away from home to find refuge with a company of players run by Carolina Neuber (Dorsch). After the troupe suffers many artistic and financial problems, Philine gets the Duchess of Weisenfels (Porten), the aunt of the man she has married, to build a theatre for Carolina. This was the first of three films Pabst made in Germany during the war, the other two being the equally ponderous *Paracelcus* and *Der Fall Molander*. Two were biopics about German geniuses, this one being about the establishment of the first German national theatre and the need to put on German plays rather than foreign 'muck'. Mechanical, melodramatic and platitudinous, it is an example of how a once-great director could be manipulated by the needs of the State. It must be remembered that Pabst's award was given by the then Fascist-controlled Venice Festival.

Best Director Venice 1941

Playing At Love

▶ **(US: The Love Game)**
▶ **Les Jeux De L'Amour**

France 1960 87 mins bw

AJYM

d **Philippe De Broca**
sc **Philippe De Broca, Daniel Boulanger**
ph **Jean Penzer**
m **Georges Delerue**
   Jean-Pierre Cassel, Geneviève Cluny,
   Jean-Louis Maury, Robert Vathier

A feckless young painter (Cassel) will not give in to his live-in girlfriend's (Cluny) desire for marriage and/or a child, but when his best friend (Maury) makes her an offer, he finally promises a wedding. This effervescent sex comedy, De Broca's first film, is dominated by the running, jumping and gesticulating Cassel, giving a performance as maddening as it is charming.

Playtime

▶ **La Récréation**

   France 1961 87 mins bw
   General-Élite/Audubon

d **François Moreuil**
sc **Daniel Boulanger, François Moreuil**
ph **Jean Penzer**
m **Georges Delerue**
   Jean Seberg, Christian Marquand,
   Françoise Prévost, Evelyn Ker

An American student (Seberg), studying at a college in Versailles, becomes fascinated to the point of obsession with the couple who live in the house next door. He (Marquand) is a sculptor, she (Prévost) his glamorous older mistress and wealthy patron. Eventually, she meets the man and they have an affair, until she recognizes his car as the vehicle that was involved in a fatal hit-and-run accident which she witnessed... The debut film of Moreuil, who was married to Seberg at the time, is not a particularly distinguished effort. Adapted from a story by Françoise Sagan, it meanders along much in the diffuse manner of that novelist, managing a little comedy, some intriguing drama and quite a lot of tedium. Seberg and Marquand are somewhat bland, leaving such honours as there are to the cool Prévost.

Playtime

   France 1967 152 mins col
   Specta Films

d **Jacques Tati**
sc **Jacques Tati, Jacques Lagrange**
ph **Jean Badal, Andreas Winding**
m **Francis Lemarque**
   Jacques Tati, Barbara Dennek, Jacqueline
   Lecomte, Henri Piccoli, Valérie Camille,
   France Romilly, Jack Gautier

Monsieur Hulot (Tati), doing battle with objects, observes a group of American tourists on their perigrinations around the Paris of modern office blocks and skyscrapers. They end up at the opening of a nightclub which is far from ready. The only glimpse of old Paris the tourists get as they scurry through the extraordinary metropolis of glass and concrete, designed by Eugène Roman, is on postcards. Tati's use of space and the possibilities of the 70mm screen have probably never been equalled. As the critic Noël Burch has written, it is the only film which must be seen 'not only several times, but at different distances from the screen'. Unfortunately, Tati's masterpiece (which appeared nine years after his previous film) did not get the recognition it deserved and was shown mainly only in versions reduced in time and space.

▶ **Pleasure Party** see Partie De Plaisir, Une

▶ **Plein Soleil** see Purple Noon

▶ **Pleure Pas La Bouche Pleine** see Spring Into Summer

Plot

▶ **L'Attentat**

   France 1972 124 mins col
   Transinter(Paris)/Terza(Rome)/Corona-Filmproduktion(Munich)

d **Yves Boisset**
sc **Ben Barzman, Basilio Franchini**
ph **Ricardo Aronovich**
m **Ennio Morricone**
   Jean-Louis Trintignant, Michel Piccoli,
   Gian Maria Volonté, Jean Seberg,
   François Périer, Philippe Noiret, Michel
   Bouquet, Bruno Cremer, Roy Scheider

Sadiel (Volonté), exiled leader of a progressive political party in a North African state, is a continuing threat to the government of his country, as well as to French and American interests. The CIA and the French Secret Service concoct an elaborate plan to get rid of Sadiel, duping Darien (Trintignant), a seedy Left-wing journalist, into luring him to Paris. When Darien discovers the betrayal, his efforts to expose the affair lead to his brutal murder. In setting out to make one film, Boisset has succeeded in making quite another. Drawing his material from such facts as are known about the notorious Ben Barka affair in 1965 – for which he suffered much harassment during and after filming – the director has failed in his ambition to create a truly realistic political document. On the level of a tough, hard-hitting and thoroughly gripping thriller, however, it works wonderfully well, and Volonté and Trintignant, very well supported, are splendid.

▶ **Plötzliche Reichtum Der Armen Leute Von Kombach, Der** see Sudden Fortune Of The Poor People Of Kombach, The

▶ **Plovec** see Swimmer, The

▶ **Plumbum Iii Opasnaya Igra** see Plumbum, Or A Dangerous Game

Plumbum, Or A Dangerous Game

▶ **Plumbum Iii Opasnaya Igra**

USSR 1986 96 mins col
Mosfilm

d   **Vadim Abdrashitov**
sc **Aleksander Mindadze**
ph **Georgi Rerberg**
m   **Vladimir Dashkevich**
    Anton Adrosov (Ruslan, alias Plumbum), Elena Dmitrieva, Elena Yakovleva, Zoya Lirova, Aleksander Feklistov, Vladimir Steklov, Aleksander Pashutin

Plumbum (Latin for lead) is the self-chosen *nom-de-guerre* of 16-year-old Ruslan, a schoolboy obsessed with stamping out crime. He worms his way into acting as an informer for a special police squad with bizarre results, such as arresting his own father for poaching. Based on a controversial best-selling novel, this movie provoked fierce debate in Russia:

some argued that Ruslan is an unacceptable product of a repressive regime which allows power to reside in hands not yet fit to exercise it, while others saw him as a paragon of virtue. An extraordinarily interesting film that offered a current picture of day-to-day life in a Russian city but, to a Western view, the moral focus is less perplexing than its sometimes unbelievable context. Ruslan (very well acted), whose doting parents don't appear to notice when he stays out all night, is obnoxious, a ghastly child whose immaturity distorts the lens of his own vision and leads, finally, to disaster. Fascinating but unsatisfying.

▶ **Plus Belles Éscroqueries Du Monde, Les** see Beautiful Swindlers, The

▶ **Plus Vieux Métier Du Monde, Le** see Oldest Profession, The

▶ **Pociag** see Night Train

▶ **Poema O Morye** see Poem Of The Sea

Poem Of The Sea

▶ **Poema O Morye**

USSR 1958 110 mins col
Mosfilm

d   **Julia Solntseva**
sc **Alexander Dovzhenko**
ph **Gavril Yegiazarov**
m   **Gavril Popov**
    Boris Livanov, Boris Andreyev, Mikhail Tsaryov, M. Romanov, Zinaida Kiriyenko

The construction of an artificial sea in the midst of the Ukraine is about to take place, necessitating the flooding of a village. Villagers past and present gather to bid farewell to their home, among them a veteran General (Livanov), his lifelong friend and the chairman of the farm collective (Andreyev), an elderly carpenter and a young boy and girl (Tsaryov and Kiriyenko). Assembling from all corners of the country, the gathering acknowledges that the past must make way for a better future. Alexander Dovzhenko died in 1956, the night before he was to begin shooting the film he had prepared for two years. Working from his detailed script, his widow fulfilled his dream. The finished product is an extremely bold venture, painted in bold colours, which attempts to marry the past, the present and the future in the form of a visual poem. Sometimes bombastic and confusing, often static, the film – which begins the vast and unique Dovzhenko- Solntseva 70mm triptych with *The Flaming Years* and *The Enchanted Desna* – is nonetheless remarkable for its confidence, grandeur and glowing beauty.

Poil De Carotte

▶ **(US: Redhead)**

France   1932   94 mins   bw
Film D'Art

d   **Julien Duvivier**
sc **Jules Renard**
ph **Armand Thirard, Emil Monniot**
m   **Alexandre Tansman**
    Harry Baur, Robert Lynen, Catherine Fonteney, Louis Gauthier, Christiane Dor

In rural France, 'Carrot Top' (Lynen), an undernourished and unloved young boy, is badly treated by his aging mother (Fonteney), but his often absent father (Baur) is unaware of this. Everything comes to a head when the child attempts suicide. Duvivier's second attempt to make Jules Renard's classic novella of childhood (the first was a silent version in 1925), turned out to be a classic film of childhood. This was thanks to the author's own screenplay, the fine photography and the wonderful key performance by the great Harry Baur. The colour remake of 1973 could not equal it.

The Pointsman

▶ **De Wisselwachter**

Netherlands   1986   96 mins   col
Jos Stelling Filmprodukties

d   **Jos Stelling**
sc **Jos Stelling, George Brugmans, Hans De Wolf**
ph **Frans Bromet, Theo Van De Sande, Paul Van Den Bos, Goert Giltaij**
m   **Michel Mulders**

Jim Van Der Woude, Stéphane Excoffier, John Kraaykamp, Josse De Pauw, Ton Van Dort

An unidentified country a few decades ago. In winter a well-dressed French woman (Excoffier), travelling by train, alights with her luggage at a remote signalling point. She is reluctantly taken in by the pointsman (Van Der Woude), who hardly ever speaks. They become lovers. The only other contacts she has are with a train driver (Kraaykamp) and his mate (Van Dort), and a postman (De Pauw) who tries to rape her. The Pointsman shoots him. Filmed mainly in the Scottish Highlands, this taciturn and eerie chronicle of the seasons beautifully captures the changing shapes of nature (unusually there are four photographers). In the foreground a duet of glances and gestures is enacted, exercising a certain hypnotic fascination, although how much of the schematic work is meant to be humorous is a moot point.

Poison

▶ **Gift**

Denmark   1966   98 mins   bw
Nordisk Films/Morten Schyberg

d   **Knud Leif Thomsen**
sc **Knud Leif Thomsen**
ph **Claus Loof**
m   **Niels Viggo Bentzon**
    Søren Strømberg, Sisse Reingard, Poul Reichhardt, Astrid Villaume, Judy Gringer

Henrik Steen (Reichhardt), middle-aged, comfortably off, and married with a teenage daughter, indulges in affairs with the maid, his secretary and other available girls. His double standards receive a jolt when his daughter's boyfriend (Strømberg) moves in, preaching and acting out an unashamed gospel of sexual liberation. An interesting and amusing idea which Thomsen renders lifeless by directing with deathly earnestness, while ignoring all but unintentional humour.

▶ **Pokjaniye,   Monanieba** see
Repentance

▶ **Pokolenie** see Generation, A

Police

France 1985 113 mins col
Gaumont/TFI

d **Maurice Pialat**
sc **Catherine Breillat, Sylvie Danton,
    Jacques Fieschi, Maurice Pialat**
ph **Luciano Tovoli**
m **Henryk Mikolaj Gorecki
    Gérard Depardieu, Sophie Marceau,
    Richard Anconina, Pascale Rocard,
    Sandrine Bonnaire, Franck Karoui**

A Parisian police inspector (Depardieu),
investigating a drug ring operating out of
Marseilles, becomes passionately involved
with a girl (Marceau) at its centre. Pialat's
first big budget film, a tremendous hit in
France, is a tough *policier* that unintentionally
(?) seems to collude with the rascist, sexist
cop played by Depardieu with his usual compelling power. Equally forceful is the direction, especially in the documentary-type
realism of police procedure in the first half.
But when the film moves away from the genre
into the central erotic relationship between
Depardieu and Marceau, it resounds with the
familiar ring of the 'cops and crooks are alike'
plot. Marceau declared Pialat a 'sado-masochistic pervert' in his treatment of her during
the shooting, and he called her 'a young
bitch'. Charmant!

▶ **Polioty Vo Sne Naiavou** see Dream
Flights

▶ **Polowanie Na Muchy** see Hunting
Flies

Ponirah

▶ **Ponirah Terpidana**

Indonesia 1983 105 mins col
Sukma Putra Film

d **Slamet Rahardjo**
sc **Slamet Rahardjo**
ph **Tantra Suryadi**
m **Eros Djarot
    Nani Vidya, Christine Hakim, Ray
    Sahetapy, Slamet Rahardjo, Bambang
    Hermanto, Lina Budiarti, Teguh Karya**

Ponirah (Vidya), whose mother died giving
birth to her, has grown up in the care of her
loving nurse (Hakim) but rejected by her
father. This denial has scarred her emotionally
and, harbouring feelings of both guilt and
resentment, she sets out to take a bitter
revenge on her past and on a society that
exploits her. Made by a well-known actor
and one of Indonesia's foremost theatre directors, Rahardjo's third excursion into film-
making demonstrates the emergence of an
original and maturing talent. What could so
easily have been a melodrama develops as a
profound tragedy, thanks to the director's
accomplished and disciplined approach which
lends the piece a grand dimension. The performances, too, are convincingly on target.
It's interesting to note that Rahardjo has
tackled Japanese Noh, a Czech play and
Brecht's *The Good Woman Of Szechuan* in
the theatre, all of which has no doubt contributed to his experimental yet formal sense of
style and structure.

▶ **Ponirah Terpidana** see Ponirah

▶ **Popiol I Diament** see Ashes And
Diamonds

▶ **Popioly** see Ashes

▶ **Porcile, Il** see Pigsty

The Pornographer

▶ **Jinruigaku Nyumon**

Japan 1966 128 mins bw
Nikkatsu

d **Shohei Imamura**
sc **Koji Numata, Shohei Imamura**
ph **Shinsaku Himeda**
m **Toshiro Mayuzumi
    Shoichi Ozawa, Sumiko Sakamoto,
    Masaomi Kondo, Keiko Sagawa, Ganjiro
    Nakamura**

Mr Ogata (Ozawa), officially a medical instruments salesman, in fact devotes his energies
to the purveyance of sex aids in the committed
belief that he is spreading happiness. He lives
with the widowed Haru (Sakamoto), towards
whose daughter he feels both guilt (for an
accident she suffered) and lust. Harassed and

put-upon, he goes to pieces when Haru, ill and mad, kills herself, and decides that man's happiness must lie in satisfying his physical needs free of women. Moving into a dilapidated houseboat, he begins work on his most dedicated pornographic project – the construction of an artificial but physically authentic woman... Imamura's film, generally shown cut by 35 minutes, borders on the bizarre but is played and photographed in a matter-of-fact style, neither prurient nor judgemental in tone. Depressing and discomfiting, it is also riveting.

▶ **Porte Aperte** see Open Doors

▶ **Porte Des Lilas** see Gates Of Paris

▶ **Portes De La Nuit, Les** see Gates Of The Night

▶ **Portes Tournantes, Les** see Revolving Doors, The

Port Of Call

▶ **Hamnstad**

Sweden 1948 100 mins bw
Svensk Filmindustri

d   Ingmar Bergman
sc Ingmar Bergman
ph Gunnar Fischer
m   Erland Von Koch
    Nine-Christine Jönsson, Bengt Eklund, Mimi Nelson, Berta Hall, Birgitta Valberg

A tormented girl (Jönsson), caught between her reformatory past and the rigid puritanism of the social workers, turns to an honest, slow-thinking young sailor (Eklund) for love. The film, belonging to Bergman's short 'realist' period, was largely shot on location in the Göteborg docks in a rare attempt to strike an almost documentary note. Against this coherent background is a bleak tale, tinged with elements of melodrama that often verge on hysteria. But Fischer's photography and Jönsson's performance hold this early work together.

▶ **Port Of Shadows** see Quai Des Brumes

▶ **Port Of Shame** see Lovers Of Lisbon, The

Portrait Of A Life

▶ **Ekti Jiban**

India 1988 130 mins col
Chalchitra Productions

d   Raja Mitra
sc Raja Mitra
ph Kamal Nayak
m   Raja Mitra
    Soumitra Chatterjee, Madhavi Chakrabarty, Avory Dutta, Munna Chakrabarty

In the 1930s, Gurudas (Chatterjee), a humble teacher of Sanskrit in a poor country school, becomes fascinated by the origin of Bengali words and decides to write the first Bengali dictionary. This he does by dedicating the rest of his life to the task, only winning official recognition on his death bed in a hovel. Not a subject to catch the film publicist's eye – 'See the Writing of the First Bengali Dictionary!' 'Thrill to the Academic Quest for Knowledge!' – nevertheless, it does make enthralling viewing. Although Mitra plainly views Gurudas as saintly, the film avoids the pitfalls of hagiography by showing him to be a very human but obsessive man (beautifully played by Satyajit Ray's favourite actor) who neglects his family as he goes about his huge undertaking. It also proves that there is no subject that cannot be turned into something cinematic when done with artistry.

Portrait Of Chieko

▶ **Chieko-Sho**

Japan 1967 125 mins col
Shochiku

d   Noboru Nakamura
sc Minoru Hirose, Noboru Nakamura
ph Hiroshi Takamura
m   Masaru Sato

Tetsuro Tamba, Shima Iwashita, Eiji Okada, Takamura Sasaki, Jin Nakayama

Chieko, the wife of poet and sculptor Kotaro Takamura (Tamba), is passionately dedicated to the creation of beauty. Her gifts, however, are unable to match her inspiration and, when her paintings come in for criticism, she withdraws, attempts suicide and finally, in spite of her husband's devoted care, becomes incurably insane. This detailed and intensely moving document of human suffering is based on the true story of Takamura, one of Japan's major artists. Directed at an appropriately measured pace, exquisitely photographed and acted at the highest level (notably by Iwashita as the tormented Chieko), the film is a profound mood piece, enhanced by the music and the use of Takamura's poetry to annotate events.

Portrait Of Teresa

▶ **Retrato De Teresa**

Cuba   1979   103 mins   col
Instituto Cubano De Arte E Industria

d **Pastor Vega**
sc **Pastor Vega, Ambrosio Fornet**
ph **Livio Delgado**
m **Carlos Fariñas**
   Daisy Granádos, Adolfo Llauradó, Raúl Pomares, Alina Sánchez

Teresa, a textile worker and mother of three, spends time after work as factory cultural secretary, much to the displeasure of her macho husband (Llauradó), who resents the household duties that fall on him. After he has an affair with a younger woman (Sánchez), Teresa resolves to make a life of her own. Part of the reconstruction of post-revolutionary Cuba was legislation for sexual equality and Vega's first feature (after making documentaries) was an effective instrument in the re-education of the Cuban male. Using his own wife (an exuberant Granádos) and sons, the director intended to 'drop a bomb' into every Cuban household. Despite being a step forward, the film still defines its heroine in terms of men, but is technically assured and benefits from Vega's attention to authenticity. Granádos, for example, spent some

months working in a textile factory before shooting began.

A Portuguese Goodbye

▶ **Um Adeus Português**

Portugal   1985   85 mins   col/bw
Um Adeus Português/João Botelho

d **João Botelho**
sc **Leonor Pinhão, João Botelho**
ph **Acácio De Almeida**
m **Messiaen , Domingos Bomtempo, Frei Manuel Cardoso, Música Popular Angolana, Conjunto Monte Cara, Anamar Rui Furtado, Isabel De Castro, Maria Cabral, Fernando Heitor, Cristina Hauser**

Fatigued soldiers trek through the jungle of a Portuguese African colony in 1973, embroiled in the last stages of war against the native inhabitants. In Lisbon in 1985, an elderly couple visit their bachelor son, and their daughter-in-law who is the widow of their other son, killed in action in Africa. Botelho's unusual film deals with the necessity of coming to terms with the past in order to live in the present. The effect of recent history on individuals who are unaware of the full implications of their country's/brother's/son's engagement in colonial warfare is delicately suggested, and the resolution of the family relationships realistic and unsentimental. The director's fluid juxtaposition of past and present, monochrome and colour, help point the way to his themes.

▶ **Poseban   Tretman** see Special Treatment

▶ **Poshchyochina** see Slap In The Face, A

▶ **Possessors, The** see Grandes Familles, Les

▶ **Postava K Podpírání** see Joseph Kilián

▶ **Posto, Il** see Job, The

▶ **Postriziny** see Short Cut

▶ **Pot-Bouille** see House Of Lovers

▶ **Potemkin** see Battleship Potemkin, The

▶ **Pote Tin Kyriaki** see Never On Sunday

▶ **Potomok Chingis-Khana** see Storm Over Asia

▶ **Potselui Meri Pikford** see Kiss Of Mary Pickford, The

▶ **Poulet Au Vinaigre** see Cop Au Vin

▶ **Poupées De Roseau** see Reed Dolls

▶ **Pourquoi Israel?** see Israel Why?

▶ **Poussière D'Ange** see Angel Dust

▶ **Povest' Plamennykh Let** see Flaming Years, The

The Power Of Men Is The Patience Of Women

▶ **Die Macht Der Männer Ist Die Geduld Der Frauen**

W. Germany 1978 80 mins col
Sphinx Filmproduktion

d   Cristina Perincioli
sc Cristina Perincioli
ph Katia Forbert Petersen, Henrietta Loch
m   Flying Lesbians
    Elisabeth Walinski, Eberhard Feik, Dora Kürten, Christa Gehrmann, Ulrich Thiel, Barbara Stanek

Addi Flemming (Walinski) sells clothes at a market stall to help support her young son, and suffers beatings at the hands of her husband (Feik), a boorish, womanizing and violent drunk. She finally leaves him, but economics force her return and the whole cycle starts again until she finds refuge in a shelter for battered wives. This is a feminist film, certainly, but one which is even-handed in its judgement, identifying the contribution of women's passivity to the retention of male power. Filmed naturalistically with much hand-held camerawork, and beginning deceptively as a tale of deprivation and underprivilege, this is a bitter, salutary and clever attack on social structures and institutions, convincingly interpreted by a group of actresses who wrote much of their own dialogue.

▶ **Po Zakonu** see By The Law

▶ **Prästänkan** see Parson's Widow, The

▶ **Pratidwandi** see Adversary, The

▶ **Prato, Il** see Meadow, The

▶ **Prénom Carmen** see First Name Carmen

▶ **Préparez Vos Mouchoirs** see Get Out Your Handkerchiefs

▶ **Prestupleniye I Nzaniye** see Crime And Punishment

The Price Of Love

▶ **I Timi Tis Agapis**

Greece 1984 110 mins col
Andromeda/Greek Film Centre/ERTI

d   Tonia Marketaki
sc Tonia Marketaki
ph Stavros Hassapis
m   Helen Karaindrou
    Toula Stathopolou, Anny Loulou, Stratis Tsopanellis, Spyros Antiochos

Andreas (Tsopanellis), the son of a formerly wealthy family, falls in love with Rini (Loulou), the poor working-class daughter of Epistimi (Stathopolou), who works in a factory to support her children and alcoholic husband. Andreas wants to marry Rini, but demands the price of his mortgage as a dowry. Epistimi's refusal begins a chain of events that ends in dishonour, betrayal and violence. The talented and intelligent Marketaki, who spent the years of the Colonels in exile in Algeria, has set her film in Corfu at the turn of the century. A well-constructed, well-acted drama of romance and revenge, played in glorious settings. However, in unfolding her tale, the director also lays bare a society where past and present overlap and clash, with modernization ruining the fabric of tradition, and women are trapped between the demands of subservience and progress.

The Priest's Wife

▶ **La Moglie Del Prete**

 Italy 1970 103 mins col
 Carlo Ponti

d **Dino Risi**
sc **Ruggero Maccari, Bernardino Zapponi**
ph **Alfio Contini**
m **Armando Trovaioli**
 Sophia Loren, Marcello Mastroianni,
 Venantino Venantini, Pippo Starnazza,
 Miranda Campa, Augusto Mastrantoni

Poor, embarassed by her height, and longing
to marry, Valeria (Loren) suffers a suicidal
depression on learning that her boyfriend has
a wife. Seeking guidance through a telephone
help line, she falls for her therapist (Mastroianni), only to discover later that he is a
priest, but pursues him nevertheless until they
become lovers, and he promises to leave the
Church. At the heart of this film lies the
primary dilemma of the Catholic priesthood:
what to do about celibacy. However, as written and directed, it is a slightly tasteless hotch-
potch of comedy and melodrama, its leads
too glamorous by half, and its compromised
plot resolution barely credible. If Loren is
sometimes touching, her Valeria is really quite
an irritating and stupid character, and
Marcello's tormented cleric is a wooden
bore.

▶ **Prima Angelica, La** see Cousin
 Angelica

▶ **Prima Della Rivoluzione** see Before
 The Revolution

Primal Fear

▶ **aka A Scream From Silence**

▶ **Mourir À Tue-Tête**

 Canada 1979 96 mins col
 National Film Board Of Canada

d **Anne Claire Poirier**
sc **Marthe Blackburn, Anne Claire Poirier**
ph **Michel Brault**
m **Maurice Blackburn**
 Julie Vincent, Germain Houde, Paul
 Savoie, Monique Miller, Micheline
 Lanctôt

While walking home from work one night, a
young nurse (Vincent) is attacked from
behind, forced at knife point into a truck and
raped. She never recovers from the experience
and, finding herself unable to make love again
with her boyfriend (Savoie), she commits suicide. The central story takes less than half the
running time of this analytical and provocative study of the nature and consequences,
but not causes, of rape. By prefacing the
narrative with the camera 'tracking' down the
rapist (Houde) in the guise of ostensibly
respectable different men, Poirier makes the
contentious point that all men are potential
rapists. The rape itself is filmed subjectively
through the victim's eyes and then commented
on by a director (Miller) and her editor
(Lanctôt). More 'alienation' techniques are
added to the argument, such as documentary
footage of women collaborators having their
hair shaved and a clitoridectomy being performed in Africa. The analogies are intellectually shaky, but the film does offer a
springboard for further debate.

The Princes

▶ **Les Princes**

 France 1982 100 mins col
 ACC/Babylone Films

d **Tony Gatlif**
sc **Tony Gatlif**
ph **Jacques Loiseleux**
m **Tony Gatlif**
 Gérard Darmon, Muse Dalbray, Céline
 Militon, Concha Tavora, Marie-Hélène
 Rudel

Nara (Darmon) is a gypsy who, having
thrown his wife out because she took the pill,
lives with his old mother and young daughter
in derelict circumstances. A series of misfortunes resulting from his own volatile temperament, drives them to a nomadic existence.
Gatlif's intended study of the gypsy plight in
urban France has lost sight of its objectives.
Technically, the film is part vérité (lots of
hand-held camera) and part stylishly photographed. In content it swings all over the
place, juxtaposing comedy and drama at ill-
chosen moments, and obscuring its message

by making Nara destructive and reactionary while caricaturing its non-gypsy participants. A well-meaning muddle.

▶ **Princes, Les** see Princes, The

▶ **Princess Yang Kwei Fei** see Empress Yang Kwei Fei, The

▶ **Prise De Pouvoir Par Louis XIV, La** see Rise Of Louis XIV, The

▶ **Prisonnière, La** see Woman In Chains

A Private Conversation

▶ **aka Without Witnesses**

▶ **Bez Svidetelei**

USSR 1983 96 mins col
Mosfilm

d   Nikita Mikhalkov
sc Nikita Mikhalkov, Sofia Prokofyeva, Ramiz Fataliyev
ph Pavel Lebeshev
m   Eduard Artemyev
    Michael Ulyanov, Irina Kupchenko

A man visits his ex-wife one winter evening and old wounds are reopened. They argue. He tries to make love to her again. She reveals she is about to remarry. A film with only two characters, which takes place entirely in one setting, is easily open to accusations of being 'too theatrical' (an accusation springing from a limited definition of 'cinematic'). The impact of the film derives as much from the discreet camerawork and cutting as from the intensity of the performances and the brillant dialogue. The whole is a fascinating, Strindberg-flavoured war of words, as the protagonists continually position, nor is it without humour.

The Private Lesson

▶ **La Leçon Particulière**

France 1968 82 mins col
Mannic Films/Francos Films/C.I.C.C.

d   Michel Boisrond
sc Claude Brûlé, Annette Wademant,

ph Michel Boisrond
m   Francis Lai
    Nathalie Delon, Renaud Verley, Robert Hossein, Bernard Le Coq, Katia Cristina, Martine Sarcey

Olivier (Verley), a senior student at a Paris lycée, becomes infatuated with beautiful, 25-year-old Frédérique (Delon), who turns out to be the mistress of a famous racing driver (Hossein) whom the boy much admires. He nonetheless pursues Frédérique and, in time, circumstances conspire to bring them together in an idyllic affair. A formula French romance, glossy, slick, trendy and superficial. However, there is some genuine tenderness and humour on offer, and a cheeky, engaging performance from Verley as the schoolboy already acquainted with sex but learning the lessons of love.

Private Life

▶ **Chastnaya Zhizn**

USSR 1982 104 mins col
Mosfilm

d   Yuli Raizman
sc Anatoly Grebnyev, Yuli Raizman
ph Nikolai Olonovsky
    Michael Ulyanov, Iya Savvina, Irina Gubanova, Tatyana Dogileva, Aleksei Blokhin, Elena Sanayeva

Sergei Abrikosov (Ulyanov), a businessman in his fifties, is not given the company directorship he expects, and resigns. At home, angry and idle, he gradually perceives the distance that has grown up between him and his wife (Savvina) and children due to his long preoccupation with his career. He turns to his former secretary (Gubanova) for sympathy but she grows impatient with him. At last, helped by a series of unforeseen events, Sergei and his family begin to communicate again. Precise and formal in its composition, striking in its images, the veteran Raizman's much admired film is at once a universally recognizable drama of mid-life crisis and a metaphor for certain Socialist ideals that have outlived their usefulness. The screenplay is let down from time to time by contrivances that have no logic and little sense, but this is an intelligent and provocative movie.

Private Vices And Public Virtues

▶ **(US: Vices And Pleasures)**

▶ **Vizi Privati, Pubbliche Virtù**

   Italy/Yugoslavia 1976 104 mins col
   Filmes (Rome)/Jadran Film (Zagreb)

d   Miklós Jancsó
sc Giovanna Gagliardo
ph Tomislav Pinter
m   Francesco De Masi
    Lajos Balázsovits, Pamela Villoresi,
    Franco Branciaroli, Teresa Ann Savoy,
    Laura Betti, Ivica Pajer

The young heir (Balázsovits) to the throne of
a Central European kingdom at the turn of
the century spends his time in wild orgies a
a country estate. After ignoring the King's
request to return to the capital, the Prince,
his friends and his lovers are faced with
troops. From 1970, Jancsó made films in his
native Hungary and inferior ones in Italy.
Because of its soft-porn elements, this erotico-
political version of the Mayerling story gained
a wider audience than his previous ritualistic
and revolutionary pictures using a minimal
number of shots. Ritual and revolutionary
sentiments are still present, but they have
been subsumed by the nudity of most of the
romping protagonists in this playful, often
childishly shocking, representation of history
in terms of an orgy.

▶ **Prix Du Danger, Le** see Prize Of
Peril, The

The Prize Of Peril

▶ **Le Prix Du Danger**

   France 1983 93 mins col
   Swanie/TF1/UGC/Top 1/Avala/Brent
   Walker

d   Yves Boisset
sc Yves Boisset, Jean Curtelin
ph Pierre William Glenn
m   Vladimir Cosma
    Gérard Lanvin, Michel Piccoli, Marie-
France Pisier, Bruno Cremer, Andréa
Ferréol

Contestants on a TV game show, hosted by
a smarmy MC (Piccoli), are invited to be
chased around Paris for four hours by paid
assassins. If they survive, they will receive a
million dollars. Robert Sheckley's black
comic novel might have made a fascinating
thriller set in a psychotic society. Alas, after
a promising build-up, Boisset has gone for
the usual violent metropolitan chase movie
so that, instead of observing and commenting
on the bloodthirsty TV audience, the cinema
audience is asked to share its perverse
pleasure.

▶ **Procès De Jeanne D'Arc, Le** see
Trial Of Joan Of Arc, The

Professor Mamlock

   USSR 1938 100 mins bw
   Lenfilm

d   Adolph Minkin, Herbert Rappaport
sc Adolph Minkin, Herbert Rappaport,
    Friedrich Wolf
ph G. Filatov
m   Y. Kochurov, N. Timofeyev
    S. Mezhinski, E. Nikitina, Otto Zhakov,
    V. Chesnokov, B. Svetlov, N.
    Shaternikova

A brilliant surgeon (Mezhinski) at a Berlin
hospital in 1933 is publicly degraded because
he is a Jew. He makes an impassioned speech
against the Nazi regime and is shot down.
Carefully recreating the Berlin setting, it was
one of the rare Soviet films of the period to
deal with a foreign subject and was initially
banned in Britain because of its anti-German
stance. The irony and understatement of the
direction make it a far more pungent work
than more rhetorical efforts. In 1961, it was
remade in East Germany by Konrad Wolf,
the son of the co-screenwriter and author of
the original play

▶ **Profumo Di Donna** see Scent Of A
Woman

▶ **Proie Pour L'Ombre, La** see Shadow Of Adultery

▶ **Proshchanie** see Farewell

▶ **Prostoi Sluchai** see Simple Case, A

The Proud Ones

▶ **Les Orgueilleux**

France 1953 105 mins bw
C.I.C.C./Reforma/Chrysaor/Iena

d Yves Allégret
sc Jean Aurenche, Pierre Bost, Jean Clouzot, Yves Allégret
ph Alex Phillips
m Paul Misraki
 Michèle Morgan, Gérard Philipe, Carlos Moctezuma, Victor Mendoza, Michèle Cardone

A young Frenchwoman (Morgan), holidaying with her husband in the Gulf of Mexico, finds herself stranded and penniless in a grubby harbour town after he dies of a contagious fever. She falls in love with a local doctor (Philipe) who has taken to the bottle since the death of his wife and, when her feelings are eventually reciprocated, she stays to help him in his work. Although adapted from a novel by Sartre (*L'Amour Rédempteur*), the screenplay reeks of banality and cliché. All the more credit then to Allégret for riveting the attention with his oppressively realistic evocation of a filthy, fly-blown tropical milieu – riveting, that is, if you can stand the uncompromising details of the sordid and unpleasant. Morgan and Philipe do their best with their unworthy roles.

The Proud Ones

▶ **Le Cheval D'Orgueil**

France 1980 118 mins col
Bela/TF1

d Claude Chabrol
sc Claude Chabrol, Daniel Boulanger
ph Jean Rabier
m Pierre Jansen
 Jacques Dufilho, Bernadette Lesache, François Cluzet, Ronan Hubert, Arnel Hubert

A young boy grows up in a poor but independent community in Britanny in the first decade of the century, playing pranks, seeing the villagers suffer economic deprivation and his father go off to war, and witnessing the struggle to maintain their Breton language and customs. Chabrol's first film, *Le Beau Serge*, was a rural melodrama and he has returned to the theme of village life from time to time, most powerfully in *Le Boucher*, most unconvincingly in this *faux naif* peasant romp. Chabrol's method is that of a museum curator meticulously and lovingly recreating the regional costumes, decoration and artefacts of the period, without an overall political or social perspective. Even the question of Breton pride in their own language is fudged by having the actors speak French (presumably for practical and commercial reasons).

▶ **Prova D'Orchestra** see Orchestra Rehearsal

▶ **Proverka Na Dorogakh** see Trial On The Road

▶ **Provincial, La** see Girl From Lorraine, A

▶ **Prozess, Der** see Trial, The

▶ **Przesluchanie** see Interrogation

▶ **Przypadek** see Blind Chance

▶ **Pugni In Tasca, I** see Fists In The Pocket

▶ **Puritain, Le** see Puritan, The

The Puritan

▶ **Le Puritain**

France 1937 87 mins bw
Derby

d Jeff Musso
sc Jeff Musso
ph Curt Courant, Charles Bauer
m Jeff Musso, Jacques Dallin
 Jean-Louis Barrault, Pierre Fresnay, Viviane Romance, Mady Berry, Jean Tissier

Francis Ferriter (Barrault) believes that 'God is dead,' and belongs to a secret society dedicated to cleansing society of its moral impurities. When a fellow member refuses to denounce his own son's affair, Ferriter kills the girl in question, only realizing much later that he was motivated by his own repressed sexual desire. In its day, Musso's film, transposed from an Irish story by Liam O'Flaherty, was considered shocking and was banned in the Irish Free State and also in the State of New York. Now it is dated, but provides a wonderful opportunity to watch the unique Barrault at work, and is interesting, too, in implying criticism of Ferriter's dangerous puritanism rather than an attack on the values of society, here represented by the probing and perceptive police chief (Fresnay).

Purple Noon

▶ **Plein Soleil**

France   1959   115 mins   col
Paris/Panitalia/Titanus

d   **René Clément**
sc   **René Clément, Paul Gégauff**
ph   **Henri Decaë**
m   **Nino Rota**
    Alain Delon, Maurice Ronet, Marie

Laforêt, Elvire Popesco, Erno Crisa, Bill Kearns

Ripley (Delon), indolent and impecunious friend of a rich playboy (Ronet), schemes to take his friend's clothes, yacht, girlfriend (Laforêt) and life. Although the plot, taken from Patricia Highsmith's *The Talented Mr Ripley*, is pure *film noir*, the picture glows with the warm hedonism of the Mediterranean, courtesy of Decaë's camera. But it's not only gorgeous to look at, it's entertainingly suspenseful as well. The film also launched the 24-year-old Delon into stardom, his beautiful face accurately reflecting both the charm and the coldness of the ambiguous character in this perverse tale. *Purple Noon*, crassly retitled *Lust For Evil* for TV in the USA, was the last ray of warmth in Clément's prestigious career.

▶ **Pursuit** see Tragic Pursuit, The

▶ **Puss Och Kram** see Hugs And Kisses

▶ **Putyovka V Zhizn** see Road To Life, The

▶ **Pyat' Vecherov** see Five Evenings

▶ **Pyshka** see Boule De Suif

▶ **Qingchun Ji** see Sacrificed Youth

Quai Des Brumes

▶ **(US: Port Of Shadows)**

France 1938 89 mins bw
Ciné Alliance/Pathé

d **Marcel Carné**
sc **Jacques Prévert**
ph **Eugen Schüfftan**
m **Maurice Jaubert**
Jean Gabin, Michèle Morgan, Michel Simon, Pierre Brasseur, Aimos, Delmont

An army deserter (Gabin) commits murder and flees to Le Havre where he meets and falls in love with Nelly (Morgan), but their plan to escape together is foiled by her guardian (Simon). This is the first film in which the distinctive melancholy poetic realism of Carné and Prévert expressed itself. The slant-eyed 18-year-old Morgan, in trench coat and beret, together with the doomed Gabin trying to grab some happiness in a sombre fog-bound port (superb sets by Alexandre Trauner) are quintessential images associated with the world-weariness prevalent in pre-war France.

Quai Des Orfèvres

▶ **(US: Jenny Lamour)**

France 1947 105 mins bw
Productions Majestic

d **Henri-Georges Clouzot**
sc **Henri-Georges Clouzot, Jean Ferry**
ph **Armand Thirard**
m **Francis Lopez**
Louis Jouvet, Suzy Delair, Bernard Blier, Simone Renant

A music hall entertainer (Delair) believes she has killed a lascivious old man. Her husband, (Blier) who *intended* to kill him, arrives to find him already dead. Each conceals the experience from the other, and the husband becomes the prime suspect. An accomplished thriller is the outer casing for an exposure of relationships and a wonderfully atmospheric portrait of a milieu. Clouzot's observation of human frailty, made with a mixture of wit and compassion, and shot with an extraordinarily fine sense of composition and lighting and use of chiaroscuro, renders the piece a classic of its kind. The great Louis Jouvet is memorable as the worldly-wise policeman – part cynic, part sentimentalist – determined to wrap up the last case before his retirement and take care of his motherless, half-caste son. The rest of the cast, too, is marvellous.

Best Director Venice 1947

▶ **Quarterly Balance** see Woman's Decision, A

▶ **Quatorze Juillet** see Fourteenth of July, The

▶ **Quatre Aventures De Reinette Et Mirabelle** see Four Adventures Of Reinette And Mirabelle

▶ **Quatre Cents Coups, Les** see Four Hundred Blows, The

▶ **Quatre Nuits D'Un Rêveur** see Four Nights Of A Dreamer

▶ **Quattro Giornate Di Napoli, Le** see Four Days Of Naples, The

▶ **Quattro Passi Fra Le Nuvole** see Four Steps In The Clouds

▶ **Queda, A** see Fall, The

Queen Bee

▶ **(US: The Conjugal Bed)**
▶ **Una Storia Moderna: L'Ape Regina**

Italy 1963 90 mins bw
Sancro Film/Fair Film/Les Films
Marceau

d Marco Ferreri
sc Goffredo Parise, Massimo Franciosa,
    Diego Fabbri, Rafael Azcona, Pasquale
    Festa Campanile, Marco Ferreri
ph Ennio Guarnieri
m Teo Usuelli
    Ugo Tognazzi, Marina Vlady, Walter
    Giller, Linda Sini, Achille Maieroni

A middle-aged car dealer (Tognazzi) marries
a young girl (Vlady) who not only wants to
have a baby as quickly as possible, but has a
voracious sexual appetite which wears him
out to the point of suffering an ultimately
fatal heart attack after his final – and successful – attempt to make her pregnant. The plot
belies an eventful entertainment, characteristic of the Italian sex comedies that were all
the rage in the 1960s. Vlady is good to look
at while Tognazzi, of course, is a dab hand
at this sort of thing. Not to be taken seriously
for a moment, it's funny and enjoyable.

Best Actress (Marina Vlady) Cannes 1963

▶ **Queen of Atlantis** see Atlantide, L'

▶ **¿Que He Hecho Yo Para Merecer Esto?!** see What Have I Done To
Deserve This?

▶ **Que La Bête Meure** see Killer!

▶ **Que La Fête Commence** see Let
Joy Reign Supreme

▶ **Quelques Jours Avec Moi** see Few
Days With Me, A

Querelle

W. Germany 1982 105 mins col
Planet/Gaumont(Paris)

d Rainer Werner Fassbinder
sc Rainer Werner Fassbinder
ph Xaver Schwarzenberger
m Peer Raben
    Brad Davis, Franco Nero, Jeanne
    Moreau, Laurent Malet, Hanno Pöschl,
    Günther Kaufmann

The crew of a marine destroyer takes its leave
of each other at the port of Brest. The captain
(Nero) worships Querelle (Davis), a handsome young sailor, from afar. Querelle,
involved in drug smuggling, murders a fellow
seaman and then goes to a famous brothel
where he meets the rapacious Madame
(Moreau) and other habitués of the place who
all succumb to his fatal allure. Jean Genet's
classic 1947 homoerotic novel *Querelle De
Brest* seemed a perfect subject for the innovative and imaginative gifts of the openly gay
Fassbinder. He opted to shoot it in a garish,
stylized studio set in which a collection of gay
icons – macho clones, sailors and men in
leather – pose against a permanently orange
sky, fight and philosophize. This is punctuated by quotes from Plutarch and an unbe-
lievably monotonous song warbled by a
ludicrous Moreau. Sadly, this was to be the
36-year-old Fassbinder's last film. He died
soon after its completion. At least he left
behind 41 better films – an astonishing output – to be remembered by.

▶ **Questione D'Onore, Una** see Question Of Honour, A

A Question Of Honour

▶ **Una Questione D'Onore**

Italy 1965 110 mins col
Mega Film(Rome)/Orphée
Productions(Paris)

d Luigi Zampa
sc Piero De Bernardi, Leo Benvenuti, Luigi
    Zampa, Ennio Gicca Palli
ph Carlo Di Palma, Luciano Trasatti
m Luis Bacalov
    Ugo Tognazzi, Nicoletta Machiavelli,
    Bernard Blier, Franco Fabrizi, Tecla
    Scarano, Lucien Raimbourg

A thick-headed, in both senses, salt-mine

worker (Tognazzi) finds himself caught in the crossfire of a vendetta between the Sannas (headed by Blier) and the Porcus (leader Fabrizi), and eventually has to kill his own wife in order to preserve his honour and hers. On the credit side, Zampa offers some dramatic locations, the effortless talents of Tognazzi and a few unexpected twists in the plot. For the rest, this is an Italian comedy utilizing the ingredients of high drama without drawing too much mirth from the spectator.

A Question Of Rape

- ▶ (US: The Rape)
- ▶ Le Viol
- ▶ aka Overgreppet

France/Sweden 1967 84 mins col
Sandrew(Stockholm)/Parc Film/
Argos(Paris)

d   Jacques Doniol-Valcroze
sc Jacques Doniol-Valcroze
ph Rune Ericson
m   Michel Portal
    Bibi Andersson, Bruno Cremer, Frédéric
    De Pasquale, Katerina Larsson

At home alone one Sunday, Marianne (Andersson) is disturbed by a stranger (Cremer) who holds her hostage at gun point. In the event, he is cultivated and sympathetic and, eventually, they make love. That night, one of her husband's dinner guests is the stranger... An absorbing film, directed with a precise, formal elegance in geometrically designed interiors that reflect its abstract nature. The Swedish Andersson, speaking her own French, is, as usual, first-class, and is well-matched by Cremer. Doniol-Valcroze's intentions remain ambiguous: is Marianne's experience the acting out of a desirable fantasy or the delusory by-product of sexual repression? More significantly, did the encounter with the stranger actually take place? A provocative exploration of illusion and reality, recalling elements of *Last Year In Marienbad*.

A Question Of Silence

- ▶ De Stilte Rond Christine M.

Netherlands 1982 96 mins col

Sigma Films

d   Marleen Gorris
sc Marleen Gorris
ph Frans Bromet
m   Lodewijk De Boer, Martijn Hasebos
    Edda Barends, Nelly Frijda, Henriette
    Tol, Cox Habbema, Eddy Brugman, Hans
    Croiset

Three women, entirely unknown to each other, and of differing backgrounds and occupations, brutally murder the male owner of a boutique. Dr Janine Van Den Bos (Habbema) is called in to assess their mental capacity and finds Christine (Barends) wedded to catatonic silence and Annie (Frijda) garrulous and cheerful, while Andrea (Tol), the most intelligent of the three, attacks Van Den Bos's motives and line of questioning. The eventual court hearing disintegrates as Van Den Bos maintains that the women are sane and walks out of the proceedings. In constructing an uncompromising feminist polemic, Gorris has made an original and powerful film, gripping in its story and in its technique. Indeed, the latter – a formalized pattern of flashback and cross-cutting both to contrast and link the protagonists – creates a world of absolute reality which overcomes the fundamental, almost surreal irrationality of the plot. The piece has its weaknesses, but is a well-written, well-acted examination of women in a men's world, taking an oblique approach to achieve a transparent and convincing thesis.

A Quiet Duel

- ▶ aka A Silent Duel
- ▶ Shizuka Naru Ketto

Japan 1949 95 mins bw
Daiei

d   Akira Kurosawa
sc Senkichi Taniguchi, Akira Kurosawa
ph Shoichi Aisaka
m   Akira Ifukube
    Toshiro Mifune, Takashi Shimura, Miki
    Sanjo, Kenjiro Uemura, Chieko Nakakita,
    Noriko Sengoku

Kyoji (Mifune), a young and idealistic doctor and still a virgin, has an understanding to marry Misao (Sanjo), who works devotedly for him and his father (Shimura) in the small hospital they run. During the war he becomes an army surgeon and contracts syphilis from the blood of a patient when he cuts himself during an operation. Six years later, treating himself in secret and tormented by his conscience and his celibacy, he rejects the heartbroken Misao without explanation and throws himself into his work. Again demonstrating another aspect of his affinity to the cinematic conventions of the West, Kurosawa has constructed an out-and-out Hollywood melodrama, tear-stained and replete with noble self-sacrifice; as well as a sub-plot concerning the moral reclamation of a trainee nurse (Sengoku), and a low-life villain in the syphilitic soldier who contaminates Kyoji. However, acting and atmosphere are both of a high standard and, ironically, the film has acquired special interest today in its unmistakable parallel with AIDS which gives it a meaningful contemporary resonance.

A Quiet Place In The Country

▶ **Un Tranquillo Posto Di Compagna**

Italy 1969 106 mins col
PEA(Rome)/Les Artistes Associés(Paris)

d **Elio Petri**
sc **Luciano Vincenzoni, Elio Petri**
ph **Luigi Kuveiller**
m **Ennio Morricone**
    Franco Nero, Vanessa Redgrave, Georges Géret, Gabriella Grimaldi, Madeleine Damien, Renato Menegotto

A successful modern artist (Nero), needful of a change, goes off to a country house rented for him by his mistress-cum-agent (Redgrave). Troubled by mysterious happenings, he learns that the ghost of the former owner's daughter supposedly haunts the place. He becomes increasingly obsessed with the vision of the girl, who materializes as Gabriella Grimaldi, transfers his affections to her and brutally murders Miss Redgrave. Or does he?... Nero performs with suitable taciturnity, Redgrave is fine, Grimaldi is a convincingly erotic nymphomaniac ghost. However, the honours belong firmly to the director and the photographer, with Kuveiller stunningly capturing the kaleidoscope of bizarre images intended by Petri. On the surface this is a carefully constructed, coldly calculated Gothic horror creepy; beneath, it is a terrifying visual realization of the onset and progress of insanity. A little pretentious, perhaps, but mysterious and chilling.

Special Jury Prize Berlin 1969

r

► **Raba Lubvi** see Slave Of Love, A

► **Rabbit Case, The** see Payment In Kind

► **Racconti Di Canterbury, I** see Canterbury Tales, The

► **Raduga** see Rainbow, The

► **Ragazza Con La Valigia, La** see Girl With A Suitcase, The

► **Ragazza Di Bube, La** see Bebo's Girl

The Railroad Man

► **aka Man Of Iron**

► **Il Ferroviere**

Italy 1956 110 mins bw
Carlo Ponti/ENIC

d **Pietro Germi**
sc **Alfredo Giannetti, Luciano Vincenzoni, Pietro Germi**
ph **Leonida Barboni**
m **Carlo Rustichelli**
Pietro Germi, Luisa Della Noce, Sylva Koscina, Saro Urzi, Giulia, Edoardo Nevola

The relationships and problems of an Italian railway worker (Germi) and his unruly family during a period when life and the world seem to be turning against him. The misfortunes begin with the pregnancy of his daughter (Koscina), who refuses to marry the baby's father and runs off with another man, and continue with setbacks in his working life which lead him to seek solace in wine with old friends. One of the last films made during actor-director-writer Germi's Neo-Realist period, this is a well-observed, warm and detailed slice of Italian domestic drama. There are uniformly excellent performances from the cast, including Saro Urzi – who would win the Best Actor award at Cannes 10 years later in *Seduced And Abandoned* – in a supporting role.

The Rainbow

► **Raduga**

USSR 1944 92 mins bw
Kiev Studios

d **Mark Donskoi**
sc **Wanda Wasilevska**
ph **Bentsion Monastirsky**
m **Lev Schwartz**
Natalia Uschvy, Nina Alisova, Yelena Tyapkina, B. Ivashova

In 1943, during the German invasion of the Soviet Union, a peasant woman Olena (Uschvy), pregnant and lightly clad, flees from the Nazis across the snow-covered wastes of the Ukrainian countryside. Everywhere there is hardship and brutality, but in the end a rainbow appears as a symbol of hope. Although Donskoi's reputation rests on the enriching *Gorky Trilogy*, this inspirational wartime drama is no less remarkable. What gives it extra poignancy and power is that it was filmed in the winter of 1943, during the horrifying events it depicts. In fact, Yelena Tyapkina, who plays a mother who sees her son shot, lost her own son in the war and others among the cast and crew suffered similar losses. The simplicity and realism of the film made it an overwhelming success in the Allied countries.

Raise Ravens

▶ **aka Cria!**

▶ **Cria Cuervos**

Spain   1975   115 mins   col
Elias Querejeta

d   **Carlos Saura**
sc   **Carlos Saura**
ph   **Teo Escamilla**
m   **Federico Mompoll**
  **Ana Torrent, Geraldine Chaplin, Conchita
  Perez, Maite Sanchez**

Nine-year-old Ana (Torrent) is a serious-minded child desperately seeking to understand the world she inhabits. Having watched her mother die a terrible death of cancer a few years earlier, and blaming her father for this tragedy, she then holds herself responsible for his subsequent death. Saura's almost dreamlike attempt to enter the mind of a deeply unhappy child moves across three periods in Ana's life and the result is a bit of a curate's egg. Agony is piled on to the point where it becomes difficult to believe and the motive force is not clear. There are some magic moments, though, with Torrent superb and Chaplin, doubling as the dying mother and Ana as an adult, terrific.

Special Jury Prize Cannes 1976

Ran

Japan   1985   162 mins   col
Herald Ace/Nippon Herald/Greenwich
Films(France)

d   **Akira Kurosawa**
sc   **Akira Kurosawa, Hideo Oguni, Masato
  Ide**
ph   **Takao Saito, Masaharu Ueda**
  **Tatsuya Nakadai, Satoshi Terao, Jinpachi
  Nezu, Daisuke Ryu, Mieko Harada,
  Yoshiko Miyazaki, Peter**

The aged Lord Hidetora (Nakadai) abdicates power in favour of his eldest son Taro (Terao), but finds himself driven out of his own kingdom which then is torn apart by greed and rivalry. Seventy-five-year-old Kurosawa's epic version of *King Lear* keeps many of the main themes and the thrust of Shakespeare's play, while turning the daughters into sons and transposing the action to 16th-century Japan. The powerful performances of Nakadai, Terao, and Harada as an evil encapsulation of Goneril and Regan, burst from the screen. There is, too, an effective rendering of the Fool by a transvestite called merely Peter. The battles are visually stunning, far more involving than in *Kagemusha*, Kurosawa's previous film made five years before. *Ran*, which means 'chaos', cost $11½ million ($7 million from Japan and the rest from France).

▶ **Rape, The** see Question Of Rape, A

▶ **Rape Of Love** see Violated Love

Rashomon

Japan   1950   83 mins   bw
Daiei

d   **Akira Kurosawa**
sc   **Akira Kurosawa, Shinobu Hashimoto**
ph   **Kazuo Miyagawa**
m   **Takashi Matsuyama**
  **Toshiro Mifune, Machiko Kyo, Masayuki
  Mori, Takashi Shimura, Minoru Chiaki**

In feudal times a samurai (Mori), travels through the woods with his wife (Kyo). She is raped and then he is killed by a bandit (Mifune). At the trial, the incident is described in conflicting versions by the bandit, the wife, a priest (Chiaki) and a woodcutter (Shimura), demonstrating the subjective nature of truth. The first Japanese film to be widely shown in the West is significant beyond its indubitable qualities because it opened the way for greater works by Mizoguchi and Ozu. Its popularity was due to its intriguing story and the forceful performances, as much as to its then unfamiliar background. It was ineffectively remade in Hollywood as a Western entitled *The Outrage*, in 1964.

Best Film Venice 1951

Raskolnikov

Germany   1923   116 mins   bw
Lionardi-Film

d   **Robert Wiene**
sc   **Robert Wiene**

ph **Willy Goldberger**
Gregory Khmara, Michael Tarkhanov,
Maria Guermanova, Maria
Kryjanovskaya, Pavel Pavlov

Raskolnikov (Khmara), an impecunious student, has written a dissertation on the relationship between the individual and the law. However, he murders an elderly pawnbroker and her sister to obtain money for the Marmeladovs, whose daughter Sonia (Kryjanovskaya) has been driven to prostitution to save the family from destitution. Making his first film since *The Cabinet Of Dr Caligari* four years earlier, Wiene again utilizes Expressionist design techniques but, overall, it is much more naturalistic. Unfortunately, this leads to a clash of styles that disturbs one's involvement, and the adaptation of Dostoevsky's *Crime And Punishment* has been limited to the narrative outline, dispensing with the psychology. Thus Porfiry, the sinister chief-of-police of the original who traps Raskolnikov into a cat-and-mouse game of unbearable tension, is here reduced to a conventional character known as The Coroner. Nonetheless, enough of the imaginative qualities of both Russian novelist and German film-maker remain to give it some interest.

The Rats

▶ **Die Ratten**

W. Germany 1955 91 mins bw
CCC/Herzog

d   **Robert Siodmak**
sc **Jochen Huth**
ph **Göran Strindberg**
m   **Werner Eisbrenner**
Maria Schell, Heidemarie Hatheyer, Curt
Jurgens, Gustav Knuth, Ilse Steppat

A pregnant refugee from East Germany (Schell) is abandoned by her lover. When her baby is born, she gives it to a woman (Hatheyer) who has always longed for a child but been unable to conceive. Inevitably, a bitter conflict between the two ensues. Adapted from a stage play by Gerhard Hauptmann, with considerable changes to the material that serve only to complicate and weaken the plot, this is nonetheless a gripping movie. Siodmak has brought all his expertise to constructing a realistic picture of the bleak underside of life in post-war West Berlin, well served by absolutely first-class performances.

Best Film Berlin 1955

▶ **Ratten, Die** see Rats, The

Rat-Trap

▶ **Elippathayam**

India 1981 121 mins col
General Pictures

d   **Adoor Gopalakrishnan**
sc **Adoor Gopalakrishnan**
ph **Ravi Varma**
m   **M.B. Srinivasan**
Karamana, Sarada, Jalaja, Rajam K.
Nair, Prakash, Sonan, John Samuel

Unni (Karamana), middle-aged and bad-tempered, lives on the family estate in a remote village with two of his sisters, Rajamma (Sarada) and teenaged Sridevi (Jalaja). The former looks after him without complaint, even though he deprives her of marriage, but the latter longs for escape. Eventually, Sridevi disappears, Rajamma falls ill and Unni, grown reclusive, allows the estate to collapse. This film is about the inevitability of change and the price to be paid for failing to adapt to it. Its social critique is conveyed through formal, symbolic images which gradually unfold the extent of Unni's social displacement, ending in his death in the river where Rajamma used to drown the rats. Made with a sharp feeling for atmosphere, the film suffers from excessive length and some rather muddled narrative detail, but Gopalakrishnan is clearly talented.

The Raven

▶ **Le Corbeau**

France 1943 92 mins bw
L'Atelier Français

d   **Henri-Georges Clouzot**
sc **Louis Chavance**
ph **Nicolas Hayer**
m   **Tony Aubain**
Pierre Fresnay, Pierre Larquey, Ginette

Leclerc, Hélène Manson, Micheline Francey

The effect on the inhabitants of a small French provincial town of a spate of poison pen letters from someone who seems to know the secrets of many of the recipients. Among the latter is a doctor (Fresnay), torn between two women (Leclerc and Francey). Clouzot's second film – an effective but sour view of French provincial life – was accused of being anti-French Nazi propaganda at the time. In fact, although made under the Occupation by a German-run company, the excellent script had been written by Chavance six years previously. Both Clouzot and the film were temporarily banned after the Liberation. As well as tight direction, it is full of telling character studies. Otto Preminger remade it, less memorably, as *The Thirteenth Letter* in 1951.

Raven's Dance

▶ **Korpinpolska**

Finland 1980 80 mins col
Suomi/Filmi Oy/SFI/Television Lulla

d **Markku Lehmuskallio**
sc **Markku Lehmuskallio**
ph **Bekka Martevo, Markku Lehmuskallio
Pertti Kalinainen, Paavo Katajsaari,
Hilka Matikainen, Eero Kemila**

In an unspoiled region of Northern Finland, an old man (Katajsaari), formerly a hunter, his young son (Kalinainen) and his daughter-in-law (Matikainen) live a challenging but simple life. The young man hunts, but with respect for the animals, and all three are in harmony with nature. When 'progress' comes with the building of a road, the young hunter is arrested and his gun confiscated. The raven, traditionally a dark omen, occupies a symbolic place in this hauntingly beautiful film, which opens with a silent half-hour prologue revealing the lakes and forests, the reindeer and elk, the birds and flowers, in images of breathtaking beauty. The dialogue is minimal, the acting thoroughly convincing in the service of a story in which little happens – until the climax in which so-called civilization heralds the destruction of nature and of the lives of the protagonists who symbolize its value. Lehmuskallio's message is poignant, painful and salutary.

Raven's End

▶ **Kvarteret Korpen**

Sweden 1963 100 mins bw
Europa Film/Svensk Filminstitutet

d **Bo Widerberg**
sc **Bo Widerberg**
ph **Jan Lindeström**
m **Giusepe Torelli, Arthur Hedström, Karl
Jularbo, Hermann Gellin, Edvard Persson
Thommy Berggren, Keve Hjelm, Emy
Storm, Ingvar Hirdwall, Christina
Frambäck,**

Anders (Berggren), a young would-be writer, lives with his drunken father (Hjelm) and worn-out mother (Storm) in a dingy apartment in Malmö in 1936 during the Depression. Each believes they can better their conditions. Widerberg's second feature, one of the first to benefit from funds given by Svenska Filminstitutet, was rather too lyrical and the poverty too picturesque to carry much of its political message. But it does have a freshness and an autobiographical feel (Widerberg was born in 1930) that is hard to resist. The film was overpraised at the time because its social realism seemed to mark a new trend away from the cerebral and visceral works of Ingmar Bergman that had dominated Swedish cinema for over a decade.

A Ray Of Sunshine

▶ **Sonnenstrahl**

Austria 1933 85 mins bw
Serge Otzoup Filmproduktion/Tobis-Sascha

d **Pál Fejós**
sc **Pál Fejós, Adolf Lantz**
ph **Adolf Weith**
m **Ferenc Farkas
Annabella, Gustav Frölich, Paul Otto,
Hans Marr**

A young couple (Annabella and Frölich) try to survive in the harsh world of the Depression in Vienna in the early 1930s. Some of the jobs they manage to find – and lose – are at a fairground, cleaning a department store and working for a hairdresser. Finally, after many ups and downs, they are able to buy a taxi. Very much in the tradition and tone of Murnau's *Sunrise* (1927) and Fejós's most celebrated Hollywood film, *Lonesome* (1928), this is an endearing urban romance, charmingly played by the two leads. As a statement of economic exploitation it lacks substance and its fairy-tale Capraesque ending, when the inhabitants of a tenement shower Annabella with money to pay the rent, is only for the sweet of tooth. Yet, the director's imaginative use of sound and free-flowing location shooting compensates for the deficiencies.

▶ **Rayon Vert, Le** see Green Ray, The

Rebellion

▶ **Joi-Uchi**

Japan   1967   121 mins   bw
Toho/Mifune

d   **Masaki Kobayashi**
sc **Shinobu Hashimoto**
ph **Kazuo Yamada**
m   **Tohru Takemitsu**
     Toshiro Mifune, Takeshi Kata, Michiko Otsuka, Yoko Tsukasa, Tatsuya Nakadai

Yogoro (Kata), a young man forced to marry his overlord's mistress (Tsukasa), is ordered to give her up when her son becomes the overlord's heir. He refuses to part with his wife and, supported by his father (Mifune), rebels against the feudal lord and his men. Kobayashi composes his shots beautifully on the Tohoscope screen, as the complex manoeuverings of early 18th-century Japanese politics are detailed. The measured pace often explodes with action, such as the intricately choreographed swordfights. As in *Harakiri*, Kobayashi shows his ability to extend the limits of the Japanese period film.

▶ **Record Of A Living Being** see I Live In Fear

▶ **Récréation, La** see Playtime

The Red And The Black

▶ **aka Scarlet And Black**
▶ **Le Rouge Et Le Noir**

France   1954   170 mins   col

Franco London/Documento

d   **Claude Autant-Lara**
sc **Jean Aurenche, Pierre Bost, Claude Autant-Lara**
ph **Michel Kelber**
m   **René Cloërec**
     Gérard Philipe, Danielle Darrieux, Antonella Lualdi, Jean Martinelli

The ambitious Julien Sorel (Philipe), a carpenter's son, chooses the black robe of the priest rather than the scarlet of the soldier to make his way up the social ladder. In his first post as tutor, he seduces Madame De Rênal (Darrieux), the mother of his pupils. He then courts and wins Mademoiselle De La Mole (Lualdi), the daughter of an aristocrat whose secretary he has become. Gérard Philipe, who had six years previously played Fabrice in *The Charterhouse At Parma*, embodied another Stendhal hero admirably in a sumptuous but rather superficial rendering of the great 1831 novel. Lacking much of the irony and psychology of the original, it is merely a prettily illustrated tale of a handsome opportunist.

The Red And The White

▶ **Csillagosok, Katonák**

Hungary/USSR   1967   90 mins   bw
Mafilm Studio/Mosfilm

d   **Miklós Jancsó**
sc **Georgy Mdivani, Gyula Hernádi, Miklós Jancsó**
ph **Tamás Somló**
     Tatyana Konyukova, Krystyna Mikolajewska, Mikhail Kasakov, Viktor Ardyushko, Bolot Beyshenaliyev

In central Russia in 1918, Hungarians fighting in the International Brigade of the Red Army are hunted by White Russian troops. Only a small group of them escapes death. The first Russian-Hungarian co-production, made to celebrate the fiftieth anniversary of the Revolution, has all the Jancsó stylistic flourishes first recognized in *The Round-Up*, his preceding film. Using the possibilities of the large screen, he orchestrates an enthralling, sweeping, large-scale drama of domination and submission with a minimum of dialogue. The original title translates as 'Stars, Soldiers'.

The Red Balloon

▶ **Le Ballon Rouge**

France   1956   36 mins   col
Montsouris

d   **Albert Lamorisse**
sc **Albert Lamorisse**
ph **Edmond Séchan**
m   **Maurice Le Roux**
    Pascal Lamorisse

On his way to school one morning, a little
boy comes upon a balloon hanging round a
lamppost. The balloon seems to have almost
human powers of communication, takes a
fancy to the child and attaches itself to him
until the sad event that ends its life. A whimsical, imaginative and thoroughly delightful
fantasy which received a standing ovation at
Cannes when it was first seen. It passed into
the small and select canon of well-remem-
bered and much-loved short features, continuing to enchant adults and children alike ever
since. There is no dialogue as such, only
random voices, street sounds and music, and
the film was shot in an old quarter of Paris
in soft hues of blue and grey against which
the bright red balloon shines – a symbol of
dreams and a poignant reminder of the cruelty
of those who destroy them.

Red Beard

▶ **Akahige**

Japan   1965   185 mins   bw
Toho

d   **Akira Kurosawa**
sc **Akira Kurosawa, Ryuzo Kukishima,**
    Hideo Oguni, Masato Ide
ph **Asaichi Nakai, Takao Saito**
m   **Masaru Sato**
    Toshiro Mifune, Yuzo Kayama, Kamatari
    Fujiwara, Tsutomu Yamakazi, Terumi Niki

Under the guidance of an aging, autocratic
doctor (Mifune), an idle and socially
ambitious new intern (Kayama) learns the
rewards of healing the poor clinic patients in
19th-century Japan. This very long, discursive, complex, often sentimental social drama,
yields rewards in its detailed reconstruction
of a feudal era, its humanitarian message,
and in the powerhouse performance of
Mifune in the title role.

The Red Desert

▶ **Il Deserto Rosso**

Italy   1964   116 mins   col
Duemila/Fracoriz

d   **Michelangelo Antonioni**
sc **Michelangelo Antonioni, Tonino Guerra**
ph **Carlo Di Palma**
m   **Giovanni Fusco**
    Monical Vitti, Richard Harris, Carlo
    Chionetti, Xenia Valderi

Giuliana (Vitti), the wife of an electronics
engineer (Chionetti) in Ravenna has an affair
with her husband's best friend (Harris), but
becomes increasingly alienated from the sou-
less industrial environment around her. The
main interest in this rather banal exercise in
modern *angst* is Antonioni's meticulous and
creative use of colour for the first time. He
even had buildings painted to serve the film's
mood. Deep reds and greens reflect the wife's
neurosis, while brighter colours appear during
her flights into fantasy. Vitti struggles to
convince in the part, and Harris merely looks
lost.

Best Film Venice 1964

▶ **Redhead** see Poil De Carotte

The Red Inn

▶ **L'Auberge Rouge**

France   1951   110 mins   bw
Memnon/Cochinor

d   **Claude Autant-Lara**
sc **Jean Aurenche, Pierre Bost**
ph **André Bac**
m   **René Cloërec**
    Fernandel, Françoise Rosay, Julien
    Carette, Grégoire Aslan, Marie-Claire
    Olivia, Lud Germain

In 1833, a monk (Fernandel), discovers that
stage-coach travellers staying at a desolate
inn are robbed and murdered by the proprietor (Carette) and his wife (Rosay). He
tries to save a coachload of stupid unsuspecting people from the same fate. This is an
extremely amusing macabre comedy, but its
'blasphemous' aspects have now dated somewhat. (It took the British censor six years to

pass it uncut.) Although it is inclined to get too hectically farcical at times, as Fernandel finds himself in more and more difficult situations, the almost ballad-like structure contains it. Yves Montand introduces the tale and the moral in song on the sound-track.

▶ **Redl Ezredes** see Colonel Redl

The Red Mantle

▶ **Den Røde Kappe**

Denmark 1967 100 mins col
Asa Film(Denmark)/Movie Art Of
Europe(Sweden)/ Edda Film(Iceland)

d   **Gabriel Axel**
sc **Gabriel Axel, Frank Jaeger**
ph **Henning Bendtsen**
m   **Per Norgaard**
    **Gitte Haenning, Oleg Vidov, Gunnar
    Björnstrand, Eva Dahlbeck, Birgitte
    Federspiel, Johannes Meyer**

After King Hamund is killed by King Sigvor (Björnstrand), his three sons, following the demands of custom, ride off to take vengeance on the victor's sons. After a day's fighting, Sigvor brings about a truce, which is just as well, since his daughter (Haenning) and Hamund's eldest son (Vidov) have fallen in love. However, due to the machinations of an evil German who covets the girl himself, everything ends in bloodshed and tragedy. The dramatically brooding and impressive Icelandic landscape against which this 11th-century saga is unfolded, soon palls in the face of the simplistic drivel of the script. It's marginally amusing to watch Gunnar Björnstrand and Eva Dahlbeck (as his Queen) making fools of themselves, and interesting to note that director Axel would put his spare approach to rather better use 20 years later in creating the Oscar-winning *Babette's Feast*.

Red Psalm

▶ **Még Kér A Nép**

Hungary 1971 88 mins col
Mafilm

d   **Miklós Jancsó**

sc **Gyula Hernádi**
ph **János Kende**
m   **Folk music and revolutionary songs
    (arranged Ferenc Sebo)**
    **Lajos Balázsovits, András Bálint, Gyöngyi
    Bürös, Andrea Drahota**

In the 1890s, on a large Hungarian estate owned by a wealthy count (Bálint), a group of striking farm workers wait for a reply to their demands. The army moves in, but there is a temporary respite from hostilities when they all join in a festive dance. Then the strikers are fired upon. Moving even further in the direction of balletic cinema (Ferenc Pesovár is credited with the choreography), Jancsó has become even more master of his inimitable style. Only 28 shots are used in the entire film to convey, almost exclusively in symbols, a pattern of tyranny and revolution. Colour, too, takes on emblematic meaning, especially red. A hand wound is turned into a red rosette, a river runs red with blood, and a woman in a red shoots down soldiers with a pistol wrapped in a red ribbon. Jancsó's cinema does not conform to narrative or psychological conventions, but opens up other areas which are usually only found in the screen musical.

Red Sorghum

▶ **Hong Gaoliang**

China 1987 92 mins col
Xi'an Film Studio

d   **Zhang Yimou**
sc **Chen Jianyu, Zhu Wei, Mo Yan**
ph **Gu Changwei**
m   **Zhao Jiping**
    **Gong Li, Jiang Wen, Teng Rujun, Liu Ji,
    Qian Ming, Ji Chunhua, Zhai Chunhua**

Eighteen-year-old Nine (Gong Li) is betrothed to a leprous 50-year-old who owns a remotely situated sorghum wine distillery. *En route* to her future husband, the travellers are attacked by the notorious bandit Sanpao (Chunhua), but Nine is saved by the chair-carrier Yu (Wen). The couple are physically attracted and, at a later opportunity, make love and conceive a child. Nine's husband is murdered, the distillery prospers under her management, and Yu claims her for his wife. All is well until the Japanese invasion brings horror and tragedy. This bare-bones synopsis omits the many intricate relationships and critical events that punctuate an unusual portrait of rural Chinese life over a period of many years. The tale is introduced by an unseen narrator – the grandson of Nine and Yu – who tells us that the account of his grandparents' meeting has passed into folk myth. And, indeed, former cameraman Zhang (*Yellow Earth*) Yimou's original and exotic film has the quality of an epic folk tale. Romantic, violent, compelling, occasionally humorous and wonderfully acted. *Red Sorghum* also offers a treat to the eye in its exceptional beauty of landscape and photography. Best seen on the big screen, but rather the little one than not at all.

Best Film Berlin 1988

▶ **Red Wedding** see Blood Wedding

Reed Dolls

▶ **Poupées De Roseau**

Morocco 1981 88 mins col
Herakles Productions

d **Jillali Ferhati**
sc **Farida Belyazid**
ph **Abdelkrim M. De Kaoui**
Chaiba Adraoui, Bisiam, Sand Thami, Ahmed Ferhati, Jillali Ferhati, Ahmed Boudouadi

Aicha (Bisiam), a poor country girl, is sent to live with her aunt in town and is married to her cousin when she is old enough (i.e. when she begins menstruating). Her husband dies suddenly, leaving her a victim of the severe social and economic difficulties of an unprotected woman with children in a traditionalist Arab community. The film is a riveting and detailed insight into Moroccan culture, and a rare exposé of the oppression of Muslim women. Brilliantly well-acted by two Aichas (Bisiam the girl, Thami the woman) and Adraoui, outstanding as the supportive aunt battling to ward off catastrophe, the film is also visually exquisite, displaying a superb sense of both colour and composition, and directed with authority and understanding.

The Refusal

▶ **Die Verweigerung**
▶ **aka Der Fall Jägerstätter**

Austria 1972 94 mins bw
Neue Thalia-Film

d **Axel Corti**
sc **Hellmut Andics**
ph **Walter Kindler**
Kurt Weinzierl, Julia Geschnitzer, Hugo Gottschlich, Helmut Wlasak, Fritz Schmiedl

In the Upper Austrian village of St Radegund in 1943, Franz Jägerstätter (Weinzierl), an anti-Nazi farmer, family man and devout Catholic, refused conscription on the grounds of conscience. Ignoring exhortations from the Church, his wife and even the sympathetic army Major who offered him a non-combatant unit as a way out, he was guillotined in Brandenburg prison. From these true facts about a remarkable man, Corti has made a restrained and dignified film in which the dramatic reconstruction is intercut with film of the survivors of the place and period who were involved with or witnessed the events. Truthful, balanced and unmelodramatic, it is a monument to a man of uncompromising integrity, though it ends on a salutary note: an old man in the village remarks that 'Wars are always unjust. When another one comes along, it will be unjust too,' implying that Jägerstätter's self-sacrifice was pointless.

▶ **Regain** see Harvest

▶ **Regi – Andrej Tarkovskij** see Directed By Andrei Tarkovsky

▶ **Règle Du Jeu, La** see Rules Of The Game, The

▶ **Rehearsal For A Crime** see Criminal Life Of Archibaldo De La Cruz, The

▶ **Reise Der Hoffnung** see Journey Of Hope

▶ **Rekopis Znaleziony W Saragossie** see Saragossa Manuscript, The

La Religieuse

▶ **aka Suzanne Simonin, La Religieuse De Diderot**

▶ **(US: The Nun)**

France 1965 140 mins col
Rome-Paris Films/Société Nouvelle De
Cinématographie

d **Jacques Rivette**
sc **Jacques Rivette, Jean Gruault**
ph **Alain Levent**
m **Jean-Claude Eloy**
**Anna Karina, Liselotte Pulver, Micheline
Presle, Christine Lenier, Francine Bergé,
Francisco Rabal**

Suzanne Simonin (Karina) is forced, through
lack of a dowry, to enter a convent where she
is subjected to semi-starvation and beatings.
Her efforts to annul her vows fail, but she is
transferred to another convent where the
Mother Superior makes Lesbian overtures to
her until she escapes with the help of a priest
(Rabal), who then attempts to rape her, and
she has to endure new sufferings on the outside. Taken from a novel by Diderot written
in 1760, this film was initially banned in
France on grounds of anti-clericalism,
although it was shown at Cannes in the
interim. It is directed with austere detachment
and an authentic sense of claustrophobia and
pain, with the suggestion that the corruption
and cruelty lurking behind the façades of
religion is a metaphor for the world at large.
If one can sit out the heavy-handed and
repetitive sequences, there is much of interest,
and the attractive Karina is adequate.

Remedy

▶ **Derman**

Turkey 1984 90 mins col
Gülsah Film

d **Serif Gören**
sc **Ahmet Soner**
ph **Erdogan Engin**
m **Yeni Türkü Gurubu**
**Hülya Koçyigit, Tarik Akan, Talat Bulut,
Nur Sürer**

Mürüvett (Koçyigit), a midwife, journeys to
a post in Anatolia. On the way, she is trapped
in a snowstorm in a nearby village and, the
place becoming entirely snowbound, is forced
to spend four months there. Before long, she
is tending the sick children and delivering the
babies, while two men, one of them (Akan)
on the run from the police, become dependent
on her. Serif Gören was responsible for
directing Güney's *Yol* while Güney was in
prison, and it is quite clear from this film that
he must share in the credit for *Yol's* success.
Working on his own account here, he not
only draws good performances from his cast,
but creates a palpable sense of the atmosphere
and daily life in a small and remote Anatolian
village. Above all, however, it is his outstanding visual flair that distinguishes this movie,
with the ever-present and constraining snow
extraordinarily photographed as both reality
and as an emblem of hardship.

▶ **Rémorques** see Stormy Waters

Le Rempart Des Béguines

▶ **aka The Beguines**

France 1972 90 mins col
Paris Film/Antheo Film(Rome)

d **Guy Casaril**
sc **Guy Casaril, Françoise Mallet-Joris**
ph **Andreas Winding**
m **Michel Delpech, Roland Vincent**
**Nicole Courcel, Anicée Alvina, Venantino
Venantini, Jean Martin, Ginette Leclerc**

Schoolgirl Hélène (Alvina) is seduced by her
father's mistress Tamara (Courcel) and a passionate affair develops, marred only by
demands of submission and a touch of violence from Tamara. When Tamara agrees to
marry Hélène's father, the girl overcomes her
jealousy through the realization that her lover
is doing it for material security and that she
herself will now have the upper hand. This
sounds like a piece of typical Lesbian sexploitation but, in fact, Mallet-Joris' successful first
novel has been brought to the screen with a
touch of class. Directed with elegance,
restraint and sensuality, and offering convincing performances from the women, its weakest
element is the absence of any social or domestic context, thus robbing it of genuine conflict. Casaril places us, together with his

protagonists, in a hothouse of sexual emotion which becomes a little too humid and enervating for comfort.

Rendez-Vous

France   1985   83 mins   col
T. Films/Films A2

d   **André Téchiné**
sc   **André Téchiné, Olivier Assayas**
ph   **Renato Berta**
m   **Philippe Sarde**
    Juliette Binoche, Lambert Wilson, Wadeck Stanczak, Jean-Louis Trintignant, Dominique Lavanant

Naive Nina (Binoche), just 18, arrives in Paris from the provinces, seeking independence and a theatrical career. She becomes enmeshed with over-idealistic Paulot (Stanczak) and destructive Quentin (Wilson), loses both of them, but gains the lead in *Romeo And Juliet*. Masquerading as a study of opposing forces in life and fate – Shakespeare's play is a symbol – Téchiné delivers a chic, well-cast, and certainly eventful, drama that rises above the level of drivel only because of the expertise with which it is put together.

Best Director Cannes 1985

Rendezvous At Midnight

▶ **Le Rendez-Vous De Minuit**

France   1961   90 mins   bw
Editions Cinégraphiques/Argos/Films Roger Leenhardt

d   **Roger Leenhardt**
sc   **Roger Leenhardt, Jean-Pierre Vivet**
ph   **Jean Badal**
m   **Georges Auric**
    Lilli Palmer, Michel Auclair, Jean Galland, Maurice Ronet, Michel De Ré, France Anglade

At the cinema Jacques (Auclair) is watching a film called *Rendez-vous De Minuit* starring Lilli Palmer and Maurice Ronet. Eva, a young woman next to him, becomes emotional and rushes out of the cinema. Concerned, he goes after her and she explains that her life is following the pattern of the film's heroine and that she is about to commit suicide as the latter does on screen. Eva is the image of Lilli Palmer... Leenhardt, in the second of his two features (the first was *The Last Vacation*) has constructed an intricate study of illusion versus reality that is difficult to describe. He constantly intercuts the film-within-a-film to contrast two different 'realities' and complicates the issue further when a third Lilli Palmer, presumably as herself, makes a brief appearance at the end. Although it's not difficult to follow the action, the director's aim and object is somewhat obscure. No matter. It's inventive and funny, with Palmer splendid in her multiple roles.

Les Rendez-Vous D'Anna

▶ **aka The Meetings Of Anna**

Belgium/France/W.
Germany   1978   122 mins   col
Hélène Films/Paradise Films/Zweites Deutsches Fernsehen

d   **Chantal Akerman**
sc   **Chantal Akerman**
ph   **Jean Penzer**
    Aurore Clément, Helmut Griem, Magali Noël, Hans Zieschler, Lea Massari, Jean-Pierre Cassel

Anna Silver (Clément), a Belgian film director in her twenties (like Chantal Akerman at the time), travels to several European cities to publicize her latest film. In Essen, she meets a German journalist (Griem), with whom she goes to bed; in Paris, she visits her mother (Massari) and goes out with an ex-lover (Cassel). She returns to her apartment alone. For those who are willing to enter Akerman's world – static camera, medium long shots, mournful monologues and solemn silences – it does bring some rewards. The cryptic style and dislocated characters, existing in impersonal hotel rooms and railway stations, get close to the heart of a modern malaise in cool and understated images.

Rendez-Vous De Juillet

France   1949   120 mins   bw
UGC/SNEG

d   **Jacques Becker**
sc   **Jacques Becker, Maurice Griffe**

ph **Claude Renoir**
m **Jean Wiener, Mezzmezzrow**
   Daniel Gélin, Bernard Lajarrige, Brigitte
   Auber, Nicole Courcel, Maurice Ronet

A group of young people planning to make an anthropological film in Africa, attempt to find maturity and happiness through love, theatre, and jazz in post-war St-Germain-des-Prés. Although very much a film of its day, the performances still have a rare freshness and the interplay of the characters is more interesting than the thin plot and sociological angles.

▶ **Rendez-Vous De Minuit, Le** see Rendezvous At Midnight

▶ **Renegade Priest, The** see Défroqué, Le

Repast

▶ **Meshi**

Japan 1951 101 mins bw
Toho

d **Mikio Naruse**
sc **Toshiro Ide, Sumie Tanaka**
ph **Masao Tamai**
m **Fumio Hayasaka**
   Setsuko Hara, Ken Uehara, Yukiko
   Shimazaki, Kan Nihonyanagi, Keiju
   Kobayashi

The empty, unfulfilled five-year marriage of Michiyo (Hara) and her husband Hatsunosuke (Uehara) is brought to a head when their flirt of a niece (Shimazaki) comes to stay. Michiyo tries to become independent, but returns to her husband in the end. The first of six works that Naruse adapted from the novels of Fumiko Hayashi, all of which deal with women who are trying to redefine their lives, but who are ultimately defeated. The ambiguous ending of *Repast* is often seen as a compromise, but it is more truthful than most happy conclusions to melodramas. The whole delicate, minutely-observed work is greatly enriched by the playing of the two leads.

Repentance

▶ **Pokjaniye, Monanieba**

USSR 1984 150 mins col
Gruziafilm/Georgian State TV

d **Tengiz Abuladze**
sc **Tengiz Abuladze, Nana Djanelidze, Rezo**
   Kveselava
ph **Mikhail Agranovich**
m **Nana Djanelidze**
   Avtandil Makharadze, Zeynab
   Botsvzadze, Edisher Giorgobiani, Katevan
   Abuladze, Iya Ninidze, Merab Ninidze

When Varlam Avaridze (Makharadze), the mayor of a small Georgian town, dies, he is buried with full pomp. But the attractive Guliko (Iya Ninidze), who had been persecuted by him, continually digs up his corpse. During her trial, the full extent of Varlam's crimes emerges. There are few Soviet films that so epitomize *glasnost* than this searing exposé of Stalinism and the 'cult of personality'. Shot in Georgian in Stalin's own republic, it was cleared for mass distribution two years after its completion. A dark, lucid, bitter film, laced with black humour, it unfolds in a series of nightmarish flashbacks and meaningful symbols.

▶ **Report On The Party And The Guests, A** see Party And The Guests, The

▶ **Repos Du Guerrier, Le** see Warrior's Rest

Republic Of Sin

▶ **La Fièvre Monte À El Pao**

France/Mexico 1960 100 mins bw
Groupe Des Quatre(Paris)/
Cinematografica Filmex(Mexico)

d **Luis Buñuel**
sc **Louis Sapin, Luis Buñuel**
ph **Gabriel Figueroa**
m **Paul Misraki**
   Gérard Philipe, Jean Servais, Maria
   Felix, Raoul Dantes, M.A. Ferriz,
   Domingo Soler

A satellite island off the coast of a Latin-American Republic has a large population of jailbirds and political prisoners from the mainland. The administration is corrupt and callous, and the governor is assassinated. Vasquez (Philipe), his former secretary and a man of ideals, takes care of matters – and falls in love with the dead man's widow (Felix) – until a new governor (Servais) is appointed. The two men do not see eye to eye, mutiny breaks out and, eventually, Vasquez becomes governor, only to find that power forces him to betray his humane principles. Buñuel here has come up with part potboiler, part acute political analysis. There is a splendid villain from Servais, and Maria Felix's sexy beauty is given rein in some well-shot bedroom scenes. However, the cruel cynicism of the director's message – that individuals are forced to bow to systems – comes through loud and clear. Gérard Philipe, making his last film before his early death, seems unable to inject life into his somewhat vaguely characterized role. A disappointing exit for the French superstar.

▶ **Restless Night** see All Night Through

▶ **Retour De Martin Guerre, Le** see Return Of Martin Guerre, The

▶ **Retrato De Teresa** see Portrait Of Teresa

The Return Of Martin Guerre

▶ **Le Retour De Martin Guerre**

France 1982 123 mins col
SFP/France Region 3/Marcel Dassault/Roissi Films

d **Daniel Vigne**
sc **Jean-Claude Carrière, Daniel Vigne**
ph **André Neau**
m **Michel Portal**
   Gérard Depardieu, Stéphane Peau, Nathalie Baye, Bernard-Pierre Donnadieu, Sylvie Meda, Maurice Barrier

In the 16th century, a man (Depardieu) comes to a French village claiming to be Martin Guerre, a youth who left his child-bride (Baye) pregnant eight years earlier. A trial is held to establish whether he is an imposter. The main strength of Vigne's 'who is it?' medieval mystery is the extraordinary re-creation of a cruel, ignorant and suspicious society. But the plot is never as intriguing as it promises and takes quite a time to get to the point. Depardieu's calm presence holds the film together.

The Return Of Maxim

▶ **Vozvrashcheniye Maksima**

USSR 1937 114 mins bw
Lenfilm

d **Grigori Kozintsev, Leonid Trauberg**
sc **Grigori Kozintsev, Leonid Trauberg, Lev Slavin**
ph **Andrei Moskvin**
m **Dmitri Shostakovitch**
   Boris Chirkov, Valentina Kibardina, A. Kuznetsov, Alexander Zrazhevsky, Mikhail Zharov

In 1914, Maxim (Chirkov), his girlfriend Natasha (Kibardina) and their comrades take part in the workers' demonstrations against the war and the operations to discover an armaments factory. With the dramatist Slavin, brought in to enliven the complicated political scenes, Kozintsev and Trauberg continued the mood of *The Youth Of Maxim* (1935), although tinged with more seriousness as the hero becomes a full-blown revolutionary. The introduction of a new character, Dimba (Zharov), St Petersburg's billiards king, good enough to worry Paul Newman, the stirring crowd scenes and the stirring music, make an impressive second part of *The Maxim Trilogy*, to be concluded by *The Vyborg Side*.

▶ **Revenant, Un** see Lover's Return, A

The Revolt Of Job

▶ **Jób Lázadása**

Hungary 1983 98 mins col
Mafilm Tarsulás Studio/Hungarian TV(Budapest)/ ZDF(Mainz)

d   **Imre Gyöngyössi, Barna Kabay**
sc **Katalin Petényi, Imre Gyöngyössi, Barna Kabay**
ph **Gábor Szabó**
m   **Zoltán Jeney**
    Ferenc Zenthe, Hédi Temessy, Gábor Fehér, Péter Rudolf, Leticia Caro

By 1943, Job and Rosa (Zenthe and Temessy), an elderly Jewish couple in an East Hungarian farming community, have outlived their seven children. Eager to hand on their heritage before they die, they adopt Lacko (Fehér), a seven-year-old orphan. The period of adjustment is difficult, with the boy rebellious and distrustful. He comes to love his adoptive parents, whereupon the Nazi round-up of the Jews begins and Job must find a way to protect Lacko... This story is told from the boy's point of view, much in the same manner as Kusturica's *When Father Was Away On Business*. Screenplay, direction and cast are workmanlike, but it's the superbly natural and committed performance of young Gábor Fehér that lends it special poignancy and distinction.

The Revolt Of The Fishermen

▶ **Vostaniye Rybakov**

USSR 1934 60 mins bw
Mezhrabpomfilm

d   **Erwin Piscator**
sc **Georgi Grebner**
ph **Pyotr Yermolov, M. Kirillov**
m   **Ferenc Sabo, Nikolai Chembendzhi, Vladimir Ferre**
    Aleksey Diky, Emma Tsesarskaya, Vera Yanukova, Nikolai Gladkov

When the fishermen on board the 'Santa Barbara' go on strike, blacklegs are brought in from a neighbouring village by the bosses to replace them. Andreas (Diky), a young sailor, joins the blacklegs in order to wreck their ship with dynamite. During a struggle between the fishermen and the blacklegs, one of the strikers is killed. At his funeral the mourners, incensed by the graveyard speech of the priest (acting on the side of authority), break out into a bloody revolt against the soldiers who have been marshalled to keep

order. The only film by Piscator, the extremely influential German theatre director, was based on the novel by Anna Seghers and filmed in the USSR during the last year of Soviet cinema's internationalist policy. It is a fascinating and rarely seen work, almost a compendium of expressionist film styles – the low-key lighting, the distorting camera work, the brooding sailor and the earthy prostitute (the superb Tsesarskaya) derive from the German silent cinema, while the shock cuts, the crowd groupings and the choral singing put one in mind of Eisenstein. Yet, although it is the result of a theatre man's pillaging of the cinematic ideas of others, it remains fervent and visually exciting.

The Revolving Doors

▶ **Les Portes Tournantes**

Canada 1988 102 mins col
Malofilm Production (Montreal)/
L'Union Générale/Cinématographique
(Paris)

d   **Francis Mankiewicz**
sc **Jacques Savoie**
ph **Thomas Vamos**
m   **François Dompierre**
    Monique Spaziani, Gabriel Arcand, Miou-Miou, François Méthé, Jacques Penot

Nearing the end of her life, Céleste Beaumont (Spaziani) sends her diary to the grown-up son (Arcand) she has never seen, himself the father of a 12-year-old boy, Antoine (Méthé), whose mother (Miou-Miou) lives apart from them. The diary tells how, in the 1920s, young Céleste became a piano accompanist for silent films. Losing her job with the coming of talkies, she married wealthy Pierre Blaudelle (Penot), but when he was killed in World War II, she left her newborn son with her in-laws, went to New York, and became a jazz pianist. The introverted Blaudelle is disturbed by the diary, but Antoine decides to go to New York and meet his grandmother. Shanghai-born Mankiewicz, a former Canadian TV cameraman and director, has made an unusual and charming feature that sends his protagonists and his audience through the revolving doors of time. There are joyous moments in the evocation of Céleste's early life and of the silent cinema, and a seductive, dream-like atmosphere permeates the film. The performances are good, too, but for all its virtues, the movie has a sketchy and superficial screenplay that leaves one vaguely dissatisfied.

▶ **Richard Tauber Story, The** see You Are The World For Me

▶ **Rideau Cramoisi, Le** see Crimson Curtain, The

Rififi

▶ **Du Rififi Chez Les Hommes**

France 1955 116 mins bw
Indus/Pathé/Prima

d Jules Dassin
sc Jules Dassin, René Wheeler, Auguste Le Breton
ph Philippe Agostini
m Georges Auric
Jean Servais, Carl Mohner, Robert Manuel, Marie Sabouret, Perlo Vita (Jules Dassin), Magali Noël

A group of criminals plan and execute a jewel robbery and then fall out over the loot. After being forced out of Hollywood by the McCarthy blacklist, Dassin settled in France where he made this clever and much imitated (in films and life) heist movie, originally assigned to Jean-Pierre Melville. The film's reputation rests on the meticulously enacted and tense 22-minute robbery sequence played in total silence, and the sleazy view of the Montmartre underworld.

Best Director Cannes 1955

▶ **Riflemen, The** see Carabiniers, Les

▶ **Rih Essed** see Man Of Ashes

The Ripening Seed

▶ **(US: The Game Of Love)**

▶ **Le Blé En Herbe**

France 1953 105 mins bw
Franco London

d Claude Autant-Lara

sc Claude Autant-Lara, Jean Aurenche, Pierre Bost
ph Robert Lefèbvre
m René Cloërec
Nicole Berger, Pierre-Michel Beck, Edwige Feuillère

While on holiday at the seaside with his childhood sweetheart (Berger), an adolescent boy (Beck) is seduced by a mysterious, attractive, much older woman (Feuillère). This tender triangular tale, intelligently adapted from Colette's novel, was condemned as 'immoral and obscene' by the Church and banned in Nice and Chicago, no doubt a contributing factor to its success. However, the grace and glamour of Feuillère was the clincher.

▶ **Ripoux, Les** see Cop, Le

▶ **Riptide** see Such A Pretty Little Beach

The Rise Of Louis XIV

▶ **aka The Rise To Power Of Louis XIV**

▶ **La Prise De Pouvoir Par Louis XIV**

France 1966 100 mins bw
ORTF

d Roberto Rossellini
sc Philippe Erlanger
ph Georges Leclerc
m Betty Willemetz
Jean-Marie Patte, Raymond Jourdan, Silvagni, Katharina Renn

The early life of Louis XIV (Patte) under the domination of the regents, his later taking over of power for himself, the building of Versailles and the centralized court life. From the mid-1960s to his death in 1977, Rossellini turned his attention almost exclusively to the making of historical and religious features for TV. This was one of the few of them to escape the confines of the small screen and obtain a wide theatrical release. His method here was not only to approach his subject in a direct and realistic manner, to reveal the man beneath the wig, but also to show that power resides in routine and ritual. Impressive is the central documentary-like section detailing life at the court, and the ending, when the little king is divested of his robes.

▶ **Rise To Power Of Louis XIV, The**
see Rise Of Louis XIV, The

▶ **Riso Amaro** see Bitter Rice

The Rite

▶ **Riten**

Sweden 1969 74 mins bw
Svensk Filmindustri/Sveriges TV/A.B. Cinematograph

d **Ingmar Bergman**
sc **Ingmar Bergman**
ph **Sven Nykvist**
   Ingrid Thulin, Anders Ek, Gunnar Björnstrand, Erik Hell

An internationally famous theatrical troupe consisting of husband (Björnstrand), wife (Thulin) and wife's lover (Ek), have their show stopped because an item, 'The Rite', is considered obscene. Summoned by a Judge, they are subjected to provocative and sadistic examinations of their private lives which ruthlessly expose their serious neuroses and misdemeanours. This was the first film that Bergman made specifically for television, but it soon received cinema release. Dealing with one of the director's major and recurring themes – the relationship of the artist to society and the dislocation between his private and public self – it shows no compromise for the small screen. A complex, disturbing, and deeply pessimistic film, with a brilliant performance from Thulin as the unhappy, alcoholic actress.

▶ **Riten** see Rite, The

▶ **Road, The** see Strada, La

The Road To Corinth

▶ **La Route De Corinthe**

France 1967 90 mins col
Les Films La Boétie(Paris)/
CGFC(Rome)/Orion Films(Athens)

d **Claude Chabrol**
sc **Claude Brûlé, Daniel Boulanger**
ph **Jean Rabier**
m **Pierre Jansen**
   Jean Seberg, Maurice Ronet, Christian Marquand, Michel Bouquet, Saro Urzi, Claude Chabrol

Robert Ford (Marquand), a NATO security officer, is shot while investigating mysterious electronic boxes that are jamming US radar installations in Greece. His wife Shanny (Seberg), falsely convicted for his murder and ordered to leave the country, sets out to find the killer, giving the slip to Dex (Ronet), whom Robert's superior (Bouquet) has detailed to chaperone her. Complications multiply as Dex becomes Shanny's ally... High-class escapist hokum with a wry undertone and magnificent Greek locations that could equally well have served Hitchcock or the James Bond team. That said, Chabrol has used his light-hearted caper as the basis for a witty, bizarre and sumptuous exercise in style, expertly photographed by Rabier.

The Road To Life

▶ **Putyovka V Zhizn**

USSR 1931 121 mins bw
Mezhrabpomfilm

d **Nicolai Ekk**
sc **Nikolai Ekk**
ph **Vaslli Pronin**
m **Yakov Stollyar**
   Maria Gonfa, Tsifan Kyria, Nikolai Batalov

In the early 1920s, during the chaotic aftermath of the Civil War, thousands of homeless orphans roam the countryside as vagabonds and petty criminals. At a children's collective, they are rehabilitated and taught a trade. The first Soviet film to be conceived and made as a talkie showed an impressive grasp of the potential of sound, while still using intertitles. Although there were also some remnants of the montage techniques Ekk had learnt from his teacher Eisenstein, the film moved towards a more personalized kind of Soviet cinema. Praised technically and dramatically at home and abroad, today it needs to be seen in its historical context to be fully appreciated.

Rocco And His Brothers

▶ **Rocco E I Suoi Fratelli**

Italy 1960 180 mins bw
Titanus/Les Films Marceau

d   Luchino Visconti
sc   Luchino Visconti, Suso Cecchi D'Amico,
    Vasco Pratolini
ph   Giuseppe Rotunno
m   Nino Rota
    Alain Delon, Renato Salvatori, Annie
    Girardot, Katina Paxinou, Roger Hanin,
    Paolo Stoppa, Suzy Delair, Claudia
    Cardinale, Spiros Focas, Rocco Vidolazzi

Rosaria Pafundi (Paxinou) and her four sons, Rocco (Delon), Simone (Salvatori), Vincenza (Focas), and Luca (Vidolazzi), come to Milan to escape the poverty of the South, but find that the streets of the unfeeling metropolis are not exactly paved with gold. Visconti's long family saga, told in four episodes bearing the name of each of the brothers, was an attempt to return to Neo-Realism, but the melodramatics and the star cast put it nearer the world of Hollywood soap. Delon as a 'wise fool' is unconvincing, especially as a boxer who wouldn't harm a flyweight. Salvatori and Girardot bring the necessary weight to their tragic roles, although placed in an operatic finale. 'Rococo And His Brothers'? Yet there is much to admire in the scale of the enterprise, the scenes of the family's arrival and the Milanese locations.

Best Director Venice 1960

▶ **Rocco E I Suoi Fratelli** see Rocco And His Brothers

▶ **Røde Kappe, Den** see Red Mantle, The

▶ **Røde Rubin, Den** see Song Of The Red Ruby, The

RoGoPaG

Italy 1962 125 mins bw/col
Arco/Cineriz/Lyre

d   Roberto Rossellini, Jean-Luc Godard,
    Pier Paolo Pasolini, Ugo Gregoretti
sc   Roberto Rossellini, Jean-Luc Godard,
    Pier Paolo Pasolini, Ugo Gregoretti
ph   Luciano Trasatti, Jean Rabier, Tonino
    Delli Colli, Mario Bernardo
m   Carlo Rustichelli
    Orson Welles, Ugo Tognazzi, Rosanna
    Schiaffino, Alexandra Stewart, Jean-Marc
    Bory, Renato Salvatori, Lisa Gastoni,
    Bruce Balabin

Rossellini (Ro): An airline hostess (Schiaffino) has to fend off an American passenger (Balabin). Godard (Go): A couple (Stewart and Bory) have an unsatisfactory love affair in a post-nuclear world. Pasolini (Pa): A man dies on the cross while acting in a religious epic directed by Orson Welles. Gregoretti (G): A couple (Tognazzi and Gastoni) comes up against modern selling techniques. 'Ragbag' might have been a better title for this quartet of sketches on the horrors of contemporary life. The most effective is Pasolini's view of the contrast between the Christian message and those who propagate it, which got him four months suspended sentence for 'public defamation'. Godard's is a disturbing and sharp premonitory essay, Gregoretti offers a familiar satire, and the first feeble sketch is unworthy of its director.

▶ **Rok Spokojnego Słońca** see Year Of The Quiet Sun, A

The Role

▶ **Bhumika**

India 1977 142 mins col
Blaze Film Enterprises

d   Shyam Benegal
sc   Girish Karnad, Pandit Satyadev Dubey,
    Shyam Benegal
ph   Govind Nihalani
m   Vanraj Bhatia
    Smita Patil, Anant Nag, Amrish Puri,
    Naseeruddin Shah, Amol Palekar

Keshav (Palekar) gets Usha (Patil), the young daughter of his mistress, into films as a singer. She falls in love with her regular co-star Rajan (Nag), but his attitude to her is ambivalent and, eventually, she finds herself marrying Keshav, who plays on a multitude of her emotions, including her sense of obligation, to get her to do so. She becomes the family breadwinner, forced to continue working against her desires. Benegal's deceptively simple seventh film, with its narrative echoes of a Hollywood-style 'woman's picture' is, in fact, a multi-layered, complex affair which reveals the difficulties and contradictions of a woman's role in India. The director cunningly combines past and present, drawing skilful correspondences between Usha's screen roles and her life, in an absorbing story which excels in all departments.

▶ **Roma** see Fellini's Roma

▶ **Roma, Città Aperta** see Rome, Open City

▶ **Roman D'Un Tricheur, Le** see Story Of A Cheat, The

▶ **Romeo, Julie A Tma** see Romeo, Juliet And Darkness

Romeo, Juliet And Darkness

▶ **Romeo, Julie A Tma**

Czechoslovakia 1959 96 mins bw
Ceskoslovensky Film

d **Jiří Weiss**
sc **Jiří Weiss, Jan Otčenásek**
ph **Václav Hanus**
m **Jiří Srnka**
   Ivan Mistrik, Dana Smutná, František Smolik, Blanka Bohdanová, Jiří Koder, Vladimir Ráž

In 1942, during the Nazi occupation of Czechoslovakia, Hana (Smutná), a Jewish schoolgirl, escapes the ghetto round-up and is given refuge by Pavel (Mistrik), a boy who hides her in his mother's attic and keeps her going as best he can until the inevitable bleak outcome. A restrained and atmospheric film in which Weiss admirably captures the daily stress and consequence of living in fear. The close relationship that grows between the two young people, and sparks off the climax of the plot, relies for its credibility on Mistrik's depth of performance. (Smutná is beautiful but blank.) The film is affecting and authentic; its director, interestingly, escaped the Occupation and spent the war years in Britain.

Rome, Open City

▶ **(US: Open City)**
▶ **Roma, Città Aperta**

Italy 1945 101 mins bw
Minerva/Excelsa

d **Roberto Rossellini**
sc **Sergio Amedei, Federico Fellini**
ph **Ubaldo Arata**
m **Renzo Rossellini**
   Aldo Fabrizi, Anna Magnani, Marcel Pagliero, Maria Michi, Harry Feist

In 1944, in the last days of the German occupation of Italy, Resistance leader Manfredi (Pagliero), fleeing the Gestapo, is given refuge by the pregnant Pina (Magnani). When she is shot, he takes shelter with a good-time girl (Michi) who betrays him. Manfredi and a priest (Fabrizzi) are arrested and executed. The film that brought the Italian Neo-Realist movement to fruition was concerned with capturing, as directly as possible, the experiences of ordinary people caught in political events. Using a documentary approach and filming with minimum resources in the streets and apartments of Rome, Rossellini achieved an immediacy and intensity that audiences had never previously witnessed. Two of the few professionals in the cast, Magnani and Fabrizzi give extremely moving performances.

Best Film Cannes 1946

Romuald & Juliette

France 1989 112 mins col
CINEA/Enilog Films/FR3 Films

d **Coline Serreau**
sc **Coline Serreau**
ph **Jean-Noël Ferragut**
m **Jerome Reese (musical research)**
   Daniel Auteuil, Firmine Richard, Pierre Vernier, Maxime Lerous, Gilles Privat, Muriel Combeau, Catherine Salviat, Sambou Tati

Romuald (Auteuil), the wealthy, dynamic president of a huge yogurt-manufacturing company, lives in the lap of luxury with his *soignée* wife and two perfect teenage children. Juliette (Richard) is the black night-cleaner of the company's Paris headquarters and struggles to raise five children (the offspring of five ex-husbands) in a couple of cramped rooms, and to feed and educate them on her meagre income. When Juliette tumbles to a conspiracy to unseat Romuald and brand him a criminal, she sets out to help him and the disparate pair forge an unlikely relationship with major consequences for both of them. Coline Serreau's film is a highly romantic, often funny and occasionally poignant screwball romance which needs to be taken at face value to be appreciated, whereupon it yields maximum enjoyment and pleasure. Packed with plot, it rackets merrily along, serviced by a first-rate cast headed by a charmingly bemused Auteuil and a buxom and beguiling Richard, making her acting debut in middle age. *Romuald*, one of France's five top box-office hits during 1989, entered 1990 facing the same fate as Serreau's previous success, *Three Men And A Cradle*, namely American recycling. The original will almost certainly remain the best, given its organically Parisian context.

La Ronde

France   1950   97 mins   bw
Sacha Gordine

d   **Max Ophüls**
sc **Jacques Natanson, Max Ophüls (from Arthur Schnitzler's play)**
ph **Christian Matras**
m   **Oscar Straus**
    Anton Walbrook, Simone Signoret, Serge Reggiani, Daniel Gélin, Danielle Darrieux, Simone Simon, Fernand Gravey, Odette Joyeux, Jean-Louis Barrault, Isa Miranda, Gérard Philipe

Ten episodes, linked by a puppet master/narrator (Walbrook), in which the protagonists ride a sexual merry-go-round in 19th-century Vienna, with one partner always connecting to the next story eg the whore and the soldier, the soldier and the maid, the maid and the master, and so forth. Schnitzler's mordant comment on sexual mores and the illusion of love, never seems to come off in performance, emerging, for the most part, as whimsical rather than piquant. Here, Ophüls has assembled a glittering cast, and the opening credits are classy, elegant and full of promise. In the event, although wonderfully photographed with a camera that, itself, acts as a carousel, and exquisitely dressed and mounted, this exercise in artifice is a soufflé that takes a long time to rise, and is distressingly quick to collapse. Gélin, Darrieux and Miranda are outstanding and almost worth the price of admission, but it is difficult, three decades on, to appreciate the rapturous reception originally accorded to the film, including the story and screenplay prize at Venice, two Oscar nominations and the British Academy's Best Film award.

La Ronde

France   1964   110 mins   col
Paris Film Production/Interopa Film(Rome)

d   **Roger Vadim**
sc **Jean Anouilh**
ph **Henri Decaë**
m   **Michel Magne**
    Marie Dubois, Claude Giraud, Anna Karina, Jean-Claude Brialy, Jane Fonda, Maurice Ronet, Catherine Spaak, Bernard Noël, Francine Bergé, Jean Sorel

A merry-go-round of lovers, for the plot of which see Ophüls' *La Ronde*, with which comparison is inevitable. Vadim and his distinguished writer, Anouilh, have left Schnitzler even further behind than did Ophüls, updating the material to the eve of World War I, transferring the Viennese setting to Paris, bringing sexual explicitness to the bedroom(s), and substituting simplistic comedy for elegant wit. The big gain is Henri Decaë's colour and 'Scope photography, but almost everything else can be counted a loss. Catherine Spaak and Francine Bergé, midinette and actress respectively, are first-class, but Fonda is too young, Brialy too gauche and the rest simply not as good as their glittering predecessors. The general tenor of the movie is uneven, but the women, and the sets, look ravishing.

Rondo

Yugoslavia   1966   94 mins   bw
Jadran Film(Zagreb)

d   **Zvonimír Berkovič**

sc **Zvonimír Berković**
ph **Tomislav Pinter**
m **Mozart**
   Stevo Zigon, Relja Basić, Milena Dravić

Fedja (Basić), a young, married man, encounters the older Mladen (Zigon) playing chess in a café and invites him home. Observed by Fedja's wife, Neda (Dravić), the two men meet regularly each week to play chess; their games echo the developing relationships as Neda grows apart from her husband and is finally seduced by Mladen. The simplicity of a synopsis gives no clue to the formal brilliance of Berković's debut film. The constantly recurring situation – the weekly chess game – undergoes subtle changes with each repetition (as do the audience's shifting sympathies), and deliberately echoes Mozart's Rondo in A Minor which gives this finely acted film its title.

The Roof

▶ **Il Tetto**

Italy 1957 101 mins bw
Titanus/Les Films Marceau

d **Vittorio De Sica**
sc **Cesare Zavattini**
ph **Carlo Montuori**
m **Alessandro Cicognini**
   Gabriella Pallotta, Giorgio Listuzzi, Gastone Renzelli, Maria Di Rollo, Giuseppe Martini

A newly-wed humble bricklayer (Listuzzi) and his bride (Pallotta) have to live with his relations in their already overcrowded quarters. A family quarrel results in his sleeping in the toolshed, while she shares with a servant-girl friend. Finally, in the course of a single night and with the help of some friends, they set about constructing a meagre dwelling that will serve as a home of their own. Apparently, by Italian law, once the roof is on a building, the occupants cannot be evicted. This fact allowed De Sica to film a race against time and the police from which he has extracted a maximum of gentle comedy, while retaining a sense of the seriousness of the young couple's plight. Unpretentious and well played, this is one of the last of the director's quality Neo-Realist films. It is no *Bicycle Thieves* or *Umberto D*, being much

lighter-weight, but it manifests the same sense of compassion for the poor.

▶ **Room Upstairs, The** see Martin Roumagnac

Rosa Luxemburg

W. Germany 1986 120 mins col
Bioskop Film

d **Margarethe Von Trotta**
sc **Margarethe Von Trotta**
ph **Franz Rath**
m **Nicolas Economou**
   Barbara Sukowa, Daniel Olbrychski, Otto Sander, Adelheid Arndt, Jurgen Holtz, Doris Schade

Rosa Luxemburg (Sukowa), the Polish-born Jewish revolutionary, falls under the spell of activist Leo Jogiches (Olbrychski), involves herself with the German Social Democratic Party, undergoes a series of imprisonments and is murdered in January 1919 by members of the Freikorps, her body thrown into a canal. Although basing the film primarily on Rosa's letters and speeches, thus somewhat limiting the perspective, Von Trotta falls into the trap of seeing the widely influential radical from a modern feminist angle. However, the material is potent enough, and Sukowa's passionate rendition of the great speeches drives the film forward.

Best Actress (Barbara Sukowa) Cannes 1986

Roselyne And The Lions

▶ **Roselyne Et Les Lions**

France 1989 137 mins col
Cargo Films/Gaumont

d **Jean-Jacques Beineix**
sc **Jean-Jacques Beineix, Jacques Forgeas**
ph **Jean-François Robin**
m **Reinhardt Wagner**
   Isabelle Pasco, Gérard Sandoz, Philippe Clevenot, Gunter Meisner, Wolf Harnisch, Gabriel Monnet

Thierry (Sandoz), bored with school but fascinated by the lion-taming act at the zoo, persuades the owner-trainer Frazier (Monnet) to teach him in return for doing odd jobs. He proves a more than apt pupil and falls in love with the talented Roselyne (Pasco), also learning to be a lion-tamer. Encouraged by Thierry's English teacher, Bracquard (Clevenot), the young couple run away from Marseilles to try for an act of their own. After various struggles and humiliations, they are engaged by Koenig's of Munich, the leading German circus and very much a grandiose five-star affair. Overcoming the fact that they have bitten off more than they can chew, and keeping the fissures in their own relationship at bay, the couple triumph, with Roselyne built into a media star by Koenig. Synopsis can offer only the barest outline of this film, which is rich in subsidiary characters and packed with incidents humorous, romantic and dramatic. A good deal of the time is taken up with the lions, scenes for which Sandoz and Pasco underwent a lengthy training. It pays off, for this is the real thing and feels like it. Beineix's familiar motifs of love, death and dreams are ever present in this highly unusual story and his visual imagination operates at full tilt in the opening sequence and, more particularly, the baroque and spectacular climax in which we watch the young couple's finished act before a huge audience. Original, intriguing and thoroughly entertaining, the movie is mercifully free of the director's indulgent excesses, familiar from his previous work (*Diva*, *Betty Blue*, *The Moon In The Gutter*), and is well worth seeing.

▶ **Roselyne Et Les Lions** see Roselyne And The Lions

▶ **Rosemary** see Girl Rosemarie, The

▶ **Rossetto, Il** see Lipstick, The

La Roue

▶ **aka The Wheel**

France   1922   144 mins (see text)   bw
Pathé

d   **Abel Gance**
sc **Abel Gance**
ph **L.H. Burel, Bujard, Duverger**
m   **Silent**

Séverin-Mars, Ivy Close, Gabriel De Gravone

Sisif (Séverin-Mars), a railwayman, and his son (De Gravone), both fall in love with Norma (Close), with tragic results. This film was originally of epic time proportions, running for eight hours, until Gance spent several months cutting it down to the practical length of approximately 144 minutes. In the 1980s, however, Marie Epstein has come up with a restored version lasting 303 mins and it's impossible to know which version one is most likely to see. As to the film itself: its interest lies not in its cheap, melodramatic plot, but in the authentic location work in the railway milieu and Gance's innovative rapid montage techniques. The most celebrated section is a rhythmic sequence on a train as Sisif drives Norma away to the big city at full speed. Jean Cocteau pronounced that, 'There is cinema before and after *La Roue*, as there is painting before and after Picasso'.

Rouge

▶ **Yanzhi Kou**

Hong Kong   1987   96 mins   col
Golden Way Films

d   **Stanley Kwan (Guan Jinpang)**
sc **Li Bihua, Qiu-Dai Anping (Qiu Gangjian)**
ph **Bill Wong (Huang Zhongbiao)**
m   **Michael Lai (Li Xiaotian)**
    Anita Mui (Mei Yanfang), Leslie Cheung (Zhang Guorong), Alex Man (Wan Ziliang), Emily Chu (Zhu Baoyi), Irene Wan (Wen Bixia)

In 1934 in Hong Kong, Fleur (Mui), a beautiful courtesan, and Chan Chen-Pang (Cheung), known as the Twelfth Master, meet in the 'flower house' where she works and fall passionately in love – a socially unacceptable alliance with no future. Over 50 years later, newspaperman Yuen (Man) is closing up for the night when a strangely old-fashioned woman arrives asking to place a classified ad. It transpires that she is Fleur, now a ghost, and seeking a rendezvous with her lover who failed to meet her in the next world after she killed herself in their suicide pact. This exquisite love story has had limited release in the West, but whenever seen is acclaimed a masterpiece. With its fantastical plot rooted in

Rouge Baiser

reality and free of any 'arty' pretension, it is thoroughly believable and gripping, erotically charged and deeply poignant. Proving that the Hong Kong film industry is not exclusively devoted to violence, *Rouge* is a beguiling piece of work, cast, directed and edited with much skill.

Rouge Baiser

France   1985   112 mins   col
Stephan Films

d   Vera Belmont
sc   Vera Belmont
ph   Ramón Suárez
m   Jean-Marie Senia
    Charlotte Valandrey, Lambert Wilson,
    Marthe Keller, Laurent Terzieff, Günther
    Lamprecht

In Paris in 1952, 15-year-old Nadia (Valandrey), ardently championing Left-wing causes, falls for an older, cynical *Paris Match* photographer (Wilson) with a taste for decadent night life. She finds she must choose between politics and her passion for him. Belmont's semi- autobiographical film convincingly conjures up the world of Communist meetings and of the girl's Stalinist Polish-Jewish parents (Terzieff and Keller), and the atmosphere of jazz clubs in the Paris of the 1950s. But the director can't leave well alone. Each scene is invested with fussy camera movements and staccato editing, and the young heroine is not interesting enough to transcend the style.

▶ **Rouge Et Le Noir, Le** see Red And The Black, The

Rough Treatment

▶ **aka Without Anaesthesia**
▶ **Bez Znieczulenia**

Poland   1978   131 mins   col
Group X/Film Polski

d   Andrzej Wajda
sc   Andrzej Wajda, Agnieszka Holland
ph   Edward Klosínski
m   Piotr Derfel, Wojciech Mlynarski

Zbigniew Zapasiewicz, Ewa Dalkowska,
Andrzej Seweryn, Krystyna Janda

A middle-aged TV personality and journalist (Zapasiewicz), returning home from yet another trip abroad, finds that his wife (Dalkowska) is leaving him for a younger man (Seweryn) whose political and cultural attitudes are diametrically opposed to his own. Wajda, in a functional and uncluttered style, charts the man's disintegration, 'without anaesthesia'. Together with *Ashes And Diamonds* and *Man Of Marble*, Wajda considers that this film most clearly mirrors the concerns and interests of the majority of Polish film audiences. The ambiguity of the characters and the understated relationship between the personal and political may make it less clear to other audiences, but the grim humour and mental agony come across forcefully.

The Round-Up

▶ **Szegénylegények**

Hungary   1965   94 mins   bw
Mafilm Studio IV

d   Miklós Jancsó
sc   Gyula Hernádi
ph   Tamás Somló
m   Popular songs
    János Görbe, Tibor Molnár, András
    Kozák, Gábor Agárdy, Zoltán Latinovits

On a bleak plain, a group of peasants is rounded up by Austro-Hungarian troops, who, by means of torture, interrogations and killings, attempt to weed out the leader of a partisan group in the Kossuth revolution 20 years before in 1848. In this film, Jancsó's very personal style blossomed, giving the tracking shot a new meaning. The camera weaves in and out like an invisible observer, as groups of people split up and realign, sometimes moving with them, sometimes tracking them down and shooting them. There is little dialogue, the characters are depersonalized, the setting is timeless. The film's hypnotic beauty and the daring technique launched Jancsó as a leading director on the international scene.

▶ **Route De Corinthe, La** see Road To Corinth, The

The Royal Hunt

▶ **Mrigaya**

India   1976   112 mins   col
Uday Bhaskar International

d   **Mrinal Sen**
sc **Mrinal Sen, Mohit Chattopadhya**
ph **K.K. Mahajan**
m   **Salil Chowdhury**
    Mithun Chakraborty, Mamata Shankar, Robert Wright, Ann Wright, Sadhu Meher

In a remote village in British India, a curious friendship is struck up between Ghenua (Chakraborty), a young tribesman, and the English District Commissioner (Robert Wright). But when Ghenua kills the money-lender (Meher) who kidnapped his wife (Shankar) in lieu of an unpaid debt, the Englishman condemns him to death and riots ensue. Sen's first film in colour is also a return to more narrative concerns after the rigour of his agit-prop 'Calcutta Trilogy' – *Interview, Calcutta '71,* and *The Guerrilla Fighter* – though it is no less political. Based on the Santhal Revolt of 1901, it is a devastating attack on colonialism, paternalism and *bourgeois* justice. But the beautifully shot tale, drawing upon local storytelling traditions and strong on generalities, fails to penetrate beneath the surface of the characters.

▶ **Rozmarné Léto** see Capricious Summer

▶ **Rue Cases Nègres** see Black Shack Alley

▶ **Rue De L'Estrapade** see Françoise Steps Out

The Rules Of The Game

▶ **La Règle Du Jeu**

France   1939   113 mins   bw
La Nouvelle Edition Française

d   **Jean Renoir**
sc **Jean Renoir, Carl Koch**
ph **Jean Bachelet**
m   **Joseph Kosma, Mozart, Monsigny, Saint-Saëns, Johann Strauss**
    Marcel Dalio, Nora Gregor, Jean Renoir, Mila Parély, Julien Carette, Gaston Modot, Roland Toutain, Paulette Dubost

The Count and Countess La Chesnaye (Dalio and Gregor) organize a lavish weekend party at their country château, where there are sexual tensions among the hosts, guests and servants. Renoir's most archetypal and perfect film, made on the eve of the outbreak of war, shows modern French society being disrupted from within. The structure, setting and plot was inspired by the works of Marivaux, Beaumarchais and Musset, and this dynamic juxtaposition of past, present, comedy, tragedy, melodrama, farce and realism gives the film its uniqueness. Apart from the wonderful performances, especially Renoir's own central one, there are two outstanding set pieces – the after-dinner entertainment and the rabbit shoot. It was a commercial disaster on its initial release and was cut to 85 minutes before being banned as 'too demoralizing'. It was only in 1956, when restored to its original length, that the film was acclaimed the masterpiece it undoubtedly is.

The Runaway

▶ **Atithi**

India   1966   103 mins   bw
New Theatres(Exhibitors)Pvt

d   **Tapan Sinha**
sc **Tapan Sinha**
ph **Dilip Ranjan Mukherjee**
m   **Tapan Sinha**
    Partha Mukherji, Basabi Banerji, Samita Biswa, Salil Dutta, Smita Sinha, Mita Mukherji

Tarapada (Partha Mukherji) is an exceptionally engaging teenager who, to the despair of his mother and brothers, is possessed of a wanderlust which takes him on several adventures – among other things, he becomes a fairground acrobat and a musician with a group of strolling players – and finally brings him into contact with a wealthy family who take him in, educate him, and arrange for his marriage to their daughter. But that's not all... Tapan Sinha, working from a story by Rabindranath Tagore and treading territory in the tradition of Satyajit Ray, has made a leisurely, detailed film, rich in nostalgic and beautiful visual resonances, full of charm and humour.

The Runner

▶ **Dawandeh**

Iran 1984 94 mins col
Tehran Institute For The Intellectual Development Of Children And Young Adults

d **Amir Naderi**
sc **Amir Naderi, Behruz Gharibpur**
ph **Firuz Malekzadeh**
m **No credit given**
   Majid Nirumand, Musa Torkizadeh, A. Gholamzadeh, Reza Ramezani, Shirzan Bechkal

At an Iranian gulf port, Amiro (Nirumand), a 13-year-old waif, scrapes a living by selling empty bottles washed in from the ships, as well as iced water to the port workers. Gradually, he collects enough money to set up a shoeshine stand at a café. Amiro's ambitions lead him to enrol in a literary class and perhaps a better future. Naderi's autobiographical account of his own deprived childhood gives an extraordinary impression of a country devastated by war and in economic crisis, the superb photography revealing a small boy against an inhospitable desolate landscape. In its unsentimental view of child labour, the almost plotless film is a worthy and more optimistic companion to *Salaam Bombay!*. There is an invigorating montage

as the boy learns the alphabet, metaphorically finding his voice for the first time. But although the film contains specific symbols, such as the climactic race towards a block of melting ice, its message is allowed to emerge naturally out of the sharply and often comically observed environment.

La Rupture

▶ **(US: The Breakup)**

France 1970 124 mins col
Films De La Boétie/Euro International/ Cinévog

d **Claude Chabrol**
sc **Claude Chabrol**
ph **Jean Rabier**
m **Pierre Jansen**
   Stéphane Audran, Jean-Claude Drouot, Michel Bouquet, Jean-Pierre Cassel, Catherine Rouvel, Jean Carmet, Annie Cordy

When a man on LSD (Drouot) attacks his wife (Audran) and child, she retaliates and he ends up in hospital. Wanting to gain custody of the child, her father-in-law (Bouquet) hires a seedy detective (Cassel) to spy on her activities. Chabrol's terse and suspenseful style works to great advantage in this neat thriller based on a Charlotte Armstrong novel. *Bourgeois* evil is well represented by Bouquet, while Audran is at her best as an innocent woman fighting to keep her son.

▶ **Rysopis** see Identification Marks: None

S

The Sacrifice

▶ **Offret**

Sweden 1986 145 mins col/bw
Swedish Film Institute/SVT2/Film Four
International/Argos/Sandrew/Josephson
and Nykvist

d **Andrei Tarkovsky**
sc **Andrei Tarkovsky**
ph **Sven Nykvist**
m **Bach, Swedish and Japanese folk music**
Erland Josephson, Susan Fleetwood, Allan
Edwall, Valérie Mairesse, Sven Wollter,
Gudrún Gísladóttir

At the start of a nuclear war, a distinguished
writer (Josephson), isolated on a Swedish
island with his wife (Fleetwood), two small
children and friends, makes a pact with God
that he will renounce his family, self and
possessions if the world is allowed to return
to normal. The opening six-minute take of a
man and child planting a tree prepares the
audience to be patient. By the time the film
reaches its brilliant climax – an unbroken 10-
minute take of a burning house seen from a
distantly-placed camera, many might have
lost that patience. In between, the mixture of
Swedish and Russian post-nuclear *angst* is
heavy going, despite the mastery of the camerawork and some impressive set pieces. It
was Tarkovsky's final film. He died of cancer
in 1987, at the age of 54.

Special Jury Prize Cannes 1986

Sacrificed Youth

▶ **Qingchun Ji**

China 1985 96 mins col

Youth Film Studio Of The Beijing Film
Academy

d **Zhang Nuanxin**
sc **Zhang Nuanxin**
ph **Mu Deyuan**
m **Liu Suola, Qu Xiaosong**
Li Fengxu, Feng Yuanzheng, Song Tao,
Guo Jianguo, Yu Da, Yu Shuai

In line with the policies of the Cultural Revolution, Li Chun (Fengxu), a shy, repressed 17-
year-old student from Beijing, is sent to work
with the peasants in the rice fields in South
China. At first she feels ill at ease with the
family where she is billeted and with her
fellow workers, and finds the physical work
gruelling. She strikes up a friendship with
fellow exile, Ren Jia (Yuanzheng), thus awakening the jealousy of 'Brother' (Jianguo), a
member of her host family. Because of it, Li
Chun leaves and becomes a teacher in another
village. This lyrical and moving tribute to
those who suffered during the days of China's
more recent dark history predates *Hibiscus
Town* (1986) and *King Of The Children* (1988),
two other contemporary films to tackle the
Cultural Revolution head on. The director
imbues the film with her personal knowledge
of the subject, having herself been sent to the
rice paddies and her father having committed
suicide at the time. Certainly there are autobiographical elements in the portrayal of the
leading character, gradually growing in sympathy for her workmates and gaining an
awareness of her own sensuality, the latter
handled with rather more discretion than
seems necessary, even in a Chinese context.

▶ **Saiehaien Bolan De Bad** see Tall
Shadows Of The Wind

▶ **Saikaku Ichidai Onna** see Life Of O-Haru, The

Salaam Bombay!

India   1988   114 mins   col
Mirabai Films/NFDC (New Delhi)/
Cadrage (Paris)/Channel 4 (London)

d   **Mira Nair**
sc **Sooni Taraporevala**
ph **Sandi Sissel**
m   **L. Subramaniam**
Shafiq Syed, Raghubir Yadav, Aneeta Kanwar, Nana Patekar, Hansa Vithal, Chanda Sharma

Twelve-year-old Krishna (Syed) owes his tyrannical brother money and runs away from his village to Bombay, determined to earn it. He becomes a tea delivery boy for a stallkeeper and is soon familiar with the city's low life. He meets the inhabitants of a brothel and is befriended by the prostitute Rekha (Kanwar) and her small daughter Manju (Vithal), and forms a close relationship with Chillum (Yadav), the drug-addicted runner for the local drug baron Baba (Patekar). After losing his job, Krishna increasingly scratches a living with the other impoverished urchins until he and Manju are picked up by the police and detained in a children's remand centre, the notorious 'chiller', from which there is little hope of escape. But escape he does, only to be plunged into further threatening circumstances... The feature debut of the distinguished documentarist Mira Nair, *Salaam Bombay!* is an impressively assembled mosaic of Bombay's street life, its harsh cruelties and the fleeting pleasures it offers its destitute inhabitants. The powerful veracity of the piece is reinforced by the casting which, but for the leading adult players, was done off the streets, and by the use of actual locations, including the brothel and the children's home. Made in record time and for little money, neither of which limitations show in the finished product, this is an absorbing film, unbearably sad and yet not without humour. Shafiq Syed, plucked from the gutters of the city to play Krishna, is irresistible, and the film, avoiding sentimentality but flirting attractively with melodrama (especially in the scenes involving the arresting Patekar's Baba), is a superb achievement.

▶ **Salaire De La Peur, Le** see Wages Of Fear, The

The Salamander

▶ **La Salamandre**

Switzerland   1971   129 mins   bw
Svociné

d   **Alain Tanner**
sc **John Berger, Alain Tanner**
ph **Renato Berta**
m   **Patrick Moraz**
Jean Luc Bideau, Jacques Denis, Bulle Ogier

A novelist and a journalist constantly interview a working-class girl suspected of shooting her guardian. This wordy, worthy study of a non-conformist seen from different angles appealed greatly to the conformist population of Switzerland who made the film into one of the country's first native box-office hits. It also enjoyed a certain success elsewhere, awakening the world to the existence of Swiss cinema. Bulle Ogier, as the focus of the investigation, helps flesh out Berger and Tanner's rather theoretical character.

▶ **Salamandre, La** see Salamander, The

Sallah

Israel   1964   105 mins   bw
Sallah Ltd(Tel Aviv)

d   **Ephraim Kishon**
sc **Ephraim Kishon**
ph **Floyd Crosby**
m   **Yohanan Zarai**
Haym Topol, Geula Noni, Gila Almagor, Arik Einstein, Esther Greenberg, Shraga Friedman, Shaika Levy

Sallah, a likeable, ebullient but bone-idle Oriental Jew, arrives in Israel with his wife and seven children in 1948. The family finds itself housed unhappily in a transit camp near the local kibbutz, and when Sallah's son (Levi) and daughter (Noni) each fall in love with a kibbutz resident, dowry difficulties result. Managing to lose all the jobs he gets, Sallah finally solves the family's problems by devious cunning. A rough-hewn, folksy, syrupy tale which tries for satire, and in one of its best scenes – some American tourists come to check on 'their' trees being planted – succeeds. The leading man, who would drop his first name to become internationally known as Topol, displays the charismatic energy that would bring him stardom (in *Fiddler On The Roof*), but is hammy in his efforts to appear at least 25 years older than he actually was. As a glimpse of the then newly created State of Israel, this early Menachem 'Cannon' Golan production is not without interest but, overall, it's naive and rambling.

▶ **Salo O Le Centiventi Giornate Di Sodoma** see Salo Or The 120 Days Of Sodom

Salo Or The 120 Days Of Sodom

▶ **Salo O Le Centiventi Giornate Di Sodoma**

　Italy　1975　117 mins　col
　PEA/UA

d　**Pier Paolo Pasolini**
sc　**Sergio Citti**
ph　**Tonino Delli Colli**
m　**Ennio Morricone**
　　Paolo Bonacelli, Giorgio Cataldi, Umberto Paolo Quintavalle, Caterina Boratto, Elsa De Giorgi, Hélène Surgère

During the days of Mussolini's Italy, in a vast mansion, a party of Fascists have rounded up a group of attractive young people to satisfy their depraved desires. Pasolini's last film before he was murdered, is an astute updating of the Marquis De Sade's novel – 'nothing more than a cinematic transposition,' the director claimed. An almost unbearable film to watch (if it weren't there'd be something wrong with both spectator and picture), it never sets out to titillate, neither does it relish its horrors while clinically exposing the exploitation of human beings by their fellow men. The last 10 minutes of executions are among the most revolting, memorable and beautiful (the camerawork, the music, the poignancy) in all cinema.

▶ **Salto Nel Vuoto** see Leap Into The Void

Salut L'Artiste

　France　1973　96 mins　col
　Gaumont/Productions De La Gueville
　Euro International

d　**Yves Robert**
sc　**Jean-Loup Dabadie**
ph　**Jean Penzer**
m　**Vladimir Cosma**
　　Marcello Mastroianni, Françoise Fabian, Jean Rochefort, Carla Gravina

Nicholas (Mastroianni), a bit part actor in plays, films and commercials, is separated from his wife (Gravina) and two children. He lives with his jealous mistress (Fabian), but when she leaves him, he tries to return to his wife, now pregnant by another man. Robert's bitter-sweet comedy, revealing the less glamorous side of show business, takes its tone from Mastroianni's amusing and melancholy performance. Sentimentalized though the character is – and actor-director Robert's view of the acting profession – there are enough sardonic sequences to balance it. Jean Rochefort as Nicholas's friend and fellow actor gives good support, and the women do their best with their underwritten roles of wife and mistress. The bit part players aren't bad either.

Salvatore Giuliano

　Italy　1961　125 mins　bw
　Lux/Vides/Galatea

d　**Francesco Rosi**
sc　**Francesco Rosi, Suso Cecchi D'Amico, Enzo Provenzale, Franco Solinas**
ph　**Gianni Di Venanzo**
m　**Piero Piccioni**
　　Frank Wolff, Salvo Randone, Federico Zardi, Pietro Cammarata (Salvatore), Fernando Cicero

The true story of how a Sicilian outlaw, whose bullet-ridden body was found in a courtyard on 5 July, 1950, had risen to become a Mafia boss. Filmed in the heart of Mafia country, with a mixed cast of amateur and professional actors, it was the first of Rosi's 'reconstructed documentaries'. Using a probing camera, flashbacks and interviews, he builds an intricate, sometimes obscure, maze of facts in an objective, uncompromising manner. The film was instrumental in getting the government in Palermo to set up an inquiry into Mafia activities. Michael Cimino remade it in 1987 as *The Sicilian*.

Best Director Berlin 1962

▶ **Samma No Aji** see Autumn Afternoon, An

▶ **Samo Jednom Se Ljubi** see You Only Love Once

▶ **Samourai, Le** see Samurai, The

Samurai

▶ **Miyamoto Musashi**

Japan   1954-1955   92 mins (Part I), 104 mins (Part II), 105 mins (Part III)   col Toho

d   Hiroshi Inagaki
sc   Hiroshi Inagaki, Tokuhei Wakao
ph   Jun Yasumoto (Parts I and II), Kazuo Yamada (Part III)
m   Ikuma Dan
     Toshiro Mifune , Rentaro Mikuni, Karuo Yashigusa, Koji Tsurata, Sachio Sakai, Akihiko Hirata

Takezo (Mifune) joins an army, lives as an outlaw, is nearly hanged but is freed by a widow (Yashigusa) who loves him, is imprisoned in a castle, studies the ways of the sword and becomes the legendary samurai Miyamoto Musashi. Of the 100 or so films turned out by Inagaki (mostly *jidai-geki* or period pictures), only a few have reached the West. This most ambitious and renowned of his works (a colour remake of his 1941 trilogy of the same name) came in on the first wave of Japanese samurai films to leave the country after the war. Much of the action is splendidly staged and impressive looking, but the style is slow and the spiritual quest for the Way may seem rather simplistic. It was some years before Western audiences could compare such epics with the masterpieces of Mizoguchi. It

won an honorary Oscar as Best Foreign Film in 1955 (competitive Foreign Oscars were not instituted by the Academy until 1956, when *La Strada* was the first winner).

The Samurai

▶ **Le Samourai**

France   1967   95 mins   col
Filmel/CICC/Fida

d   Jean-Pierre Melville
sc   Jean-Pierre Melville, Georges Pellegrin
ph   Henri Decaë
m   François De Roubaix
     Alain Delon, François Périer, Nathalie Delon, Cathy Rosier, Jacques Le Roy

A hired killer (Alain Delon) goes about his fatal business with a watertight alibi, but makes the mistake of falling in love with a girl (Rosier) who inadvertently betrays him. With little dialogue, muted colours, a meticulous eye for atmospheric detail – the killer's dingy room, the chromium night club, the Paris Métro – Melville reached the peak of his romantic and ritualistic gangster movies. Alain Delon's expressionless but riveting performance is the focus of each formal scene.

Sandakan-8

▶ **Sandakan Hachiban Shokan: Bokyo**

Japan   1975   120 mins   col
Toho

d   Kei Kumai
sc   Kei Kumai, Sakae Hirosawa
ph   Mitsuji Kaneo
m   Akira Ifukube
     Kinuyo Tanaka (Saki as old woman), Yoko Takahashi (Saki as young woman), Komaki Kurihara, Eitaro Ozawa

This impressive Oscar-nominated film on the exploitation of women is told in the framework of an old woman telling her story to a woman journalist (Kurihara). Sandakan-8 is the brothel in Borneo where the young Saki works so that she can send money back to her relatives in Japan. After many years and much hardship, she marries and has a son.

She now lives as a poor widow in Japan. The flashback within a flashback technique, and the juxtaposition with modern Japan allows Kumai, one of the most political of the younger Japanese directors, to set the story in historical context and gives ideological reasons for Saki's suffering. More intellectually than emotionally involving, the film has the advantage of Tanaka, perhaps Japan's greatest screen actress, in the central role.

Best Actress (Kinuyo Tanaka) Berlin 1975

▶ **Sandakan Hachiban Shokan: Bokyo** see Sandakan-8

▶ **Sandra** see Of A Thousand Delights

▶ **Sang Des Bêtes, Le** see Blood Of The Beasts

▶ **Sang D'Un Poète, Le** see Blood Of The Poet, The

▶ **Sangen Om Den Røde Rubin** see Song Of The Red Ruby, The

Sanjuro

▶ **Tsubaki Sanjuro**

Japan 1962 96 mins bw
Toho

d   Akira Kurosawa
sc Akira Kurosawa, Ryuzu Kikushima, Hideo Oguni
ph Fukuzo Koizumi, Kozo Saito
m   Masaru Sato
Toshiro Mifune, Tatsuya Nakadai, Masao Shimizu, Yunosuke Ito, Takako Irie

Sanjuro (Mifune), an unwashed, lonely wandering samurai, joins up with eight young warriors to fight corruption and treachery, and rescue a kidnapped chancellor from a wicked war lord. Virtually a sequel to the previous year's *Yojimbo* (on which *A Fistful Of Dollars* was based), this Eastern-Western is the nearest Kurosawa came to spoofing the samurai genre. Apart from the humour, there is plenty of sparkling sword-play and an exciting final duel ending with a fountain of gushing blood.

▶ **Sans Famille** see Adventures of Rémi, The

▶ **Sanshiro Sugata** see Judo Saga

▶ **Sansho Dayu** see Sansho The Bailiff

Sansho The Bailiff

▶ **Sansho Dayu**

Japan 1954 125 mins bw
Daiei

d   Kenji Mizoguchi
sc Yahiro Fuji, Yoshikata Yoda
ph Kazuo Miyagawa
m   Fumio Hayasaka, Kanahichi Odera, Tamekichi Mochizuki
Kinuyo Tanaka, Yoshiaki Hanayagi, Kyoko Kagawa, Masao Shimizu, Eitaro Shindo, Akitare Kawano

The son (Hanayagi) and daughter (Kagawa) of a noble family in feudal Japan are kidnapped and sold as slaves to a tyrannical bailiff (Shindo). Years later, the son escapes and is reunited with his mother (Tanaka), now blind, crippled and living in abject poverty. Set in a barbaric period, authentically re-created, Mizoguchi's sublime work transforms the ancient Japanese legend, as related by the novelist Ogai Mori, into a timeless, humanist statement of injustice and suffering. The long takes, lingering long shots and the weaving camera create an elegiac mood and a deep involvement in the unfolding tale, making it often unbearably moving and yet never sentimental. This is one of the director's most awesome achievements.

▶ **Sans Lendemain** see No Tomorrow

▶ **Sans Soleil** see Sunless

▶ **Sans Toit Ni Loi** see Vagabonde

Santa Sangre

Italy 1989 118 mins col
Intersound

d   Alejandro Jodorowsky

sc Alejandro Jodorowsky, Roberto Leoni,
    Claudio Argento
ph Daniele Nannuzzi
m   Simon Boswell
    Axel Jodorowsky, Blanca Guerra, Guy
    Stockwell, Thelma Tixou, Sabrina
    Dennison, Adan Jodorowsky, Faviola
    Elenka Tapia, Teo Jodorowsky

Fenix (Adan Jodorowsky) is a child conjurer
in a circus, where Orgo (Stockwell), his macho
father, is a knife-thrower, and Concha
(Guerra), his religious maniac mother, is the
trapeze artiste. His only real friend is the
deaf-mute Alma (Dennison). Concha has
both arms severed by her husband after she
throws acid on his genitals to punish his
adultery with the Tattooed Lady (Tixou).
When Fenix, now aged twenty (Axel Jodorowsky) leaves a mental asylum, he joins his
mother in a cabaret act in which she sings
while he provides her arms and hands from
behind, but he is led to murder. The Chilean-
born, Paris-based Jodorowsky's first release
since *The Holy Mountain* in 1973 – a film
called *Tusk* (1979) was never shown publicly –
reveals him still wallowing in the baroque
images and heavy symbols of yesteryear. 'I
like to take reality and put it into an imaginative context and it becomes a masterwork,' the
director modestly admits. It certainly has
pretensions to grandeur, and tiresome as
much of it is, some of the hallucinatory images
do carry an impact, while making striking
allusions to horror films in the line of *Night
Of The Living Dead*. Nevertheless, the result
makes one long to watch anything by Geoge
Romero instead, or, better still, Buñuel and
Fellini, to whom Jodorowsky also owes a
great deal.

▶ **Santos Inocentes, Los** see Holy
Innocents, The

São Bernardo

Brazil 1972 110 mins col
Saga Filmes

d   **Leon Hirszman**
sc **Leon Hirszman**
ph **Lauro Escorel**
m   **Caetano Veloso**
    **Othon Bastos, Isabel Ribeiro, Nildo
    Parente, Vande Lacerda, Mario Lago**

An old plantation owner (Bastos), who started
life as a humble labourer, sits alone in his
decaying mansion reflecting on his acquisition
of wealth, property and a wife (Ribeiro) who
later committed suicide. Based on a novel by
Graciliano Ramos (*Barren Lives, Memories Of
Prison*), the film tries to retain the book's first
person perspective, organized as it is around
the old man at his desk writing and narrating.
However, Hirszman has cleverly rendered a
literary mode into a cinematic experience, shot
with a painterly sense of colour and composition, evolving in long shots and lengthy
takes. Despite its stylization and slightly hermetic atmosphere, the military dictatorship in
Brazil still saw it as a criticism of the regime
and delayed its release for seven months –
enough time to bankrupt the independent
company that financed it.

The Saragossa Manuscript

▶ **Rekopis Znaleziony W
Saragossie**

Poland 1964 175 mins bw
Kamera Film Unit/Film Polski

d   **Wojciech Has**
sc **Tadeusz Kwiatkowski**
ph **Mieczyslaw Jahoda**
m   **Krzysztof Penderecki**
    **Zbigniew Cybulski, Iga Cembrzynska,
    Joanna Jedryka, Slawomir Linder**

Early in the 19th century, a Belgian army
officer (Cybulski) travelling to Madrid meets
two beautiful princesses who send him on a
fantastic journey to prove himself worthy of
them. Probably the Chinese-box effect (a story
within a story within a story) worked better
in the 1813 Polish novel written in French by
Jan Potocki, who thereafter committed suicide. However, the adept use of the wide
screen, and the amiable performance by Cybulski, looking rather like Bob Hope on the
road to somewhere or other, made this
ambitious undertaking watchable.

Sarajevo

▶ **(US: Mayerling To Sarajevo)**

▶ **De Mayerling À Sarajevo**

France   1940   89 mins   bw
B.U.P. Française

d   **Max Ophüls**
sc **Kurt Alexander**
ph **Curt Courant, Otto Heller**
m   **Oscar Straus**
    Edwige Feuillère, John Lodge, Aimé
    Clariond, Jean Worms, Gabrielle Dorziat,
    Aimos

A morganatic marriage takes place between
the Countess Sophie (Feuillère) and the Arch-
duke Franz-Ferdinand (Lodge), despite opposition from the Austro-Hungarian court. They
lead a happy and uneventful married life until
their assassination in Sarajevo that led to the
outbreak of World War I. Ophüls' last completed film before his departure for the USA
(he had begun *L'École Des Femmes*) found
him relishing the sort of thing he did best –
casting an ironic eye on the extravagances
and absurdities of the aristocracy and portraying a bitter-sweet romance against a background of operas, balls, and rides through
the woods. However, the film has rather a
jaded air about it, and neither Feuillère nor
Lodge (rhymes with stodge) are at ease, but
Dorziat as the Archduchess Maria Theresa
reigns supreme.

Sarraounia

Burkino Faso   1986   121 mins   col
Films Soleil Ô

d   **Med Hondo**
sc **Med Hondo, Abdoulaye Mamani**
ph **Guy Famechon**
m   **Pierre Akendengué, Abdoulaye Cissé,**
    Issouf Compaore
    Aï Keïta, Jean-Roger Milo, Féodor
    Atkine, Jean Edmond, Roger Mirmont,
    Aboubacar Traoré, Tidjani Ouedraogo

Sarraounia (Keïta), Queen of the Aznas of
Lugu and well-schooled in the arts of herbal-
ism and warfare, leads her people to victory
against a neighbouring tribe. However, she
loses her valued general and former lover,
Baka (Traoré), who is jealous of the poet-
musician with whom she is involved. Now
the Queen must defend her territory against
the advancing French army, led by Captain

Voulet (Milo), as well as combat the hostility
of certain neighbouring tribes who consider
her a 'witch and an infidel'. Med Hondo's
fluid and visually striking film, with its echoes
of the classic Japanese cinema in its treatment
of tradition and custom, is a jewel in the
expanding crown of Third World cinema. The
story, which can be enjoyed at the level of a
superior war epic, unfolds on a foundation
of strong themes which juxtapose resistance
and resignation, the colonial expansionist
oppression against the contradictions in tribal
society, the differing roles and attitudes
between men and women in the African tribes.
Sarraounia herself, played with awe-inspiring
dignity and presence, is a symbol of courage
and epic resistance to colonialism.

▶ **Săsom I En Spegel** see Through A
Glass Darkly

▶ **Satansbraten** see Satan's Brew

Satan's Brew

▶ **Satansbraten**

W. Germany   1976   100 mins   col
Albatros/Trio

d   **Rainer Werner Fassbinder**
sc **Rainer Werner Fassbinder**
ph **Michael Ballhaus, Jürgen Jürgens**
m   **Peer Raben**
    Kurt Raab, Margit Carstensen, Helen
    Vita, Volker Spengler, Ingrid Caven, Y
    Sa Lo

A written-out poet (Raab) murders his mistress, then plagiarizes and takes on the identity of the symbolist poet Stefan George, even
down to his idol's homosexual tastes. The
title well describes this diabolical mixture of
the Theatre of the Absurd, Hollywood screwball comedy, German Expressionism and
Fassbinder's own sexual politics. It is all
rather difficult to swallow, but there is some
amusement to be had in the excess, and Raab
and company hold the attention.

▶ **Satyricon** see Fellini Satyricon

▶ **Sauvage, Le** see Savage, The

► **Sauve Qui Peut (La Vie)** see Slow Motion

The Savage

► **(US: Lovers Like Us)**
► **Le Sauvage**

France 1978 110 mins col
Lira/PAI

d   Jean-Paul Rappeneau
sc Jean-Paul and Elizabeth Rappeneau,
    Jean-Loup Dabadie
ph Pierre Lhomme
m   Michel Legrand
    Yves Montand, Catherine Deneuve, Luigi
    Vannucchi, Dana Wynter, Tony Roberts

A businessman (Montand), who is fleeing from his wife (Wynter), ends up on a small tropical South American island alone with a runaway heiress (Deneuve). A strained French attempt to make a romantic comedy on the lines of those made in Hollywood in the 1930s. Despite their attractiveness and talent, Montand and Deneuve are not Cary Grant and Carole Lombard but, even so, they help to make it reasonable escapist fare.

► **Savage Princess** see Aan

Sawdust And Tinsel

► **aka The Naked Night**
► **Gycklarnas Afton**

Sweden 1953 95 mins bw
Sandrew/Svensk Filmindustri

d   Ingmar Bergman
sc Ingmar Bergman
ph Sven Nykvist, Hilding Bladh
m   Karl-Birger Blomdahl
    Harriet Andersson, Åke Grönberg, Hasse
    Ekman, Anders Ek, Annika Tretow,
    Gudrun Brost

The owner and ring master (Grönberg) of a circus troupe passing through a provincial town, tries to make up with his wife (Tretow) who left him years before, and has his jealousy aroused when his mistress (Andersson) is seduced by a suave actor (Ekman). Reviled by both Swedish and foreign critics at the time, the film is now seen as a *tour de force*, a landmark in Bergman's *oeuvre*. Perhaps the Baroque style is rather too self-conscious, purposefully based on the Expressionism of German silent cinema (particularly the 1925 *Variety* with Emil Jannings), but the technique is masterful. The silent dream sequence in which the clown (Ek) is humiliated by his wife (Brost), is one of the director's most brilliant moments.

► **Sayat Nova** see Colour Of Pomegranates, The

Scandal

► **Shuban**

Japan 1950 105 mins bw
Shochiku

d   Akira Kurosawa
sc Akira Kurosawa, Ryuzo Kikushima
ph Toshio Ubukata
m   Fumio Hayasaka
    Toshiro Mifune, Yoshiko Yamaguchi,
    Takashi Shimura

A handsome young artist (Mifune) and a beautiful concert singer (Yamaguchi) become the innocent victims of a libellous article in a scandal magazine. He decides to sue but, being a soft touch, hires a questionable lawyer (Shimura) because the man's small daughter has TB. Made just before *Rashomon*, which established his international reputation, but only released in the West 30 years later, this is a fascinating movie for Kurosawa collectors. Borrowing, as he frequently has, from the American model, the director has made, at one level, a soap opera from which every last tear is shamelessly wrung by his accomplished cast. Look more closely, however, and you'll detect a caustic parody of the genre it appears to ape and a satire on the Japanese willingness to accept the alien culture thrust upon them by America. All the iconography is there, from the hero's motorbike, to the elaborately decorated Christmas tree the lovers take the dying child, and Yamaguchi warbles a collection of Western songs, including 'Auld Lang Syne' and 'Silent Night' (in Japanese).

► **Scandale, Le** see Champagne Murders, The

The Scandalous Adventures Of Buraikan

► **Buraikan**

Japan 1970 104 mins col
Ninjin Club/Toho

d **Masahiro Shinoda**
sc **Shuji Terayama**
ph **Kozo Okazaki**
m **Masaru Sato**
Tatsuya Nakadai, Tetsuro Tamba, Shima Iwashita, Suisen Ichikawa, Shoichi Ozawa

In 1842, in Tokyo's pleasure district of Edo, the lives of three people cross: a good-for-nothing layabout (Nakadai) who dreams of becoming a Kabuki actor, a man (Ozawa) who has left his wife and child and the shogun's tea master (Tamba), who is really the notorious outlaw Buraikan. Shinoda and Terayama (a year before *his* first feature as director) have plainly made a political parallel between the Tempo Reformation, when the long established shogunate was threatened by rebellion, and the student movements of the 1960s. This is done in a boisterous, erotic and blackly humorous manner, aided by wide screen, lavish colour, and an anachronistic jazz score, capturing some of the subversive spirit of the earliest Kabuki.

► **Scandals of Clochemerle, The** see Clochemerle

► **Scarlet And Black** see Red And The Black, The

The Scarlet Letter

► **Der Scharlachrote Buchstabe**

W. Germany 1972 89 mins col
Filmverlag Der Autoren/WDR/Elias Querejeta (Madrid)

d **Wim Wenders**
sc **Wim Wenders, Bernardo Fernández**
ph **Robby Müller**
m **Jürgen Knieper**

Senta Berger, Hans Christian Blech, Lou Castel, Yelena Samarina, Yella Rottländer

When Dr Roger Prynne (Blech) arrives in New England after two years of captivity by Indians, he finds that his wife Hester (Berger) is the object of public scorn, forced to display a scarlet letter 'A' for adulteress on her dress. Prynne, who changes his name, becomes obsessed with proving that the Reverend Arthur Dimmesdale (Castel) is the father of his wife's child (Rottländer). Wenders' version of Nathaniel Hawthorne's classic was not as authentic as the director had wished. Budget limitations forced him to film in Spain with rather artificial New England sets, Senta Berger was not his choice for the lead and he was asked to truncate his extended takes and go for a snappier editing style. These restrictions tell on the finished product, and yet there is a fascination in the way Wenders has brought a modern sensibility to bear on the puritanism in the novel. Still, Victor Sjöström's silent 1926 version, starring Lillian Gish, gives more satisfaction.

► **Sceicco Bianco, Lo** see White Sheik, The

► **Scener Ur Ett Aktenskap** see Scenes From A Marriage

Scenes From A Marriage

► **Scener Ur Ett Aktenskap**

Sweden 1974 168 mins col
Cinematograph AB Sweden

d **Ingmar Bergman**
sc **Ingmar Bergman**
ph **Sven Nykvist**
Liv Ullmann, Erland Josephson, Bibi Andersson, Jan Malmsjö, Gunnel Lindblom

Marianne (Ullmann) has to cope with the infidelity of her husband (Josephson) who is seriously involved with a younger woman (Andersson). The trauma of a beleaguered marriage is played largely in close-up, creating a claustrophobic, hermetically sealed atmosphere, while the terse exchanges and bitter silences convey a sense of bleak aridity. Originally conceived as a six-part television series running 300 minutes (and subsequently shown in that form and medium), Bergman himself edited the film for cinematic release. It is undeniably absorbing, with the hand of the director everywhere evident, especially in the use of his uniquely accomplished actresses, but it is, finally, sterile and unrewarding.

Scent Of A Woman

▶ **Profumo Di Donna**

Italy   1974   103 mins   col
Dean

d   **Dino Risi**
sc   **Dino Risi, Ruggero Maccari**
ph   **Claudio Cirillo**
m   **Armando Trovaioli**
    Vittorio Gassman, Alessandro Momo, Agostina Belli, Moira Orsei

A blind, one-armed ex-Army captain (Gassman), who is a proud and arrogant ladies' man, travels to Naples with a young army cadet (Momo) who acts as his eyes, describing beautiful women, but the officer cannot declare his love for the woman (Belli) whose portrait he keeps beside a pistol. For a great deal of the film there is a sharp serio-comic interplay between the aristocratic soldier and his naive guide, but sentimentality, melodrama and a dubious attitude to women encroach upon the latter part of the plot.

Best Actor (Vittorio Gassman) Cannes 1975

▶ **Scharlachrote Buchstabe, Der** see Scarlet Letter, The

▶ **Schaste** see Happiness

▶ **Schatten** see Warning Shadows

▶ **Schaukel, Die** see Swing, The

▶ **Scherben** see Shattered

▶ **Schloss Vogelöd** see Haunted Castle, The

▶ **Schlussakkord** see Final Chord

Le Schpountz

▶ **(US: Heartbeat)**

France   1938   140 mins   bw
Marcel Pagnol

d   **Marcel Pagnol**
sc   **Marcel Pagnol**
ph   **Willy**
m   **Casimir Oberfeld**
    Fernandel, Charpin, Odette Roger, Jean Castan, Orane Demazis, Léon Bélières, Maupi

A film-fan grocer (Fernandel) is a victim of a practical joke played on him by a film crew touring his district of Provence. He arrives at the studio in Paris on their false promises, but reveals himself as a successful comic. The title of this ironic, very amusing, self-mocking satire is Slav argot used by the photographer Willy (Faktorovitch) meaning a simple or screwy person. Fernandel is wonderfully 'Schpountzy', surrounded by a rich gathering of movie characters. When accusations of anti-Semitism were levelled at Pagnol for his depiction of the producer Meyerboom (Bélières), he cut a whole scene from the film, which had already been in the cinemas for a few weeks.

▶ **Schreckliche Mädchen, Das** see Nasty Girl, The

▶ **Schweizermacher, Die** see Swissmakers, The

▶ **Schwestern Oder Die Balance Des Glücks** see Sisters Or The Balance Of Happiness

▶ **Sciuscia** see Shoeshine

The Scoundrel

▶ **Les Mariés De L'An Deux**

France   1971   100 mins   col
Gaumont International(Paris)/Rizzoli Film(Rome)/ Bucuresti Film(Bucharest)

d   **Jean-Paul Rappeneau**
sc   **Jean-Paul Rappeneau, Daniel Boulanger**
ph   **Claude Renoir**

m **Michel Legrand**
Jean-Paul Belmondo, Marlène Jobert,
Michel Auclair, Sami Frey, Laura
Antonelli, Pierre Brasseur

Nicolas Philibert (Belmondo), an 18th-century anti-Royalist who fled to America, returns to France some years later to seek out his wife Charlotte (Jobert) and obtain a divorce. He finds her living with a Marquis (Frey) while being wooed by a Prince (Auclair) but, after numerous complications and adventures, she and Nicolas are reunited and live happily as titled aristocrats of Napoleon's Empire. Rappeneau's swashbuckling comedy, very Gallic, very tongue-in-cheek, is loaded with high-spirited action, charm and plenty of laughs. It is also polished in execution with an appealing performance by Belmondo. The film even survives the American dubbed version.

▶ **Scream From Silence, A** see Primal Fear

▶ **Sea, The** see Mare, Il

The Seagull

▶ **Chaika**

USSR 1971 98 mins col
Mosfilm

d **Yuli Karasik**
sc **Yuli Karasik, from the play by Anton Chekhov**
ph **Mikhail Suslov**
m **A. Schnitke**
Ludmila Savelyeva, Vladimir Tchetverikov, Alla Demidova, Yuri Yakovlev, Nikolai Plotnikov, Valentina Telichkina, Armen Djigarkhanyan, Sofia Pavlova, S. Torchachevsky

Guests at a country house party the actress Arkadina (Demidova) and her lover Trigorin (Yakovlev), a famous writer. They gather to watch a play by Arkadina's son, Konstantin (Tchetverikov), starring Nina (Savelyeva) whom Konstantin loves, but who loves Trigorin. Three years later, the unhappy group reassembles, its members having undergone certain changes in their lives. A synopsis cannot do justice to the complexities and subtleties of Chekhov's famous play. Alas, neither does this film. Karasik directs with respectful restraint, utilizing a skilful ensemble cast, but his tone is so hushed and his pace so uniform as to deprive the piece of its essential drama. There are one or two moments when he frees himself to take advantage of the medium, thus demonstrating the missed opportunities.

The Seashell And The Clergyman

▶ **La Coquille Et Le Clergyman**

France 1928 45 mins bw
Germaine Dulac

d **Germaine Dulac**
sc **Antonin Artaud**
ph **Paul Guichard**
m **Silent**
Alex Allin, Gerica Athanasiou, Bataille

The dream imagery of a frustrated celibate clergyman (Allin). 'This film is so cryptic as to be almost meaningless. If there is a meaning, it is doubtless objectionable,' commented the British censor on the film's being refused a certificate. It is now considered to be the first surrealist film, just as Dulac's *The Smiling Madame Beudet* (1923), is recognized as the first feminist film. Artaud had intended to direct it and play the lead, but he later withdrew and repudiated it. It would have been fascinating to see how he would have managed the automatic associations and the projection of his hypnotic personality into the role of the priest, but he might not have had the extraordinary technical skill that Dulac brought to this pioneering *avant-garde* classic.

The Season For Love

▶ **La Morte-Saison Des Amours**

France 1960 100 mins bw
Jad Film/Europa/Beaux Arts/Gaston Hakim

d **Pierre Kast**
sc **Pierre Kast, Alain Aptekman**
ph **Sacha Vierny**
m **Georges Delerue**

Daniel Gélin, Françoise Arnoul, Pierre Vaneck, Françoise Prévost

Sylvain (Vaneck), a writer, and his young wife Geneviève (Arnoul) leave Paris to seek idyllic fulfilment in the (actual) beautiful village of La Saline Des Chaux. Once there, Sylvain's creativity dries up and Geneviève, feeling betrayed, becomes involved with the local lord of the manor (Gélin), a libertine who falls genuinely in love with her, while Sylvain has an affair with his wife (Prévost). Kast has made a penetratingly observant film about crisis of self and crisis in relationships, to which he brings the surface glitter of a comedy of manners while allowing a compassionate examination of his characters to emerge. The cast is skilful and polished, and the haunting locations are exquisitely caught by Vierny's camera.

The Second Awakening Of Christa Klages

▶ **Das Zweite Erwachen Der Christa Klages**

W. Germany   1977   93 mins   col
Bioskop-Film/West Deutsches Rundfunk

d   Margarethe Von Trotta
sc   Margarethe Von Trotta, Luise Francia
ph   Franz Rath
m   Klaus Doldinger
   Tina Engel, Sylvia Reize, Katharina Thalbach, Marius Müller-Westernhagen, Peter Schneider

Christa Klages (Engel), deeply comitted to the progressive nursery she opened three years previously and which is now threatened by lack of funds, robs a bank, together with her lover Werner (Müller-Westernhagen). This desperate act turns them into fugitives, leads to Werner's violent death and drives Christa temporarily out of the country with her friend Ingrid (Reize) who has harboured her. The first of Von Trotta's non-collaborative works but, confusingly, not shown abroad until after her maturer works, this film presages all the themes to come: the limitations of the German *bourgeoisie*, the struggles of the socially aware, the bonding of women and the catastrophic consequences of misguided acts. It is a film which conjoins despair with comic

irony, and is jam-packed with plot, within which is buried the director's characteristic needle-sharp observation.

Second Breath

▶ **Le Deuxième Souffle**

France   1966   150 mins   bw
Productions Montaigne

d   Jean-Pierre Melville
sc   Jean-Pierre Melville
ph   Marcel Combes
m   Bernard Gérard
   Lino Ventura, Paul Meurisse, Raymond Pellegrin, Christine Fabrega, Marcel Bozzufi

A gangster (Ventura) breaks out of jail and joins a gang that carries out a daring robbery outside Marseilles, but he is trapped by a police inspector (Meurisse) into betraying his partners in crime and his honour. The key to Melville's attitude to his gangster heroes lies in a reference to the character played by Ventura: 'He is a danger to society, but he has preserved a sort of purity'. Underneath the surface thrills of the realistic crime movie is a romantic meditation on the nature of friendship and betrayal told in images of almost Bressonian restraint. (The pre-credit sequence is a homage to *A Man Escaped*.) But perhaps it was the exciting execution of the hold-up on a winding mountain road and the power of the trench-coated figure of Ventura that were major factors in making it Melville's biggest box-office success.

Second Chance

▶ **Si C'Était A Refaire**

France   1976   99 mins   col
Les Films 13

d   Claude Lelouch
sc   Claude Lelouch
ph   Jacques Lefrançois
m   Francis Lai, Pierre Barouh
   Catherine Deneuve, Anouk Aimée, Charles Denner, Francis Huster, Jean-Jacques Briot

Catherine (Deneuve) has a baby son, whom she calls Simon, while she is in prison on a charge of being an accessory to murder. On her release 18 years later she and Simon (Briot) are reunited, he falls in love with her friend from the prison (Aimée), and engineers a happy match for his mother with his history teacher. Typical Lelouch tosh, redolent with 'meaningful' musings which lead nowhere, woven into a woman's magazine story filmed with a largesse of gloss and glamour.

The Secret

▶ **Le Secret**

> France 1974 102 mins col
> President/Euro International

d   **Robert Enrico**
sc **Pascal Jardin**
ph **Etienne Becker**
m   **Ennio Morricone**
    Jean-Louis Trintignant, Marlène Jobert, Philippe Noiret, Jean-François Adam, Solange Pradel

Escaping from prison, David (Trintignant) goes on the run and finds refuge with Thomas and Julia (Noiret and Jobert), a couple living in seclusion in the mountains. He tells them that he has been tortured in a mysterious asylum and is under threat of death because he is in possession of a state secret. Thomas believes him, Julia has her doubts, and the audience is kept in suspense wondering whether he is a dangerous maniac or a victim of ruthless chicanery. This thriller, with its political overtones, may occasionally strain credibility, but it's full of incident and surprise, is well acted, and ties up its sinister loose ends with satisfying clarity.

▶ **Secret, Le** see Secret, The

▶ **Secret Game, The** see Forbidden Games

Secrets Of A Soul

▶ **Geheimnisse Einer Seele**

> Germany 1926 95 mins bw
> UFA/Hans Neumann

d   **G.W. Pabst**
sc **G.W. Pabst, Hans Neumann, Colin Ross**

ph **Guido Seeber, Kurt Oertel, Walter Robert Lach**
m   **Silent**
    Werner Krauss, Jack Trevor, Ruth Weyher, Pawel Pawlow

A professor (Krauss) consults a psychoanalyst (Pawlow) because he has nightmares whenever he sees or thinks of a knife, a phobia which leads to an attempt to stab his wife (Weyher). The film's reputation rests not on its uninteresting surface domestic drama, but on the stunning depiction of the dreams told to the analyst, fine examples of Expressionist cinema. They contain multi-layer superimpositions, cut-out figures against blank backgrounds, and menacing images of razors and knives. Werner Krauss, the face of German Expressionism, gives another powerful performance. Although Pabst was assisted in the script by two of Freud's collaborators, the Viennese doctor repudiated the final film.

▶ **Secrets Of Women** see Waiting Women

Secret Wedding

▶ **Boda Secreta**

> Argentina 1989 95 mins col
> Allarts Enterprizes/Cinéphile/Movie Centre

d   **Alejandro Agresti**
sc **Alejandro Agresti**
ph **Ricardo Rodriguez**
m   **Paul M. Van Brugge**
    Tito Haas, Mirtha Bushnelli, Sergio Poves Campos, Nathan Pinson, Floria Bloise, Elio Marchi, Carlos Roffe

A middle-aged man (Haas) runs naked through the streets of Buenos Aires, is picked up by the police, interrogated and found suffering from amnesia. They learn that he is Fermin Garcia, 'disappeared' thirteen years previously and, in the new climate of post-junta 'democracy', release him. He returns to the small, dusty village of his youth in search of Tota (Bushnelli), the woman he has never ceased to love, and finds her waiting for him but so lost in memories of the past that she fails to recognize him. Calling himself Alberto, Fermin is befriended by Pipi

(Campos), an ex-torture victim, and inn-keeper Dona Patricia (Bloise), but he becomes the object of suspicion and hostility to the other villagers, notably the priest. Following on *Love Is A Fat Woman* (1987), the 29-year-old Agresti has confirmed himself as a major Argentinian talent. The superb actors, some familiar from the earlier film, smoothly bear the burden of playing for real in tragi-comic situations which often border on the surreal. Still pursuing the themes of *Fat Woman*, but in a strong and straightforward narrative, he has constructed a powerful political parable in tandem with a heart-rending love story, beautifully photographed and highly original in its method of criticizing hypocrisy, bigotry and the establishment.

Section Spéciale

► **aka Special Section**

> France   1975   118 mins   col
> Reggane Films/Les Productions Artistes Associés (Paris)/Goriz Films(Rome)/ Janus Film(Frankfurt)

d   **Costa-Gavras**
sc   **Jorge Semprun**
ph   **Andreas Winding**
m   **Eric De Marsan, Takis**
     Louis Seigner, Michel Lonsdale, Ivo Garrani, François Maistre, Pierre Dux, Claude Piéplu, Heinz Bennent, Michel Galabru, Jacques Rispal, Julien Bertheau

When a group of young Communists shot a German naval officer in Paris in 1941, the Vichy government placated the Nazis by offering the execution of six Frenchmen. Costa-Gavras, continuing his interest in the poisonous effects of State complicity in the perversion of justice, records the setting up of the Special Section which was detailed to select the victims from already imprisoned Jews, Communists and anarchists, and follows the bizarre legal entanglements, compromises and protests that marked the ensuing trials. This is an unavoidably sober and salutary tale, but characterization, motivation and conflict are all rather superficial and academic, leaving one with little more than a grand display of the mechanics of power, enacted by a vast, proficient and well-directed cast.

Best Director Cannes 1975

► **Sedmikrásky** see Daisies

► **Sedotta   E   Abbandonata** see Seduced And Abandoned

Seduced And Abandoned

► **Sedotta E Abbandonata**

> Italy   1963   123 mins   bw
> Lux/Ultra/Vides/Lux C.C. De France

d   **Pietro Germi**
sc   **Pietro Germi, Luciano Vincenzoni, Age, Furio Scarpelli**
ph   **Aiace Parolin**
m   **Carlo Rustichelli**
     Stefania Sandrelli, Aldo Puglisi, Saro Urzi, Lando Buzzanca, Leopoldo Trieste

Fifteen-year-old Agnese (Sandrelli) is seduced by her sister's fiancé (Puglisi) and becomes pregnant. His engagement is broken off, but he abandons Agnese because she is no longer a virgin. Germi's follow-up to *Divorce – Italian Style* is a somewhat frenzied farce in which genuine wit and pointed satire only occasionally surface. The director has concocted an efficient farrago of authentic Sicilian passions, but it lacks the appeal of its predecessor.

Best Actor (Saro Urzi) Cannes 1964

► **Seduction Of Julia, The** see Adorable Julia

The Seduction Of Mimì

► **Mimì Metallurgico Ferito Nell'Onore**

> Italy   1972   120 mins   col
> Vera Film

d   **Lina Wertmüller**
sc   **Lina Wertmüller**
ph   **Blasco Giurato**
m   **Piero Piccioni**
     Giancarlo Giannini, Mariangela Melato, Agostina Belli, Elena Fiore, Turri Ferro

Mimì (Giannini), a simple labourer in Southern Italy, finds himself caught between the local Mafia on the one hand and the Communist party on the other. All he wants is a decent living for his family and a contented personal life, but manages to sabotage himself on both counts: he offends the Mafia and has an affair with a liberated and anarchic girl (Melato), thus driving his wife into the arms of another man and himself to some grotesquely ill-judged behaviour. Cooking up her usual stew of sex and politics, Wertmüller here seasons it with humour to come up with a comment on Sicilian society that is both bitter and funny. Some sequences demonstrate the director's penchant for the erotic, but unfortunately serve to undercut the suggestion of feminist argument, and there are several longueurs. Giannini delivers a terrific performance, well matched by Melato, and by Turri Ferro, who plays six different characters – all Mafia men.

The Seedling

▶ **Ankur**

India   1974   131 mins   col
Blaze

d Shyam Benegal
sc Shyam Benegal
ph Govind Nihalani, Kamath Ghanekar
m Vanraj Ram Mohan
    Anant Nag, Shabana Azmi, Sudhu Meher, Priya Tendulkar, Mirza Qadir Ali Baig

A servant girl (Azmi) with a deaf-mute husband (Meher) is seduced by an arrogant young man (Nag), sent by his father to manage a remote farm on the family estate. The landlord's son leaves her pregnant and beats her husband out of fear, an act which only plants the seed of revolution. This brilliantly assured feature film debut by former documentary-director Benegal was based on a story he had written when he was 16, revolving around an incident of which he had firsthand knowledge. Made in Hindi, the dominant language of Indian commercial cinema, it succeeds in being accessible to a mass audience while carrying a political message. The beautiful images contrast vividly with the exposure of the brutal feudalism still prevalent in parts of India today.

See Here My Love

▶ **Écoute Voir...**

France   1978   110 mins   col

Prospectacle

d Hugo Santiago
sc Claude Ollier, Hugo Santiago
ph Ricardo Aronovitch
m Edgardo Canton, Michel Portal
    Catherine Deneuve, Sami Frey, Florence Delay, Anne Parillaud, Didier Haudepin, Antoine Vitez, Gilbert Adair

A bisexual private eye (Deneuve) is hired by the mysterious owner of a château (Frey) to investigate a break-in. She discovers a strange Right-wing sect operating from the château, using a machine that interferes with radio waves to brainwash the population. The film starts out as a parody of Raymond Chandler, with a female Philip Marlowe, but gradually moves away from the thriller into more metaphysical, sexual and political preoccupations, none of which is particularly engaging. The film's quality lies in the stereo soundtrack (écoute), which contains clues to the mystery (if one cares), the photography and creative use of the 'Scope screen (voir). The ending, a technically expert telescoping of time and space, is merely further obfuscation.

▶ **Seemabaddha** see Company Limited

See You Tomorrow

▶ **Do Widzenia Do Jutra**

Poland   1960   85 mins   bw
Film Polski-Kadr Film Unit

d Janusz Morgenstern
sc Zbigniew Cybulski, Bogumil Kobiela, Wilhelm Mach
ph Jan Laskowski
m Krzysztof T. Komeda
    Zbigniew Cybulski, Teresa Tuszynska, Grazyna Muszynska, Jacek Fedorowicz, Roman Polanski

Jacek (Cybulski), who runs a student theatre in Gdansk, falls in love with Marguerite (Tuszynska), the daughter of a foreign diplomat. He neglects his work to court her, although they can barely communicate because of language difficulties, and she is unreceptive to the seriousness of his intentions. The slightest of interludes, this film offers a series of incidental pleasures – the sharply evoked sense of a sleepy summer, fine photography, an exuberantly youthful Polanski as one of Jacek's friends – but there's not enough material to support a full-length film.

▶ **Sehnsucht Der Veronika Voss, Die** see Veronika Voss

▶ **Semaine De Vacances, Une** see Week's Holiday, A

Senilità

Italy 1961 110 mins bw
Zebra (Rome)/Aera (Paris)

d   **Mauro Bolognini**
sc **Mauro Bolognini, Tullio Pinelli, Goffredo Parise**
ph **Armando Nannuzzi**
m   **Piero Piccioni**
   Anthony Franciosa, Claudia Cardinale, Betsy Blair, Philippe Leroy, Raimondo Magni

Emilio (Franciosa), a mild-mannered, middle-aged clerk whose intellect controls his passions, lives with his lonely spinster sister, Amalia (Blair). He becomes infatuated with the beautiful but amoral Angiolina (Cardinale, sporting a Louise Brooks hair-do), who humiliates and destroys him. Based on a novel by Italo Svevo and set in a graphically well-reproduced, rain-drenched Trieste in the 1920s, Bolognini's low-keyed film accurately conveys the stultifying atmosphere of lives lived in a state of repression (Amalia) and frustration (Emilio), but finally misses the mark. The acting is not quite good enough, and there is a failure of clarity on the part of both screenplay and leading man in expressing the degree of Emilio's intellectual arrogance which reduces him to the one condition he is determined to avoid – that of emotional slavery.

▶ **Señora De Nadie** see Nobody's Wife

Senso

▶ **aka The Wanton Contessa**

Italy 1954 115 mins col
Lux

d   **Luchino Visconti**
sc **Luchino Visconti, Suso Cecchi D'Amico, Giorgio Prosperi, Carl Alianello, Giorgio Bassani**
ph **G.R. Aldo, Robert Krasker**
m   **Bruckner, Verdi**
   Alida Valli, Farley Granger, Massimo Girotti, Heinz Moog, Rina Morelli, Christian Marquand

In 1866 in Venice, a married Italian noblewoman (Valli), working for the cause of independence, falls in love with an Austrian officer (Granger) in the army of occupation, but she denounces him for desertion after he has been unfaithful to her. Working through the conventions of Italian grand opera – the film opens sumptuously at the opera house at a performance of *Il Trovatore* – Visconti creates a lush melodramatic historical romance. Inferior to *The Leopard* (1963), the other of his films set during the Risorgimento, the colour photography is no less stunning (Aldo died in a car crash during the shooting). A cut version with dubbed dialogue by Tennessee Williams and Paul Bowles was inflicted on American audiences.

Sensualità

▶ **aka Barefoot Savage**

Italy 1952 93 mins bw
Ponti/DD

d   **Clemente Fracassi**
sc **Alberto Moravia, Ennio De Concini**
ph **Aldo Tonti**
m   **Enzio Masetti**
   Eleonora Rossi Drago, Amedeo Nazzari, Marcello Mastroianni, Francesca Liddi

Franca (Rossi Drago), a seductive Slav immigrant in Italy, is tired of working in the fields and marries the owner (Nazzari) of the farm although she actually prefers his brother (Mastroianni). Desirable as the smouldering Rossi Drago is, this steamy melodrama still leaves a lot to be desired. The hand of co-writer Moravia is sometimes in evidence, and the settings are convincing even if the plot triangle is not.

▶ **Senza Pietà** see Without Pity

▶ **Se Permuta** see House For Swap

▶ **Seppuku** see Harakiri

▶ **Septième Juré, Le** see Seventh Juror, The

▶ **Sept Péchés Capitaux, Les** see Seven Deadly Sins, The

▶ **Sept Péchés Capitaux, Les** see Seven Deadly Sins, The

▶ **SER** see Freedom Is Paradise

▶ **Serdtze Materi** see Heart Of A Mother

▶ **Seryozha** see Splendid Days, The

Seven Beauties

▶ **Pasqualino Settebellezze**

Italy 1975 115 mins col
Medusa

d Lina Wertmüller
sc Lina Wertmüller
ph Tonino Delli Colli
m Enzo Iannacci
Giancarlo Giannini, Fernando Rey, Shirley Stoler, Enzo Vitale, Piero Di Iorio

Pasqualino (Giannini), a small-time crook and ladykiller, lives in Naples with his mother and seven fat sisters (the 'beauties' of the title). After killing a pimp while defending the honour of the eldest of them, he is put into an insane asylum where he rapes an inmate, then joins the Italian army, deserts, is captured by the Germans and sent to a concentration camp where he seduces a large sadistic female commandant...*The New York Times* called this grotesque, cacophonous comic-strip 'Miss Wertmüller's *King Kong*, her *Nashville*, her *8½*, her *Navigator*, her *City Lights*'. Another comparison might be with the vat of excrement in which a Spanish anarchist (Rey) drowns himself.

The Seven Deadly Sins

▶ **Les Sept Péchés Capitaux**

France/Italy 1952 150 mins bw

Franco London/Costellazione

d Eduardo De Filippo, Jean Dréville, Yves Allégret, Roberto Rossellini, Carlo Rim, Claude Autant-Lara, Georges Lacombe
sc Charles Spaak, Carlo Rim, Pierre Bost, Jean Aurenche, Roberto Rossellini, Claude Autant-Lara
ph Enzo Serafin, André Thomas, Roger Hubert, Robert Le Fevre, André Bac
m Yves Baudrier, René Cloërec
Eduardo De Filippo, Isa Miranda, Paolo Stoppa, Louis De Funès, Jean Richard, Françoise Rosay, Gérard Philipe, Noël-Noël, Viviane Romance, Michèle Morgan

Sketches illustrating 1) 'Avarice and Anger' 2) 'Sloth' 3) 'Lust' 4) 'Envy' 5) 'Gluttony' 6) 'Pride' 7) 'The Eighth Sin'. Gérard Philipe introduces each of the sinful tales, or collection of dirty jokes, which reveal a lot about attitudes to sex in the early 1950s. Because of its irreverance towards the then taboo subjects in English-speaking films, it was a tremendous hit. A few of the sketches still survive in their own right, especially Rossellini's 'Lust' and Rim's 'Envy'. The latter was based on a story by Colette about a wife who was jealous of her husband's cat. The stellar cast also reaps rewards. A number of *Nouvelle Vague* directors had a go at interpreting the seven sins in a similar, multi-episode format in 1961.

The Seven Deadly Sins

▶ **Les Sept Péchés Capitaux**

France 1961 113 mins bw
Franco London/Gibe/Titanus

d Sylvain Dhomme, Eugene Ionesco, Max Douy, Edouard Molinaro, Philippe De Broca, Jacques Demy, Jean-Luc Godard, Roger Vadim, Claude Chabrol
sc Eugene Ionesco, Claude Mauriac, Roger Peyrefitte, Daniel Boulanger, Jacques Demy, Jean-Luc Godard, Roger Vadim, Felicien Marceau
ph Jean Penzer, Louis Miaille, Henri Decaë, Jean Rabier
m Michel Legrand, Sacha Distel, Pierre Jansen
Marie-José Nat, Claude Brasseur, Georges Wilson, Laurent Terzieff, Jean-Louis Trintignant, Micheline Presle,

Corinne Marchand, Jean-Pierre Aumont, Sami Frey, Jean-Claude Brialy, Claude Rich, Claude Berri, Eddie Constantine

1) 'Gluttony' – a family stops to eat once too often on the way to a funeral 2) 'Pride' – a cheating wife finds her husband having an affair 3) 'Envy' – a chambermaid falls in love with a millionaire 4) 'Sloth' – a movie star is too lazy to undress for sex 5) 'Lust' – a man finds he can see through girls' clothes 6) 'Anger' – flies pop up in bowls of soup around town 7) 'Greed' – 25 students pool their money to buy one of their number some time with a high-class prostitute. An inconsequential collection of modern parables, unworthy of the names involved, the best being Godard's 'Sloth'. The eighth sin was making the film in the first place.

Seven Samurai

▶ **Shichinin No Samurai**

Japan   1954   200 mins   bw
Toho

d   **Akira Kurosawa**
sc **Shinobu Hashimoto, Hideo Oguni, Akira Kurosawa**
ph **Asaichi Nakai**
m   **Fumio Hayasaka**
    Takashi Shimura, Yoshio Inaba, Isao Kimura, Seiji Miyaguchi, Toshiro Mifune, Minoru Chiaki, Daisuke Kato, Keiko Tsushima, Ko Kimura, Kuniniri Kodo

A farming community of meagre resources decides to hire samurai to fight off the annual incursion of brutal bandits who steal the harvest. After many travails, they persuade one warrior (Shimura) to take it on, and he sets about recruiting his chosen minimum of six more men – with the greatest difficulty, since the job offers neither money nor glory, but only the challenge of the fight. The samurai band moves into the village with the inept and frightened inhabitants to plan their strategy, and finally routs the 40 bandits. On this simple framework, Kurosawa has constructed a superb narrative, bursting with incident that is by turns exciting, absorbing, moving and funny. Carefully and lovingly reconstructing medieval Japan, he reveals the entire spectrum of human strength and weakness with absolute clarity of vision. The warrior heroes are seen as a shabby, lonely band of outcasts, retaining dignity, courage and good humour, but no glamour. Shimura's wise leader and Mifune's half-crazed, self-appointed samurai dominate a brilliant cast, while the lighting and photography are unforgettable. The film, on which Hollywood based the Western *The Magnificent Seven* (1960), remains one of the greatest achievements in cinema history.

Seventeen

▶ **Sytten**

Denmark   1965   88 mins   col
Palladium

d   **Annelise Meineche**
sc **Bob Ramsing**
ph **Øle Lytken**
m   **Øle Hoyer**
    Øle Soltøft, Ghita Norby, Hass Christensen, Øle Monty, Bodil Steen, Lise Rosendahl

In the summer of 1913, a 17-year-old schoolboy (Soltøft) loses his virginity with his pretty cousin (Norby) and learns the art of lovemaking from the maid (Rosendahl). This predictable, heavy-humoured piece was popular when Scandinavia still had a sexy reputation. Only 17-year-old virgins, if any still exist in the world, would find anything to entertain them in this piece.

The Seventh Juror

▶ **Le Septième Juré**

France   1964   90 mins   bw
Orex/Trans-Lux

d   **Georges Lautner**
sc **Jacques Robert, Pierre Laroche**
ph **Maurice Fellous**
m   **Jean Yatove**
    Bernard Blier, Danièle Delorme, Francis Blanche, Jacques Riberolles

A middle-aged, married, and popular pillar of the community, Grégoire Duval (Blier) kills a provocative girl who spurns his advances. When her disreputable boyfriend is charged with the crime, Duval finds himself on the jury and, troubled by conscience, engineers an acquittal. Later, he confesses his guilt, but nobody will believe him. . . . Full of nice twists and turns of plot, and with a splendidly ironic ending, this makes a diverting little film for addicts of the genre, and for admirers of the excellent Blier.

The Seventh Seal

▶ **Det Sjunde Inseglet**

Sweden   1957   90 mins   bw
Svensk Filmindustri

d   **Ingmar Bergman**
sc **Ingmar Bergman**
ph **Gunnar Fischer**
m   **Erik Nordgren**
    **Max Von Sydow, Gunnar Björnstrand,
    Bengt Ekerot, Nils Poppe, Bibi Andersson**

A knight (Von Sydow) returns from the Crusades to find Sweden ravaged by plague. In his search for God he meets a group of strolling players, suffering peasants and Death (Ekerot), with whom he plays a deadly game of chess. Shot in only 35 days, this powerful morality tale depicts the cruelty of medieval life – witch burning, flagellation – as well as the joys and noble aspirations of people in luminous images derived from early church paintings. Bergman's seventeenth film set him firmly in the pantheon of great directors.

Special Jury Prize Cannes 1957

▶ **Several Interviews On Personal Matters** see Interviews On Personal Problems

Sex Shop

France   1972   105 mins   col
Renn Productions/Les Artistes
Associés(Paris)/ P.E.A.
Cinematografica(Rome)/Regina
Films(Munich)

d   **Claude Berri**
sc **Claude Berri**
ph **Pierre Lhomme**
m   **Serge Gainsbourg**
    **Juliet Berto, Claude Berri, Nathalie
    Delon, Jacques Martin, Grégoire Aslan,
    Jean-Pierre Marielle, Béatrice Romand**

Business is bad for Paris bookseller Claude (Berri). With an extravagant wife (Berto) and two children to support, he follows a friend's suggestion and turns the premises into a sex shop stocking erotic literature, movies and gadgets. The enterprise leads him to try and inject some experimental excitement into his marriage and complications proliferate until the police close the shop and he and his wife settle back into their comfortable routine. Berri here makes a comic excursion into fantasy and permissiveness that is harmless and also pointless. The action takes place in prettified exteriors and Art Deco interiors and is overlaid with excessively lush music, the cast lacks vitality and the director's usual commitment to subject and gift for observation are missing.

Shadowman

▶ **aka The Man Without A Face**

▶ **L'Homme Sans Visage**

▶ **aka Nuits Rouges**

France   1974   105 mins   col
Terra/SOAT

d   **Georges Franju**
sc **Jacques Champreux**
ph **Guido Renzo Bertoni**
m   **Georges Franju, Berlioz**
    **Jacques Champreux, Gayle Hunnicutt,
    Gert Fröbe, Josephine Chaplin, Ugo
    Pagliai**

A sinister masked criminal attempts to mastermind the stealing of the treasure of the Knights' Templar, but he has to overcome members of the 12th-century sect that still guards it. Franju's first film for four years was a pitiful return to the shadowy serial world of his magical *Judex* (1963). However, whereas the earlier film was a remake of a Feuillade serial, this is cod Feuillade which, lacking in visual flair and atmosphere, and offering only listless performances, is diabolical in both senses.

Shadow Of Adultery

▶ **La Proie Pour L'Ombre**

France   1960   99 mins   bw

Marceau/Cocinor

d Alexandre Astruc
sc Alexandre Astruc
ph Marcel Grignon
m Bach, Richard Cornu
   Annie Girardot, Daniel Gélin, Christian
   Marquand, Anne Caprile, Michèle
   Gerbier

The wife (Girardot) of a rich building contractor (Gélin), beginning to tire of being merely a social asset to her husband, finds an outlet by running an art gallery and taking a lover (Marquand). In the end, she sacrifices both men for her independence. White sports cars, cocktail parties, an art gallery, a recording studio, modern skyscapers, jazz and Bach on the soundtrack and quick, slick cross-cutting, give Astruc's contribution to the *Nouvelle Vague* an over-riding air of chic. The main interest of the film lies in the conflict of the woman (superbly played by Girardot) and her place in a man's world.

Shadows In Paradise

▶ Varjoja Paratiisissa

Finland 1986 76 mins col
Villealfa Filmproductions

d Aki Kaurismäki
sc Aki Kaurismäki
ph Timo Salminen
m Pop songs
   Matti Pellonpää, Kati Outinen, Saku
   Kuosmanen, Mato Valtonen, Kylli Köngäs

A shy and lonely garbage-truck driver (Pellonpää) courts a supermarket cashier (Outinen) who, when sacked, steals a cashbox. She accepts his help to get out of the ensuing jam but walks out on him before they come together again. Kaurismäki's third film is the first in his so-called 'working-class' trilogy, completed by *Ariel* (1988) and *The Match Factory Girl* (1989). Very short, very sparse but not very sweet, it lays down the director's markers which were to become familiar to his cult following: silent, put-upon losers working at soulless jobs in bleak surroundings. The ending is not, however, without hope, as Ilona, the seemingly self-destructive heroine, finally allows herself the possibility of happiness. Pellonpää and Outinen, both excellent,

would become familiar regulars in Kaurismäki's future work. An interesting but not a compelling film.

Shadows Of Our Forgotten Ancestors

▶ Teni Zabytykh Predkov

USSR 1964 100 mins col
Dovzhenko Studio

d Sergo Paradjanov
sc Sergo Paradjanov, Ivan Chendei
ph Viktor Bestayeva
m Y. Shorik
   Ivan Nikolaychuk, Larisa Kadochnilova,
   Tatiana Bestayeva, Spartak Bagashvili

In a primitive community in the Carpathian mountains at the turn of the century, a young peasant falls in love with the daughter of the man responsible for the death of his father, but marries a woman who indulges in sorcery. Paradjanov's first film to be shown in the West (UK 1968, USA 1967) revealed his remarkable talent for lyrical extravagance which reached its peak five years later with *The Colour Of Pomegranates*. Perhaps the latter story of a poet and his works lent itself better to his swirling, kaleidoscopic camera style than this rural folk tale. However, it exerts a greater fascination than most Soviet films of the period.

▶ Shadows Of The Yoshiwara, The
see Crossways

▶ Shakha Proshakha see Branches Of
The Tree, The

The Shame

▶ Skammen

Sweden 1968 103 mins bw
Svensk Filmindustri

d Ingmar Bergman
sc Ingmar Bergman
ph Sven Nykvist
   Liv Ullmann, Max Von Sydow, Gunnar
   Björnstrand, Birgitta Valberg, Sigge Furst

In the year 1971, on an island off an unnamed

country, an apolitical couple are unwillingly caught up in, and gradually corrupted by, a bitter civil war. 'Sometimes it's like a dream. Not mine. I'm forced into someone else's dream,' says Ullmann, exactly describing the spectators' experience in entering Bergman's powerful parable illustrated in stark, realistic images, static camera movements, and sharp sounds (there is no music, although the couple are musicians). The two leads, especially Von Sydow's big gangling baby forced to face reality, are superb, having been allowed by the director for the first time to improvise some of their dialogue.

The Shameless Old Lady

▶ **La Vieille Dame Indigne**

France   1965   94 mins   bw
SPAC

d **René Allio**
sc **René Allio**
ph **Denys Clerval**
m **Jean Ferrat**
   Sylvie, Malka Ribovska, Victor Lanoux, Etienne Bierry

A septuagenarian grandmother has lived a quiet life devoted to her large family but, on becoming a widow, she begins a new life by buying a *deux chevaux*, joining a political group, befriending a prostitute, and going on holiday, before dying happy. Sylvie, a character actress in the cinema for over 50 years, grasped her first starring role brilliantly before her death in 1970 aged 87. She is the principal reason for seeing this tale based on a story by Bertolt Brecht about his grandmother, but Allio's approach is traditional rather than Brechtian, laying on both the charm and the message rather thickly.

The Shanghai Drama

▶ **Le Drame De Shanghai**

France   1938   100 mins   bw
Marc Sorkin

d **G.W. Pabst**
sc **Leo Laniz, Alexandre Arnoux**
ph **Eugen Schüfftan**
m **Ralph Erwin**

Louis Jouvet, Christiane Mardayne, Raymond Rouleau, Dorville, Elina Labourdette

A group of White Russian refugees in Shanghai, just prior to the Sino-Japanese war, are drawn into the network of a terrorist society promoting the Japanese cause. One of them, a cabaret singer (Mardayne), wants to get out because ˇ she fears for her daughter's safety which, in the end, is secured with the help of a journalist (Rouleau). More a character study than an action drama, Pabst made this stylized film during his brief sojourn in Paris before returning to work in Nazi Germany. It was vividly photographed by Schüfftan – later a leading Hollywood cinematographer and Oscar-winner for *The Hustler* – but the top-billed Jouvet was wasted in a minor role as a villainous member of a spy ring.

▶ **Shatranj Ke Khilari** see Chess Players, The

Shattered

▶ **Scherben**

Germany   1921   62 mins   bw
Rex Film

d **Lupu Pick**
sc **Carl Mayer**
ph **Friedrich Weimann**
m **Silent**
   Werner Krauss, Edith Posca, Paul Otto

A railway worker's daughter (Posca) is seduced by her father's superior. The couple are discovered by the girl's mother who, shocked and distraught, runs out into the cold and freezes to death. Further destruction comes when the girl's seducer abandons her and is killed by her father. This grim, small-scale film is one of the important works of Lupu Pick, a theatre director who rose to prominence as the chief exponent of *kammerspiel* (chamber play) on the screen – sparse, naturalistic, dealing in a minimum number of characters and observing the unities of time, place and action. After this, Pick quarrelled with Mayer whose *The Last Laugh* he was due to direct, and his work deteriorated over the years. He died of poisoning in 1931, aged 45.

▶ **Shattered** see Passagers, Les

Shchors

▶ **aka Shors**

USSR   1939   140 mins   bw
Kiev Film Studio

d   **Alexander Dovzhenko**
sc   **Alexander Dovzhenko**
ph   **Yuri Ekelchik**
m   **Dmitri Kabalevsky**
     Evgeni Samailov, Ivan Skuratov, F.
     Ishchenko, L. Liashenko, O. Khvylia

Under the leadership of the young Nikolai Shchors (Samailov), a regiment of pro-Bolshevik Ukrainian partisans liberate Kiev from the Germans in 1918. After reversals and victories, Shchors founds a school for Red Army officers. Stalin asked Dovzhenko to make a 'Ukrainian *Chapayev*' and the director came up with a vivid, heroic epic of the regiment in which he had served for a short while as a young man. In the tradition of 'the cult of personality' Soviet films of the period, which extolled the achievements of one man, the idealized title character is seldom off the screen. Discursive, episodic and, at times, wordily didactic, it contains some of Dovzhenko's renowned poetic imagery, and shows his ability to use characters to embody ideas without taking away their humanity.

She And He

▶ **Kanojo To Kare**

Japan   1963   115 mins   bw
Iwanami

d   **Susumu Hani**
sc   **Susumu Hani, Kunio Shimizu**
ph   **Juichi Nagano**
m   **Tohru Takemitsu**
     Sachiko Hidari, Eiji Okada, Kikuji
     Yamashita, Mariko Igarashi

Fire destroys rag-pickers' shacks next to the comfortable apartment block where Naoko (Hidari) and her husband Eiichi (Okada) live. They encounter Ikona (Yamashita), one of the victims, who was once at the university with Eiichi, but now lives in poverty with his dog and a blind orphan. Fascinated by Ikona's world, Naoko encourages a friend-ship which only leads to terrible discord. A minutely observed, intimate and unsentimental drama of social consciousness that uncovers the spiritual wasteland of suburbia, and explores the barriers erected by differences of class, money and, above all, aspiration. Naoko (sensitively played by Hidari) is perceived as a woman drawn to wider human contact, but deprived of it by virtue of her social position.

Best Actress (Sachiko Hidari) Berlin 1964

The Sheep Has Five Legs

▶ **Le Mouton À Cinq Pattes**

France   1954   100 mins   bw
Cocinor

d   **Henri Verneuil**
sc   **Albert Valentin**
ph   **Armand Thirard**
m   **Georges Van Parys**
     Fernandel, Françoise Arnoul, Delmont,
     Louis De Funès, Noël Roquevert, René
     Genin

A crusty old vintner holds a grudge against his quintuplet sons who have never come home to the farm after their schooling. The town doctor (Delmont) sets off to find them and surprise the old man with a reunion. He unearths a prissy, rich beautician, a poor, hypochondriac window-cleaner with a flock of children, a dour sea captain, a village *curé* and a lonely hearts columnist. No more than a series of sketches, this variable entertainment was made as a vehicle to display the versatility of Fernandel, who plays the father and all five sons. Rather broad and vulgar at times, it does contain some very funny scenes, the best of which concern the window-cleaner being dogged by an undertaker (De Funès). There is also a droll in-joke which finds the *curé* becoming a laughing stock due to his resemblance to a certain film star famous for his role as the priest Don Camillo.

▶ **Shestoe Iulya** see Sixth Of July, The

The She-Wolf

▶ **La Lupa**

Italy   1953   90 mins   bw

Ponti/De Laurentiis
d   Alberto Lattuada
sc Alberto Lattuada, Luigi Malerba, Antonio
    Pietrangeli, Ivo Perilli, Ennio Concini
ph Aldo Tonti
m   Felice Lattuada
    Kerima, Ettore Manni, Maj Britt, Mario
    Passante, Maresa Gallo

Although kept by her rich, factory-owning lover, a woman with a passionate hunger for men has an affair with a young soldier. He then falls in love with and marries her daughter. When the couple has a baby, mother moves in and seduces her son-in-law all over again, creating havoc and destruction. Another offering from the lust-obsessed end of the Neo-Realist spectrum, with Lattuada expertly capturing the heat and dust of a Sicilian village. Whether the swarthy Kerima convinces in the title role is a matter of opinion but, like several similar Italian offerings of the period, it caused some excitement at the time.

▶ **Shichinin No Samurai** see Seven Samurai

▶ **Shina Ningyo** see Fruits Of Passion, The

▶ **Shinel** see Overcoat, The

▶ **Shin Heike Monogatari** see New Tales Of The Taira Clan

▶ **Shinjo Ten No Amijima** see Double Suicide

▶ **Shinjuku Dorobo Nikki** see Diary Of A Shinjuku Thief

A Ship Bound For India

▶ **aka The Land Of Desire**

▶ **(US: Frustration)**

▶ **Skepp Till Indialand**

Sweden 1947 102 mins bw
Sveriges Folkbiografer
d   Ingmar Bergman
sc Ingmar Bergman
ph Göran Strindberg

m   Erland Von Koch
    Holger Löwenadler, Anna Lindahl, Birger
    Malmsten, Gertrud Fridh, Lasse Krantz,
    Jan Molander, Erik Hell,

Alexander Blom (Löwenadler), the captain of a salvage ship, treats his hunchback son Johannes (Malmsten) with cruelty and contempt. The enmity between them comes to a head when Blom brings Sally (Fridh), a back-street dancer, to the ship and Johannes falls in love with her, provoking his father to an attempt on his life. Bergman's third film as director has, in fact, a complicated plot, and a melodramatic one at that – a tone which is emphasized by the high-pitched direction and playing (although Löwenadler is first-class in a difficult role). The murky events are unfolded in one long flashback as Johannes, reunited with Sally after seven years, recalls past events. It is an interesting movie for Bergman followers because it sows so many seeds of the concerns and techniques that would flower later – human beings battling with illness, emotional isolation and frustration, the fascination of the theatre, and a magic moment of release from inner and outer claustrophobia, as when Johannes and Sally temporarily escape the oppressive confines of the ship.

▶ **Shivers** see Dreszcze

▶ **Shizuka Naru Ketto** see Quiet Duel, A

▶ **Shlosha Yamim Ve Yeled** see Three Days And A Child

Shoah

France 1985 9 hrs 43 mins col
Les Films Aleph/Historia Films
d   Claude Lanzmann
ph Dominique Chapuis, Jimmy Glasberg,
    William Lubtchansky

Survivors of the Nazi extermination camps at Treblinka, Auschwitz and elsewhere, plus witnesses, Polish bystanders and a handful of German officials, recall the Holocaust. Under Lanzmann's unwavering and detailed questioning they reveal the inconceivable horror and obscenity of the atrocities, and the minutiae of the detached planning that was the

Final Solution. Lanzmann spent 10 years travelling and visiting the scenes of humanity's greatest crime to amass his towering document edited from 350 hours of film. Marcel Ophüls terms *Shoah* (meaning annihilation) 'the greatest documentary about contemporary history ever made, bar none'; Lanzmann maintains that it is neither a documentary nor a historical film. Be that as it may, it is certainly a work of art as well as a unique and disturbing testament. The images are made manifest without using a single frame of archive material, and are all the more powerful for that: the Jewish barbers sent to cut the hair of their own wives and daughters at the entrance to the gas chambers; the Jews of the *sonderkommando* forced to shovel the crushed bodies of their fellows into ovens as the price of their own survival; the nightmarish conditions of the Warsaw ghetto. This landmark in film-making is, perhaps, most significant of all in reminding us that anti-Semitism is still alive and well.

Shoeshine

▶ **Sciuscia**

Italy 1946 93 mins bw
Alfa/ENIC

d   **Vittorio De Sica**
sc   **Vittorio De Sica, Cesare Zavattini, Sergio Amedei, Adolfo Franci, Cesare Giulio Viola**
ph   **Anchise Brizzi**
m   **Alessandro Cicognini**
     Rinaldo Smordoni, Franco Interlenghi, Aniello Mele, Bruno Ortensi, Pacifico Astrologo

In post-war Rome, Giuseppe (Smordoni) and Pasquale (Interlenghi), two shoeshine boys, dream of buying a horse with the little extra money they make out of dealing in black market goods, but they end up in reform school. One of the first pictures to come out of Italy after the war, it created an international sensation. It was also the first foreign-language movie to win an honorary Academy Award for proving 'to the world that the creative spirit can triumph over adversity'. (Until 1956, foreign films were given special, non-competitive awards.) Its impact was due to the powerful and touching

semi-documentary treatment of poverty in post-war Italy, the main theme of the Neo-Realists.

▶ **Shokutaku No Nai Ie** see Empty Table, The

▶ **Shonen** see Boy

Shoot The Pianist

▶ **(US: Shoot The Piano Player)**
▶ **Tirez Sur Le Pianiste**

France 1960 80 mins bw
Films De La Pleiade

d   **François Truffaut**
sc   **François Truffaut, Marcel Moussy**
ph   **Raoul Coutard**
m   **Georges Delerue**
     Charles Aznavour, Marie Dubois, Nicole Berger, Michèle Mercier, Albert Rémy

An ex-concert pianist (Aznavour), working in a seedy bar in the outskirts of Paris, gets involved with gangsters when he helps his two petty-crook brothers escape from them, an action culminating in the death of his girlfriend (Dubois). 'A pastiche of the Hollywood B film,' said Truffaut of his second picture. The plot, derived from a pulp novel by David Goodis, has the elements of American *film noir*, but the style is pure *Nouvelle Vague* with its mobile camera, mood changes and visual gags. Aznavour's sad-eyed figure at the centre gives depth to the light-hearted proceedings.

▶ **Shoot The Piano Player** see Shoot The Pianist

▶ **Shop On Main Street, The** see Shop On The High Street, The

The Shop On The High Street

▶ **aka The Shop On Main Street**
▶ **Obchod Od Na Korze**

Czechoslovakia 1965 128 mins bw

Barrandov

d **Jan Kadar**
sc **Jan Kadar, Elmar Klos**
ph **Vladimir Novotny**
m **Zdeněk Liška**
   Jožef Kroner, Ida Kaminska, Hana
   Slivková, František Zvarik

In Nazi-occupied Czechoslovakia, a lowly carpenter (Kroner) becomes the 'Aryan comptroller' of a button shop owned by an old Jewish lady (Kaminska). She turns out to be stone deaf, unaware there's a war on, and has barely a button in the place. Caught between self-interest and his growing affection for her, his bungled attempts to protect her lead to tragedy for them both. Kadar conveys the political climate with absolute clarity (and comedy) and Kaminska's performance is a miracle. Don't miss it – but be prepared to shed tears of sorrow.

Best Foreign Film Oscar 1965

▶ **Shors** see Shchors

Short Cut

▶ **Postriziny**

Czechoslovakia 1981 98 mins col
Barrandov Studios

d **Jiří Menzel**
sc **Bohumil Hrabal, Jiří Menzel**
ph **Jaromír Šofr**
m **Jiří Šust**
   Jiří Schmitzer, Magda Vašáryová,
   Jaromír Hanzlík, Rudolf Hrušínsky,
   František Rehák, Oldřich Vlach

Francin (Schmitzer), shy and serious, manages the local brewery in a small provicial town prior to World War I and attempts to cope with the high spirits of his beautiful and extrovert wife, Marja (Vašáryová), who is universally adored by the locals. The coming of sound radio is the 'short cut' that projects the lifestyle of the village into the present. On this flimsy foundation, popular Czech novelist Bohumil Hrabal, drawing on the life of his parents in the days of the Austro-Hungarian empire, has constructed a funny and affectionate exercise in nostalgia to which Jiří Menzel brings the full measure of his gifts for warmth, humour, and satirical observation. The period is evoked with atmosphere, enhanced by a lyrical camera, and the townsfolk are given authentic life by cast and director.

Short Encounters

▶ **aka Short Meetings**
▶ **aka Brief Encounters**
▶ **Korotkie Vstrechi**

USSR 1967 88 mins bw
Odessa Feature Film Studio

d **Kira Muratova**
sc **Kira Muratova, Leonid Zhukovitsy**
ph **G. Kariuk**
m **Oleg Karavaichuk**
   Nina Ruslanova, Kira Muratova, Vladimir
   Vysotsky

A young village girl and her employer, the latter the dedicated organizer of the town's housing committee, are in love with the same man, a free-wheeling, guitar-strumming geologist. A simple love story, simply shot in unglamourized black-and-white and utilizing flashback techniques, it gives a picture of daily life in the Russian provinces, revealing the existence of free love, bureaucratic inefficiency and fiddling the system. These facts, coupled with the presence of Vysotsky, theatre idol and composer of protest songs who was regarded as a dissident, resulted in the multi-talented Muratova's film being suppressed for 20 years. Vysotsky, who died at the age of 42, and the stunning Ruslanova, were both making their screen debuts.

A Short Film About Killing

▶ **aka Thou Shalt Not Kill**
▶ **Krótki Film O Zabijaniu**

Poland 1988 84 mins col
Film Polski, Tor Unit

d **Krzysztof Kieslowski**
sc **Krzysztof Piesiewicz, Krzysztof**
   Kieslowski
ph **Slawomir Idziak**
m **Zbigniew Preisner**

Miroslaw Baka, Krzysztof Globisz, Jan
Tesarz

A young and aimless drifter (Baka) kills an
ill-natured taxi driver by repeatedly bashing
in his head with a stone. He is caught, arrested
and condemned to death, and the authorized
killing is as horribly disturbing as the senseless
and brutal crime. Kieslowski's powerful and
purposefully shocking film was made as part
of a TV series based on the Ten Command-
ments. It differs from most other anti-capital
punishment films in that its treatment of the
subject starkly refuses to sentimentalize the
situation, with the director determined to
show both killings in the most graphic detail.
Shot in bleached out greenish- browns, utilizing eerie camera angles and sudden cuts to
discomforting images, it's made with a masterly hand that cannot fail to shake any sense
of audience complacency. Whether it will
make conversions, either to its cause or the
style of its director, is another matter entirely.

Special Jury Prize Cannes 1988

A Short Film About Love

▶ Krótki Film O Milości

Poland 1988 90 mins col
Polish Film Producers' Corporation

d Krzysztof Kieślowski
sc Krzysztof Kieślowski, Krzysztof
Piesiewicz
ph Witold Adamek
m Zbigniew Preisner
Grażyna Szapolowska, Olaf Lubaszenko,
Stefania Iwińska, Piotr Machalika

Postal worker Tomek (Lubaszenko), a
reclusive 19-year-old virgin, studies langages
in the evening, until the woman in the apartment opposite comes home, whereupon he
watches her every move through his telescope.
His interest in Magda (Szapolowska) becomes
obsessive infatuation and he contrives a series
of unwittingly cruel ploys in order to meet
her. The resulting relationship between the
innocent boy and the experienced, cynical
woman who no longer believes in love, brings
near-tragedy to him and grief to her. Following on his extraordinary A Short Film About
Killing (1988), this film is the second of two
in Kieślowski's otherwise made-for-TV Deca-

logue, inspired by the Ten Commandments,
to be made for the cinema. The director,
generally regarded by 1990 as Poland's foremost contemporary film-maker, here gives us
another superbly assembled work. From its
ironic title to its plangent denouement, the
movie exemplifies its maker's approach: to
X-ray and then wield his precise scalpel to
open up and explore the habits of human
existence and the scars of damaged emotions.
Szapalowska, well known in her native
Poland, and newcomer Lubaszenko both give
superb performances.

▶ **Short Meetings** see Short Encounters

▶ **Shuban** see Scandal

▶ **Shura** see Pandemonium

▶ **Siberiada** see Siberiade

Siberiade

▶ Siberiada

USSR   1979   190 mins   col
Mosfilm

d Andrei Mikhalkov-Konchalovsky
sc Valentin Yezhov, Andrei Mikhalkov-
Konchalovsky
ph Levan Paatashvili
m Eduard Artemyev
Vladimir Samoilov, Vitaly Solomin,
Nikita Mikhalkov, Ludmila Gurchenko,
Nathalia Andretchenko

The lives of the wealthy Solomins and the
poor Ustyuzhanins in a Siberian village from
1909 to 1969, and how the many changes in
Soviet society affect them. There are certain
parallels between the wastes of Siberia and
those of the wide open spaces of the American
West, and this saga showing the republic's
'progress' from forests to oil rigs has similarities to an Edna Ferber epic. However, Konchalovsky's sometimes confusing and rambling
narrative is far more symbolic and concerned
with how individuals are the tools of history.
Forceful performances by Samoilov as the
woodman grandfather Solomin, Nikita Mikhalkov (the director's actor-director brother)
as a flamboyant oilman, and Gurchenko, the
girl he loves from the other family, shine in

Sign Of Disaster   581

a fine cast that brings the characters sharply into focus.

Special Jury Prize Cannes 1979

Siberian Lady Macbeth

▶ **Sibirska Ledi Magbet**

Yugoslavia 1962 95 mins bw
Avala

d **Andrzej Wajda**
sc **Sveta Lukić**
ph **Aleksandar Sekulović**
m **Dušan Radić adapted from Dimitri Shostakovitch**
   Olivera Marković, Ljuba Tadić, Miodrag Lazarvić, Bojan Stupica

The bored wife (Marković) of a merchant takes an itinerant workman (Tadić) as a lover while her husband is away. She then gives her father-in-law rat poison and, aided by her lover, strangles the husband on his return. Wajda, working outside Poland for the first time, went uncharacteristically for a passionate melodrama based on Nikolai Leskow's 1865 story, which also served for Shostakovitch's opera *Lady Macbeth Of Mtsensk*. Much of the film is operatic, as well as being influenced by the work of Kurosawa whose 'Japanese Lady Macbeth' (*Throne Of Blood*) had appeared a few years before. Wajda then returned to Poland and sobriety.

▶ **Sibirska Ledi Magbet** see Siberian Lady Macbeth

▶ **Si C'Était A Refaire** see Second Chance

The Sicilian Clan

▶ **Le Clan Des Siciliens**

France 1968 120 mins col
Fox-Europa/Les Films Du Siècle

d **Henri Verneuil**
sc **Henri Verneuil, José Giovanni, Pierre Pelégri**
ph **Henri Decaë**
m **Ennio Morricone**
   Jean Gabin, Alain Delon, Lino Ventura,

Irina Demick, Amedeo Nazzari, Sydney Chaplin

Roger Sartet (Delon) escapes from a French jail and joins forces with Manalese (Gabin), an aging Sicilian looking for a last coup which Sartet proposes in the form of an audacious jewel robbery in Venice. All goes well until Manalese discovers that Sartet has been having an affair with his daughter-in-law. The pairing of Delon and Gabin was obviously intended to spark off an atmosphere of dramatic conflict. In the event, the stars give mechanical performances in what is no more than a competent, routine crime thriller, enlivened by a couple of first-class action sequences and lent a touch of class by Decaë's atmospheric photography.

▶ **Siddharta And The City** see Adversary, The

▶ **Sierra De Teruel** see Man's Hope

▶ **Signe Du Lion, Le** see Sign Of Leo, The

Sign Of Disaster

▶ **aka III Omen**

▶ **Znak Bedy**

USSR 1986 145 mins col
Byelerus Film

d **Mikhail Ptashuk**
sc **Yevgeni Grigoryev, Oskai Nikich**
ph **Tatyana Loganova**
m **Oleg Yanchenko**
   Nina Ruslanova, Gennady Garbuk, Vladimir Ilin, Aleksandr Timoshkin, Kaspar Putse, Slava Soldatenko

A troop of Germans is billeted on the little farm of Stepanida (Ruslanova) and Petrok (Garbuk) but, finally, it is the hatred and brutality of the local collaborators that destroys them. Based on Vasil Bykov's best-selling novel, this controversial and relentlessly harrowing work depicts the chilling injustices that arose from the collectivization programme as well as the horrors of the Nazi occupation, and amply demonstrates the pervasive influence of fear that leads to corruption. At the centre is Stepanida who remains courageously and defiantly committed to the original principles of Bolshevism. Filmed in the vast spaces of Byelorussia, and moving skilfully back and forth in time, *Sign Of Disaster* was a political landmark in Soviet cinema – a clear indication that *glasnost* was no myth. In spite of an unconvincing and melodramatic ending, it is also a moving and powerful document, wonderfully well acted, particularly by Ruslanova.

The Sign Of Leo

▶ **Le Signe Du Lion**

France 1959 90 mins bw
AJYM Productions

d **Eric Rohmer**
sc **Eric Rohmer**
ph **Nicolas Hayer**
m **Louis Saguer**
Jess Hahn, Van Doude, Michèle Girardon, Jean Le Poulain, Stéphane Audran, Françoise Prévost

An impoverished 40-year-old American composer (Hahn) lives on the Left Bank in Paris. Hearing that he has inherited a fortune, he borrows money to hold a party, only to learn that the money has gone to a cousin. The ensuing crises lead him by subtle degrees into becoming a tramp, begging outside cafés, until an unexpected turn of events brings rescue. Rohmer (born Maurice Schérer) was the editor of the influential *Cahiers Du Cinéma* when he made this, his modest first full-length feature, a perceptive portrait of a good-natured but hopelessly irresponsible man slowly disintegrating in the face of reality. Only the pat ending strikes a false note. However, what makes the film particularly watchable is the detailed and vivid evocation – brilliantly captured by Nicolas Hayer's camera – of a sweltering Paris in August, deserted by its regular inhabitants. Rohmer would not make another feature for eight years, when his style would develop in another direction.

La Signora Di Tutti

Italy 1934 89 mins bw
Novella

d **Max Ophüls**
sc **Max Ophüls, Hans Wilhelm, Kurt Alexander**
ph **Ubaldo Arata**
m **Daniele Amfitheatrof**
Isa Miranda, Memo Benassi, Tatiana Pavlova, Federico Benfer, Nelly Corradi, Franco Coop

A famous Italian film star (Miranda) recalls the events leading up to her suicide attempt. Expelled from school because of a scandal involving the music teacher, she becomes the mistress of a banker (Benfer), whose son (Benassi) really loves her, but she only learns of this too late. Shooting in Italy on a contemporary subject, Ophüls retained the hallmarks of his style – extensive use of flashbacks, flowing camera movements, stunning crosscuts and lilting music – which suited the romantic tale admirably. Like *Lola Montes*, the heroine is a *femme fatale* and an innocent victim, a woman who publicly has everything and privately nothing. These ambiguities are securely handled by the director and by Miranda in her first leading role.

▶ **Signora Senza Camelie, La** see Lady Without Camellias, The

▶ **Signore E Signori** see Birds, The Bees And The Italians, The

Signs Of Life

▶ **Lebenszeichen**

W. Germany 1968 90 mins bw
Werner Herzog Filmproduktion

d **Werner Herzog**
sc **Werner Herzog**
ph **Thomas Mauch**
m **Stavros Xarchakos**
Peter Brogle, Wolfgang Reichmann, Athina Zacharopoulou, Wolfgang Von Ungern-Sternberg, Wolfgang Stumpf

Stroszek (Brogle), a German soldier wounded during the Occupation of Crete, is sent with two other soldiers and his Greek wife to the peaceful island of Kos to recuperate. Once there, the men have nothing to do other than guard a deserted fortress and a store of redundant Greek ammunition, and the enforced idleness and isolation drive Stroszek to inner reflections which finally result in madness. Herzog's first feature foreshadows his later preoccupation with outsiders unable to conform to a prescribed structure. Photographed with an impressive feel for the hot and dusty landscape, the film employs images as narrative and as emblems of inner states of being, and does so with remarkable command.

Special Prize Berlin 1968

▶ **Si Jolie Petite Plage, Une** see Such A Pretty Little Beach

The Silence

▶ **Tystnaden**

Sweden 1963 96 mins bw
Svensk/Janus

d Ingmar Bergman
sc Ingmar Bergman
ph Sven Nykvist
m Bo Nilsson, Bach
   Ingrid Thulin, Gunnel Lindblom, Jörgen Lindström, Eduardo Futierrez, Haken Jahnberg

Ester (Thulin), a Lesbian intellectual, is physically attracted to her sister Anna (Lindblom), herself the sexually vibrant mother of a 10-year-old boy. While the carefree Anna indulges in casual sex, her son briefly falls in with a troupe of dwarfs, and Ester wastes away from alcohol and tuberculosis. Bleak, dense, puzzling, and heavy with symbolism, the film is explicitly erotic. Certain scenes (Thulin masturbating, a couple copulating in a cinema) were profoundly shocking at the time – all the more so, perhaps, for the unadorned frankness with which they were presented. Impeccably interpreted by two of the best actresses in Bergman's impressive stable, this is a dark, passionate, elusive and disturbing work.

Silence And Cry

▶ **Csend Es Kiáltás**

Hungary 1968 79 mins bw

Mafilm

d Miklós Jancsó
sc Gyula Hernádi
ph János Kende
   A. Kozák, Zoltán Latinovits, Mari Töröcsik, Andrea Drahota, József Madáras

After the defeat of the first Hungarian Communist regime in 1919, István (Kozák), a fugitive from the White terror of Admiral Horthy's regime, is sheltered on a farm among peasants demoralized by the cruelty of the police. Photographed in a series of long sequences, with each cut representing a time lapse, the film depicts the cruelty, dehumanization and claustrophobia that comes from oppression. Jancsó's ritualistic style manages to make the particular Hungarian situation into a universal parable of evil, ending with a cry of hope.

Le Silence De La Mer

France 1947 86 mins bw
Melville

d Jean-Pierre Melville
sc Jean-Pierre Melville
ph Henri Decaë
m Edgar Bischoff
   Howard Vernon, Jean-Marie Robian, Nicole Stéphane

During the Occupation, a German officer (Vernon), a musician and an intellectual, is billeted in the countryside in the home of an old French farmer (Robian) and his niece (Stéphane). They have sworn never to speak to the invader and listen in silence as the German pours out his ideas and feelings about music, the war and his love of France. Melville's first feature succeeds in transposing Vercors' almost unfilmable parable of the Resistance to the screen. 'I wanted to attempt a language composed entirely of images and sounds, and from which movement and action would be more or less banished,' commented the director. The film is virtually a monologue by the German officer, but a great deal of what is going on beneath the surface is suggested by look and gesture. This sensitive and intense film on the Occupation, a theme the director would return to in *Léon Morin, Priest* and *The Army In The Shadows*, was an influence on the style of Robert Bresson.

Le Silence Est D'Or

▶ **aka Silence Is Golden**

▶ **(US: Man About Town)**

France 1947 100 mins bw
Pathé/RKO

d René Clair
sc René Clair
ph Armand Thirard
m Georges Van Parys
Maurice Chevalier, François Périer,
Marcelle Derrien

In 1906 a middle-aged ex-comedian, now a film-maker (Chevalier), tutors his young assistant (Périer) in the arts of seduction, unaware that they are both in love with the same girl (Derrien). Clair's first French film for over a decade was a bitter-sweet regretful look at the silent cinema in which he began his career. It also reunited him with Chevalier (showing rare depth) with whom he had worked on *Break The News* in 1937. The recreation of the era is more entertaining than the rather strained, leisurely plot.

▶ **Silence Is Golden** see Silence Est D'Or, Le

▶ **Silencieux, Le** see Silent One, The

▶ **Silent Duel, A** see Quiet Duel, A

The Silent One

▶ **(US: Escape To Nowhere)**

▶ **Le Silencieux**

France 1973 113 mins col
S.N.E.G./Trianon (Paris)/Medusa (Rome)

d Claude Pinoteau
sc Jean-Loup Dabadie, Claude Pinoteau
ph Jean Collomb
m Jacques Datin, Alain Goraguer
Lino Ventura, Leo Genn, Robert Hardy,
Lea Massari, Suzanne Flon, Pierre-
Michel Le Conte, Bernard Dhéran

Russian nuclear scientist Haliakov (Ventura) arrives in London, is involved in a car accident, and hospitalized. In fact, it's a put-up job by MI5 who know that he is really Frenchman Clément Tibère, kidnapped by the Russians some years before. The British offer him a new identity in exchange for certain information. . . This plot seems so familiar as to make it appear redundant, but don't be fooled. If spy thrillers are to your taste, you'll enjoy this one for its taut building of suspense, its intelligent exposé of the illusory nature of freedom and, of course, the immaculate Lino Ventura who brings nuances of depth to the character of a man trapped by both past and present circumstances.

The Silent World

▶ **Le Monde Du Silence**

France 1956 86 mins col Filmad/
F.S.J.Y.C.

d Jacques-Yves Cousteau, Louis Malle
sc Jacques-Yves Cousteau, Louis Malle
ph Edmond Séchan
m Yves Baudrier
Frédéric Duman, Albert Falco, Jacques-
Yves Cousteau

The exploration of the fauna and flora of the oceans' depths by Jacques-Yves Cousteau, the famous French oceanographer, diver and documentary film-maker. This extraordinary voyage into an unknown (before all those TV programmes of which Cousteau's were the best), silent (except for music and commentary by Cousteau) world, had no less than four underwater cameramen (including the co-directors) to frighten the most frightening fish. Although 24-year-old Louis Malle had worked with Bresson as assistant on *A Man Escaped* and had participated on Cousteau's voyages for some years, this was his first credit as director. Apart from the boardwalk in *Atlantic City*, he never seemed to go near the sea again in his own films. The film won the documentary Oscar in 1956.

Best Film Cannes 1956

Silken Skin

▶ **(US: The Soft Skin)**

▶ **La Peau Douce**

> France   1964   118 mins   bw
> Films Du Carrosse/SEDIF

d   **François Truffaut**
sc **François Truffaut, Jean-Louis Richard**
ph **Raoul Coutard**
m   **Georges Delerue**
    Jean Desailly, Françoise Dorléac, Nelly
    Benedetti, Daniel Ceccaldi, Laurence
    Bady

A married, middle-aged literature professor (Desailly) falls in love with an air stewardess (Dorléac) after a trip to Lisbon and leaves home for her. When she rejects him, he seeks reconciliation with his wife (Benedetti) who shoots him in a restaurant. After the triumph of *Jules And Jim* (1961), Truffaut followed with another triangle story, this time, as he stated, 'a truly modern love; it takes place in planes, elevators, it has all the harassments of modern life'. Like the title, it has a brilliant surface, but, despite patches of warmth and wit, is uncharacteristically cool with rather remote characters.

▶ **Simón Del Desierto** see Simon Of The Desert

Simon Of The Desert

▶ **Simón Del Desierto**

> Mexico   1965   45 mins   bw
> Gustavo Alatriste

d   **Luis Buñuel**
sc **Luis Buñuel**
ph **Gabriel Figueroa**
m   **Raúl Lavista**
    Claudio Brook, Silvia Pinal, Hortensia
    Santovena, Enrique Alvarez Felix

For six years, six weeks and six days, Simon (Brook), emulating St Simon Stylites, has stood on a pillar in the Mexican desert as an inspiration and example to the peasants who crowd below. The Devil tries to tempt him down, first in the guise of a young woman

(Pinal) and then disguised as Jesus, but Simon will not be moved. Originally conceived as a full-length feature, the film had to be truncated when the money ran out. What another hour might have done to this economical, pointed and wry anecdote can only be surmised, but it stands, like its hero, high above most films with a theological theme. It makes a good companion piece to *Nazarín*, also about the impossibility of absolute piety.

Special Jury Prize Venice 1965

Simon The Swiss

▶ **(US: The Crook)**

▶ **Le Voyou**

> France   1970   120 mins   col
> Les Films Ariane/Les Films 13/Artistes Associés

d   **Claude Lelouch**
sc **Claude Lelouch, Pierre Uytterhoeven,**
    Claude Pinoteau
ph **Jean Collomb**
m   **Francis Lai**
    Jean-Louis Trintignant, Danièle Delorme,
    Charles Gérard, Christine Lelouch, Yves
    Robert, Charles Denner

A crooked lawyer (Trintignant), imprisoned for 20 years for stealing $1 million, escapes, hides in the apartment of a girl (Delorme) he meets at the movies, and leads the police a merry chase through Europe. The antithesis of the sombre gangster films being made in France at the time by Jean-Pierre Melville, this slick caper offers colourful locations, a plug for Simca cars, contrived plot twists, and an appearance by Sacha Distel.

A Simple Case

▶ **Prostoi Sluchai**

> USSR   1932   96 mins   bw
> Mezhrabpomfilm

d   **Vsevolod Pudovkin**
sc **Alexander Rzheshevsky**
ph **G. Bobrov, G. Kabalov**
m   **Silent**
    Aleksandr Baturin, Yevgeniya Rogulina,

A. Gorchilin, A. Chekulaeva, I.
Novoseltsev, Alexander Chistyakov

A Red Army commander (Baturin) and his
wife (Rogulina) endure the danger and deprivation of the Russian Civil War together.
Afterwards, while his wife is away recuperat-
ing in the country, he meets and falls in love
with another woman. He is condemned by
his friends for betraying their 'comrade citizen' and returns to her. In the early 1930s,
the great classics of the Russian cinema,
including those by Pudovkin, were condemned as élitist. This may explain why the
director's last silent film contains such a banal
triangular love conflict, lacking depth or
development. Yet it was criticized as 'overly
abstract and pseudo-significant'. Despite the
restrictions placed on him, Pudovkin achieved
much visual poetry and some virtuoso montage sequences, including a powerful and passionate battle scene and an impressionistic
vision of nature erupting.

A Simple Story

▶ **Un Histoire Simple**

  France 1978 110 mins col
  Renn Productions/Sara Films/
  FR3(Paris)/ Rialto-Film(Berlin)

d **Claude Sautet**
sc **Claude Sautet, Jean-Loup Dabadie**
ph **Jean Boffety**
m **Philippe Sarde**
  **Romy Schneider, Bruno Cremer, Claude
  Brasseur, Arlette Bonnard, Sophie
  Daumier, Roger Pigaut**

Marie (Schneider), divorced and with a teenage son, a lover (Brasseur), a high-powered
job and a circle of women friends, seems
successful and content but is, in fact, questioning the meaning of her life as she
approaches the big Four-0. Her self-examination leads her to break off with her lover
and abort his child, whereupon she has a
reunion of sorts with her ex-husband
(Cremer) and becomes pregnant by him. Pursuing his preoccupation with the 'things of
life' as they affect the fashionable French
middle classes, Sautet has made a fashionable
French middle-class film, in which attractive
people prepare and eat a lot of attractive
food, while grappling with life and love. It's

all superficially agreeable, particularly if
you're a fan of Romy Schneider who gives a
convincing performance, but the director's
aim and object remain rather vague and the
film fails to live up to its pretensions.

The Sin

▶ **aka The Outcast**
▶ **aka The Broken Commandment**
▶ **Hakai**

  Japan 1961 119 mins bw
  Daiei

d **Kon Ichikawa**
sc **Natto Wada**
ph **Kazuo Miyagawa**
m **Yasushi Akutagawa**
  **Raizo Ichikawa, Rentaro Mikune,
  Hiroyuki Nagato, Eiji Fujimura, Ganjiro
  Nakamura**

Segawa (Ichikawa, no relation to the director), born of an *eta* family (the very bottom
of the social scale in 19th-century Japan) and
educated far from his roots, promises his
dying father to hide his class origins forever.
A popular teacher, Segawa finds the strain of
living a lie too much and follows in the
footsteps of the murdered *eta* writer Rentaro
Inoko (Mikune) in campaigning for the rights
of the social outcasts. Although the nuances
of the social background may elude most
Western audiences, there is no escaping the
impact of the situation in which the hero finds
himself, nor the beauty and passion with
which it is expressed. There are dollops of
sentimentality, but fewer than to be found in
Keisuke Kinoshita's 1948 version of the same
novel by Toson Shimazaki.

▶ **Sinbad** see Sindbad

Sindbad

▶ **aka Sinbad**
▶ **Szindbád**

  Hungary 1971 98 mins col
  Mafilm

d **Zoltán Huszárik**

sc Zoltán Huszárik
ph Sándor Sára
m   Zoltán Jeney
    Zoltán Latinovits, Margit Dayka, Éva
    Ruttkai, Erika Szegedi, Bella Tanay

The dying Sindbad (Latinovits), a lifelong
hedonist, thinks back over all the beautiful
women he has loved and all the wonderful
food and drink he has consumed. This startlingly original, impressionistic work, based on
Gyula Krúdy's classic stories in Hungarian
literature, owes a great deal to the director's
recreation of sensuality, aided by Sára's
superb camerawork and Latinovits' performance. The parade of female pulchritude, gastronomic delights, rich costumes and colour
tends to cloy after a while, but that is, after
all, the thematic point of the film.

The Sin Of Father Mouret

▶ (US: The Demise Of Father
  Mouret)
▶ La Faute De L'Abbé Mouret

    France 1970 93 mins col
    Stéphan/Valoria/Les Films Du Carrosse/
    New Films Production (Rome)

d   Georges Franju
sc Georges Franju, Jean Ferry
ph Marcel Fradetal
m   Jean Wiener
    Francis Huster, Gillian Hills, Tino
    Carrero, André Lacombe, Hugo
    Fausto

Father Mouret (Huster), a young parish
priest in a remote area of France, devotes
his life to the worship of the Virgin Mary.
But when he meets a wild young girl (Hills),
the priest gives in to lust with tragic consequences. The purple prose of Zola's novel is
matched by the lush colour photography of
the floral landscape of Provence – the girl
dies smothered by the fragrance of flowers –
a sensuous contrast to the self-abnegatory
nature of the tale. In fact, the overheated
erotic sections work less well than the harshness and violence of the religious scenes
loomed over by Lacombe's fanatic Friar.
Huster and Hills make a pretty pair in
Franju's first colour feature, made near the
end of his career.

Sir Arne's Treasure

▶ aka The Three Who Were
  Doomed
▶ Herr Arnes Pengar

    Sweden 1919 114 mins bw
    Svensk Biografteatern

d   Mauritz Stiller
sc Mauritz Stiller, Gustaf Molander
ph J. Julius Jaenzon
m   Silent
    Hjalmar Selander, Richard Lund, Mary
    Johnson

In 16th-century Denmark, three Scottish mercenaries steal Pastor Arne's treasure, massacre
everyone in the household except his adopted
daughter Elsalill (Johnson) and burn the
house to the ground. Later Elsallil unwittingly
falls in love with the gang's leader Sir Archie
(Lund), but betrays him when she discovers
the truth. Under the influence of his friend
Victor Sjöström, Stiller moved from sophisticated comedies nearer the more sombre Swedish literary tradition with the first of his films
based on the novels of Selma Lagerlöf, in
which the close relation between the landscape
and the characters is explored. Particularly
impressive in this regard is the climax, when
a procession of black-robed figures follow a
coffin across a frozen lake.

▶ Sirène Du Mississippi, La see Mississippi Mermaid, The

▶ Sissi see Forever My Love

▶ Sissi-Die Junge Kaiserin see Forever My Love

▶ Sissi-Schicksalsjahre Einer Kaiserin see Forever My Love

Sisters Of The Gion

▶ Gion No Shimai

    Japan 1936 69 mins bw
    Daiichi Eiga

d   Kenji Mizoguchi
sc Kenji Mizoguchi, Yoshitaka Yoda
ph Minoru Miki

Isuzu Yamada, Yoko Umemura, Benkei Shiganoya, Eitaro Shindo, Taizo Fukami, Fumio Okura

Two Geisha sisters, the elder (Umemura) faithful to the old traditions, the younger (Yamada) more modern in her attitudes, both end up being hurt, the one injured by a jealous ex-lover and the other deserted by a man to whom she had given her love. Mizoguchi's most famous pre-war film, made at the time when realism was entering Japanese cinema, is full of beautifully composed contrasting scenes, gentle humour and pathos. The director condemns neither woman but the society that exploits them.

Sisters Or The Balance Of Happiness

▶ **Schwestern Oder Die Balance Des Glücks**

W. Germany   1979   95 mins   col
Bioskop-Film/Westdeutscher Rundfunk

d   Margarethe Von Trotta
sc Margarethe Von Trotta, with Luise Francia, Martje Grohmann
ph Franz Rath, Thomas Schwan
m   Konstantin Wecker
    Jutta Lampe, Gudrun Gabriel, Jessica Früh, Konstantin Wecker, Heinz Bennent, Agnes Fink

Efficient, high-powered secretary Maria (Lampe) shares a comfortable flat with dreamy, introspective Anna (Gabriel), her younger biology-student sister whom she is supporting – and encouraging, controlling and dominating. When the emotionally fragile Anna can no longer bear her dependency on Maria, she kills herself. Maria takes up with Miriam (Früh), a girl at her office, and starts repeating the pattern of her disastrous sibling relationship. Made two years earlier than Von Trotta's *The German Sisters* (but released later in Britain and the US), this is, in fact, a more coherent and finely controlled work. An intimate study – very well acted – of sibling and 'mother-daughter' relationships, the film also explores the implications of the materialistic society of post-war Germany and the suffocating stranglehold of family guilt. The director's eye for detail and her sensitivity

to the psychology of her characters, make for some telling and visually brilliant moments.

▶ **Siuzhet Dlya Nebloshova Ras-skaza** see Lika, Chekhov's Love

Six In Paris

▶ **Paris Vu Par...**

France   1965   98 mins   col
Films Du Losange/Barbet Schroeder

d   1) Jean Douchet 2) Jean Rouch 3) Jean-Daniel Pollet 4) Eric Rohmer 5) Jean-Luc Godard 6) Claude Chabrol
sc 1) Jean Douchet, Georges Keller 2) Jean Rouch 3) Jean-Daniel Pollet 4) Eric Rohmer 5) Jean-Luc Godard 6) Claude Chabrol
ph 1) Nestor Almendros 2) Etienne Becker 3) and 4) Alain Levent 5) Albert Maysles 6) Jean Rabier
    1) Barbara Wilkind 2) Nadine Ballot, Barbet Schroeder 3) Micheline Dax, Claude Melki 4) Jean- Michel Rouzière, Marcel Gallon 5) Joanna Shimkus 6) Claude Chabrol, Stéphane Audran

1) An American girl is dropped by one French boy only to be picked up by another. 2) After quarrelling with her husband, a wife encounters a wealthy stranger who intends to kill himself. 3) A timid dishwasher brings a prostitute back to his room. 4) A salesman hits a tramp with his umbrella and imagines he has killed him. 5) A girl fears she has mixed up letters to her two lovers. 6) A small boy is so tired of hearing his parents arguing that he buys earplugs and, later, cannot hear his mother's cries for help. These slight but entertaining sketches, of which the one by Chabrol is the best, were shot in 16 mm in different parts of the city.

The Sixth Of July

▶ **Shestoe Iulya**

USSR   1968   112 mins   bw
Mosfilm

d   Yuli Karasik

sc **Mikhail Shatrov**
ph **Mikhail Suslov**
m   **A. Shnitke**
    Yuri Kayurov, Alla Demidova, Vladimir
    Tatosov, Vassily Lanovoi, Vyacheslav
    Shalevich, B. Rizhukhin

In July 1918 (about 10 days before the assassination of the Tsar), under the Treaty of Brest-Litovsk, the newly-born Soviet Republic under the leadership of Lenin (Kayurov) ceded the Ukraine and the Baltic States to Germany in return for peace. An opposing Russian faction, led by Maria Spiridovna (Demidova), opposed the move without success, murdered the German ambassador in Moscow and attempted to overthrow the Bolsheviks. Lenin quelled this uprising by force. Resuscitating an incident little-known or remembered in the West, Karasik has combined a political thriller with a somewhat sketchy history lesson that ignores the welter of political complications surrounding the period, and fails to make clear just how strong Spiridovna's Left Socialist-Revolutionaries were and how close they came to overthrowing Lenin. The film is, nonetheless, well paced and absorbing, notably in the second half when events gather momentum.

▶ **Sjecas Li Se Dolly Bell** see Do You Remember Dolly Bell?

▶ **Sjunde Inseglet, Det** see Seventh Seal, The

▶ **Skammen** see Shame, The

▶ **Skepp Till Indialand** see Ship Bound For India, A

Skin Skin

▶ **Käpy Selän Alla**

Finland 1967 88 mins bw
Mikko Niskanen

d   **Mikko Niskanen**
sc **Marja-Leena Mikkola**
ph **Esko Nevalainen**
m   **Kaj Chydenius**
    Kristina Halkola, Eero Melasniemi, Kirsti
    Wallasväära, Pekka Autiovuori

Four Helsinki students take a camping holiday together. Leena (Wallasväära), hoping to become a writer, is hungry for experience but frightened of sex and not helped by the timidity of her boyfriend (Autiovuori); for Rita, sex is no problem, but she's looking for marriage, which doesn't suit *her* boyfriend. The four learn something of themselves and return home a little sadder and wiser. A lightweight offering, it still has much charm and insight. Niskanen paints an accurate picture of young people searching, often painfully, for identity, the atmosphere of the beautiful Finnish lakes is well caught and the performances are convincing.

▶ **Skønheden Og Udyret** see Beauty And The Beast, The

▶ **Skulpjaci Perja** see Happy Gypsies

Skyline

▶ **La Linea Del Cielo**

Spain 1983 90 mins col
La Salamandra

d   **Fernando Colomo**
sc **Fernando Colomo**
ph **Angel Luis Fernandez**
m   **Miguel Angel Santamaria**
    Antonio Resines, Beatriz Perez-Porro,
    Patricia Cisarano, Jaime Nos, Roy
    Hoffman

Gustavo (Resines), a Spanish photographer, arrives in New York hoping to make it as a photo-journalist. He rents a sumptuous loft, but is short of professional contacts and speaks virtually no English. He goes to English classes, acquires an agent, battles with enforced idleness and, being a bit of a wet, goes home. The movie is not without interest as a bird's eye view of a foreigner's difficulties in the Big Apple, but it is really no more than a vignette suitable for a TV documentary. Shot almost entirely in the small streets and large lofts of Manhattan, the skyline of the title is barely in evidence, and the lack of visual interpretation of the world's most famous modern city is doubly bizarre in a movie concerned with a photographer of buildings.

A Slap In The Face

▶ **Poshchyochina**

USSR 1980 col 90 mins
Armenfilm Studio

d **Genrikh Malyan**
sc **Stepan Aldzhadzhyan**
ph **Sergei Israelyan**
m **Tigran Mansurian**
  **Ashot Adamian, Mger Mkrtchyan, Sofico
  Chiaureli, Galina Belyaeva, Tigran
  Voskonyan**

A simple Armenian saddlemaker
(Mkrtchyan) and his wife (Chiaureli) adopt a
young orphan, Torik (Adamian). The boy,
shy and slightly slow-witted, finally masters
his foster father's trade, but marrying him off
proves insurmountable until three prostitutes
come to town... Malyan's film is reminiscent
of the best French rural comedies of the
1930s. It is beautifully acted; the efforts of
the concerned mother (now widowed) to find
a wife for her boy are both hilarious and
moving. The exposure of *bourgeois* hypocrisy
in the village folk's outraged reaction when
Torik weds a pretty, orphaned whore (Belyaeva), lends an added dimension to this thoroughly charming romance.

A Slave Of Love

▶ **Raba Lubvi**

USSR 1976 94 mins col
Mosfilm

d **Nikita Mikhalkov**
sc **Andrei Mikhalkov-Konchalovsky,
  Friedrich Gorenstein**
ph **Pavel Lebeshev**
m **Eduard Artemyev**
  **Elena Solovei, Rodion Nakhapetov,
  Alexander Kalyagin, Oleg Basilashvili**

In Odessa in 1917, an impoverished film crew
is attempting to complete a dreadful melodrama. They are only dimly aware that the
government has fallen to the Revolution in
Moscow, but distant events become meaningful when the cameraman who has secretly
filmed White Guard atrocities is shot before
the eyes of his lover, the leading actress.

Milhalkov, who had acted in other people's
pictures for 10 years before directing, brought
his knowledge of both sides of the camera to
bear on this bitter-sweet, atmospheric, rather
self-conscious film about filming. The director's obvious affection for his feckless characters is realized in the performances, notably
those of Solovei and Kalyagin as bitchy
actress and batty director respectively.

▶ **Slavnosti A Hostech, O** see Party
And The Guests, The

The Sleeping Car Murders

▶ **Compartiment Tueurs**

France 1965 95 mins bw
PECF

d **Costa-Gavras**
sc **Costa-Gavras**
ph **Jean Tournier**
m **Michel Magne**
  **Yves Montand, Simone Signoret, Pierre
  Mondy, Catherine Allégret, Jacques
  Perrin, Jean-Louis Trintignant, Michel
  Piccoli, Charles Denner, Daniel Gélin,
  Claude Dauphin, Claude Mann**

During the investigation of the murder of a
woman on the overnight express from Marseilles to Paris, some of the suspects are killed.
Costa-Gavras, the maker of distinguished political thrillers such as *Z* (1969), started his
career with this commercially successful, non-
political thriller on the Hollywood model of
the 1940s. Its entertainment value lies mainly
in the starry cast headed by Montand, his
wife Signoret, and her daughter by director
Yves Allégret.

▶ **Slingrevalsen** see Stepping Out

Slow Attack

▶ **Endstation Freiheit**

W. Germany 1980 112 mins col
Bioskop-Film/Planet Film(Munich)/
ZDF(Mainz)

d **Reinhard Hauff**

sc **Burkhard Driest**
ph **Frank Brühne**
m   **Irmin Schmidt**
    Burkhard Driest, Rolf Zacher, Katja
    Rupé, Carla Egerer, Kurt Raab, Eckehard
    Ahrens, Irm Hermann

Nik Dellman (Driest), released after eight years in prison for robbery, decides to write a novel. As his girlfriend Eva (Rupé) has acquired another man and a child, he takes refuge with a friend (Egerer) and, when his prison mate (Zacher) turns up and proposes a heist, Nik refuses, planning a huge crime on paper instead of in fact – until the manuscript is repeatedly turned down... Reinhard Hauff's concern with outsiders and violence surfaces in an imaginative plot, set in a world of subways, bunkers, hermetic rooms and night streets, crisply and atmospherically photographed. A penetrating and absorbing study of character and morals, the film is often strongly reminiscent of Hollywood *film noir* in tone and style.

Slow Motion

▶ **(US: Every Man For Himself)**

▶ **Sauve Qui Peut (La Vie)**

France   1980   87 mins   col
Sonimage/Sara/MK2/Saga/Zoetrope

d   **Jean-Luc Godard**
sc **Jean-Claude Carrière, Anne Marie**
    Miéville
ph **William Lubtchansky, Renato Berta**
m   **Gabriel Yared**
    Isabelle Huppert, Jacques Dutronc,
    Nathalie Baye, Roland Amstutz, Anna
    Baldaccini

Three different characters move between the city and the countryside: Isabelle (Huppert), a country girl, comes to the city and becomes a prostitute, Denise (Baye) seeks out an idyllic pastoral life, and Paul (Dutronc) finds it difficult either to exist in or escape from urban life. 'My second first film,' Godard called it after 12 years away from 'commercial' filmmaking. Using stars, a narrative of sorts, and a somewhat banal theme of the role of sexuality in the consumer society, he retains his artistic integrity by the masterful manipu-

lation of his material, continually re-educating the audience to see and hear differently.

▶ **Smaak Van Water, De** see Taste Of
Water, The

Small Change

▶ **L'Argent De Poche**

France   1976   105 mins   col
Films Du Carrosse/Artistes Associés

d   **François Truffaut**
sc **François Truffaut, Suzanne Schiffman**
ph **Pierre William Glenn**
m   **Maurice Jaubert**
    Geory Desmouceaux, Philippe Goldman,
    Claudio and Franck Deluca, Jean-
    François Stevenin

A series of happenings in the lives of a group of young schoolchildren in a small provincial town, revolving around their wise, protective teacher (Stevenin). Truffaut's way with children was proven in *The Four Hundred Blows* (1959) and *Wild Child* (1970), neither of which sentimentalized or idealized childhood. In contrast, *Small Change*, the English title suggested by Steven Spielberg, tends to lean towards cuteness. Not that there aren't some amusing vignettes such as the boy telling his first dirty joke, and the girl, who has been locked up as punishment, using a loud-hailer to procure food.

Smiles Of A Summer's Night

▶ **Sommarnattens Leende**

Sweden   1955   105 mins   bw
Svensk Filmindustri

d   **Ingmar Bergman**
sc **Ingmar Bergman**
ph **Gunnar Fischer**
m   **Erik Nordgren**
    Gunnar Björnstrand, Eva Dahlbeck, Ulla
    Jacobsson, Harriet Andersson, Margit
    Carlquist, Jarl Kulle, Björn Bjelvenstam

A middle-aged lawyer (Björnstrand), his still-virgin, young wife (Jacobsson) and her stepson (Bjelvenstam) are invited to a country mansion for a summer weekend. Also invited are a beautiful actress (Dahlbeck) who is the lawyer's ex-mistress and the current lover of another guest, and a count (Kulle), there with his wife (Carlquist). During the course of the weekend, couples meet, separate and exchange partners. Beneath the bubbly surface and behind the sensuous light of the Swedish summer of this charmed and charming comedy of manners, the illusions and pretentions of the turn-of-the-century *haute bourgeois* are sharply exposed. The plot, in the tradition of Marivaux, formed the basis of Stephen Sondheim's musical *A Little Night Music*, and was the inspiration behind Woody Allen's *A Midsummer Night's Sex Comedy* (1982). The film was a milestone in Bergman's career, bringing him the prestige and independence to do virtually anything he desired.

The Smiling Madame Beudet

▶ **La Souriante Madame Beudet**

France   1923   32 mins   bw
Film D'Art/Vandal/Dulac-Aubert

d   **Germaine Dulac**
sc **André Obey**
ph **A. Morrin**
m   **Silent**
    Germaine Dermoz, Alexandre C. Arquillière, Madeleine Guitty, Jean D'Yd

The bored wife (Dermoz) of a pompous, bullying merchant (Arquillière), always teasing her by putting a gun to his head, decides to take her revenge. One of the first woman directors in French films (and elsewhere for that matter), Dulac could lay claim to having made the first feminist film with this little gem with an ironic title – Madame Beudet, in fact, only ever smiles in her daydreams. Based on a one-act play by Denys Amiel and André Obey, it uses imaginative techniques such as superimposition, distorted close-ups, and dream images. *The Seashell And The Clergyman* was the other short masterpiece by Dulac, who gave up directing with the coming of sound.

▶ **Smultronstället** see Wild Strawberries

Snares

▶ **(US: Personal Column)**
▶ **Pièges**

France   1939   115 mins   bw
Speva

d   **Robert Siodmak**
sc **Jacques Companeez, Ernst Neubach, Jacques Gantillon**
ph **R. Voinquel, Ted Pahle, Michel Kelber**
m   **Michel Michelet**
    Maurice Chevalier, Marie Déa, Pierre Renoir, Erich Von Stroheim

When a series of young women go missing after replying to advertisements in the personal column of a newspaper, the police enlist the aid of the latest victim's roommate (Déa) to act as a decoy. She meets and falls in love with a prime suspect (Chevalier), but he is arrested. All, however, ends happily. Siodmak's last French-made film before his departure for Hollywood is not his best, but prefigures his American period. With Chevalier cast as a nightclub owner and given a couple of songs to deliver, the piece is an unsatisfying mixture of crime chiller and love story, and somewhat run-of-the-mill in both directions. It is also overlong, but was not improved by 26 minutes of cuts made by the American censors on its first release. The film was remade by Douglas Sirk as *Lured* in 1947.

Snobs

France   1961   90 mins   bw
UFA Comacico/Investissements Overseas Service

d   **Jean-Pierre Mocky**
sc **Jean-Pierre Mocky**
ph **Marcel Weiss**
m   **Joseph Kosma**
    Michel Lonsdale, Gérard Hoffman, Véronique Nordy, Noël Roquevert, Francis Blanche

The president of a milk co-operative is drowned in a vat of milk while inspecting a dairy plant. Four directors become rivals for his post, each playing on the snobbery and foibles of the electors. Mocky continued to live up to his name in his third film, an iconoclastic comedy which he milks unmercifully for laughs. Some good gags can be salvaged from the bawdy slapstick, but not enough to satisfy. Very few of Mocky's many later comedies have made it to the English-speaking world.

So Close To Life

▶ **(US: Brink Of Life)**

▶ **Nara Livet**

Sweden 1957 84 mins bw
Nordisk Tonefilm

d Ingmar Bergman
sc Ingmar Bergman, Ulla Isaksson
ph Max Wilen
   Ingrid Thulin, Eva Dahlbeck, Bibi
   Andersson, Max Von Sydow, Erland
   Josephson, Barbro Hiort Af Ornäs

Three women in a maternity ward: one (Thulin) has had a miscarriage and feels it's a punishment for her marriage break-up; the second (Dahlbeck) is happily married and desperately wanting a child, but loses it; the youngest (Andersson), unmarried, decides to keep her baby after trying an abortion. Mothers-to-be or not to be, that is the question in Bergman's clinical, pessimistic film that hardly strays outside the maternity ward. Although the treatment of birth is realistic, the script is over-literary at times and two of the stories have too-neatly tied endings. However, there are three good reasons for seeing the film – the female leads.

Best Actress (Collective Prize – Thulin, Dahlbeck, Andersson, Ornäs) Cannes 1958

▶ **Sodrásban** see Current

▶ **Soeurs Brontë, Les** see Brontë Sisters, The

▶ **Soft Skin, The** see Silken Skin

▶ **Soir Sur La Plage, Un** see Violent Summer

Un Soir, Un Train

Belgium 1968 90 mins col
Fox Europa/Films Du Siècle/Parc

d André Delvaux
sc André Delvaux
ph Ghislain Cloquet
m Frédéric Devreese
   Yves Montand, Anouk Aimée, Adriana
   Bogdan, Hector Camerlynck, François
   Beukelaers

Mathias (Montand), a rationalist Flemish professor living with Anne (Aimée), a French-speaking theatrical designer, seldom questions his way of life or their relationship. One autumn evening, on a train journey, Anne disappears, and Mathias, set down in an unknown region, begins to look for her while being forced to come to terms with himself. Delvaux's second film is a sensitively photographed and melancholy story of lost love, intermingling past and present, reality and fantasy. As in most of his films, there is an elusive image of womanhood, here ideally embodied by the beautiful Anouk Aimée. Montand drifts enigmatically through the symbol-cluttered screenplay.

Solaris

USSR 1972 165 mins col
Mosfilm/Magna

d Andrei Tarkovsky
sc Andrei Tarkovsky, Friedrich Gorenstein
ph Vadim Yusov
m Eduard Artemyev
   Natalya Bondarchuk, Donatas Banionis,
   Yuri Yarvet, Anatoly Solonitsin

An astronaut travels to a distant space station orbiting the planet of Solaris, to investigate the many deaths occuring there, and the phenomenon whereby people in the thoughts of the space travellers materialize. This visually striking Soviet sci-fi film, based on a novel by Stanislav Lem, manages to convince technologically without reliance on special effects. However, Tarkovsky does take his time in space, and weighs the movie down with somewhat turgid philosophical discussions as the cosmonauts are forced into self-examination.

▶ **Soldiers, The** see Carabiniers, Les

▶ **Soleil Des Voyous, Le** see Action Man

Soleil Ô

▶ aka Oh, Sun

Mauritania 1970 105 mins bw
Shango Production

d Med Hondo
sc Med Hondo
ph François Catonne
m Georges Anderson
   Robert Liensol, Theo Legitimus, Yane
   Barry, Bernard Fresson, Gabriel Glissand,
   Ambroise M'Bia, Jean Baptiste Tiemele

In an unnamed French colony in West Africa,
black men line up before a white priest for
baptism and re-naming – the first step in a
process which simultaneously deracinates and
subjugates them. In France, encouraged by
propaganda, colonial blacks arrive to seek a
better life. What they find is unemployment
but for a handful of 'dirty' jobs, unacceptable
living conditions, naked racism and bureaucratic indifference. Searching for a new form,
Med Hondo has eschewed all conventional
narrative. From the stylized and surreal opening sequences to the episodic adventures of a
particular man (Liensol) – an educated black
who conducts dialogues with a Frenchman
(Fresson) and who functions as a collective
emblem for the immigrant – the director
presents a series of imaginative set-pieces,
linked by voice-over narrative, to investigate
and dramatize a complex web of inter-related
themes. A scathing attack on colonialism, the
film is also a shocking exposé of racism and
a brutal and ironic indictment of Western
capitalist values. If the imagery and sentiments are sometimes crude, simplistic or
heavy-handed, it is nonetheless a gripping and
startlingly original work.

▶ Soliti Ignoti, I see Persons Unknown

Solo Sunny

E. Germany 1979 102 mins col
Deutsche Film Aktien Gesellschaft/
Babelsberg Group

d Konrad Wolf, Wolfgang Kohlhaase
sc Wolfgang Kohlhaase
ph Eberhard Geick
m Günther Fischer

Renate Krössner, Alexander Lang, Dieter
Montag, Heide Kipp, Klaus Brasch

Ex-factory worker Sunny (Krössner) sings
and travels with a pop group called The
Tornadoes, but wants to go solo. She also
has trouble with the men in her life – a
saxophone player (Brasch), a taxi-driver
(Montag) and a musician-philosopher (Lang).
An interesting, perceptive and sometimes
amusing portrait of a young woman trying
to find independence against the uncapti-
vating background of East German bars and
cabarets. It greatly appealed to East German
youth, the theme song became a hit and it
seemed to steer the cinema of the GDR into
a less restricted direction. The film's main
strength lies in the terse script and the vibrant
performance from the pretty and petite
Krössner.

Best Actress (Renate Krössner) Berlin 1980

Somewhere In Europe

▶ (US: It Happened In Europe)
▶ Valahol Európában

Hungary 1947 90 mins bw
Mafirt-Radványi

d Géza Radványi
sc Géza Radványi, Béla Bálazs, Judit Fejér,
   Félix Máriássy
ph Barnabás Hegyi
m Dénes Buday
   Arthur Somlay, Zsuzsa Bánki, Miklós
   Gábor, Laci Horváth, György Bárdy

A band of thieving and begging orphans takes
refuge in a castle inhabited by an orchestra
conductor (Somlay), and find a new way of
life in contrast to the bitter realities of post-
war Hungary. Hungary's first international
success for many years led to the cinema
becoming a nationalized industry, and
marked the return to creative work in his
homeland (after wartime exile in the USSR)
of Béla Bálazs, the great film theorist and
author. The Neo-Realist-influenced film
addresses the problems facing a new generation with directness and optimism.

▶ Sommaren Med Monika see Summer With Monika

▶ **Sommarlek** see Summer Interlude

▶ **Sommarnattens Leende** see Smiles Of A Summer's Night

▶ **Söndag I September, En** see Sunday In September, A

▶ **Song of Bwana Toshi, The** see Bwana Toshi

The Song Of The Red Ruby

▶ **Sangen Om Den Røde Rubin**

▶ **aka Den Røde Rubin**

Denmark   1970   106 mins   col
Palladium

d   **Annelise Meineche**
sc   **Annelise Meineche, John Hilbard**
ph   **Erik Wittrup Willumsen**
m   **Øle Hoyer**
     Øle Soltøft, Ghita Norby, Lotte Horn, Annie Birgit Garde, Gertie Jung, Lizzi Varencke, Eva Weinreich

Ash Burlefoot (Soltøft) dreams of becoming a great musician but is constantly waylaid by his insatiable appetite for women, two of whom he makes pregnant. Eventually, he falls in love with a teacher (Norby), settles down, and realizes his ambitions. Trumpeted as a frank account of a young man's journey to maturity, and taken from a best-selling novel by Agnar Mykle, this film is, in fact, a series of undernourished sexual and romantic clichés. Mediocre acting and pedestrian direction fail to improve matters.

▶ **Sonnenstrahl** see Ray Of Sunshine, A

▶ **Sorcières De Salem, Les** see Witches of Salem, The

▶ **Sorok Pervyi** see Forty First, The

The Sorrow And The Pity

▶ **Le Chagrin Et La Pitié**

France   1971   270 mins   bw
Télévision Rencontre (France)/
Norddeutscher
Rundfunk (Hamburg)/S.S.R.(Lausanne)

d   **Marcel Ophüls**
sc   **Marcel Ophüls, André Harris**
ph   **André Gazut, Jürgen Thieme**
m   **Popular songs of the period**

Four-and-a-half hours of footage largely consists of interviews with inhabitants of the city of Clermont-Ferrand who lived through World War II. A probing, incisive and fluent interviewer, as well as a brilliantly accomplished documentary director, Ophüls (son of Max) ruthlessly exposes the degree of collaboration among the French citizenry. He also talks to former members of the Resistance and some of the Nazi occupiers, inter-cutting archive material of Hitler in Paris and famous figures of the day going about their business – for example, Danielle Darrieux blithely setting off to tour Germany. The soundtrack, featuring Maurice Chevalier, is a masterstroke in setting period and ironically counterpointing the realities of the subject. Made for French TV which then refused to show it, it went on cinema release where its ugly revelations courted both acclaim and bitter controversy. In finally uncovering the still unwelcome topic of collaboration, Ophüls opened the way for feature film-makers to re-examine the war, beginning notably with Louis Malle's *Lacombe Lucien*.

▶ **Soshun** see Early Spring

▶ **S.O.S. Mediterranean** see Hell's Cargo

▶ **Souffle Au Coeur, Le** see Dearest Love

▶ **Sound Of Trumpets, The** see Job, The

▶ **Soupirant, Le** see Suitor, The

▶ **Souriante Madame Beudet, La** see Smiling Madame Beudet, The

▶ **Sous Le Soleil De Satan** see Under Satan's Sun

Sous Les Toits De Paris

▶ **aka Under The Roofs Of Paris**

France   1929   92 mins   bw

Tobis

d **René Clair**
sc **René Clair**
ph **Georges Périnal**
m **Armand Bernard**
Albert Préjean, Pola Illery, Gaston Modot, Edmond Gréville

A street singer (Préjean) falls for a pretty Romanian girl (Illery) whom he protects from her lecherous lover (Modot), but he is accused of theft. Although this is one of the very first French talkies, it doesn't have a great deal of talk. What it has is a wisp of a story with sound effects and street noises (studio created), sometimes purposefully drowning out the dialogue for effect, and a number of pleasant songs. The title song is rendered by various Parisians, with the camera moving from singer to singer, from house to house. Creaky as much of it seems today, it still retains considerable charm and is a good example of the more fluent, early French sound films.

The South

▶ **El Sur**

Spain 1983 94 mins col
Elias Querejeta/Chloe/Spanish Radio Television

d **Victor Erice**
sc **José Luis Lopez Linares**
ph **José Luis Alcaine**
Omero Antonutti, Lola Cardona, Sonsoles Aranguren, Iciar Bollan, Rafaela Aparicio

A young girl grows up in the 1950s away from her enigmatic Republican father, imagining things about him, including an affair with a famous actress, and the South where he lives. Erice's second film came an astonishing 10 years after the much-acclaimed *The Spirit Of The Beehive*. It was worth the wait. Like the previous film, the world is seen through the sensibility of a child – poetic, elusive and mysterious. There is also a wonderful rapport between the director and the two young actresses (Aranguren aged eight, Bollan aged 15) who play the daughter. Unfortunately, because of a disagreement with the producer, a second part was abandoned.

South

▶ **Sur**

Argentina 1988 127 mins col
Cinesur(Buenos Aires)/Pacific/Canal Plus(Paris)

d **Fernando E Solanas**
sc **Fernando E Solanas**
ph **Felix Monti**
m **Astor Piazzola**
Miguel Angel Sola, Susu Pecoraro, Philippe Léotard, Lito Cruz, Ulises Dumont

In 1983, after five years in prison on charges of subversion, Floreal (Sola) is released, but finds he must reckon with the past before he can find the strength to return home and face the future. His wife (Pecoraro), meanwhile, has her own adjustments to make, having endured the nightmare of his absence, with the help of his best friend (Léotard) who, in her loneliness, she allowed to become her lover. Following on *Tangos, The Exile Of Gardel*, Solanas (himself a former exile) again deals with the theme but, this time, it's the exile of imprisonment which tears life and relationships apart, and it's a far more sombre film than its predecessor. The lead performances are beautifully controlled and the film is magnificent to look at as Floreal wanders through dreams and memories in the neighbourhood from which he was cruelly removed. As with *Tangos*, the music once again plays a cardinal role in the evocation of emotion and atmosphere but the piece suffers from a profusion of incidental characters and occurrences that serve only to confuse.

Best Director Cannes 1988

▶ **Sparkling Winds** see Confrontation, The

The Sparrow

▶ **Al Asfour**

Egypt 1973 120 mins col
Misr-International(Cairo)/ONCIC(Algeria)

d **Youssef Chahine**
sc **Lofti El Kholly, Youssef Chahine**

ph **Mustapha Imam**
m **Sheikh Imam, Ali Ismaïl, N. Bahgat**
   Mahmoud El Miligui, Habiba, Mohsena
   Tewfik, Meriam Fakhreddine, Salah
   Kabil, Aly El Sharif, Seif El Dine

It is 1967 and the Arabs have lost the war
with Israel. Several parallel stories bring their
Left- wing protagonists together at the house
of Bahiah who releases a sparrow – symbol
of the Egyptian people – from its cage and
leads his fellow men into the streets of Cairo
in a surge of proud defiance. Stylistically
adventurous and politically explosive, Chahine's uncompromising attack on corruption
and weakness among the ruling classes was
banned for several years in most Arab countries. This film is a cry for solidarity, not just
among oppressed classes but among Arab
nations, and attempts to show how the war
was lost from within. Chahine's pleas, first
made in the narrower context of *The Land*
(1969), are couched in dramatic, powerful and
imaginative cinematic language that grips the
attention and makes this one of the most
acclaimed works in the Arab cinema.

The Sparrow Of Pigalle

▶ **Piaf**

   France   1974   105 mins   col
   Films Feuer/Ernie Martin Films

d **Guy Casaril**
sc **Françoise Ferley, Guy Casaril**
ph **Edmond Séchan**
m **Ralph Burns plus the Piaf song repertoire**
   Brigitte Ariel, Pascale Christophe, Guy
   Tréjean, Pierre Vernier, Jacques Duby,
   Anouk Ferjac

In the first 20 years of her life, Edith Piaf,
born in the gutter, faced poverty, illness and
degradation, before her magical voice, extraordinary presence and spirited determination
hauled her up to stardom. Based on the book
by Piaf's half-sister Simone Berteaut, Casaril's film does little either to illumine or
enhance the Piaf legend, being an absolutely
superficial account of the disasters that dogged her young life. Musically, too, it's a
mishmash, using stills of the real Piaf with
her voice over, Ariel miming to some of the
songs, and with yet others sung by Betty
Mars. On the credit side, the colourful sleaze
of pre-war Pigalle is very well caught, Ariel

looks suitably waif-like and Christophe is
excellent as Momone (otherwise Berteaut),
Edith's self-appointed protector.

A Special Day

▶ **Una Giornata Particolare**

   Italy   1977   105 mins   col
   Champion/Canafox

d **Ettore Scola**
sc **Ettore Scola, Ruggero Maccari, Maurizio**
   Costanzo
ph **Pasqualino De Santis**
m **Armando Trovaioli**
   Sophia Loren, Marcello Mastroianni,
   John Vernon, Françoise Berd, Nicole
   Magny

Two lonely residents of a seedy apartment
building – the weary mother of six children
and a homosexual radio announcer – are
drawn together on a day in 1938 while the
populace is in the streets cheering Hitler's
visit to Mussolini in Rome. Some of the minor
appeal of this depressing, contrived piece is
in the casting against type of Loren as a
frumpish housewife, and Mastroianni as a
gay man. The political background is merely
an excuse to show that repression is a common bond between two differing people, even
to the point of making love.

▶ **Special Section** see Section Spéciale

Special Treatment

▶ **Poseban Tretman**

   Yugoslavia   1980   93 mins   col
   Centar Film

d **Goran Paskaljević**
sc **Dušan Kovačević, Filip David, Goran**
   Paskaljević
ph **Aleksandar Petković**
m **Vojislav Kostić, Wagner, Dvořák**
   Ljuba Tadić, Dušica Žegarac, Milena
   Dravić, Danilo Stojković, Petar Kralj,
   Milan Srdoć

Dr Ilich (Tadić) runs a sanatorium for
alcoholics where his cure consists of strict diet
and exercise, extensive playing of Wagner's
music and, above all, the use of psychodrama.

His supposedly progressive methods, however, mask his own moral decline and disaster strikes his group during a visit to a brewery. This is a well-made and expertly acted allegory about authoritarianism and the imprisonment of the individual will, but a lot of heavy-handed symbolism is tacked on to a somewhat meagre plot. It remains in the memory more because it is so depressing than for any other reason.

▶ **Speriamo Che Sia Femmina** see Let's Hope It's A Girl

Spetters

Holland   1983   109 mins   col
VSE

d   **Paul Verhoeven**
sc **Gerard Soeteman**
ph **Jöst Vacano**
m   **Ton Scherpenzeel, Kayak**
    Toon Agterberg, Maarten Spanjer, Hans
    Van Tongeren, Renée Soutendijk,
    Marianne Boyer

Three young men, involved with a scheming blonde who runs a hot-dog stand, dream of winning the motor-cross championships, but disillusion sets in after one is beaten up and another is crippled in an accident. Despite the explicit sex, gay and straight, graphic violence and motor-bike action, *Spetters*, which means grease spots or whizz-kids, is not your average teen exploitation movie. Using its elements and delirious visuals, Holland's leading director pulls out all the stops but also peels off the leather-jacketed characters to reveal the hollowness of their dreams.

Spices

▶ **Mirch Marsala**

India   1986   125 mins   col
National film Development Corp.

d   **Ketan Mehta**
sc **Ketan Mehta, Shafi Hakim**
ph **Jenhangir Choudhury**
m   **Rajat Dholakia**
    Naseeruddin Shah, Smita Patil, Om Puri,
Suresh Oberoi, Deepti Naval, Benjamin Gillani

A brutal tax collector (Shah) arrives in a small rural community in the early 1940s where he takes a shine to Sonbai (Patil), a married woman whose husband is away seeking work in Bombay. She refuses him and when his soldiers try to capture her, she takes refuge in a spice factory with other girls and an old watchman (Puri), who closes the gates and defends her. The film starts off as a populist piece of Hindu cinema interspersed with songs and dances, a colourful melodrama with stereotyped characters – the evil villain stroking his curling moustache, the ignorant and exploited peasants, the bespectacled, idealistic schoolmaster, the young lovers wanting to elope to avoid an arranged marriage, the outraged father and a beautiful, wronged and faithful heroine. However, it is soon apparent that the fast-paced and exciting film asks serious questions about the role of women in society, using its village setting as a microcosm. It is really the story of three women rebelling against their oppression. The wife of the village chief takes her small daughter to school where only boys are permitted to attend; the young girl makes love to a boy before marriage; Sonbai will not accept the *droit de seigneur*, and it is the collective will of the women which settles the issue at the climax. There are also tragi-comic scenes involving the men, especially an episode which shows the tax collector (the Subedar) playing his phonograph to the astonishment of the villagers. The passionate tale is told against the background of a blue lake and fields of red chillies. It was the last of the superb actress Smita Patil's 70 films. She died in childbirth soon after filming was complete, the knowledge of which lends the film an added tragic dimension.

Spicy Rice

▶ **aka Dragon's Food**

▶ **Drachenfutter**

W. Germany   1987   75 mins   bw
Novoskop Film Jan Schütte (West Germany)/Probst Film (Switzerland)

d   **Jan Schütte**
sc **Jan Schütte, Thomas Strittmatter**

ph **Lutz Konermann**
m **Claus Bantzer**
   Bhaskar, Ric Young, Buddy Uzzaman,
   Wolf-Dieter Sprenger, Ulrich Wildgruber,
   Peter Fitz

Two young immigrants in Germany, a Pakis-
tani (Bhaskar) without a work permit, and a
Chinese waiter (Ric Young), decide to start
their own restaurant where they employ a
mixture of struggling immigrants like themselves. Thirty-year-old Schütte manages a
delightful new slant on the oft-treated immigrant problem in Germany through affectionate observation of his melting pot of
characters. The fact that very few of them
can understand each other – they communicate in Urdu, Swahili, Mandarin, Gujarati
and pidgin German – puts the spectator in
their position, yet doesn't obscure what is
happening. A film that enriches and enter-
tains, and possibly creates more tolerance
than more strident projects – and all the more
praiseworthy for succeeding at an unfashion-
ably short length and in black-and-white.

The Spiders

▶ **Die Spinnen**

   Germany   1919-1920   80 mins (Part I);
   94 mins (Part II)   bw
   Decla-Bioscop

d **Fritz Lang**
sc **Fritz Lang**
ph **Emil Schünemann (Part I), Karl Freund**
   (Part II)
m **Silent**
   Carl De Vogt, Lil Dagover, Ressel Orla,
   Paul Morgan, Georg John, Rudolf
   Lettinger, Thea Zander

I. 'The Golden Lake': Hoog (De Vogt) is
pitted against Lio-Shah (Orla) and the criminal gang, The Spiders, all rivals in a search
for Inca treasure in a subterranean city. II.
'The Diamond Ships': Hoog, Lio-Shah and
The Spiders are after a diamond, shaped like
the head of Buddha, the wearer of which will
rule Asia. One of Fritz Lang's earliest works
seems to have been inspired by the German
pulp writer Karl May and the serials of Louis
Feuillade, but Langian elements are already
implanted – the use of mirrors, hypnosis,
underground chambers and arch criminals –

that would reappear frequently throughout
his *oeuvre*. 'I simply wanted to film adventurous subjects...I loved everything that was
exuberant and exotic', Lang stated. The two
stories, broken up into many episodes in the
serial structure, are certainly exuberant and
exotic, filmed against gigantic architectural
sets with ordinary German sunshine providing the lighting effects.

The Spider's Stratagem

▶ **Strategia Del Ragno**

   Italy   1970   110 mins   col
   Radiotelevisione Italiana

d **Bernardo Bertolucci**
sc **Bernardo Bertolucci, Eduardo De**
   Gregorio, Marilu Parolini
ph **Vittorio Storaro, Franco Di Giacomo**
m **Verdi, Schoenberg**
   Alida Valli, Giulio Brogi, Tino Scotti,
   Pino Campanini

A young man (Brogi) revisits the village in
the Po valley where his father was murdered
by the Fascists in 1936, but gradually discovers that the hero he thought his father to
be, was really a traitor. Jorge Luis Borges'
story, *Theme Of The Traitor And The Hero*,
transposes easily from Ireland to Italy, though
it comes across on screen as an over-elaborate
piece of Oedipal plotting. However, much of
it is intriguing and the photography, sometimes evoking the paintings of De Chirico, is
memorable.

The Spies

▶ **Les Espions**

   France   1957   120 mins   bw
   Filmsonor/Vera Films

d **Henri-Georges Clouzot**
sc **Henri-Georges Clouzot, Jérôme Jeronimi**
ph **Christian Matras**
m **Georges Auric**
   Curt Jurgens, Gérard Séty, Peter Ustinov,
   Sam Jaffe, Vera Clouzot, O.E. Hasse

A second-rate psychiatrist (Séty), running a
shabby sanatorium with only a couple of
patients in residence, is offered a generous
sum of money by the American military to

harbour a mystery personage. The bemused doctor accepts and a stranger (Jurgens) – purportedly a top-level German physicist – arrives, followed by a bevy of international spies and some rather curious replacements for the hospital staff... Leaving the ingenuity of *Les Diaboliques* behind him, Clouzot ventured into the formula territory of the espionage thriller and came up with a formula entertainment. The director's command of atmosphere and gift for suspense is laid on a bit too thickly, but there is some good acting, especially from Vera Clouzot, very moving as a genuine patient.

▶ **Spinnen, Die** see Spiders, The

The Spirit Of The Beehive

▶ **El Espiritu De La Colmene**

Spain 1973 98 mins col
Elias Querejeta

d **Victor Erice**
sc **Francisco J. Querejeta**
ph **Luis Cuadrado**
m **Luis De Pablo**
  Ana Torrent, Isabel Telleria, Fernando Fernan Gomez, Teresa Gimpera

In a remote Castilian village in 1940, eight-year-old Ana (Torrent) becomes obsessed with Boris Karloff's good-bad monster in *Frankenstein* seen at a travelling film show, and believes that a fugitive whom she befriends is the spirit of the monster. Most of what happens in this sensitive, cryptic film is reflected in the wide, brown eyes of the lonely little girl, creating the world of a child's imagination, more effective for being shot realistically. A profoundly impressive first film by Erice, it drew beautifully underplayed performances from the non-professional cast. For those willing to look, it also says something about Franco's Spain.

Spirits Of The Dead

▶ **Histoires Extraordinaires**
▶ **aka Tre Passi Nel Delirio**

France/Italy 1968 117 mins col

Les Films Marceau/Cocinor/P.E.A.

d 1) **Roger Vadim** (*Metzengerstein*),
   2) **Louis Malle** (*William Wilson*),
   3) **Federico Fellini** (*Toby Dammit*)
sc 1) **Roger Vadim, Pascal Cousin, Clement Biddle Wood** 2) **Louis Malle, Daniel Boulanger, Clement Biddle Wood**
   3) **Federico Fellini, Bernardino Zapponi, Clement Biddle Wood**
ph 1) **Claude Renoir** 2) **Tonino Delli Colli**
   3) **Giuseppe Rotunno**
m 1) **Jean Prodromidès** 2) **Diego Masson**
   3) **Nino Rota**
   1) **Jane and Peter Fonda, Carla Marlier, James Robertson Justice** 2) **Alain Delon, Brigitte Bardot, Katia Christina**
   3) **Terence Stamp, Salvo Randone**

1) In the Middle Ages, a young woman believes that the spirit of the cousin she loved, killed in a stable fire that she had ignited, was transferred to a horse that escaped. 2) A mean-spirited, gambling Austrian officer murders his *doppelgänger*, confesses and kills himself. 3) A famous British film star, after making a movie in Rome, gets very drunk at the end-of-shooting party and is beheaded while speeding in his Maserati. All three episodes are based on the macabre tales of Edgar Allan Poe; the third, the only one updated, is far and away the best, though pretty familiar Fellini territory. Malle's telling is handsome and straightforward and the detail gruesome; while Vadim saw to it that his wife (Fonda) wore revealing clothes, and caused an incestuous *frisson* by casting her brother as her lover.

The Splendid Days

▶ **Seryozha**

USSR 1960 80 mins bw
Mosfilm

d **G. Danieli, Igor Talankin**
sc **Vera Panova, G. Danieli, Igor Talankin**
ph **A. Nitochkin**
m **B. Chaikovsky**
  Boria Barchatov, Sergei Bondarchuk, Irina Skobotseva, Natasha Chechetkina, Seryosha Metelitsin, Yura Kozlov

Five-year-old Seryozha (Barchatov) lives on

a farm with his widowed mother (skobtseva). One summer's day, she brings home the burly Korostelyov (Bondarchuk) and introduces him as the boy's new father. The summer passes in the typical activities of childhood but, as Seryozha rides his bicycle or plays with his friends, he is constantly under a cloud of unease. Two young directors, working from a story by Panova, a well-known Russian children's novelist, have come up with an intimate, detailed and often charming observation of childhood and a child's psychology. Seryozha's gradual perception of his stepfather's sterling qualities and the way in which the family becomes a welded and loving whole is conveyed with simplicity and truth. Unfortunately, it is also heavily garnished with sentimentality and 'poetic' effects and, nowadays, has an even more curiously old-fashioned air than it already suffered from on its original release.

Splendor

Italy 1989 110 mins col/bw
Cecchi Gori Group/Tiger
Cinematografica/Studio E.L./Gaumont
(Paris)/R.A.I.

d **Ettore Scola**
sc **Ettore Scola**
ph **Luciano Tovoli**
m **Armando Trovaioli**
Marcello Mastroianni, Marina Vlady, Massimo Troisi, Paolo Panelli, Pamela Villoresi

Jordan (Mastroianni), owner of the cinema in a small provincial town, has fallen victim to declining audiences and resulting debt, and is forced to sell out to a commercial property developer. On the night of the final performance he, his loyal usherette and former mistress (Vlady), and his heartbroken projectionist, Luigi (Troisi), remember the past... Scola's nostalgic homage to the cinema and its artists is also a cry of rage at the philistinism of television. It coincided with Tornatore's *Cinema Paradiso* and was torpedoed by the success of the latter – unfairly so. Certainly his competitor's film is smoother, glossier and more epic, but *Splendor* achieves a greater coherence of theme and is much the richer in characterization. Mastroianni is perfectly

cast, as is Marina Vlady, matured into attractive middle age. But the triumph is the larger-than-life character of Luigi, both as conceived by Scola and performed by the ebullient and uninhibited Massimo Troisi. Luigi is the extreme, indeed somewhat alarming, exemplar of the powerful hold that the cinema can have, and to him are given some of the film's best moments. The scene where he attempts to put the small son of his girlfriend to sleep by recounting the plot of Billy Wilder's *Ace In The Hole* is the most sparkling of the film's several comic gems. Scola's handling of switches in time, and between colour and black and white, are not always easily handled and his exposition is sometimes over-leisurely, but with its poignant story and its massive collection of clips from films ranging far and wide in period and nationality, *Splendor* is an irresistible collector's piece for all movie-lovers.

Spoiled Children

▶ **Des Enfants Gâtés**

France 1977 113 mins bw
Films 66/Little Bear/Sara Film/Gaumont

d **Bertrand Tavernier**
sc **Christine Pascal, Charlotte Dubreuil, Bertrand Tavernier**
ph **Alain Levent**
m **Philippe Sarde**
Michel Piccoli, Christine Pascal, Michel Aumont, Gérard Jugnot, Arlette Bonnard

A famous film director (Piccoli), unable to concentrate on his new script at home with his family, rents a high rise apartment. Instead of finding peace and quiet, he gets involved in the tenants' fight against an exploitative landlord, and with a girl (Pascal) half his age. Tavernier, staunch defender of *Le Cinéma De Papa*, the more traditional style of narrative in pre-*Nouvelle Vague* days, has come up with another of his own examples. This 'dramatic comedy' of a 'blocked' artist exchanging an ivory tower for a tower block never goes much below the surface of the issues it raises – feminism, art vs life, modern Paris vs the Paris of the past – but Piccoli brings credence to the central role.

▶ **Spoorloos** see Vanishing, The

Spring Into Summer

▶ **Pleure Pas La Bouche Pleine**

France 1973 117 mins col
Renn Productions/Les Films Du Chef-
Lieu/ORTF

d **Pascal Thomas**
sc **Pascal Thomas, Roland Duval, Suzanne
Schiffman**
ph **Colin Monnier**
m **Vladimir Cosma**
   **Annie Cole, Frédéric Duru, Jean Carmet,
Christiane Chamaret, Bernard Menez,
Daniel Ceccaldi**

Annie (Cole) and Frédéric (Duru), aged 16
and 19 respectively, are courting during the
summer in Poitou where they live. Secretly,
Annie yearns for some excitement and when
Alexandre (Menez), superficially more sophisticated than the local boys, comes to Poitou,
she gets it. Fragile and charming, this is,
refreshingly, a female rites of passage film,
played in the context of happy family relationships and everyday people doing everyday
things. Annie's sexual initiation, the centre of
a story in which nothing much happens, is
handled with matter-of-fact truth, and
Thomas brings to the whole enterprise an
observant eye for the details of village life.

Spring River Flows East

▶ **Yijiang Chunshui Xiang Dong
Liu**

China 1947 188 mins bw
LinHua Film Company

d **Cai Chusheng, Zheng Junli**
sc **Cai Chusheng, Zheng Junli**
ph **Zhu Jimming**
m **Zhang Zhengfan**
   **Tao Jin, Pai Yang, Wu Yin, Yan
Gongshang, Shu Xiuwen**

An initially idealistic schoolteacher (Jin),
leaves his father and mother (Gongshang and
Yin), his young wife (Yang) and his child to
join the Red cross and take part in the struggle
against the Japanese in 1931. He is captured,
but escapes to the Kuômintang capital

Chongqing, where he is seduced by *bourgeois*
life and bigamously marries a high-society
woman (Xiuwen), while his family suffers
extreme deprivation in occupied Shanghai.
Made in two parts, titled 'Wartime Separation' and 'Darkness And Dawn', this is one
of Chinese cinema's greatest pre-Revolution-
ary achievements. Sprawling, often sentimental and simplistic, it is also richly entertaining,
illuminating the whole tumultuous era it
covers, and immensely involving. The cross-
cutting between parallel stories not only demonstrates the social contradictions in the
country, but allows Junli (the director of
Crows And Sparrows) and the veteran Chusheng (who apparently worked mainly on the
script) to present both powerful drama and
sophisticated comedy sequences.

▶ **Spring Shower** see Marie – A Hungarian Legend

Spring Symphony

▶ **Frühlingssinfonie**

W. Germany/E. Germany 1983 103
mins col
Allianz/Peter Schamoni/ZDF/DEFA/
Greentree

d **Peter Schamoni**
sc **Peter Schamoni**
ph **Gerard Vandenberg**
m **Schumann**
   **Nastassja Kinski, Herbert Grönemeyer,
Rolf Hoppe, Anja-Christine Preussler,
Bernhard Wicki, Edda Seipel, André
Heller, Gideon Kremer**

The love affair of composer Robert Schumann (Grönemeyer) and the gifted pianist Clara
Wieck (Kinski), from their meeting in adolescence (the younger Clara played by Preussler) when Wieck's father (Hoppe) taught
Schumann the piano, until their wedding.
Schamoni's film is an ambitious failure. It
paints a vivid picture of Clara's relationship
with her over-possessive father who tries to
prevent the marriage; it wanders, in typical
biopic fashion, through the concert halls of
Europe with Clara as she is hailed a virtuoso
by everybody from Goethe to Chopin. What
Schamoni fails to do is bring the complexities,

excitement and difficulty of genius to life. The movie is dull, reverent and superficial, leaving little besides the glorious outpouring of music, interpreted by several great artists such as Dietrich Fischer-Dieskau, Wilhelm Kempff and Ivo Pogorelich.

▶ **Sreo Sam Cak I Srecne Cigane** see Happy Gypsies

▶ **Stachka** see Strike

Stalker

USSR   1979   161 mins   col/bw
Mosfilm

d   **Andrei Tarkovsky**
sc **Boris and Arkady Strugatsky**
ph **Aleksandr Knyazhinsky**
m   **Eduard Artemyev**
    Aleksandr Kaidanovsky, Anatoly Solonitsin, Nikolai Grinko

The stalker (Kaidanovsky) guides a writer (Solonitsin) and a scientist (Grinko) to the centre of a dangerous, overgrown, forbidden area called the Zone where a room is said to contain the Truth. One wonders if the long (almost three hours of screen time) journey was really necessary when the writer and scientist, on reaching their destination, discuss their differing viewpoints in terms of bad didactic drama reminiscent of the 1930s, and little truth is revealed to them or to the spectator. But Tarkovsky's strength lies in startling images and the creation of mystical *milieux* rather than in narrative, and the nightmarish trip undertaken by the shaven-headed stalker and his companions, shot in eerie sepia colour, haunts the memory.

Stammheim

W. Germany   1986   107 mins   col
Bioskop-Film/Thalia Theater/Filmverlag Der Autoren

d   **Reinhard Hauff**
sc **Stefan Aust**
ph **Frank Brühne**
m   **Marcel Wengler**
    Ulrich Tukur, Therese Affolter, Sabine Wagner, Hans Kremer, Ulrich Pleitgen,
    Marina Wandruszka, Hans Christian Rudolph, Gunther Flesch, Horst Mendroch

A dramatized account of the notorious Baader-Meinhof trial that shook Germany from 1975 to 1977. One of the defendants dies at the outset as a result of a hunger strike; during the trial Ulrike Meinhof (Affolter) is found dead in her cell, an apparent suicide; the chief prosecutor is murdered before the end of the proceedings at which Andreas Baader (Tukur) and the other two defendants are sentenced to life imprisonment, only to be found dead shortly afterwards. Director Hauff, who had already demonstrated his concern with man's relationship to authority in *Knife In The Head* and *Slow Attack*, has brought this most controversial of political trials to the screen with gripping and powerful conviction. That the screenplay is largely taken from the trial transcript and the action confined mainly to the courtroom at Stammheim prison (recreated in an old Hamburg warehouse), does not limit the sense of action. Made on a tiny budget with the help of the Thalia Theater Ensemble – it was refused official funding – the film caused a major furore at the Berlin Festival.

Best Film Berlin 1986

▶ **Stärker Als Die Nacht** see Stronger Than The Night

▶ **Staroye I Novoye** see General Line, The

Stars

▶ **Sterne**

E. Germany/Bulgaria   1959   95 mins   bw
DEFA(Berlin)/Studiya Za Igralni Filmi(Sofia)

d   **Konrad Wolf**
sc **Anzhel Wagenstein**
ph **Werner Bergmann**
m   **Simeon Pironkov**
    Sascha Kruscharska, Jürgen Frohriep, Erik S. Klein, Stefan Pejtschew, Milka Tujkowa

A small Bulgarian town in 1943. In the

schoolyard, now a barbed-wire prison, a consignment of Greek Jews awaits deportation to the death camps. A young Jewess (Kruscharska) and a German soldier (Frohriep) fall in love and he determines to save her. When he fails, his new awareness of his country's atrocities and his guilt at his own complicity fuel his decision to join the Partisans and fight the Nazi regime. Written by a Bulgarian Jew and directed by a former Red Army officer, *Stars* – the badge of the doomed Jewish fate as well as the romantic canopy for the lovers – is a convincing re-creation of a specific time and place. Wolf, one of East Germany's finest directors, has admirably avoided the pitfalls of melodrama and maudlin sentimentality, offering instead haunting and graphically realistic images of despair in a film that is both moving and thought provoking.

Special Jury Prize Cannes 1959

State Of Siege

▶ **État De Siège**

France   1973   120 mins   col
Reggana/Cinema 10/Unidis/Euro International/Dieter Geissler/Cinema 5

d   **Costa-Gavras**
sc   **Costa-Gavras, Franco Solinas**
ph   **Pierre William Glenn**
m   **Mikis Theodorakis**
Yves Montand, Renato Salvatori, O.E. Hasse, Jacques Weber, Jean Luc Bideau

In an unnamed repressive South American country, an American CIA agent (Montand) is held hostage by a Left-wing guerrilla group demanding the release of 150 political prisoners. Using the manipulatively skilful cinematic techniques of *Z* (1969) and *The Confession* (1970), Costa-Gavras convincingly indicts the USA's clandestine involvement with dictatorships in Latin America, which caused the film to be withdrawn from Washington D.C.'s American Film Institute Theater in 1973. Filmed in Chile under Allende, the setting for the same director's *Missing* (1982) after the coup, it was also criticized by the Left for representing the CIA in the sympathetic guise of Montand. Either way it made money.

The Station

▶ **La Stazione**

Italy   1990   92 mins   col
Fandango

d   **Sergio Rubini**
sc   **Umberto Marino, Filippo Ascione, Sergio Rubini**
ph   **Alessio Gelsini**
m   **No credit given**
Sergio Rubini, Margherita Buy, Ennio Fantastichini

During a party at a smart villa, Flavia (Buy) quarrels with her arrogant lover, Danilo (Fantastichini). On impulse she decides to go to Rome and finds herself passing the rainy night, waiting for the 6 a.m. train, in company with Domenico (Rubini), the stationmaster at a small stopover. The relationship between the simple provincial and the rich city girl develops with warmth and humour through the long hours, but is violently disturbed by the arrival of Danilo, drunk and on the rampage... Italian theatre actor and director Rubini made his film debut with this fresh, charming and bitter-sweet romantic comedy, adapted from a stage play by Umberto Marini which ran successfully for three years with the same cast. If the screenplay's origins are recognizably rooted in the theatre, the piece still makes for an entertaining movie, expertly played by Rubini and Buy, and offering some subtle observations on class differences.

A Station For Two

▶ **Vokzal Dlya Dvoikh**

USSR   1983   133 mins   col
Mosfilm

d   **Eldar Ryazanov**
sc   **Emil Braginsky, Eldar Ryazanov**
ph   **Vadim Alisov**
m   **Andrei Petrov**
Ludmila Gurchenko, Oleg Basilashvili, Nikita Mikhalkov, Nonna Mordinkova, Mikhail Kononov

A former concert pianist (Basilashvili), held in a Siberian labour camp on a manslaughter charge, is sent off to visit his wife by the kindly (*sic*) commandant. During the journey he is delayed at a stopover by an argument with a waitress, misses his train, falls in love with the waitress (Gurchenko) and finds her waiting for him when he returns to the camp. Although made by one of the USSR's best-known satirical directors, the film is no more than a gently amusing and oddly incoherent romantic comedy.

Stavisky

France   1974   117 mins   col
Cerito Films/Les Films Ariane/Euro International

d   **Alain Resnais**
sc **Jorge Semprun**
ph **Sacha Vierny**
m   **Stephen Sondheim**
Jean-Paul Belmondo, Charles Boyer, François Périer, Anny Duperey, Michel Lonsdale, Claude Rich, Silvia Badesco

Serge Alexandre (Belmondo), born Sacha Stavisky, a Russian Jew, is a financier and swindler whose powerful allies and connections politicians and police. These desert him when a major fraud is unmasked, and he dies in mysterious circumstances. Basing his film on the real-life Stavisky who provoked a scandal which almost toppled the French government in 1934, Resnais has combined fact and fiction into what one critic aptly described as 'a tone poem to the 1930s'. The director's first feature after a six-year break, of which he himself said, 'It is not a political or historical document but rather an entertainment,' it is, in spite of its political context, an empty exercise beneath its glittering exterior. Resnais' characteristic approach is evident in the symbolic use of colour – white as a romantic emblem of death – and in his employment of shifting time scales. *Stavisky* is visually breathtaking in its evocation of period, and expertly acted. Finally, however, coming from Resnais, a disappointment.

▶ **Stazione, La** see Station, The

Stella

Greece   1955   94 mins   bw
Millas Films

d   **Michael Cacoyannis**
sc **Michael Cacoyannis**
ph **Costa Theodorides**
m   **Manos Hadjidakis**
Melina Mercouri, Yiorgo Fountas, Alekos Alexandrikis, Sophia Vembo

Men are wild about Stella (Mercouri), singer in a bouzouki hall and a free spirit who will not be caged. Her involvement with a middle-class writer and a football hero leads to tragedy for all three. Only the second film made by Cacoyannis, it hints at his particular talent for capturing a sense of pre-ordained doom and is characterized by effective low-key photography, punctuated with some lively set-pieces. Mercouri, Greece's Minister of Culture in the 1980s, was here making her screen debut, and holds nothing back in exhibiting her narrow range of gifts: sex appeal, a generous smile, a captivating wink, uninhibited earthiness and an ouzo-soaked singing voice. All of which makes for a reasonably entertaining melodrama of uneven quality.

▶ **Stem Van Het Water, De** see Voice Of The Water, The

Stepfather

▶ **Beau-Père**

France   1981   120 mins   col
Sara Films/Antenne 2

d   **Bertrand Blier**
sc **Bertrand Blier**
ph **Sacha Vierny**
m   **Philippe Sarde**
Patrick Dewaere, Ariel Besse, Maurice Ronet, Nicole Garcia, Nathalie Baye, Maurice Risch

A bar pianist (Dewaere), widowed when his wife is killed in a motor accident, is left with his adolescent stepdaughter (Besse), who decides that he should be her first lover. Further complications arise when her real father (Ronet) comes to claim her. Working from his own novel, Blier's overlong and *Lolita*-like tale is played largely for comedy. It manages to stay just this side of tastelessness thanks to a strand of tenderness and the performances of the leads, notably newcomer Besse, who conveys an appealing mixture of childlike qualities and sensuality.

Stepping Out

▶ **Slingrevalsen**

Denmark 1981 104 mins col
Metronome Productions A/S

d **Esben Høilund Carlsen**
sc **Nils Schou**
ph **Dirk Brüel**
m **Bent Fabricius-Bjerre**
  Solbjørg Højfeldt, Kurt Dreyer, Ole Ernst, Ulf Pilgaard, Lisbeth Lundquist, Nikolaj Harris, Anne- Stine Lier

Karen (Højfeldt) leaves Søren (Ernst) for Jens (Dreyer) who leaves Lis (Lundquist) who is married to Blom (Pilgaard) who...'How many combinations do you think are left – mathematically speaking?' asks a puzzled guest at a party attended by all the various couples in this 'Divorce Danish Style' comedy. There is a lot in it that compares favourably with serious American films such as *Kramer Vs Kramer*, plus some Scandinavian sexual insights. The humour in the marital discords may escape many – cornflakes are emptied over a husband's head – but the innumerable plot complications are well-handled, and the playing is amiable, especially by the two children (Harris and Lier) caught up in the battle of the sexes.

▶ **Sterne** see Stars

▶ **Stilte Rond Christine M., De** see Question Of Silence, A

▶ **Stir Patra** see Letter From The Wife

Stolen Kisses

▶ **Baisers Volés**

France 1968 91 mins col
Films Du Carrosse/Artistes Associés

d **François Truffaut**
sc **François Truffaut, Claude De Givray, Bernard Revon**
ph **Denys Clerval**
m **Antoine Duhamel**
  Jean-Pierre Léaud, Delphine Seyrig, Michel Lonsdale, Claude Jade, Harry-Max

Antoine Doinel (Léaud), aged 20 and discharged from the army, returns to Paris where he is employed variously as a hotel clerk, private detective, salesman in a shoe store, where he has a brief affair with the owner's wife (Seyrig), and TV repair man, before proposing to his long-time girlfriend (Jade). The light tone of 1930s romantic comedies is set immediately by Charles Trenet singing 'Que Reste T'il De Nos Amours?' on the sound track at the start of this third episode in the life of Doinel, Truffaut's alter-ego. It is difficult to believe that while Truffaut was being true to the spirit of the endearing Paris of the films of René Clair and Jacques Becker, the city was in turmoil with the student riots of May 1968.

Stone Wedding

▶ **Nunta De Pietra**

Romania 1973 83 mins bw
Bucuresti Studios

d **1) Mircea Veroiu 2) Dan Pita**
sc **1) Mircea Veroiu 2) Dan Pita**
ph **Iosif Demian**
m **Dorin Liviu Zaharia, Dan Andrei**
  1)Leopoldina Bălănută, Nina Domiga 2) Mircea Dianconu, Radu Boruzescu, Ursula Nussbächer

Two tales of peasant life in the Carpathian Mountains. In the first, a poor widow (Bălănută) sells everything to buy a wedding dress for the burial of her teenage daughter (Domiga), her last remaining child, who never lived to marry. In the second, an itinerant fiddler (Boruzescu), playing at a village wedding, runs off with the bride (Nussbächer). Both stories, one dark, the other lighter in tone, take place against a spectacular mountain setting captured in elegant and atmospheric black and white images. A successful blend of the realistic peasant life with Romanian folk myth, this unusual and striking film debut by two young directors helped launch a new wave in Romanian cinema.

▶ **Stora Aventyret, Det** see Great Adventure, The

▶ **Storia Moderna: L'Ape Regina, Una** see Queen Bee

Storm Over Asia

▶ **aka The Heir To Genghis Khan**

▶ **Potomok Chingis-Khana**

USSR 1928 93 mins bw
Mezhrabpomfilm

d **V.I. Pudovkin**
sc **Osip Brik**
ph **Anatoli Golovnya**
m Silent
    **Valeri Inkizhinov, A. Dedintsev, V.
    Tzoppi, Paulina Belinskaya**

Bair (Inkizhinov) a nomadic fur-trapper claiming to be the heir to Genghis Khan, is set up as a puppet monarch by the occupying British interventionist forces in Mongolia in 1918 but, realizing his national identity, he rouses the Asian hordes against their oppressors. A film of great visual beauty, dynamic montage, humour and compassion, it was banned in the UK for some years because the British are portrayed as the baddies. It was the last great silent film by Pudovkin, who was never really happy in the sound era, but a new version with a sound track added under his supervision was released in 1950.

▶ **Storm Within, The** see Parents Terribles, Les

Stormy Waters

▶ **Rémorques**

France 1941 80 mins bw
Sedis

d **Jean Grémillon**
sc **Jacques Prévert, André Cayatte**
ph **Armand Thirard, Louis Née**
m **Roland Manuel**
    **Jean Gabin, Michèle Morgan, Madeleine
    Renaud, Jean Marchat**

The captain of a tugboat (Gabin) is happily married but, when he rescues a boat from stormy waters, he falls in love with the wife (Morgan) of its captain, a hateful boor. He leaves her to keep a vigil at the bedside of his own wife (Renaud) who is mortally ill. An intimate and perceptive study of passion and the nature of fidelity which benefits from a Prévert script and a trio of France's top stars. Filmed partly on location at Brest – Grémillon wanted only authentic sea and storm footage – work began in 1939, was hampered by the restrictions imposed by the Nazis, and was completed two years later in a Paris studio.

The Story Of A Cheat

▶ **Le Roman D'Un Tricheur**

France 1936 85 mins bw
Cinéas

d **Sacha Guitry**
sc **Sacha Guitry**
ph **Marcel Lucien**
m **Adolphe Borchard**
    **Sacha Guitry, Jacqueline Delubac, Rosine
    Déréan, Marguerite Moreno, Pauline
    Carton, Serge Grave, Pierre Assy**

An aging gentleman (Guitry) settles himself at a table of a pavement café and commences writing his memoirs. As he scribbles, his voice-over narrates the tale which begins when, as a young boy (Grave, later Assy), he is sent to bed without supper as punishment for stealing a few sous. That evening, his whole family dines on poisonous mushrooms and dies, thus setting him on a dishonest course on the basis that cheating pays. Guitry's most internationally celebrated film is a masterpiece of wit, style and invention in which we see the events acted out without dialogue, except for one scene in which a countess (Moreno) joins The Cheat at the café and is permitted a few words which reveal that he had been a passing lover of hers in his youth. Amoral to be sure and slightly repetitious, but charm and cleverness keep it constantly entertaining. With its masterly cutting back and forth between past and present, the film influenced such directors as Truffaut, Godard and Alain Resnais.

The Story Of Adèle H

▶ **L'Histoire D'Adèle H**

France 1975 98 mins col
Films Du Carrosse/Artistes Associés

d   François Truffaut
sc François Truffaut, Jean Gruault, Suzanne
    Schiffman
ph Nestor Almendros
m   Maurice Jaubert
    Isabelle Adjani, Bruce Robinson, Sylvia
    Marriott, Reubin Dorey, Joseph Blatchley

Adèle (Adjani), Victor Hugo's daughter, falls
madly in love with a young English lieutenant
(Robinson) in Guernsey and, despite his
indifference to her, follows him to Nova Sco-
tia and then to Barbados where she becomes
a vagrant. Based on Adèle's diary written in
code and decoded in 1955, the film is 'a
musical composition for one instrument,' as
Truffaut called it. That instrument is the
exquisite 19-year-old Adjani (Adèle was in
her thirties at the time) seldom off the screen
and having to portray a passionate woman
in the throes of *amour fou*. But because of
the director's ironic detachment, both she and
the film are muted and uninvolving. It was
finely shot, partly in English, on location in
Guernsey and Dakar.

▶ **Story Of A Love Affair** see Chronicle
of A Love

The Story Of Sin

▶ **Dzieje Grezechu**

Poland   1975   128 mins   col
TOR

d   Walerian Borowczyk
sc Walerian Borowczyk
ph Zygmunt Samosiuk
m   Mendelssohn
    Grazyna Dlugolecka, Jerzy Zelnik,
    Olgierd Lukaszewicz

In turn-of-the-century Poland, a teenage girl
of strict upbringing falls in love with a married
man. When he leaves her pregnant, she
drowns the child and sinks into degradation
and prostitution. Borowczyk's brief return to
his homeland from France produced a creaky
period melodrama, based on a popular sentimental novel by Stefan Zeromski, and overlaid with his usual highly decorative style (art
direction by Teresa Barska), erotic fetishism
(shoes and underwear) and narrative slug-
gishness.

The Story Of The Late Chrysanthemums

▶ **Zangiku Monogatari**

Japan   1939   142 mins   bw
Shochiku

d   Kenji Mizoguchi
sc Yoshitaka Yoda
ph Shigeto Miki
m   Senji Ito
    Shotaro Hanayagi, Kakuko Mori,
    Gonjuro Kawarazaki, Kokichi Takada,
    Ryotaro Kawanami

The actor Kikunosuke (Hanayagi) is criticized
for ineptitude by the other members of a
Kabuki troupe. Despondent, he returns home
and starts an affair with Otoku (Mori), one
of his family's maids. They marry and live in
poverty, until Kikunosuke, with the help and
sacrifices of his wife, becomes a successful
actor. The only obstacle to Western audiences'
appreciating one of Mizoguchi's finest middle-
period films is the need to distinguish between
good and bad acting in the Japanese theatrical
traditions of *kabuki* and *shinpa* (popular
melodrama), but the poignant tale of a woman's sacrifice for the man she loves can be
appreciated in any language. The successful
film, made up mostly of a single, long, mobile
take per sequence, was originally shown in
the West in a cut version running 115 minutes.

La Strada

▶ **aka The Road**

Italy   1954   115 mins   bw
Trans-Lux

d   Federico Fellini
sc Federico Fellini, Tullio Pinelli, Ennio
    Flaiano
ph Otello Martelli
m   Nino Rota
    Giulietta Masina, Anthony Quinn,
    Richard Basehart, Aldo Silvani, Marcella
    Rovere, Livia Venturini

Gelsomina (Masina), a simple-minded girl,
loves the whoring, drunken itinerant circus
strong-man, Zampano (Quinn), who bought
her for a few lire, put her to work as a clown,
and ignores her. When Zampano fights and

kills the gentle tightrope-walker (Basehart) who befriended her, she dies of a broken heart. Simplicity itself, *La Strada* is a magical tale and an unbearably painful account of loneliness which will always be associated with the sublimely Chaplinesque Masina (here given her first starring role by her husband, Fellini), but Quinn, too, is superb, particularly in the final revelation of his own heartbreak and isolation. The inherent sentimentality of the plot is off-set by the realistically desolate provincial towns in which it is played out, often effectively filmed at night.

Best Foreign Film Oscar 1956

Straight Through The Heart

▶ **Mitten Ins Herz**

W. Germany 1983 91 mins col
WDR (Cologne)/Olga Film (Munich)

d **Doris Dörrie**
sc **Jelena Kristl**
ph **Michael Goebel**
m **Paul Shigihara**
Beata Jensen, Sepp Bierbichler, Gabrielle Litty, Jens-Muller Rastede, Joachim Hoepner

Anna (Jensen), a lonely 20-year-old whose attempts to assert herself have gone no further than dying her hair blue, attracts the attention of Armin (Bierbichler), a middle-aged and reclusive dentist. He persuades her to live with him in return for money, but turns out to want absolutely nothing from her other than her presence. Her increasingly determined efforts to involve him with her emotionally inevitably doom them both. Essentially a two-hander, best described as Absurdist in style, this drama explores the themes of role-play in male-female relationships. An original, imaginative and commendably assured first feature from a director who would lighten her tone, if not the weight of her meaning, with the highly successful *Men* two years later.

Straits Of Love And Hate

▶ **Aien Kyo**

Japan 1937 88 mins bw

Shinko Kinema

d **Kenji Mizoguchi**
sc **Yoshitaka Yoda,**
ph **Minoru Miki**
Fumiko Yamaji, Seizaburo Kawazu, Masao Shimizu, Haruo Tanaka

A servant (Yamaji) is seduced by the weak son (Shimizu) of the household and becomes pregnant. She parts with her baby, takes to the streets, and then joins a theatrical troupe. Some years later, the man tries to make amends. Mizoguchi, forced for commercial reasons, since 1922, to make many films in which he had little interest, now began to develop his own style and subject matter, although ostensibly the idea for this story came from Tolstoy's *Resurrection*. The melodrama is continually undercut by realism and humour. There is also a tragicomic rendering of 'My Blue Heaven' by the heroine.

▶ **Strange Adventure Of David Gray, The** see Vampyr

▶ **Strange Masquerade** see Improperly Dressed

The Strange Ones

▶ **Les Enfants Terribles**

France 1949 100 mins bw
Gaumont/Continentale/Concord

d **Jean-Pierre Melville**
sc **Jean-Pierre Melville, Jean Cocteau**
ph **Henri Decaë**
m **Vivaldi, Bach**
Nicole Stéphane, Edouard Dermithe, Renée Cosima, Jacques Bernard

Paul (Dermithe) and Elisabeth (Stéphane), a teenage brother and sister unhealthily obsessed with each other, create a private enclosed world in their untidy, shared single room, but the intrusion of others leads to suicide. Written in the late 1920s, Cocteau's strange novel would have seemed unfilmable except by the author himself. (Not that he is not overly present as narrator.) But Melville's severe style and craftsmanship combined with the bejewelled prose of the screenplay retains much of the claustrophobic spirit of the original. Made on a small budget, it was shot almost entirely on the stage of the Théâtre Pigalle with the then unusual use of baroque music on the sound track. The passionate performance of Stéphane makes up for the deficiencies of Dermithe, Cocteau's adopted son.

A Strange Place To Meet

▶ **Drôle D'Endroit Pour Une Rencontre**

France 1988 98 mins col
Hachette Première et Cie/Hachette Productions/Films A2/DD Productions/ Deneuve SA/Orly Films/Éditions Sidonie

d François Dupeyron
sc François Dupeyron, Dominique Faysse
ph Charlie Van Damme
m Selection of songs by Richard Strauss, Serge Gainsbourg and others
   Catherine Deneuve, Gérard Depardieu, André Wilms, Nathalie Cardone, Alain Rimoux

While driving along a motorway one rainy night, France (Deneuve) quarrels with her husband. He abandons her in a lay-by where Charles (Depardieu), a doctor, is attempting to mend his car. France, against Charles' will, attaches herself to him and spends the night in his car, which the police tow away in the morning. The couple repair to a motorway café where the waitress tells France her husband has been and she decides to wait for him there. Meanwhile, Charles has fallen in love with her... It's difficult to know what on earth Deneuve and Depardieu (in the words of critic Geoff Brown, *la belle et la bête* of contemporary French cinema) are doing in this tedious and hollow film in which nothing happens, no explanations are given for the little that does and the characters are entirely without flesh or interest. A first feature by a maker of shorts and documentaries, it looks good and its leads do their best, but it would be difficult to imagine a more futile way of spending one's movie viewing time.

The Stranger

▶ **Lo Straniero**

Italy 1967 104 mins col

DD/Master/Marianne/Casbah

d Luchino Visconti
sc Luchino Visconti, Suso Cecchi D'Amico, Georges Conchon, Emmanuel Robles
ph Giuseppe Rotunno
m Piero Piccioni
   Marcello Mastroianni, Anna Karina, Bernard Blier, Georges Wilson, Bruno Cremer

Meursault (Mastroianni), a French clerk living in Algiers who shot and killed a young Algerian for no apparent reason, reflects on his existence while awaiting the guillotine. The flamboyant Visconti was particularly unsuited to the astringency of Albert Camus' psychological and philosophical modern classic novel about an outsider and, though Mastroianni approached this role intelligently, it really needed a Gérard Philipe to carry it off. The steamy atmosphere of 1938 Algeria is quite well caught, but the film was one of the director's biggest flops.

The Stranger And The Fog

▶ **Gharibeh-Va-Meh**

Iran 1974 140 mins col
Rex Cinema Theater Company

d Bahram Beyzai
sc Bahram Beyzai
ph Mehrdad Fakhimi
m Bahram Beyzai
   Khosrow Shojazadeh, Parvaneh Ma'soumi, Esmat Safavi, Manuchehr Farid

One day, a stranger (Shojazadeh) arrives out of the fog at a small, tightly-knit fishing community. He cannot recall where he came from and the villagers are suspicious of him. Gradually he is accepted and marries a young widow (Ma'soumi) whose husband presumably died a year earlier. But the 'dead' husband returns and a group of men come in search of the stranger. The film is heavily infused with symbolic elements and themes (intolerance, injustice, martyrdom) from traditional Persian theatre, of which the director is a major scholar. This may prove an obstacle to Western audiences, since the film only occasionally manages to go beyond the specific culture in its allegorical depiction of the oppression of the innocent. Certainly the atmosphere comes across potently in Beyzai's economical visual style, and the enigmas are the more haunting for not being understood. There is no problem, though, with the expertly staged, ten-minute, brutal climactic battle in the woods.

▶ **Strangers** see Journey To Italy

▶ **Straniero, Lo** see Stranger, The

▶ **Strategia Del Ragno** see Spider's Stratagem, The

Stray Dog

▶ **Nora Inu**

Japan 1949 122 mins bw
Shin Toho

d Akira Kurosawa
sc Akira Kurosawa, Ryuzo Kikushima
ph Asakazu Kakai
m Fumio Hayasaka
Toshiro Mifune, Takashi Shimura, Ko Kimura, Keiko Awaji

A young policeman (Mifune) has his gun stolen from him in a bus, resulting in a long search for the thief (Kimura) through the underworld, during which the cop has to face his own criminal impulses. Kurosawa, always the most Western-influenced of older generation Japanese directors, made this atmospheric thriller on location with the contemporary Hollywood model in mind, but the pace is slower due to some of the techniques such as slow dissolves and double exposures. However, an interesting picture of post-war Japan emerges.

Street Angel

▶ **Malu Tianshi**

China 1937 100 mins bw
Mingxing

d Yuan Muzhi
sc Yugu Muzhi
ph Wu Yinxiang
m He Luting

Zhao Dan, Wei Heling, Qian Qianli, Zhou Xuan

In one of the poorest areas of Shanghai in the 1930s, the owners of a teahouse have pressed two women into prostitution. A young man (Dan) from the run-down lodgings opposite carries on a chaste affair with the younger woman (Xuan). Around them life is hard, money and work are short and street violence prevails. One of the last and most celebrated of pre-war Chinese films (Shanghai fell to the Japanese in the same year) derives its title and much of its sentimental urban poetic style from Frank Borzage's Hollywood movie of 1928 starring Janet Gaynor. But it has a tragicomic vein of its own, is more firmly rooted in reality and more explicit in its social criticism. The 28-year-old director's only subsequent film was a war documentary.

Street Of Shame

▶ **Akasen Chitai**

Japan 1956 88 mins bw
Daiei Kyoto

d Kenji Mizoguchi
sc Masashige Narusawa
ph Kazuo Miyagawa
m Toshiro Mayazumi
Machiko Kyo, Ayako Wakao, Aiko Mimasu, Michiyo Kogure

The night-by-night existence of a group of prostitutes working in a bordello called Dreamland in the red light district of Tokyo. In his last completed film, Mizoguchi returned to an earlier contemporary subject to illustrate his major theme – the exploitation of women throughout the ages. Perhaps commercial pressure influenced some of the melodramatic and vulgar lapses, but the insight, humour and humanity still shine through. The greatest of all Japanese directors died of leukemia at the age of 58 in the year of the film's release.

▶ **Street Of Sorrow, The** see Joyless Street

▶ **Streghe, Le** see Witches, The

Strike

▶ **Stachka**

USSR 1924 82 mins bw
Goskino

d Sergei Eisenstein
sc Sergei Eisenstein, Valeri Pletniov, I.
Kravchinovski
ph Edouard Tissé
m Silent

Maxim Shtraukh, Grigori Alexandrov,
Mikhail Gomorov, I. Ivanov, I. Klukvin

In 1912, after peaceful efforts to settle a
strike caused by the suicide of a sacked
worker fail, strikers and their families are
brutally slaughtered by cavalrymen sent by
the state. Made with members of the Prolet-
kult theatre, Eisenstein's first feature was a
vital part of the *avant-garde* Constructivist
art movement in the Soviet Union of the
1920s. Already much in evidence was his
'dialectic montage' *viz* the use of caricature,
visual metaphor and shock cutting. For
example, a factory boss uses a lemon
squeezer as police move in on the striking
workers, and shots of a slaughterhouse are
cut in as they are mown down.

▶ **Strohfeuer** see Summer Lightning

▶ **Stroke of Midnight, The** see Phantom Carriage, The

Stromboli

▶ **Stromboli, Terra Di Dio**

Italy 1950 107 mins bw
Be-Ro/RKO

d Roberto Rossellini
sc Roberto Rossellini, Art Cohen, Renzo
Cesana, Sergio Amedei, C.P. Callegari
ph Otello Martelli
m Renzo Rossellini

Ingrid Bergman, Mario Vitale, Renzo
Cesana, Mario Sponza

A Lithuanian refugee (Bergman), interned in
Italy after the war, gains her freedom by
marrying a simple fisherman (Vitale), but
finds only loneliness and hostility on his barren, volcanic island. When she becomes pregnant, she flees as the volcano erupts. Moral
indignation erupted from puritan groups in
the USA who boycotted the film because of
Bergman's 'wanton ways' in leaving her husband for Rossellini. But more harm was done
to the film by the indifferent narration, sloppy
pace and the uneasy teaming of Bergman
(although stripped of the trappings of Hollywood stardom) with non-actors. Further
damage was perpetrated by routine director
Alfred Werker who edited the English version
down to 81 minutes and changed the ending
for RKO.

▶ **Stromboli, Terra Di Dio** see
Stromboli

Stronger Than The Night

▶ **Stärker Als Die Nacht**

E. Germany 1954 117 mins bw
Deutsche Film

d Slatan Dudow
sc Jeanne Stern, Kurt Stern
ph Karl Plintzner, Horst Brandt
m Ernst Roters

Wilhelm Koch-Hooge, Helga Göring,
Kurt Oligmüller, Rita Gödikmeier

When Hitler comes to power in Germany,
Hans Löning (Koch-Hooge) is imprisoned
for seven years for his Communist activities.
Released in 1940, he immediately forms an
underground group, but is informed upon
and executed. One of the best East German
films of the 1950s was based on an original
script by Communist party activists Jeanne
and Kurt Stern, who participated in the
Spanish Civil War and worked for the
French Resistance. Although it has its share
of rhetorical gestures, especially in the closing paean to its martyr hero, and a slight
bending of history to suit the argument,
Dudow, who worked with Fritz Lang, G.
W. Pabst and Bertolt Brecht, is too sophisticated a director to be content with simplist-
ics. The characters are finely nuanced, and
the bitter denunciation of Nazism is forcefully expressed by some expressionist tech-

niques, voice-over interventions and newsreel shots.

Stroszek

W. Germany   1977   108 mins   col
Werner Herzog

d   **Werner Herzog**
sc **Werner Herzog**
ph **Thomas Mauch**
m   **Tom Paxton, Chet Atkins, Sonny Terry**
    Eva Mattes, Bruno S, Clemens Scheitz

An ex-con (Bruno S), his unemployed neighbour (Scheitz) and a prostitute (Mattes) leave Germany for America where they settle in Wisconsin in a mobile home bought on credit. After a bungled robbery, they split up. Another of Herzog's ventures off the beaten track finds him in Middle America with Bruno S, his curious lead from *The Enigma Of Kaspar Hauser* (1974), virtually playing himself. Unhappily, though the location shooting is interesting, the acting is stilted and the outsider's view of the barrenness of American life is obvious.

The Structure Of Crystals

▶ **Struktura Krysztalu**

Poland   1969   137 mins   bw
Tor Film Unit

d   **Krzysztof Zanussi**
sc **Krzysztof Zanussi, Edward Zebrowski**
ph **Stefan Matjaszkiewicz**
m   **Wojciech Kilar**
    Barbara Wrzesińska, Andrzej Żarnecki,
    Jan Myslowicz, Wladyslaw Jarema,
    Daniel Olbrychski

A metropolitan member of the scientific élite (Zarnecki) visits an old friend and colleague (Myslowicz) who has retreated with his wife (Wrzesińska) to a remote meteorological station, and tries to persuade him to return to the city. Zanussi's first feature, after a number of documentaries, showed considerable intelligence and maturity. It was the first of a series of films that looked at the scientific community, (mainly uncharted territory in

the cinema except for science fiction) to make general philosophical points. Rather too long and cerebral, despite the sex scenes, it might not seem as clear as the title suggests.

▶ **Struktura Krysztalu** see Structure Of Crystals, The

Stubby

▶ **Fimpen**

Sweden   1974   87 mins   col
Bo Widerberg Film

d   **Bo Widerberg**
sc **Bo Widerberg**
ph **John Olsson, Hanno Fuchs, Roland**
    Sterner, Åke Åstrand
m   **Prokofiev**
    Johan Bergman (Stubby), Monica
    Zetterlund, Ernst-Hugo Jaeregard

An amazing six-year-old soccer wizard becomes a national hero as anchor man on the senior Swedish team in the World Cup series, but he quits when his school work suffers and he still can't even sign autographs. Little Johan's soccer skills were spotted by Widerberg while the director was waiting to play in a match between two teams of film technicians, and he resolved to make a film around him. This reasonable family entertainment, with the boy's real-life parents and top international players as themselves, basically has only one visual joke.

The Student Of Prague

▶ **Der Student Von Prag**

Germany   1913   56 mins   bw
Bioskop

d   **Stellan Rye**
sc **Hanns Heinz Ewers**
ph **Guido Seeber**
m   **Silent**
    Paul Wegener, John Gottowt, Grete
    Berger, Lyda Salmonova, Lothar Körner

A penniless student (Wegener), sells his reflection to the mysterious Scapinelli (Gottowt) to obtain the means to woo the girl of his choice. The reflection, however, haunts him, driving him to kill it and, eventually, himself. This film lit the early spark which flamed into the German cinema's love of supernatural subjects, leading in turn to the making of classics in the Expressionist tradition. Filmed on location, it capitalized on the medieval quarters of the city and it has been suggested that it was there that Wegener (one of whose five wives was Salmonova) first heard the legend of *The Golem* which he would film three times.

The Student Of Prague

▶ **Der Student Von Prag**

Germany   1926   116 mins   bw
H.R. Sokal-Film

d **Henrik Galeen**
sc **Henrik Galeen, Hanns Heinz Ewers**
ph **Günther Krampf, Erich Nitzschmann**
m **Silent**
   Conrad Veidt, Werner Krauss, Agnes Esterhazy, Elizza La Porta, Ferdinand Von Alten

In return for a large sum of money, Balduin (Veidt), a poor student, agrees that the sinister Scapinelli (Krauss) may remove an item of his choice from his room. Scapinelli takes Balduin's reflection, which dogs the young man until he and it meet their end. If the 1913 version of this tale is a landmark and effective in its own right, this studio-bound version, reflecting the full flowering of German Expressionism, is certainly the more accomplished. It is rich in atmosphere and some memorable images – such as Scapinelli's shadow looming over a tryst between the doomed lovers – and both leads, who had made so strong an impact in *The Cabinet Of Dr Caligari*, do themselves and their roles full justice.

The Student Of Prague

▶ **Der Student Von Prag**

Germany   1935   87 mins   bw
Cine-Allianz

d **Arthur Robison**
sc **Arthur Robison, Hans Kyser**
ph **Bruno Mondi**
m **Theo Mackeben**
   Adolf Wohlbrück, Dorothea Wieck, Theodor Loos, Erich Fiedler, Edna Greyff

As in previous versions, Balduin (Wohlbrück) sells his reflection. This time the buyer is Dr Carpis (Loos) and Balduin uses the cash to pursue Julia (Wieck), a beautiful singer. Here, Balduin discovers that he has sold his better half and, deprived of it, he grows unscrupulous, becomes a murderer and finally goes insane. This sound production, though packed with plot, is the weakest of the three attempts. The Chicago-born German director died before its completion, and the star (to become internationally known as Anton Walbrook) lacked the intensity of his predecessors, especially Conrad Veidt. Quite simply, the film fails to frighten. But it has been acknowledged as the last of the pre-Nazi period films in style, of interest as a kind of throwback to the great era of the German silent cinema.

▶ **Student Von Prag, Der** see Student Of Prague, The

▶ **Stützen Der Gesellschaft** see Pillars Of Society

▶ **Subida Al Cielo** see Mexican Bus Ride

▶ **Subject For A Short Story** see Lika, Chekhov's Love

Subway

France   1985   102 mins   col
Films Du Loup/TSF/TF1

d **Luc Besson**
sc **Luc Besson, Alain Le Henry, Pierre Jolivet, Sophie Schmit, Marc Perrier**
ph **Carlo Varini**
m **Eric Serra**
   Christopher Lambert, Isabelle Adjani, Richard Bohringer, Michel Galabru, Jean-Hugues Anglade

Fred (Lambert) steals some important documents from the crooked businessman-husband of Helena (Adjani), and flees to the Paris Métro where he lives in the labyrinthine passages with various other outcasts. Twenty-six-year-old Besson's underground film (only in the sense of its setting) has the advantage of high-tech art work from the veteran Alexandre Trauner, and an audacious use of 'Scope and Dolby. But not even the intensity of Lambert in dinner-jacket and yellow hair (Sting was the first choice), and the beauty of Adjani (in her first film for two years) could make the characters and situations less preposterous. Breathless and flashy, it is a film for the pop video generation.

▶ **Such A Gorgeous Kid Like Me**
see Gorgeous Bird Like Me, A

Such A Pretty Little Beach

▶ **(US: Riptide)**

▶ **Une Si Jolie Petite Plage**

France 1949 97 mins bw
CICC/Dormer/Films Corona

d Yves Allégret
sc Jacques Sigurd
ph Henri Alekan
m Maurice Thiriet, Jacques Sigurd
Madeleine Robinson, Gérard Philipe, Jane Marken, Jean Servais, Julien Carette, Mona Dol

A young man (Philipe) registers at a dismal hotel at a desolate seaside resort in Normandy in winter. He had worked here as a kitchen boy some years before and run off with a famous singer, recently murdered. He is suspected by a mysterious fellow guest (Servais) of committing the *crime passionel*. Rain falls incessantly in this archetypal romantic, fatalistic post-war French drama, dominated by the boyish, sensitive, intense face of Philipe, perfectly cast as the melancholy fugitive. Far too schematically doom-laden, the film does have superb photography and wonderful all-round performances.

▶ **Sudba Cheloveka** see Destiny Of A Man

The Sudden Fortune Of The Poor People Of Kombach

▶ **Der Plötzliche Reichtum Der Armen Leute Von Kombach**

W. Germany 1971 102 mins bw
Hessischer Rundfunk/Hallelujah

d Volker Schlöndorff
sc Volker Schlöndorff, Margarethe Von Trotta
ph Franz Rath
m Klaus Doldinger
Reinhard Hauff, Georg Lehn, Karl Joseph Cramer, Wolfgang Bachler, Margarethe Von Trotta, Rainer Werner Fassbinder

In 1821, seven poor peasants rob the monthly tax-money cart. They are arrested and executed after they have spent much of their ill-gotten fortune. One of Schlöndorff's most forceful films, this is a stark, analytical depiction of 19th-century social irrationalism without any period embellishments. The accomplished narrative reaches a pessimistic conclusion about the nature of rebellion that fits modern times. Fassbinder, then beginning to make a name for himself as a director of a very different type of film, plays a peasant.

Sugarbaby

▶ **Zückerbaby**

W. Germany 1984 86 mins col
Pelemele Film/BMI/Bayerischen Rundfunks

d Percy Adlon
sc Percy Adlon
ph Johanna Heer
m Dreier, Franz Erlmeier, Fritz Köstler, the Paul-Würges Combo
Marianne Sägebrecht, Eisi Gulp, Manuela Denz, Toni Berger

An overweight, plain woman in her late thirties, leading a boring existence as a mortician's assistant, is smitten with a handsome young subway train driver. She tracks him down and takes advantage of his wife's absence to draw him into a brief but rewarding encounter. A boost for fat women, this idiosyncratic romantic comedy is full of mischievous wit, cleverly avoiding both mockery and pathos.

Sometimes Adlon decorates the slight story with too many stylistic devices, but Sägebrecht's gently nuanced performance holds the picture together.

▶ **Sugata Sanshiro** see Judo Saga

The Suitor

▶ **Le Soupirant**

France   1962   85 mins   bw
CAPAC/Cocinor

d   Pierre Étaix
sc   Pierre Étaix, Jean-Claude Carrière
ph   Pierre Levant
m   Jean Paillaud
     Pierre Étaix, Laurence Lignères, France Arnell, Karin Vesely

A shy and studious young man (Étaix), urged by his mother to marry, proposes to a Swedish girl who fails to understand him, meets a drunken beauty, becomes obsessed with a music-hall star, and returns to the Swede – who accepts him. This first, and most successful, feature by Étaix, who had been an assistant to Jacques Tati on *Mon Oncle* (1958), relies almost exclusively on physical humour and is constructed, like all his films (and Tati's), around a series of comic set-pieces. Yet, though often amusing, his comedy is too derivative, similar jokes having been better executed by Buster Keaton, and Max Linder whom Étaix resembles.

▶ **Sult** see Hunger

▶ **Summer** see Green Ray, The

A Summer Affair

▶ **(US: One Wild Moment)**

▶ **Un Moment D'Égarement**

France   1977   100 mins   col
Renn Productions/Société Française De Production

d   Claude Berri
sc   Claude Berri

ph   André Neau
m   Michel Stelio
     Jean-Pierre Marielle, Victor Lanoux, Christine Dejoux, Agnes Soral, Martine Sarcey

Divorced Pierre (Marielle), his friend Jacques (Lanoux) and their 17-year-old daughters holiday on the Côte D'Azur. Pierre, and Jacques' daughter Françoise (Soral) have an affair, with initially comic results as Jacques tries to discover the identity of his daughter's seducer and assaults the wrong man. The ending is more sober as Jacques learns the truth, and Pierre must face both the damage to their friendship and unresolved problems posed for himself by his relationship with Françoise. Berri's film, although it has its excellent moments, the glamour of the Riviera and polished performances from the two lead men, seems uncertain of its intention. It comes out as a confused mix of love story, moral tale, exploration of the generation gap and exposé of the dangers beneath the surface of the holiday mood. It was remade by Stanley Donen in 1984 as *Blame It On Rio*, starring Michael Caine.

A Summer At Grandpa's

▶ **Dongdong De Jiaqui**

Taiwan   1984   102 mins   col
Marble Road Productions

d   Hou Hsiao-hsien
sc   Zhu Tianwen
ph   Chen Kunhou
m   Edward Yang
     Wang Qiguang, Zhou Shengli, Gu Jun, Mei Fang, Lin Xiuling

When the mother of a 12-year-old boy (Qiguang) and his little sister (Shengli), who live in Taipei, has surgery, the children are sent, escorted by an irresponsible uncle, to spend the summer with their grandfather (Jun) who is an old-fashioned country doctor. Once there, a variety of experiences and adventures, from the amusing to the frightening, befall them. It is rare to see a quality film from Taiwan, which this is in terms of charm, good performances and a story that provides some delightful moments. Gentle and enjoyable, but lightweight.

Summer Interlude

► **aka Illicit Interlude**

► **Sommarlek**

Sweden 1950 97 mins bw
Svensk Filmindustri

d **Ingmar Bergman**
sc **Ingmar Bergman, Herbert Grevenius**
ph **Gunnar Fischer, Bengt Järnmark**
m **Erik Nordgren**
   **Maj-Britt Nilsson, Birger Malmsten, Alf
   Kjellin, Stig Olin**

A prima ballerina (Nilsson) looks back on
the idyllic summer she spent several years
before on an island near Stockholm with the
boy (Malmsten) she loved. But the affair
comes to an abrupt and tragic end when he
is killed in an accident. This heartbreaking
loss leaves her bitter and without emotion
until she meets a young journalist (Kjellin).
Bergman's first mature film deals with adolescent love, the subject of much of his early
work, also revealing the psychological dangers of dwelling on the past. The Swedish
summer is wonderfully captured in the early,
lyrical love scenes.

► **Summer Light** see Lumière D'Été

Summer Lightning

► **Strohfeuer**

W. Germany 1972 100 mins col
Hallelujah Films

d **Volker Schlöndorff**
sc **Volker Sclöndorff, Margarethe Von
   Trotta**
ph **Sven Nykvist**
m **Stanley Myers**
   **Margarethe Von Trotta, Friedhelm Ptok,
   Martin Lüttge, Walter Sedlmayer**

Elisabeth (Von Trotta) feels wonderfully free
after her divorce from her husband (Ptok),
although a decision on the custody of their
five-year-old son is still pending. But the feeling does not last as she struggles from one job
to another and attempts to regain her child.
This portrait of a woman trying to make it in

a male world in the early days of women's liberation seemed pretty loaded over a decade
later, though many of the problems raised had
yet to be solved. Schlöndorff's wife, Von
Trotta, who would become a director herself
a few years later, gives a performance that
sometimes transforms the tract into drama.

Summer Manoeuvres

► **(US: The Grand Manoeuver)**

► **Les Grandes Manoeuvres**

France 1955 106 mins col
Filmsonor/Rizzoli

d **René Clair**
sc **René Clair**
ph **Robert Lefèbvre**
m **Georges Van Parys**
   **Gérard Philipe, Michèle Morgan, Yves
   Robert, Brigitte Bardot, Jean Desailly,
   Pierre Dux**

In a pre-World War I garrison town, a handsome dragoon (Philipe) wagers he can seduce
a stand-offish divorcée (Morgan). In the process, he falls in love with her, but his reputation as a Don Juan has destroyed his
credibility. Clair stated that 'love is the only
concern of the film . . . a very serious matter'.
This gently ironic romantic comedy, Clair's
first in colour, has more genuine emotion
than any of his previous work. The leads play
with charm and intelligence.

The Summer of Aviya

► **Hakayitz Shel Aviya**

Israel 1988 96 mins col
H.S.A. Ltd

d **Eli Cohen**
sc **Eli Cohen, Gila Almagor, Chaim Buzaglo**
ph **David Garfinkel**
m **Shem-Tov Levi**
   **Gila Almagor, Kaipo Cohen, Eli Cohen,
   Marina Rossetti, Avital Dicker, Dina
   Avrech, Ya'kov Ayali**

Isreal 1951. Henya (Almagor), a 43-year-old
woman who has been released from a mental
hospital after a breakdown as a result of her

experiences in the war and the loss of her husband, lives with her nine-year-old daughter Aviya (Kaipo Cohen) in a cabin in a small settlement where she works as laundress and seamstress. Delivering laundry to the Abramsons, Aviya meets their daughter Maya (Dicker), the local ballet teacher, who opens up a new world to her. But problems arise when Aviya fantasises that a married neighbour, Mr Gantz (Eli Cohen), is her father. Based on the autobiographical, best-selling novel by Gila Almagor about her childhood, this second feature by the actor and ex-documentary director Cohen, allows the distinguished Israeli actress to play her own mother, powerfully suggesting the traumas of the recent past. The acting throughout is remarkable, from the dark-eyed child of the title to each member of the closed community. Eli Cohen's achievement is in the creation of rounded characters, never shirking from the unsympathetic sides of mother or daughter, and his balancing of a rites of passage comedy-drama with subtle references to the Holocaust. The scene when Henya shaves her daughter's head to avoid lice brings the two strands together in an imaginative way. Although it is never made clear why the villagers are so antagonistic towards the mother, the expression of their ostracism – reflected in the tragi-comic scenes where she has to bring children in from the street to attend Aviya's birthday party and her gatecrashing of a ball – comes across with cruel irony.

Best Director Berlin 1989

Summer Paradise

▶ **aka Paradise Place**

▶ **Paradistorg**

Sweden   1977   113 mins   col
Cinematograph AB/Swedish Film Institute/Svensk Filmindustri

d   **Gunnel Lindblom**
sc   **Ulla Isaksson, Gunnel Lindblom**
ph   **Tony Forsberg**
m   **Georg Riedel**
     Birgitta Valberg, Sif Ruud, Solveig Ternström, Per Myrberg, Margareta Byström, Holger Löwenadler, Pontus Gustafson, Göran Stangertz, Agneta Ekmanner

Katha Wilk (Valberg), a doctor and divorced grandmother, is the centre of a large family group and assorted friends of all ages, who gather at her lakeside house to enjoy the Midsummer holiday. Once there, tensions mount, particularly between the generations, and the sojourn ends in tragedy. No surprise that the producer was Ingmar Bergman, whose protegée, Gunnel Lindblom, was making her debut film as director. The title is ironic: scenery aside, here is no paradise but a focal point for the meeting of unhappiness, futility, frustration and madness. Intended to expose the underside of 'progressive' Swedish society, this is a depressing and all-too-convincing film.

Summer Soldiers

Japan   1971   103 mins   col
Teshigahara Productions

d   **Hiroshi Teshigahara**
sc   **John Nathan**
ph   **Hiroshi Teshigahara**
m   **Tohru Takemitsu**
     Keith Sykes, Lee Reisen, Kazuo Kitamura, Toshiko Kobayashi, Shoichi Ozawa, Greg Antonacci

An American GI (Sykes), stationed in Japan, deserts in order to avoid being sent to Vietnam. He and other American deserters hide out with Japanese families, constantly moving from one household to the next to avoid arrest. John Nathan, screenwriter and scholar of Japanese literature, and Teshigahara, have created an interesting culture-clash drama out of a topical situation. Questions about the American action in Vietnam are raised that were ignored by American films of the time. In *cinéma vérité* style, its cast of amateurs includes members of the Tokyo Deserters Aid Committee and Japanese host families. The film's main weakness lies in the passive, bland performance of Sykes, a folk-rock singer from Kentucky, in the main role.

Summer Vacation 1999

▶ **1999-Nen No Natsu Yasumi**

Japan   1988   90 mins   col
New Century Producers/CBS-Sony Group

d   Shusuke Kaneko
sc Rio Kishida
ph Kenji Takama
m   Yuriko Nakamura
    Eri Miyajima, Tomoko Otakara, Miyuki
    Nakano, Rie Mizuhara

Four teenage boys remain on at a deserted boarding-school in the countryside during the summer vacation of 1999. They are the sensitive Yu (Miyajima); Naoto (Nakano), the oldest at sixteen and their leader; thirteen-year-old Norio (Mizuhara), the youngest and most impressionable, and Kazuhiko (Otakara), the most beautiful. One midnight, Yu apparently drowns himself in the school's lake. Norio blames the suicide on Kazuhiko, who had rejected Yu's love. A new boy arrives and is the image of the dead Yu. The four boys play a strange game of adolescent love, jealousy and death. By casting young girls in the boys' roles, Kaneko obviously wanted to introduce a stronger androgynous element into this poetic tale of schoolboy crushes. Transvestism is part of the tradition of Japanese theatre, but Western audiences might find it rather more difficult to accept. In fact, the film was inspired by a story in a comic book for girls, and the director used dialogue from the source (which may account for some of its silliness). The lush soft-focus photography and long takes give the film a dreamy quality, and there is some poignancy in the depiction of growing pains.

Summer With Monika

▶ (US: Monika)

▶ Sommaren Med Monika

    Sweden   1952   97 mins   bw
    Svensk Filmindustri

d   Ingmar Bergman
sc Ingmar Bergman, Per-Anders Fogelström
ph Gunnar Fischer
m   Erik Nordgren
    Harriet Andersson, Lars Ekborg, Åke
    Grönberg, Naemi Briese, Åke Fridell

An irresponsible teenage girl (Andersson) spends a summer island holiday with a young clerk (Ekborg), but she gets pregnant and later literally leaves him holding the baby. Bergman sees little hope for these adolescents in the winter of their discontent after a summer made glorious by Fischer's camera. The two young leads give this simple tale a remarkable veracity. Thereafter, until *Fanny And Alexander* (1982), adults, principally women, took centre stage in the director's work.

▶ **Suna No Onna** see Woman Of The Dunes

Sunday Daughters

▶ Vasárnapi Szülok

    Hungary   1979   100 mins   col
    Mafilm

d   János Rósza
sc István Kardos
ph Elemér Ragályi
m   Levente Szorényi
    Julianna Nyakó, Julianna Balogh, Andrea
    Blizik, Melinda Szakács, Erzsi Pásztor,
    Agnes Kakassy, Sergei Elistratov

Teenage girls in a reformatory dream of, and attempt, escape. Eventually one of them, Juli (Nyakó), makes it to her sister's distant home, but is forced to leave. She finds refuge with Aranka (Pásztor), her one-day (Sunday) foster mother appointed by the institution, where she makes love with Aranka's son, but must leave there, too ... In common with Yugoslavia's *Special Treatment*, this film looks at the methods and consequences of repressive, bureaucratic correctional institutions where no attempt is made to understand the inmates. Rósza directs with exemplary judgement of action and character, allowing the natural and high spirits of the girls to emerge in the otherwise bleak atmosphere: in a memorable sequence, a dormitory party spills over into hysteria and a suicide attempt. Both engaging and salutary, the film ends with recaptured Juli and the others watching *The Four Hundred Blows*, the final scenes of which are a poignant echo of their plight.

Sunday In August

▶ Domenica D'Agosto

    Italy   1950   75 mins   bw

Colonna

d **Luciano Emmer**
sc **Franco Brusati, Luciano Emmer, Cesare Zavattini, Giulio Macchi**
ph **Domenica Scala, Leonida Barboni, Ubaldo Marelli**
m **Roman Vlad**
Anna Baldini, Franco Interlenghi, Elvy Lissia, Massimo Serato, Correda Verga, Marcello Mastroianni, Ave Ninchi

One August Sunday, five groups of ordinary people leave Rome to spend the day at the beach resort of Ostia. Former documentary film-maker Emmer's first and most successful feature was a gentle, perceptive and humorous look at Italian *petit bourgeois* mores, made on location in the Neo-Realist vein. The script was purposefully diffuse – there is little or no connection between the five groups – but is given form by skilful editing. The little-known, 26-year-old Mastroianni appeared in Emmer's next two films.

A Sunday In September

▶ **En Söndag I September**

Sweden 1963 113 mins bw
Europa Film

d **Jörn Donner**
sc **Jörn Donner**
ph **Tony Forsberg**
m **Bo Nilsson**
Harriet Andersson, Thommy Berggren, Barbro Kollberg, Harry Ahlin, Axel Düberg, Jan-Erik Lindqvist

Stig and Birgitta (Berggren and Andersson) fall in love, marry – by which time she is pregnant – survive her miscarriage and gradually drift apart. Within this framework, the debut film of Finnish writer, political reporter and critic Donner, highlights the incompatabilities of his young couple, while attempting a serious examination of the social background to marriage and relationships, concluding on a downbeat note. The piece is divided into four distinct segments – romance, marriage, estrangement and divorce – each one introduced by a montage of shots of landscape and life in contemporary Sweden. The leads are excellent (the gifted Andersson would become the director's wife) and the

film won the Opera Prima at Venice. There are definite echoes of Bergman, particularly in Donner's treatment of Birgitta – fascinating in view of his public criticism of the Swedish master's work as irrelevant to contemporary society.

Sunday In The Country

▶ **Un Dimanche À La Campagne**

France 1984 94 mins col
Sara Films/Films A2/Little Bear

d **Bertrand Tavernier**
sc **Bertrand Tavernier, Colo Tavernier**
ph **Bruno De Keyzer**
m **Fauré**
Louis Ducreux, Sabine Azéma, Michel Aumont, Geneviève Mnich, Monique Chaumette, Claude Winter, Thomas Duval

On a Sunday in 1912, the widowed, 76-year-old artist, Monsieur Ladmiral (Ducreux), who lives in the country looked after by his housekeeper (Chaumette), awaits a visit from his son Edouard (Aumont), daughter-in-law and grandchildren. They arrive, later joined by Ladmiral's unattentive but adored daughter Irène (Azéma) of whom Edouard, feeling cheated of his father's love, is jealous. The day passes, the family leaves, and Ladmiral returns to his easel... The film is stylish, good-looking and beautifully played, dealing in nuances and thoroughly beguiling. However, its deeper themes are dealt with superficially and, like so much of Tavernier's work, there is more show than substance, making for ephemeral pleasure.

Best Director Cannes 1984

The Sunday Of Life

▶ **Le Dimanche De La Vie**

France 1965 100 mins bw
Sofracima/Doxa(Paris)Taurus(Munich)/Schermi(Rome)

d **Jean Herman**
sc **Olivier Hussenot, Georges Richard, Raymond Queneau**
ph **Jean-Jacques Tarbes**
m **Georges Delerue**

Danielle Darrieux, Jean-Pierre Moulin,
Françoise Arnoul, Olivier Hussenot,
Berthe Bovy, Jean Rochefort

Julia (Darrieux) and her sister (Arnoul) run a hat shop in provincial France during the 1930s. On his discharge from the army, Valentin (Moulin) marries Julia but goes off and becomes a picture framer in Paris. Julia joins him and, discovering that she can foresee events, sets herself up as Madame Saphir, clairvoyant. Her success is laced with sadness as the threat of war grows and begins to affect the future.... This first feature is a gently satirical series of vignettes revealing the life in a Parisian *quartier* between two world wars, when time seems to be standing still. Director, writer and actors achieve an authentic and nostalgic atmosphere and some vivid and witty characterization through imaginative moments that speak volumes. However, these moments are fleeting and without a solid foundation, leaving an impression of contrivance that begins to pall and reduces the film to a forgettable exercise in charm.

A Sunday Romance

▶ **Bakaruhaban**

Hungary 1957 92 mins bw
Hunnia Studio

d Imre Fehér
sc Miklós Hubay
ph János Badal
m Tibor Polgár
Margit Bara, Iván Darvas, Sándor Pécsi,
Maria Lázár, Vali Korompai, Adám
Szirtes

World War I has just begun. In a small Hungarian town, Sándor (Darvas), a comfortably off journalist and gentleman, dons a humble private's uniform every Sunday and goes out walking. He meets Vilma (Bara), a delightful and naive girl who falls in love with him. It turns out that she works as a maid for the lawyer whose daughter Sándor is courting but, by the time he finds the courage to admit to his feelings for Vilma, it is too late. A beautifully controlled first film from a director who has a fine sense of irony, a gift for intimacy and an eye for detail. The bitter-sweet love story is told in a well-observed social context in which the character

of provincial life is beautifully delineated. Well-acted and splendidly photographed, its weakness is that the narrative intermittently runs out of steam.

Sundays And Cybèle

▶ **Cybèle Ou Les Dimanches De Ville-D'Avray**

France 1962 110 mins bw
Terra/Fides/Orsay/Trocadero

d Serge Bourgignon
sc Serge Bourgignon, Antoine Tudal
ph Henri Decaë
m Maurice Jarre
Hardy Kruger, Patricia Gozzi, Nicole
Courcel, Daniel Ivernel

In a small town near Paris, a former German pilot, now suffering from amnesia, forges a friendship with a 12-year-old girl from the convent orphanage, but when they innocently spend Christmas together in the woods, he is suspected of assaulting her. The warm playing of Kruger and Gozzi as the odd couple helps to counteract some of the self-conscious charm and aesthetics of the direction. Bourgignon, who won an Oscar with this debut film, has done nothing to merit much attention since.

Best Foreign Film Oscar 1962

Sunflower

▶ **I Girasoli**

Italy 1970 107 mins col
Champion/Concordia/Mosfilm

d Vittorio De Sica
sc Tonino Guerra, Cesare Zavattini, Georgy
Mdivani
ph Giuseppe Rotunno
m Henry Mancini
Sophia Loren, Marcello Mastroianni,
Ludmila Savelyeva, Galina Andreyeva,
Germano Longo

An Italian couple, married for 12 days, are separated when the husband is sent to the Russian front and reported missing, but they find each other again after the war. A sad example of how much De Sica's work had declined since the 1950s. The sentimentality incipient in his earlier films has here taken over, and any social message is wrapped in a glossy package containing a predictable plot and lifeless characters. Interesting sidelight: this was the first Italian film to be shot mainly in Russia, and Loren's child in the film was her own by producer Carlo Ponti, her husband.

Sunless

▶ **Sans Soleil**

> France 1982 100 mins col
> Argos

d **Chris Marker**
sc **Chris Marker**
ph **Chris Marker, Sana Na N'Hada, Jean-Michel Humeau, Mario Marret, Eugenio Bentivoglio, Daniel Tessier, Haroun Tazieff**
m **Moussorgsky, Sibelius**

A fictional cameraman tries to make sense of the cultural dislocation he sees and feels in Japan, West Africa and Iceland. Using diverse images, letters, quotes and musings, Marker continues to extend the limits of the 'documentary'. Here, he makes use of new video technology and image-processing provided by Hayao Yamaneko, credited with special effects. The result is a poetic, philosphical and political collage, which Marker describes as like 'a musical composition, with recurrent themes, counterpoints and mirror-like fugues'.

▶ **Sur** see South

▶ **Sur, El** see South, The

▶ **Sürü** see Herd, The

Susana

▶ **(US: The Devil And The Flesh)**
▶ **Demonio Y Carne**

> Mexico 1951 82 mins bw
> Internacional Cinematografica/Oscar Dancigers

d **Luis Buñuel**
sc **Jaime Salvador**
ph **José Órtiz Ramos**

m **Raúl Lavista**
    Rosita Quintana, Fernando Soler, Victor Manuel Mendoza, Matilde Palau

Susana (Quintana) begs God to work a miracle and free her from prison. He does so. After wandering over the mountains, she is taken in by a kindly rich family that employs her as a maid on its ranch, but she repays her benefactors by seducing every man in sight. 'A perfectly routine film,' Buñuel called this rehearsal for his more mature excursions into the world of sex and power games and, despite an inspired opening scene, his estimation is about right. Yet no film by the Spanish master is without interest and this cheaply-made melodrama contains many of his anything-but-routine trademarks, including the amoral vamp and an ironic anti-religious ending.

▶ **Süsuz Yaz** see Waterless Summer

▶ **Suzanne Simonin, La Religieuse De Diderot** see Religieuse, La

Swann In Love

▶ **Un Amour De Swann**

> France 1983 110 mins col
> Gaumont/Bioskop/FR3/SFPC

d **Volker Schlöndorff**
sc **Peter Brook, Jean-Claude Carrière, Marie-Hélène Estienne**
ph **Sven Nykvist**
m **Hans-Werner Henze**
    Jeremy Irons, Ornella Muti, Alain Delon, Fanny Ardant, Marie-Christine Barrault, Anne Bennent

Charles Swann (Irons), received into aristocratic circles despite the fact that he is a Jew, has a passionate affair with Odette (Muti), a beautiful demi-mondaine over whom he is racked with insane jealousy. Elegant, refined and well played – especially, and unexpectedly, by Delon as the decadent Baron Charlus – with turn-of-the-century Paris exquisitely caught by Nykvist's camera, the film nonetheless cannot begin to approach the richness of Swann's Way, the first volume of Marcel Proust's great novel. The elimination of the narrator is only one essential dimension that is lost.

Swan Song

▶ **Juexiang**

China　1985　100 mins　col
Pearl River Film Studio – Youth
Division

d　**Zhang Zeming**
sc　**Zhang Zeming**
ph　**Zheng Kangzhen, Zhao Xiaoshi**
m　**Zhou Xiaoyuan**
　　Kong Xianzhu, Chen Rui, Mo Shaoying,
　　Liang Yujin, Feng Diqing, Liu Qianyi, Li
　　Jianjun

A Cantonese musician (Xianzhu), a composer
and master of the *qin* (Chinese zither), finds
himself out of favour in the New China of
1949, mainly because of an opium addiction
that led to the breakdown of his marriage.
He lives on a pittance trying to raise his son
(Rui) to be a musician, while his estranged
daughter (Yujin) is being educated at the
music academy. During the Cultural Revolution, forbidden to write or play music, the
father hears a travestied arrangement of his
'A Wild Goose Soars High' as a grandiose
piano concerto played by his daughter and
passed off as her own composition. This debut
feature is a bitter-sweet chronicle of the life
of an artist buffeted by the upheavals of
modern Chinese history. A deserted back
alleyway serves as a motif to underline that
the events witnessed take place outside the
glare of publicity. It certainly touches on
aspects unseen in recent Chinese films and
makes a stark contrast between the past and
the vulgar, 'Westernized' present where the
characters seem more and more alienated.
The occasionally rambling screenplay and
direction benefit from the haunting Cantonese
music and the nuanced performance from
Xianahu in the leading role.

The Swedish Mistress

▶ **aka The Mistress**

▶ **Älskar Innan**

Sweden　1962　77 mins　bw
Svensk Filmindustri/Janus

d　**Vilgot Sjöman**
sc　**Vilgot Sjöman**
ph　**Lasse Björne**
　　Bibi Andersson, Max Von Sydow, Per

Myrberg, Ølegard Welton, Birgitta
Valberg

A young woman (Andersson), who already
has a regular boyfriend (Myrberg), meets an
older married man (Von Sydow) at a scientific
conference. They have an involved affair, but
his refusal to leave his wife causes her much
pain and leads to a reassessment of her life.
This was the first feature from Ingmar
Bergman's former assistant, who would make
his own mark by causing a sensation with *I
Am Curious – Yellow* five years later. It is
conventional in both subject and treatment,
but helped no end by the high-powered lead
casting.

Best Actress (Bibi Andersson) Berlin 1963

The Sweet Body Of Deborah

▶ **Il Dolce Corpo Di Deborah**

Italy　1967　95 mins　col
Zenith Cinematografica/Flora Film
(Rome)/Lux (Paris)

d　**Romolo Guerrieri**
sc　**Ernesto Gastaldi**
ph　**Marcello Masiocchi**
m　**Nora Orlandini**
　　Carroll Baker, Jean Sorel, George Hilton,
　　Ida Galli, Luigi Pistilli

Returning to Geneva from their honeymoon,
Deborah (Baker) and Marcel (Sorel) encounter unpleasant accusations from Marcel's friend Philip (Pistelli) concerning the death of
his former fiancée, and are hounded by threatening phone calls. They seek respite in Nice,
but things go from bad to worse, culminating
in murder. The title of this film, together with
its erotic opening sequence of lovemaking in
the shower, suggests a salacious sex movie.
In fact, it is a superior and ingenious suspense
thriller, full of surprise twists in the tradition
of *Les Diaboliques*.

Sweet Hours

▶ **Dulces Horas**

Spain　1981　103 mins　col
Elias Querejeta Productions

d　**Carlos Saura**
sc　**Carlos Saura**
ph　**Teo Escamilla**

Assumpta Serna, Iñaki Aierra, Alvaro De Luna, Jacques Lalande, Luisa Rodrigo, Pedro Samson

A playwright (Aierra), rehearsing a play about his own childhood during the Franco era, finds himself falling in love with the actress (Serna) who is playing his beloved mother, a vivacious woman whose sudden death shocked him profoundly. Using his favourite (and now rather worn) device of the melding of memories, dreams, fantasies, the past and the present, Saura adds the more interesting Pirandellian twist of breaking down the boundaries of reality and the theatre. We are seldom sure whether we are watching the play, the playwright's memories, or both. What is certain and rather banal is that, having the sensuous and attractive Assumpta Serna (an impressive debut) playing both the mother and actress, the shade of Oedipus is not far away.

▶ **Sweet Life, The** see Dolce Vita, La

Swept Away...By An Unusual Destiny In The Blue Sea Of August

▶ **Travolti Da Un Insolito Destino Nell'Azzurro Mare D'Agosto**

Italy 1975 120 mins col
Medusa Cinematografica

d **Lina Wertmüller**
sc **Lina Wertmüller**
m **Ennio Guarnieri**
m **Piero Piccioni**
Giancarlo Giannini, Mariangela Melato, Riccardo Salvino, Aldo Puglisi, Isa Danieli

A Sicilian deck-hand (Giannini), working on a yacht, and his boss's wife (Melato) find themselves adrift on a dinghy. After two nights, they reach an island on which they carry out a series of sexual and class strategies. Reality intrudes when the castaways are rescued. Wertmüller's twee title and desert island plot disguise a simple-minded determinist parable. If the message is that people's sexual attitudes are governed by economics and class, then the medium shows a director working in gender stereotypes. The two leads

play the puppet characters with as much conviction as is possible in the circumstances, and there are successful moments of bitter irony.

The Swimmer

▶ **Plovec**

USSR 1981 105mins bw/sepia/col
Gruzia Film

d **Irakli Kvirikadze**
sc **Irakli Kvirikadze**
ph **Turam Tugushi**
m **Teimuraz Bakuradze**
Elgudzha Burduli, Ruslan Mikaberidze, Baadur Tsuladze, Guram Pirtskhalava, Nana Kvachantiradze, Gia Lezhava

Three generations of a family – grandfather, father, grandson – are obsessed with swimming. This passion destroys the first two, while the middle-aged surviving member tries to keep it at bay. Made in Georgia, this is an original piece of work, constructed as a film within a film, and shot as distinct segments intercut with the activities of the crew which is supposed to be making it. Grandfather's tale is photographed in sepia, intriguingly beautiful and lyrical; son's episode is black and white, and redolent with the atmosphere of the post-war Stalinist period; grandson's story takes place on the contemporary film set and is in colour. There is little dialogue, voice-over commentary being largely used, and it is difficult to appreciate why the film's release was withheld for a few years. An interesting, often absorbing curiosity, that falls apart in the third segment.

▶ **Swindle, The** see Swindlers, The

The Swindlers

▶ **(US: The Swindle)**

▶ **Il Bidone**

Italy 1955 114 mins bw
Titanus/SGC

d **Federico Fellini**
sc **Federico Fellini, Ennio Flaiano, Tullio Pinelli**
ph **Otello Martelli**

m Nino Rota
   Broderick Crawford, Richard Basehart,
   Franco Fabrizi, Giulietta Masina

Three small-time crooks fleece the poor by
disguising themselves as priests, but when one
of them tries to double-cross the others, he is
beaten up and left to die alone on a stony
hillside. In answer to criticism from the Left
about his betrayal of Neo-Realist principles
in *La Strada* (1954), Fellini made his starkest
and most bitter social drama, but failed to
please the general public. Seriously lacking
his natural exuberance, the film does reach
tragic dimensions in the remarkable final
scene when Crawford finds salvation prior to
his death.

The Swing

▶ **Die Schaukel**

   W. Germany 1983 133 mins col
   Pelemele Film/Pro-ject Film/Roxy Film

d **Percy Adlon**
sc **Percy Adlon**
ph **Jürgen Martin**
m **Peer Raben, Johann Strauss**
   Anja Jaenicke, Lena Stolze, Joachim
   Bernhard, Rolf Illig, Suzanne Herlet,
   Christine Kaufmann

In Munich during the 1880s, the Lautenschlag
family – singing teacher mother (Kaufmann),
father (Illig) who is the Royal Bavarian landscape gardener, four teenage children – lives
a madcap existence, pawning antiques and
entertaining the Crown Prince at a musical
recital in its shabby home. In contrast to the
stuffy Prussian Von Zwingers who frown
upon them, the Lautenschlags are short of
money, enthusiastic about art, high-spirited
and unconventional. This is an affectionate,
charming, nostalgic and humorous portrait
of a madcap family, one of whose daughters
(Jaenicke) records the events in her diary and,
in later years, becomes a novelist who writes
the story we see. As in his earlier *Céleste*,
Adlon reveals a striking gift for evoking period through authentic visual detail.

The Swissmakers

▶ **Die Schweizermacher**

   Switzerland 1978 108 mins col

Lyssy/Rex/Willora/Schoch/Ecco

d **Rolf Lyssy**
sc **Rolf Lyssy, Beatrice Kessler**
ph **Fritz E. Maeder**
m **Jonas C. Haefeli**
   Walo Lüond, Emil Steinberger, Beatrice
   Kessler, Wolfgang Stendar, Hilde Ziegler,
   Claudio Caramaschi

A pair of policemen (Lüond and Steinberger)
in the naturalization section of the government have to investigate the suitability of
three candidates who have applied for Swiss
citizenship – an Italian baker (Caramaschi),
a German doctor (Stendar) and a Yugoslavian ballet dancer (Kessler), whom one of the
policeman falls for. An amusing and trenchant social comedy on 'How To Be A Swiss',
it is realized with a much lighter touch than
many of the other satires by Swiss directors
on their 'clean, conservative and complacent'
country. The opening lecture is influenced by
the Swiss-born Jean-Luc Godard.

The Switchboard Operator

▶ **aka The Tragedy Of A
   Switchboard Operator**

▶ **(US: Love Affair: Or The Case
   of The Missing Switchboard
   Operator)**

▶ **aka An Affair Of The Heart**

▶ **Ljubavni Slucaj**

▶ **aka Tragedija Sluzbenice P.T.T.**

   Yugoslavia 1967 69 mins bw
   Avala

d **Dušan Makavejev**
sc **Dušan Makavejev**
ph **Aleksandar Petković**
   Eva Ras, Slobodan Aligrudić, Ruzica
   Sokić, Miodrag Andrić

A young independent switchboard operator
(Ras) sets up house with a Turkish ratcatcher
(Aligrudić), who becomes jealous and accidentally kills her after she is seduced by a
postman (Andrić). Using hand-held cameras
in the streets, newsreels, asides, and ironic
juxtapositions between traditional and modern Yugoslavia, Makavejev invests his second
feature with vitality and an anarchic spirit.
However, the interruptions of the narrative

by a criminologist and a sexologist have dated, as has the director's obvious attempt to affront a conservative audience.

▶ **Swords Of Blood** see Cartouche

Sylvia And The Ghost

▶ **(US: Sylvia And The Phantom)**

▶ **Sylvie Et Le Fantôme**

France   1945   93 mins   bw
Écran Français/André Paulve

d Claude Autant-Lara
sc Jean Aurenche
ph Philippe Agostini
m René Clöerec
   **Odette Joyeux, François Périer, Jean
   Desailly, Jacques Tati, Louis Salou**

Sixteen-year-old Sylvia (Joyeux) is enamoured of a nobleman in a portrait which hangs in her castle home. Her father pays someone to impersonate the dead man, but two of her suitors have the same idea until the real ghost pops up. Less whimsical than it sounds, the film is an entertaining light comedy romance with a chance to see Jacques Tati as the ghost making his first appearance – and disappearance – in a feature. The 28-year-old Joyeux was made to look younger by her husband, photographer Agostini.

▶ **Sylvia And The Phantom** see Sylvia And The Ghost

▶ **Sylvie Et Le Fantôme** see Sylvia And The Ghost

Symphonie Fantastique

France   1947   90 mins   bw
L'Atelier Français

d Christian-Jaque
sc J.P. Feydeau, H.A. Legrand
ph Armand Thirard
m Berlioz
   **Jean-Louis Barrault, Renée Saint-Cyr,
   Lise Delamare, Bernard Blier, Gilbert-Gil**

The struggles of French composer Hector Berlioz as he climbs from obscurity to fame.

En route, domestic discord drives him to leave his wife for a more understanding woman, whereupon he creates his masterpieces. As this romantic hero of a romantic age, Jean-Louis Barrault, agonized and posturing, is not very sympathetic in a biopic which, while meticulously reproducing the elegance of the age, fails to capture its excitement, remaining tedious and pedestrian. The film does, however, provide a feast of musical extracts from some of Berlioz's most famous works, 'conducted' by Barrault, sometimes to the accompaniment of quite dramatic effects, such as storms raging without.

La Symphonie Pastorale

France   1946   110 mins   bw
Pathé/Les Films Gibe

d Jean Delannoy
sc Jean Aurenche, Jean Delannoy
ph Armand Thirard
m Georges Auric, Beethoven
   **Michèle Morgan, Pierre Blanchar, Jean
   Desailly, Line Noro, Louvigny, Andrée
   Clément, Rosine Luguet**

Gertrude (Morgan), a blind orphan girl, is taken in and raised by Pastor Martin (Blanchar) and his wife. He imbues her with a sense of the world as a place of beauty and harmony and eventually falls in love with her, as does his son Jean (Desailly). Jean wants to marry Gertrude and arranges an operation to restore her sight but, although this is successful, disillusion and tragedy follow. This is a sensitive if sombre adaptation of André Gide's heartbreaking novella, capturing the ironically beautiful and serene atmosphere of the mountain village where it is set. Delannoy directs with taste and discretion and Morgan, her beautiful and expressive eyes communicating Gertrude's innermost thoughts, is superb.

**Best Film Cannes 1946
Best Actress (Michèle Morgan) Cannes 1946**

▶ **Symphony Of The Don Basin** see Enthusiasm

▶ **Syskonbädd 1782** see My Sister, My Love

▶ **Sytten** see Seventeen

▶ **Szegénylegények** see Round-Up, The

▶ **Szerelem** see Love

▶ **Szerelmem, Elektra** see Elektreia

▶ **Szerencsés Daniel** see Daniel Takes A Train

▶ **Sziget A Szárazföldön** see Lady From Constantinople, The

▶ **Szindbád** see Sindbad

Tabataba

Madagascar 1988 94 mins col
Films Du Volcan/La SECAE/La Sept

d **Raymond Rajaonarivelo**
sc **Raymond Rajaonarivelo, Robert Archer, Jèrome Tonnerre**
ph **Bruno Privat, Gilles Arnaud, Véronique Patte**
m **Eddy Louis**
   François Botozandry, Lucien Dakadisy, Soatody, Soavelo, Rasoa, Philippe Nahoun

Set around the 1947 insurrection against the French in Madagascar (which only gave way to independence in 1960 after 100,000 people had been killed), this film is a portrait of a village gradually coming to understand liberation and the injustice of colonialism. The title is a word to describe the leaves of the trees rustling in the wind, which also is taken to mean that changes will come. Against the background of a wonderfully poetic tropical landscape, an old lady observes it all, watching history evolve in the microcosmic village. This dignified and controlled first feature by 40-year-old Rajaonarivelo, is also the first film to be produced in his country (with French financial participation). Seen from the point of view of the colonized, the film reveals a tragic situation, making its points effectively and calmly, offering no false hope. Yet the restrained style never diminishes the passion behind it or the drama inherent in the circumstances. One of the few flaws is the rather inappropriate jazzy music.

▶ **Ta' Det Som En Man, Frue!** see Take It Like A Man, Ma'am

▶ **Tagebuch Einer Verloren** see Diary Of A Lost Girl

▶ **Taiheiyo Hitoribochi** see Alone On The Pacific

▶ **Tailor's Maid, The** see Like Father, Like Son

Take It Like A Man, Ma'am

▶ **Ta' Det Som En Man, Frue!**

Denmark 1975 96 mins col
Rode Soster

d **Elizabeth Rygard, Mette Knudsen, Li Vilstrup**
sc **Elizabeth Rygard, Mette Knudsen, Li Vilstrup**
ph **Katia Forbert Petersen, Judy Irola, Lene Føg-Moller, Leni Schou**
m **Fuzzy, Nina Larsen, Gudrun Steen-Andersen, Maria Marcus**
   Tove Maës, Alf Lassen, Berthe Quistgard, Hans Kragh Jacobsen, Dough Crutchfield, Asta Esper Andersen

A middle-aged married woman (Maës), whose children have grown up, leads an unfulfilled existence with a neglectful, patronizing husband (Lassen). In a dream she sees a society in which there is a complete gender reversal. Waking up to the depressing reality, she determines to get a job and regain some independence and happiness. A cooperative venture by an all-woman production team, the film boldly and lucidly declares itself strongly feminist, but it succeeds in working both as propaganda and entertainment. At the centre is a long, trenchantly amusing dream sequence in which men and women swap roles and attitudes – men are sex objects, bring up the children, work as secretaries to female bosses, have to be asked to dance and are generally oppressed. On either side of the dream is a more documentary-style analysis of the difficulties that women of 'a certain age' have in getting worthwhile employment. The film ends hopefully, although things have not changed enough since 1975 to invalidate the points it makes.

A Tale Of Springtime

▶ **Conte De Printemps**

France   1990   112 mins   col
Les Films Du Losange

d   **Eric Rohmer**
sc   **Eric Rohmer**
ph   **Luc Pagès**
m   **Beethoven, Schumann**
   Anne Teyssèdre, Hugues Quester, Florence Darel, Eloise Bennett, Sophie Robin, Marc Lelon, François Lamore

Jeanne (Teyssèdre), a philosophy graduate, meets Natasha (Darel), a piano student, at a party. As both their boyfriends are away from Paris, Natasha invites Jeanne to stay with her at the flat of her divorced father Igor (Quester), who lives elsewhere with his girlfriend Eve (Bennett). The four of them spend an awkward weekend at the family's country house near Fontainebleau. When Eve leaves after an argument and Natasha goes off with her boyfriend, Igor and Jeanne find themselves alone and mutually attracted. After the sequence of 'Six Moral Tales' and 'Six Comedies and Proverbs', Rohmer embarked on 'Tales Of The Four Seasons', though this spring did not seem to provide him with a new beginning. Once again we are in the delicate and intricate world of human relationships where the main characters move restlessly from place to place and from person to person, analysing themselves as they do so. However, the master of enticing comedies of manners seems to have delivered a comedy of mannerisms this time. Previously, as tiresome as many of his personages have been, the director's ironic distance has rendered their ethical choices interesting. Here, the empty, small-talking, well-heeled quartet strain the patience as they ramble on about gardens and kitchens on the same level as they do about their lovers. Nevertheless, there is always some pleasure to be had in seeing Rohmer's behaviourist actors doing so much with so

little and in watching as they weave a fine web around a trivial centre – on this occasion, a missing necklace.

The Tall Blond Man With One Black Shoe

▶ **Le Grand Blond Avec Une Chaussure Noire**

France   1972   89 mins   col
Gaumont International/Productions De La Guéville/ Madeleine Films

d   **Yves Robert**
sc   **Yves Robert, Francis Véber**
ph   **René Mathelin**
m   **Vladimir Cosma**
   Pierre Richard, Bernard Blier, Jean Rochefort, Mireille Darc, Jean Carmet, Colette Castel

When secret service agency chief Toulouse (Rochefort) suspects that Milan (Blier) is after his job, he sets him up by sending him to tail a dangerous agent who, in reality, is somebody picked at random from a crowd. The innocent victim, a naive and clumsy violinist (Richard), is engaged in an affair with his friend's wife, whose apartment is bugged by Milan's men. A brilliantly ironic idea, but muddled in its realization. Everything points to a wild comedy but the humour is only sporadically injected into what is played as a straight spy thriller. The acting, particularly from new comic discovery Richard, is accomplished, and there are a number of clever elements, but the sum of the parts is greater than the whole, even though it spawned a sequel, *The Return Of The Tall Blond*, in 1974.

Special Jury Prize Berlin 1973

Tall Shadows Of The Wind

▶ **Saiehaien Bolan De Bad**

Iran   1978   110 mins   col
Telfilm/Iran Biograph Film Centre

d   **Bahman Farmanara**
sc   **Hushang Golshiri, Bahman Farmanara**
ph   **Alireza Zarindast**
m   **Ahmad Pejman**
   Faramaz Gharibian, Saiid Nikpour, Nadia Khalilpur

A bus driver (Gharibian), plying a route between remote villages, draws a face on a scarecrow and puts his own hat on its head. Various mysterious events take place thereafter, and the villagers, believing the scarecrow to be an evil deity, blame the bus driver. Working through visually striking symbols in a folk tale format, Farmanara and the short story writer Golshiri, have created an arresting film which implicitly attacks superstition and authoritarianism. The film came into disfavour under the Shah and then under Khomeini, each regime seeing itself represented by the scarecrow. The vivid colours and the lush musical score add to the atmosphere of the piece, and there is a memorable dream sequence.

▶ **Tamas** see Darkness

Tampopo

Japan 1986 117 mins col
Itami Productions/New Century Producers

d **Juzo Itami**
sc **Juzo Itami**
ph **Masaki Tamura**
m **Kinihiko Murai**
   Tsutomu Yamazaki, Nobuko Miyamoto, Koji Yakusho, Ken Watanabe, Rikiya Yasuoka

An all-night truck driver (Yamazaki) pulls in for a snack at a wayside noodle shop run by the widowed Tampopo (Miyamoto, Itami's wife). Finding the food uneatable, he stays to help her turn the place into one of the best restaurants in the country. This gorgeous gastronomic comedy of table manners satirizes Japanese social mores in a series of vignettes, mostly set in the *ramen* (noodle) shop. The director calls it a '*ramen* western', due to some similarities to *Shane* and co. – wandering trouble shooter rides into town and then rides off alone. The film satisfies like a good meal, although it should not be seen on an empty stomach.

Tango Bar

Argentina 1988 90 mins col

Zaga Films (Puerto Rico)/Beco Films (Argentina)

d **Marcos Zurinaga**
sc **Marcos Zurinaga, José Pablo Feinnman, Juan Carlos Cordazzi**
ph **Marcos Zurinaga**
m **Atilio Stampone**
   Raùl Julia, Valeria Lynch, Ruben Juarez

Ricardo (Julia) and Elena (Lynch) meet their old friend Antonio (Juarez) in the Buenos Aires cabaret where they had jointly presented a successful tango show before Antonio's 10-year political exile. The flashbacks show the pressures put upon them by the dictatorship of the military junta, while demonstrating the history of the tango from the *milonguitas* to the modern forms with the use of film clips, including Valentino in *The Four Horsemen Of The Apocalypse* and Gene Kelly in *Anchors Aweigh*. This episodic film relies almost solely on the dance numbers for any interest or pleasure it provides, the perfunctory story forming a flimsy framework. Derived and performed by the cast members of Broadway's *Tango Argentino*, it still has the whiff of the stage clinging to it. Lovers of the tango, however, will enjoy many of the vintage film glimpses of past maestros of the seductive dance step and the fancy footwork of their heirs.

▶ **Tangos, L'Exil De Gardel** see Tangos, The Exile Of Gardel

Tangos, The Exile Of Gardel

▶ **Tangos, L'Exil De Gardel**

Argentina/France 1985 130 mins col
Cinesur(Buenos Aires)/Terciné(Paris)

d **Fernando E Solanas**
sc **Fernando E Solanas**
ph **Felix Monti**
m **Astor Piazzola**
   Marie Laforêt, Philippe Léotard, Miguel Angel Sola, Marina Vlady, Georges Wilson, Lautaro Murua, Anna Maria Picchio

A group of Argentinian exiles in Paris must battle with nostalgia, problems of national identity and the practicalities of making ends meet. They decide to stage a tango ballet inspired by the memory and music of Carlos Gardel, the legendary Argentinian tango star who was killed in 1935. Coming from the radically politicized director of, among other things, *The Hour Of The Furnaces*, this movie is something of a surprise. Solanas displays humour and a gift for the staging of dance numbers, unfolding a tale about the pain of exile through the relationships and incidents that attend the rehearsals and production of the show. The movie is marred by its undisciplined structure and inordinate length, but the lighting photography, music and dance are a triumph.

Special Jury Prize Venice 1985

▶ **Tanin No Kao** see Face Of Another, The

▶ **Tant Qu'on A La Santé** see As Long As You're Healthy

▶ **Tanu, A** see Witness, The

▶ **Tartüff** see Tartuffe

Tartuffe

▶ **Tartüff**

Germany 1925 70 mins bw
UFA

d **F.W. Murnau**
sc **Carl Mayer**
ph **Karl Freund**
m **Silent**
  Emil Jannings, Werner Krauss, Lil Dagover, Lucie Höflich

Having ingratiated himself with the wealthy Orgon (Krauss), the rascally and hypocritical Tartuffe (Jannings) comes to dominate the man's household. Orgon's eyes are finally opened when he catches Tartuffe trying to make love to his attractive young wife (Dagover). This heavily Germanic adaptation of Molière's classical comedy was turned into a chamber film, eliminating the secondary characters in order to concentrate on the central triangle of relationships. Murnau also added a superfluous prologue to introduce the story. Stylishly made, the picture benefited

from an outstanding team behind the camera which included top art directors Walter Röhrig and Robert Herlth, but it is best remembered for the performances of its stellar cast.

The Taste Of Water

▶ **De Smaak Van Water**

Netherlands 1982 100 mins col
Maya Film

d **Orlow Seunke**
sc **Orlow Seunke, Dirk Ayelt Kooiman**
ph **Albert Van Der Wildt**
m **Jan Musch**
  Gerard Thoolen, Dorijn Curvers, Joop Admiraal, Hans Van Tongeren, Olga Zuiderhoek

A social worker (Thoolen), efficient, but seemingly indifferent after years of dealing with poverty and suffering, dedicates himself to the education and rehabilitation of a neglected, dirty, animal-like 14-year-old girl (Curvers), who hardly leaves the cupboard in which she was raised. In the tradition of *The Miracle Worker* and Truffaut's *Wild Child*, Seunke's film deals with the civilizing process while, at the same time, attacking Dutch bureaucracy. Directed in a straightforward manner, without seeking sympathy, the film gains its emotional impact both from the subject matter and from the extraordinary performance from Dorijn Curvers, who worked on the material with the director for over four years before shooting began.

Tatie Danielle

France 1990 110 mins col
Telema/FR3 Films

d **Etienne Chatiliez**
sc **Florence Quentin**
ph **Philippe Welt**
m **Gabriel Yared**
  Tsilla Chelton, Catherine Jacob, Isabelle Nanty, Neige Dolsky, Eric Prat

Tatie Danielle (Chelton) is a wealthy old woman, living only to die and join the husband to whose portrait she talks. She is also a vile and tyrannical monster, who torments her even older companion-housekeeper literally to death, whereupon her only family, a great nephew, his wife and two children, take her to live with them in their Paris apartment, where she insidiously proceeds to destroy their equilibrium and their home. Following his debut film, *Life Is A Long Quiet River* (1989), Chatiliez confirms that he has an offbeat casting sense and a wicked eye for the foibles of human behaviour – especially among the *bourgeoisie*. However, this film self-destructs as a result of being much too long, too slow to get under way, weak in its plot resolution and, above all, presents a main character of such monumental awfulness that the joke is not really funny. It does, however, have its moments and is sporadically intriguing and entertaining.

▸ **Tausend Augen Des Dr Mabuse, Die** see Thousand Eyes Of Dr Mabuse, The

▸ **Tavaszi Zapor** see Marie – A Hungarian Legend

▸ **Taxidi Sta Kithira** see Voyage To Cythera

A Taxing Woman

▸ **Marusa No Onna**

Japan   1987   127 mins   col
Itami Productions/New Century Producers

d   **Juzo Itami**
sc **Juzo Itami**
ph **Yoneza Maeda**
m   **Toshiyuki Honda**
    Nobuko Miyamoto, Tsutomu Yamazaki, Masahiko Tsugawa, Hideko Murota

The day-to-day life of an eager-beaver female tax inspector (Miyamoto, Itami's wife) determined to track down every small-scale tax fraud, despite being harassed, humiliated and harmed by the people she pursues, although a certain sympathy develops between her and a petty criminal (Yamazaki). The bright new meteor of the Japanese cinema followed up his 'noodle Western' *Tampopo* with an equally successful comedy on the unlikely subject of tax returns (to be followed by *A Taxing*

Woman 2, dealing with million-dollar tax evasions). The detailed observation of the heroine's profession is as obsessive as that of Bresson's *Pickpocket*, but to more satiric ends. Itami's legerdemain allows him to easily from comedy to the realism of the gangster movie, ending in a tender, tense and surprising manner.

A Taxing Woman's Return

▸ **Marusa No Onna 2**

Japan   1988   127 mins   col
Itami Productions

d   **Juzo Itami**
sc **Juzo Itami**
ph **Yonezo Maeda**
m   **Toshiyuki Honda**
    Nobuko Miyamoto, Rentaro Mikuni, Masahiko Tsugawa, Tetsuro Tamba, Toru Masuoka, Takeya Nakamura

Continuing where *A Taxing Woman* left off, the brave female tax collector (Miyamoto), this time accompanied by a young, bumbling graduate (Mikuni), tackles a powerful politician, greedy real estate speculators, gangsters and a wealthy religious cult. As the first film was the third most successful in Japanese history, Itami could not resist falling into the numerical sequence mode so prevalent in the USA. Unfortunately, his previous box-office success and a bigger budget led the director, known for his innovative techniques, into a slick repetition of the formula and a more conventional narrative structure. Nevertheless, there are some good examples of Itami's offbeat humour and the occasional scathing sideswipe at Japanese capitalism. But the falling off can be put down to the fact that the marvellous Miyamoto has far less to do than her idiotic partner and Tsutomu Yamazaki, her splendid foil from earlier films, is missing.

Taxi Zum Klo

W. Germany   1981   92 mins   col
Frank Ripploh, Horst Schier, Laurens Straub

d   **Frank Ripploh**
sc **Frank Ripploh**
ph **Horst Schier**

m **Hans Wittstadt**
   Frank Ripploh, Bernd Broaderup,
   Magdalena Montezuma, Tabea
   Blumenschein, Gitte Lederer

A gay teacher (Ripploh), having a bad time with his jealous, home-making lover (Broaderup), spends his nights looking for pick-ups at public lavatories and loses his job. The director, whose debut film this is, plays himself as an amusing, randy and lovable rogue, supported by real-life friends and lovers. Despite the self-indulgence, some misogyny, and scenes 'of an explicit nature that might offend', it is a touching, humorous and generally positive view of homosexual life on the eve of the AIDS scare. Especially good are Ripploh in front of his class, and a tragicomic fancy dress party. The title could be translated as 'Taxi To The Loo'.

Tchaikovsky

USSR   1970   191 mins   col
Mosfilm(Moscow)/Warner Bros.-7
Arts(Hollywood)

d **Igor Talankin**
sc **Budimir Metalnikov, Yuri Nagibin, Igor Talankin**
ph **Margarita Pilikhina**
m **Tchaikovsky**
   Innokenti Smoktunovsky, Antonina Shuranova, Evgeni Leonov, Maya Plisetskaya, Vladislav Strzeltchik, Alla Demidova, Kirill Lavrov, Bruno Friendlikh, Evgeni Evstigneev, Lidiya Yudina

The childhood memories, adult struggles, loneliness and despair of Peter Ilyich Tchaikovsky (Smoktunovsky), culminating in his death a week after conducting the first performance of the Sixth symphony *(Pathétique)*. The making of this film realized a long-cherished dream of the celebrated Russian-born composer, Dimitri Tiomkin, who served as executive producer. However, all he came up with was a respectable and dull biopic, which ignores the composer's homosexuality and puts the collapse of his marriage down to a trivial social incident. Made with an eye to the West, where it is generally shown cut by about an hour-and-a-half and with an English commentary

spoken by Laurence Harvey, the film offers a few splendid visuals, and the great Smoktunovsky manages to rise above the generally static script. The music, of course, is glorious.

▶ **Teen Kanya** see Two Daughters

▶ **Telefteo Psemma, To** see Matter of Dignity, A

▶ **Téléphone Rose, Le** see Pink Telephone, The

▶ **Tema** see Theme, The

▶ **Tempos Dificeis, Este Tempo** see Hard Times

▶ **Tempo Si È Fermato, Il** see Time Stood Still

▶ **Ten Days That Shook The World** see October

The Tender Age

▶ **aka Adolphe Or The Awkward Age**

▶ **Adolphe Ou L'Âge Tendre**

France   1968   103 mins   col
Prisma Films/Oceanic

d **Bernard T. Michel**
sc **Bernard T. Michel, Jean Moal**
ph **Jean Charvein**
m **Michel Damase**
   Ulla Jacobsson, Philippe Noiret, Jean-Claude Dauphin, Claude Giraud, Nathalie Nell

A young man (Dauphin), making a film of Benjamin Constant's 19th-century novel about an older woman's love for a youth, finds a parallel situation between himself and Hélène (Jacobsson), the mistress of the count (Noiret), whose château is being used for the film. The attractive location photography does not make up for this misconceived, miscast film-within-a-film. Constant's classic novel has subtlety and grace, two qualities lacking in this pointless updating.

The Tender Enemy

▶ **La Tendre Ennemie**

France 1936 69 mins bw
Eden/SELF

d Max Ophüls
sc Max Ophüls, Kurt Alexander
ph Eugen Schüfftan, Lucien Colas
m Albert Wolff
Simone Berriau, Georges Vitray,
Jacqueline Daix, Maurice Devienne,
Catherine Fonteney, Valbel

Three men meet for the first time after death and discuss the woman (Berriau) who had cheated them in life. It is revealed that she destroyed their lives because her mother (Fonteney) had refused to allow her to elope with the only man she ever loved. Ophüls' sweet tooth makes him sugar the sour play by André-Paul Antoine, while still retaining some of its bite. Not one of his better romances, but there are enough gags and nicely executed camera movements to give pleasure.

Tenderness Of Wolves

▶ **Zärtlichkeit Der Wölfe**

W. Germany 1973 83 mins col
Tango Film

d Ulli Lommel
sc Kurt Raab
ph Jürgen Jürges
m Peer Raben
Kurt Raab, Jeff Roden, Margit
Carstensen, Hannelore Tiefenbrunner,
Tanara Schanzara, Wolfgang Schenk,
Rainer Werner Fassbinder, Brigitte Mira

During the depression in Germany in the 1920s, Fritz Haarman (Raab), apparently a charming, friendly, inoffensive man, works as a police informer. Actually, he is the 'Vampire of Düsseldorf' – the murderer of at least 25 young boys, whose remains he sells as meat on the black market. The actual case depicted had been the basis of Fritz Lang's *M* (in which Peter Lorre killed young girls) and other German horror films, but it had never been so explicitly or chillingly portrayed. The film has the mark of its producer, Fassbinder, all over it; many of the cast and the technical crew belong to the Fassbinder 'family' and he was also one of the editors. Despite its nasty subject, there is a certain tongue-in-cheek humour and a distancing stylization that prevents it from becoming too distasteful. Raab gives quite a good imitation of Peter Lorre.

▶ **Tendre Ennemie, La** see Tender Enemy, The

▶ **Tendre Poulet** see Dear Inspector

▶ **Tengoku To Jigoku** see High And Low

▶ **Teni Zabytykh Predkov** see Shadows Of Our Forgotten Ancestors

The Ten Thousand Suns

▶ **Tízezer Nap**

Hungary 1967 112 mins bw
Mafilm Studio

d Ferenc Kosá
sc Sándor Csoóri, Imre Gyöngyössi, Ferenc Kosá
ph Sándor Sárá
m András Szöllösy
Tibor Molnár, Gyöngyi Bürös, János Koltai, András Kozák, Ida Simenfalvi

István Széles (Molnár), a successful landowning farmer who started life as a poverty-stricken peasant, is prompted by his son's optimistic departure from home, and his own necessity to adapt to the new Communist society, to look back over the past 30 years of his life. Director Kosá made his feature debut with this startlingly mature and expert piece of film-making. His themes embrace the clash of ideologies as personified by the serious disagreement between István and his one-time friend Fulop (Koltai), and he gives a detailed view of 20th-century Hungarian history. The exemplary camerawork is out of the school of Jancsó, but Kosá's choice of surprise images is very much his own. If the subtleties of argument elude the English-speaking viewer, this fine, well-acted film is nonetheless richly rewarding.

Best Director Cannes 1967

▶ **Tenue De Soirée** see Evening Dress

▶ **Teorema** see Theorem

Terminus

France 1986 83 mins col
Les Films Du Cheval De Fer/Cat
Production/Initial Group/CBL/Films A2

d   **Pierre William Glenn**
sc **Pierre William Glenn**
ph **Jean-Claude Vicquery**
m   **Stan Ridgeway**
    Johnny Hallyday, Jürgen Prochnow,
    Karen Allen, Gabriel Damon, Julie Glenn,
    Louise Vincent

A computer-guided juggernaut zig-zags across
country in an elaborate race where the losers
forfeit their lives. The players are a tough
jailbird (Hallyday), an American woman
truck-driver (Allen) and an evil doctor
(Prochnow) who wants to take over the world.
Pierre William Glenn's disappointing directorial debut confirmed the general rule that
fine cinematographers, of whom he is one of
France's best, seldom make fine directors.
This tortuous science fiction road-race movie
has an impassive performance from Hallyday
and three ham ones from Prochnow as a mad
doctor in black leather, a mad scientist and
a mad driver. *Terminus* is the end.

▶ **Terra Em Transe** see Land In
Anguish

La Terra Trema

Italy 1948 160 mins bw
Universalia

d   **Luchino Visconti**
sc **Luchino Visconti**
ph **G.R. Aldo**
m   **Luchino Visconti, Willy Ferrero**
    The inhabitants of Aci Trezza, Sicily

An account of the hard life of a group of
Sicilian fishermen, in particular the young
'Ntoni Valastro, who have to struggle not
only against nature, but against unscrupulous
middlemen. Visconti originally intended an
epic trilogy about the exploitation of Sicilian

fishermen, peasants and miners, but only the
first part (inspired by Verga's 1881 novel) was
made. Visconti himself speaks the commentary in standard Italian (added after the film
had flopped) because the population, playing
themselves, speak in their own Sicilian dialect.
Although Visconti initially gained his reputation as a Neo-Realist – the term coined to
describe his first film, *Ossessione* – only this
film comes close to the movement's ideals. It
is difficult to remain unmoved by this human
document, shot entirely on location, despite
some operatic notions on the part of the
director and the beautiful camera compositions at odds with the harsh world depicted.
It won a special prize at Venice for its 'choral
qualities and style'.

▶ **Terre Sans Pain** see Land Without
Bread

The Terroriser

▶ **Kongbufenzi**

Taiwan 1986 109 mins col
Sunny Overseas Corporation (Taipei)/
Golden Harvest (Hong Kong)

d   **Edward Yang (Yang Dechang)**
sc **Xiao Ye (Li Yuan), Edward Yang (Yang
    Dechang)**
ph **Zhang Zhan**
m   **Weng Xiaoliang**
    **Cora Miao (Miu Quianren), Li Liqun, Jin
    Shijie, Gu Baoming, Wang An, Ma
    Shaojun**

Zhou Yufen (Miao), a novelist in Taipei and
unhappy with her husband, is offered a job
and a resumption of their affair by a former
lover (Shijie). Elsewhere in the city, a man is
lying dead in the street and police raid an
apartment, capturing a gang. One member, a
Eurasian girl (Wang An), escapes with a
broken leg and ultimately is locked up by her
mother with only a telephone for contact with
the world; a photographer (Shaojun) records
these incidents on film. Using these parallel
incidents as a starting point for a complicated
plot in which all these paths cross, sometimes
as in a dream, Yang delivers a dazzlingly
accomplished film. A director of the Taiwanese New Wave, a group little known in

the West but for the very differently toned work of Hou Hsiao-Hsien (e.g. *A Summer At Grandpa's*). The structure and technique here are occasionally more reminiscent of certain *avant-garde* European film-makers and Yang utilizes a bustling urban landscape whose lurking terrors (hence the title) nestle in the souls of the various protagonists. The movie examines the relationship between life and fiction, and demonstrates the deceptions on which most modern lives rest, and although sometimes elliptical and obscure, it is an interesting and entertaining piece, presenting a varied gallery of characters across the social spectrum.

▶ **Testament, Le** see Verdict

▶ **Testament Des Dr Mabuse, Das** see Testament Of Dr Mabuse, The

▶ **Testament D'Orphée, Le** see Testament Of Orpheus, The

▶ **Testament Du Dr Cordelier, Le** see Testament Of Dr Cordelier, The

The Testament Of Dr Cordelier

▶ **(US: Experiment In Evil)**

▶ **Le Testament Du Dr Cordelier**

France 1959 100 mins bw
ORTF/Sofirad/Renoir

d   **Jean Renoir**
sc **Jean Renoir**
ph **Georges Leclerc**
m   **Joseph Kosma**
    Jean-Louis Barrault, Michel Vitold, Teddy Billis, Jean Topart, Micheline Gary

A series of brutal attacks, mainly on women and children, are traced to a mysterious Monsieur Opale, whom the respected Dr Cordelier (Barrault) claims as a friend. One day, the doctor's lawyer (Billis) discovers that his client and Opale are one and the same, the doctor having created an evil alter ego by means of a drug. Renoir's reworking of *The Strange Case Of Dr Jekyll And Mr Hyde*, gave him a wonderful opportunity to return to the anarchy and freedom of the eponymous tramp

hero of *Boudu Saved From Drowning*. Renoir, using up to eight cameras and 12 microphones, which gives the film a fluid, rough-edged, spontaneous appeal, first conceived it as a live TV play. The director's method of cutting only after each sequence and allowing the actors to determine their own speed was completely vindicated by the wonderfully unique performance by Barrault as the jaunty, twitching, shaggy, prancing Opale, his finest film work since *Les Enfants Du Paradis*.

The Testament Of Dr Mabuse

▶ **aka The Last Will Of Dr Mabuse**

▶ **Das Testament Des Dr Mabuse**

Germany 1932 122 mins bw
Nero

d   **Fritz Lang**
sc **Thea Von Harbou, Fritz Lang**
ph **Fritz Arno Wagner**
m   **Hans Erdmann**
    Rudolf Klein-Rogge, Otto Wernicke, Gustav Diessl, Oscar Beregi, Vera Liessem

The arch-criminal Dr Mabuse (Klein-Rogge), confined to a lunatic asylum, uses his hypnotic powers – and the asylum director as the agent of those powers – to operate his plan to master the world. But he is finally foiled by Inspector Lohmann (Wernicke). Or is he? Lang continued the *pfennig* dreadful adventures of *Dr Mabuse, The Gambler*, saturating the film with the same atmosphere of decadence and evil, but with the added layer of sound which he uses forcefully. The mad villain expressed sentiments too close for Nazi comfort, provoking Goebbels to ask Lang politely to change the last reel. The director realized that the monster he had created could now control him, so he fled to France and then to the USA for a second career, leaving behind his wife, Thea Von Harbou, who had joined the Nazi party.

The Testament Of Orpheus

▶ **Le Testament D'Orphée**

France 1960 83 mins bw
Les Éditions Cinégraphiques

d Jean Cocteau
sc Jean Cocteau
ph Roland Pointoizeau
m Georges Auric
   Jean Cocteau, Edouard Dermithe, Maria
   Casarès, François Périer, Yul Brynner,
   Jean Marais, Pablo Picasso, Jean-Pierre
   Léaud, Charles Aznavour

Jean Cocteau as The Poet wanders weightlessly through a dream landscape peopled by his friends, and the characters and images from his works, including The Princess (Casarès), Heurtebise (Périer) and Cégeste (Dermithe) from his *Orpheus*. Made on a shoestring, Cocteau's valedictory film is a self-indulgent, self-mocking self-portrait, mystifying but intriguing to those who have no previous knowledge of his films, plays, poems and novels, fascinating and illuminating to those who have. Yet the whole of his unique *oeuvre* is allusive and personal. As he says, 'A film, whatever it may be, is always its director's portrait'. In this film, he is penetrated by a sword, but pops up from his grave uttering the words, 'A poet can never die'. Cocteau's body died in 1963, but his art lives on.

▶ **Tête Contre Les Murs, La** see Keepers, The

▶ **Tetto, Il** see Roof, The

▶ **Teufel's General, Des** see Devil's General, The

▶ **Thank Heaven For Small Favors** see Heaven Sent

▶ **Thank You, Aunt** see Grazie Zia

▶ **That Cat** see When The Cat Comes

That Man From Rio

▶ **L'Homme De Rio**

   France 1964 120 mins col
   Ariane/ Artistes Associés/Dear/Vides

d Philippe De Broca
sc Jean-Paul Rappeneau, Ariane
   Mnouchkine, Daniel Boulanger, Philippe
   De Broca
ph Edmond Séchan
ph Georges Delerue

Jean-Paul Belmondo, Françoise Dorléac,
Jean Servais, Adolfo Celi, Simone Renant

An airline pilot (Belmondo) becomes involved in a wild adventure that takes him from Paris to Rio, Brasilia and the Amazon in order to help his archaeologist fiancée (Dorléac) search for stolen treasures. Since 007 hit the screens in 1962, a deluge of spy spoofs followed in the USA and Europe, many of them rating double zero. This is one of the best in that it uses the cheeky, bouncy persona of Belmondo, the beauty of Dorléac and exotic Brazilian locations to good effect. De Broca directs in his early frenetic style, not always sharing his fun with the audience.

That Obscure Object Of Desire

▶ **Cet Obscur Objet Du Désir**

   France 1977 103 mins col
   Greenwich/Galaxie/In Cine

d Luis Buñuel
sc Luis Buñuel, Jean-Claude Carrière
ph Edmond Richard
m Wagner
   Fernando Rey, Carole Bouquet, Angela
   Molina, Julien Bertheau, André Weber,
   Piéral

A rich businessman (Rey) falls under the spell of his maid Conchita, who refuses to give herself to him, although she continues to feed his hopes. He, therefore, does everything in his power to persuade her. When Maria Schneider left the project after three weeks' shooting, Buñuel, with the surreal logic that runs through his career, decided to cast two actresses (Bouquet and Molina) to alternate the role of Conchita. At first, the dual casting is disconcerting, but it gradually becomes strangely normal – revealing two different sides of the same woman which the man fails to notice. In the background to the activities of this discreetly charming *bourgeois* (Rey perfect), are those of a revolutionary group. Buñuel's last film (based like the Sternberg-Dietrich 1935 movie, *The Devil Is A Woman*, on Pierre Loüys' novel *La Femme Et Le Pantin*) is another sly and witty bomb placed under the privileged classes. The great Spanish-born director died in 1983, the same age as the century.

The Theme

▶ **Tema**

USSR 1979 98 mins col
Mosfilm

d **Gleb Panfilov**
sc **Gleb Panfilov, Aleksander Cervinski**
ph **Leonid Kalashnikov**
m **Vadim Bibergan**
  Inna Churikova, Michael Ulyanov,
  Stanislav Lyubshin, Evgeny Vesnik,
  Sergei Nikonenko, Natalya Selezneva

Esenin (Ulyanov) is a successful but mediocre
Moscow writer, having sold out to the easy
plaudits and privileges that come from kowtowing to the regime. In need of fresh inspiration, he visits his native village where he
meets Sasa Nikolaeva (Churikova) and falls
in love with her. An artist who has refused
to compromise, she is involved with a poet
with the same views, rebuffs Esenin, and is
frank in expressing her low opinion of him.
The Berlin award for Panfilov's film was also
a tacit honour conferred upon glasnost, which
allowed The Theme to come off the shelf
where it had been languishing for eight years.
Unlike some other Soviet films, the reasons
why this one was repressed are not hard to
discern, for Panfilov airs the two very thorny
themes of artistic freedom and emigration.
The latter arises with the determination of
Sasa's lover, reduced by his integrity to digging graves, to settle in Israel. Aside, however,
from the didactic worthiness of the enterprise,
it is well made, intelligent and – thanks to
the director's skilful sense of irony and two
wonderful performances from Churikova and
Ulyanov – entertaining.

Best Film Berlin 1987

Themroc

France 1972 110 mins col
Filmanthrope/FDL Productions

d **Claude Faraldo**
sc **Claude Faraldo**
ph **Jean-Marc Ripert**
  Michel Piccoli, Béatrice Romand, Marilù
  Tolo, Francesca R. Coluzzi, Mme
  Herviale, Members of the Café De La
  Gare Théâtre Troupe

Factory worker Themroc (Piccoli) lives in a
squalid flat with his mother and sister and
pursues an existence of repetitive routine
and urban grind. He suddenly rebels, causing
havoc in the factory, making love to his
sister, smashing down the apartment walls
and drawing all comers into his web of
anarchy. Faraldo's controversial film has its
roots in the French tradition of comedy as a
social weapon, but his approach is uniquely
original in abandoning language and having
his characters communicate in a series of
formless noises (their meaning is clear).
Initially using the hand-held cameras of
cinéma vérité to evoke the nightmare of city
life, he switches techniques to unfold the
bizarre goings-on that result from Themroc's
rebellion. Faraldo's attack on robot-like conformity is surreal, absurdist and funny, holding up to ridicule our pitiful rituals, our
authority figures and the passivity of the
workers.

Theorem

▶ **Teorema**

Italy 1968 98 mins col
Aetos Film

d **Pier Paolo Pasolini**
sc **Pier Paolo Pasolini**
ph **Giuseppe Ruzzolini**
m **Ennio Morricone**
  Terence Stamp, Silvana Mangano,
  Massimo Girotti, Anne Wiazemsky,
  Laura Betti, Andrés José Cruz

A handsome young man (Stamp) ingratiates
himself into the home of a rich industrialist
(Girotti) and sleeps with every member of
the family – the father, the mother (Mangano), the daughter (Wiazemsky), the son
(Cruz) and the maid (Betti) – completely
changing their lives. This fable on the middle
classes was banned and Pasolini charged
with obscenity by the Italian government
(he was acquitted), although it contains no
recognizable human beings. The director sets
out to prove that, once the family was
liberated from its bourgeois existence by the
young stranger (long-haired English actors
were very fashionable in European films of
the 1960s), it goes mad because sex is the
one thing it cannot control.The QED of
Pasolini's theorem may be unconvincing, but

there is a certain mathematical beauty in his efforts to reach it.

Best Actress (Laura Betti) Venice 1968

▶ **Thérèse** see Thérèse Desqueyroux

Thérèse

France   1986   90 mins   col
AFC/Films A2/CNC

d   **Alain Cavalier**
sc **Alain Cavalier, Camille De Casabianca**
ph **Isabelle Dedieu**
    Catherine Mouchet, Hélène Alexanderis, Aurore Prieto, Sylvia Habault, Clémence Massart, Ghislaine Mona

Fifteen-year-old Thérèse (Mouchet), at her own request, leaves her father to enter the strict Carmelite Order at Lisieux. Her love of life and God help her to endure the deprivations and inspire those around her. She contracts TB and dies aged 24 in 1897. She was canonized 27 years later. A series of tableaux of convent life containing little drama and less dialogue sounds as if the film might be a chastening experience in itself. But each scene has much to tell about the simple faith of Thérèse, beautifully played by stage actress Mouchet, and the various other nuns. What comes through is not religiosity but an almost mundane domesticity and humanity, and an underlying eroticism.

Thérèse Desqueyroux

▶ **aka Thérèse**

France   1962   109 mins   bw
Filmel

d   **Georges Franju**
sc **François Mauriac, Claude Mauriac, Georges Franju**
ph **Christian Matras**
m   **Maurice Jarre**
    Emmanuele Riva, Philippe Noiret, Edith Scob, Sami Frey

Thérèse (Riva), finding herself stifled by provincial life and a dull marriage, decides to poison her boring but gentle and inoffensive husband (Noiret). Emanuele Riva was at the height of her film career when she took on the role of the dissatisfied heroine in this updated version of François Mauriac's novel. She subtly portrays the psychological and physical deterioration of Thérèse, while director Franju succeeds in capturing the oppressiveness of the natural world around her.

Best Actress (Emanuele Riva) Venice 1962

Thérèse Raquin

▶ **(US: The Adulteress)**

France   1953   110 mins   bw
Paris Films/Lux Films

d   **Marcel Carné**
sc **Charles Spaak, Marcel Carné**
ph **Roger Hubert**
m   **Maurice Thiriet**
    Simone Signoret, Raf Vallone, Jacques Duby, Sylvie, Roland Lesaffre

Thérèse Raquin (Signoret), the bored, unhappy and love-starved wife of a weak, flabby and petulant railway worker (Duby), becomes involved with a handsome Italian truck driver (Vallone), an affair that leads to murder and blackmail. For what was his last notable film, Carné updated Émile Zola's famous novel of destructive sensual passion, and set it in the bleak provincial back streets of Lyons. It is redolent with brooding atmosphere but, somehow, it is a cold film in which the leads are efficient rather than passionate, leaving the acting honours to Sylvie as Thérèse's crippled, unpleasant and vigilant mother-in-law. The famous version of this tale, made in 1928 by Jacques Feyder is, alas, no longer extant.

There Was A Father

▶ **Chichi Ariki**

Japan   1942   94 mins   bw
Shochiku/Ofuna

d   **Yasujiro Ozu**
sc **Tadao Ikeda, Takao Yanai, Yasujiro Ozu**
ph **Yushun Atsuta**
m   **Gyoichi Saiki**
    Chishu Ryu, Shuji Sano, Haruhiko Tsuda, Mitsuko Mito, Takeshi Sakamoto, Shin Saburi

A widowed schoolteacher (Ryu) is very close

to his son (Tsuda young, Sano older), but circumstances make them live separate lives with the son at boarding school and then university. However, the father has the pleasure of seeing him married to the daughter (Mito) of his best friend (Sakamoto) before he dies. Although made at the height of World War II, and subject to a range of restrictions, among them the necessity to some propaganda, Ozu managed to make one of his most affecting films. Chishu Ryu, Ozu's favourite actor, is outstanding, giving a sensitive and appealing performance. Unusual for Ozu are the many locations and the long time span of the plot, but his special insights into the parent-child relationship and the attention to the details of ordinary existence remain intact.

They Don't Wear Black Tie

▶ **Eles Nao Usam Black Tie**

> Brazil   1981   120 mins   col
> Embrafilme

d **Leon Hirszman**
sc **Leon Hirszman, Gianfrancesco Guarnieri**
ph **Lauro Escorel**
m **Radamés Gnatelli, Adoniram Barbosa**
   Fernanda Montenegro, Gianfrancesco
   Guarnieri, Carlos Alberto Ricelli, Bete
   Mendes

In São Paulo, a working-class family is deeply divided over a strike at the factory in which father (Guarnieri), son (Ricelli), and the latter's pregnant fiancée (Mendes) work. The father resists the police and is sent to prison, but the son crosses the picket line. Scrupulously avoiding stereotypes, Hirszman, with the help of exceptional ensemble playing, gives an unidealized and wide-ranging view of the working classes. Unlike his earlier more Brechtian approach, the director has gone for a more popular style which he calls 'democratic realism'. A little too glossy for the subject, the film nevertheless gets its point across effectively.

Special Jury Prize Venice 1981

▶ **They Were Five** see Belle Équipe, La

▶ **Thiassos, O** see Travelling Players, The

The Thief Of Paris

▶ **Le Voleur**

> France   1967   120 mins   col
> Nouvelles Éditions/Compania
> Cinematografica

d **Louis Malle**
sc **Jean-Claude Carrière, Daniel Boulanger,**
   Louis Malle
ph **Henri Decaë**
   Jean-Paul Belmondo, Geneviève Bujold,
   Marie Dubois, Julien Guiomar, Françoise
   Fabian, Charles Denner

A young man (Belmondo), taught to despise poverty by his guardian uncle who then fleeces him of his inheritance, takes to crime as an act of revenge. By the time he is a fully-fledged thief, he knows no other way of earning a living. After the frivolity of *Viva Maria*, Malle, for his seventh film, turned his attention to a solid period thriller-cum-romance, which also contains an incisive comment on hypocrisy, injustice, anarchy and corruption, examining the causes of crime without condoning it. If the director's stance is a little cold and detached, he has nonetheless lovingly and in lavish detail re-created the glory and the squalor of turn-of-the-century Paris. Flashback is effectively used to reveal the thief's past and Belmondo, carrying an aura of suppressed violence which occasionally erupts, is excellent; so is Guiomar's criminal priest, while Bujold makes a suitably fragile and pretty object of the protagonist's affections.

The Things Of Life

▶ **Les Choses De La Vie**

> France   1969   89 mins   col
> Lira Films(Paris)/Fida
> Cinematografica(Rome)

d **Claude Sautet**
sc **Paul Guimard, Jean-Loup Dabadie,**
   Claude Sautet
ph **Jean Boffety**
m **Philippe Sarde**
   Michel Piccoli, Romy Schneider, Lea
   Massari, Gérard Lartigau, Jean Bouise

Pierre (Piccoli), separated from his wife (Massari) and having an affair with Hélène (Schneider), still retains an attachment to, and an interest in, his wife, his son, his friends, the places he has known – in short, the 'things' of life – and consequently finds it difficult to make the absolute commitment that Hélène requires. Sautet and his cast bring fluent expertise to a subtle and universally interesting subject. However, too much weight is given to the details of Pierre's car accident, which is the fulcrum of an essentially plotless film, and the characters are insufficiently explored, leaving an impression of coldness and superficiality.

The Third Generation

▶ **Die Dritte Generation**

W. Germany 1979 111 mins col
Tango Film (Berlin)/Pro-ject
Filmproduktion/Filmverlag Der Autoren

d **Rainer Werner Fassbinder**
sc **Rainer Werner Fassbinder**
ph **Rainer Werner Fassbinder, Hans Günther Bücking**
m **Peer Raben**
    Volker Spengler, Bulle Ogier, Hanna Schygulla, Margit Carstensen, Harry Baer, Udo Kier, Hark Bohm, Eddie Constantine

The cell of a Berlin terrorist group includes Suzanne (Schygulla), who is secretary to international computer dealer Lurz (Constantine), and Petra (Carstensen), a banker's wife. Step by step the group is destroyed by a combination of internal tensions and betrayal by August (Spengler), leader of the group. Fassbinder's terrorists, however, are largely middle-class radical chic individuals, far from the usual stereotype, although the introduction of a hardened professional to the group triggers the chain of disasters. The effect of the director's approach results in an intriguing, semi-satirical thriller, but the political clues are oblique and the message blunted for all but the most acute viewer.

The Third Lover

▶ **L'Oeil Du Malin**

France 1962 80 mins bw
Rome-Paris Films/Lux Films

d **Claude Chabrol**
sc **Martial Matthieu, Claude Chabrol**
ph **Jean Rabier**
m **Pierre Jansen**
    Jacques Charrier, Stéphane Audran, Walther Reyer, Daniel Boulanger, Badri

A second-rate French journalist (Charrier), visiting West Germany to write a series of articles, meets a successful author (Reyer) and his French wife (Audran), who appear to be an exceptionally happy couple. He insinuates himself into their lives, becomes obsessed with their relationship and attempts to seduce the wife, thereby causing destruction. One of the most elegant of Chabrol's early works, the film presents an intriguing situation that develops with Hitchcockian undertones, even though the warped behaviour of the journalist remains somewhat of a puzzle. However, Chabrol's Peeping Tom camera is effectively used to suggest a study in voyeurism.

Thirst

▶ **aka Three Strange Loves**

▶ **Törst**

Sweden 1949 88 mins bw
Svensk Filmindustri

d **Ingmar Bergman**
sc **Herbert Grevenius**
ph **Gunnar Fischer**
m **Erik Nordgren**
    Eva Henning, Birger Malmsten, Birgit Tengroth, Mimi Nelson, Hasse Ekman

Rut (Henning) and Bertil (Malmsten) are locked into a badly disintegrating marriage, exacerbated by her inability to bear children because of a botched abortion after an earlier affair. We follow them on a journey to Stockholm, trapped in the claustrophobic confines of a train compartment where they reach the nadir of their disillusion and misery. Taking its material from stories by Birgit Tengroth, Rut and Bertil's tale is intercut with the story of Bertil's ex-wife Viola (Tengroth), whose own desperation drives her to consult a psychiatrist (Ekman) and to turn to a sympathetic female ballet dancer (Nelson) for friendship, both with disastrous consequences. The two stories are unfolded in parallel time, together with a lot of flashback.

This approach leads to a measure of confusion, while some of the connections made between the protagonists are tenuous and the arm of coincidence occasionally stretches too far. That said, this ambitious but uneven work brilliantly reflects the inner desolation of the married couple in powerful exterior images.

▶ **Thirst For Love, The** see Longing For Love

▶ **37°2 Le Matin** see Betty Blue

▶ **This Man Must Die** see Killer!

This Special Friendship

▶ **Les Amitiés Particulières**

France   1964   105 mins   bw
Christine Gouze Renal

d   **Jean Delannoy**
sc **Jean Aurenche, Pierre Bost**
ph **Christian Matras**
m   **Jean Prodromidès**
    Michel Bouquet, Didier Haudepin, Louis Seigner, Lucien Nat, Francis Lacombrade

In a boys' Catholic boarding school, the 'special friendship' between an older boy (Lacombrade) and a young cherub (Haudepin) is discouraged in a heavy-handed manner by most of the priest-teachers, which inevitably leads to tragedy. Roger Peyrefitte's sensitive novel of youthful homo-eroticism has become rather sentimental and pussy-footing under Delannoy's pedestrian direction. Among the adults, Bouquet is best as a more tolerant priest, but the elder boy is poorly played. Nevertheless, it has its affecting moments and the well-worn subject of emotional repression in an all-male environment is reasonably explored in the screenplay.

▶ **This Strange Passion** see El

This Sweet Sicknees

▶ **Dites-Lui Que Je L'Aime**

France   1977   107 mins   col

Prospectacle/Filmoblic/FR3(Paris)

d   **Claude Miller**
sc **Claude Miller, Luc Béraud**
ph **Pierre Lhomme**
m   **Alain Jomy, Mozart, Schubert**
    Gérard Depardieu, Miou-Miou, Dominique Laffin, Claude Piéplu, Christian Clavier

On the surface, David Martinaud (Depardieu) is a hardworking, solitary man who visits his ailing parents every weekend. Juliette (Miou-Miou) falls in love with him and discovers he has no parents but goes to a mountain chalet he has built for Lise (Laffin),the object of his obsessional love who is married to someone else, but whom he deludes himself will one day be his. Ensuing events lead to tragedy. Miller, in his second film, evokes several deliberate, well-chosen echoes of Hitchcock (and a direct reference in the use of a clip from *Rebecca*) in his approach to the suspense elements but, overall, this is a study of the destructive possibilities of sexual passion and contradictory faces of love to which the title refers. Well-photographed on location in the French Alps and with superb leads, it's an uncomfortable but gripping movie, adapted from Patricia Highsmith's novel.

The Thistles Of Baragan

▶ **Ciulinii Baraganului**

Romania   1957   140 mins   bw
Bucuresti Studios

d   **Louis Daquin**
sc **Louis Daquin, Antoine Tudal, Alexandru Struteanu**
ph **André Dumaître**
m   **Radu Palade**
    Nuta Chirlea, Ana Vladescu, Florin Piersic, Ruxandra Ionescu

In 1907, a poor orphan boy (Chirlea), unofficially adopted by a young peasant girl (Vladescu), witnesses poverty and violence in a small village on the harsh plain of the Baragan. After a bitter winter, the peasants rise up against the repressive village boyar, but are slaughtered by soldiers. To commemorate the 50th anniversary of the peasants' uprisings, the ten-year-old Romanian film industry invited the French director, known principally for his *Nous Les Gosses* (1941) about children, to direct this adaptation of a well-known novel (written in French) by the proletarian writer Panait Istrati. With telling camerawork and an imaginative use of sound and music, Daquin captures the atmosphere of the dusty and windy Baragan and vividly re-creates the life of the Romanian peasant at the beginning of the century. Pity about the cardboard characters and some weak acting.

This Wonderful Crook

▶ **Pas Si Méchant Que Ça**

Switzerland 1974 110 mins col
Citel-Films/Artco Films (Geneva)/Action Films/M.J. Productions (Paris)

d   **Claude Goretta**
sc   **Claude Goretta**
ph   **Renato Berta**
m   **Arié Dzierlatka, Patrick Moraz**
     Gérard Depardieu, Marlène Jobert,
     Dominique Labourier, Philippe Léotard

When his father, the owner of a small craftsmanship furniture factory, has a stroke, hitherto carefree Paul (Depardieu) takes over the running of the business, only to discover that it is in dire financial straits. In an effort to rescue the situation, he takes to holding up banks and post-offices and, although happily married, becomes romantically involved with one of his victims, a postmistress (Jobert). Filmed in a Swiss locale of flat fields and provincial towns, Goretta's tale begins with a clever idea but steadily loses both credibility and focus, leaving the ever ebullient Depardieu as the only real attraction.

▶ **Thomas Graals Bästa Film** see
Thomas Graal's Best Film

Thomas Graal's Best Film

▶ **Thomas Graals Bästa Film**

Sweden 1917 62 mins bw
Svenska Bio

d   **Mauritz Stiller**
sc   **Harald B. Harald (pseudonym for Stiller**
     & Gustaf Molander)

ph   **Henrik Jaenzon**
m   **Silent**
     Victor Sjöström, Karen Molander, Albin
     Laven, Jenny Tschernichin-Larsson

Scriptwriter Thomas Graal (Sjöström) is suffering from writer's block and decides to invent a story about his secretary (Molander) with whom he is infatuated. These imagined events, fantasies and flashbacks intermingle with the reality of Graal's romantic involvement. This relatively early and extremely inventive use of the film-within-a-film format is a witty pastiche of early film-making, with a charming performance from actor-director Sjöström, a close friend and associate of Stiller's at the time. It was so successful that Stiller reassembled the same cast and production team for an equally entertaining sequel, *Thomas Graal's Best Child*, the following year.

▶ **Thomas L'Imposteur** see Thomas
The Imposter

Thomas The Imposter

▶ **Thomas L'Imposteur**

France 1965 93 mins bw
Filmel

d   **Georges Franju**
sc   **Jean Cocteau, Michel Worms, Georges**
     Franju
ph   **Marcel Fradetal**
m   **Georges Auric**
     Emmanuele Riva, Fabrice Rouleau, Jean
     Servais, Edith Scob, Michel Vitold,
     Gabrielle Dorziat, Edouard Dermithe

Guillaume (Rouleau), a romantic adolescent calling himself Thomas, sets off happily for the battle front in World War I and meets up with a princess (Riva) who is helping the wounded. But the horror of war begins to intrude on his dreams. 'In him, fiction and reality became one,' is Cocteau's epitaph on his young hero (derived from his novel). It might well apply to the visual style which Franju uses to interpret Cocteau's last work for the cinema – the often surreal depiction of the war (a horse with its mane on fire) and the realism of mutilated men and corpses.

But the characters lack substance and the film is too cold and decorative to be moving.

▶ **Those Wonderful Men With A Crank** see Those Wonderful Movie Cranks

Those Wonderful Movie Cranks

▶ **(US: Those Wonderful Men With A Crank)**

▶ **Báječni Muži S Klikou**

Czechoslovakia 1978 90 mins col
Studio Barrandov

d   Jiří Menzel
sc Jiří Menzel, Oldřich Vlček
ph Jaromír Šofr
m   Jiří Šust
    Rudolf Hrušinský, Jiří Menzel, Blažena Holišová, Vlasta Fabiánová, Vladimír Menšík

In 1907, an itinerant showman (Hrušinský) goes around the country towns of Czechoslovakia, screening one-reel films, before returning to Prague where he obtains funds to set up the city's first real film theatre. Menzel's noted charm, wit and melancholy are all in abundant evidence in this affectionate re-creation of the early days of his country's cinema. Despite some anachronisms, the period atmosphere is well created, particularly in the sepia hues that conjure up early photography. The director must have found it easy to play the role of the showman's enthusiastic assistant.

▶ **Thousand And One Nights, A** see Arabian Nights, The

The Thousand Eyes Of Dr Mabuse

▶ **Die Tausend Augen Des Dr Mabuse**

W. Germany 1960 103 mins bw
CCC/CEI/Criterion

d   Fritz Lang
sc Fritz Lang, Heinz Oskar Wutting
ph Karl Löb
m   Bert Grund
    Wolfgang Preiss, Gert Fröbe, Peter Van Eyck, Dawn Addams, Andrea Checchi, Werner Peters

A police detective (Fröbe) investigates a series of crimes that all seem to be connected with the Luxor Hotel, particularly a murder which bears the mark of arch criminal Dr Mabuse, thought to be dead. In his last film, Fritz Lang returned to the villain he created over 30 years earlier in *Dr Mabuse, The Gambler*, now using TV monitors (the 'thousand eyes' of the title) to aid him in his heinous crimes. However, although Mabuse is up-to-date, the cheaply made, badly acted film seems a trifle old-fashioned. There are elements from the earlier Mabuse films, such as a two-way mirror and a séance, but the sense of evil is less strong and much of the plot is a whodunnit. Some fun can be got from the improbable goings-on, but Lang's memory is best served by his films of the 1920s and early 1930s.

▶ **Thou Shalt Honour Thy Wife** see Master Of The House

Thou Shalt Not Kill

▶ **Non Uccidere**

▶ **aka Tu Ne Tueras Point**

France/Yugoslavia/Italy 1961 129 mins bw
Moris Ergas/Lovcen Film (Belgrade)/
Gold Film Anstalt (Vaduz)

d   Claude Autant-Lara
sc Jean Aurenche, Pierre Bost, Claude Autant-Lara
ph Jacques Natteau
m   Charles Aznavour
    Laurent Terzieff, Horst Frank, Suzanne Flon, Mica Orlović, Majan Lovrić

Cordier (Terzieff), a French conscientious objector, and Adler (Frank), a German priest who killed a Resistance fighter during the war, are both put on trial. Cordier is found guilty under French law of evading his duty, while Adler is acquitted because his action was part of his duty. The story takes place in 1949, the year Autant-Lara (inspired by a newspaper article) set up the production but lost his finance because of his controversial theme. The project suffered similarly in Italy, was finally made 12 years later in Yugoslavia, and was denied commercial release in France and Italy for some time. In spite of the director's dedication to the material, the finished product is disappointing. Although the arguments are intriguing and the situation occasionally comes to life, the schematic and rambling narrative is unexciting and the characters lack depth which the actors largely fail to supply.

Best Actress (Suzanne Flon) Venice 1961

▶ **Thou Shalt Not Kill** see Short Film About Killing, A

Three Brothers

▶ **Tre Fratelli**

Italy 1981 111 mins col
Iter/Gaumont(Paris)

d Francesco Rosi
sc Francesco Rosi, Tonino Guerra
ph Pasqualino De Santis
m Piero Piccioni
   Philippe Noiret, Vittorio Mezzogiorno, Michele Placido, Charles Vanel, Andréa Ferréol

Three very different brothers return to their rural childhood home to attend their mother's funeral and to comfort their aged father (Vanel). Each brother represents a contrasting social and geographical strain in Italian society – a judge (Noiret) from Rome, a teacher (Mezzogiorno) of maladjusted children in Naples, and a factory worker (Placido) in Turin. Rosi's film is no mere family chronicle, but a symbolic meditation on the cultural split between northern and southern Italy. Some ponderous political points are made and no conclusion is reached. The best parts are those that take on a more elegiac tone and concentrate on the relationship of the teacher, Rocco, and his brothers with the father, movingly played by Vanel.

Three Crowns Of The Sailor

▶ **Les Trois Couronnes Du Matelot**

France 1982 117 mins col/bw
Société Du Cinéma Du Panthéon/INA/Antenne 2

d Râúl Ruiz
sc Râúl Ruiz, Emilio De Solar, François Ede
ph Sacha Vierny
m Jorge Arriagada
   Jean-Bernard Guillard, Philippe Deplanche, Jean Badin, Nadège Clair, Lisa Lyon

A student, after committing a brutal murder, is persuaded to spend the night listening to a drunken sailor's tales of brothels, Latin American ports and a ship with a ghost crew. Râúl Ruiz, a Chilean exile living in Paris, is one of the most prolific (he makes about four features a year) and exciting of new directors, yet this was one of his first films to get a theatrical release outside France. Ruiz is a storyteller who conjures up a series of vivid surreal images out of the slender movie resources at his disposal. This mixture of *The Ancient Mariner*, Orson Welles and his own distinctive modern voice makes for a film that takes one, like the haunted sailor, off the beaten track.

Three Days And A Child

▶ **Shlosha Yamim Ve Yeled**

Israel 1967 87 mins bw
S.Y.V. Tel Aviv

d Uri Zohar
sc Uri Zohar
ph David Gurfinkel
   Oded Kottler, Germaine Unikovski, Illy Gorlitzky, Judith Soleh, Misha Asherov

Eli (Kottler), has left the kibbutz to become a student in Jerusalem where he is involved in a triangular relationship with his best friend's girl (Unikovski). He is visited by Noa (Soleh), a girl with whom he had the briefest of liaisons on the kibbutz, who asks him to look after her three-year-old son for three days. Uri Zohar's film, while displaying a hotch-potch of influences, including some rather well-done Scandinavian-style sex scenes, is nevertheless one of Israel's better efforts. The story has charm, the action energy, and the characters and situations carry conviction. The flavour of Israeli life is well caught and, as Eli is led a merry dance by the child with whom he develops a love-hate relationship, we are left to join him in wondering whether he is, in fact, the boy's father. An ending that both intrigues and irritates.

Best Actor (Oded Kottler) Cannes 1967

▶ **Three From The Gas Station** see Three Men And Lilian

▶ **Three Loves** see Woman That Men Yearn For, The

Three Men And A Cradle

▶ **Trois Hommes Et Un Couffin**

France 1985 106 mins col
Floch Film/Soprofilm/T.F.1 Films
d   Coline Serreau
sc Coline Serreau
ph Jean-Yves Éscoffier, Jean-Jacques Bouhon
m   Schubert
    Roland Gireaud, Michel Boujenah, André Dussollier, Philippine Leroy Beaulieu, Dominique Lavanant

Three outwardly macho men-about-town who share an apartment have a baby thrust upon them. Initial panic turns to 'maternal' devotion as they school themselves in child care and grow genuinely attached to the tiny girl. An efficient, enjoyable and well-acted comedy, the film has added interest in that it subverts traditional notions of role playing. Serreau presents events from the male point of view and, in so doing, she throws up some provocative observations as to how men view women and parenthood. Hollywood subsequently remade it as *Three Men and a Baby*, and followed that with a poor sequel.

Three Men And Lilian

▶ **(US: Three From The Gas Station)**

▶ **Die Drei Von Der Tankstelle**

Germany 1930 80 mins bw
UFA
d   Wilhelm Thiele
sc Frantz Schultz, Paul Frank
ph Franz Planer
m   Werner R. Heymann
    Willy Fritsch, Lilian Harvey, Oskar Karlweis, Heinz Rühmann, Olga Tschechowa

Into the lives of three young petrol station attendants (Fritsch, Karlweis and Rühmann) comes the enchanting Lilian (Harvey), but three into one won't go. This is one of the best examples of the type of frothy, sentimental musical romance, with lilting songs and lively dances, with which Germany delighted the world in the early 1930s. It also shows Lilian Harvey at the peak of her popularity, although she might seem a trifle too ingratiating for today's tastes.

The Threepenny Opera

▶ **Die Dreigroschenoper**

Germany 1931 114 mins bw
Tobis/Nero/Warner Bros.

d   G.W. Pabst
sc Leo Lania, Béla Balázs, Laszlo Wajda
ph Fritz Arno Wagner
m   Kurt Weill
    Rudolf Forster, Lotte Lenya, Carola Neher, Valeska Gert, Fritz Rasp, Ernst Busch, Vladimir Sokoloff

In Victorian London, Mack the Knife (Forster), ladies' man, gentleman and thief, is loved by Jenny (Lenya), his favourite whore, Polly Peachum (Neher), daughter of the Beggar King (Rasp), and Lucy the jailor's daughter, but comes to a bad end. Bertold Brecht and Kurt Weill were engaged in 1929 to adapt their successful transposition of John Gay's *The Beggar's Opera* to the screen. Brecht, however, wanting to give his libretto even more anti-*bourgeois* bite than in the stage version, changed Mackie into a banker. This proved too strong for the capitalist producers. Brecht sued them and lost. Also lost were some of the songs and the disenchanted irony which was replaced by charm. The mixture of realism with stylized settings (an effectively foggy and decadent Soho designed by André Andreiev), doesn't really work either, but the performances, particularly from the inimitable Lenya (Weill's wife), and the wonderful score and lyrics retain much of the pungency of the original. The film, using a substantially different cast, was simultaneously shot in French. It was also remade in colour with an international cast in 1963.

Three Sisters

▶ **Paura E Amore**

Italy   1987   112 mins   col
Erre Produzioni-Reteitalia (Rome)/
Bioskop Film (Munich)/Cinémax-
Générale D'Images (Paris)

d   **Margarethe Von Trotta**
sc **Dacia Maraini, Margarethe Von Trotta**
ph **Giuseppe Lanci**
m   **Franco Piersanti**
    Fanny Ardant, Greta Scacchi, Valeria Golino, Peter Simonischek, Sergio Castellito, Agnes Soral, Paolo Hendel, Gila Von Weitershausen

Three sisters live in the northern Italian university town of Pavia. Velia (Ardant), the eldest and an academic, resides in the family home with the youngest, Sandra (Golino), an idealistic medical student, and their brother Roberto (Castellito), an aspiring musician. Maria (Scacchi), the middle sister, is married to a rich and successful TV comic (Hendel) and is dying of boredom. When Roberto marries a grasping and faithless wife (Soral), Velia and Maria fall in love with the same married man (Simonischek) and Sandra is courted by her young biology professor, the balance of all their lives shifts. Von Trotta is well known for her handling of women on screen and she does a superb job with an ambitiously multi-national cast. Drawing her title, family structure and certain emotional nuances from Chekhov's famous play, she and co-writer Maraini have composed a screenplay about dreams and disillusion, love and reconciliation, and the nature of family ties. Gentle, leisurely and visually beautiful, the film is a civilized and cultivated work enhanced by its classical music score, and superbly cast and acted all round. Ardant has

never been better, Castellito is outstanding and Golino confirms that she is one of Italy's finest younger actresses.

▶ **Three Strange Loves** see Thirst

▶ **Three Who Were Doomed, The** see Sir Arne's Treasure

Three Women In Love

▶ **Der Philosoph**

West Germany   1988   83 mins   col
Moana Film Produktion

d   **Rudolf Thome**
sc **Rudolf Thome**
ph **Reinhold Vorschneider**
m   **Hanno Rinné**
    Johannes Herrschmann, Adriana Altaras, Friederike Tiefenbacher, Claudia Matschulla, Jürgen Wink

Georg Hermes (Herrschmann) lives a hermit-like existence in a one-room Berlin apartment. On the publication of his first book, he decides to go out and buy himself new clothes at a shop run by three women – Franziska (Altaras), Beate (Tiefenbacher) and Martha (Matschulla). After he gets involved emotionally and sexually with all three of them, they reveal to him that they are 'Time Agents', goddesses sent to find him and look after him. Like Wim Wenders' *Wings Of Desire* (1987), which asked audiences to take angels literally, Thome's realistic fantasy, also well photographed in Berlin, presents us with the Three Graces in the most flesh-and-blood manner. The German title is far closer to the feel and subject of the film than the English one suggests. The hero is a Greek scholar, a student of Heraclitus, and his book is called *The Love Of Wisdom: An Introduction To Thinking*; the women, who provide him with all his needs, could be seen as a product of masculine wishful thinking. Unfortunately, the film never bothers to develop the many interesting conceits it sets up, leaving a number of philosophic musings hanging amidst the whimsy. Herrschmann wanders expressionlessly through it, taking time off from his philosophising to enjoy the physical pleasures offered by the three women.

Throne Of Blood

▶ **(US: Castle of The Spider's Web**

▶ **aka Cobweb Castle)**

▶ **Kumonosu-Jo**

Japan 1957 110 mins bw
Toho

d   Akira Kurosawa
sc Hideo Oguni, Shinobu Hashimoto, Ryuzo
    Kikushima, Akira Kurosawa
ph Asaichi Nakai
m   Masaru Sato
    Toshiro Mifune, Isuzu Yamada, Minoru
    Chiaki, Akira Kubo, Takamaru Sasaki,
    Yoichi Tachikawa, Takashi Shimura,
    Chieko Namira

In medieval Japan, a samurai (Mifune) is spurred on by his wife (Yamada) and a spirit (Namira) to murder his friend (Chiaki) and his lord (Shimura). Kurosawa found close parallels between feudal Japan and feudal Scotland in the first of two versions of Shakespearean plays – *Ran* (based on *King Lear*) came 28 years later. Although *Macbeth* is reduced mainly to action, images and gestures – many elements deriving from the Noh theatre – the film retains much of the original's power and momentum. An eerie mood is created, especially in the mist-shrouded forests and the castle. The climactic moments as Mifune is pierced with arrows is startlingly effective. Incidentally, it was said to have been the favourite film of the poet T.S. Eliot.

Through A Glass Darkly

▶ **Såsom I En Spegel**

Sweden 1961 91 mins bw
Svensk Filmindustri

d   Ingmar Bergman
sc Ingmar Bergman
ph Sven Nykvist
m   Bach
    Harriet Andersson, Gunnar Björnstrand,
    Max Von Sydow, Lars Passgård

On a remote island live a coldly detached novelist (Björnstrand), his son (Passgård) repulsed by women, his daughter (Andersson) lapsing into insanity, and her anguished husband (Von Sydow). Happy Families this isn't!

Bergman moved into a more *angst*-ridden and intimate world with the first (and least good) of his uncompromising trilogy – Winter Light and *The Silence* were to follow. Where this fails, despite the intense performances and probing camerawork, is in the almost parodic piling up of symbols and suffering. There is a danger that the emptiness that the characters feel communicates itself only too well to the audience.

Best Foreign Film Oscar 1961

▶ **Thy Soul Shall Bear Witness** see
Phantom Carriage, The

▶ **Tiefland** see Lowland

Tie Me Up, Tie Me Down

▶ **¡Atame!**

Spain 1989 105 mins col
Eldeseo S.A.

d   Pedro Almodóvar
sc Pedro Almodóvar
ph José Luis Alcaine
m   Ennio Morricone
    Victoria Abril, Antonio Banderas, Lolés
    Leon, Francisco Rabal, Julieta Serrano,
    Maria Barranco, Rossy De Palma

Ricky (Banderas), a young man recently released from a psychiatric hospital, is obsessed by Marina (Abril), a soft-porn actress, at present filming 'Midnight Phantom', a horror movie directed by the aging, wheelchair-bound Maximo (Rabal). Ricky follows Marina to her apartment, but she will have none of him, so he kidnaps her, beats her up and ties her to the bed. A strange, powerful and erotic relationship is built up between the man and his victim. If there were awards for the most outrageous films, this would certainly be in the running. Taking a plot reminiscent of John Fowles's *The Collector*, the prolific Spanish director has come up with a bizarre black comedy that hovers on the edge of the kind of schlocky sex movie he lampoons in the film-within-the-film, and by taking no ethical position, almost colludes with the reprehensible attitude of the brooding hero. Almodóvar's strength lies in his technical expertise and his direction of the actors, who are always able to tread the thin line between melodrama and comedy. It is a pity that in this case the piquant style cannot eliminate the distasteful content.

▶ **Tiempo De Morir** see Time To Die, A

▶ **Tiempo De Revancha** see Time For Revenge, A

The Tiger Of Eschnapur/ The Indian Tomb

▶ **Der Tiger Von Eschnapur/ Das Indische Grabmal**

W. Germany 1958 101 mins (Part I), 95 mins (Part II) col
CCC Film (West Berlin)/Rizzoli Film (Rome)/Régina/Critérion Film (Paris)

d Fritz Lang
sc Werner Jörg Lüddecke, Fritz Lang
ph Richard Angst
m Michel Michelet (Part I), Gerhard Becker (Part II)
Debra Paget, Walther Reyer, Paul Hubschmid, Claus Holm, Sabine Bethmann

1) An architect (Hubschmid), on his way to act as adviser to Chandra, the Maharajah of Eschnapur (Reyer), recues Seeta (Paget), a dancer, from a tiger. They become lovers, despite the fact that the Maharajah has proposed to her, and escape the palace together. 2) Chandra recaptures Seeta and threatens to bury her alive in a massive tomb but, after a revolt against him is put down, he allows the lovers to leave. Lang, in his penultimate film and after over 20 years in Hollywood, returned to the exotic pulp serial he scripted for Joe May in 1921 and the world of his own earliest works like *The Spiders*. The authentic Indian settings, fine decor and colour, the use of 'Scope, and a refusal to send up this comic strip material compensate for some of the stiff acting and erratic stylization. The two parts played as a double bill in Europe, but were dubbed and shown as one film of 94 minutes under the titles *Tigress Of Bengal* in Britain, and *Journey To The Lost City* in the USA.

▶ **Tiger Von Eschnapur, Der** see Tiger Of Eschnapur, The

▶ **Tikhi Don** see And Quiet Flows The Don

▶ **Till Glädje** see To Joy

A Time For Revenge

▶ **Tiempo De Revancha**

Argentina 1981 112 mins col
ARIES Cinematografica Argentina

d Adolfo Aristarain
sc Adolfo Aristarain
ph Horacio Maira
m Enrique Kauderer
Federico Luppi, Haydée Padilla, Julio De Grazia, Rudolfo Ranni, Ulises Dumont

A demolition expert (Luppi), who has been blacklisted because of his radical union work, adopts a new identity and gets a job in a multi-national company. Confronted with exploitation, he decides to fight back. Good political thrillers in the style of *Z* are rare, particularly when produced under a repressive regime, so it is all the more remarkable that Aristarain carried it off under the noses of the Junta. A rapidly moving but somewhat over-contrived *film noir* plot, a surprise ending and a splendid leading performance from Luppi (Best Actor at the Chicago Film Festival) make the film work on the purely entertainment level; the theme of an idealist fighting a corrupt system works on the political plane.

Time Of The Gypsies

▶ **Dom Za Vesanje**

Yugoslavia 1989 142 mins col
Forum Film/Sarajevo TV

d Emir Kusturica
sc Emir Kusturica, Gordon Mihic
ph Vilko Filac
m Goran Bregović
Davor Dujmović, Bora Todorović, Ljubica Adzović, Husnija Hasmović, Sinolicka Trpkova, Elvira Sali

Perhan (Dujmović), a teenage gypsy orphan

with telekinetic powers, lives in a rambling Yugoslav village with his adored and adoring grandmother Baba (Adzović), his crippled younger sister Daca (Sali) and his unstable layabout of an uncle (Hasmović). He is in love with Azra (Trpkova) but the girl's mother refuses to allow marriage because Perhan is poor. The village's richest gypsy, Ahmed (Todorović) visits from Italy and Baba uses her healing powers to cure his little son. In return Ahmed promises to finance an operation for Daca. Perhan accompanies them to look after her, but is forced away to become a member of Ahmed's band of 'beggars', thieves and prostitutes who work for him in Milan. In due course Ahmed promotes Perhan, whose nefarious life makes him sufficient money to return home for Azra's hand. The journey reveals a series of terrible happenings, which he sets out to avenge with tragic consequences. Aside from Kusturica's mastery of the medium, this film from the director of the very fine *When Father Was Away On Business*, voted Best Film at Cannes in 1985, is quite different from its predecessor. Noisy, rumbustious and by turns funny, romantic and horrifying, it is a superlative evocation of an unfamiliar people and place, and is photographed and acted with impeccable quality throughout. Dujmović and Todorović in particular stand out in a cast otherwise composed largely of illiterate gypsies rather than actors, who give their all to the telling of a true story. Best seen on the big screen, it astonishes with its operative sweep and scale – indeed, the use of music is integral to its mood and rich textures. This is highly original and absorbing entertainment.

Best Director (Emir Kusturica) Cannes 1989

Time Stands Still

▶ **Megáll Az Idó**

Hungary 1982 99 mins col
Mafilm/Budapest Studio Production

d   **Péter Gothár**
sc **Péter Gothár, Géza Bereményi**
ph **Lajos Koltai**
m   **György Selmeczi**

István Znamenák, Henrik Pauer, Sándor Sóth, Péter Galfy

In 1963, Gabor (Pauer) and Denes (Znamenák), two teenage brothers and the sons of a man who escaped Hungary only steps ahead of the Russians in 1956, try to adjust to the restrictions imposed upon them. Gabor, the elder brother, is the more conventional, concerned that his father's past will prevent his going to medical school, but Denes finds escape in rock music. Time may stand still for these energetic adolescents trying to find expression through American music, but the camera is continually on the move in an attempt to keep up with them. But this is no youth movie on the Western model. It is given a political context by being topped and tailed by newsreel footage of the 1956 uprising, and the return of the father in 1967 to what he hopes is a better society. Athough an interesting and entertaining blend of themes, the film, like its young heroes, also seems to be searching for an identity.

Time Stood Still

▶ **Il Tempo Si È Fermato**

Italy 1959 80 mins bw
22 Dicembre

d   **Ermanno Olmi**
sc **Ermanno Olmi**
ph **Carlo Bellero**
m   **Pier Emilio Bassi**
    Natale Rossi, Roberto Seveso, Paolo Quadrubbi

Isolated high in the mountains, a taciturn older man (Rossi) and a raw boy (Seveso) live out the long winter months, guarding an unfinished hydro-electric dam until the workers can return to complete it in the spring. Gradually their initial mutual mistrust turns to respect and affection. Olmi had shot over 40 industrial shorts for the Edison-Volta company (for which he worked) before making his first feature, partly financed by the firm. Using non-professionals, and filming in winter in the mountains, he meticulously describes the routine job of the two men with warmth and humour, managing the trick of portraying tedium without being tedious.

▶ **Time To Die, A** see Amelia Or The
Time For Love

A Time To Die

▶ **Tiempo De Morir**

Colombia   1985   94 mins   col
FOCINE (Colombia)/ICAIC (Cuba)

d   Jorge Ali Triana
sc Gabriel García Márquez
ph Mario García Joya
m   Leo Brouwer, Nafer Duran
    Gustavo Angarita, Sebastian Ospina,
    Jorge Emilio Salazar, Maria Eugenia
    Davila, Lina Botero

After serving 18 years in jail for killing a man
in a gunfight, Juan Sayago (Angarita) returns
to his native Colombian village hoping to
resume his once peaceful life as a horse
breeder. Unfortunately, his victim's sons seek
to avenge their father's death. Using a traditional revenge tragedy plot and the theme
from countless Westerns, Triana, in his debut
film as director, builds in a criticism of Latin
American *machismo*. Although familiar and
less impressive than one would have expected
from Nobel Prize-winning author Gabriel
García Márquez's first screenplay, it is intelligently paced, finely photographed and well
acted.

▶ **Time To Live And A Time To Die,
A** see Feu Follet, Le

The Time To Live And The
Time To Die

▶ **Tongnian Wangshi**

Taiwan   1985   137 mins   col
Central Motion Picture
Corporation,Taipei

d   Hou Hsiao-hsien
sc Zhu Tianwen
ph Li Pingbin
m   Wu Chuchu
    You Anshun, Tian Feng, Mei Fang, Tang
    Ruyun, Xiao Ai, Xin Shufen, Hu
    Xiangping

In 1947, seeking fresh opportunities, Fem-
ming (Tian Feng), his wife, children and
elderly mother leave the Chinese mainland
for a village in Taiwan. The sojourn is
intended as temporary, but the revolution
comes and they remain. With this autobiographical piece, the director of *A Summer At
Grandpa's* has enhanced and expanded his
international reputation. It is an understated,
intimate family saga which spans several years
of everyday life, recalled through the childhood memories of Ah-Ha-Gu (Anshun),
otherwise Hou Hsiao-hsien himself. The quiet
ordinariness of content and the spare simplicity of style make this an eloquent, sometimes humorous document, memorable for
the discreet detail with which illness and
several deaths are movingly chronicled. The
tone and approach is reminiscent of the early
films of Satyajit Ray, creating a world of
small events into which we are irresistibly
drawn.

▶ **Timi Tis Agapis, I** see Price Of Love,
The

The Tin Drum

▶ **Die Blechtrommel**

W. Germany   1979   142 mins   col
UA/Franz Seitz/Bioskop/GGB 14 KG/
Hallelujah/ Artemis/Argos/Jadran/Film
Polski

d   Volker Schlöndorff
sc Jean-Claude Carrière, Franz Seitz, Volker
    Schlöndorff
ph Igor Luther
m   Maurice Jarre
    David Bennent, Mario Adorf, Angela
    Winkler, Daniel Olbrychski, Katharina
    Thalbach, Berta Drews, Tina Engel,
    Heinz Bennent, Charles Aznavour, Andréa
    Ferréol

The teenage Oskar (David Bennent), stopped
growing at the age of three by an act of will.
Naturally, he is a concern to his parents
(Adorf and Winkler) because he has tantrums,
constantly bangs a toy tin drum and has a
scream that shatters glass. He acts as a sort
of conscience to the inhabitants of Danzig

when the Nazis come to power and the war rages. The film is often a disturbing look at German history through the relentless gaze of a weird child – an amazing performance from 12-year-old David Bennent, son of the actor Heinz Bennent. However, although much of the complexity of Günther Grass's allegorical novel has been lost, it hasn't gained in clarity.

Best Foreign Film Oscar 1979
Best Film Cannes 1979

Tire-Au-Flanc

France   1928   80 mins   bw
Néo-Film

d   **Jean Renoir**
sc **Jean Renoir, Claude Heymann**
ph **Jean Bachelet**
m   **Silent**
    Georges Pomiés, Michel Simon, Félix Oudart, Jeanne Helbling, Jean Storm, Paul Velsa, Manuel Raaby

Jean (Pomiés), an aristocratic, absent-minded and bungling poet, lives a sheltered life with his wealthy mother and his faithful valet and companion, Joseph (Simon). The men are called up for national service during which Jean, ill-prepared for life in the barracks, constantly finds himself in trouble. There have been four screen versions of this stage farce–which translates as 'The Malingerer'–by Mouézy-Eon and Sylvane, the most recent directed by Claude De Givray in 1961. Filmed with refreshing spontaneity, Renoir's loose adaptation avoids any suggestion of theatricality, and links the silent comedy tradition of Chaplin and Keaton with the early sound films of Vigo *(Zéro De Conduite)* and his own *Boudu Saved From Drowning.* While satirizing *bourgeois* life and institutions, the film is perhaps most worth watching for its fine ensemble acting.

▶ **Tirez Sur Le Pianiste** see Shoot The Pianist

▶ **Tizezer Nap** see Ten Thousand Suns, The

▶ **To Bed... Or Not To Bed** see Devil, The

To Begin Again

▶ **Volver A Empezar**

Spain   1981   92 mins   col
Nickel Odéon

d   **José Luis Garci**
sc **José Luis Garci, Angel Llorente**
ph **Manuel Rojas**
m   **Pachelbel's 'Canon', Cole Porter's 'Begin The Beguine'**
    Antonio Ferrándis, Encarna Paso, José Bódalo, Agustín González, Pablo Hoyos, Marta Fernandez Muro

Antonio Albajara (Ferrándis), one-time Republican soldier in the Spanish Civil War and now a professor at a Californian university, wins the Nobel Prize for Literature and visits his birthplace at Gijon. There, he relives the past, reminiscing with his great love (Paso), and his best friend (Bódalo) to whom he confides that he is dying. After receiving many honours, he returns to unhappy exile. Spain's first Oscar winner is lushly sentimental and self-consciously poetical, and it's difficult to understand – or care – why Albajara keeps abandoning all that is dearest to him. The director has made much of his choice of music, and perhaps the curious idea that Pachelbel and Porter make comfortable and significant bedfellows best sums up the confused thinking that bedevils this well-meant film.

Best Foreign Film Oscar 1983

▶ **Toda Nudez Sera Castigada** see All Nudity Shall Be Punished

▶ **Tod Der Maria Malibran, Der** see Death Of Maria Malibran, The

To Die In Madrid

▶ **Mourir À Madrid**

France   1962   87 mins   bw
Ancinex

d   **Frédéric Rossif**
sc **Madeleine Chapsal**
ph **Georges Barsky**
m   **Maurice Jarre**

Newsreel and documentary footage of the Spanish Civil War from the archives of six countries is combined with more recent sequences shot in contemporary Spain. This often facile, but still forceful, emotive and subjective compilation film generally won great praise, but also opened up old wounds. East Germany replied with *Untameable Spain* in the same year, attacking the Allied governments' apathy, and *Morir En España* (1965) gave Franco's side of the story. Rossif's film, some footage of which was used at the opening of Fred Zinnemann's *Behold A Pale Horse*, had a commentary spoken in English by John Gielgud and Irene Worth for the original British and American releases.

▶ **To Homa Vaftike Kokkino** see Blood On The Land

To Joy

▶ **Till Glädje**

Sweden 1949 98 mins bw
Svensk Filmindustri

d **Ingmar Bergman**
sc **Ingmar Bergman**
ph **Gunnar Fischer**
m **Beethoven, Mozart, Mendelssohn, Smetana**
   Victor Sjöström, Maj-Britt Nilsson, Stig Olin, Margit Carlquist, Birger Malmsten

Two young musicians (Olin and Nilsson) in a provincial orchestra get married and dream of becoming soloists. Years later, the husband carries on an affair with a married woman (Carlquist) which leads to disaster. Students of Bergman's *oeuvre* will find plenty of clues to his more mature work in this early minor drama – married couples devouring one another, the duties of an artist and music as a unifying force, while the avuncular appearance of Victor Sjöström as the conductor looks forward to his commanding role in *Wild Strawberries*. The title derives from the choral movement of Beethoven's Ninth Symphony that ends the film on a note of hope.

▶ **Tokyo Boshoku** see Tokyo Twilight

Tokyo Chorus

▶ **Tokyo No Gassho**

Japan 1931 91 mins bw
Shochiku/Kamata

d **Yasujiro Ozu**
sc **Kogo Noda**
ph **Hideo Shigehara**
m **Silent**
   Tokihiko Okada, Hideo Sugawara, Emiko Yagumo, Mitsuo Ichimura, Takeshi Sakamoto

A married man (Okada) loses his job when he objects to the unfair dismissal of a fellow worker. After many misadventures while searching for work, he gets into the restaurant business. Although Ozu seldom criticized social conditions directly, this Depression-set satire says a lot about the pettiness of certain aspects of society. It is done with a deft comic touch – and what the director called 'his darker side' in the second half. Ozu here uses a great deal of camera movement and several exteriors, not prevalent in his more mature work. The film contains two of his funniest sequences, focusing, in turn, on the workers on a parade ground, and the office clerks in a washroom.

▶ **Tokyo Monogatari** see Tokyo Story

▶ **Tokyo No Gassho** see Tokyo Chorus

Tokyo Olympiad

▶ **Tokyo Orinpikku**

Japan 1965 130 mins col
Toho

d **Kon Ichikawa**
sc **Natto Wada, Yoshio Shirasaka, Shuntaro Tanikawa, Kon Ichikawa**
ph **Shigeo Hayashida, Kazuo Miyagawa, Juichi Nagano, Kinji Nakamura, Tadashi Tanaka, plus 159 more**
m **Toshiro Mayuzumi**

A documentary on the 1964 Olympic Games in Tokyo. 'I have attempted to capture the solemnity of the moment when man defies his limits...I have tried to penetrate human nature not through fiction, but in the truth of the

Games.' Unlike Leni Riefenstahl's view of the 1936 Berlin Games, Ichikawa presents the human rather than the god-like qualities of the participants, although they are no less heroic. Not much factual information is given – TV and the Press were there for that – but it does get nearer the body and soul of the athlete than any previous attempt. This the director achieved with the help of 164 cameramen who used 232 different lenses. The result was a crystallization of Japanese technical wizardry and creative genius.

▶ **Tokyo Orinpikku** see Tokyo Olympiad

Tokyo Story

▶ **Tokyo Monogatari**

Japan   1953   136 mins   bw
Shochiku

d   **Yasujiro Ozu**
sc **Yasujiro Ozu, Kogo Noda**
ph **Yushun Atsuta**
m   **Senji Ito**
    Chishu Ryu, Chiyeko Higashiyama,
    Setsuko Hara, Satoshi Yamamura,
    Haruko Sugimura

An elderly couple (Ryu and Higashiyama), paying a visit to their children and grandchildren in Tokyo, begin to feel a burden on them and return home where the woman dies. Ozu claimed this was his most melodramatic film, yet in Western terms, this radiant, gentle, heartbreaking, perceptive investigation into the tensions within a family is far from our definition of melodrama. As usual, there are remarkable performances all round, and a unique use of sound and exteriors punctuating the subtle interior sequences. One of the finest films of Ozu's last decade, it was the one that belatedly made his name in the West.

Tokyo Twilight

▶ **Tokyo Boshoku**

Japan   1957   141 mins   bw
Shochiku/Ofuna

d   **Yasujiro Ozu**
sc **Yasujiro Ozu, Koga Noda**
ph **Yuharu Atsuta**

m   **Takanobu Saito**
    Setsuko Hara, Isuzu Yamada, Ineko
    Arima, Chishu Ryu, Masami Taura

Two daughters, the elder (Hara) having left her husband and the younger (Arima) having an affair that results in an abortion, live with their father (Ryu). But they are shattered when they discover that the mother (Yamada) they thought dead is still alive and living with another man. This is the nearest that Ozu ventured towards Western ideas of melodrama, although he is still more restrained than the plot suggests. His last black-and-white film is also one of his darkest and most intense. The dialogue and acting are superb and it's interesting to note the difference between the subtle performance Isuzu Yamada gives for Ozu, and the stylized one she gives as 'Lady Macbeth' for Kurosawa in *Throne Of Blood*.

▶ **To Live** see Living

To Love

▶ **Att Älska**

Sweden   1964   95 mins   bw
Sandrew

d   **Jörn Donner**
sc **Jörn Donner**
ph **Sven Nykvist**
m   **Bo Nilsson, and Eje Thelin's Jazz Quintet**
    Harriet Andersson, Zbigniew Cybulski,
    Isa Quensel, Tomas Svanfeldt, Jane
    Friedmann, Nils Eklund

Louise (Andersson), the attractive mother of a young son, is suddenly widowed. At her late husband's funeral she meets Frederik (Cybulski), a foreigner working in Stockholm and, before long, they embark on a relationship and he moves in with her. In his second film, Donner paints an observant portrait of a developing relationship in which the temperamental balance of the partners subtly shifts so that serious Louise is infected by Frederik's insouciance, whereas he becomes sober and wants stability and permanence. The director is helped immeasurably by his expert actors but, for all this, the film disappoints because a slight story has been padded out with generalizations about life in Sweden, which are no doubt meant to be illuminating but serve only to jar.

Best Actress (Harriet Andersson) Venice 1964

▶ **Tomorrow Is My Turn** see Crossing Of the Rhine, The

Tomorrow's Warrior

▶ **Avrianos Polemistis**

Cyprus 1981 95 mins col
Cyprian(MP)Films

d **Michael Papas**
sc **Michael Papas**
ph **John McCallum**
m **Nicos Mamangakis**
   Christos Zannides, Aristodemos Fessas, Dimitri Andreas, Jenny Lipman, Joanna Shafkali, Antonis Katsaris

Orestes (Zannides), a young Greek Cypriot, and his parents, flee their mountain village to escape the Turkish invasion of July 1974, but are caught and imprisoned in a dispiriting refugee camp. Months later, Orestes escapes and begins to make his way back to the mountains where his grandfather (Fessas), a former guerrilla fighter, has remained and where he will, presumably, become 'tomorrow's warrior'. Papas begins imaginatively, using flashback and fantasy to recall the history of Cyprus since independence, and the personal memories of the freedom fighters, as Orestes' grandfather recounts his experiences. A chronicle of the cruel fate suffered by Greeks at the hands of the Turks, the film contains a couple of sequences of real power. However, the uncompromisingly pro-Greek, anti-Turk bias, while perhaps understandable, succeeds in turning it into a piece of blatant and sentimental nationalistic propaganda, thereby reducing its impact.

▶ **Tongnian Wangshi** see Time To Live And The Time To Die, The

Toni

France 1935 95 mins bw

Films D'Aujourd'hui

d **Jean Renoir**
sc **Jean Renoir, Carl Einstein**
ph **Claude Renoir**
m **Paul Bozzi**
   Charles Blavette, Jenny Hélia, Célia Montalvan, Edouard Delmont, Andrex, Max Dalban

Toni (Blavette), an immigrant Italian worker in Provence, falls in love with Josépha (Montalvan) but is unable to marry her. They meet up years later, each unhappily married. The result is a *crime passionnel*. Following the example of Marcel Pagnol, Renoir completely abandoned the studio and filmed exclusively outdoors and in genuine interiors in the Midi, using authentic sound and actors drawn from the region. The film is remarkable for its avoidance of the melodramatic, the depth and fluidity of the camerawork and the feeling for figures in a landscape. This important film was not appreciated in its time.

▶ **Ton Kero Ton Hellinon** see When The Greeks

▶ **Too Beautiful For You** see Trop Belle Pour Toi!

To Our Loves

▶ **À Nos Amours**

France 1983 102 mins col
Les Films Du Livradois/Gaumont/FR3

d **Maurice Pialat**
sc **Arlette Langmann, Maurice Pialat**
ph **Jacques Loiseleux**
m **Purcell**
   Sandrine Bonnaire, Dominique Besnehard, Maurice Pialat, Christophe Odent, Cyr Boitard, Maïté Maillé

Suzanne (Bonnaire), aged 15, leaves her gentle boyfriend (Boitard) because she is unable to feel love and becomes increasingly promiscuous in her quest for it. Meanwhile, her father (Pialat), to whom she is attached, leaves home, where her hysterical mother and camp, ambitious brother (Besnehard) vent their own frustrations on her in the form of physical blows. At 17, she marries a man she doesn't love, and leaves him only days later for yet another lover (Odent). Brilliantly well acted by a mixed cast of professionals and amateurs, it is directed with style, commitment and compassion. Albeit that Pialat's incessant pursuit of naturalism becomes self-defeating at moments, his film is a painful and perceptive study of fragmented psyches. Suzanne, played with vitality and intensity by Bonnaire, is the focus of a screenplay that deals with the chasm between romantic yearnings and the ability to realize them; it is not about aimless youth or adolescent growing pains. If the movie tends to end somewhat vaguely, it is nonetheless thoroughly absorbing and good to look at.

Topaze

France   1933   103 mins   bw
Paramount

d   **Louis Gasnier**
sc   **Marcel Pagnol**
ph   **Fred Langenfeld**
Louis Jouvet, Edwige Feuillère, Pauley, Simone Heliard, Pierre Larquey

Monsieur Topaze (Jouvet), a shy and idealistic provincial schoolteacher, is hired as a front by a disreputable financier (Pauley) to sign cheques and take the rap if necessary. But he catches on fast, and ends up by appropriating both his boss's organization and his mistress (Feuillère). The combination of Jouvet's magisterial performance and the pungent dialogue of the play that made Pagnol famous is irresistible. Pagnol himself would direct it, with Arnaudy in 1936 and Fernandel in 1951 in the title role, and in 1961, Peter Sellers directed himself disastrously in *Mr Topaz*. Gasnier, who made this first and choicest of the versions, gained his reputation in America directing *Pearl White* serials.

Topaze

France   1936   110 mins   bw
Films Marcel Pagnol

d   **Marcel Pagnol**
sc   **Marcel Pagnol**
ph   **Willy**
m   **Vincent Scotto**

Arnaudy, André Pollack, Sylvie Bataille, Pierre Asso, Jean Arbuleau, Henri Poupon

Topaze (Arnaudy), a naive schoolmaster, discovers that he is being manipulated by a crooked businessman (Pollack). This revelation leads him to quit his post and enter into dubious business deals himself. Pagnol was disappointed that the 1933 French film version of his hit play, starring the incomparable Louis Jouvet, had cut much of his dialogue and rearranged some of his scenes, nor was he happy with the John Barrymore Hollywood adaptation of the same year. Therefore, after he had directed a number of films, he decided to remake it himself in 1936 (and again in 1951) restoring most of the original text. But the memory of Jouvet was too strong in the public mind and it flopped, despite its having the more authentic Pagnol touch.

Topaze

France   1951   135 mins   bw
Les Films Marcel Pagnol

d   **Marcel Pagnol**
sc   **Marcel Pagnol**
ph   **Philippe Agostini**
m   **Raymond Legrand**
Fernandel, Marcel Vallée, Jacqueline Pagnol, Pierre Larquey, Jacques Morel

Topaze (Fernandel), an idealistic schoolmaster, soon learns from his boss (Vallée) that there are more profitable (and less legal) ways of making a living. The third French version of the popular and still topical satire gave Fernandel the chance to follow in the footsteps of Jouvet, Arnaudy and John Barrymore (in the 1933 RKO production), bringing more affection to the role. Of the string of Topazes, this one pleased Pagnol most, as it is nearest to his original play and is technically superior to the others.

▶ **Topio Stin Omichli** see Landscape In The Mist

▶ **Torment** see Frenzy

▶ **Törst** see Thirst

La Tosca

Italy   1940   91 mins   bw
Scalera

d   **Carl Koch**
sc **Jean Renoir,**
ph **Ubaldo Arata**
m   **Puccini**
**Imperio Argentina, Michel Simon,
Massimo Girotti, Rossano Brazzi**

In Rome in 1800, the opera singer Floria
Tosca (Argentina) is in love with the painter
Cavaradossi (Brazzi), who has helped her
rebel brother Angelotti (Girotti) to escape the
clutches of Scarpia (Simon), the dreaded chief
of police. When Cavaradossi is taken prisoner, Tosca is prepared to give herself up to
Scarpia in exchange for his release. Jean
Renoir, invited to Rome by Mussolini, a fan
of *La Grande Illusion*, to lecture on film-
direction, started shooting this version of the
Sardou play – best known as Puccini's opera
version – at the same time. But he only got
to film a few scenes (two horsemen galloping
through the night) before war was declared
and he had to leave Italy. Koch, Renoir's
German assistant, completed it with the Italian cast and the Swiss Simon. The latter's
contribution is virtually the sole reason for
seeing this uninspired 'nasty little shocker',
although there are some well-used views of
the Eternal City.

▶ **Tosen Fran Stormytorpet** see Girl
From Stormycroft, The

▶ **Touchez Pas Au Grisbi** see Grisbi

A Touch Of Zen

▶ **Hsia Nu**

Taiwan   1969   180 mins   col
International Film

d   **King Hu**
sc **King Hu**
ph **Hua Hui-Ying, Chou Yeh-Hsing**
m   **Wu Ta-Chiang**
**Hsu Feng, Shih Chun, Pai Ying, Hseuh
Han, Roy Chiao**

A young woman (Feng), fleeing the army of
her father's enemies, takes refuge in an old
fort and seeks the aid of a young scholar
(Chun) who loves her. They frighten the
troops away by making the fort appear to be
haunted. Some months later, the adversaries
meet again in a bamboo forest. Because of
the 'chop-socky' films of Bruce Lee in the
1970s, martial arts films have been devalued.
Hu's ravishing and exciting three-hour epic,
set during the Ming dynasty, is in a higher
realm altogether, being the finest example of
the genre. Much of the choreographic art of
the Peking Opera has been brought to bear
on the breathtaking sword fights, stunningly
filmed in 'Scope using zooms, pans and tracks.
The director has also succeeded in showing
the philosophy of Zen in practice rather than
in theory.

▶ **Toute Une Nuit** see All Night Long

▶ **Toute Une Vie** see And Now My Love

▶ **Tout L'Or Du Monde** see All The
Gold In The World

Tout Va Bien

France   1972   95 mins   col
Anouchka/Vicco/Empire

d   **Jean-Luc Godard, Jean-Pierre Gorin**
sc **Jean-Luc Godard, Jean-Pierre Gorin**
ph **Armand Marco**
**Jane Fonda, Yves Montand, Vittorio
Caprioli, Jean Pignol, Anne Wiazemsky**

During a strike, the workers occupy the factory and hold the bosses prisoner. An American journalist (Fonda) and her lover
(Montand), a film director now forced to
make TV ads for a living, come to report the
sit-in, but are themselves held. In an attempt
to get their Marxist ideas across to a wider
public, the team of Godard and Gorin
returned to 'commercial' cinema after four
years making 16mm and video movies to be
shown in work places and youth clubs. During
that period, Godard had made TV ads for
Dim stockings, as the Montand character does
here. The film comments directly on the need
to sign up stars in order to raise money from

producers and cleverly plays on Fonda's radical image. The message of the film is also radical, but the medium is more conservative than Godard's previous work. Now it seems a marvellous monument to the revolutionary spirit of 1968. The composite set is used as brilliantly as in Jerry Lewis's *The Ladies' Man*, although for a vastly different purpose.

Traffic

▶ **Trafic**

France   1970   96 mins   col
Corona/Gibe/Selenia

d   **Jacques Tati**
sc   **Jacques Tati, Jacques Lagrange**
ph   **Eduard J.R. Van Der Enden, Marcel Weiss**
m   **Charles Dumont**
Jacques Tati, Maria Kimberley, Marcel Fraval, Honoré Bostel, François Maisongrosse, Tony Kneppers

Monsieur Hulot (Tati), entrusted with taking a newly invented camping car from Paris to a motor show in Amsterdam, encounters a multitude of problems on the way. In Tati's deeply suspicious view of the motorcar, many of the gags go beautifully, some run out of gas or stall and others come a cropper. Both during the production of his masterpiece, *Playtime*, and since, Tati suffered great financial difficulties, and *Traffic*, a Dutch co-production, did not give him the amount of time and freedom he needed. Nevertheless, Tati's last feature (leaving aside the dismal *Parade* made for TV) is a fond farewell to the incomparable Monsieur Hulot.

▶ **Trafic** see Traffic

▶ **Tragedia Di Un Uomo Ridicolo, La** see Tragedy Of A Ridiculous Man, The

▶ **Tragédie De La Mine, La** see Kameradschaft

▶ **Tragedija Sluzbenice P.T.T** see Switchboard Operator, The

The Tragedy Of A Ridiculous Man

▶ **La Tragedia Di Un Uomo Ridicolo**

Italy   1981   116 mins   col
Fiction Cinematographica

d   **Bernardo Bertolucci**
sc   **Bernardo Bertolucci**
ph   **Carlo Di Palma**
m   **Ennio Morricone**
Ugo Tognazzi, Anouk Aimée, Laura Morante, Victor Cavallo, Olympia Carlisi, Ricardo Tognazzi

Primo Spaggiari (Ugo Tognazzi), a factory owner and a self-made man, sees his son being forcibly hustled into a car. The police suspect the victim of colluding in his own kidnapping because of his far-Left sympathies, Primo's wife (Aimée) determines to pay the ransom demand, and he begins to realize he never knew his own son. This elliptical, elegantly shot semi-thriller, the reverse of *The Spider's Stratagem* in which a son investigates his father's life , was Bertolucci's first film for many years to deal with contemporary Italy. Its ambiguous view of terrorism suggests that in politics he prefers to be lost in a maze than find his way out. It is more interesting on the psychological level, but it failed critically and commercially, mainly because the crime remains unsolved.

Best Actor (Ugo Tognazzi) Cannes 1981

▶ **Tragedy Of A Switchboard Operator, The** see Switchboard Operator, The

▶ **Tragic Hunt** see Tragic Pursuit, The

The Tragic Pursuit

▶ **aka Pursuit (US: Tragic Hunt)**

▶ **Caccia Tragica**

Italy   1947   89 mins   bw
Lux/ANPI

d   **Giuseppe De Santis**
sc   **Giuseppe De Santis, Michelangelo**

Antonioni, Cesare Zavattini, Carlo
Lizzani, Umberto Barbaro
ph **Otello Martelli**
m **Giuseppe Rosati**
**Massimo Girotti, Andrea Checci, Vivi
Gioi, Carla Del Paggio, Vittorio Duse,
Checcho Rissone, Guido Della Valle**

After the Liberation, a young couple (Girotti
and Del Paggio) get involved with two bandits
(Checci and Gioi) who steal money that was
to be used to buy farming implements for a
collective farm in the Po Valley. The peasants
unite to hunt them down. The frequent crane
shots, expressionist lighting and echoes of
pre-war Marcel Carné with whom Antonioni,
one of the quintet of screenwriters, had
worked, hardly qualify De Santis's debut feature as Neo-Realist. It does have elements of
the latter in its social concerns but topples
too often into melodrama and sentimentality
to be entirely convincing. It was voted Best
Italian Film at Venice in 1947.

▶ **Trances** see Transes

▶ **Tranquillo Posto Di Compagna,
Un** see Quiet Place In The Country, A

Transes

▶ **aka Trances**
▶ **El Hal**

Morocco 1981 87 mins col
SOGEAV/Interfilms(France)

d **Ahmed El Maanouni**
sc **Ahmed El Maanouni**
ph **Ahmed El Maanouni**
m **Nass El Ghiwane**
**Boujema Hgour, Omar Sayed, Allal
Yaala, Aberrahman Paco, Larbi Batma**

Nass El Ghiwane (People of Song), a group
of five singing musicians are idolized and
mobbed by the young of the Maghreb. Here
they are interviewed and seen in concert,
cross-cut with historical and ethnological
material and views of the reality of life in
Morocco. An unusual musical documentary
to Western eyes and ears, it shows not only
a Third World Beatlemania, but analyses the

group's appeal and sets them in a historical
and cultural context. Their aim to bring modern electronic techniques to bear on traditional Moroccan music is brought home in
a scene where the folk tradition of trance
dancers merges into that of the contemporary
musicians. However, to the untutored spectator, much of the music and lyrics are as
banal as the images illustrating the songs.

Trans-Europ Express

France 1966 90 mins bw
Como
ph **Alain Robbe-Grillet**
sc **Alain Robbe-Grillet**
ph **Willy Kurant**
m **Verdi**
**Jean-Louis Trintignant, Marie-France
Pisier, Nadine Verdier, Christian Barbier,
Alain Robbe- Grillet, Catherine Robbe-
Grillet**

A film director (Alain Robbe-Grillet), on the
Trans-Europ Express from Paris to Antwerp,
decides to write a script about a sadistic drug
smuggler (Trintignant) on his way to Antwerp
to collect a shipment of cocaine. There, the
character gets involved with a prostitute (Pisier) and is caught up in a series of perilous
situations. To an extent, Robbe-Grillet prepared audiences for the kind of film he was
to direct with his screenplay for *Last Year At
Marienbad*, in that they were asked, in a
certain sense, to participate in the films, which
could take any number of paths and be open
to any number of interpretations. In his
second film, he plays the creator in the course
of creation, far more concerned with form
than content. Everything has a double perspective – a film-within-a-film about double-
crossing, double agents, and a double murder.
It is a game with a serious purpose – rein-
venting stereotypes – which excludes those
who don't know the rules.

A Trap For Cinderella

▶ **Piège Pour Cendrillon**

France 1965 118 mins bw
S.N.E.G.(Paris)/Jolly Film(Rome)

d **André Cayatte**

sc **André Cayatte, Jean-Baptiste Rossi, Jean Anouilh**

ph **Armand Thirard**

m **Louiguy**
   Dany Carrel, Madeleine Robinson, Hubert Noël, Jean Gaven, Francis Nani, René Dary

A girl burnt in a fire undergoes plastic surgery and finds herself suffering from amnesia. Determined to trace her identity, she learns that her name is Michèle, that she lived with her cousin Dominique in the South of France in a house that exploded and that the orphaned Dominique was cared for by Jeanne, an older companion. On meeting Jeanne, Michèle uncovers revelations that lead her to suicide. Leaving the French judicial system behind him for a while, Cayatte delivers a quest-for-identity mystery that is neat and ingenious until it plunges into absurdity. However, like most of his films it is, even at its most melodramatically idiotic, entertaining – not least in Madeleine Robinson's delicious over-the-top portrayal of the sinister Jeanne, and the clever use of Dany Carrel doubling as Michèle and Dominique.

▶ **Träumende Mund, Der** see Melo

The Travelling Players

▶ **O Thiassos**

   Greece 1975 230 mins col
   George Papalios

d **Theo Angelopoulos**

sc **Theo Angelopoulos**

ph **Ghiorgos Arvanitis**

m **Loukianos Kilaidonis**
   Eva Kotamandiou, Petros Zarkadis, Maria Vassiliou, Statos Pachis, Aliki Georgoulis

In Egion in 1952, on the eve of the election of Papagos, the field marshal who won the Civil War against Left-wing forces, a troupe of travelling players recall Greek political history and their own personal histories since they last visited the place in 1939. Angelopoulos emerged on to the international scene after the seven years of military dictatorship in Greece with one of the most ambitious Greek films to date, partly filmed during the last months of the colonels' regime. Knowledge of Greek history, politics and culture – allusions are made to the *Oresteia* – and plenty of patience are required to appreciate this extremely slow but ultimately impressive epic drama.

▶ **Traversée De Paris, La** see Pig Across Paris, A

La Traviata

   Italy 1982 105 mins col
   Accent Films B.V./R.A.I./UNIV

d **Franco Zeffirelli**

sc **Franco Zeffirelli (Libretto by Francesco Maria Piave)**

ph **Ennio Guarnieri**

m **Guiseppe Verdi (conducted by James Levine)**
   Teresa Stratas (Violetta), Placido Domingo (Alfredo), Cornell MacNeil (Germont), Alan Monk (The Baron), Axelle Gall (Flora)

Dumas' novel, *The Lady Of The Camellias*, in its operatic incarnation by Verdi. The ill-fated lovers, Marguerite and Armand, were rechristened Violetta and Alfredo by the great composer, but the story of the consumptive courtesan who sacrifices her happiness to protect her lover's reputation is intact. Zeffirelli adds an imaginative prologue and epilogue and skilfully opens out the action away from stagy confines, while his collaboration with designer and cameraman, though sometimes over-prettified, is ravishing to the eye, as is the music to the ear. The beautiful and gifted Teresa Stratas delivers a moving Violetta, well-matched by Domingo's attractively mature Alfredo. Opera-goers, however, will be disconcerted by cuts in the score.

▶ **Travolti Da Un Insolito Destino Nell'Azzurro Mare D'Agosto** see Swept Away...By An Unusual Destiny In The Blue Sea Of August

The Tree Of Wooden Clogs

▶ **Albero Degli Zoccoli**

   Italy 1978 186 mins col

RAI/Italnoleggio Cinematografica/
GPC(Milan)

d **Ermanno Olmi**
sc **Ermanno Olmi**
ph **Ermanno Olmi**
m **Bach, Mozart**
   Luigi Ornaghi, Francesca Morrigi, Omar
   Brignoli, Antonio Ferrari, Teresa
   Brescianini, and the peasants and people
   of the Bergamo countryside

The lives of four peasant families, all living
in the same Lombardy farmhouse at the end
of the 19th century, are slowly revealed in a
mosaic of small incidents: the cultivation of
prize tomatoes, the sending of a child to
school, a wedding, the recovery of a sick cow.
Almost documentary in style (shot in 16mm
with non-professional players), this lovingly
constructed work is perfectly paced, deeply
spiritual, and a moving tribute to the enduring
relationship between the earth and those who
work it. Using the simplest of narratives, the
film re-established the international reputation of Olmi, who brilliantly sustains the
Biblical symbolism of the expulsion from
Eden, as well as his political and religious
sub-texts.

   Best Film Cannes 1978

▶ **Tre Fratelli** see Three Brothers

▶ **Tre Passi Nel Delirio** see Spirits Of
  The Dead

▶ **Tretia Mecht Chanskaya** see Bed
  And Sofa

▶ **Trêve, La** see Truce, The

The Trial

▶ **Der Prozess**

   Austria 1948 108 mins bw
   Oesterreicheische Wecheschau/
   Filmproduktion A.G.

d **G.W. Pabst**
sc **Rudolf Branngraber, Kurt Heuser,**
   Emmerich Roboz
ph **Oscar Schnrich**
m **Alois Melichar**
   Ewald Balser, Ernst Deutsch, Albert

Truby, Heinz Moog, Gustav Diessl,
Maria Eis, Aglaja Schmid

In a Hungarian village in 1882, the disappearance and suicide of a young servant girl is
construed as a Jewish-organized ritual murder, and several Jews are arrested and tried.
The defending lawyer (Balser), dedicated to
religious freedom, eloquently proves their
innocence. Presumably attempting to atone
for his work with the Nazis, Pabst here made
a telling case against anti-Semitism, drawing
the material from an actual incident that was
something of a *cause célèbre*. The skilled
director creates some powerful moments, and
the use of traditional Jewish music – notably
in a synagogue scene where it is sung by the
famous cantor Ladislaus Morgenstern – is
affecting. However, the film is weakened by
needless   sentimentality,   flashy   effects,
emotional manipulation and the outrageously
caricatured anti-Semites, led by a virulent
Baron (Moog). The portrayals of the Jewish
defendants, notably Deutsch, are much better
handled.

   Best Director Venice 1948
   Best Actor (Ernst Deutsch) Venice 1948

The Trial Of Joan Of Arc

▶ **Le Procès De Jeanne D'Arc**

   France 1962 65 mins bw
   Agnès Delahaie

d **Robert Bresson**
sc **Robert Bresson**
ph **L.H. Burel**
m **Francis Seyrig**
   Florence Carrez, Jean-Claude Fourneau,
   Marc Jacquier, Roger Honorat, Jean
   Gillibert, André Régnier, Philippe Dreux,
   E.R. Pratt, Harry Sommers

The period of Joan of Arc's imprisonment
and trial, during which she is relentlessly
interrogated by the court and persecuted by
her gaolers. Eventually shaken, she recants,
but only briefly, and is burned at the stake.
In theory, Bresson would appear the ideal
film-maker to undertake this subject with its
medieval context and religious themes. However, he carries his austerity and detachment
to such an extreme that the whole business is
actually rather a bore, its restraint interrupted

only by the regular English shouts of 'Burn the Witch'. With Bresson drawing the trial scenes from the actual transcripts, Joan herself, especially as impersonated by Florence Carrez, is no more than a one-dimensional mouthpiece for the utterance of her faith. There are details to admire, notably the sombre opening and the dramatic and horrifying closing images of the charred stake, but perhaps the subject needs dramatic licence after all. The Cannes Festival jury clearly held a different opinion.

Special Jury Prize Cannes 1962

Trial On The Road

▶ **Proverka Na Dorogakh**

USSR   1971   98 mins   bw
Lenfilm

d   **Alexei Gherman**
sc   **Eduard Volodarsky**
ph   **L. Kolganov, B. Aleksandrovsky**
m   **Isaak Shvarts**
     Rolan Bykov, Anatoly Solinitsin, Vladimir Zamansky, Oleg Borisov, Fyodor Odinokov, Anda Zaitse

Lazarev (Zamansky), a German soldier, is captured by Russian partisans but reveals that he is a former Red Army sergeant who was forced to serve the Nazis. Major Petushkov (Solinitsin) wants Lazarev shot, but Lieutenant Erofeyich (Odinokov) prevails on him to take the man into the fighting unit. There, he is treated with suspicion and, from Petushkov, vindictiveness, but distinguishes himself by bravery. Gherman's first film, restrained and assured, was banned for 15 years for reasons which are not at all evident – indeed, even difficult to guess at. The director's choice of monochrome, effectively evoking the atmosphere of the landscape, together with his focus on individuals who are committed to their own course (Lazarev, Erofeyich), set both the style and the theme for his future work. Here, the context is that of an excellent combat movie.

▶ **Tribulations D'Un Chinois En Chine, Les** see Up To His Ears

▶ **Tricheurs, Les** see Youthful Sinners

Trip To The Moon

▶ **Le Voyage Dans La Lune**

France   1902   14 mins   bw or tinted
Châtelet Productions

d   **Georges Méliès**
sc   **Georges Méliès**
ph   **Georges Méliès**
m   **Silent**
     Georges Méliès, Bluette Bernon, Victor André, Henri Delannoy, Farjaux, Kelm, Brunnet

Six members of the Astronomers' Club take off in a rocket to the moon. They land in the Plain of Craters, are attacked by an army of creatures, but manage to get back to the spaceship in time to return to Earth. 'A film that people will talk about for 30 years. It made a deep impression, being the first of its kind. In brief, it was considered a masterpiece – I don't agree with that,' said Méliès, conjuror, cartoonist, mechanic and pioneer film-maker about one of the most famous of his 100 or so innovative short films. Based partly on Alfred De Neuville's illustrations for the Jules Verne novel of the same name and Méliès' own inventions, such as the rocket landing in the right eye on the face of the moon causing it to shed a tear, it still astonishes and amuses. The film was available at a higher price in the hand-tinted version, as were almost all of his later works, including another Verne adaptation, *20,000 Leagues Under The Sea* (1907).

Tristana

Spain   1970   105 mins   col
Epoca/Talía/Selenia Cinematografica/Les Films Corona(Paris)

d   **Luis Buñuel**
sc   **Luis Buñuel, Julio Alejandro**
ph   **José F. Aguayo**
     Catherine Deneuve, Fernando Rey, Franco Nero, Lola Gaos, Antonio Casas

Don Lope (Rey), a progressive, liberal, agnostic Spanish gentleman, is laid low by his reactionary and hedonistic code towards women and the lust he feels for his ward, the gentle and innocent Tristana (Deneuve). By transferring the story – by Benito Pérez

Galdós, the author of *Nazarín* – to the Spain of the 1920s and from Madrid to provincial Toledo, Buñuel was able to relate to the time of his youth and create a stifling provincial atmosphere that traps the two main characters. One of the least complicated and symbolic of the director's films, it is also one of his most assured. Without wasting a single shot, he goes to the heart of his subject, while keeping a sly and ironic distance. Both Rey and Deneuve give their finest performances – he the volcano, she the iceberg.

▶ **Triumph Des Willens** see Triumph Of The Will

Triumph Of The Will

▶ **Triumph Des Willens**

Germany   1934   120 mins   bw
NSDAP

d   **Leni Riefenstahl**
sc **Leni Riefenstahl**
ph **Sepp Allgeier (supervisor)**
m   **Herbert Windt**

The preparations for the 1934 Nuremberg Rally, the arrival of Hitler, the marches and the speeches. Riefenstahl was given over 40 cameramen and many technicians by the Nazi Party to make this documentary under a title suggested by Hitler. Despite her later protestations that it was merely a record of an historical event and not a propaganda film, the rally was shaped into a great, mythic spectacle, with the Führer as a Wagnerian hero descending upon the medieval town to save *das volk*. Ecstatic faces stare up at him as the sun catches his head like a halo. Using dramatic editing, the people become a dehumanized mass moving through Busby Berkeley routines in a 'Springtime for Hitler' show.

▶ **Trois Couronnes Du Matelot, Les** see Three Crowns Of The Sailor

▶ **Trois Hommes Et Un Couffin** see Three Men And A Cradle

▶ **Trollflöjten** see Magic Flute, The

Trop Belle Pour Toi!

▶ **aka Too Beautiful For You**

France   1989   91 mins   col
Ciné Valse/DD Productions/Orly Films/
SEDIF/TF1 Films

d   **Bertrand Blier**
sc **Bertrand Blier**
ph **Philippe Rousselot**
m   **Franz Schubert (recordings of various works)**

Gérard Depardieu, Josiane Balasko, Carole Bouquet, Roland Blanche, François Cluzet

Successful car salesman Bernard (Depardieu) lives in some opulence with his wife Florence (Bouquet) and two perfect children, and enjoys a social life with a close-knit group of friends. Above all, he is the envy of the men in their circle since Florence is a specimen of perfect beauty. All the more surprising, then, when he finds himself irresistibly attracted to his new secretary, Colette (Balasko), a somewhat plain, dumpy and dowdy woman, with whom he embarks on an intensely sensual affair. Blier's central notion is an intriguing one: a man may relish cool perfection in a mistress but requires something more comfortable in a wife. Working from this premise, he constructs a film whose sum is, alas, not at all equal to its parts. Mixing fantasy with reality without distinguishing between the two or attributing the fantasies to any particular protagonist, the movie confuses and irritates where it should clarify and illumine. Nonetheless, there are some perfectly judged moments which linger in the mind long afterwards and Josiane Balasko gives a ripe and delicious performance as the plain Jane aflame with desire.

Special Jury Prize Cannes 1989

▶ **Trou, Le** see Hole, The

The Truce

▶ **La Trêve**

France   1968   90 mins   col
T.E.C.

d   **Claude Guillemot**

sc **Claude Guillemot**
ph **Denys Clerval**
m   **Jorge Milchberg, Armand Mijiani**
    Daniel Gélin, Charles Denner, Caroline
    Car, Virginie Vignon, Marc Lamole, Jean
    Mondain, Eric Husberg

Paris nightclub owner Arno (Gélin) is invited to an exclusive high-stakes gambling party at a country manor one weekend. He decides to enjoy some fishing *en route*, accompanied by Laura, the club's stripper (Car). They bump into Julien (Denner), an old underworld rival of Arno's, and his girlfriend Fifine (Vignon) and team up with them, but fall into arguments and one-upmanship while, at the same time, being tailed by a gangster and his henchmen. An energetic and unusual treatment of the popular French gangster genre, featuring beguilingly 'ordinary' protagonists in Arno and Julien. The tale zips along, combining tension with comedy in an appealing mix.

The Truth

▶ **La Vérité**

France 1960 130 mins bw
Iéna/C.E.L.A.P

d   **Henri-Georges Clouzot**
sc **Henri-Georges Clouzot, Jérôme Géronimi,**
    Simone Drieu, Michèle Perrein,
    Christiane Rochefort
ph **Armand Thirard**
m   **Beethoven, Stravinsky**
    Brigitte Bardot, Marie-José Nat, Sami
    Frey, Charles Vanel, Paul Meurisse

Dominique (Bardot) and her sister Annie (Nat) arrive in Paris where Annie settles in at the music conservatoire and falls in love with Gilbert (Frey). Dominique, however, finds it impossible to settle to anything other than a tempestuous affair with her sister's lover, which ends in her shooting him when he's had enough. Set in the court during Dominique's trial, the events that brought her there are told in flashback, but it is the court scenes themselves (shades of Cayatte) that work best. For the rest, this meeting of H-G and BB, the Old Guard and the New Wave, is a disappointment. Working from an undistinguished script, Clouzot seems lost in his wanderings through the new generation, and Bardot, trying hard, despite having to cha-

cha in the nude, portrays a character so two-dimensional and tedious as to be hardly worth the bother.

▶ **Tsubaki Sanjuro** see Sanjuro

▶ **Tsuma Yo Bara No Yo Ni** see Wife, Be Like A Rose

▶ **Tsvet Granata** see Colour Of Pomegranates, The

▶ **Tulipää** see Flame Top

▶ **Tulipe Noir, La** see Black Tulip, The

▶ **Tu Ne Tueras Point** see Thou Shalt Not Kill

▶ **Turbulent Years, The** see Flaming Years, The

Turkish Delight

▶ **Turks Fruit**

Netherlands 1973 106 mins col
Rob Houwer Film Holland

d   **Paul Verhoeven**
sc **Gerard Soeteman**
ph **Jan De Bont**
m   **Rogier Van Otterloo**
    Monique Van De Ven, Rutger Hauer,
    Tonny Huurdeman, Wim Van Den Brink

Eric (Hauer), a young sculptor and rebel, marries Olga (Van De Ven), a girl from a *bourgeois* family. When the pressures of married life drive them apart, he tries to forget her by sleeping with as many girls as he can, but they meet again in sad circumstances. Paul Verhoeven burst on to the tranquil and somewhat sparse Dutch cinema scene with this aggressive, juvenile, alienating, emetic and erotic movie, based on a 1969 bestseller by Jan Wolkers. The box-office success at home and abroad for this 'love story for today' must be attributable to the full-frontal sex and not to its heavy-handed attempts to satirize Dutch middle-class mores.

▶ **Turks Fruit** see Turkish Delight

Turksib

USSR   1929   60 mins   bw
Vostok Kino

d   **Victor Turin**
sc **Victor Turin, Alexander Macheret, Viktor Shklovsky, Y. Aron**
ph **E. Slavinski, B. Frantzisson**
m   **Silent**

A documentary following the building of the Turkestan-Siberian Railway, a tremendous engineering feat, climaxing with the men hastening to lay the last tracks to meet the first Five Year Plan. This exuberant, splendidly pictorial morale-booster was, in fact, completed before the railway. It made a great impact on documentary film-makers in Britain, such as John Grierson.

▶ **Tutto A Posto** see All Screwed Up

▶ **Tuzolto Utca 25** see 25 Fireman's Street

Twenty Days Without War

▶ **Dvadtsat Dnei Bez Voini**

USSR   1976   100 mins   bw
Lenfilm

d   **Alexei Gherman**
sc **Konstantin Simonov**
ph **Valery Fedosov**
m   **V. Lavrov**
    Yuri Nikulin, Ludmila Gurchenko, R. Sadykov, Nikolai Grinko, A. Stepanova

Major Lopatin (Nikulin), novelist and war correspondent, has 20 days leave after the Battle of Stalingrad and visits his home town in Tashkent where a film based on his articles is being made. Once there, he visits his ex-wife and her new husband, addresses the workers at an armaments factory and, above all, spends time with the film unit, only to discover that their perceptions of the war are very different from what he has tried to convey. Gherman's second film, like his first (*Trial On The Road*, 1971), was banned for several years, and for reasons almost as obscure. The director's assurance and eye for detail displayed in his debut is confirmed in

this study of people's attitudes to war: Lopatin learns that those who stayed at home need romantic and heroic illusions, and the film's subject broadens into an examination of the nature of truth.

25 Fireman's Street

▶ **Tuzolto Utca 25**

Hungary   1973   97 mins   col
Budapest Studio

d   **István Szabó**
sc **István Szabó**
ph **Sándor Sára**
m   **Zdenkó Tamássy**
    Rita Békés, Lucyna Winnicka, Péter Müller, András Bálint, Mari Szémes

The dreams and memories of the inhabitants of an old house on the eve of its demolition, particularly those of the baker's wife (Békés), who helped shelter fugitives from the Nazis in her attic, and Mária (Winnicka), who was arrested during World War II. The memories move through the socialization in the late 1940s and the 1956 uprising to the relative stability of the present day. Szabó was born in 1938 and most of his restrained and reflective films are concerned with the German occupation of Hungary and the events of 1956 from the perspective of his own generation. By using one specific location circumscribing a small group of characters and a fragmentary, non-chronological structure, he has successfully protrayed public and private events stretching over 40 years. At the haunting climax, the director's alter ego, András Bálint, who plays Mária's son, looks back at the house and sees the previous inhabitants, alive and dead, arrayed as if for a photograph.

Twenty-Four Hours In A Woman's Life

▶ **Vingt-Quatre Heures De La Vie D'Une Femme**

France   1968   84 mins   col
Progefi/Consortium Pathé(Paris)/Roxy Film(Munich)

d   **Dominique Delouche**

sc **Dominique Delouche, Albert Valentin, Marie-France Rivière**
ph **Walter Wottitz**
m **Brahms, Jean Podromidès**
Danielle Darrieux, Robert Hoffman, Romina Power, Marthe Alycia, Lena Skerla

During 1914, a society widow (Darrieux) encounters a handsome young man (Hoffman) losing heavily in the casino of an Italian resort. In spite of their age difference, they become lovers for that night, during which she learns that he is a deserter from the Austrian army who has become a compulsive gambler. Delouche began life as a painter, moved into film as Fellini's assistant, and much admired Max Ophüls, three facts which exercised a clear influence on his first feature: Ophüls had intended to make Stefan Zweig's short story (originally set in 1890) with Darrieux, and Delouche strives to achieve the composition and camera style of the great director. Some bedroom scenes are redolent of Fellini at his worst, but the overall look of the film glows with the exquisite painterly colours and textures of the Impressionists. In all, a period romance which doesn't fulfil its promise, but with the advantage of Darrieux's always magical and dignified presence in a role played by Merle Oberon in English in 1952.

Twenty Six Days In The Life Of Dostoevsky

▶ **Dwadzat Schest Dnej Is Shisni Dostojewskogo**

USSR 1981 87 mins col
Mosfilm

d **Alexander Zarkhi**
sc **Vladimir Vladimirov, Pavel Finn**
ph **Vladimir Klimov**
m **Irakli Gabeli**
Anatoly Solinitsin, Evgenia Simonova, Eva Szykulska

In the winter of 1866, Dostoevsky (Solinitsin), his genius as yet unrecognized, has just suffered the death of his first wife and that of his beloved brother and collaborator. He has family dependants, is a compulsive gambler and badly in debt. When his publisher sends the police chief to pressure him for repayment of a loan, he hires a stenographer (Simonova) and dictates a novel to her in 26 days. It is *The Gambler*, drawing on his own experiences during a European trip four years earlier. The film brings these to life and traces the growing bond between the writer and the stenographer, who became his second wife. An intriguing idea with a complex structure and much of interest, but screenplay and direction are erratic, and it is left to the power of Solinitsin's performance to carry it through.

Best Actor (Anatoly Solinitsin) Berlin 1981

Twin Sisters Of Kyoto

▶ **aka The Old Capital**
▶ **Koto**

Japan 1963 107 mins col
Shochiko

d **Noboru Nakamura**
sc **Toshihide Gondo**
ph **Toshiro Narushima**
m **Tohru Takemitsu**
Shima Iwashita, Seiji Miyaguchi, Teruo Yoshida, Tamotsu Hayakawa, Hiroyuki Nagato, Michiyo Tamaki

Chieko, the adopted daughter of a comfortably off Kyoto merchant, suspects that her parents are concealing something of her history. In fact, she is one of a pair of twins, abandoned at birth because twins are considered an omen of ill-fortune, and, for the twin, it is a shame and disgrace to be so born. In due course, Chieko meets a poor village girl who is her double and, gradually, they both have to face the traumatic truth that they are twin sisters. A splendid film, boasting breathtaking photography, and a *tour de force* of acting from Iwashita in the dual roles of both girls. Nakamura brings much sensitivity to handling the conflicts and eventual resolution of feelings in the sisters. He also contrasts the lifestyles between rich and poor and vividly evokes Kyoto, an ancient city where custom dies hard.

▶ **Two Cents Worth Of Hope** see Two Pennyworth Of Hope

Two Daughters

▶ **Teen Kanya**

India 1961 114 mins bw
Satyajit Ray productions

d **Satyajit Ray**
sc **Satyajit Ray**
ph **Soumendou Roy**
m **Satyajit Ray**
   1) Anil Chatterji, Chandana Banerji,
   Nriparti Chatterji, Kagen Rathak, Gopal
   Roy
   2) Soumitra Chatterjee, Aparna Das
   Gupta, Sita Mukherji, Gita Dey, Santosh
   Dutt, Mihir Chakravarty

Two separate episodes, based on stories by
Tagore, made as Ray's salute to the centenary
of the author's birth. In 'The Postmaster', a
new postmaster (Anil Chatterji) in an isolated
village is taken care of by a little orphan girl
(Banerji). He begins to give her the basics of
the education she longs for; she nurses him
through a malaria bout. But the life is too
dull for him and he leaves. In 'Samapti', a
student (Soumitra Chatterjee) returns home
to his village to find his mother has arranged
a marriage for him. Rejecting her choice, he
marries the local tomboy (Das Gupta) who
causes a scandal by running away on her
wedding night. These gentle, graceful and
observant tales owe as much to the eye and
ear of the director and the gifts of his actors
as to their distinguished literary origins. Combining humour and pathos, Ray's rich tapestry of the emotions and behaviour of
ordinary people is revealed at a leisurely pace,
drawing us into their world. *Teen Kanya*, in
fact, means 'Three Daughters', but Ray cut
the third story 'Monihara', when the film was
sent abroad for release.

▶ **Two English Girls** see Anne And
Muriel

Two Lions In The Sun

▶ **Deux Lions Au Soleil**

France 1980 110 mins col
Asta Films/F.R.3

d **Claude Faraldo**

sc **Claude Faraldo**
ph **Bernard Lutic**
m **Albert Marcoeur, François Ovide**
   Jean-François Stevenin, Jean-Pierre
   Sentier, Catherine Lachens, Jean-Pierre
   Tailhade, Martine Sarcey, Michel Robin

Paul (Stevenin) and René (Sentier) are two
middle-aged factory workers, respectively divorced and widowed. Fed up with their low
pay and humdrum routine, and convinced
that life should hold excitement and pleasure,
they temporarily become conmen until they
have enough ill-gotten gains to run away from
Paris and enjoy a final fling. The director of
Themroc (1972) has come up with an uneven
entertainment, often interesting, sometimes
poignant, but occasionally teetering on the
edge of crassness. What makes it unmistakably off-beat and original is that the heroes,
beautifully played by both actors, are bisexual
live-in lovers who, in the most charming
sequence, share the favours of a love-starved
barmaid.

The Two Of Us

▶ **Le Vieil Homme Et L'Enfant**

France 1966 90 mins bw
P.A.C./Valoria/Renn Productions

d **Claude Berri**
sc **Claude Berri**
ph **Jean Penzer**
m **Georges Delerue**
   Michel Simon, Alain Cohen, Charles
   Denner, Luce Fabiole, Roger Carol, Paul
   Préboist, Zorica Lozice

During the Nazi occupation of Paris, an
irrepressible eight-year-old Jewish boy,
Claude (Cohen), is sent to stay with an elderly
couple in the country. Since Pepé, the old
man (Simon), is a rabid anti-Semite, the boy
is instructed to conceal his origins (and his
circumcision) and is taught the Lord's prayer.
Once there, Claude and Pepé forge a close
relationship – beautifully realized in the playing – in which the boy is amused by the old
man's bigoted outbursts and delights in provoking him, while Pepé comes to dote on the
child. The complex situation is sensitively and
charmingly handled and made simple by being
seen through a child's eyes. Berri's film is a
reconstruction of his own childhood experi-

ence and he described it as 'a love affair between a Jew and an anti-Semite'. Made with warmth, humour and an accurate eye for the atmosphere of the period, it does occasionally lapse into sentimentality and overstatement. However, this can be forgiven in a debut feature, particularly from the director who, 20 years later and rather more ambitiously, would tackle *Jean De Florette* and *Manon Des Sources*.

Best Actor (Michel Simon) Berlin 1967

Two Or Three Things I Know About Her

▶ **Deux Ou Trois Choses Que Je Sais D'Elle**

France 1966 95 mins col
Anouchka/Argos/Les Films Du Carrosse/Parc Film

d **Jean-Luc Godard**
sc **Jean-Luc Godard**
ph **Raoul Coutard**
m **Beethoven**
   Marina Vlady, Anny Duperey, Roger Montsoret, Jean Narboni, Raoul Lévy

Juliette (Vlady) lives with her husband (Montsoret) and young child in a new high-rise building in the suburbs of Paris. She spends one day a week in the city centre where she prostitutes herself to obtain consumer durables. Godard makes it clear that the '*Elle*' or 'Her' of the title of his 'sociological essay' refers to Paris and not to his practical heroine. Inspired by a magazine article on housewife prostitutes, the film moves into the wider political sphere, at the same time Godard's voice on the soundtrack questions his own choice of images. The film is an important milestone on the way to Godard's total political commitment and his attempt to find an alternative to '*bourgeois* cinema'. For those who care, this is a particularly stimulating exercise.

Two Pennyworth Of Hope

▶ **(US: Two Cents Worth Of Hope)**
▶ **Due Soldi Di Speranza**

Italy 1952 98 mins bw

Universalcine

d **Renato Castellani**
sc **Renato Castellani, Titina De Filippo**
ph **Arturo Gallea**
m **Alessandro Cicognini**
   Vincenzo Musolino, Maria Fiore, Filumena Russo, Luigi Astarita

A young man (Musolino) returns from the war to his village on the slopes of Vesuvius. Here he tries his hand at a number of jobs while trying to impress his future father-in-law who dislikes him. The rest of the villagers seem to be divided between the Church and Communism, and spend their time squabbling. Castellani, a minor figure in the Neo-Realist movement, brought a great deal of humour and vivacity to this comedy-drama, making it one of his best films. It completes an optimistic post-war trilogy of Italian life, following *Under The Sun Of Rome* and *It's Forever Springtime*.

Best Film Cannes 1952

Two Stage Sisters

▶ **Wutai Jiemei**

China 1964 114 mins col
Tianma Film Studio(Shanghai)

d **Xie Jin**
sc **Lin Gu, Xu Jin, Xie Jin**
ph **Zhou Daming**
m **Huang Zhun**
   Xie Fang, Cao Yindi, Feng Ji, Li Wei, Deng Nan, Wu Baifang, Shangguan Yunzhu, Shen Hao, Gao Yuansheng

Chunhua (Fang), a runaway, finds refuge with a travelling opera troupe and grows very close to Yuehong (Yindi). Life on the road is cruel, and the two girls are in bondage to Ax'in (Nan), the troupe's owner, who takes them to Shanghai. There, they impress manager Tang (Wei) and become stars, but Yuehong, seduced by materialism, gives up singing, marries Tang and drifts into misery. The distraught Chunhua commits herself to the Revolution and forms a women's co-operative opera company. This is a marvellous film. One of the last made before the Cultural Revolution, it was suppressed for reasons that can only be put down to extreme and irrational puritanism, since its political bias –

anti-Capitalist corruption, pro-Feminist – is of the correct hue. However, while putting its revolutionary message across forcefully, it takes the form of theatrical melodrama with which the West is totally familiar, doing so at the highest level of skill. An involved and involving story, spanning the years 1935–50, it is superbly well acted (Xie Fang gives an outstanding performance), and photographed with a breathtaking sense of colour, composition, and inventive camera angles. The music beguiles, too, particulary the sung melodies that form part of the narration.

Two Women

▶ **La Ciociara**

Italy 1960 110 mins bw
Champion/Marceau/Cocinor/SGC

d   **Vittorio De Sica**
sc **Cesare Zavattini, Vittorio De Sica**
ph **Gabor Pogany**
m   **Armando Trovaioli**

Sophia Loren, Eleonora Brown, Jean-Paul Belmondo, Raf Vallone, Renato Salvatori

A widow (Loren) and her 13-year-old daughter (Brown), fleeing south after the Allied bombing of Rome in 1943, survive dangers, deprivation and ultimately rape by soldiers. The title refers to mother and daughter, but it was Loren's all-stops-out performance which gained her the rare distinction of being the first (and last?) actress (or actor) to win an Oscar for a foreign-language film, proving that Hollywood never knew how to make use of her dramatic talents. The film itself, based on a story by Alberto Moravia, was greeted, in the main, with less rapture by the critics, although it was a commercial success. De Sica's usual warmth and insight gave way too often to melodrama, but it has its touching and harrowing moments.

Best Actress (Sophia Loren) Oscar 1961

Best Actress (Sophia Loren) Cannes 1961

▶ **Tystnaden** see Silence, The

▶ **Uccellacci E Uccellini** see Hawks And The Sparrows, The

▶ **Ucho** see Ear, The

▶ **Udienza, L'** see Audience, The

▶ **Ugetsu** see Ugetsu Monogatari

Ugetsu Monogatari

▶ **(US: Ugetsu)**

Japan 1953 96 mins bw
Daiei

d Kenji Mizoguchi
sc Matsutaro Kawaguchi, Yoshitaka Yoda
ph Kazuo Miyagawa
m Fumio Hayasaka
Masayuki Mori, Kinuyo Tanaka, Sakae Ozawa, Machiko Kyo

Genjuro (Mori), a poor potter trying to make a living in a war-torn medieval village, is lured away from his devoted wife (Tanaka) and young son by the mysterious Lady Wasaka (Kyo) who turns out to be a ghost. When Genjuro returns home repentant, his wife, too, has become a ghost. The first film to introduce Mizoguchi to the West (translated as *Tales Of The Pale And Silvery Moon After The Rain*, but known under its original title), it was immediately acclaimed as one of the masterpieces of world cinema. Based on two 18th-century ghost stories by Akinari Veda and one by Guy De Maupassant, it is told in lyrical, haunting and intense images which never ignore the human element. Mizoguchi's artistry is best demonstrated by the trip across the lake as the boat emerges from the mist, hinting at the supernatural; Genjuro and Wasaka on the grass beside a shimmering lake, and the final sequence, when the potter see the phantom of his dead wife where there was emptiness before, giving the film an emotional impact that has seldom been equalled.

▶ **Ugly, Dirty and Mean** see Down And Dirty

▶ **Ukigumo** see Floating Clouds

▶ **Ukigusa** see Floating Weeds

▶ **Ulica Graniczna** see Border Street

▶ **Ultima Cena, La** see Last Supper, The

▶ **Ultima Donna, L'** see Last Woman, The

▶ **Ultimas Imagenes Del Naufragio** see Last Images Of The Shipwreck

▶ **Uma** see Horse

▶ **Umarete Wa Mita Keredo** see I Was Born, But...

Umberto D

Italy 1952 89 mins bw
Dear Films

d Vittorio De Sica
sc Cesare Zavattini, Vittorio De Sica
ph G.R. Aldo
m Alessandro Cicognini
Carlo Battisti, Maria Pia Casilio, Lina Gennari

An old-age pensioner (Battisti), unable to pay his rent, has only his dog and a pregnant housemaid (Casilio) for friends. He is forced to consider begging and suicide. Dedicated to his father, the film marked the end of De Sica's great Neo-Realist period. Using non-professionals in real locations – Umberto was played by an elderly professor of philology – one of the director's most affecting films avoids sentimentality by its truth, harshness and accuracy. From child neglect in *Shoeshine* to discarded old age in *Umberto D*, De Sica's films showed, in his own words, 'the indifference of society towards suffering. They are a word in favour of the poor and unhappy.'

The Umbrellas Of Cherbourg

▶ **Les Parapluies De Cherbourg**

France   1964   92 mins   col
Parc/Madeleine/Beta(Munich)

d   **Jacques Demy**
sc **Jacques Demy**
ph **Jean Rabier**
m   **Michel Legrand**
    Catherine Deneuve, Anne Vernon, Nino Castelnuovo, Ellen Farner, Marc Michel

Geneviève (Deneuve), who works in the umbrella shop of her widowed mother (Vernon), loves Guy (Castelnuovo), a garage mechanic. She discovers that she is pregnant after he has gone on military service, so she marries a young diamond merchant (Michel) for security. Demy, a lover of the Hollywood musical (his first feature *Lola* owed much to *On The Town*), attempted to distil the genre through his own French sensibility. The originality of the film lies in the fact that all the dialogue is sung (the cast is dubbed) in a kind of recitative. Filming in colour for the first time, Demy had both the exterior and interior of houses in Cherbourg painted in an array of colours, matching the clothes of the characters. It's all very pretty-pretty and insubstantial, and Legrand's tinkly music makes it more chanting than enchanting. The film's immense popularity proves how much tastes differ.

Best Film Cannes 1964

Under Satan's Sun

▶ **Sous Le Soleil De Satan**

France   1987   98 mins   col

Erato/Films A2/Flach/Action

d   **Maurice Pialat**
sc **Sylvie Danton**
ph **Willy Kurant**
m   **Henri Dutilleux**
    Gérard Depardieu, Sandrine Bonnaire, Maurice Pialat, Alain Artur, Yann Dedet, Brigitte Legendre

Father Donissan (Depardieu), a simple and devout priest, senses Satan everywhere, especially in the heart of Mouchette (Bonnaire), a wild young woman who has killed a man. She cuts her throat when he declares that she is possessed. In another village, he gains the reputation of a saint. Pialat, who also plays Donissan's superior, has constructed this uncompromisingly bleak, claustrophobic and humourless film as a series of long duologues. Obviously influenced by Bresson's method – based, like *Diary Of A Country Priest* and *Mouchette*, on a novel by Georges Bernanos – the narrative suffers from a number of ellipses that provoke unanswered questions. The performances of Depardieu and Bonnaire (both of whom had worked with Pialat more than once before) are riveting, but it might leave one agreeing with Buñuel's statement: 'Thank God, I'm an atheist'.

Best Film Cannes 1987

▶ **Under The Roofs Of Paris** see Sous Les Toits De Paris

▶ **Une Chante, L'Autre Pas, L'** see One Sings, The Other Doesn't

▶ **Unfaithful Wife, The** see Femme Infidèle, La

Unfinished Piece For Mechanical Piano

▶ **(US: An Unfinished Piece For Player Piano)**

▶ **Neokonchennaya Pyesa Dlya Mekhanicheskogo Pianin**

USSR   1977   100 mins   col
Mosfilm

d   **Nikita Mikhalkov**

sc **Aleksander Adabashyan, Nikita Mikhalkov**
ph **Pavel Lebeshev**
m **Eduard Artemyev**
   Alexander Kalyagin, Elena Solovei, Eugenia Glushenko, Antonina Shuranova, Yuri Bogatyrev, Nikita Mikhalkov

Schoolteacher Platanov (Kalyagin), is married to the unintellectual Sasha (Glushenko). At the country estate of the widow Anna Petrovna (Shuranova), he again meets Sophia (Solovei), a girlfriend of seven years previously, just married to Sergei (Bogatyrev), a complete fool. Their attempt to recapture their past only leads to tragic farce. Mikhalkov (who plays the drunken doctor) has splendidly adapted *Platanov*, Chekhov's rambling first play, to give his stock company ample opportunity to display its acting skills. The atmosphere of the lazy summer's day is beautifully caught by Lebeshev's cinematography, although there are times when the pictorial distracts from the text and the sweet takes over too often from the bitter.

▶ **Unfinished Piece For Player Piano, An** see Unfinished Piece For Mechanical Piano

▶ **Unholy Love** see Alraune

▶ **Unruhige Nacht** see All Night Through

▶ **Unser Kurzes Leben** see Our Short Life

▶ **Unsichtbare Gegner** see Invisible Adversaries

▶ **Unvanquished, The** see Aparajito

▶ **Uomo A Meta, Un** see Almost a Man

▶ **Uomo Di Paglia, L'** see Man Of Straw

The Uprising

▶ **Der Aufstand**

W. Germany   1980   96 mins   col
Joachim Von Vietinghoff

d   **Peter Lilienthal**

sc   **Peter Lilienthal, Antonio Skármeta**
ph   **Michael Ballhaus**
m   **Claus Bantzer**
     Águstin Pereira, Carlos Catanía, María Lourdes Centano De Zelaya, Oscar Castillo

Nicaragua in the last days of the dictator Somoza and his brutal National Guard. In the university town of Léon, a young man (Pereira) in the Guard, sides with the Sandinistas, to which his father (Catanía) belongs, and participates in the taking of the government stockade. The West German director, who spent his adolescence in Uruguay and lived in Allende's Chile, shot the film in Léon four months after the Sandinista victory, using the people themselves in place of actors. As a result, this is a simple, direct, hot-off-the- press document, re-enacted with fervour by the participants. However, given the youth of the revolution, it would have been too much to expect that Lilienthal and the exiled Chilean novelist Skármeta should go deeper into the political and economic questions rather than deal mainly on the level of the undoubted solidarity and heroics of the people.

Up To A Point

▶ **Hasta Cierto Punto**

Cuba   1983   68 mins   col
ICAIC

d   **Tomás Gutiérrez Alea**
sc   **Juan Carlos Tabío, Serafin Quiñones, Tomás Gutiérrez Alea**
ph   **Mario García Joya**
m   **Leo Brouwer**
     Oscar Alvarez, Mirta Ibarra, Omar Valdés, Coralia Veloz, Rogelio Blaín, Ana Viña

Oscar (Alvarez), a writer married to an actress, is researching a film about Latin-American *machismo*. While interviewing workers of both sexes at the Havana docks, he falls in love with one of them, the attractive Lina (Ibarra). As their involvement deepens, it becomes clear that under his veneer of acquired liberated views, Oscar is as much trapped in notions of maleness as the workers he talks to. Juxtaposing video interviews with workers – one of whom says that women should be free 'up to a point' – with artistic and working-class life, the film demonstrates the difficulties of resolving those traditional sexual and social conflicts that are at odds with the political ideology by which the characters are governed and to which they willingly subscribe. As an account of a dead-end love affair, the story is banal, but is lent conviction by the well-chosen cast.

Up To His Ears

▶ **Les Tribulations D'Un Chinois En Chine**

France   1965   110 mins   col
Les Films Ariane/Artistes
Associés(Paris)/Vides(Rome)

d   **Philippe De Broca**
sc   **Daniel Boulanger, Philippe De Broca**
ph   **Edmond Séchan**
m   **Georges Delerue**
Jean-Paul Belmondo, Ursula Andress, Valérie Lagrange, Maria Pacôme, Valery Inkijinoff, Jean Rochefort

Arthur Lempereur (Belmondo) is so bored by his colossal wealth that he wants to die. His Chinese advisor Mr Goh (Inkijinoff) persuades him to suspend his suicide attempts for insurance purposes, and rather have himself killed after a suitable interval. Arthur embarks on a yacht trip round the world with an entourage that includes his fiancée (Lagrange), meets an alluring striptease dancer (Andress) in Hong Kong and decides he doesn't want to die after all... So far, so good. In a plot derived from a novel by Jules Verne, the film offers attractive Far Eastern locations, Belmondo's unique charm and a splendidly inscrutable performance from Inkijinoff. However, when Arthur sets off to look for Mr Goh and intercept the plans for his own assassination, we get an inferior re-run of *That Man From Rio*, so jam-packed with comic-book escapades played at a frenzied pace, that the film grows very tiresome well before its ironic resolution.

▶ **U Samovo Sinyevo Morya** see By The Bluest Of Seas

▶ **Usual Unidentified Thieves, The** see Persons Unknown

▶ **Utamaro And His Five Women** see Five Women Around Utamaro

▶ **Utamaro O Meguru Gonin No Onna** see Five Women Around Utamaro

▶ **Utvandrarna** see Emigrants, The

▶ **Už Zase Skáču Přes Kaluže** see I'm Jumping Over Puddles Again

▶ **Vacances De Monsieur Hulot, Les** see Monsieur Hulot's Holiday

▶ **Vache Et Le Prisonnier, La** see Cow And I, The

Vagabonde

▶ **Sans Toit Ni Loi**

France 1985 104 mins col
Cine-Tamaris/Films A2/Ministère De La Culture

d   Agnès Varda
sc Agnès Varda
ph Patrick Blossier
m   Joanna Bruzdowicz
    Sandrine Bonnaire, Macha Meril,
    Stéphane Freiss, Eliane Cortadellas,
    Marthe Jarnias, Joel Fosse

The body of a young woman, Mona (Bonnaire), is found frozen to death in a ditch. Various 'witnesses' tell of their encounters with her and of how she threw up an office job for life on the open road. Agnès Varda's first feature for nine years is also one of her best. It is a telling study of an aimless existence upon which the director imposes a rigorous form. It is to the credit of both Varda and the magnificent Bonnaire that such an unsympathetic central character manages to reach tragic stature as she moves further and further into degradation against a cruel but beautiful wintry landscape.

Best Film Venice 1985

▶ **Vaghe Stelle Dell'Orsa** see Of A Thousand Delights

▶ **Valahol Európában** see Somewhere In Europe

Valerie And Her Week Of Wonders

▶ **Valerie A Tyden Divu**

Czechoslovakia 1970 77 mins col
Barrandov Studio

d   Jaromil Jires
sc Jaromil Jires, Ester Krumbachová
ph Jan Curík
m   Jan Klusák
    Jaroslava Schallerová, Helena
    Anýzková, Petr Kopriva, Jírí Prymek,
    Jan Klusák

Innocent Valerie (Schallerová), aged 13, lives in small town with her young-looking grandma (Anýzková), who becomes a vampire and is tried for witchcraft. However, the magic earrings given to Valerie by a young man called the Eagle – who turns out to be her brother – and which have protected her from the Weasel and from rape by a priest, save granny from the stake. These are, in fact, Valerie's baroque, Gothic fairytale dreams, in which images mystical, religious, sexual, brutal and romantic, jostle for position. Jires has moved a great distance from his simple early narratives (e.g. *The Cry*, 1963), to join that school of Czech film-makers with a penchant for the bizarre and fantastical. Unfortunately, although the form of this one is visually spectacular, the content is an irritating jumble.

▶ **Valerie A Tyden Divu** see Valerie And Her Week Of Wonders

▶ **Valseuses, Les** see Making It

▶ **Vámmentes Házasság** see Duty Free Marriage

Les Vampires

France 1915–1916 420 mins bw
Gaumont

d **Louis Feuillade**
sc **Louis Feuillade**
ph **Manichoux**
m **Silent**
**Musidora, Edouard Mathé, Marcel
Lesque, Jean Aymé, Jacques Feyder**

'The Vampires', a gang of brilliant jewel thieves led by The Grand Vampire (Aymé) and the anagrammatically named Irma Vep (Musidora), are tracked down by a crusading journalist (Mathé). This visually compelling, 10-part serial is generally considered Feuillade's best work. It's certainly the most typical, with its strange combination of fantasy, realism, thrills and comedy. And at its centre the electrifying Musidora in black tights and cloak as the arch-villainess. Although the gang is finally vanquished, the Ministry Of the Interior temporarily banned a couple of episodes for what it deemed the glamorization of crime.

Vampyr

▶ **aka The Strange Adventure Of
David Gray**

France/Germany 1932 83 mins bw
Tobis Klangfilm/Carl Dreyer

d **Carl Dreyer**
sc **Carl Dreyer, Christen Jul**
ph **Rudolph Maté, Louis Née**
m **Wolfgang Zeller**
**Julian West, Henriette Gérard, Sybille
Schmitz, Maurice Schutz, Jan Hieronimko**

David Gray (West), a young traveller, witnesses the effects of vampires on the lord of a remote castle and on his two daughters. Financed by the Baron Nicolas De Gunzberg, a Dutch amateur actor (it shows), on condition that he should play the leading role under a pseudonym, Dreyer's first sound film was shot entirely on location near Paris in French, German and English. Despite or because of the necessity of keeping dialogue to a minimum, the shooting restrictions and the money limitations, Dreyer went far beyond the purely Gothic, creating a horror film that makes most

others pale into insignificance. The eerie mood was partly due to the luminous photography, achieved by reflecting light off gauze. The supernatural gives way to the magnificent 'natural' climax when the villain is buried alive by flour in a mill. The disturbing tale was based on a short story by Sheridan Le Fanu.

▶ **Vangelo Secondo Matteo, Il** see Gospel According To Saint Matthew, The

Vanina Vanini

▶ **aka The Betrayer**

Italy 1961 130 mins col
Zebra Film(Rome)/Orsay Film(Paris)

d **Roberto Rossellini**
sc **Roberto Rossellini, Diego Fabbri, Franco
Solinas, Antonello Trombadori**
ph **Luciano Trasatti**
m **Renzo Rossellini**
**Sandra Milo, Laurent Terzieff, Martine
Carol, Paolo Stoppa, Isabelle Corey,
Fernando Cicero**

Pietro Missirilli (Terzieff), a Carbonari revolutionary, travels to Rome to kill a traitor and is given refuge by a sympathetic Countess (Carol). She passes him on to her lover, Prince Vanini (Stoppa), who places him in hiding where he is discovered by the prince's daughter Vanina (Milo). The couple fall in love and, when Pietro leaves to rejoin his comrades, Vanina secretly accompanies him, beginning a chain of events whereby, in her efforts to hold him, she ends up betraying him. This excursion into period politics and romance richly evokes the conflicts and contradictions of the time. Rossellini uses colour to brilliant effect and his handling of several different interlocking strands of action is admirable. Social inequality, religious and political corruption, intrigue, guilt and betrayal are everywhere palpable in this high romance of the Risorgimento. Only some mediocre acting lets it down.

The Vanishing

▶ **Spoorloos**

Netherlands/France 1988
106 mins col

Golden Egg Film (Amsterdam)/Ingrid
Productions (Paris)

d   **George Sluizer**
sc **Tim Krabbé**
ph **Toni Kuhn**
m   **Henny Vrienten**
    **Bernard-Pierre, Donnadieu, Gene
    Bervoets, Johanna Ter Steege, Gwen
    Eckhaus**

A Dutch couple, Rex (Bervoets) and Saskia
(Ter Steege), are motoring in France *en route*
to Provence. At a motorway stop Saskia goes
to fetch drinks and is never seen again. Meanwhile, Raymond Lemorne (Donnadieu), a
science teacher in Nîmes, happily married and
the father of two daughters, has been per-
fecting a plan to abduct a young woman.
Three years later Rex is still obsessively
searching for an explanation to Saskia's fate
when Donnadieu presents himself and promises, under certain conditions, to give it...
George Sluizer's film, constructed, photographed and acted with the utmost expertise
and discretion, is a totally chilling portrait of
a psychopath and a gripping study of twin
obsessions. The horror of its unexpected and
shocking ending is, like Donnadieu's masterly, self-confessed monster, unforgettable.
An original and compelling psychological
thriller, subtly weaving and intersecting its
parallel threads and its travelling time span,
it is a must for fans of the genre.

The Vanishing Corporal

▶ **Le Caporal Épinglé**

France 1962 110 mins bw
Les Films Cyclope

d   **Jean Renoir**
sc **Jean Renoir, Guy Lefranc**
ph **Georges Leclerc**
m   **Joseph Kosma**
    **Jean-Pierre Cassel, Claude Brasseur,
    O.E. Hasse, Claude Rich, Jacques
    Jouanneau, Mario David**

The majority of French soldiers in a German
P.O.W camp adjust to the life in spite of their
homesickness and grumbles, but one young
corporal (Cassel), good-looking, educated
and off-beat, dedicates himself to escape.
Although his repeated attempts fail, he keeps
trying, even managing a romantic interlude

with the receptionist daughter of a female
German dentist. It is an unusual film in which
Renoir treats his subject from a perspective
of gentle comedy and with great charm, yet
manages to suggest, by a series of subtle shifts
of mood, the reality beneath the surface of
the situation. Cassel is perfectly cast, supported by a gallery of sharply observed
characters who demonstrate the melting pot
of backgrounds that is the army. Finely
photographed in misty winter landscapes that
are evocative without being depressing, it's
wry, touching and entertaining, while suggesting echoes of Renoir's World War I masterpiece, *La Grande Illusion*.

▶ **Vargtimmen** see Hour Of The Wolf

▶ **Variété** see Variety

Variety

▶ **aka Vaudeville**

▶ **Variété**

Germany 1925 104 mins bw
UFA

d   **E.A. Dupont**
sc **E.A. Dupont, Leo Birinsky**
ph **Karl Freund**
m   **Silent**
    **Emil Jannings, Lya De Putti, Maly
    Delschaft, Warwick Ward**

An aging trapeze artist (Jannings) kills the
newcomer (Ward) who seduced his wife and
partner (De Putti). This conventional melo of
passion and jealousy was notable for its
unconventional impressionistic use of swirling
light and movement and spectacular camera
effects. It was a tremendous success, stylistically influential, and brought Dupont to the
attention of Hollywood, where he ended up
making mostly B-movie trash.

▶ **Variety Lights** see Lights Of Variety

▶ **Varjoja Paratiisissa** see Shadows In
Paradise

▶ **Vasárnapi Szülok** see Sunday
Daughters

Vassa

USSR 1983 136 mins col
Mosfilm

d   Gleb Panfilov
sc Gleb Panfilov
ph Leonid Kalashnikov
m   Vadim Bibergan
    Inna Churikova, Vadim Medvedev,
    Nikolai Skorobogatov, Valentina
    Yukeninia, Valentina Telichkina,
    Vyacheslav Bogachov

Vassa (Churikova) rules her family and its
shipping empire with a rod of iron, but when
her efforts to save her husband from prosecution for molesting young girls fail, she
persuades him to commit suicide. But even
the formidable Vassa, locked in mortal combat with her political-activist daughter-in-law
(Yukeninia), cannot stay the gathering forces
of revolution. In adapting Maxim Gorky's
mainstay of Soviet repertory theatre, *Vassa
Zhelevnova*, as a vehicle for his wife and
regular leading lady, Panfilov has shifted the
work's emphasis to make the eponymous
heroine a reasonably sympathetic character.
He brings the story to life as an accessible
domestic drama, but with an overlay of fascinating political ambiguity. The splendid Churikova convinces, as does the richly detailed
re-creation of the life lived by the Russian
provincial *bourgeoisie* in 1913, when the Bolsheviks began to beat at the door of the
merchant classes.

▶ **Vaudeville** see Variety

▶ **Ved Vejen** see Katinka

▶ **Veiviseren** see Pathfinder

▶ **Velikii Uteshitel** see Great Consoler,
The

▶ **Vem Dömer?** see Love's Crucible

Verdict

▶ **aka Jury Of One**

▶ **Le Testament**

France 1974 97 mins col

Les Films Concordia/P.E.C.F./
Champion Cinematografica

d   André Cayatte
sc André Cayatte, Henri Pierre Dumayet,
    Paul Andreota
ph Jean Badal
m   Louiguy
    Sophia Loren, Jean Gabin, Henri Garcin,
    Michel Albertini, Gisèle Casadessus,
    Muriel Catala

A young law student is charged with rape
and murder, but his adoring mother (Loren),
the wealthy widow of a gangster, is convinced
of his innocence. To secure his acquittal, she
intimidates the trial judge (Gabin) by kidnapping his seriously ill wife. What starts out as
a respectable courtroom drama quickly
degenerates into a salacious, lurid, ugly and
fanciful melodrama of confused and questionable moral focus. One keeps watching,
though, held by the *gravitas* of the aged Gabin
in the penultimate film before his death, and
the irresistible sight of the beautiful Loren as
a ruthless tigress protecting her less than
endearing cub.

▶ **Verdugo, El** see Executioner, The

▶ **Vérité, La** see Truth, The

▶ **Verkaufte Braut, Die** see Bartered
Bride, The

▶ **Verlorene, Der** see Lost One, The

▶ **Verlorene Ehre Der Katharina
Blum, Die** see Lost Honour Of Katharina Blum, The

▶ **Verlorene Sohn, Der** see Lost Son,
The

Veronico Cruz

▶ **La Deuda Interna**

▶ **aka Veronico Cruz**

Argentina 1987 96 mins col
Yacoraite Film (Buenos Aires)/
Mainframe Films (London), in
association with BFI and Channel 4

d   Miguel Pereira
sc Eduardo Leiva Muller, Miguel Pereira

ph **Gerry Feeny**
m **Jaime Torres**
  **Juan José Camero, Gonzalo Morales,
  René Olaguivel, Guillermo Delgado, Don
  Leopolda Abán, Ana Maria Gonzales,
  Fortunato Ramos, Juana Daniela Cáceres**

When the wife of Castulo Cruz (Ramos) dies in childbirth, he leaves the isolated, poor and primitive village of Chorcan to seek work. The baby son, Veronico, is cared for by his frail grandmother and grows into a shy and lonely child (Morales) until a teacher (Camero) arrives to open a school. He forms a bond with Veronico and takes him in when the grandmother dies. Together they journey to the city to look for Castulo, but the military junta is now in control and the man has 'disappeared'. The teacher is transferred and loses touch with the boy during the Falklands War. Returning to Chorcan to look for Veronico, he learns that he has joined the navy... Made, interestingly enough, with a substantial investment of British money, this Argentinian film is a tale of simple people, simply told. The gradual awakening of aspirations and optimism in the children of a backward community, thanks to the efforts of the teacher (a marvellously sympathetic, restrained and attractive Camero), the hamfisted encroachment of the dictatorship on the ways of the villagers and the tragedy of the Falklands War subtly emerge in a gentle unfolding of the story. The bold landscape and atmosphere are evoked with clarity and discretion to enhance a poignant and instructive film. On the debit side, it is perhaps a mite too slow, demanding some initial determination to stay with it.

Veronika Voss

▶ **Die Sehnsucht Der Veronika Voss**

W. Germany   1981   104 mins   bw
Maura/Tango/Rialto/Trio/Maran

d   **Rainer Werner Fassbinder**
sc **Peter Märthesheimer, Pea Frölich**
ph **Xaver Schwarzenberger**
m   **Peer Raben**
    **Rosel Zech, Hilmar Thate, Anne Marie
    Düringer, Cornelia Froeboess, Doris
    Schade, Armin Müller-Stahl**

In the 1950s, a journalist (Thate) becomes involved in the life of Veronika Voss (Zech), a screen idol of the previous decade but now at the end of her career and under the influence of a doctor (Düringer) who supplies her with drugs. Fassbinder's striking use of black and white evokes in different ways the atmosphere of Germany in the dour post-war years and – in dreams – the brashness of the Nazi era. One of the director's last films, it is a flamboyant tribute to the UFA Studios with a nod towards *Sunset Boulevard* by the great Billy Wilder.

Best Film Berlin 1982

▶ **Verweigerung, Die** see Refusal, The

▶ **Very Curious Girl, A** see Dirty Mary

▶ **Very Happy Alexandre** see Alexandre

A Very Moral Night

▶ **Egy Erkölcsös Éjszaka**

Hungary   1979   99 mins   col
Dialög Filmstudio

d   **Károly Makk**
sc **István Örkény, Péter Bacsó**
ph **János Tóth**
m   **Chopin, Offenbach, Délibes, Johann
    Strauss, Leo Fall, Ferenc Erkel, György
    Forrai, István Major, Béla Radics
    Margit Makay, Irén Psota, Carla
    Romanelli, Györgyi Tarján, György
    Cserhalmi**

Kelepey (Cserhalmi), a young student in a small Hungarian town early in the century, frequents the local brothel where he is a great favourite of the girls, particularly Darinka (Tarján), with whom he shares a chaste bed. Eventually, he moves into the brothel. When his mother turns up to visit him, Madame and the girls encourage her assumption that the place is a boarding house. A pleasant enough film, sweet, gentle and rather old-fashioned, but missing out on its obvious comic potential. Well-acted and directed, and boasting photography of outstanding quality, it is nonetheless disappointing coming, as it does, from the distinguished Károly Makk whose usual sense of commitment to painful situations has been abandoned here.

A Very Private Affair

▶ **Vie Privée**

France 1961 103 mins col
Progefi/Cipra(Paris)/CCM(Rome)

d   **Louis Malle**
sc **Jean-Paul Rappeneau, Louis Malle**
ph **Henri Decaë**
m   **Fiorenzo Carpi**
    Brigitte Bardot, Marcello Mastroianni, Grégoire Von Rizzori, Ursula Kubler, Dirk Sanders

In love with Fabio (Mastroianni), her best friend's husband, Jill (Bardot) goes to Paris where she becomes a film actress. Ill from the pressures of stardom, she returns to Geneva, meets the now separated Fabio again and enjoys an idyllic affair with him until her life ends in tragedy. Louis Malle's fifth feature is one of his least distinguished. Bardot is called upon to give a sort of parody of herself, while Mastroianni battles with his two-dimensional role as a soulful theatre director straight out of magazine fiction – as is the story, which never reaches a seriously credible level. However, what the director lacks in material, he compensates for in detailed visuals, breath-takingly photographed by Decaë, particularly the final dramatic sequences at Spoleto.

▶ **Vesničkó Má Středisková** see My Sweet Little Village

▶ **Vesyolye Rebyata** see Jazz Comedy

▶ **V Gorodye S** see In The Town Of S

▶ **Viaccia, La** see Love Makers, The

▶ **Viaggio In Italia** see Journey To Italy

Vice And Virtue

▶ **Le Vice Et La Vertu**

France 1963 100 mins bw
SNE/Gaumont/Trianon

d   **Roger Vadim**

sc **Roger Vailland, Claude Choublier, Roger Vadim**
ph **Marcel Grignon**
m   **Michel Magne**
    Annie Girardot, Catherine Deneuve, Robert Hossein, O.E. Hasse, Philippe Lemaire, Serge Marquand, Luciana Paluzzi

In Nazi-occupied France, sisters Juliette (Girardot) and Justine (Deneuve) are arrested. At the opulent German headquarters in Paris they are ordered to dispense their sexual favours to the High Command. Justine, a Resistance worker, somehow manages to keep her honour intact, while Juliette becomes the mistress of an SS officer, and thus they exemplify the 'vice' and 'virtue' of the title. Vadim has drawn his material from two novels of the Marquis De Sade, updating them in an attempt to give an impression of contemporary relevance. However, this intention is but a thin veneer overlaying a wallow in decadence, torture and hysteria, occasionally relieved by a measure of stylish eroticism. The classy leading ladies, some wildly baroque sets and a pseudo-Wagnerian score cannot disguise that this is a superficial exercise in sensationalism, albeit quite cleverly manipulated by the director.

▶ **Vice Et La Vertu, Le** see Vice And Virtue

▶ **Vices And Pleasures** see Private Vices And Public Virtues

▶ **Victoire En Chantant, La** see Black And White In Colour

▶ **Vidãs Sêcas** see Barren Lives

▶ **Vie, Une** see One Life

▶ **Vie À L'Envers, La** see Life Upside Down

▶ **Vie Conjugale, La** see Anatomy Of A Marriage

La Vie De Château

France 1965 93 mins bw
Ancinex/Cobela/La Guéville

d   **Jean-Paul Rappeneau**
sc **Jean-Paul Rappeneau, Alain Cavalier,
    Claude Sautet**
ph **Pierre Lhomme**
m   **Michel Legrand**
    **Catherine Deneuve, Pierre Brasseur,
    Philippe Noiret, Henri Garcin, Carlos
    Thompson**

World War II is raging but the Normandy château of Jérôme (Noiret) and Marie (Deneuve) is a haven of peace – if not of marital bliss. When Marie discovers Julien (Garcin), a mysterious stranger who claims to be in love with her but who is, in fact, a Free French agent on a mission, hiding in the château, events take a complicated turn. In his debut directorial effort, Rappenau manages a dose of charm and a sense of the comic which he would seldom repeat. There is the odd lapse in pace and, indeed, in credibility, but director, writers (would it be more appropriate to call them co-directors?) and the accomplished Lhomme create a good-natured, good-looking fairy story in which even Klopstock (Thompson), the German C.O. in love with Marie, is not noticeably villainous. Garcin and Noiret give superior performances.

▶ **Vie Devant Soi, La** see Madame Rosa

La Vie Est À Nous

▶ **(US: The People Of France)**

France   1936   66 mins   bw
Partie Communiste Français

d   **Jean Renoir, Jean-Paul Le Chanois,
    Jacques Becker, André Zwoboda, Pierre
    Unik, Henri Cartier-Bresson**
sc **Jean Renoir, Jean-Paul Le Chanois,
    Pierre Unik, Paul Vaillant-Couturier**
ph **Claude Renoir, Jean-Serge Bourgoin,
    Jean Isnard, Alain Douarinou**
m   **Songs of the Front Populaire
    Gaston Modot, Jean Dasté, Julien
    Berthot, Madeleine Sologne, Jacques
    Brunius, Roger Blin, Charles Blavette,
    Madeleine Dax, Jean Renoir, Jacques
    Becker, Vladimir Sokoloff**

A number of sketches, newsreels and political speeches put forward the policies of the French Communist Party. The staged scenes a bailiff being driven off a farm by peasants, an unemployed intellectual joining the Party and a newspaper vendor selling L'Humanité being beaten up by Fascist thugs. Asked by the Communist Party to make a propaganda work, Renoir merely supervised the film, which was shot and edited principally by his youthful assistants. Given that it was a collaborative effort, filmed in a few weeks in order to be ready in time for the 1936 election, Renoir's warm-hearted realism comes flooding through much of it, especially, it must be said, in the less directly political scenes. Later forbidden by the censors and then thought lost, it resurfaced again after May 1968.

La Vie Est Belle

Zaire   1987   72 mins   col
Lamy Films (Brussells/Stéphan Films (Paris)/Sol'Oeil Films (Kinshasa)

d   **Benoit Lamy, Ngangura Nweze**
sc **Benoit Lamy, Ngangura Mweze, Maryse
    Léon**
ph **Michel Baudour**
m   **Papa Wemba, Zaïko Langa Langa,
    Tshala Muana, Klody**
    **Papa Wemba, Bibi Krubwa, Landu
    Nzunzimbu Matshia, Kanku Kasongo,
    Lokinda Mengi Feza, Mazaza Mukoko**

Kourou (Wemba), a village musician, travels to Kinshasa in the hope of becoming a record star, but finds himself working as a houseboy. Meanwhile, he meets and falls in love with Kabibi (Krubwa) who gives him money to start his own band, but Kabibi's mother (Mukoko) wants her daughter to marry a rich club owner (Kasongo), and locks her up. Kourou is desperate, but things improve due to the intervention of a witch doctor. A rare film from Zaire, co-directed by Zairean Mweze and Belgian-born Lamy, it reveals, with a certain irony, fascinating aspects of life (polygamy, magic, feminism, class differences) in the former Belgian colony, and adds to the rich diversity of the growing African cinema. A further interest comes from the leading role, played with great charm by Papa Wemba, an internationally-known pop musician who now lives in Paris. The title, a phrase that is continually repeated by a dwarf street vendor to cheer up the hero, reflects the optimistic tone of this lively and populist film.

▶ **Vie Est Une Longue Fleuve Tranquille, La** see Life Is A Long Quiet River

▶ **Vie Est Un Roman, La** see Life Is A Bed Of Roses

▶ **Vie Et Rien D'Autre, Le** see Life And Nothing But

▶ **Vieil Homme Et L'Enfant, Le** see Two Of Us, The

▶ **Vieille Dame Indigne, La** see Shameless Old Lady, The

La Vieille Fille

▶ **aka The Old Maid**

France 1972 85 mins col
Lira Films(Paris)/Praesidens SPA(Rome)

d   Jean-Pierre Blanc
sc Jean-Pierre Blanc
ph Pierre Lhomme
m   Michel Legrand
    Annie Girardot, Philippe Noiret, Michel Lonsdale, Edith Scob, Jean-Pierre Darras, Marthe Keller

Gabriel (Noiret), a carefree, womanizing bachelor, is on his way to Spain when his car breaks down, forcing him to put up at a small seaside hotel on the French border. Taking the only available chair at dinner, he finds himself sitting with Muriel (Girardot), a shy, self-effacing single woman in her thirties. Both are ill-at-ease but, as the days pass, a sympathetic relationship develops between them. This charming vignette slyly and comically observes the idiosyncracies of life in this kind of establishment – man-eating maids, skirt-chasing waiters, highly eccentric guests – while gently delineating the fragile central relationship, which ends on a note of hope, but not certainty, for Muriel. The stars are excellent, the supporting cast superior.

Best Director Berlin 1972

▶ **Vie, L'Amour, La Mort, La** see Life, Love, Death

▶ **Vie Privée** see Very Private Affair, A

▶ **Vierde Man, Die** see Fourth Man, The

Une Vie Sans Joie

▶ **aka Catherine**

France 1924 75 mins bw
Jean Renoir

d   Albert Dieudonné
sc Jean Renoir
ph Jean Bachelet, Gibory
m   Silent
    Catherine Hessling, Albert Dieudonné, Louis Gauthier, Pierre Philippe, Eugénie Naud, Oléo, Pierre Champagne

Catherine, a young servant girl (Hessling), accompanies the tubercular Maurice (Dieudonné) and his family when they move from their village to Nice for the sake of Maurice's health. After his dramatic death, Catherine is forced to fend for herself, helped by a sympathetic prostitute and her pimp. She returns to the village and her former employer, M. Mallet (Gauthier) the Mayor, but when he is vilified for employing a fallen woman she runs away. Caught in a storm, Catherine is forced to shelter in a deserted tram car which breaks loose... Unimaginatively directed by Dieudonné (remembered as Gance's Napoleon), the picture nonetheless offers a climactic romantic rescue in the vein of D.W. Griffith and some outstanding location photography by Bachelet, who would become Renoir's regular cameraman. It is noteworthy as Renoir's first venture into film-making, with a script that anticipates such films as *Nana, La Chienne and Diary Of A Chambermaid* (made in Hollywood) in its sympathetic treatment of low-life characters, contrasted with the hypocrisy of the *bourgeoisie*. Renoir appears in a small role as a dandyish and adulterous member of the latter class.

▶ **Vieux Pays Où Rimbaud Est Mort, Le** see Old Country Where Rimbaud Died, The

Viktor Und Viktoria

> Germany 1933 101 mins bw
> UFA

d Reinhold Schünzel
sc Reinhold Schünzel
ph Konstantin Irmen-Tschet
m Franz Doelle
   Renate Müller, Hermann Thimig, Adolf
   Wohlbrück, Hilde Hildebrand, Fritz
   Odemar, Aribert Wäscher

Viktor (Thimig), a would-be tragedian down on his luck, is reduced to performing in vaudeville as a female impersonator. He meets Susanne (Müller), an equally hapless aspiring singer, and, feeling unwell, persuades her to don drag and appear for him. She is a huge hit, Viktor becomes her manager and they tour their star act through Europe. Needless to say, complications multiply due to the constant switches of gender and wreak havoc with their personal lives. An extremely well-paced and funny comedy, directed with a light touch and lots of *echt* backstage atmosphere. The performances are excellent and Renate Müller, wonderfully relaxed and confident in drag, also has a pleasing singing voice. It was simultaneously made in French as *Georges Et Georgette* with Julien Carette and Meg Lemonnier. Of several subsequent remakes, the best known is Blake Edwards's *Victor/Victoria*, starring his wife Julie Andrews.

Village In The Mist

▶ Angemaeul

> South Korea 1983 90 mins col
> Hwa-Chun Trading Co

d Lim Kwon-Taek
sc Song Kil-Han
ph Jong Il-Song
m Kim Jong-Kil
   Ahn Song-Ki, Chong Yun-Hee, Lee Yea-Min, Kim Ji-Yung, Choi Dong-Jun, Jin Bong-Jin

Su-ok (Yun-Hee), a graduate teacher engaged to be married, takes up her first post in a village far from her fiancé and the urban custom and comfort of her home town. She learns that the villagers comprise one large clan, the only outsider being Kae-chol (Song-Ki), a mysterious layabout whose presence disturbs her. Lim Kwon-Taek made his reputation with *Mandala*, a controversial film about Buddhist monks, that was shown at Berlin in 1982. Here he deals with the hidden emotional behaviour and sexual problems that arise in a closed and inbred community. Filming in 'Scope, he calls on a dazzling array of camera and editing effects to give a compelling picture of a way of life that is vanishing in Korea, as well as drawing a perceptive portrait of his young schoolteacher, through whose eyes the life is observed. The movie was made on location in a picturesque village, detailed to be swallowed up by the construction of a dam.

▶ **Ville Des Pirates, La** see City Of Pirates

Vincent, François, Paul And The Others

▶ **Vincent, François, Paul...Et Les Autres**

> France 1974 118 mins col
> Lira Films/President Produzione

d Claude Sautet
sc Jean-Loup Dabadie, Claude Neron,
   Claude Sautet
ph Jean Boffety
m Philippe Sarde
   Yves Montand, Michel Piccoli, Serge
   Reggiani, Gérard Depardieu, Stéphane
   Audran, Marie Dubois, Antonella Lualdi,
   Umberto Orsini, Catherine Allégret,
   Ludmilla Mikael

Machine-shop owner, Vincent (Montand), successful doctor, François (Piccoli), and failed novelist, Paul (Reggiani), are old friends who are pushing fifty; the 'others' are Vincent's young protegé (Depardieu), a boxer, and the men's assorted wives and mistresses, most of whom are leaving or have left their partners. The story, if such it can be termed, deals with a period of mid-life crisis for the protagonists, during which they fall back on one another for emotional support. This movie is a paradigm of all that is best and worst about the work of Claude Sautet. It looks very good, boasts clever performances and chronicles middle-class Parisian lifestyle with deft accuracy, but it is overwhelmed by its superficial perfection and the powerful glamour of its all-star cast. The real issues of pain, fear and failure are thus left to lie buried in the hollow at its centre.

▶ **Vincent, François, Paul...Et Les Autres** see Vincent, François, Paul And The Others

▶ **Vingt-Quatre Heures De La Vie D'Une Femme** see Twenty-Four Hours In A Woman's Life

▶ **Viol, Le** see Question Of Rape, A

Violated Love

▶ **(US: Rape Of Love)**

▶ **L'Amour Violé**

France   1977   110 mins   col
Equinoxe/Dragon/MK2

d **Yannick Bellon**
sc **Yannick Bellon**
ph **Georges Barsky, Pierre William Glenn**
m **Aram Sedefian**
   Nathalie Nell, Alain Fourès, Michèle Simonnet, Pierre Arditi, Daniel Auteuil, Bernard Granger

After the initial trauma of being brutally raped by four young men, a nurse (Nell) starts to ask questions of herself and others, and tries to find a meaning to the crime. The film can be accused of predictability and didacticism, but not of pussyfooting, and it effectively emphasizes the banality of evil.

Violent Summer

▶ **Un Soir Sur La Plage**

France   1961   85 mins   bw
Francos/Mannic/Cocinor-Marceau

d **Michel Boisrond**
sc **Annette Wademant**
ph **L.H. Burel**
m **Michel Durand**
   Martine Carol, Jean Desailly, Daliah

Lavi, Henri-Jacques Huet, Michel Galabru

Successful author Michel (Huet) goes to stay with rich widow Georgina (Carol) on the Riviera, where she lives with her doctor lover (Desailly) and two children. His visit is marked by strange and sinister happenings, culminating in the beach murder of a retarded girl with whom he has had a fleeting and anonymous sexual encounter. Some intriguing ideas, atmospherically presented, together with an attractive cast, promise a good entertainment. However, both style and content depart a third of the way through, leaving a disappointingly flaccid and unconvincing thriller, foundering on its lost opportunities.

▶ **Violette** see Violette Nozière

Violette Et François

France   1977   99 mins   col
Président Films/FR3

d **Jacques Ruffio**
sc **Jean-Loup Dabadie**
ph **Andreas Winding**
m **Philippe Sarde**
   Isabelle Adjani, Jacques Dutronc, Serge Reggiani, Lea Massari, Françoise Arnoul

Violette (Adjani), François (Dutronc) and their baby son live together in a highly unsuitable liaison given their extreme differences of background and, more seriously, of temperament. François, a drifter and a dreamer, shoplifts – first for fun, then seriously, then compulsively. They marry, but nothing changes and, for a while, Violette becomes his accomplice... Goodness only knows what the point of this film is. Half delighting in the youthful high spirits of its protagonists and half aspiring to a moral tale, it's best viewed as a slick, superficial romance, worth watching for the ever-delightful Adjani.

Violette Nozière

▶ **(US: Violette)**

France   1977   122 mins   col
Filmel/Cinevideo/FR3

d   **Claude Chabrol**
sc   **Odile Barski, Herve Bromberger, Frédéric Grendel**
ph   **Jean Rabier**
m   **Pierre Jansen**
     Isabelle Huppert, Jean Carmet, Stéphane Audran, Bernadette Lafont, Jean-François Garreaud

In 1933, 18-year-old Violette (Huppert), a lower-middle-class Parisian girl, leads a promiscuous life, contracts syphilis, and poisons her mother (Audran) and putative father (Carmet). The mother survives to accuse her daughter of murder. After another bad spell, Chabrol popped back into critical and box-office favour with his sordid but excellently crafted and acted tale based on a true case history. Huppert is particularly impressive in expressing Violette's mixture of innocence and evil. The backgrounds – the parents' small apartment and the Left Bank cafés – are well delineated. It is, however, one of Chabrol's most impersonal films.

Best Actress (Isabelle Huppert) Cannes 1978

Les Violons Du Bal

France   1974   108 mins   col/bw
Port Royal/Planfilm

d   **Michel Drach**
sc   **Michel Drach**
ph   **William Lubtchansky (col) Yan Le Masson (bw)**
m   **Jean Manuel De Scareno, Jacques Monty**
     Michel Drach, Jean-Louis Trintignant, Marie-José Nat, David Drach, Christian Rist, Nathalie Roussel, Gabrielle Doulcet

Michel Drach attempts to persuade producers to back a film about his own childhood as a Jewish boy in Nazi-occupied France. They demand a star name, whereupon Trintignant materializes as both Drach and his father, while Drach's real-life wife, Nat, plays his wife and his mother, and his son David plays him as a child. Action shifts constantly between past and present in a complex pattern of filmic tricks which, combined with the doubling, make the film at times difficult to follow (or swallow). However, Drach has a firm grasp of his technical manoeuvres as well

as drawing a winning performance from his son. For the rest, it's rather old-fashioned – the climactic escape of young Michel, his mother and grandmother on foot to Switzerland the kind of thing that has been done countless times before – but it is sometimes amusing and occasionally inspired, as in the beautifully handled sequences where school-boy Michel learns that to be Jewish is to invite insult and assault.

Best Actress (Marie-José Nat) Cannes 1974

Virgin

France   1987   88 mins   col
CB Films/Sofica/CNC

d   **Catherine Breillat**
sc   **Catherine Breillat with Roger Salloch**
ph   **Laurent Dailland**
m   **Maxime Schmitt (consultant)**
     Delphine Zentout, Etienne Chicot, Olivier Parnière, Jean-François Stevenin, Stéphane Moquet

Fourteen-year-old Lili (Zentout), on holiday with her family in Biarritz, is bored to screaming pitch. She meets Maurice (Chicot), a middle-aged man of questionable occupation and morals, who attempts to seduce her. Desirous of losing her virginity but unable to bring herself to do so, she embarks on a protracted and unsatisfactory relationship with the older man before cold-bloodedly giving herself to an unattractive youth. Working from her own novel, *36 Fillette*, Breillat (who wrote the novel and screenplay of the sleazy *Police* (1985), filmed by Pialat), set out to make a film with absolute realism as its keynote. This she has succeeded in doing, but whether or not you want to spend the best part of two hours in the company of a sullen, foul-mouthed teenager and be a fly on the wall to her ghastly sexual exploits is another matter. Chicot is excellent and the nubile Zentout appropriate, but the movie is discomfiting and unpleasant without revealing anything of particular value or meaning.

The Virgin Spring

▶ **Jungfrukällan**

Sweden   1960   88 mins   bw

Svensk Filmindustri

d **Ingmar Bergman**
sc **Ulla Isaksson**
ph **Sven Nykvist**
m **Erik Nordgren**
   Max Von Sydow, Brigitta Valberg,
   Gunnel Lindblom, Brigitta Pettersson

In 14th-century Sweden, a young virgin (Pettersson) is raped and murdered by three swineherds after her half-sister (Lindblom) has invoked a pagan curse. When her father (Von Sydow) avenges his daughter's death, a spring bubbles up from the spot where she died. As in *The Seventh Seal*, Bergman meticulously conjures up a cruel and superstitious medieval world, but with heavier symbols and more unrelieved gloom than in the previous film. The performers, too, have less room to breathe, but there are some haunting visual images created by Nykvist (replacing Gunnar Fischer as Bergman's constant cameraman). Although the film won the International Critics Prize at Cannes, it was, curiously, announced as too good to be judged for the Best Film award.

Best Foreign Film Oscar 1960

Viridiana

Spain 1961 91 mins bw
Uninci/Films 59/Gustavo Alatriste

d **Luis Buñuel**
sc **Luis Buñuel, Julio Alajandro**
ph **José Agayo**
m **Handel**
   Silvia Pinal, Fernando Rey, Francisco Rabal, Margarita Lozano, Victoria Zinny

Out of Christian charity, Viridiana (Pinal), a novice about to take her vows who has been abused and cheated by her uncle (Rey) and his bastard son (Rabal), opens up the former's house to a collection of cripples and beggars. As Buñuel's first film made in his native land for 29 years is a savage attack on Catholic mentality and rituals, it was also his last in Spain for many more years. Although the script had been unaccountably passed by Franco's censors, the film itself was banned outright in Spain. The notorious set-piece of The Last Supper being enacted by the scum of the earth also caused the Vatican to con-

demn it. In general, however, the public and critics enjoyed the mordant humour and anticlericalism, and welcomed Buñuel back to the centre stage of world cinema.

Best Film Cannes 1961

Les Visiteurs Du Soir

▶ **(US: The Devil's Envoys)**

France 1942 120 mins bw
André Paulvé

d **Marcel Carné**
sc **Jacques Prévert, Pierre Laroche**
ph **Roger Hubert**
m **Joseph Kosma, Maurice Thiriet**
   Arletty, Jules Berry, Marie Déa, Alain Cuny, Fernand Ledoux, Marcel Herrand

In 1485, Gilles (Cuny) and Dominique (Arletty), two minstrels, arrive during the celebrations of the betrothal of a baron's daughter (Déa) to a knight (Herrand). But they are really servants of the devil (Berry). Gilles seduces the bride, but forgetting the devil's work, falls in love with her. The first of the two 'escapist' films that Carné and Prévert made during the Occupation (the other was *Les Enfants Du Paradis*) was seen by the French at the time as an allegory of their situation, with the devil as Hitler. None of this comes through today in this stilted, whimsical, medieval fairytale. But there are pleasures in the art design (Alexandre Trauner and Georges Wakhevitch), the photography and (the too long in arriving) Berry in another of his ingratiating villain roles.

▶ **Viskingar Och Rop** see Cries And Whispers

▶ **Visszaesök** see Forbidden Relations

I Vitelloni

▶ **(US: The Young And The Passionate)**

Italy 1953 109 mins bw
Peg/Cité

d **Federico Fellini**

sc **Federico Fellini, Ennio Flaiano, Tullio
    Pinelli**
ph **Otello Martelli**
m   **Nino Rota**
    **Franco Fabrizi, Franco Interlenghi,
    Eleonora Ruffo, Alberto Sordi, Leopoldo
    Trieste, Riccardo Fellini**

A group of five layabouts in their late twenties
hang around a small Italian seaport, playing
pool, drinking, getting up to mischief and
day-dreaming. Only Moraldo (Interlenghi)
manages to break away and go to Rome. In
his second film as solo director, Fellini
revisited and recreated, with acute observation and ambivalence, the place and friends
he grew up with. (His brother Riccardo plays
one of them.) Although critical of these 'overgrown calves' (vitelloni), Fellini and the insep-
arable music of Rota, lend the whole film an
aura of nostalgia, regret and loss of innocence.
He would follow his alter-ego Moraldo (who
becomes Marcello) to the big city in *La Dolce
Vita.*

Viva La Muerte

Tunisia/France 1971 90 mins col
Isabelle Films/SATPEC

d   **Fernando Arrabal**
sc **Fernando Arrabal, Claudine Lagrive**
ph **Jean-Marc Ripert**
m   **Jean-Yves Bosseur**
    **Mahdi Chaouch, Nuria Espert, Anouk
    Ferjac, Ivan Henriques, Jazia Klibi**

Fando (Chaouch), a 12-year-old boy living
with his mother (Spanish stage director
Espert) and aunt (Ferjac), tries to discover
the fate of his gentle father (Henriques) who
disappeared. Memories and visions intrude
upon his mind as he finds out that his mother
betrayed his father to Franco's police for
being a 'Red' and an atheist. The *avant-garde*
Spanish novelist and playwright Arrabal's
first film might have had a serious intent, an
indictment of tyranny, but it is drowned in
an excessive flow of grotesque, ugly, visceral
and perverse images. Among these are a priest
being forced to eat his own genitals, a city
drowned in urine, female masturbation, the
biting off of a lizard's head...The film, therefore, can only be recommended to those who
find these examples appealing, or are inter-

ested in the outer reaches of the Surrealist
movement. There were enough of them to
make it a cult midnight movie in New York
at the time.

Viva Maria!

France 1965 120 mins col
Nouvelles Éditions/Artistes Associés/
Vides

d   **Louis Malle**
sc **Louis Malle, Jean-Claude Carrière**
ph **Henri Decaë**
m   **Georges Delerue**
    **Jeanne Moreau, Brigitte Bardot, George
    Hamilton, Paulette Dubost, Claudio
    Brook**

The Two Marias (Moreau and Bardot), a
double song 'n' dance act working in an
unspecified Central American state, both fall
for a revolutionary leader (Hamilton) whom
they help in the struggle to overthrow the
country's dictator. The gaiety of this large
scale extravaganza was in complete contrast
to the solemnity of *Le Feu Follet* (1963).
Filmed in colour and on location in Mexico,
it wittily takes off the kind of big production
it is. France's two top female stars seemed to
relish the zestful occasion, as did the public.
A great many critics enjoyed it less.

▶ **Vivement Dimanche** see Finally
Sunday

▶ **Vivre Pour Vivre** see Live For Life

▶ **Vivre Sa Vie** see It's My Life

▶ **Vizi Privati, Pubbliche Virtù** see
Private Vices And Public Virtues

▶ **Vlyudyakh** see My Apprenticeship

▶ **Voce Della Luna, La** see Voice Of
The Moon, The

The Voice Of The Moon

▶ **La Voce Della Luna**

Italy 1989 115 mins col

Cecchi Gori Group/Tiger
Cinematográfica/Cinémax/RAI-TV

d **Federico Fellini**
sc **Federico Fellini, Ermanno Gavazzoni,
Tullio Pinelli**
ph **Tonino Delli Colli**
m **Nicola Piovani**
    **Roberto Benigni, Paolo Villaggio, Nadia
    Ottaviani, Marisa Tomasi, Sim, Syusy
    Blady, Uta Schmidt**

Salvini (Benigni), poet, dreamer and visionary, communing with nature, finds himself in
a cemetery where ghosts come to haunt him.
At a chaotic beauty pageant organized by the
paranoid village prefect (Villaggio) he dreams
of waltzing with a beautiful duchess. He then
returns to the fields to contemplate the moon.
Made for $25 million to mark the director's
seventieth birthday, Fellini called this very
free adaptation from the Ermanno Gavazzoni
novel, *The Poem Of Lunatics*, 'a little movie
with just a skeleton of a scenario'. It contains
many of the themes and obsessions that have
been familiar in Fellini's special world for
over three decades – the memories of youth,
the pains of love, the escape into dreams and
the circus motif. As episodic as many of his
films, this haunting, sad and funny work is
really one long dream, intruded upon by the
worst aspects, as Fellini sees it, of the modern
world, represented mainly by deafening pop
music. Ironically, despite the inherent praise
of silence and poetic contemplation, the film
is as noisy as can be and the late Nino Rota's
evocative music is sorely missed. Among the
magnificent set pieces is a rumbustious pizza
festival in stark contrast to the fairy-tale
elements that run through it.

The Voice Of The Water

▶ **De Stem Van Het Water**

Netherlands 1966 82 mins col
Haanstra's Filmproductie

d **Bert Haanstra**
sc **Bert Haanstra**
ph **Anton Von Munster**
m **Robert Heppener**

Haanstra's acclaimed film, three years in the
making, observes the relationship of the
Dutch people with the water that is their main

ally and their greatest threat. Using a simple,
clear-cut approach, matched by vivid and
unpretentious camerawork, the director
shows us all manner of ordinary people
engaged in all manner of activities connected
with water: eel fishermen, brave tugboat sailors, children skating. The people are viewed
with affection, the water with respect, and not
all the incidents are happy ones. A little gem
of documentary film making, accompanied
by an economical and charming English commentary spoken in a beguiling Dutch accent,
it is alas, sometimes screened shorn of a good
half-hour.

▶ **Voici Les Temps Des Assassins**
see Murder À La Carte

▶ **Voie Lactée, La** see Milky Way, The

▶ **Voile Bleu, Le** see Blue Veil, The

▶ **Voina I Mir** see War And Peace

▶ **Vokzal Dlya Dvoikh** see Station For
Two, A

▶ **Voleur, Le** see Thief Of Paris, The

Volpone

France 1940 98 mins bw
Ile de France Productions

d **Maurice Tourneur**
sc **Jules Romains, Stefan Zweig**
ph **Armand Thirard**
m **Marcel Delannoy**
    **Harry Baur, Louis Jouvet, Fernand
    Ledoux, Marion Dorian**

Volpone (Baur), a wealthy Venetian merchant, with the aid of his servant Mosca
(Jouvet), decides to pretend to be dying in
order to watch the reactions of his 'friends'
as they jostle to inherit his money. One of
the few of Maurice Tourneur's sound films of
interest, this Gallic version of Ben Jonson's
classic comedy boasts two memorable performances from Baur and Jouvet. The director's eye for pictorial composition and décor
that so suited his Hollywood fantasies, such
as *The Blue Bird* (1918), and his taste for

literature are fairly well satisfied in this lav-
ishly presented production.

▶ **Volver A Empezar** see To Begin
Again

▶ **Voskhozhdenie** see Ascent, The

▶ **Vostaniye Rybakov** see Revolt Of
The Fishermen, The

Voyage Beyond

▶ **Antarjali Yatra**

India 1987 118 mins col
National Film Development Corporation

d **Gautam Ghose**
sc **Gautam Ghose, Sunil Gongopadhaya**
ph **Gautam Ghose**
m **Gautam Ghose**
  **Shatrughan Sinha, Shampa Ghose,
  Promode Ganguli, Robi Ghosh, Mohan
  Agashe**

In the India of the 1830s an old Brahmin
(Ganguli), who is near death, is brought to
the banks of the Ganges where an astrologer
tells him it is imperative that he takes a wife
with him to the afterlife. A young virgin
(Ghose) is offered to him by her father, who
stands to inherit the dead man's estate. However, the ancient bridegroom revives and
demands his marital rights. Meanwhile, the
girl makes friends with an untouchable
(Sinha), who is waiting to light the funeral
pyre for the couple. Although suttee (the
ritual whereby widows have to follow their
husbands on to the pyre) was outlawed by
the reigning colonial government, it was still
practised illegally until recently in certain
quarters. The film condemns it as barbaric,
but in a tone of black comedy moving towards
tragedy. This virtual three-hander all takes
place on the sands of the riverbank – there
is not one interior shot – the setting of which
is explored with intricate camera movements
manipulated by the director himself. The performance of Ganguli as the dying man is
pitched at the right absurdist level, while the
Untouchable shouts a lot and the girl weeps
throughout the film's rather protracted
length. But it is an unusual work on a rarely
considered subject.

▶ **Voyage Dans La Lune, Le** see Trip
To The Moon

Voyage Surprise

France 1946 85 mins bw
Pathé-Consortium Cinema

d **Pierre Prévert**
sc **Jacques Prévert, Pierre Prévert**
ph **Sinoël**
m **Joseph Kosma**
  **Jean Bourgoin, Maurice Baquet, Brevant,
  Pierre Prévert, Piéral, Martine Carol**

The life-long dream of an old man (Bourgoin)
is to organize a 'voyage surprise' or mystery
tour by coach. In spite of the machinations
of wicked competitors, he is finally able to
carry it off with results that neither he nor
his eccentric passengers could ever have
imagined. The third and final feature made
by the Brothers Prévert is a fast and furious
fantasy, a delightful *voyage surprise* in itself,
featuring anarchists, evil Grand Duchesses
and comic cops. Pierre Prévert died in his
82nd year in 1988, eleven years after his writer
brother.

Voyage To Cythera

▶ **Taxidi Sta Kithira**

Greece 1984 149 mins col
Cinema Centre of Greece/RAI/Channel
4/ Greek TV/ZDF/Angelopoulos
Productions

d **Theo Angelopoulos**
sc **Theo Angelopoulos, Theo Valtinos, Tonino
  Guerra**
ph **Giorgios Triantafyllou**
m **Helen Karapiperis**
  **Manos Katrakis, Giulio Brogi, Mary
  Chronopoulou, Dionyssis
  Papayannopoulos, Dora Volanaki**

An old man (Katrakis), a Communist fighter
in the Civil War, returns to Greece after more
than 30 years' exile in the Soviet Union. He
attempts to come to terms with his country
and the wife and family he hardly knows. A
knowledge of Greek politics would be a help
in understanding this lengthy, oblique and
taciturn drama. In fact, it is so understated

that the spectator has to fill in a great deal. Yet the long takes against urban landscapes have a mesmeric effect and the man's plight is genuinely moving. The last impressive long shot of him and his wife adrift on a raft has a strong symbolic impact.

▶ **Voyage Vers L'Espoir** see Journey Of Hope

▶ **Voyou, Le** see Simon The Swiss

▶ **Vozvrashcheniye Maksima** see Return Of Maxim, The

▶ **Vrazda Po Cesky** see Murder Czech Style

▶ **Vredens Dag** see Day Of Wrath

▶ **Všichni Dobří Rodaci** see All My Good Countrymen

The Vyborg Side

▶ **Vyborgskaya Storona**

USSR 1939 120 mins bw
Lenfilm

d   **Grigori Kozintsev, Leonid Trauberg**

sc **Grigori Kozintsev, Leonid Trauberg**
ph **Andrei Moskvin, G. Filatov**
m   **Dmitri Shostakovitch**
    Boris Chirkov, Valentina Kirbardina,
    Mikhail Zharov, Natalia Uzhvi, Maxim
    Strauch, Mikhail Gelovani

After the Revolution in 1917 and the capture of the Winter Palace, Maxim (Chirkov) is put in charge of the State Bank as political commissar and has meetings with Lenin (Strauch) and Stalin (Gelovani). His comrade Natasha (Kirbardina) becomes a judge and Dimba (Zharov), the billiards-playing clerk, an 'anarchist activist.' The responsibilities of the characters in the new state also seemed to weigh more heavily on the shoulders of Kozintsev and Trauberg, whose direction lost some of the sparkle of *The Youth Of Maxim* and *The Return Of Maxim*. However, there are still some memorable scenes – Maxim's embarrassment when offered his position – fine pictorial compositions and the finely etched portraits of Lenin and Stalin. The character of Maxim became so popular that Chirkov was called upon to play him in further pictures.

▶ **Vyborgskaya Storona** see Vyborg Side, The

▶ **Vzlomshchik** see Burglar

W

► **Wachsfigurenkabinett, Das** see Waxworks

► **Waga Ai** see When A Woman Loves

► **Waga Koi Wa Moenu** see My Love Has Been Burning

The Wages Of Fear

► **Le Salaire De La Peur**

France 1953 140 mins bw
Filmsonor/CICC/Vera

d Henri-Georges Clouzot
sc Henri-Georges Clouzot
ph Armand Thirard
m Georges Auric
Yves Montand, Folco Lulli, Peter Van Eyck, Charles Vanel, Vera Clouzot, William Tubbs

Four down-and-outs in a sleazy South American town agree to risk their lives transporting two truckloads of highly dangerous nitroglycerine over treacherous roads to an oil field 300 miles away. One of the most successful French films of all time, it is also one of the most suspenseful ever made. Clouzot, shooting on location in the South of France, brilliantly creates the sweaty atmosphere of the tropics where his disenchanted and greedy characters are put through the mill. A high-octane thriller in every sense.

Best Film Cannes 1953
Best Actor (Charles Vanel) Cannes 1953
Best Film Berlin 1953

Waiting Women

► **(US: Secrets Of Women)**

► **Kvinnors Väntan**

Sweden 1952 107 mins bw
Svensk Filmindustri

d Ingmar Bergman
sc Ingmar Bergman
ph Gunnar Fischer
m Erik Nordgren
Anita Björk, Maj-Britt Nilsson, Eva Dahlbeck, Gerd Andersson, Aino Taube, Jarl Kulle, Birger Malmsten, Gunnar Björnstrand

While a group of women wait for their husbands to join them for the summer, three of them relate decisive incidents in their married lives. Rakel (Björk) recalls a friend who wanted to seduce her while her husband was away; Marta (Nilsson) remembers a Swedish artist she met in Paris; and Karin (Dahlbeck) recounts the time she was stuck in a lift with her husband. A good example of Bergman's early concern with relations between the sexes, particularly from a woman's point of view. The first two tales belong on the dark side, but the last episode is a sardonic comedy, beautifully written and delightfully played by Dahlbeck and Björnstrand.

► **Walking, Walking** see Camminacammina

Walkover

► **Walkower**

Poland 1965 78 mins bw
Syrena/Film Polski

d Jerzy Skolimowski
sc Jerzy Skolimowski
ph Antoni Nurzynski

m Andrzej Trzaskowski
Aleksandra Zawieruszanka, Jerzy
Skolimowski, Krzystof Chamiec, Elzbieta
Czyżewska, Andrzej Herder

On the eve of his thirtieth birthday, rootless
amateur boxer Andrzej (Skolimowski) meets
Teresa (Zawieruszanka), a girl he had known
at university before he was expelled. After
spending the night with her, he enters a
boxing tournament at a factory, winning it
by a walkover. Skolimowski, a former amateur boxer himself, had made a documentary
called *Boxing* (1961). Following his first feature, *Identification Marks: None*, he presents
here another picture of an equivocal outsider.
Making use of a moving camera and long
takes, the entire film consists of only 29 shots.
The film has a brittle energy, creates a feeling
for the industrial locale and poses questions
about competition and aging.

▶ **Walkower** see Walkover

The Wall

▶ **aka Güney's The Wall**

▶ **Duvar**

▶ **aka Le Mur**

France 1983 117 mins col
Güney Productions/MK2 Productions/
TF1 Films/Ministère De La Culture

d   Yilmaz Güney
sc Yilmaz Güney
ph İzzet Akay
m   Ozan Garip S&ahin, Setrak Bakirel
Tuncel Kurtiz, Ayse Emel Mesci,
SelahattirKuzuoğluS&abanS&is&oZiya,
Garip, Zapata, Mankafa, Malik Berrichi,
Nicolas Hossein

A Turkish prison is full of both criminal and
political prisoners. In Dormitory 4 the young
boys are treated like slaves by the sadistic
guards. When they revolt, the riot is brutally
quelled. This searing, almost unbearably
powerful film was the first directed by Güney
in person since 1974 when he was imprisoned.
It was made in Turkish in France where
Güney lived in exile until his death in 1984.
He based his screenplay on an actual revolt
of children in Ankara prison in March 1976,

and claimed to have softened the facts. 'In
blood, fire and tears, walled in, they sought
water and light. I dedicate this film to these
young friends in this quest' – Yilmaz Güney.

The Walls Of Malapaga

▶ **Au-Delà Des Grilles**

▶ **aka Le Mura Di Malapaga**

France/Italy 1949 91 mins bw
Francinex

d   René Clément
sc Jean Aurenche, Pierre Bost
ph Louis Page
m   Roman Vlad
Jean Gabin, Isa Miranda, Vera Talchi,
Andrea Checchi, Robert Dalban

Having killed his mistress, a Frenchman
(Gabin) stows away aboard a ship to Italy.
Suffering from toothache, he gets off in Genoa
only to have his money and papers stolen.
He meets up with a lonely waitress (Miranda)
and her young daughter (Talchi) and realizes
he loves her – too late, for the authorities
catch up with him. Clément's almost plotless,
bilingual film with its understated script that
nonetheless speaks volumes, is a simple and
honest slice of life in which two lost and
lonely people find temporary solace together –
in this instance, complicated by the bewildered jealousy of the little girl, played with
remarkable expressiveness by Talchi. Gabin,
trading in his familiar mix of tenderness and
cynicism, is perfectly cast, while Miranda
brings subtlety and complexity to the waitress.
It is a sad film, played against the awful
reality of the war-torn Genoese slums and
ending on a note of hopelessness.

Best Director Cannes 1949
Best Actress (Isa Miranda) Cannes 1949

The Wanderer

▶ **Le Grand Meaulnes**

France 1967 104 mins col
Madeleine

d   Jean-Gabriel Albicocco
sc Jean-Gabriel Albicocco, Isabelle Rivière
ph Quinto Albicocco

m   Jean-Pierre Bourtayre
     Jean Blaise, Alain Libolt, Brigitte Fossey,
     Alain Noury, Juliette Villard

In the small town of Sologne at the turn of
the century, the young Augustin Meaulnes
(Blaise) falls deeply in love with Yvonne De
Galais (Fossey), a beautiful and mysterious
girl whom he meets at a strange house party.
When she disappears, he searches for her and
for his lost adolescence. Alain Fournier's
popular young people's classic waited 30 years
before Isabelle Rivière agreed to allow her
brother's work to be filmed. Despite her participation in the screenplay, it is a far too
frenetic and flashy attempt to re-create the
fairy-tale atmosphere of the novel in visual
terms, but it remains the director's only film
to make an impact outside France.

▶ **Wanderers, The** see Gens Du Voyage,
Les

The Wandering Jew

▶ **L'Ebreo Errante**

   Italy 1948 97 mins bw
   Distributori Indipendenti

d   **Goffredo Alessandrini**
sc   **Goffredo Alessandrini, Ennio De Concini,**
     Anton Giulio Majano
ph   **Vaclav Vich**
m   **Enzio Masetti**
     Vittorio Gassman, Valentina Cortese,
     Noelle Norman, Pietro Sharoff

A young and wealthy Jew (Gassman) collab-
orates with the Nazis when they take over
Paris but, realizing his treachery, allows himself to be sent to a concentration camp. He
escapes with the girl he loves (Cortese), but
returns in order to save others from execution.
Director Alessandrini had made several
award-winning propaganda films for Mussolini and must here have been exorcising his
guilt. In so doing, he came up with a poignant
film, well acted and using a big budget to
good effect. However, the symbol of the Wandering Jew is clumsily and not too coherently
woven into the plot.

The Wanton

▶ **(US: The Cheat)**

▶ **Manèges**

   France 1950 90 mins bw
   Films Modernes/Discina

d   **Yves Allégret**
sc   **Jacques Sigurd**
ph   **Jean Bourgoin**
m   **Paul Misraki**
     Simone Signoret, Bernard Blier, Frank
     Villard, Jane Marken

A dull middle-aged owner of a riding school
(Blier) marries a much younger woman (Signoret), and is bled dry by her and her greedy
mother (Marken). When she is paralyzed in
an accident, both her husband and lover
(Villard) desert her. A moody, glum but
accomplished little melodrama, it finally fails
to involve because of its lack of any sympathetic characters. The flashback is quite cleverly
used to reveal the truth after we first see the
minx (Signoret, languorous) through the eyes
of her devoted husband (Blier, dogged). Signoret's subsequent divorce from first husband
Allégret made this their last film together.

▶ **Wanton Contessa, The** see Senso

▶ **Wan Zhong** see Evening Bell

War And Peace

▶ **Voina I Mir**

   USSR 1966–1967 507 mins col
   Mosfilm

d   **Sergei Bondarchuk**
sc   **Sergei Bondarchuk, Vasily Solovyov**
ph   **Anatoli Petritsky**
m   **Vyacheslav Ovchinnikov**
     Ludmila Savelyeva, Sergei Bondarchuk,
     Vyacheslav Tikhonov, Anastasia
     Vertinskaya, Vasily Lanovoi, Irina
     Skobotseva

How Napoleon's invasion of Russia in 1812
affected the lives of two upper-class families,
centering on the love of clumsy, myopic Pierre
(Bondarchuk) for his vivacious young cousin
Natasha (Savelyeva), and her marriage to
army officer Andrei (Tikhonov). This four-
part, eight-hour, 70mm, $100 million epic is
a remarkable achievement. Never just content
to use the vast resources at his disposal to
illustrate the literary masterpiece, Bondar-

chuk attempts to find visual equivalents of Tolstoy's prose. The Battle of Borodino is not only a breathtaking spectacle, but Pierre becomes the spectator's surrogate in the midst of the horror. The film's frequent lapses into grandiloquence and its reliance on the dissolve don't detract from the stunning use of over-head tracking shots, split-screen techniques and the subjective camera.

Best Foreign Film Oscar 1968

The War Is Over

▶ **La Guerre Est Finie**

France   1966   122 mins   col
Sofracima/Europa Film

d   **Alain Resnais**
sc **Jorge Semprun**
ph **Sacha Vierny**
m   **Giovanni Fusco**
    Yves Montand, Ingrid Thulin, Geneviève
    Bujold, Michel Piccoli, Paul Crauchet,
    Jean Bouise, Jean Dasté

An aging and tired Spanish revolutionary exile in Paris (Montand) remembers his experiences during the Civil War but has to face the fact that his 25 years of struggle against Franco have achieved nothing. Resnais' masterly technique of shifting between temporal and mental states does not disguise the fact that this portrait of a man imprisoned by his past is simplistic and mon-otonous. The sensual sex scenes seem to have been influenced by Godard's *A Married Woman* (1964). The screenplay by Spanish exile Semprun received an Oscar nomination.

Warning Shadows

▶ **Schatten**

Germany   1923   62 mins   bw
Pan Film/Dafu Film Verlieh

d   **Arthur Robison**
sc **Rudolf Schneider, Arthur Robison**
ph **Fritz Arno Wagner**
m   **Silent**
    Fritz Kortner, Ruth Weyher, Alexander
    Granach, Gustav Von Wangenheim, Fritz
    Rasp

A travelling showman (Granach) enters a country mansion and introduces himself to

the host (Kortner), his wife (Weyher) and their four guests, one of them the wife's effete young lover (Von Wangenheim). He puts them all under hypnosis so that they can act out their subconscious desires, which has a beneficial effect on the marriage. One of the most celebrated of the films of the period of German Expressionism called Caligarism (after the first manifestation of the genre, *The Cabinet Of Dr Caligari*), was subtitled 'A Nocturnal Hallucination'. The shadowy cam-erawork and the strange settings by Albin Grau (credited with the 'idea' for the film) create an atmosphere in which the highly erotic pschyodrama takes place. The acting is in keeping with some of the over-the-top effects.

▶ **Warnung Vor Einer Heiligen Nutte** see Beware Of A Holy Whore

The War Of The Buttons

▶ **La Guerre Des Boutons**

France   1962   95 mins   bw
Productions De La Guéville

d   **Yves Robert**
sc **Yves Robert, François Boyer**
ph **André Bac**
m   **José Berghmans**
    André Treton, Michel Isella, Martin
    Lartigue, Jean Richard, Yvette Etievant,
    Jacques Dufilho

Two rival gangs of small boys wage a daily battle in a sandpit between their two villages, taking prisoners whose belts, braces and but-tons are cut off. Lebrac (Treton), leader of one gang, conceives the idea of surprising the other side by going into battle naked and chalks up a victory. As the war games become more elaborate, the parents have to intervene and Lebrac and his rival counterpart (Isella) end up in a reformatory. Robert's film, inar-guably picturesque, occasionally satirical and sometimes humorous, is also cutesy-cutesy and a little insipid (which didn't stop the British censor X-rating it on the grounds of some mild bad language), although the direc-tor coaxes good performances from the boys. The movie was a huge commercial success on initial release, but it's unlikely to appeal much to those more interested in the infinitely complex and unequivocally nasty *The Lord Of The Flies.*

Warrior's Rest

▶ **Le Repos Du Guerrier**

> France 1962 101 mins col
> Francos Films(Paris)/Incei(Rome)

d **Roger Vadim**
sc **Claude Choublier, Roger Vadim**
ph **Armand Thirard**
m **Michel Magne**
> **Brigitte Bardot, Robert Hossein, James Robertson Justice, Jean-Marc Bory, Jacqueline Porel**

Geneviève (Bardot), young, beautiful and wealthy, is suitably engaged to Pierre (Bory). In Dijon on business, she wanders into the wrong hotel room by mistake and finds Renaud (Hossein), an alcoholic, collapsed after attempting suicide. The encounter leads to a passionate affair in which he initiates her into the joys of uninhibited sex and the pain of abuse and degradation. Eschewing the subtleties of the novel by Christiane Rochefort on which this is based, Vadim and Choublier have come up with a superficial screenplay which, while allowing Bardot to flex her acting muscles a little and casting her in the unusual role of emotional and moral redeemer, offers more than its fair share of titillation and nudity. The resolution is both mawkish and ludicrous. Nevertheless, it was a huge hit in Paris on release.

▶ **Warui Yatsu Yoku Nemuru** see Bad Sleep Well, The

▶ **Warum Läuft Herr R Amok?** see Why Does Herr R Run Amok?

The Watchmaker Of St Paul

▶ **L'Horloger De St-Paul**

> France 1973 105 mins col
> Lira

d **Bertrand Tavernier**
sc **Jean Aurenche, Pierre Bost, Bertrand Tavernier**
ph **Pierre-William Glenn**
m **Philippe Sarde**
> **Philippe Noiret, Jean Rochefort, Sylvain Rougerie, Christine Pascal**

A watchmaker (Noiret), living a quiet life in a suburb of Lyons, is stunned when he learns that his son is wanted for the murder of a factory owner. He is then forced to reconsider his life as a man and father. Former critic Tavernier made his name with this well-crafted, intelligent debut feature based on a story by Georges Simenon, transferred from the USA to the director's home town. The social detail and the interplay between Noiret and Rochefort, as a police inspector, are the best parts of the rather clockwork plot.

Special Jury Prize Berlin 1974

Waterless Summer

▶ **aka I Had My Brother's Wife**

▶ **(US: Dry Summer)**

▶ **Süsuz Yaz**

> Turkey 1964 84 mins bw
> Hitit Film

d **Ismail Metin**
sc **Jim Lehner**
ph **Ali Ugur**
m **Manos Hadjidakis**
> **Ulvi Dogan, Errol Tash (Erol Tas), Julie Kotch (Hülya Kocyigit), members of the Jerusalem Theatre Arts Players, The Athens Hellenic Theatre, The Istanbul Theatre Of Performing Arts**

During a drought, tyrannical landowner Osman (Tash) shuts off the water supply to neighbouring farmers, in opposition to his brother Hassan (Dogan). He spies on Hassan and his wife making love. Violent protest springs up in the district, in the course of which Osman kills a farmer, but Hassan takes the blame. While he is in prison, Osman tries to alienate Hassan's wife after whom he lusts. Metin's film is, overwhelmingly, about sexual frustration, for which the drought and its consequences become an extended metaphor. The action and images are deliberately repetitive and the music insistent, but it is a hypnotic rather than a monotonous experience.

Best Film Berlin 1964

Waxworks

▶ **Das Wachsfigurenkabinett**

    Germany 1924 93 mins bw
    Neptun-Film

d Paul Leni
sc Henrik Galeen
ph Helmar Lerski
m Silent
    Wilhelm Dieterle, Emil Jannings, Conrad
    Veidt, Werner Krauss, Olga Belajeff

A young poet (Dieterle) in a fairground wax museum tells the story of three of the exhibits – Haroun-al-Raschid (Jannings), Ivan the Terrible (Veidt) and Jack the Ripper (Krauss). 'I have tried to create sets so stylized that they evince no ideas of reality,' wrote Paul Leni, the director of one of the best examples of German Expressionism on film. The lighting and the remarkable designs by Leni, Alfred Junge and Ernst Stern are symbolic of character and plot, creating a sinister atmosphere. It was Leni's last film as a director in Germany (he continued to design) before continuing his contribution to the horror genre at Universal Studios in Hollywood. He died of blood poisoning in 1929 aged 44.

▶ **Ways In The Night** see Night Paths

▶ **Ways Of Love** see Amore, L'

The Way To Bresson

▶ **De Weg Naar Bresson**

    Netherlands 1984 54 mins col/bw
    Frans Rasker

d Jurrien Rood, Leo De Boer
sc Jurrien Rood, Leo De Boer
ph Deen Van Der Zaken
    Robert Bresson, Louis Malle, Dominique
    Sanda, Paul Schrader, Andrei Tarkovsky

A series of interviews, interspersed with short illustrative clips from his films, on the work of the highly individualistic French director, Robert Bresson. It is divided, not altogether satisfactorily, into segments with subtitles such as 'camera', 'actors', 'theory', and so forth, which tend to disturb the flow and, on occasion grow a little portentous. Unsurprisingly, perhaps, the tone is one of undiluted veneration and the film frustrates in being too short to explore its subject with sufficient thoroughness. However, the documentary's great triumph is the rare presence of the great director himself, an elusive man who, by 1984, had made just 13 films in a 40-year long career.

We All Loved Each Other So Much

▶ **C'Eravamo Tanto Amati**

    Italy 1975 136 mins col/bw
    Dean Cinematografica/Delta

d Ettore Scola
sc Age, Furio Scarpelli, Ettore Scola
ph Claudio Cirillo
m Armando Trovaioli
    Nino Manfredi, Vittorio Gassman,
    Stefania Sandrelli, Stefano Satta Flores,
    Giovanna Ralli, Aldo Fabrizi

Three men from different backgrounds have been bound by their friendship for 30 years since they met as partisans in World War II, and through their love for the beautiful Luciana (Sandrelli). The lives of Antonio (Manfredi), a good-natured, politically active proletarian, Gianni (Gassman), a *bourgeois* opportunist, and Nicola (Flores), a radical intellectual film buff, are paralleled by the history of Italian cinema over the years. This often moving, sometimes sentimental, amusing and humanistic study of friendship offers an added pleasure to the film fan: there are extracts from films by Antonioni, Rossellini, Visconti, De Sica (to whom the film is dedicated) and Fellini, the last two appearing as themselves, and there are also film pastiches, some good, some crass.

▶ **We Are All Murderers** see Are We All Murderers?

Web Of Passion

▶ **aka Leda**

▶ **À Double Tour**

    France 1959 110 mins col

Paris/Panitalia

d   Claude Chabrol
sc Paul Gégauff
ph Henri Decaë
m   Paul Misraki
    Jacques Dacqmine, Madeleine Robinson,
    Jean-Paul Belmondo, Bernadette Lafont,
    Antonella Lualdi, André Joselyn

When the beautiful mistress (Lualdi) of a
wealthy wine merchant (Dacqmine) is murdered, tensions grow in the man's Provençal
house among his neurotic wife (Robinson),
mother-fixated son (Joselyn), wilful daughter
(Lafont) and her uncouth Hungarian fiancé
(Belmondo). Chabrol, using colour for the
first time, seems dazzled by its decorative
possibilities, particularly in the Japanese style
of the mistress' home. Beneath the gloss is a
gimmicky second-rate thriller, told in a banal
flashback form with a Hollywood ending.
Only a glimpse of Belmondo's *Breathless*
character of the following year holds the
interest.

**Best Actress (Madeleine Robinson) Venice
1959**

The Wedding

▶ **Wesele**

Poland 1972 110 mins col
Film Polski/Plan Film Unit

d   Andrzej Wajda
sc Andrzej Kijowski
ph Witold Sobocinski
m   Stanislaw Radwan
    Ewa Zietek, Daniel Olbrychski, Andrzej
    Lapícki, Wojciech Pszoniak, Franciszek
    Pieczka, Maja Komorowska

When a girl (Zietek) in a small village near
Cracow marries a poet (Olbrychski), her
painter brother-in-law gives a wedding party
to which he invites artists, intellectuals, a city
journalist, a priest, and a mystically 'possessed' Jewish girl (Komorowska). The celebrations give way to rumours of border war,
the headman arms the peasants, and the wedding guests fall prey to visions. Wajda,
working from a famous stage play by Stanislaw Wyspianski, made this film during his
'literary' period when censorship threatened
his contemporary political dramas. Here, he

deliberately fuses fantasy and reality, dreams
and legends, bringing some 20 years of experience to his masterly control of changing pace
and mood, but failing to avoid a certain
confusion.

▶ **Wedding In Blood** see Blood Wedding

Weekend

France 1967 105 mins col
Lira/Comacico/Copernic/Ascot Cineraid

d   Jean-Luc Godard
sc Jean-Luc Godard
ph Raoul Coutard
m   Mozart, Antoine Duhamel
    Mireille Darc, Jean Yanne, Jean-Pierre
    Léaud, Juliet Berto, Anne Wiazemsky

A *bourgeois* couple (Darc and Yanne), driving
into the country from Paris, find themselves
in a nightmare of traffic jams, car crashes,
murder, destruction and cannibalism. A virtuoso piece of film-making and the most devastating of attacks on modern society and the
motor car. This is best captured in the famous
10-minute tracking shot along miles of immobile vehicles, irate drivers, and the injured
and dead victims of accidents. The impact is
occasionally lessened when Godard decides
to explore some of the byways of the main
theme.

Weekend At Dunkirk

▶ **Week-End À Zuydcoote**

France 1964 119 mins col
Paris Film(Paris)/Interopa(Rome)

d   Henri Verneuil
sc François Boyer
ph Henri Decaë
m   Maurice Jarre
    Jean-Paul Belmondo, Catherine Spaak,
    Georges Géret, Jean-Pierre Marielle,
    Pierre Mondy, Marie Dubois, François
    Périer, Kenneth Haigh, Ronald Howard

In June 1940, thousands of French and
English troops are trapped on the Dunkirk
beaches as the Germans advance. Four
Frenchman camp in an abandoned ambu-
lance: a courageous sergeant (Belmondo), a

man only interested in saving his own skin (Mondy), a chaplain (Marielle) and a resourceful fellow who finds them supplies (Périer). What befalls them and the sergeant's efforts to save a local girl (Spaak) in danger form the substance of the action. Based on a novel by Robert Merle, this French view of a famous episode in World War II which has provided so much film fodder for Britain and America, is distinguished by the truthfulness of the battle scenes and the exceptional photography by Decaë. The personal stories, however, in spite of the cast's best efforts, are banal and melodramatic.

▶ **Week-End À Zuydcoote** see Weekend At Dunkirk

A Week's Holiday

▶ **Une Semaine De Vacances**

France 1980 103 mins col
Sara Films/Antenne 2/Little Bear

d **Bertrand Tavernier**
sc **Bertrand Tavernier, Marie-Françoise Hans, Colo Tavernier**
ph **Pierre William Glenn**
m **Pierre Papadiamandis**
   Nathalie Baye, Michel Galabru, Flore Fitzgerald, Gérard Lanvin

A Lyons schoolteacher (Baye) in her early thirties suffers from severe depression as a result of a crisis of faith in her work and unresolved differences in her relationship with her lover. On doctor's orders she takes a week's holiday, during which she visits her parents and has several encounters, notably with the father of one of her pupils, and decides to return to teaching. Placed specifically in time – winter, 1980 – and place – Lyons, its landscapes filmed with loving detail – this is a somewhat glib and self-satisfied comment on the life it reveals, with everything sliding rather too neatly into place. Nonetheless, it is reasonably entertaining and, on the surface at least, intelligent.

▶ **Wege In Der Nacht** see Night Paths

▶ **Weg Naar Bresson, De** see Way To Bresson, The

▶ **Weib Des Pharao, Das** see Wife Of Pharaoh, The

▶ **Weisse Hölle Vom Piz Palü, Die** see White Hell Of Pitz Palu, The

Welcome, Mr Marshall

▶ **Bienvenido, Mr Marshall**

Spain 1952 75 mins bw
UNINCI

d **Luis Berlanga**
sc **Luis Berlanga, Juan Antonio Bardem**
ph **Manuel Berenguer**
m **Jesús García Leoz**
   Lolita Sevilla, Manolo Moran, José Isbert, Alberto Romea, Elvira Quintilla

The news that a Marshall Plan commission intends to visit a poor village in Castile causes the inhabitants to make what they can of their surroundings in order to create a good impression on the visiting Americans in the hope of getting financial aid. American diplomats and Edward G. Robinson, a member of the Cannes Festival jury, mistakenly denounced the film for its anti-American bias, for it is far more a sardonic look at Spanish foibles and greed. Pointedly written and observed, the film is an example of 'Spanish Neo-Realism', taking the style from the Italians but without the freedom to criticize the system directly. It was one of Spain's biggest international successes during the Franco years.

The Well-Digger's Daughter

▶ **La Fille Du Puisatier**

France 1940 131 mins bw
Marcel Pagnol

d **Marcel Pagnol**
sc **Marcel Pagnol**
ph **Willy**
m **Vincent Scotto**
   Raimu, Fernandel, Charpin, Josette Day

A crusty old well-digger (Raimu) is shocked to discover that his daughter (Day) has been seduced and abandoned. His simple assistant (Fernandel) agrees to marry her and accept the child as his own. 'The subjects of my films are simple, for I find there is no art outside ordinary places and people,' stated Pagnol. But one of his achievements was to show that the subjects and forms of *bourgeois* drama could be transposed to peasant life. Melodrama it may be, but it is laced through with piquant dialogue, heady Provençal settings, and towering performances from his single-named male stars. The film originally ended with father and daughter being reconciled by listening to a speech by Pétain on the radio. After the Liberation, Pagnol substituted the voice of De Gaulle.

▶ **Wend Kuuni** see Gift Of God, The

Werther

France   1938   85 mins   bw
Nero Film

d   **Max Ophüls**
sc **Hans Wilhelm**
ph **Eugen Schüfftan**
m   **Henri Herblay (on classical themes)**
    Pierre-Richard Willm, Annie Vernay,
    Jean Galland, Paulette Pax, Henri Guisol

Young Werther (Willm) falls in love with Charlotte (Vernay), whom he discovers is to be married to his best friend Albert (Galland). He leaves her and begins to lead a dissipated life. Seeing Charlotte again gradually forces him to suicide. Ophüls seemed unsympathetic towards Goethe's *Sorrows Of Young Werther*, as witness his turning of the pre-Romantic 18th-century drama into a wild 19th-century romance, shifting the tragedy from the hero to the heroine and also adding a comic-relief aunt (Pax). There are some pretty country scenes, moments of bravura with the camera and some good acting from the charming Vernay, soon to die tragically.

▶ **Wesele** see Wedding, The

Westfront 1918

▶ **aka Comrades Of 1918**

Germany   1930   96 mins   bw
Nero-Film

d   **G.W. Pabst**
sc **Laszlo Wajda, Peter Martin Lampel**
ph **Fritz Arno Wagner, Charles Métain**
    Gustav Diessl, H.J. Moebis, Fritz
    Kampers, Claus Clausen, Jackie Monnier

The horror and futility of life in the trenches in general, and for four soldiers in particular, and the ignorance at home of the reality at the Front. Released in the same year as the superior *All Quiet On The Western Front*, Pabst's film also caught the anti-war mood of the times. It captures the monotony and chaos of trench warfare through a series of short scenes and long tracking shots over the battleground. Much of it is now too familiar and the plea for universal brotherhood is expressed in a naive manner.

We The Living

▶ **Noi Vivi**

Italy   1942   174 mins   bw
Scalera Films

d   **Goffredo Alessandrini**
sc **Anton Giulio Majano**
ph **Giuseppe Caracciolo**
m   **Renzo Rossellini**
    Alida Valli, Rossano Brazzi, Fosco
    Giachetti, Giovanni Grasso, Emilio Cigoli,
    Cesarina Gheraldi

Russia in the early 1920s. Kira (Valli), a young engineering student, falls in love with Leo (Brazzi), anti-Communist scion of an aristocratic family and wanted for questioning by the secret police. Leo falls ill with TB but is denied medical attention because of his politics, so Kira helps him by having an affair with Taganov (Giachetti), a leading figure in the secret police who is unaware of her relationship with Leo. He finds out, of course, paving the way for the film's dramatic climax. Adapted from a novel by Ayn (*The Fountainhead*) Rand, who herself grew up in St Petersburg, *We The Living* represents a significant coup of rediscovery and restoration that was not given as wide a release as it deserved when it re-emerged in 1988. Made during the Mussolini era, it enjoyed five months of success in Italy and won the Volpi Cup before it occurred to the authorities that its anti-Communist message could equally be read as anti-Fascist, whereupon it was withdrawn and disappeared. Many years later Rand's legal advisers, Erika and Henry Holzer, traced a print and, with Rand's participation, commenced restoring it to the present version. What we have is a historically interesting and highly entertaining romantic drama in luminous black and white, enhanced by a first-class cast. Alida Valli, aged 21 and blossoming into her Garboesque beauty, shows all the promise which she was to fulfil, and it is a pleasure to see Brazzi at the peak of his youthful matinée-idol good looks. Giachetti, less known to English-speaking audiences, convinces as the committed Party official.

We Were One Man

▶ **Nous Étions Un Seul Homme**

France   1978   90 mins   col
Sou Mau

d   **Philippe Vallois**
sc **Philippe Vallois**
ph **François About**
m   **Jean Jacques Ruhlmann**
    Serge Avédikian, Piotr Stanislas,
    Catherine Albin

Guy (Avédikian), a patient escaped from a mental hospital, lives in an isolated cottage during 1943. When he discovers Rolf, a wounded German soldier, in the woods, he takes him home and a complex friendship develops through which Rolf becomes a deserter since Guy prevents him leaving. Their relationship develops into a homosexual affair until Rolf is captured. Vallois has created an unnerving study of isolation, madness, passion, guilt and betrayal. He eloquently conveys the claustrophobic emotions of his characters, and draws a superb performance from Avédikian, but he presents gay men as a doomed species, here represented by a disturbed neurotic and a Nazi.

We Will Not Grow Old Together

▶ **Nous Ne Vieillerons Pas Ensemble**

France   1972   107 mins   col
Lido Film

d   **Maurice Pialat**
sc **Maurice Pialat**
ph **Luciano Tovoli**
m   **Haydn**
    Marlène Jobert, Jean Yanne, Macha
    Meril, Jacques Galland, Christine
    Fabrega, Muse Dalbray

A selfish and domineering married man (Yanne), estranged from his wife (Meril) but still living with her, has been having an affair for six years with a much younger woman (Jobert). Now, inevitably, the relationship is disintegrating, causing pain and confusion to the girl and involving her distressed friends and parents. Pialat's disturbing and truthful film unfolds in a series of perceptive episodes in which the couple alternately indulges in damaging recriminations and tearful reconciliations before finally breaking off the liaison. Script and direction probe and reveal the intricacies of the dying days of a long love affair, lent extra conviction by the uncompromising performances of forceful Yanne and wistful Jobert.

Best Actor (Jean Yanne) Cannes 1972

What Have I Done To Deserve This?

▶ **¡¿Que He Hecho Yo Para Merecer Esto?!**

Spain   1984   101 mins   col
Tesauro/Kaktus

d   **Pedro Almodóvar**
sc **Pedro Almodóvar**
ph **José Luis Martinez**
m   **Bernardo Bonezzi**
    Carmen Maura, Luis Hostalot, Angel De
    Andres-López, Gonzalo Suarez, Verónica
    Forqué, Juan Martinez, Anabela
    Hilomann, Ampara Soler Leal

In a depressing working-class Madrid apartment block live Gloria (Maura), a cleaner, her husband Antonio (Andres-López), a chauvinistic taxi-driver, her mother-in-law and her two sons, one of whom (Martinez), aged 14, deals in cannabis. Impinging on their lives are assorted other tenants, including prostitute Cristal (Forqué). Antonio picks up a middle-aged, middle-class writer (Suarez) in the course of his work, which leads to a complex involvement in attempted blackmail, fraud and forgery and Gloria killing her husband by administering a kendo-chop with a ham bone. Almodóvar seems to specialize in plots of indescribable complexity, serviced by crossing the paths of an ever-increasing cast of characters, and the short synopsis here only conveys fifty percent of the film's story. Released in English-speaking countries only after *Women On The Verge Of A Nervous Breakdown* and *Law Of Desire* had brought him acclaim, this earlier film suffers by comparison. Once again, the superlative Carmen Maura shines at the centre of events and the director effectively uses black comedy to highlight the injustices suffered by poor, working-class women. However, the proceedings, which grow ever more bizarre, are handled with insufficient discipline and an emotional detachment which finally alienates where it should involve.

▶ **Wheel, The** see Roue, La

The Wheel

▶ **Moul Le Ya, Moul Le Ya**

South Korea 1983 105 mins col
Han Lim Cinema Corp

d **Lee Doo-Yong**
sc **Lim Chung**
ph **Lee Sung-Choon**
m **Chung Yun-Ju**
   Won Mi-Kyung, Shin Il-Yong, Choi Sung-Kwan, Mun Chung-Sook, Choi Sung-Ha, Mun Mi-Bong

Gil-rye (Won Mi-Kyung), the beautiful daughter of an impoverished scholar, is sold to the wealthy and aristocratic Kim family. They marry her posthumously to their dead son, remind her to protect her chastity and set her to work at a spinning wheel. One day she sees her brother-in-law Han making love with his wife and her own dormant sexual needs are awakened. Han subsequently rapes her and forces her into a regular illicit relationship, the discovery of which leads to his execution and her banishment... The tragedy of Gil-rye is carefully detailed, echoing the style of Mizoguchi. With a perfectly judged central performance from the victim-heroine, it is a period piece which exposes the appalling subjugation of women in a society dominated by men and by rigid social codes and traditions. The title is well-chosen, for Gil-rye is literally broken by the wheel of unhappy fortune on which her fate relentlessly turns.

The Wheelchair

▶ **El Cochecito**

Spain 1959 81 mins bw
Films 59

d **Marco Ferreri**
sc **Marco Ferreri, Rafael Azcona**
ph **Juan Julio Baeña**
m **Miguel Asins Arbó**
   José Isbert, Pedro Porcel, José Luis Lopez Vázquez, Maria Luisa Ponte, Lepe, Antonio Gavilán, Angel Alvarez

Don Anselmo (Isbert) lives with his lawyer son and the latter's family. Elderly but fit, he spends much of his time going on outings with a group of cripples in motorized wheelchairs, of whom his best friend is one. He becomes obsessed by the desire to own such a contraption himself and, to this end, does some very strange things. This grotesque and perverse one-joke farce wears very thin very quickly. On the credit side, a couple of scenes are of such absurdity as to become funny in spite of themselves, Isbert plays his ridiculous role with dignity and the evocation of Spanish life, particularly in a middle-class home, is interesting.

When A Woman Loves

▶ **Waga Ai**

Japan 1959 97 mins col
Shochiku

d **Heinosuke Gosho**
sc **Toshio Yasumi**
ph **Haruo Takeno**
m **Yasushi Akutagawa**
   Ineko Arima, Shin Saburi, Yatsuko Tanami, Nobuko Otowa

At the funeral wake of a renowned journalist and war correspondent (Saburi), a mysterious young girl briefly appears, offering prayers and incense. Afterwards, she reflects on her relationship with the dead man which we see in flashback – a meeting before the war when she is too young for him, another during the war and, several years later, a few months of happiness together in a mountain retreat before he returns to his family. Firmly in the popular tradition of Japanese 'women's pictures', this is a full-blooded weepie romance, backed by a lush Western-style score that would do justice to Hollywood. However, within its genre, it's a superior piece of filmmaking in every department, displaying the skills of Gosho who, having reached his peak in the mid-1950s, notably with *Where Chimneys Are Seen*, entered a period of unashamed commercial film-making.

When Father Was Away On Business

▶ **Otac Na Službenom Putu**

Yugoslavia 1985 136 mins col
Forum/Sarajevo Film

d   **Emir Kusturica**
sc **Abdulah Sidran**
ph **Vilko Filač**
m   **Zoran Simjanović**
     Manolo De Bartoli, Miki Manojlović, Mirjana Karanović, Mustafa Nadarević, Mira Furlan, Predrag Laković

In 1950, six-year-old Malik (De Bartoli) lives a normal family life in Sarajevo until Mešac (Manojlović), his womanizing father, is denounced by his mistress as a Stalinist and sentenced to three years' exile. Kusturica's surprise Festival winner gets off to an intolerably slow start. However, once underway, it lives up to its reputation, offering an absorbing, absolutely naturalistic portrait of Yugoslavian customs and politics of the period. Key incidents – among them circumcision, one of Mešac's whoring expeditions, and his avenging rape of his ex-mistress – are seen largely through Malik's young eyes (and reported through his voice-over narrative), lending freshness, poignancy and a deal of comedy to the proceedings. The performances are terrific, especially from Mirjana Karanović as Malik's struggling mother, and the photography first rate.

Best Film Cannes 1985

When Joseph Returns...

▶ **Ha Megjön József**

Hungary 1975 88 mins col
Hungarofilm

d   **Zsolt Kézdi-Kovács**
sc **Zsolt Kézdi-Kovács**
ph **János Kende**
     György Pogány, Lili Monori, Éva Ruttkai, Gábor Koncz, Mária Ronyecz

Mária (Monori), a newly-wed country girl working in a Budapest factory, is left with her mother-in-law Agnes (Ruttkai) when her sailor husband returns to his ship. Agnes takes casual lovers in an attempt to get over her broken marriage while Mária, insecure and lonely, becomes involved in an affair, leaves her job, becomes pregnant and miscarries. Her plight moves Agnes to awareness and concern and, strengthened, the women await Joseph's return. This story of personal suffering and recovery is observed with an unsentimental and accurate eye. Acted with an almost documentary-like veracity, particularly by Monori, it's well photographed, detailing the unhappy life in the women's small flat and the landscape without, with atmospheric precision.

▶ **When Moscow Laughs** see Girl With The Hatbox

When The Cat Comes

▶ **aka That Cat**
▶ **Až Přijde Kocour**

Czechoslovakia 1963 110 mins col
Czech State Film

d   **Vojtěch Jasný**
sc **Jiří Brdečka, Vojtěch Jasný**
ph **Jaroslav Kučera**
m   **Svatopluk Havelka**
     Jan Werich, Vlastimil Brodský, Jiří Sovák, Emilie Vašáryová

A magician (Werich) comes to a small town, bringing his bespectacled cat who is able to see people in their true colours. Thus, cheats appear grey, adulterers yellow, and so forth, while those with nothing to hide remain the same. This inventive film is humorous Czech fantasy at its best (notwithstanding some repetitive sequences), made with lightness and charm by one of Prague's favourite directors of the period. Song, dance and sentiment are adroitly woven into the tale, making it appealing to children, while, for adults, it cocks a cleverly veiled but unmistakable snook at the politics of totalitarianism.

Special Jury Prize Cannes 1963

When The Greeks

▶ **Ton Kero Ton Hellinon**

> Greece 1981 100 mins col
> Cinetic/Greek Film Centre

d **Lakis Papastathis**
sc **Lakis Papastathis**
ph **Theodoros Margas**
m **Georges Papadakis**
   Alexis Damianos, Kostas Arzoglou, George Sampanis, Stavros Mermighis

A rich, young landowner (Damianos) is kidnapped by a gang of nationalist bandits at the turn of the century. For the first time, he sees the ancient landscape and culture of his own country, and learns to identify with his captors, who seem to be like ancient Greek warriors. Papastathis's debut feature is a poetic meditation on class and culture but, most of all, on what it is to be Greek. Stunningly filmed against splendid landscapes, its highpoints are two beautifully staged rituals – a wedding and a funeral.

When We Were Young

▶ **Kak Molody My Byli**

> USSR 1985 92 mins col
> Dovzhenko Studio

d **Mikhail Belikov**
sc **Mikhail Belikov**
ph **Vasily Trushkovsky**
m **Chopin, Gershwin, Y. Vinnik**
   Taras Denisenko, Elena Shkurpelo, N. Sharolapova, Aleksander Pashutin, A. Sviridovsky

Teenage Sasha (Denisenko) training as a sanitary engineer while doing a part-time labour-

ing job, is sexually initiated by an older woman, and then marries his childhood friend Yulka (Shkurpelo) who is suffering from a rare blood disease. Spanning a few years from sometime in the 1950s to the day of Gagarin's space flight in 1961, Belikov's film is a muddled exercise in nostalgia which suggests that the protagonists are the 'lost' generation, bridging the gap between the old Russia and the new, whose children will ignite the society of the 1980s. Quite touching, but it suffers from anachronisms and, to a non-Russian viewer, domestic references that are meaningless.

Where Chimneys Are Seen

▶ **aka Four Chimneys**
▶ **Entotsu No Mieru Basho**

> Japan 1953 108 mins bw
> Studio 8 Productions/Shin Toho

d **Heinosuke Gosho**
sc **Hideo Oguni**
ph **Mitsuo Miura**
m **Yasushi Akutagawa**
   Ken Uehara, Kinuyo Tanaka, Hiroshi Akutagawa, Hideko Takamine

A struggling, childless, middle-aged couple (Uehara and Tanaka) find themselves having to look after an abandoned baby. The responsibility and the effort required puts a great strain on them and their upstairs neighbours (Akutagawa and Takamine). The baby, however, becomes a positive force in their lives. One of the best surviving examples of 'Goshoism', a distinctive blend of comedy and pathos among a wide range of characters in *shomin-geki*, stories of everyday life. Unlike the other great masters of the genre, Ozu and Naruse, Gosho uses a swift cutting style and mobile camera. In this 'tenement' film, beginning with shots of the chimneys of a smoggy Tokyo, the interior scenes are always resourceful and the ensemble playing is perfect.

The White-Haired Girl

▶ **Pai Mao Nu**

> China 1970 90 mins col

Shanghai Film Studio

d   **Sang Hu**
sc   **Shanghai Dance School, 'White-Haired Girl' Unit**
ph   **Shen Xilin**
m   **Revolutionary music and songs Mao Huifang, Ling Jiaming, Wang Guojun, Dong Xilin**

Xi'er (Huifang), the daughter of a peasant (Xilin) beaten to death by the henchmen of a wicked landlord, is now held prisoner by the landlord. She escapes to the mountains where hardship turns her hair white (the symbol of purity and righteousness). Her boyfriend (Jiaming), who is in the army, comes with his battalion to the town, liberates the peasants, hangs the landlord and is reunited with Xi'er. She joins him in the army to take part in the class struggle. This ballet version of the celebrated Chinese opera of 1944, filmed previously as a realistic drama in 1950, was supervised by Mao Tse-tung's wife, the former film actress and dancer Chiang Ching, at the height of the Cultural Revolution. It was typical of film ballets such as *The Red Detachment Of Women* (1960) and *The East Is Red* (1964), influenced by Western classical choreography, but instilled with revolutionary fervour. Although much of it is naive and monotonous, the heavily made-up faces, the heroic gestures, the distinctive goodies and the baddies have the visual appeal of pop art as well as being able to inspire.

The White Hell Of Pitz Palu

▶ **Die Weisse Hölle Vom Piz Palü**

Germany   1929   121 mins   bw
UFA

d   **Arnold Fanck, G.W. Pabst**
sc   **Arnold Fanck, G.W. Pabst**
ph   **Sepp Allgeier, Richard Angst, Ladislaus Vajda, Hans Scheeberger**
m   **Silent**
     Gustav Diessl, Leni Riefenstahl, Ernst Petersen, B. Spring

A famous mountain climber (Diessl) returns every year to the place on the 12,000 ft Pitz Palu in the Alps where his wife disappeared on their honeymoon. One day, caught in a storm, he finds himself reunited with his young bride. This most celebrated of 'Mountain Films' – a popular German genre in the 1920s and early 1930s – was both a vivid documentary and a symbolic melodrama. It was shot in conditions of extreme cold by technicians who were expert alpinists and skiers over five months of location work in the Alps. Universal, who bought it for release in the United States, later used much of the footage in many B-movies and serials.

White Nights

▶ **Le Notti Bianche**

Italy   1957   107 mins   bw
Vides/Intermondia/CIAS

d   **Luchino Visconti**
sc   **Suso Cecchi D'Amico, Luchino Visconti**
ph   **Giuseppe Rotunno**
m   **Nino Rota**
     Maria Schell, Marcello Mastroianni, Jean Marais, Clara Calamai

A young man of slender means (Mastroianni) falls in love with a mysterious girl (Schell) who spends her days dreaming of the lover (Marais) who will one day return to her. In contrast to his first two 'Neo- Realist' films and the operatic-style colour spectacle of *Senso*, Visconti here moved into the misty, dreamlike world of the Dostoevsky story also tackled by Pyriev in 1959 and Bresson in 1971. Whereas those versions were set in 19th-century St Petersburg and modern-day Paris respectively, Visconti's takes place in what passes for contemporary Livorno. But an emphasis on the artificiality of the theatrical settings and the soft-textured photography, gives it an air of feyness despite some magic moments. Only Calamai (Visconti's lead in *Ossessione*) injects some reality into the proceedings.

White Nights

▶ **Beliye Nochi**

USSR   1959   97 mins   col
Mosfilm

d   **Ivan Pyriev**
sc   **Ivan Pyriev**
ph   **Valentin Pavlov**

m Rachmaninov, Glazounov, Rossini,
   Scriabin
   Oleg Strizhenov, Ludmila Marchenko,
   U.N. Popova

A poor young man (Strizhenov) in love with an enigmatic, gullible girl (Marchenko), dreams every night that he is a romantic hero fighting single-handedly against tyrants and villains and winning the heroine. This was the second of Pyriev's three adaptations from the works of Dostoevsky, the others being *The Idiot* and *The Brothers Karamazov*. It comes off better than the other two because the original is more suited to transference to the screen; it is more compact, and has fewer characters. Unlike Visconti's and Bresson's updating to modern Italy and France respectively, Pyryev retained the 19th-century St Petersburg setting, recreating Dostoevsky's visionary view of the city. The tragicomic dreams themselves tend towards the fey but the performances of the two leads are admirable.

The White Sheik

▶ **Lo Sceicco Bianco**

   Italy   1952   88 mins   bw
   Luigi Rovere/PDC/OFI

d   Federico Fellini
sc Federico Fellini, Ennio Flaiano, Tullio
    Pinelli
ph Arturo Gallea
m   Nino Rota
    Alberto Sordi, Brunella Bovo, Leopoldo
    Trieste, Giulietta Masina, Lilia Landi,
    Ernesto Almirante

A *petit-bourgeois* couple (Trieste and Bovo) arrive in Rome on their honeymoon, but the bride spends most of the time with her idol (Sordi), an egocentric, womanizing star of *fumetti*, romantic magazine picture stories. Fellini's first solo film, based on a story by Michelangelo Antonioni, is an ironic and touching satire on marriage, illusions, and popular culture. It is already recognizably a Fellini work, although he might have deepened the one-dimensional characters later in his career. It is interesting to note his wife Masina in the small role of the prostitute Cabiria, the subject of *Nights of Cabiria* four years later.

▶ **White White Boy . . ., A** see Mirror

▶ **Whither   Germany?**   see Kühle
Wampe

Whity

   W. Germany   1970   95 mins   col
   Antiteater-X Film

d   Rainer Werner Fassbinder
sc Rainer Werner Fassbinder
ph Michael Ballhaus
m   Peer Raben
    Günter Kaufmann, Hanna Schygulla, Ulli
    Lommel, Harry Baer, Katrin Schaake,
    Rainer Werner Fassbinder, Ron Randall

Half-black Whity (Kaufmann) is overworked by the Nicholson family until Hanna (Schygulla), a sexually exploited barmaid, incites him to murder his white masters. They end up together in the desert. After putting his new boyfriend Kaufmann in *Gods Of The Plague*, Fassbinder wrote a Western with his 'Bavarian Negro' in the misspelt title role. The tensions and tantrums during the 20-day shoot in Spain became the basis for *Beware The Holy Whore* the following year. Some of this spills over into the atmosphere of this bizarre, sadistic and playful pastiche. However, there are so many personal obsessions on display that audiences may feel excluded at times.

Who Looks For Gold

▶ **Kdo Hledá Zlaté Dno**

   Czechoslovakia   1975   98 mins   col
   Barrandov Studio

d   Jiří Menzel
sc Vojtěch Měštan, Rudolf Ráž, Jiří Menzel
ph Jaromír Šofr
m   Jiří Šust, Angelo Michajlov
    Jan Hrušínsky, Jana Giergielová, Julius
    Pántik, František Husák, Míla
    Mystíková, Otakar Dadák

Returning to Prague after his military service, Lada (Hrušínsky) finds it difficult to adjust to civilian society. Gifted with his hands and able to repair anything from a wristwatch to a motor car, he is put in the way of easy-money jobs by his knowing girlfriend Petra (Giergielová). But Lada is an idealist and, although he loses both Petra and his illusions as a result, he takes a job out in the country with a dam construction outfit. Jiří Menzel's first film after a six-year break has little plot to speak of. However, the director's gift for the telling nuance, his perceptive control of the performances which touch subtle depths of character, and the impact of Šofr's swirling camera (particularly in the dam sequences) make this an absorbing experience.

Whom The Gods Wish To Destroy

▶ **Die Nibelungen (Part I: Siegfried Von Xanten Part II: Kriemhilds Rache)**

W. Germany   1966   Part I: 91 mins
Part II: 104 mins   col
CCC/Avala

d   **Harald Reinl**
sc **Harald G. Petersson**
ph **Ernst W. Kalinke**
m   **Rolf Wilhelm**
    Uwe Beyer (Siegfried), Maria Marlow (Kriemhild), Karin Dor (Brunhild), Rolf Henninger (Gunther), Herbert Lom (Attila), Siegfried Wischnewski (Hagen)

After killing a dragon, Siegfried gains magic powers, undergoes many trials and adventures in winning the hand of Brunhild on behalf of Gunther, and bringing tragedy to his wife Kriemhild. Director Reinl, whose previous claim to fame rested in the odd Karl May Western and cheap Dr Mabuse spin-offs, has gone to town with this colour version of the 13th-century poem which boasts the use of 8,000 extras in one battle scene alone. Slick, spectacular and offering an impressive Dragon, it is nonetheless a fairly ludicrous enterprise which will either amuse or offend fans of Fritz Lang's 1920s epic. It is generally shown in Britain and America as one film lasting 153 mins.

Who Saw Him Die?

▶ **aka Eeny Meeny Miny Moe**

▶ **Ole Dole Doff**

Sweden   1967   110 mins   bw
Svensk Filmindustri

d   **Jan Troell**

sc **Claes Engström, Bengt Forslund, Jan Troell**
ph **Jan Troell**
m   **Erik Nordgren**
    Per Oscarsson, Kerstin Tidelius, Anne-Marie Gyllenspetz, Bengt Ekerot, Harriet Forssell

Martensson (Oscarsson), a schoolteacher at odds with the education system, is able neither to communicate with nor discipline his pupils. Sensing his weakness, they torment him cruelly and highlight his sense of failure, which extends to his unhappy marriage. Inevitably, events terminate his career in a tragic climax. Former schoolteacher Troell shot his second film entirely on location in a Malmö school, using the actual pupils and a fluid 16mm camera, thus lending it a documentary veracity. Although the root causes of Martensson's problems remain unexplored and his point of view is left one-sided, this is an accurate picture of a bleak life in bleak surroundings, lent weight by Oscarsson's powerfully truthful and understated performance.

Best Film Berlin 1968

Who's That Singing Over There?

▶ **Ko To Tamo Peva**

Yugoslavia   1980   83 mins   col
Centar Film

d   **Slobodan Šijan**
sc **Dušan Kovačević**
ph **Božidar Nikolić**
m   **Vojislav Kostić**
    Pavle Vuisić, Aleksandar Berček, Dragan Nikolić, Danilo Stojković, Miodrag and Nenad Kostić

'Somewhere in Serbia, April 5, 1941', a rickety old bus, crammed with a motley group of passengers, tries to make it to Belgrade before the Nazis arrive. This stylish, manic, picaresque, black comedy is an impressive debut feature by director Šijan. The answer to the question of the title is two Gypsies (Miodrag and Nenad Kostić) who act as a chorus by singing the narration. The rest of the travellers are seen purposefully as comic stereotypes, which the splendid cast, nevertheless, present as fully-rounded personages.

Why?

▶ **Detenuto In Attesa Di Giudizio**

Italy 1971 102 mins col
Documento

d **Nanni Loy**
sc **Sergio Amedei, Amilio Sanna**
ph **Sergio D'Offizi**
m **Carlo Rustichelli**
    Alberto Sordi, Elga Andersen, Lino Banfi,
    Giuseppe Anatrelli, Tano Cimarosa

Giuseppe Di Noi (Sordi), Italian head of a
Swedish civil engineering firm, returns to Italy
for a holiday with his Swedish wife (Andersen)
and two children, but he is arrested at the
border by the Italian police for an unspecified
crime. He goes from one tough jail to another,
suffering physically and mentally, until his
case finally comes up. With the popular comic
actor Sordi in the lead and the jaunty opening,
it comes as a shock when the film moves into
the harsh area of a prison exposé. Loy builds
up a relentless, rather over-emphatic indictment of a horrific system and cleverly uses
Sordi's persona to gain sympathy and a large
audience.

Best Actor (Alberto Sordi) Berlin 1972

Why Does Herr R Run Amok?

▶ **Warum Läuft Herr R Amok?**

W. Germany 1970 88 mins col
Antiteater-Produktion for Maran-Film

d **Rainer Werner Fassbinder, Michael**
    Fengler
sc **Rainer Werner Fassbinder, Michael**
    Fengler (improvised)
ph **Dietrich Lohmann**
m **'Geh' Nicht Vorbei' by Christian Anders**
    Kurt Raab, Lilith Ungerer, Amadeus
    Fengler, Franz Maron, Hanna Schygulla

Middle-class and comfortably married with
one child, Kurt Raab represents a typical
urban species. He has his share of domestic
problems, and mars his chances of promotion
with an ill-judged speech at the office
Christmas party, but no matter. One night,
watching TV while his wife chatters to a
visiting neighbour, he suddenly picks up a
heavy candelabrum, smashes in the women's
skulls, and similarly kills his son. A favourite
Fassbinder theme – ordinary man destroyed
by his inability to cope with modern life – is
here based on a case history. The film calls
its characters by the actors' names, thus
further distancing the audience from any
sense of artifice in what is a painfully realistic
study. Close examination, however, reveals
the characters as stereotypes, and it is a matter
of opinion whether Raab's outbreak of violence and subsequent suicide have a valid
cause in his rather everyday frustrations.

Why Not?

▶ **Eijanaika**

Japan 1981 151 mins col
Shochiku

d **Shohei Imamura**
sc **Shohei Imamura, Ken Miyamoto**
ph **Masahisa Himeda**
m **Shinichiro Ikebe**
    Kaori Momoi, Shigeru Izumiya, Ken
    Ogata, Shigeru Tsuyuguchi, Masao
    Kusakari

Genji (Japanese rock star Izumiya) returns to
19th-century Japan from a six-year absence
in the USA to find his wife (Momoi) has
become the mistress of a gangster(Tsuyugu-
chi). The population around them consists of
wandering samurai, murderers, entertainers,
whores and gamblers who rise up in revolt
against the ruling shogunate screaming the
anarchist slogan 'Why not?'. Imamura isn't
one to do things by halves and this period
film is full of bustling energy, sexuality and
violence, captured in bright colours and with
a mobile camera. The style suits the subject,
though the plot gets a bit hazy at times.

Wife, Be Like A Rose

▶ **Tsuma Yo Bara No Yo Ni**

Japan 1935 83 mins bw
PCL/Toho

d **Mikio Naruse**
sc **Mikio Naruse**
ph **Hiroshi Suzuki**
m **Noburu Itoh**
    Sachiko Chiba, Sadao Maruyama, Yuriko
    Hanabusa, Kamatari Fujiwara

On the eve of her marriage, an office worker (Chiba), hoping to reunite her father (Maruyama) with her poet mother (Hanabusa) whom he had left some time before, finds he is perfectly happy with his mistress (Fujiwara) and second family in the country. The 1930s and 1950s were Naruse's two great creative periods and this is a masterwork from the first epoch. The framing, editing and playing are all elegantly controlled in this poignant yet humorous study of a disrupted family, which leads to a shattering climax. Many of Naruse's best films, such as *Repast* (1951), are about marriage break-ups.

The Wife Of Pharaoh

▶ **(US: The Loves Of Pharaoh)**

▶ **Das Weib Des Pharao**

> Germany 1921 115 mins bw
> EFA/UFA/Ernst Lubitsch

d **Ernst Lubitsch**
sc **Norbert Falk, Hans Kräly**
ph **Théodor Sparkühl, Alfred Hansen**
m **Silent**
> **Emil Jannings, Harry Liedtke, Dagny Servaes, Paul Wegener, Lyda Salmonova**

War between Egypt and Ethiopia ensues when the tyrannical Pharaoh Amenes (Jannings) falls in love with Theonis (Servaes), the Greek serving girl of the Ethiopian Princess (Salmonova) he had arranged to marry. Theonis, in turn, loves Ramphis (Liedtke), who eventually becomes Pharaoh. Made on a huge scale, it had 126,000 extras and took ten months to shoot. Considering that the narrative is somewhat confused and the lavish sets tend to overwhelm the players, Lubitsch managed to sustain the atmosphere throughout. The only weak link in the cast was Dagny Servaes who got the part because Pola Negri was unavailable.

▶ **Wildcat, The** see Mountain Cat, The

The Wild Child

▶ **L'Enfant Sauvage**

> France 1970 84 mins bw
> Films Du Carrosse/Artistes Associés

d **François Truffaut**
sc **François Truffaut, Jean Gruault**
ph **Nestor Almendros**
m **Vivaldi**
> **Jean-Pierre Cargol, Jean Dasté, François Truffaut, Françoise Seigner, Paul Ville**

In 1798, a boy (Cargol) who resembles a wild beast is discovered in the woods in central France. He is sent to the Institute for the Deaf and Dumb in Paris where Dr Jean Itard (Truffaut) struggles to make him walk upright, wear clothes and give him speech. Dedicated to Jean-Pierre Léaud, the remarkable child in Truffaut's first feature *The Four Hundred Blows*, this coolly made but very moving film has another extraordinary performance from a young boy. Cargol, of gypsy parentage, is directed by Truffaut (playing the doctor without any emotion) from in front of the camera instead of behind it. Based on a true case, the film meticulously charts each fascinating step in the boy's education, making an interesting comparison with *The Miracle Worker*.

The Wild Duck

▶ **Die Wildente**

> Austria 1976 100 mins col
> Solaris

d **Hans W. Geissendörfer**
sc **Hans W. Geissendörfer**
ph **Robby Müller**
m **Nils Janette Walen**
> **Jean Seberg, Peter Kern, Bruno Ganz, Anne Bennent, Heinz Moog**

Hjalmar (Kern), a dreaming egoist who can barely feed his wife, Gina (Seberg), and 14-year-old daughter, Hedwig (Bennent), attempts in vain to better his situation with the Consul Werle (Moog). Geissendörfer's faithful adaptation of the first of Ibsen's symbolist plays was shot in seven weeks in a studio in Vienna. In as much as the play can be made cinematic, and without being *The Quintessence Of Ibsenism* in Shaw's terms, it is a well-acted, satisfactory version. It was Jean Seberg's last film before her suicide three years later. *The Wild Duck* was filmed in a silent German version in 1925, and was made again in Norway in 1963 – astonishingly, the first indigenous screen adaptation of an Ibsen work.

▶ **Wildente, Die** see Wild Duck, The

▶ **Wild Flowers** see Fleurs Sauvages, Les

Wild Game

▶ **Wildwechsel**

W. Germany 1972 102 mins col
Intertel

d **Rainer Werner Fassbinder**
sc **Rainer Werner Fassbinder**
ph **Dietrich Lohmann**
m **Beethoven**
    Jörge Von Liebenfels, Ruth Drexel, Eva
    Mattes, Kurt Raab, Harry Baer

Although 19-year-old Franz (Baer) and 14-year-old Hanni (Mattes) are in love, he is sent to prison for seducing an under-age girl. When he is released a few months later, Hanni goads him into killing her repressive father (Liebenfels). Franz Kroetz protested violently against Fassbinder's interpretation of his play, but by playing up the Nazism and incipient incestuousness of the girl's father, the director-writer gives an extra dimension to this depiction of distorted social values. The cool distance from which Fassbinder views his subject, and the somewhat stylized performances, allow the spectator to assess the rather melodramatic tale with a certain objectivity.

Wild Strawberries

▶ **Smultronstället**

Sweden 1957 93 mins bw
Svensk Filmindustri

d **Ingmar Bergman**
sc **Ingmar Bergman**
ph **Gunnar Fischer**
m **Erik Nordgren**
    Victor Sjöström, Ingrid Thulin, Gunnar
    Björnstrand, Bibi Andersson, Naima
    Wifstrand, Max Von Sydow

An aged professor (Sjöström) travels by car with his daughter-in-law (Thulin) to Lund to receive an honorary doctorate. A visit to the family home and various encounters on the way inspire reminiscences, insights into his own shortcomings and intimations of mortality. Bergman's smiles and tears on a summer's day make for a mellow modern morality, with the action shifting skilfully between past and present, dream and reality. Most memorable of all is the extraordinary farewell performance of 78-year-old Victor Sjöström, Bergman's predecessor as the greatest Swedish film director.

Best Film Berlin 1958

▶ **Wildwechsel** see Wild Game

▶ **Will O' The Wisp** see Feu Follet, Le

The Wind

▶ **Finyé**

Mali 1982 100 mins col
Les Films Cissé

d **Souleymane Cissé**
sc **Souleymane Cissé**
ph **Etienne Carton De Grammont**
m **Pierre Gorse, Mali folk music**
    Fousseyni Sissoko, Goundo Guisse, Balla
    Moussa Keïta, Ismaïla Sarr, Oumou
    Diarra

Two university students from very different backgrounds fall in love, to the chagrin of their families. He fails his exams because of his poor background, and she passes hers because she is the daughter of the repressive military governor. Together they join other students in a fight for equality. Although Cissé's third feature (in seven years) is a bitter attack on the 'haves' on behalf of the 'have nots' in his country, he demonstrates subtlety, perception and humour. Sissoko and Guisse, as the young couple, are a delight.

The Windbreaker

▶ **Il Petomane**

Italy 1983 101 mins col
Filmauro

d **Pasquale Festa Campanile**
sc **Leo Benvenuti, Piero De Bernardi, Enrico**
    Medioli
ph **Alfio Contini**
m **Carlo Rustichelli, Paolo Rustichelli**
    Ugo Tognazzi, Mariangela Melato,

Vittorio Caprioli, Anna Maria Gherardi, Ricardo Tognazzi

Joseph Pujol, or Le Petomane, is famous for his music hall act which consists of farting in an amazing variety of sounds and styles, and to music. Slighted by some deprecating remarks from Paris society, he determines to present a Haydn symphony to the accompaniment of his farts and, after a period in the wilderness and some complications in a love affair, achieves his ambition. The film, inspired by the existence of the actual Pujol, is a tiresome imbroglio of fact, fiction and caricature, somewhat redeemed by Tognazzi's courtly, comic and touching performance in the title role.

Windfall In Athens

▶ **Kyritiko Xyprima**

> Greece   1956   112 mins   bw
> Millas Film

d **Michael Cacoyannis**
sc **Michael Cacoyannis**
ph **Alvize Orphanelli**
m **André Ryder**
  Elli Lambetti, George Pappas, Dimitri Horn, Tasso Kavadia, Chris Pateraki, Margarita Georgiou

A pretty Athens salesgirl (Lambetti) has a lottery ticket stolen and, in her distress, is befriended by a middle-aged lawyer (Pappas) who becomes infatuated with her. When the lottery is drawn, the stolen ticket wins and turns out to be in the possession of a penniless young musician (Horn) who bought it from the thieves. Needless to say, the ensuing battle between him and the girl leads to romance. Overlong for its featherweight subject and utterly predictable, this is nonetheless a good-natured and pleasant little entertainment. Of note as Cacoyannis' debut feature and, although moderately successful outside Greece, it does not really point to the particular gifts of the former English-educated lawyer and actor which would soon show in more substantial and interesting films.

Wings Of Desire

▶ **Der Himmel Über Berlin**

> W. Germany   1987   127 mins   bw/col

Road Movies (Berlin)/Argos Films(Paris)

d **Wim Wenders**
sc **Wim Wenders in collaboration with Peter Handke**
ph **Henri Alekan**
m **Jürgen Knieper**
  Bruno Ganz, Solveig Dommartin, Otto Sander, Curt Bois, Peter Falk

Two angels, Damiel (Ganz) and Cassiel (Sander) descend to earth to observe and minister to the people of Berlin, but Damiel falls in love with a trapeze artist (Dommartin) and decides to give up his immortality and become human. For the first hour, this angel's eye view of a modern and crumbling Berlin inhabited by a melancholy population in need of hope holds the attention. Gradually, the enterprise becomes more spurious as Damiel, benignly smiling throughout, is drawn towards life in the shape of a performer (an unexciting film debut from the French Dommartin) at a tatty circus. It also ludicrously turns out that Peter Falk, making a film in Berlin, is himself a fallen angel. The only real magic comes from the masterful, mostly black-and-white photography of the great 78-year-old Henri Alekan. It is to be noted that the Circus in the film is called the Cirque Alekan.

Best Director Cannes 1987

▶ **Winifred Wagner Und Die Geschichte** see Confessions Of Winifred Wagner, The

Winter Light

▶ **aka The Communicants**

▶ **Nattvardsgasterna**

> Sweden   1962   80 mins   bw
> Svensk Filmindustri

d **Ingmar Bergman**
sc **Ingmar Bergman**
ph **Sven Nykvist**
m **Extracts from Swedish psalms**
  Max Von Sydow, Ingrid Thulin, Gunnar Björnstrand, Gunnel Lindblom

A village pastor (Björnstrand) begins to doubt his beliefs, and his sermons fail to give comfort to his mistress (Thulin), a widow (Lindblom), and a man (Von Sydow) afraid of nuclear annihilation. The central drama in Bergman's despairing trilogy of the 1960s, between *Through A Glass Darkly* and *The Silence*, is probably his most austere and solemn film on the silence of God. The opening church service brilliantly suggests the hollowness behind the ritual and the joylessness of the congregation by a juxtaposition of stark images. The excellent cast expose the characters' suffering in revealing close-ups.

▶ **Wir Wunderkinder** see Aren't We Wonderful?

The Wishing Tree

▶ **Drevo Zhelanya**

USSR 1976 107 mins col
Grusiafilm (Georgia)

d **Tengiz Abuladze**
sc **Revaz Inanishvili, Tengiz Abuladze**
ph **Lomer Ahvlediani**
m **Bidzina Kvernadze, Yakov Bobohidze
Lika Kavzharadze, Soso Dzachvliani,
Zaza Kolelishvili, Kote Daushvili, Sofiko
Chiaureli**

An account of life in a Georgian village at the beginning of the century where the village elder decrees rules which, in the case of two young lovers, leads to tragedy. Among the gallery of village eccentrics is a man who, in the process of searching for the legendary wishing tree, freezes to death. A curious film, visually elaborate and employing a primitive camera style to capture its *faux-naïf* approach to colour and composition, but unfolding a series of somewhat random incidents at too leisurely a pace to hold one's interest.

▶ **Wisselwachter, De** see Pointsman, The

Witchcraft Through The Ages

▶ **Häxan**

Sweden 1922 83 mins bw

Svensk Filmindustri

d **Benjamin Christensen**
sc **Benjamin Christensen**
ph **Johan Ankarstjerne**
m **Silent**
**Oscar Stribolt, Clara Pontoppidan, Karen
Winther, Maren Pedersen, Elith Pio,
Benjamin Christensen**

Christensen conducts a documentary-style investigation into the practice of witchcraft from medieval times using etchings, manuscripts and re-enacted episodes, in which he also plays the Devil. His most famous film, three years in the making, sees the witch as the victim of a superstitious and repressive Church. An array of cinematic devices creates a film that is illuminating, frightening and amusing. In 1968, an unnecessary sound version was released with a commentary by William Burroughs and a jazz score.

The Witches

▶ **Le Streghe**

Italy 1966 104 mins col
Dino De Laurentiis Cinematografica
(Rome)/ Les Productions Artistes
Associés (Paris)

d **1) Luchino Visconti 2) Mauro Bolognini
3) Franco Rossi 4) Pier Paolo Pasolini
5) Vittorio De Sica**
sc **1) Giuseppe Patroni Griffi 2) Age,
Scarpelli, Bernardino Zapponi 3) Franco
Rossi, Luigi Mani 4) Pier Paolo Pasolini
5) Cesare Zavattini**
ph **Giuseppe Rotunno**
m **Piero Piccioni, Ennio Morricone
Silvana Mangano and 1) Annie Girardot
2) Alberto Sordi 3) Pietro Tordi, 4) Totò,
Ninetto Davoli, 5) Clint Eastwood**

1) A film star, on holiday in the Swiss Alps, is miserable and lonely despite being surrounded by many people. 2) A woman drives an injured truckdriver to hospital, but makes a fatal detour. 3) When a Sicilian woman cannot marry the man of her choice, her father starts a civil war. 4) Two tramps invent a maid servant. 5) The bored wife of a banker imagines her husband competing for her favours with comic-book heroes. This not uninteresting portmanteau picture displays

the undoubted versatility of La Mangano (Mrs De Laurentiis) in five different roles. Pasolini's wonderful little wordless fable emerges the winner, with Visconti, among the others, riding the clichés best. Look out for a young Helmut Berger (then Steinberger), playing his first movie role in the first story.

The Witches of Salem

▶ aka The Crucible

▶ Les Sorcières De Salem

France   1957   143 mins   bw
Borderie/CICC/Pathé/DEFA (E.
Germany)

d   Raymond Rouleau
sc   Jean-Paul Sartre
ph   Claude Renoir
m   Georges Auric
Simone Signoret, Yves Montand, Mylène Demongeot, Jean Debucourt

In Massachusetts in 1692, a servant girl (Demongeot) accuses her mistress Elizabeth Proctor (Signoret) of witchcraft to hide her guilt for having slept with her master (Montand), thus leading to multiple trials and executions. It is a pity that the McCarthy witch-hunt prevented this adaptation of *The Crucible* from being filmed in America because its author Arthur Miller was blacklisted at the time. It is a pity, too, that his superb play was not given less lethargic direction or a less plodding screenplay. It was the first co-starring of Montand and Signoret, who had played the Proctors on stage the previous year.

Witch Hunt

▶ Forfolgelsen

Norway   1981   93 mins   col
Norsk Film AS/Svensk Filminstitutet

d   Anja Breien
sc   Anja Breien
ph   Erling Thurmann-Andersen
m   Arne Nordheim
Lil Terselius, Björn Skagestad, Anita Björk, Erik Mørk, Ella Hval

During the 17th-century, a Swedish woman

(Terselius), who has left her husband, comes to a remote mountain community in Norway in search of work. Her arrival coincides with a witch hunt and, soon, her foreignness, her independence and her frankness (she openly has an affair with a farmhand) place her under suspicion of being a witch. Anja Breien made Norway's biggest international success, *Wives*, and returns here, albeit in a very different context, to the theme of non-conformist women and their place in society. It's a fascinating piece, superbly photographed on location, and with a persuasively strong central performance from Terselius.

▶ Witch Woman, The see Parson's Widow, The

▶ Without Anaesthesia see Rough Treatment

Without Pity

▶ Senza Pietà

Italy   1949   94 mins   bw
Lux Films

d   Alberto Lattuada
sc   Tullio Pinelli, Federico Fellini, Alberto Lattuada
ph   Aldo Tonti
m   Nino Rota
Carla Del Poggio, John Kitzmiller, Pierre Claudé, Giulietta Masina, Folco Lulli

A prostitute (Del Poggio), working for a ruthless bootlegger (Claudé), falls in love with a black American soldier (Kitzmiller) on the run from the military police. They arrange to hold up the bootlegger in order to get enough money to go to America, but things go wrong. While the film seems to be part of the Neo-Realist movement then at its peak – an almost documentary view of post-war Livorno – it draws its inspiration from American *film noir*. The stylistic balance is well struck, and it looks forward to the early films of Fellini (here a co-writer).

▶ Without Witnesses see Private Conversation, A

The Witness

▶ A Tanu

Hungary 1968 108 mins col
Mafilm Studio One

d Péter Bacsó
sc Péter Bacsó
ph János Zsombolyai
m György Yukán
   Ferenc Kállai, Lajos Öze, Zoltán Fabri,
   Béla Both, Lili Monori

Loyal Party member József Pelikán (Kállai) illegally slaughters the family pig and is imprisoned, but swiftly released. He puts it down to his long friendship with Zoltán Daniel (Fabri), a government minister who has, in fact, disappeared. His successor takes an interest in József, constantly promoting and protecting him, and finally grooming him to be a prosecution witness at Zoltán's trial on a trumped-up treason charge. The Hungarian authorities withheld *The Witness* for nine years, a compliment to its ability to wound official political sensibilities. Bacsó has opted to transmit his message through comedy but, although the film, set in 1949, is an interesting and often funny document, it suffers from a clash of styles – farce, satire, the odd dash of symbolism – which leaves it ultimately less satisfying than it ought to be.

Wives

▶ Hustruer

Norway 1975 84 mins col
Norsk Film

d Anja Breien
sc Anja Breien (with the cast)
ph Halvor Naess
m Finn Ludt
   Anne Marie Ottersen, Frøydis Armand,
   Katja Medbøe, Nøste Schwab, Helge
   Jordal, Sverre Anker Ousdal

Former schoolmates Mie, Heidrun and Kaja (Ottersen, Armand and Medbøe), married and in their late twenties, meet for the first time since leaving school. The occasion is an all-night reunion party for their former teacher, at which they indulge in heady reminiscence and decide to go off and kick over the traces together. After sobering up in a sauna, they pool resources, send postcards to their husbands and embark on a series of irresponsible adventures that getting themselves picked up. Breien's episodic and improvisational film, very well photographed and appealingly acted, is pro-feminist in its sympathies, accurate in its portrait of female companionship and quite clever in asking questions about responsibility. It's a good-natured escapade, too, but one in which the women's behaviour sometimes seems contrived and irritatingly immature.

Wives (10 Years After)

▶ Hustruer Ti Ar Etter

Norway 1985 88 mins col
Norsk Film

d Anja Breien
sc Anja Breien, Knut Faldbakken
ph Erling Thurmann-Andersen
   Anne Marie Ottersen, Frøydis Armand,
   Katja Medbøe, Henrik Scheele, Per
   Frisch, Jon Eikemo, Nøste Schwab

Ten years after their reckless spree together (see *Wives* above), the three friends meet again, this time at a fancy dress party just before Christmas, and decide to repeat history. Times, however, have changed. Heidrun (Armand) is divorced and involved with Jens (Scheele), himself estranged from his wife but not ready for another commitment; Kaja (Medbøe) is still married to Kristian (Frisch), who comes after her in a rage at having been abandoned; Mie's husband is remarried and she (Ottersen), too, has a lover (Eikemo). Using the same narrative structure as the previous film, Breien uncompromisingly exposes the changes that age and failure in marriage have made to her protagonists. This time, their friendship almost founders as the result of the tensions each is suffering in relation to her need for men. The three end up spending Christmas in a deserted hotel in Malmö where the manager waits on them hand and foot, but this time there is little joy to be had. If the atmosphere of female *angst* grows a little hard to take, the film is undeniably truthful and the return of the same actresses is a bonus.

▶ **Woman** see Amore, L'

The Woman From Africa

▶ **L'Africana**

Italy/Germany/France 1990 104 mins col
Scena Group (Rome)/Bioskop Film (Munich)/Rachel Productions (Paris) in association with RAI 2

d   **Margarethe Von Trotta**
sc **Margarethe Von Trotta**
ph **Tonino Delli Colli**
m   **Eleni Karaindrou**
    Barbara Sukowa, Stefania Sandrelli, Sami Frey, Jan Biczycki, Alexandre Mnouchine, Jacques Sernas

Some years earlier, Victor (Frey) left his lover Martha (Sukowa), a German doctor, in favour of marrying her best friend, Anna (Sandrelli). Bitter in her rejection, Martha went to live in Africa. Now Anna falls ill and, in her debilitated state, imagines that Martha has cast a vengeful spell on her. She prevails on Victor to write and ask Martha to come to Paris in the hope that her presence will break the spell and lead to her recovery. The intellectually indefatigable Von Trotta has constructed a characteristically complex and thoughtful screenplay in which familiar themes of love, friendship and betrayal are present. Centrally, however, she deals in the ambivalent relationship between Martha and Anna, attempting to demonstrate that friendship between women can survive the tensions that are generated by their relationships with the same man. If the film occasionally falters, it is nonetheless challenging and there is a distinct bonus in the performances of Sukowa and Sandrelli, two of Europe's finest actresses, here playing starkly contrasting characters, and the splendid, moody photography of Delli Colli. The score, too, as in the director's *Three Sisters*, is an enhancement.

▶ **Woman From Nowhere, The** see
Femme De Nulle Part, La

Woman In Chains

▶ **(US: The Female Prisoner)**
▶ **La Prisonnière**

France 1968 110 mins col
Films Corona/Vera Films(Paris)/Fono Roma(Rome)

d   **Henri-Georges Clouzot**
sc **Henri-Georges Clouzot, Monique Lange, Marcel Moussy**
ph **Andreas Winding**
m   **Gilbert Amy, various classical pieces**
    Laurent Terzieff, Elizabeth Wiener, Bernard Fresson, Dany Carrel, Dario Moreno

Film editor José (Wiener) and her artist husband Gilbert (Fresson) are frank about their extra-marital affairs, although they don't seem too happy about it. When José becomes involved with gallery-owner Stan (Terzieff), seemingly a morose loner but who turns out to indulge in photographing women in poses of masochistic submission, Gilbert's equilibrium deserts him. After his only half successful attempt to climb on the bandwagon of modernity with *The Truth* some 10 years earlier, Clouzot did not make another film until this one. (Ill-health prevented him from completing *L'Enfer* in 1964). Here, the French master of the dark-toned thriller has left all his familiar ground behind him and the result is an uncomfortable, unconvincing and rather tawdry sex drama which serves no purpose other than to tarnish his reputation.

A Woman In Flames

▶ **Die Flambierte Frau**

West Germany 1983 105 mins col
Robert Van Ackeren Filmproduktion/ Dieter Geissler Film/Planet Film/Pik 7 Film Produktions

d   **Robert Van Ackeren**
sc **Robert Van Ackeren, Catharina Zwerenz**
ph **Jürgen Jürges**
m   **Peer Raben**
    Gudrun Landgrebe, Mathieu Carrière, Hanns Zischler, Gabriele Lafari, Matthias Fuchs

Eva (Landgrebe) walks out on her middle-class husband and fashionable friends and turns to prostitution with the help of Yvonne (Lafari), an experienced call girl. She meets Chris (Carrière), a male prostitute, and they set up house together. But tensions creep into the relationship when Chris, afraid of growing too old for the job, becomes resentful of Eva's superior earning power. The film, anti-*bourgeois* decadent in tone, set almost entirely in fashionable interiors and stylishly photographed, makes comparisons with Fassbinder inevitable. These are emphasized further by the music of Raben, the more famous director's regular composer. Van Ackeren's aims and targets are far less lucid than was usual in Fassbinder's work and there is a certain insecure hovering on the border between voyeurism and social criticism. What does come out forcefully is a mordant analysis of the differences between the genders in sex games and an interesting view of prostitution as a profession like any other. Landgrebe's cool, dark allure and conviction in the title role – so named because she is set alight by kirsch *flambée* thrown on her during one of the many meals that punctuate the screenplay – lend the film an extra and fascinating dimension.

▶ **Woman In The Dunes** see Woman Of The Dunes

The Woman In The Moon

▶ **(US: By Rocket To The Moon)**

▶ **Die Frau Im Mond**

Germany 1929 107 mins bw
UFA

d   **Fritz Lang**
sc **Thea Von Harbou, Fritz Lang**
ph **Curt Courant, Oskar Fischinger, Otto Kanturek**
m   **Silent**
    Willy Fritsch, Klaus Pohl, Gustav Von Wangenheim, Gerda Maurus, Fritz Rasp

A scientist (Pohl), who believes the moon is rich in gold, has a rocket flight financed by a group of five capitalists hoping to corner the gold market. The other passengers a young rocket designer (Fritsch), the woman he loves (Maurus), and her fiancé (Von Wangenheim). Films made about moon landings long before the actual event are often quaint and misguided. Lang's comic-strip fantasy is no exception, and the plot is both melodramatic and farcical. However, the best moments come from the few elements of clairvoyance, such as the take-off, portrayed in dramatic montage and camera angles. Later, the Nazis thought the film authentic enough to take it out of distribution because the rocket design seems to have been close to one they were working on at the time. One of the film's technical advisors, Professor Hermann Oberth, was, in fact, a contributor to the V2 programme.

Woman In White

▶ **Le Journal D'Une Femme En Blanc**

France 1965 110 mins bw
Sopac/S.N.E.G. (Paris)/Arco Film (Rome)

d   **Claude Autant-Lara**
sc **Jean Aurenche, René Wheeler**
ph **Michel Kelber**
m   **Michel Magne**
    Marie-José Nat, Jean Valmont, Claude Gensac, Robert Benoît, Paloma Matta, Jean-Pierre Dorat

Claude Sauvage (Nat) is a senior medical student specializing in gynaecology. She becomes especially involved in the plight of an unmarried patient, ill from a self-induced abortion, and fights, side by side with resident specialist Pascal (Valmont) to save the girl's life, but to no avail. Claude herself ends up pregnant by Pascal and determines to have the baby out of wedlock. Another controversial piece of didacticism from Autant-Lara, this time arguing for the rights of women, particularly the right to contraception. The thematic focus is, however, slightly befuddled and the points are made by implication rather than directly. The film's professional gloss is high and the world of the hospital is portrayed with clinical realism, but the plot and surface characterization is pure *Dr Kildare*.

A Woman Is A Woman

▶ **Une Femme Est Une Femme**

France 1961 85 mins col
Rome Paris

d   Jean-Luc Godard
sc   Jean-Luc Godard
ph   Raoul Coutard
m   Michel Legrand
     Jean-Paul Belmondo, Jean-Claude Brialy,
     Anna Karina, Marie Dubois

A nightclub stripper (Karina) wants to have
a baby and settle down with her lover (Brialy).
When he refuses, she turns to his best friend
(Belmondo). Godard's third film is also one
of his lightest hearted, his first in colour and
'Scope, and the first in which Karina played
a dominant role. In fact, the camera is so
besotted by her that it's no surprise that the
director behind it married her soon after.
There are the usual literary references, jump
cuts and film quotes, but it seems to be
Godard's homage to the MGM musical, set
mainly in a Paris apartment with three characters. Jeanne Moreau appears briefly as herself.

Best Actress (Anna Karina) Cannes 1961

The Woman Next Door

▶ **La Femme D'À Côté**

France 1981 106 mins col
Les Films Du Carrosse/T.F.1 Films
Production

d   François Truffaut
sc   François Truffaut, Suzanne Schiffman,
     Jean Aurel
ph   William Lubtchansky
m   Georges Delerue
     Gérard Depardieu, Fanny Ardant, Henri
     Garcin, Michèle Baumgartner, Véronique
     Silver, Roger Van Hool

Bernard Coudray (Depardieu), a marine
engineer, lives with his wife and child in a
village near Grenoble where social life
revolves round the tennis club. When the
Bauchards move in next door, Bernard discovers that Mathilde (Ardant) is none other
than the old flame of his youth. The pair
resurrect their affair with disastrous and,

finally, fatal consequences. Doubtless
intended as a sophisticated study of an *amour
fou* among the professional middle classes,
Truffaut's film emerges as an old-fashioned,
lazy and somewhat boring soap opera. The
protagonists are sketchy and superficial, and
Depardieu (wooden) and Ardant (petulant)
walk through their roles, failing to lend them
any interest. Sad to see Truffaut's gifts as
badly tarnished as this.

▶ **Woman Of Antwerp** see Dédée

Woman Of Darkness

▶ **Yngsjömordet**

Sweden 1966 120 mins bw
Svensk Filmindustri

d   Arne Mattsson
sc   Eva Dahlbeck
ph   Lasse Björne
     Gunnel Lindblom, Gösta Ekman, Christina
     Schollin, Rune Lindström, Heinz Hopf

On a chilly morning in 1890, Anna
Mansdotter (Lindblom) is taken from her prison cell to the executioner's yard where she is
to be decapitated for committing incest and
murder. As she awaits the axe, Anna recalls
the trial where, in the face of local outrage but
lack of evidence, she and her son and lover Per
(Ekman) were found guilty of the murder of
his wife. Her recollections then move further
back to the events that led up to the crime.
One of Sweden's most prolific directors of
thrillers (and the romantic *One Summer Of
Happiness*) here turned his attention to the
notorious real-life case of the last woman to
suffer the death penalty in Sweden. Not surprisingly, the film is grimly doom-laden, but
superbly photographed and with a powerful
central performance from Lindblom. A bit
overloaded with gloomy visual clichés, it is
nonetheless absorbing and disturbing.

Woman Of The Dunes

▶ **(US: Woman In The Dunes)**

▶ **Suna No Onna**

Japan 1964 127 mins bw

Teshigahara

d   **Hiroshi Teshigahara**
sc **Kobo Abe**
ph **Hiroshi Segawa**
m   **Tohru Takemitsu**
    Eiji Okada, Kyoto Koshoda

An entomologist (Okada) finds an attractive young widow (Koshoda) living at the bottom of an enormous sandpit on a deserted beach. He becomes her prisoner, endlessly shovelling sand to avoid being engulfed. Teshigahara's best known film is a heavily symbolic erotic drama which effectively uses extreme close-ups until the characters almost become part of the landscape. Produced independently and made for a mere $100,000, it made a great impression on Western audiences.

Special Jury Prize Cannes 1964

Woman Of The River

▶ **La Donna Del Fiume**

Italy 1954 95 mins col
Les Fils De Centaur

d   **Mario Soldati**
sc **Basilio Franchini, Giorgio Bassani, Pier Paolo Pasolini, Florestano Vancini, Antonio Altoviti, Mario Soldati**
ph **Otello Martelli**
m   **Angelo Lavagnino**
    Sophia Loren, Gérard Oury, Rik Battaglia, Lise Bourdin, Enrico Olivieri

A girl (Loren) working in a village factory is loved by the local policeman (Oury), but her heart belongs to a handsome smuggler (Battaglia). When he deserts her, refusing to believe she is carrying his child, she betrays him. Years pass, bringing only disaster to all concerned. The usual excess of screenwriters so beloved of the Italian cinema – working from a story by no less than Alberto Moravia and Ennio Flaiano – dreamed up no more than a familiar potboiler, reminiscent in particular of *Bitter Rice*. What it's got going for it, of course, is sexy, smouldering Sophia, showcased by producer Carlo Ponti whom she would soon marry. Interesting, too, to note the first screenplay credit of Pasolini, who would move on to more profound topics.

A Woman Or Two

▶ **Une Femme Ou Deux**

France 1985 97 mins col
Hachette Première/Philippe Dussart/FR3 Films/DD Productions

d   **Daniel Vigne**
sc **Daniel Vigne, Elizabeth Rappenau**
ph **Carlo Varini**
m   **Kevin Mulligan, Evert Verhees, Toots Thielemans**
    Gérard Depardieu, Sigourney Weaver, Ruth Westheimer, Michel Aumont, Zabou, Jean-Pierre Bisson

Archeologist Julien (Depardieu) unearths the two million-year-old remains of the 'first Frenchwoman' and, as a result becomes embroiled with American advertising executive Jessica (Weaver) and follows her to New York. What starts out as a latter day French-flavoured screwball comedy, in which Jessica and Julien meet only because she's pretending to be somebody else, steadily disintegrates into a contrived and irritating farce without much point or purpose. One would have expected more from the director of *The Return Of Martin Guerre*.

A Woman's Decision

▶ **aka Quarterly Balance**

▶ **Bilans Kwartalny**

Poland 1974 99 mins col
Film Polski

d   **Krzysztof Zanussi**
sc **Krzysztof Zanussi**
ph **Slawomir Idziak**
m   **Wojciech Kilar**
    Maya Komorowska, Piotr Franczewski, Marek Piwowski

Marta (Komorowska) combines marriage and motherhood with a career as an accountant. She is the union representative at her office, and a reliable friend in solving other people's problems. Her strengths desert her, however, in facing difficulties in her own marriage which crystallize in having to decide whether to leave with her lover (Piwowski). This is an accessible and straightforward exercise from Zanussi, dealing perceptively and sympathetically with its subject. An enjoyable film, enhanced by a marvellous performance from Komorowska, but it reduces the sharpness of its impact by its intrusively lush and over-romantic photography.

A Woman's Face

▶ **En Kvinnas Ansikte**

Sweden 1937 100 mins bw
Svensk Filmindustri

d   Gustaf Molander
sc Gösta Stevens
ph Äke Dahlquist
m   Eric Bengtson, Chopin
    Ingrid Bergman, Anders Henrikson,
    Georg Rydeberg, Karin Carlsson-Kavil,
    Goran Bernhard, Tore Svennberg

Anna Holm (Bergman), hideously disfigured since childhood by a facial scar received in an accident, has become an embittered and remorseless woman. A successful operation transforms her into a beauty and softens her nature, so that she shoots the man she loves rather than commit a murder on his behalf. Bergman working, as in *Intermezzo*, with Molander, is breathtaking in what is essentially high melodrama, adapted from a French play by De Croisset and here given effectively solemn and well-controlled treatment. An extremely entertaining piece of hokum, it surfaced again in Hollywood in 1941 and became a hit for Joan Crawford, directed by George Cukor.

A Woman's Life

▶ **aka A Woman's Story**
▶ **Onna No Rekishi**

Japan 1964 120 mins bw
Toho

d   Mikio Naruse
sc Ryozo Kasahara
ph Asaichi Nakai
m   Ichiro Saito
    Hideko Takamine, Tatsuya Nakadai,
    Akira Takarada, Yuriko Hoshio

Nobuko (Takamine) is widowed when her husband is killed in the war. Later, her beloved son marries a girl of whom she disapproves, and is then killed in a car accident. She comes to terms with her grief only when she learns to accept her daughter-in-law, pregnant with the dead husband's child. This moving film has been directed and acted with sensitivity, perception, and a delicacy that is characteristic of the Japanese cinema when it deals with intimate subjects on a small canvas. Nobuko's struggle with her inner self is timeless and universal.

▶ **Woman's Story, A** see Woman's Life, A

▶ **Woman That Men Long For, The** see Woman That Men Yearn For, The

The Woman That Men Yearn For

▶ **aka The Woman That Men Long For**
▶ **(US: Three Loves)**
▶ **Die Frau, Nach Der Man Sich Sehnt**

Germany 1929 2360 metres bw
Terra Film AG (Berlin)

d   Kurt Bernhardt
sc Ladislaus Vajda
ph Kurt Courant, Hans Scheib
m   Silent
    Marlene Dietrich, Fritz Lörtner, Uno
    Henning, Frida Richard, Oskar Sima,
    Bruno Ziener

A young Frenchman (Henning) marries a girl (Richard) whom he does not really love in order to save his firm from bankruptcy. On his honeymoon he meets a fascinating woman (Dietrich) accompanied by a sinister man (Lörtner). The woman, with whom he falls instantly in love, seems terrified of her escort and begs the young man to save her. Leaving his bride, he follows the pair to an hotel, from where he plans to arrange an escape during a masked ball. 'Discovery of a female star is something for a German film to accomplish,' wrote *Variety* in May 1929. 'Here Marlene Dietrich shows herself as a strong contender for international honours.

At the moment she is imitating Greta Garbo's half-closed eyes and langorous eroticism, but there is enough individuality in her work to show that the girl is there. She has the right face and figure and she can troupe.' Dietrich had made over a dozen films before Von Sternberg and audiences outside Germany discovered her. Yet this splendid example of late German silent cinema romance spiced with perversity dispels the myth that the Dietrich look was created by Sternberg. One scene in particular – her first appearance looking through a frosted train window – makes one wonder how the director of *The Blue Angel*, the following year, could not have seen this film and been influenced by the way Kurt Bernhardt (Curtis from 1940 in Hollywood) treated the 'woman that men yearn for'.

▶ **Woman Who Dared, The** see Ciel Est À Vous, Le

The Women On The Roof

▶ **Kvinnorna På Taket**

Sweden 1989 90 mins col
Filmhuset/Swedish Film Institute/Svensk Filmindustri

d   **Carl-Gustaf Nykvist**
sc **Carl-Gustaf Nykvist, Lasse Summanen**
ph **Jörgen Persson, Ulf Brantas**
m   **Håkan Möller**
    Amanda Ooms, Helena Bergström, Stellan Skarsgård, Percy Brandt

Linnea (Ooms), young and shy, takes lodgings in 1914 Stockholm and works as a general dogsbody in a photographic shop. Anna (Bergström), a sophisticated photographer, moves into a disused studio in Linnea's lodging house, befriends the girl and gets her to pose for the mythological photographs she is working on. When Anna's former lover Willy (Skarsgård) arrives unexpectedly, a complex situation develops which culminates in a disastrous row. This is the debut feature of cinematographer Sven Nykvist's son, whose heritage is evident in every painterly frame. Other than its visual quality, however, this film has a long debit column. The narrative is unfocused, the characters blank and uninteresting, the pace mind-numbingly slow and the heavily enigmatic hints at deep and dark meanings lead nowhere. Director Nykvist is evidently fascinated by photographs and the people who take them: this is the first of an intended trilogy about 'pictures as the magic mirrors of man's fate'. One can only hope they improve.

Women On The Verge Of A Nervous Breakdown

▶ **Mujeres Al Borde De Un Ataque De Nervios**

Spain 1988 89 mins col
El Deseo/Lauren Film

d   **Pedro Almodóvar**
sc **Pedro Almodóvar**
ph **José Luis Alcaine**
m   **Bernardo Bonezzi**
    Carmen Maura, Antonio Banderas, Fernando Guillén, Julieta Serrano, Maria Barranco, Guillermo Montesinos

Pepa (Carmen Maura), a volatile and attractive television actress, is pregnant by her married and philandering lover. Unaware of her condition, he blithely abandons her via a message on her telephone answering machine. As all her efforts to contact him fail, Pepa grows totally distraught and hysterical, and is precipitated into a series of increasingly bizzare and surreal situations. In company with Finland's Aki Kaurismäki and Poland's Krzysztof Kieslowski, Spain's Pedro Almodóvar found himself the critics' darling in English-speaking countries, as well as throughout Europe, during the late 1980s and early 1990s. It was this film, set in fashionable Madrid, that broke through the barriers, attracting large and enthusiastic audiences for his trendy and distinctive visual style (influenced, in this case at least, by 1950s' Hollywood) and his anarchic brand of humour. The director described it as high comedy, but it is actually farce in its arrangement of irrational happenings held together by an internal logic that is very funny. There is a feminist message struggling to escape from the screwball events as Pepa – a superb performance from the smouldering Maura – gradually comes to see her lover for what he is and to bury her self-pity. But *Women On The Verge*, for all that is is largely diverting, adroitly handled and often clever, lacks the depth its subject might have allowed it and grows a little tedious before the end.

The Wonderful Lie Of Nina Petrovna

▶ aka (US: The Wonderful Lies Of Nina Petrovna)

▶ Die Wunderbar Lüge Der Nina Petrovna

1929   80 mins   bw
UFA

d   Hans Schwarz
sc Hans Szekely
ph Carl Hoffmann
m   Silent
Brigitte Helm, Franz Lederer, Warwick Ward, Lya Jan, Harry Hardt, Ekkehard Arendt

Nina Petrovna (Helm), the blonde mistress of an army general (Ward), living in luxury, falls in love with a penniless young lieutenant (Lederer). She gives up her jewels and villa to live modestly with her lover, but when the general challenges his young rival to a game of poker with Nina as the stake, she makes a sacrifice to save the officer's life. This splendidly sophisticated triangular love affair, played to perfection by Helm, Lederer and Ward, and smoothly directed by Schwarz, is played out against sumptuous settings. Carl Hoffmann, Fritz Lang's favourite photographer, uses an excitingly mobile camera, especially in a scene which moves us through the corridors and rooms of the villa to a discovery of the tragic heroine.

▶ Wonderful Lies Of Nina Petrovna, The see Wonderful Lie Of Nina Petrovna, The

▶ Word, The see Ordet

The Working Class Go To Heaven

▶ (US: Lulu The Tool)

▶ La Classe Operaia Va In Paradiso

Italy 1972 126 mins col

Euro International Films

d   Elio Petri
sc Elio Petri, Ugo Pirro
ph Ubaldo Terzano
m   Ennio Morricone
Gian Maria Volonté, Mariangela Melato, Salvo Randone, Gino Pernice, Luigi Diberti, Donato Castellaneta

Lulu Massa (Volonté), a factory piece-worker, is obsessed with achieving the highest daily output, thus arousing the resentment of his fellow-workers, inviting exploitation by the shop stewards and frustrating his mistress (Melato) with whom he lives. Crisis and change come when he is temporarily laid off as a result of an accident at work and he visits a retired worker (Randone), now in a mental hospital, who gives him a different perspective. Returning to work, he attempts to become a leader in the Left's fight for better conditions. A plot synopsis cannot possibly convey the complex layers of Petri's film. He explores the corruption of capitalism with ingenuity and imagination, at the same time revealing the innate weaknesses of Lulu the man, whose working and domestic lives become destructively reversed. The film has its flaws, particularly in failing to flesh out anybody who represents the system that is under attack, but it's an intelligent and provocative work, boasting a magnificent performance from Volonté, and from Melato as the person who appears the quickest to grasp reality.

Best Film Cannes 1972

The World Of Apu

▶ Apu Sansar

India 1959 117 mins bw
Satyajit Ray-West Bengal Government

d   Satyajit Ray
sc Satyajit Ray
ph Subrata Mitra
m   Ravi Shankar
Soumitra Chatterjee, Sharmila Tagore, Shapan Mukerjee

Apu (Chatterjee), a young man in Calcutta, comes to love his wife of an arranged marriage, but when she dies in childbirth, he refuses to see his son. They are reconciled some years later. The final part of the 'Apu

Trilogy' is taken at a less leisurely pace and is more conventionally structured than the previous two (*Pather Panchali*, 1955 and *Aparajito*, 1956), but it is still imbued with the same keen observation, beautiful playing, and memorable scenes such as Apu's scattering of the pages of his novel over a mountain at dawn. The triptych, a humanist masterpiece of cinema begun in Ray's mind almost 10 years before, ends on a note of hope.

World Without Pity

▶ **Un Monde Sans Pitié**

France   1989   88 mins   col
Alain Rocca/Les Productions Lazennec/
FR3 Films

d   **Eric Rochant**
sc **Eric Rochant**
ph **Pierre Novion**
m   **Gérard Torikian**
    **Hippolyte Girardot, Mireille Perrier,
    Yvan Attal, Jean Marie Rollin, Cécile
    Mazan**

Good-looking, raffish Hippo (Girardot), unemployed and seemingly content to be so, lives in an ill-kempt apartment with his younger brother (Rollin) who supports him from the proceeds of cannabis dealing. When Hippo, who spends his time playing poker and womanizing, pursues the lovely Nathalie (Perrier), he gets more than he bargained for. She is a middle-class Jewish intellectual, committed to her academic career, and is irresistibly attracted to Hippo while being repelled by his empty lifestyle and lack of interests. This very talented feature debut was garlanded with awards – Césars for Best First Film and Most Promising Young Actor – and boasts an excellent cast in which Perrier, especially, shines. But for all its virtues in capturing a particular *milieu*, it is likely to hold most appeal for younger audiences; the more mature might find the central character's aimlessness, self-absorption and unfocused rebellion somewhat irritating.

Woyzeck

W. Germany   1978   80 mins   col
Herzog/ZDF

d   **Werner Herzog**
sc **Werner Herzog**
ph **Jörg Schmidt-Reitwein**
m   **Vivaldi, Benedetto Marcello**
    **Klaus Kinski, Eva Mattes, Wolfgang
    Reichmann, Willy Semmelrogge, Josef
    Bierbichler, Paul Burian**

Franz Woyzeck (Kinski), a poor, simple-minded, brow-beaten soldier, takes on a variety of jobs in order to support his common-law wife Maria (Mattes) and their young child. When he suspects Marie of betraying him with the handsome Drum Major (Bierbichler), Woyzek stabs her to death. Although prettily shot in Czechoslovakia, and sticking as closely as possible to the 27 short scenes of Georg Büchner's remarkable 1836 play, the film rings hollow, and Kinski, in his third role for Herzog, fails to elicit sympathy for the character. It was filmed more imaginatively in 1947 by Georg Klaren.

**Best Supporting Actress (Eva Mattes)
Cannes 1979**

▶ **WR – Misterije Organizma** see
WR – Mysteries Of The Organism

WR – Mysteries Of The Organism

▶ **WR – Misterije Organizma**

Yugoslavia   1971   86 mins   col
Neoplanta (Yugoslavia)/Telepool (W.
Germany)

d   **Dušan Makavejev**
sc **Dušan Makavejev**
ph **Pega Popović, Aleksandar Petković**
m   **Bojana Makavejev**
    **Milena Dravić, Jagodar Kaloper, Zoran
    Radmilović, Ivica Vidović, Miodrag
    Andrić, Tuli Kupferberg**

A documentary and fictional examination of the theories of sexologist Wilhelm Reich and the actions of two of his Yugoslav disciples (Dravić and Kaloper). Using a fusion of styles, the anarchic Makavejev ambiguously compares the West with the Eastern bloc countries and Reich with Stalin. While seeming to admire Reich, he gives him and his followers, including porn merchants, enough rope to beat each other with. This shocking, amusing and exasperating movie caused offence wherever it was shown and made a lot of money.

Wrong Movement

▶ **Falsche Bewegung**

W. Germany 1975 103 mins col
Solaris Film/Peter Genée-Bernd Eichinger

d **Wim Wenders**
sc **Peter Handke**
ph **Robby Müller**
m **Jürgen Knieper**
   Rüdiger Vogler, Hanna Schygulla, Ivan Desny, Marianne Hoppe, Hans-Christian Blech, Peter Kern, Nastassja Nakszynski (Nastassja Kinski)

Wilhelm (Vogler), a discontented writer, leaves on a journey through Germany. On his travels he gets involved with Laertes (Blech), an old singer, Therese Farmer (Schygulla), an actress, a suicidal industrialist (Desny) and a poet (Kern). Inspired by *Wilhelm Meister's Apprenticeship,* Goethe's renowned *Bildungsroman*, Wenders and Handke derived a typically bleak and cryptic road movie which set Rüdiger Vogler in melancholy motion again. (It is the second of a trilogy between *Alice In The Cities* and *Kings Of The Road*.) The vision of a figurative and literal wasteland that is Germany and its suggestions of the Nazi past are effective, if rather obvious, milestones on the journey. Nastassja Kinski makes a non-speaking screen debut in the role of an adolescent mute juggler.

▶ **Wszystko Na Sprzedaz** see Everything For Sale

▶ **Wunderbar Lüge Der Nina Petrovna, Die** see Wonderful Lie Of Nina Petrovna, The

▶ **Wunder Des Malachias, Das** see Miracle Of Malachias, The

▶ **Wutai Jiemei** see Two Stage Sisters

Wuthering Heights

▶ **Abismos De Pasión**

Mexico 1953 90 mins bw
Producciones Tepeyac

d **Luis Buñuel**
sc **Luis Buñuel**
ph **Augustín Jiménez**
m **Raúl Lavista**
   Jorge Mistral, Irasema Dilian, Lilia Prado, Ernesto Alonso

Having been adopted by his master when a young orphaned servant boy, the adult Alexandro (Mistral), returns to the family home having made his fortune. He resumes his close, passionate and almost mystical relationship with his adopted sister Cataline (Dilian), to the discomfort of her husband whose sister Isabelle (Prado) falls in love with him. Driven by motives of revenge, he marries her, while Cataline, now desperately ill, dies, and Alexandro is killed by Isabelle's brother. Played in harsh, white light against a dry and stony Mexican landscape which bears little resemblance to the murky Yorkshire moors of Emily Brontë's celebrated novel, Buñuel's adaptation nonetheless successfully and imaginatively captures the dark heart of the original. This is a skilfully made and intimate melodrama with deeper resonances than the surface would suggest. Although remaining true to the spirit of the novel, a favourite of the Surrealists, the director makes the work very much his own: a relentless celebration of *l'amour fou*, combined with a strongly implied critique of class differences. Mistral, an utterly ruthless Alexandro/Heathcliffe, is, together with the rest of the cast, adequate.

▶ **Wuya Yu Maque** see Crows And Sparrows

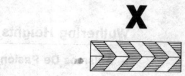

X

Xala

▶ **aka The Curse**

Senegal 1974 123 mins col
Filmi Domireew/Société Nationale De
Cinématographie

d **Ousmane Sembène**
sc **Ousmane Sembène**
ph **Georges Caristan**
m **Samba Diabara Samb**
   Tierno Leye, Seune Samb, Miriam Niang,
   Younouss Seye, Dieynaba Niang, Fatim
   Diagne

A rich and powerful businessman (Leye) is
about to take a third wife (Dieynaba Niang).
Neither of his other two wives (Samb and
Seye) nor his daughter (Miriam Niang) is
happy with the situation. On his wedding
night, his usual prowess lets him down. Someone has evidently bestowed a Xala on him –
a curse rendering the victim impotent. It is
only a matter of time before his financial
affairs start to crumble. Sembène sees the
impotence of the man as the impotence of
Senegal, a country that has failed to remove
class injustices and has 'formed new classes
that only know how to imitate Western *bour-
geoisies*'. Based on the director's own widely
praised novel, this savage and funny satirical
film was equally extolled, except by the Senegalese government which cut the last 10
minutes.

▶ **Xiaozi Bei** see Bus Number Three

Y

Yaaba

Burkino Faso 1989 90 mins col
Les Fils De L'Avenir (Ouagadougou)/
Thelma Film (Zurich)/Arcadia Films
(Paris)

d **Idrissa Ouedraogo**
sc **Idrissa Ouedraogo**
ph **Matthias Kalin**
m **Francis Bebey**
   **Fatima Sanga, Noufou Ouedraogo, Barry
Roukietou, Adama Oudraogo, Amade
Toure, Sibidou Ouedraogo**

In a remote tribal village in Burkino Faso, two
young cousins, Nopoko and Bila (Roukietou,
Ouedraogo), are in the cemetery conducting a
ritual in memory of Nopoko's dead mother.
They are watched by Sana (Sanga), a very old
woman who, having been orphaned in childhood, lives as an outcast and is thought to be
a witch. At first fearful of the woman, the children strike up a relationship with her and she
is moved when the boy Bila calls her Yaaba
(grandmother)... Although taken at a leisurely
pace consonant with the vast and beautiful
landscape and the lazy hum of insects, *Yaaba*
is filled with incident. Larger issues of superstition, custom and the gradual encroachment
of new thinking into tribal life are subtly presented through the myriad details of domestic
routine and relationships. The tale of Yaaba
herself, cruelly treated, is desperately sad,
while Bila's growing understanding of her is
compassionate and optimistic. Ouedraogo
evokes a fascinating world of 'otherness' for a
Western viewer with this well-acted and much-
praised film.

The Yankee

▶ **Jänken**

Sweden 1970 95 mins bw

Svensk Filminstitutet

d **Lars Forsberg**
sc **Lars Forsberg**
ph **Petter Davidson**
   **Anita Ekström, Lars Green, Mona
Dan-Bergman, Louise Hedberg, Inger
Ekström, Tommy Sernling**

Inger (Anita Ekström) has grown up in a
slum, is bored by her factory job and ill-
equipped to deal with the pregnancy that
results from an affair with a boy visiting from
America. She moves in with Mascot (Green),
an old friend and small-time crook, and lands
in all kinds of uninvited trouble. Lars
Forsberg's debut film is assured in execution,
well photographed, sympathetic and secures
an excellent performance from Ekström.
However, the story of an underprivileged girl
as society's victim offers no new angles or
insights and is thus numbingly familiar.

▶ **Yanzhi Kou** see Rouge

▶ **Yawar Mallku** see Blood Of The
Condor

A Year Of The Quiet Sun

▶ **Rok Spokojnego Słońca**

Poland 1984 108 mins col
Tor Film Unit(Warsaw)/Teleculture(New
York)/ Regina Ziegler(W.Berlin)

d **Krzysztof Zanussi**
sc **Krzysztof Zanussi**
ph **Slawomir Idziak**
m **Wojciech Kilar**
   **Maja Komorowska, Scott Wilson, Hanna
Skarżanka, Ewa Dalkowska, Vadim
Glowna**

In the Poland of 1946, an American soldier

(Wilson) and a Polish widow (Komorowska) strike up a relationship, even though neither speaks the other's language. He is under orders to go to Berlin where he hopes she will join him, but he waits in vain. The drab and bitter aftermath of the war in East Europe is visited once again and so is the story of unfulfilled love in Zanussi's circumspect, stoical and rather conventional film. Yet there are interesting details – Polish profiteers, the problems of crossing the border – and two tender performances from Wilson and Zanussi's favourite actress, Komorowska.

Best Film Venice 1984

▶ **Yeelen** see Brightness

Yellow Earth

▶ **Huang Tudi**

     China   1984   89 mins   col
     Guangxi Film Studio

d   **Chen Kaige**
sc   **Zhang Ziliang**
ph   **Zhang Yimou**
m   **Zhao Jiping**
     Xue Bai, Wang Xueqi, Tan Tuo, Liu Qiang

In the spring of 1939, a soldier arrives in a small community to research folk songs. He becomes involved in the life of one family – an old man, his 14-year-old daughter about to make an arranged marriage, and the younger son – and finds himself unable to alter their traditional, superstitious ways. *Yellow Earth* came like a bolt from the blue in the West, altering received ideas of Chinese cinema. A heady mixture of music, poetry, dance and drama, it is set against the vividly evoked dusty, barren landscape of the title. Although it has a rather pessimistic ending – the people do not heed the soldier's exhortation that 'all of China must change' – audiences know that it finally did.

Yerma

     Hungary   1984   104 mins   col
     Starfilm; Martin Moszkowicz/Makropus

Film/Hunnia Filmstudio/Sefel Pictures/ Channel 4

d   **Imre Gyöngyössi, Barna Kabay**
sc   **Imre Gyöngyössi, Barna Kabay, Katlalin Petenyl**
ph   **Gabor Szabo**
m   **Zoltan Pesko**
     Gudrun Landgrebe, Mathieu Carrière, Titusz Kovacs, Mareike Carrière

After three years of marriage to the shepherd Juan (Mathieu Carrière), Yerma (Landgrebe) has still not had the child she yearns for. She desperately seeks a solution from older women and even consults a sorceress, but to no avail. The obsession with her barrenness leads to tragedy. Federico Garcia Lorca's play about frustrated maternal instincts successfully combines poetic and dramatic elements. In transposing it to the screen, the same director-writing-photography team as the previous year's *The Revolt Of Job* have lost much of the inherent theatricality of the piece. When set against real backgrounds, stylized scenes, such as the chorus of laundresses, take on an artificial air. Although shot in Spain, the film also lacks authenticity because of the mixed German and Hungarian cast, led by Gudrun Landgrebe and Mathieu Carrière, the two stars of *A Woman In Flames* (1983), as rather unconvincing Spanish peasants. The picture-postcard locations, however pleasing to the eye, seem inappropriate to the stark symbolic drama of barrenness played out in them.

▶ **Ye Shan** see In The Wild Mountains

Yesterday Girl

▶ **Abschied Von Gestern**

     W. Germany   1966   90 mins   bw
     Kairos Film/Alexander Kluge/ Independent

d   **Alexander Kluge**
sc   **Alexander Kluge**
ph   **Edgar Reitz, Thomas Mauch**
     Alexandra Kluge, Günther Mack, Hans Korte, Eva Marie Meinecke

Anita G. (Kluge), a completely amoral and rebellious East German girl, escapes to West

Germany only to find herself still at odds with a different but equally conservative society. Alexander Kluge's first feature was based on the case of a woman he encountered during his work as a lawyer. Greatly influenced by Godard, he uses documentary-style interviews, combined with jump cuts, inserts, and other fragmenting techniques, to get to the heart of his subject. It came as a breath of fresh air to the moribund German film industry. Kluge was instrumental in setting up the Young German Film Fund which would help finance quality productions, and *Yesterday Girl* received over 60 per cent of its budget from it. The director's sister made a superb film debut as Anita G.

Special Jury Prize Venice 1966

Yesterday, Today And Tomorrow

▶ **Ieri, Oggi, Domani**

Italy 1963 119 mins col
CCC(Rome)/Les Films Concordia(Paris)

d   **Vittorio De Sica**
sc **1) Eduardo De Filippo, Isabella Quarantotti**
    2) Cesare Zavattini, Billa Billa Zanuso
    3) Cesare Zavattini
ph **Giuseppe Rotunno**
m   **Armando Trovaioli**
    Sophia Loren, Marcello Mastroianni, Aldo Guiffre, Agostino Salvietta, Tina Pica, Armando Trovaioli, Giovanni Ridolfi, Gennaro Di Gregorio

Three separate stories, 'Adelina Of Naples', 'Anna Of Milan', and 'Mara Of Rome', utilize the services of a distinguished director, two superstars, a leading dramatist (De Filippo), a highly skilled screenwriter (Zavattini), and one of the world's best colour cameramen. What a waste! The threadbare and slightly vulgar content is neither especially romantic nor particularly amusing, though the film looks handsome. The best segment is the first, in which Loren plays Adelina, a wife who avoids imprisonment for black-marketeering by keeping herself continuously pregnant by Mastroianni's sexy husband. It was clearly thought more highly of at the time (see below).

Best Foreign Film Oscar 1964

▶ **Yeux Sans Visage, Les** see Eyes Without A Face

Yiddle With His Fiddle

▶ **Yidl Mitn Fidl**

Poland 1936 92 mins bw
Greenfilm

d   **Joseph Green, Jan Nowina-Przybylski**
sc **Joseph Green**
ph **Seweryn Steinwurzel**
m   **Abraham Ellstein, Itzik Manger**
    Molly Picon, Simche Fostel, Max Bozyk, Leon Liebgold, Dora Fakiel

A young woman (Picon) disguises herself as a boy and travels with a group of itinerant musicians in order to help support her aging father (Fostel). She falls in love with one of them (Liebgold). but must keep her real identity a secret. The first international Yiddish hit had all the essential ingredients. Technically superior to many of the cheap Yiddish films made in the USA at the time, it was full of well-known Jewish songs, comic vaudeville routines, a dose of tears, a wedding scene and a strong-willed heroine. The popular Yiddish comedienne, Molly Picon, at the height of her career, made the most of this role. The charming film also offers a glimpse of Jewish society in Poland before it was tragically destroyed.

▶ **Yidl Mitn Fidl** see Yiddle With His Fiddle

▶ **Yijiang Chunshui Xiang Dong Liu** see Spring River Flows East

▶ **Yngsjömordet** see Woman Of Darkness

▶ **Yoidore Tenshi** see Drunken Angel

Yojimbo

Japan 1961 110 mins bw
Toho

d   **Akira Kurosawa**

sc   **Ryuzo Kikushima, Akira Kurosawa**
ph   **Kazuo Miyagawa**
m   **Masaru Sato**
     Toshiro Mifune, Eijiro Tono, Kamatari
     Fujiwara, Takashi Shimura, Seizaburo
     Kawazu, Isuzu Yamada, Hiroshi
     Tachikawa

Yojimbo (Mifune), a masterless samurai, wanders into a town to find it terrorized by two rival factions. He offers his services to the highest bidder but, uncovering treachery, he arranges events so that both sides will destroy each other. Kurosawa's love of the Western shows itself in the plot and in some of the set-ups (the small town with its wide street) and effective use of the wide 'Scope image – a compliment that was repaid by Sergio Leone's 'Spaghetti Western' remake, *A Fistful Of Dollars* (1964). Yet the film is also in the tradition of the *jidai-geki* (samurai action film), although the graphic violence and black humour tend to subvert the more stylized and serious examples of the genre. The big scenes leading up to the showdown between the cynical hero and villain are well staged, despite the over-use of the telephoto lens. *Sanjuro*,a semi- sequel of this popular film, was released the following year.

▶ **Yokihi** see Empress Yang Kwei Fei, The

Yol

Turkey   1982   114 mins   col
Güney/Cactus/Maran/Antenne 2/Swiss
Television

d   **Serif Gören**
sc   **Yilmaz Güney**
ph   **Erdogan Engin**
m   **Sebastian Argol, Kendal**
     Tarik Akan, Halil Ergün, Necmettin
     Cobanoglu, Serif Sezer, Meral Orhonsoy,
     Semra Ucar, Tuncay Akca, Hikmet Celik

The story of five prisoners on a week's parole. Yusuf (Akca) is arrested at the outset because he has lost his papers; Mevlut (Celik) is kept from his fiancée by patriarchal customs; Mehmit (Ergün) flees with his wife from her vengeful family; Omer (Cobanoglu), a Kurd, returns to his village to find it devastated by the Turkish army ; and Seyit (Akan) is required by tradition to kill his wife (Sezer) for having been unfaithful to him during his absence. *Yol* ('the road of life' being the nearest translation) was based on an extremely detailed script written by Güney when he was in jail and directed in Turkey by his long-time assistant. The negatives were smuggled out to Europe where Güney, following his 1981 escape from prison, edited it. Acted with great conviction, against vividly realized landscapes, the film is an exceptionally powerful condemnation of an oppressive society.

Best Film Cannes 1982

You Are The World For Me

▶ **aka The Richard Tauber Story**
▶ **Du Bist Die Welt Für Mich**

Austria   1953   107 mins   bw
Erma

d   **Ernst Marischka**
sc   **Ernst Marischka**
ph   **Sepp Ketterer**
m   **The Tauber Repertoire (Musical director**
     Anton Profes)
     Rudolf Schock, Anne Marie Düringer,
     Richard Romanowsky, Fritz Imhof,
     Dagny Servaes

An account of the rise to fame of the world-famous tenor and operetta star, Richard Tauber (Schock). On his way to the top, he neglects the ballerina (Düringer) he loves and so loses her. And that is about as eventful as this conventional biopic ever gets. Efficiently made by Marischka, the doyen writer-pro-ducer-director of German musicals, Schock's singing is dubbed by recordings of Tauber himself (he died in 1948), making this a good bet for any extant fans, but rather dull and old-fashioned for anybody else.

The Young And The Damned

▶ **Los Olvidados**

Mexico   1950   88 mins   bw
Ultramar/Oscar Dancigers

d   **Luis Buñuel**
sc   **Luis Buñuel, Luis Alcoriza, Oscar Dancigers**
ph   **Gabriel Figueroa**
m   **Gustavo Pittaluga**
    Alfonso Mejía, Miguel Inclán, Estela Inda, Roberto Cobo

Pedro (Mejía), a pure young boy, becomes corrupted and destroyed by Jaibo (Cobo) and a group of juvenile delinquents living a violent life in the slums of Mexico City. After making a couple of trashy commercial films in his first years of exile in Mexico, Buñuel was able to return to serious film-making. His last great film had been *Land Without Bread*, the stark documentary on the contrast between the poverty of the Spanish peasants and the wealth of the church. He continued where he had left off 18 years before and became famous once more. This powerful yet detached view of slum conditions and their effect on children was made in only 21 days but 'for several months I toured the slums...I came to know these people and much of what I saw went unchanged into the film'. The harsh realism – note the beating up of the blind musician (Inclán) – is mixed with Buñuel's surrealism in the dream sequences.

Best Director Cannes 1951

▶ **Young And The Passionate, The**
see Vitelloni, I

Young Aphrodites

▶ **Mikres Aphrodites**

    Greece   1962   98 mins   bw
    Minos Films/Anzervos Studios

d   **Nikos Koundouros**
sc   **Costas Sphikas, Vassilis Vassilikos**
ph   **Giovanni Variano**
m   **Yiannis Markopoulos**
    Takis Emmanouel, Vangelis Joannides, Cleopatra Rota, Eleni Prokopiou, C. Papaconstantinou

In Ancient Greece, a group of mountain shepherds in search of pasture come upon a fishing village where the inhabitants are all women. Skymnos (Joannides), fascinated by this strange world, strikes up a tentative friendship with Chloë (Rota), a young girl he sees fishing in a rock pool. Meanwhile, Tsakalos (Emmanouel), seduces Arta (Prokopiou). Skymnos's dreams are shattered when Lykas (Papaconstantinou), a dumb shepherd boy, ravishes the innocent Chloë. Koundouros drew his material from the tale of *Daphnis And Chloë* and the *Idylls* of Theocritus. The result is a film of magical, mythological atmosphere, quite breathtaking in its settings and photography, primitive and poetic in tone. Nonetheless, although it was well received on release and won prizes, it is, frankly, very thin in content, sometimes slow and often twee.

Best Director Berlin 1963

The Young Have No Morals

▶ **(US: The Chasers)**
▶ **Les Drageurs**

France   1959   78 mins   bw
Lisbon Films/Films Fernand Rivers

d   **Jean-Pierre Mocky**
sc   **Jean-Pierre Mocky**
ph   **Edmond Séchan**
m   **Maurice Jarre**
    Jacques Charrier, Charles Aznavour, Dany Robin, Anouk Aimée, Nicole Berger, Belinda Lee, Margit Saad, Inge Schoener, Dany Carrel

Freddy (Charrier), aged 20 and experienced, and Joseph (Aznavour), 25 but shy and green, spend an evening in Paris searching for their ideal girl. Before ending up at a society orgy where Freddy has a disillusioning encounter with an aimless beauty (Lee) while Joseph finds a sympathetic nurse (Berger), they encounter a string of women who a cripple (Aimée) and a couple of Swedish Lesbians. In making his first film, actor Mocky adopts a New Wave approach and a subject reminiscent of Carné's *The Cheaters* (1958) but does so with more conviction. It is efficiently made and very well photographed, but both character development and moral centre are left underdeveloped and vague, leaving only surface attractions – pleasing ironies, a noticeably good score, and some lively acting.

The Young Ladies Of Wilko

▶ **Panny Z Wilka**

Poland 1979 116 mins col
Zespól Filmowy(Warsaw)/Les Films
Molière(Paris)

d Andrzej Wajda
sc Zbigniew Kamínski
ph Edward Klosínski
m Szymanowski (First Violin Concerto)
    Daniel Olbrychski, Anna Seniuk,
    Christine Pascal, Maja Komorowska,
    Stanislawa Celínska, Krystyna
    Zachwatowicz, Zofia Jaroszewska,
    Tadeusz Bialoszczynski

Viktor Ruben (Olbrychski), a solitary bachelor who saw service in World War I, is advised by his doctor to take a vacation. He visits his aunt and uncle in Wilko where the neighbouring estate belongs to five sisters (six until one died), in all of whose lives Viktor once featured as a romantic fantasy. The reunion rekindles new hopes in each now disillusioned breast, but they fade with the collective realization that all of them have changed. Wajda, temporarily deserting topical political statement, has made an exquisite period piece which lays bare the futility of attempting to resurrect the past. Wonderfully photographed and perfectly cast, the film has an engaging theatrical charm, but is overloaded with wearisome Chekhovian yearning.

Young Törless

▶ **Der Junge Törless**

W. Germany 1966 85 mins bw
Franz Seitz/Nouvelles Éditions De Film

d Volker Schlöndorff
sc Volker Schlöndorff
ph Franz Rath
m Hans Werner Henze
    Matthieu Carrière, Bernd Fischer, Marian
    Seidowsky, Alfred Dietz, Barbara Steele

At a semi-military boarding school, Törless (Carrière), an intelligent pupil, is the silent witness to the dreadful bullying of his friend Basini (Seidowsky) by the sadistic Beineberg (Fischer) and Reiting (Dietz). By the time he realizes his moral responsibility it is too late. Twenty-seven-year-old Schlöndorff's first feature, which won the International Critics award at Cannes, is an accomplished transposition of the Robert Musil novel of embryonic Nazis at the turn of the century. It marks the beginning of the director's obsession with modern German history. Among the excellent young actors, is Barbara Steele, English queen of Italian horror movies, as a waitress who teaches the boys things that are not on the school curriculum.

The Young Wolves

▶ **Les Jeunes Loups**

France 1968 111 mins col
S.N.C.(Paris)/West Film(Rome)

d Marcel Carné
sc Marcel Carné, Claude Accursi
ph Jacques Robin
m Jack Arel, Guy Magenta, Cyril
    Haydée Politoff, Christian Hay, Roland
    Lesaffre, Yves Benyeton, Maurice Garrel,
    Bernard Dhéran

Alain Langlois (Hay), good-looking and ruthlessly ambitious, exploits the affections of wealthy older women, at the same time becoming involved with Sylvie (Politoff), a girl of his own age. When Ugo (Garrel), a wealthy property owner in a position to employ Alain, is attracted to Sylvie, the young man passes her off as his sister and they move in to Ugo's mansion, until Sylvie grows jealous of Alain's ambiguous relationship with his employer. There is little in this clichéd, determinedly 'with it' account of youthful amorality to link it with Marcel Carné other than its technical competence. The characters are superficial stereotypes and the director lacks a point of view, failing even to inject the energy of his first disappointing attempt to move with the times, *Youthful Sinners* (1958).

You Only Love Once

▶ **(US: The Melody Haunts My Memory)**

▶ **Samo Jednom Se Ljubi**

Yugoslavia 1980 103 mins col
Jadran Film

d   Rajko Grlić
sc Rajko Grlić, Branko Šömen, Srdjan
    Karanović
ph Tomislav Pinter
m   Branislav Živković
    Predrag Manojlović, Vladica
    Milosavljević, Zijah Sokolović, Mladen
    Budiščak, Erland Josephson

Just after World War II, Tomislav
(Manojlović), a Partisan hero with Communist ideals, becomes obsessed with and marries
Baby (Milosavljević), a middle-class ballerina
with traditional views. The tempestuous
relationship leads him to prison and a mental
hospital. On one level, the film reflects the
difficult and complex post-war period when
Yugoslavia was searching for a new identity –
the class conflict is compellingly revealed –
and on another level, it can be seen as a study
of a destructive relationship. However, the
hero's macho behaviour and the woman's
shallow passivity – only she is seen nude in
the graphic sex scenes – reveal a rather dubious ambiguity of purpose.

Youthful Sinners

► aka The Cheats
► Les Tricheurs

    France   1958   117 mins   bw
    Silver Films/Cinétel/Zebra Film/CD

d   Marcel Carné
sc Marcel Carné, Jacques Sigurd
ph Claude Renoir
    Jacques Charrier, Pascale Petit, Andrea
    Parisy, Jean-Paul Belmondo

A middle-class Parisian student (Charrier)
becomes involved with a crowd dedicated to
defying social and moral convention. Nonetheless, he and one of the young crowd
(Petit) fall in love, until blackmail, infidelity
and group pressures sabotage the relationship
which ends in tragedy. Carné, who had
reached the peak of his creativity with Les
Enfants Du Paradis in 1945, was making a
bid to keep up with the youth movement by
dealing with contemporary subject matter.
Alas, in spite of some good moments and the
introduction of some new stars, his efforts
resulted in an overlong and somewhat tedious
film.

The Youth Of Maxim

► Yunost Maksima

    USSR   1935   97 mins   bw
    Lenfilm

d   Grigori Kozintsev, Leonid Trauberg
sc Grigori Kozintsev, Leonid Trauberg
ph Andrei Moskvin
m   Dmitri Shostakovitch
    Boris Chirkov, Stepan Kayukov,
    Valentina Kibardina, Michael Tarkhanov

In 1910, Maxim (Chirkov), a young worker,
falls in love with Natasha (Kibardina) and
through a militant Bolshevik (Kayukov)
becomes a revolutionary. He is drawn into
the struggle against workers' exploitation and
is arrested. The team of Kozintsev and Trauberg, dissatisfied with contemporary represen-
tations of the Bolsheviks as 'heroes of
adventure fiction', created the most human
of revolutionary films, a study of a flesh-and-
blood unromanticized individual caught up
in the struggle. There is plenty of humour
mixed with the message and Maxim is no
mean accordian player (his theme tune is still
a favourite in the Soviet Union). The lively
episodic structure, Chirkov's natural performance (he spent months working in a factory
and talking to old Bolsheviks prior to filming)
and Moskvin's photographic compositions
are at their best in the first of what became
The Maxim Trilogy, followed by The Return
Of Maxim and The Vyborg Side.

Yoyo

    France   1965   97 mins   bw
    C.A.P.A.C(Paris)

d   Pierre Étaix
sc Pierre Étaix, Jean-Claude Carrière
ph Jean Boffety
m   Jean Paillaud
    Pierre Étaix, Luce Klein, Philippe
    Dionnet, Claudine Auger

A millionaire, bored by the solitude and idle
luxury of his life, yearns for his former sweetheart (Klein). Later, he recognizes her as the
equestrienne in a visiting circus and, when
the Wall Street crash robs him of his wealth,
he joins her and her clown child, Yoyo, who
is his son. Yoyo grows up to be a star and

takes steps to restore his father's now decaying château, but... In his second feature, Étaix pays tribute to the tone and technique of the silent cinema with a nostalgic and enchanting comedy romance, filming the first half-hour or so without dialogue (but with splendid sound effects, such as the creaking of the vast château doors). As both the adult Yoyo and the millionaire, Étaix brings the same control and individual sense of style to his performance as to his direction.

▶ **Yuanlizhanzhengde Niandai** see Far From the War

▶ **Yukinojo Henge** see Actor's Revenge, An

▶ **Yunost Maksima** see Youth Of Maxim, The

Z

Z

France 1968 125 mins col
Reggane Films/ONCIC(Algiers)

d **Costa-Gavras**
sc **Jorge Semprun, Costa-Gavras**
ph **Raoul Coutard**
m **Mikis Theodorakis**
Yves Montand, Irene Papas, Jean-Louis Trintignant, Jacques Perrin, François Périer, Charles Denner, Bernard Fresson, Jean Bouise

In an unidentified Mediterranean country, support is growing for 'Z' (Montand), the leader of the pacifist opposition party. Following a meeting, 'Z' is knocked down by a van and dies after undergoing brain surgery. An investigating magistrate (Trintignant) assigned to the case, treats the death as murder when he uncovers a secret organization supported by the government and police. Based on a novel by Vassili Vassilikos, this very slick and effective political thriller, shot in Algeria by the Greek-born Costa-Gavras, plainly points its finger at the Colonels' regime in Greece. Despite the topicality, and the simple treatment of complicated issues, the film's message and passion still communicate to an audience because, though the specifics have altered, the generality of totalitarian regimes has not. Its popularity and awards rocketed the director into world prominence and enabled him to continue making the kind of political thrillers which mark his speciality.

Best Foreign Film Oscar 1969
Best Actor (Jean-Louis Trintignant) Cannes 1969

▶ **Zacharovannaya Desna** see Enchanted Desna, The

▶ **Zamach** see Answer To Violence

▶ **Zangiku Monogatari** see Story Of The Late Chrysanthemums, The

▶ **Zärtlichkeit Der Wölfe** see Tenderness Of Wolves

Zazie

▶ **Zazie Dans Le Métro**

France 1960 88 mins col
Nouvelles Éditions

d **Louis Malle**
sc **Louis Malle, Jean-Paul Rappeneau**
ph **Henri Raichi**
m **Fiorenzo Carpi**
Catherine Demongeot, Philippe Noiret, Carla Marlier, Vittorio Caprioli, Hubert Deschamps, Annie Fratellini, Yvonne Clech

Precocious, foul-mouthed pre-teen Zazie (Demongeot) spends 36 hours with her female impersonator uncle Gabriel (Noiret) in Paris with the sole intention of going for a ride on the Métro, but everything seems to conspire to prevent this. Malle's brave attempt to find visual equivalents to the eccentric syntax of Raymond Queneau's novel by using a series of cinematic tricks, quotes from other movies and silent comedy techniques, was more frenetic than funny, more hectic than hilarious. The surreal view of Paris in bright colours gives much pleasure, but even that burns itself out.

▶ **Zazie Dans Le Métro** see Zazie

▶ **Zbehovia A Poutníci** see Deserter And The Nomads, The

▶ **Zemlya** see Earth

▶ **Zénu Ani Kvêtinou Neuhodis** see Never Strike A Woman – Even With A Flower

▶ **Zerkalo** see Mirror

Zéro De Conduite

France   1933   45 mins   bw
Gaumont/Franco/Aubert

d   **Jean Vigo**
sc   **Jean Vigo**
ph   **Boris Kaufman**
m   **Maurice Jaubert**
Jean Dasté, Louis Lefèvre, Gilbert Pruchon, Robert Le Flon, Delphin, Coco Goldstein

At a dreadful boarding school in a Paris suburb, four schoolboys organize an uprising because of the petty restrictions imposed on them. Little money and not much experience account for the rough edges of Vigo's iconoclastic masterpiece, but these only add to its strange, anarchic poetry. It has a fresh, child's-eye view of authority from which adults are seen as hypocritical, oppressive and corrupt. The headmaster, played by the long-bearded dwarf Delphin (who killed himself in 1938), is looked down upon by the boys, whereas the only likeable teacher (Dasté) does handstands and imitations of Chaplin. The most celebrated sequence is the dormitory pillow fight that becomes a snowy wonderland of feathers, and a mock Catholic procession. After its first showing, the film was banned on political grounds until 1945. Its influence on Truffaut and Godard is noticeable, and it was the direct inspiration behind Lindsay Anderson's *If* ... (1968).

▶ **Zezowate Szczescie** see Bad Luck

▶ **Zhivoi Trup** see Living Corpse, The

▶ **Zhonghua Nuer** see Daughters Of China

▶ **Ziemia Obiecana** see Land Of Promise

▶ **Znak Bedy** see Sign Of Disaster

▶ **Zoo De La Nuit, Un** see Night Zoo

Zouzou

France   1934   100 mins   bw
Arys Films

d   **Marc Allégret**
sc   **Carlo Rim**
ph   **Michel Kelber**
m   **George Van Parys, Vincent Scotto**
Josephine Baker, Jean Gabin, Pierre Larquey, Yvette Lebon, Palau, Madeleine Guitry

Zouzou (Baker) adores her foster-brother (Gabin), a womanizing sailor. They go to Paris and find work in a music hall where Zouzou, given an opportunity to step into the star's shoes, becomes one herself. This stock yarn is an unashamed showcase for the considerable gifts of the legendary black American entertainer who became the toast of Paris, and includes her memorable rendition of 'Pour Moi Y'a Qu'un Homme Dans Paris'. Incidental pleasures in Marc Allégret's workmanlike film a good evocation of the backstage atmosphere at the music hall and a clutch of showy production numbers at the finale which are best described as Busby Berkeley out of *Folies Bergère*. But it is the extraordinary dynamism of singer-dancer Baker that holds everything together.

▶ **Zückerbaby** see Sugarbaby

▶ **Zuihou Yige Dongri** see Last Day Of Winter, The

▶ **Zur Chronik Von Grieshuus** see Chronicles Of The Grey House, The

Zvenigora

USSR   1927   66 mins approx   bw
VUFKU

d   **Alexander Dovzhenko**
sc   **Alexander Dovzhenko**
ph   **Boris Zavelev**
m   **Silent**
Mikola Nademsky, Polina Otava, Semyon

Svashenko, Alexander Podorozhin, Mikhail Barbe, Astafiev

An old man (Nademsky) and his two grandsons, one revolutionary (Svashenko), one reactionary (Podorozhin), go in search of treasure buried in the hill of Zvenigora. On the way, the grandfather dreams of early Ukrainian history, and the reactionary grandson advertises his own suicide at a theatre to raise money. The first of Dovzhenko's films in which he had total freedom was experimental and allegorical, changing from dream to reality, past to present, an example of the last flowering of the exciting *avant-garde* Soviet cinema of the 1920s, the product of a young, revolutionary society. When Eisenstein and Pudovkin saw it, they gave 'a joyful welcome to our new colleague,' and the three directors celebrated with an all-night drinking session.

► **Zweite Erwachen Der Christa Klages, Das** see Second Awakening Of Christa Klages, The

► **Zwischen Zeit Und Ewigkeit** see Between Time And Eternity

► **Zwischen Zwei Kriegen** see Between Two Wars

► **Zycie Rodzinne** see Family Life

Index of Directors

Aagren, Gösta 57
Abashidze, Dodo 44, 365
Abdelsalam, Shadi 462
Abdrashitov, Vadim 495, 517
Abuladze, Tengiz 542, 710
Ackeren, Robert Van 713
Adlon, Percy 115, 615, 625
Agostini, Philippe 110
Agresti, Alejandro 388, 567
Akerman, Chantal 20, 264, 329, 541
Albicocco, Jean-Gabriel 261, 691
Alea, Tomás Gutiérrez 164, 360, 426, 672
Alessandrini, Goffredo 247, 692, 698
Alexandrov, Grigori 328
Allégret, Marc 207, 219, 273, 351, 484, 732
Allégret, Yves 167, 256, 526, 571, 615, 692
Allio, René 575
Almodóvar, Pedro 157, 420, 648, 699, 718
Amar, Denis 4
Amaral, Suzana 297
Ambesser, Axel Von 267
Amelio, Gianni 85, 483
Ammar, Abdel-Latif Ben 53
Andrien, Jean-Jacques 204
Angelopoulos, Theo 16, 67, 161, 303, 356, 660, 688
Annaud, Jean-Jacques 79
Antonioni, Michelangelo 52, 124, 151, 195, 259, 307, 353, 388, 470, 474, 537
Aragón, Manuel Gutiérrez 79, 168, 277
Arcand, Denys 167, 330
Archibugi, Francesca 429
Ardavin, Cesar 363
Aristarain, Adolfo 649
Armiñán, Jaime De 457
Arrabal, Fernando 686
Askoldov, Aleksandr 138
Astruc, Alexandre 149, 480, 574
Audry, Jacqueline 258, 314, 436, 467, 479
August, Bille 505
Aurel, Jean 19
Autant-Lara, Claude 173, 187, 244, 249, 272, 344, 389, 413,

478, 512, 536, 537, 545, 571, 626, 644, 714
Axel, Gabriel 54, 538

Babenco, Hector 514
Bacsó, Péter 712
Baghdadi, Maroun 378
Baky, Josef Von 8
Balayan, Roman 189
Ballmann, Herbert 260
Baratier, Jacques 263
Barbash, Uri 74
Bardem, Juan Antonio 106, 165
Barnet, Boris 103, 262, 299
Barreto, Bruno 184
Barreto, Lima 59
Batalov, Aleksei 489
Baudin, Jean 327
Beaucler, André 4
Becker, Jacques 7, 17, 37, 196, 216, 243, 265, 268, 274, 292, 440, 541
Becker, Jean 479
Beineix, Jean-Jacques 73, 180, 440, 550
Belikov, Mikhail 702
Bellocchio, Marco 122, 233, 318, 363
Bellon, Yannick 683
Belmont, Vera 552
Bemberg, Maria Luisa 106, 466
Benegal, Shyam 43, 127, 338, 547, 569
Benoît-Lévy, Jean 421
Bergenstrahle, John 402
Bergman, Ingmar 51, 147, 174, 175, 215, 216, 220, 222, 246, 298, 334, 367, 403, 461, 472, 500, 508, 520, 546, 562, 563, 573, 574, 577, 583, 591, 593, 617, 619, 641, 648, 653, 685, 690, 708, 709
Berković, Zvonimir 549
Berlanga, Luis (Garcia) 212, 372, 697
Bernard, Raymond 25, 120, 433, 434
Bernhardt, Kurt 717
Berri, Claude 328, 331, 411, 417, 573, 616, 667
Bertolucci, Bernardo 67, 140,

273, 385, 397, 465, 498, 599, 658
Besson, Luc 357, 464, 614
Beyer, Frank 326, 453
Beyzai, Bahram 610
Blanc, Jean-Pierre 681
Blasetti, Alessandro 7, 198, 241
Blier, Bertrand 99, 211, 257, 404, 448, 488, 605, 663
Blom, Per 305
Bodrov, Sergei 243
Boer, Leo De 695
Boese, Carl 266
Boisrond, Michel 385, 496, 524, 683
Boisset, Yves 143, 516, 525
Bokóva, Jana 296
Böll, Heinrich 255
Bolognini, Mauro 13, 188, 189, 279, 314, 353, 389, 428, 461, 478, 570, 710
Bondarchuk, Sergei 171, 692
Borderie, Bernard 31
Borowczyk, Walerian 64, 82, 268, 311, 608
Botelho, João 281, 521
Bourgignon, Serge 621
Bouzid, Nouri 409
Boyer, Jean 394
Bozzetto, Bruno 19
Bozzuffi, Marcel 25
Braun, Vladimir 405
Breien, Anja 494, 711, 712, 712
Breillat, Catherine 684
Bresson, Robert 32, 41, 59, 155, 173, 176, 241, 255, 354, 407, 443, 511, 661
Brialy, Jean-Claude 395
Bringmann, Peter F. 284
Broca, Philippe De 113, 162, 173, 313, 332, 383, 478, 516, 571, 637, 673
Brocka, Lino 63, 89, 316, 399, 408
Brook, Peter 436
Bruckberger, R. 110
Brusati, Franco 95, 238
Brustellin, Alf 255
Brynych, Zbyněk 229
Bugajski, Ryszard 317
Bulajić, Veljko 290
Buñuel, Juan 48
Buñuel, Luis 12, 69, 99, 115,

120, 149, 176, 179, 198, 212,
213, 357, 428, 430, 456, 510,
542, 585, 622, 637, 662, 685,
721, 727

Cacoyannis, Michael 199, 260,
321, 422, 605, 709
Campanile, Pasquale Festa 7,
708
Camus, Marcel 80
Camus, Mario 293, 298
Carax, Leos 93, 461
Carlsen, Esben Hoilund 606
Carlsen, Henning 302
Carné, Marcel 79, 160, 205,
252, 296, 329, 338, 414, 528,
639, 685, 728, 729
Carow, Heiner 138
Casaril, Guy 46, 540, 597
Castellani, Renato 105, 668
Cavalcanti, Alberto 288
Cavalier, Alain 284, 639
Cavani, Liliana 74
Cayatte, André 28, 40, 150,
339, 387, 392, 434, 660, 677
Chabrol, Claude 18, 64, 65, 75,
84, 90, 102, 118, 143, 145,
226, 283, 317, 339, 345, 356,
373, 419, 453, 483, 498, 526,
546, 554, 571, 588, 641, 684,
696
Chahine, Youssef 4, 17, 105,
197, 354, 596
Chalonge, Christian De 181,
405
Chanois, Jean-Paul Le 113,
385, 501
Charrell, Erik 141
Chatiliez, Etienne 371, 631
Chenal, Pierre 17, 132, 148,
357, 362
Chmielewski, Tadeusz 212
Chouikh, Mohamed 129
Christensen, Benjamin 710
Christian-Jaque 6, 54, 81, 92,
219, 385, 392, 454, 504, 626
Chukrai, Grigori 57, 131
Chusheng, Cai 602
Chytilová, Véra 39, 155
Ciampi, Yves 288
Cissé, Souleymane 54, 96, 708
Ciulei, Liviu 382
Clair, René 22, 35, 66, 172,
207, 227, 241, 252, 323, 359,
385, 431, 460, 584, 596, 617
Clausen, Erik 158
Clément, Magali 329
Clément, René 63, 155, 237,
257, 527, 691
Cloche, Maurice 440
Cloos, Hans Peter 255
Clouzot, Henri-Georges 175,
410, 432, 445, 511, 528, 534,
599, 664, 690, 713
Cocteau, Jean 65, 84, 193, 485,
496, 637
Cohen, Eli 617
Colomo, Fernando 589
Colpi, Henri 381

Comencini, Luigi 66, 88, 95,
95, 435
Corbiau, Gérard 446
Corneau, Alain 239
Cornell, Jonas 300
Corti, Axel 539
Costa-Gavras 139, 568, 590,
604, 731
Cousteau, Jacques-Yves 584
Coutard, Raoul 292
Cozarinsky, Edgardo 480
Czinner, Paul 393, 425

Damiani, Damiano 43, 203,
376
Danelia, Georgy 51
Danieli, G. 600
Daquin, Louis 642
Darène, Robert 72
Dassin, Jules 289, 457, 545
Decoin, Henri 2, 114, 385
Delannoy, Jean 3, 61, 71, 322,
331, 385, 386, 404, 626, 642
Delluc, Louis 226
Delouche, Dominique 665
Delvaux, André 2, 69, 70, 412,
593
Dembo, Richard 156
Demy, Jacques 64, 222, 380,
403, 571, 671
Denham, Reginald 34
Denis, Claire 123
Depardon, Raymond 110
Deray, Jacques 91, 250, 286
Deruddere, Dominique 147
De Seta, Vittorio 22, 60
De Sica, Vittorio 75, 96, 121,
251, 265, 416, 432, 550, 578,
621, 669, 670, 710, 725
Devers, Claire 467
Deville, Michel 6, 70, 163, 186,
364, 492
Dhéry, Robert 20, 69
Dhomme, Sylvain 571
Diegues, Carlos 102
Dieudonné, Albert 681
Dinov, Todor 306
Djordjević, Purisa 441
Doniol-Valcroze, Jacques 530
Donner, Jörn 10, 33, 80, 620,
654
Donskoi, Mark 121, 285, 447,
452, 532
Doo-Yong, Lee 700
Dörrie, Doris 426, 609
Douchet, Jean 588
Douy, Max 571
Dovzhenko, Alexander 10, 42,
194, 324, 576, 732
Drach, Michel 24, 684
Dréville, Jean 105, 571
Dreyer, Carl 161, 257, 363,
430, 484, 497, 501, 675
Dreyer, Carl Theodor 420
Duarte, Anselmo 262
Dudow, Slatan 350, 612
Dudrumet, Jean-Charles 392
Dulac, Germaine 565, 592
Dupeyron, Francois 610

Dupont, E.A. 28, 676
Durant, Alberto 405
Duras, Marguerite 313
Duvivier, Julien 69, 112, 204,
266, 266, 293, 299, 378, 414,
414, 445, 493, 506, 518
Dziedzina, Julian 93

Edel, Ulrich 124
Edwall, Allan 14
Eguino, Antonio 126
Eisenstein, Sergei 16, 63, 253,
324, 475, 612
Ekk, Nicolai 546
Elek, Judit 352
Emmer, Luciano 620
Enrico, Robert 567
Epstein, Jean 217, 231
Epstein, Marie 421
Erice, Victor 596, 600
Ermler, Friedrich 242, 504
Esway, Alexander 422
Étaix, Pierre 45, 269, 616, 729
Eustache, Jean 442
Export, Valie 320

Fanck, Arnold 703
Faraldo, Claude 638, 667
Farmanara, Bahman 629
Farocki, Harun 73
Fassbinder, Rainer Werner 25,
74, 78, 122, 197, 225, 242,
255, 263, 312, 321, 343, 374,
380, 416, 417, 427, 443, 529,
561, 641, 678, 704, 706, 708
Fehér, Imre 621
Fejós, Pál 414, 535
Felice, Lionello De 12
Fellini, Federico 24, 30, 88,
113, 130, 134, 183, 197, 225,
226, 258, 318, 338, 373, 388,
463, 484, 600, 608, 624, 685,
687, 704
Fengler, Michael 706
Feng-Liang, Yeng 337
Ferét, René 450
Ferhati, Jillali 539
Fernández, Emilio 413
Ferreri, Marco 38, 49, 85, 177,
248, 361, 529, 700
Feuillade, Louis 220, 336, 675
Feyder, Jacques 47, 112, 146,
254, 270, 273, 471, 505
Filippo, Eduardo De 239, 571
Fong, Allen 224
Ford, Alexsander 91, 233, 348
Forman, Miloš 83, 231, 509
Forsberg, Lars 723
Forst, Willi 419
Fracassi, Clemente 14, 570
Franju, Georges 83, 214, 336,
344, 573, 587, 639, 643

Gaál, István 153, 216
Gábor, Pál 32, 294
Gabrea, Radu 408
Galeen, Henrik 23, 614
Gallaga, Peque 265
Gallone, Carmine 370, 400

Gance, Abel 50, 154, 305, 369,
    455, 551
Garci, José Luis 652
Gary, Romain 77
Gasnier, Louis 656
Gatlif, Tony 523
Gaup, Nils 502
Gazdag, Gyula 301
Geissendörfer, Hans W. 707
Genée, Heidi 481
Genina, Augusto 286
Georgiades, Vassilis 84
Georgiyev, Viktor 307
Gerasimov, Sergei 29
Gerima, Haile 282
Gerlach, Arthur Von 126
Germi, Pietro 17, 77, 181, 383,
    410, 532, 568
Ghatak, Ritwik 129, 424
Gherman, Alexei 448, 662, 665
Ghose, Gautam 688
Glenn, Pierre William 635
Godard, Jean-Luc 23, 95, 110,
    123, 142, 171, 222, 232, 249,
    276, 323, 377, 385, 403, 416,
    418, 471, 472, 478, 489, 500,
    512, 547, 571, 588, 591, 657,
    668, 696, 715
Godoy, Armando Robles 272
Gogoberidze, Lana 318
Gómez, Sara 482
Gopalakrishnan, Adoor 534
Gören, Serif 540, 726
Goretta, Claude 166, 259, 321,
    351, 643
Gorin, Jean-Pierre 657
Gorris, Marleen 97, 530
Gosho, Heinosuke 68, 700, 702
Gothár, Péter 650
Gout, Alberto 4
Grangier, Gilles 39, 144
Granier-Deferre, Pierre 119,
    468, 497
Grede, Kjell 282, 300
Green, Joseph 725
Gregoretti, Ugo 65, 458, 547
Gregorio, Eduardo De 45
Grémillon, Jean 127, 397, 607
Gremm, Wolf 215, 341
Griffi, Giuseppe Patroni 413
Grlić, Rajko 729
Grospierre, Louis 98
Grosse, Nina 263
Grote, Alexandra Von 471
Groulx, Gilles 114
Grousset, Didier 341
Gubenko, Nikolai 52
Gudmundsson, Ágúst 355
Guerra, Ruy 208, 217, 222,
    274, 483
Guerra, Tonino 421
Guerrieri, Romolo 623
Guillemot, Claude 663
Guissart, René 135
Guitry, Sacha 391, 455, 504,
    607
Güney, Yilmaz 691
Guzman, Patricio 62
Gyöngyössi, Imre 544, 724

Haanstra, Bert 687
Hallström, Lasse 449
Handke, Peter 364
Hani, Susumu 102, 313, 576
Hansen, Rolf 11
Harlan, Veit 331
Harnack, Falk 21
Hartl, Karl 264
Has, Wojciech 183, 560
Hauff, Reinhard 347, 590, 603
Heifits, Josef (Joseph) 59, 76,
    319, 354
Herman, Jean 620
Hermosillo, Jaime Humberto
    184, 418
Herzog, Werner 13, 134, 206,
    211, 233, 285, 469, 582, 613,
    720
Hirszman, Leon 560, 640
Hjulström, Lennart 291
Hochbaum, Werner 210
Hoffmann, Kurt 40
Holland, Agnieszka 228
Hondo, Med 561, 594
Honkasalo, Pirjo 235
Horikawa, Hiromichi 65
Hristov, Hristo 306
Hsiao-hsien, Hou 94, 130, 159,
    616, 651
Hu, King 657
Hu, Sang 703
Hubert, Jean-Loup 269
Huillet, Danièle 131
Hunebelle, André 221
Huszárik, Zoltán 586

Ichikawa, Kon 3, 22, 100, 140,
    232, 475, 586, 653
Imai, Tadashi 101
Imamura, Shohei 58, 80, 316,
    512, 519, 706
Imhoof, Markus 87
Inagaki, Hiroshi 558
Indovini, Franco 478
Ionesco, Eugene 571
Iosseliani, Otar 224
Ishihara, Shintaro 386
Ishii, Sogo 146
Itami, Juzo 247, 630, 632, 632
Ivens, Joris 9, 222

Jabor, Arnaldo 21
Jacoby, Georg 67, 360
Jacopetti, Gualtiero 12, 438
Jaeckin, Just 202
Jakubisko, Juro 170
Jakubowska, Wanda 359
Jancsó, Miklós 13, 141, 199,
    452, 525, 536, 538, 552, 583
Jasný, Vojtěch 20, 701
Jessner, Leopold 55
Jessua, Alain 137, 182, 372
Jiang, Zhai 159
Jianxin, Huang 79
Jiayi, Wang 101
Jin, Xie 289, 668
Jíres, Jaromil 152, 503, 674
Joannon, Léo 167, 287

Jodorowsky, Alejandro 201,
    559
Joffé, Alex 219
Jügert, Rudolf 229
Junli, Zheng 150, 602
Juráček, Pavel 333
Jutra, Claude 451
Jutzi, Phil 71

Kabay, Barna 544, 724
Kaboré, Gaston J.M. 257
Kachyna, Karel 134, 193, 310
Kadar, Jan 6, 579
Kaige, Chen 76, 346, 724
Kalatozov, Mikhail 146
Kaneko, Shusuke 619
Kaplan, Nelly 118, 178
Karanović, Srdjan 242
Karasik, Yuli 565, 588
Karnad, Girish 238
Kast, Pierre 565
Katakouzinos, George 31
Kaurismäki, Aki 41, 278, 365,
    421, 574
Käutner, Helmut 109, 133,
    174, 357
Kawalerowicz, Jerzy 50, 173,
    463, 511
Kermadec, Liliane De 22
Keusch, Erwin 56
Kézdi-Kovács, Zsolt 238, 701
Kieslowski, Krzysztof 82, 106,
    466, 579, 580
Kimiavi, Parviz 251
Kinoshita, Keisuke 58, 111,
    210, 327
Kinugasa, Teinosuke 150, 252,
    491
Kirsanov, Dimitri 426
Kishon, Ephraim 556
Klein, William 222
Klimov, Elem 13, 137, 221
Kluge, Alexander 42, 255, 502,
    724
Knudsen, Mette 628
Kobayashi, Masaki 203, 281,
    301, 350, 536
Koch, Carl 657
Kohlhaase, Wolfgang 594
Kok, Marja 314
Koller, Xavier 334
Komarov, Sergei 183, 346
Korda, Alexander 415, 437
Kosá, Ferenc 634
Kotulla, Theodor 164
Koundouros, Nikos 727
Kovács, András 135
Kozintsev, Grigori 277, 345,
    458, 543, 689, 729
Krejčík, Jiří 180
Kuleshov, Lev 103, 166, 213,
    271
Kulidzhanov, Lev 148
Kulle, Jarl 91
Kumai, Kei 558
Kümel, Harry 439
Kunert, Joachim 9
Kurahara, Koreyoshi 381
Kurosawa, Akira 55, 170, 182,

189, 191, 289, 290, 308, 309,
337, 340, 379, 395, 530, 533,
533, 537, 559, 562, 572, 611,
648, 725
Kurys, Diane   47, 117, 134, 507
Kusturica, Emir   188, 649, 701
Kutz, Kazimierz   64
Kvirikadze, Irakli   624
Kwan, Stanley   551
Kwon-Taek, Lim   682

Lacombe, Georges   373, 418,
571
Lakhdar-Hamina, Mohammed
125
Lamorisse, Albert   229, 537
Lampin, Georges   148, 308
Lamprecht, Gerhard   201, 400
Lamy, Benoit   680
Lang, Fritz   171, 182, 375, 399,
428, 459, 599, 636, 644, 649,
714
Lang, Michel   36, 295
Lanzmann, Claude   322, 577
Lasticati, Carlo   34
Lattuada, Alberto   33, 373,
388, 407, 431, 577, 711
Lautner, Georges   249, 572
Lauzon, Jean-Claude   464
Leconte, Patrice   439
Leduc, Paul   245
Leenhardt, Roger   169, 541
Lefèbvre, Jean Pierre   186, 236,
478
Legoshin, Vladimir   381
Lehmann, Maurice   244
Lehmuskallio, Markku   535
Lehto, Pekka   235
Lelouch, Claude   29, 35, 90,
114, 196, 222, 371, 379, 388,
406, 406, 566, 585
Leni, Paul   55, 695
Leroy, Serge   499
Leszczlowski, Michal   178
Levy, Jean-Benoît   231
L'Herbier, Marcel   6, 40, 137,
220, 362, 451, 508
Lilienthal, Peter   159, 672
Lindblom, Gunnel   618
Lindgren, Lars Magnus   162
Littín, Miguel   24, 326
Litvak, Anatole   423
Lizzani, Carlo   301, 385, 388
Lombardi, Francisco J.   375
Lommel, Ulli   634
Lopushansky, Konstantin   368
Lorre, Peter   382
Losey, Joseph   185, 444
Loubignac, Jean   227
Loy, Nanni   240, 402, 706
Lubitsch, Ernst   33, 213, 401,
443, 489, 707
Luchetti, Daniele   323
Luntz, Edouard   454
Lyssy, Rolf   625

Maanouni, Ahmed El   659
Maas, Dick   27
Machaty, Gustav   195

Mainka, Maximiliane   255
Mainka-Jellinghaus, Beate   255
Makavejev, Dušan   315, 408,
625, 720
Makharam, Ababacar Samb
333
Makhmalbaf, Mohsen   505
Makk, Károly   35, 115, 384,
678
Malaparte, Curzio   237
Malle, Louis   49, 49, 161, 227,
351, 373, 391, 431, 584, 600,
640, 679, 686, 731
Malmros, Nils   65
Malraux, André   411
Malyan, Genrikh   590
Mankiewicz, Francis   544
Marczewski, Wojciech   190
Marischka, Ernst   238, 726
Marker, Chris   14, 152, 222,
333, 368, 622
Marketaki, Tonia   522
Marquand, Christian   477
Martin, Paul   83, 389
Maselli, Francesco   388
Masumura, Yasuzo   500
Matsumoto, Toshio   493
Mattsson, Arne   481, 715
May, Joe   45
Medvedkin, Alexander   280
Meerapfel, Jeanine   405
Mehboob   1
Mehrjui, Daryush   145, 153
Mehta, Ketan   598
Mehta, Vijaya   509
Mei, Hu   222
Meideros, Richard De   458
Meineche, Annelise   572, 595
Méliès, Georges   662
Melville, Jean-Pierre   42, 87,
179, 187, 366, 558, 566, 583,
609
Menshov, Vladimir   441
Menzel, Jiří   109, 132, 451, 579,
644, 704
Mészáros, Márta   5, 175, 176,
465
Metin, Ismail   694
Michel, André   9
Michel, Bernard T.   633
Mikhalkov, Nikita   157, 233,
474, 524, 590, 671
Mikhalkov-Konchalovsky,
Andrei   46, 232, 457, 580
Mikkelsen, Laila   376
Milkina, Sofia   349
Miller, Claude   72, 312, 316,
509, 642
Minkin, Adolph   525
Miró, Pilar   149
Mitra, Raja   520
Mitrani, Michel   252
Mizoguchi, Kenji   151, 203,
234, 258, 372, 390, 396, 435,
449, 459, 486, 559, 587, 608,
609, 611, 670
Mizrahi, Moshe   310, 401
Mnouchkine, Ariane   437

Mocky, Jean-Pierre   15, 286,
394, 592, 727
Moguy, Leonid   11
Molander, Gustaf   317, 717
Molinaro, Edouard   105, 513,
571
Monicelli, Mario   163, 184,
271, 367, 374, 485, 508
Moreau, Jeanne   5
Moreuil, Francois   516
Morgenstern, Janusz   569
Morin, Edgar   125
Morita, Yoshimitsu   218
Munk, Andrzej   55, 208, 499
Muratova, Kira   579
Murer, Fredi   23
Murnau, F.W.   100, 224, 230,
283, 359, 468, 631
Musso, Jeff   526
Muzhi, Yuan   611

Naderi, Amir   554
Nair, Mira   556
Nakamura, Noboru   520, 666
Naruse, Mikio   236, 361, 542,
706, 717
Němec, Jan   498
Nichetti, Maurizio   306
Nichev, Ivan   91
Niermans, Edouard   30, 36
Nihalani, Govind   158, 277
Niskanen, Mikko   589
Niskanen, Tuija-Maija   222
Nowina-Przybylski, Jan   725
Nuanxin, Zhang   555
Nuytten, Bruno   107
Nweze, Ngangura   680
Nykvist, Carl-Gustaf   718

Ogorodnikov, Valery   100
Oguri, Kohei   444
Ökten, Zeki   205, 288
Oliveira, Manoel De   32, 108,
243
Olivera, Hector   247
Olmi, Ermanno   107, 191, 206,
332, 365, 381, 480, 650, 661
Olsson, Stellan   133
Ophüls, Marcel   296, 386, 595
Ophüls, Max   62, 180, 369, 380,
400, 469, 515, 549, 561, 582,
634, 698
Oshima, Nagisa   93, 116, 163,
177, 202, 319, 423
Otomo, Katsuhiro   15
Ouedraogo, Idrissa   723
Oury, Gérard   9, 186
Ozep, Fedor   379
Ozu, Yasujiro   50, 194, 194,
205, 207, 235, 236, 267, 325,
361, 362, 639, 653, 654, 654

Pabst, G.W.   11, 48, 177, 186,
326, 335, 340, 360, 390, 493,
494, 515, 567, 575, 646, 661,
698, 703
Pagnol, Marcel   31, 56, 116,
127, 282, 332, 368, 410, 427,
564, 656, 656, 697

Palcy, Euzhan 81
Panayotopoulos, Nikos 136
Panfilov, Gleb 68, 638, 677
Papas, Michael 655
Papastathis, Lakis 702
Papić, Krsto 278
Papoušek, Jaroslav 72
Paradjanov, Sergo 44, 136, 365, 574
Paskaljević, Goran 597
Pasolini, Pier Paolo 2, 39, 109, 166, 268, 284, 385, 406, 424, 476, 513, 547, 557, 638, 710
Passendorfer, Jerzy 36
Passer, Ivan 320
Pastrone, Giovanni 104
Patellière, Denys De La 41, 112, 270
Pattrea, Purnendu 368
Patwardhan, Anand 89
Pereira, Miguel 677
Perelman, Pablo 362
Peries, Sumitra 261
Perincioli, Cristina 522
Petersen, Wolfgang 87, 141
Petri, Elio 45, 320, 531, 719
Petrović, Aleksander 281, 419
Pfleghar, Michel 478
Philipe, Gérard 9
Pialat, Maurice 384, 453, 499, 519, 655, 671, 699
Pichul, Vasili 378
Pick, Lupu 575
Pietrangeli, Antonio 302
Pinoteau, Claude 584
Pirès, Gérard 3, 209
Piscator, Erwin 544
Pita, Dan 606
Podskalsky, Zdeněk 457
Poirier, Anne Claire 523
Polanski, Roman 65, 347
Polidoro, Gian Luigi 172
Poligny, Serge De 510
Pollet, Jean-Daniel 588
Pontecorvo, Gillo 62, 342
Pool, Léa 34
Pottier, Richard 112
Prado, Guilherme De Almeida 352
Prévert, Pierre 4, 11, 688
Prosperi, Franco 12
Protazanov, Yakov 10, 239
Ptashuk, Mikhail 581
Ptoushko, Alexander 459
Pudovkin, Vsevolod (V.I.) 204, 442, 585, 607
Puenzo, Luis 476
Pyriev, Ivan 98, 308, 703

Queysanne, Bernard 391

Rabenalt, Arthur Maria 73
Rademakers, Fons 46, 181, 347, 423
Radev, Vulo 504
Radványi, Géza 402, 594
Rahardjo, Slamet 519
Raizman, Yuli 524
Rajaonarivelo, Raymond 628

Rappaport, Herbert 525
Rappeneau, Jean-Paul 153, 562, 564, 680
Ray, Satyajit 8, 10, 38, 75, 94, 119, 120, 138, 161, 172, 179, 200, 212, 250, 293, 341, 429, 446, 502, 667, 719
Reiniger, Lotte 8
Reinl, Harald 705
Reitz, Edgar 255, 287
Renoir, Jean 82, 92, 121, 149, 160, 199, 244, 264, 269, 300, 376, 377, 395, 397, 400, 417, 454, 472, 482, 553, 636, 652, 655, 676
Resnais, Alain 26, 222, 291, 330, 361, 370, 425, 446, 447, 460, 605, 693
Rey-Coquais, Cyrille 255
Richard, Jean-Louis 420
Riefenstahl, Leni 86, 395, 479, 663
Rim, Carlo 571
Rios, Humberto 152
Ripploh, Frank 632
Risi, Dino 68, 388, 523, 564
Rivers, Fernand 404
Rivette, Jacques 27, 116, 250, 390, 496, 540
Robbe-Grillet, Alain 311
Robert, Yves 16, 66, 144, 495, 557, 629, 693
Robison, Arthur 614, 693
Rocha, Glauber 12, 37, 80, 355, 375
Rochant, Eric 720
Rödl, Josef 15
Rodriguez, Ismael 59
Rohmer, Eric 51, 130, 135, 240, 246, 266, 272, 387, 415, 448, 450, 503, 507, 582, 588, 629
Romm, Mikhail 92, 366, 366, 465
Rondi, Brunello 168
Rood, Jurrien 695
Room, Abram 67
Rose, Hubert-Yves 285
Rosenbaum, Marianne S.W. 507
Rosi, Francesco 111, 124, 124, 128, 279, 309, 421, 438, 557, 645
Rossellini, Renzo 386
Rossellini, Roberto 26, 210, 225, 253, 256, 335, 386, 492, 545, 547, 548, 571, 612, 675
Rossi, Franco 165, 245, 710
Rossif, Frédéric 652
Rósza, János 619
Rouch, Jean 125, 588
Rouleau, Raymond 392, 711
Rouquier, Georges 223
Rozier, Jacques 5
Rubini, Sergio 604
Ruffio, Jacques 683
Ruiz, Râúl 129, 304, 645
Runze, Ottokar 290
Rupé, Katja 255

Ruttmann, Walter 71
Ryazanov, Eldar 604
Rye, Stellan 613
Rygard, Elizabeth 628

Sagan, Leontine 401
Salce, Luciano 377
Saleh, Tewfik 191
Salerno, Enrico Maria 34
Saless, Sohrab Shahid 20
Samperi, Salvatore 208, 270
Sanders-Brahms, Helma 248, 256, 467
Sándor, Pál 156, 311
Sanjines, Jorge 83
Santiago, Hugo 569
Santis, Giuseppe De 78, 658
Santos, Nelson Pereira Dos 19, 61, 425
Sathyu, M.S. 297
Saura, Carlos 28, 37, 52, 85, 110, 145, 169, 198, 200, 294, 302, 386, 506, 533, 623
Sautet, Claude 56, 117, 228, 422, 586, 640, 682
Sayyad, Parviz 434
Schamoni, Peter 602
Schell, Maximilian 415, 504
Schenkel, Carl 488
Schlöndorff, Volker 128, 144, 168, 255, 382, 615, 617, 622, 651, 728
Schmidt, Jan 333
Schroeter, Werner 165, 492
Schubert, Peter 255
Schünzel, Reinhold 27, 682
Schütte, Jan 598
Schwarz, Hans 719
Schweitzer, Mikhail 349
Scola, Ettore 57, 188, 217, 328, 462, 501, 597, 601, 695
Sembène, Ousmane 108, 115, 202, 438, 722
Sen, Mrinal 29, 254, 316, 489, 553
Serreau, Coline 548, 646
Seunke, Orlow 631
Shaji 78
Shapiro, Mikhail 353
Shengalaya, Eldar 86
Shengelaya, Georgy 514
Shepitko, Larisa 43
Shimazu, Yasujiro 97
Shindo, Kaneto 122, 322, 371, 482
Shinoda, Masahiro 187, 563
Siddik, Khalid 151
Sidelov 16
Sierck, Detlef 230, 276, 513
Šijan, Slobodan 705
Simenon, Marc 103
Sinha, Tapan 553
Sinkel, Bernhard 255, 375
Siodmak, Robert 174, 221, 437, 506, 534, 592
Sjöberg, Alf 223, 244, 435
Sjöman, Vilgot 87, 305, 450, 623

Sjöström, Victor 259, 343, 393, 488, 510
Skarmeta, Antonio 101
Skolimowski, Jerzy 61, 169, 307, 690
Sluizer, George 676
Sointseva, Julia 235
Solanas, Fernando E 297, 596, 630
Solas, Humberto 396
Soldati, Mario 716
Solntseva, Julia 204, 235, 517
Solum, Ola 485
Sow, Thierno Faty 108
Staudte, Wolfgang 445
Steinhoff, Hans 477
Stelli, Jean 86
Stelling, Jos 518
Stemmle, Robert 58
Sternberg, Josef Von 85
Štiglic, France 466
Stiller, Mauritz 48, 209, 274, 385, 587, 643
Stöcklin, Tania 255
Straub, Jean-Marie 125, 131, 441, 470
Subielo, Eliseo 358
Sucksdorff, Arne 271, 449
Svankmajer, Jan 18
Swaim, Bob 57
Syberberg, Hans Jürgen 140, 292, 396, 497
Sydow, Max Von 343
Szabó, István 99, 136, 140, 223, 280, 426, 665
Szlingerbaum, Samy 98

Tabio, Juan Carlos 298, 514
Tacchella, Jean-Charles 145, 209
Tai, Luo 101
Talankin, Igor 600, 633
Tanner, Alain 118, 234, 319, 333, 427, 429, 556
Tarkovsky, Andrei 29, 324, 433, 469, 555, 593, 603
Tassios, Pavlos 495
Tati, Jacques 334, 439, 451, 494, 516, 658
Tavernier, Bertrand 131, 336, 367, 370, 601, 620, 694, 697
Taviani, Paolo and Vittorio 21, 342, 424, 462, 491
Téchiné, André 60, 97, 541
Terayama, Shuji 93, 246
Teshigahara, Hiroshi 215, 618, 716
Tessari, Duccio 164

Thiele, Rolf 260
Thiele, Wilhelm 646
Thomas, Pascal 602
Thomas, Robert 90
Thome, Rudolf 647
Thomopoulos, Andreas 195
Thomsen, Christian Braad 162, 352
Thomsen, Knud Leif 518
Tianming, Wu 478
Törhönen, Lauri 100
Tornatore, Giuseppe 128
Torre-Nilsson, Leopoldo 216, 278, 299
Tourneur, Maurice 687
Trauberg, Leonid 458, 543, 689, 729
Trenker, Luis 202, 383
Triana, Jorge Ali 651
Troell, Jan 201, 459, 705
Trotta, Margarethe Von 245, 255, 382, 550, 566, 588, 647, 713
Truffaut, Francois 34, 66, 96, 160, 230, 240, 267, 272, 337, 359, 386, 390, 412, 435, 578, 585, 591, 606, 608, 707, 715
Turin, Victor 665
Tzavellas, George 37

Ulmer, Edgar 506

Vadim, Roger 28, 185, 285, 369, 549, 571, 600, 679, 694
Vajda, Ladislao 46, 412
Vallois, Philippe 699
Varda, Agnès 89, 132, 222, 481, 674
Vasiliev, Georgi 118
Vasiliev, Sergei 118
Vega, Pastor 521
Verbong, Ben 262
Verhoeven, Michael 456
Verhoeven, Paul 242, 344, 598, 664
Verneuil, Henri 76, 146, 237, 385, 391, 576, 581, 696
Veroiu, Mircea 606
Vertov, Dziga 206, 412
Vigne, Daniel 543, 716
Vigo, Jean 39, 47, 732
Vilstrup, Li 628
Visconti, Luchino 70, 142, 156, 164, 315, 366, 396, 476, 486, 547, 570, 610, 635, 703, 710
Vollmar, Wolf 429
Voulgaris, Pantelis 280

Wachsman, Daniel 194
Wajda, Andrzej 44, 77, 139, 157, 211, 254, 303, 315, 341, 348, 355, 356, 383, 386, 387, 409, 409, 552, 581, 696, 728
Warmerdam, Alex Van 1
Warneke, Lothar 487
Wasynski, Michael 192
Watkins, Peter 196
Wegener, Paul 266
Weidenmann, Alfred 6, 30
Weiss, Jiří 445, 548
Weisz, Franz 283
Wenders, Wim 18, 25, 38, 346, 563, 709, 721
Wertmüller, Lina 21, 107, 380, 384, 568, 571, 624
Wicki, Bernhard 96, 432
Widerberg, Bo 3, 201, 393, 407, 411, 535, 613
Wiene, Robert 104, 279, 533
Wilder, Billy 422
Wirth, Franz Peter 42
Wolf, Konrad 325, 594, 603
Woo, John 345

Xavier, Nelson 217
Xueshu, Yan 320

Yamamoto, Kajiro 295
Yanagimachi, Mitsuo 231
Yang, Edward 635
Yimou, Zhang 337, 538
Yutkevitch, Sergei 374, 487

Zadek, Peter 310
Zafranovic, Lordan 474
Zampa, Luigi 31, 38, 529
Zanussi, Krzysztof 108, 141, 142, 218, 309, 463, 613, 716, 723
Zaorski, Janusz 60
Zarkhi, Alexander 33, 59, 666
Zavattini, Cesare 388
Zeffirelli, Franco 487, 660
Zeman, Karel 61, 330
Zeming, Zhang 623
Zetterling, Mai 26, 260, 394, 461
Zhifeng, Ling 159
Zhuangzhuang, Tian 295
Zidi, Claude 143
Ziniu, Wu 211, 358
Zohar, Uri 645
Zsombolyai, János 192
Zurinaga, Marcos 630
Zurlini, Valerio 218, 261
Zuylen, Erik Van 314